FROMMER'S
COMPREHENSIVE TRAVEL GUIDE
AUSTRALIA '92-'93

by Elizabeth Hansen
Assisted by Richard Adams

PRENTICE HALL TRAVEL

NEW YORK • LONDON • TORONTO • SYDNEY • TOKYO • SINGAPORE

FROMMER BOOKS

Published by Prentice Hall General Reference
A division of Simon & Schuster Inc.
15 Columbus Circle
New York, NY 10023

ISBN 0-13-334798-2
ISSN 1040-9408

Design by Robert Bull Design
Maps by Geografix Inc.

Manufactured in the United States of America

FROMMER'S AUSTRALIA '92-'93

Editor-in-Chief: Marilyn Wood
Senior Editors: Judith de Rubini, Alice Fellows
Editors: Paige Hughes, Sara Hinsey Raveret, Lisa Renaud, Theodore Stavrou
Assistant Editor: Peter Katucki
Contributing Editors: Lisa Legarde, Pamela Marshall

CONTENTS

LIST OF MAPS

For Rick,

for being there

ACKNOWLEDGMENTS

The author gratefully acknowledges the assistance of the Australian Tourist Commission, Australian Airlines, Qantas Airways, the Queensland Tourist and Travel Corporation, the Northern Territory Tourist Commission, the Western Australian Tourism Commission, Tourism South Australia, the Victorian Tourism Commission, Tourism Tasmania, and the ACT Tourism Commission. Thanks also to Sandra Swan who provided assistance in Sydney.

INVITATION TO THE READERS

In researching this book, I have come across many wonderful establishments, the best of which I have included here. I am are sure that many of you will also come across appealing hotels, inns, restaurants, guesthouses, shops, and attractions. Please don't keep them to yourself. Share your experiences, especially if you want to comment on places that have been included in this edition that have changed for the worse. You can address your letters to:

Elizabeth Hansen
Frommer's Australia '92–'93
c/o Prentice Hall Travel
15 Columbus Circle
New York, NY 10023

A DISCLAIMER

Readers are advised that prices fluctuate in the course of time and travel information changes under the impact of the varied and volatile factors that affect the travel industry. Neither the author nor the publisher can be held responsible for the experiences of readers while traveling. Readers are invited to write to the publisher with ideas, comments, and suggestions for future editions.

SAFETY ADVISORY

Whenever you're traveling in an unfamiliar city or country, stay alert. Be aware of your immediate surroundings. Wear a moneybelt and keep a close eye on your possessions. Be particularly careful with cameras, purses, and wallets, all favorite targets of thieves and pickpockets.

CHAPTER 1

GETTING TO KNOW AUSTRALIA

Australia's wonders attract visitors from all over the world. Some come to see the desolate beauty of the outback; others travel halfway around the globe to witness for themselves the Great Barrier Reef. Many want to cuddle a koala or stroke the head of a joey poking up out of a mother kangaroo's pouch. Birders are fascinated by Australia's colorful winged life, and other people are intrigued by the mysterious Aboriginal culture.

Whatever your reason for heading down under, keep in mind that Australia is about the same size as the 48 contiguous U.S. states, and wandering about without a game plan will get you nowhere—literally. Instead, I hope you'll use this guide to help you decide which areas you want to visit and plan your means of getting there. And while I wouldn't for a minute suggest that you skip Sydney, the Reef, and the Rock, I also hope you'll let me lead you off the beaten path to at least a couple of the small towns and country areas that aren't promoted as tourist destinations.

Australia is a great, big, wonderful country, and it's one I've covered extensively. I want you to enjoy your trip as much as I've enjoyed all of mine, and to that end I look forward to sharing what I've learned with you. My hope is that you will get not only the best possible value for your time and money, but some wonderful memories as well.

1. GEOGRAPHY, FLORA & FAUNA

GEOGRAPHY

The facts belie Australia's youthful appearance. Scientists have determined that the continent dates back 130 million years. Ayers Rock is composed of material deposited in the Precambrian era—over 600 million years ago. The Aborigines have been in residence for at least 40,000 years.

0 | 500 km
0 | 310 mi

Indian Ocean

Timor Sea

Bathurst Island
Melville Island
DARWIN
Katherine

Kununurra
Victoria Hwy.
Lake Argyle
Ord River
KIMBERLEY PLATEAU

Broome
Coastal Hwy.

GREAT SANDY DESERT
TANAMI DE

Port Hedland
West
North

MACDONNELL RANG

GIBSON DESERT
Tropic of Capricorn

Mt Olga
Yular
Ayers R

95
WESTERN AUSTRALIA

Great Northern Hwy.

GREAT VICTORIA DESERT

Brand Hwy.

Geraldton
Kalgoorlie
Nullarbor P

1
94
Great Eastern Hwy.
Eyre Hwy.
1

Rottnest Island
PERTH
Fremantle
Esperance Hwy.
Great Australian Bi

South Coast Hwy.
Esperance

Albany

TASMANIA
Bass Strait
Devonport
Launceston
Tasmania
HOBART

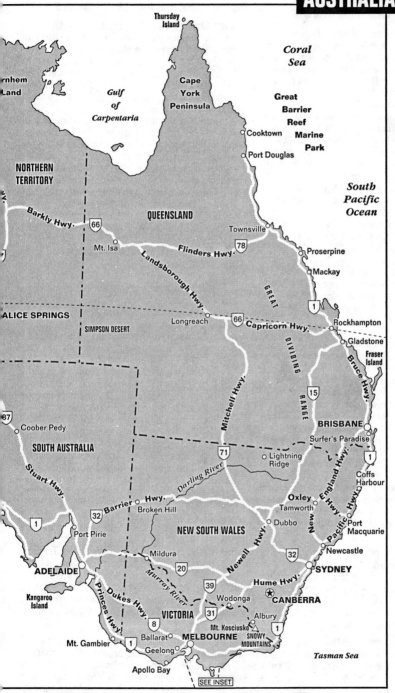

AUSTRALIA

Thursday
Island

Coral
Sea

Cape
York
Peninsula

Great
Barrier
Reef
Marine
Park

Gulf
of
Carpentaria

rnhem
Land

Cooktown
Port Douglas

NORTHERN
TERRITORY

South
Pacific
Ocean

Barkly Hwy.
66
QUEENSLAND
Townsville

Mt. Isa
Flinders Hwy.
78
Proserpine
Mackay

Landsborough Hwy.

ALICE SPRINGS
Longreach
66
Capricorn Hwy.
Rockhampton
Gladstone

SIMPSON DESERT
1
Fraser
Island

87
Coober Pedy

SOUTH AUSTRALIA

Mitchell Hwy.
15
BRISBANE
Surfer's Paradise
1

Stuart Hwy.
71
Lightning
Ridge
Coffs
Harbour

1
Barrier Hwy.
32
Broken Hill
Oxley
Tamworth
Port
Macquarie

Port Pirie
NEW SOUTH WALES
Dubbo

Darling River

ADELAIDE
Mildura
20
Newell Hwy.
32
Newcastle

Murray River
39
Hume Hwy.
SYDNEY

Kangaroo
Island
Dukes Hwy.
Wodonga
CANBERRA

Princes Hwy.
VICTORIA
31
Albury

8
Mt. Kosciusko
1

Mt. Gambier
1
Ballarat
MELBOURNE
SNOWY
MOUNTAINS

Geelong
Tasman Sea

Apollo Bay

SEE INSET

GREAT DIVIDING RANGE

New England Hwy.

Pacific Hwy.

Bruce Hwy.

? DID YOU KNOW . . . ?

- "Waltzing Matilda" is *not* Australia's national anthem. This honor goes to "Advance Australia Fair," a patriotic song composed by Peter Dodds McCormick in about 1878.
- Australia's legendary rabbit problem started when a nostalgic settler let loose 24 English rabbits for hunting in Victoria in 1859.
- The Northern Territory is the only place in Australia where it's legal to keep a dingo as a pet.
- Australia is the largest diamond-producing country in the world.
- Australia has the largest population of free-ranging camels in the world (about 200,000).
- The secret ballot box was pioneered in Victoria in 1856.
- The world's largest cattle station, Strangeray Springs in South Australia, is almost the same size as Belgium.
- Voting is compulsory in Australia.
- Rupert Murdoch, the newspaper/television magnate, was born in Australia in 1931. He became a U.S. citizen in 1985.
- Granny Smith apples were originally grown in New South Wales in the 1860s.
- Before he made it big in the movies, Paul Hogan worked as a bridge rigger and a racetrack bookmaker's assistant.
- The Royal Flying Doctor Service, which provides urgent medical care to outback residents, flies almost 5 million kilometers (3,125,000 miles) annually.

THE REGIONS IN BRIEF

The Outback   When I think of the Australian landscape, I visualize vast expanses of dry reddish-brown earth, punctuated by stately ghost gums whose branches are host to large colorful birds. The sun is shining and the sky is robin's-egg blue. Not all of Australia looks like this, but a lot of it does, and it makes a lasting impression.

The rust color, which comes from iron in the soil, is the predominant hue in the outback. Because of it the middle of the country around Ayers Rock and Alice Springs is commonly called the Red Centre. The clear sky reflects the lack of pollution in the air.

These vast arid expanses extend for great distances without so much as a hill to add variety to the horizon. Australia has the distinction of being not only the driest continent but also the flattest. The average elevation is less than 300 meters (990 ft.), compared with the world's mean of about 700 meters (2,310 ft.).

Ghost gums and other varieties of eucalyptus trees manage to survive the harsh conditions in some areas, but they aren't sufficiently drought-resistant for the most barren places, such as the Nullarbor Plain, whose name means "without trees." Passengers on the Indian Pacific train, which crosses the Nullarbor on the longest stretch of straight track in the world, can look out the windows for hours and not see a living thing, except perhaps a fleeting glimpse of a kangaroo.

Every mainland state except Victoria has its share of this outback wilderness. In addition to the Nullarbor Plain, Western Australia has the Gibson Desert and the Great Sandy Desert. The Simpson Desert covers an area about the size of South Carolina in the adjacent corners of the Northern Territory, Queensland, and South Australia. The huge Great Victoria Desert is close to the Red Centre and also spills into more than one state.

Except for mining towns like Coober Pedy, Mount Isa, Broken Hill, Tennant Creek, and Andamooka, actual settlements do not exist. Instead, families live on large sheep and cattle stations (ranches), where they receive their medical care from the Royal Flying Doctor Service and their children, through two-way radio contact, attend classes via the School of the Air. One of these cattle stations, Strangeray Springs in South Australia, covers 30,028 square kilometers (11,954 square miles) and is almost the same size as Belgium.

The Green Rim   In contrast to the inhospitable outback terrain, a fertile band extends inward from the perimeter of the country, providing an agreeable environment for both humans and animals. In fact, 82% of the population live within 20 kilometers (12½ miles) of the coast. Australians like to joke that their founding fathers knew that future generations would love the beach, so they built all the state capitals near the coast; but they couldn't put Canberra, the federal capital, there because the politicians wouldn't get any work done.

Australia is about the same size as the "lower 48" U.S. states, but because it occupies an entire continent, it has much more coastline—36,700 kilometers (22,754 miles) as compared with 19,812 kilometers (12,283 miles) in the United States. The beaches created by the Indian Ocean on the west and the South Pacific Ocean on the east are some of the most beautiful in the world.

The Great Barrier Reef   The Great Barrier Reef lies off the Queensland coast and extends for some 2,000 kilometers (1,240 miles) from Gladstone to the Gulf of Papua near New Guinea. It is the largest coral structure in the world and is considered one of the great wonders. The reef and its unique array of bird, plant, and marine life are discussed in Chapter 10.

Mountains & Rivers   In addition to beaches and barren outback, Australia also has mountains and rivers. The highest point in the country is New South Wales's Mount Kosciusko, which reaches a height of 2,228 meters (7,352 ft.). This peak is in the Snowy Mountains region of the Great Dividing Range. It is from the southern portion of these mountains that the Murray River, one of the nation's longest, emerges. The other major river, the Darling, has its headwaters in the eastern highlands of New South Wales and southern Queensland. The Murray-Darling system flows for a total of 5,300 kilometers (3,286 miles) until it enters the ocean in South Australia.

FLORA

The fertile coastal strip that nearly encircles the country contains not only beaches but also the "bush," or what non-Australians would call "forest." In most zones the woodland areas are dominated by eucalyptus trees. Approximately 550 varieties of gum (eucalyptus) trees thrive in Australia, and their identification has been the subject of several books. Some notable examples include the jarrah in Western Australia, the messmate stringybark in Victoria, and the spotted gum in New South Wales and Queensland.

Like the gum trees, about 600 species of wattle (acacia) are found in Australia. These colorful shrubs provide vivid yellow flowers that can be seen throughout the country; the golden wattle is the unofficial national floral emblem. Red bottlebrushes and grevilleas, dramatic banksias, and pretty baronias, which are native only to Australia, are other prominent wildflowers. While all the states have endemic flowering plants, Western Australia has by far the greatest number.

Rain forests, another feature of the coastal strip, are located in damp areas on the eastern side of the mainland as well as in Tasmania; they range from temperate in the south to tropical in the north. Rain forests teem with plant and bird life and are the antithesis of the arid outback. National parks such as Lamington near the New South Wales–Queensland border provide an opportunity for visitors to witness the dark, dense, humid splendor of this special kind of forest, with its characteristic strangler figs, bird's-nest ferns, staghorn ferns, and native orchids.

IMPRESSIONS

Here I am happy to say we are in full enjoyment of peace and plenty. The colony has improved equal to my most sanguine expectations. My situation is one of considerable fatigue and exertion but this I do not consider any hardship.
—LETTER FROM LACHLAN MACQUARIE, GOVERNOR OF THE NEW SOUTH WALES COLONY, 1812

Australia has a marvellous sky and air and blue clarity and a hoary sort of land beneath it, like a Sleeping Princess on whom the dust of ages has settled. Wonder if she'll ever get up.
—D. H. LAWRENCE, 1922

FAUNA

The variety and drama of the country's landscape are rivaled only by the animals that inhabit it. Nowhere else but in Australia do kangaroos and emus dash across the highway, and nowhere else is home to as many large, colorful, noisy birds.

NATIVE ANIMALS

Most of the unique native animals are marsupials, whose young are born at a very early stage of development and are carried and nursed in an external abdominal pouch while they continue to mature. Kangaroos are marsupials, as are their equally well known cousins, the koalas. Other members of the family include sugar gliders, possums, quokkas, wallabies, bandicoots, Tasmanian devils, and wombats—this last animal being almost as cute as the koala but, lacking a good press agent, not nearly as popular.

Most everyone knows koalas *aren't* bears, in spite of their cuddly, teddy-bear appearance. These marsupials eat only the tender stems, shoots, and leaves of eucalyptus trees. Because of their diet, koalas have a distinctive body odor that isn't as appealing as their countenance.

Much less is commonly known about kangaroos, and many people are surprised to learn that there are 45 species in Australia. I find it fascinating that mama roos have a continuous flow of reproduction: one joey outside the pouch, one inside, and one embryo on hold. In this way the female can produce offspring long after the male has disappeared. She is also capable of limiting reproduction during droughts.

There are two species of crocodiles in Australia: the freshwater type and the saltwater, or estuarine, variety. It is important to know the difference between the two, especially if one is fond of swimming: The freshwater type is generally not a problem, but the saltwater croc can make a quick meal of a horse, cow, or human.

Snakes, too, can make their presence known. Many, like the death adder, the taipan, and the brown snake, are poisonous. Since most travelers will not have the time or interest to learn the identity of each type of snake, it's a good idea to leave *all* of them alone.

And on the subject of danger, it's important to know that Australian waters are home to about 20 different kinds of sharks. While some of these are harmless, white pointers, blue pointers, tiger sharks, and whaler sharks have been involved in attacks on humans. The eastern seaboard, particularly, is heavily infested; therefore, most swimming areas are not only carefully patrolled but also protected with shark nets.

Not everything that swims in Australia is ferocious. You'll be lucky to catch a glimpse of the shy platypus; fairy penguins come ashore nightly on Victoria's Phillip Island without paying any attention to the human entourage assembled to watch them; the seals on South Australia's Kangaroo Island don't disturb visitors who roam through their colony as long as they keep a respectful distance from any pups; Monkey Mia, on the coast of Western Australia, is the only place in the world where you can pet wild dolphins; and most of the marine life on the Great Barrier Reef is perfectly safe.

In addition to aquatic animals, more than 700 species of birds live in Australia. Emus are the largest and, like the strange-looking cassowaries, can't fly. But they aren't as colorful as galahs, sulfur-crested cockatoos, rainbow lorikeets, or king parrots. Other notable birds are the kookaburra, known for its raucous laugh, and the black swan, the symbol of Western Australia.

IMPORTED WILDLIFE

Some of the animals associated with Australia are not indigenous to the continent. They have been introduced, and several have caused unexpected problems. The dingo, or wild dog, is thought to have been brought in by the Aborigines 3,000 to 8,000 years ago. In spite of fences thousands of miles long, dingoes continue to prey on sheep and are classified as a noxious pest. Rabbits, imported by early British settlers, reproduce at such a rate that they still threaten the livestock industry by eating grass intended for cattle and sheep, a serious depredation where rain and water are scarce. And water buffalo, introduced in the north during the first half of the 19th century, are currently the target of an eradication program because their presence threatens the natural ecology. Camels were brought in and used by early explorers as a means of traversing the island continent's vast deserts.

2. HISTORY, POLITICS & THE ECONOMY

HISTORY

To begin at the beginning would mean going back 40,000 years to the time when Australia's first inhabitants, the Aborigines, arrived from Asia. For our purposes, however, it will suffice to start with the 17th-century explorations of Dutch, Portuguese, and British navigators. These ambitious sailors confirmed a theory that had been proposed in the 2nd century: that an unknown southern landmass, a *terra australis incognita,* lay to the south of Asia.

EUROPEAN DISCOVERY

Willem Jansz, a Dutch explorer, was the first white man to set foot on the mysterious land when he went ashore on the Queensland coast in 1606. Another Dutchman, Abel Tasman, discovered Tasmania in 1642; however, it was the British who actually took possession of the land when Capt. James Cook sailed the *Endeavour* into Botany Bay (near present-day Sydney) in 1770, claimed the east coast of the island continent, and named it New South Wales.

THE FIRST FLEET

For King George III, Captain Cook's timing couldn't have been better. Britain was having a hard time controlling rebellious colonists in America, and the monarch was looking for a new place to deposit the overflow from English jails; after America won the War of Independence in 1781, the situation became critical. On May 13, 1787, Capt. Arthur Phillip was dispatched from England with 1,030 people, 736 of whom were convicts. He and his fleet of 11 ships arrived in Botany Bay on January 18, 1788. However, they found conditions unsuitable and left after 8 days, finally settling nearby at Port Jackson, commonly known now as Sydney Harbour. Today Australia Day, the anniversary of the arrival of the First Fleet on January 26, is an important holiday celebrated throughout the nation.

RELUCTANT SETTLERS

Between 1788 and 1868, 160,000 criminals were transported from England. Some of these men and women had committed minor acts of thievery or disobedience and were really victims of the social conditions in their home country. The convicts were used to build the new settlement, and without their labor, modern-day Sydney would

DATELINE

- **40,000 B.C.** *Terra australis incognita* is inhabited by Aboriginal people.
- **1606** Dutch explorer Willem Jansz lands on Queensland coast.
- **1642** Abel Tasman discovers Tasmania.
- **1770** Capt. James Cook sails the *Endeavour* into Botany Bay and takes possession of the land for Britain.
- **1781** America wins War of Independence.
- **1787** Capt. Arthur Phillip dispatched from England with first convicts.
- **1788** Captain Phillip and the First Fleet arrive in Port Jackson.
- **1788–1868** Convicts transported from England to the colony of Australia.
- **1793** The first free settlers arrive.
- **1797** John Macarthur introduces merino sheep.
- **1807** First ship-

(continues)

be lacking some of its most impressive structures. Francis Greenway, who was transported for forgery and arrived in Port Jackson in 1814, was one of the colony's important architects. Since he had trained as an architect, he was given a "ticket of leave" and allowed the freedom to ply his trade. He subsequently designed the lighthouse at the south entrance to Sydney Harbour, St. James Church in Sydney, Hyde Park Barracks in Sydney, the Court House in Windsor, and the building that is now the home of the New South Wales Conservatorium of Music.

Like Greenway, many of the convicts elected to remain in the new colony when they finally attained their freedom. Some of them participated in the exploration of the interior, which, because of the rugged terrain, proceeded slowly. In 1813 Gregory Blaxland, William Charles Wentworth, and William Lawson crossed the Blue Mountains west of Sydney and in so doing provided the colony access to the fertile western plains. In 1860 Robert O'Hara Burke and William Wills were the first Europeans to cross the continent from south to north; their journey ended tragically when they starved to death during the return trip.

When gold was discovered in Victoria in 1851 and in Western Australia in 1863, the original settlers were joined by droves of pioneers from all over the world. By 1860 the population of Australia was over one million.

FEDERATION & THE GREAT WARS

The colony announced its intention to become independent of Britain in 1900, and on January 1, 1901, the Commonwealth of Australia was proclaimed. Nevertheless, in 1914 Australia followed Britain into World War I and, along with New Zealand, sustained devastating casualties on the Gallipoli Peninsula. A large display in the War Memorial in Canberra tells the moving story of this terrible siege.

As part of the ANZAC (Australian and New Zealand Army Corps) forces, Australia again followed Britain into war in 1939. Australia also hosted over a million U.S. servicepeople during their respites from the war in the Pacific. Among these was Gen. Douglas MacArthur, who held some of his important strategy meetings in the Australia Hotel in Melbourne.

The Japanese bombing of Darwin in February 1942 brought the war close to home, and the help of the American forces in the decisive Battle of the Coral Sea in May 1942 solidified the already warm relationship between the United States and Australia. To date, in this century, Australia and New Zealand are the only allies that have fought alongside America in every major war.

Australia entered the Vietnam conflict in 1965 and was a popular R&R destination for thousands of American service personnel during those years.

AUSTRALIA TODAY

In 1972 the White Australia Policy, which had prevented Asians and other nonwhites from immigrating to Australia, formally ended. In 1986, during a visit to Canberra, Queen Elizabeth II signed a proclamation that severed some of Australia's legal and political ties with Britain. Finally, on January 26, 1988, Australia celebrated the 200th anniversary of the landing of the First Fleet at Port Jackson.

POLITICS

Australia's government is an interesting amalgam of British tradition and American format. While the official head of state is Queen Elizabeth II, the three-tier system of federal, state, and local governments closely resembles that of the United States.

THE FEDERAL GOVERNMENT

The country's official name is the Commonwealth of Australia. It is an independent self-governing member of the Commonwealth of Nations. All of the members of this group were at one time part of the former British Empire, and they continue to recognize the British monarch as their titular head. The queen is represented at the federal level by a governor-general and at the state level by governors.

Parliament, the legislative body, consists of the House of Representatives, where the number of members depends on the population of each state, and the Senate, with 12 senators for each state and 2 for each territory.

National elections are held at least every 3 years and voting is compulsory. The two major political parties are Labour and Liberal; the minor parties are National and Democrat. The leader of the party or coalition that gets the majority in the House of Representatives becomes the prime minister, or head of government.

THE STATES

Australia consists of six states (New South Wales, Queensland, Western Australia, South Australia, Victoria, and Tasmania) and two internal territories (the Australian Capital Territory and the Northern Territory). The federal capital, Canberra, is in the Australian Capital Territory. Several external territories are also under Australia's control, including Norfolk Island, Christmas Island, Macquarie Island, Cocos Island, Lord Howe Island, and part of Antarctica.

Each state has its own parliament, which, with the exception of Queensland's, consists of two chambers. The leader at the state level is called the premier.

Originally there were six separate colonies, but they became a federation of states in 1901. When Australia's founding fathers wrote the constitution and designed the system of government, they were able to pick and choose what they thought best from the examples of other countries. Their Anglo-American blend is unique and seems to be working well.

THE ECONOMY

The financial management of the island continent also represents a combination of styles. Founded "on the

DATELINE

tion is 3,773,801. Aborigines are not counted.

- **1902** Women granted the right to vote.
- **1908** Canberra chosen as the site for the federal capital.
- **1911** American Walter Burley Griffin designs Canberra.
- **1914** Australia enters World War I.
- **1920** QANTAS founded.
- **1927** Federal capital moved from Melbourne to Canberra.
- **1928** The Flying Doctor Service is founded.
- **1932** Sydney Harbour Bridge opens.
- **1939** Australia enters World War II.
- **1942** Darwin bombed. Japanese submarines detected in Sydney Harbour. The Battle of the Coral Sea takes place.
- **1950** Australian troops join U.N. forces in Korea.
- **1950s** Humane treatment of Aborigines becomes an issue.
- **1951** ANZUS Security Treaty signed in Washington, D.C., by Australia, New Zealand, and the United States.
- **1956** Olympic Games held in Melbourne.
- **1960** Aborigines
(continues)

DATELINE

granted citizenship.
- **1961** Extensive iron ore deposits found in Western Australia.
- **1965** Australia enters Vietnam conflict.
- **1966** Decimal currency introduced.
- **1967** Aborigines included in the national census for the first time.
- **1969** Arbitration Commission grants equal pay to women.
- **1970** Large anti-war demonstrations take place.
- **1971** Australia ends fighting role in Vietnam.
- **1972** White Australia Policy formally ended.
- **1973** Sydney Opera House completed.
- **1974** Cyclone Tracy devastates Darwin.
- **1978** Aboriginal Land Rights Act returns some tribal territory to native people.
- **1983** Ayers Rock handed back to Aborigines.
- **1983** *Australia II* wins America's Cup Race.
- **1986** Queen Elizabeth II signs proclamation that severs some of Australia's ties with Britain.
- **1988** Australia celebrates 200th anniversary of the landing of the First
(continues)

sheep's back" and known as a leading producer of wool, beef, lamb, wheat, sugar, and dairy products, Australia has more recently turned its attention to export-oriented mining and energy products. The nation's mineral resources include silver, lead, zinc, oil, gas, bauxite, coal, iron ore, uranium, copper, nickel, and gold. Manufacturing is also a major source of income.

In Australia the free-enterprise system is moderated by protective tariffs and controlled marketing of agricultural products. Considerable taxes are imposed on imported goods. Less than 10% of the federal budget is spent on defense, and more than half goes for social security, health, education, and general public services.

The majority of employed people in Australia belong to trade unions, which are extremely powerful. Nearly everyone works a 38-hour week and receives 4 weeks annual vacation. Some Aussies complain that taxes are too high, the unions are too strong, and too much welfare money is doled out. Others rejoice in the opportunity to "have a go," to improve their status in life via the free-enterprise system.

3. FAMOUS AUSTRALIANS

Sir Joseph Banks (1743–1820) English botanist who accompanied Capt. James Cook aboard the *Endeavour*. He served as a government consultant on the colony of New South Wales, overseeing the survey of the Australian coastline and influencing significant political appointments.

William Bligh (1754–1817) Appointed governor of New South Wales in 1806, but probably better known as the protagonist in the mutiny aboard the HMS *Bounty* while the vessel was under his command in 1789.

Evonne Fay Cawley [née Goolagong] (1951–) One of Australia's best-known tennis players. In 1971 she became the first Aborigine to compete at Wimbledon. She won the women's singles title that year and again in 1980.

Ian, Gregory & Trevor Chappell (1943– , 1948– , and 1952– , respectively) Three brothers who all became great Australian cricketers.

Margaret Court [née Smith] (1942–) The first Australian to win the women's singles at Wimbledon. She was ranked number one women's seed in the world for 3 years from 1962. In 1967 Court retired from tennis to marry, but returned the following year.

Peter Ingle Finch (1916–77) Star of dozens of movies and stage plays. He won an Oscar for best actor for his performance in *Network*. The award was made posthumously in 1977.

Errol Flynn (1909–59) Film actor who achieved international recognition in Hollywood from the mid-1930s while under contract to Warner Brothers. He was often cast as a swashbuckling hero.

Miles Franklin (1879–1954) Author of *My Bril-*

liant Career (1901) and several other novels. She lived in the United States in the early 1900s where she became involved with the feminist movement. She also lived in England for a short time, returning to Australia in 1933. Under the terms of her will the Miles Franklin Award is made annually for an outstanding Australian novel.

Dawn Fraser (1937–) Swimming champion who competed in 1956, 1960, and 1964 Olympic Games. She has won more medals in competition than any other swimmer. In 1972 she became the first Australian to be inducted to the Swimming Hall of Fame in Fort Lauderdale, Florida.

DATELINE

Fleet at Port Jackson.
• **1991** Australia's population reaches 17 million.

Germaine Greer (1939–) Author and academic who achieved prominence in the feminist movement with the publication of *The Female Eunuch* (1970).

Dame Nellie Melba (1861–1931) World-renowned soprano who received her first training in her native Melbourne before leaving for Europe. She made her operatic debut in Brussels in 1887 and later appeared at Covent Garden and in Paris and New York. She returned to Australia several times for concert tours and gave singing lessons at the University of Melbourne in 1913. She was appointed DBE (Dame of the British Empire) in 1918.

Albert Namatjira (1902–59) Aboriginal artist who spent most of his life at the Hermannsburg Mission near Alice Springs in the Northern Territory. His watercolor landscapes brought him financial success and national recognition. In 1954 he was presented to Queen Elizabeth II.

Sir Sidney Nolan (1917–) Internationally recognized artist best known for his series depicting events in the life of bushranger Ned Kelly. He was knighted in 1981.

Dame Joan Sutherland (1926–) One of the world's great operatic sopranos. She made her Sydney debut in 1947 and joined the Covent Garden Opera Company in 1952. Her final performance before entering retirement was at the Sydney Opera House in 1990.

Sir Charles Edward Kingsford Smith (1897–1935) Pioneer of Australian aviation who established a number of ambitious records. These included the first flight across the Pacific and the first trans-Tasman flight between New South Wales and New Zealand (both in 1928). He received a knighthood in 1932 and disappeared off the coast of Burma in 1935. Sydney's international airport is named in his honor.

Peter Weir (1944–) Film director and writer whose successes include *Picnic at Hanging Rock* (1975), *The Last Wave* (1977), *Gallipoli* (1981), *The Year of Living Dangerously* (1982), and *Witness* (1985).

Patrick White (1912–90) Nobel Prize–winning novelist whose books include *Voss* (1957), *The Vivisector* (1970), *A Fringe of Leaves* (1976), and *The Twyborn Affair* (1979). He has also written numerous short stories, a screenplay, and six plays.

4. ART, ARCHITECTURE & LITERATURE

For a long time the majority of Australia's cultural efforts reflected the dominance of England. Artists and performers strove to imitate styles popular in Britain and the rest

IMPRESSIONS

It does not read like history, but like the most beautiful lies. And all of a fresh new sort, no mouldy old stale ones. It is full of surprises, and adventures, and incongruities, and incredibilities: but they all are true, they all happened.
—MARK TWAIN, ON HIS VISIT TO AUSTRALIA IN 1895

of Europe, and when one of them became successful, he or she often failed to claim the island continent as home. Anything written, painted, designed, or produced in Australia was considered inferior to creations coming from abroad.

Eventually a few brave pioneers began working in a style that reflected the country's unique historical and geographical background, and when their efforts received world acclaim, the local population reluctantly accepted the idea that something done "Aussie style" could have merit. Today there is great enthusiasm for the arts in Australia as writers, artists, filmmakers, actors, and composers continue to experiment with and refine the country's cultural style.

ART

Australia's first artists were the Aborigines. They painted characters from their spiritual Dreamtime on the walls of caves, on rocks and bark, and even on their bodies. Though their art is a ritual part of their beliefs and will never fully be understood by outsiders, it is greatly admired for its haunting beauty. Recently some Aboriginal artists at the Papunya settlement near Alice Springs have started painting their traditional earth-tone designs on canvas, and these have been well received at galleries around the world. The best known of the Aboriginal landscape artists is Albert Namatjira, whose richly toned watercolors gained worldwide attention in the 1930s and 1940s.

The first European-Australian art emerged in the 1880s, when artists Tom Roberts, Frederick McCubbin, Charles Conder, and Arthur Streeton established the Heidelberg School and created dramatic impressionist paintings of Australia's landscape. These differed from the French impressionist style in frequently including a dramatic incident such as a cattle stampede or a bush fire.

Other, more recent artists have retold the nation's legends by painting in series. Best known for this method is Sidney Nolan, who, through his work, has shared the stories of the ill-fated Burke and Wills expedition, the tragedy of Gallipoli, and the adventures of the popular folk hero and outlaw Ned Kelly.

The Trial of Ned Kelly is on display at the Australian National Gallery in Canberra, one of the best places in the country to see Australian art. The National Gallery of Victoria in Melbourne houses another excellent collection. It's not surprising, given its beauty, that many artists, including Sidney Nolan, have painted realistic images of Australia's rugged outback.

In the fashion field, contemporary artist Ken Done (rhymes with phone) has won international attention. His popular colorful designs, which depict Australia, particularly Sydney, at its happiest, adorn everything from T-shirts to bed linens. Done started his professional life in advertising after studying at the East Sydney Technical College, where he was told he'd never make it as an artist. Today, at shops all over Australia and in several other countries, people are standing in line to buy his designs. They might even push, grab, and bump, as I discovered recently when I attended the half-price sale at the Done Art and Design shop in The Rocks area of Sydney.

ARCHITECTURE

Australia's climate, terrain, and local building materials lend a distinctive character to the country's architecture. Take, for example, the Sydney Opera House. Though designed by Danish architect Joern Utzon, this famous structure is very much an

---

IMPRESSIONS

In Australia alone is to be found the Grotesque, the Weird, the strange scribblings of nature learning how to write . . . the subtle charm of this fantastic land of monstrosities.
—Marcus Clarke, Journalist, 1846–81

Australian building. The unique series-of-sails construction suits its position on the water and mirrors the boats that continuously cross the harbor. The white tiles that cover the roof reflect the warm Australian sun, and the bold character of the building reflects the Australian spirit.

In Canberra, the nation's capital, one finds a similar emphasis on the local landscape. Designed by American architect Walter Burley Griffin in 1911, the city is built on a plain and has the expansive, open feel typical of much of the country. Low-rise buildings complement the natural topography; commercial and housing tracts are decentralized like the mini-settlements that dot the outback. Even the new Parliament House, designed by the American firm of Mitchell, Giurgola, and Thorp, and opened in 1988 as part of the bicentennial festivities, is built into a hill so that it blends with the environment rather than dominates it.

Environmental conditions also loomed large for Philip Cox & Partners, who within the last decade designed the Yulara Tourist Village, located between Ayers Rock and the Olgas in central Australia. The self-contained village, catering to 5,000 visitors a day, has its own power, water, communications, and waste-disposal systems. Because of the harsh, desert environment, tentlike fabric roofs providing shade from the strong sun were incorporated into the design.

The early pioneers were quick to realize the need to create architecture suitable for their new surroundings. Their original efforts consisted of "wattle and daub" huts—logs and saplings covered with mud, pipe clay, and lime. Later they modified the Georgian, Victorian, and Edwardian homes popular in England to suit Australia's climate. Galvanized iron roofs collected precious moisture from the night air—moisture that could be routed to and stored in barrels—and verandas provided shade. Wide eaves and bull-nosed iron hoods over windows were other attempts to keep things cool. In hot, humid Queensland, the settlers built houses on raised platforms supported by stilts for protection against the heat as well as floods and snakes.

Many of the early homes boasted cast-iron railings, balustrades, and trim that had originally come out to the colony as ship's ballast on sailing ships. Later ironwork was done by skilled craftspeople who emerged from the gold rush and other mining endeavors. The majority of colonial buildings in Sydney were constructed of local sandstone; native timbers, such as cedar and jarrah, and marble from New South Wales and Queensland lent character to the emerging Australian architecture.

HIGH-RISE PIONEERS

The first tall buildings appeared in the 1920s, but it wasn't until the arrival of Austrian architect Harry Seidler in 1948 that skyscraper construction really blossomed. From 1961 to 1967 Seidler designed the 170-meter (561-ft.) glass-and-concrete Australia Square tower, which for many years dominated Sydney's skyline. Today this building is overshadowed by others that have grown up around it, such as Sydney's Centrepoint, which stands at 305 meters (1,006 ft.).

As Australia's buildings have become taller, shinier, and more sophisticated, architects have found new ways to cater to the prevailing climatic conditions. One way is by providing open spaces at ground level, often with a cooling fountain and shady places for the public to sit. These plazas and courtyards have created an Aussie institution: the open-air lunch. From noon to about 1:30pm, office workers and vendors selling snacks fill these areas to capacity; the addition of free concerts in many cities adds to the carnival atmosphere. At the end of the lunch break everyone disappears, and the canyons created by surrounding tall buildings seem somber and citified once again.

LITERATURE

Is there a person alive who hasn't heard of *The Thorn Birds?* Colleen McCullough's blockbuster novel about the Cleary clan has sold 14 million copies since it first appeared in 1977 and became a television miniseries. While the popularity of this book was unusual, its subject matter is typical of much of Australian literature.

"We live on the perimeter and are obsessed by the centre," explains one of the country's best-known literary critics. The theme of striving to understand the rest of the country, to bridge the psychological gaps created by great distances, runs throughout the nation's writing. This longing has replaced the homesickness for Britain that characterized Australia's earliest novels.

Patrick White addressed "the vacancy at the centre of Australia" in his 1957 novel *Voss*, and David Malouf and Richard Meale readdressed it when they turned *Voss* into an opera. In 1973 White won the Nobel Prize in Literature for his work *The Eye of the Storm*. Popular adventure writer Jon Cleary tells about a year in the life of a sheep drover's family in *The Sundowners*, later made into a movie. Xavier Herbert's *Poor Fellow, My Country*, published in 1980, seeks to help us understand the life and values of the Aborigines. Thomas Keneally writes about the mysterious Northern Territory in *Outback* (1984). In 1982 Keneally won Britain's prestigious Booker McConnell prize for *Schindler's Ark* (U.S. title, *Schlinder's List*).

BUSH POETS

While White, Cleary, Herbert, and Keneally tell about the rural areas of Australia in contemporary terms, much can be learned by reading the works of another group of writers—one that emerged in the 1890s. Andrew Barton "Banjo" Patterson, Henry Lawson, Harry "Breaker" Morant, and others wrote "bush ballads" that appeared in *The Bulletin*, a literary journal. These rough-and-ready guys wrote from personal experience and extolled the superiority of bush life. Patterson is best known for *The Man from Snowy River and Other Verses*, which was published in 1895, and for "Waltzing Matilda," Australia's favorite song.

SUCCESSFUL EXPATRIATES

The patriotic bush poets never wanted to live anywhere other than Australia, but many of the country's writers have felt the need to go overseas to gain perspective on their homeland. Christina Stead (1904–83) was born and educated in Australia but spent most of her life abroad. She lived in London when she wrote *Seven Poor Men of Sydney* and continued writing during the time she lived in Paris and America. Randolph Stow (*Tourmaline, Visitants, The Girl Green as Elderflower*), has lived in England since 1966. George Johnston (1912–70), who won the Literary Guild Award (U.S.) for his novel *Closer to the Sun*, lived in Greece for 10 years. Colleen McCullough lives on Norfolk Island. Robert Hughes, author of the best-seller *The Fatal Shore*, lives in America.

CONTEMPORARY AUSTRALIAN WRITERS

A subtle resentment exists between the Australian writers who stay at home and those who choose to become expatriates. Another not-so-subtle war is waged between the men and women of Australian literature. Let me say that Helen Garner, Elizabeth Jolley, and Kate Grenville are easily three of the country's most interesting writers. Garner's *Monkey Grip* won a National Book Award and was made into a film in 1981. Jolley is best known for her highly praised *Milk and Honey*. Grenville's first novel, *Lilian's Story*, won the Australian/Vogel Literary Award. Germaine Greer achieved worldwide fame in 1970 with *The Female Eunuch*. These women are following in the tradition of excellence established by Henry Handel Richardson (Henrietta Robertson, 1870–1946) and by Miles Franklin (1879–1954) who wrote about the outback in *My Brilliant Career*, a book that made her famous.

Before I am accused of prejudice, let me add that contemporary novelists Peter Carey and David Malouf are also very exciting writers. Carey's *Bliss* won the Miles Franklin Award and was made into a controversial Australian film. David Malouf has penned six volumes of verse, two novels, and four novellas.

Among cnildren's books, Pamela Travers's *Mary Poppins* (1934) and Norman Lindsay's *The Magic Pudding* (1918) are classics.

5. RELIGION, MYTH & FOLKLORE

RELIGION

The majority of Australians are Christians, and of these, most belong to the Anglican Church and the Roman Catholic Church. The chaplain of the First Fleet conducted a Church of England (Anglican) service in the fledgling colony on February 3, 1788, 8 days after the ships landed. The first church was built at Sydney Cove in 1793. Today there are about four million Anglicans (Episcopalians) in Australia; in 1981 the denomination officially changed its name to the Anglican Church of Australia.

The Uniting Church, formed in 1977 by a union of Methodists, Presbyterians, and Congregationalists, is another major Protestant denomination.

Although there were Catholics aboard the First Fleet, there were no priests in the colony for more than a decade. The first authorized mass was celebrated in 1803 by an Irish convict. About four million Australians are members of the Catholic Church.

The Mormons (the Church of Jesus Christ of Latter-day Saints) and the Brethren were both established in the 1850s. Other religious groups in Australia since the 19th century include: the Christadelphians, the Christian Scientists, and the Seventh-Day Adventists.

The first Muslims also arrived in the 19th century. They came to Australia from India, Pakistan, and Afghanistan. Their ability to work with camels and their experience in arid environments was valuable to the early explorers. Today, Muslims comprise the largest non-Christian religion in Australia.

Large-scale immigration of Jewish people began as a result of their persecution in Europe in the 1930s. The largest Jewish communities are in the capital cities, particularly Melbourne and Sydney.

MYTH & FOLKLORE

ABORIGINAL BELIEFS

In Aboriginal Dreamtime myths, the mountains, oceans, springs, sky, sun, moon, stars, and all other natural features were formed by spirits, who afterward returned to the Dreamtime, a sort of Aboriginal heaven. "Dreaming places" are sacred spots associated with a particular mythical ancestor; some can be visited only by initiated males. According to Aboriginal tradition, man can draw on the power of the Dreamtime by the reenactment of various myths and the practice of certain rituals and ceremonies.

One of the most potent of the Aboriginal religious beliefs involved "pointing the bone." In this procedure, an animal or human bone (the forearm of a dead medicine man was preferred) was pointed toward a victim while those doing the pointing sang ritual chants. It was believed that the bone would travel invisibly to the victim and pierce his body. So strongly was this belief held that once someone learned that the bone had been pointed at him, death actually followed.

MODERN HEROES

Burke & Wills While spiritual ancestors are held in high esteem by the Aborigines, other Australians have their own heroes. Two of these, Robert O'Hara Burke and William John Wills, were the first Europeans to cross Australia from south to north. Their expedition left Melbourne in August 1860 and established a supply camp at Cooper's Creek, nearly the north-south midpoint. From the camp Burke, Wills, and two others set out for the Gulf of Carpentaria on the north coast. After they had reached their goal, it took them 2 months to journey back to the supply camp; when the three of them arrived (one had died en route), they discovered that the men who had been ordered to wait for them had left that morning. Burke, Wills, and John King, desperate for supplies, attempted to reach a distant police outpost at Mount Hopeless. In the meantime, part of the original expedition returned to Cooper's Creek and, because they didn't find the message left by Burke, set off for Melbourne. In the end, Burke and Wills starved to death at the base camp, while King was saved by Aborigines.

Ned Kelly   Like the tale of the ill-fated Burke and Wills expedition, the story of Ned Kelly, Australia's most famous outlaw, or "bushranger," has been retold in paintings, literature, and film. In April 1878 Ned shot a trooper who was arresting his brother Dan for horse stealing. The two Kellys fled into the bush, where they were joined by Joe Byrne and Stephen Hart. The Kelly Gang, as they were known, proceeded to ambush and kill three police constables, rob banks, hold up stage-coaches, and generally wreak havoc. These men became folk heroes much the way Jesse James did in America. Ned Kelly was hanged in Melbourne at the age of 26.

Breaker Morant   Harry "Breaker" Morant also became an Aussie hero, but for entirely different reasons. Morant, a bush poet and contemporary of "Banjo" ("Waltzing Matilda") Patterson, was sent to South Africa to fight in the Boer War, Britain's conflict with Dutch colonists. During the war Britain needed a scapegoat to resolve the controversial shooting of several Boer prisoners. Lieutenant Morant was court-martialed for his supposed role in the incident, and was executed.

Kingsford Smith   A pioneer in the field of aviation, Kingsford Smith represents yet another type of hero. In 1928 Smith and Charles Ulm flew from California to Brisbane in 83 hours and 38 minutes. They later made a nonstop flight across Australia and the first trans-Tasman flight to New Zealand. Smith continued to break records, making the first solo flight from England to Australia. He was knighted in 1932 and disappeared while flying in 1935.

Phar Lap   Can a horse be a hero? If so, Phar Lap, winner of the 1930 Melbourne Cup, would certainly qualify. Although he is considered Australia's most famous racehorse, Kiwis are quick to point out that he was actually born in New Zealand. Phar Lap won 37 of 51 starts in his career, later dying mysteriously in the United States. A movie, entitled simply *Phar Lap,* was made about his life, and his stuffed body is on display in the Museum of Victoria in Melbourne.

Although Australians are not quick to idolize public figures, they make an exception in the area of sports—many of the country's contemporary heroes are, like Phar Lap, outstanding athletes.

6. CULTURAL & SOCIAL LIFE

THE PEOPLE

Australia's 17 million people comprise one of the most multicultural societies on earth. In addition to the native Aborigines, immigrants and descendants of immigrants from 163 different nations make up the total population. This variety creates many advantages and is generally considered to be a positive factor. At the same time, many Aussies feel uncomfortable with the lack of a clear-cut national identity, an issue that receives frequent coverage in the popular press, usually under a headline such as "Who Are We?"

THE ABORIGINES

At the time of the first white settlement in Australia, more than 300,000 Aborigines were living on the land. Their traditional society had complex systems of religion, law, and social organization, and tribal groups lived a nomadic hunter-gatherer existence. Each tribe's territory was connected to its mythical ancestors through features of the landscape, and because of this spiritual relationship, little incentive existed for one group to take over the territory of another. The Aborigines had no concept of ownership; instead, they considered themselves caretakers of the land. Their ability to survive in Australia's harsh environment was most remarkable. They dealt imaginatively with a scant water supply, and were expert in stalking game over long distances before killing it with a spear or boomerang.

According to Aboriginal religious beliefs, creation of the world took place in the "Dreamtime," an undefined period when their ancestors emerged from the night, carried out their tasks, and sank back into the earth, leaving their spirits to live on in people and in such places as rock formations, watering holes, and plants. Various rituals and ceremonies reenacted Dreamtime myths and were potent sources of power.

The advent of European settlement had a devastating effect on the natives, and their numbers declined drastically because of disease, alcohol, and the ruthless manner in which they were treated. Conflict arose when the colonists attempted to move tribes off the land to which they had strong spiritual ties. The Aborigines were considered subhuman pests and in some areas, most notably Tasmania, were actually hunted like animals. By 1947 their count had declined to 76,000.

It wasn't until the late 1950s that humane treatment of Aborigines became an issue in Australia. In 1960 Aborigines were granted citizenship, and in 1967 a change in the constitution permitted them to be included in the national census. The Aboriginal Land Rights Act of 1978 returned significant tribal territory to its former owners, and in 1983 the government handed back the title to Uluru National Park (Ayers Rock), one of the most sacred Aboriginal sites.

Today, with improved health and welfare programs, the Aborigines account for about 1% of the population, approximately 160,000 people. Nearly half of them live in cities and towns, although many still remain in remote areas and prefer a traditional, tribal-oriented way of life. In spite of their equal rights and legally improved status, the Aborigines, in general, still have low levels of education, relatively poor health, inadequate housing, and high unemployment rates.

The plight of the Aborigine is an embarrassment to some Australians and a source of resentment for others, who disapprove of the government's aid and assistance efforts. In spite of this controversy, the native people are rebuilding their traditional social systems, and their rich culture, with its music, dance, painting, carving, and mythology, is being revitalized.

THE AVERAGE AUSTRALIAN

Are Paul Hogan and Bryan Brown typical Aussies? Some Australians might like you to think so, but facts show that less than 15% of the population live in rural areas. Instead, the average Australian lives in one of eight capital cities, has never seen native fauna anywhere but in a zoo or wildlife park, is much more comfortable in trendy imported clothing than in a Driza-bone coat or Akubra hat, and prefers cappuccino to

IMPRESSIONS

They're very friendly people, people not prone to, as we say 'dip your lid', to others in a sense of recognizing a superiority in one class of people. There is a phrase we have in Australia—the 'fair go'. The fair go really means that all people are created with the right to develop and express themselves.
—FORMER PRIME MINISTER ROBERT HAWKE ON THE AUSSIE CHARACTER

billy tea. Given the choice, garden-variety Aussies would rather vacation in California than explore the rest of their own country. The "ocker" Aussie, or stereotypical uncultured Australian, does exist outside the movies, but not in the numbers one might think. If you're determined to find such a person, head for an isolated sheep or cattle station in the outback.

In cities and towns the people you'll meet may say "G' day, mate," but chances are their pronunciation will have a foreign flavor. About 22% of Australians were born overseas and a further 44% have at least one parent born in another country. These arrivals have doubled the population since World War II. The British Isles are the largest source—80%—with Italy, Greece, and Yugoslavia close behind. Many Asians have settled in Australia, starting with the Chinese who came out during the gold rush in the mid- and late 19th century and including a significant number of recent Indochinese refugees. Unlike its neighbor New Zealand, which identifies with Mother England, Australia has a waning interest in things British and tends to see itself as a part of Australasia.

Though the question of who is a true-blue Aussie may plague many Australians in search of a national identity, it doesn't really affect visitors. What we notice are personality traits—and these, surprisingly, seem to transcend ethnic origin, tenure in the country, and habitat.

The friendliness of the people—not to mention their sense of humor—is the first thing travelers usually notice. Though Aussies may be descended in good part from English stock, they sure don't exhibit the traditional British reserve. They seem to like just about everyone and they don't try to hide it. For example, it's quite common for the passenger to sit in front with the taxi driver—so they can talk. Can you imagine that in London or in New York?

Love of sports is yet another trait that unites Australians. Whether it's rugby league, Aussie Rules football, cricket, tennis, sailing, surfing, soccer, golf, car racing, or horse racing, the vast majority of people either participate or are avid spectators. Involvement is especially high on weekends, when seemingly every playing field hosts some sort of a competition and the major radio and television stations devote long hours to coverage.

Gambling, another great passion, goes hand-in-hand with the interest in sports. However, most Aussies don't need a team to bet on; they can get very enthusiastic over the toss of a coin. Anyone who doubts my word should go to one of the country's casinos and watch the crowd play two-up.

Some say the consuming interest in sports accounts for the sparsely filled pews in Australia's churches, but others suggest that the lack of interest in organized religion stems from the nation's origins as a convict colony, from the era when representatives of the church doled out some of the harshest punishments.

A strong sense of independence and an innate irreverence and resentment of authority are other characteristics that stem from the country's origins as a convict colony. Aussies love to make fun of their political leaders, law enforcement officers, and any others who try to set themselves above others. The person who offends the national spirit of egalitarianism is open to a raft of good-hearted verbal ribbing.

If you're getting the idea that the average Australian is dedicated to the enjoyment of life, you're absolutely right. "No worries" is not only a common expression, it's also a prevalent attitude. Even now, with the country suffering the discomfort of economic recession, most people are managing to maintain a positive attitude.

Aussies dress casually and enjoy a relaxed life-style characterized by backyard barbecues and high pub attendance. They even speak casually, adding "y" or "ie" to nearly everything, so that "football" becomes "footy," "biscuit" becomes "bickie," "mosquito" is "mossie," "postie" is the person who delivers the mail, and "barby" is what you slip a shrimp on (except that Australians call them prawns).

Basic to this way of life is a high regard for the family unit. Parents include their children in most social occasions (and vacations) and only infrequently leave them at home with a sitter. The average Australian couple has 2.2 children, lives in a major urban center, and owns a home. Women comprise 40% of the total work force and about half of these are married.

How is it possible that a population of people from such diverse backgrounds shares so many common attitudes? Why is it that the new arrival from southern Europe who has barely mastered English already loves sports, gambling, barbecues, and going to the pub as much as the descendants of the early settlers? I think it has something to do with pride. Australia has long been known as the "lucky country," and those who are able to immigrate consider themselves lucky people. Australia is still the land of opportunity, and the newest of the new Aussies are pleased to embrace its traditions. They happily watch footy on telly, have a barby with their mates, and smile when they say "G'day."

7. PERFORMING ARTS & EVENING ENTERTAINMENT

PERFORMING ARTS

OPERA, CONCERTS, THEATER & DANCE

Australia is home to some of the most beautiful and technically perfect theater complexes in the world. The Sydney Opera House, with its five stages, is the best known, but Brisbane's Performing Arts Complex, Adelaide's Festival Centre, and Melbourne's Victorian Arts Centre are also very impressive.

Australia's most famous performing artist was soprano Dame Nellie Melba. She made her European debut in 1887, and between then and her death in 1931 she sang in virtually every major opera house in the world. (In 1893 French chef Auguste Escoffier created a dessert in her honor and named it peach Melba.) Joan Sutherland, another Aussie opera star, became as well known as her illustrious predecessor. During her career she regularly appeared at the Sydney Opera House, in addition to fulfilling the overseas demand for her talent. Dame Joan's final performance was in 1990.

In the area of conducting, Australians Charles Mackerras and Richard Bonynge (the latter married to Joan Sutherland) have both earned excellent international reputations.

Australian theater has come a long way since 1789, when 12 convicts performed a comedy called *The Recruiting Officer* as part of the birthday celebration for King George III. The theater was lit by candles stuck into mud walls, and tickets were purchased with rum, tobacco, or even turnips. Today plays written and performed by Australians are regularly presented throughout the country. David Williamson is one of the country's most successful playwrights.

Barry Humphries is easily the king of Aussie comedy. A sometimes biting satirist, Humphries comments on local politics, fashions, and follies via the now-famous character he created: Dame Edna Everage, a frumpy, pretentious, outspoken housewife.

Since Anna Pavlova's famous Australian tour, there has been an interest in dance in

IMPRESSIONS

There has long been this element in Australia of delighting in life for its vigour and activity, without asking questions about it.
—DONALD HORNE, THE LUCKY COUNTRY (1978)

Australia. Robert Helpmann was one of the best-known Australian dancers, who emigrated to Europe. Today there is a lively dance scene in Australia, and the Sydney Dance Company has won an international reputation.

MUSIC

Australia's popular music, with its fresh, vital and imaginative sounds, is attracting world attention.

Rock & Pop

The Bee Gees were one of the first Australian groups to become popular overseas. The Little River Band, the Seekers, Olivia Newton-John, and Rick Springfield were other successful exports in the 1970s. More recently, Men at Work, INXS, John Farnham, Icehouse, Midnight Oil, Jason Donovan, and Kylie Minogue have also scored big hits, making Australia the third-largest supplier of repertoire to the world's charts, behind the United States and Britain.

Classical, Jazz & Country

Sadly, the vitality of the rock and pop industry is lacking in other types of music in Australia. Classical composers, for instance, have not been nearly as well received in foreign markets. Percy Grainger, a gifted pianist and composer, was one of the few who won international recognition (he became an American citizen and died in New York in 1961). Malcolm Williamson, who has spent much of his professional life in England, is another talented Australian composer. Alfred Hill is yet another. For many years Australian opera companies performed predominantly European works. In recent years, however, local composers have created their own success stories. The first was *Voss*, a grand opera composed by Richard Meale and given its premiere at the 1986 Adelaide Festival. *Metamorphosis*, a chamber opera, is another locally written work.

Jazz musicians and composers have received even less acclaim than their classical counterparts. The one exception is Don Burrows, the nation's top jazzman, who has been awarded an MBE, has hosted his own television program, and is a well-known composer, instrumentalist, and public figure.

Country music is relatively popular, especially around Tamworth in New South Wales. Every January a music festival is held in this town, 453 kilometers (280 miles) north of Sydney, which calls itself the "Nashville of Australia." Slim Dusty, Chad Morgan, and Reg Lindsay are the top performers.

Native Sounds

Only one type of music is purely Australian, of course, and that is Aboriginal. These songs tell of Dreamtime legends, tribal rituals, and heroic deeds. The didgeridoo, a wind instrument made from a slender tree trunk hollowed out by termites, lends a haunting sound to these stories. Unfortunately, many Aborigines have lost interest in their traditional music, and opportunities to witness it being performed in public are infrequent. For better or for worse, Australia's native people seem to prefer rock and roll.

FILM

What do Errol Flynn and Paul Hogan have in common? Nothing, if you visualize the suave and debonair Flynn standing next to rough-and-ready Hogan. But there's more here than meets the eye. To begin with, both are Australian and both made their fame in film. However, one major difference exists between the careers of the two men. Tasmanian-born Flynn's career started before the movie industry in Australia had a strong national identity. As a result, the actor defected to Hollywood only 2 years after making his 1933 debut in Charles Chauvel's *In the Wake of the Bounty*. Hogan, on the other hand, entered the scene after stars like Chips Rafferty, and later, Bryan Brown and Jack Thompson, had popularized the role of the rugged outback male. As Crocodile Dundee, Paul Hogan took over where the others left off and has raised being an ocker Aussie to an art form.

Early Moviemaking

The success of *Crocodile Dundee, Mad Max*, and the "surfie" drama *Puberty Blues* is ironic when one considers that the first feature-length movie in the world was the religious epic *Soldiers of the Cross*, produced by the Australian Salvation Army in 1900. This film was followed in 1906 by *The Story of the Kelly Gang*, but after an auspicious start, the movie industry failed to keep up the pace. Australia was used as the setting of *The Overlanders* in 1946, *On the Beach* in 1959, and *The Sundowners* in 1960, but it wasn't until the 1970s that Aussie filmmaking really came into its own. In the meantime, actor Peter Finch had left for London, where he made the now-classic 1956 version of *A Town Like Alice*.

Australian Success Stories

Picnic at Hanging Rock, released in 1975, was the first significant contemporary film to feature both a domestic story line and a homegrown director, in the person of Peter Weir. *The Last Wave*, another Weir success, introduced the world to Aboriginal folklore. *My Brilliant Career, Breaker Morant*, and *Mad Max* further improved the fortunes of the Australian film industry. Judy Davis, the star of *My Brilliant Career*, was named Best Actress and Best Newcomer in a Leading Role at the 1981 British Academy Awards. Jack Thompson won a Best Supporting Actor Award for *Breaker Morant*, and Bryan Brown also received praise for his part in the film. Breaker also brought acclaim to Aussie director Bruce Beresford. *Mad Max*, a worldwide smash hit, grossed over $100 million and launched Mel Gibson to international stardom.

Peter Weir followed with *Gallipoli*, the moving story of Australia's World War I tragedy, and the political suspense thriller *The Year of Living Dangerously*, based on the novel by Australian writer Christopher Koch. George Miller's *The Man from Snowy River* was equally successful. Gillian Armstrong, the first woman director in Australia since the 1930s, established her reputation with *My Brilliant Career*, and secured it with *Mrs. Soffel*, starring Mel Gibson and Diane Keaton. *Careful He Might Hear You* was voted one of the top 10 films of 1984 by American critics.

In 1986 Australia topped its string of critical successes with the commercial blockbuster *Crocodile Dundee*, which irrevocably proved the popularity of the country's national characteristics. *Crocodile Dundee II* and *A Cry in the Dark*, with Meryl Streep, attracted more attention. It's now clear that in the movie industry, not only is it okay to be Australian, it seems to be a requirement for success.

NIGHTLIFE

If, after a day of sightseeing or sporting activity, you still have the energy for nightlife, you'll be able to find something of interest in any of Australia's cities.

PUBS

Pubs are also listed under "Where to Stay" in Chapter 2, but their main function is the dispensing of alcoholic beverages, primarily—but not limited to—beer. The word "pub" is shorthand for "public licensed hotel," that is, a place where it is legal to sell "spirituous liquors" to the public. We normally think of pubs as noisy, smoky, jovial places where no one would notice if you used the floor for an ashtray; actually, asking for an ashtray would probably cause more of a stir. However, lots of Hiltons, Sheratons, and the like are also public licensed hotels. They each have a public bar that keeps the legal pub hours, and anyone can drink there; the public bar in one of these top-class hotels has an ambience which is a cross between a traditional pub and a cocktail lounge. Obviously, these hotels also have piano bars and other posher places to drink. These areas are open later than the public bar, and the dress code prohibits jeans, thongs, and singlets (sleeveless undershirts that are part of the "Aussie uniform").

There are also hotels with liquor licenses that limit the dispensing of alcohol to their registered guests and people who are dining in their restaurants. You will know you have wandered into such a place when you order a drink and the barmaid asks, "Do you intend to dine?" Legally she can't serve you unless you respond in the affirmative. Likewise, restaurants are licensed to serve drinks only to their dining patrons.

Pub hours vary but usually run from 10am to 11pm Monday through Saturday; some places are closed on Sunday, and those that are open don't get started until noon and close by 10pm, an hour earlier than during the week. The drinking age throughout the country is 18.

Pub etiquette is simple. If you're drinking with a group, each one takes a turn at buying a round. This is called "shouting."

DISCOS

Unlike the pub scene, where "shouting" refers to the opening of one's wallet, shouting in a disco is what's usually required for conversation. If this is your cup of tea, you'll be happy to know that every capital city in Australia has at least a couple of these high-decibel dancing dens. The better ones are located in the big hotels. Discos are often closed on Sunday and Monday and stay open until the wee hours other nights; cover charges range from A$8 to A$15 (U.S. $6.40 to U.S. $12).

CASINOS & CLUBS

Most major cities have a casino. Craps, roulette, blackjack, minidice, poker, and two-up are the favorite games. Poker machines (slots) are illegal in some states, but are found in private clubs.

In addition to being venues for gambling, casinos often have cabarets (nightclubs) with floor shows or a band for dancing.

Private clubs are an important part of the nightlife scene, especially in areas outside the big cities, where there is often a dearth of evening entertainment. Places like RSL (Returned Services League) Clubs provide a legal way around Australia's sometimes parochial drinking and gambling laws. Visitors are welcome at any of these clubs as long as they are properly dressed and sign in at the door.

In addition to RSLs, football-leagues clubs offer the same facilities: poker machines, bars, restaurants, floor shows, and sometimes discos. It's also not unusual for the clubs to have weight rooms, aerobics classes, and other gym facilities. The cost of dining and drinking in these clubs is normally quite reasonable, probably because the overhead expenses are subsidized by gambling revenues.

OTHER EVENING ENTERTAINMENT

In addition to the nightlife options already mentioned, Australian cities offer a wide range of cultural performances—everything from grand opera to intimate dramatic works. There are also comedy clubs, venues for listening to particular types of music (such as jazz), and lots of movie theaters. Overseas visitors also often enjoy after-dark harbor cruises and restaurants with Australiana entertainment.

Lastly, like all the world's major cities, Australian capitals offer pornographic movie houses and miscellaneous sexual sideshows. The area best known for this is Sydney's Kings Cross, where those willing to pay the price can see just about everything from women-who-used-to-be-men doing the cancan to women-who-still-are-women performing in seedy striptease shows. American servicemen who took their R and R in Sydney during the Vietnam era helped make Kings Cross what it is today; the country's other red-light districts pale by comparison.

IMPRESSIONS

The most Australian thing you can do is to lie on a clean, wide beautiful beach.
—ROSS TERRILL

8. SPORTS & RECREATION

The Aussies' passion for sports is almost legendary. They play cricket, rugby union, rugby league, golf, tennis, squash, Australian Rules football, soccer, and hockey. They sail, cycle, surf, swim, box, balloon, run, row, race horses, and waterski—with gusto. It seems that everyone either plays sports or is an avid fan, and the enthusiasm for these various activities goes hand-in-hand with the national love of betting (Aussies are great gamblers, or "punters" as they're known down under).

In 1962 *Sports Illustrated* rated Australia as the world's top sporting nation on a per capita basis. And that was *before* Rod Laver, Ken Rosewall, Margaret Smith Court, Roy Emerson, John Newcombe, and Evonne Goolagong made names for themselves in tennis; Dawn Fraser became the first swimmer to win gold medals in three successive Olympic Games; Heather McKay became the world's greatest-ever woman squash player; and Peter Thompson distinguished himself in golf.

More recently, John Bertrand has captured the America's Cup, Pat Cash has won at Wimbledon, Greg Norman has become a top dollar-earner on the American professional golf circuit, and Rob de Castella has won the Boston Marathon.

While these victories are impressive, it's the success of the national cricket and rugby union teams that really makes heroes out of outstanding players. Dennis Lillee, Greg Chappell, and Rodney Marsh were elevated to star status for their performances on the cricket pitch. Likewise, the Aboriginal Ella brothers—Mark, Glen, and Gary—gained great respect for their prowess on the rugby field.

Australia competes against other members of the Commonwealth in most sports, but since Australian Rules football is played only at home, the competition is between various domestic clubs. Victoria is the hotbed of Aussie Rules, or "footy," as it's called by the locals, but other states share the passion to a lesser extent.

Horse racing also captures the country's attention, especially on the first Tuesday in November when the Melbourne Cup is run. I'd heard the event referred to as "the race that stops the nation," but I didn't believe it until I saw it with my own eyes. I was in Sydney, in the public bar of the Regent Hotel. It was midday and the room was crowded with office workers hovering over the "Cup Day" buffet, talking about the big race, and placing wagers. A half dozen television sets brought in for the occasion relayed the happenings at the Flemington Racecourse in Melbourne, including lavish parties, women dressed to the nines, and interviews with international jet setters and others for whom this was the highlight of the social season.

Through the windows of the pub I could also watch the activity on Sydney's busiest street. Buses and taxis were bumper to bumper, while pedestrians vied for space on the sidewalk.

And then the race started, and George Street suddenly became an empty canyon. The buses disappeared; the taxis stopped; not one person remained outside the window. For 3 minutes Sydney and, I assume, the rest of the nation were transfixed by

IMPRESSIONS

This is really a wonderful Colony; ancient Rome in her imperial grandeur would not have been ashamed of such an offspring.
—LETTER FROM CHARLES DARWIN, 1836

horses galloping around the track at the Flemington Racecourse in Melbourne. For 3 minutes the only audible sound was the pounding of horses' hooves and the pounding of punters' hearts.

9. FOOD & DRINK

FOOD

Dining down under has become quite a varied and sophisticated affair, which pleasantly surprises most visitors. Likewise, the local wine industry has blossomed and today offers many exciting options. I tend to think of Australia's cuisine as falling into three categories.

COLONIAL FARE

The dishes that either came out from Britain with the settlers or were created by them after they arrived are sometimes referred to as colonial fare. Certainly, roast-lamb and roast-beef dinners belong in this category, as do fish-and-chips, and the delicious scones served with morning and afternoon tea. On the other hand, damper bread was created early on by men who lived in the bush. It was originally cooked in the coals of a campfire or in a camp oven, not unlike the sourdough bread that was once a staple in the American West. Life on the frontier also produced billy tea, and the now-famous Aussie barbecue. Australians also invented the carpetbag steak, a thick cut of beef stuffed with oysters.

Lamingtons, tasty cubes of sponge cake covered with chocolate icing and shredded coconut, were invented by colonists and named after one of their governors. Pavlova, another sweet concoction, was first prepared by a local chef in Perth in 1935 and named in honor of Anna Pavlova, the Russian ballerina. A large soft-centered meringue filled with whipped cream and garnished with fruit, pavlova has become the unofficial national dessert.

It's easy to understand the Australian passion for pavlova, but not the fondness for Vegemite, a yeast-based spread for toast that most Aussies (and Kiwis, too) seem to crave. Be forewarned: Should you decide to try it, it may be several days before your taste buds forgive you.

Because of Australia's varied climate, which ranges from temperate to tropical, the early settlers found they were able to grow an extensive variety of fruits and vegetables. Canned plums were one of Australia's first exports, and with today's modern transportation it is possible to enjoy a wide range of fresh produce anywhere in the country throughout the year.

INDIGENOUS FOOD

Australia's abundant waters provide large and varied quantities of seafood. Sydney is known for its rock oysters; also popular are barramundi, coral trout, mud crab, jewfish, and John Dory. Moreton Bay bugs and Balmain bugs sound awful, but the lobsterlike shellfish are really delicious.

While the above-mentioned "bugs" aren't of the creepy-crawly type, insects do feature in Australia's indigenous food. Witchetty grubs, giant-size larvae, were consumed by the Aborigines in days past. If you're dying to try one, I suggest you head for Rowntrees Restaurant in Hornsby, a suburb of Sydney. This is one of the few places in the country that serves them. It's easier to find restaurants that offer kangaroo, crocodile, and water buffalo; some even serve kangaroo-tail soup. Macadamia nuts, also a native food, find their way into many dishes.

ETHNIC FOOD

The large numbers of recent immigrants account for Australia's vast array of ethnic food. For example, one block of Oxford Street in Sydney boasts restaurants serving the cuisines of 16 different countries. In Carlton, a neighborhood of Melbourne, both sides of Lygon Street are lined with Italian restaurants. Adelaide and Melbourne both have excellent Greek restaurants. Nationally, Chinese—Cantonese to be specific—is the most popular ethnic food. Recent arrivals also run delis throughout the country, and at lunchtime it's possible to buy wonderful thick sandwiches and treats like gyros in pita.

And what has America contributed to the Aussie dining experience? According to a song written by Australian folk singer Judy Small, "Every 17 hours another McDonald's opens up . . .," and, by all appearances, what she says is true. For better or for worse, the golden arches stand tall throughout the land and have proven to be incredibly popular. If the lines are any indication, quarter-pounders with cheese are more popular than the nation's traditional meat pies.

DRINK

SOFT DRINKS & WATER

Coca-Cola has been made in Australia since 1938 and is widely available throughout the country, as are a full array of other soft drinks. Aussies also frequently quench their thirst with fruit-juice beverages, and quite a variety of these are also on sale. The water is safe to drink in all parts of the nation.

BEER & WINE

If your idea of the perfect ending to a day of sightseeing is a nice cold beer or a glass of wine, you'll find both quantity and quality readily available in Australia. You'll also find plenty of company, as Aussies are the largest consumers of alcohol in the English-speaking world.

Beer

Fosters is the country's most popular beer, but each state also has its favorite. In New South Wales, Tooheys is the most popular; in Western Australia, Swan Lager is tops; according to the locals in Queensland, Fourex (XXXX) "isn't a beer, it's a religion." Other Aussies will swear by Carlton Crown Lager or Reschs.

Beer is served in 20-ounce pints, half pints (also called "middies"), and 15-ounce schooners. Light drinkers might order a "seven," which is a 7-ounce glass. Regardless of the size of the vessel, Australian beer is always served ice cold.

Wine

Australians are justifiably proud of their wine industry, which in recent years has won some impressive awards. The main grape-growing regions are the Hunter Valley in New South Wales, the Yarra Valley in Victoria, the Barossa and Clare valleys and the Coonawarra district in South Australia, and the Swan Valley and Margaret River area in Western Australia. Overall, South Australia is the state with the greatest wine production.

Penfolds and Lindemans rank as two of the biggest wineries, but smaller houses have won many of the most coveted prizes. In 1986 Philip Shaw of the Rosemont Estate in the Upper Hunter Valley won the Robert Mondavi Winemaker of the Year Award at the International Wine and Spirit Competition in London. This highly regarded recognition went to Greg Clayfield of Lindemans in the Coonawarra district in 1988, and to the Penfolds Group in 1990. Peterson's Hunter Valley chardonnay won in its category in the 1987 Qantas Wine Cup and tied for best white of the show. The Australians beat the Americans overall in this internationally judged competition.

Altogether, the 400 producing wineries in Australia sell about five times more white than red. They also make a great many dessert wines, especially port, and sparkling-wine production is on the increase. The famous French champagne company Domaine Chandon started growing grapes in Victoria's Yarra Valley in 1985 and released its first bubbly late in 1988.

Australian vintners have only recently begun actively marketing their wines overseas. "Before that," one winemaker told me, "we knew it was good enough, but we didn't make huge quantities; and we were afraid if we exported it, there wouldn't be enough to go around at home."

This philosophy still exists to some degree, and the traveler in Australia is in the enviable position of being able to visit the wineries and sample the country's best wines—the ones the Aussies keep for themselves.

10. RECOMMENDED BOOKS, FILMS & RECORDINGS

BOOKS

Veteran travelers agree that reading about a destination adds to the enjoyment of a trip. If "know before you go" is your motto, here are some suggestions:

Archaeology of the Dreamtime by Josephine Flood (Honolulu: University of Hawaii, 1983). The author paints an interesting portrait of past and present Aboriginal life.

The Australians by Ross Terrill (New York: Simon & Schuster, 1987). The author is a distinguished scholar-journalist, and the book is a personal, richly anecdotal essay on his native land.

Cooper's Creek by Alan Moorehead (New York: Harper & Row, 1963). The author retraced the ill-fated Burke and Wills expedition in a Land Rover.

Down Under All Over by Barbara Marie Brewster (Oregon: Four Winds Publishing, 1991). This is a very personal account of an American woman's love affair with Australia.

The Eye of the Storm by Patrick White (New York: Viking, 1973). White won the Nobel Prize in Literature for this 1973 effort. His earlier works include *Voss, The Tree of Man,* and *The Vivisector.*

The Fatal Shore by Robert Hughes (New York: Knopf, 1986). The author provides good background on early life in the colony, complete with gruesome accounts of prisoners' punishments.

Four-legged Australians: Adventures with Animals and Man in Australia by Bernhard Grzimek (New York: Hill & Wang, 1967). Good information on the unique animal life down under.

Games of the Strong and *The Hottest Night of the Century* by Glenda Adams (Cane Hill Press, 1989). The author of these two collections of stories won the Miles Franklin Award in 1987 for *Dancing on Coral.*

Great Barrier Reef by Isobel Bennett (London: Mereweather, 1982). A must for anyone with a serious interest in Australia's greatest wonder.

Kings in Grass Castles by Mary Durack (New South Wales: Transworld Publishers, 1989). This true story tells of the author's grandfather and his descendants and their struggle to settle the Kimberley district of Western Australia. It was first published in 1959. Like its sequel, *Sons in the Saddle,* this book is an Australian classic.

My Brilliant Career by Miles Franklin (New York: St. Martin's, 1980). First published in 1901, this book about a young woman who must choose between marriage and a career became the basis of the movie of the same title.

Outback by Thomas Keneally (Chicago: Rand-McNally, 1984). This book, written by one of Australia's best-known authors, tells about the history, geology, and culture of the Northern Territory.

The Ribbon and the Ragged Square by Linda Christmas (New York: Viking, 1986). An entertaining study of contemporary Australian society written by an English journalist.

The Road from Coorain by Jill Ker Conway (New York: Vintage Books, 1989). This autobiography traces the life of a girl raised on a remote New South Wales sheep station who becomes the president of Smith College.

Songlines by Bruce Chatwin (New York: Viking, 1987). The author explores Dreamtime legends and sacred places.

The Thorn Birds by Colleen McCullough (New York: Harper & Row, 1977). While the story is fiction, the outback character she describes is real.

Walkabout by James V. Marshall (New York: Doubleday, 1961). A classic Australian tale of two children who are the sole survivors of a plane crash in the outback and their relationship with the Aborigines who save them. The book was made into an excellent movie, by Nicholas Roeg, in 1970.

Also well worth a look: *National Geographic* magazine, February 1988. The entire issue is devoted to Australia and contains good background information as well as travel ideas. Also see *National Geographic,* January 1991, which features Northwest Australia, and October 1991, which features Lord Howe Island.

If your local bookstore doesn't have a good selection of Aussie books, contact **The Australian Book Source,** 1309 Redwood Lane, Davis, CA 95616 (tel. 916/753-1519; fax 916/753-6491).

FILMS

The following films are available on video. Each provides a very different view of Australia.

COMEDY

Crocodile Dundee (1986). Paul Hogan and Linda Kozlowski star in the story of a free-spirited Aussie who hunts crocodiles with his bare hands until he comes to the attention of an American reporter who brings him to the jungles of New York.

Crocodile Dundee II (1988). Crocodile Dundee finds himself up against a gang of ruthless Colombian drug dealers.

COMEDY/DRAMA

Down Under (1984). Two adventurous types travel to Australia in search of gold. They find a lot more than they bargained for as seen in this film of their year-long odyssey. Forsaking the beaches of California, they chase kangaroos and beautiful women, feast on goannas, and still find time to prospect for gold.

Quigley Down Under (1990). Tom Selleck and Laura San Giacomo (*Pretty Woman*) star in this adventure set in Western Australia in the 1860s. The movie provides some great laughs, but also an all-too-realistic look at the relationship between the Aborigines and the colonial ranchers.

DRAMA

A Town Like Alice (1980). This Australian miniseries, winner of many international awards, stars Bryan Brown and Helen Morse as lovers separated in Malaya during World War II. The movie is based on the novel by Nevil Shute.

Burke & Wills (1987). Jack Thompson stars in this docudrama about the first white men to cross the vast desert of central Australia. A true and gripping story.

My Brilliant Career (1981). Judy Davis and Sam Neill star in the touching story of a young woman, daughter of a poor ranch family, who has aspirations of artistic greatness and finds she must choose between her dream and her love affair. The film is directed by Gillian Armstrong.

Phar Lap (1984). Based on a true story, this movie tells the tale of a champion racehorse that won an incredible number of races in the 1930s.

MUSIC & SPORTS

Australia Now. Australia's most popular rock bands are featured in this collection of interviews and performances.

Aussie Rules Football (1987). This sports flick promises to be "full of bone-crushing highlights." It also includes a simplified explanation of the rules.

RECORDINGS

Because Aussie rock groups are often at the top of the charts, their recordings are readily available around the globe. It is a bit more difficult, however, to find recordings of other types of Australian music. If you have trouble locating what you want, contact The Australian Catalogue Company, 7408 Grist Mill Road, Raleigh, NC 27615 (tel. 919/848-9977; fax 919/872-2132).

COUNTRY/FOLK

G'Day G'Day, Slim Dusty. One of Australia's most popular country stars sings "Up the Old Nulla Road," "Sittin' on the Old Front Verandah," and others.
Now I'm Easy, Eric Bogle. This gold seller includes "And the Band Played Waltzing Matilda," and "Leaving Nancy."
Seven Creeks Run. This anthology includes popular songs such as "Click Go the Shears," "Ballad of the Kelly Gang," and "The Fire at Ross Farm."

NATIVE

Proud to Be Aborigine, Tjapukai Dance Theatre. This album combines traditional Aboriginal music with contemporary tunes. The Tjapukai Dance Theatre performs throughout the year in Kuranda, Queensland (near Cairns), and has traveled around the world representing Australia.

CHAPTER 2
PLANNING A TRIP TO AUSTRALIA

"**B**e prepared" is more than just a motto for Boy Scouts. It's also good advice for travelers who want to get the most possible enjoyment for the time and money they spend on a trip. Careful planning pays off in successful sojourns, and since I want your Australian experience to be a good one, I've compiled a whole chapter of nuts-and-bolts background information.

1. INFORMATION, ENTRY REQUIREMENTS & MONEY

SOURCES OF INFORMATION

TRAVEL AGENTS

Since the services provided by a travel agent are free, I suggest that you take advantage of them when planning your trip. If you don't already have an agent that you especially like, ask well-traveled friends who they use. Then phone two or three of those recommended and ask the same questions about Australia, making note of who seems the best informed. A good consultant is both patient and competent.

Be careful that he or she doesn't talk you into a package tour if you really want to travel independently. This would save the agent a lot of trouble, but in the end you'd be settling for something you didn't want. The same is true when it comes to accommodations: It's easier for an agent to book you into one of the large international chain hotels that have worldwide toll-free telephone numbers than to ferret out the quaint country inn or B&B you've heard about. Also, keep an eye on the travel section of your local newspaper for information on bargain promotional fares—and be sure your agent knows about them.

AUSTRALIAN TOURIST COMMISSION

The Australian Tourist Commission is extremely helpful, and maintains the following offices in North America, Britain, and New Zealand: **Chicago:** 150 North Michigan Avenue, Suite 2130, Chicago, IL 60601 (tel. 312/781-5150); **Los Angeles:** 2121 Avenue of the Stars, Suite 1200, Los Angeles, CA 90067 (tel. 213/552-1988); **New York:** 489 Fifth Avenue, 31st Floor, New York, NY 10017 (tel. 212/687-6300); **Toronto:** 2 Bloor Street West, Suite 1730, Toronto, ON M4W 3E2 (tel. 416/925-9575); **Britain:** 20 Savile Row, 4th floor, London W1X 1AE (tel. 01/434-4371); **New Zealand:** Quay Towers, 15th floor, 29 Customs Street West, Auckland 1 (tel. 09/799-594).

In addition, Americans and Canadians can request a complimentary copy of the ATC's 130-page booklet *Destination Australia* by calling toll free 800/678-8022 in the U.S., 800/225-9100 in Canada.

STATE TOURIST OFFICES

If you'd like to request information from individual states, the following addresses may be useful: **New South Wales Tourism Commission,** 2121 Avenue of the Stars, Suite 450, Los Angeles, CA 90067 (tel. 213/552-9566); **Northern Territory Tourist Commission,** 2121 Avenue of the Stars, Suite 1230, Los Angeles, CA 90067 (tel. 213/277-7877, or toll free 800/4-OUTBAC); **Queensland Tourist & Travel Corporation,** 611 North Larchmont Boulevard, Los Angeles, CA 90004 (tel. 213/465-8418, or toll free 800/333-6050); **Tourism South Australia,** 2121 Avenue of the Stars, Suite 1210, Los Angeles, CA 90067 (tel. 213/552-2821); **Australia Naturally,** representing the states of Tasmania and Victoria, 2121 Avenue of the Stars, Suite 1270, Los Angeles, CA 90067 (tel. 213/553-6352); **Western Australian Tourism Commission,** 2121 Avenue of the Stars, Suite 1210, Los Angeles, CA 90067 (tel. 213/557-1987).

ENTRY REQUIREMENTS

Everyone must have a **passport** in order to visit Australia. In addition, everyone except holders of Australian and New Zealand passports also needs a **visa.** The passport must be valid for a period longer than the intended length of stay. *The visa must be obtained prior to arriving in Australia.* Application forms are available from the consulate or embassy closest to you (see list below). Visas are free of charge and can be valid for stays of up to 6 months; they are generally good for 12 months. Do not wait until the last minute to apply for your visa, because in peak periods of travel it can take a month or more to process your application by mail. It's possible to obtain a visa in less time, but this requires that you deliver and pick up the documents in person. You must submit one recent passport-size photo with the application, and a self-addressed, stamped envelope is necessary if you're applying by mail.

Following are the Australian visa-issuing offices in the United States: **Chicago:** Australian Consulate-General, 321 North Clark Street, Suite 2930, Chicago, IL 60610 (tel. 312/645-9444); **Honolulu:** Australian Consulate-General, 1000 Bishop Street, Penthouse, Honolulu, HI 96813-4299 (tel. 808/524-5050); **Houston:** Australian Consulate-General, 1990 Post Oak Boulevard, Suite 800, Houston, TX 77056-9998 (tel. 713/629-9131); **Los Angeles:** Australian Consulate-General, 611 North Larchmont Boulevard, Los Angeles, CA 90004 (tel. 213/469-4300); **New York:** Australian Consulate-General, 636 Fifth Avenue, New York, NY 10111 (tel. 212/245-4000); **San Francisco:** Australian Consulate-General, 360 Post Street, San Francisco, CA 94108-4979 (tel. 415/362-6160); **Washington, D.C.:** Australian Embassy, 1601 Massachusetts Avenue NW, Washington, DC 20036-2273 (tel. 202/797-3222).

In Canada, contact one of the following offices: **Ottawa:** Australian High Commission, 50 O'Connor Street, Suite 710, Ottawa, ON K1P 5M9 (tel. 613/236-

0841); **Toronto:** Australian Consulate-General, 175 Bloor Street East, Suite 314, Toronto, ON M5W 3R8 (tel. 416/323-1155); **Vancouver:** Australian Consulate-General, Oceanic Plaza, 1066 West Hastings Street, Suite 800 (P.O. Box 12519), Vancouver, BC V6E 3X1 (tel. 604/684-1177).

In Britain and Ireland, contact one of the following offices: **Dublin:** The Australian Embassy, Fitzwilliam House, Wilton Terrace, Dublin 2 (tel. 01/76-1517); **Edinburgh:** Australian Consulate, Hobart House, 80 Hanover Street, Edinburgh EH2 2DL (tel. 031/226-6271); **London:** Australian High Commission, Australia House, The Strand, London WC2B 4LA (tel. 01/836-7161); **Manchester:** Australian Consulate, Chatsworth House, Lever Street, Manchester M1 (tel. 061/228-1344).

Upon landing in Australia, you will be required to produce both your passport with the visa stamped in it and a completed incoming passenger card (which is distributed on all ships and aircraft prior to arrival). You may also be asked to show your outbound airline ticket. It is not permissible to work or go to school in Australia if you have entered the country on a Visitor Visa, but young people (ages 18 to 25) from some Commonwealth countries are eligible for Working Holiday Visas.

Vaccination certificates are required only of travelers who have within six days been in areas infected with yellow fever.

Be sure that you don't bring fresh or packaged food of any kind, or such things as fruit, vegetables, or seeds. These items, as well as the importation of plants and animals, are strictly controlled.

MONEY
CASH/CURRENCY

Australians use a decimal currency. The Australian dollar (A$) is made up of 100 cents. Notes come in $5, $10, $20, $50, and $100 denominations. Coins are minted in 5¢, 10¢, 20¢, 50¢, $1, and $2 units.

THE AUSTRALIAN DOLLAR & THE U.S. DOLLAR

At this writing, U.S. $1 = approximately A$1.25 (or A$1 = U.S. 80¢), and this was the rate of exchange used to calculate the dollar values given in this book. These rates fluctuate from time to time and may not be the same when you travel to Australia. Therefore the accompanying table should be used only as a guide:

A$	$ U.S.	A$	$ U.S.
.25	.20	30.00	24.00
.50	.40	35.00	28.00
1.00	.80	40.00	32.00
2.00	1.60	45.00	36.00
3.00	2.40	50.00	40.00
4.00	3.20	60.00	48.00
5.00	4.00	70.00	56.00
6.00	4.80	80.00	64.00
7.00	5.60	90.00	72.00
8.00	6.40	100.00	80.00
9.00	7.20	125.00	100.00
10.00	8.00	150.00	120.00
15.00	12.00	175.00	140.00
20.00	16.00	200.00	160.00
25.00	20.00	250.00	200.00

TRAVELER'S CHECKS & CREDIT CARDS

When you look for a bank to cash traveler's checks, keep in mind that service charges vary widely. The National Australia Bank charges A$5 (U.S. $4) to cash a foreign-currency traveler's check. The ANZ Bank charges A$2 (U.S. $1.60) or more for the same service, and most Westpac Banks charge nothing.

If you run out of traveler's checks, you can buy more at any American Express office provided you are one of their cardmembers and have remembered to bring a personal check on your home account. The **headquarters of American Express** in Australia is 388 George Street, Sydney, NSW 2000 (tel. 02/239-0666).

It can be awkward to purchase items at a shop or pay for meals with foreign-currency traveler's checks because the personnel involved will probably not know the value of your check in Australian dollars. During banking hours this dilemma is easily solved, but after hours it can be a real problem. The simplest way to buy things and pay the tab in restaurants and hotels is to use a credit card.

Another alternative is to buy Aussie-dollar traveler's checks. You could get a cash advance against your MasterCard or VISA and use the money to buy traveler's checks in the local currency. Then you'd have the convenience of cash and the security of traveler's checks.

American Express, Bankcard, Diners Club, MasterCard, and VISA are widely accepted at hotels, restaurants, and stores throughout Australia. Carte Blanche can also be used in some places. Since some establishments take one card and not another, I suggest that you carry two.

You can get a cash advance with a credit card at banks in Australia. If you carry VISA, the ANZ Bank should be able to help you. With MasterCard, head for a Westpac Bank.

WHAT THINGS COST IN SYDNEY	U.S. $
Taxi from the airport to the city center	14.50
Bus from Central Station to downtown	1.00
Local telephone call from a pay phone	.25
Double at the Park Hyatt Sydney (deluxe)	300.00
Double at the Park All-Suite Hotel (moderate)	182.00
Double at Harbour Rocks Hotel (budget)	84.00
Lunch for one at Bobby McGee's (moderate)	13.00
Lunch for one at the Harbour Takeaway (budget)	6.00
Dinner for one, without wine, at Bilson's (deluxe)	52.00
Dinner for one, without wine, at Virgin Video Cafe (moderate)	17.00
Dinner for one, without wine, at·the Craig Brewery Bar & Grill (budget)	7.00
Can of Fosters (beer)	2.40
Coca-Cola (375ml)	1.45
Cup of coffee	1.20
Roll of ASA 100 Kodacolor film, 36 exposures	6.00
Admission to the Sydney Aquarium	10.00
Movie ticket	9.20
One liter unleaded petrol (gas)	.50

WHAT THINGS COST IN MUDGEE, NSW	U.S. $
Taxi from the airport to the city center	4.40
Local telephone call from a pay phone	.25
Double at Country Paradise Resort (deluxe)	88.00
Double at Winning Post Motel (moderate)	51.00
Double at Riverside Caravan Park (budget)	22.40
Lunch for one at Colonial Eatery (moderate)	6.40
Lunch for one at Fran's Fast Foods (budget)	3.45
Dinner for one, without wine, at Craigmoor Restaurant (deluxe)	28.00
Dinner for one, without wine, at Augustine Winery (moderate)	14.00
Dinner for one, without wine, at the Soldiers' Club (budget)	6.40
Can of Fosters (beer)	1.85
Coca-Cola (375ml)	.90
Cup of coffee	.80
Roll of ASA 100 Kodacolor film, 36 exposures	6.00
Admission to the Colonial Inn Museum	2.00
Movie ticket	4.40
One liter unleaded petrol (gas)	.57

2. WHEN TO GO — CLIMATE, HOLIDAYS & EVENTS

CLIMATE

The time of year you visit Australia will be determined chiefly by the type of weather you hope to encounter and the activities you'd like to pursue. Keep in mind that the seasons are reversed in the Southern Hemisphere: Winter is June through August, spring is September through November, summer is December through February, and fall is March through May. Also, remember that the northern part of the country is the warmest and that the southern states, particularly Tasmania, are where you might encounter some cool weather during their winter months.

The skiing in Victoria and southern New South Wales is good between June and September, but snow almost never falls in any of the cities. Wildflower buffs should head to Western Australia when it's spring down under—September through November. Prime time on the Great Barrier Reef for those who like hot weather is September through December, and for those who prefer more temperate days, May through August is better.

In general, the northern half of the country is at its best from April to October; during other times of the year it can be *very* hot and *very* wet. The southern states are most pleasant from October to April. The ideal situation would be to arrive in Australia in August and travel through Queensland and the Northern Territory before the weather gets unbearably hot. Then head to Western Australia in time for the wildflowers and continue on to South Australia, Victoria, and Tasmania in October. Sydney's temperatures are pleasant year round, but February to June can be rainy. Consult the table of average temperatures that follows when you do your planning.

Australia's Average Temperatures (°F) and Rainfall (")*

	Winter			Spring			Summer			Fall		
	June	July	Aug	Sept	Oct	Nov	Dec	Jan	Feb	Mar	Apr	May
Adelaide												
Max. Temp.	60	59	61	66	72	77	82	85	85	80	73	66
Min. Temp.	47	45	46	48	52	55	59	61	62	59	55	51
Rainfall (in.)	3	3	2	2	2	1	1	1	1	1	2	3
Alice Springs												
Max. Temp.	68	67	71	79	88	93	95	98	96	91	83	73
Min. Temp.	43	40	44	51	60	65	68	72	70	65	56	48
Rainfall (in.)	1	1	1	1	1	1	0	1	2	1	1	1
Brisbane												
Max. Temp.	69	69	71	75	79	82	84	85	84	82	79	74
Min. Temp.	51	49	50	55	60	64	67	69	69	67	62	56
Rainfall (in.)	3	2	2	2	3	4	5	7	6	6	4	3
Cairns												
Max. Temp.	78	77	80	82	85	87	88	89	88	87	84	81
Min. Temp.	65	62	64	66	69	72	74	74	75	72	71	68
Rainfall (in.)	2	1	1	1	1	3	7	16	17	18	7	4
Canberra												
Max. Temp.	54	52	55	60	66	72	79	82	80	76	67	59
Min. Temp.	34	33	33	37	42	47	52	56	55	51	44	37
Rainfall (in.)	2	2	2	2	3	3	2	2	2	2	2	2
Darwin												
Max. Temp.	88	87	89	91	92	93	92	90	89	90	92	90
Min. Temp.	69	67	69	74	77	78	78	77	77	77	76	72
Rainfall (in.)	0	4	0	1	2	5	10	15	13	10	4	1
Hobart												
Max. Temp.	53	53	55	59	62	65	68	71	71	68	63	58
Min. Temp.	41	40	41	43	45	48	51	53	53	51	48	44
Rainfall (in.)	2	2	2	2	3	2	2	2	2	2	2	2
Melbourne												
Max. Temp.	57	56	59	63	67	71	75	78	78	75	68	62
Min. Temp.	44	42	44	46	49	51	55	57	58	55	51	47
Rainfall (in.)	2	2	2	3	3	2	2	2	2	2	3	2
Perth												
Max. Temp.	65	63	64	67	70	76	81	85	86	82	76	69
Min. Temp.	50	48	48	50	53	57	61	64	64	62	57	53
Rainfall (in.)	7	7	5	3	2	1	1	1	3	1	2	5
Sydney												
Max. Temp.	62	60	63	67	71	74	77	78	78	76	72	67
Min. Temp.	48	46	48	51	56	60	63	65	65	63	58	52
Rainfall (in.)	5	4	3	3	3	3	3	4	5	5	5	5

*Source: Australian Tourist Commission, *Destination Australia*.

HOLIDAYS

It's a good idea to avoid traveling in Australia from mid-December to the end of January. That's when Aussies take their summer holidays; accommodations become both scarce and expensive, and traffic delays can be a real nuisance. Easter vacation (from the Thursday before Easter through the Tuesday after) is another period it's wise to avoid.

In addition to checking the list of holidays in "Fast Facts: Australia," below, consult the following schedules of school vacation periods when planning a trip:

NEW SOUTH WALES

	1992	**1993**
Summer:	Dec 14 (1991)–Jan 27	Dec 18 (1992)–Jan 31
Fall:	Apr 11–26	Apr 9–18
Winter:	July 4–19	June 26–July 11
Spring:	Sept 26–Oct 11	Sept 25–Oct 10

QUEENSLAND

	1992	**1993**
Summer:	Dec 13 (1991)–Jan 28	Dec 19 (1992)–Feb 1
Fall:	Apr 18–27	Apr 9–18
Winter:	June 20–July 6	June 19–July 4
Spring:	Sept 19–Oct 5	Sept 18–Oct 3

NORTHERN TERRITORY

	1992	**1993**
Summer:	Dec 13 (1991)–Jan 28	Dec 12 (1992)–Jan 26
Fall:	Apr 4–12	Apr 3–12
Winter:	June 20–July 19	June 19–July 18
Spring:	Sept 26–Oct 4	Sept 25–Oct 3

WESTERN AUSTRALIA

	1992	**1993**
Summer:	Dec 18 (1991)–Jan 28	Dec 17 (1992)–Feb 2
Fall:	Apr 11–27	Apr 9–26
Winter:	July 4–19	July 10–25
Spring:	Sept 26–Oct 11	Oct 2–17

SOUTH AUSTRALIA

	1992	**1993**
Summer:	Dec 20 (1991)–Jan 27	Dec 19 (1992)–Jan 24
Fall:	Apr 11–26	Apr 9–26
Winter:	July 4–19	July 3–18
Spring:	Sept 26–Oct 12	Sept 25–Oct 11

VICTORIA

	1992	**1993**
Summer:	Dec 20 (1991)–Jan 27	Dec 18 (1992)–Jan 24
Fall:	Apr 10–26	April 8–25
Winter:	July 3–21	July 2–18
Spring:	Sept 18–Oct 4	Sept 17–Oct 3

AUSTRALIA CAPITAL TERRITORY [ACT]

	1992	**1993**
Summer:	Dec 13 (1991)–Jan 27	Dec 18 (1992)–Jan 31
Fall:	Apr 11–26	Apr 9–18
Winter:	July 4–19	June 26–July 11
Spring:	Sept 26–Oct 11	Sept 25–Oct 10

TASMANIA

	1992	**1993**
Summer:	Dec 20 (1991)–Feb 17	Dec 23 (1992)–Feb 15
Fall:	(no holiday)	(no holiday)
Winter:	May 30–June 14	May 29–June 14
Spring:	Aug 29–Sept 13	Aug 28–Sept 12

AUSTRALIA CALENDAR OF EVENTS

JANUARY

☐ **Australia Day.** National day of celebration, rather like a down-under Fourth of July. January 26.

MARCH

☐ **Canberra Festival.** Ten days of performing arts and sporting events culminating in Canberra Day hoopla. Canberra Day is the third Monday in March.

☐ **Moomba Festival.** Melbourne's 10-day festival includes street theater, films, parades, and exhibitions. Early March.

○ *ADELAIDE FESTIVAL OF ARTS. Australia's major arts festival takes place in Adelaide in even-numbered years. Dance, theater, opera, and music are included, as are the literary and visual arts. More than a million attendances were recorded at the 40-plus venues around the city in 1990.*

Where: Adelaide. When: February 28–March 21, 1992. How: For more information, write to the General Manager, Adelaide Festival Centre, GPO Box 1269, Adelaide, SA 5001, or phone 08/213-4788 (enquiries) or 08/213-4777 (bookings).

MAY

☐ **Camel Cup.** Camel races are the highlight of this event which takes place in Alice Springs in May every year.

SEPTEMBER

☐ **Warana.** Brisbane's 2-week fête includes parades, concerts, and lots of outdoor entertainment.

☐ **Australian Rules Grand Final.** The Super Bowl of Aussie Rules footy is held in Melbourne every September.

OCTOBER

☐ **Henley-on-Todd Regatta.** This race, in which contestants run up a dry riverbed carrying homemade boats, takes place in Alice Springs every year. Late September or early October.

NOVEMBER

☐ **Australian Formula One Grand Prix.** Adelaide hosts the country's most exciting car race every year in November. It is the last race on the international Formula One racing calendar and often the most crucial one.

☐ **Melbourne Cup.** "The race that stops the nation" takes place at Flemington Racecourse in Melbourne. First Tuesday in November.

SYDNEY CALENDAR OF EVENTS

JANUARY

☐ **Festival of Sydney.** Performing arts, sporting events, and fireworks are included in this month-long festival. Many of the free concerts are held in the Domain and at Harbourside in Darling Harbour.

FEBRUARY

☐ **Gay and Lesbian Mardi Gras.** This celebration includes theatrical events and the highlight, a parade. Last 3 weeks.

MARCH/APRIL

☐ **Royal Easter Agricultural Show.** Home arts, farming equipment, games, contests, and agricultural products share the spotlight at this 2-week-long popular annual event. Begins 10 days before Easter.

JUNE

☐ **Sydney Film Festival.** For 2 weeks a full schedule of movies is shown at various venues.

DECEMBER

☐ **Sydney-Hobart Yacht Race.** Sailors and nonsailors alike turn out to see the participants off on this exciting race. December 26.

---

3. HEALTH & INSURANCE

HEALTH

There are few health hazards to worry about in Australia. The water is safe to drink, and high standards regulate food handling and preparation. Doctors and dentists are highly trained and hospitals well equipped. Your hotel will locate a doctor for you if necessary.

Visitors are permitted to import reasonable quantities of prescription medication. It's also a good idea to bring along a copy of your written prescription using the generic name for the medication in case a question arises, although local pharmacies (chemists) can fill prescriptions written by Australian doctors only. Pack all medication in your carry-on luggage, so you will still have it with you even if your checked suitcase is lost.

In addition to prescription medication, ask your doctor for recommendations for headaches, head colds, indigestion, motion sickness, constipation, diarrhea, and difficulty sleeping—all maladies which can affect travelers.

Be sure to pack sunscreen, sunglasses, and a visor or hat. Don't underestimate the strength of the Australian sun. It's no coincidence that Aussies have the highest rate of skin cancer in the world.

Vaccinations are not required if you are traveling direct from the U.S., Canada, Britain, or New Zealand unless you have come from or visited a yellow fever–infected country or zone within 6 days prior to arrival. You do not need any other health certificate to enter Australia.

INSURANCE

Check your policy to make sure your health/accident insurance covers you while traveling abroad, and if it doesn't, buy a short-term policy that will.

Likewise, check that your homeowners or renter's policy covers your possessions while you're away. It's also possible that the credit card to which you charge your airline ticket automatically provides some sort of baggage insurance.

If you will be driving down under, check to see if your auto insurance will cover you in case of accident or other loss. Also find out if the credit card with which you pay for the rental car provides any coverage. Many do these days.

4. WHAT TO PACK

Deciding what to take to Australia is not a complicated matter. The life-style is relaxed, and unless you're planning to do a great deal of formal dining and evening activities, casual clothing will do. Be sure to take some sort of waterproof coat or jacket in case you encounter showers, and a wool sweater is also recommended unless you go in the middle of their summer and plan to be only in the northern part of the country. You may want a folding umbrella and definitely should have comfortable walking shoes. Clothing with an elastic waistband is great for traveling—especially on long flights. You should include one slightly dressy outfit for nights at the theater or dining at a special restaurant. If you intend to visit the southern states during their winter, I suggest investing in a spencer after you arrive. Over the years these lightweight wool undershirts have been my salvation when traveling in places where central heating is not *de rigueur.*

The best bet is to take a selection of sweaters, shirts, and jackets and layer them according to the weather. This way you'll be comfortable and have a variety of different outfits. Try to avoid white and pastel clothing, because it shows soil quickly; I highly recommend that everything you take be machine-washable.

You'll want to take the appropriate recreational clothing, which may include a swimsuit (which Aussies call "bathers," "cozzie," or "swimmers"), hiking boots, beach sandals, riding breeches, or a tennis outfit.

You might also consider taking the following items: adapter plug and dual-voltage appliances; address book; alarm clock; camera and accessories; a face cloth; more film than you think you'll need; plastic bags to keep cameras dry and dust-free; corkscrew; insect repellent; necessary medication, copies of prescriptions, and extra contact lenses and prescription glasses; travel diary (journal). If you'll be driving long distances, you also might want some favorite cassette tapes. Take an ample supply of cosmetics and makeup because the imported ones are very expensive in Australia. Fluids should be transferred to plastic bottles with good seals, and nail polish–remover pads substituted for the liquid kind.

5. TIPS FOR THE DISABLED, SENIORS, SINGLES, FAMILIES & STUDENTS

FOR THE DISABLED

The Australian tourism industry is very conscientious in providing facilities for handicapped people. Easy access at attractions, appropriate rest room facilities in public areas, and specially designed hotel rooms make it possible for the disabled person to enjoy a holiday down under.

General information and news about special tours is available from the **Travel Industry and Disabled Exchange (TIDE),** 5435 Donna Avenue, Tarzana, CA 91356 (tel. 818/343-6339). It may also be helpful to contact the **Australian Council for Rehabilitation of the Disabled (ACROD),** 33 Thesiger Court, Deakin, ACT 2600 (P.O. Box 60, Curtin, ACT 2605), Australia (tel. 06/282-4333; fax 06/281-3488), or 55 Charles Street, Ryde, NSW 2112, Australia (tel. 02/809-4488).

FOR SENIORS

In most cases, senior citizens from other countries are not eligible for posted "pensioner" prices. These reduced admission costs are just for older Australians. However, if you're a member of an organization such as the American Association of Retired Persons (AARP), bring along your card, and give it a try.

It should also be noted that members of AARP, 1909 K Street NW, Washington, DC 20049 (tel. 202/872-4700), are eligible for discounts on car rentals, hotels, and airfares.

FOR SINGLE TRAVELERS

The good news is that Aussies are gregarious, and solo travelers can easily strike up conversations and make new friends; the bad news is that hoteliers price their rooms as if they were renting out the ark. About the only way to avoid paying for a double when traveling alone is to stay at youth hostels, in private homes, or on farms, where charges are per person, not per room. Even though bed-and-breakfast inns don't charge much less for a single than for a double, I usually favor them when I'm on my own because I like the homey environment and a chance to meet fellow travelers.

I also suggest that you join a short adventure tour (see "Adventure/Specialty Tours," below) when you feel like hiking, riding a camel, sailing, or other activities where having a buddy is a definite advantage. Otherwise you'll be perfectly safe, provided you use common sense and stay out of dark alleys and spooky parks late at night.

From time-to-time, **Travelin' Singles** (tel. 213/920-9009 or 818/902-9945) offers trips to Australia.

FOR FAMILIES

Australia is the ideal place for a family vacation. If you have any doubts, ask your offspring if they'd rather tour the churches and museums of Europe or romp with 'roos down under. You can easily focus a trip to Australia on beaches, wildlife, forests, sports, and adventure—all of which appeal to the younger set. Another advantage is the relative safety. If children go "walkabout" at the beach, parents needn't worry that they'll never see them again. Also, the informal life-style is comfortable with kids.

Because family travel is common in Australia, a good selection of suitable accommodations is available. Serviced apartments are very convenient because meals can be prepared "at home," thus saving the expense of a restaurant. Campgrounds provide handy facilities for people traveling in campers or motor homes. Those who prefer to stay in hotels will be happy to note that most hostelries allow children to stay in the same room with their parents at no additional charge. Another important fact: Hotels and motels will help arrange for baby-sitters. Some resorts even have separate supervised children's meals and almost all have cots (cribs) on hand.

Even the airlines make it easy for families to travel together. On Qantas, children aged 2 through 11 are charged 67% of the adult fare; infants are charged 10%. On Australian Airlines and Ansett (the two biggest domestic carriers), children 2 through 11 are given a 50% discount and infants are free of charge. Eastwest Airlines, another domestic line, extends the same discount. Railways of Australia also offers a child's fare.

Half-price admission for children is standard at sightseeing attractions; "mother's rooms" for changing babies' nappies (diapers) are found adjacent to public rest rooms (disposable diapers are more expensive, and most Aussie parents still use cloth); picnic and barbecue areas are plentiful. Most car-rental companies supply baby and child seats at a slight charge.

And what if the kids get homesick? No worries if they're American—just take them to McDonald's.

FOR STUDENTS

It's not surprising that Australia is a popular destination for traveling students. While backpackers are shunned in some countries, they're welcomed with open arms in Oz. Youth hostels, campgrounds, and other types of budget accommodations help keep costs down; sports and adventure opportunities abound; and the pubs are lots of fun.

The **Student Travel Network** (also known as STA Travel), with its West Coast headquarters at 7202 Melrose Avenue, Los Angeles, CA 90046 (tel. 213/934-8722, 212/986-9470 in New York, or toll free 800/777-0112 in the rest of the U.S.; 071/737-9921 in London; 09/399-995 in Auckland; 604/682-9136 in Vancouver), offers discounted international airfares on the major carriers for students under age 26. These favorable rates sometimes extend to recent graduates or academic staff. Contact the Student Travel Network for other ways they can save you money. They have 37 offices in Australia, too; national headquarters are in Melbourne: 220 Faraday Street, Carlton, VIC 3053 (tel. 03/347-6911).

The Student Travel Network or any good travel agent will be able to tell you about specialty-tour operators who cater to the 18-to-35 crowd. See also "Adventure/Specialty Tours," below.

6. ALTERNATIVE TRAVEL

STUDY ABROAD

Australian universities and other institutions of higher education accept overseas students—both from within the Commonwealth and from the United States. In 1990, nearly 2,000 U.S. students attended school in Australia. Marine biology majors relish the opportunity to study the proliferation of sea life around the Great Barrier Reef. Australia is also the obvious place to study the Aboriginal culture and related archeology. Other students study the same subjects they would have taken at their home universities. If you are interested in attending school in Australia, write to the Student Enquires Officer at the nearest Australian consulate (see above).

HOMESTAYS & FARM STAYS

Many families throughout Australia, in big cities and small towns, would love to have an overseas visitor stay overnight or for a few days. **Bed & Breakfast Australia,** P.O. Box 408, Gordon, NSW 2072 (tel. 02/498-5344; fax 02/498-6438), has been operating successfully for 12 years, matching up guests and hosts. All homes have been personally visited by Clare and Adrian Webster, owners of the company. **Australian Home Accommodation,** 1st floor, Albert Park Hotel, 83 Dundas Place, Albert Park, VIC 3206 (tel. 03/696-0422; fax 03/696-0329), is another good firm to work through.

The best way to experience rural life down under is to stay on a farm or station with a family, and there are many places around Australia to do this. Guests can try their hand at mustering or shearing or can simply lie back and enjoy the beautiful countryside and the hospitality of their hosts. Several companies specialize in arranging farm stays. If you're interested contact: **Bed & Breakfast Australia** (see above); **Australian Home Accommodation** (see above); or **Host Farms Asso-**

ciation, c/o SO/PAC, 7080 Hollywood Blvd., Suite 201, Hollywood, CA 90028 (tel. 213/393-8262, or toll free 800/551-2012 in the U.S. and Canada; fax 213/395-2061). If you decide to try a farm stay after arriving in Australia, you can contact the offices listed above or make your reservations through any of the tourist offices listed in the city and state chapters.

MEET THE PEOPLE

Friends Overseas-Australia, 68-01 Dartmouth Street, Forest Hills, NY 11375 (tel. 718/261-0534), is a nonprofit organization that operates a meet-the-people program in Australia. It puts visitors in touch with residents who have expressed an interest in meeting Americans with similar interests and backgrounds. This is a great opportunity to experience Australia—off the tourist track. Visitors spend time with local residents, but don't stay in their homes. There is a $25 membership fee (individual or family). Send a self-addressed, stamped, business-size envelope for more information.

HOME EXCHANGES

For an authentic taste of living in Australia, you might like to exchange homes for a period of time. If that's the case, contact **Vacation Exchange Club,** P.O. Box 820, Haleiwa, HA 96712 (tel. toll free 800/638-3841; fax 808/638-5184).

CAMPING & CARAVAN PARKS

If you're one of the many people who choose to rent a campervan or motor home down under and stay at caravan parks and campgrounds, you'll probably be pleasantly surprised by the facilities. Clean rest rooms, communal kitchens, barbecues, electricity hookups, and laundry facilities are almost always provided. Many also have children's playgrounds, a small grocery store, and a recreation room. Nonpowered sites (without electrical hookup) are available for tent camping, and on-site caravans (mobile homes) can be rented.

7. GETTING THERE

Whoever said "getting there is half the fun" was not talking about journeying down under. Unlike Dorothy, who woke up and found herself in the mythical land of Oz, the airborne North American or European visitor crosses the equator and several time zones before reaching the Oz we know of today.

"Getting there consumes half the budget for the trip" would be a more accurate statement. Even with the least expensive fares, the cost of an airline ticket is still a major expense, so the savvy traveler will take the time to study all options carefully.

BY PLANE

More than two dozen airlines fly to Australia from North America, Asia, Britain, and the rest of Europe. **Qantas,** the national carrier, has the most convenient schedule, offers the most nonstops, and allows for the most flexibility.

Other airlines also have very good in-flight service, but the advantage of flying Qantas is that passengers are immersed in Aussie ambience as soon as they step on board. They are also treated to in-flight videos of Australian current events and up-to-date "what's on" entertainment and sports information, as well as Aussie newspapers. All this gives the new arrival a valuable leg up.

In addition, Qantas's safety record is unblemished. Do you remember the scene in

Rain Man when Raymond refuses to board the flight his hustler brother has booked for them, citing the statistics on air crashes and fatalities? At least 15 major airlines excised the airport scene before showing the movie aboard their planes, and it isn't surprising that Australia's national carrier was the only one to show it with the 4-minute sequence intact.

To contact **Qantas,** call toll free 800/227-4500 in the U.S. Other international carriers flying to Australia include the following (telephone numbers are toll free in the U.S.): **American Airlines** (tel. 800/433-7300), **British Airways** (tel. 800/247-9297), **Canadian Airlines International** (tel. 800/426-7000), **Continental Airlines** (tel. 800/231-0856); **Air New Zealand** (tel. 800/262-1234), **Northwest** (tel. 800/447-4747), and **United Airlines** (various local numbers).

TYPICAL REGULAR FARES

Airlines change their rates more often than some people change their socks. Your best bet is to query the airlines directly to find out what they're selling *today,* or work with a travel agent who stays abreast of current fares.

First of all, each airline has at least a half dozen fare levels, ranging from first class down to various advance-purchase tickets. The least expensive fares come with the most restrictions: They have to be purchased ahead of time (usually 14 days, but sometimes 21), and maximum and minimum stays are stipulated. The time of year you travel also affects the price of your ticket. Presently, Qantas's round-trip Los Angeles–Sydney **Anniversary Fare,** which requires a 21-day advance purchase, a minimum stay of 10 days, and allows a maximum stay of 1 month, costs U.S. $1,130 in the low season (May through August), U.S. $1,361 in the shoulder season (March, April, and September through November), and U.S. $1,592 in the peak season (December through February).

Passengers wishing to stay longer than 1 month could use Qantas's **APEX fare** which allows a 3-month stay or the **excursion fare,** which allows stays of up to a year. The price of the round-trip excursion ticket (Los Angeles–Sydney) is U.S. $1,707 for the low season, U.S. $1,893 in the shoulder period, and U.S. $2,205 during the high season. The Anniversary, APEX, Super APEX, and excursion fares all have cancellation penalties and allow various numbers of stopovers. Full economy, business, and first class do not require an advance purchase, do not have cancellation penalties, and are not seasonal. Qantas's regular round-trip **full economy fare** (Los Angeles–Sydney) is U.S. $2,798; **business class** costs U.S. $4,644; **first class** costs U.S. $7,582.

Qantas flies to Australia from three points in North America: Los Angeles, San Francisco, and Vancouver. All flights from Canada go via Honolulu, but nonstops operate out of the two California cities. Australia's national carrier also flies down under from five European cities: London, Amsterdam, Rome, Frankfurt, and Athens. Flights from North America land in Sydney, Melbourne, Brisbane, and Cairns. Flights from Europe and the U.K. arrive in Sydney, Melbourne, Perth, Cairns, and Darwin.

Other airlines also offer nonstop flights to Australia and have three fare seasons. Each has its own assorted fares, different restrictions, and varying stopover policies, so it's important to inquire about these factors before reserving a flight.

Preselect your seat when you book your flight to Australia. Otherwise you'll get to the airport and find that the only spots available are in the middle of the center section. If you are a member of an airline mileage club, look into the possibility of using your points to upgrade to a higher class of service. For the best arrival view of Sydney Harbour and the Opera House, request a window seat on the left side of the plane. Special meal requests must be made ahead of time.

IN-FLIGHT COMFORT

No matter how you look at it, Australia is a long way from anywhere except Indonesia and New Zealand, and scheduled flying times always mean double-digit numbers.

FROMMER'S SMART TRAVELER: AIRFARES

1. Tickets are considerably less expensive when you fly off-season. The cheapest period is May through August, which I think is an excellent time to travel down under.
2. Shop all the airlines that fly to Australia. Watch your newspaper travel section for special promotions.
3. Don't be afraid to ask lots of questions when you phone the airlines or talk to your travel agent. It may be that you qualify for a lower-priced fare by only slightly adjusting your travel plans.
4. Buy your ticket as far ahead as possible. Only a certain number of less expensive seats are allocated for each flight.
5. Take advantage of stopovers which are offered at no additional charge.
6. If you are a member of an airline mileage club, look into the possibility of getting a free ticket or earning bonus miles.

The nonstop flight from Los Angeles to Sydney, for instance, is 14 hours and 45 minutes.

I suggest bringing along a good book and a travel-size board game if you know your seat partner. Wear loose clothing and comfortable shoes that will still fit even if your feet swell a bit. Apply moisturizing lotion during the flight to counteract high-altitude dryness. Keep alcohol consumption to a minimum; drink an 8-ounce glass of water for each hour in the air, and get as much exercise and sleep as possible. The airlines will do the rest by feeding you more often than most infants dine and by running movies almost back to back.

BY SHIP

Long-distance ship voyages are rare these days, but for those with a real fear of flying or a love of cruising, **Cunard Line,** 555 Fifth Avenue, New York, NY 10017 (tel. toll free 800/528-6273), often includes Australia on the world-cruise itineraries of the *QE 2* and the *Sagafjord*. **Princess Cruises,** 10100 Santa Monica Boulevard, Los Angeles, CA 90067 (tel. toll free 800/421-0522), and the **Royal Viking Line,** 95 Merrick Way, Coral Gables, FL 33134 (tel. toll free 800/422-8000), position vessels in the South Pacific, and passengers who fly down and join the ships visit several Aussie ports.

ADVENTURE/SPECIALTY TOURS

If you don't want to travel independently, you might be interested in the plethora of specialty tours that are available. These excursions range from general adventure, cycling, nature, and horseback-riding trips to luxury tours in chartered planes. Some are all-inclusive and some are short group experiences that can be incorporated into an independent itinerary.

In addition to these specialty trips, your travel agent should be able to show you a selection of brochures about general-interest group tours and fly-drive packages. Some are fully inclusive escorted tours; others are short trips of only a few days' duration that can be mixed and matched with periods of independent travel. Dollarwise travelers will read all brochures carefully to determine which is the best value. **Questers Worldwide Nature Tours,** 257 Park Avenue South, New York, NY 10010 (tel. 212/673-3120, or toll free 800/468-8668), as its name implies, designs excursions for birders, wildlife photographers, and anyone "curious about the world." Prices vary according to the duration of the tour; the 39-day trip called "Complete Australia" costs U.S. $10,683 including international airfare from Los Angeles. Questers' 22-day Australia tour costs U.S. $7,457 including airfare.

A 10-day mountain bike tour of Far North Queensland is offered by **Backroads Bicycle Touring,** 1516 5th Street, Berkeley, CA 94710-1740 (tel. 510/527-1555 in California, or toll free 800/245-3874; fax 510/527-1444). The experience includes a quick trip to the reef for snorkeling and overnights at some off-the-beaten-path properties. The cost is U.S. $2,195, plus bike rental of U.S. $155. Airfare is extra. Trips depart in November and May.

Contiki Holidays offers special tours for those in the 18-to-35 age group. Trips last from 8 to 21 days and cost from U.S. $530 to U.S. $1,500. Ask your travel agent to contact Contiki Holidays, 1432 East Katella Avenue, Anaheim, CA 92805 (tel. 714/937-0611, or toll free 800/624-0611 in California, 800/626-0611 in the rest of the U.S.; fax 714/937-1615).

FITS Equestrian, 2011 Alamo Pintado Road, Solvang, CA 93463 (tel. 805/688-9494, or toll free 800/666-FITS; fax 805/688-2943), offers three different riding vacations in Australia. One trip includes a 5-day pub crawl in New South Wales and riding in the Snowy Mountains. Another combines the pub crawl with the Hunter Valley, and the third combines the pub crawl with riding on Fraser Island in Queensland. Each 2-week tour includes 9 days of actual riding. There are several departures throughout the year. The cost varies from U.S. $2,100 to U.S. $2,700 not including airfare.

Equitour, P.O. Box 807, Dubois, WY 82513 (tel. 307/455-3363, or toll free 800/545-0019; fax 307/455-2354), also offers horseback riding holidays down under. The trips take place from early November to late April and cost from U.S. $600 to U.S. $700 for 5- to 7-day rides.

Baird Reynolds, 13544 Ventura Boulevard, Sherman Oaks, CA 91423 (tel. toll free 800/228-8727; fax 818/995-4973), offers air tours of Australia—an ideal way for those with limited time to see this enormous country. Their luxurious 12-day "aircruising" holiday costs from U.S. $4,500 and uses a private jet-powered, 40-seat Fokker F27 to carry passengers to visit a sheep station, an underground mine, Katherine Gorge, Kakadu National Park, the Kimberley region, and many other beauty spots. The planes are equipped with first-class seats and full beverage and meal service is included. Four- 6- and 13-day trips are also available.

Devil Four Wheel Drive Tours, c/o Lemonthyme Lodge off Cradle Mountain Road, Sheffield, Tasmania 7306 (tel. 004/92-1112; fax 004/92-1113), is an adventure company owned by Darryl "Devil" Stafford—Tassie's version of Crocodile Dundee. Darryl is very enthusiastic about Tasmania and loves showing it off to his guests. Trips last from 4 to 6 days and cost from U.S. $300 to U.S. $428.

Travelabout, 61 Brady Street, Glendalough, Perth, WA 6016 (tel. 09/242-2243; fax 09/242-1448), offers four-wheel-drive tours around Western Australia. Their 16-day trip through the beautiful Kimberley region costs U.S. $1,056. The 4-day Monkey Mia excursion to see the dolphins costs U.S. $230. Travelabout also journeys to the Hammersley Ranges and the scenic southwestern portion of the state.

8. GETTING AROUND

Transportation is an important element of any vacation, but because of the considerable miles between Australia's cities, it becomes critical when planning a trip down under. Crisscrossing the continent uses up valuable time and money, so practical itineraries and economical modes of travel are a must.

Your mode of interstate transportation will be determined by the amount of time and money you have to spend and whether you're interested more in cities or in the countryside between them. Renting a car and driving from point to point consumes a lot of time and a fair amount of money, but it's the best way to see the scenery. Taking a coach (bus) is less expensive but also less flexible. Trains are fun but don't allow for stopovers at places that strike your fancy. Flying from place to place is the fastest way to get around, but it's relatively expensive and excludes the possibility of touring rural environs on the way. Interstate ferry service comes into play only on the Melbourne-Tasmania route.

BY PLANE

In a country as big as Australia, a certain amount of flying is required for those who want to see a good cross section of sights in a limited amount of time. Since you can't see the scenery from 30,000 feet, a well-planned itinerary will use flights for the greatest distances and some sort of ground transportation for the shorter spans.

The two major Aussie carriers are **Australian Airlines** (tel. toll free 800/922-5122 in the U.S., 800/448-9400 in Canada) and **Ansett** (tel. toll free 800/366-1300 in the U.S. and Canada). Both have extensive networks of routes throughout the country. As far as I can tell, the only difference between the two is that the Australian Airlines personnel are consistently friendlier and more helpful. (I think of Australian Airlines as the Nordstrom of Australian domestic travel.) In addition to the two chief airlines, **Eastwest Airlines** (c/o Ansett; tel. toll free 800/366-1300 in the U.S. and Canada) covers the eastern half of the nation. Many smaller lines service particular regions.

Compass Airlines is Australia's newest airline, having attracted a lot of attention when they entered the transport scene at the end of 1990 with fares that are considerably cheaper than the competition's. Their six wide-body planes provide service to and from Sydney, Melbourne, Perth, Adelaide, Brisbane, and Cairns. Full-fare Compass flights can be booked outside Australia through the international carrier you choose to use, but their cheapest fares have to be purchased after arrival. If you're willing to wait and to be flexible, you could save a bundle by flying this fledgling airline.

Because of their country's vastness and sparse population, Aussies use planes as often as Londoners use the tube. But don't let the casual attitude of a bush pilot in a little plane fool you—Australian aviation standards are high. In-flight services are also very good. Federal regulations prohibit smoking on all domestic flights.

AIR PASSES & SPECIAL FARES

Overseas visitors should take advantage of the bargain airfares available to them, some of which require purchase prior to leaving home, rather than buying regular point-to-point air tickets after arriving in Australia.

Australian Airlines offers an **Australian Air Pass** which gives visitors 25% to 40% discount off full economy fares, depending on the total number of flights flown. The Air Pass can be purchased outside Australia or at an Australian Airlines office in Australia within 30 days of arrival. Australian Airlines also offers **Blue Roo Fares** which provide a 35% discount on selected routes regardless of the total number of sectors flown. Like the Air Pass, Blue Roo Fares can be purchased outside Australia or within 30 days of arrival.

Ansett's **See Australia Airfare** offers overseas travelers a 25% discount off regular economy fares, and their **Explore Australia Airpass** provides discounts of 30% to 40%, depending on the total number of domestic sectors flown. Tickets must be issued outside Australia.

Eastwest offers four passes: **System Wide, Northern Skies, Sun Airpass,** and **Southern Skies.** These passes must be sold outside of Australia and travel must be completed within 21 days from the start of use.

Because of the changing nature of air travel, the wise traveler will confirm the information provided here at the time of booking or before heading down under.

BY TRAIN

Australian rail service falls somewhere between the fast, efficient mode of transportation available in Europe and the almost-nonexistent, mediocre passenger-railroad system found in America. A dozen train routes link cities on the east coast of the continent with Melbourne, Mildura, Broken Hill, Adelaide, Alice Springs, Kalgoorlie, and Perth. Each state operates its own rail service, and they join together under the **Railways of Australia** umbrella to provide interstate transportation.

Except for the few routes on which the **XPT (Express Passenger Train)** operates, none of the trains could be described as fast, but they do provide a safe, economical, out-of-the-ordinary way to get from place to place without missing the scenery. It's even possible to combine train and car travel because many routes offer "motorail service," which means that your vehicle can ride the rails with you.

The **Indian Pacific,** which traverses the country from Sydney to Perth, is one of Australia's most popular trains. Despite the fact that the trip takes 65 hours, reservations are sometimes hard to come by and should therefore be made well in advance. The Indian Pacific leaves Sydney on Monday, Thursday, and Saturday and departs Perth on Sunday, Tuesday, and Thursday.

Recently refurbished, **The Ghan** is Australia's most deluxe train. In fact, in 1990 it won the Australian Tourist Commission's top award for tourist transportation. The train travels between Adelaide and Alice Springs, a trip which takes 22 hours and provides passengers with a good view of the outback from the lap of luxury. The Ghan leaves Adelaide on Thursday year round and on Monday and Thursday from April to October. It departs Alice Springs on Friday year round and on Tuesday and Friday from April to October.

The Queenslander carries passengers in comfort between Brisbane and Cairns, and XPTs operate on the Sydney-Brisbane route and the Sydney-Murwillumbah route. The **Trans Australian** travels between Adelaide and Perth; the **Overland** between Adelaide and Melbourne; and the **Melbourne Express, Sydney Express,** and **Intercapital Daylight** connect Australia's two largest cities.

COMFORT & ACCOMMODATIONS

First-class sleeping compartments are available on all the long-distance trains. The smallest of these accommodations are "roomettes," which provide you with a place to put your head and also give you a chance to experience how Clark Kent must have felt when he changed clothes in a phone booth. There is a bed, a sink, and a toilet and, in spite of their minuscule size, they are surprisingly comfortable.

Larger cabins, called "twinettes," have two beds and their own shower. Both types of compartments have picture windows, hot and cold water, electrical outlets for shavers, and comfortable beds with crisp linens. "Deluxe compartments" are the most spacious and feature three-quarter beds. Economy-class twinettes do not include private toilets and showers. The trains are kept spotlessly clean by a staff of ever-present porters. Since there is an extra charge for compartments, budget-conscious travelers might prefer to ride in a chair car where the seats recline for sleeping. In either case, all interstate rail passengers are allowed up to 80 kilograms (176 lb.) of luggage, which can be checked, carried in your cabin, or kept by your seat. If you wish to check luggage, keep in mind that the baggage counter closes half an hour before the train leaves.

In addition to sleeping facilities, the majority of long-distance trains in Australia have dining cars with full meal service. The food is good, and the wine list adequate (though not extensive). Dining-car stewards routinely serve and clear four-course dinners in less than an hour.

Another popular feature is the club car, which offers abundant opportunities for socializing. Aussie senior citizens and overseas visitors, the two groups with whom Australian train travel seems the most popular, often play cards and chat their way across the continent.

Smoking is permitted in club, lounge, and sleeping cars, but not in dining cars.

SPECIAL PASSES/DISCOUNTS

Visitors who intend to use trains as a major form of transportation in Australia should consider buying an **Austrailpass,** available in first class or economy for anywhere from 2 weeks to 3 months. The pass, which allows unlimited travel, must be purchased prior to arrival down under and does not include charges for berths

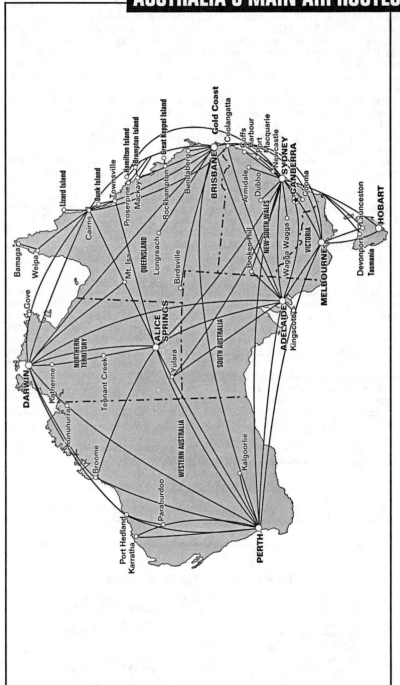

AUSTRALIA'S MAIN AIR ROUTES

(compartments) and meals. A 14-day Austrailpass costs A$690 (U.S. $552) in first class and A$415 (U.S. $332) in economy. The 21-day pass is A$850 (U.S. $680) in first class and A$535 (U.S. $428) in economy. The price of a 1-month pass is A$1,050 (U.S. $840) in first class and A$650 (U.S. $520) in economy. A 2-month pass is A$1,460 (U.S. $1,168) in first class and A$930 (U.S. $744) in economy; for 3 months, the cost is A$1,680 (U.S. $1,344) in first class and A$1,070 (U.S. $856) in economy. Seven-day extensions cost A$350 (U.S. $280) in first class and A$225 (U.S. $180) in economy.

Railways of Australia also sells a **Kangaroo Road 'n Rail Pass** which offers unlimited rail travel and unlimited travel on Greyhound buses. The 14-day pass costs A$825 (U.S. $660) in first class and A$520 (U.S. $416) in economy; the 21-day pass costs A$990 (U.S. $792) in first class and A$715 (U.S. $572) in economy. The 28-day pass costs A$1,210 (U.S. $968) in first class and A$910 (U.S. $728) in economy.

In addition to the above-mentioned passes, Railways of Australia sells **Caper Fares,** 7-day advance-purchase fares which provide a discount of 30% off the full fare. These good-value tickets can be purchased after arrival in Australia.

To make reservations and to buy either of these dollarwise passes, contact ATS/Tour Pacific (tel. toll free 800/232-2121 in California, 800/423-2880 in the rest of the U.S.). In Canada, phone Goway Travel Ltd. (tel. 416/322-1034 in Toronto, 800/663-9418 in B.C., 800/663-9107 in Alta. and Sask., 800/668-1427 in Ont., and Que., and 800/387-8850 in Man. and the Maritimes).

BY BUS

Interstate bus service in America is often a case of dingy bus stations and questionable traveling companions—but not so in Australia. Clean motorcoaches, equipped with adjustable seats, air conditioning, and bathrooms, provide economical express transportation between cities. They also ply an extensive network of minor roads, carrying passengers to small towns and out-of-the-way places. Smoking is not allowed on coaches; the terminals are modern, and seatmates are likely to be companionable Australians or other overseas tourists. In addition, coach captains (drivers) are traditionally very friendly and informative.

Pioneer, Greyhound, and **Bus Australia** are the largest express-coach companies. In addition, many smaller lines provide service within certain regions. Pioneer's **Silver Service** trips offer deluxe features such as stereo sound systems, en route videos, and seats which are more comfortable than usual. This luxury is only available on some routes.

Reservations should be made in advance on main express routes and during school holidays. Two pieces of luggage per person are carried free of charge.

SPECIAL PASSES/DISCOUNTS

Each of the coach companies offers travel passes that represent considerable savings when compared to the cost of purchasing individual tickets.

SAMPLE TRAVEL TIMES & FARES

Route	Hours	Fares
Sydney-Adelaide	24	A$125 (U.S. $100)
Sydney-Canberra	4½	A$25 (U.S. $20)
Sydney-Melbourne	14½	A$52 (U.S. $41.60)
Adelaide–Alice Springs	24	A$153 (U.S. $122.40)
Cairns-Brisbane	27	A$139 (U.S. $111.20)
Brisbane-Sydney	17	A$63 (U.S. $50.40)

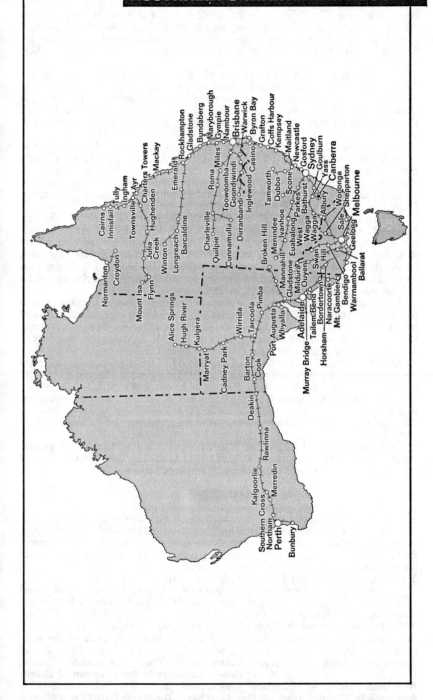

AUSTRALIA'S MAIN TRAIN ROUTES

The **Bus Australia Pass** provides unlimited coach travel on any of the company's routes. The 7-day pass costs A$302 (U.S. $241.60), the 10-day pass costs A$384 (U.S. $307.20), the 15-day pass costs A$486 (U.S. $388.80), the 21-day pass costs A$661 (U.S. $528.80), the 30-day pass costs A$814 (U.S. $651.20), the 60-day pass costs A$1,337 (U.S. $1,069.60), and the 90-day pass costs A$1,802 (U.S. $1,441.60).

Bus Australia also offers a **Flexi Pass** which provides travel, without backtracking, over one of 20 specific itineraries. Passengers are allowed 6 months to complete their journey, except in the case of the three longest routes where 12 months is allowed and the Tasmanian Wilderness route which must be completed in 14 days. Flexi Pass prices start at A$139 (U.S. $111.20) and go as high as A$857 (U.S. $685.60), although most are in the A$200 to A$400 (U.S. $160 to U.S. $320) range.

Either of Bus Australia's good-value passes can be purchased overseas or in Australia; however, prices are lower if purchased overseas. Contact Bus Australia, c/o the Australian Destination Centre, 3471 Via Lido, Suite 206, Newport Beach, CA 92663 (tel. toll free 800/227-5317 on the U.S. West Coast, 800/635-5488 in the U.S. Midwest/East Coast, or 714/675-7306 in California, 604/734-7725 in western Canada, or 416/924-1112 in eastern Canada).

Australian Coachlines, which owns both Pioneer and Greyhound, offers an **Aussie Pass** which allows unlimited travel on both coachlines. Prices vary according to duration. A 7-day pass costs A$302 (U.S. $241.60), a 10-day pass costs A$384 (U.S. $307.20), a 15-day pass costs A$486 (U.S. $388.80), a 21-day pass costs A$661 (U.S. $528.80), a 30-day pass costs A$814 (U.S. $651.20), a 60-day pass costs A$1,337 (U.S. $1,069.60), a 90-day pass costs A$1,802 (U.S. $1,441.60), and a 120-day pass costs A$1,980 (U.S. $1,584.00).

Australian Coachlines also offers an **Aussie Explorer Pass** which allows you to travel on your choice of 22 preset itineraries. No backtracking is permitted and travel must be completed within 6 or 12 months, depending on the distance to be covered. Fares range from A$60 to A$855 (U.S. $48 to U.S. $684), depending on the extent of the travel involved, with most in the A$200 to A$400 (U.S. $160 to U.S. $320) range.

Australian Coachlines also offers a **Tassie Pass** which provides unlimited travel around Tasmania on the coachlines which serve the island state. This pass costs A$99 (U.S. $79.20) for 7 days, A$120 (U.S. $96) for 14 days, and A$140 (U.S. $112) for 21 days. And don't forget about the Kangaroo Road 'n Rail Pass, sold in conjunction with Railways of Australia, mentioned earlier. The Aussie Pass, the Aussie Explorer Pass, and the Tassie Pass can be purchased in Australia, but they're less expensive abroad.

To purchase any of the Australian Coachlines passes contact Greyhound International, c/o SO/PAC (tel. toll free 800/551-2012 in the U.S. and Can.). In Canada contact Goway Travel (see "Special Passes/Discounts," above).

BY CAR

The availability of good public transportation makes cars superfluous in most Australian cities, but they're wonderful for wandering rural backroads and proceeding from city to city at your own pace. Tourists can drive with their valid foreign licenses for up to 3 months, and the various motoring organizations provide maps and other information to card-carrying members of overseas auto clubs. For stays of longer than 3 months, an international driving permit would have to be obtained.

For help with the rules of the road Aussie style, advice on outback motoring, and other questions, contact one of the following: **National Roads & Motorists Association (NRMA)**, 151 Clarence Street, Sydney, NSW 2000 (tel. 02/260-9222); **Royal Automobile Club of Victoria (RACV)**, 422 Little Collins Street, Melbourne, VIC 3000 (tel. 03/607-2137); **Royal Automobile Club of Queensland (RACQ)**, 190 Edward Street, Brisbane, QLD 4000 (tel. 07/253-2444); **Royal Automobile Club of Western Australia (RACWA)**, 228 Adelaide Terrace, Perth, WA 6000 (tel. 09/421-4444); **Royal Automobile Association of South Australia (RAA)**, 41 Hindmarsh Square, Adelaide, SA 5000 (tel. 08/223-4555); **Automobile Association of the Northern Territory (AANT)**, 79 Smith

Street, Darwin, NT 0800 (tel. 089/81-3837); or the **Royal Automobile Club of Tasmania (RACT),** corner of Patrick and Murray streets, Hobart, TAS 7000 (tel. 002/38-2200).

CAR RENTALS

The big four—**Hertz, Avis, Budget,** and **Thrifty**—have offices in all the big cities, many small towns, and most of the airports. All of them are reliable and offer a wide range of vehicles; however, I've found that **Ansa International** offers something the others don't: personal service. Because Ansa doesn't have staffed counters in Aussie airports, they send someone out from their city office to greet the new arrival. In my opinion, it's much nicer to get off a plane and see a smiling face holding a card with your name on it than to deplane and then get in line at a car-rental counter. They will also deliver cars to hotels and motels. Ansa has offices throughout Australia with the exception of the Northern Territory, and their rates are lower than the big four's.

After driving many different rented cars in Australia, I've concluded that my favorite is the Holden Commodore built by General Motors. I couldn't tell you what's under the hood, but I do know that this large sedan gets very good mileage, that its body is extremely sturdy, that its boot (trunk) is commodious, and that its interior is well designed. Ansa has many Commodores; they rent for A$55 to A$95 (U.S. $44 to U.S. $76) per day, depending on the length of the hire. A manual Mazda without air conditioning rents for A$42 to A$59 (U.S. $33.60 to U.S. $47.20) per day. A Toyota Camry with air conditioning, power steering, and so forth rents for A$52 to A$85 (U.S. $41.60 to U.S. $68) per day. These rates include unlimited kilometers and insurance.

It's sometimes possible to save money on a car rental by getting a fly-drive package, such as the "Deals on Wheels" offer made by Qantas and Avis. Airline mileage clubs also offer their members bargains with their car-rental partners.

In addition to the major car-rental companies, many local firms rent vehicles, sometimes at lower rates. The disadvantage of the smaller independents is that since they don't have many offices, they generally don't offer one-way rentals, and can't provide the backup services of the larger companies.

The minimum age for renting a car in Australia is 21, but many companies impose their own limit of 25 or over. Thrifty's minimum age is 23. Ansa's is 21.

Reservations for rental cars in Australia can be made by calling the following toll-free numbers: **Ansa** (c/o SO/PAC, tel. toll free 800/445-0190 in California, 800/551-2012 in the rest of the U.S., 800/235-8222 in Canada), **Avis** (tel. toll free 800/331-1084 in the U.S.), **Budget** (tel. toll free 800/472-3325 in the U.S. and Canada), **Hertz** (tel. toll free 800/654-3001 in the U.S., 800/268-1311 in Canada), **National** (tel. toll free 800/227-3876 in the U.S. and Canada), and **Thrifty** (tel. toll free 800/367-2277 in the U.S. and Canada).

BUYING A CAR

If your stay in Australia will be a long one, you might want to think about buying a car instead of renting one. While recommending used-car dealers is risky business, there's one in a Sydney suburb that I feel I should mention. **Mach I Autos,** 495 New Canterbury Road, Dulwich Hill, NSW 2203 (tel. 02/569-3374), is owned by Frank McCorquodale, a friendly fellow who has become well known for his guaranteed buy-back price agreement. Here's how it works: You buy a car from Mach I, and drive it as much as you want for as long as you want. When you're ready to leave the country, he buys the vehicle back at a previously agreed upon price—that is, assuming it's still in driveable condition. The buy-back price is usually about 50% of what you originally paid.

GAS

The price of gas (petrol) varies from state to state but tends to be cheapest on the east coast and highest in the Northern Territory. Presently it's selling for approximately A62¢ to A70¢ a liter.

Petrol stations accept credit cards and are generally open during business hours and the early part of the evening. *Note:* Some stations are closed on weekends, and few stay open around the clock.

ROAD CONDITIONS

Australian roads are no great shakes. The main highway between Sydney and Brisbane, for instance, is a two-lane road. In some places little shoulder exists and passing can be treacherous. Conditions in Queensland are slightly better; the motorway to Surfers Paradise stands out in my mind as one of the best in the country. The Hume Highway between Sydney and Melbourne is another good road. Generally speaking, drivers should expect nondivided, one-lane-in-each-direction highways and be pleasantly surprised when they encounter something more spiffy.

"You can't get there from here" is another principle to keep in mind. One doesn't jump in the car and drive from Cairns to the tip of the Cape York Peninsula, for instance. Not without a four-wheel-drive vehicle and someone who knows the way, because there isn't a road. The same is true in other parts of the country, so consult a recent road map before planning your itinerary.

You should also consider the weather. In the Northern Territory they don't have many roads, and the ones that exist are often closed during "the wet," the monsoon season that descends upon the area from December to April.

Another thing to watch for in the Northern Territory: "road trains," up to three truck trailers linked together forming one major hazard. They are nearly impossible to pass on a narrow road, and the drivers have been known to be less than chivalrous.

Don't drive on Australian highways at night. That's when kangaroos hop across the road, and drivers who swerve to miss them can end up in considerable strife. Locals who live in rural areas attach "roo bars" to the front of their cars. In some areas wandering camels and water buffalo also pose a problem.

DRIVING RULES

Australians drive on the left, give way (yield) to the car on the right, and turn left on red only where signs indicate that it is permissible. It's all very straightforward, and the average competent driver should not be afraid of driving down under. Roundabouts (traffic circles) are one of the few areas that cause concern to North American drivers. Just remember, give way to any vehicle already in the traffic circle.

Also, wearing seat belts is compulsory for both drivers and passengers. Drinking-and-driving laws are strict ("under .05 or under arrest"). Random-stopping breath tests are common, and the police officers involved certainly don't seem to be concerned with public relations. The speed limit in built-up areas is 60 kilometers per hour (35 m.p.h.); on the open highway it's 100 to 110 kilometers per hour (60 to 66 m.p.h.).

MAPS

The best maps are those available at the auto clubs listed earlier in this section. They are free of charge if you present your membership card from your home-country club.

BREAKDOWNS/ASSISTANCE

If you experience difficulty while driving a rental car in Australia, phone the company from which you hired the car. The other alternative would be to call the nearest auto club. The phone numbers for their breakdown service are listed in all telephone directories.

BY FERRY

While many vessels provide transfers to and from Great Barrier Reef islands, and a boat that carries both passengers and vehicles links Adelaide with Kangaroo Island, the only regularly scheduled interstate ferry service in Australia operates from Victoria to Tasmania. The **MV Abel Tasman** makes regular trips between Melbourne and Devonport; **SeaCat Tasmania** departs from Port Welshpool, Victoria, and arrives in George Town, Tasmania. Details on these services can be found in Chapter 18.

HITCHHIKING

Regardless of how much success you've had with thumbing in other parts of the world, don't plan on it in Australia. It's illegal in Queensland and Victoria and frowned upon by the police in other states. In addition, given Oz's great distances and sometimes less-than-temperate weather, hitching is highly impractical.

9. SUGGESTED ITINERARIES

CITY HIGHLIGHTS

The majority of overseas visitors include Sydney on their itinerary, and this is as it should be. The city has one of the most beautiful harbors in the world and provides a plethora of enjoyable activities. However, it would be a mistake to visit Australia's largest city and not any of the others. Adelaide, Perth, and Hobart are three of my favorites, and I hope you will consider stopping in at least one of them. These smaller cities offer something Sydney doesn't have: residents who haven't been inundated with tourists over the past few years and are therefore extremely friendly and helpful.

This is not to say that Sydneysiders are always rude, but because coastal New South Wales and Queensland are very popular with overseas visitors, the locals have become a little jaded. To experience real Aussie hospitality, venture into South Australia, Western Australia, or Tasmania. These are also three of the best places for good food and wine at less than sky-high prices.

Alice Springs in the Northern Territory is another spot I heartily recommend. There's nowhere else like it in the country, and the surrounding scenery is breathtaking.

Likewise, it's a mistake to overlook Canberra, the national capital. This beautiful city is a treasure trove of the country's accomplishments.

PLANNING YOUR ITINERARY
IF YOU HAVE 1 WEEK

I don't think anyone would or should plan to go to Australia on a 1-week vacation. It's just too far. On the other hand, you may find yourself with a spare week in Oz after attending a conference or conducting business. If this is the case, I suggest you limit your exploration to one state. You might, for instance, spend a few days in Sydney, followed by an overnight visit to Canberra, and then finish up with a stay on an outback New South Wales cattle station.

Alternatively, you could base yourself in Cairns, Queensland, and do a different day-trip every day for a week. This way you would experience the Great Barrier Reef, the rain forest of Daintree National Park, and the contrasting climate of the Atherton Tablelands.

IF YOU HAVE 2 WEEKS

If you have 2 weeks, try to confine your travels to either a northern route or a southern one. Late autumn, winter, and spring visitors (May to November) can fly into Sydney, spend a few days, and then fly to Ayers Rock. After a day or two at the rock, bus transportation to Alice Springs provides an eye-level look at the Red Centre. From "the Alice," a flight to Cairns puts you within striking distance of the Great Barrier Reef and in the heart of one of Australia's most exciting tourist areas. Since Cairns has an international airport, it won't be necessary to return to Sydney to get your homebound flight.

If your 2 weeks happen to come during Australia's late-spring to mid-autumn months (November to April), why not try a southern circuit, starting at Sydney and including Canberra, Melbourne, Tasmania, and Adelaide? This itinerary works well with train and coach schedules.

IF YOU HAVE 3 WEEKS

With more time, combine these shorter plans, or add a week in Western Australia to either of them.

HIGHLIGHTS OUTSIDE THE CITIES
EXPLORING THE GREAT BARRIER REEF

For some people, witnessing the wonders of the Great Barrier Reef is a life's ambition. If this applies to you, let me suggest a few places on which to focus your attention.

Heron Island, off the coast of Gladstone, 528 kilometers (327 miles) north of Brisbane, is one of the few coral cays with its own resort. Whether you want to snorkel, scuba, or walk on the reef at low tide, this is the place. Farther north, **Orpheus Island** (reached via Townsville) and **Lizard Island** (out of Cairns) both have excellent coral viewing on fringe reefs and launch trips to the outer reef.

While Heron, Orpheus, and Lizard prohibit day-trippers, regular catamaran service shuttles visitors back and forth between Cairns and **Green Island,** one of the other true coral cays. Since accommodations on the islands are relatively pricey, this convenient service makes Green Island the best bet for budget-conscious barrier buffs. The *Quicksilver* boat trip from Port Douglas (just north of Cairns) is another way to see the reef without having to pay for a room in a luxury resort.

A Safety Note: Keep in mind when planning your itinerary that northern Queensland's coastal waters are hazardous from October to May, when deadly marine stingers can be present. The beaches are safe, but swimming should be restricted to a pool. This condition also affects the closer Barrier Reef islands, such as Hinchinbrook and Magnetic, but it's okay to swim around the islands that are farther out.

OUTBACK OZ

The most interesting and accessible spots in the outback—**Broken Hill, Coober Pedy, Alice Springs,** and **Ayers Rock**—can easily be linked into a workable itinerary. Those who like train travel can ride the Indian Pacific from Sydney to Adelaide, a trip that includes a sightseeing stop in Broken Hill. The Ghan, the train from Adelaide to Alice Springs, doesn't go to Coober Pedy, but this odd opal-mining town is on the route of those who choose to drive between the two places.

If your time is limited, taking the train or driving is out of the question. However, **Kendell Airlines** has a flight that goes from Adelaide to Ayers Rock on Saturday, with a stop for sightseeing in Coober Pedy. The complete itinerary for those who want to see a lot of the outback would start with this flight and would include a coach trip to Alice Springs from Ayers Rock. Coaches from Sydney to Alice Springs travel via Broken Hill and Coober Pedy.

WILDLIFE WANDERING

If Australia's native fauna are the focus of your trip and you want to see them in their natural habitat, you should probably rent a car. It's nearly impossible, for instance, to get to **Lamington National Park** by public transportation, and this wonderful spot on the New South Wales–Queensland border is a treasure trove for birdwatchers and fauna fans. **Cradle Mountain National Park** in Tasmania and **Kakadu** in the Northern Territory are accessible by coach, but you'll want a car for looking around once you get there.

If you don't want to drive or go on an all-inclusive escorted tour, a few parks are still handy. You can easily fly to **Kangaroo Island** from Adelaide, and once on the island, it's possible to pick up bus tours that go to **Flinders Chase National Park.** In one memorable afternoon there I saw koalas, emus, Cape Barren geese, and many colorful birds; I also petted kangaroos, wallabies, and their joeys, and walked through a seal colony. "K.I.," as the locals refer to it, is a not-to-be-missed experience for those who enjoy wildlife.

If time doesn't permit touring national parks, you can look at native animals in one of the country's many wildlife reserves. **Healesville Sanctuary** outside of Melbourne is one of the best.

10. WHERE TO STAY

Australia offers a wide range of accommodations, from pricey international-standard hotels to modest motels and bed-and-breakfast inns. Some of the terms used down under are unusual, but the following overview should help to clarify things.

HOTELS

Australia has its fair share of the big hotels found in all the world's major cities. Travelers who enjoy the familiarity, predictability, and high standards offered by these international hostelries will be glad to know that **Sheratons, Hiltons, Regents, Hyatts, Ramadas, Holiday Inns,** and **Inter-Continentals** are available down under.

Many other hotels, of course, are part of regional chains. These are often less expensive, while offering standards similar to those found in the internationals. In this category, look for **Parkroyals, Travelodges,** and **Olims.** By the way, Travelodge Hotels in Australia are owned by a different corporation, and offer a much higher standard of accommodation than the motels of the same name in the United States.

In addition to hotels that are part of a chain, numerous independent properties are available. These often represent good value, but have remained a local secret because they don't advertise overseas. Many of them have a charming atmosphere that reflects the surrounding environment, as well as personal service the big hotels may lack. I discovered many such spots while doing the research for this book and was delighted to include them. Since their rates are lower than those of the internationals, you'll find most of these gems listed in the "Moderate Accommodations" categories of the city chapters.

All rooms in modern Australian hotels have private bathrooms, heating, air conditioning, telephones, TVs, radios, and minibars. In addition, coffee- and tea-making facilities and a small refrigerator are almost always supplied. Meals are served in a dining room or restaurant, with drinks available in at least one bar. Most places also offer room service and provide laundry facilities.

SAVING MONEY

City hotels can be very accommodating to tourists on weekends, when the business travelers who occupy most of the rooms during the week have gone home. Discounts of 40% to 50% are not unusual, but *you have to ask for them.* In hotel parlance, a weekend is Friday, Saturday, and Sunday nights. Sometimes you can also get off-season specials and long-stay rates that are much lower than the standard room rates. It's also possible to get "the corporate rate" just for asking, and an "early-bird discount" when a room is booked and paid for a week in advance. When business is slow, hotels offer special packages which might include breakfast, champagne, or a similar enticement. These can represent very good value, assuming you want whatever the extras are that are being included.

Another way to save a bit on accommodations is to present your auto-club card at one of the **Aussie motoring clubs** (see "By Car," above) and ask them to make reservations in the hotels and motels that give their members a discount. Some properties will even give discounts to auto-club members on the spot, even if the room wasn't prebooked through one of the clubs.

In addition, your airline mileage club membership might entitle you to hotel discounts.

HOTEL PASSES

Three companies offer prepaid coupons that represent a discount on their regular room rates. One of these, the Southern Pacific Hotel Corporation, sells an **SPHC Downunder Hotel Pass,** which may be used at any of their 60 deluxe and first-class Parkroyal, Centra, THC, or Travelodge hotels in Australia, New Zealand, Asia, Tahiti, and Fiji, as well as the Sydney Boulevard, the Gold Coast International in Surfers Paradise (Queensland) and the Launceston International in Tasmania.

Each coupon costs U.S. $42, and the number of coupons required at each hostelry varies from two to four. A minimum of 12 vouchers must be purchased at one time, but they do not need to be used consecutively. The hotel pass can be purchased only by U.S. and Canadian residents prior to departure. To order an SPHC Downunder Hotel Pass, contact the Southern Pacific Hotel Corporation, 1901 Avenue of the Stars, Suite 1045, Los Angeles, CA 90067 (tel. toll free 800/441-3847 in the U.S. and Can.).

Another hotel discount voucher system is offered by Flag International, which has 400 properties in Australia. Flag hotels and motels are graded into six categories, and the **Flag Hotel Pass** costs U.S. $49 to U.S. $177 per room, single or double occupancy, per night depending on which category you choose. To get a copy of the Flag directory, purchase a pass, or make reservations, call toll free 800/624-3524 in the U.S. and Canada. Reservations can be made before departing down under or as you travel through Australia via Flag's nationwide toll-free number.

The Rydges Hotel Group also offers a pass which must be purchased prior to departure. Their **Hi-Style Hotel Pass** costs U.S. $115 per room per night (single or double occupancy). For more information or reservations, phone toll free 800/878-2929.

RESERVATIONS

Many people like the flexibility of making hotel reservations as they need them, instead of reserving ahead of time. This system works well in most cases, but I strongly recommend that Sydney lodging, which is often in short supply, be organized in advance. I also think it's a good idea to prearrange the first couple of nights in the country, regardless of where you arrive. There's nothing worse than trying to find a home away from home while suffering from jet lag.

It's possible to make reservations at many Australian hotels and motels by making toll-free calls in North America. If you want to do this, you can contact the following chains: **Best Western International** (tel. toll free 800/528-1234 in the U.S. and Canada), **Flag International Hotels and Resorts** (tel. toll free 800/624-3524 in the U.S. and Canada), **Hilton International** (tel. toll free 800/445-8667 in the U.S., or 800/268-9275 in Canada), **Holiday Inns** (tel. toll free 800/HOLIDAY in the U.S. and Canada), **Hyatt Hotels** (tel. toll free 800/233-1234 in the U.S. and Canada), **Inter-Continental Hotels** (tel. toll free 800/332-4246 in the U.S. and Canada), **Regent International Hotels** (tel. toll free 800/545-4000 in the U.S. and Canada), **Sheraton Corporation** (tel. toll free 800/325-3535 in the U.S. and Canada), and **Southern Pacific Hotel Corp.** (Travelodges and Parkroyals) (tel. toll free 800/835-SPHC in the U.S. and Canada).

COUNTRY PUBS

Hotels in Australia were originally built as places for dispensing "grog," but to comply with the licensing laws, they had to have a certain number of guest bedrooms as well. Most of the pubs built during the era of these regulations are functioning today as "grog shops" only. However, some of them—primarily in country towns—offer inexpensive, atmospheric accommodations to travelers. Some of the old public licensed hotels in the city also offer overnight stays.

If you're interested in staying in a pub, contact **Australian Pubstays Pty. Ltd.,** 1st floor, Albert Park Hotel, 83 Dundas Place, Albert Park, VIC 3206 (tel.

03/696-0433; fax 03/696-0329). Prices vary from approximately A$38 to A$83 (U.S. $30.40 to U.S. $66.40) for a single and from A$55 to A$100 (U.S. $44 to U.S. $80) for two people, including breakfast.

MOTELS & MOTOR INNS

While hotels are licensed to serve alcoholic beverages and usually furnish all meals, most motels limit themselves to lodging and breakfast only. Further, while hotels often provide both showers and bathtubs, motels frequently offer only showers. Because they cater to motorists, motels and motor inns have ample free parking available. The majority of them also provide laundry facilities, telephones, TVs, radios, and heating and air conditioning, as well as coffee- and tea-making facilities and a small refrigerator.

SERVICED APARTMENTS

Overseas visitors to Australia are usually surprised to find a large number of fully furnished apartments for rent on a daily basis. These convenient places have all the kitchen equipment necessary for preparing a meal and often have a lounge (living room) in addition to one or two bedrooms. Sometimes meals are available, but rarely are serviced apartments licensed to serve alcohol. Daily cleaning service is usually included (but they don't wash dishes); all linens are supplied. Rates are generally lower than they would be for the same space at a comparable hotel. A "holiday flat" is basically the same thing as a serviced apartment, but without the daily cleaning service. Aussies are starting to use the term "all suite hotel" to describe certain serviced apartments, and they are, in fact, very similar.

FARM STAYS

Several companies specialize in arranging farm stays. Rates range from A$98 to A$115 or more (U.S. $78.40 to U.S. $92) per person per night including all meals. See "Alternative Travel," above, for more information.

YOUTH HOSTELS

The YHA has 130 hostels spread around Australia. For information on this economical form of lodging open to all ages, contact either the **American Youth Hostels National Office,** P.O. Box 37613, Washington, DC 20013-7613 (tel. 202/783-6161), or the **Canadian Hostelling Association, National Office,** 1600 James Naismith Drive, Room 608, Gloucester, ON K1B 5N4 (tel. 613/748-5638). Once in Australia, questions should be directed to the **Australian Youth Hostel Association,** 60 Mary Street, Surry Hills, NSW 2010 (tel. 02/212-1151). Fees are around A$15 (U.S. $12) a night.

BED-AND-BREAKFAST INNS

I have to confess a partiality toward these cozy inns where rooms sometimes come without a private bath, but where you get a wonderful breakfast. Every city in Australia has at least a few, although finding them requires diligent sleuthing: They often don't advertise and aren't promoted by travel agents because some of them don't pay commissions. Not only are B&Bs cozier and less expensive than hotels, but they also provide a level of hospitality matched only by that experienced at farm and home stays. Bed-and-breakfast inns in Australia are sometimes called "private hotels" because they aren't licensed to serve alcohol.

HOMESTAYS

Staying with an Australian family is a great way to get to know the country. Companies such as **Bed & Breakfast Australia,** P.O. Box 408, Gordon, NSW

2072 (tel. 02/498-5344; fax 02/498-6438), can help you find just the right host. Rates range from A$40 to A$50 (U.S. $32 to U.S. $40) per night for a single and from A$68 to A$80 (U.S. $54.40 to U.S. $64) per night for two people sharing a room, including breakfast. Bed & Breakfast Australia offers three categories of rooms; in the top two categories guests normally have their own bathroom. In economy rooms, hosts and guests share the facilities. For more information, see "Alternative Travel," above.

11. WHERE TO DINE

Australian dining spots are almost identical to restaurants in other parts of the world, but a few cultural differences are worth mentioning. To begin with, most menus are à la carte and every desired dish must be specifically ordered. This confuses some Americans, who are accustomed to finding bread and soup or salad included with all meals. Another caution for my compatriots: Don't ask for "doggie bags;" Aussies don't call them that, and they use them less frequently than we do. Don't be surprised when you have to ask for ice water, and remember that no-smoking sections are rare.

We Yanks are sometimes accused of being surly over what we consider slow service. Just keep in mind that if you want everything just the way it is at home, then home is where you should stay.

Labor costs are high in Australia, and many restaurants add a surcharge on weekends and holidays when they must pay overtime wages to their staff. On the positive side, these highly paid employees don't necessarily expect a gratuity. The Aussies who choose to tip leave a maximum of 10% for exceptionally good service, 5% for average, and nothing when they are unhappy.

Many restaurants, especially ethnic ones, offer take-away (take-out) meals. Because there is less labor involved, these are sometimes considerably less expensive than the sit-down variety.

Another way to save money on meals is to dine in BYO (Bring Your Own) restaurants. In these places diners bring their own wine or beer, purchased at a bottle shop (liquor store) and avoid paying inflated restaurant prices. It's important to find out ahead of time if an establishment is licensed to sell spirits or if it's BYO. In all restaurant write-ups in this book, I've stated which places are BYO, but it's a good idea to confirm my information when you phone to make reservations. BYOs tend to be fairly casual, as are bistros and brasseries.

The mini-Aussie/Yankee lexicon found in the appendix of this book will provide you with most of the dining definitions you'll need, but before you read any further, I want to point out a few major vocabulary differences. An "entrée" in Australia is a smallish first course, similar to an "appetizer" in the United States. A "main course" down under is an "entrée" in America. "Tea" is sometimes used as a synonym for dinner. A "salad bar" does not consist of ingredients for making a tossed green salad, but is instead a buffet of already-mixed salads, such as coleslaw, three bean, potato, pasta, and so forth. And, on the subject of salad, if you order a mixed green one, it will be served with your meal, not before it.

A "counter tea" is a casual meal served in a pub from 6 to 7:30 or 8pm. The cost is in the vicinity of A$5 to A$7 (U.S. $4 to U.S. $5.60). Pubs are also agreeable places to have lunch, but keep in mind that they serve food for only a limited time, usually from noon to 2:30pm, but sometimes just until 2pm. Pub lunches can be quite economical; curry and rice or roast-of-the-day frequently costs only A$4 (U.S. $3.20). Meat pies and sandwiches can be had for even less. Every traveler should try a pie-and-a-pint pub lunch at least once. It's a significant part of the Australian dining scene—and they don't charge extra for the ambience.

Pub meals are very good value, as are lunches and dinners at RSL clubs. Another way to economize is to picnic in one of the country's many parks; most areas have barbecue facilities and clean rest rooms.

If you stay in serviced apartments, you can do your own cooking, which is cheaper than dining out. Even if you stay in regular hotels or motels, you can avoid paying for breakfast by buying a box of cereal and a carton of milk. Refrigerators and coffee- and tea-making facilities are standard features of accommodations down under.

12. SHOPPING

There was a time when opals were about the only exciting purchase available to visitors in Australia, but that was before Aussie designers caught the attention of the world with their appealing colors and patterns. Nowadays, shoppers have fun buying traditional outback garments, contemporary fashions, and attractive souvenir items, as well as the pretty precious and semiprecious stones.

WHAT TO BUY

Australian movies have helped popularize the **work clothes** worn by rugged bushmen and drovers. *The Man From Snowy River* launched Driza-bone riding coats onto the international fashion scene. Akubra hats and moleskin pants gained wide exposure in *A Town Like Alice, Phar Lap,* and *Crocodile Dundee.* These items and a variety of sturdy boots are manufactured and sold throughout Australia by the firms of R. M. Williams and Morrisons.

Sheepskin products are also popular, but I think that travelers who are visiting both Australia and New Zealand will find that Kiwi shops offer more variety and better selection. On the other hand, Aussie designers can't be beat when it comes to colorful, creative **wool sweaters.** Ken Done and his contemporaries also turn T-shirts, sweatshirts, tea towels, aprons, and coasters into works of art.

Aboriginal arts and crafts—artifacts and paintings, bark pictures, wood carvings, and watercolors—make good investments as well as attractive mementos. You may have to go to the Northern Territory to buy Aboriginal art directly from the tribe that created it, but it is also sold at galleries throughout the country. Likewise, handcrafts produced in various states are available in craft shops in all the capital cities. **Glass** and **pottery** from Tasmania and South Australia are especially interesting. And don't overlook **Australian books** as good souvenir and gift items. Also **Australian wine.**

Melbourne is the best place for buying desinger clothing. Australia's top fashion designers are Prue Acton, Carla Zampatti, Adele Palmer, Trent Nathan, Perri Cutten, and Anthea Crawford.

OPALS

While opals can be purchased in almost every country, the best values are to be found in Australia, which produces 95% of the world's supply. Stores that sell opal jewelry are located in all the major cities and provide the best shopping for the majority of visitors. Those who prefer to travel to the remote areas where the gemstones are mined might get a good buy on unset stones if they are knowledgeable and drive a hard bargain. Lightning Ridge, New South Wales, is the home of the black opal. Coober Pedy, South Australia, is the major center for white or milk opals. Other fields are located at Mintabie, South Australia, and Quilpie in Western Queensland.

When purchasing opals, three factors should be considered: color, brightness, and pattern. Very expensive stones should have a lot of red showing. Other visible hues, in descending order of value, are orange, green, and blue. A valuable opal should also be bright, and large splashes of strong color are preferable to numerous small ones.

The most expensive opals are solid, but doublets and triplets are usually found in souvenir-quality jewelry. Be sure you know what you're buying. Triplets consist of a thin veneer of opal glued on a plastic backing and topped with a clear quartz dome. A doublet is the same thing without the quartz top.

Most stores will deduct the Australian sales tax levied on opal jewelry when overseas purchasers show their passport and airline ticket. This can result in substantial savings.

WHERE TO BUY IT

Nearly every city in Australia has a pedestrian **shopping mall** in the center of the downtown area. These handy precincts are usually dominated by one or two major department stores, like David Jones, which caters to the carriage trade, and Grace Bros., which appeals more to the middle market. Seemingly endless small shops surround the department stores and fill attractive arcades.

In addition to traditional shopping venues, there are large **public markets.** These bargain barns sell everything from fruits and vegetables to clothing, costume jewelry, and household goods. Some markets are similar to American swap meets and others are more reminiscent of European flea markets. Like the markets, **factory outlets** offer savings to the shopper with a good eye.

In all these cases, the Australian sales tax is included in the price of all goods and is not added at the time of purchase.

Duty-free stores, which sell imported jewelry, perfume, porcelain figurines, handbags, liquor, cameras, and other items, intrigue many travelers because they sound like a great place to save money. However, while these stores are popular with Aussies and Kiwis, who must normally pay high rates of Customs duty on these luxury goods, the average American tourist will not find bargains in these shops. I encourage you to exercise caution when you feel yourself lured by the words "duty free." The best bet is to call around before you leave home and find out what you'd pay for the items in your local stores. I've yet to find a perfume in a duty-free store at a lower price than I pay for the exact same thing in the States.

 AUSTRALIA

American Express Available services at American Express offices through-out Australia include: reconfirmation, rerouting, and reissuing of airline tickets; emergency check cashing; emergency card replacement; traveler's check sales and refunds; sightseeing reservations; and client letter service. The head office is at 388 George St., Sydney (tel. 02/239-0666; fax 02/235-0192).

Business Hours In general, city banks are open Mon–Thurs 9:30am–4pm and Fri 9:30am–5pm. Most businesses are open Mon–Fri 9am–5pm. Stores are generally open Mon–Fri 9am–5:30pm and Sat 9am–12:30pm; in addition, stores are open one night a week, either Thurs or Fri, until 9pm, and some shops are open Sat 9am–4pm (in tourist areas, it's not uncommon to find some stores that are open 7 days a week).

Camera/Film Most major brands and types of film are available in the larger cities. Prices are reasonable considering that most of them include processing, which can be done anywhere in the world. Prints can be developed quickly, but slides, especially Kodachrome, take much longer.

Cigarettes Smokes in Australia are expensive compared with their Yankee counterparts. I suggest that you bring your own. Each traveler over the age of 18 is allowed to bring in 250 cigarettes or 250 grams (8.75 oz.) of cigars or tobacco.

Climate See "When to Go," above.

Crime See "Safety," below.

Currency See "Information, Entry Requirements, and Money," above.

Customs Visitors may bring their personal effects into Australia without paying duty. These include cigarettes (see above) and 1 liter of liquor. Don't even think about bringing in narcotics and other controlled substances.

Dates Aussies, like Europeans, put the day before the month and year; therefore, 8/12/45 in the U.S. is equivalent to 12/8/45 down under.

Documents Required See "Information, Entry Requirements, and Money," above.

Driving Rules See "Getting Around," above.

Drugstores The down-under equivalent of the North American drugstore is called a "chemist shop."

Electricity The electric current in Australia is 220-240 volts AC, 50 hertz. North American and Japanese visitors can't use the same 110-voltage appliances they use at home. I recommend dual-voltage hairdryers, curling irons, and other implements. In addition, everyone except New Zealanders will need an adapter plug because the power outlets require a socket with three flat prongs. Universal outlets for 240-volt and 110-volt shavers are found in the better hotels. In order to get power from an electrical outlet, it is necessary to turn the adjacent switch to the on (down) position.

Embassies/Consulates Since Canberra is the capital, that's where you'll find the foreign embassies. In case of an emergency, the following information may be helpful: Canadian High Commission, Commonwealth Ave., Yarralumla, ACT 2600 (tel. 06/273-3844); Embassy of Ireland, 20 Arkana St., Yarralumla (tel. 273-3022); New Zealand High Commission, Commonwealth Ave., Yarralumla, ACT 2600 (tel. 06/273-3611); Embassy of the United Kingdom, Commonwealth Ave., Yarralumla, ACT 2600 (tel. 06/270-6666); United States Embassy, Moonah Place, Yarralumla, ACT 2600 (tel. 06/270-5000).

The following countries have consulates in Sydney: Canada, 50 Bridge St. (tel. 231-6522); New Zealand, 25th floor, State Bank Bldg., 52 Martin Place (tel. 233-8388); United Kingdom, 1 Alfred, Circular Quay (tel. 247-7521); United States, corner Elizabeth and Park streets (tel. 261-9200).

Emergencies Dial 000 anywhere in Australia to summon the fire department, police, or ambulance.

Etiquette One of the few vestiges of their British ancestry is the Australians' propensity to queue (line up) for things. Other than that, be polite, keep your voice down (but always return a shout in the pub), and you'll be right, mate.

Hitchhiking See "Getting Around," above.

Holidays See "When to Go," above.

Information See "Information, Entry Requirements, and Money," above, and individual city chapters for local information offices.

Language Aussie English has to be heard to be believed. For a sampling, see the lexicon in the appendix of this book.

Laundry Many hotels and motels in Australia have coin-operated washing machines and dryers for guests' use (irons are also widely available). For laundries, see the individual city chapters for details.

Liquor Laws Pub (bar) hours vary, but usually run Mon–Sat 10am–11pm; some places are closed Sun, and those that are open don't get started until noon and close down by 10pm. The drinking age throughout the country is 18. And remember that Aussie laws are very strict about drinking and driving, so don't.

Mail Letters can be sent to you in care of General Delivery (poste restante) at any post office in Australia. For example: Ms. H. Traveler, c/o General Delivery, GPO, Sydney, Australia. The GPO is the main post office in each city.

A postcard to the United States costs A85¢ (U.S. 70¢); a letter to the United States costs A$1 (U.S. 80¢). A postcard to New Zealand costs A65¢ (U.S. 55¢); a letter to New Zealand costs A70¢ (U.S. 60¢). A postcard to the U.K. costs A90¢ (U.S. 75¢) and a letter to the U.K. costs A$1.20 (U.S. $1).

If you send packages home or buy quantities of stamps, you can use MasterCard or VISA to pay for purchases. If you post any domestic mail, be sure to use the **postal code,** which is the equivalent of the American ZIP Code. A postcard within Australia costs A43¢ (U.S. 35¢), and a letter costs the same.

You can also receive mail in care of the local American Express office if you are a cardmember or carry their brand of traveler's checks.

Maps For information on obtaining the best maps, see "Getting Around," above.

Newspapers The most widely read daily newspapers are listed in the "Fast Facts" section of every city chapter.

Passports See "Information, Entry Requirements, and Money," above.

Pets Animals entering Australia from North America have to be quarantined in Britain for 6 months.

Police Dial 000 anywhere in Australia to summon the police.

Safety   One of Australia's attractions is its relative safety. Crime is not a big worry here, and generally you can feel safe wherever you go. However, whenever you're traveling in an unfamiliar city or country, stay alert. Be aware of your immediate surroundings. Wear a moneybelt and don't sling your camera or purse over your shoulder. Men should carry their billfolds in an inner pocket. This will minimize the possibility of your becoming a victim of crime. Every society has its criminals: It's your responsibility to be aware and alert in even the most heavily touristed areas.

Taxes   A A$10 (U.S. $8) departure tax, payable in local currency, is levied on all persons aged 12 and over when they leave Australia. (Many travelers check in for their flight, convert the balance of their cash, and then find that they lack the money to pay the tax. To prevent this from happening, I suggest that you fold an Australian $10 bill in your passport when you first enter the country, and leave it there until you depart.)

Telephone/Telex/Fax   Most hotels in Australia (and in the world, for that matter) place high surcharges on calls made from guest rooms, so you should use pay phones whenever possible, call collect, or use a credit card. The easiest way to make an overseas call is to dial the appropriate "country direct" number. This will put you in touch with an operator in that country who will handle your call. The following are country direct numbers: 0014-881-150 (Canada); 0014-881-640 (New Zealand); 0014-881-011 (U.S. AT&T); 0014-881-100 (U.S. MCI); 0014-881-440 (United Kingdom).

Toll-free numbers within Australia begin with 008.

When dialing long distance in Australia, be sure to use the right city code: 02 for Sydney, 03 for Melbourne, 07 for Brisbane, and so forth. When dialing these places from overseas, omit the zero.

Telex and fax messages can be sent from post offices or, if you're willing to pay a service charge, from your hotel.

A local call from a pay phone costs 30¢; from a hotel, the charge can be as high as 95¢ (costs are in local currency).

Time   There are three time zones in Australia. When it's noon (standard time) on the east coast, it's 11:30am in the center of the country, and 10am in Western Australia. Daylight saving time starts the last Sun in Oct and ends the first Sun in Mar in all states except Queensland, Northern Territory, and Western Australia. (During daylight saving time, Brisbane is 1 hour behind Sydney, Darwin is 1½ hours behind, and Perth is 3 hours behind.)

Tipping   Restaurant employees don't necessarily expect a gratuity; the Aussies who choose to tip leave a maximum of 10% for exceptionally good service, 5% for average, and nothing when they are unhappy. In addition, Aussies usually leave a small amount of change for bar service, give taxi drivers 5% to 10% of the fare, and A$1 (U.S. 80¢) or more to porters. It is not customary to tip hairdressers and barbers.

Tourist Offices   See "Information, Entry Requirements, and Money," above, and also the individual city chapters.

Visas   See "Information, Entry Requirements, and Money," above.

Water   You can drink the water without any worry.

CHAPTER 3
GETTING TO KNOW SYDNEY

Sydney is a collage, a patchwork of colors and textures. The sparkling waters of the harbor splash against the seawall that surrounds the Royal Botanic Gardens. The lush green surface of the park abuts the downtown core, where smooth chrome-and-glass office towers turn the streets into shady canyons. The neon lights of Kings Cross create a small rainbow at one side of the picture; while in The Rocks area, the vivid hues of redevelopment have brightened the somber tones of working warehouses and convict-cut stone cottages.

The city's 3.5 million inhabitants present contrasts no less dramatic than the background against which they live. Women in English woolens take afternoon tea at one of the old, traditional hotels, while down the street the lines at McDonald's stretch out the door.

The parks are popular with "new" Australians, and on Sunday scores of extended families can be seen strolling and picnicking, with grandma in the same black dress she'd be wearing were she still in Greece or Italy. On the same day, the harbor will be full of pricey sailboats whose occupants could be models for trendy sportswear.

1. ORIENTATION

ARRIVING
BY PLANE

Kingsford Smith Airport is well equipped to meet the needs of travelers. In the international terminal you will find: banks (open 5:30am to 11pm or until the last flight is in), baggage lockers (A$1/U.S. 80¢ for the first 24 hr., A$2/U.S. $1.60 per day thereafter), car-rental companies (Avis, Budget, Hertz, Thrifty), elevators, information, mail boxes, a message board, a post office (open Monday through Saturday from 7am to 5pm and on Sunday from 8am to 5pm), shops (Australiana, Australian produce, duty-free, and pharmacy), restaurants and bars, showers, strollers, wheelchairs, and trolleys (luggage carts).

In addition to their counters at the airport, the following airlines have offices in Sydney: **Air New Zealand,** 8 Martin Place (tel. 965-4111); **Ansett,** at the corner of Oxford Street and Riley Street (tel. 268-1111 or 268-1555); **Australian Airlines,** 70 Hunter Street (tel. 693-3333); **British Airways,** 64 Castlereagh Street (tel. 258-3300); **Canadian Airlines International,** 30 Clarence Street (tel. 299-7843); **Compass,** 50 Margaret Street (tel. 299-1977); **Continental,** 321 Kent Street (tel. 249-0111); **Eastwest Airlines,** 54 Carrington Street (tel. 268-1166); **Qantas,** at the corner of George Street and Jamison Street (tel. 236-3636 or 957-0111); **United,**

☑ # WHAT'S SPECIAL ABOUT SYDNEY

Beaches
- ☐ Manly Beach, just a short ferry ride from the central business district, where Norfolk pines line the boardwalk.
- ☐ Bondi Beach, known for great waves, with many trendy spots to eat nearby.

Museums
- ☐ Hyde Park Barracks, designed by convict architect Francis Greenway in 1818.
- ☐ Australian National Maritime Museum, in Darling Harbour, with an exhibit on U.S.-Australian links.

For Kids of All Ages
- ☐ Sydney Aquarium, in Darling Harbour, where sharks swim inches away.
- ☐ Featherdale Wildlife Park, where you can cuddle a koala or kiss a kangaroo.

Ace Attractions
- ☐ Sydney Harbour, surely one of the world's most beautiful.
- ☐ Sydney Opera House, a world-famous landmark.

Activities
- ☐ Harbour cruise, where you can admire the city from the water.
- ☐ *The Story of Sydney*, a wide-screen introduction to Australia's oldest city.

After Dark
- ☐ Sydney Opera House, offering drama, orchestral concerts, opera, and more.

Shopping
- ☐ Queen Victoria Building, a restored Victorian beauty, open 7 days a week.

Sunday Selections
- ☐ Free entertainment around the Opera House, popular with locals and visitors alike.

Wonderful Walks
- ☐ From Circular Quay to Mrs. Macquarie's Chair, along the waterfront and around the Opera House.
- ☐ Through The Rocks, admiring cottages of convict-cut stone—lots of good shops and atmospheric pubs.

---

10 Barrack Street (tel. 237-8888); and **UTA French Airlines,** 12 Castlereagh Street (tel. 233-3277).

You can travel to the city center either on the **Kingsford Smith Airport Coach** or on the **Airport Express** operated by State Transit. Both cost about A$5.00 (U.S. $4) one-way for adults, half price for children under 12, and leave the airport every 20 minutes for the ½-hour trip into town. The buses start running at 6am and serve both the international and the domestic terminals.

The Kingsford Smith bus drops its passengers at the door of their hotel or motel; the Airport Express delivers people to one of nine predetermined points in the city, from which they must walk or take a taxi. A **taxi** to Sydney from the airport costs about A$18 (U.S. $14.40).

Departing passengers can arrange for the Kingsford Smith Airport Coach to pick them up at their hotel if they call at least an hour in advance (tel. 667-3221).

BY TRAIN

Should you arrive by train from another state, it's a short taxi ride from **Central Station** at the end of Pitt Street to the city center.

BY BUS

The **Pioneer coach terminal** is on the corner of Oxford and Riley, and this is also where Greyhound buses come in; the **Bus Australia terminal** is near Central Station on Rawson Place and George Street.

BY CRUISE SHIP

Should you arrive by cruise ship, you'll find that the **Overseas Passenger Shipping Terminal** is ideally located near The Rocks and Circular Quay and only a short distance from the Opera House.

BY CAR

The **Pacific Highway** brings visitors from the north; the **Great Western Highway** is the main route to Sydney from the west, and the **Hume Highway** and **Princes Highway** enter Sydney from the south.

TOURIST INFORMATION

A plethora of information is available to Sydney's visitors. The **Travellers' Information Service** at the international airport terminal is open 365 days a year from 6am until the last flight arrives. These folks are helpful with hotel reservations and can sometimes arrange favorable rates for those who did not reserve lodgings in advance. They can also arrange cruises and coach tours. A free telephone information service is in operation 7 days a week from 8am to 6pm (tel. 669-1583 or 669-5111).

In the city center, information is available at the **New South Wales Travel Centre,** 19 Castlereagh Street near Martin Place (tel. 231-4444). This well-stocked office is open Monday through Friday from 9am to 5pm, and the staff is ready and willing to answer questions and make reservations for you. The **Sydney Visitors Information Booth** (shared with Halftix), in Martin Place between Castlereagh and Elizabeth streets (tel. 235-2424), is also a good place to get information—Monday through Friday from 9am to 5pm.

On weekends, as well as during the week, the people at **The Rocks Visitor Centre,** 104 George Street (tel. 247-4972), answer questions about their part of town. They're open Monday to Friday from 8:30am to 5:30pm and on weekends and public holidays from 9am to 5pm (closed Good Friday and Christmas). Also in The Rocks, **Tourist Newsfront,** 22 Playfair Street (tel. 247-7197), offers free tourist services and booking facilities 7 days a week from 9am to 5pm, excluding Good Friday and Christmas.

You can get good tourist information at the **National Roads and Motorists' Association (NRMA),** 151 Clarence Street (tel. 260-9222), if you are a member of an affiliated club. They're open Monday through Friday 8:30am to 5pm and Saturday 8:30 to 11:30am.

For information about the seaside suburb of Manly, contact **Manly Tourist Promotions,** South Steyne Street, Manly (tel. 977-1088). They're open 7 days a week from 10am to 4pm and are closed public holidays.

Interstate information is available by contacting: **Canberra Tourist Bureau,** 14 Martin Place (tel. 233-3666); **Northern Territory Tourist Bureau,** 345 George Street (tel. 262-3744); **Queensland Government Travel Centre,** 75 Castlereagh Street (tel. 232-1788); **South Australian Government Travel Centre,** 143 King Street (tel. 232-8388); **Tasmanian Government Tourist Bureau,** 149 King Street (tel. 233-2500); **Victorian Tourism Commission,** 61 Market Street (tel. 233-5499); and **Western Australian Tourist Centre,** 92 Pitt Street (tel. 233-4400).

CITY LAYOUT

Sydney is Australia's largest and oldest city. Founded at the harbor, it has gradually spread inland, so that the metropolitan region now covers 1,730 square kilometers (668 sq. miles)—an area considerably greater than that of sprawling Los Angeles. Sydney is about the same distance from the equator as San Diego and enjoys a similar sunny climate.

Two major bodies of water—the South Pacific Ocean and the harbor, which is a major inlet of the ocean—have given Sydney its shape. The **harbor** divides the downtown core on the south from the suburbs, which stretch out to the north. The **Sydney Harbour Bridge** connects the two sides. The inland waterway's irregular coastline has determined where the most expensive real estate is, and where the most picturesque neighborhoods have developed. The harbor has dozens of bays, separated by arms of land. From the bridge eastward are marinas filled with private yachts. West of the bridge is commercial and industrial activity. Just 11 kilometers (7 miles) to the east, large surf rolls up onto some of the most beautiful beaches in the world.

MAIN ARTERIES & STREETS

Downtown Sydney has grown from **Circular Quay** (pronounced "key"), the terminal for dozens of ferries and fast catamarans that regularly cross the harbor, to the south along Macquarie, Elizabeth, Castlereagh, Pitt, and George streets. The major east-west thoroughfares are Bridge, Hunter, King, Market, and Park. The twisted maze of streets near the quay evolved from ruts created by bullock carts in colonial days. Now taxis, buses, and cars inch their way through the area. **Martin Place,** a pedestrian mall that runs from Macquarie Street to George Street, is the heart of the city center. While sleek, modern buildings predominate here, some beautiful examples of colonial architecture remain on Macquarie Street. **Centrepoint Tower,** on Market Street between Pitt and Castlereagh, is a lofty, easy-to-spot landmark.

NEIGHBORHOODS IN BRIEF

Circular Quay   Because of the harbor ferries, which come and go frequently, the train station, and bus stop, Circular Quay is a major transport hub. It is also a picturesque spot for strolling and has both indoor and outdoor eateries. The Opera House is only steps away at the end of Bennelong Point. From Circular Quay there is a good view of the Sydney Harbour Bridge, also known as "the coat hanger."

North Sydney   Once a repository for the overflow of Sydney's office buildings and now an important business district in its own right. Located at the north end of the Harbour Bridge.

Northern Suburbs   Beyond North Sydney, Chatswood, Lindfield, Killara, and other suburbs are strung out along Pacific Highway. The easiest way to get there is by train.

North-shore Communities   Kirribilli and Neutral Bay are only two of the popular neighborhoods located on the north side of the harbor. The Taronga Park Zoo is also here. Ferries provide frequent access.

Manly & the Northern Beaches   Easily reached by ferry or fast catamaran, the seaside suburb of Manly is known for its good beach. Other beaches along the coast north of the harbor entrance: Curl Curl, Dee Why, Collaroy, Avalon, and Whale.

The Rocks   A historic area of colonial stone buildings that now house myriad shops and popular pubs, as well as a string of excellent restaurants. The Rocks area is located west of Circular Quay.

Darling Harbour   Located at the southwest edge of the main business district is a former industrial area that now hosts many sights of interest to tourists. Darling Harbour's convention center, Sydney Aquarium, exhibition center, waterfront promenade, Harbourside Marketplace, and Chinese garden were opened in 1988 as part of the bicentennial celebrations. The Australian National Maritime Museum has opened since then. Easily reached by monorail.

Kings Cross & Beyond   About a mile from the city center, lies the infamous red-light district called Kings Cross. Beyond "the Cross," attractive suburbs—Elizabeth Bay, Double Bay, Rose Bay, and Watsons Bay—hug the waterfront.

Paddington   Inland from Double Bay, this Sydney neighborhood is a down-under version of New York's Greenwich Village.

Bondi & Other Southern Beaches Sydney's famous beaches face the South Pacific Ocean on both sides of the harbor entrance: to the south, Bondi, Bronte, Clovelly, and Coogee.

Parramatta This major manufacturing area lies within the metropolitan region, about 45 minutes by train from the central business district.

STREET MAPS

Get maps of Sydney and the surrounding area from the New South Wales Travel Centre, 19 Castlereagh Street (tel. 231-4444), or, if you're a member of an affiliated club, get maps from the NRMA, 151 Clarence Street (tel. 260-9222).

---

2. GETTING AROUND

BY PUBLIC TRANSPORTATION

State Transit operates an excellent network of buses and ferries in Sydney, coordinated with the urban and suburban trains run by CityRail. For **timetable information** on all State Transit lines, call Metrotrips (tel. 954-4422) daily from 6am to 10pm. In addition, a monorail connects the city center to Darling Harbour.

MONEY-SAVING PASSES Visitors who will be using public transportation frequently would be wise to purchase the **SydneyPass,** which includes 3 days' unlimited use of all the following: the Sydney Explorer Bus (described below), all State Transit buses, The Rocks–Darling Harbour Shuttle, all Sydney ferries and JetCats (including Manly), the harbor cruises operated by State Transit, and the Airport Express Bus (round-trip). The price is A$39 (U.S. $31.20) for adults and A$20 (U.S. $16) for children under 16. The SydneyPass is for sale only to interstate and overseas residents. You can buy the pass in Sydney (proof of residence required) from the New South Wales Travel Centre, 19 Castlereagh Street (tel. 231-4444), on board the Airport Express Bus, on board the Sydney Explorer Bus, at the Ansett Gift Shop in the Domestic Terminal, at the Travellers' Information Service office in the International Terminal, and anywhere else the SydneyPass logo is displayed.

State Transit's **One Day Sydney Network Bus Tripper** is also a good deal. It costs A$6 (U.S. $4.80) and provides unlimited bus travel for 1 day. Buy it on the bus, and get more information from Metrotrips (tel. 954-4422).

BY PUBLIC BUS

Bus routes cover a wide area of metropolitan Sydney. The minimum fare is A$1.20 (U.S. $1) for a 4-kilometer (2½-mile) "section." The farther you go the cheaper it gets. For example, the 44-kilometer (27-mile) trek to Palm Beach costs A$3.80 (U.S. $3.05). Tickets are purchased directly from the driver, and exact change is not needed. In peak periods, a "queue conductor" near the bus stop sells tickets. Try to avoid using public transportation during the morning and evening rush hours.

Buses bound for the suburbs leave from Circular Quay, Railway Square next to Central Station, York Street at Wynyard Park, and a few other places. Buses heading south and west travel along George Street from the quay, while those going east travel along Elizabeth or Pitt Street, turning east after Park Street. Northbound buses leave from Carrington Street beside Wynyard Park and head across the Harbour Bridge. Since the system is somewhat confusing, your best bet is to ask for some assistance before making a trip. Buses run from 4am to 11:30pm during the week, less frequently on weekends and public holidays.

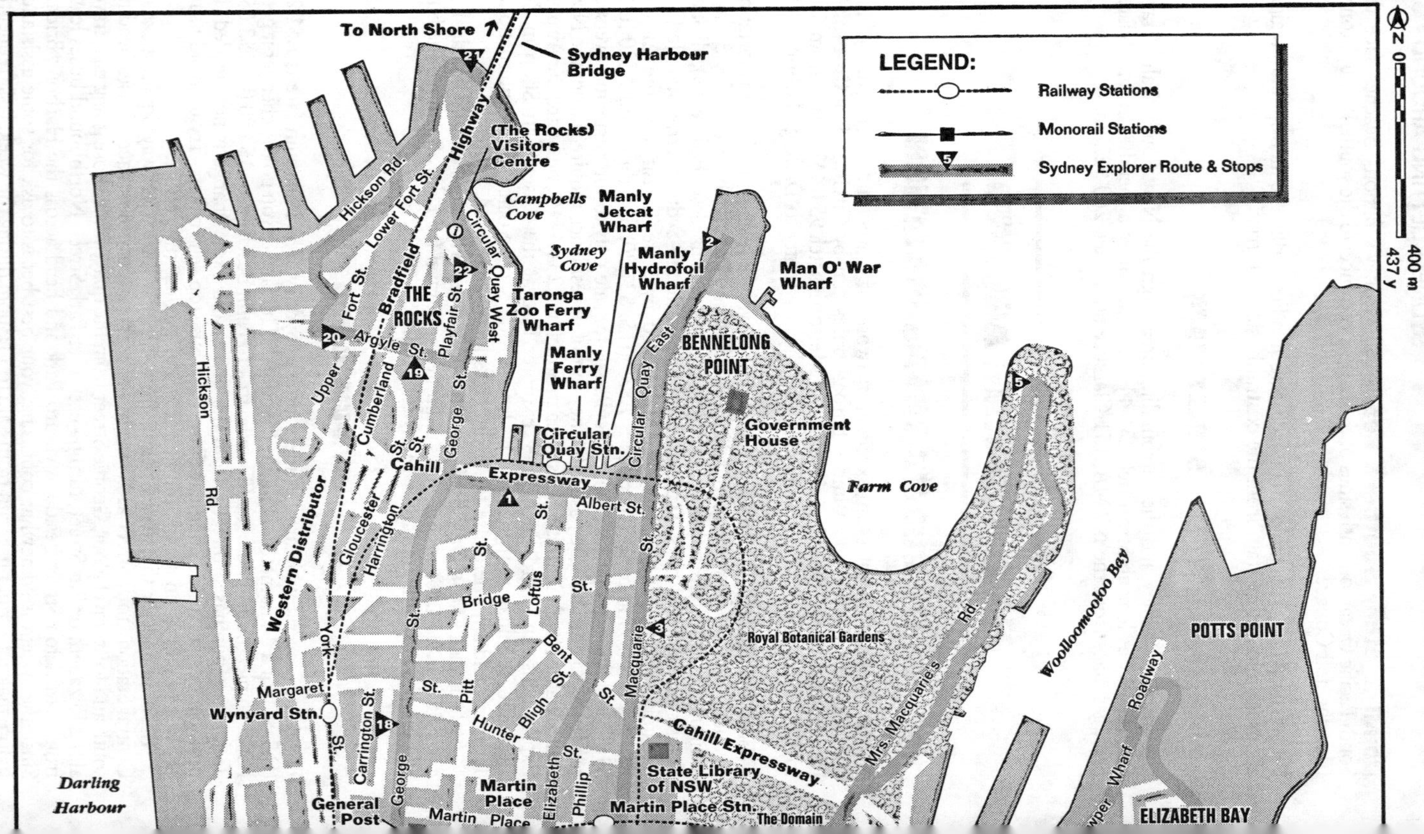

400 m
437 y
LEGEND:
Railway Stations
Monorail Stations
Sydney Explorer Route & Stops
To North Shore
Sydney Harbour Bridge
(The Rocks) Visitors Centre
Campbells Cove
Manly Jetcat Wharf
Sydney Cove
Manly Hydrofoil Wharf
Man O' War Wharf
Taronga Zoo Ferry Wharf
Manly Ferry Wharf
THE ROCKS
BENNELONG POINT
Government House
Circular Quay Stn.
Circular Quay West
Circular Quay East
Farm Cove
Royal Botanical Gardens
Woolloomooloo Bay
POTTS POINT
ELIZABETH BAY
Cahill Expressway
State Library of NSW
Martin Place Stn.
The Domain
Martin Place
General Post
Wynyard Stn.
Darling Harbour
Hickson Rd.
Lower Fort St.
Bradfield Highway
Fort St.
Argyle St.
Playfair St.
Upper
Cumberland St.
George St.
Cahill Expressway
Albert St.
Western Distributor
Gloucester St.
Harrington St.
Bridge St.
Loftus St.
Bent St.
Macquarie St.
Mrs. Macquarie's Rd.
Roadway
Wharf
York St.
Margaret St.
Carrington St.
Pitt St.
Hunter St.
Bligh St.
Elizabeth St.
Phillip St.

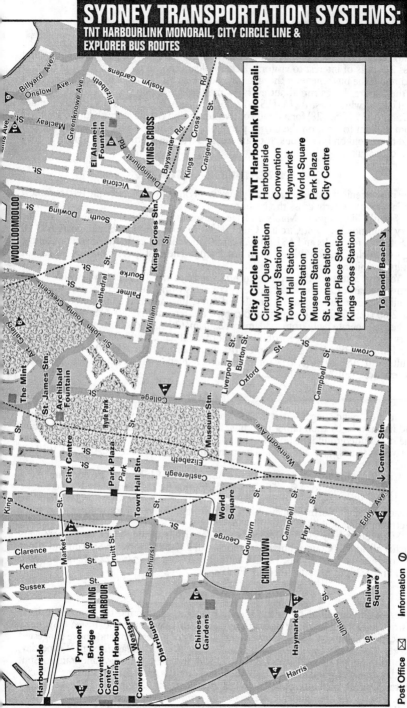

BY SYDNEY EXPLORER BUS

Also operated by State Transit, the Sydney Explorer is a great value for tourists. The easily recognizable red buses follow a 20-kilometer (12-mile) loop around the city and pass 22 spots of interest to visitors. Ticket holders can get off at any point in the trip and rejoin the bus whenever they like; they can visit all 22 points of interest or as few as they desire. Buses run about every 17 minutes.

Tickets, which cost A$15 (U.S. $12) for adults, A$10 (U.S. $8) for children under 16, and A$35 (U.S. $28) for a family of two adults and two or more children, are good from 9:30am to 5pm on the day of purchase. The buses operate 7 days a week and tickets are sold on board. Bus stops are marked with distinctive red-and-green Sydney Explorer signs.

BY FERRIES & JETCATS

The most scenic way to get around Sydney is on one of the picturesque ferries or new JetCats that regularly cross the harbor.

If you'd like to go to Manly and see the seaside suburb's ocean beach, take the ferry from no. 3 jetty at Circular Quay. The trip takes 35 minutes and costs A$3.20 (U.S. $2.60) for adults and A$1.60 (U.S. $1.30) for children each way. If you opt for the high-speed JetCat, you'll leave from no. 2 jetty. The cost is A$4.30 (U.S. $3.45) for adults or children each way.

You can also take the ferry from no. 5 jetty to the Taronga Zoo, which is just across the harbor. At the wharf the ferry connects with a bus which carries passengers uphill to the entrance gates. A combined ferry, bus, and zoo admission ticket costs A$12.60 (U.S. $10.10) return (round-trip). Children pay A$5.80 (U.S. $4.65).

Ferries operate daily from 5:30am to 12:30am. Other places that can be reached by ferry include Neutral Bay, Kirribilli, Cremorne, Balmain, Grenwich, Cockatoo Island, and Hunters Hill. A one-way trip on the inner harbor costs A$2.40 (U.S. $1.95) for adults and A$1.20 (U.S. $1) for children. Frequency of service varies. For ferry information, call 256-4670 or 256-4672.

BY TRAIN

Because of traffic congestion, it is usually quicker to get to your destination in Sydney and its suburbs by train rather than bus. In the central region, the **City Circle** train line runs underground. Stations on this route: Central, Town Hall, Wynyard, Circular Quay, St. James, and Museum. The minimum one-way tickets costs A$1.10 (U.S. 90¢).

CityRail's **CityHopper pass** costs A$2.10 (U.S. $1.70) and provides unlimited off-peak train travel for 1 day. Tickets are half price for children under 16 and can be used after 9am weekdays and all day weekends around the City Circle, including Milson's Point, North Sydney, Martin Place, and Kings Cross. Information from Metrotrips (tel. 954-4422).

State Rail operates CityRail service and Countrylink trains which carry passengers farther afield. For Countrylink reservations, call 217-8812 between 6:30am and 10pm or stop in at the Countrylink Travel Centre, 11-31 York Street (tel. 224-4744), between 8am and 5:30pm Monday through Friday.

BY MONORAIL

Like the underground train, the speedy monorail connecting the central business district to Darling Harbour doesn't compete with vehicular traffic. Instead, Sydney's sleek, state-of-the-art system glides over the heads of pedestrians and above congested streets. The system usually operates from 7am to 10pm Monday through Wednesday, 7am to midnight Thursday and Friday, 9am to midnight Saturday, and 9am to 8pm Sunday, but it's a good idea to check the hours on signs posted in the stations. The city center/Darling Harbour round-trip takes approximately 12 minutes. Tickets cost A$2 (U.S. $1.60); children under 5 are free. The monorail connects with trains at Town Hall Station. For more information call TNT Harbourlink (tel. 552-2288).

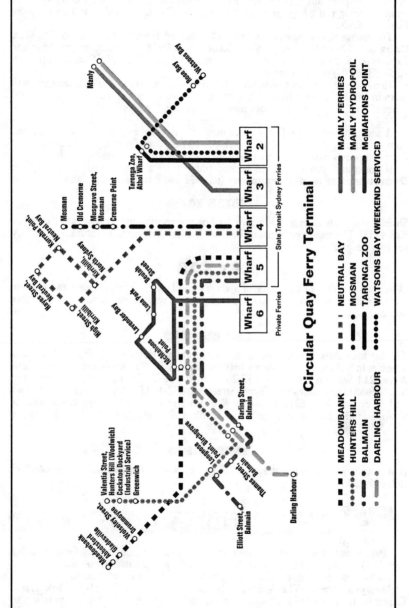

SYDNEY FERRIES

Circular Quay Ferry Terminal

Wharf 2 | **Wharf 3** | **Wharf 4** | **Wharf 5** — State Transit Sydney Ferries

Wharf 6 — Private Ferries

Manly
Rose Bay
Watsons Bay

Taronga Zoo, Athol Wharf

Mosman
Old Cremorne
Musgrave Street, Mosman
Cremorne Point

Kurraba Point, Neutral Bay
Neutral Bay
Bayes Street, Neutral Bay
High Street, Kirribilli
Kirribilli
North Sydney

Lavender Bay
Luna Park
South Street
McMahons Point

Darling Street, Balmain
Longnose Point, Birchgrove

Valentia Street, Hunters Hill (Woolwich)
Cockatoo Dockyard (Industrial Service)
Greenwich

Meadowbank
Abbotsford
Gladesville
Drummoyne
Wolseley Street
Elliott Street, Balmain

Thames Street, Balmain
Darling Harbour

Legend:

- ■ ■ ■ MEADOWBANK
- HUNTERS HILL
- BALMAIN
- DARLING HARBOUR
- ■ ■ ■ NEUTRAL BAY
- MOSMAN
- TARONGA ZOO
- WATSONS BAY (WEEKEND SERVICE)
- MANLY FERRIES
- MANLY HYDROFOIL
- McMAHONS POINT

BY TAXI

Sydney and its suburbs are well served by taxis. Fares are set by the Department of Motor Transport, and all cabs are metered. Extra charges apply for a taxi request by phone, waiting time, luggage weighing over 25 kilograms (55 lb.), and crossing the Harbour Bridge.

The main cab companies are **Taxis Combined Services** (tel. 332-8888), **RSL Cabs** (tel. 699-0144), and **Legion Cabs** (tel. 2-0918). All three accept American Express or Diners Club credit cards. Fares start at A$1.65 (U.S. $1.35) and go up about A85¢ (U.S. 70¢) per kilometer.

Taxis line up at ranks throughout the city, but I personally find it easiest to catch them in front of the big hotels. A light on the roof of the car indicates whether it is "vacant" or "engaged." To order modified vehicles for people with disabilities, call 339-0200.

A *word of warning:* The shift change of drivers takes place between 2:30 and 3pm, and during this time cabs will pick you up only if you're going in the direction of their company's base. Taxis also become scarce as soon as it starts to rain.

If you think you have been treated unfairly by a Sydney taxi driver, call the **Department of Motor Transport** (tel. 662-5403) to file a complaint.

WATER TAXIS

Should you wish to rent your own harbor transportation, try **Taxis Afloat** (tel. 922-4252). The trip from Watsons Bay to Circular Quay costs about A$30 (U.S. $24) for two people.

BY CAR

Wise visitors will take advantage of Sydney's good public transportation and not rent a car. Traffic congestion is a problem and parking very limited (and expensive when you can find it).

CAR RENTALS

The big four (Avis, Budget, Hertz, and Thrifty) have desks at the airport. Car-rental agencies in Sydney include: **Ansa International,** 51 William Street (tel. 361-3366), **Avis,** 214 William Street (tel. 357-2000 or 516-2877); **Budget,** 93 William Street (tel. 339-8811); **Dollar,** 80 William Street (tel. 332-1033); **Hertz,** corner of William and Riley (tel. 360-6621); **Letz,** 80 William Street (tel. 331-3099); **National,** 16 Oxford Street, Darlinghurst (tel. 332-1233); and **Thrifty,** 85 William Street (tel. 357-5399).

LIMOUSINES

If you want your own chauffeur and limo, call **Astra Chauffeured Limousines** (tel. 699-2233).

FAST FACTS SYDNEY

American Express Traveler's checks can be cashed at 388 George St. (tel. 239-0666 or 886-1111), Mon–Fri 8:30am–5:30pm and Sat 9am–noon.

Area Code Sydney telephone numbers are in the 02 area code.

Baby-sitters The Sydney City Council operates the Hyde Park Family Centre on the corner of Park and Elizabeth streets (tel. 265-9411). Child-minding, up to 6 hours per week, costs A$2.50 (U.S. $2) for 1 hour. Hours are Mon–Fri 7:30am–6pm. The All Sydney Baby Sitting Service (tel. 521-3333) comes to your hotel and charges about A$6 (U.S. $4.80) per hour plus traveling charges.

Bookstores Dymocks (pronounced *Dim*-icks) Book Arcade, 426 George St., (tel. 235-0155) just north of Market St., is open daily: Mon–Tues and Fri 8:30am–

5:30pm, Wed 9am–5:30pm, Thurs 8:30am–9pm, Sat 9am–5pm, and Sun 10am–5pm.

Angus & Robertson Bookstore, in the Imperial Arcade, 168 Pitt St. (tel. 235-1188) is open Mon–Wed and Fri 8:30am–6pm, Thurs 8:30am–9pm, Sat 9am–5:30pm, and Sun 10:30am–5pm.

Business Hours Banks are open Mon–Thurs 9:30am–4pm and Fri 9:30am–5pm. Stores are generally open Mon–Fri 9am–5:30pm (Thurs to 9pm) and Sat 9am–5pm. Some shops stay open later on Fri (David Jones is open until 7pm, for instance) and some are open only until noon on Sat.

Car Rentals See "Getting Around," above.

Climate See "When to Go," in Chapter 2.

Currency See "Information, Entry Requirements, and Money," in Chapter 2.

Currency Exchange In addition to at the American Express office, traveler's checks can be cashed at Thomas Cook, Kingsgate Shopping Centre, Kings Cross (tel. 356-2211), Mon–Fri 8:45am–5:30pm and Sat–Sun 8:45am–1pm. The Interforex Money Exchange at no. 6 jetty, Circular Quay (tel. 247-2082), is open Mon–Fri 8am–9pm, Sat 8am–8pm, and Sun 9am–6pm.

While there are many Westpac banks in Sydney, one of the most convenient for tourists is located at 47 George St., The Rocks (tel. 226-2388); it's open during regular bank hours (see "Business Hours," above).

Dentist For dental problems, contact the Dental Emergency Information Service, an official service of the Australian Dental Association (tel. 267-5919).

Doctor Look under "Medical Practitioners" in the yellow pages of the Sydney directory.

Drugstores Most pharmacies (called chemist shops) keep regular shopping hours, but Wu's Pharmacy, 629 George St. (tel. 211-1805), is open Mon–Sat 9am–9pm and Sun 9am–7pm.

Embassies/Consulates All embassies are in Canberra, the capital. Sydney is home to the following consulates: Canada, 50 Bridge St. (tel. 231-6522); New Zealand, 25th floor, State Bank Bldg., 52 Martin Place (tel. 233-8388); United Kingdom, 1 Alfred, Circular Quay (tel. 247-7521); United States, at the corner of Elizabeth St. and Park St. (tel. 261-9200).

Emergencies In an emergency, dial 000 to summon an ambulance, the fire department, or the police.

Eyeglasses Replace lost or broken prescription glasses at OPSM Express, 383 George St. opposite Strand Arcade (tel. 299-3061). They're open Mon–Wed and Fri 8:30am–5:15pm, Thurs 8:30am–7:15pm, and Sat 8:30am–2:30pm. One-hour service is available.

Hairdressers/Barbers Fuss on the 9th floor of the Inter-Continental Hotel, 117 Macquarie St. (tel. 247-2083), offers ladies and gents hairdressing and a full range of other beauty services. A woman's haircut costs A$40 (U.S. $32) and a man's is A$25 (U.S. $20). Closed Sun.

Holidays See "When to Go," and "Fast Facts: Australia" in Chapter 2. In addition, New South Wales observes Labour Day the first Mon in Oct.

Hospitals You'll find Sydney Hospital on Macquarie St. (tel. 228-2111).

Hotlines The following numbers may be useful in an emergency: Crisis Centre (tel. 358-6577), Poison Information (tel. 519-0466), and the Rape Crisis Centre (tel. 819-6565).

Information See "Tourist Information," above.

Laundry/Dry Cleaning Wash on the Rocks, 9 Argyle Place, The Rocks (tel. 247-4917), is open Mon–Fri 7am–6pm and Sat 8am–3pm. If they do the laundry for you the cost is A$15 (U.S. $12) for two loads.

One-hour dry-cleaning service is available at Lawrence Dry Cleaners, Wynyard Station (tel. 262-1583), and Maurice Dry Cleaners, 11 AMP Centre (tel. 231-2498).

Library The State Library of New South Wales is on Macquarie St. (tel. 230-1414).

Lost Property At the airport: go to the Federal Airport Corporation's administration office, second floor, International Terminal (tel. 667-9583). In taxis: Phone the office of the taxi company. On ferries: Phone 256-4655 or 256-4656. On trains: Go to 470 and 490 Pitt St. near the Central Railway Station (tel. 219-4757 and 211-1176). On buses: Each bus depot has its own lost property office. There is no general lost property bureau in Sydney. Other than the above suggestions, go to the police station closest to where you lost the item.

Luggage Storage/Lockers   There are baggage lockers at the Kingsford Smith Airport: A$1 (U.S. 80¢) for the first 24 hours, A$2 (U.S. $1.60) per day thereafter. The lockers in Central Station cost A$1.10 (U.S. 90¢) a day.

Newspapers   The *Sydney Morning Herald* is the major metropolitan paper. *The Australian,* distributed across the country, is also widely read.

Photographic Needs   Paxton's Photographics, 285 George St. (tel. 299-2999), is open Mon–Fri 8:30am–5:30pm (Thurs to 7:30pm) and Sat 8:30am–2:30pm. Whilton Camera Service, Shop 533 in the Royal Arcade, under the Hilton Hotel (tel. 267-8429), is open Mon–Fri 8am–6pm and Sat 8am–2pm.

Police   In an emergency, dial 000 to reach the police.

Postal Code   Central Sydney addresses have a 2000 postal code.

Post Office   The General Post Office (GPO), on Martin Place (tel. 230-7033), is open Mon–Fri 8:15am–5:30pm and Sat 8:30am–noon.

Radio   Classical, ABC.FM (92.9); news/talk, 2GB.AM (87); album-oriented rock, 2MMM.FM (104.9); current affairs, 2BL.AM (702); easy listening, 2CH.AM (1170); news, sports, 2VE.AM (954).

Religious Services   Sydney is well supplied with places of worship: Anglican, St. Andrew's Cathedral, Sydney Sq. (tel. 269-0642 or 264-8834); Baptist, Central Baptist Church, 619 George St. (tel. 211-1833); Buddhist, 144 Walker St., North Sydney (tel. 929-8643); Christian Scientist, Liverpool St. and Forbes St., Darlinghurst (tel. 357-5721); Greek Orthodox, 242 Cleveland St., Redfern (tel. 699-5811); Jewish, Elizabeth St. (tel. 267-2477 or 358-3726); Lutheran, St. Paul's Church, 3 Stanley St. (tel. 419-6586); Muslim, 13 John St., Erksineville; Presbyterian, Scots Church, at York and Margaret Sts. (tel. 29-1804 or 92-1259); Roman Catholic, St. Mary's Cathedral, College St. (tel. 232-3788); Seventh-Day Adventist, 219 Edgecliffe Rd., Wollahra (tel. 858-4061); Unitarian, 15 Francis St. (tel. 33-4863); Uniting Church, St. Stephen's, 197 Macquarie St. (tel. 221-1688).

Rest Rooms   In the central business district, you can avail yourself of the facilities in the Queen Victoria Building, any department store, or outside of business hours, any hotel. In Darling Harbour, there are nice rest rooms in the Harbourside Marketplace.

Safety   Avoid The Rocks on Fri and Sat around 11pm when the pubs close, and Kings Cross in the wee hours. And of course, stay out of parks and gardens after dark.

Shoe Repair   You'll find The Cobbler's Last at Shop P42, on the lower level of Centrepoint (tel. 233-5228), open Mon–Fri 8am–5:30pm (Thurs to 9pm), and Sat 8am–noon. While-you-wait service is available.

Taxes   Sales tax is not added to purchases anywhere in Australia, and there is no GST. Sydney does not have a hotel tax.

Taxis   See "Getting Around," above.

Telegrams/Telex   The least expensive way to send these is from a post office. Hotels will do it, too, but will probably add a service charge.

Telephones   The Telecom Phone Centre, 100 King St. (tel. 233-2252), is open 24 hours a day and has more than 100 pay phones for local or overseas calls.

Television   Sydney has five television stations: three commercial networks and two government-owned. Channel 1, SBS TV, offers multicultural programming; Channel 2, ABC (Australian Broadcasting Company), is the equivalent to PBS in the U.S.; Channel 7, ATN, runs a variety of programs including the NBC "Today" show with Bryant Gumbel at 11:35pm; Channel 9, TCN, shows excerpts from CBS and ABC news from the States, as well as "Murphy Brown," "The Cosby Show," and "Matlock." This channel also airs an Australian version of "60 Minutes." Channel 10, TEN TV, has varied programming during the day and runs CNN from midnight to dawn. The stations are required to run at least 40% Australian programming, but manage to include a large number of U.S. shows.

Transit Information   Call Metrotrips (tel. 954-4422) daily from 6am to 10pm.

Useful Telephone Numbers   You might find the following useful: news (tel. 1199), telephone directory assistance (information) (tel. 013), time (tel. 1194), Traveller's Aid Society (tel. 211-2469).

Weather   For the local weather forecast, dial 1196.

3. NETWORKS & RESOURCES

FOR STUDENTS

The phone number of the Student Travel Association is 519-9866. The general information number at the University of Sydney is 692-2222.

FOR GAY MEN & WOMEN

To reach the gay and lesbian hotline, call 319-2799 between 4pm and midnight. For the Gay What's On line call 319-6320 (24-hour recorded information). *OutRage* is Australia's leading monthly magazine for gay men. *The Sydney Star Observer* is a free fortnightly newspaper for gays. To reach the AIDS hotline call 332-4000. The Bookshop, 207 Oxford Street, Darlinghurst (tel. 331-1103) is a good source of information.

Note: Tasmania is the only Australian state where male homosexuality is illegal. Lesbian sex has never been outlawed in Australia.

FOR WOMEN

Please read "Safety" in "Fast Facts: Sydney," above. The number of the rape crisis hotline is 819-6565. You might also want to contact the Women's Resource Centre, 23 Sheriff, Ashcroft (tel. 607-7536). The YWCA, 5-11 Wentworth Avenue (tel. 264-2451), offers women and couples low-cost, centrally located accommodation.

CHAPTER 4

WHERE TO STAY & DINE IN SYDNEY

A room with a view? A cozy B&B? Traditional? Modern? No worries—Sydney and its suburbs has them all, in all price ranges. Whether you want to be completely pampered, cook your own meals, or stay in a more homey environment, Sydney can accommodate you.

And with more than 2,000 available dining spots, offering dozens of different ethnic cuisines as well as indigenous Australian specialties, Sydney's restaurant scene presents a challenge for the short-term visitor.

I'll help you sort out the possibilities below.

1. SYDNEY ACCOMMODATIONS

General lodging information can be found in "Where to Stay," in Chapter 2. Note that most hotel rates are the same for a single or double occupancy, and where there is a single rate, it's usually only slightly less than the double rate. Unless otherwise stated, tariffs given below are for a double/twin room being shared by two people.

The following price categories apply in this chapter: very expensive—more than A$250 (U.S. $200) a night; expensive—A$151 to A$250 (U.S. $120.80 to U.S. $200); moderate—A$100 to A$150 (U.S. $80 to U.S. $120); inexpensive—A$50 to A$99 (U.S. $40 to U.S. $79.20); budget—less than A$50 (U.S. $40).

IN THE CITY CENTER
VERY EXPENSIVE

HOLIDAY INN MENZIES, 14 Carrington St., Sydney, NSW 2000. Tel. 02/299-1000, or toll free 008/221-066 in Australia. Fax 02/290-3819. 441 rms, 15 suites. A/C MINIBAR TV TEL **Train:** Wynyard.

$ Rates: A$264 (U.S. $211.20) standard room; A$330–A$850 (U.S. $264–U.S. $680) suite; A$319 (U.S. $255.20) executive floor (including breakfast and special services); A$20 (U.S. $16) extra person. Children under 18 stay free in parents' room. No-smoking rooms available. AE, BC, DC, MC, V. **Parking:** A$10 (U.S. $8).

Ideally located in the central business district, the Menzies was Sydney's first five-star hotel when it opened in 1963. It wasn't part of the Holiday Inn chain then; that came about in 1986. Happily, it has been able to maintain its traditional, slightly staid identity, which would no doubt please the hotel's namesake, Archibald Menzies. This Scotsman arrived in Australia in 1852 and, through his good fortune in the gold-rush days, built one of the foremost hotels in Melbourne.

The 14-story Menzies has spacious bedrooms, decorated with colonial-style furnishings and either king-size beds or a pair of doubles. Only the lobby, with its polished black marble floor, Queen Anne chairs, mirrored walls, and antique Coromandel screen behind the reception desk, deviates from the conservative approach.

Dining/Entertainment: Meals are served in the informal Carrington Restaurant and Coffee House, open 7 days a week from 6am to midnight (lunchtime buffet costs A$28/U.S. $22.40). The Park Lounge is open 24 hours a day. The Gallery Grill is open for lunch and dinner weekdays. Japanese chefs prepare traditional dishes in The Keisan, which is open every day but Sunday.

Services: Concierge, 24-hour room service, shoeshine, laundry, valet, baby-sitting, massage, in-room movies, free daily newspaper, and turn-down service.

Facilities: Indoor pool, sauna, gym, spa, gift shop, and newsagent.

HOTEL INTER-CONTINENTAL SYDNEY, 117 Macquarie St., Sydney, NSW 2000. Tel. 02/230-0200, or toll free 008/221-828 in Australia. Fax 02/251-2342. 460 rms, 42 suites. A/C MINIBAR TV TEL **Train or ferry:** Circular Quay.

$ **Rates:** A$285–A$350 (U.S. $228–U.S. $280) single or double depending on view; A$530–A$2,100 (U.S. $424–U.S. $1,680) suite; A$350–A$400 (U.S. $280–U.S. $320) executive floor (including breakfast); A$30 (U.S. $24) extra person. Children under 18 stay free in parents' room. Lower weekend tariffs. No-smoking rooms available. AE, BC, CB, DC, MC, V. **Parking:** A$15 (U.S. $12).

The Inter-Continental illustrates the principle that historic buildings need not be destroyed to make way for new ones. The architects who designed this hostelry, which reopened in 1985, incorporated into their plans the beautiful old Treasury building, built in 1849, and added a 31-story high-rise tower to accommodate the guest bedrooms. The restaurants and other public areas are located in the restored area. Throughout the hotel, the ambience is one of tradition and luxury.

The hotel is located opposite the Royal Botanic Gardens, and is less than a 5-minute walk from the Opera House and Circular Quay. Half the spacious bedrooms have a harbor view. Regular rooms have queen-size or twin beds, while king-size beds are found only in the suites. In addition to the standard refrigerator and coffee- and tea-making facilities, bedrooms come equipped with toasters. All bathrooms have telephones and hairdryers, and two rooms are designed to accommodate handicapped guests.

Dining/Entertainment: Teas, light lunches, and cocktails are served in the skylit central Cortile, a lobby bar surrounded by the sandstone arcades and arches of the Treasury's old-world facade. Lunch is served in this area from noon to 3pm and teas are available from 3 to 5:30pm; snacks may be ordered from 5:30 to 11pm. The Treasury is the hotel's fine-dining venue. The Top of the Treasury Cocktail Lounge on the 31st floor is a good spot for a drink with a panoramic view. Café Opera offers informal dining daily from 6:30am to midnight (breakfast buffet A$23/U.S. $18.40, luncheon buffet A$29/U.S. $23.20, dinner buffet A$29/U.S. $23.20, and supper buffet A$22.50/U.S. $18).

Services: Concierge, 24-hour room service, turn-down service, baby-sitting, shoeshine, laundry, valet, massage, free daily newspapers, and in-room movies.

Facilities: The Inter-Continental offers its guests one of the best hotel fitness clubs in the city. Available in the Clark Hatch Fitness Centre are an indoor pool, a sauna, a spa, a gymnasium with exercise equipment, power-walking classes, and massage therapists. The hotel also has a business center, hair/beauty salon, gift shop, newsagent, and an early arrivals/late departures lounge.

REGENT OF SYDNEY, 199 George St., Sydney, NSW 2000. Tel. 02/238-0000, or toll free 008/022-800 in Australia. Fax 02/251-2851. 596 rms, 66 suites. A/C MINIBAR TV TEL **Train or ferry:** Circular Quay.

$ **Rates:** A$295–A$440 (U.S. $236–U.S. $352) depending on whether city, Opera House, or harbor view; A$550–A$600 (U.S. $440–U.S. $480) junior suite; A$715–A$2,200 (U.S. $572–U.S. $1,760) suite. Children under 16 stay free in parents' room. Weekend packages available. No-smoking rooms available. AE, BC, CB, DC, MC, V. **Parking:** A$12 (U.S. $9.60).

⭐ The Regent established a new benchmark for hotel luxury and service when it opened in 1982, and it isn't surprising that it has subsequently won the Australian government's National Tourism Award for Excellence in Accommodation several years in a row. All rooms feature Italian marble bathrooms, blackout curtains for those who wish to sleep during the day, a choice of king-size or twin beds, three dual-line telephones, modern Tasmanian oak furnishings, fresh flowers, remote-control TVs and videos, fax machines, lights on dimmers, and towels that are weighed regularly to ensure adequate thickness for the hotel's pampered guests. In addition, each suite has its own telescope.

A three-story atrium rises from a lobby floor of gleaming South Australian granite, and each level is rimmed with brass balustrades and a profusion of greenery. In addition to luxury and service, the 36-story hotel has a great location near Circular Quay and The Rocks, and expansive views from the majority of its rooms.

Dining/Entertainment: Kable's, the Regent's fine dining restaurant, is considered one of the best eating spots in the city. The cuisine and service here are truly outstanding. The Club Bar has an elegant country-club ambience. The Mezzanine Lounge is a delightful place for light lunches and afternoon teas. The Lobby Restaurant is open from 6:30am to 1am. The George Street Bar is an upmarket pub. For more details on these dining venues, see "Sydney Dining," below.

Services: A Mercedes-Benz limousine stands ready for airport transfers (A$50/U.S. $40); 24-hour room service; turn-down service, shoeshine, laundry, valet, concierge, baby-sitting, massage, free daily newspapers, and complimentary in-room movies. In addition, floor stewards greet guests, pack/unpack, reconfirm airline reservations, and provide myriad other services.

Facilities: Outdoor pool, health club, business center, hair salon, gift shop, and newsagent.

RITZ-CARLTON SYDNEY, 93 Macquarie St., Sydney, NSW 2000. Tel. 02/252-4600, or toll free 008/252-888 in Australia. Fax 02/252-4286. 92 rms, 14 suites. A/C MINIBAR TV TEL **Train or ferry:** Circular Quay.

$ Rates: A$358–A$468 (U.S. $286.40–U.S. $374.40) depending on size of room and view; A$495 (U.S. $396) Club Level (including breakfast, tea, and cocktails); from A$660 (U.S. $528) Parlour Room. Children under 18 stay free in parents' room. Lower weekend tariffs and weekend packages. No-smoking rooms available. AE, BC, CB, DC, MC, V. **Parking:** A$12 (U.S. $9.60).

Open since 1990, the Ritz-Carlton Sydney was the prestigious hotel chain's first Australian property (since joined by the Ritz-Carlton Double Bay, which housed George Bush in January, 1992). The hotel, which feels like a grand mansion, is conveniently located less than a 5-minute walk from the Opera House and across the street from the Royal Botanic Gardens. Crystal chandeliers in every public room and in the lifts (elevators), antiques, original works of art, and damask wall coverings create an elegant atmosphere.

Well-appointed rooms include remote-control TVs, two-line phones, and marble bathrooms (most with double sinks and the shower separate from the tub). The majority of rooms have balconies and French doors. CD players are standard in suites; VCRs and fax machines are available.

Dining/Entertainment: The Dining Room is an elegant venue offering continental cuisine and an extensive wine list. The Café Restaurant serves both hearty fare and fitness food (Sunday brunch including a glass of champagne costs A$29.50/U.S. $23.60). The Bar has an English Club ambience created by large oil paintings in gilded frames, Persian rugs, and a polished mahogany floor. Afternoon tea is served in The Lounge.

Services: Personal shopping service, concierge, 24-hour room service, turn-down service, shoeshine, laundry, valet, baby-sitting, massage, free daily newspapers, and in-room movies.

Facilities: Outdoor pool, gift shop, fitness center, gym, sauna, newsagent/gift shop.

SYDNEY HILTON, 259 Pitt St., Sydney, NSW 2000. Tel. 02/266-0610.
Fax 02/265-6065. 585 rms, 28 suites. A/C MINIBAR TV TEL **Train:** Town Hall.
$ Rates: A$285 (U.S. $228) standard room; A$395 (U.S. $316) room on Executive
Floor (including breakfast and cocktails); A$650 (U.S. $520) suite; A$30 (U.S.
$24) extra person; A$200 (U.S. $160) weekend rate. Children free of charge in
parents' room. No-smoking rooms available. AE, BC, DC, MC, V. **Parking:** A$14
(U.S. $11.20).

Dedicated shoppers will love the Sydney Hilton, located in the heart of the business
and shopping district. Dozens of stores line the Royal Arcade, which runs under the
hotel, and another 200 are just across the street in the Queen Victoria Building. The
hotel's guest rooms occupy the top 24 floors of a 44-story high-rise. Standard rooms
have queen-size or twin beds and very attractive modern furnishings. King-size beds
are available. The Alcove Suites have sleeping and sitting areas separated by a curtain,
while the Royal Suite has its own sauna, wet bar, and circular bathtub.

The Hilton is also ideal for business travelers with its three Executive Floors, which
provide a club-style lounge where complimentary continental breakfasts, hors
d'oeuvres, and cocktails are served. Traveling executives who stay on these special
floors enjoy upgraded rooms and amenities.

Dining/Entertainment: The Hilton offers a wide range of dining and drinking
facilities, including the elegant San Francisco Grill, America's Cup Bar, and the
Marble Bar. The Market Place is the hotel's 24-hour coffee shop.

Services: Concierge, 24-hour room service, turn-down service, shoeshine,
laundry, valet, baby-sitting, free daily newspapers, in-room movies, and massage. On
the Executive Floors, there is a business center which offers secretarial service,
photocopying, word processing, 24-hour news update, and free local phone calls.

Facilities: Outdoor pool, gym, sauna, spa, gift shop, and newsagent.

EXPENSIVE

**WYNYARD TRAVELODGE, 7-9 York St., Sydney, NSW 2000. Tel. 02/
299-3000.** Fax 02/262-2416. 201 rms, 1 suite. A/C MINIBAR TV TEL **Train:**
Wynyard.
$ Rates: A$190 (U.S. $152) standard room; A$400 (U.S. $320) suite. Children
under 15 stay free in parents' room. Weekend discounts. No-smoking rooms
available. AE, BC, CB, DC, MC, V. **Parking:** Free.

The convenience of being steps from Wynyard Station and a 5-minute walk from
Circular Quay makes this Travelodge a popular choice for business travelers, who
comprise 80% of the hotel's guests.

Rooms feature dusty-rose upholstered chairs and headboards, white-oak woodwork, and pale-gray carpeting. All have double or queen-size beds (no king-size) and
tub/shower combinations. Shutters provide total darkness for daytime sleepers, and
solid masonry walls ensure quiet. Unfortunately, the lobby level of the Travelodge isn't
as handsome as its bedrooms, and readers who choose this hostelry sight unseen
shouldn't be put off by the modest reception area.

Dining/Entertainment: Casual meals are served daily in the Café on York
coffee shop from 6:30am to 11:30pm. For fancier fare, head to Kache, on the 21st
floor.

Services: 24-hour room service, laundry, concierge, baby-sitting, and free daily
newspaper (on request).

Facilities: Gift shop/newsagent.

Serviced Apartments

**HYDE PARK PLAZA, 38 College St., Sydney, NSW 2000. Tel. 02/331-
6933,** or toll free 008/22-2442 in Australia. Fax 02/331-6022. 136 rms, 46 suites.
A/C MINIBAR TV TEL **Train:** Museum.
$ Rates: A$175 (U.S. $140) single; A$185 (U.S. $148) double; A$195 (U.S. $156)
suite; A$210 (U.S. $168) executive floor; A$10 (U.S. $8) extra person. Lower
weekend tariffs. AE, BC, DC, MC, V. **Parking:** Free.

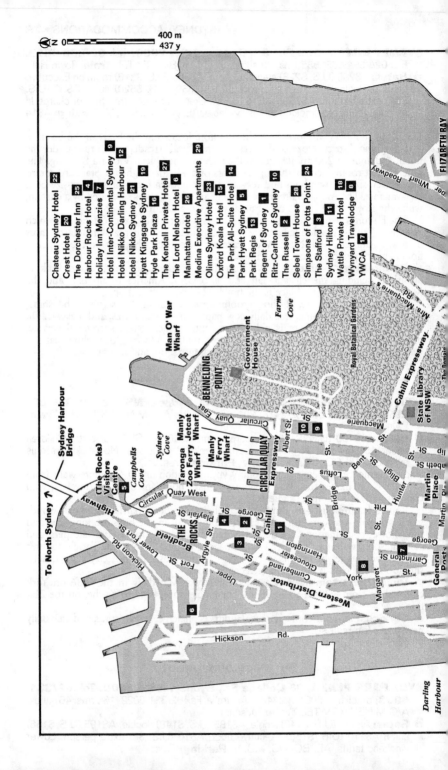

400 m
437 y

Chateau Sydney Hotel **22**
Crest Hotel **20**
The Dorchester Inn **25**
Harbour Rocks Hotel **4**
Holiday Inn Menzies **7**
Hotel Inter-Continental Sydney **9**
Hotel Nikko Darling Harbour **12**
Hotel Nikko Sydney **21**
Hyatt Kingsgate Sydney **19**
Hyde Park Plaza **16**
The Kendall Private Hotel **27**
The Lord Nelson Hotel **6**
Manhattan Hotel **26**
Medina Executive Apartments **29**
Olims Sydney Hotel **23**
Oxford Koala Hotel **15**
The Park All-Suite Hotel **14**
Park Hyatt Sydney **5**
Park Regis **13**
Regent of Sydney **1**
Ritz-Carlton of Sydney **10**
The Russell **2**
Sebel Town House **28**
Simpsons of Potts Point **24**
The Stafford **3**
Sydney Hilton **11**
Wattle Private Hotel **18**
Wynyard Travelodge **8**
YWCA **17**

Sydney Harbour Bridge

To North Sydney

Highway

(The Rocks) Visitors Centre **5**

Campbells Cove

Circular Quay West

Sydney Cove

Man O' War Wharf

BENNELONG POINT

Farm Cove

Government House

Royal Botanical Gardens

Taronga Zoo Ferry Wharf

Manly Ferry Wharf

Manly Jetcat Wharf

Circular Quay East

CIRCULAR QUAY

Expressway

Albert St.

Cahill Expressway

Mrs. Macquaries Rd.

State Library of NSW

Cahill Expressway

The Domain

Macquarie St.

Bent St.

Bligh St.

Hunter St.

Elizabeth St.

Martin Place

Martin Pl.

Phillip St.

George St.

Pitt St.

Loftus St.

Bridge St.

Macquarie St.

General Post Office

York St.

Margaret St.

Carrington St.

Gloucester St.

Harrington St.

Cumberland St.

George St.

Playfair St.

Argyle St.

Fort St.

Upper Fort St.

Lower Fort St.

THE ROCKS

Bradfield Highway

Hickson Rd.

Western Distributor

Hickson Rd.

Darling Harbour

ELIZABETH BAY

Billyard Ave.

Roadway

4 **2** **1** **3** **6** **10** **9** **7** **8**

SYDNEY ACCOMMODATIONS

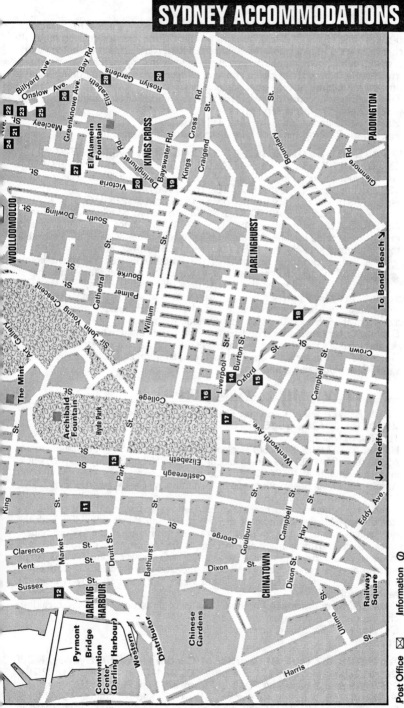

Post Office ☒   Information ❶

The rooms at the Hyde Park Plaza range in size from studios to "executive flexi-suites" that accommodate up to eight people. All the spacious quarters have full kitchens, either a dining table or a breakfast bar, very attractive contemporary furnishings, tub/shower combinations, and windows that open. The two-bedroom apartments also have walk-in closets, full-size refrigerators, irons, and ironing boards. Rooms on the Oxford Street side have balconies.

Dining/Entertainment: Hyde Park Plaza has a licensed restaurant open 7 days a week, but offers no room service.

Services: Laundry, concierge, free daily newspaper.

Facilities: Rooftop sun deck with a spa, sauna, and heated pool.

THE PARK ALL-SUITE HOTEL, 16-32 Oxford St., Sydney, NSW 2010. Tel. 02/331-7728, or toll free 008/22-1813 in Australia. Fax 02/360-2583. Reservations through Flag International, toll free 800/624-3524 in U.S. and Can. 135 apartments. A/C MINIBAR TV TEL **Train:** Museum.

$ Rates: A$195 (U.S. $156) one person in a 1 bedroom; A$228 (U.S. $182.40) two people in a 1 bedroom; A$250 (U.S. $200) one or two people in a 2-bedroom; A$15 (U.S. $12) extra person; A$8 (U.S. $6.40) child under 12. Lower weekend rates. Lower rates in June and July. Lower weekly rates. Lower rates available through Aussie auto clubs. AE, BC, DC, MC, V. **Parking:** Free.

The Park is the most luxurious of the centrally located apartment hotels described in this chapter. Each of the one- or two-bedroom units has a spacious, fully equipped kitchen with a dishwasher, oven, and full-size refrigerator. In addition, every apartment has its own washing machine, dryer, iron, ironing board, and balcony with table and chairs. "Harbourside" apartments are located from the 7th to 16th floors and overlook the water.

Dining/Entertainment: The licensed Park Lane restaurant is open 7 days a week, and Clancy's supermarket is conveniently located across the street.

Services: Room service from 7am to 11pm, laundry, and baby-sitting.

Facilities: Pool, sauna, and spa.

MODERATE

OXFORD KOALA HOTEL, corner Oxford and Pelican Sts., Sydney, NSW 2010. Tel. 02/269-0645. Fax 02/267-6107. 267 rms, 76 apartments. A/C TV TEL **Train:** Museum.

$ Rates: A$127 (U.S. $101.60) single room; A$139 (U.S. $111.20) double room; A$177 (U.S. $141.60) one person in apartment; A$187 (U.S. $149.60) two people in an apartment; A$10 (U.S. $8) extra person. Lower rates available through Aussie auto clubs. Reservations can be made through Best Western. AE, BC, DC, MC, V. **Parking:** A$5 (U.S. $4).

This property contains both hotel accommodations and serviced apartments. It's located about 4 blocks southeast of the city center and shares a building with the Pioneer coach terminal and the other shops and businesses in the Oxford Square complex. Each apartment has a full kitchen, a dining counter with four stools, a bedroom separate from the living room, and tub/shower combinations (some standard rooms have shower only). All accommodations are spacious and attractive. Apartments on the upper floors have good views, but the best view is from the 13th-floor pool deck.

Dining/Entertainment: The hotel's Cafe Koala is open daily for breakfast, lunch, and dinner. A piano bar is adjacent.

Services: 24-hour room service, laundry.

Facilities: Pool.

PARK REGIS, 27 Park St. (corner of Castlereagh St.), Sydney, NSW 2000. Tel. 02/267-6511, or toll free 008/22-1138 in Australia. Fax 02/264-2252. 119 rms, 8 suites. A/C TV TEL **Monorail:** Park Plaza. **Train:** Town Hall.

$ Rates: A$108 (U.S. $86.40) single; A$121 (U.S. $96.80) double; A$143 (U.S. $114.40) suite; A$10 (U.S. $8) extra person. Children under 18 stay free in parents' room. AE, BC, DC, MC, V. **Parking:** Free.

S The hotel occupies the first 15 floors of a 45-story city-center high-rise. Condominiums fill the rest of the building, and a licensed restaurant is next door. Hyde Park, the Queen Victoria Building, and Sydney Tower are all nearby.

The average-size bedrooms are light, attractive, and modern. All have the standard coffee- and tea-making and fridge facilities; bathrooms have shower only. Front rooms have park and city views, but even without a view, the room rate is a good value.

Dining/Entertainment: The restaurant offers a continental breakfast buffet at a reasonable price.

Services: Room service from 7am to 10pm, laundry, and concierge.

Facilities: Outdoor pool.

INEXPENSIVE

YWCA, 5-11 Wentworth Ave., Sydney, NSW 2010. Tel. 02/264-2451. Fax 02/283-2485. 124 rms, 14 suites. **Train:** Museum.

$ Rates: A$39 (U.S. $31.20) single with shared bath, A$65 (U.S. $52) single with private bath; A$65 (U.S. $52) twin with shared bath, A$93 (U.S. $74.40) twin with private bath; A$17 (U.S. $13.60) per person in dormitory (four people sharing, maximum stay 3 nights); A$10 (U.S. $8) extra person, including children under 12. Children under 4 stay free in parents' room. No-smoking rooms available. BC, MC, V. **Parking:** Moderate charge.

Central Sydney's YWCA (Young Women's Christian Association) has convenient, inexpensive accommodations for women traveling alone, couples, or families. In other words, no solo men. Rooms are a bit on the Spartan side, but those familiar with college dormitories should feel right at home. Rooms with private bathroom have tub/shower combinations and coffee- and tea-making facilities; all beds are twins, and one room and three bathrooms are equipped for handicapped travelers. TV lounges and laundry facilities are available. A cafeteria adjacent to the lobby is open daily.

A Bed-and-Breakfast Inn

WATTLE PRIVATE HOTEL (formerly Waratah House), 108 Oxford St. (corner of Palmer St.), Darlinghurst (Sydney), NSW 2010. Tel. 02/ 332-4118. Fax 02/331-2074. 12 rms (all with bath). MINIBAR TV TEL **Bus:** Taylor Square.

$ Rates (including continental breakfast): A$85 (U.S. $68) single; A$95 (U.S. $76) double; A$10 (U.S. $8) extra person. BC, MC, V. **Parking:** None.

S I visited this place on Melbourne Cup Day and found a merry group of guests gathered around a television set in the breakfast room. Michael Wu, the Wattle's congenial host, was enjoying the prerace program as much as the others, and I had the feeling of being in a big family home.

The Wattle's attractive exterior is best described as "remodeled Edwardian." The house, built between 1900 and 1910, has been altered more than once. Luckily, the Federation-period stained-glass windows remain in the breakfast room. Upstairs (four stories, no elevator or "lift"), the bedrooms each have large windows that make them bright. The decor is a hodgepodge of French provincial headboards, Chinese vases, tropical fans, Victorian high ceilings, and contemporary bedspreads, but all quarters are clean and comfortable, and the mattresses are firm. Each room has its own coffee- and tea-making facilities, and small refrigerator. There are laundry facilities on the premises.

KINGS CROSS & VICINITY

VERY EXPENSIVE

HOTEL NIKKO SYDNEY, 81 Macleay St., Potts Point, NSW 2011. Tel. 02/368-3000, or toll free 008/02-3665 in Australia. Fax 02/358-6631. 457 rms, 13 suites. A/C MINIBAR TV TEL **Train:** Kings Cross about 1km (½ mile). **Bus:** No. 311 from Circular Quay.

FROMMER'S SMART TRAVELER: HOTELS

VALUE-CONSCIOUS TRAVELERS SHOULD TAKE ADVANTAGE OF THE FOLLOWING:

1. Weekend discounts, corporate rates, long-stay rates, off-season rates, and lower rates available through Australian auto clubs, such as the National Roads & Motorists' Association (NRMA).
2. Special packages, such as ones that include breakfast and a bottle of champagne for the normal room rate.
3. Serviced apartments, which are generally good value and help save on dining costs.
4. Hotel passes, such as the ones described in "Where to Stay," in Chapter 2.

VALUE-CONSCIOUS TRAVELERS SHOULD AVOID THE FOLLOWING:

1. Minibars, where every item costs about 50% more than it would elsewhere.
2. Hotel laundry service (you could buy new underwear for what some of them charge to wash it).
3. Making telephone calls from hotel rooms. A local call can cost as much as A95¢ (U.S. 76¢).
4. Breakfast in hotel. Continental can cost A$16 (U.S. $12.80); cooked A$25 (U.S. $20). Instead, pick up muffins or similar and "picnic" in your room, taking advantage of the ever-present tea- and coffee-making facilities.
5. Room-service meals.
6. Hotel parking garages, which can cost up to A$18 (U.S. $14.40) a day.

$ Rates: A$290 (U.S. $232) single or double; A$325–A$765 (U.S. $260–U.S. $612) Nikko Floor (including continental breakfast, cocktails, and business amenities); A$985 (U.S. $788) Presidential Suite, Nikko Floor; A$25 (U.S. $20) extra bed. Children under 19 stay free in parents' room. Weekend packages available. No-smoking rooms available. AE, BC, DC, MC, V. **Parking:** A$9 (U.S. $7.20). Open since late 1990, the Hotel Nikko Sydney is located in the pleasant suburb of Potts Point about 3 kilometers (almost 2 miles) east of central Sydney and offers excellent views of both the city and Elizabeth Bay. In addition to public transportation, those using the Explorer Bus will find that stop no. 10 is right in front of the hotel. Extensive use of beige marble creates a spacious feel in the lobby.

The bedrooms, which are bright and airy, feature modern Tasmanian oak furnishings and pastel decors. Both king- and queen-size beds are available. Like the lodging in all of Sydney's five-star properties, rooms at the Nikko include clock radios, hairdryers, tea- and coffee-making facilities, small refrigerators, in-room movies, and free daily newspaper; terry robes are provided at no charge if requested. All suites feature walk-in closets, a shower separate from the tub, and double sinks. Facilities for handicapped travelers have been provided throughout the hotel.

Dining/Entertainment: The hotel's several food and beverage outlets are all located on the ground floor. Cafe Serena is open until midnight 7 days a week and is a popular spot for Sunday brunch (A$28/U.S. $22.40 includes a glass of champagne). Benkay serves authentic Japanese cuisine. The Point, with its tile floor, mahogony doors with stained-glass transoms, and dark wooden chairs has the feel of a San Francisco bistro.

Services: 24-hour room service, turn-down service, shoeshine, laundry, valet, concierge, and baby-sitting.

Facilities: Outdoor pool, gift shop.

SEBEL TOWN HOUSE, 23 Elizabeth Bay Rd., Elizabeth Bay, NSW 2011.

Tel. 02/358-3244, or toll free 008/222-266 (reservations only) in Australia. Fax 02/357-1926. 168 rms, 9 suites. A/C MINIBAR TV TEL **Train:** Kings Cross.

$ **Rates:** A$305–A$335 (U.S. $244–U.S. $268) standard double; from A$650 (U.S. $520) suite; A$1,300 (U.S. $1,040) Presidential Suite; A$20 (U.S. $16) extra person. Children under 12 stay free in parents' room. No-smoking rooms available. AE, BC, DC, MC, V. **Parking:** Free.

Located in the inner suburb of Elizabeth Bay, about a block from the bright lights of Kings Cross, the hotel has long been the choice of the theatrical set. It has hosted such luminaries as Elton John, Bob Hope, Rex Harrison, Lauren Bacall, Rod Stewart, Glenda Jackson, and Bette Davis, to name a few.

The stars are attracted by the hostelry's reputation for excellent personal service. For Richard Harris, a certain type of rolled oats was imported from Britain; Elton John's wedding reception was held in the hotel's ballroom, and cases of his favorite champagne are always kept on hand when he's in residence. Rex Harrison lived in the Sebel for 3 months while he performed locally. Happily, it isn't just recognizable guests who receive this mollycoddling. Everyone is called by name; restaurant and bar hours can be adjusted to suit individual needs; shoes left outside the door are shined overnight. More important, security is very tight. The Beatles wanted to stay at the Sebel, but were asked to go elsewhere because it was feared that their entourage of fans would disturb the other guests.

The spacious rooms have traditional furnishings, including built-in mahogony cabinets, windows that open, and terry robes. In the junior suites, luxury suites, and magnificent penthouse, the decor is "theatrical" and facilities include mini-kitchens, VCRs, and audiocassette systems. Guests have a choice of queen- or king-size beds, and everyone receives a free daily newspaper. About half of the accommodations offer a view of the marina at Rushcutters Bay, and a nearby park is ideal for jogging.

Dining/Entertainment: An à la carte restaurant and cozy bar are on the premises.

Services: 24-hour room service, turn-down service, shoeshine, laundry, valet, concierge, and baby-sitting.

Facilities: Hairdressing salon, outdoor pool, gym, sauna, business center, and gift shop.

EXPENSIVE

CHATEAU SYDNEY HOTEL, 14 Macleay St., Potts Point, NSW 2011. Tel. 02/359-2500. Fax 02/358-1959. Reservations can be made through Flag International, toll free 800/624-3524 in the U.S. or Canada. 94 rms, 2 suites. MINIBAR TV TEL **Train:** Kings Cross about 1km (½ mile). **Bus:** No. 311 from Circular Quay.

$ **Rates:** A$175–A$195 (U.S. $140–U.S. $156) single or double, depending on view; A$195 (U.S. $156) executive floor; A$375 (U.S. $300) suite; A$15 (U.S. $12) extra person. Children under 15 stay free in parents' room. Lower weekend rates include continental breakfast. Lower winter rates. Lower rates through Aussie auto clubs. AE, BC, DC, MC, V. **Parking:** Free.

Many of the rooms here offer expansive views of peaceful sailboats on Elizabeth Bay. All quarters have been recently renovated and redecorated in light neutral colors. Each has a tub/shower combination. Queen- and king-size beds are available. In-room movies, hairdryers, clock radios, bathroom scales, tea- and coffee-making facilities, and free daily newspapers are provided.

Dining/Entertainment: The Poolside Brasserie, which is licensed, offers a view and provides casual dining day and night.

Services: 24-hour room service, shoeshine, laundry, valet, concierge, and baby-sitting.

Facilities: Outdoor pool.

HYATT KINGSGATE SYDNEY, William St., Kings Cross, NSW 2011. Tel. 02/356-1234. Fax 02/356-4150. 389 rms, 14 suites. A/C MINIBAR TV TEL **Train:** Kings Cross.

$ Rates: A$230 (U.S. $184) single or double; A$280 (U.S. $224) executive floor (including continental breakfast); A$460 (U.S. $368) suite; A$30 (U.S. $24) extra person. Children under 18 stay free in parents' room. Weekend and off-season (May–Aug) discounts. No-smoking rooms available. AE, BC, DC, MC, V. **Parking:** A$15 (U.S. $12).

The surrounding colorful nightlife makes this 33-story hotel a great lodging option for late-night revelers. It's also an ideal stopping place for those who wish handy access to the good eating spots in the area. The city center is about 2 kilometers (1 mile) to the west. The train provides frequent, inexpensive transportation. Those who opt for a taxi will pay about A$4 (U.S. $3.20).

In any case, the Hyatt is a three-tower complex whose rooms are connected by a maze of corridors and elevators. The quarters are spacious, and each has a tub/shower combination, a king-size bed or twin beds, and windows that open.

Dining/Entertainment: Chitose is a Japanese restaurant; Craigend is a fine-dining, à la carte room; Trumpets is an attractive coffee shop, done in an eye-catching black-and-white decor, which is open from 6:30am to 10:30pm.

Services: 24-hour room service, turn-down service, laundry, valet, concierge, and baby-sitting.

Facilities: Outdoor pool, business center, hair salon, gift shop, and newsagent.

OLIMS SYDNEY HOTEL, 26-34 Macleay St., Potts Point, NSW 2011.
Tel. 02/358-2777. Fax 02/358-3186. 118 rms, 3 suites. A/C MINIBAR TV TEL **Train:** Kings Cross about 1km (½ mile). **Bus:** No. 311 from Circular Quay.
$ Rates: A$155 (U.S. $124) single; A$165 (U.S. $132) double; A$230 (U.S. $184) suite; A$13 (U.S. $10.40) extra person. Children under 12 stay free in parents' room. Weekend tariffs on application. No-smoking rooms available. AE, BC, DC, MC, V. **Parking:** Free.

Situated on an appealing tree-lined street in a mixed commercial/residential neighborhood, the Olims is 5 blocks from Kings Cross and close to Elizabeth Bay. This is an ideal spot for travelers who want attractive accommodations slightly outside the city center. The hotel's reception foyer, with high-backed velveteen wing chairs and glass-and-brass coffee tables, looks so smart that people used to come in off the street thinking it was a furniture store.

Two-thirds of the hotel's modern-style bedrooms have queen-size beds; the rest have doubles and twins. All rooms have showers, windows that open, refrigerators, and coffee- and tea-making facilities. The suites have such additional amenities as wet bars, bathtubs, and walk-in closets. The majority of rooms have harbor views. Everyone gets a free daily newspaper.

Dining/Entertainment: Popular barman Paul Williams presides over Trinkets Cocktail Bar, which is open daily from 4pm. This old-style drinks venue is appropriately named—the walls are covered with postcards sent by former guests, as well as hats, paper money, flags, and military insignia.

Services: Room service (not 24 hours), laundry, and baby-sitting.

Facilities: Outdoor pool, business center.

A Bed-and-Breakfast Inn

SIMPSONS OF POTTS POINT, 8 Challis Ave., Potts Point, NSW 2011.
Tel. 02/356-2199. Fax 02/356-4476. 14 rms (all with bath). A/C MINIBAR TV TEL **Train:** Kings Cross about 1km (½ mile). **Bus:** No. 311 from Circular Quay.
$ Rates (including continental breakfast): From A$170 (U.S. $136) one person; from A$190 (U.S. $152) two people; A$240 (U.S. $192) The Cloud Suite (including private spa); A$15 (U.S. $12) children 12–18 in parents' room (children under 12 are not allowed); A$25 (U.S. $20) extra person. Lower weekend rates. BC, MC, V. **Parking:** Free. **Closed:** Christmas–New Year's Day.

Simpsons was designed in 1892 by John Bede Barlow, one of Sydney's best-known colonial architects. It was built to be the family residence of John Lane-Mullins, MLC, a member of the New South Wales Colonial Parliament. The elegant mansion was carefully restored in 1988 and, not surprisingly, won the

New South Wales State Tourism Award the following year for excellence in accommodation.

The house is imbued with the genteel ambience usually associated with bygone eras. Beautiful stained-glass windows grace the lounge, hallways, and some of the bedrooms. Imported English fabrics have been used on upholstered pieces, for bedspreads, and draperies. Most of the furniture is antique. A French Pleyel piano is in the lounge, and every room has framed reproductions of Ellis Rowan's paintings of Australian wildflowers (copied from the originals which are on display in Sydney's Powerhouse Museum). Classical music is played in the lounge and dining area.

Bedrooms are furnished with clock radios, hairdryers, ceiling fans, and small refrigerators; some have queen-size beds. Four rooms have tub/shower combinations. The others have showers only. Terry robes are available on request, and everyone receives a free daily newspaper. Tea- and coffee-making facilities are provided throughout the day in a picturesque courtyard conservatory.

Dining/Entertainment: Continental breakfast can be enjoyed in guest bedrooms or in the conservatory.

Services: Laundry.

MODERATE

CREST HOTEL, 111 Darlinghurst Rd. (corner of Victoria St.), Kings Cross, NSW 2011. Tel. 02/358-2755, or toll free 008/221-805 in Australia. Fax 02/358-2888. Reservations can be made through Best Western. 214 rms, 5 suites. A/C TV TEL **Train:** Kings Cross.

$ Rates: A$137–A$143 (U.S. $109.60–U.S. $114.40) single or double; A$15 (U.S. $12) extra person. Children under 12 stay free in parents' room. No-smoking rooms available. AE, BC, DC, MC, V. **Parking:** Free.

The Crest, occupying a busy corner across the street from the Hyatt, is in the same block as much of the area's X-rated activity. This allows guests a good view of the bright lights and human sideshows for which Kings Cross is legendary.

The rooms in the 25-year-old hotel are spacious and pleasant. Most have showers, instead of tub/shower combos, and all have coffee- and tea-making facilities as well as small refrigerators. Some quarters have queen-size beds.

Dining/Entertainment: Four of the hotel's bars are located on the ground floor, and there is a cocktail lounge one level up. The restaurant is open daily.

Services: Limited room service and secretarial service.

Facilities: Outdoor pool, gift shop, and chemist shop (drugstore).

MANHATTAN HOTEL, 8 Greenknowe Ave., Potts Point, NSW 2011. Tel. 02/358-1288, or toll free 008/22-1562 in Australia. Fax 02/357-3696. 165 rms (135 with bath). TV TEL **Bus:** No. 311. **Train:** Kings Cross.

$ Rates: A$57 (U.S. $45.60) single without bath, A$90 (U.S. $72) single with bath; A$78 (U.S. $62.40) double without bath, A$102 (U.S. $81.60) double with bath; A$12 (U.S. $9.60) extra person. Children under 3 stay free in parents' room. AE, BC, DC, MC, V. **Parking:** A$5 (U.S. $4).

The Manhattan Hotel is located on a relatively quiet street about 3 kilometers (2 miles) from central Sydney and a couple of blocks from the neon glow of Kings Cross. The eight-story property was built more than half a century ago, but because of renovations completed in the late 1980s, the attractive bedrooms have a modern peach-and-gray decor and offer TVs, telephones, clock radios, tea- and coffee-making facilities, and small refrigerators. With any luck, the remaining soft mattresses will have been replaced by the time you get there. Some rooms have views of east Sydney Harbour, and others have balconies that overlook nearby Elizabeth Bay. In spite of the large number of rooms, the hotel's friendly staff manage to create a homey atmosphere.

Dining/Entertainment: The Fifth Avenue Restaurant offers a breakfast buffet daily from 7 to 9am (A$6.50/U.S. $5.20 continental, A$8/U.S. $6.40 cooked) in an art deco atmosphere complete with potted palms and arched windows. It also offers two-course dinners for about A$17 (U.S. $13.60). Both the restaurant and bar are open daily.

Services: Laundry, concierge, and baby-sitting.

A Bed-and-Breakfast Inn

THE KENDALL PRIVATE HOTEL, 122 Victoria St., Potts Point, NSW 2011. Tel. 02/357-3200. Fax 02/357-7606. 22 rms (all with bath). TV TEL **Train:** Kings Cross.
$ Rates (including continental breakfast): A$120 (U.S. $96) single; A$140 (U.S. $112) double; A$155–A$175 (U.S. $124–U.S. $140) deluxe double with sun deck or "honeymooners" with balcony; A$10 (U.S. $8) extra person. AE, BC, DC, MC, V. **Parking:** Free.

Two stately Victorian homes have been joined and restored to create this B&B located on the edge of Kings Cross. The property is named after Australian poet Henry Kendall (1830–82), an ancestor of one of the current owners.

All rooms have ceiling fans, showers (no tubs), and clock radios. Four rooms have small refrigerators. Queen- and king-size beds are available. The honeymoon suite has a four-poster queen-size bed and a private balcony. Tea- and coffee-making facilities are located in a pretty plant-filled conservatory and adjacent cozy sitting room. Comments in the visitors' book reflect guests' appreciation of the Kendall's old-world character and friendly service.

Dining/Entertainment: Breakfast is served in guest bedrooms or in the conservatory with quarry-tile floor, glass ceiling, and bubbling fountain.
Services: Laundromat next door.
Facilities: Spa.

A Serviced Apartment

MEDINA EXECUTIVE APARTMENTS, 70 Roslyn Gardens, Elizabeth Bay, NSW 2011. Tel. 02/356-7400, or toll free 008/25-1122 in Australia. Fax 02/357-2505. 58 studio apartments. A/C TV TEL **Train:** Kings Cross.
$ Rates: A$105 (U.S. $84) single; A$125 (U.S. $100) double; A$12 (U.S. $9.60) extra person. Lower rates through Aussie auto clubs. No-smoking rooms available. AE, BC, DC, MC, V. **Parking:** Free, in a security area.

The Medina Apartments are located in Elizabeth Bay, a residential neighborhood between Kings Cross and scenic Rushcutters Bay about 3 kilometers (2 miles) from central Sydney.

The studio apartments are decorated in a modern color scheme of gray and black or cream and red. Rooms open onto a six-story atrium with cascading green plants. Each unit has a kitchenette, a small dining table and two chairs, and double, queen-size, or twin beds. Twelve apartments have tub/shower combinations.

Dining/Entertainment: Medina lacks a restaurant or bar, but the Dining In service, which delivers meals from more than 40 local restaurants, is available, and there is a grocery shop nearby. Guests may use the rooftop barbecue.
Services: Laundry, valet, concierge, and baby-sitting.
Facilities: Guest laundry.

INEXPENSIVE

A Serviced Apartment

THE DORCHESTER INN, 38 Macleay St., Potts Point, NSW 2011. Tel. 02/358-2400. Fax 02/357-7579. 14 apartments. A/C TV TEL **Train:** Kings Cross. **Bus:** No. 311.
$ Rates: A$85 (U.S. $68) single; A$95 (U.S. $76) double; A$120 (U.S. $96) 1 bedroom; A$135 (U.S. $108) 2 bedroom; A$15 (U.S. $12) extra person. AE, BC, DC, MC, V. **Parking:** A$5 (U.S. $4).

In this 106-year-old mansion on the same block as the Olims Sydney Hotel, the tiny reception desk consumes most of the space in an equally tiny lobby. The inn's decor is colonial, its charm clearly old world. Each of the apartments is spacious, bright, and cheerful. Ten studio, two one-bedroom, and two two-bedroom units are available. Some have tub/shower combinations, but most have showers only. All have full kitchens and some have queen-size beds. The management can arrange baby-sitting.

THE ROCKS
VERY EXPENSIVE

PARK HYATT SYDNEY, 7 Hickson Rd., The Rocks, Sydney, NSW 2000. Tel. 02/241-1234, or toll free 008/222-188 in Australia. Fax 02/256-1555. 159 rms and suites. A/C MINIBAR TV TEL **Train or ferry:** Circular Quay.

$ **Rates:** A$415–A$465 (U.S. $332–U.S. $372) single or double; A$640 (U.S. $512) executive studio; A$935 (U.S. $748) premier suite; A$2,300 (U.S. $1,840) Governor Suite; A$30 (U.S. $24) extra bed. Children under 18 stay free in parents' room. Lower weekend rates and packages. No-smoking rooms available. AE, BC, DC, MC, V. **Parking:** A$15 (U.S. $12).

The Park Hyatt opened in 1990 and occupies an enviable position in the Campbell's Cove area of Sydney Harbour. This location affords spectacular views of the Opera House, harbor, and city and has attracted such guests as Billy Joel and Frank Sinatra.

Seemingly every possible luxury has been incorporated into the bedrooms. Guests have a choice of either king-size or twin beds; all quarters have remote-control curtains (sheer and blackout), water views, double-glazed windows for total quiet, three two-line phones, stereo systems including CD players, VCRs, walk-in closets, dressing rooms, safes, and a shower separate from the tub in a marble bathroom. Daily newspapers, and the loan of videos and compact discs is complimentary. Fax machines are available. The 33 executive studios have two balconies and a telescope.

Dining/Entertainment: Verandah at The Park, the hotel's casual dining area, is open daily from 6:30am to 1am. Formal dining is done in No. 7 at The Park which has a spectacular waterfront view. The Bar, which has a fireplace, resembles an English club. There's also a juice bar in the health club.

Services: Butler (several on each floor), 24-hour room service, turn-down service, shoeshine, laundry, valet, concierge (on every floor), baby-sitting, and massage.

Facilities: Outdoor pool, health club, gym, steam room, sauna, spa, lobby shop, and business center.

EXPENSIVE
A Serviced Apartment

THE STAFFORD, 75 Harrington St., The Rocks, Sydney, NSW 2000. Tel. 02/251-6711. Fax 02/251-3458. 61 apartments. A/C TV TEL **Train or ferry:** Circular Quay.

$ **Rates:** A$187 (U.S. $149.60) studio; A$203 (U.S. $162.40) executive studio; A$231 (U.S. $184.80) 1 bedroom; A$302 (U.S. $241.60) executive 1 bedroom; A$253 (U.S. $202.40) terrace house; A$15 (U.S. $12) extra person. Children under 16 stay free in parents' room. Weekly rates lower. AE, BC, DC, MC, V. **Parking:** A$15 (U.S. $12).

Ideally located in the historic Rocks area, where atmospheric pubs, shops, and dining spots abound, the six-story Stafford offers views of the harbor and Opera House from the top three floors. The property, which opened in 1989, consists of seven two-story terrace houses dating from 1870 to 1895 and 54 modern apartments.

All units have modern furnishings, tub/shower combinations, and full kitchens, although the 49 studio apartments lack dishwashers. Some queen-size beds are available. Everyone receives a free daily newspaper. Half of the lodgings have a balcony.

Dining/Entertainment: The Stafford lacks a restaurant, but the nearby Clocktower Coffee Lounge provides room-service breakfasts.

Facilities: Complimentary self-service laundry, outdoor pool, gym, sauna, and spa.

MODERATE

HARBOUR ROCKS HOTEL, 34-52 Harrington St., The Rocks, Sydney, NSW 2000. Tel. 02/251-8944, or toll free 008/25-1210 in Australia. Fax 02/251-8900. 55 rms (30 with bath). TV TEL **Train or ferry:** Circular Quay.
$ Rates: A$180 (U.S. $144) single or double with bath; A$115 (U.S. $92) single, double, or family room without bath; A$20 (U.S. $16) extra person. Children under 16 stay free in parents' room. AE, BC, DC, MC, V. **Parking:** A$10 (U.S. $8), across the road.

Location is the biggest advantage of this four-story hotel. Many of Sydney's premier attractions are within a short walk. The building is over 100 years old, and some of the rooms were once workmen's cottages. It became a hotel in 1989. Because of its popularity, it is often necessary to book a room in this hostelry several months in advance.

"Deluxe" quarters have private bathrooms (showers, no tubs); "standard" rooms use shared facilities labeled "wenches" and "convicts." All rooms are clean and tidy and have ceiling fans, small refrigerators, tea- and coffee-making facilities, clock radios, and either twin or double beds. There is a luggage lift (elevator), but guests climb the stairs. Some rooms are equipped for handicapped travelers.

Dining/Entertainment: Cellar's Restaurant, where convict-cut block walls and lots of greenery create a pleasant atmosphere, serves all meals daily. A continental breakfast costs A$8.50 (U.S. $6.80), cooked costs A$14.50 (U.S. $11.60). Scarlett's Lounge Bar is open until midnight and frequently offers live entertainment.

Services: Laundry, baby-sitting, and limited room service.
Facilities: Coin-operated laundry.

A Bed-and-Breakfast Inn

THE RUSSELL, 143A George St., The Rocks, Sydney, NSW 2000. Tel. 02/241-3543. Fax 02/252-1652. 30 rms and suites (19 with bath). TEL **Train or ferry:** Circular Quay.
$ Rates (including continental breakfast): A$98–A$190 (U.S. $78.40–U.S. $152) single; A$109–A$200 (U.S. $87.20–U.S. $160) double; A$235 (U.S. $188) suite; A$15 (U.S. $12) extra person. No-smoking rooms available. AE, BC, DC, MC, V. **Parking:** None.

The Russell offers Victorian-style accommodations in the heart of the historic Rocks area. All rooms are decorated with Laura Ashley spreads and upholstery, wicker and cane furniture, ceiling fans, and antique iron beds. An open fire warms the reception area, and a rooftop garden provides views over Circular Quay and the harbor. With its cozy atmosphere, it isn't surprising that the Russell is popular with honeymooners and romantic overseas visitors who have no problem overlooking a few worn furnishings. Narrow stairs make this 100-year-old inn a poor choice for elderly or handicapped travelers.

All guests are provided bathrobes and free daily newspapers. Rooms with private facilities (showers, no tubs) have tea- and coffee-making facilities, and seven rooms have TVs. The 11 rooms without en suite facilities share five bathrooms. Suites include kitchenettes.

Breakfast is served in a picturesque café or in bed. Nonhouseguests may also enjoy breakfast in Café Russell between 7:30 and 9am (A$8.50/U.S. $6.80).

Services: Turn-down service, laundry, baby-sitting, and massage.

INEXPENSIVE
Pub Lodging

THE LORD NELSON BREWERY HOTEL, corner of Kent and Argyle Sts., The Rocks, Sydney, NSW 2000. Tel. 02/251-4044. Fax 02/251-1532. 6 rms (none with bath). TEL **Train or ferry:** Circular Quay.
$ Rates (including continental breakfast): A$65–A$110 (U.S. $52–U.S. $88) single or double, depending on size of room; A$10 (U.S. $8) extra person. AE, BC, DC, MC, V. **Parking:** None.

The Lord Nelson is a wonderful old atmospheric pub located in The Rocks area of Sydney. Downstairs, crowds of happy folks eat and drink surrounded by sandstone block walls and brewery bric-a-brac. Upstairs, the six bedrooms are decorated in Laura Ashley–type prints and antique furniture. Tea- and coffee-making facilities are provided and shared by guests. The overall atmosphere is one of colonial charm. Since the Lord Nelson is Sydney's oldest licensed hotel, you couldn't sleep in a more historic setting.

MANLY

EXPENSIVE

MANLY PACIFIC PARKROYAL, 55 N. Steyne, Manly, NSW 2095. Tel. 02/977-7666. Fax 02/977-7822. 145 rms, 24 suites. A/C MINIBAR TV TEL **Ferry:** Manly.
$ **Rates:** A$242–A$286 (U.S. $193.60–U.S. $228.80) single or double; A$395–A$630 (U.S. $316–U.S. $504) suite; A$15 (U.S. $12) extra person. Reservations can be made through the Southern Pacific Hotel Corporation. AE, BC, DC, MC, V.
Parking: Free.

The only top-class hotel on the Sydney beachfront, the Manly Pacific Parkroyal has an atmosphere entirely different from that of the city hotels I've already described. Everything in this seven-story building is spacious and bright, which is one of the reasons it feels more like a resort than a metropolitan-area hotel. Wide hallways lead to standard rooms that have two double beds, generous closet space, and balconies. On the ocean side, lower floors have a better view because the pines that line the boardwalk aren't in the way; upper floors are quieter. All oceanview rooms have tub/shower combinations, and the king-size studios have king-size beds and an ocean view. Facilities for handicapped travelers are available.

Taxi fare to the hotel from the Manly side of the ferry is about A$1.50 (U.S. $1.20), but most people without luggage prefer the short walk.

Dining/Entertainment: Gilbert's Restaurant, the fine-dining venue, is located one level above the street, overlooking the water. Breakfast, lunch, and dinner are served daily except Saturday, when lunch isn't available. Devonshire tea and light meals are served in the coffee shop, Nells Garden Restaurant. The Charlton Bar and Grill and Dallys Night Club are also located in the hotel.

Services: 24-hour room service, concierge, and laundry.
Facilities: Rooftop spa, pool, gym, and sauna.

INEXPENSIVE

A Motel

MANLY PARADISE MOTEL AND BEACH PLAZA APARTMENTS, 54 N. Steyne, Manly, NSW 2095. Tel. 02/977-5799. Fax 02/977-6848. 20 rms, 16 apartments. TV TEL **Ferry:** Manly.
$ **Rates:** A$76–A$93 (U.S. $60.80–U.S. $74.40) single or double motel unit Mon–Thurs; A$87–A$104 (U.S. $69.60–U.S. $83.20) single or double motel unit Fri–Sun and public holidays. A$170 (U.S. $136) 2-bedroom apartment Mon–Thurs; A$180 (U.S. $144) 2-bedroom apartment Fri–Sun and public holidays; A$10 (U.S. $8) extra person. Lower long-stay rates. AE, BC, DC, MC, V.
Parking: Free, undercover security.

For midprice accommodations just steps from the beach, the Manly Paradise is the best choice. The motel units are air-conditioned and have showers, tea- and coffee-making facilities, small refrigerators, toasters, and clock radios. Some have ocean views. The spacious apartments have two bedrooms, two bathrooms, full kitchens with dishwashers, laundry facilities, tub/shower combinations, and large balconies overlooking the beach. Motel units receive daily chamber service; apartments are cleaned weekly (or daily for a small additional charge).

Manly Paradise lacks a restaurant and bar, but these abound in the surrounding commercial area and next door at the four-star Manly Pacific Parkroyal. Breakfast can be served to units. A rooftop pool and sun deck are available to guests. Ferries and JetCats provide frequent service to central Sydney.

A Guesthouse

PERIWINKLE—MANLY COVE GUESTHOUSE, 19 East Esplanade, Manly, NSW 2095. Tel. 02/977-4668. Fax 02/977-6308. 18 rms (none with bath). **Ferry:** Manly.

$ Rates (including continental breakfast): A$70 (U.S. $56) single; A$78 (U.S. $62.40) double; A$8 (U.S. $6.40). Lower weekly rates. No-smoking rooms available. BC, MC, V. **Parking:** Free.

The Periwinkle is a homey guesthouse where visitors prepare their own meals in a communal kitchen, often barbecue together in the central courtyard, and gather around the fireplace in the cozy lounge (living room) during cool spells. The inn occupies an 1895 harborside house in the suburb of Manly. The present owner, Peter Cameron, added a wisteria-covered pergola on the front of the Periwinkle to hide an unflattering 1920s addition and chose a name for his guesthouse that "sounded friendly." Each of the spacious rooms has a refrigerator and ceiling fan; most have sinks. Accommodations at the front of the two-story house have a harbor view. A self-serve laundry is available. Hosts provide free daily newspapers and will arrange baby-sitting.

DARLING HARBOUR

EXPENSIVE

HOTEL NIKKO DARLING HARBOUR, 161 Sussex St. (corner of Market St.), Sydney, NSW 2000. Tel. 02/299-1231, or toll free 008/222-700 in Australia. Fax 02/299-3340. 649 rms and suites. A/C MINIBAR TV TEL **Train:** Town Hall. **Ferry:** Darling Harbour.

$ Rates: A$240–A$300 (U.S. $192–U.S. $240) single or double, depending on view; A$450–A$550 (U.S. $360–U.S. $440) suite; A$1,000 (U.S. $800) deluxe suite; A$1,600 (U.S. $1,280) Presidential Suite; A$25 (U.S. $20) extra bed. AE, BC, DC, MC, V. **Parking:** Available.

Situated on the city side of Darling Harbour, the Nikko opened in late 1991 and is, at least for now, Australia's largest tourist hotel. The hotel incorporates the Corn Exchange building built by Sydney's City Council in 1887, the Dundee Arms Hotel, and two sandstone maritime warehouses from the 1850s. The interior of the hotel has a nautical art deco decor. To reach Darling Harbour's National Maritime Museum, Harbourside Marketplace, and Convention Centre, guests take the short walk across the Pyrmont Bridge; the Sydney Aquarium and ferries to Circular Quay are even closer.

Most rooms in the 15-story hotel have harbor views, and all offer polished granite bathrooms, in-room movies, and music and radio systems. Nikko Floor residents rate special services. Rooms for handicapped travelers are available.

Dining/Entertainment: The Corn Exchange Brasserie, Lobby Bar, Kamogawa Japanese Restaurant, Dundee Arms Tavern, and a disco are all located on the ground floor.

Services: 24-hour room service, laundry, valet, and concierge.

Facilities: Takashimaya Department Store, business center, early-arrival lounge, roof garden, and duty-free shops.

NOVOTEL SYDNEY ON DARLING HARBOUR, 100 Murray St., Pyrmont, NSW 2009. Tel. 02/934-0000. Fax 02/934-0099. 530 rms and suites. A/C MINIBAR TV TEL **Monorail:** Harbourside.

$ Rates: A$198–A$230 (U.S. $158.40–U.S. $184) single or double; A$286 (U.S. $228.80) junior suite; A$435–A$525 (U.S. $348–U.S. $420) 2-story penthouse; A$15 (U.S. $12) extra bed. Children under 16 stay free in parents' room and receive free breakfast. Weekend packages available. AE, BC, DC, MC, V. **Parking:** Security parking available.

Located just behind the Harbourside Marketplace and steps from the National

Maritime Museum and Convention Centre, the Novotel Sydney is linked to the central business district by the city's sleek monorail.

Open since mid-1991, the hotel's guest rooms feature remote-control TV, radio, tea- and coffee-making facilities, small refrigerators, in-house movies, and tub/shower combinations. Many rooms have harbor and city-skyline views. Fax machines are available.

Dining/Entertainment: Food and beverage outlets include the Pool Bar, Baudin's (all-day dining with a great view), and La Terrasse Lounge Bar. Reflecting the ownership of the hotel, all cuisine has a Gallic flavor.

Services: 24-hour room service and laundry.

Facilities: Business center, outdoor pool, gym, sauna, nightlit tennis courts, and sundries shop.

SUBURBAN SYDNEY
VERY EXPENSIVE

RITZ-CARLTON DOUBLE BAY, 33 Cross St., Double Bay, NSW 2028. Tel. 02/362-4455. Fax 02/362-4744. (Preopening telephone and fax numbers; check with Ritz-Carlton toll free 800/241-3333 in the U.S. for current information.) 140 rms and suites. A/C MINIBAR TV TEL

$ Rates: A$265 (U.S. $212) single or double; rates for suite on application. AE, BC, DC, MC, V. **Parking:** Available.

Scheduled to open about the time this book is published, the Ritz-Carlton Double Bay will offer the first five-star accommodations in Sydney's most posh suburb. "Double Bay, double pay," has often been said in referring to the area's chic boutiques and shops. Designed in the French provincial style, the six-story property is situated in the heart of the community, which is 4 kilometers (2½ miles) east of central Sydney.

Each spacious bedroom offers a marble bathroom with separate shower and toilet compartments. There are also three phones per room, remote-control TVs, radios, small refrigerators, and fluffy robes. All rooms have French doors leading to private balconies. Most have water views. Quarters on the Ritz-Carlton Club floor offer additional comfort and privacy.

 FROMMER'S COOL FOR KIDS: HOTELS

The Park All-Suite Hotel *(see p. 82).* No other central city property feels more like a home away from home. Each roomy unit has a full kitchen and its own washing machine and dryer. The heated pool is popular with kids, and the management can organize baby-sitters.

Manly Paradise Motel and Beach Plaza Apartments *(see p. 91).* What kid wouldn't want to be right across the street from the beach! The apartments are spacious and have full kitchens, balconies, and laundry facilities—and there's also a pool on the roof. Another fun bonus: going back and forth to Sydney on a ferry or JetCat.

Novotel Sydney on Darling Harbour *(see p. 92).* A swimming pool and tennis courts add to the "kid appeal" of this place, but the biggest factor is location. The adjacent Darling Harbour development boasts dozens of quick and casual places to dine, a playground for small fry, the National Maritime Museum, the Powerhouse Museum (with lots of hands-on exhibits designed for the younger set), and the Sydney Aquarium. The Novotel likes families so much that children under 16 get a free breakfast daily, and a children's menu is available in the restaurant. Another plus: Access is by monorail or ferry.

Dining/Entertainment: Try The Dining Room for continental cuisine in an intimate, elegant environment. The Café for breakfast, lunch, and dinner daily. The Bar for lunch or cocktails. The Lobby Lounge for continental breakfast, cocktails, or afternoon tea.

Services: 24-hour room service, turn-down service, concierge, valet, baby-sitting, and "water limousine."

Facilities: Business center, sundries shop, fitness center, and exclusive shops.

EXPENSIVE

CENTRA HOTEL NORTH SYDNEY, 17 Blue St., North Sydney, NSW 2060. Tel. 02/955-0499, or toll free 008/22-466 in Australia. Fax 02/922-3689. 220 rms, 2 suites. A/C MINIBAR TV TEL **Train:** North Sydney. **Ferry:** Lavendar Bay.

$ **Rates:** A$195 (U.S. $156) single or double; A$350 (U.S. $280) suite; A$15 (U.S. $12) extra person. Lower weekend rates. No-smoking rooms available. AE, BC, CB, DC, MC, V. **Parking:** Free.

The Centra Hotel North Sydney (formerly North Sydney Travelodge) is your best bet if you want to locate across the Harbour Bridge. Because of the hotel's semicircular design, almost all its guest rooms have breathtaking harbor views—back across the water to the Opera House and Sydney's impressive skyline. The hotel is especially popular with business travelers.

The train ride to central Sydney takes 10 minutes; the bus takes about 5 minutes longer. Adventurous folks, of course, could walk across the bridge (not recommended for the fainthearted).

All rooms have clock radios, tea- and coffee-making facilities, and small refrigerators; queen-size beds and in-room movies are available. Guests receive free daily newspapers.

Dining/Entertainment: Meals are available in Blues Bar and Restaurant.

Services: 24-hour room service, shoeshine, laundry, valet, concierge, and baby-sitting.

Facilities: Outdoor pool and business center.

A Serviced Apartment

OAKFORD EXECUTIVE APARTMENTS, 400 Glenmore Rd., Paddington, NSW 2021. Tel. 02/361-9000, or toll free 008/338-111 in Australia. Fax 02/332-3484. 48 apartments. A/C TV TEL **Train:** Edgecliff.

$ **Rates** (including continental breakfast on first day): A$226 (U.S. $180.80) apartment for four people; A$278 (U.S. $222.40) apartment for six people. Children under 18 stay free in parents' room. Discounts for weekly and monthly stays. AE, BC, DC, MC, V. **Parking:** Free.

Situated on the edge of the White City Tennis Complex, Sydney's answer to Wimbledon, these sleek, spacious, low-rise apartments are the tennis buff's delight. They are also well located for travelers who wish easy access to the posh shops in Double Bay or the bohemian cafés and markets in Paddington. Central Sydney is a little more than 3 kilometers (2 miles) away.

At the Oakford, the two- and three-bedroom apartments built in 1987 are appointed with attractive furnishings, including decorative prints, large sprays of fresh flowers, leather couches, and lacquer tables. Some units have expansive city-skyline views, and all have patios or balconies, large kitchens with dishwashers, and laundry facilities. The Dining In service brings meals from a variety of restaurants and the management provides a grocery- and liquor-shopping service. Laundry and baby-sitting can also be arranged. The facilities include an outdoor pool, business center, and barbecue. Tennis courts, some of the best in the country, are steps away.

MODERATE

A Bed-and-Breakfast Inn

THE PENSIONE SYDNEY, 25-27 Georgina St., Newtown, NSW 2042.

Tel. 02/550-1700, or toll free 800/223-0888 in the U.S. and Canada. Fax 02/550-1021. 14 rms (all with bath). TV TEL **Bus:** No. 422, 423, 426, 428, or 448 from city.

$ Rates (including continental breakfast): A$130 (U.S. $104) single; A$150–A$175 (U.S. $120–U.S. $140) double; A$15 (U.S. $12) extra person. Children 12 to 18 stay free in parents' room; those under 12 are not accepted. No-smoking rooms available. AE, BC, DC, MC, V. **Parking:** Not available.

Proprietors Robert George and Dallas Bayly have lovingly restored this three-story Victorian house located in a blue-collar suburb about 5 kilometers (3 miles) outside the city center and close to the campus of Sydney University. Complimentary wine, perked coffee, and other drinks are served in a charming drawing room, where Oriental carpets, antiques, high ceilings with ornamental plaster cornices, a marble fireplace, and a pianola create an old-world atmosphere.

The guest rooms are equipped with coffee- and tea-making facilities, small refrigerators, clock radios, and bathrobes. King- and queen-size beds are available. Evening meals are served in an intimate restaurant Thursday through Saturday, and guests are encouraged to use the sun deck at the back of the house.

Pensione Sydney can be reached by public buses which run along King Street every 10 minutes. It takes about 15 minutes to get to the city center (A$2.50/U.S. $2). A taxi costs about A$5.50 (U.S. $4.40). Courtesy transfers to and from the airport are provided. Laundry and valet service are available.

BUDGET

For those on a budget, **YHA Hostels** are dotted around the Sydney suburbs. **Forest Lodge,** 28 Ross Street, Forest Lodge, NSW 2037 (tel. 02/692-0747), is near Sydney University. **Dulwich Hill,** 407 Marrickville Road, Dulwich Hill, NSW 2203 (tel. 02/569-0272), is 3½ miles from Central Station and 2½ miles from the airport. **Glebe Point,** 262 Glebe Point Road, Glebe, NSW 2037 (tel. 02/692-8418), is near the water. **Hereford Lodge,** 51 Hereford Street, Glebe, NSW 2037 (tel. 02/660-5577; fax 02/552-1771), is YHA's Australian flagship. Forest Lodge and Dulwich Hill cost A$14 (U.S. $11.20) per person in a twin room. Charges at Glebe Point and Hereford Lodge are A$19 to A$20 (U.S. $15.20 to U.S. $16). Weekly rates are lower. Children are half price.

2. SYDNEY DINING

It would be a mistake to leave the harborside metropolis before sampling local seafood, such as Sydney rock oysters, Balmain bugs (rock lobster), or John Dory. It would also probably be an error not to try Chinese dining at least once, since the area's Cantonese restaurants are some of the best outside Asia.

In the following listings you'll find restaurants that float and others that are perched on top of a tower. A handful are out of doors and several are in pubs. Some have harbor views, a few offer entertainment, many have excellent wine lists, and some are BYOs. Almost all the very expensive and most of the moderately priced places accept major credit cards, weekend and public-holiday surcharges are *de rigueur,* and reservations are recommended in all but the most casual eateries.

In this chapter, restaurants in which a three-course dinner for one would cost A$50 (U.S. $40) or more are categorized very expensive. Places where the same number of courses would cost A$38 to A$49 (U.S. $30.40 to U.S. $39.20) are expensive; A$25 to A$37 (U.S. $20 to U.S. $29.60), moderate; A$15 to A$24 (U.S. $12 to U.S. $19.20), inexpensive; less than A$15 (U.S. $12), budget.

CITY CENTER
VERY EXPENSIVE

KABLE'S, in the Regent Hotel, 199 George St. Tel. 238-0000.

Cuisine: AUSTRALIAN. **Reservations:** Recommended. **Train or ferry:** Circular Quay.

$ Prices: Fixed-price two-course lunch A$29.50 (U.S. $23.60); three-course lunch A$34.50 (U.S. $27.60); fixed-price four-course dinner A$55 (U.S. $44). Also à la carte. AE, BC, DC, MC, V.

Open: Lunch Mon–Fri noon–2:30pm; dinner Mon–Sat 6:30–11pm.

Kable's is generally regarded as Sydney's finest hotel dining venue and one of Australia's best restaurants. It has won numerous awards including the New South Wales Tourism Award for Best Restaurant in 1990.

Ironically named after the first convict to step ashore in the new colony (he carried Governor Phillip to land on his shoulders), Kable's is extravagant and elegant in every detail. Expensive tableware and crystal complement the stylish black, white, and gray art deco decor, and the service is flawless.

Executive chef Serge Dansereau oversees the preparation of the dishes on a menu that changes daily to take advantage of the best available produce. You might order grilled rainbow trout filets on spinach and mango compote, stuffed quail with foie gras, or venison médaillons. In addition to superb cuisine, the restaurant has an extensive wine list. You won't be disappointed.

LEVEL ONE—SYDNEY TOWER RESTAURANT, in Centrepoint Tower, Market St. between Pitt St. and Castlereagh. Tel. 233-3722.

Cuisine: INTERNATIONAL. **Reservations:** Recommended. **Train:** St. James. **Monorail:** City Centre.

$ Prices: Appetizers A$9.50–A$18 (U.S. $7.60–U.S. $14.40); main courses A$22.50–A$29.50 (U.S. $18–U.S. $23.60); fixed-price lunch or early dinner A$29.50–A$32.50 (U.S. $23.60–U.S. $26); fixed-price dinner A$37.50–A$45.50 (U.S. $30–U.S. $36.40). Minimum per person A$21 (U.S. $16.80). Sat surcharge 10%. AE, BC, DC, MC, V.

Open: Lunch Mon–Fri 11am–3pm; dinner Mon–Sat 5–10:30pm. **Closed:** Public holidays.

Rotating 85 stories above the city, this restaurant provides a spectacular view as well as excellent food and service. The Tower, whose restaurants opened in 1981, is the tallest public building in the Southern Hemisphere, and diners are treated to a 360° view of the city, harbor, and suburbs. Restaurant patrons don't pay the A$3.50 (U.S. $2.80) normally charged for the 40-second ride to the observation level; instead, they enter via Market Street, take the elevator to the Gallery Level, and proceed to the reception lounge, where they are given tokens for the "lift up" to the restaurant.

Level One's international à la carte menu, served in an intimate, candlelit environment, includes local seafood as well as a variety of carefully prepared meat dishes. A special menu for children aged 3 to 12 is available for lunch and early dinner, which finishes at 7:30pm. A less expensive, self-service dining spot is located on Level Two (see below).

EXPENSIVE

BENNELONG RESTAURANT, in the Sydney Opera House. Tel. 250-7548 or 250-7578.

Cuisine: MODERN AUSTRALIAN. **Reservations:** Recommended. **Train or ferry:** Circular Quay.

$ Prices: Appetizers A$8.50–A$14.50 (U.S. $6.80–U.S. $12.40); main courses A$23–A$28 (U.S. $18.40–U.S. $22.40); fixed-price two-course lunch A$29.50 (U.S. $23.60); fixed-price three-course pretheater dinner A$32.50 (U.S. $26). AE, BC, DC, MC, V.

Open: Lunch Mon–Sat noon–2:30pm; pretheater meal Mon–Sat 5:30–7pm; dinner Mon–Sat 8–10:30pm.

I would not miss dining in the Bennelong Restaurant any more than I'd visit Paris without having lunch or dinner aloft in the Eiffel Tower. Travelers more pragmatic than me may also elect to have a pretheater meal at the Bennelong because of its convenient location and quality cuisine.

If you dine here you'll find an attractive restaurant with a cathedral-style interior created by the landmark's sail-shaped exterior. Views of the bridge and harbor are spectacular both day and night. If your heart is willing, but the budget can't be stretched to accommodate the Bennelong, try the Opera House's less pricey dining venues: the Forecourt Restaurant and the Harbour Restaurant, both with waiter service; or Café Mozart and the Harbour Takeaway, both self-service.

MERRONY'S, 2 Albert St., Circular Quay. Tel. 247-9323.
   Cuisine: MODERN AUSTRALIAN WITH FRENCH INFLUENCE. **Reservations:** Recommended, especially for lunch any day, and dinner Fri–Sat. **Train or ferry:** Circular Quay.
$ Prices: Appetizers A$8–A$13.50 (U.S. $6.40–U.S. $10.80); main courses A$15.50–A$18 (U.S. $12.40–U.S. $14.40). Sun and public holiday surcharge A$2.50 (U.S. $2) per adult. AE, BC, DC, MC, V.
   Open: Lunch Mon–Fri noon–2:30pm; dinner daily 5:45–11:45pm.

Chef Paul Merrony has all Sydney talking about his bistro-style restaurant where the food is nothing short of divine. In other establishments it might be the view overlooking Circular Quay which rated attention, but at Merrony's, the focus is on creative cuisine. Favorite appetizers include goat cheese tart, pigeon salad, and raw tuna with cucumber and dill. Mains include braised cabbage stuffed with pork, steak tartare, and snapper with a parsley and mushroom crust. The not-to-be-missed dessert is "death by chocolate." The chef trained in London and Paris, and his dishes rate kudos for presentation as well as flavor.

A popular site for power lunches since it opened in mid-1990, the 40-table eatery is also ideal for pretheater and posttheater meals. There's a good wine list; a bottle of 1988 Evans Family chardonnay from the Hunter Valley will add A$28 (U.S. $22.40) to your tab. Request a window table with a water view.

PARAGON CAFE, in the Paragon Hotel, Loftus St., Circular Quay. Tel. 241-3888.
   Cuisine: MODERN AUSTRALIAN. **Reservations:** Recommended. **Train or ferry:** Circular Quay.
$ Prices: Appetizers A$12 (U.S. $9.60); main courses A$18 (U.S. $14.40). AE, BC, MC, V.
   Open: Lunch Mon–Fri noon–3pm; dinner Mon–Sat 6–10pm.

The Paragon Cafe opened in mid-1990 on the second floor of the Paragon Hotel, which dates from 1865. The restaurant's art deco decor reflects a 1930s refurbishment and provides a pleasant atmosphere for dining.

Chef Chris Manfield oversees the only all-woman kitchen in Sydney, and her partner, Margy Harris, looks after the noncooking details. The menu changes continuously based on seasonal availability. Typical appetizers include whiting and coconut pancake with coriander-yogurt sauce; spiced duck and asparagus salad; and seared beef with lemongrass and pickled papaya. On the day you dine there mains might be: braised baby chicken, boned and stuffed with onion and sage risotto or grilled veal filet with mustard cream sauce and spiced cabbage. Wonderful bread rolls are served with meals, and there's a good wine list.

MODERATE

CLUB BAR, in the Regent Hotel, 199 George St. Tel. 238-0000.
   Cuisine: LIGHT LUNCHES/COCKTAILS. **Reservations:** Recommended for lunch. **Train or ferry:** Circular Quay.
$ Prices: Lunch A$10.50 (U.S. $8.40). AE, BC, DC, MC, V.
   Open: Mon–Thurs 11:30am–1am, Fri 11:30am–2am, Sat 5pm–2am, Sun 5pm–1am. Lunch served Mon–Fri noon–2:30pm.

As the name implies, this comfortable lounge off the hotel lobby has the furnishings and ambience of a country club or cruise ship rather than a typical bar. Adult games such as Trivial Pursuit, backgammon, chess, and draughts (checkers), together with a selection of newspapers and magazines, are available to patrons.

The Upper Crust Lunch, consisting of salads, cheese, fruit, and freshly baked

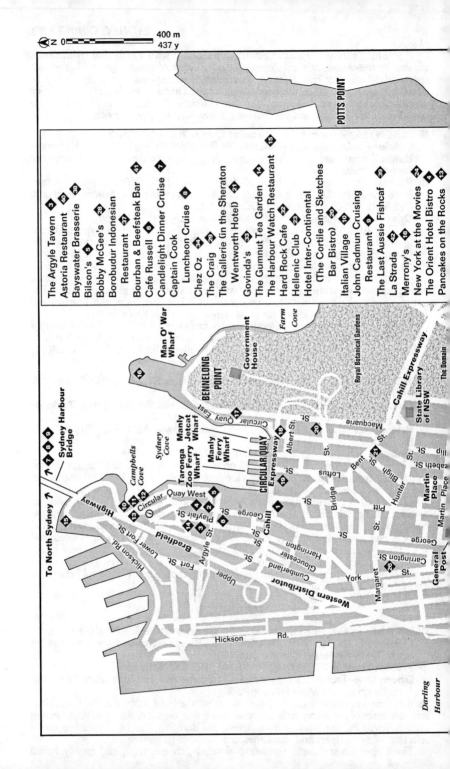

400 m
437 y

POTTS POINT

The Argyle Tavern 3
Astoria Restaurant 44
Bayswater Brasserie 38
Bilson's 5
Bobby McGee's 28
Borobudur Indonesian Restaurant 47
Bourban & Beefsteak Bar 41
Cafe Russell 6
Candlelight Dinner Cruise 7
Captain Cook Luncheon Cruise 8
Chez Oz 15
The Craig 29
The Gallerie (in the Sheraton Wentworth Hotel) 27
Govinda's 43
The Gumnut Tea Garden 1
The Harbour Watch Restaurant 22
Hard Rock Cafe 23
Hellenic Club 25
Hotel Inter-Continental (The Cortile and Sketches Bar Bistro) 26
Italian Village 2
John Cadmun Cruising Restaurant 9
The Last Aussie Fishcaf 39
La Strada 42
Merrony's 40
New York at the Movies 24
The Orient Hotel Bistro 4
Pancakes on the Rocks 45

Sydney Harbour Bridge

To North Sydney

Man O' War Wharf

BENNELONG POINT

Government House

Farm Cove

Royal Botanical Gardens

Campbells Cove

Sydney Cove

Circular Quay East

Circular Quay West

Taronga Zoo Ferry Wharf

Manly Jetcat Wharf

Manly Ferry Wharf

CIRCULAR QUAY

Cahill Expressway

Albert St.

Loftus St.

Bridge St.

Bent St.

Bligh St.

Hunter St.

Phillip St.

Elizabeth St.

Macquarie St.

State Library of NSW

The Domain

Cahill Expressway

Martin Place

General Post

George St.

Carrington St.

Margaret St.

York St.

Harrington St.

Gloucester St.

Cumberland St.

Western Distributor

Cahill Expressway

George St.

Playfair St.

Argyle St.

Fort St.

Upper Fort St.

Lower Fort St.

Hickson Rd.

Bradfield Highway

Hickson Rd.

Darling Harbour

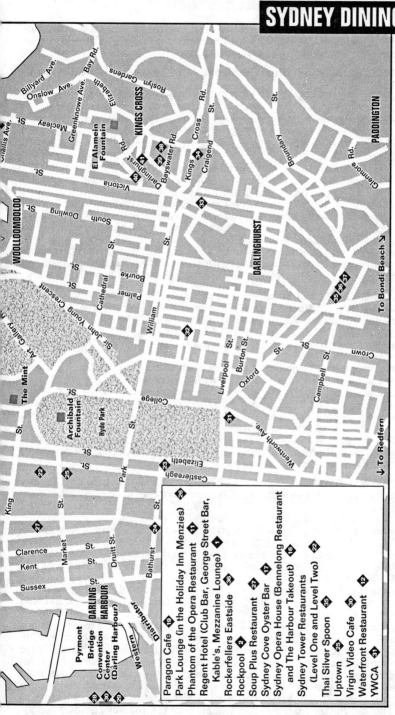

SYDNEY DINING

Paragon Cafe ◆

Park Lounge (in the Holiday Inn Menzies) ◆

Phantom of the Opera Restaurant ◆

Regent Hotel (Club Bar, George Street Bar,
Kable's, Mezzanine Lounge) ◆

Rockerfellers Eastside ◆

Rockpool ◆

Soup Plus Restaurant ◆

Sydney Cove Oyster Bar ◆

Sydney Opera House (Bennelong Restaurant
and The Harbour Takeout) ◆

Sydney Tower Restaurants
(Level One and Level Two) ◆

Thai Silver Spoon ◆

Uptown ◆

Virgin Video Cafe ◆

Waterfront Restaurant ◆

YWCA ◆

Post Office ⊠   Information ⓘ

breads, is popular. So are selections from the long list of exotic beverages. The Regent's proximity to the Opera House makes this a great spot for an after-theater nightcap.

CORTILE, in the Hotel Inter-Continental, 117 Macquarie St. Tel. 230-0200.

Cuisine: SNACKS & LIGHT MEALS/TEA. **Reservations:** None. **Train or ferry:** Circular Quay.

$ **Prices:** All dishes A$7–A$16 (U.S. $5.60–U.S. $12.80); breakfast A$18 (U.S. $14.40); afternoon tea A$15 (U.S. $12). AE, BC, DC, MC, V.

Open: Sun–Thurs 10am–11pm; Fri–Sat 10am–midnight; afternoon tea 3–5:30pm.

★ The skylit Cortile, the Inter-Continental's lovely lobby bar, is surrounded by the sandstone arches of Sydney's beautiful old Treasury Building which dates from 1849. This is a delightful site for light meals, teas, and cocktails.

The traditional English afternoon tea includes a selection of finger sandwiches, freshly baked scones with King Island cream and strawberry preserves or a gâteau slice of your choice. You could also have toasted crumpets, English butter cake, or English fruitcake. A string quartet accompanies.

For lunch you could have a croissant with a choice of fillings, or other light dishes such as soup or quiche. Dinner offerings include smoked Tasmanian salmon, an Australian farmhouse cheese platter, or roast beef, pickles, and horseradish cream.

HELLENIC CLUB, 251 Elizabeth St., 5th floor. Tel. 264-5883.

Cuisine: GREEK. **Reservations:** Recommended at lunch. **Train:** Museum.

$ **Prices:** Appetizers A$4–A$8.50 (U.S. $3.20–U.S. $6.80); main courses A$10.50–A$13 (U.S. $8.40–U.S. $10.40). AE, BC, DC, MC, V.

Open: Lunch Mon–Fri noon–3pm; dinner Mon–Fri 5–9pm, Sat 5–10pm. **Closed:** Public holidays.

The large room which comprises the Hellenic Club is where Sydney's Greek residents dine and where they hold their daughters' wedding receptions. It's also where Kitty, Michael, and Olympia Dukakis ate when they were in town. The decor, which includes a mural of Greek gods behind the bar and oil paintings of scenes of Greece, is a little dated, but for authentic lamb dishes and traditional favorites such as moussaka, this place is a real winner. The waiters—many of them newly arrived from the old country—are friendly and contribute to the overall congenial ambience of the place.

Six window tables allow diners a wonderful view over Hyde Park. Ask for one of these when you call to make reservations.

LEVEL TWO SYDNEY TOWER RESTAURANT, in Centrepoint Tower, Market St. between Pitt and Castlereagh Sts. Tel. 233-3722.

Cuisine: BUFFET (GRILLS, ROASTS, SEAFOOD, & ASIAN). **Reservations:** Recommended. **Train:** St. James. **Monorail:** City Centre.

$ **Prices:** Lunch A$22.50–A$27.50 (U.S. $18–U.S. $22); early dinner A$25–A$27.50 (U.S. $20–U.S. $22); dinner A$29.50–A$32.50 (U.S. $23.60–U.S. $26). Reduced prices for children aged 3–12 are offered for lunch and early dinner. Weekend and public holiday surcharge of 10%–15% is added on drinks only. AE, BC, DC, MC, V.

Open: Lunch Tues–Sun 11am–3:30pm (last booking 2:15pm); early dinner Tues–Sun 5–last booking 6pm; dinner Tues–Sat 5–11:45pm (last booking 9:15pm).

Level Two is one floor up from Level One, the more expensive dining spot I described earlier. The view from these two places is obviously the same—spectacular. Both complete an entire rotation in about an hour, providing diners with the best bird's-eye view in town. The main difference is that Level Two is self-service, sans tablecloths. The extensive buffet consists of three different appetizers, at least a dozen main courses, and four desserts. Should you choose this Sydney Tower restaurant, you can heap your plate with just-carved roast, steak, Chinese dishes, and specialties such as pork knuckle, chicken Maryland, and lasagne. Trust me, you won't go away hungry.

Restaurant patrons purchase a voucher at the gallery-level reception area and receive a complimentary "lift up" instead of paying the regular charge for the fast elevator ride up the tower. *Note:* If budget or time constraints make this aerial carvery out of the question, light refreshments and drinks are available before 5pm at a snack bar, the Sydney Tower Sky Lounge, on Level Three.

MEZZANINE LOUNGE, in the Regent Hotel, 199 George St. Tel. 238-0000.

Cuisine: LIGHT MEALS/AFTERNOON TEA. **Reservations:** Not usually necessary. **Train or ferry:** Circular Quay.

$ **Prices:** Afternoon tea A$15 (U.S. $12). AE, BC, DC, MC, V.

Open: Breakfast daily 7–10:30am; all-day menu daily 10:30am–late; afternoon tea daily 3–5pm.

A three-story atrium rises from the polished marble floor of the Regent's lobby. Each level is trimmed with brass railings and cascading green plants. On the second floor, the Mezzanine Lounge provides a bird's-eye view of the hotel's front doors and the activity in the elegant entrance foyer. Surely there isn't a better perch in all of Sydney for a quick breakfast, light lunch, afternoon tea, after-work cocktail, or after-theater supper.

The set price for afternoon tea includes sandwiches, scones, French pastries, an assortment of cakes, sorbets, ice cream, and a selection of Twinings teas. A classical ensemble provides accompaniment.

PARK LOUNGE, in the Holiday Inn Menzies, 14 Carrington St. Tel. 299-1000.

Cuisine: SNACKS & LIGHT MEALS. **Reservations:** Recommended. **Train:** Wynyard.

$ **Prices:** Appetizers A$5–A$17 (U.S. $4–U.S. $13.60); main course A$7.50–A$22 (U.S. $6–U.S. $17.60). AE, BC, DC, MC, V.

Open: Daily 9am–1am (24 hours a day for house guests).

Tapestry, brass lamps, and heavy timber paneling give this room an elegant, old-world air. This is a good spot for coffee, snacks, and cocktails. Harpist Ulpia Erdos provides accompaniment.

UPTOWN, Skygarden shopping arcade, Level 3, 77 Castlereagh St. Tel. 223-4211.

Cuisine: MULTICULTURAL. **Reservations:** Recommended, especially at lunch. **Train:** St. James. **Monorail:** City Centre.

$ **Prices:** Appetizers A$6–A$7 (U.S. $4.80–U.S. $5.60); main courses "small appetite" A$7–A$12 (U.S. $5.60–U.S. $9.60), "large appetite" A$9.50–A$18.50 (U.S. $7.60–U.S. $14.80). AE, BC, MC, V.

Open: Lunch Mon–Fri 11:30am–3pm; dinner Mon–Sat 6pm–midnight.

Both the menu and the decor of this trendy spot are best described as eclectic. The designer of the interior created "a metaphorical cityscape," a place where diners can view "images of urban life through the ages." The walls boast assorted facades of buildings from various parts of the world and from differing periods in history. The result is very colorful and very avant-garde.

Like the decor, the menu also comes from various corners of the globe. When I last dined there, the daily specials were Creole lasagne with meat and eggplant, North Indian lamb curry, and antipasto with caponata, marinated peppers, artichoke, and tuna. Chinese, Thai, and German dishes are also offered, along with local specialties such as Sydney rock oysters.

Uptown is both a restaurant and a bar, so even if you aren't hungry, you can go in, have a drink and ogle the "cityscape." A draft beer costs A$2.80 (U.S. $2.25).

INEXPENSIVE

THE GALLERIE, in the Sheraton Wentworth Hotel, 61-101 Phillip St. Tel. 230-0700.

Cuisine: LIGHT MEALS & COFFEE. **Reservations:** None. **Train:** Martin Place.
$ Prices: Lunch A$10–A$12 (U.S. $8–U.S. $9.60); coffee A$3.80 (U.S. $3.05). AE, BC, DC, MC, V.
Open: Mon–Fri 9am–6:30pm, Sat 10am–4pm.

Coffee is the specialty of the house in this casual café. Java fans can sample Kona style, Blue Mountain style, royal blend, Colombian, mocha and Kenya blend, or European style. Teas, juices, soft drinks, and milk shakes are also offered. These can be accompanied by pastries, muffins, or scones. The lunchtime menu consists of salads, sandwiches, a cheese and fruit plate, or a hot dish such as cannelloni.

GEORGE STREET BAR, in the Regent Hotel, 199 George St. Tel. 238-0000.
Cuisine: PUB FARE. **Reservations:** Not usually required. **Train or ferry:** Circular Quay.
$ Prices: Lunch and snacks from A$7 (U.S. $5.60). AE, BC, DC, MC, V.
Open: Mon–Thurs 11am–11pm, Fri noon–11:45pm; lunch Mon–Fri noon–2:30pm.

The Regent's George Street Bar has a lively atmosphere and classic pub decor including brass railings, brick floor, and lots of wood. The bar has two entrances directly on the main thoroughfare from which it gets its name. Large windows allow patrons a view of the city's hustle and bustle. The handsome interior, together with the relative brightness of the place, puts the George Street Bar a cut above the majority of public bars. A full range of drinks, wines, and draft beers are offered, in addition to hearty pub lunches such as meat pies and roasts from a blackboard menu.

SKETCHES BAR AND BISTRO, in the Hotel Inter-Continental, 117 Macquarie St. Tel. 230-0200.
Cuisine: PASTA. **Reservations:** Not usually required. **Train or ferry:** Circular Quay.
$ Prices: Small dishes of pasta A$8.50 (U.S. $6.80); large dishes of pasta A$12.50 (U.S. $10); salads A$4.50 or A$7 (U.S. $3.60 or U.S. $5.60). AE, BC, DC, MC, V.
Open: Mon–Fri 11am–11pm; lunch noon–2:30pm; dinner 5:30–7:30pm.

Large blackboard menus proclaim the daily choices in this lively, create-your-own-plate dining venue. Guests pay at the cashier, then wander over to the pasta bar where they choose from close to a dozen different types of freshly made pasta and a variety of sauces. While waiting for their fettuccine, tortellini, or agnolotti to be cooked, they can start on the salad bar. A jug (pitcher) of draft beer costs A$7.90 to A$9.75 (U.S. $6.32 to U.S. $7.80). This eatery is so named because the work of the Australian Black & White Artists Club decorates its walls. The cartoons and caricatures of the country's politicians, sports figures, and other celebrities are for sale.

SOUP PLUS RESTAURANT, 383 George St. Tel. 299-7728.
Cuisine: INTERNATIONAL. **Reservations:** Recommended. **Train:** Town Hall.
$ Prices: Appetizers A$4–A$7 (U.S. $3.20–U.S. $5.60); main courses A$7–A$12 (U.S. $5.60–U.S. $9.60). AE, BC, MC, V.
Open: Mon–Thurs noon–midnight, Fri–Sat noon–1:30am, Sun 6–11:30pm.
Closed: Christmas, New Year's Day, Good Friday, and Easter Sunday.

Located opposite the Strand Arcade between King Street and Market Street, Soup Plus offers live jazz between 7:30 and 11:30pm during the week and until 1:30am Friday and Saturday nights. The quality of the performances is quite high, as is the volume, so don't plan on an intimate conversation during your meal. As the name implies, at least four soups are offered daily, some hot and some chilled. The blackboard menu also usually lists several kinds of pastas, salads, steak, chicken, and vegetarian dishes. The food is good, and the plain pine furniture, basement location, and self-service setup create a simple, yet pleasant, atmosphere. This place is very good value and it's not surprising that it's been voted one of the best "cheap eats" in Sydney. Be aware, however, that a cover charge of A$3 to A$5 (U.S. $2.40 to U.S. $4) applies after 7:30pm, that the minimum purchase if you want to pay by credit card is

A$20, and that when I last dined there they were charging A50¢ (U.S. 40¢) for a glass of water.

SYDNEY COVE OYSTER BAR, 1 E. Circular Quay. Tel. 247-2937.

Cuisine: MODERN AUSTRALIAN. **Reservations:** Not usually required. **Train or ferry:** Circular Quay.

$ Prices: Snacks A$5–A$9 (U.S. $4–U.S. $7.20); glass of wine A$2.90 (U.S. $2.35); 10-oz. midi of beer A$2.90 (U.S. $2.35); 15-oz. schooner of beer A$3.80 (U.S. $3.05). AE, BC, DC, MC, V.

Open: Mon–Thurs 11am–11pm, Fri 11am–midnight, Sat 10am–midnight, Sun 10am–9pm.

You couldn't ask for a better setting for enjoying a drink and a light meal. The Sydney Cove Oyster Bar is located *right* on the water, a stone's throw from the Opera House, in a building which dates from 1906. Ferries and JetCats pass back and forth while patrons seated at umbrella tables enjoy the view and live jazz Friday 6 to 9pm, Saturday 8 to 11pm, and Sunday 3 to 6pm. Those who get hungry can munch on smoked trout pâté, oysters, selections from a cheese platter, or other dishes chosen from a blackboard menu. This is one of the few places you can drink Hahn beer, a local specialty. The other tap brew is Coopers Ale from South Australia.

THE YWCA OF SYDNEY, 5-11 Wentworth Ave. Tel. 264-2451.

Cuisine: HOME-STYLE. **Reservations:** None. **Train:** Museum.

$ Prices: Appetizers A$2.50–A$5 (U.S. $2–U.S. $4); main courses A$6.25–A$7.50 (U.S. $5–U.S. $6). No credit cards.

Open: Mon–Fri 7:30am–7pm, Sat–Sun breakfast and dinner only.

The setting might not be exciting, but you can't beat the Y for economical meals. Remember, it isn't licensed to serve alcoholic beverages and you can't bring your own. High chairs are provided for children, and Hyde Park is right across the street.

BUDGET

In addition to the economical eatery listed below, more cheap eats are included in "Casual, Fast Food, and 24-Hour Eateries," below.

THE HARBOUR TAKEAWAY, on the north side of the Sydney Opera House. Tel. 250-7191.

Cuisine: SEAFOOD. **Reservations:** None. **Train or ferry:** Circular Quay.

$ Prices: Fish-and-chips A$5.50 (U.S. $4.40); seafood box A$9.50 (U.S. $7.60); tea or coffee and cake A$3.50 (U.S. $2.80); glass of house wine A$2.50 (U.S. $2). No credit cards.

Open: Daily 11am–7pm.

Walk around the back of the Opera House, past the small theaters and recital rooms on the side, and you will find two dining spots with million-dollar views. The Harbour Restaurant is a moderately priced seafood place with waiter service. However for a quick bite, I heartily recommend its budget-priced, self-service neighbor, the Harbour Takeaway. Seating is indoors or out, and the parade of ferries and other vessels on the harbor is almost constant.

KINGS CROSS & VICINITY
VERY EXPENSIVE

LA STRADA, 95 Macleay St., Potts Point. Tel. 358-1160.

Cuisine: ITALIAN. **Reservations:** Recommended. Children under 12 "discouraged." **Train:** Kings Cross.

$ Prices: Appetizers A$15–A$67 (U.S. $12–U.S. $53.60; top price for caviar and pâté de foie gras); main courses A$25–A$45 (U.S. $20–U.S. $36). AE, BC, DC, MC, V.

Open: Dinner Mon–Sat 6–11:30pm (last orders 10:30pm). **Closed:** Public holidays.

A monument to the 1954 Fellini film of the same name, La Strada is located on the edge of Kings Cross, about 3 kilometers (2 miles) from the center of Sydney. Its walls

FROMMER'S SMART TRAVELER: RESTAURANTS

1. Eat your main meal at noon when some of Sydney's best restaurants offer fixed-price lunches designed to attract business diners.
2. Take advantage of food courts (see "Casual, Fast Food & 24-Hour Eateries," below), where many one-course meals cost only about A$5 (U.S. $4).
3. Don't overlook the inexpensive ethnic eateries along Oxford Street.
4. Dine in BYOs which allow you to bring your own wine and beer.
5. Be aware of which restaurants add a surcharge on weekends and public holidays. Eat in these places during the week.
6. Don't overtip. Australians generally leave 5% to 10%.

are adorned with giant photos of Anthony Quinn and others from the movie. The rest of the decor is black-and-white art deco, the overall ambience that of an Italian nightclub.

The restaurant's owner and chef, Giovanna Toppi, has created a dining spot that is popular with touring superstars such as Bruce Springsteen, David Bowie, and Bob Hope as well as with sophisticated Sydney residents. The menu, written in a combination of Italian and English, offers an extensive food list—antipasto of Russian caviar, mussels marinara, and prosciutto e melone, veal and beef prepared in more than a dozen ways, and pastas, poultry, salads, and omelets. The wine list is extensive. In 1991 maître d' Frank Aranda won *The Sydney Morning Herald* special award for outstanding service to the restaurant industry.

EXPENSIVE

CHEZ OZ, 23 Craigend St., Darlinghurst. Tel. 332-4866.
    Cuisine: MODERN MULTICULTURAL. **Reservations:** Recommended. **Train:** Kings Cross.
$ Prices: Appetizers A$8.50–A$10.50 (U.S. $6.80–U.S. $8.40); main courses A$18.50 (U.S. $14.80). AE, BC, DC, MC, V.
    Open: Lunch Tues–Fri 12:30–3pm; dinner Mon–Sat 7pm–midnight (last orders 10pm).

Chez Oz has been a haven for serious diners since it opened in 1985. The restaurant is located adjacent to Kings Cross, about 2 kilometers (1 mile) from the city center. Chef Peter Maresch likes to prepare his own interpretation of various ethnic cuisines. Therefore the menu contains such items as Thai chicken and papaya salad; tomato fettuccine with roasted shallot mushroom sauce; and green curry noodles with beef and Chinese chives. This is also the spot for duck and white-bean chili with warm tortillas or prawn and red-pepper pot stickers with cucumber and basil.

Diners sit on bentwood chairs at tables covered with crisp white linens. Candles and fresh flower arrangements contribute to the intimate environment.

MODERATE

BAYSWATER BRASSERIE, 32 Bayswater Rd., Kings Cross. Tel. 357-2177.
    Cuisine: MODERN MULTICULTURAL. **Reservations:** None. **Train:** Kings Cross.
$ Prices: Appetizers A$6–A$8 (U.S. $4.80–U.S. $6.40); main courses A$10–A$17 (U.S. $8–U.S. $13.60). Weekend and public holiday surcharge A$2.50 (U.S. $2) per person. BC, MC, V.
    Open: Mon–Fri noon–midnight, Sat–Sun 10am–midnight. Bar open until 2am Fri–Sat (light snacks available).

S The popularity of this brasserie is not hard to understand: good food, reasonable prices, friendly service, and convenient hours. In addition, the drop-in-and-eat-what-you-like policy and casual ambience are very appealing to locals and visitors alike. You might want to try spicy seafood fritters, duck liver mousse and brioche, or linguine with field mushrooms, cream, and parsley. It would also be perfectly okay to sit in the garden area and nurse a couple of Bloody Marys over the course of an afternoon or drop in for nothing more substantial than pastry and coffee. A disc jockey holds forth in the bar on Monday, Friday, and Saturday nights.

BOURBON & BEEFSTEAK BAR, 24 Darlinghurst Rd., Kings Cross. Tel. 358-1144.

Cuisine: INTERNATIONAL. **Reservations:** Recommended on weekends. **Train:** Kings Cross.

$ Prices: Appetizers A$4.95–A$15.95 (U.S. $4–U.S. $12.80); main courses A$9.50–A$21.50 (U.S. $7.60–U.S. $17.20). Weekend and public holiday surcharge A$2 (U.S. $1.60). AE, BC, DC, MC, V.

Open: Daily 24 hours. Happy hour daily 4–7pm.

This restaurant came into its own during the late 1960s when U.S. servicemen took their R and R in Sydney and frequented the Cross. Even today, the Bourbon & Beefsteak specializes in American breakfasts of Denver omelets, hash browns, pancakes, or eggs Benedict. There's even a chili con carne omelet, which must have brought tears to the eyes of homesick GIs from Texas. Dinners range from a variety of huge steaks to such gourmet dishes as "son-of-a-bitch cowpoke beef stew" and "gawdammit J.R.'s chili." Mexican, Italian, Chinese, and vegetarian dishes are also offered.

Food may be served around the clock at the B&B, but drinks and dancing are just as important to its clientele of tourists, locals, and the colorful transients who work in the "lively half mile" of Darlinghurst Road, where the bar is located. Vying for tables by the picture window near the street, some watch the seedy side of life without having to be part of it, while others crowd onto the dance floor and gyrate to the bands that play daily from 5pm to 4am.

HARD ROCK CAFE, 121-129 Crown St., Darlinghurst. Tel. 331-1116.

Cuisine: AMERICAN. **Reservations:** None. **Train:** Museum.

$ Prices: Appetizers A$3.95–A$7.95 (U.S. $3.20–U.S. $6.40); main courses A$7.95–A$16.50 (U.S. $6.40–U.S. $13.20). Weekend and public holiday surcharge 10%. AE, BC, MC, V.

Open: Sun–Thurs noon–midnight, Fri–Sat noon–2am. **Closed:** Christmas Day and Good Friday.

In 1989, almost 20 years after the first Hard Rock Cafe opened in London, Sydney finally got its long-awaited rock-and-roll, burger eatery. The memorabilia which adorns the walls and ceiling includes costumes worn by Elvis, Elton John, and John Lennon, as well as items from Australian groups such as INXS and Icehouse. As per the other locations, a Cadillac rides overhead and the menu features bulging burgers with a variety of toppings, salads, chicken, ribs, and the like. And, as at the other Hard Rocks around the world, the queue (line) to get in is ever-present.

THE LAST AUSSIE FISHCAF, 24 Bayswater Rd., Kings Cross. Tel. 356-2911.

Cuisine: SEAFOOD. **Reservations:** Recommended, especially on weekends. Book *well ahead* Fri–Sat nights. **Train:** Kings Cross.

$ Prices: All à la carte dishes A$8.50–A$15.50 (U.S. $6.80–U.S. $12.40). Fri and Sat fixed-price two-course dinner A$31 (U.S. $24.80); Fri–Sat fixed-price three-course dinner A$36 (U.S. $28.80). Surcharge for entertainment A$2 (U.S. $1.60) per person. AE, BC, DC, MC, V.

Open: Dinner Tues–Sun 6–11:30pm; lunch only in the summer.

The '50s are alive and well at The Last Aussie Fishcaf. An authentic Wurlitzer jukebox plays "Peggy Sue," "Love Potion No. 9," and other favorites from that era of rock and roll. Neon bobby-soxers decorate the walls, and the costumed wait staff periodically take over the stage and lipsync songs. During the course of the evening there is usually a limbo contest and lots of games—1950s birthday-party games. If you don't want to join the crowd on stage doing the hokey pokey, you can sit back and watch the exhibition dancers jitterbug. Real nostalgia buffs may want to purchase their own "Lost in the 50s" T-shirt. This place is heaven for the young and young at heart.

Appetizers include oysters, fish felafel, and spice-dusted squid. Typical mains are fish-and-chips, fishcaf curry, and a hot pot of seafood in a tomato fish stock.

INEXPENSIVE

BOROBUDUR INDONESIAN RESTAURANT, 263 Oxford St., Darlinghurst. Tel. 331-3464.
   Cuisine: INDONESIAN. **Reservations:** Recommended. **Bus:** Taylor Sq., then walk 1 block east.
$ Prices: Appetizers A$4.50–A$4.80 (U.S. $3.60–U.S. $3.85); main courses A$7.20–A$14.90 (U.S. $5.80–U.S. $11.95). Public holiday surcharge A$1 (U.S. 80¢). AE, BC, MC, V.
   Open: Mon–Sat 6–10pm.
This informal BYO (bring your own beer or wine) restaurant serves traditional Indonesian cuisine including marinated chicken pieces in a spicy coconut milk sauce, curry puffs, and deep-fried fish filets with Balinese sauce. The tables are covered with batik cloths.

ROCKERFELLERS EASTSIDE, 225 Oxford St., Darlinghurst. Tel. 361-6968.
   Cuisine: AMERICAN. **Reservations:** Recommended. **Bus:** Taylor Sq., then walk 1 block east.
$ Prices: Appetizers A$3.90–A$8.90 (U.S. $3.15–U.S. $7.15); main courses A$9.90–A$15.90 (U.S. $7.95–U.S. $12.75). Sun surcharge A50¢ (U.S. 40¢) per person. AE, BC, MC, V.
   Open: Mon–Sat 6pm–midnight, Sun 6–11pm.
Seemingly every symbol of the U.S. has been incorporated into the decor of this restaurant. This includes Mickey and Minnie Mouse, "grid-iron" (football) players suspended from the ceiling, and jelly beans on the counter. The food is also stereotypical Yank: burgers, ribs, barbecue chicken, and so forth. This eatery is licensed to serve alcohol, but you may bring your own if you wish.

THAI SILVER SPOON, 203 Oxford St., Darlinghurst. Tel. 360-4669.
   Cuisine: THAI. **Reservations:** Recommended on weekends. **Bus:** No. 380 to Darlinghurst Court House. Restaurant is across the street.
$ Prices: Appetizers A$3.60–A$5.80 (U.S. $2.90–U.S. $4.65); main courses A$7.90–A$11.90 (U.S. $6.35–U.S. $9.55). Public holiday surcharge A$1 (U.S. 80¢). AE, BC, MC, V.
   Open: Lunch Tues–Fri noon–2:30pm; dinner daily 6–11pm.
This is the place if you like green curry chicken, pork chili dip, garlic squid, or whole chili fish. Two soups are offered: tom khar kai, chicken with coconut milk, and tom yum, prawn or chicken soup with lemongrass and galangal. Like many of the ethnic eateries located along Oxford Street, the Thai Silver Spoon is BYO.

BUDGET

ASTORIA RESTAURANT, 7 Darlinghurst Rd., Kings Cross. Tel. 358-6327.
   Cuisine: TRADITIONAL AUSTRALIAN. **Reservations:** Not necessary. **Train:** Kings Cross.
$ Prices: Main courses A$4.70–A$5.50 (U.S. $3.80–U.S. $4.40); desserts A90¢–A$1.20 (U.S. 75¢–U.S. $1). Public holiday surcharge A40¢ (U.S. 35¢) per person. No credit cards.
   Open: Lunch Mon–Sat 11am–2:30pm; dinner Mon–Sat 4–8:30pm.
Located right across the street from the Bourbon & Beefsteak Bar (see above), the Astoria is a welcome sight for those whose budgets have worn thin. Roast dinners with

vegetables cost less than A$5 (U.S. $4), as do other home-style dishes such as pork chops and apple sauce, and American fried chicken. Jelly (Jello), ice cream, tinned (canned) fruit salad, and trifle are all offered for dessert. The decor is dated, but at these prices, who cares? The Astoria is BYO.

GOVINDA'S, 112 Darlinghurst Rd., Darlinghurst. Tel. 357-5162.
   Cuisine: VEGETARIAN. **Reservations:** None. **Train:** Kings Cross.
$ **Prices:** Lunch A$5.90 (U.S. $4.75); dinner A$7.90 (U.S. $6.35). AE, BC, MC, V.
   Open: Lunch Mon–Fri noon–2:30pm; dinner daily 5:30–9pm.

Govinda's is located on the second floor in the Hare Krishna Centre, but diners are not exposed to doctrine. Instead, they are treated to a delicious, all-you-can-eat buffet of vegetarian dishes, some of which have an Indian flavor. The decor, including a tile floor and black lacquer tables, is simple and pleasant. There are nine tables inside and four on a balcony. No alcohol is allowed on the premises. A takeaway (take-out) counterpart is open downstairs Monday to Friday from 11:30am to 8:30pm. The Hare Krishnas also operate Mukunda's on Victoria Street where free meals are distributed nightly at 5pm.

THE ROCKS
VERY EXPENSIVE

BILSON'S, Upper Level, International Passenger Terminal, Circular Quay West, The Rocks. Tel. 251-5600.
   Cuisine: MODERN AUSTRALIAN. **Reservations:** Recommended well in advance. **Train or ferry:** Circular Quay.
$ **Prices:** Appetizers A$14–A$23 (U.S. $11.20–U.S. $18.40); main courses A$26–A$32 (U.S. $20.80–U.S. $25.60); fixed-price three-course lunch A$35 (U.S. $28); table d'hôte dinner A$50 (U.S. $40). AE, BC, DC, MC, V.
   Open: Lunch Mon–Fri noon–2pm; dinner Mon–Sat 7–10pm.

Bilson's occupies two glass-walled levels at the northern end of the cruise-ship terminal and offers its patrons the finest view in all of Sydney. By day, diners take in the sparkling water of the sun-drenched harbor, the Opera House, north-shore suburbs, ferries bustling to and from Circular Quay, and the Harbour Bridge. At night, the scene becomes a fairyland of reflected lights. It's no surprise that Bilson's is "a must" for many visitors. INXS dined here when they were in town, as did Mick Jagger and the king and queen of Spain.

The creative cuisine prepared by chef Peter Kuruvita is equally as spectacular as the view. The menu changes daily in order to take advantage of seasonal specialties. Popular appetizers include crisp veal sweetbreads with spinach and cheese triangles; paupiette of John Dory with oscietra caviar; and roast jumbo quail breast with spring onions and onion bread. Main courses include roast jewfish filet, baby leeks and fried Jerusalem artichokes; saddle of hare, blueberries and cassis sauce; and shellfish pot au feu. The extensive wine list includes Australian and French vintages that complement the magic Kuruvita works in the kitchen.

In deference to North American visitors who expect such things, manager Michael McMahon provides a no-smoking section and will organize quick service for guests that are in a hurry. However, I can't imagine wanting to leave this beautiful spot in less than 2 or 3 hours.

ROCKPOOL, 109 George St., The Rocks. Tel. 252-1888.
   Cuisine: SEAFOOD. **Reservations:** Necessary. **Train or ferry:** Circular Quay.
$ **Prices:** Appetizers A$14–A$22 (U.S. $11.20–U.S. $17.60); main courses A$25 (U.S. $20). AE, BC, DC, MC, V.
   Open: Lunch Mon–Fri noon–2:30pm; dinner Mon–Sat 6:30–10pm.

This two-story restaurant across the street from the Museum of Contemporary Art has a '50s-modern decor, which includes crisp white tablecloths.

Chef Neil Perry prepares Australian seafood like no one else. His innovative menu includes such dishes as crayfish ravioli with burnt butter and yogurt, red curry of blue-eye cod, and herb and spice crusted tuna with braised eggplant. Some nonfish dishes are: roasted Illabo milk-fed lamb with fried artichoke and aïoli, and veal with potato and fennel gratin and pea purée. A bottle of 1989 Paulette Polish River chardonnay from South Australia, which I highly recommend, will add A$25 (U.S. $20) to your tab.

EXPENSIVE

THE ARGYLE TAVERN, in the Argyle Center, 12-18 Argyle St., The Rocks. Tel. 247-7782.

Cuisine: AUSTRALIAN. **Reservations:** Recommended. **Train or ferry:** Circular Quay.

$ Prices: Dinner and show A$59.50 (U.S. $47.60). AE, BC, DC, MC, V.

Open: Dinner daily 7:30pm; show starts 8pm.

The Argyle Centre, where the tavern is located, was built in 1828 as a bond store and warehouse. It served this purpose until 1966, when it was converted to its present use. The original walls have been retained, making an ideal setting for the "Jolly Swagman Show," which includes folk songs, sheepshearing, a large dollop of cornball humor, and horseplay.

The three-course, fixed-price meal consists of a seafood appetizer, prime rib with all the trimmings, traditional damper bread, and Australia's national dessert—pavlova. An alternative main course is available for non–meat eaters. This place lives up to its promise to be "a feast of Aussie food, fun, and folklore." So go along, say "G'day," and learn the words to "Waltzing Matilda."

THE HARBOUR WATCH RESTAURANT, top level, Pier One, Hickson Rd. and Lower Fort St., The Rocks. Tel. 241-2217.

Cuisine: SEAFOOD. **Reservations:** Recommended. **Train or ferry:** Circular Quay, then free bus to Pier One.

$ Prices: Appetizers A$7.90–A$14.90 (U.S. $6.35–U.S. $11.95); main courses A$19.20–A$37 (U.S. $15.40–U.S. $29.60); fixed-price three-course lunch A$24.90 (U.S. $19.95); children's menu A$8 (U.S. $6.40). Weekend and public holiday surcharge from A$2.50 (U.S. $2). AE, BC, DC, MC, V.

Open: Lunch daily noon–2:30pm; dinner daily 6–10pm.

Because it's located on the upper level of Pier One, the Harbour Watch is provided with an ever-changing and panoramic backdrop for an enjoyable meal. Ferries, large container ships, and various private craft continuously ply the waters in front of the restaurant. The 300-seat room is divided into three levels, so that nearly every table shares the remarkable vista.

The very good menu consists almost entirely of fish and shellfish, although three kinds of steak are offered as a concession to those who prefer meals from the turf rather than the surf. A list of daily specials heralds the seasonal availability of Queensland mud crab, lobster, Moreton Bay sand crab, Hawkesbury silver bream, mussels, and pearl perch (found only off the coast of northern New South Wales and southern Queensland). The regular, tabloid-style menu enumerates such dishes as whole trout, snapper filets, blue-eye cod, and green prawns, which are obtainable year round.

WATERFRONT RESTAURANT, in Campbell's Storehouse, 27 Circular Quay West, The Rocks. Tel. 247-3666.

Cuisine: SEAFOOD. **Reservations:** Recommended. **Train or ferry:** Circular Quay.

$ Prices: Appetizers A$10.95–A$13.95 (U.S. $8.80–U.S. $11.20); main courses A$16.95–A$32.50 (U.S. $13.60–U.S. $26). Weekend surcharge A$2 (U.S. $1.60); public holiday surcharge A$5 (U.S. $4). AE, BC, DC, MC, V.

Open: Lunch daily 11:30am–4pm; dinner daily 5:30pm–midnight.

The Waterfront is located in the historic Campbell's Storehouse, Sydney's first commercial building, on the harbor's edge. Adjacent to the restaurant stands a monument to Robert Campbell, who constructed the building in the colonial period. Both the large inside and outside seating areas are decorated in a 19th-century nautical motif. The open-air plaza is shaded by sails suspended from a tall ship's mast;

indoors, three levels of tables are surrounded by brass lanterns, fish nets, tea chests, barrels, and halyards.

It isn't surprising that fresh seafood is the specialty of the house. John Dory, sole, barramundi, baby schnapper (snapper), bream, rainbow trout, and gemfish are served either grilled or pan-fried. In addition, Sydney rock oysters, fresh ocean prawns, blue swimmer crabs, and Moreton Bay bugs (rock lobster) are regularly available. Though most of the fish is caught locally, some, like the barramundi, is flown in from Queensland. Live lobsters also arrive daily from Tasmania. The food is very good, as is the service.

MODERATE

ITALIAN VILLAGE, in Campbell's Storehouse, 7 Circular Quay West, The Rocks. Tel. 247-6111.
   Cuisine: ITALIAN. **Reservations:** Recommended. **Train or ferry:** Circular Quay.
$ **Prices:** Appetizers A$8.50–A$12.50 (U.S. $6.80–U.S. $10); main courses A$18.50–A$19.95 (U.S. $14.80–U.S. $16). Weekend surcharge per person A$2 (U.S. $1.60); public holiday surcharge per person A$5 (U.S. $4). AE, BC, DC, MC, V.
   Open: Daily 11:30am–midnight.

Like the Waterfront Restaurant described above, the Italian Village is located in the historic Campbell's Storehouse, on the harbor. The decor of the three-story dining spot includes blue-and-white checked cloths, a quarry-tile floor, and rustic bric-a-brac, all of which combine to create a country-taverna ambience. The waiters' uniforms are not unlike those of Venetian gondoliers. Seating is both indoors and out.

Appetizers include calamari fritti, penne alla marinara, and lasagne al forno. Sample mains: saltimbocca alla romana, cozze e marinara (mussels cooked in a traditional Sardinian sauce), and scaloppine vino bianco.

PHANTOM OF THE OPERA RESTAURANT, in Campbell's Storehouse, 17-21 Circular Quay West, The Rocks. Tel. 247-2755.
   Cuisine: FRENCH/MODERN AUSTRALIAN. **Reservations:** Recommended. **Train or ferry:** Circular Quay.
$ **Prices:** Appetizers A$5–A$10.50 (U.S. $4–U.S. $8.40); main courses A$15–A$17.50 (U.S. $12–U.S. $14); brunch A$11.50 (U.S. $9.20). Weekend and public holiday surcharge A$2 (U.S. $1.60). AE, BC, MC, V.
   Open: Brunch Sat–Sun 10am–noon; lunch daily noon–4pm; dinner Mon–Sat 6pm–midnight (last orders 10pm).

⭐ Phantom of the Opera is located on the waterfront in Campbell's Storehouse. The owners are Jean Gatellier, a Frenchman educated at Stanford, and Susana Sam-Vargas, a Peruvian/Chinese who lived in California for 20 years, studied at UCLA, and graduated from Harvard. Consequently, the menu reflects the influence of several continents. While the pair may hail from different lands, they share an interest in opera and a particular affection for the old *Phantom of the Opera* movie. The Phantom's menu includes such dishes as homemade vermicelli pasta with chargrilled octopus, filet of beef Rossini, and roast crispy duck breast and confit of duck leg.

Gatellier and Sam-Vargas also own the adjacent Australian Wine Centre, where hundreds of Aussie vintages are sold by the bottle or glass, so Phantom of the Opera's wine list is particularly extensive. (For more on the wine center see "Sydney Savvy Shopping," in Chapter 5.)

Seating is both indoors and out, with views of the Opera House and the ferries coming and going from Circular Quay. In short, Phantom of the Opera is a very special restaurant in a most picturesque setting. They also operate a bistro in the wine center, in all but winter months, where lunches run about A$6 to A$8 (U.S. $4.80 to U.S. $6.40). Seating is outdoors on the harborside.

INEXPENSIVE

THE ORIENT HOTEL BISTRO, 89 George St., The Rocks. Tel. 251-1255.

Cuisine: AUSTRALIAN BARBECUE. **Reservations:** Not necessary. **Train or ferry:** Circular Quay.

$ **Prices:** Appetizers A$6–A$7.50 (U.S. $4.80–U.S. $6); main courses A$6–A$11 (U.S. $4.80–U.S. $8.80). AE, BC, CB, DC, MC, V.

Open: Lunch Sun–Fri noon–2:30pm.

This is an historic Aussie pub with simple, good-value meals. Patrons can choose and grill their own steak or select other dishes from a blackboard menu. Meat pies, moussaka, lasagne, quiche, and an extensive salad bar are offered at affordable rates. Seating is outdoors at large wooden tables on a walled brick patio.

BUDGET

CAFE RUSSELL, 143 George St., The Rocks. Tel. 241-3543.

Cuisine: LIGHT MEALS & TEA. **Reservations:** Not usually required. **Train or ferry:** Circular Quay.

$ **Prices:** Breakfast A$3.50–A$8.50 (U.S. $2.80–U.S. $6.80); light lunches A$4.50–A$10.50 (U.S. $3.60–U.S. $8.40); morning or afternoon tea (including selection of sweets) A$3.50 (U.S. $2.80). Weekend and public holiday surcharge 10%. AE, BC, DC, MC, V.

Open: Daily 7:30am–3:30pm.

This charming little eatery is on the ground level of the Russell B&B described above. Lunchtime offerings include salad and damper (Australian bush bread) with a choice of lamb, beef, ham, chicken, salmon, or cheese filling. If you want wine with lunch, you'll have to BYO.

THE GUMNUT TEA GARDEN, 28 Harrington St., The Rocks. Tel. 247-9591.

Cuisine: LIGHT MEALS & TEA. **Reservations:** Recommended for lunch Mon–Fri. **Train or ferry:** Circular Quay.

$ **Prices:** Light lunch from A$5 (U.S. $4); pot of Twinings tea A$2.20 (U.S. $1.80); order of scones ("enough to share") A$4.70 (U.S. $3.80). Weekend and public holiday surcharge 10%. BC, MC.

Open: Daily 11am–5pm. **Closed:** Good Friday, 3 days at Christmas, and New Year's Day.

This wonderful little cottage, with its crooked windows, sloping floor, and uneven plaster walls, was built in 1835 by an Irish blacksmith convict named William Reynolds. He had been sent to Australia as punishment for stealing a horse in Dublin. The original fireplace is still used during cool winter months. Diners have a choice of sitting in one of several tiny rooms inside or outside at an umbrella table on a leafy brick patio. The Gumnut's scones, made only on weekends, are legendary, and their recipe for lemon-hazelnut meringue was requested by the editors of *Gourmet* and printed in the magazine. BYO.

MANLY

INEXPENSIVE

CAFE STEYNE, 14 S. Steyne, Manly. Tel. 977-0116.

Cuisine: BREAKFAST ANYTIME/SANDWICHES/BURGERS/PASTA. **Reservations:** Not necessary. **Ferry or JetCat:** Manly.

$ **Prices:** Breakfast (cooked) A$6.80–A$9.60 (U.S. $5.45–U.S. $7.70); burgers A$7.20–A$10.90 (U.S. $5.80–U.S. $8.75); children's menu A$3.50 (U.S. $2.80). AE, BC, MC, V.

Open: Daily 8am–11pm.

The beachfront location makes this eatery ideal for a casual meal or a cold beer. The menu is much like an American coffee shop, offering everything from cooked and continental breakfasts to steaks and ribs. A cobb salad or a Greek salad might appeal if you're watching your waistline; otherwise try one of their super sundaes. Children under 12 can have junior-size burgers, hot dogs, or fish-and-chips.

DARLING HARBOUR

MODERATE

BOBBY MCGEES, in the Harbourside Festival Marketplace, Level 2, South Pavilion, Darling Harbour. Tel. 281-3944.
Cuisine: AMERICAN. **Reservations:** Recommended. **Monorail:** Harbourside.

$ **Prices:** Appetizers A$4.50–A$8.50 (U.S. $3.60–U.S. $6.80); main courses A$9.50–A$21.95 (U.S. $7.60–U.S. $17.60). Weekend and public holiday surcharge 10%. AE, BC, DC, MC, V.

Open: Mon–Sat noon–3am, Sun noon–midnight (last food order 10pm weekdays, 11pm weekends).

Bobby McGee's calls itself, "The world's best place to celebrate anything," and it's not hard to see why. The waiters and waitresses wear zany costumes and periodically break into song. Everyone is unusually friendly and a lively atmosphere prevails. The decor consists of old movie posters and black-and-white glossies of movie stars. Floor-to-ceiling windows provide a view of city lights reflected in the water.

The menu is eclectic and includes prime rib, southern fried chicken, Bobby's gourmet cheeseburger, catch of the day, and a huge salad bar. Kids under 12 are catered for with a special menu (which they can color) and a free "big squeeze" beverage container. Anyone celebrating a special occasion gets their picture taken.

VIRGIN VIDEO CAFE, in the Harbourside Festival Marketplace, Space 429, Darling Harbour. Tel. 281-3807.
Cuisine: CASUAL MEALS/SNACKS. **Reservations:** Recommended Fri–Sat nights. **Monorail:** Harbourside.

$ **Prices:** Brunch from A$7.50 (U.S. $6); burgers and pasta A$8–A$12 (U.S. $6.40–U.S. $9.60); desserts A$6 (U.S. $4.80); cocktails A$6.50–A$8.50 (U.S. $5.20–U.S. $6.80); shooters A$4.50 (U.S. $3.60); beer A$2.80–A$6 (U.S. $2.25–U.S. $4.80). Sun and public holiday surcharge 10%. AE, BC, DC, MC, V.

Open: Mon–Wed 9am–10pm, Thurs 9am–12:30am, Fri–Sat 9am–2am, Sun 9am–10pm. **Closed:** Christmas Day.

This place is nirvana for the 18 to 25 crowd and anyone else who's interested in contemporary rock music. Music videos run continuously on TV screens suspended over the bar, and taped music plays from morning until closing. Cocktails and shooters bear the names of popular groups: INXS (gin, vodka, white curaçao, Bacardi, tequila, lemon juice, and Coke), AC/DC (Tia Maria and vodka), and the Beatles (Bailey's Kahlúa, and peppermint schnapps) for example. Fourteen kinds of beer are offered.

Ten tables inside around the bar have a view of the water through floor-to-ceiling windows; the 20 or so umbrella tables outside enjoy an ambience not unlike a sidewalk café. Three associated businesses are just steps away: the Virgin Clothing Co., Virgin Record Co., and Virgin Video Co.

BUDGET

THE CRAIG BREWERY BAR & GRILL, in the Harbourside Festival Marketplace, Darling Harbour. Tel. 281-3922.
Cuisine: AUSTRALIAN BARBECUE. **Reservations:** Advisable Thurs–Sat nights. **Monorail:** Harbourside.

$ **Prices:** Lunch or dinner Mon–Fri A$4.90 (U.S. $3.95); lunch or dinner Sat–Sun A$6.90 (U.S. $5.55). Surcharge on public holidays. AE, BC, MC, V.

Open: Mon–Sat 10am–midnight or later, Sun 11am–midnight. **Closed:** Good Friday and Christmas Day.

In spite of the fact that it can accommodate up to 1,500 people, the Craig is often chockablock. It isn't surprising when you see the menu, the three bars, the waterfront location, the poker machines, and the live bands on Friday and Saturday nights. Where else can you have beef satay, rump steak, half a chicken, lasagne, or a fisherman's basket for A$4.90 (U.S. $3.95) during the week and A$6.90 (U.S. $5.55) on weekends. Nine beers are on tap, including Craig ale and lager. A pint (20 oz.) will set you back A$4 (U.S. $3.20).

SUBURBAN SYDNEY & FARTHER AFIELD
VERY EXPENSIVE

BEROWRA WATERS INN, Berowra Waters. Tel. 456-1027.
   Cuisine: MODERN WITH FRENCH INFLUENCE. **Reservations:** Imperative, well in advance. **Transportation:** Hornsby, then taxi; or driving, take Pacific Hwy. to Berowra, follow signs to Berowra Waters. Wait at public wharf for pickup by the restaurant's boat. Do not cross river on car-ferry.
 $ Prices: Fixed-price three-course lunch or dinner including one glass of French champagne and coffee A$85 (U.S. $68). AE, BC, MC, V.
   Open: Lunch Fri–Sat from 12:30pm; dinner Fri–Sat from 7:30pm; lunch Sun from noon.

This much-talked-about spot is generally acknowledged to be Sydney's—and possibly Australia's—finest restaurant. Chef/owner Gay Bilson is well known throughout the country for the innovative cuisine she serves her guests. The setting of Berowra Waters Inn is also spectacular and contributes to its popularity.

You might try brioche with poached bone marrow and red-wine butter; salad of stuffed squid, black noodles, and pancetta; grilled rare tuna with sorrel, lemon, olives, and oil. Desserts include crème brûlée, chocolate mousse sandwich, baked orange and cardamom custard with caramel sauce, and passion-fruit Bavarian crème. It's all delicious. The extensive wine list includes a wide selection of domestic vintages.

About an hour's drive north of Sydney on the shore of Berowra Creek, a tributary of the Hawkesbury River, the restaurant is reachable by car, by boat, or by seaplane.

EXPENSIVE

THE COACHMEN RESTAURANT, 763 Bourke St., Redfern. Tel. 319-7705.
   Cuisine: INTERNATIONAL. **Reservations:** Recommended. **Transportation:** Taxi from city center costs about A$10 (U.S. $8).
 $ Prices: Appetizers A$7.95–A$14.95 (U.S. $6.40–U.S. $12); main courses A$21.95 (U.S. $17.60). Weekend surcharge A$2 (U.S. $1.60) per person; public holiday surcharge A$5 (U.S. $4) per person. AE, BC, DC, MC, V.
   Open: Lunch Mon–Fri noon–2:30pm; dinner daily 6–11pm.

The Coachmen is housed in an 1826 building constructed by convicts. The home originally belonged to Thomas Campbell and was a Sydney landmark. The nine rooms used for guest dining reflect its colonial heritage; wagon wheels, barrels, antique farm implements, exposed brick and stone walls, original Australian oil paintings, and wood paneling are complemented by subdued lighting. A band provides soft music for dancing 6 nights a week.

The menu includes such seafood and meat dishes as grilled barramundi, rack of lamb, veal Oscar, and steak au poivre. "Crêpes fruit de mer"—prawns, scallops, and oysters cooked in white wine sauce and rolled in a thin pancake—is the house specialty. Herb bread, baked on the premises, makes a delicious accompaniment. The Coachmen has a good wine list.

MODERATE

BARRENJOEY HOUSE, 1108 Barrenjoey Rd., Palm Beach. Tel. 974-4001.
   Cuisine: CONTEMPORARY AUSTRALIAN. **Reservations:** "Appreciated."
   Bus: Palm Beach; or seaplane.
 $ Prices: Appetizers A$8–A$12.50 (U.S. $6.40–U.S. $10); main courses A$17–A$20 (U.S. $13.60–U.S. $16). AE, BC, MC, V.
   Open: Lunch Sat–Sun from noon; dinner Wed–Sun from 7pm.

A perfect spot for a summer lunch, the restaurant's canvas-covered outdoor dining space has a conservatorylike feel; airy indoor seating is available, too. The well-prepared cuisine puts its emphasis on fresh ingredients. Main courses might include venison saddle with celeriac rémoulade, glazed apples, and turnips; leg of lamb roasted with herb crust, beetroot, and yams; and fresh fish from the market. The chef and his staff bake the bread served in the restaurant, cure olives, and dry tomatoes grown in the kitchen garden.

Since Palm Beach is a waterfront community about 40 kilometers (25 miles) from Sydney, most folks without a car opt for the seaplane flights offered by Aquatic Air (tel. 974-5966) from Rose Bay near the city or take the public bus from Sydney to Palm Beach. The bus costs A$3.80 (U.S. $3.05) one-way.

SPECIALTY DINING

DINING WITH A VIEW

The Sydney Tower Restaurants provide the best lofty viewpoints. The Bennelong, Merrony's, Bilson's, and Harbour Watch each offer a harbor vista. The Sydney Cove Oyster Bar and the Harbour Takeaway are al fresco on the water. Berowra Waters Inn is sited on a river.

WATERBORNE DINING

JOHN CADMAN CRUISING RESTAURANT, No. 6 Jetty, Circular Quay. Tel. 922-1922.
Cuisine: INTERNATIONAL. **Reservations:** Imperative. **Train or ferry:** Circular Quay.
$ Prices: 3½-hour cruise, three-course dinner, and entertainment A$72 (U.S. $57.60). AE, BC, DC, MC, V.
Open: Dinner daily 7:30–11pm.
"Sydney's cruising restaurant" departs Circular Quay every evening at 7:30pm and meanders around Sydney Harbour for 3½ hours while passengers enjoy drinks, dinner, and dancing to live music. Visitors staying on the north shore can join the boat at the Jeffrey Street wharf, Kirribilli.

CANDLELIGHT DINNER CRUISE, No. 6 Jetty, Circular Quay. Tel. 251-5007.
Cuisine: INTERNATIONAL. **Reservations:** Recommended. **Train or ferry:** Circular Quay.
$ Prices: Three-course dinner, disco, and 4-hour cruise A$59 (U.S. $47.20). AE, BC, DC, MC, V.

 FROMMER'S COOL FOR KIDS: RESTAURANTS

Bobby McGee's (see p. 111). Waiters and waitresses in zany costumes, staff who periodically break out in song, balloons, stunts, and placemats they can color will keep kids entertained.

The Last Aussie Fishcaf (see p. 105). Even if mom and dad don't get up and jitterbug, youngsters will love this lively spot with its limbo contests, exhibition dancers, and general silliness.

Hard Rock Cafe (see p. 105). The teen and preteen set thrive on these rock-and-roll eateries. The music is loud, and that's how they like it.

Argyle Tavern (see p. 108). Where else can kids see a sheep shorn while they eat dinner and sing "Waltzing Matilda"?

Open: Dinner Fri–Sat 7–11pm.

Like the John Cadman, the Candlelight Dinner Cruise is operated by Captain Cook Cruises. This company, the granddaddy of waterborne sightseeing and dining, operates nine vessels on Sydney Harbour. The Candlelight Cruise docks at 9:30pm for those who wish to disembark early.

CAPTAIN COOK LUNCHEON CRUISE, No. 6 Jetty, Circular Quay. Tel. 251-5007.

Cuisine: INTERNATIONAL. **Reservations:** Recommended. **Train or ferry:** Circular Quay.

$ Prices: Buffet lunch and cruise A$36 (U.S. $28.80) for adults, A$30 (U.S. $24) for children. AE, BC, DC, MC, V.

Open: Daily 12:30–2pm.

In addition to the dinner cruise there is a 1½-hour luncheon cruise with a commentary on passing sights, allowing busy tourists to do some sightseeing while they enjoy a very good buffet. The meal includes oysters, trout, ham, roast beef, chicken, a variety of salads, lots of fresh fruit, and a cheese platter. Beer and wine can be purchased separately.

DINING CLUSTERS

Oxford Street, from Crown Street to South Dowling Street, in Darlinghurst is a paradise for fans of ethnic food. In these 4 blocks about 2 kilometers (1 mile) from the city center, no fewer than 16 restaurants serve the fare of faraway places. Nearly all the eateries are smallish mon-and-pop operations. Some of these spots are listed above in the inexpensive category of the "Kings Cross and Vicinity" section, above, but if you're feeling adventurous you might just stroll down Oxford Street and stop wherever strikes your fancy.

LIGHT MEALS/TEA & COFFEE

The Cortile in the Hotel Inter-Continental and the Mezzanine Lounge in the Regent are attractive spots for traditional afternoon tea. The Gumnut Tea Garden and Café Russell, both in The Rocks, have a cozy, colonial ambience and are a less formal site for a morning or afternoon cuppa. The Sheraton's Gallerie offers a wide variety of freshly brewed coffee. The Sydney Cove Oyster Bar is understandably popular for al fresco snacks. The Club Bar in the Regent is great for a light lunch.

The best places for a snack or dessert after the theater are the Mezzanine Lounge, the Cortile, the Park Lounge in the Holiday Inn Menzies, Soup Plus, and Bayswater Brasserie. All of these dining venues are described above.

In addition, **New York at the Movies,** 543 George Street (tel. 264-9912), is in the perfect location for an after-movie sweet. This Big Apple–style coffee lounge is open daily from noon to midnight and serves American sandwiches and light meals, too.

CASUAL, FAST FOOD & 24-HOUR EATERIES

Sydney's food courts provide welcome relief to the city's visitors who would prefer that their credit-card statement not resemble the national debt. These clusters of stall-like mini-kitchens can be found at several places around town. Inexpensive, mostly ethnic, food is sold take-out style and consumed at tables provided in a central area.

One of the best of these food courts is on the bottom level of the **Queen Victoria Building,** on George Street between Market and Druitt; another good one is on the Pitt Street level at **Centrepoint,** on Market Street between Pitt and Castlereagh. Similar spots are located on the waterfront in the **Pier One** complex, at Darling Harbour in the **Harbourside Festival Marketplace,** and in the **Skygarden** shopping arcade on level 3.

For better or for worse, American fast food is available in Sydney. If you're pining for a really good chocolate-chip cookie, you'll be glad to know there's a **Mrs. Field's** on the lower level of Martin Place (tel. 221-5596). A **Kentucky Fried Chicken** graces the corner of Bathhurst and George streets in the central business district. And there are golden arches—yes, **McDonald's**—at 375, 505, 600, and 863 George Street, as well as on the corner of Pitt and Park, on the Wynyard Station concourse, and across from Circular Quay.

The **Bourbon & Beefsteak Bar** and **Pancakes on the Rocks,** 10 Hickson Road, The Rocks (tel. 247-6371), are open 7 days a week, 24 hours a day.

CHAPTER 5

SYDNEY ATTRACTIONS

Kangaroos don't hop through the central business district, but that's about the only disappointment visitors to Sydney are likely to experience. If your ideas about Australia's largest city are even just *slightly* more down to earth, you'll be pleased with what you encounter.

Public transportation is inexpensive and easy to use. Sightseeing attractions are truly interesting and rarely evoke the "We really should visit this church because it's famous" syndrome. (Most museums, for instance, are designed to be hands-on experiences.) Shopping is also fun, as are the many spectator and participatory sporting opportunities. After-dark options range from high-brow to red-light.

SIGHTSEEING STRATEGIES

IF YOU HAVE 1 DAY

Confine your sightseeing to a limited area, such as The Rocks, Circular Quay, and the Opera House. Start with the show at The Story of Sydney (100 George Street, The Rocks), which provides good background on the history of the city. Then pick up a map of the area at The Rocks Visitors Centre and browse around the Argyle Centre and surrounding lanes with their cottages of convict-cut stone. Wander along Circular Quay and then over to the Opera House for a guided tour. If there's time, take a ferry or JetCat over to Manly and back. Another option would be to take the Captain Cook Luncheon Cruise, so you can dine and savor the sights at the same time. For information on this cruise, see "Waterborne Dining" in Chapter 4.

IF YOU HAVE 2 DAYS

Your first day should be The Rocks, Circular Quay, and the Opera House, as suggested above. The second day could take in the several attractions in the Darling Harbour area, formerly a main shipping area of Sydney's port known as Cockle Bay. These include: the Sydney Aquarium, the National Maritime Museum, the Powerhouse Museum, and the Chinese Garden. The myriad eateries in the Harbourside Festival Marketplace provide a logical lunch stop. Use the monorail to get here.

? DID YOU KNOW . . . ?

- It takes 30,000 liters (7,800 gal.) of paint to cover the Sydney Harbour Bridge with one coat.
- When it first opened in 1932 the toll on the Sydney Harbour Bridge was 6 pence for a car and 3 pence for a horse and rider.
- The first road from Sydney to Liverpool was paid for with 400 gallons of rum.
- Sydney Harbour, also known as Port Jackson, covers an area of 55 square kilometers (22 sq. miles).
- From 1897 to 1905 Sydney's Kings Cross was called Queen's Cross.
- The *Sydney Morning Herald* is the oldest daily newspaper in the Southern Hemisphere, founded in 1831.

IF YOU HAVE 3 DAYS

Follow my suggestions above for days 1 and 2, and add the Sydney Tower, Hyde Park Barracks, the Australian Museum, the Queen Victoria Building, and a walk in the Royal Botanic Gardens on day 3.

IF YOU HAVE 5 DAYS OR MORE

In addition to what's already been suggested, the visitor with more time could spend a day at Manly or Bondi exploring the area and experiencing an Australian beach and another day at one of the wildlife parks, such as Featherdale or the Australian Wildlife Park.

1. THE TOP ATTRACTIONS

SYDNEY OPERA HOUSE, Bennelong Point. Tel. 250-7111 (general inquiries), 250-7250 (tours), or 250-7777 (box office).

⭐ Whether you think it looks like a cleverly folded dinner napkin or, as some say, like a pair of armadillos in heat, you'll be impressed by the size and drama of Sydney's—and Australia's—top attraction.

Most visitors are surprised to learn that this famous landmark isn't really an opera house per se. In fact, it's a performing arts center and contains four main auditoriums. In addition, the complex houses a reception hall, five restaurants, six theater bars, a library, archives, and extensive foyer and lounge areas.

The largest and most impressive theater is the 2,690-seat **Concert Hall,** in which 18 adjustable acrylic rings are suspended over the performance platform. These "clouds" contribute to the room's excellent acoustics. The Concert Hall is used for symphony concerts, chamber music, opera, dance, and choral performances, as well as for pop, jazz, and folk music shows. The **Opera Theatre,** which seats 1,547, is used for opera, ballet, and dance. The **Drama Theatre,** seating 544, accommodates drama and dance performances. The **Playhouse,** which seats 398, is used for plays with small casts, as well as lectures and seminars.

The New South Wales government built the Opera House with funds raised in a lottery. The original cost projections were A$7 million (U.S. $5.6 million), but by the time the building was finished the total cost came to A$102 million (U.S. $81.6 million), not a cent of which came from taxpayers. Designed by Danish architect Joern Utzon, the Opera House was completed in 1973 and was paid for by 1975.

If you're in Sydney on a Sunday, enjoy the **free open-air entertainment** presented on the patios along the back and sides of the building. These range from high school band concerts to solo performances of interpretive dance to mimes and jugglers. The minishows are popular with Sydneysiders, who often spend the afternoon there with friends, a sack lunch, a book, and the breeze off the harbor.

Tours: Hour-long guided tours of foyers and theaters not in use are given daily (except Christmas and Good Friday) from 9am to 4pm; cost is A$8 (U.S. $6.40) for adults and A$5 (U.S. $4) for children. Backstage tours, including the stages and rehearsal areas, are given on Sunday from 9am to 4pm at a cost of A$12 (U.S. $9.60). Children under age 12 are not allowed on the backstage tours. Both tours involve quite a bit of walking.

To organize tours and tickets before leaving North America, contact **ATS/Sprint** (tel. toll free 800/232-2121 in California, 800/423-2880 in the rest of the U.S.). They sell an "Evening at the Opera House" package that includes a tour, dinner in the

Bennelong restaurant, and a performance. Prices vary from U.S. $121 to U.S. $136, depending on which concert, drama, ballet, or opera you select. Saturday nights are the most expensive, and the package is not available on Sunday nights. Another option is to buy tickets only; for U.S. $71 you get your seat and a glass of champagne during the interval. **Qantas** passengers can buy the same "Evening at the Opera House" package for U.S. $83 to U.S. $112. Tickets and champagne purchased through Qantas range from U.S. $37 to U.S. $66. A third option is to phone the box office directly, charge the tickets to your credit card, and pick them up after you arrive in Sydney.

Admission: See tours and tickets, above.
Open: Box office Mon–Sat 9am–8:30pm. **Train or ferry:** Circular Quay. **Bus:** No. 438. **Sydney Explorer Bus:** Stop 2.

SYDNEY TOWER AT CENTREPOINT, Market St. between Pitt and Castlereagh. Tel. 229-7444.

Rising 305 meters (1,006 ft.) above Centrepoint Shopping Complex, Sydney Tower is the city's tallest, and one of Australia's most spectacular buildings. Visitors ride one of the three double-decker elevators for the 41 seconds it takes to get to the top, and there they are treated to a spectacular 360° view. The tower houses two revolving restaurants and an observation area. This is Sydney's version of the Eiffel Tower and well worth the fee.

Admission: A$5 (U.S. $4) adults, A$2 (U.S. $1.60) children.
Open: Mon–Sat 9:30am–9:30pm, Sun 10:30am–6:30pm. **Train:** St. James.
Monorail: City Centre. **Sydney Explorer Bus:** Stop 17.

HYDE PARK BARRACKS, Queen's Sq. at the top of Macquarie St. Tel. 223-8922.

This classic Georgian-style building was designed by the convict architect Francis Greenway in 1818. Over the years it has served as convict barracks, a female immigration depot, legal offices, and a museum. In 1990 it was taken over by the Historic Houses Trust of New South Wales, and by the time you get there it will be open again in yet another role. This time the building is going to be allowed to speak for itself. Various periods of social history are demonstrated by the structure and the alterations that have been made to it. Actual Victorian color schemes have been restored on the second floor; the original whitewashed brick walls can be seen on the third floor which was a dormitory for convicts. This top floor also provides rare insight into the daily lives of the convicts; visitors can see the 2-by-7-foot space they were allotted and the burlap hammocks in which they slept. Throughout this significant historic building exhibits address the various contrasting groups of people who have lived and worked within its walls.

The relationship between the barracks and the colonial buildings and parks around it are also addressed. These neighboring entities include: St. James Church, the Mint, the Supreme Court, Hyde Park, and the Domain.

The Barracks Café, located in the courtyard, is open daily from 10am to 4pm.

Admission: Free.
Open: Daily 10am–5pm. **Closed:** Christmas Day and Good Friday. **Train:** St. James. **Sydney Explorer Bus:** Stop 4.

SYDNEY HARBOUR

Officially designated "Port Jackson," Sydney's harbor is certainly one of the most spectacular in the world. It is also one of the busiest, playing host to an almost constant parade of container ships, cruise ships, ferries, JetCats, water taxis, and private yachts. The extensive waterway, with a shoreline of 240 kilometers (149 miles),

IMPRESSIONS

We got into Port Jackson in the afternoon, and had the satisfaction of finding the finest harbour in the world, in which a thousand sail of the line may ride in the most perfect security.
—CAPT. ARTHUR PHILLIP, RECOUNTING HIS ARRIVAL WITH THE FIRST FLEET IN 1788

is the focal point of the city. Major streets lead to it, the Opera House is perched above it, the Royal Botanic Gardens abut it, and homes, hotels, and office buildings are designed to face it.

A small island located in the middle of the harbor was once used to confine convicts and got the nickname Pinchgut from prisoners who were kept there on short rations. **Fort Denison**, as it is properly known, provides superb water and city views. Captain Cook Tours conducts excursions to the isle (see "Organized Tours," below).

Until about 60 years ago, the only way to cross the harbor was by boat—a scenic, but not always convenient, mode of transportation. However, in 1932 construction of the **Harbour Bridge,** known locally as the "coat hanger," was completed. The 1,150-meter (3,795-ft.) bridge spans the 503-meter (1,660-ft.) distance between Dawes Point on the south and Milson's Point on the north. Accommodated on the bridge are an eight-lane road, two train tracks, a bicycle path, and a pedestrian walkway. The **Pylon Lookout** (tel. 218-6451), where you can view displays relating to the history of the bridge, can be visited daily from 10am to 5pm mid-October to mid-February and Saturday through Tuesday during the rest of the year. Admission is about A$1 (U.S. 80¢). *Note:* Touring the pylon involves climbing 200 steps.

No tourist should leave Sydney without taking a cruise on the harbor. Several possibilities have been detailed in "Organized Tours," below.

THE STORY OF SYDNEY, 100 George St., The Rocks. Tel. 247-7777.

Through the use of multidimensional walk-through galleries and two wide-screen theaters, The Story of Sydney introduces visitors to the city's history and some of the colorful personalities associated with it. The audiovisual portion of the experience takes about an hour, and as much time as desired can be spent in the museum exhibition area. The delightful cantata which accompanies the cinematic show was especially composed for this unusual attraction which opened in 1991.

The Macquarie Terrace Café, which is open from 8:30am to 5pm, serves Devonshire teas and light meals. A very nice gift shop is also on the premises.

Admission: A$10 (U.S. $8) adults, A$6 (U.S. $4.80) children under 14, A$22.50 (U.S. $18) family ticket (two adults and two children).

Open: Daily 9am–5pm. **Train or ferry:** Circular Quay. **Sydney Explorer Bus:** Stop 22.

WESTPAC MUSEUM, 6-8 Playfair St., The Rocks. Tel. 251-1419.

The Westpac Museum details the history of Australia's oldest Bank, the Bank of New South Wales, and the economic growth of the country. A dateline around the main gallery traces major events in the financial history. A computer answers banking related questions such as "Why is a cashier called a teller?" You can even cash a traveler's check in an 1890s-style bank.

Admission: Free.

Open: Mon 1:30–4pm, Tues–Fri 10:30am–4pm, Sat 1–4pm, Sun noon–4pm. **Closed:** Christmas Day and Good Friday. **Train or ferry:** Circular Quay. **Sydney Explorer Bus:** Stop 19 or 22.

THE SYDNEY OBSERVATORY, Watson Rd., Observatory Hill, The Rocks. Tel. 241-2478.

The observatory was built in 1858 and included a dome for an equatorial telescope, a room with slits in the roof for a transit telescope, an office, a time-ball tower, and a residence for the astronomer. In those days the time ball would drop at exactly 1pm every day to signal the correct time to the city and harbor below. Today, visitor's can use the observatory's telescopes to discover the wonders of the southern sky. The evening program includes a short talk and tour of the building, films or videos, and telescope viewing of the night sky.

Admission: Daytime free; night visits A$2.50 (U.S. $2) adults, A$1.50 (U.S. $1.20) children, A$6 (U.S. $4.80) family.

Open: Mon–Fri 2–5pm, Sat–Sun 10am–5pm, also Thurs–Tues from 6:30pm. Bookings made well in advance are essential for the evening sessions. **Closed:**

Christmas Day and Good Friday. **Train or ferry:** Circular Quay. **Sydney Explorer Bus:** Stop 20.

NATIONAL TRUST CENTRE, Observatory Hill, The Rocks. Tel. 247-5374.

The building that houses the National Trust was built in 1815 as the colony's military hospital. From 1850 until 1974 it was Fort Street High School. The center includes the S. H. Ervin Gallery, a café, and a bookshop.

Admission: Free. Admission to gallery A$4 (U.S. $3.20) adults, A$2 (U.S. $1.60) children.

Open: Tues–Fri 11am–5pm, Sat–Sun 2–5pm. **Train or ferry:** Circular Quay. **Sydney Explorer Bus:** Stop 20.

THE MUSEUM OF CONTEMPORARY ART, Circular Quay West. Tel. 252-4033.

This museum is dedicated to contemporary visual arts and houses the J. W. Power Collection, which includes more than 4,000 works including artists such as Marcel Duchamp, Christo, Robert Rauschenberg, Andy Warhol, and a special representation of Aboriginal art. The MCA opened in late 1991.

Admission: A$6 (U.S. $4.80) adults, A$4 (U.S. $3.20) children.

Open: Wed–Mon 11am–7pm. **Train or ferry:** Circular Quay. **Sydney Explorer Bus:** Stop 22.

SYDNEY AQUARIUM, Darling Harbour—East Side. Tel. 262-2300.

Shaped like a great breaking wave, the aquarium stands 15 meters (50 ft.) high and 140 meters (462 ft.) long and is listed in the *Guinness Book of Records* as the largest aquarium in the world. Inside are extensive exhibits of purely Australian aquatic species. A major feature is the "Open Ocean" oceanarium where many species of sharks and rays can be observed at very close range from underwater transparent tunnels. There is also a marine mammal sanctuary for dolphins and seals, and a touch pool where children can pick up live specimens. The Great Barrier Reef display, live crocodiles, and exhibits relating to Australian fish are other good reasons to come here.

The Aquarium Restaurant serves breakfast, lunch, and dinner, and a gift shop is located in the main lobby.

Admission: A$15 (U.S. $12) adults, A$10 (U.S. $8) seniors and students, A$8 (U.S. $6.40) children under 16; under 3 free.

Open: Daily 9:30am–9pm. **Ferry:** Darling Harbour. **Monorail:** Harbourside. **Bus:** Rocks–Darling Harbour Shuttle.

THE AUSTRALIAN NATIONAL MARITIME MUSEUM, Darling Harbour. Tel. 552-7777.

Scheduled to open at the end of 1991, this museum will house historic vessels, artifacts, and displays depicting Australia's relationship with the sea, from the Aboriginal seafarers to modern mariners.

Admission: A$7 (U.S. $5.60) adults; A$3.50 (U.S. $2.80) children.

Open: Daily 10am–5pm. **Monorail:** Harbourside.

POWERHOUSE MUSEUM, 500 Harris St., Ultimo, Darling Harbour. Tel. 217-0111.

The largest museum in the Southern Hemisphere, the Powerhouse Museum is notable for the innovation of its displays. Formerly the Ultimo Power Station, the museum's attractive architectural space is filled with information about science, transportation, technology, decorative arts, and social history. Participation is encouraged here. Video games, computers, and experiments capture the attention of people who think they don't like museums. This place is a treasure house of Australia's past and present. The Kids Interactive Discovery Spaces (KIDS) are designed to appeal to children under 8.

The Switch Cafe on level 5 and the kiosk in the Grace Bros. Courtyard on level 2 serve light lunches and snacks.

Admission: Free. Highlight tour daily at 1:30pm A$3 (U.S. $2.40).
Open: Daily 10am–5pm. **Closed:** Christmas Day and Good Friday. **Monorail:** Haymarket. **Sydney Explorer Bus:** Stop 14.

CHINESE GARDEN, Darling Harbour. Tel. 281-6863.

This is the largest traditional Chinese garden of its type outside of China. It embodies principles dating back to the 5th century and is a refreshing hideaway in the heart of Sydney. The garden was designed by Guangdong Landscape Bureau in Guangzhou, China—Sydney's sister city.

Admission: A$2 (U.S. $1.60) adults, A50¢ (U.S. 40¢) children.
Open: Mon–Fri 9:30am–5pm, Sat–Sun 9am–5pm. Closing time is later in the summer. **Monorail:** Haymarket. **Sydney Explorer Bus:** Stop 16.

TARONGA ZOO, Bradleys Head Rd., Mosman. Tel. 969-2777.

Located in a suburb on the north side of the harbor, this zoo claims to have the world's finest collection of native fauna and has a wonderful harbor and city view. Animals are displayed in 30 hectares (74 acres) of gardens that slope down to the water's edge.

Highlights for overseas visitors include the koala exhibit, where a spiral staircase permits good viewing; the nocturnal house; the rain-forest aviary; and the platypus display area. Phone ahead to find out the koalas' feeding time or you're likely to see just their little furry bodies asleep in the forks of trees. Also, for the best look at the platypus, try to be there between 11am and noon or between 2 and 3pm. Travelers with young children won't want to miss the Friendship Farm, where the zoo displays its baby animals, or the seal show (daily at 1:15 and 3:15pm, with an extra performance on Sunday at 11:15am).

Zoo train and guided walking tours are available at a small charge, and a large souvenir shop is located near the zoo exit.

Admission: A$12 (U.S. $9.60) adults, A$5.50 (U.S. $4.40) children 4–16, A$28 (U.S. $22.40) family.
Open: Daily 9am–5pm. **Ferry:** Taronga Zoo, then bus or aerial tramway uphill to entrance gate. Combination ferry, bus, and zoo admission tickets are sold at Circular Quay. **Bus:** No. 247.

FEATHERDALE WILDLIFE PARK, 217 Kildare Rd., Doonside. Tel. 622-1644.

If you've got a bit more time, it's well worth the effort to make your way to Featherdale Wildlife Park, located 41 kilometers (25 miles) west of Sydney. The park is the home of Syd, the Qantas koala, and dozens of his adorable furry friends. If you want to cuddle, be there between 10 and 11:30am or between 2:30 and 3:30pm. (Phone to confirm these hours if it's really important to you.) Kangaroos and wallabies can be petted all day. Allow time for admiring the colorful native birds and wincing at the ferocious Tasmanian devil. There are also lots of wonderful wombats—animals that, in my opinion, would be as popular as koalas if they had a better press agent.

Snacks are sold from a kiosk on the premises.

Admission: A$6.50 (U.S. $5.20) adults, A$3.25 (U.S. $2.60) children 4–14.
Open: Daily 9am–5pm. **Closed:** Christmas Day. **Train:** Blacktown, then bus no. 725. Featherdale is also included on many sightseeing coach tours.

THE AUSTRALIAN WILDLIFE PARK, Wallgrove Rd., Eastern Creek. Tel. 675-0187 or 953-0899.

The newest of the three fauna parks described here, the Australian Wildlife Park opened at the end of 1990. It is located 1 hour west of Sydney on the way to the Blue Mountains. Visitors can have their picture taken with a koala and can hand-feed emus and kangaroos. There's also a 5-meter (15-ft.) crocodile named Maniac. Another exhibit features goannas and there is a walk-through aviary.

Admission: A$7.50 (U.S. $6) adults, A$5.50 (U.S. $4.40) children 4–10; under 4 free.

Open: Daily 9am–5pm. **Closed:** Christmas Day. **Driving:** Follow the F4 freeway.

2. MORE ATTRACTIONS

HISTORIC HOUSES

VAUCLUSE HOUSE, Wentworth Rd., Vaucluse. Tel. 337-1957.

Vaucluse House is a 15-room mansion built in the Gothic style and splendidly sited on Sydney Harbour. From 1827 to 1853 it was the home of William Charles Wentworth, father of the Australian constitution. Vaucluse House Tearooms is a fully licensed restaurant serving à la carte lunches and morning and afternoon teas.

Admission: A$5 (U.S. $4) adults, A$3 (U.S. $2.40) children.
Open: Tues–Sun 10am–4:30pm. **Closed:** Good Friday and Christmas Day.
Bus: No. 325 from Circular Quay or Castlereagh St.

ELIZABETH BAY HOUSE, 7 Onslow Ave., Elizabeth Bay. Tel. 358-2344 or 358-2719.

An elegant mansion built in 1835, Elizabeth Bay House was described at the time as the "finest house in the colony." A domed ceiling covers a central oval foyer, and an impressive winding staircase leads to rooms on the second floor. Located close to the harbor, Elizabeth Bay House commands some of the best views in Sydney.

Admission: A$5 (U.S. $4) adults, A$3 (U.S. $2.40) children.
Open: Tues–Sun 10am–4:30pm. **Closed:** Good Friday and Christmas Day.
Bus: No. 311. **Sydney Explorer Bus:** Stop 9.

 FROMMER'S FAVORITE SYDNEY EXPERIENCES

Sunday Around the House   Every Sunday there is free entertainment on the patios around the Opera House, but it's not just the mimes and musicians that make the scene special. Sydneysiders of all ages gather for this happening, and it's fun to see how people from another nation play. The breeze off the harbor and the continuous parade of sailboats and ferries add to the experience.

An Evening at the House   There's something magical about attending a performance at the Opera House; maybe it's the wonderful view of lights sparkling on the harbor that you have from the bar and lounge areas during the interval.

Collecting Ken   I find Ken Done's exuberant designs very hard to resist, so it isn't surprising that Done Art & Design on George Street in The Rocks is my favorite place to shop in Sydney. His prints, posters, and original works of art are sold nearby at the Ken Done Gallery. If I have any money left when I've been to these two places, I stop at Dorian Scott, also on George Street, and admire the wonderful handknit sweaters they stock.

Afternoon Tea at the Regent Hotel   Tea in the Mezzanine Lounge is a memorable experience. The scones are fluffy, the service impeccable, and it's fun to watch the comings and going in the lobby one level below. You're sure to see a few tycoons, some famous faces, and maybe even a head of state.

MUSEUMS & GALLERIES

ART GALLERY OF NEW SOUTH WALES, Art Gallery Rd., The Domain. Tel. 225-1700.
The gallery houses a comprehensive collection, including various Australian schools. There are continuous temporary exhibitions.
Admission: Free.
Open: Mon–Sat 10am–5pm, Sun noon–5pm. **Train:** Martin Place. **Sydney Explorer Bus:** Stop 6.

MINT MUSEUM, Macquarie St. opposite Queen's Sq. Tel. 217-0122.
In addition to stamps and coins, various decorative arts are displayed in the museum, which is housed in Sydney's oldest public building. It's next to Hyde Park Barracks.
Admission: Free.
Open: Thurs–Tues 10am–5pm, Wed noon–5pm. **Closed:** Good Friday and Christmas Day. **Train:** St. James. **Sydney Explorer Bus:** Stop 4.

AUSTRALIAN MUSEUM, 6 College St. Tel. 339-8111.
The Australian Museum holds the country's largest natural-history and anthropology collection, including many Aboriginal artifacts. Take advantage of the free guided tours. Children enjoy the hands-on activities in the Discovery Space. A restaurant with low-cost meals is open from 10am to 4pm.
Admission: Free.
Open: Daily 10am–5pm. **Closed:** Christmas Day. **Train:** Museum. **Sydney Explorer Bus:** Stop 11.

THE STATE LIBRARY OF NEW SOUTH WALES, Macquarie St. Tel. 230-1414.
In addition to containing a huge amount of reference material, the library is also a venue for literature-related exhibits and films. Be sure to notice the marble mosaic Tasman Map on the floor in the vestibule. It depicts the discoveries made by Abel Tasman on his voyages to terra australis in 1642–43 and 1644.
Admission: Free.
Open: Mon–Fri 9am–9pm, Sat 9am–5pm, Sun 11am–5pm. **Closed:** Christmas Day, Boxing Day, New Year's Day, and Good Friday. **Train:** Martin Place. **Sydney Explorer Bus:** Stop 3.

LUNCHTIME PERFORMANCES, Martin Place Amphitheatre, Martin Place. Tel. 265-9110 (Sydney City Council).
Martin Place is a delightful spot for a brief lunchtime infusion of culture. A varied program of performing arts and music is presented. You can phone the Sydney City Council to find out what's planned. A variety of take-outs, snack bars, and cafés are nearby at the MLC Centre.
Admission: Free.
Performances: Mon–Fri 12:15–2pm. **Train:** Martin Place, then walk 1 block west.

PARKS & GARDENS

Look at a map of Sydney and you'll quickly recognize the important role that parks and gardens play in the city's profile. **Hyde Park,** bordered by Elizabeth, College, and Liverpool streets and St. James Road, is the most central. Named after the well-known Hyde Park in London, it has at various times served as a military training reserve, a cricket ground, and a racecourse. Today it provides a shady spot for office workers' lunchtime retreats, and it's a popular spot for chess games. During the Sydney Festival in January, Hyde Park is the site of frivolity and free entertainment. At the northern end the **Archibald Fountain,** designed by French artist François Sicard, commemorates the Australian-French alliance of 1914–18.

The **Domain,** adjacent to the Royal Botanic Gardens, is the home of the Art Gallery of New South Wales and the Boy Charlton Pool (public), but the area most

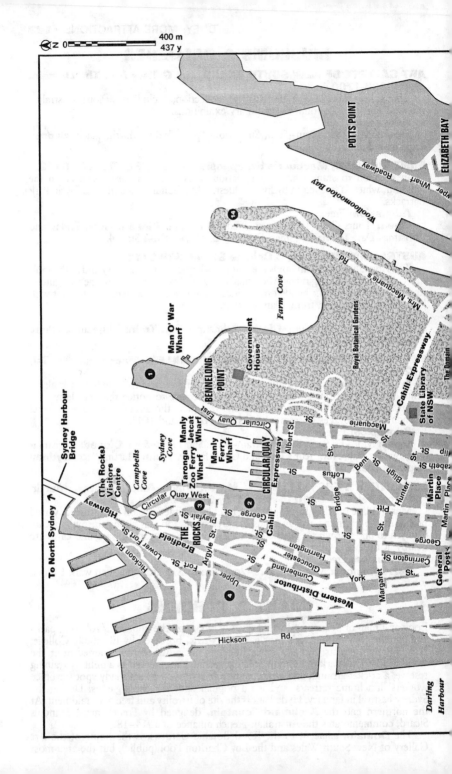

SYDNEY ATTRACTIONS

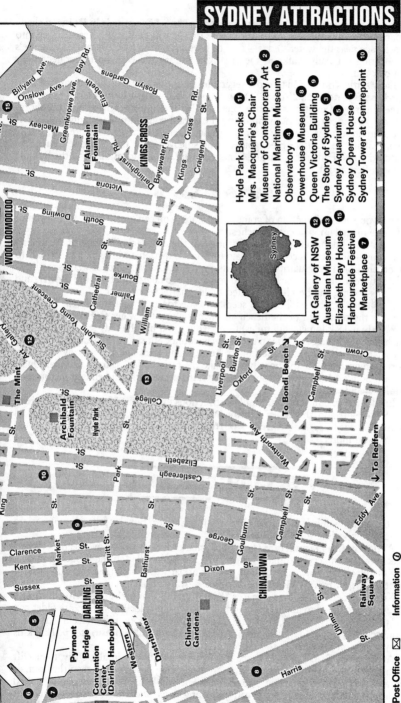

Hyde Park Barracks 11
Mrs. Macquarie's Chair 14
Museum of Contemporary Art 2
National Maritime Museum 6
Observatory 4
Powerhouse Museum 8
Queen Victoria Building 9
The Story of Sydney 3
Sydney Aquarium 5
Sydney Opera House 1
Sydney Tower at Centrepoint 10

Art Gallery of NSW 12
Australian Museum 13
Elizabeth Bay House 15
Harbourside Festival Marketplace 7

Post Office ⊠   Information ⊘

visited by Sydneysiders and overseas travelers is **Mrs. Macquarie's Point,** a shady expanse of lawn with sweeping harbor views that gets its name from a seat carved into a rock face near the water's edge—said to have been used by Governor Macquarie's wife during her daily walks in the area. On Sunday the Domain is frequented by soapbox orators.

Early settlers once tried to grow vegetables on the land where the **Royal Botanic Gardens Sydney** (tel. 231-8125) now bloom. Today they would surely be surprised to see the array of exotic and native trees, shrubs, and flowers thriving near the shores of Sydney Harbour. The herbarium and the pyramid glasshouse (greenhouse) are of special interest, as is the new Sydney Tropical Centre. The gardens are open daily from 6:30am to sunset. Free guided walks leave from the Visitors Centre on Wednesday and Friday at 10am and Sunday at 1pm. Meals are available at the Botanic Gardens Restaurant.

SURF & SAND

Even if you have no intention of going in the water, you can't leave Sydney until you've seen one of its famous ocean beaches.

Located 8 kilometers (5 miles) southeast of the city, **Bondi** is one of Australia's best-known beaches. Access is via train to Bondi Junction and then a no. 380 bus to the beach. Bondi's popularity is due to its good surf and fine sand, as well as the lively pubs and trendy bistros nearby. Should you decide to take a dip, there are showers and changing rooms; the beach is patrolled by lifeguards year round.

If you like walking, follow the scenic seaside footpath that starts near the baths (pool) at the south end of the beach and winds along the water to **Bronte Beach.**

Manly is 15 kilometers (9 miles) from Sydney and has the only surf beach on the north side of the harbor that is patrolled year round, but safety isn't the only drawing card at this well-patronized beach. Its beauty is in part due to the row of stately Norfolk pines that line the boardwalk. Take the ferry or JetCat from Circular Quay. As with Bondi, a lovely waterfront walkway starts at the baths and ends at picturesque **Shelly Beach.**

In addition to a nice beach, Manly's attractions include the **Manly Oceanarium** (tel. 949-2644) and the **New Manly Wharf,** which has restaurants, shops, and amusement facilities. The **Manly Visitors Information Bureau** (tel. 977-1088) can tell you more.

3. COOL FOR KIDS

Almost all of Sydney's attractions are fun for families, but the following places are especially appealing for youngsters.

At the **Sydney Aquarium** (see p. 120) sharks and rays swim overhead as visitors walk through an acrylic tunnel. Marine life can be handled in the "touch pool."

Kids of all ages are sure to enjoy going aboard the ships that are part of **The Australian National Maritime Museum** (see p. 120).

Kids Interactive Discovery Spaces (KIDS) at the **Powerhouse Museum** (see p. 120) are designed to appeal to children under 8 years old. Those who are older can use the computers, videos, and other hands-on aspects of this museum to learn about science, technology, and more. At the **Australian Museum** (see p. 123) kids enjoy hands-on activities in the Discovery Space.

At **Taronga Zoo** (see p. 121) first it's the ferry ride from Circular Quay, then a lift in an aerial tram to the entrance gates. Your offspring haven't even seen the animals yet, and they're already having a good time. The whole family can be photographed holding a koala, and the kids can pet kangaroos and other native animals at **Featherdale Wildlife Park** (see p. 121) and **The Australian Wildlife Park** (see p. 121).

I've yet to meet a child who doesn't think a day spent at the beach is a day well spent. **Bondi Beach** (*see p. 126*) and **Manly Beach** (*see p. 126*) are both good ones.

The Earth Exchange, 18 Hickson Road, The Rocks (tel. 251-2422), is a fun place to visit if traveling with children. They can experience a Sydney earthquake, walk through a volcano, and learn about geology and mining through interactive computer games. The Earth Exchange is open daily from 10am to 5pm; admission is A$6.50 (U.S. $5.20) for adults and A$5 (U.S. $4) for children. There's a café on the premises.

4. SPECIAL-INTEREST SIGHTSEEING

FOR THE LITERARY ENTHUSIAST

The **Writers Walk** which starts at the east end of Circular Quay and proceeds toward the Opera House is of interest to both readers and writers. A project of the New South Wales Ministry for the Arts, round bronze plaques set in the brick footpath recognize Australian authors or authors from other countries who wrote about Australia.

The first disk commemorates the completion of the project: "What we are and how we see ourselves evolves fundamentally from the written and spoken word. The Writers Walk demonstrates that this evolutionary process continues to channel the thoughts and perceptions, the hopes and the fears of writers who have known this great city and its people. Dedicated 13 February 1991."

Authors included on the walk are: Miles Franklin, Eleanor Dark, Charles Darwin, David Williamson, A. B. "Banjo" Patterson, C. J. Dennis, Christopher Brennan, Oodgeroo Noonuccal, Kenneth Slessor, D. H. Lawrence, Jack London, and Henry Lawson.

Miles Franklin's circle contains a quote from *My Brilliant Career,* and Eleanor Dark's a passage from *The Timeless Land.* David Williamson, who is still living, is Australia's best-known 20th-century dramatist. Oodgeroo Noonuccal is the adopted Aboriginal name of poet Kath Walker. She adopted the name of her tribe in 1988 to honor the Aboriginal people's cause.

FOR THE ARCHITECTURE ENTHUSIAST

Sydney's architecture is a case of majestic colonial buildings successfully juxtaposed with contemporary high-rises. The following structures are of particular interest:

The **Mint** and **Hyde Park Barracks** stand next to each other on Macquarie Street, a testimonial to the colonial period. The Mint was originally the south wing of the 1816 Rum Hospital which was converted into the Royal Mint in 1856. It has been restored to its 1870 appearance. The convict architect Francis Greenway designed the Hyde Park Barracks in 1818 for Governor Macquarie and it, too, has been restored to its original appearance. **The Strand Arcade,** 412 George Street, was first opened in 1892. It was destroyed by fire in the 1970s and was subsequently restored. The **Queen Victoria Building,** 455 George Street, was built in 1883 and is probably Sydney's best example of adaptive reuse. More than 150 specialty shops and dining venues have been sensitively fitted into the grand old structure.

Other good examples of successful reuse include the **Powerhouse Museum,** once the Ultimo Power Station where the electricity to run the city's tram system was generated, and the **Hotel Nikko Darling Harbour** which incorporates the Corn Exchange building built by Sydney's City Council in 1887. Architecture enthusiasts will also want to stop in at the **Hotel Inter-Continental,** 117 Macquarie Street, and admire the way the facade of the old Treasury Building was incorporated into the present use.

On the modern side of things, of course the **Sydney Opera House,** designed by

Danish architect Joern Utzon, is of great interest. Likewise, **Sydney Tower**—the tallest building in the Southern Hemisphere—is notable. The **MLC Centre,** surrounded by Martin Place, Castlereagh and King streets, was designed in 1977 by Harry Seidler, the Austrian-born architect who introduced the high-rise to Australia in the 1960s when he designed the **Australia Square** tower, located between George, Bond, and Pitt streets. The MLC Centre is one of the tallest reinforced concrete towers in the world.

More recently, the **Sydney Aquarium** and the **Australian National Maritime Museum** in Darling Harbour were both designed by Phillip Cox Richardson Taylor and Partners. **Chifley Tower,** 92-122 Phillip Street, a 49-story office building, is due to be completed in 1992. The **World Square Development,** surrounded by Liverpool, Pitt, Goulburn, and George streets, will be the largest consolidated development to date in Sydney when it is completed.

5. WALKING TOURS

In addition to the communities I will describe below a few other areas are worth a wander. For instance, nice restored terrace houses trimmed with cast-iron "lace" are found along tree-lined residential streets in **Paddington.** The New Edition Bookshop, 328 Oxford Street, Paddington (tel. 360-6913), distributes a free booklet on "Paddo," as the locals call it. Bus no. 378, 380, or 389 will get you there, but the no. 389 (from Circular Quay) is best for an overview of the restored houses. Paddington is only 4½ kilometers (less than 3 miles) from the city center.

Sydney doesn't have a huge Chinatown, but **Dixon Street** near the Darling Harbour Development has lots of Chinese restaurants and some Asian shops.

If **Kings Cross** is too seedy for you after dark, you can get the general idea by strolling through there during the day.

Here are three self-guided tours that can be done separately or linked together into one long one. For guided walking tours, see "Organized Tours," below.

WALKING TOUR 1 — George Street

Start: Bathurst and George streets.
Finish: Alfred and George streets.
Time: Allow at least ½ hour, not including shopping stops and viewing time at Sydney Tower.
Best Times: Weekdays, but not during business rush hours when the sidewalks are chockablock with office workers.
Worst Times: Sunday, when services are held in St. Andrew's Cathedral and shops in the Strand Arcade are closed.

Sydney's main street starts near Central Station and ends in The Rocks. A walk from one end to the other, a distance of about 2½ kilometers (1½ miles), takes you past a good selection of historic buildings—and four McDonald's restaurants! The most interesting section, the 1½ kilometers (1 mile) from Bathurst to Alfred Street is detailed here. George Street was named by Governor Macquarie in 1810 in honor of King George III of England. Australia's oldest thoroughfare, it was originally called Sergeant Major's Row, Spring Row, and High Street.
Begin at:
1. **St. Andrew's Cathedral,** at Sydney Square on the northwest corner of Bathurst and George. It dates from 1868 and is the oldest Anglican cathedral in Australia. It was constructed from Hawkesbury sandstone and built in the Gothic style. Adjacent to St. Andrew's is the:
2. **Town Hall,** which opened in 1889 and is still an impressive site for welcoming

WALKING TOUR—GEORGE STREET

N

Cahill
finish here
Alfred St.
Circular Quay Expressway
Regent Hotel

Cumberland
Essex St.
Gloucester
Jenkins St.
Sussex St.
Loftus St.
Young St.
Phillip St.
Macquarie St.

Grosvenor St.
Dalley St.
Bridge

Lang St.
York St.
George St.
Jamison St.
Pitt St.
Spring St.
O'Connell St.
Bent

Margaret
St.
Curtin Pl.
7
Hunter
Bligh
Phillip St.
St.

Kent St.
Clarence St.
York St.
Carrington St.
Wynyard Ln.
6
General Post Office ✉
St.

Erskine St.
Martin Place
Hospital Rd.

Ln.
Barrack St.
Martin Pl.
Castlereagh St.
Elizabeth St.
Phillip
Macquarie St.

King St.
King St.

George St.
5
Pitt St.
St James Rd.

4
Market
Market St.

Market St.
City Centre
Castlereagh St.
Elizabeth St.
Hyde Park
College St.

Sussex St.
Kent St.
Clarence St.
York St.
3
Park Plaza ▪

Druitt St.
2
Park St.

1
start here

Cinemas
Bathurst St.

Sydney

1 St. Andrew's Cathedral
2 Town Hall
3 The Queen Victoria Building
4 Sydney Tower
5 Strand Arcade
6 Martin Place
7 Australia Square

visiting dignitaries. The Lord Mayor holds official receptions in this grand building, which is also used for exhibitions and public meetings. After crossing Druitt Street, you will see:

3. **The Queen Victoria Building,** known locally as the QVB. This huge Romanesque edifice, covering an entire city block, housed the city's main produce markets when it opened in 1898. Allowed to deteriorate from the 1930s on, it reopened in 1986 with all its Byzantine splendor restored and containing nearly 200 shops, cafés, and restaurants. Pierre Cardin is supposed to have called the QVB "the most beautiful shopping center in the world," and I can understand why. The spacious interior is characterized by tall arches, intricate tile patterns, and magnificent stained-glass windows. A curved glass roof allows natural light to illuminate ornate plasterwork, grand columns, and a unique clock that displays scenes of English history on the hour. The building is open for shopping 7 days a week. The statue of Queen Victoria in the plaza at the south end of the building was donated by the government and people of Ireland. Until 1947 it stood in front of Leinster House in Dublin—the seat of the Irish Parliament. The sculptor was John Hughes, RHA, Dublin (1865–1941).

REFUELING STOP "Eat Street," the food court on the lower level of the QVB, offers an array of dining options. Fast food can be purchased take-out style and eaten in a central area where tables and chairs are provided. A dozen moderately priced cafés also sell light meals and snacks.

As you leave the Queen Victoria Building, head east on Market Street to:

4. **Sydney Tower** where you can zoom 305 meters (1,006 ft.) to the top in one of three double-decker lifts (elevators). The cost is A$5 (U.S. $4) for adults and A$2 (U.S. $1.60) for children, and the view is fantastic. Leaving Sydney Tower, walk north through the Pitt Street Mall until you come to the:

5. **Strand Arcade,** which runs from Pitt Street through to George Street. When this shopping area opened in 1892, it was described in the *Daily Telegraph* as "the finest public thoroughfare in the Australasian Colonies." Today it boasts 80 shops on three levels and a charming 19th-century atmosphere. Continue walking north on George Street past the American Express Tower to:

6. **Martin Place.** The General Post Office (GPO) occupies the corner. As you pass it, note the large clock tower. Martin Place is a popular midday spot for office workers, who share their brown-bag lunches with the pigeons and enjoy free concerts presented Monday through Friday at 12:15pm in the amphitheater. In contrast to the historic buildings found along the upper reaches of George Street, the:

7. **Australia Square** high-rise between Hunter Street and Bond Street is a young whippersnapper. Constructed in 1968, the tower is 170 meters (561 ft.) high. At the Opal Skymine on level 6, there is a large-scale model of an opal mine (open Monday through Friday from 9am to 5pm, Saturday from 10am to 3pm, and Sunday by appointment).

REFUELING STOP If you've walked all this way, you must be thirsty. Go just a bit farther and you can wander into the **8. Regent Hotel** and have a drink or meal. (See "Sydney Dining" in Chapter 4 for information on the Regent's Club Bar, George Street Bar, and Mezzanine Lounge.)

WALKING TOUR 2 — Around The Rocks

Start: The Rocks Visitors Centre, 104 George Street.
Finish: Museum of Contemporary Art, Circular Quay West.
Time: Allow a minimum of an hour, much more if you stop to shop or visit any of the attractions.
Best Times: Any day.

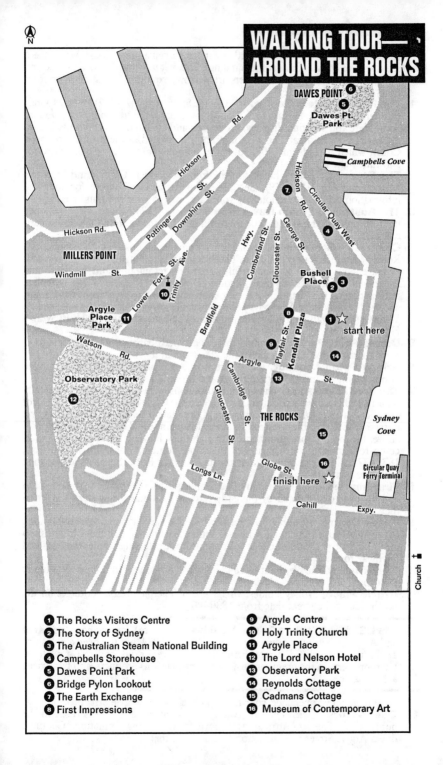

WALKING TOUR— AROUND THE ROCKS

N

DAWES POINT 6
5
Dawes Pt. Park

Campbells Cove

Hickson Rd.

7

4

Circular Quay West

MILLERS POINT

Windmill St.

Bushell Place
2 3

† 10

Argyle Place Park 11

8

1 ★ start here

Watson Rd.

9

14

Argyle

13

St.

Observatory Park

12

THE ROCKS

Sydney Cove

15

16

Globe St.

Circular Quay Ferry Terminal

Longs Ln.

finish here ★

Cahill Expy.

Church

1 The Rocks Visitors Centre
2 The Story of Sydney
3 The Australian Steam National Building
4 Campbells Storehouse
5 Dawes Point Park
6 Bridge Pylon Lookout
7 The Earth Exchange
8 First Impressions

9 Argyle Centre
10 Holy Trinity Church
11 Argyle Place
12 The Lord Nelson Hotel
13 Observatory Park
14 Reynolds Cottage
15 Cadmans Cottage
16 Museum of Contemporary Art

The site of the first European settlement in Australia, The Rocks was once a neglected area of convict-built stone buildings. Today it is Sydney's most historic and lively neighborhood. Because the streets are narrow, exploring is best done on foot. Start your tour at:

1. **The Rocks Visitors Centre,** 104 George Street (tel. 247-4972), open Monday through Friday from 8:30am to 5:30pm and on Saturday and Sunday from 9am to 5pm. Here you will find displays, brochures, and an audiovisual presentation on the history of the area. The Visitors Centre is located in the former Coroner's Court, which dates from 1907. After you've looked around, walk out the door and turn right where you will see:

2. **The Story of Sydney** housed in the former Mariners Church and Seaman's Mission Building (1856–59). (See "The Top Attractions," above, for complete information on this attraction.) As you leave, stay to your right and pass:

3. **The Australian Steam Navigation Building** (1883) whose tower was once used for sighting ships. Cross the road and descend the Custom Officers Stairs to reach:

4. **Campbell's Storehouse,** Sydney's first commercial building. A monument to Robert Campbell is near the stairs. These colonial warehouses have been restored and are now a row of wonderful waterfront restaurants and home to the Australian Wine Centre. (See "Sydney Dining" in Chapter 4 for complete information on the Phantom of the Opera Restaurant, the Waterfront Restaurant, and the Italian Village. See "Savvy Shopping," below, for details on the Australian Wine Centre.) Walk in front of the restaurants and around the Park Hyatt Sydney Hotel to:

5. **Dawes Point Park** from which there is a superb harbor view. This is a good place to rest if you plan to climb the 200 stairs in the:

6. **Bridge Pylon Lookout.** (See "The Top Attractions," above, for complete information.) Return to George Street and proceed to:

7. **The Earth Exchange.** The building that houses this attraction was originally built in 1902 as an electric light station, but was never used as such. (See "Cool For Kids," above, for more information.) Continue up George Street past historic terrace houses and the Westpac Banking Museum (see "The Top Attractions," above, for more information) and turn right into Playfair Street. You will soon come to a row of terrace houses that now contain shops. They date from 1875–77 and were once workmen's cottages. In the Rocks Square is a sandstone sculpture named:

8. **First Impressions.** Created by Bud Dumas, it tells the story of the hardship and bondage experienced by the early settlers. Continue a few steps farther to the:

9. **Argyle Centre,** a group of four restored warehouses surrounding a cobblestone courtyard. Today the complex houses shops, restaurants, and bars. If you shop until you drop you won't be able to continue up Argyle Street under the Bradfield Highway to:

10. **Holy Trinity Church,** built in 1848. When you leave the church walk 1 block west to:

11. **Argyle Place,** Sydney's oldest village green. The picturesque cottages on the north side of the street date from 1830–80.

REFUELING STOP   12. The Lord Nelson Hotel, on the corner of Kent and Argyle streets, was originally a home, built in 1834, but has been a pub since 1842. It is a delightful, atmospheric place to have a drink and rest a while. A microbrewery on the premises turns out some delicious products, and bar snacks are available.

When you've quenched your thirst go back down Argyle Street to:

13. **Observatory Park.** The observatory was built in 1858 and is open to the public. (See "The Top Attractions," above, for complete information.) Continue down Argyle Street to Harrington Street where the:

14. **Reynolds Cottage,** built in the 1830s by a colonial blacksmith, now houses the Gumnut Tea Garden. (For details on this quaint spot for lunch or tea, see "Sydney Dining" in Chapter 4.) Continue down Argyle Street and turn left onto George Street. On the right-hand side of the street you will see:

15. **Cadman's Cottage,** the oldest house in Sydney. Built in 1816, it once fronted onto a sandy inlet. John Cadman, a convict, lived here for 19 years with his wife and two daughters. He was given a pardon and rose to chief superintendent of the governor's boats. Walk down the stairs next to the cottage, cross Circular Quay West, and turn right, following the pedestrian walkway until you see the:

16. **Museum of Contemporary Art,** which is housed in the old Martime Services Board building. (See "The Top Attractions," above, for complete information on the MCA.)

WALKING TOUR 3 — Around The House

Start: On the pedestrian walkway just south of the cruise-ship terminal and east of John Cadman's cottage.
Finish: Mrs. Macquarie's Chair, The Domain.
Time: 1–2 hours, depending on your pace.
Best Times: Weekends, when the harbor is dotted with sailboats.
Worst Times: There isn't a bad time to do this walk.

This walk isn't described in "Frommer's Favorite Sydney Experiences," above, only because I wanted to avoid being redundant. It is, in fact, my *very favorite* thing to do in Sydney. Walking from one side of the Opera House to the other imparts a precious familiarity with this great landmark. Along the way there are wonderful views of the bridge, harbor, city, and Royal Botanic Gardens.

Start this walk in the shade of the fig tree growing in a raised planter just south of the cruise-ship terminal and east of Cadman's Cottage. Admire the view of the Opera House from this angle before proceeding south past the MCA to the:

1. **Commemorative Map** at the west end of Circular Quay near the intersection of Alfred and Pitt streets. The brass and terrazzo map has a diameter of about 12 feet and is raised about 18 inches off the brick footpath. It shows how Sydney Cove looked in 1808. The ferry information booth is nearby. Proceed along Circular Quay, past the buskers and sidewalk musicians, to the beginning of:

2. **The Writers Walk,** which starts just past no. 2 jetty. This series of round brass plaques set into the footpath acknowledges the contributions of Australian authors and others who have written about Australia. It is described fully in "Special-Interest Sightseeing," above. You might want to get an ice-cream cone at the Portobello Caffè or have a beer at the Sydney Cove Oyster Bar (see "Sydney Dining" in Chapter 4) before continuing to:

3. **The Opera House.** Walk around the side, past the recital rooms and rehearsal halls, stopping to drink in the view of the Harbour Bridge and the myriad vessels on the water. When you reach the back of the Opera House, you can stop for tea or a light meal at the Harbour Takeaway (see "Sydney Dining" in Chapter 4), or just sit and admire the panorama. Continue on around, keeping the water on your left. You will soon come out at the front of "the House." Walk a bit farther to the:

4. **Man O' War Steps.** According to a plaque posted there, "For 150 years the Man O' War Steps served as a landing and embarkation point for men of the British and Australian fleets in peace and war." Enter the:

5. **Royal Botanic Gardens** through a gate across from the steps. Enjoy the flowers, shrubs, and trees along the path. The mansion to your right is Government House, the official residence of the Governor-General. Continue to:

6. **Seawall,** which follows the shoreline around Farm Cove. From here there are great views of the central business district. Continue to:

7. **Mrs. Macquarie's Point** (exiting the gardens through the Yurong Gate), and

admire the Opera House from this new angle. This is a great sunset view if you time it right. Continue uphill along an asphalt footpath to:

8. **Mrs. Macquarie's Chair,** a bench carved in stone which was used by Governor Macquarie's wife on her daily walks. From here you have a choice of retracing your steps or continuing on through The Domain.

6. ORGANIZED TOURS

WALKING TOURS

Because Sydney is compact, it's an ideal place for those who like exploring on foot. If you enjoy guided excursions, try **The Rocks Walking Tour** (tel. 247-6678) Monday through Friday at 10:30 and 11:30am and 12:30, 1:30, and 2:30pm and Saturday and Sunday at 10:30am and 12:30 and 2:30pm. Tours depart from 39 Argyle Street or 5 minutes later from The Rocks Visitors Centre and last 1 hour and 15 minutes. The cost is A$7 (U.S. $5.60) for adults and A$4.50 (U.S. $3.60) for children.

For other escorted walks, contact **Maureen Fry Guided Tours** (tel. 660-7157). Her 2-hour tours operate daily, cover various parts of the city, and cost A$12 (U.S. $9.60).

BUS TOURS

If you don't want to use public transportation and you do want to see the sights, organized bus tours are available. Some of these are operated by **Newmans** (tel. 225-8061), **AAT King's** (tel. 252-2788 or 667-4918), and **Australian Pacific Tours** (tel. 693-2222 or 233-2744).

CRUISES

No tourist should leave Sydney without taking a cruise on the harbor. In addition to the ones listed below, a variety of cruises are operated by **State Transit** (tel. 954-4422 or 247-4738). You can also cruise Sydney Harbour on a paddle wheeler; **Sydney Showboat** (tel. 247-5189 or 552-2722) departs from Campbells Cove in The Rocks. Buy tickets at No. 2 Jetty, Circular Quay. Another option: Sail the harbor in a replica of Captain Bligh's **Bounty** (tel. 251-6568).

CAPTAIN COOK CRUISES, No. 6 Jetty, Circular Quay. Tel. 251-5007 or 247-2723.

The granddaddy of cruise operators on Sydney Harbour, Captain Cook Cruises offers a 2½-hour Coffee Cruise, a 1¼-hour Budget Cruise, a Luncheon Cruise and a Candlelight Dinner Cruise (both described in "Sydney Dining" in Chapter 4), a Sundowner Cruise, an Aquarium Cruise, and a trip to Fort Denison. All excursions include full commentary.

Tickets: Coffee Cruise (including coffee/tea and cake) A$24 (U.S. $19.20), adults, A$16 (U.S. $12.80) children 5–14; Budget Cruise A$14 (U.S. $11.20) adults, A$10 (U.S. $8) children 5–14; Sundowner Cruise A$16 (U.S. $12.80) adults, A$10 (U.S. $8) children 5–14; Aquarium Cruise (combines Budget Cruise with entry into Sydney Aquarium) A$26 (U.S. $20.80) adults, A$16 (U.S. $12.80) children 5–14; Fort Denison Tour A$9 (U.S. $7.20) adults, A$6.50 (U.S. $5.20) children 5–14.

Departures: Coffee Cruise daily 10am and 2:15pm; Budget Cruise daily 9:30 and 11am, 2:30 and 4pm; Aquarium Cruise daily 9:30 and 11am, 2:30 and 4pm; Sundowner operates Oct–Apr 5:30pm; Fort Denison Tour Tues–Sun 10am, 12:15 and 2pm.

MATILDA CRUISES, Aquarium Wharf, Darling Harbour. Tel. 264-7377.

The second-largest cruise operator on Sydney's waters is based at Darling Harbour. Matilda Cruises has four modern motorized catamarans and a 125-foot gaff-rigged topsail schooner named *Solway Lass*. This classic tall ship, with 10 working sails, was built in 1902 and accommodates up to 60 passengers. Two-hour

WALKING TOUR—
AROUND THE HOUSE

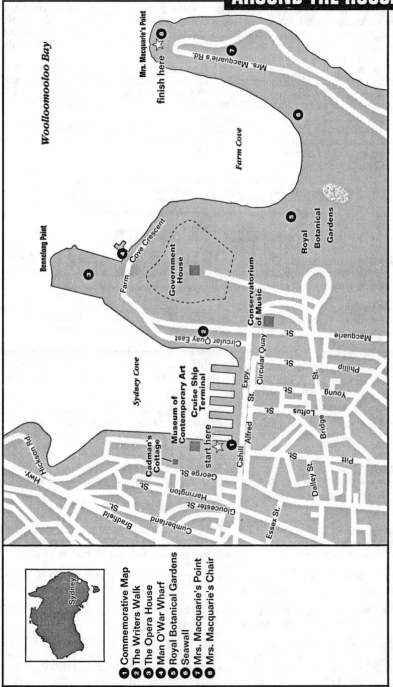

Woolloomooloo Bay

Mrs. Macquarie's Point

finish here

Mrs. Macquarie's Rd.

Bennelong Point

Farm Cove

Farm Cove Crescent

Government House

Royal Botanical Gardens

Conservatorium of Music

Sydney Cove

Circular Quay East

Museum of Contemporary Art

Cruise Ship Terminal

Cadman's Cottage

start here

George St.

Harrington St.

Gloucester St.

Cumberland St.

Bradfield Hwy.

Hickson Rd.

Essex St.

Dalley St.

Pitt

Bridge St.

Loftus St.

Young St.

Phillip St.

Macquarie St.

Circular Quay St.

Alfred St.

Cahill Expy.

Sydney

1. Commemorative Map
2. The Writers Walk
3. The Opera House
4. Man O'War Wharf
5. Royal Botanical Gardens
6. Seawall
7. Mrs. Macquarie's Point
8. Mrs. Macquarie's Chair

Discovery cruises are offered daily on the catamarans; luncheon and dinner cruises as well as afternoon sails utilize *Solway Lass*. All trips include full commentary. In addition, Matilda Cruises offers a good-value package: The **Darling Harbour Superticket,** valid for 3 months, includes a Discovery Cruise, a ride on the monorail, entrance to the Sydney Aquarium, entrance to the Chinese Gardens, lunch or dinner at the Craig Brewery Bar & Grill, and 10% off at participating stores in the Harbourside Festival Marketplace.

Tickets: Discovery Cruise or afternoon sail on *Solway Lass* (including tea or coffee) A$22 (U.S. $17.60) adults, A$15 (U.S. $12) children under 12; luncheon cruise A$40 (U.S. $32) adults, A$28 (U.S. $22.40) children under 12; dinner cruise A$50 (U.S. $40) adults or children; Darling Harbour Superticket A$36.50 (U.S. $29.20) adults, A$26.50 (U.S. $21.20) children under 12.

Departures: Discovery Cruise daily 11:30am, 1:30 and 3:30pm; *Solway Lass* luncheon cruise daily 12:15pm; *Solway Lass* dinner cruise Fri–Sat 7pm; *Solway Lass* afternoon sail daily 2pm.

7. SPORTS & RECREATION

SPECTATOR SPORTS

Cricket Played from October through March. The Sydney Cricket Ground (SCG) is the city's best-known site. Phone the New South Wales Cricket Association (tel. 274-053) for more information.

Football This sport (rugby, rugby league, soccer, and Aussie Rules) draws large crowds from May through September. Each club has its own playing field. The Manly Warringah Rugby League Ground is the best known in the Sydney area.

Horse Racing Races take place on Saturday throughout the year. Sydney's four tracks are: Randwick, Canterbury, Rosehill, and Warwick Farm. Admission is about A$8 (U.S. $6.40) per person. Call the **Australian Jockey Club** if you have questions (tel. 663-8400).

Surfing Carnivals These are a uniquely Australian phenomenon where volunteer life savers (lifeguards) demonstrate their talents at ocean beaches; these events take place from November through March. Call the **Surf Life Saving Association** (tel. 663-4298) for times and locations.

Yacht Racing The start of the **Sydney-to-Hobart Yacht Race** is a not-to-be-missed sight if you're in town on Boxing Day (the day after Christmas).

RECREATION

Playing games and keeping up your fitness routine while you travel not only means that you stand a chance of returning home in good shape, it can also be a pleasant way to meet local people. This is certainly true in Australia, where sport is king.

Ballooning You can float over Sydney's rural environs with **Balloon Aloft** (tel. 607-2255). The cost is about A$170 (U.S. $136), with city hotel pickup available.

Boomerang Throwing What could be more Australian? Lessons are available from **Bennelong Boomerangs** (tel. 241-1121).

Cycling Rent bikes from **Centennial Park Cycles** (tel. 398-5027). Cost is A$6 (U.S. $4.80) for the first hour; A$10 (U.S. $8) for 2 hours; A$14 (U.S. $11.20) for 3 hours and the fourth hour is free. There are no cycle pathways around the city. Ride in Centennial Park.

Golf There are dozens of courses to choose from because this is one of Sydney's favorite sports. You might like the **Lakes Golf Club,** near the airport (tel. 669-1311; A$80/U.S. $64 for 18 holes). The **Royal Sydney Golf Club** at Rose Bay (tel. 371-4333) and the **Australian Golf Club** (tel. 663-2273) are prestigious private clubs, but they sometimes allow members of "recognized" overseas golf clubs to play provided arrangements are made in advance. No matter where you play, reservations must be made ahead of time. Club rental costs about A$25 (U.S. $20). The **New South Wales Golf Association** (tel. 264-8433) can answer any other questions. Travelers who plan to play golf in Australia may want to purchase *Golf Courses of Australia* (available from The Australian Expatriate, 3809 Plaza Drive, Suite 107-307, Oceanside, CA 92056).

Grass Skiing Long hot summers and short warm winters are responsible for the popularity of this somewhat strange sport (literally skiing with special skis on grass). You can try it any weekend in **Moore Park,** at the corner of South Dowling Street and Cleveland Street (tel. 663-2070). Cost is about A$12 (U.S. $9.60) an hour.

Gym Workouts The **Clark Hatch Fitness Centre** in the Hotel Inter-Continental (tel. 251-3486) is one of the best in the city.

Horseback Riding Centennial Park is the best place to ride near the city center. Rent your steed from **Centennial Park Horse Hire** in Paddington (tel. 332-2770) or the **Challis Riding School** (tel. 399-9942). Both charge about A$15 (U.S. $12) an hour.

Jogging The Domain, Hyde Park, and the Royal Botanic Gardens are scenic spots for stretching your legs.

Surfing Bondi, Cronulla, Long Reef, and Manly are just a few of Sydney's best surfing spots. The **NSW Surfboard Riders' Association** (tel. 977-7453) can tell you about other places and also has the scoop on the various surfing competitions. You can rent a board at the **Bondi Surf Beat,** 78 Campbell Parade, Bondi (tel. 365-0870). The rate of about A$22 (U.S. $17.60) per day includes a wet suit.

Swimming Both **harbor and ocean beaches** abound, and between October and March seemingly every Sydneysider takes to his or her favorite sandy spot and stays there. Lady Jane Beach at Watsons Bay is popular with nude bathers.

The **Andrew (Boy) Charlton Pool** (tel. 358-6686) in The Domain is open every day from 6:30am to 7:15pm from September to June. For winter workouts the **North Sydney Olympic Pool** (tel. 955-2309) is preferable.

Tennis National and international tournaments, including the Davis Cup, are held on the **White City courts** (tel. 357-4111), 3 kilometers (1.8 miles) from the city, and visitors can play there too, subject to availability. You might also try **Rushcutters Bay Tennis Centre,** Waratah Street, Rushcutters Bay (tel. 357-1675), or **Moore Park Tennis Courts** in Paddington (tel. 662-7005). The **NSW Tennis Association** can advise you on the location of other courts (tel. 331-4144).

Windsurfing Rent your gear from **Balmoral Marine** (tel. 969-6006) or **Longreef Sailboard & Surf** (tel. 982-4829), and head for Long Reef Beach, the premier spot for wave jumping. It costs about A$15 (U.S. $12) an hour to hire a windsurfer.

Yachting If you'd like to be on one of the beautiful white boats in the harbor rather than admiring them from the shore, contact the **Cruising Yacht Club of Australia** (tel. 363-9731) about the possibility of crewing for one of their members. You can also rent a sailboat, powerboat, rowboat, canoe, or dinghy from **Balmoral Marine** at Balmoral Beach (tel. 969-6006). Catamaran hire cost about A$20 (U.S. $16) an hour. The **Yachting Association of New South Wales** (tel. 247-5163) may also be helpful.

8. SAVVY SHOPPING

Sydney is a shopper's delight. Whether you're interested in Australian fashions, opals, local wines, quality souvenirs, or gifts, you'll find a wide selection in the city's hundreds of stores. (This would be a good time to reread "Shopping" in Chapter 2.)

THE SHOPPING SCENE
GREAT HUNTING GROUNDS

A good place to start is the **Queen Victoria Building,** which occupies an entire block in the city center. The QVB, bounded by George, Market, York, and Druitt streets, is open 7 days a week. The beautifully restored Victorian center has nearly 200 shops, including many fashion specialty stores with Pierre Cardin and lots of other high-fashion moguls. **The Strand Arcade,** which dates from 1892, runs from the Pitt Street Mall through to George Street between King and Market and shares the QVB's Victorian grace and elegance. Like the majority of Sydney's stores, the three levels of shops in the Strand Arcade are open Monday to Saturday from 9am to 5:30pm, and on Thursday until 9pm. Some places close at noon or 4pm on Saturday, and a few stay open a bit later on Friday.

   Centrepoint, on Market Street between Pitt and Castlereagh, has a colorful array of places to spend money, as do the nearby **Imperial Arcade** and **Mid City Centre.** The **Royal Arcade** under the Hilton Hotel, **Sydney Square** between the Town Hall and St. Andrews Cathedral on George Street, and the **Pitt Street Mall** between King and Market offer hundreds more opportunities to browse boutiques, search for souvenirs, and generally shop until you drop. The **Skygarden** arcade which runs from the Pitt Street Mall through to Castlereagh Street, is Sydney's newest, most-talked-about shopping venue.

   A short distance from the city center, many unusual stores are dotted around **The Rocks,** and most of them are open 7 days a week. More purchases await at Darling Harbour's **Harbourside Festival Marketplace** and at the shops on the **Manly Wharf.**

   Most suburbs have their own shopping meccas, but probably the only one worth trekking out to is **Double Bay,** about a mile east of the city center, also known as "double pay" because of the posh designer boutiques that line Knox Street, Cross Street, and Transvaal Avenue.

BEST BUYS

There was a time when opals were about the only exciting purchase available to visitors in Australia. Nowadays, shoppers have fun buying traditional outback garments, contemporary Australian fashions, Aboriginal artwork and crafts, and attractive souvenir items, as well as the pretty precious and semiprecious stones.

SHOPPING A TO Z
ABORIGINAL ARTIFACTS & CRAFTS

ABORIGINAL ARTIST GALLERY, 477 Kent St. Tel. 261-2929.
   This shop has a large selection of Aboriginal arts and crafts, including boomerangs, paintings, bark paintings, and wood carvings.

COO-EE ABORIGINAL ART, 88 George St., The Rocks. Tel. 241-3800.
   The proprietors collect items from more than 30 different Aboriginal communities throughout Australia and sell them at this store and their others: Coo-ee Emporium, 98 Oxford Street, Paddington (tel. 361-4986), and Coo-ee Art Gallery, 202 Oxford Street, Paddington (tel. 332-1544). These are the places to find prints by traditional and urban Aboriginal artists, hand-printed fabrics, didgeridoos, books, sculptures, and more. The store in The Rocks is open daily.

BINDI ABORIGINAL GALLERY, on the top level of the Queen Victoria Building. Tel. 261-5402.
Aboriginal paintings and authentic craft items are sold in this shop.

ART PRINTS & ORIGINALS

THE KEN DONE GALLERY, 21 Nurses Walk, The Rocks. Tel. 247-2740.
A complete range of originals, limited-edition prints, and posters by artist/designer Ken Done are sold here. Done's work, which is colorful and exuberant, captures the essence of Sydney and reflects the city's high energy level. Nurse's Walk is a quaint little lane 1 block west of George Street. Open daily.

THE ORIGINAL AUSTRALIAN ART GALLERY, Shop 100, Argyle Centre, The Rocks. Tel. 247-7037.
Original paintings and prints are sold here, including the work of Paul Ching Bor. Ken Done silk screens are a popular item. Only Australian artists are represented. Open daily.

BOOKS

In addition to the following emporia, the various museum gift shops also sell a good selection of books; try the ones listed below under "Gifts and Souvenirs."

ANGUS & ROBERTSON BOOKSTORE, Imperial Arcade, 168 Pitt St. Tel. 235-1188.
One of the granddaddies of Australian bookselling, this bookstore in the Pitt Street Mall is open 7 days a week.

DYMOCKS BOOK ARCADE, 426 George St. Tel. 235-0155.
Like Angus & Robertson, Dymocks (pronounced *Dim*-icks) sells a complete range of books, and the sales staff are very helpful. Open daily.

CRAFTS

ARGYLE ARTS CENTRE, 18 Argyle St., The Rocks. Tel. 241-1853.
Lots of small craft shops are located in and around the center.

AUSTRALIAN CRAFTWORKS, 127 George St., The Rocks. Tel. 247-7156.
Here you'll find the products of more than 300 Aussie craftspeople who work in glass, leather, textiles, clothing, wood, ceramics, and jewelry. The building which houses the shop was once a police station and dates from 1882. It's interesting to see even if you aren't shopping for crafts. Some of the old gaol (jail) cells are used as exhibit spaces. Open daily.

CRAFT GALLERY, Shop 2, Metcalfe Arcade, 80-84 George St., The Rocks. Tel. 241-1673.
This shop is run by The Society of Arts and Crafts of NSW, an organization which has been in existence since 1906, and only the work of members is exhibited. Each individually crafted piece was made in New South Wales. The shop is open 7 days a week and staffed by members.

THE CRAFT CENTRE, 88 George St., The Rocks. Tel. 247-7984.
In this store the work of members of the Crafts Council of NSW is sold. Look for blown-glass pieces, wood turnings, pottery, textiles, silk screening, and jewelry.

DEPARTMENT STORES

Sydney's major department stores are **David Jones,** at Castlereagh Street and Market Street, and **Grace Bros.,** on the corner of Pitt and Market streets.

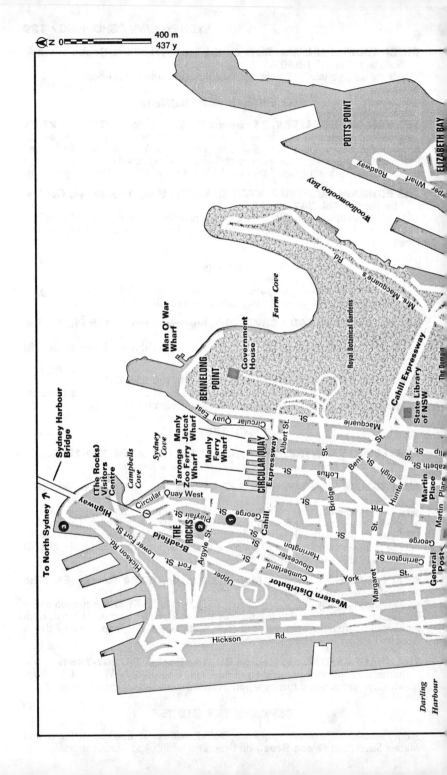

SAVVY SHOPPING IN SYDNEY

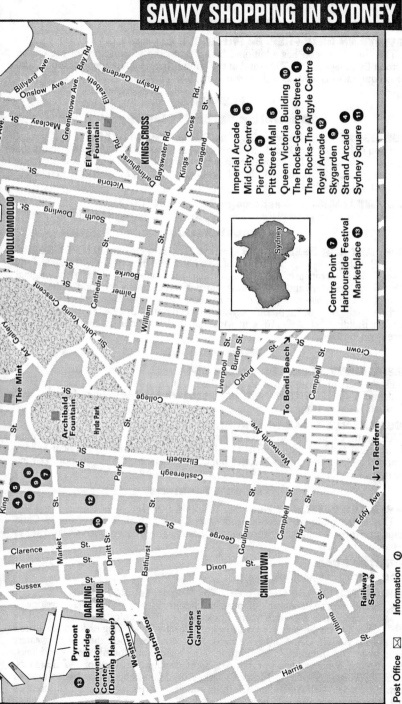

Imperial Arcade **8**
Mid City Centre **6**
Pier One **3**
Pitt Street Mall **5**
Queen Victoria Building **10**
The Rocks-George Street **1**
The Rocks-The Argyle Centre **2**
Royal Arcade **12**
Skygarden **9**
Strand Arcade **4**
Sydney Square **11**

Centre Point **7**
Harbourside Festival Marketplace **13**

Post Office ⊠   Information ❶

DUTY-FREE SHOPS

DOWNTOWN DUTY FREE, 84 Pitt St. Tel. 221-4444.

This duty-free shop has additional branches on the second floor of the Queen Victoria Building (tel. 267-7944) and in the Strand Arcade. Photographic, sound, and video equipment is sold, as well as souvenirs, leather goods, and the like.

FASHIONS

Australian Outback Clothing

MORRISONS, 105 George St., The Rocks. Tel. 241-1596.

If you're looking for Driza-bone coats, moleskin pants, or Akubra hats, this is the place. It's one of the oldest companies in the country selling this type of outback wear. Another branch is located in the Harbourside Festival Marketplace in Darling Harbour (tel. 281-3923).

R. M. WILLIAMS, 71 Castlereagh St. Tel. 233-1347.

This is the other good place to look for Man from Snowy River clothes.

Casual Clothing

DONE ART AND DESIGN, 123 George St., The Rocks. Tel. 251-6099.

This shop sells only the designs of Ken Done and his wife, Judy. These include T-shirts, sweatshirts, children's clothing, and housewares. This is the original Ken Done store and has the most current and complete selection. Other Done Art and Design stores are located in the Harbourside Festival Marketplace in Darling Harbour (tel. 281-3818), in the Skygarden center (tel. 232-6625), in the Queen Victoria Building (tel. 283-1167), in Mosman, and in Bondi Junction. The Rocks' store is open daily.

Men's Fashions

DAVID JONES, Market St. Tel. 266-5544.

Established in 1838, David Jones (called DJs by locals) is Australia's premier department store. Designers such as Giorgio Armani, Valentino, Ungaro, and Christian Dior are featured.

COUNTRY ROAD, 142-146 Pitt St. Tel. 232-6299.

There are Country Road stores all over Australia and in quite a few U.S. cities. Their casual fashions are popular with both men and women. Additional Sydney locations include: the Queen Victoria Building, Skygarden, Bondi Junction, Darling Harbour, Double Bay, Manly, Mosman, and Chatswood.

Women's Fashions

CARLA ZAMPATTI, 437 Kent St. Tel. 264-8244.

This is the place for "stylish, understated high fashion." There are 29 Carla Zampatti stores throughout Australia, and her designs are also sold in David Jones Department Store.

COUNTRY ROAD.

See "Men's Fashions," above.

DORIAN SCOTT, 105 George St., The Rocks. Tel. 247-4090.

Handknit sweaters—or "jumpers," as they are known in Australia—are one of the specialties at Dorian Scott. Look for the clever, colorful ones designed by Click Go the Shears. My favorites sport cuddly flag-waving or formally attired koalas (and A$350/U.S. $280 price tags). Also, don't overlook the Coogi sweaters made by an Italian family in Melbourne. They're sold at Bloomingdale's and Saks, too, at much higher prices. In total, Ms. Scott displays the work of 147 designers, including Maggie Shepherd, Moreen Clark, Amy Hamilton, Robyn Malcolm, and Ruth Fitzpatrick—all Australian. Clothing and accessories for men and children, as well as women, are also sold here. Open daily.

FLAMINGO PARK, in the Strand Arcade. Tel. 231-3027.

This is the exclusive outlet for designer Jenny Kee, who is best known for her vibrant handknits featuring Australian motifs.

FOOD

DAVID JONES DEPARTMENT STORE, Market St. Tel. 266-5544.

⭐ The food hall here has everything you could ever want for a picnic in the park or a midnight snack in your hotel room. This place is a real feast for the senses—all of them.

HARRIS COFFEE AND TEAS, on the concourse level in the Strand Arcade. Tel. 231-3002.

You won't want to miss this emporium. Believe it or not, this shop is one of the originals in the arcade, which means it has been around since 1892.

GIFTS & SOUVENIRS

In addition to the following stores, there are also excellent shops for quality souvenirs and gifts, including books, at the Opera House, the Taronga Zoo, the Australian Museum, and the Hyde Park Barracks.

BLUEGUM DESIGNS, Level 2, Queen Victoria Building. Tel. 264-8070.

This shop sells a wide range of quality Australian crafts and souvenirs including T-shirts, soft toys, and designer accessories. Be sure to notice the Australian floral fragrances and the hand-painted koalas and kangaroos. Most items are made in Australia. Open daily.

KOALA BEAR SHOP, top level, Queen Victoria Building. Tel. 267-3187.

All types of souvenirs are sold here, including toys, T-shirts, sheepskin products, and opal jewelry. The Koala Bear Shop also stocks Driza-bone coats and Thomas Cook clothing. Open daily.

NATIONAL TRUST GIFT AND BOOKSHOP, Observatory Hill, The Rocks. Tel. 258-0123.

This is a good place for souvenirs, placemats, stuffed animals, T-shirts, and so forth. Many items are specifically designed for the National Trust. The shop is housed in a historic building. Open daily.

MARKETS

PADDY'S MARKET, on Garden St. near Redfern Railway Station, Redfern. Tel. 764-3522.

If you like big public markets, you'll love Paddy's Market. This swap meet–like place sells an assortment of farm produce, plants, food, clothing, crafts, household goods, and general merchandise. Open Saturday and Sunday from 9am to 4:30pm. Easy access by train from the city center. Another Paddy's Market is held in Flemington on Friday and Sunday.

PADDINGTON MARKET, at the corner of Newcombe and Oxford Sts., Paddington.

This is the other popular bargain mart, also known as the Paddington Village Church Bazaar because it's held on the grounds of the Village Church in Paddington. The specialties here are crafts, costume jewelry, funky clothing (new and used), curios, and other items of interest to devotees of alternative life-styles. This is a great place for people-watching—bizarre dress is standard at this bazaar. The 200 or so stalls of the Paddington Market set up shop on Saturday from 9am to 4pm.

OPALS

This is a good time to reread the information about opals in "Shopping" in Chapter 2.

FLAME OPALS, 119 George St., The Rocks. Tel. 247-3446.

Only solid opals from the major mining fields are sold here. These include boulder opal, black opal, and white, or "milk," opal. A wide range of handcrafted opal jewelry in 18-carat gold and sterling silver are available, too. Flame Opals is known for its straight talk and fair prices, and several readers have commented on the knowledgeable and helpful service they received. Open daily.

THE OPAL SKYMINE, sixth level, Australia Square, George St. Tel. 247-9912.

If you stop in here you can tour a replica of a working opal mine, complete with animated miners, and enjoy an audiovisual presentation that will tell you all about opals. Both loose stones and designer jewelry are for sale, as well as accessories such as name-card holders and letter openers. A worldwide moneyback guarantee is provided. Open Monday to Saturday.

SHEEPSKIN PRODUCTS

LAMBSWOOL TRADER, 80-84 George St., The Rocks. Tel. 247-9174.

The Lambswool Trader sells sheepskin coats, boots, and rugs, as well as general souvenirs. Open daily.

AUSFURS, Shop 4, Clocktower Sq., Argyle St. (corner of Harrington St.), The Rocks. Tel. 247-3160.

This shop sells the products they manufacture at their factory in suburban Sydney, so they have real quality control. Sheepskin coats and rugs are their most popular items, and they also sell footwear, car-seat covers, and little sheepskins for babies. There is another Ausfurs in the Queen Victoria Building (tel. 264-6072). You can sometimes buy bargain-priced seconds at the factory: 414 Bourke Street, Surry Hills (tel. 361-3075). Stores open daily.

WINE

AUSTRALIAN WINE CENTRE, 17-21 Circular Quay West, Campbell's Storehouse, The Rocks. Tel. 247-2755.

This is probably the best place in the country to buy cases of wine to send home. The proprietors stock an extensive selection of fine Australian wines, and the staff are completely clued in to each state's liquor laws and the shipping procedures. Their packing is almost breakage free, and they provide competent, personal service. Premium wine from all the major growing areas in the country are sold, including vintages from some boutique wineries that don't export overseas. One of New South Wales' largest stocks of Penfolds Grange Hermitage and other rare wines are on hand. Informal tastings are held throughout the day, 7 days a week.

9. EVENING ENTERTAINMENT

Whether your idea of after-dark entertainment is an atmospheric pub, some hot jazz, or a lively disco, you'll find something that pleases you in Sydney. For a review of licensing restrictions and pub hours, look at "Performing Arts and Evening Entertainment" in Chapter 1. For up-to-date information on current shows and appearances, check *The Sydney Morning Herald* (especially the "Metro" section included in the paper on Friday) or look for a complimentary copy of *Where* magazine in your hotel.

For any of the theaters mentioned here and many more, you can get half-price, day-of-performance tickets at the **Halftix** booth in Martin Place between Elizabeth Street and Castlereagh Street (tel. 235-1412). Tickets must be purchased in person, and sales are made in cash only. No refunds or exchanges are allowed. Halftix is open Monday through Friday from noon to 5:30pm and Saturday from noon to 5pm. The booth sells full-price tickets to all events in Sydney Monday through Friday from 9am. Halftix also sells half-price bus tours and harbor cruises.

THE PERFORMING ARTS

MAJOR PERFORMING ARTS COMPANIES

The **Australian Chamber Orchestra**, the **Sydney Philharmonia Choir**, the **Sydney Symphony Orchestra**, the **Australian Ballet**, and the **Australian Opera** are all based at the Sydney Opera House. The **Sydney Theatre Company** and the **Sydney Dance Company** are associated with the Wharf Theatre, but sometimes perform in the Opera House. **One Extra Dance Company** is usually at the Belvoir Street Theatre.

MAJOR CONCERT HALLS & ALL-PURPOSE AUDITORIUMS

SYDNEY OPERA HOUSE, Bennelong Point. Tel. 250-7111.
   Performances are held in four different theaters—opera, ballet, dance, symphony and chamber concerts, drama, experimental theater, and pop, jazz, and folk-music shows. Consult the *Sydney Morning Herald* to find out what's on or stop by the Opera House and pick up a copy of the bimonthly *Diary,* which lists all events. Buy your tickets at the box office (tel. 250-7777) or phone and charge them to a credit card and have them held for you. For information about ordering tickets before arrival in Australia, see the Opera House listing in "The Top Attractions," above. It's important to arrive on time for performances at the Opera House because the ushers are very sticky about seating latecomers—and don't bother too much about dressing up; Australians are fairly casual. The box office is open Monday to Saturday from 9am to 8:30pm. Prices vary. Opera is the most expensive, followed by major ballet performances; plays and concerts are less costly.

SEYMOUR CENTRE, Cleveland St. and City Rd., Chippendale. Tel. 692-3511 (box office), 692-0555 (general inquiries).
   Across from Sydney University, this center, which opened in 1976, is another notable complex of theaters which contains the York, Everett, and Downstairs theaters. Music, dance, musicals, and dramas are performed. Many productions are held here during the Festival of Sydney.

THEATERS

BELVOIR STREET THEATRE, 25 Belvoir St., Surry Hills. Tel. 699-3273.

THE MAJOR CONCERT & PERFORMANCE HALLS

   Belvoir Street Theatre, 25 Belvoir St., Surry Hills (tel. 699-3257 or 699-3273).
   Footbridge Theatre, Parramatta Rd. (tel. 692-9955).
   Her Majesty's Theatre, Quay St. (tel. 212-3411).
   New Theatre, 542 King St., Newtown (tel. 519-3403).
   Seymour Centre, corner of Cleveland St. and City Rd., Chippendale (tel. 692-3511 box office, 692-0555 general inquiries).
   Sydney Opera House, Bennelong Point (tel. 250-7777).
   Sydney Entertainment Centre, Harbour St., Haymarket (tel. 211-2222).
   Theatre Royal, on King St. near Pitt St. (tel. 231-6111).
   Wharf Theatre, Pier 4, Hickson Rd., The Rocks (tel. 250-1700).

Innovative, often "political," theater is staged here, including many performances which are part of Sydney's annual Gay and Lesbian Mardi Gras. Ticket prices are about A$25 (U.S. $20).

FOOTBRIDGE THEATRE, Sydney University, Parramatta Rd., Broadway. Tel. 692-9955.

The Footbridge is used by professional theater companies, except once a year when the various departments within Sydney University put on revues. The theater seats about 600 and specializes in musical comedy.

HER MAJESTY'S THEATRE, 107 Quay St. Tel. 212-3411.

42nd Street was held here during the 1990 season. Before that Her Majesty's hosted *Evita, Sweeney Todd, 9*, and other musicals. Ticket prices are in the vicinity of A$30 to A$44 (U.S. $24 to U.S. $35.20).

NEW THEATRE, 542 King St., Newtown. Tel. 516-5025 (general inquiries), 519-3403 (box office).

This comfortable fringe theater, which opened in 1932, seats 150 in a raked auditorium. The New Theatre was started in the depression of the 1930s and continues to do plays which reflect the "problems confronting mankind." Dramas, comedies, musicals, and classics performed by the resident company tend to have a left-wing point of view. Ticket prices vary from A$8 to A$12 (U.S. $6.40 to U.S. $9.60).

THEATRE ROYAL, in the MLC Centre, King St. Tel. 224-8444 (general inquiries), 231-6111 (box office).

Major musicals, such as *Cats* and *Les Misérables* are performed here. The theater accommodates 1,133 in continental seating: 731 in the stalls (orchestra section) and 402 in the dress circle (mezzanine). Since it opened in 1976, Peter O'Toole, Deborah Kerr, Peter Ustinov, and Vincent Price have graced its stage. Ticket prices are usually in the A$35 to A$42 (U.S. $28 to U.S. $33.60) range.

WHARF THEATRE, Pier 4, Hickson Rd., The Rocks. Tel. 250-1700.

Home of the Sydney Theatre Company, the Wharf Theatre is—literally—located on a refurbished wharf on the edge of Sydney Harbour.

DINNER THEATER/COMEDY SHOWS

ARGYLE TAVERN, 12-18 Argyle St., The Rocks. Tel. 247-7782.

This place is listed in "Sydney Dining," in Chapter 4, but it's worth repeating because the "Jolly Swagman Show" is really fun. You couldn't get better authentic Australian entertainment and dining value. The Aussie bush ballads and colonial songs, sheepshearing demonstration, and skit about convicts add up to a lot of laughs and a good time. And where else are you likely to see an Aborigine play a didgeridoo?

Prices: Dinner and show A$59.50 (U.S. $47.60).

THE CLUB & MUSIC SCENE

NIGHTCLUBS/CABARET

LES GIRLS, 2C Roslyn St., corner of Darlinghurst Rd., Kings Cross. Tel. 358-2333.

Les Girls has a slightly macabre feel to it. The dinner show is an "all-male revue," but all of the men are female impersonators who look like Las Vegas–type showgirls. They lipsync songs, parade around in extravagant gowns, and one even does a striptease. The master (?) of ceremonies tells some good jokes and makes lots of sexual wisecracks. Funny, but definitely not a family show. For example, the customers' rest rooms are labeled "gents," "ladies," and "shims." Explain that to your kids. Shows are Wednesday through Saturday at 9:15 and 11:15pm.

Admission: Show only A$25 (U.S. $20); dinner and show A$35 (U.S. $28).

COMEDY CLUBS

THE COMEDY STORE, 278 Cleveland St., Surry Hills. Tel. 699-5731.
This is Sydney's original comedy nightclub. Dinner shows Wednesday through Saturday and late shows on weekends feature stand-up comics.

FOLK, COUNTRY & ROCK

In addition to the Hard Rock Cafe and Virgin Video Cafe, see "Dance Clubs/Discos," below, for more nightspots featuring rock.

ROSE, SHAMROCK AND THISTLE, 193 Evans St., Rozelle. Tel. 555-7755.
Known locally as "the three weeds," this popular place features blues, as well as folk music. The Rose Café, specializing in Australian cuisine, is open Thursday through Sunday from 6:30pm. The entertainment area opens at 6pm; 8pm Sunday.

HARD ROCK CAFE, 121-129 Crown St., Darlinghurst. Tel. 331-1116.
This is a great spot to listen to *loud* rock while you dine and/or drink. Rock memorabilia hangs from the ceilings and walls. For more information see "Sydney Dining" in Chapter 4.

VIRGIN VIDEO CAFE, in the Harbourside Festival Marketplace, Darling Harbour. Tel. 281-3807.
Rock music and videos play continuously here. For more information, see "Sydney Dining" in Chapter 4.

JAZZ & BLUES

Sydney is the jazz capital of Australia. Serious aficionados should know about the Jazz Hotline: 0055-22814.

TOP OF THE TREASURY in the Hotel Inter-Continental, 117 Macquarie St. Tel. 230-0200.
Live jazz and other contemporary music is offered Friday and Saturday nights at this sophisticated cocktail lounge which occupies the top floor of the 31-story hotel. There are wonderful vistas of the city and harbor. The intimate space accommodates a maximum of 60 people.
Admission: Cover charge A$5 (U.S. $4).

SOUP PLUS, 383 George St. Tel. 299-7728.
Not all of Sydney's settings for jazz are elegant and sophisticated. Soup Plus is a casual self-service eatery where hot jazz is performed between 7:30pm and midnight 5 nights a week and until the wee hours on Friday and Saturday. For details on the restaurant, see "Sydney Dining" in Chapter 4.
Admission: Cover charge A$3–A$5 (U.S. $2.40–U.S. $4).

SYDNEY COVE OYSTER BAR, 1 E. Circular Quay. Tel. 247-2937.
★ This delightful waterfront spot is described under "Sydney Dining" in Chapter 4, but it's also a great place for listening to jazz Friday and Saturday night and Sunday afternoon.
Admission: No cover charge.

REAL ALE CAFE, 66 King St. Tel. 262-3277.
The largest venue for jazz in Australia, this popular place is also known for its excellent food. Patrons choose from over 183 beers from 32 countries. Listen to live jazz Tuesday through Saturday from 8pm.

PHANTOM OF THE OPERA RESTAURANT, in Campbell's Storehouse, 17-21 Circular Quay West, The Rocks. Tel. 247-2755.
This wonderful dining spot, described in "Sydney Dining" in Chapter 4, serves jazz with dinner several nights a week.

THE CRAIG BREWERY BAR & GRILL, in the Harbourside Festival Marketplace, Darling Harbour. Tel. 281-3922.

Live rock bands make this a popular place on Friday and Saturday nights, while jazz brings 'em in on Saturday afternoon from 3 to 6pm. The scenic waterfront location is great, too. For more information see "Sydney Dining" in Chapter 4.

Admission: Free before 10pm.

PARAGON II, in the Paragon Hotel, Loftus St., Circular Quay. Tel. 241-3522.

This historic hotel, built around 1865, is the site of the Paragon Café described in "Sydney Dining," in Chapter 4, and Paragon II also on the second floor. Live jazz, played here Monday through Thursday from 6 to 11pm, is popular with the after-work crowd.

Admission: No cover charge.

DANCE CLUBS/DISCOS

BOURBON & BEEFSTEAK BAR, 24 Darlinghurst Rd., Kings Cross. Tel. 358-1144.

This is a hot spot for dancing—their ad reads: "Two bands on two floors, 5pm to 4am." There's also a piano bar, and the restaurant serves food 24 hours a day. If you need a breather, snag a window table and watch the parade of humanity on Darlinghurst Road. The Bourbon & Beefsteak is in the heart of the red-light district. For details on the restaurant, see "Sydney Dining," in Chapter 4.

Admission: Fri–Sat A$2–A$5 (U.S. $1.60–U.S. $4).

JULIANA'S, in the Hilton International, 259 Pitt St. Tel. 266-0610.

If you prefer discos, the glittery Juliana's is a good choice. The club is open Tuesday through Saturday from 9pm to 3am. If you don't feel like dancing go to watch the disco-dressed people or have supper. Popular with the over-25 crowd.

Admission: Nonguests, Tues–Thurs A$10 (U.S. $8), Fri–Sat A$20 (U.S. $16).

WILLIAMS, in the Boulevard Hotel, 100 William St. Tel. 356-2222.

This is the most sophisticated of Sydney's discos, where chrome, mirrors, and polished black marble create a sleek, urbane atmosphere. The clientele are equally sleek and ultra well dressed; many worldly Sydneysiders have annual memberships. It's open for dancing Wednesday through Saturday from 8pm to 3am.

Admission: Nonguests A$15 (U.S. $12).

STUDEBAKERS, 33 Bayswater Rd., Kings Cross. Tel. 358-5656.

This lively spot, with its red diner motif, caters to the 21- to 35-year-old crowd with an interest in '50s and '60s rock and roll. It's show time once every half hour and entertainers lipsync songs and do dance routines. No live music here, but good DJs. Studebakers is open Saturday through Monday from 8pm to 2 or 3am and Tuesday through Friday from 5pm to 2 or 3am. A buffet supper is included in the cover charge up until 9pm. Free hot dogs and chips are offered after 9pm. This place promises "nonstop bop"—and delivers. Look for the 1951 red bullet-nose Studebaker in the entrance.

Admission: Weekdays before 9pm A$4 (U.S. $3.20), after 9pm A$6 (U.S. $4.80); Fri–Sat after 8pm A$10 (U.S. $8).

SPECIALTY CLUBS

Most of Sydney's **gay nightspots** are located on Oxford Street between Whitlam Square in Darlinghurst and Centennial Park in Paddington—known as "the Golden Mile." For more information pick up a copy of the city's free gay newspaper, the *Sydney Star Observer.*

DON'T CRY MAMAS, 33 Oxford St. Tel. 267-7380.

Also known as "D.C.M." this place is popular with both gay men and women of all ages. There's a disco downstairs and a bar upstairs. It's open nightly from 11pm to 6am.

Admission: Cover charge A$5 (U.S. $4).

MIDNIGHT SHIFT, 85 Oxford St. Tel. 360-4319.

This nightspot is popular with gay men and women in the 25- to 45-year-old crowd. Open daily from 10am to 5am, there's a disco upstairs and a bar downstairs.
Admission: Cover charge during the week A$3 (U.S. $2.40), Fri–Sat A$7 (U.S. $5.60).

THE BAR SCENE
PUBS/BARS

In addition to the pubs mentioned here, the **George Street Bar** is described in "Sydney Dining" in Chapter 4.

AMERICA'S CUP BAR, in the Hilton International, George St. Tel. 266-0610.

With its nautical decor featuring mementos of the famous yacht race, the America's Cup Bar is a must for sailing buffs and sports fans who want to watch cricket, rugby, and so forth on the pub's wide-screen TV. It's open Monday through Thursday from noon to midnight, Friday and Saturday from noon to 1am, and Sunday from 2:30pm to midnight.
Prices: Draft beer A$3 (U.S. $2.40); bottled beer A$4.10 (U.S. $3.30).

HERO OF WATERLOO HOTEL, 81 Lower Fort St., The Rocks. Tel. 252-4553.

Built during the years 1843–44 and granted a license in 1845, the Hero of Waterloo is an atmospheric colonial pub. A tunnel which runs from the cellar of the hotel to the harbor was used for smuggling rum and the "involuntary recruitment" of sailors. This sandstone landmark is classified by the National Trust. Live music adds to the ambience on the weekends. The Hero of Waterloo is open normal pub hours: Monday to Saturday from 10am to 11pm, and Sunday from 10am to 10pm.
Prices: Schooner of draft beer A$2.60 (U.S. $2.10); can of beer A$2.70 (U.S. $2.20).

LORD DUDLEY HOTEL, 236 Jersey Rd., Woollahra. Tel. 327-5399.

Outside of the city center on a tree-lined street near Paddington, this pub has an Olde English atmosphere and a trendy following. It's open Monday to Wednesday from 11am to 11pm, Thursday to Saturday from 11am to midnight, and Sunday from noon to 10pm.
Prices: Schooner of draft beer A$2.20 (U.S. $1.80); can of beer A$2.65 (U.S. $2.15).

LORD NELSON, corner of Kent and Argyle Sts., The Rocks. Tel. 251-4044.

The Lord Nelson was granted a license in 1842, which makes it the city's oldest hotel. The thing that's particularly interesting here is that the proprietor, Blair Hayden, makes his own beer, and patrons can sample this as well as established brands. Blair's brews include Old Admiral, Victory Bitter, Trafalger Pale Ale, and Nelson's Blood. Substantial bar snacks are available 7 days a week, and there's a brasserie upstairs, so there's no risk of going hungry while you soak up the historic ambience and some suds. The "pub that restored Nelson's eyesight" is a gathering point for yuppies and similar friendly, fun-loving types. I highly recommend it. There's more information on the Lord Nelson in "Walking Tours," above, and in "Sydney Accommodations" in Chapter 4.
Prices: Beer A$2–A$4 (U.S. $1.60–U.S. $3.20).

MARBLE BAR, in the Hilton International, George St. Tel. 266-0610.

The bar was originally built in 1893 at a cost of 32,000 pounds sterling and was, at that time, part of Adams' Hotel, which stood on the site where the Hilton is now. The decoration of the bar was carried out in the style of the 15th-century Italian Renaissance. (The capitals of the Corinthian columns are solid bronze.) Artist Julian Ashton was commissioned to paint 18 rural scenes with nudes, for which the bar became famous.

In 1968 the decision was made to sell and demolish the old Adams' Hotel while preserving as much as possible of the Marble Bar. In 1969 the bar closed, the paintings were removed, the marble was tagged and photographed, casts were taken of the plasterwork, and the stained-glass windows were carefully packed away. On July 19, 1973, the rebuilt Marble Bar was opened as part of the Hilton International. The main difference between the original and the present-day bar is that it now boasts a carpeted floor. Some 14 of the big paintings remain, and it is still a significant watering hole for Sydneysiders—as it has been for nearly 100 years. It's open Monday through Thursday from 4pm to midnight, Friday from 4pm to 2am, and Saturday from 5pm to 2am. There's live entertainment Tuesday through Saturday.

Prices: Schooner of draft beer A$2.80 (U.S. $2.25); bottle of beer A$3.90 (U.S. $3.15).

OAKS HOTEL, 118 Military Rd., Neutral Bay. Tel. 953-5515.

Over in Neutral Bay on the north shore of the harbor, the Oaks Hotel is a place where upscale singles mix and mingle while they down a few beers and cook their own steaks. There are six different drinking areas, including a beer garden and the Tramway Bar, which actually contains the front half of a real tram. To get there, take a ferry from no. 4 jetty, Circular Quay, a bus from Wynyard, or a taxi. The bar is open Monday through Saturday from 10am to midnight and Sunday from noon to 10pm.

Prices: Schooner of beer A$2.40 (U.S. $1.95); can of beer A$2.60 (U.S. $2.10).

COCKTAIL LOUNGES

For a quiet drink with a beautiful view, head to **The Lounge** on top of the Boulevard Hotel, 100 William Street (tel. 356-2222). Soft piano music adds to the sophisticated surroundings. The **Garden Court Lounge** on the fifth floor of the Sheraton Wentworth Hotel, 61 Phillip Street (tel. 230-0700), is another romantic setting, where a trio provides music and floodlights illuminate an attractive garden area. While you're there, notice the fountain made from a horse's trough brought out from England during the colonial period. The **Club Bar** in the Regent Hotel, 199 George Street (tel. 238-0000), is a great spot for people-watching.

MORE ENTERTAINMENT

The **John Cadman Cruising Restaurant** and the **Candlelight Dinner Cruise** described in "Sydney Dining" in Chapter 4 and the **Sydney Showboat** and Matilda Cruises' *Solway Lass* **Dinner Cruise** described above in this chapter are all pleasant options for an evening in Sydney.

Three multiscreen **cinemas** are located cheek-to-jowl on George Street between Liverpool and Bathurst streets. The **Village Cinema 6 Plex** is next to the **Greater Union** multiscreen, which is next to the **Hoyts Centre** which has 7 screens. The cost is about A$11.50 (U.S. $9.20) for adults and A$6 (U.S. $4.80) for children.

In addition, art and classic films are shown nightly at 7:30pm in a small theater in the **Hare Krishna Centre** in Darlinghurst. Govinda's, the wonderful dining spot in the same place, is described in "Sydney Dining" in Chapter 4. The cost is A$9.50 (U.S. $7.60). Woody Allen movies are especially popular.

The "dirty half mile" of Darlinghurst Road in Kings Cross offers a plethora of sex shows, porn movies, adult book shops, and prostitutes. Places like the **Pink Panther Club**, 41 Darlinghurst Road (tel. 358-5070), advertise nude dancers, strippers, and "live sex on stage," and they mean what they say. Admission is officially A$20 (U.S. $16), but if they aren't busy it's negotiable.

10. EASY EXCURSIONS FROM SYDNEY

In addition to the destinations described here, it is also possible to do day-trips to the **Blue Mountains** and the **Hunter Valley**. These places are profiled in Chapter 6, "New South Wales."

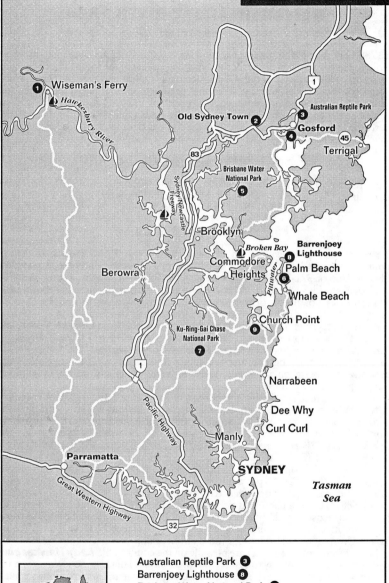

GREATER SYDNEY

Wiseman's Ferry **1**

Hawkesbury River

Old Sydney Town **2**

Australian Reptile Park **3**

Gosford

4

45

Terrigal

83

Brisbane Water National Park **5**

Sydney–Newcastle Freeway

Brooklyn

Broken Bay

Commodore Heights

Berowra

Barrenjoey Lighthouse **8**

Palm Beach **6**

Pittwater

Whale Beach

Church Point **9**

Ku-Ring-Gai Chase National Park **7**

1

Narrabeen

Dee Why

Curl Curl

Manly

Pacific Highway

Parramatta

SYDNEY

Tasman Sea

Great Western Highway

32

Sydney

Australian Reptile Park **3**
Barrenjoey Lighthouse **8**
Brisbane Water National Park **5**
Church Point **9**
Gosford **4**
Ku-ring-gai Chase National Park **7**
Old Sydney Town **2**
Palm Beach **6**
Wiseman's Ferry **1**

THE HAWKESBURY RIVER AREA

43km (27 miles) N of Sydney

In 1788 Governor Phillip discovered the Hawkesbury River and was grateful for its fertile soil needed to grow food for the struggling colony to the south. The river enters the ocean at Broken Bay about 43 kilometers (27 miles) north of Sydney and was named for Baron Hawkesbury who was president of the Board of Trade and Plantations in England at the time. As a result of Phillip's discovery, the earliest farming settlements in Australia were along the Hawkesbury River. To this day, the riverlands have remained rural and provide the background for a peaceful, picturesque respite from the rigors of urban existence.

GETTING THERE

To Palm Beach: Drive or take State Transit (tel. 954-4422) bus no. 190. To Brooklyn: Drive up the Sydney-Newcastle Freeway or Pacific Highway or take a train from Central Station to the Hawkesbury River Railway Station.

WHAT TO SEE & DO

You might start your exploration of the area in scenic **Palm Beach,** a genteel community perched on the end of the Barrenjoey Peninsula. From here, Aquatic Air (tel. 974-5966 or 371-7700) operates scenic flights over **Pittwater,** a long, sheltered inlet popular with yachtsmen. It's possible to rent catamarans and paddleboats from the Barrenjoey Boathouse, or you can have lunch at Barrenjoey House (see "Sydney Dining" in Chapter 4).

At the southern end of Pittwater, there are good vistas from **Church Point,** and from there it's a short drive into the bushland of **Ku-ring-gai Chase National Park** and more sweeping views from **Commodore Heights.** The wildflowers in the park are at their best during September and October. The water views are especially impressive on weekends, when millions of dollars' worth of sailboats become part of the picture.

Another approach to the Hawkesbury, is to drive or take the train to **Brooklyn,** on the south shore of the river. The sentimental American workers who built the railroad bridge across the Hawkesbury at this spot named the town, which is 50 kilometers (31 miles) north of Sydney, after their borough in New York. The **Hawkesbury River Ferries** (tel. 985-7566), which leave the Brooklyn wharf Monday through Friday at 9:30am, distribute mail and other necessities to people who live along the banks and, in so doing, share a slice of Australiana with visitors (cost is A$18/U.S. $14.40 per adult, half price for children). The boat returns at 1:15pm after passing countless sheltered bays and miles of bush-clad shore. **CityRail** (tel. 217-8811) offers a combined ticket that includes the river cruise and the train up from Sydney (cost is A$23/U.S. $18.40 per adult, half price for children); the trip is also on the itineraries of several sightseeing coaches. Contact the **New South Wales Travel Centre** (tel. 231-4444) for more information.

Longer sojourns on the river are possible on the comfortable *Lady Hawkesbury* cruise ship—a leisurely way to explore the waterway and the historic towns around it. Accommodations are in deluxe staterooms, regular staterooms, or cabins; waiter-served meals are available in an attractive dining room. Lounge chairs on the sun deck near the swimming pool allow guests to sit back, relax, and watch the scenery float by. The Windsor Heritage cruise retraces early explorers' tracks upriver to the historic town of **Windsor.** Stops are made at **Wiseman's Ferry,** one of the oldest towns on the river (named after Solomon Wiseman, who was deported from England for hiding spies in his boat during the Napoleonic wars) and at other scenic spots, such as the gorges of **Berowra Waters** and the beautiful yacht-filled inlet of **Pittwater.** Passengers have a choice of 2-, 4-, or 6-night cruises, starting either in Brooklyn or Windsor.

Rates are seasonal: The January-April and October-December periods are the most expensive. May and September are midprice; the June-August period is the least expensive time to go. Rates range from A$266 to A$451 (U.S. $212.80 to U.S. $360.80) for a 2-night midweek cruise, to A$745 to A$1,255 (U.S. $596 to U.S. $1,004) for a 6-night excursion. All rates are per person, based on two adults sharing a cabin. Round-trip coach transfer between Sydney and Brooklyn or Windsor is an additional A$46 (U.S. $36.80) per person. In North America, contact the *Lady Hawkesbury* via **SO/PAC** (tel. toll free 800/551-2012 in the U.S. or Canada). The prices quoted here are valid if purchased directly from Captain Cook Cruises in Australia (No. 6 Jetty, Circular Quay, Sydney; tel. 247-4548 or 251-5007).

GOSFORD

84km (52 miles) N of Sydney

Gosford is a picturesque town on the edge of **Brisbane Water National Park,** an area renowned for its beaches and waterways.

GETTING THERE

Drive up the Pacific Highway and the Sydney-Newcastle Freeway, take the train, or catch the Central Coast Airbus (tel. 043/32-8655). Several Sydney sightseeing companies, such as Australian Pacific Tours and Newmans Coaches, run excursions to Old Sydney Town (see below).

INFORMATION

You can get information from the Gosford City Visitors Information Centre, 200 Mann Street, Gosford, NSW 2250 (tel. 043/25-2835). Open daily.

WHAT TO SEE & DO

OLD SYDNEY TOWN, Pacific Hwy., Somersby, 9km (5½ miles) south of Gosford. Tel. 043/40-1104.
   This attraction is a must if you're traveling with children (and maybe even if you aren't). Old Sydney Town is where Australia is re-created as it was 200 years ago. Costumed characters live out colonists' lives against a backdrop of historic buildings. Kids particularly enjoy the reenactment of activities that took place in 1806–07. These include floggings and hangings, as well as wagon rides. Allow an hour to drive to Old Sydney Town from Sydney. There's a connecting bus from the Gosford train station. Meals are available at Rosetta's Eating Establishment, the King's Head Tavern, and a snack bar.
   Admission: A$12.80 (U.S. $10.25) adults, A$6.80 (U.S. $5.45) children 5–16; under 5 free.
   Open: Wed–Sun 10am–5pm and daily during NSW school and public holidays. **Closed:** Christmas Day.

AUSTRALIAN REPTILE PARK, Pacific Hwy., Gosford. Tel. 043/28-4311.
   Besides a plethora of snakes, lizards and other reptiles, this fauna park has koalas, birds, and three platypuses (named Eb, Flo, and Ripple). There are also turtles, iguanas, and funnel web spiders. Visitors who are game can hold a python.
   Admission: A$7.50 (U.S. $6) adults, A$3 (U.S. $2.40) children.
   Open: Daily 9am–5pm. **Closed:** Christmas Day.

WHERE TO STAY & DINE

PEPPERS HOTEL, 26-40 The Esplanade, Terrigal, NSW 2260. Tel. 043/84-9111, or toll free 008/02-4966 in Australia. Fax 043/84-5798. 196 rms and suites. A/C MINIBAR TV TEL **Directions:** Bus or taxi from Gosford. Central Coast Airbus from Sydney.

$ Rates: A$240 (U.S. $192) single or double; A$430–A$475 (U.S. $344–U.S. $380) suite; A$30 (U.S. $24) extra person. Children under 12 stay free in parents' room. AE, BC, DC, MC, V. **Parking:** A$3 (U.S. $2.40).

Terrigal is a beach community about 1½ hours north of Sydney and 15 to 20 minutes east of Gosford. This attractive resort hotel was built at a cost of A$60 million (U.S. $40 million) and opened mid-1989. It provides a getaway for harried Sydneysiders who flock to it on weekends. From the outside the eight-story property looks a bit like a Mediterranean villa. All but six rooms face the ocean and have bougainvillea-trimmed balconies. Rooms have either two double beds or a queen. In-room movies, free daily newspapers, bathrobes, tea- and coffee-making facilities, small refrigerators, and radios are provided.

Dining/Entertainment: The hotel offers a wide range of dining venues—from very casual to quite formal. The thing they have in common is great tasting food, attractively presented. La Mer is the formal, à la carte restaurant for gourmet dining. Fresh seafood and French cuisine are featured, and the wine list is very extensive. Men are required to wear jackets. La Mer is open Tuesday to Saturday from 7pm to 1am. The Norfolk Brasserie is a casual dining spot where the hardwood floor, bouquets of garden flowers, ceiling fans, and blue-and-white tablecloths create a chic country decor. This eatery is open for breakfast, lunch, and dinner daily. The Conservatory overlooks the ocean and is also open daily. On the ground floor, Scoozi is a sidewalk café for teas and snacks. Pepper's also has a disco: the Key Largo Nightclub.

Services: 24-hour room service, turn-down service, laundry, valet, concierge, baby-sitting, and massage.

Facilities: Outdoor pool, extensive health club, gym, sauna, spa, Captain Pepper Club for children's activities, children's center, hair salon, gift shop, and newsagent.

KIM'S, Toowoon Bay, NSW 2261. Tel. 043/32-1566. Fax 043/33-1544. 34 individual bungalows. TV TEL **Directions:** 20 minutes' drive from Gosford.

$ Rates (including all meals): A$145–A$250 (U.S. $116–U.S. $200) per person midweek; A$165–A$275 (U.S. $132–U.S. $220) per person weekends. Minimum stay 2 days on weekends, 3 days on public-holiday weekends, and 5 days at Easter. AE, BC, DC, MC. **Parking:** Free.

For more than 100 years this beachfront site has been a stopping place for vacationers, but up until 5 years ago when Kim's bungalows were built, accommodation was limited to camping. Now guests relax in comfortable, but not self-consciously posh, surroundings. This is very much an adult retreat and families are not encouraged. Instead, the privacy and natural beauty of the area appeals to honeymooners and others with a need to get away. The lush tropical foliage (all imported) makes this place look more like Queensland than New South Wales. About a third of the quarters are right on the beach; others are just a short stroll away. Many rooms have fireplaces, all have balconies, most have outdoor spa pools or indoor spa baths, and one has a private swimming pool. All have tea- and coffee-making facilities and small refrigerators, the majority also have video players. Some beds are king-size, the rest queens.

Dining/Entertainment: A bell rings to call guests to meals which are served buffet style.

Services: Limited room service.

YERRANDERIE

96km (60 miles) NW of Sydney

During the silver-mining boom of 1907 to 1914, Yerranderie had a population of 2,000. Most of its workers worked for the Tonalli Mining and Engineering Company. In those days the richest silver in Australia came from these mines bordered by the Blue Mountains National Park. However, the mines closed in 1928 and the place became a ghost town. It was further isolated when the Sydney Water Board flooded the nearby Burragorang Valley in 1957, cutting the direct-access road from Sydney.

At this point Yerranderie was officially removed from most maps of the area and would have disappeared completely had it not been for the interest of one of Tonalli's former stockholders, Val Lhuede. This stalwart lady bought the ghost town and the 462 hectares (1,141 acres) of bushland surrounding it and is gradually restoring the original buildings. The town now has a permanent population of one, caretaker Bill Chisholm. Kangaroos, wallabies, and other native animals thrive in the peaceful environment, making it an ideal location for nature study. Conducted tours of the site cost A$2 (U.S. $1.60). Admission to Yerranderie is A$2 (U.S. $1.60).

GETTING THERE

You can drive to Yerranderie from Sydney in about 6 hours, from Katoomba in 4 hours, or from the Jenolan Caves in just under 3 hours. However, the easiest way is probably with the 4-wheel-drive tours from Sydney offered by **AAT King's** (tel. 666-3899 or 252-2788) from October through April. These cost A$95 (U.S. $76) for a day tour or A$330 (U.S. $264) for a 2-day tour with overnight accommodation. Penrith Air Charter also provides transfers from the Sydney area.

INFORMATION

If you have questions or would like to book accommodations, get in touch with **Val Lhuede,** Yerranderie Village Project, 81/2 Parkes Street, Kirribilli, NSW 2061 (tel. 046/59-6165, or 02/955-8083 in Sydney).

WHERE TO STAY

Overnight guests can sleep in a rustic lodge that formerly housed the post office at a cost of A$32 (U.S. $25.60) per adult; camping costs A$8 (U.S. $6.40). Children under 12 are half price. Guests must bring their own provisions, as there are no food shops or petrol (gas) stations. No credit cards.

CHAPTER 6

NEW SOUTH WALES

"**I**t's more than a bridge and an Opera House," residents of New South Wales remind visitors. And they're right. Their state has many wonders. Beyond the borders of Sydney lie beaches, mountains, bushland, vineyards, rivers, mining country, and outback wilderness.

Because New South Wales is relatively small (it occupies only 10% of the continent), travelers can sample its assorted features with relative ease without putting an inordinate strain on time and dollar budgets. It would be possible, for instance, to fossick for opals in Lightning Ridge, stay overnight on an outback cattle station, tour Hunter Valley wineries, pick bananas in Coffs Harbour, and bushwalk through a forest of eucalyptus within a week. And, depending on the time of year, sunbathing or skiing could be added to the itinerary.

The four main geographical regions are: the fertile coastal strip, the high tablelands and peaks of the Great Dividing Range, pastoral farmland on the western slopes of the range, and the sparsely populated western plains that cover two-thirds of the state. The climate varies from subtropical to alpine.

New South Wales is the home of Sydney, the country's largest city; Mount Kosciusko, the highest peak; and the only Australian island registered on the World Heritage List (Lord Howe). The Australian Capital Territory (Canberra) is contained within its borders.

Besides this wealth of diversity, New South Wales is also economically the richest of Australia's six states because it is the country's main wheat, coal, and sheep producer. In addition, the Newcastle-Sydney-Wollongong region is the industrial heart of the nation. New South Wales is the oldest state and the most populous. Approximately 35% of all Australians live within its borders.

SEEING NEW SOUTH WALES

Good highways link the major cities and towns in New South Wales. The **Pacific Highway** heads north over Sydney's Harbour Bridge and follows the coast north. The **Princes Highway** meanders along the south coast. The **New England Highway,** which passes through Tamworth and Armidale, is parallel to and inland from the Pacific Highway. The **Great Western Highway** heads west from Sydney and through the Blue Mountains. The **Hume Highway** connects Sydney and

WHAT'S SPECIAL ABOUT NEW SOUTH WALES

Beaches
☐ Byron Bay, the most easterly point in Australia, with some of the country's best beach. Great surfing.
☐ Coffs Harbour, just one of the places on the coast north of Sydney where the beaches stretch for miles.

Events/Festivals
☐ Bathurst, in the Golden West, hosts the "Toohey's 1000" auto race in October and the "James Hardie 12-Hour Race" at Easter.
☐ Bowral, in the Southern Highlands, hosts a Tulip Festival every spring (September/October).
☐ Tamworth, in the New England region, hosts the Australasian Country Music Awards and a music festival each January.

Natural Spectacles
☐ Mount Kosciusko, in the Snowy Mountains, the highest point in the country. Good skiing June through September.
☐ The Blue Mountains—superbly scenic, with good hiking trails and lodging in cozy guesthouses.

Ace Attractions
☐ The Hunter Valley, the oldest commercial wine-producing area in Australia, with dozens of wineries open for tours and tasting.
☐ The Jenolan Caves, slightly southwest of the Blue Mountains, open to the public. Guided tours take place daily.

Offbeat Places
☐ Lord Howe Island, due east of Port Macquarie, one of only three islands in the world on the World Heritage List. Rare plants, birds, and marine life abound.

Unusual Activities
☐ A pub crawl on horseback through the New England region—a great way to meet the locals.
☐ Fossicking for opals in Lightning Ridge.

Galleries
☐ Broken Hill's "Brushmen of the Bush" exhibit their work at several galleries in this outback town.

Melbourne. Travelers should consult the **National Roads & Motorists' Association** (NRMA), 151 Clarence Street, Sydney, NSW 2000 (tel. 02/260-9222), before setting out by car across the state.

If you aren't driving, **Ansett Express, Hazelton Airlines, Eastern Australia Airlines, Oxley Airlines,** and **Eastwest Airlines** provide intercity air service. If you'd rather get into training, **CityRail** and **Countrylink** can get you to most areas of the state. **Bus Australia, Pioneer,** and **Greyhound** also cover major routes.

INFORMATION

The **New South Wales Travel Centre,** 19 Castlereagh Street, Sydney, NSW 2000 (tel. 02/231-4444), is the best source of tourist information.

1. THE SOUTHERN HIGHLANDS & THE SOUTH COAST

Two main roads lead south from Sydney: the Hume Highway and the Princes Highway. Both connect Australia's two biggest cities, but the Hume is the faster and is therefore popular with truck drivers and others who must get to their destinations quickly. Using this road one can get to Melbourne in 12 hours. The Princes Highway, following the coast and passing small towns and beachfront resorts, requires at least 2 days.

Many travelers, taking the most scenic route, start out on the Hume, which goes through the picturesque Southern Highlands, and then cross over to the Princes via the Illawarra Highway, which connects the two roads about 140 kilometers (87 miles) south of Sydney. By following this path, they can enjoy the gardens and forests of the highlands; the route reaches the ocean just in time for the most beautiful beach vistas. Berrima, Bowral, Mittagong, Moss Vale, and other quaint towns in the highlands make pleasant overnight destinations for those who lack the time or desire for the full trip along the coast. Those wishing to follow the Hume all the way to Melbourne will find information in "Along the Hume Highway" in Chapter 17.

BERRIMA

122km (98 miles) SW of Sydney

GETTING THERE   By Train, Bus, or Car   You'll need your own vehicle if you want to go to Berrima. The closest train station and bus depot are in Mittagong 18 kilometers (11 miles) to the northeast. The bus ride from Sydney to Mittagong takes 2½ hours. If you're driving, you'll find the village on the Hume Highway.

ESSENTIALS   The **Southern Highlands Tourist Centre** (tel. 048/71-2888), in Winifred West Park on the Hume Highway in Mittagong, is open daily from 9am to 5pm. Ask for the "Two Foot Tour" booklet if you'd like to do a self-guided walking tour past Berrima's historic buildings. The **area code** is 048.

The historic village of Berrima was founded in 1829 by settlers attracted to the fertile farmlands that surround it. A courthouse, jail, public school, inn, and other buildings were constructed of local sandstone, and the town was expected to become a major center in this part of the state. However, the railroad bypassed Berrima in the 1860s, and thereafter the town failed to thrive. Today it retains its 19th-century appearance and has a population of 685.

WHAT TO SEE & DO

The colonial sandstone buildings that give Berrima its charm are open to the public. Of special note are the **Surveyor General Inn**, the **Court House**, the **Gaol** (jail), the **Church of Holy Trinity**, and **St. Francis Xavier Roman Catholic Church**. Also of interest are the many antiques and craft shops and the scenic countryside surrounding the village.

WHERE TO STAY

BERRIMA BAKEHOUSE MOTEL, corner of Hume Hwy. and Winge-carribee St., Berrima, NSW 2577. Tel. 048/77-1381. 18 units. TV TEL
$ Rates: A$60–A$80 (U.S. $48–U.S. $64) double; A$15 (U.S. $12) extra person. AE, BC, DC, MC, V.
Each unit has a shower and coffee- and tea-making facilities. The two-story property also offers laundry facilities, a playground, and a pool.

WHERE TO DINE

THE COLONIAL INN RESTAURANT, Hume Hwy. Tel. 77-1389.
   Cuisine: AUSTRALIAN. **Reservations:** Recommended.
$ Prices: Appetizers A$6–A$14 (U.S. $4.80–U.S. $11.20); main courses A$12.50–A$25.50 (U.S. $10–U.S. $20.40). Sun and public holiday surcharge A$2.50 (U.S. $2) per adult. AE, BC, DC, MC, V.

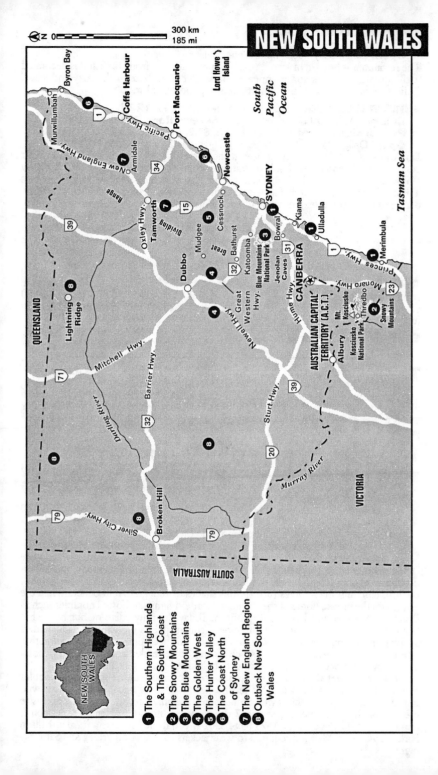

NEW SOUTH WALES

300 km
185 mi

South Pacific Ocean

Tasman Sea

Byron Bay
Murwillumbah
Coffs Harbour
Port Macquarie
Lord Howe Island
Pacific Hwy.
New England Hwy.
Armidale
34
Range
Oxley Hwy.
Tamworth
15
Dividing
Great
Mudgee
Cessnock
Newcastle
SYDNEY
Kiama
Bowral
Ulladulla
Bathurst
Katoomba
Blue Mountains National Park
31
Jenolan Caves
CANBERRA
Merimbula
Princes Hwy.
Dubbo
32
Great Western Hwy.
Newell Hwy.
Hume Hwy.
Monaro Hwy.
23
Mt. Kosciusko
Thredbo
Snowy Mountains
AUSTRALIAN CAPITAL TERRITORY (A.C.T.)
Albury
Kosciusko National Park
QUEENSLAND
Lightning Ridge
39
71
Mitchell Hwy.
Barrier Hwy.
Darling River
32
Sturt Hwy.
39
20
Murray River
VICTORIA
Broken Hill
Silver City Hwy.
79
79

1
6
34
7
15
5
6
1
3
31
4
32
4
4
2
23
8
8
8
8
8

SOUTH AUSTRALIA

NEW SOUTH WALES

1 The Southern Highlands & The South Coast
2 The Snowy Mountains
3 The Blue Mountains
4 The Golden West
5 The Hunter Valley
6 The Coast North of Sydney
7 The New England Region
8 Outback New South Wales

Open: Lunch daily noon–3pm; dinner daily 6–9:30pm.
The restaurant is housed in an old coaching inn that dates from 1842 and is decorated with antiques. Candles and an open fire in winter contribute to the cozy ambience. Children's meals are available, and there is a good wine list.

SURVEYOR GENERAL INN, Hume Hwy. Tel. 77-1226.
  Cuisine: AUSTRALIAN BARBECUE. **Reservations:** Not necessary.
$ **Prices:** Main courses A$9–A$11 (U.S. $7.20–U.S. $8.80). No credit cards.
  Open: Daily 10am–11pm. **Closed:** Christmas Day and Good Friday.
Don't miss the chance to have a beer at the Surveyor General Inn, Australia's oldest continuously licensed hotel still operating within its original walls. It was built by William Harper in 1834. Diners select from the choice of steaks—which includes T-bone, rump, and Scotch filet—and grill their own. The bistro also offers hot damper bread and an extensive salad bar. Wine is available, and Guinness is on tap.

BOWRAL

5km (3 miles) S of Mittagong, 109km (87 miles) SW of Sydney

GETTING THERE By Train, Bus, or Car Countrylink trains provide regular service to Bowral (A$19.10/U.S. $15.30 first class; A$13.50/U.S. $10.80 economy); Bus Australia, Pioneer, and Greyhound coaches stop in Mittagong. It takes just under 2 hours to drive from Sydney.

ESSENTIALS The **area code** is 048.

The annual **Tulip Festival** in late September or early October draws thousands of visitors to Bowral. During this time 60,000 tulips bloom along with other spring flowers, trees, and shrubs, turning this part of the Southern Highlands into a picture-postcard sight. The town's parks and gardens, established in the late 1800s when it was developed as a tourist resort, are also worthwhile at other times of the year.

WHERE TO STAY & DINE

MILTON PARK COUNTRY HOUSE HOTEL, Horderns Rd., Bowral, NSW 2576. Tel. 048/61-1522, or toll free 008/028-954 in Australia. Fax 048/61-4716. 46 rms, 5 suites. MINIBAR TV TEL
$ **Rates** (including continental breakfast): A$210–A$260 (U.S. $168–U.S. $208) double; A$430 (U.S. $344) suite; A$45 (U.S. $36) extra person. Children under 12 not allowed. Midweek discounts, depending on occupancy level. AE, BC, DC, V.
  This is the grandest lodging to be found in all the Southern Highlands. Its artistically landscaped gardens are judged to be the finest in Australia and were once rated in the world's top 10. In the spring, lilacs, dogwoods, rhododendrons, azaleas, and daffodils are at their peak; in the fall (March to May), the leaves of the ash, elm, and maple trees turn various shades of red, gold, and ocher. When the estate was the private home of the Anthony Hordern family, it hosted notables such as Princess Margaret and Lyndon B. Johnson. Today the Edwardian manor house has been remodeled and expanded. The most frequent guests are affluent Sydneysiders soaking up the ambience of peace and luxury. All accommodations are attractive, offering king-size beds, plenty of space, heated towel racks, and plush terry robes. Suites have fireplaces, spa baths, and coffee- and tea-making facilities.
  Dining/Entertainment: The French-style gourmet cuisine is another popular feature. Poached spatchcock, hare terrine, warm salad of squab pigeon with wild mushrooms, and sea-fish filets with fennel purée are only a few items on the extensive menu. Lunch and dinner are served 7 days a week and nonresidents are welcome; main courses start at around A$25 (U.S. $20). If you decide to have a meal at Milton Park, *book early*. Men are required to wear jackets to dinner on Friday and Saturday night.

Services: Limited room service.

Facilities: Guests at Milton Park can play tennis or croquet, swim, cycle, ride horses, and wander through the spectacular gardens (open to the public only during the 10-day Tulip Festival).

LINKS HOUSE, 17 Links Rd., Bowral, NSW 2576. Tel. 048/61-1408. 16 rms. TV

$ Rates (including breakfast and dinner): A$125 (U.S. $100) per person. AE, BC, MC, V.

This small hotel is in a relaxing setting in the country surrounded by attractive gardens. An open fire warms the guest lounge. Rooms have showers (no tubs); there are a few queen beds, but most are doubles.

Dining/Entertainment: The cuisine at Links House is Californian with French influence.

Facilities: Tennis courts, spa, and swimming pool. Bowral Golf Course is across the road.

KIAMA

119km (74 miles) S of Sydney

GETTING THERE   By Train or Bus   There is regular train and coach service from Sydney. The bus trip with either Greyhound or Pioneer takes about 3 hours (A$32/U.S. $25.60).

By Car   If you take the Illawarra Highway from Moss Vale in the Southern Highlands down to the coast, you will come out just north of Kiama. The other alternative, if you're driving, is to head straight south from Sydney through Wollongong on the Princes Highway.

ESSENTIALS   The **Kiama Visitors Centre,** Blowhole Point (tel. 042/32-3322), can answer your questions. The **area code** is 042.

Kiama is located on the **Illawarra Coastline,** which stretches 295 kilometers (183 miles) from Sydney to Bateman's Bay.

WHAT TO SEE & DO

Kiama (pop. 7,716) is known for its **blowhole.** Although its performance is anything but consistent, jets of water spurting up through this rock fissure *can* reach heights of 60 meters (198 ft.). The blowhole is floodlit until 1am.

A **Heritage Walk** is available here, too. It takes visitors around the historic precinct of this pretty harborside village including the timber terraces built in 1896 as workers' cottages. They are now classified by the National Trust and house craft and gift shops (most open daily from 10am to 5pm). Kiama's **beaches** are good for surfing, swimming, and fishing.

WHERE TO STAY & DINE

KIAMA TERRACE MOTOR LODGE, 51 Collins St., Kiama, NSW 2533. Tel. 042/33-1100. Fax 042/33-1235. 50 rms. A/C TV TEL

$ Rates: A$90 (U.S. $72) double; A$10 (U.S. $8) extra person. Reservations can be made through Best Western. Lower rates through Aussie auto clubs. Weekend packages. AE, BC, DC, MC, V.

Kiama's newest motor inn is three stories and has a restaurant on the premises. All rooms have bathtubs as well as showers, and 22 have roomy spa tubs. Videos, clock radios, queen-size beds, coffee- and tea-making facilities, and small refrigerators are standard throughout.

Dining/Entertainment: Meals can be brought to the room or eaten in the restaurant.

Facilities: Self-service laundry, barbecue, and saltwater pool.

ULLADULLA

233km (140 miles) S of Sydney

GETTING THERE   By Bus   A daily bus transports passengers from the railhead at Nowra. The trip from Sydney on either Pioneer or Greyhound takes about 5 hours (A$38/U.S. $30.40).

ESSENTIALS   The **area code** is 044.

Farther along the Illawarra Coast, Ulladulla (pop. 6,016) is a picturesque fishing port whose catch more often than not ends up on a menu in Sydney. If you're in the area at Easter, don't miss the colorful **Blessing of the Fleet ceremony.** Surfing, swimming, golf, and fishing are popular local activities, and bushwalkers can make the trek to **Pigeon House Mountain,** a rocky outcrop at the south end of Morton National Park. It's easy to net prawns in season, and the rock and offshore fishing is good.

WHERE TO STAY

PIGEON HOUSE MOTOR INN, 156 Princes Hwy., Ulladulla, NSW 2539.
   Tel. 044/55-1811. Fax 044/55-5256. 16 rms. TV TEL
$ **Rates:** A$65 (U.S. $52) double; A$15 (U.S. $12) extra person. Holiday sur-
   charges at Christmas, in Jan, and at Easter. Reservations can be made through
   Flag Inns. AE, BC, DC, MC, V.
This motor inn is located ½ kilometer (a few blocks) south of the center of town. All rooms have the standard coffee- and tea-making facilities and refrigerators, plus toasters and clock radios. There's also an outdoor pool.

MERIMBULA

480km (384 miles) S of Sydney, 580km (464 miles) NE of Melbourne

GETTING THERE   By Plane, Bus, or Car   Kendell Airlines and Hazelton Airlines operate flights to Merimbula. The Pioneer or Greyhound bus trip from Sydney takes 8 hours and 40 minutes (A$52/U.S. $41.60). The drive from Sydney takes about 7 hours; from Melbourne the trip takes about 7½ hours; from Canberra figure on 3 hours.

ESSENTIALS   The **Tourist Information Centre,** Beach Street, Merimbula, NSW 2548 (tel. 064/95-1129), is open daily from 9am to 5pm. The **area code** is 064.

The focal point for the coastal country between Bega and Eden, Merimbula (pop. 4,000) has developed into a successful seaside resort. It's also the last point of interest before the Princes Highway crosses the state border into Victoria.

WHAT TO SEE & DO

Eden, near Merimbula, was once a major whaling port, and the town's **Killer Whale Museum,** on Imlay Street (tel. 064/96-2094), displays an array of maritime relics relating to the whaling industry. It's open from 11am to 4pm daily. The admission is A$2.50 (U.S. $2) for adults and A$1 (U.S. 80¢) for children.
   You may be interested in seeing the **Brogo Valley Rotolactor,** 16 kilometers (10 miles) north of Bega, where cows are milked on a rotary turnstile at 3pm daily. There are also tours at the **Bega cheese factory** Monday through Friday.

Golf is the main game in Merimbula, and the most popular venue in the area is the **Pambula-Merimbula Golf Club** (tel. 064/95-6154), where kangaroos regularly graze on the fairways of the 27-hole course. Another favorite place to play is the **Tura Beach Country Club** (tel. 064/95-9002) located at **Tura Beach,** 4 kilometers (2½ miles) north of town. This course is known for its excellent coastline views. (Greens fees are A$15/U.S. $12.) Besides golf, Merimbula has good **beaches** for surfing and windsurfing. Fishing, oystering, and prawning are also popular.

WHERE TO STAY

OCEAN VIEW MOTOR INN, at Princes Hwy. and View St., Merimbula, NSW 2548. Tel. 064/95-2300, or toll free 008/02-8293 in Australia. Fax 064/95-3443. 19 rms. A/C TEL TV
$ Rates: A$66–A$100 (U.S. $52.80–U.S. $80) double; A$10 (U.S. $8) extra person. AE, BC, DC, MC, V.
All quarters in this two-story motor inn have showers (no tubs), clock radios, coffee- and tea-making facilities, and small refrigerators. Ten rooms have queen-size beds. Kitchenettes are available in 13 of the units. A saltwater swimming pool, recreation room, barbecue, and self-service laundry are provided for guests' use.

SEA HORSE INN, Boydtown, NSW 2551. Tel. 064/96-1361. Fax 064/96-3447. 13 rms, 2 suites (none with bath). TV
$ Rates (including cooked breakfast): A$65 (U.S. $52) single; A$80 (U.S. $64) double; A$20 (U.S. $16) extra person. AE, BC, DC, MC, V.
The Sea Horse Inn is located 8 kilometers (5 miles) south of Eden at Boydtown in a Tudor-style building that was built in 1842 and has been classified by the National Trust. The inn is a licensed hotel in a wonderful beachfront location. All quarters have tea- and coffee-making facilities, small refrigerators, and clock radios. There are tennis courts on the premises.

2. THE SNOWY MOUNTAINS

In a country like Australia, best known for its beaches and outback barrenness, the Snowys are a rarity. While snow falls in other places, these mountains have the only ski facilities. Aussies love the Snowys and flock to the area for both winter and summer sports.

The loftiest point is Mount Kosciusko, which reaches a height of 2,173 meters (7,171 ft.) and dominates **Kosciusko National Park.** The major ski areas—Thredbo, Perisher Valley, Smiggen Holes, Guthega, Charlotte Pass, Mount Blue Cow, and Mount Selwyn—are all in the park. In addition to their fame as a winter-sports venue, the Snowys are also known for high-country horseback riding, an activity that got great exposure in the movie *The Man from Snowy River.* The ballad on which the film was based was written by the bush poet Banjo Patterson in 1895 and set in the area around Kiandra in the northern part of the park.

Some of the action in the movie also takes place in the neighboring state of Victoria, which borders Kosciusko National Park on the south and is separated from New South Wales by the Murray River.

THREDBO

519km (322 miles) SW of Sydney, 208km (129 miles) SW of Canberra, 534km (331 miles) NE of Melbourne

GETTING THERE **By Plane** Travelers coming from Sydney can fly to **Cooma,** 95 kilometers (59 miles) to the northeast, on Ansett Express or Eastern Australia Airlines.

By Bus   The connecting bus trip to Thredbo takes 1½ hours. From June to October Pioneer and Greyhound offer two trips a day from Sydney to Thredbo (duration: 8 hr.). Cost is A$48 (U.S. $38.40). You could also take a Countrylink train from Sydney to Canberra and catch a Pioneer or Greyhound coach from there to Thredbo.

By Train   The Sydney-Canberra train ride takes 5 hours; the Canberra-Thredbo bus trip lasts 3 hours.

By Car   Motorists follow the Hume Highway through Goulburn, connecting with the Federal Highway to Canberra. From there the Monaro Highway leads to Cooma, and a lesser road through Jindabyne ends in Thredbo Village.

ESSENTIALS   Tourist information is available at the **Thredbo Resort Centre** (tel. 064/57-6360, or toll free 008/02-6333 in Australia), which is open daily from 9am to 6pm. **Snow reports** are as close as the phone in Sydney (tel. 02/11-544) and Melbourne (tel. 03/11-544). Information is also available from the U.S. (tel. toll free 800/876-6983).

The village, which feels more like Switzerland than Australia, is a compact cluster of lodges, restaurants, and a hotel; a **free shuttle bus** operates to the valley terminal, even though the lifts are within easy walking distance. An underground **Skitube** links Thredbo to the ski areas at Perisher, Blue Cow, and Smiggens.

The **area code** is 064.

Easily the area's most popular ski resort, this alpine village has facilities on a par with those of similar resorts around the world. Thredbo is the site of international skiing events and offers a wide range of accommodations and dining options.

WHAT TO SEE & DO

In spite of efforts to promote summer activities in the village, **skiing** is still the sport that brings most people to Thredbo and other resorts in the Snowy Mountains. The season runs from June through September. Equipment rental (skis, poles, boots, and clothing) is available in the valley terminal. Lift tickets cost A$49 (U.S. $39.20) a day, lessons are available, and there are over 100 kilometers (62 miles) of trails.

Summer attractions include bushwalking, canoeing, fishing, golf, tennis, horseback riding, and swimming. The chair lift runs year round, and at the top you can have a beer and a bite in the cafeteria or head for the top of Mount Kosciuski, which is a 13-kilometer (8-mile) trek round-trip. Brochures available from the Resort Centre describe other alpine hikes of varying degrees of difficulty.

Tennis courts can be rented in the village, as can fishing rods. You can also play golf.

Horseback riding is available in the village, but for that real *Man from Snowy River* experience, you should contact Roslyn and John Rudd at **Reynella Safaris,** Adaminaby, NSW 2630 (tel. 064/54-2386 or 54-2469). They lead alpine horseback trips into Kosciusko National Park and host guests at their Reynella Country Lodge, which is nestled in the foothills of the Snowy Mountains. The riding season is November to April.

WHERE TO STAY

KARA'S APARTMENTS, Bobuck Lane, Thredbo, NSW 2627. Tel. 064/ 57-6385. Fax 064/57-6060. 9 apartments. TV

$ Rates: A$1,290 (U.S. $1,032) a week for two people in a bed-sitter (studio); A$1,800 (U.S. $1,440) a week for four people in a 1-bedroom apartment; A$2,400 (U.S. $1,920) for six people in a 2-bedroom apartment. These rates are for the high season (late June–early Sept); rates are lower and daily tariffs are available before and after this period. **Closed:** Oct–May. No credit cards.

Ⓢ Kara's is a good choice for those who want self-contained living with daily chamber service. Each studio, one-bedroom, or two-bedroom unit has its own fully equipped kitchen and all the necessary bed and bath linens. All have balconies from which there is a view of Crackenback Mountain; a sauna is shared by guests.

THREDBO ALPINE HOTEL, Thredbo, NSW 2627. Tel. 064/57-6333. 64 rms, 2 suites. MINIBAR TV TEL

$ Rates: A$48–A$135 (U.S. $38.40–U.S. $108) per person in summer; A$78–A$154 (U.S. $62.40–U.S. $123.20) per person for bed-and-breakfast in winter. Weekly rates available. Lower rates through Aussie auto clubs. AE, BC, DC, MC, V.

The three-story Thredbo Alpine Hotel has comfortable rooms, a heated pool, sauna, spa, licensed restaurant and bistro, and several bars. The hotel is the social center of the community since it is the only licensed hotel in the village, and the ideal place for people who like being in the thick of things.

BERNTI'S MOUNTAIN INN, Mowamba Place, Thredbo, NSW 2627. Tel. 064/57-6332. 27 rms, 4 apartments. TV TEL

$ Rates (including breakfast): A$85–A$162 (U.S. $68–U.S. $129.60) per person. BC, MC, V.

The inn is a cozy stone-and-timber alpine lodge operated by Tricia and Bernd Hecher. It features a pleasant lounge with an open fire, a popular bar and licensed restaurant, an open-air café, a sauna, a spa, and attractive rooms. The apartments have cooking facilities, and the whole place has rustic charm.

3. THE BLUE MOUNTAINS

They were an unwelcome obstacle for the explorers who tried to cross them in the early 1800s, but for the past century the Blue Mountains have provided a scenic retreat for harried Sydneysiders in search of peace and quiet. Waterfalls now run down the sandstone plateaus that thwarted colonists' westward movement, and some of the eroded cliffs have taken on fanciful shapes. The area is heavily timbered with eucalyptus, and it's the oil vapor from these trees that makes the mountains look blue. While superb scenery is the major draw, the hospitality and good food at the region's cozy guesthouses also contribute to its popularity.

The mountains are most popular in winter (June through August), when the thermometer registers an average daytime winter maximum of 7°C (45°F) and guesthouse proprietors, celebrating Yule Fest, serve traditional English-style Christmas dinners, accompanied by caroling. Summer temperatures average 27°C (80°F).

Katoomba is the largest of the 26 townships in the Blue Mountains area. Other resort communities along the Great Western Highway include Wentworth Falls, Leura, Medlow Bath, Blackheath, and Mount Victoria. The combined Katoomba–Wentworth Falls area has a population of 13,942.

KATOOMBA

100km (62 miles) W of Sydney

GETTING THERE By Train There is frequent train service between Sydney and Katoomba; the trip takes about 2 hours. In addition, CityRail offers a Blue

Mountains Special Tour (A$34/U.S. $27.20 adults, A$14/U.S. $11.20 children) which includes return (round-trip) transportation to Katoomba and a bus tour of the area (Monday to Friday only).

By Bus or Car One-day coach tours are operated by AAT King's, Australian Pacific Tours, Newmans, Murrays, and others. Pioneer and Greyhound provide regular bus service (duration: 2 hr., 45 min.). Cost is A$23/U.S. $18.40. Those who opt to drive can make it in slightly less than 2 hours on the Great Western Highway.

ESSENTIALS Tourist information is dispensed at centers staffed by the **Blue Mountains Tourism Authority,** centrally located at Echo Point, Katoomba, NSW 2780 (tel. 047/82-0756), and on the Great Western Highway at Glenbrook (tel. 047/39-6266); both places are open daily from 9am to 5pm. The **area code** is 047.

In the late 1870s the first vacationers made the lengthy trip in Cobb & Co. stagecoaches, but today's visitors can hop on a train or bus, or get behind the wheel, and be in the mountains in only 2 hours. One-day tours are available, too, but to fully appreciate the area, more time is required.

WHAT TO SEE & DO

Mountain scenery is the main attraction in Katoomba. **The Three Sisters** is the best-known and most popular sight. The trio of pinnacles is best viewed from Echo Point off Cliff Drive, near the Visitor Information Centre. Other good viewpoints include **Evans Lookout, Govetts Leap,** and **Hargreaves Lookout.** Serious scenery buffs with their own cars should pick up a brochure giving details of the 10 self-guided drives in the area. These routes are signposted and easy to follow. If you take drive no. 4, be sure to include the 20-minute walk from the parking lot at Falls Reserve to **Princes Rock Lookout** for the best view of **Wentworth Falls.**

The **Skyway,** a cable car that glides 300 meters (990 ft.) above the floor of the Jamison Valley and provides a breathtaking view of **Orphan Rock** and **Katoomba Falls,** and the **Scenic Railway,** the world's steepest, are two popular rides. Each costs A$3 (U.S. $2.40). Both the Skyway and railway (tel. 82-2699) operate daily from 9am to 5pm (last trip 4:50pm). The Skyway Revolving Restaurant (tel. 82-2577) is open daily from 9:30am to 4:30pm.

Carless visitors who take the train to Katoomba can connect with the **Explorer Bus,** which operates on weekends, and goes to the major attractions (A$12.50/U.S. $10 adults, A$5/U.S. $4 children) or take the 3-hour Blue Mountains Highlights Tour offered Monday through Friday (A$25/U.S. $20 adults, A$12.50/U.S. $10 children). Both are operated by **Fantastic Aussie Tours** (tel. 82-1866).

In addition to the various viewpoints, the **Norman Lindsay Gallery,** 14 Norman Lindsay Crescent (via Chapman Parade), Faulconbridge, east of Katoomba (tel. 51-1067), is a worthwhile stop. Lindsay was an imaginative Australian artist and writer who lived from 1879 to 1969. The gallery, his former home, is a National Trust property and open on Friday, Saturday, and Sunday from 11am to 5pm; admission is A$3 (U.S. $2.40) for adults and A$1 (U.S. 80¢) for children. Lindsay's best-known work is *The Magic Pudding,* a children's classic, and his drawings of the book's characters are displayed in one room. The landscaped gardens around the gallery are dotted with 15 of his fountains. The tea garden serves Devonshire teas and boasts "we bake the best scones in town."

WHERE TO STAY & DINE

FAIRMONT RESORT, 1 Sublime Point Rd., Leura, NSW 2780. Tel. 047/82-5222. Fax 047/84-1685. 210 rms, 16 suites. A/C MINIBAR TV TEL
$ Rates: A$242 (U.S. $193.60) single or double; A$341–A$726 (U.S. $272.80–

U.S. $580.80) suite; A$35 (U.S. $28) rates extra person. Lower Sun–Fri, with 2-night minimum stay. AE, BC, DC, MC, V.

Compared to the cozy guesthouses found in the area, the Fairmont Resort seems like a gigantic palace. The modern four-story hotel overlooking the beautiful Jamison Valley opened in 1988, giving the Blue Mountains area its first deluxe accommodations. Each room has tea- and coffee-making facilities, a small refrigerator, a clock radio, and a fluffy bathrobe. In-room videos are provided, and queen-size beds are available. The resort was built at a cost of A$52 million (U.S. $42 million) and has won numerous awards.

Dining/Entertainment: Embers is a cozy lounge with a huge stone fireplace and an expansive mountain view; Jamison's is the fine-dining room; and the Terrace Restaurant is a casual brasserie with inside and outside seating. A tavern/disco, supper club, and coffee shop are also available.

Services: 24-hour room service, turn-down service, laundry, valet, concierge, baby-sitting, and massage.

Facilities: Indoor pool, outdoor pool, health club, gym, sauna, business center, children's center and supervised activity program, gift shop, four floodlit tennis courts, two glass-backed squash courts, and spas. The Leura Golf Course is adjacent.

AVONLEIGH GUEST HOUSE, 174 Lurline St., Katoomba, NSW 2780. Tel. 047/82-1534. Fax 047/82-5688. 12 rms.

$ Rates (including dinner and breakfast): A$95 (U.S. $76) per person midweek; A$110 (U.S. $88) per person weekend. Rates based on two people sharing. AE, BC, DC, MC, V. **Closed:** Late Dec–early Jan.

This cozy Federation period (1900–15) mountain home has comfortable bedrooms, a cozy ambience created by open fires and classical music, and cuisine that could compete favorably with that of the best city restaurants. Hosts Belinda and Ivan Harris are responsible for the success of the inn, which they renovated in 1986. While Belinda acts as hostess, Ivan, who trained as a chef in Lausanne and London, works his magic in the kitchen.

The home is a mixture of Edwardian and Victorian decor. Bedrooms feature double beds with antique headboards. Tufted velvet chairs, double cameo couches, sprays of dried flowers, and a high ceiling of white ornamental pressed metal create a Victorian air in the living room. Guests enjoy a complimentary glass of sherry before dinner, as well as free coffee and tea in the lounge day and night. Avonleigh is only a 5-minute walk from Echo Point; the hosts provide transfers to the railway station. Because of the delicate decor and peaceful nature of their inn, Belinda and Ivan don't encourage guests to bring children, and stairs make it an unlikely choice for handicapped travelers.

Ivan's gourmet dinners start with an entrée such as leek, mushroom, and sherry soup, or vegetable timbale with tomato coulis. The main course might be turkey with green peppercorns and avocado. Delicious desserts include vanilla bavarois or apple-and-banana brûlée followed by homemade chocolates. Popular Christmas dinners are served on Saturday nights throughout July. The dining room is open to nonresidents on a space-available basis; dinners cost A$35 (U.S. $28) per person. Diners bring their own wine.

THE LITTLE COMPANY GUEST HOUSE, 2 Eastview Ave., Leura, NSW 2781. Tel. 047/84-4023. Fax 047/82-5361. 35 rms, 5 suites. TV TEL

$ Rates (including dinner and breakfast): A$120 (U.S. $96) per person Mon–Thurs, A$140 (U.S. $112) per person Fri–Sun. Reduced rates for children under 12. AE, BC, DC, MC, V.

A few kilometers east of Katoomba in the community of Leura, the Little Company Guest House sits on parklike grounds surrounded by tennis courts, gardens, putting green, croquet lawn, barbecue area, and swimming pool. Hosts Margaret and Alan Hair have converted the original house, which was built in 1906 and for 50 years served as a retreat for nuns from the Little Company of Mary, into a charming inn. Ten front bedrooms have views of Mount Hay and Mount Wilson. There are also five country houses of four bedrooms each suitable for small groups. One room is set up to accommodate handicapped travelers. Soufflés, croissants, homemade yogurt, and eggs cocotte are served for breakfast, and three-course "home-style gourmet" dinners are served nightly in a delightful dining room with turn-of-the-century decor. Yule Fest dinners enliven Saturday nights during June, July, and August. Regular evening meals for nonresidents cost A$35 (U.S. $28). BYO.

BLACKHEATH

14km (9 miles) W of Katoomba, 114km (71 miles) W of Sydney

GETTING THERE   By Train or Car   CityRail trains provide frequent service from Sydney to Blackheath. Motorists proceed west from Katoomba on the Great Western Highway.

ESSENTIALS   The **area code** is 047.

Like neighboring Katoomba, Blackheath is surrounded by scenic rock formations and waterfalls. Four kilometers (2½ miles) further west, the township of Mount Victoria, perched on the highest peak in the Blue Mountains, is known for its antiques and craft shops and adventurous bushwalks.

WHAT TO SEE & DO

You don't have to be an experienced rider to enjoy the "holidays on horseback" offered by **Mountain River Riders,** c/o P.O. Box 95, Oberon, NSW 2787 (tel. 063/36-1890). All you need is an appreciation of the wilderness and a desire to see part of the real Australia. Warwick and Beryl Armstrong come from families who first bought property in this region when the country was only 70 years old; now they want to share the beauty of the bush they know so well with visitors. Pack trips can be tailored to suit individual needs, but typically last 3 days. They start at River Downs, the Armstrongs' home on the edge of Blue Mountains National Park, 20 kilometers (12 miles) south of Blackheath. From there, two experienced guides lead six to eight riders into a remote cattleman's outstation in the bush, making 17 river crossings along the way. Guests spend 2 nights in huts equipped with a fireplace, and during the day they fish (trout season is October to June), hike, swim, or just enjoy the silence afforded by the location. The 3-day/2-night experience costs about A$420 (U.S. $336) per person, or more if helicopter transfers from Sydney are required. Alternatively, day rides cost A$70 (U.S. $56) and include morning and afternoon tea, lunch in the bush, and 5 hours of riding.

Mountain River Riders has recently extended its operation to include four-wheel-drive trips, too. These day excursions are designed for a minimum of four people and a maximum of six; costs vary from A$75 to A$125 (U.S. $60 to U.S. $100) per person and offer lots of beautiful scenery, morning and afternoon tea, and a barbecue lunch. Horseback riding is included in the tour they call "River Downs Roamer." Highly recommended.

WHERE TO STAY

JEMBY-RINJAH LODGE, 336 Evans Lookout Rd., Blackheath, NSW 2785. Tel. 047/87-7622. 9 cabins (2 1-bedroom, 7 2-bedroom).
$ Rates: Cabin (occupied by up to two adults and two children) A$72 (U.S. $57.60) Mon–Thurs; A$90 (U.S. $72) Fri–Sun; A$10 (U.S. $8) extra adult; A$5 (U.S. $4) extra child; A$30 (U.S. $24) bunkhouse bed. BC, MC, V.

Jemby-Rinjah Lodge consists of nine deluxe cabins sleeping up to six people and a bunkhouse in a lovely wooded setting on the edge of the Grose Valley section of Blue Mountains National Park. This is a wonderful place for those who like hiking; the start of the grand canyon and clifftop walk are nearby. The two-bedroom/one-bath cabins are carpeted, have wood stoves in the living rooms, and boast fully equipped kitchens. Feather doonas grace each bed. Owners Peter and Margaret Quirk have a high regard for the fragility of the bush and designed the accommodations accordingly. Composting toilets and passive solar heating protect the environment, while the lovely wooden cabins provide guests all the comfort they could possibly expect. Hosts provide courtesy pickup from Blackheath Rail Station and can arrange baby-sitting.

JENOLAN CAVES

182km (113 miles) W of Sydney

GETTING THERE   By Train or Bus   Travelers using public transport can take a CityRail train to Katoomba and link up with daily Jenolan Caves excursions conducted by Fantastic Aussie Tours (tel. 047/82-1866). The CityRail combination train/coach tour ticket costs A$49 (U.S. $39.20) for adults and A$19 (U.S. $15.20) for children. The tour alone costs A$40 (U.S. $32) for adults and A$20 (U.S. $16) for children. These prices don't include cave tours.

One-day round-trip coach tours that include the Jenolan Caves are operated by AAT King's and Australian Pacific Tours. Pioneer and Greyhound provide regular bus service to Katoomba from Sydney.

By Car   It takes about 1½ hours to drive to the Jenolan Caves from Katoomba (turning left onto Jenolan Caves Road just after the township of Hartley).

ESSENTIALS   The **area code** is 063.

Underground limestone caves can be found in several places in New South Wales, but the best known are the Jenolan Caves, situated a short distance from the Kanangra Boyd National Park on a spur of the Great Dividing Range. Several million people have visited the caves since they were first opened in 1866, and I doubt that many have been disappointed. Stalactites and stalagmites combine with underground rivers to create a magical scene.

WHAT TO SEE & DO

Nine different caverns are open to the public and guided tours are conducted by the staff of the Jenolan Caves Reserve Trust (tel. 063/59-3311). The first cave tour starts at 9:45am weekdays and 9:30am weekends and holidays. The final tour starts at 5pm every day. Each costs A$8 to A$10 (U.S. $6.40 to U.S. $8) and lasts 1½ to 2 hours. Children under 16 pay half price. A kiosk sells snacks, and meals are available at Peppers Jenolan Caves House (see below).

WHERE TO STAY & DINE

PEPPERS JENOLAN CAVES HOUSE, Jenolan Caves, NSW 2790. Tel. 063/59-3304, or toll free 008/02-7927 in Australia. Fax 063/59-3227. 101 rms (some with bath).

$ Rates (including breakfast and dinner): A$70–A$105 (U.S. $56–U.S. $84) per adult. Rates are based on two adults sharing. A$28 (U.S. $22.40) per child under 12; children under 2, free. Three-day/2-night packages available. AE, BC, DC, MC, V.

The three-story hotel was built between 1888 and 1906 and is a classic example of late Victorian architecture. Constructed of limestone blocks, its grandness is strictly old world. Residents of New South Wales feel "100 years of affection" for this property, so there was great concern when the Peppers Hotel Group bought the historic structure from the state government in 1990. Watchful eyes kept track of the renovations, and there was great relief when it became apparent that Peppers would preserve—and in some cases restore—the integrity of the building while adding the conveniences today's travelers expect.

The wildlife reserve surrounding the hotel is ideal for walking and scenic drives. Blooming wildflowers makes it especially pretty in the spring.

Dining/Entertainment: Peppers' properties, which include a guesthouse in the Hunter Valley and a seaside resort hotel in Terrigal, all have one thing in common: great food. Therefore, it wasn't surprising that their first move at Caves House was to install a new chef (whom they stole from one of the best restaurants in the Hunter Valley). Given the quality of the traditional country cuisine, the dinner-bed-and-breakfast tariffs and 2-night/6-meal packages are incredibly good value. In addition to the grand dining room, with its 16-foot ceiling and huge antique sideboards, a café lounge on the ground floor serves light lunches and Devonshire teas.

4. THE GOLDEN WEST

West of the Blue Mountains and the Great Dividing Range is a region of New South Wales called the Golden West, so named because Australia's first assayable gold was found there in 1851.

The discovery of the precious metal brought diggers and Chinese workers into an area that was previously not heavily populated. Towns grew overnight, and many fine homes were constructed with goldfield money. Some 13 tons of gold were found around Gulgong within 5 years; today Gulgong is known as "the town on the 10-dollar note."

While for all practical purposes mining has come to a halt, this part of the state continues to thrive as an important agricultural area. The city of Orange is known as "Australia's Big Apple," not because it in any way resembles its U.S. namesake, but because two-thirds of all the apples in New South Wales are grown there. Mudgee has emerged in the last few years as an important grape-growing district; sheep and cattle thrive in the region's fertile pastures.

For visitors, the main points of interest are relics of the gold-mining days—and a chance to understand this important part of Australia's history a bit better.

BATHURST

211km (131 miles) W of Sydney

GETTING THERE By Plane, Train, Bus, or Car Eastern Australia Airlines has flights to Bathurst from Sydney. Countrylink offers direct rail service from Sydney's Central Station (A$23/U.S. $18.40 economy, A$32/U.S. $25.60 first class). The bus trip, on either Pioneer or Greyhound, takes 3 hours and 45 minutes (A$28/U.S. $22.40). Motorists follow the Great Western Highway through the Blue Mountains.

ESSENTIALS Tourist information is available in the **Court House,** Russell Street, Bathurst, NSW 2795 (tel. 063/33-6288), open Monday through Friday from 9am to 4:30pm and on Saturday and Sunday from 10am to 4pm. The **area code** is 063.

I t's ironic that the two main attractions in this sedate old city (pop. 27,500) are its historic connections to the past and its very modern racing circuit.

WHAT TO SEE & DO

The modern **Mount Panorama Circuit** is the site of major car races, including the Toohey's 1000 held in October and the James Hardie 12-Hour Race at Easter. Visitors who aren't here at these times can drive the circuit (no charge) and visit the **Bathurst Motor Racing Museum** (tel. 32-1872) in the pit area. It's open Saturday through

Monday, Wednesday, and Thursday from 9am to 4:30pm, and Tuesday and Friday from 9am to 2pm (A$3/U.S. $2.40 for adults, A$1/U.S. 80¢ for children).

At the **Bathurst Sheep and Cattle Drome** (tel. 37-3634), you can learn about milking and shearing and watch sheepdog demonstrations. Shows are daily at 11:30am.

Bathurst has more than its fair share of attractive historical buildings. Of particular interest: **Abercrombie House,** a huge mansion built in the late 1870s (open Wednesday afternoon), the **Court House** (which contains a small museum as well as a tourist-information office), and **Miss Traill's House,** a colonial Georgian cottage built in 1845 (open Sunday from 11am to 4:30pm).

Bathurst Gold Diggings, located at Karingal Village, Mount Panorama (tel. 31-3319), is an authentic reconstruction of an 1860s gold mine, complete with restored machines in action and a film on gold discoveries. Visitors can try their luck at panning, and while I can't promise you good results, it sometimes still happens in the Golden West: at Ophir, near Orange, a nugget worth more than A$100,000 (U.S. $80,000) was found in 1979.

WHERE TO STAY & DINE

GOVERNOR MACQUARIE MOTOR INN, 11-21 Charlotte St., Bathurst, NSW 2795. Tel. 063/31-2211. Fax 063/31-4754. 37 rms, 2 suites. A/C MINIBAR TV TEL

$ Rates: A$60–A$75 (U.S. $48–U.S. $60) single; A$75–A$87 (U.S. $60–U.S. $69.60) double; A$10 (U.S. $8) extra person. AE, BC, DC, MC, V.

The Governor Macquarie Motor Inn is a centrally located two-story motel. All units have showers, coffee- and tea-making facilities, and small refrigerators; 19 have bathtubs. Other features include a guest laundry and swimming pool. A la carte meals are served in The Governors and drinks are available in the Ribbon Gang Bar.

MUDGEE

264km (164 miles) NW of Sydney

GETTING THERE   By Plane, Bus, or Car   Hazelton Airlines flies between Sydney and Mudgee. A Countrylink coach—not train—ticket costs about A$30 (U.S. $24). Take the Great Western Highway and connect with Highway 86 if you're driving; allow about 4 hours.

ESSENTIALS   Take your questions to the **Tourist Information Centre,** 64 Market Street, Mudgee, NSW 2850 (tel. 063/72-5874 or 72-5875), open weekdays from 8:30am to 4:30pm, on Saturday from 9:30am to 4pm, and Sunday from 9:30am to 2pm; pick up a free visitors' guide.

The **area code** is 063.

SPECIAL EVENTS   The **Mudgee Wine Festival,** which includes eating, drinking, listening to good music, and enjoying spring weather, takes place in September. The **Rose Festival** is held every April.

Once known for its "Mudgee mud," beer with sediment in the bottom of the bottle, this attractively laid-out town (pop. 7,500) has become known for its vineyards and the fine wines they produce. Besides grapes, the area produces stud cattle and sheep, fine wool, and honey.

WHAT TO SEE & DO

Mudgee's meadery and 18 wineries are open daily and welcome visitors. For the most part, they are small operations, and often it is the proprietor who conducts the tastings in the cellar. **Craigmoor Winery,** Craigmoor Lane (tel. 72-2208), is open Monday through Saturday from 10am to 4:30pm and on Sunday from 11am to 4pm. **Montrose Winery,** on Henry Lawson Drive (tel. 73-3853), is open Monday through Friday from 9am to 4pm and on Saturday and Sunday from 10am to 4pm. **Miramar,** also on Henry Lawson Drive (tel. 73-3874), is open daily from 9am to 5pm. The wineries are clustered together only a short way out of town; they're easy to find using the map in the visitors' guide supplied free of charge at the Tourist Information Centre.

After you've learned about the local vino, you may want to investigate the two major honey factories. At the **Mudgee Honey Company,** 28 Robertson Street (tel. 72-2359), visitors can see bees working under glass and taste various types of the pure natural product; it's open on weekdays from 9am to 5pm and on weekends from 9am to 4pm. At **Honey Haven,** Gulgong Road (tel. 72-4478), they sell 70 different flavors of honey, conduct tours, and offer tasting.

After looking around Mudgee, you may want to take a side trip to **Gulgong,** an atmospheric town 27 kilometers (17 miles) to the north. The quaint place has been described as "a Walt Disney set." The Pioneers Museum, 73 Herbert Street, Gulgong (tel. 063/74-1513), is worth a peek.

WHERE TO STAY

COUNTRY PARADISE RESORT, Cassilis Rd., Mudgee, NSW 2850. Tel. 063/72-4500, or toll free 008/02-7916 in Australia. Fax 063/72-4525. 70 rms, 4 suites. A/C TV TEL

$ Rates: A$120 (U.S. $96) double; A$185 (U.S. $148) suite; A$10 (U.S. $8) extra person. AE, BC, DC, MC, V.

This two-story property is the newest lodging in Mudgee. Each room has a clock radio, coffee- and tea-making facilities, and a small refrigerator. Meals are served in the à la carte Paradise Restaurant or in the Country Bistro. Limited room service is also available. The cocktail lounge, Holtermanns, is named after Bernardt Holtermann who found the largest gold specimen in the world. There's also a public bar on the premises. Guests can use the heated indoor pool, spa, and sauna.

WINNING POST MOTOR INN, 101-105 Church St., Mudgee, NSW 2850. Tel. 063/72-3333, or toll free 008/02-7915 in Australia. Fax 063/72-1208. 32 rms, 2 suites. A/C MINIBAR TV TEL

$ Rates: A$70–A$80 (U.S. $56–U.S. $64) double; A$88–A$110 (U.S. $70.40–U.S. $88) suite; A$8 (U.S. $6.40) extra person. Surcharge Sat night and public holidays. No-smoking rooms available. Reservations can be made through Flag Inns. AE, BC, DC, MC, V.

This motor inn has all the usual modern amenities, plus a licensed restaurant, laundry, outdoor pool, spa, half-court tennis, and playground. In-room videos, clock radios, coffee- and tea-making facilities, and small refrigerators are in all quarters. Limited room service is available.

WHERE TO DINE

AUGUSTINE VINEYARD RESTAURANT, George Campbell Dr. Tel. 72-3880.

Cuisine: AUSTRALIAN. **Reservations:** Essential for dinner.

$ Prices: Appetizers A$5–A$6 (U.S. $4–U.S. $4.80); main courses A$12–A$13 (U.S. $9.60–U.S. $10.40); Devonshire tea A$5 (U.S. $4); cheese-and-fruit plate A$5 (U.S. $4) per person. AE, BC, MC, V.

Open: Morning tea daily 10am–noon; lunch daily noon–2pm; afternoon tea daily 2–4pm; dinner Fri–Sat by advance reservation only; wine tasting daily 10am–4pm.

Light lunch or Devonshire teas can be enjoyed here at picnic tables in a patio shaded by grape vines, giving credence to their slogan: "Dine beneath the vines at Augustine Wines." The view of the vineyard on two sides is delightful. In addition to the al fresco dining, meals are served inside is a large room with a colonial ambience. Main courses include chargrilled Mudgee sirloin of beef, roast rack of lamb, or baked rainbow trout. The tasting room is nearby, and there's a children's play area.

DUBBO

420km (260 miles) NW of Sydney

GETTING THERE **By Plane** Ansett Express Airlines and Hazelton Airlines provide air service between Sydney and Dubbo. The flight lasts 55 minutes and costs A$133 (U.S. $106.40).

By Train or Bus Countrylink trains take 6½ hours and cost A$63.50 (U.S. $50.80) first class and A$45 (U.S. $36) economy. Dubbo is a popular stopover point for many coach companies, including Greyhound, Pioneer, and Bus Australia, on the routes between Melbourne and Brisbane, Adelaide and Brisbane, and Sydney and Adelaide.

By Car If you're driving, Dubbo lies at the intersection of the Newell and Mitchell highways.

ESSENTIALS Tourist information is available at the **Dubbo Visitors Centre,** corner of Darling and Erskine streets, Dubbo, NSW 2830 (tel. 068/84-1422), open daily from 9am to 5pm. Another information center is located at the **Dubbo Museum,** 232-234 Macquarie Street (tel. 068/82-5359). The **area code** is 068.

Sited on the Macquarie River, Dubbo (pop. 34,000) is the regional capital for this part of the state. The city is best known to tourists as the home of the Western Plains Zoo.

WHAT TO SEE & DO

WESTERN PLAINS ZOO, 5km (3 miles) south of town. Tel. 82-5888.

This is by far the largest open-range zoo in the country. Animals from six continents, including giraffes, elephants, rhinoceroses, tigers, zebras, and monkeys, are displayed in natural settings throughout the wildlife park's 300 landscaped hectares (741 acres). Since the animals are contained by moats and other subtle means, they give the illusion of roaming free; the absence of cages and bars is much appreciated by visitors. Native Australian fauna, such as koalas, kangaroos, dingoes, and emus, are also included in the collection. Because of the zoo's size, you have a choice of walking, renting a bike or Jeep, or driving your car past the exhibits. Children can pet young animals in the Friendship Farm. A bistro and fast-food kiosk overlook a lake.

Admission: A$13 (U.S. $10.40) adults, A$6 (U.S. $4.80) children 4–16; under 4, free.

Open: Daily 9am–4pm. **Directions:** Newell Hwy. south; turn left on Obley Rd.

OLD DUBBO GAOL [JAIL], Macquarie St. Tel. 82-8122.

Located in the center of the city between the State and Commonwealth banks, the old gaol has been restored. It was actually in use until 1966, and a tour of the gallows, padded cells, and hangman's kit gives some insight into Australia's slightly gruesome past. Animated models of prisoners reveal their lives of crime to visitors.

Admission: A$3.50 (U.S. $2.80) adults, A$1.50 (U.S. $1.20) children.

Open: Daily 9am–5pm (no admission after 4:30pm).

WHERE TO STAY

ASHWOOD COUNTRY CLUB MOTEL, Whylandra St. (Newell Hwy.), Dubbo, NSW 2830. Tel. 068/81-8700, or toll free 008/33-5005 in Australia. Fax 068/81-8930. Reservations can be made through Flag Inns. 39 rms and suites. A/C MINIBAR TV TEL

$ Rates: A$75 (U.S. $60) single; A$85 (U.S. $68) double; A$95 (U.S. $76) suite; A$10 (U.S. $8) extra person. AE, BC, DC, MC, V.

This motel is a cut above the average. To begin with, each room has a queen-size bed, a toaster and an ironing board, in addition to the usual coffee- and tea-making facilities and small refrigerator. For an extra A$7 (U.S. $5.60) guests can rent a VCR and as many videos as they choose. The facilities include a guests' laundry, an outdoor pool, spa, tennis court, and playground. Meals are served in a licensed restaurant or delivered to units. Some quarters have water beds; eight have bathtubs. Handicapped facilities are available. This lodging is conveniently located 1 kilometer (½ mile) from the zoo.

CASCADES MOTOR INN, 147 Cobra St., Dubbo, NSW 2830 Tel. 068/ 82-3888, or toll free 008/02-7256 in Australia. Fax 068/82-0906. 36 rms. A/C MINIBAR TV TEL

$ Rates: A$60–A$79 (U.S. $48–U.S. $63.20) single; A$65–A$85 (U.S. $52–U.S. $68) double; A$8 (U.S. $6.40) extra person. Reservations can be made through Flag Inns. AE, BC, DC, MC, V.

This two-story property has all the normal amenities, plus bathtubs in 14 units and a spa bath in one. There's a licensed restaurant on the premises and limited room service. Guests can use the laundry facilities and pool.

WHERE TO DINE

MATILDA'S FAMILY STEAKHOUSES, corner of Mitchell and Newell highways. Tel. 84-3333.
Cuisine: CONTEMPORARY AUSTRALIAN. **Reservations:** Strongly recommended for dinner Thurs–Sun.
$ Prices: Appetizers A$3.99–A$5.49 (U.S. $3.20–U.S. $4.40); main courses A$8.45–A$13.99 (U.S. $6.80–U.S. $11.20); children's meals A$3.99–A$4.49 (U.S. $3.20–U.S. $3.60). Public holiday surcharge 10%. BC, MC, V.
Open: Lunch daily noon–2:30pm; dinner daily 6–9:30pm.

If you've ever eaten at a Sizzler in the U.S., you might have a spell of déjà vu at Matilda's. The two places are a great deal alike: Both offer wholesome, inexpensive meals and both welcome families. Dubbo's Matilda's (there's another one in Orange) has an attractive Australiana decor, which includes bentwood chairs, wooden tables, exposed-brick walls painted mushroom, and forest-green woodwork. All very smart and clean.

Sample main courses include lemon and tandoori chicken, rump steak, and a seafood platter. All main-course prices include a trip to the extensive salad bar. Matilda's is licensed to serve alcohol, but diners can bring their own if they wish. The slogan here is "Good times, good tucker."

5. THE HUNTER VALLEY

The Hunter Valley is the oldest commercial wine-producing area in Australia. The first vines were planted more than 150 years ago after attempts at establishing vineyards around Sydney Cove proved fruitless. South Australia produces more wine, but with its rich, fertile soil and its pleasant, often sunny climate, the Hunter Valley is the second most important region and has the advantage, from the traveler's point of view, of being relatively close to Sydney. Since this is the Southern Hemisphere, the harvest months are February and March.

The Hunter Valley is an area of beautiful rolling countryside, with sections of farmland interspersed between the vineyards. If you have transportation, it's easy to get around during the day; but at night, signposts on the rural roads aren't lit, so you have to go slowly and take care as you make your way back to your accommodations after dinner.

In addition to wine-related activities, the Hunter also presents opportunities for gallery browsing, craft shopping, and even hot-air ballooning.

CESSNOCK & POKOLBIN

190km (118 miles) N of Sydney

GETTING THERE **By Plane** Yanda Airlines flies between Sydney and Cessnock.

By Train or Bus Countrylink coaches and trains go to Maitland, which is about 30 kilometers (19 miles) away. The coach costs A$15.50 (U.S. $12.40). The train costs A$27 (U.S. $21.60) first class and A$19 (U.S. $15.20) economy. A taxi from Maitland to Cessnock will set you back about A$20 (U.S. $16). Several Sydney sightseeing companies, such as AAT King's and Australian Pacific Tours, operate 1- and 2-day excursions to the Hunter Valley.

By Car If you drive from Sydney, the trip will take about 2 hours via the Pacific Highway, the Sydney-Newcastle Freeway, and Highway 82.

ESSENTIALS The **Cessnock Tourist Information Centre,** on the corner of Wollombi Road and Mount View Road, Cessnock, NSW 2325 (tel. 049/90-4477), is open Monday through Friday from 9am to 5pm, Saturday from 9:30am to 5pm, and Sunday from 9:30am to 3:30pm. The **area code** is 049.

A few wineries are located in the Upper Hunter Valley, but tourists with only a day or two for tasting and touring would do well to confine themselves to the 35 places found in the lower part. Cessnock is the only town of any size (pop. 16,916), and provides commercial support for the wineries that dot the rolling countryside of the Lower Hunter Valley. Most of the wineries are located nearby in an area that spreads out from the village of Pokolbin. Cessnock and Pokolbin are so close together it's hard to tell where one ends and the other begins.

WHAT TO SEE & DO
Attractions

The best place to start your exploration of the area is at the **Hunter Valley Wine Society,** 4 Wollombi Road, Cessnock, NSW 2325 (tel. 049/90-6699), where 38 wineries are represented under one roof. This is a good place to get an overview before you start out on your own because the staff consists of local people who know each company's products. It's open daily from 9am to 4:30pm for tastings and bottle sales. There's a small charge for tasting.

Of the 46 wineries operating in the valley, 35 welcome visitors to their cellars, where generous tasting policies prevail. Some operations, like Petersons (see below), are family businesses producing small quantities of exceptionally good wine. On the other extreme, **Hungerford Hills** has created an entire "wine village," including a children's playground, Cellar Restaurant, a picnic area, and a shopping complex.

Tyrrell's, established in 1858, is the oldest family-owned Hunter Valley winery; it's open 8am to 5pm Monday through Saturday. The **Rothbury Estate,** which is open daily, is a good example of a successful, fairly new operation.

There's always one member of the family in the tasting room at **Petersons,** whose chardonnays have won some impressive awards. Ironically, Shirley and Ian Peterson never dreamed of growing grapes when they bought their Hunter Valley property in 1964. They intended to run cattle, but by 1971 the pharmacist and his wife were planting their first crop. In 1974 they crushed some grapes and squeezed them through pantyhose to make wine for themselves. Their 1986 chardonnay won the 1987 Qantas Cup, a prestigious America vs. Australia competition.

In addition to tasting, **Lindeman's Winery** provides picnic tables, barbecues, a children's play area, a small museum of wine-making equipment, and an educational video. Other well-known companies include **Wyndham Estate, Tulloch's, McWilliams,** and **Draytons.**

If you don't have your own car, you can tour the area in a limousine with **Top Hat Tours** (tel. 049/90-1699). The most romantic means of travel are the elegant horse-drawn carriages operated by **Somerset Carriages** (tel. 049/98-7591). They offer an all-day excursion which includes a gourmet picnic, with wine served by a lake, and transportation to four wineries for tasting.

Hot-air ballooning takes place daily at sunrise from February through November. If you'd like to glide over the Hunter Valley, call **Balloon Aloft** in Cessnock (tel. 049/38-1955, or toll free 008/02-8568 in Australia). The cost is about A$180 (U.S. $144) for adults and A$120 (U.S. $96) for children aged 8 to 12 and includes a champagne breakfast.

Shopping

Don't miss **Butterflies Gallery,** Broke Road, Pokolbin (tel. 98-7724), where Allen Black displays the paintings and crafts of some of Australia's most talented artists. Much of the artwork, pottery, glass, wood, and hand-painted silk is the work of New South Wales craftspeople. Look for Peter Crisp's glass pieces, Alan Williams' wood work, Pat Cahill's pottery, and Jim Trier's cattle-horn objects and pewter ware. All work is by Australians. Allen will ship your purchases if necessary. Open daily from 10am to 5pm. Butterflies Tea Room is adjacent (see below).

Peppers Creek Antiques, at the corner of Broke and Ekerts roads, Pokolbin, near Peppers Guest House (tel. 98-7532), sells antique jewelry, Georgian and Victorian furniture, and old-world bric-a-brac; open Wednesday through Sunday from 10am to 5pm.

WHERE TO STAY

Dollarwise travelers will plan to be in the Hunter Valley during the week when the rates for lodging are *significantly lower* than they are on weekends.

PEPPERS HUNTER VALLEY, Ekerts Rd., Pokolbin, NSW 2321. Tel. 049/98-7596. Fax 049/98-7739. 49 rms. TEL

$ **Rates:** A$185–A$205 (U.S. $148–U.S. $164) single or double; A$25 (U.S. $20) extra person. Children under 12 stay free in parents' room. Lower midweek rates and packages. AE, BC, DC, MC, V.

Peppers exudes a country-colonial ambience in perfect accord with the 24 hectares (60 acres) of verdant rolling hills that surround it. Each of the inn's three wings is built in the style of an early Australian home, painted maize (with dark green shutters) and topped by a typical tin roof. One could easily believe that Peppers had been the residence of a wealthy settler, but, in truth, it's only a few years old. Inside, each of the bedrooms has antique cedar furniture and old paintings. Skylights and the lack of bathtubs are the only telltale signs of modern construction (all guest rooms have showers). Throughout the inn, large windows and French doors frame the surrounding country views. Considering the fine accommodations, good food, and other facilities offered, it isn't surprising that the country house hotel won the New South Wales Tourism Award in 1991 and that it's filled with sophisticated Sydneysiders nearly every weekend. Overseas visitors should either make their reservations well ahead of time or plan on a midweek stay.

Dining/Entertainment: In the Georgian colonial dining room (open to the public), copper pots and wicker baskets hang on brick walls painted blue-green. Dinner for two costs about A$80 (U.S. $64), plus wine. The big open fire and Sanderson upholstery in the bar and lounge are reminiscent of an English manor house.

Services: Massage, laundry.

Facilities: Tennis courts, a jogging/walking track, pool, spa, gym, sauna, and beauty shop.

THE HUNTER RESORT, Hermitage Rd., Pokolbin, NSW 2321. Tel. 049/98-7777. Fax 049/98-7787. 30 rms. A/C TV TEL
$ Rates: A$110 (U.S. $88) single or double; A$10 (U.S. $8) extra person. Lower midweek rates. Lower rates through Aussie auto clubs. AE, BC, MC, V.
All units at this motel have a view of vineyards in the foreground and the Brokenback Mountain Range in the distance. The place has a natural-log look on the outside, but features modern amenities inside. These include clock radios, coffee- and tea-making setup, small refrigerators, and queen-size beds. Additional facilities include a self-service laundry, an outdoor swimming pool, spa, children's playground, tennis courts, and barbecue area with picnic benches and covered pergola. The management can arrange baby-sitting.

POKOLBIN VILLAGE MOTEL, 188 Broke Rd., Pokolbin, NSW 2320. Tel. 049/98-7670. Fax 049/98-7670. 16 2-bedroom units. A/C MINIBAR TV TEL
$ Rates: A$105–A$150 (U.S. $84–U.S. $120) double; A$20 (U.S. $16) extra person. Lower midweek rates. Lower rates through Aussie auto clubs. BC, MC, V.
This motel is part of a village-style commercial area which also includes a general store, coffee shop, and licensed restaurant. All units have two bedrooms and one bathroom with a shower, except one has a bathtub, and one has a spa bath. Three units have full kitchens, and all quarters have tea- and coffee-making facilities, small refrigerators, toasters, and microwaves. There's a saltwater pool, playground, volleyball court, tennis court, and picnic area on the premises.

THALGARA ESTATE, Debeyers Rd., Pokolbin, NSW 2320. Tel. 049/98-7717. 6 units (3 studio and 3 1-bedroom). TV TEL
$ Rates: A$85 (U.S. $68) studio double; A$140 (U.S. $112) 1-bedroom for two to four people. Lower midweek rates. Lower rates for stays of more than 2 nights. BC, MC, V.

Ⓢ Steve and Sue Lamb have built six units near their home in a countryside setting surrounded by many acres of vineyards. The three studios and three one-bedroom units can sleep from two to four guests; each has a bathroom, a fully equipped kitchen, open-beam ceilings, contemporary furnishings, and a patio with table and chairs. Hosts can arrange baby-sitting and enjoy showing guests around their winery.

WHERE TO DINE

In addition to the restaurant at Peppers (see "Where to Stay," above), you might try the following:

BLAXLAND'S RESTAURANT, Broke Rd., Pokolbin. Tel. 98-7550.
Cuisine: INTERNATIONAL. **Reservations:** Recommended.
$ Prices: Appetizers A$9.60–A$11.20 (U.S. $7.70–U.S. $9); main courses A$15–A$18 (U.S. $12–U.S. $14.40). Weekend and public holiday surcharge A$2 (U.S. $1.60) per person. AE, BC, DC, MC, V.
Open: Lunch daily from 2pm; dinner daily from 7pm.

★ The restaurant was constructed from the remains of the original Blaxland homestead built in the nearby town of Broke in 1827. It was the restaurant's proprietor, Chris Barnes, who had the idea of recycling the convict-made sandstone blocks and bricks when the colonial house was razed. In spite of the unusual architecture and historic atmosphere, the most outstanding feature of Blaxland's is its extensive wine list. Chris manages to keep more than 100 wines available, and he has a license to sell wine by the bottle or the case.
On a typical evening the blackboard menu may list such main courses as rack of lamb with mint sauce, duckling with orange sauce, and trout with roasted almonds. Typical desserts include raspberry crumble, pavlova, and pecan nut pie. Be sure you have some damper bread. I also suggest that you make a point of meeting the host, who's very knowledgeable about the area and wines.

CASUARINA RESTAURANT, Hermitage Rd., Pokolbin. Tel. 98-7888.

Cuisine: INTERNATIONAL WITH ASIAN OVERTONES. **Reservations:** Recommended.
$ Prices: Appetizers A$7.50–A$13.50 (U.S. $6–U.S. $10.80); main courses A$16–A$23 (U.S. $12.80–U.S. $18.40). Children's meals 50% discount. Public holiday and weekend surcharge A$3 (U.S. $2.40) per person. AE, DC, MC, V.
Open: Lunch Sat–Sun from noon; dinner daily from 7pm.

The Casuarina is a very special dining venue. The restaurant is housed in a building owner/chef Peter Meier bought and enlarged in 1982. He named it after a native Australian tree because "when the wind blows through casuarinas, it makes a beautiful sound." A cozy bar with sofas and easy chairs is adjacent to the dining room, where a dozen huge white paper lanterns hang from cathedral ceilings. The sandstone block walls have been painted peach, and large flower arrangements rest on antique mahogany sideboards.

Peter believes that "the greatness of food lies in its simplicity," so he prepares food that is light and healthful. This surprises many people who know that Peter is German and learned his trade in hotels in Salzburg and Paris. "I also believe in custom-made food and food that is cooked very quickly," he says, so many dishes are flambéed at the table. Typical entrées might include stir-fried prawns, pan-fried duck livers, or sugar-cured Atlantic salmon. Some popular main courses are: roast filet of veal, rolled chicken breast, and rack of lamb. Flambés include chili lobster and prawns, and seafood Thai style. Because the Casuarina is popular with local vintners, the wine list often includes vintages unobtainable at other dining spots.

The Casuarina Country Inn, comprised of eight suites, is adjacent to the restaurant and also owned and personally supervised by Peter Meier. Guests have the use of a swimming pool, tennis court, sauna, and croquet lawn.

POKOLBIN KIOSK, in the Hungerford Hill Wine Village, Broke Rd., Pokolbin. Tel. 98-7518.
Cuisine: LIGHT LUNCHES. **Reservations:** Not required.
$ Prices: About A$5 (U.S. $4) per person. No credit cards.
Open: Mon–Fri 10am–4pm, Sat–Sun 10am–5pm.

Located in the Hungerford Hills complex, Pokolbin Kiosk sells unusual sandwiches such as smoked salmon, caper, onion, sprouts, and lettuce. More traditional fare such as pumpkin soup with hot crusty damper bread is also available. You might also like to try Australian ANZAC biscuits or homemade carrot and banana cake. Picnic tables are provided. BYO.

BUTTERFLIES TEA ROOM AND ART GALLERY, Broke Rd., Pokolbin. Tel. 98-7724.
Cuisine: HOME-STYLE AUSTRALIAN. **Reservations:** Recommended at lunch.
$ Prices: Devonshire tea A$6 (U.S. $4.80); light lunch about A$8 (U.S. $6.40). BC, DC, MC, V.
Open: Daily 10am–5pm.

Everything Sue and Allen Black serve is made in their kitchen. My mother's meat loaf is wonderful, but it can't compare with Sue's, which she serves with damper bread and salad. Butterflies' version of a ploughman's lunch contains cheese, salami, and roast beef. This is also a great place for tea: The sideboard holds tins of Twinings and cakestands bearing mouth-watering delights. Part of the pleasure of stopping at this pretty place, with its light blue walls, open fire, and view of the countryside, is meeting jolly Sue and her congenial husband. Highly recommended. BYO.

6. THE COAST NORTH OF SYDNEY

The **Pacific Highway** leads travelers over Sydney's Harbour Bridge, through white-collar northern suburbs, and to the bushland at the edge of the metropolitan region. Farther on, it passes the Hawkesbury River and the resort district around Gosford. The highway skirts the recreation areas of Tuggerah Lake and Lake Macquarie and the city of Newcastle, and then it hugs the coast, while the other major north-south road, the **New England Highway,** heads inland. Many people elect to follow the Pacific Highway all the way to Brisbane, a distance of 1,000 kilometers (620 miles), which is best covered in at least 2 days and could easily occupy a week at a leisurely pace. The popularity of this route can be attributed both to the varied scenery and to the good lodging and dining facilities found along the way. The beach vistas are excellent, and when the highway leaves the coast at places like Taree and Kempsey, travelers encounter heavily timbered terrain, as well as inland lakes, rivers, and green mountain slopes. Most of the ocean viewpoints require a detour of at least a few kilometers, which can add to the time the journey takes. Even if your time is limited, don't miss the views from **Crescent Head, Nambucca Head, Yamba,** and—best of all—**Byron Bay,** where a picturesque lighthouse marks the most easterly point in Australia.

The biggest coastal resort centers are Port Macquarie and Coffs Harbour. Murwillumbah, near the Queensland border, is the gateway to the beautiful Tweed Valley and Mount Warning National Park. In between these places are great surf, several outstanding fishing spots, an award-winning resort, a down-under dude ranch, and a banana 10 meters (33 ft.) long. How's that for a trip?

PORT MACQUARIE

423km (262 miles) N of Sydney

GETTING THERE   By Plane   Eastern Australia Airlines flies between Sydney and Port Macquarie. The one-way fare is about A$143 (U.S. $114.40). The airport is close to town and a taxi should cost about A$5 (U.S. $4).

By Bus or Car   The coach fare from Sydney is A$39 (U.S. $31.20), and the trip takes 7 hours. The trip from Brisbane takes almost 11 hours and costs A$45 (U.S. $36). Motorists follow the Pacific Highway north from Sydney.

ESSENTIALS   The **Visitor Information Centre,** located at the water end of Horton Street near Clarence Street (tel. 065/83-1293, or toll free 008/02-5935 in Australia), is open Monday through Friday from 8:30am to 5pm and on Saturday and Sunday from 8:30am to 4pm. The **area code** is 065.

Located roughly midway between Sydney and the border with neighboring Queensland, "Port," as the locals call it (pop. 26,000) is at the mouth of the Hastings River, an ideal spot for boating. There are also very good ocean beaches, including Flynn's, which is exceptionally good for surfing. Horton Street is the main shopping area.

WHAT TO SEE & DO

Timbertown, 23 kilometers (14 miles) west of Port Macquarie on the Oxley Highway (tel. 85-2322), is a re-creation of a turn-of-the-century timber-cutting and logging settlement, and visitors walk through and watch timber workers splitting logs, blacksmiths at work, and a steam train that still runs. Timbertown is open daily from 9am to 5pm; the entrance fee is A$13 (U.S. $10.40).

Old World Timber Art, 120 Hastings River Drive (tel. 83-2502), presents an opportunity to watch the Cruthers family turning wood into goblets, canisters, bowls, vases, and other items for sale. Artisans work Monday through Friday from 8:30am to 3:30pm. The shop is open Monday through Friday from 8:30am to 5pm and Saturday and Sunday from 10am to 4pm. Admission is free of charge and complimentary coffee and tea are served.

River cruises are another popular Port Macquarie activity. The 257-passenger vessel *Port Venture* (tel. 83-3058) departs daily from the foot of Clarence Street at 10am and 2pm. Tickets cost A$11.50 (U.S. $9.20) for the 2-hour cruise on the scenic Hastings River.

WHERE TO STAY

PELICAN SHORES RESORT, Park St., Port Macquarie, NSW 2444. Tel. 065/83-3999, or toll free 008/02-5271 in Australia. Fax 065/84-0397. 83 suites. A/C MINIBAR TV TEL

$ Rates: A$130 (U.S. $104) single; A$160 (U.S. $128) double; A$185 (U.S. $148) family suite; A$260 (U.S. $208) executive suite; A$24 (U.S. $19.20) extra person. High-season rates (Christmas to mid-Jan) 30% more. Children under 12 stay free in parents' room. BC, DC, MC, V.

Pelican Shores offers the most luxurious accommodations in town. As its name implies, the resort is located on the waterfront, and seabirds, as well as boats of all sizes and shapes, pass back and forth in front of the two-story property. Each room has either a queen-size bed or two twins, coffee- and tea-making facilities, a small fridge, toaster, and various other amenities. The family suites have kitchenettes and queen-size beds, with twin beds in screened-off areas; the executive suites offer king-size beds, expansive water views, kitchenettes, and spa baths. All quarters have private balconies, ceiling fans, free in-house movies, and tub/shower combinations. Two rooms have been specially equipped for the disabled.

Dining/Entertainment: The Shores restaurant and bar overlook the water.

Services: 24-hour room service, turn-down service, baby-sitting, massage, and laundry.

Facilities: Indoor and outdoor spas, heated seawater pool, children's pool, sauna, tennis courts, volleyball court, children's playroom and playground, bicycle rental, and mini-golf. Boats and canoes can be rented next door at the marina.

EL PASO MOTOR INN, 29 Clarence St., Port Macquarie, NSW 2444. Tel. 065/83-1944, or toll free 008/02-7965 in Australia. Fax 065/84-1021. 55 rms, 2 suites. A/C MINIBAR TV TEL

$ Rates: A$70 (U.S. $56) single; A$79 (U.S. $63.20) double; A$93 (U.S. $74.40) suite; A$9 (U.S. $7.20) extra person. A$15 (U.S. $12) surcharge Easter, Christmas, and holiday weekends. BC, DC, MC, V.

This establishment is on the waterfront in the heart of town. Many of the rooms in the three-story building have kitchenettes, and they all have the standard Aussie motel amenities. There are also a heated pool, sauna, spa, recreation room, licensed restaurant, and a cocktail bar. Water beds and facilities for handicapped travelers are offered.

Nearby Places to Stay & Dine

MOUNT SEAVIEW RESORT, near Yarras, NSW 2446. Tel. 065/87-7144. Fax 065/87-7195. 26 motel rms, 24 lodge rms. A/C TEL **Transportation:** Guests are picked up from the train station in Wauchope or at the Port Macquarie coach depot or airport.

$ Rates: A$37 (U.S. $29.60) single in lodge; A$42 (U.S. $33.60) double in lodge; A$56 (U.S. $44.80) single motel unit; A$66 (U.S. $52.80) double motel unit; A$76 (U.S. $60.80) single suite; A$90 (U.S. $72) double suite; A$10 (U.S. $8) extra person; A$300 (U.S. $240) per person (based on double occupancy) for a 3-day/2-night package including accommodations, meals, four-wheel-drive safari, horseback riding, and transfer from Port Macquarie. Children under 12 are half price. AE, BC, MC, V.

Mount Seaview is 80 kilometers (50 miles) west of Port on the Oxley Highway (and 55km/34 miles west of Wauchope, which the locals inexplicably pronounce "war hope"). Here, guests can ride horses, swim in the Hastings River, hike, or take four-wheel-drive safaris. The resort is situated on a beautiful 1,200-hectare (2,964-acre) cattle-breeding ranch with majestic hills, pockets of rain forest, a crystal-clear river, and "fair dinkum" Aussie bush. Strangler figs, staghorn ferns, wild orchids, and flame trees give the rain forest a wondrous storybook appearance. Native animals thrive throughout the area.

Accommodations are in comfortable motel-type rooms, a bunkhouse, a rustic lodge, and a camping/caravan area. Hearty home-cooked meals are available in the lodge (licensed or BYO), or guests can prepare their own food in a communal kitchen. Hosts Ralph and Eric Clissold join guests around the big log fire at night and create a welcoming, friendly atmosphere.

Facilities: Pool table, table tennis, a putting green and driving range, a tennis court, indoor bowling, and playground. Horseback riding is an additional A$12 (U.S. $9.60) an hour and full-day safaris cost about A$35 (U.S. $28). The cost of four-wheel-drive trips varies from A$12 to A$50 (U.S. $9.60 to U.S. $40) per person.

HAY STREET DELICATESSEN, on the waterfront at Hay St. and Sunset Parade. Tel. 83-5094.
Cuisine: LIGHT LUNCHES. **Reservations:** None.
$ Prices: Lunch for two about A$10 (U.S. $8). No credit cards.
Open: Mon–Fri 7:30am–5:45pm, Sat 7:30am–12:45pm.

This is a mom-and-pop operation with wonderful homemade casseroles, soups, sandwiches, and desserts. Everything is take-out, which is great with a park only steps away. I highly recommend the rissole (meatball) sandwiches and carrot cake.

EVENING ENTERTAINMENT

Visitors are welcome at the three-story **Port Macquarie RSL Club,** Short Street (tel. 83-1999), the focal point of Port's nightlife. It covers an entire block and, in addition to one fancy restaurant and four casual eateries, it has five bars, floor shows, and a disco. Dining and drinking in RSLs are generally very good values because costs are subsidized by poker (slot)-machine revenues. This particular club also has an indoor swimming pool, gym, and aerobics classes.

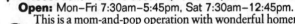

LORD HOWE ISLAND

702km (435 miles) NE of Sydney, due E of Port Macquarie

GETTING THERE By Plane Access to Lord Howe is via **Oxley Airlines** from Sydney, Port Macquarie, and other New South Wales cities, and **Eastern Australia Airlines** from Sydney.

ESSENTIALS The **New South Wales Travel Centre,** 19 Castlereagh Street, Sydney, NSW 2000 (tel. 02/231-4444), is the best source of information. The **area code** is 065.

Little known even to Australians, this tiny island is 11 kilometers (less than 7 miles) long and no more than 2 kilometers (about 1¼ miles) wide. Lord Howe has the southernmost coral reef in the world and boasts some of the rarest flora, birds, and marine life to be found anywhere. The Kentia palm, which is indigenous to the island, provides the only income, apart from tourism. Seeds from these palms have been collected and sold throughout the world for more than 100 years. Lord Howe is one of only three islands in the world on the World Heritage List.

Lord Howe is a good destination for those wishing to truly get away from it all and experience a friendly, casual island where visitors find themselves on a first-name basis with one another and with the locals after a very short period of time. There are refreshingly few cars and not very many telephones. And where else in the world is it still safe to leave the key in your car or front door? (Anyone interested in this destination should read the feature on Lord Howe Island in the October 1991, edition of *National Geographic* magazine.)

WHAT TO SEE & DO

Lord Howe's subtropical climate, which varies from 16°C in winter to 26°C in summer (61°F to 79°F), and its unspoiled water and land make it a virtual playground. Visitors can swim, surf, snorkel, scuba dive, play tennis, golf, fish, hike, and birdwatch. It's also possible to hand-feed the fish at Ned's Beach. The most common form of transport on the island is bicycle. Glass-bottom boats make it possible for nonswimmers to view the sea life, and 2-hour cruises circle the island, providing a good look at its mountains, which rise straight from the ocean. Golf sticks (clubs), tennis rackets, bicycles, masks and flippers for snorkeling, and all scuba gear can be rented.

WHERE TO STAY & DINE

Lodging on the island is mainly at guesthouses such as the one described below. Self-contained apartments are also available. Lord Howe doesn't have a pub, but bars are located in the various accommodations houses and in several restaurants. Hosts provide transport to and from the airport.

PINETREES, Lord Howe Island, NSW 2898. Tel. 065/63-2177, or toll free 008/22-6142 in Australia. Fax 065/63-2156. Sydney booking office: 72 Erskine St. (tel. 02/262-6585). 27 rms, 7 cottages.

$ Rates (including all meals): From A$225 (U.S. $180) single; from A$150 (U.S. $120) per person double; from A$320 (U.S. $256) per person suite. Higher rates in the summer (Dec–Mar). No credit cards.

Pinetrees is the largest and oldest guesthouse resort on the island, having first opened its doors in 1900. It is run by descendants of the first hosts, and the original family homestead, built in 1884, still stands as part of the lounge-, bar-, dining-room complex. Accommodation is in motel-style units, one-bedroom garden cottages, a four-bedroom/three-bath cottage, and a "two-and-a half"-bedroom cottage. There are also a tennis court, small library, and billiard table. The lagoon beach is just across the road. Guests ride bicycles to the golf course and surf beach.

COFFS HARBOUR

150km (93 miles) N of Port Macquarie, 572km (355 miles) N of Sydney, 427km (265 miles) S of Brisbane

GETTING THERE   By Plane   Ansett Express Airlines flies nonstop to Coffs Harbour from Sydney and Melbourne; Oxley Airlines flies to Coffs from Lord Howe Island.

By Train or Bus   A Countrylink train from Sydney costs A$54 (U.S. $43.20) economy class and A$75.50 (U.S. $60.40) first class. Several coach companies, including Pioneer, Greyhound, and Bus Australia, make the trip from Sydney in about 9 hours. A ticket costs about A$45 (U.S. $36). A bus from Brisbane takes 7 hours and costs A$39 (U.S. $31.20).

By Car   Travel time by car up the Pacific Highway from Sydney is at least 7 hours without stops; the trip from Brisbane takes 5 hours.

ESSENTIALS   The **Tourist Information Centre** (tel. 066/52-1522) is located in Urara Park next to the Fitzroy Hotel on Pacific Highway 2 blocks south of the city center. It's open daily from 9am to 5pm. The **area code** is 066.

As you drive north in Australia, the pace at which people move slows down and their life-style relaxes. Melburnians have little in common with residents of far-north Queensland, and were you to travel between those two places by road, you'd see a gradual loosening of dress standards and general reduction of formalities.

My husband and I drove up the coast from Sydney to Cairns while doing the research for this book, and I remember thinking when we got to Coffs Harbour (pop. 52,000) that it was our initial contact with an area that felt tropical. It certainly isn't steamy and lush like Cairns or Port Douglas, but banana plantations are a common sight, the beaches stretch for miles, the weather is warmer, and it's the first place I remember seeing houses built up on poles the way they are in Queensland.

High Street is the main drag in Coffs Harbour. Most stores are east of Pacific Highway, the main north-south street.

WHAT TO SEE & DO

The sight you want to be sure not to miss is the 10-meter (33-ft.) banana I mentioned earlier. You'll find it alongside the highway at **The Big Banana** theme park (tel. 066/52-4355), 3 kilometers (2 miles) north of town. This pièce de résistance is constructed of reinforced concrete.

At the Big Banana you can take a ride in an air-conditioned shuttle train around the 25-acre banana plantation on which a variety of exhibits have been built. The theme park is open daily from 9am to 4pm. Admission is A$10 (U.S. $8) for adults and A$6 (U.S. $4.80) for children. A coffee shop and restaurant serve banana bread, banana cake, banana splits, banana shakes—you get the idea. The local favorite seems to be chocolate-covered bananas.

You might also be interested in **George's Gold Mine,** 38 kilometers (23 miles) inland from Pacific Highway on Bushman's Range Road (tel. 54-5355). It's open Wednesday through Sunday from 10am to 4pm, and admission is A$7.50 (U.S. $6) for adults and A$2.50 (U.S. $2) for children. At the **Clog Barn** (also known as Holland Downunder), 1.6 kilometers (1.3 miles) north of the Coffs post office on the highway (tel. 52-4633), visitors can watch traditional Dutch wooden shoes being made daily at 11am and 4pm. The attraction is open 8am to 5pm; admission to the model village display is A$2.50 (U.S. $2) for adults and A$1.50 (U.S. $1.20) for children.

Gary Rollans of **Orara Carriages,** Island Loop Road, Upper Orara (tel. 53-8488), will take you on a leisurely horse-drawn carriage ride in the countryside, including either a picnic in a peaceful spot by the river or a jaunt through the scenic Orara Valley. Costs range from A$18 (U.S. $14.40) for the 2-hour trot to A$50 (U.S. $40) for a full day with catered picnic; 3- and 4-day tours are also offered. Gary represented Australia at the World Pair Driving Championship in England in 1985.

If you don't have your own car, **Coffs Harbour Coach and Travel,** 42 Moonee Street (tel. 52-2686), operates full- and half-day tours of the surrounding area.

Some 50 kilometers (31 miles) south of Coffs Harbour, a **Nambucca River cruise** (tel. 68-6922) operates several days a week. The morning trips last 3 hours and include a smörgåsbord lunch. The afternoon excursions take 2 hours; complimentary tea and coffee are served. Cost is A$13 (U.S. $10.40) for adults and A$6.50 (U.S. $5.20) for children. The luncheon cruise costs A$27 (U.S. $21.60) for adults and A$13.50 (U.S. $10.80) for children.

If you drive north of Coffs during the last week in October or the first week in November, allow time for enjoying the **Jacaranda Festival** in Grafton. Past Grafton at Yamba, the **Surf Carnival** takes place in January and the **Family Fishing Festival** in July.

Big Foot Adventure Safaris (tel. 52-3924) operates exciting 1-day canoe trips on the lower portion of the Nymboida River. Cost is A$75 (U.S. $60) a day for adults and A$40 (U.S. $32) for children; trips operate on weekends only. The tariff includes a bush barbecue with good ol' Aussie billy tea.

Wildwater Adventures, Lot 4, Butlers Road, Bonville, NSW 2441 (tel. 53-4469), will take you white-water rafting on the Upper Nymboida River or the Gwydir River for A$85 (U.S. $68) per person. These adventurous 1-day expeditions operate most days, year round, depending on water levels. Extended 2-, 3-, and 4-day rafting experiences cost from A$245 (U.S. $196) to A$425 (U.S. $340). Prices include all meals; participants camp out by the river on overnight trips. Rafting is especially exciting from November through June, when the water is rougher. The minimum age for participants is 12 years. Bonville is 14 kilometers (9 miles) south of Coffs Harbour, and the operators provide transfers.

WHERE TO STAY

PELICAN BEACH RESORT, Pacific Hwy., Coffs Harbour, NSW 2450. Tel. 066/53-7000, or toll free 008/02-8882 in Australia. Fax 066/53-7066. 112 suites. A/C MINIBAR TV TEL

$ Rates: A$143–A$190 (U.S. $114.40–U.S. $152) single; A$175–A$235 (U.S. $140–U.S. $188) double; A$190–A$400 (U.S. $152–U.S. $320) family and executive suite; A$25 (U.S. $20) extra person. The higher rates are for holiday periods. AE, BC, DC, MC, V.

Located 7 kilometers (4 miles) north of Coffs Harbour, Pelican Beach is the award-winning big brother of Port Macquarie's Pelican Shores. The 7½ acres of landscaped grounds that surround the resort are adjacent to a lovely stretch of long white sandy beach. The outdoors is brought into interior hallways with the effective use of large container gardens, streams diverted from the pool, and natural light streaming through the glass ceiling of a multistory atrium.

The accommodations are arranged on six levels that have been terraced into a hillside so that many rooms have a view over the lagoonlike pool to the beach. Each room has its own balcony and spacious, modern decor, with a tub/shower combination. Family suites have kitchenettes, and three rooms are equipped for handicapped travelers.

Dining/Entertainment: The hotel's dining options include The Shores, an à la carte restaurant that overlooks the pool area and offers an extensive menu and wine list (about A$85/U.S. $68 for a three-course dinner for two, plus wine), and the less expensive Waves Bistro. Lunch is served at the Beach Grill by the pool.

Services: 24-hour room service.

Facilities: Outside there's a 46-meter (50-yd.) free-form heated seawater pool, a glass-enclosed spa, a children's pool, nine holes of mini-golf (not free of charge), three full-size floodlit tennis courts (not free of charge), a volleyball court, and a cricket pitch. Inside are a gym, sauna, spa, and children's games room.

NAUTILUS ON-THE-BEACH, Pacific Hwy., Coffs Harbour, NSW 2450. Tel. 066/53-6699, or toll free 008/02-9966 in Australia. Fax 066/53-7039. 18 rms, 50 apartments. MINIBAR TV TEL

$ Rates: A$140 (U.S. $112) single or double hotel room; A$192 (U.S. $153.60) junior suite; A$220 (U.S. $176) 1-bedroom suite for up to four people; A$275 (U.S. $220) 2-bedroom suite for up to seven; A$300 (U.S. $240) 3-bedroom suite for up to eight. Children under 18 stay free in parents' room. Rates 25% higher during NSW school holidays. Reservations can be made through Flag Inns. AE, BC, DC, MC, V.

Nautilus on-the-Beach enjoys a "beaut pozzie" on a long stretch of white sand 7 kilometers (4.2 miles) north of Coffs Harbour. Nautilus's beach, in fact, is a continuation of the one belonging to its next-door neighbor, Pelican Beach. In spite of the resorts' proximity to each other, their personalities are quite different. At Nautilus the emphasis is on do-it-yourself living and family activities. Only the "deluxe hotel rooms" lack a full kitchen. The junior suites and the one-, two-, and three-bedroom suites all have completely equipped kitchens (including dishwashers) and laundry facilities. All units are modern, spacious, and bright with high-quality furnishings; all bathrooms have tub/shower combos. Queen- and king-size beds are available. Guests receive a free daily newspaper. Under-cover parking is adjacent to each low-rise duplex. The apartments are set on 9 acres of landscaped grounds.

During school holidays, the rates are significantly higher, the minimum stay is 1 week, and the resort is fully booked a year in advance.

Dining/Entertainment: Tucked around the property are the casual Deck Chairs Bar and Grill (breakfast and snacks) and Cocos Restaurant (à la carte dining, A$67/U.S. $53.60 for dinner for two).

Services: Baby-sitting, massage.

Facilities: Two full-size "mod grass" tennis courts, three heated pools, a barbecue area, sauna, spa, small gym, and children's games room and playground.

SANCTUARY RESORT, Pacific Hwy., Coffs Harbour, NSW 2450. Tel. 066/52-2111. 37 rms. TV TEL

$ Rates: A$75 (U.S. $60) single; A$85 (U.S. $68) double; A$10 (U.S. $8) extra person. Holiday surcharges. Lower rates through Aussie auto clubs. AE, BC, MC, V.

The Sanctuary Resort is a 37-unit low-rise motel located about 2 kilometers (1¼ miles) south of town and situated in an animal sanctuary where kangaroos, peacocks, and native birds roam. The resort has all the "mod cons" (modern conveniences), including pool, spa, sauna, rec room, playground, tennis and squash courts, and gym. The Treehouse Restaurant is a lofty retreat overlooking the gardens and sanctuary.

READERS RECOMMEND

Ranch Guesthouse, 4 *Wellington Dr., Nambucca Heads, NSW 2448. Tel. 065/68-6386.*
—*"My husband and I visited this old converted guesthouse. The Irish couple who own and run it are delightful and made us feel at home immediately. As a B&B it is ideal for those who want to be close to the ocean, but away from the busy, touristy coast. We would recommend it to anyone who wants a slower pace, with the sounds of the birds and surf and great walks from the front door. Their rate for bed and breakfast is A$40 (U.S. $32) for two people."*
—E. Hope Stewart, Nanaimo, B.C., Canada. *Author's note:* Nambucca Heads is 44 kilometers (27 miles) south of Coffs Harbour.

WHERE TO DINE

The jetty end of High Street is Coffs Harbour's restaurant row, with 15 restaurants in 1 block. Since they post their menus in the window, you can easily peruse the scene and make your decision on the spot. And if you like fast food, there's a huge, 530-seat **McDonald's** on Pacific Highway at North Boambee Road (tel. 52-7200).

In addition to these and the dining spots I described above in "Where to Stay," I want you to know about two other special places:

SEAFOOD MAMA'S, Pacific Hwy. Tel. 53-6733.
Cuisine: ITALIAN/SEAFOOD. **Reservations:** Recommended.
$ Prices: Appetizers A$5–A$11.95 (U.S. $4–U.S. $9.60); main courses A$11.50–A$18 (U.S. $9.20–U.S. $14.40). AE, BC, DC, MC, V.
Open: Lunch Wed–Fri noon–2pm; dinner daily from 6pm.

⭐ This restaurant overlooking the Pacific Ocean near the Pelican Beach and Nautilus resorts, 7 kilometers (4 miles) north of Coffs Harbour, was named by the jazz-fan proprietors after Fats Waller's song "Hold Tight." The present mama-in-residence is Diane Strachan, who looks nothing at all like the plump fishwife on the menu. As you might guess from the restaurant's name, the specialty here is local—and therefore very fresh—seafood done in a tasty Southern Italian style, as well as pasta and veal dishes. Favorite items on the menu include scaloppine del mare, spaghetti chili octopus, and fettucine marinara. The atmosphere is cheerful, friendly, and informal, and the food is great, so it's not surprising that Seafood Mama's has recently won several awards. The restaurant also delivers and does take-out.

PIZZA MAMA'S, at The Jetty, 382 High St. Tel. 51-3000.
Cuisine: PIZZA/PASTA/STEAK/SALAD. **Reservations:** Not required.
$ Prices: Appetizers A$2.50–A$10.50 (U.S. $2–U.S. $8.40); main courses A$5.50–A$15.50 (U.S. $4.40–U.S. $12.40). A$1 (U.S. 80¢) surcharge per person weekends and holidays. BC, MC, V.
Open: Dinner daily from 6pm until "whenever people want to leave."

Ⓢ As you might have guessed, Pizza Mama's is owned and operated by the same friendly folks who run Seafood Mama's, the difference being that this is a less-expensive, family-oriented spot. They advertise "Real food—real quick" and deliver on their promise. Twelve kinds of pizza are on the menu, as well as a half dozen types of pasta, and lots of other goodies. Take-out food costs 10% less than meals eaten on the premises. BYO.

EVENING ENTERTAINMENT

COFFS HARBOUR EX-SERVICES CLUB, at Pacific Hwy. and Vernon St. Tel. 52-3888.

This is one of the popular local nightlife spots. Live bands often perform in Crystal's Disco and the Mural Lounge. This place also has poker (slot) machines, if you're feeling lucky, and six bars, a bistro, and an à la carte dining room.

OSCAR'S, in the High Street Mall. Tel. 51-2266.

Oscar's is the other hot disco/nightclub/restaurant. Lunch is served Monday through Friday from noon, and dinner is available nightly except Sunday. The Supper Club operates until 3am 7 nights a week.

MURWILLUMBAH

321km (200 miles) N of Coffs Harbour, 893km (554 miles) N of Sydney,
30km (19 miles) S of Queensland border

GETTING THERE   By Plane   Ansett Express Airlines flies from Sydney to Lismore (81km/50 miles southwest of Murwillumbah) and to Ballina (94km/58 miles southeast of Murwillumbah). The Coolangatta airport is just north of the Queensland border, 34 kilometers (21 miles) away. An Australian Airlines Sydney-Coolangatta ticket costs from A$131 to A$166 (U.S. $104.80 to U.S. $132.80).

By Train or Bus   Direct Countrylink XPT trains link Murwillumbah to Sydney. A first-class ticket costs A$91 (U.S. $72.80); economy class costs A$65 (U.S. $52). The trip takes 12 hours and 40 minutes. By coach, the trip takes 13 hours and 50 minutes and costs A$63 (U.S. $50.40).

By Car   Murwillumbah is inland from the coast on the Pacific Highway which connects Sydney and Brisbane.

ESSENTIALS   Check in at the **Visitors Centre,** at Pacific Highway and Alma Street, Murwillumbah, NSW 2484 (tel. 066/72-1340), before heading out through more of the Tweed Valley or east to the beaches. There's another **Tourist Information Office** at 69 Jonson Street, Byron Bay (tel. 066/85-8050), which is 78 kilometers (48 miles) southeast. The **area code** is 066.

The beautiful beaches at **Byron Bay,** the forested slopes of **Mount Warning,** picturesque country towns, and the razzmatazz of licensed clubs near the Queensland border are all within a short drive of Murwillumbah (pop. 8,000), which is the focal point of the scenic **Tweed Valley.** In addition to being a good base for touring, Murwillumbah is also an important commercial center. Throughout the area you will see evidence of the sugarcane, banana, and timber industries.

WHAT TO SEE & DO

Avocadoland, on Pacific Highway (tel. 77-7222), 15 kilometers (9 miles) north of Murwillumbah and 15 kilometers south of Coolangatta, is the home of The Big Avocado. Tractor-train safaris across the 200-acre tropical fruit plantation, four-wheel-drive rain-forest adventure rides, and river boat rides are offered. A plantation restaurant, kiosk, fruit market, and gift shop are also available. Avocadoland is open daily from 10am to 5pm. Admission is free of charge. Rides cost A$5 (U.S. $4) for adults, A$2.50 (U.S. $2) for children, and A$10 (U.S. $8) for a family. This is the Tweed Valley's top attraction.

Many good bushwalks circle and lead to the top of 1,156-meter (3,815-ft.) **Mount Warning,** from where there is a good view of the caldera formed from volcanic action 20 to 23 million years ago. Mount Warning National Park is one of four World Heritage Parks in the area.

Attractions at Byron Bay

⭐ The **Byron Bay Lighthouse** on Cape Byron is one of Australia's most powerful—its beacon is visible more than 40 kilometers (25 miles) out to sea. The lofty, sparkling white tower is not open for inspection, but the point on which it's located affords visitors a spectacular ocean view 7 days a week, weather permitting.

Watego's Beach, under Cape Byron, is one of the best surfing beaches on the east coast. **Julian Rocks,** in the same vicinity, is a good area for skin- and scuba diving.

WHERE TO STAY

In addition to the more costly options listed below, those sticking to a tight budget will appreciate the **Murwillumbah YHA Backpackers Lodge,** 1 Tumbulgum Road, Murwillumbah, NSW 2484 (tel. 066/72-3763), with two eight-bed dorms and four double/twin rooms. Charges are A$11.50 to A$12.50 (U.S. $9.20 to U.S. $10) per person.

MIDGINBIL HILL HOLIDAY FARM, Uki, NSW 2484 via Murwillumbah. Tel. 066/79-7158. Fax 066/79-7120. 8 lodge rms, 1 on-site van, 30 tent sites.
  Transportation: One-way transfers from Coolangatta Airport A$25 (U.S. $20).
$ **Rates:** Lodge rooms (including all meals) A$78 (U.S. $62.40) adult; A$39 (U.S. $31.20) children 4–15; free for children under 4. Tent sites A$6 (U.S. $4.80) adults; A$3 (U.S. $2.40) children. Horseback riding is A$12/U.S. $9.60 extra; a wildlife canoeing safari costs A$20/U.S. $16. No credit cards.

Midginbil Hill is a holiday farm designed for relaxed family fun. Located 30 kilometers (19 miles) west of Murwillumbah and surrounded by beautiful views of the Tweed Valley, the 160-hectare (395-acre) cattle property (ranch) is great for folks who want to ride horses, go on four-wheel-drive safaris, try their hand at canoeing, or, depending on the time of year, help out with mustering livestock. Proprietors Annette and John Flower create a welcoming, friendly atmosphere and encourage kids to help feed the farm animals. Archery, swimming, tennis, pool, and table tennis keep even the most active youngsters happy. "Mountain morning tea" provides a real Aussie-style experience: One group rides out into the bush on horseback and another goes on a four-wheel-drive safari. They meet, boil the billy for morning tea, and then switch conveyances to return to the farm.

Healthful home-cooked meals are enjoyed in the original colonial homestead, which is sometimes also used for bush dances. Accommodations are in rustic lodges with bunk beds and private bathrooms, in an on-site van, or in tents.

Places to Stay at Byron Bay

Three accommodation properties in the Byron Bay vicinity have won New South Wales Tourism Commission awards. In addition to the beach retreat described below, you might be interested in **The Wheel Resort,** 39-51 Broken Head Road, Byron Bay, NSW 2481 (tel. 066/85-6139), which is comprised of comfortable self-contained cabins with screened verandas, and **The Taylor's,** McGettigan's Lane, Ewingsdale, Byron Bay, NSW 2481 (tel. 066/84-7436; fax 066/84-7526), which is a charming five-room country house.

There is also a hostel at Byron Bay. The **Cape Byron Lodge,** 78 Bangalow

Road, Byron Bay, NSW 2481 (tel. 066/85-6445; fax 066/85-6445), charges A$11 (U.S. $8.80) for one person and A$30 (U.S. $24) for two.

BYRON BAY BEACH RESORT, Bayshore Dr., Byron Bay, NSW 2481. Tel. 066/85-8000, or toll free 008/02-8927 in Australia. Fax 066/85-6916. 78 units. TV

$ Rates: A$87 (U.S. $69.60) studio; A$98 (U.S. $78.40) villa; A$115 (U.S. $92) 2-bedroom chalet. Holiday rates are 30%-40% higher. AE, BC, DC, MC, V.

Located right on Byron Bay Beach, this spot is a great venue for recreation and relaxing. Kangaroos are often seen on the nine-hole golf course, and you might also catch a glimpse of other wildlife as you stroll about the 230-acre site. There are also several lakes, a swimming pool, horses for riding, and tennis courts. You can go canoeing, play cricket or volleyball. Children are catered for with a supervised program. Tennis and bicycles are free. Horse riding costs A$15 (U.S. $12) an hour.

Meals are served in the Bayshore Restaurant, which sits high on the foreshore with a view out over the surf, and in the Poolside Coffee Shop. In addition, all units have cooking facilities.

WHERE TO DINE

PULLMAN'S RETREAT, Coolman St., Tyalgum. Tel. 79-3415.
   Cuisine: LIGHT LUNCHES/TEA. **Reservations:** Not necessary.
$ Prices: Light lunches A$5–A$10 (U.S. $4–U.S. $8). No credit cards.
   Open: Fri–Sun 10am–4pm.

Located in the tiny village of Tyalgum, 22 kilometers (13 miles) west of Murwillumbah, Pullman's Retreat is a lovely place to stop for tea or lunch. The restaurant is housed in a former bank building that dates from 1911 and today provides a casual dining venue with historic ambience. Owner/chef Les Pullman displays watercolors and pencil sketches, which are for sale. The town's hotel, nearby, is an authentic Aussie country pub and a good spot for a cold beer. The veranda sports a most amazing collection of staghorn ferns.

EVENING ENTERTAINMENT

Because New South Wales's gambling and drinking laws are less stringent than neighboring Queensland's, several clubs thrive on the border at Tweed Heads.

TWIN TOWNS SERVICES CLUB, Wharf St., Tweed Heads. Tel. 075/36-2277.

As with most clubs like this in Australia, food and beverages at Twin Towns are very good value. Dining options range from a snack bar to an à la carte restaurant. In the Bistro/Carvery a roast dinner with four veggies costs A$8 (U.S. $6.40). Entertainment and dancing go on every afternoon and evening. On Monday nights they show free movies in the auditorium. Casual dress is acceptable during the day at this poker-machine palace, but after 7:30pm shorts and thongs are prohibited. Children under 18 are not allowed in the gambling area, but may be left in the children's lounge on level three. Open Monday to Thursday from 9am to 12:30am, Friday from 9am to 1am, Saturday from 9am to 1:30am, and Sunday from 9am to midnight.
   Admission: Free.

SEAGULLS RUGBY LEAGUE FOOTBALL CLUB, Gollan Dr., Tweed Heads. Tel. 075/36-3433.

This is another popular spot for dining, entertainment, drinking, and gambling. Top-name stars often perform in the club's Stardust Room, which seats up to 1,600 people. In the past few years Seagulls has hosted such performers as Tom Jones, Joe Cocker, and Bob Hope. There are also five eateries, three lounges, nine bars, and a casino with 522 poker machines. A three-course meal in the Char Grill costs A$25 (U.S. $20); you could have steak, seafood, or lasagne for lunch or dinner in Julios Cafe for A$8 (U.S. $6.40); Seagulls Chinese Restaurant costs about A$18 (U.S. $14.40) per person; a roast dinner in the Bistro will set you back all of A$8 (U.S. $6.40). The

Bargain Breakfast, served in the Bistro daily from 5 to 9am is very good value at A$2.99 (U.S. $2.40). Open daily 24 hours.
Admission: Free.

7. THE NEW ENGLAND REGION

If you've ever wanted to sample autumn in New England, you might like to visit Tamworth, Armidale, or Glen Innes between April and June, when trees in the area turn lovely shades of gold, red, and orange. Unlike the north-coast region on the other side of the Great Divide, New England is about 1,000 meters (3,300 ft.) above sea level and has four distinct seasons—and fall is one of the nicest.

Armidale is the center of the area, which spreads out on either side of the New England Highway from the Hunter Valley to the Queensland border. This highway roughly parallels the coastal Pacific Highway from Sydney to Brisbane and, instead of beaches, offers rugged gorges, lofty waterfalls, dense forests, wide green paddocks, and bracing highland air. If you want to sample a real variety of scenery, start out on one highway and cross the Great Dividing Range to the other road part way up. Three highways, the Oxley, the Gwydir, and the Bruxner, make it possible to do this. And wherever you are in New England, keep your eyes on the ground. The area is rich in gemstones, and it's quite possible to stumble across jasper, serpentine, quartz, crystal, and chalcedony. If you were very lucky, you might even find sapphires, diamonds, and gold.

TAMWORTH
453km (281 miles) NW of Sydney

GETTING THERE   By Plane   The fare for flights from Sydney on **Eastwest Airlines** is A$149 (U.S. $119.20). **Eastern Australia Airlines** also stops in Tamworth.

By Train or Bus   A **Countrylink** XPT train ticket from Sydney to Tamworth costs A$45 (U.S. $36) economy class and A$63.50 (U.S. $50.80) first class. Several coach companies, including Pioneer, Greyhound, and McCafferty's, travel the New England Highway. A one-way ticket from Sydney to Tamworth costs about A$44 (U.S. $35.20). The trip takes 8 hours and 15 minutes or more.

By Car   Tamworth is about a 5½-hour drive from Sydney, north on the Pacific Highway and then west and north on the New England Highway. Motorists traveling from Brisbane should allow 6½ hours.

ESSENTIALS   Tourist information is dispensed at the **Visitors Centre,** on the corner of the New England Highway and Kable Avenue, Tamworth, NSW 2340 (tel. 067/68-4462), open Monday through Friday from 8:30am to 4:45pm, Saturday from 9:30am to 4pm, and Sunday from 9am to 3pm.
The **area code** is 067.

SPECIAL EVENTS   Known as the "country music capital of the nation," Tamworth hosts the **Australasian Country Music Awards** and 11-day **music festival** every January. More than 600 shows, concerts, and talent quests are staged during this time, and the city is packed with musicians and their fans.

E xcept during the music festival in January, Tamworth (pop. 34,500) is an attractive, quiet city in the center of a rich pastoral and agricultural area. Before its musical identity was established by a radio program called "Hoedown," which was popular in the 1960s, Tamworth was known as the "city of lights" because it was the first place in

Australia to have electric streetlights. Because it is situated at the junction of the New England and Oxley highways, it makes a good stopover on the route from Sydney or Melbourne to Brisbane.

WHAT TO SEE & DO

If you're feeling lucky, drive the **Fossicker's Way** from Tamworth to Glen Innes. The route was so named after numerous gemstones were found in its vicinity.

If you like country music, you won't want to miss **Hands of Fame Park,** at the New England Highway and Kable Avenue, where country and western musicians have their handprints recorded in concrete à la Mann's Chinese Theater in Hollywood. At the **Hall of Fame Wax Museum,** models of Chad Morgan, Frank Ifield, Buddy Williams, and Slim Dusty, to name just a few, tell their stories via tape. The clothes on the wax figures are the real thing, donated by the performers or their families.

The **Powerstation Museum,** Peel Street (tel. 66-1999), is the first working steam-powered electricity-generating museum in Australia. It commemorates the fact that Tamworth had the first electric streetlights in the nation. Open 9am to 1pm Tuesday through Friday. No admission charge.

Oxley Park at the top of Brisbane Street (tel. 66-3641) is a sanctuary for kangaroos and other native wildlife. It's open daily from 8am to 5pm. Nice picnic area. Free admission.

WHERE TO STAY & DINE

POWERHOUSE MOTOR INN, New England Hwy., Tamworth, NSW 2340. Tel. 067/66-7000. Fax 067/66-7748. 60 rms, 10 suites. A/C MINIBAR TV TEL

$ **Rates:** A$85 (U.S. $68) single; A$100 (U.S. $80) double; A$135–A$155 (U.S. $108–U.S. $124) suite; A$10 (U.S. $8) extra person. Reservations can be made through Flag Inns. AE, BC, DC, MC, V.

In addition to the standard amenities, the two-story Powerhouse offers queen-size beds, water beds, ironing boards, hairdryers, spa baths, a gym, and 24-hour room service. A licensed restaurant, large swimming pool, sauna, hot spa, children's playground, and self-service laundry are also available. Two rooms have cooking facilities, and there are specially equipped quarters for disabled travelers. Baby-sitting can be arranged.

Staying on a Farm

LALLA ROOKH COUNTRY HOUSE, Duri, NSW 2344. Tel. 067/68-0216. Fax 067/68-0330. 4 rms (2 with bath).

$ **Rates** (including breakfast): A$65 (U.S. $52) single; A$90 (U.S. $72) double. BC, MC. **Closed:** Christmas week.

Ⓢ Bob and Sue Moore welcome guests to Lalla Rookh and treat them like members of the family. Their 160-hectare (395-acre) grazing property is 20 kilometers (12 miles) south of Tamworth, and visitors are accommodated in the guest wing of the Moores' modern home. This is a great spot for gaining insight into Australian agricultural production and enjoying warm country hospitality. Both hosts have traveled widely; Sue is a potter. Two twin rooms have their own bathrooms, while the other twin and a double share another (guests-only) bathroom. Breakfast is included in the tariff, and other meals are available at an extra charge. Only children over the age of 15 are accepted. Hosts will pick up guests in Tamworth if necessary. I recommend you treat yourself to Lalla Rookh and the Moore's hospitality.

ARMIDALE

110km (68 miles) N of Tamworth, 563km (349 miles) NW of Sydney, 464km (288 miles) S of Brisbane

GETTING THERE By Plane The Sydney-to-Armidale flight on **Eastern**

Australia Airlines costs A$163 (U.S. $130.40). An **Oxley Airlines** ticket from Brisbane costs A$156 (U.S. $124.80).

By Train, Bus, or Car   A Countrylink, Pioneer, or Greyhound coach ticket from Sydney costs A$48 (U.S. $38.40). The coach fare from Brisbane is A$44 (U.S. $35.20). From Tamworth it's about a 2-hour drive on the New England Highway; about a 7½-hour drive from Sydney.

ESSENTIALS   Your questions will be answered if you take them to the **Visitors Centre and Coach Station,** 82 Marsh Street, Armidale, NSW 2350 (tel. 067/ 73-8527). It's open Monday through Friday from 8:30am to 5pm. The **area code** is 067.

Being both a major commercial center and a university city, Armidale (pop. 22,000) is the focal point of the New England region. Its university, cathedral, parks, and gardens are reminiscent of old England, an impression reinforced by the cool weather often experienced at the city's 1,035-meter (3,416-ft.) elevation. Several other educational institutions are located in Armidale, giving it the bookish appearance of Cambridge—Massachusetts or England. The surrounding area is known for its merino wool, cattle, apples, stone fruit, and vegetables. Spring and fall are the best times to visit.

WHAT TO SEE & DO
Attractions

You can tour the 260-hectare (642-acre) campus of the **University of New England** (tel. 73-3333) daily from 9am to 4:30pm. The "Uni" is located off Queen Elizabeth Drive, 5 kilometers (3 miles) northwest of the city. Be sure to notice Booloominbah, which was built between 1883 and 1888 as a homestead for Frederick White. The impressive building, with its gables, stained-glass windows, and great cedar staircase, was purchased and donated to the University of Sydney in 1937; this eventually resulted in the founding of the University of New England in Armidale. Today "Bool" is an administrative center, and the relatively new campus with its many historic buildings has a strong traditional feel. Fallow deer, kangaroos, and wallabies wander nearby in **Deer Park,** adding to the peaceful atmosphere.

Some 39 kilometers (24 miles) east of Armidale on the road to Ebor, the 220-meter (726-ft.) **Wollomombi Falls** plunge into a rugged gorge. These falls are one of the highest in Australia and well worth a look. Good picnic facilities are nearby.

NEW ENGLAND REGIONAL ART MUSEUM, Kentucky St. Tel. 72-5255.

This museum houses the famous Hinton Art Collection, the Armidale City Art Collection, and the Coventry Collection. The Howard Hinton Collection, which contains over 1,100 pictures, bronzes, medallions, and craft works, is the most valuable provincial collection in the country.

Admission: A$3 (U.S. $2.40) adults; children, free.

Open: Mon–Sat 10am–5pm, Sun 1–5pm.

ARMIDALE AND DISTRICT FOLK MUSEUM, at Rusden and Faulkner Sts. Tel. 72-8666, ext. 236.

Set in a National Trust building, this folk museum contains a display of pioneer relics and room settings from a 19th-century parlor, bedroom, and kitchen.

Admission: Free.

Open: Daily 1–4pm.

A New England Adventure

Here's something you can't do at home: **a pub crawl on horseback.** Congenial host Steve Langley, P.O. Box 379, Glen Innes, NSW 2370 (tel. 067/32-1599), conducts 6-day trips that start at Boolabinda, his homestead located 113 kilometers (70 miles) north of Armidale near Glen Innes. Riders traverse the beautiful New

England countryside and stay overnight in historic country pubs. Along the way they meet local stockmen, farmhands, miners, prospectors, horse breakers, and other colorful people. Steve welcomes children as well as adults, as long as they have "a smattering of horsemanship"—6 hours a day is spent in the saddle. One night is spent in the town of Emmaville (pop. 500, two hotels), 2 nights in Torrington (pop. 80, one hotel), and yet another in Deepwater (pop. 350), where the original Cobb & Co. stagecoaches stopped. Groups are kept to a maximum of 16 participants; horses range from docile to spirited. The tariff of A$800 (U.S. $640) includes horses, accommodations, and all meals. If you like horses, beautiful scenery, getting off the beaten path, and cold beer, this could really be fun. Don't forget to pack your broad-brimmed hat and riding boots. If you don't have one, stockman's coats can be hired (A$20/U.S. $16). Steve picks guests up upon arrival in Glen Innes. Shorter rides are also available.

This trip can also be arranged through **FITS Equestrian.** See "Adventure/ Specialty Tours" in Chapter 2.

WHERE TO STAY & DINE

Both farm stay and bed-and-breakfast accommodation are popular in the Armidale area. If you're interested in savoring the local hospitality, contact **Tourism New England,** P.O. Box 1221, Armidale, NSW 2350 (tel. 067/72-8155; fax 067/72-4564).

CATTLEMAN'S MOTOR INN, 31 Marsh St. (New England Hwy.), Armidale, NSW 2350. Tel. 067/72-7788, or toll free 008/02-8910 in Australia. 54 units. A/C TV TEL
$ Rates: A$85–A$110 (U.S. $68–U.S. $88) single; A$95–A$120 (U.S. $76–U.S. $96) double; A$130–A$170 (U.S. $104–U.S. $136) suite; A$10 (U.S. $8) extra person. Reservations can be made through Best Western. AE, BC, DC, MC, V.
Set in a modern two-story building, guest rooms have toasters in addition to the standard coffee- and tea-making facilities; 14 rooms have tubs as well as showers. A licensed restaurant, guest laundry, barbecue, pool, spa, sauna, and facilities for disabled travelers are also available.

COTSWOLD GARDENS MOTOR INN, 34 Marsh St. (New England Hwy.), Armidale, NSW 2350. Tel. 067/72-8222. Fax 067/72-5139. 25 rms. MINIBAR TV TEL
$ Rates: A$64 (U.S. $51.20) single; A$70 (U.S. $56) double; A$6 (U.S. $4.80) extra person. Reservations can be made through Flag Inns. AE, BC, CB, DC, MC, V.
What could be more appropriate in this town with its English feel than this single-story hostelry with its gabled roof and colonial appearance? Rooms have modern amenities, and a licensed restaurant, cocktail bar, and games room are on the premises. Baby-sitting can be arranged.

8. OUTBACK NEW SOUTH WALES

The western two-thirds of New South Wales consists of arid, rust-colored plains periodically broken by low, rocky ranges and dry, or nearly dry, riverbeds. It is inhospitable terrain and only the most rugged souls can live there. Heat, distance, and low rainfall are a constant threat, even to visitors, who must be careful to stay on main roads and carry water with them at all times. If it weren't for the discovery of valuable minerals and gemstones, the outback would probably have remained unsettled.

As it is, large deposits of silver, lead, and zinc have put Broken Hill on the map, and black opals draw residents to Lightning Ridge. Other towns, like Bourke for instance, serve as commercial centers for the surrounding sheep or cattle country, where vast stations (ranches) go on for miles.

To many overseas visitors, the outback is the real Australia, a land of harsh conditions, great expanses, kangaroos, Aborigines, miners, sheep and cattle stations, and the Flying Doctor Service. While this is true, I encourage you to be realistic and careful about traveling in this region, especially during the period from November to March, when temperatures often reach 38°C (100°F) and flies and dust are thick and annoying. Running out of petrol, food, or water can be a very serious matter. On the other hand, if you're cautious, your experience could be one of watching Aussie folklore come to life, meeting some unusual outback characters, and having a fair dinkum good time.

BROKEN HILL

1,157km (717 miles) W of Sydney, 508km (315 miles) NE of Adelaide

GETTING THERE   By Plane   There are regular flights on Kendell Airlines to/from Adelaide. Hazelton Airlines goes back and forth from Sydney. Sunstate Airlines connects Broken Hill to Melbourne, Adelaide, and Mildura.

By Train   The Indian Pacific train stops on its way to Perth and passengers have time for a quick sightseeing tour. A Countrylink rail ticket from Sydney to Broken Hill costs A$73 (U.S. $58.40) economy class and A$102 (U.S. $81.60) first class.

By Bus   Pioneer, Greyhound, and Stateliner provide coach service; the trip from Adelaide takes 6½ hours and costs A$40 (U.S. $32). A Sydney–Broken Hill bus ticket costs A$100 (U.S. $80), and the journey lasts nearly 16 hours.

By Car   If you're driving from Sydney, take the Great Western Highway to Dubbo, then the Mitchell Highway to the Barrier Highway, and the Barrier Highway on to Broken Hill, but I don't recommend it unless you're familiar with driving in the outback and your vehicle is fully equipped for the rigorous—and long—trip.

ESSENTIALS   Tourist information is available at the **Broken Hill Tourist and Travellers Centre,** at Blende Street and Bromide Street, Broken Hill, NSW 2880 (tel. 080/87-6077), open daily from 8:30am to 5pm. In the same location are a car-rental desk, a souvenir shop, bus terminal, and cafeteria. The **area code** is 080.

More than 100 years ago, Charles Rasp, a German boundary rider, found what he thought was tin ore on a broken hill in the vicinity of the Mount Gipps Station. Instead of tin, Rasp's samples turned out to be silver and lead, and by 1885 the Broken Hill Proprietary Company had been launched. The ore deposits turned out to be the largest and richest of their kind in the world, and through the years BHP has played a major role in transforming Australia from a pastoral nation to an important industrial force. The mines continue to operate and produce two million tons of ore annually, although BHP, Australia's largest company, pulled out of the community in 1940.

Broken Hill (pop. 24,450) is very close to the South Australian border. The fact that it operates on South Australian time (central standard time, a half hour behind eastern standard time), though located in New South Wales, is symbolic of its proximity to Adelaide and distance from Sydney. Access to this outback oasis is surprisingly easy.

WHAT TO SEE & DO

If you arrive in Broken Hill without a car, **Silver City Tours,** 328 Argent Street (tel. 080/87-6956), conducts coach and minicoach tours to most of the places mentioned below.

Major Attractions

BROKEN HILL CITY ART GALLERY, Chloride St. between Blende and Beryl Sts. Tel. 88-9252.

This gallery, located in the modern Entertainment Centre, is the state's oldest gallery outside Sydney and houses an extensive collection. Of particular interest is the

Silver Tree, wrought from pure silver from the Broken Hill mines for Charles Rasp, discoverer of the rich mineral deposits. This is a good place to see the work of the **Brushmen of the Bush,** a well-known group of artists who live in the outback and attempt to capture its unique scenery on canvas. Look for paintings by Pro Hart, Jack Absalom, Eric Minchin, Hugh Schulz, and John Pickup. Their pictures of the local landscape have been exhibited worldwide.

Other galleries scattered around town include the **Hugh Schulz Gallery,** 51 Morgan Street (tel. 87-6624), and the **Pro Hart Gallery,** 108 Wyman Street (tel. 87-2441). Both are open daily.

Admission: A$2 (U.S. $1.60) adults, A$1 (U.S. 80¢) children.
Open: Mon–Sat 9am–4pm, Sun 1–4pm. Guided tours are given Mon–Fri at 11:30am. **Closed:** Dec 25–26, Jan 1, Good Friday, Easter Sunday.

RAILWAY AND HISTORICAL MUSEUM, at Blende and Bromide Sts. Tel. 88-4660.

This technical museum, opposite the Tourist Information Centre, has displays that explain how the railway lines from Sydney and Melbourne, together with the wealth of the mining industry, transformed Broken Hill into a relatively modern oasis in the middle of the otherwise desolate outback. On display in the stone railway station, built about 1905, are old photos and books relating to the Silverton Tramway Co.

Admission: A$1.50 (U.S. $1.20) adults, A$1 (U.S. 80¢) children.
Open: Daily 10am–3pm.

GLADSTONE MINING MUSEUM, at South and Morish Sts., South Broken Hill. Tel. 87-6277.

Here you can visit a replica of a mine that has been built in an old hotel. Displays in six rooms, including a 35-minute taped description, explain mining procedures.

Open: Mon, Wed, Fri–Sat 2–5pm.

BROKEN HILL'S MOSQUE.

The mosque was built around 1891 by Afghan and Indian camel drivers on the site of the camp where they loaded and unloaded their camel teams.

Admission: Free.
Open: Sun 2:30pm.

Mine Tours

Underground mine tours are conducted at **Delprat's Mine** (tel. 88-1604) Monday through Friday at 10:30am and on Saturday at 2pm. Visitors go 120 meters (396 ft.) below the surface and gain an understanding of what it's like to work in one of Broken Hill's mines. Children under age 12 are not permitted. Cameras are okay. Tours last 2 hours and cost A$18 (U.S. $14.40).

The School of the Air & the RFDS

You might also like to visit the **School of the Air** and the **Royal Flying Doctor Service** base. Both of these places provide real insight into the "tyranny of distance" that historian Geoffrey Blainey speaks of when describing Australia's remote regions. The School of the Air, which conducts lessons via two-way radio for children on isolated stations, requires that visits be booked by the Tourist Information Centre. The Royal Flying Doctor Service base is located at the Broken Hill Airport (tel. 88-0777). The RFDS maintains communication with over 400 outback stations, providing long-range diagnosis of problems and, if necessary, dispatching a physician by air. The Broken Hill base covers 25% of New South Wales, as well as parts of Queensland and South Australia. Explanatory sessions lasting 45 minutes are held at the base Monday through Friday at 10:30am and 3:30pm and on Saturday and Sunday at 10:30am. Admission is A$2 (U.S. $1.60) for adults; children under 12 are free.

A Side Trip to a Ghost Town

Silverton (pop. 50), a ghost town 23 kilometers (14 miles) northwest of Broken Hill, is a popular location for moviemakers. *A Town Like Alice, Mad Max II (The Road*

Warrior), and many other films have been shot there. Silverton was home to a population of 3,000 after silver chlorides were discovered there in 1882, but the field closed in 1889 and nearly everyone left. Its restored buildings include a hotel and a jail.

An Outback Adventure

If you really want to get a feel for the outback, join an airborne postman as he flies the Saturday and Tuesday bush mail run to a string of about 16 isolated sheep stations along a 560-kilometer (347-mile) loop outside Broken Hill. The tour departs at 7am and can carry five sightseers in addition to the pilot. Along the way you'll see lots of kangaroos and other native animals, land at strips on remote stations, and meet some quite out-of-the-ordinary people. The experience costs A$165 (U.S. $132), including tea and lunch. To book your seat on this adventure, contact **Lindon Aviation,** P.O. Box 811, Broken Hill, NSW 2880 (tel. 080/88-5257).

WHERE TO STAY

BROKEN HILL OVERLANDER MOTOR INN, 142 Iodide St., Broken Hill, NSW 2880. Tel. 080/88-2566. Fax 080/88-4377. 15 rms. A/C TV TEL

$ **Rates:** A$56–A$62 (U.S. $44.80–U.S. $49.60) single; A$62–A$70 (U.S. $49.60–U.S. $56) double; A$8 (U.S. $6.40) extra person. Reservations can be made through Best Western. AE, BC, DC, MC, V.

Barry and Kerry Josephs offer 15 modern units, as well as an outdoor pool, sauna, and spa. Each room has a clock radio, tea- and coffee-making facilities, and a small refrigerator. Handicapped facilities are available, as are in-house movies and a guest laundry. Baby-sitting can be arranged.

TOURIST LODGE, 100 Argent St., Broken Hill, NSW 2880. Tel. 080/88-2086. 33 rms (none with bath).

$ **Rates:** A$20 (U.S. $16) single; A$32 (U.S. $25.60) double. AE, BC, MC, V.

The centrally located Tourist Lodge has both private rooms and dormitory facilities, all at budget prices. Shared coffee- and tea-making facilities are provided, as are continental breakfasts (A$4/U.S. $3.20), laundry facilities, and a communal television lounge. Evening meals cost an additional A$10 (U.S. $8).

DINING & EVENING ENTERTAINMENT

BROKEN HILL MUSICIANS CLUB, 276 Argent St. Tel. 88-1777.
   This spot is open daily for lunch and dinner and is licensed to serve alcohol. Live entertainment is provided.

RSL CLUB, 2 Chloride St. Tel. 87-2653.
   This club provides meals, drinks, and a chance to play one-arm bandits.

LIGHTNING RIDGE

765km (474 miles) NW of Sydney, 572km (355 miles) SW of Brisbane

GETTING THERE   By Plane, Train, or Bus   Lightning Ridge is most easily accessible via Hazelton Airlines. A Countrylink coach/rail ticket costs A$80 (U.S. $64); travel is via Dubbo.

ESSENTIALS   Tourist information is available from the **Lightning Ridge Tourist Association,** P.O. Box 251, Lightning Ridge, NSW 2834 (tel. 068/29-0429). The **area code** is 068.

While most people move to Lightning Ridge with the hopes of finding a large vein of black opal, it's the frontier atmosphere and relaxed life-style that keep them there. The township is home to 4,000 people who have chosen an unorthodox way of life over urban conformity. In the town pub, the Digger's Rest Hotel, locals tantalize visiting fossickers with tales of great strikes and legendary riches, but their wealth isn't as apparent as their love of the "great Aussie leg pull." Consider yourself lucky if you find even one or two dirt-encrusted opal pebbles. Lightning Ridge is one of three main opal fields in Australia and the only source of black opals in the world. The other two important fields are Quilpie, Queensland, and Coober Pedy, South Australia.

WHAT TO SEE & DO

The **Artesian Bore Baths,** 2 kilometers (1 mile) from the post office on Pandora Street (tel. 29-0429), are free of charge and open 24 hours a day. The artesian hot water is believed to be of therapeutic value.

At the **Opal Bazaar,** on Three Mile Road (tel. 29-0247), you can watch cutting demonstrations free of charge daily at 2pm. Also known as the Big Opal, this place sells loose stones and jewelry. You can also visit **Spectrum Opal Mines, 1** kilometer (½ mile) north of the post office on Bald Hill Road (tel. 29-0581), where admission is free and films are shown daily. Also on display here: black opals from their mines. Nice picnic area.

WHERE TO STAY

BLACK OPAL MOTEL, Opal St., Lightning Ridge, NSW 2834. Tel. 068/29-0518. Fax 068/29-0884. 12 rms. A/C TV TEL
$ Rates: A$49 (U.S. $39.20) single; A$57–A$59 (U.S. $45.60–U.S. $47.20) double; A$10 (U.S. $8) extra person. AE, BC, MC, V.

The rooms in the Black Opal Motel have showers and are equipped with coffee- and tea-making facilities, small refrigerators, and clock radios.

CHAPTER 7

BRISBANE

"Send the worst convicts somewhere else" was a demand often voiced by the free settlers in New South Wales in the 1820s. As a result, Gov. Sir Thomas Macdougall Brisbane sent explorers north to find a suitable spot for a new penal colony. They searched the coast for a site on a river, for in those days all long-distance transport was by sea, and it was Lt. John Oxley in the cutter *Mermaid* who discovered the waterway extending inland from Moreton Bay, 1,031 kilometers (639 miles) north of Sydney. The location was ideal. Fresh water was plentiful, grazing land was lush, and it was a long way from the free settlers. Within a year a colony had been established on the Brisbane River (pronounced "*Briz*-bun" by Aussies), named after the governor who had precipitated its discovery.

The Australian colony continued to expand, and in 1837 free settlers joined the convicts at Brisbane Town. In 1842 the original penal settlement was closed. The fledgling community remained under the control of New South Wales until 1859, when the state of Queensland was declared. By 1891 more than 104,000 people, attracted by gold, rich farmland, and local industries such as shipbuilding, had chosen to live in Brisbane.

During World War II, Gen. Douglas MacArthur set up his South Pacific headquarters in Brisbane, and thousands of American troops were housed in the area. By the early 1960s Brisbane had amassed a city-size population, but still had a reputation throughout Australia of being "just an overgrown country town." This bothered forward-thinking civic leaders, who set about to use the wealth of the state's newly developed mineral resources to change their community's image.

When Brisbane hosted the Commonwealth Games in 1982, Australians and others became aware that the Queensland capital was no longer a Sleepy Hollow down under. Even more people were attracted to the area, the population figures rising nearly as fast as the height of the office towers that appeared on the skyline. In the mid-1980s Brisbane's voters took their modern ideas to the ballot box and elected a woman, the popular Sallyanne Atkinson, Lord Mayor. In 1991 Atkinson was succeeded by Alderman Jim Soorley, who earned his M.A. in Organizational Development at Loyola University in Chicago in 1983–84.

Today Brisbane has a population of 1.2 million; only Sydney and Melbourne are larger. It has a slower pace and doesn't take itself as seriously as the southern capitals. Like Sunbelt cities in North America, Brisbane attracts young people who enjoy and perpetuate the area's relaxed life-style. Sports clothes are commonplace in the city center and a do-your-own-thing atmosphere prevails. However, the close to 15 million visitors who attended the highly successful World Expo 88 will be the first to tell you that this is Australia's most "go ahead" metropolis.

WHAT'S SPECIAL ABOUT BRISBANE

Ace Attractions
☐ The Australian Woolshed, a chance to learn about sheep, milk a cow, and generally become conversant in the agricultural side of life in Australia. Highly recommended.

Architectural Highlights
☐ The Queensland Cultural Centre, a low-rise complex of buildings surrounded by imaginative pools and fountains—a visual treat.

Regional Food
☐ Excellent opportunities for savoring seafood at the city's dining spots. Don't miss the Moreton Bay bugs.

For Kids of All Ages
☐ Lone Pine Koala Sanctuary, containing the world's largest population of the cuddly creatures.
☐ Bunya Park—also a great place to see and hold a koala.

Shopping
☐ The only city in Australia to offer 7-day shopping in the central business district.

Sunday Selections
☐ The Cats Tango Pure Crafts Market, held in the plazas and boardwalks around the Riverside Centre every Sunday from 8:15am to 3pm.

1. ORIENTATION

ARRIVING

BY PLANE

Qantas, Air New Zealand, Continental, and **British Airways** operate direct flights to Brisbane from Europe, New Zealand, and North America; passengers on other international carriers may have to change to a domestic airline in another gateway city.

If you are traveling to the Queensland capital from within Australia, you'll find there are frequent air, rail, and bus services. **Ansett, Australian Airlines, Compass,** and **Eastwest** fly in and out several times a day. Australian Airlines' Sydney-Brisbane Blue Roo Fare is A$145 (U.S. $116). The Australian Air Pass fares range from A$136 to A$170 (U.S. $108.80 to U.S. $136).

Brisbane's international airport provides a **Westpac Bank,** mailbox, bar, restaurant, and shops, but lacks lockers and showers.

Brisbane has separate international and domestic airport terminals located 5 minutes apart and 11 kilometers (7 miles) from the city center. The domestic terminal, built in 1987, is one of the most modern in Australia. **Coachtrans** (tel. 236-1000 or 236-1400) operates a half-hourly shuttle bus service from each terminal to the city center (A$5/U.S. $4) and between terminals; taxis are also available (about A$15/U.S. $12). The major car-rental companies have desks in both buildings.

BY TRAIN

The Spirit of Capricorn brings visitors from Rockhampton; the trip takes almost 10 hours and costs A$62.90 (U.S. $50.35) economy-class sitting and A$140.60 (U.S. $112.50) for a first-class berth. The **Sunlander** and **Queenslander** carry passengers from Cairns. That journey lasts about 33 hours and costs A$114.70 (U.S. $91.80) for an economy-class seat—more for a berth and meals. A ticket on the Sydney-Murwillumbah XPT (with coach connection to Brisbane) costs A$130 (U.S. $104) first class and A$90 (U.S. $72) economy class. Children are charged almost half price.

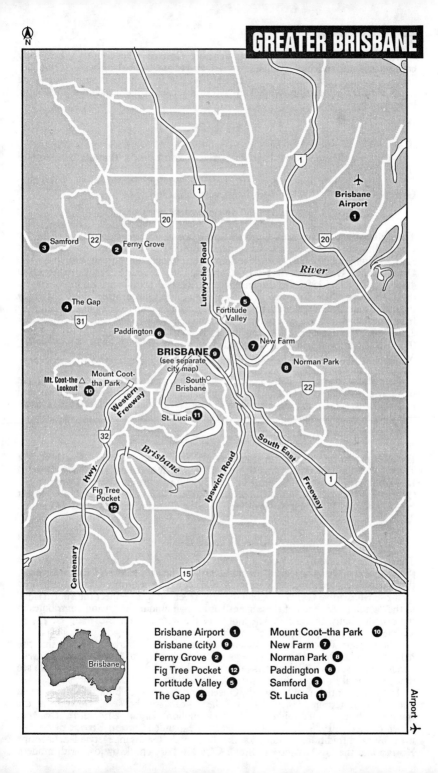

GREATER BRISBANE

Brisbane Airport ①
Brisbane (city) ⑨
Ferny Grove ②
Fig Tree Pocket ⑫
Fortitude Valley ⑤
The Gap ④

Mount Coot–tha Park ⑩
New Farm ⑦
Norman Park ⑧
Paddington ⑥
Samford ③
St. Lucia ⑪

Airport ✈

Trains arrive at Brisbane's spiffy **Transit Centre,** the country's first fully coordinated rail and bus terminal, located on **Roma Street** adjacent to the city center. Facilities here include an extensive food hall with inexpensive take-out-style meals, showers, a pharmacy, while-you-wait shoe repair, post office, florist, and tourist information.

BY BUS

If you take the bus to Brisbane from Sydney, the 17-hour trip costs A$63 (U.S. $50.40). Long-distance coach trips also arrive at **Brisbane's Transit Centre** (see above).

For intercity bus information, call these bus services: **Pioneer** (tel. 840-9350), **Greyhound** (tel. 840-9343), **Bus Australia** (tel. 236-2272).

TOURIST INFORMATION

The **Brisbane Visitors and Convention Bureau** operates information centers at City Hall, King George Square, Brisbane, QLD 4000 (Monday through Friday from 9am to 5pm; tel. 07/221-8411), and in the international airport terminal. The **Queensland Government Travel Centre**, 196 Adelaide Street, Brisbane, QLD 4000 (tel. 07/833-5255), also dispenses advice. There is an information booth run by the **Brisbane City Council** in the middle of the Queen Street Mall (Monday through Thursday from 8:30am to 5pm, Friday from 8:30am to 8:30pm, and Saturday from 9am to 4pm). You can phone them between 8:30am and 5pm weekdays (tel. 225-4360). The **Cultural Centre** makes news available on a 24-hour tape (tel. 07/11-632). Information is also provided at the **Transit Centre,** Roma Street, Monday through Friday from 7:30am to 5pm and on weekends from 7:30am to 12:30pm (tel. 236-2020).

Sunstate Tours (tel. 236-3355) and **Boomerang Tours** (tel. 236-3614) operate half-day city-sights tours (A$20/U.S. $16 for adults, A$10/U.S. $8 for children) and full-day trips north to the **Sunshine Coast** or south to the **Gold Coast** (A$35/U.S. $28 for adults, A$18/U.S. $14.40 for children).

INTERSTATE INFORMATION

For information on other states, contact the following offices: **New South Wales Travel Centre,** 40 Queen Street (tel. 229-8833); **Northern Territory Tourist Commission,** 48 Queen Street (tel. 229-5799); **Tasmanian Travel Centre,** 217 Queen Street (tel. 221-2744); **Victorian Tourist Commission,** 45 Queen Street (tel. 221-4300); **Western Australian Tourist Centre,** 243 Edward Street (tel. 229-5794).

CITY LAYOUT

The Brisbane River follows a curved course through the city. It wanders leisurely past the spectacular **Queensland Cultural Centre,** the former **World Expo 88 site,** the **Botanic Gardens,** cliffs fortified with convict-cut stone, and the mirrored high-rise **Riverside Centre.** Along the way, seven bridges connect the "north side" to the "south side." Each of these spans has its own unique design and contributes to the overall beauty of the city. The mouth of the waterway on **Moreton Bay** is 16 kilometers (10 miles) east, as the crow flies.

The city sprawls over a wide area and is encircled by suburbs and parks that rise from low hills. One of the best views of Brisbane is from **Mt. Coot-tha Park,** perched on a summit 7 kilometers (4 miles) to the west. From this point one can see that the central business district is triangular, with the river on two sides.

In the residential neighborhoods, Queenslanders—houses built on stilts to avoid flood danger, termite destruction, and heat—can still be seen. Downtown, the standard-setting A$480-million (U.S. $384-million) **Myer Shopping Centre,** which opened in 1988, dominates the recently expanded **Queen Street pedestrian mall,** and traditional landmarks like the French Renaissance–style **Parliament House** and the Queensland sandstone **City Hall** are cheek by jowl with modern high-rises. **Queen Street** is the main thoroughfare, and parallel streets are named after royal women: **Ann, Adelaide, Elizabeth, Charlotte, Mary.** Cross streets are named after royal men: **George, Albert,** and **Edward.**

  South Brisbane, across the **Victoria Bridge** from the city, was extensively developed as the site of World Expo 88 and boasts the **Queensland Cultural Centre** with its wonderful **Performing Arts Complex,** art gallery, and museum. **Spring Hill** is an inner suburb on a rise just north of the city center. **Chinatown** is located in **Fortitude Valley,** another close-in area. **Paddington,** a popular suburb northwest of the central business district, is known for historic buildings that house boutiques, craft shops, and restaurants.

2. GETTING AROUND

BY PUBLIC TRANSPORTATION

Brisbane is well served by public buses, suburban trains, cross-river ferries, and taxis. In addition, a **Citysights** specialty bus makes the rounds of the major sightseeing attractions. This handy transport operates Sunday through Friday from 9am to 4pm and costs A$9 (U.S. $7.20) for adults and A$5 (U.S. $4) for children. See also "Organized Tours" in "Brisbane Attractions," below.

BY BUS

The Brisbane City Council operates a bus service throughout the city and suburban areas. Buses operate Monday through Friday from 5:30am to 11pm, with reduced frequency on weekends. Timetables and information are available from the **Public Transport Information Centre,** Brisbane Administration Centre, corner of George and Ann streets (tel. 225-4444). A single-zone ticket costs A90¢ (U.S. 75¢) for adults and A45¢ (U.S. 40¢) for children. A special reduced-price **City Heart fare** of A45¢ (U.S. 40¢) is available in the central business district; bus stops in this zone display a sign with a red heart in a black triangle. **Day Rover** tickets cost A$5.50 (U.S. $4.40) when purchased from a driver, A$5 (U.S. $4) when purchased from a ticket agent, and they provide unlimited bus travel for 1 day.

BY TRAIN

Brisbane's suburban trains service a wide area and operate daily from 4:30am to 1:30am. Maps and timetables are available from the information desk at the **Central Railway Station,** Ann Street (tel. 235-2222). Tickets cost A$1.20 (U.S. $1) per sector except in the City Circle, where they cost A90¢ (U.S. 75¢). **Day Rover** tickets are available.

BY FERRY

Cross-river ferries operate from Edward Street, Waterfront Place, and the Riverside Centre at approximately 15-minute intervals. Individual tickets cost A80¢ (U.S. 65¢) and a book of 10 adult tickets, the **Ferry Fare Saver,** is A$6.40 (U.S. $5.15). For information, call the **Brisbane City Council Ferries** (tel. 399-4768).

BY TAXI

The three major cab companies are **Ascot Taxi Service** (tel. 831-3000), **Black and White Cab Company** (tel. 238-1000), and **Yellow Cab Company** (tel. 391-0191). These operate 24 hours a day.

BY CAR

The following car-rental agencies have offices in Brisbane: **Ansa International,** 925 Ann Street, Fortitude Valley (tel. 257-1622, or toll free 008/07-4116 in Australia);

Avis, 275 Wickham Terrace, Fortitude Valley (tel. 252-7111); **Budget,** St. Paul's Terrace, Fortitude Valley (tel. 252-0151); **Hertz,** 55 Charlotte Street (tel. 221-6166); **National,** 388 Wickham Terrace, Fortitude Valley (tel. 854-1499); **Thrifty,** 325 Wickham Terrace, Fortitude Valley (tel. 252-5994).

For dealings with the **RACQ** (Royal Automobile Club of Queensland), 190 Edward Street (tel. 253-2444), you must present your home-country membership card.

FAST FACTS *BRISBANE*

Airline Offices   The following have offices in Brisbane: Air New Zealand, 288 Edward St. (tel. 07/229-3044); Australian Regional Airlines, c/o Australian Airlines (tel. 07/260-3311); Ansett, corner of George and Queen Sts. (tel. 07/854-2828); Australian Airlines, 247 Adelaide St. (tel. 07/260-3311 or 07/223-3333); British Airways, 243 Edward St. (tel. 07/232-3000); Compass Airlines (tel. 834-1444); Continental, 123 Eagle St. (tel. 07/221-7961); Eastwest Airlines, 195 Adelaide St. (tel. 07/854-2296); Qantas Airways, 241 Adelaide St. (tel. 07/234-3747); Sunstate Airlines, Brisbane Airport (tel. 07/223-3333); United Airlines, 307 Queen St. (tel. 07/221-7477); UTA French Airlines, 1st floor, 201 Edward St. (tel. 07/221-5655).

American Express   Perry House, 131 Elizabeth St. (tel. 07/229-0022). Open regular business hours.

Area Code   Brisbane telephone numbers are in the 07 area code.

Baby-sitters   Between the hours of 8am–5pm Mon–Fri, children under 6 years of age may be left at Kindercraft Childcare Centre on the 3rd floor of the City Hall, King George Sq. (tel. 221-7639 or 221-0145). The cost is A$2.50 (U.S. $2) an hour. At other times, it is best to check with the concierge at your hotel or look in the local newspaper for ads.

Business Hours   Banks are generally open Mon–Thurs 9:30am–4pm and Fri 9:30am–5pm. Stores are generally open Mon–Thurs 9am–5:30pm, 9am–9pm, Sat 8:30am–4pm, and Sun 10:30am–4pm. Suburban shops stay open until 9pm Thurs instead of Fri.

Car Rentals   See "Getting Around," above, in this chapter.

Currency   See "Information, Entry Requirements, and Money" in Chapter 2.

Dentist   Contact Dentists Emergency Service (tel. 252-2793).

Doctor   For 24-hour medical service, call 378-6900 or 831-8311.

Drugstores [Chemist Shops]   T & G Corner Day and Night Pharmacy, Queen Street Mall, corner Albert St. (tel. 221-4585), is open Mon–Sat 8am–9pm and Sun 10am–5pm.

Embassies/Consulates   The following countries have consulates in Brisbane: New Zealand, 288 Edward St. (tel. 221-9933); United Kingdom, 193 North Quay (tel. 236-2575); United States, 383 Wickham Terrace (tel. 839-8955).

Emergencies   Dial 000 to summon ambulance, fire department, or police in an emergency.

Eyeglasses   Eyewear Now, 184 Albert St., opposite Albert Cinemas (tel. 221-4055), is open Mon–Thurs 8:30am–5:30pm, Fri 8:30am–9pm, and Sat 8:30am–4pm. They can make new prescription lenses in 1 hour.

Hairdressers/Barbers   Antoine's Hair and Beauty Salon, 323 Brunswick St., Fortitude Valley (tel. 252-2985), caters to men and women.

Holidays   See "When to Go" in Chapter 2.

Hospitals   Royal Brisbane Hospital, Herston Rd., Herston (tel. 253-8111), is about 10 minutes from the city center.

Hotlines   Brisbane Crisis Line (tel. 252-1111); Lifeline (tel. 252-1213); Rape Crisis Line (tel. 844-4008).

Laundry/Dry Cleaning   Alex's Laundromat, corner of Gympie Rd. and Boothby St., Kedron (tel. 359-3059), is open daily 5:30am–10pm. Same-day service is available from the dry cleaner in the Myer Centre, Shop 18 (tel. 221-5742).

Libraries Try the State Library of Queensland, Cultural Centre (tel. 840-7880). It's open Sun–Fri 10am–5pm.

Luggage Storage/Lockers There are lockers on the third floor of the Transit Centre, Roma St. (tel. 236-1400).

Newspapers/Magazines The *Courier-Mail* is the major metropolitan daily. *The Australian* is a nationwide daily. A wide range of overseas and domestic newspapers and magazines is available at Currans Corner Souvenirs, corner of Adelaide and Edward streets (tel. 229-3690). Currans is open 8am–9pm daily.

Photographic Needs Camera Tech, 270 Adelaide St. (tel. 229-5406), does repairs on the premises and gives free estimates.

Police Dial 000.

Postal Code Central Brisbane addresses have a 4000 postal code.

Post Office The General Post Office (GPO), 261 Queen St. (tel. 224-1202), is open Mon–Fri 7am–7pm. Other post offices in the city, such as the one in the Transit Centre, are open Mon–Fri 9am–5pm. Use the GPO for general delivery (poste restante).

Radio Classical, 106.1 FM or 103.7 FM; country western, 101.1 FM; news and weather, 612 AM; rock, 105.3 FM, 104.5 FM, or 1008 AM.

Religious Services You'll be able to attend services at the following locations: Anglican, St. John's Cathedral, 417 Ann St. (tel. 839-2420); Baptist, City Tabernacle, Wickham Terrace (tel. 831-1613); Christian Scientist, First Church of Christ Scientist, 273 North Quay (tel. 236-2023); Greek Orthodox, Church of the Assumption, Creek Rd., Mount Gravatt (tel. 343-7304); Jewish, Brisbane Synagogue, Margaret St. (tel. 229-3412); Lutheran, St. Andrews, 25 Wickham Terrace (tel. 831-9106); Muslim, 309 Nursery Rd., Holland Park (tel. 343-4748); Presbyterian, 145 Ann St. (tel. 221-0238); Roman Catholic, St. Stephen's Cathedral, Elizabeth St. (tel. 229-4827); Uniting Church, corner of Albert and Ann streets (tel. 221-6788); Seventh-Day Adventist, corner of Eagle and Quay streets (tel. 221-7972).

Shoe Repairs Mister Minit, Shop 14, Myer Centre, Queen Street Mall (tel. 221-2547), is open Mon–Fri 9am–5:30pm.

Taxes No sales tax or Goods and Services Tax (GST) is added to purchases. Neither is there a hotel tax.

Taxis See "Getting Around," above, in this chapter.

Telegrams/Telex These can be sent from the GPO.

Television Brisbane receives channels 2, 7, 9, 10, and SBS. For information on their content see "Fast Facts: Sydney" in Chapter 3.

Transit Info For information on public buses, call the Bus Hotline 225-4444; address queries about suburban train service to 235-2222; questions about Brisbane's ferry service will be answered if you call 399-4768.

Useful Telephone Numbers For weather information, call 1196. Time: 1194. Tourist Infoline: 11-654. B105 FM News Service: 1197. Brisbane Entertainment Centre: 11-611. Women's Community Health Centre: 844-1935. Women's Information Service: 229-1580. Gay and Lesbian Counselling and Information Service: 844-2967.

3. BRISBANE ACCOMMODATIONS

Hotels and motels in Brisbane are a sight for sore pocketbooks if you're coming from Sydney, where accommodations costs are generally higher. Standards are still quite good, and a wide range—from top-class to budget—is available.

If you'd like to stay with a local family in their home, contact **Aussie Home**

Stays, P.O. Box 1277, Broadbeach, QLD 4218 (tel. 075/72-5826). Prices, which include a cooked breakfast, are A$44 to A$50 (U.S. $35.20 to U.S. $40) single, A$76 to A$84 (U.S. $60.80 to U.S. $67.20) for two people sharing a room. Bed-and-breakfast in city and country homes in and around Brisbane, the Gold Coast, and Cairns can be arranged. Children aged 3 to 14 are charged half the adult rate.

IN THE CITY CENTER

EXPENSIVE

BRISBANE CITY TRAVELODGE, Roma St., Brisbane, QLD 4000. Tel. 07/238-2222. Fax 07/238-2288. 169 rms, 22 king suites. A/C MINIBAR TV TEL

$ Rates: A$160 (U.S. $128) standard single or double; A$170 (U.S. $136) superior room; A$180 (U.S. $144) king suite; A$20 (U.S. $16) extra person. Children under 16 stay free in parents' room. Weekend discounts available. Lower rates through Aussie auto clubs. No-smoking rooms available. AE, BC, DC, MC, V. **Parking:** Free.

Though the hotel is located on top of the Transit Centre, where coaches and trains come and go, rooms are well insulated against noise. The center's shoe-repair shop, dry cleaner, tourist information desk, and food hall are just steps from the hotel. State-of-the-art elevators give time and weather information via an electronic readout, announce other messages with the aid of a computer-operated voice, and whisk guests between floors in a matter of seconds.

Not only is the Travelodge one of the most attractive hotels in town, but it's also Brisbane's best value. I would describe it as a five-star hotel with four-star prices. This 18-story hotel, open since 1986, offers spacious rooms with large windows that frame lofty city views. All quarters feature contemporary blond wood built-in desks and dressers, his-and-hers closets, and pleasing teal-and-light-brown decors. The staff is unusually helpful and friendly.

Dining/Entertainment: The Sunlander Cocktail Lounge is just off the lobby foyer, and the Queenslander public bar is accessed from the Transit Centre; the Drawing Room restaurant and bar are on the fifth floor, and the casual Verandah Café is on the second floor.

Services: 24-hour room service, turn-down service, laundry, concierge, and baby-sitting.

Facilities: Two hot spas, a gym, and a sauna; self-service laundry.

BRISBANE HILTON, 190 Elizabeth St., Brisbane, QLD 4000. Tel. 07/231-3131, or toll free 008/22-2255 in Australia. Fax 07/231-3199. 321 rms and suites. A/C MINIBAR TV TEL

$ Rates: A$245 (U.S. $196) single; A$255–A$295 (U.S. $204–U.S. $236) double; A$750 (U.S. $600) suite; A$305 (U.S. $244) executive floor; A$40 (U.S. $32) extra person. Children under 18 stay free in parents' room. Lower weekend rates. No-smoking rooms available. AE, BC, CB, DC, MC, V. **Parking:** A$10 (U.S. $8).

The hotel's entrance opens onto the Queen Street pedestrian shopping mall. Inside, glass elevators run from the 6th to the 25th floor under Australia's largest glass-domed atrium.

All bedrooms have hairdryers, videos, clock radios, coffee- and tea-making facilities, and attractive furnishings. Accommodations on the north side have a city view; south-side rooms have river vistas. Like the Sheraton, the Hilton offers extra pampering and facilities for guests who pay a premium rate. Executive Floor residents are provided with fresh flowers and terry robes, free local calls, and a complimentary breakfast.

Dining/Entertainment: The Atrium Lounge, with its cane chairs and potted palms, is popular with locals as well as visitors. Situated just off the lobby, it's a convenient and agreeable spot for a drink. The Hilton also offers a piano bar, the open-air Tropicana Bar, America's Cup Bar with wide-screen TV for watching sporting events, the Prince Edward Pub, and Her Majesty's Lounge Bar. Dining options range from the casual Atrium Café to Victoria's Fine Dining Room.

Service: 24-hour room service, turn-down service, laundry, valet, concierge, baby-sitting, and massage. Executive Floors have a butler on call.

Facilities: Everyone has access to the outdoor pool on the eighth floor (free), the Nautilus Health Club one level down (free for Executive Floor guests, A$6 to A$11/U.S. $4.80 to U.S. $8.80 for others), and the tennis court (free for Executive Floor guests, A$18/U.S. $14.40 for others).

SHERATON BRISBANE HOTEL & TOWERS, 249 Turbot St., Brisbane, QLD 4000. Tel. 07/835-3535. Fax 07/835-4960. 410 rms, 25 suites. A/C MINIBAR TV TEL

$ Rates: A$262 (U.S. $209.60) single or double; A$352 (U.S. $281.60) executive floor; A$429 (U.S. $343.20) suite; A$55 (U.S. $44) extra person. Children under 18 are free in parents' room. Lower weekend rates. No-smoking rooms available. AE, BC, CB, DC, MC, V. **Parking:** Free.

The hotel is built over the Central Railway Station in the heart of the city and, as with the Travelodge above the Transit Centre, the train noise cannot be heard. I assumed a hotel over a train station would have a mundane atmosphere, but I was wrong. The lobby is glamorous, with Oriental-pattern carpets, potted palms in brass planters, and overstuffed chairs. A doorman in top hat and tails welcomes guests at the porte cochère.

The Sheraton is really two hotels in one. Aside from the regular rooms, Tower accommodations constitute a kind of hotel within a hotel. These premium quarters are ideal for those guests who wish special treatment and are happy to pay for it. Personalized stationery, terry robes, upgraded amenities, daily newspaper, and nightly turn-down service are all provided. In addition, Tower residents can use a special lounge where a butler is on duty from 6am to 1am, hors d'oeuvres and cocktails are served for an hour each evening, local calls are free, and a complimentary breakfast buffet is offered every morning. Rooms in the main part of the Sheraton are also luxurious. Sixteen rooms are specially outfitted for handicapped visitors.

Dining/Entertainment: Breakfast, lunch, and dinner are served 7 days a week in the Sidewalk Café, where large windows overlook the city and Post Office Square. The breakfast buffet costs A$20 (U.S. $16), and the weekday buffet lunch is the same price. Denison's, the hotel's fine-dining venue, is open for dinner Tuesday through Saturday. There are six bars including Someplace Else—which has to be seen to be believed.

Services: 24-hour room service, turn-down service, shoeshine, laundry, valet, concierge, baby-sitting, and massage.

Facilities: Outdoor pool, health club, squash courts, sauna, and spa. The club is free to Tower guests and costs others A$9 (U.S. $7.20). There are also a business center, hair salon, and gift shop.

MODERATE

GATEWAY HOTEL, 85 North Quay, Brisbane, QLD 4000. Tel. 07/236-3300. Fax 07/236-1036. 175 rms, 15 suites. A/C MINIBAR TV TEL

$ Rates: A$99 (U.S. $79.20) single or double; A$130–A$340 (U.S. $104–U.S. $272) suite; A$10 (U.S. $8) extra person. AE, BC, DC, MC, V. **Parking:** Free.

Situated on the Brisbane River with views across the water to the beautiful Queensland Cultural Centre and the former site of World Expo 88, this 13-story hotel's guest rooms all feature AM/FM clock radios, coffee- and tea-making facilities, toasters, small fridges, and tub/shower combinations. The hotel, built in 1971, was completely remodeled in 1988. Floors 9 and 10 are reserved for nonsmokers. Rooms on floors four and five lack minibars. The hotel also provides in-house movies, 24-hour room service, a pool, a sauna, and a spa.

Gillies Restaurant, an à la carte seafood eatery with an old-world atmosphere created by crystal chandeliers and Louis XVI chairs, is open daily for breakfast and dinner. The garden terrace area of Gillies's piano bar is a great spot for a drink with a river view. The Wiggs Grill is so named because the Supreme Court is next door to the hotel and many judges dine there. Portraits of jurists and shelves of law books line the walls.

GAZEBO HOTEL, 345 Wickham Terrace, Brisbane, QLD 4000. Tel. 07/831-6177, or toll free 008/77-7789 in Australia. Fax 07/832-5919. 167 rms, 13 suites. A/C MINIBAR TV TEL

$ **Rates:** A$125–A$152 (U.S. $100–U.S. $121.60) single or double; A$176–A$220 (U.S. $140.80–U.S. $176) suite; A$15 (U.S. $12) extra person. Children under 12 stay free in parents' room. Reservations can be made through Flag Inns. Lower weekend rates. No-smoking rooms available. AE, BC, DC, MC, V. **Parking:** Free.

Located between the city and the inner suburb of Spring Hill, the hotel is out of the hustle and bustle but within walking distance of shops and sights. Because of the building's contemporary terraced architecture, every room at the 11-story Gazebo Hotel has its own balcony. These provide lots of fresh air and good views of either the city or the surrounding hills. Only ground-floor quarters lack views. Rooms on two floors lack minibars; 90 rooms have bath tubs; 13 offer cooking facilities. The hotel has 24-hour room service, but if you'd rather dine out, the Terrace Bistro is a pleasant coffee shop with indoor and outdoor seating. The Gazebo's other dining option, Wickham's Restaurant on the 10th floor, has a wonderful city-lights view at night. Laundry facilities and a swimming pool are also provided.

REGAL PARKVIEW MOTEL, 128-132 Alice St., Brisbane, QLD 4000. Tel. 07/229-7000. Fax 07/229-7000. 49 rms. A/C TV TEL

$ **Rates:** A$60 (U.S. $48) single; A$65 (U.S. $52) double; A$10 (U.S. $8) extra adult; A$5 (U.S. $4) extra child. Senior citizen discount offered. AE, BC, DC, MC, V. **Parking:** Free.

The Regal Parkview is a modest two-story motel adjacent to the Botanic Gardens and 4 blocks from the heart of downtown. At one time, there were two separate adjacent properties, the Motel Regal and the Parkview Motel, but they became one in early 1990. Nine rooms have views of the park, and all quarters offer large windows which make the rooms bright. Amenities include radios, coffee- and tea-making facilities, and small refrigerators. No bath tubs, only showers. A small swimming pool, laundry room, and a licensed restaurant called Barney Barnard are on the premises; there is limited room service. What the family-owned-and-operated Regal Parkview lacks in flashy amenities it makes up for with location and friendly, personal service.

SPRING HILL
MODERATE

ALBERT PARK MOTOR INN, 551 Wickham Terrace, Spring Hill, QLD 4004. Tel. 07/831-3111, or toll free 008/77-7702 in Australia. Fax 07/832-1290. 95 rms. A/C TV TEL **Bus:** No. 23 or 61.

$ **Rates:** A$85 (U.S. $68) single or double; A$90 (U.S. $72) executive floor; A$10 (U.S. $8) extra person. Children under 18 stay free in parents' room. Lower weekend rates. Reservation can be made through Flag Inns. No-smoking rooms available. AE, BC, DC, MC, V. **Parking:** Free.

This hotel's pleasant rooms overlook Albert Park about a 10-minute walk from the city center. It's located in the inner suburb of Spring Hill, an interesting older area with many restored terrace houses. The Transit Centre is 1 kilometer (½ mile) to the south. By the time you arrive, an ambitious building program, more than doubling the size of the property, will have been completed. Rooms have showers, no tubs, clock radios, coffee- and tea-making facilities, small refrigerators, and queen-size or double beds. Room service is available 24 hours a day. Guests also have use of the pool and business center. Albert Park's restaurant serves all meals during the week, but is closed Sunday.

HOTEL RIDGE, 189 Leichardt St. (corner of Henry St.), Brisbane, QLD 4000. Tel. 07/831-5000, or toll free 008/07-7777 in Australia. Fax 07/832-2589. 63 rms, 21 suites. A/C MINIBAR TV TEL **Bus:** City precinct express bus.
$ Rates: A$103 (U.S. $82.40) single or double; A$131 (U.S. $104.80) suite; A$10 (U.S. $8) extra person. Weekend discounts. AE, BC, DC, MC, V. **Parking:** Free.

Located on the edge of the city center near the inner suburb of Spring Hill, this 10-story hotel has large family suites which are ideal if there are four or five of you traveling together. Each large unit has a kitchenette, well stocked with dishes and cutlery; a table and chairs; and a generous amount of closet space. There are also regular hotel rooms without cooking facilities. Most quarters have showers only, and beds are either queens or twins. Every room has a safe-deposit box, clock radio, coffee- and tea-making facilities, and a small refrigerator. Guests are also provided with 24-hour room service and use of the hotel's laundry room, pool, and sauna.

The Rooftop Restaurant, with a great city view, is one of the few dining spots in Brisbane with live dance music: Tuesday through Saturday nights a band and vocalist present traditional music. Breakfast is served daily in this room, and à la carte meals are offered at lunch Monday through Friday and at dinner nightly.

BUDGET

ANNIE'S SHANDON INN, 405 Upper Edward St., Brisbane, QLD 4000. Tel. 07/831-8684. Fax 07/831-3073. 19 rms (4 with bath).
$ Rates (including continental breakfast): A$35–A$45 (U.S. $28–U.S. $36) single; A$45–A$55 (U.S. $36–U.S. $44) double; A$10 (U.S. $8) extra adult; A$5 (U.S. $4) extra child. AE, BC, MC, V.
Parking: Free.

Located on the edge of the city center, Annie's Shandon Inn is owned by Carmel Nicholson, whose grandmother came out from Ireland in 1888. "She worked as a maid in this hotel, which was just called 'Shandon' then," the proprietor told me. "Later she borrowed money from Irish bank managers and bought the place." The property is one of the oldest in Brisbane, having been built in 1854, and has an eye-catching blue stucco exterior with pink shutters. Inside, Carmel has decorated the B&B's bedrooms with coordinated country-print curtains, bedspreads, and sheets. Rooms are charming, but not large; eight have sinks; four have en suite shower, sink, and toilet. A no-smoking policy prevails in the communal breakfast and TV rooms. The downstairs hallway is lined with old family photos, and the proprietress, who is exceptionally friendly and cheerful, never seems to tire of telling guests about them.

SOUTH BRISBANE

MODERATE

HILLCREST CENTRAL APARTMENTS, 311 Vulture St., South Brisbane, QLD 4101. Tel. 07/846-3000. Fax 07/846-3578. 80 units. A/C TV TEL **Bus:** No. 160, 170, or 180.
$ Rates: A$88–A$98 (U.S. $70.40–U.S. $78.40) single; A$126–A$160 (U.S. $100.80–U.S. $128) double. Weekly and monthly discounts. AE, BC, DC, MC, V.
Parking: Free.

These spacious, modern apartments are very good value for folks who wish all the comforts of home when they travel. All but 16 units have full kitchens, and the two-bedroom apartments have their own washing machines and dryers. Some quarters have tub/showers, some just showers, and a choice of either one queen-size bed or two singles is offered. The contemporary pale-gray and aqua-blue decors include stylish furnishings imported from Italy. All two-bedroom apartments have balconies, and all but a few units have wonderful city/river outlooks. All guests have access to the pool, tennis court, sauna, spa, games room, and children's playground. One apartment in the nine-story building is equipped for handicapped travelers.

A bistro in the lobby is open for breakfast and casual dinners. Some guests take their meals up to their apartments, while others carry them out to the swimming pool area.

KANGAROO POINT

MODERATE

OLIMS BRISBANE, 355 Main St., Kangaroo Point, QLD 4169. Tel. 07/391-5566. Fax 07/391-8715. 91 rms. A/C MINIBAR TV TEL **Bus:** No. 30, 31, or 367. **Ferry:** From the foot of Edward St. to Thornton St.

$ Rates: A$82–A$88 (U.S. $65.60–U.S. $70.40) single or double; A$12 (U.S. $9.60) extra person. No-smoking rooms available. AE, BC, DC, MC, V. **Parking:** Free.

This eight-story motor inn is located right on the south bank of the Brisbane River, and many of the rooms have excellent views across the water to the city and Botanic Gardens. Accommodations at Olims are divided between the riverside block, with the best views, and a tall building behind it. Rooms are spacious and have contemporary decors. Ladies' quarters, with special accessories for women, are available. Guests have the use of a pool and laundry room.

The Restaurant, located above the riverside section, affords a breathtaking view and is open for breakfast daily, lunch during the week, and dinner nightly. Limited room service is also offered.

4. BRISBANE DINING

I have to confess that I expected Australia's best restaurants to be in Sydney and Melbourne, an idea that was reinforced by talking to residents of those southern cities, so I was very pleasantly surprised to stumble onto some incredibly good dining spots in Brisbane. For the most part, they are unpretentious, but dish for dish, they more than hold their own. The seafood places are especially wonderful and offer an opportunity to sample local specialties like Moreton Bay bugs (a delectable shellfish with a flavor similar to that of lobster), Queensland mud crabs, and fresh fish from the Great Barrier Reef. The Sunshine State's tropical products—pawpaws (papayas), mangoes, pineapples, and avocados—also come as a pleasant, unexpected treat, as does excellent beef.

IN THE CITY CENTER

EXPENSIVE

DENISON'S, in the Sheraton Brisbane Hotel, 249 Turbot St. Tel. 835-3535.

Cuisine: MODERN INTERNATIONAL. **Reservations:** Recommended at all times, imperative on weekends. **Train:** Central Station.

$ Prices: Appetizers A$11–A$24.50 (U.S. $8.80–U.S. $19.60); main courses A$29.50–A$45 (U.S. $23.60–U.S. $36). AE, BC, DC, MC, V.

Open: Dinner Tues–Sat 6–10pm.

Located on the 30th floor of the Sheraton Brisbane Hotel and approached by way of glass-walled elevators, this eatery provides mountain views from the dining area and city vistas from the cocktail lounge. The decor is formal and yet warm; imported linen and silver and fine crystal appear on every table. Tropical Queensland foliage is the subject of an etched-glass panel that forms one wall of the restaurant.

The menu includes such dishes as barramundi filets baked in parchment and flavored with lemongrass, and king prawns braised in young cabbage leaves. Beluga caviar served in ice with Russian vodka; roast wild duck with green apple Rösti and a cassis sauce; and venison médaillons with morel cream sauce and candied chestnuts are also available. The restaurant's extensive wine list includes a large number of domestic and imported vintages. After dinner, patrons choose from a selection of complimentary liqueurs served in handmade chocolate cups.

RUMPOLES ON THE QUAY, corner of Turbot St. and North Quay. Tel. 236-2877.

Cuisine: INNOVATIVE. **Reservations:** Recommended.

$ **Prices:** Appetizers A$9.50–A$15.50 (U.S. $7.60–U.S. $12.40); main courses A$20–A$27 (U.S. $16–U.S. $21.60). AE, BC, DC, MC, V.

Open: Lunch Mon–Fri noon–2pm (desserts until 3pm); dinner Mon–Sat 6:30–10pm; dessert and coffee 10–11pm; bar until midnight.

Doug Flockhart is Australia's answer to Wolfgang Puck, and Rumpoles is Brisbane's answer to L.A.'s Spago. The eatery is located across the river from the cultural center, and "modern international" is the way Flockhart describes his restaurant's fare. He is especially proud of the designer pizzas, which include smoked salmon, chives, salmon pearls, and sour cream (on one); grilled eggplant, fragrant garlic, Italian baked cheese, and kalamata olives (on another). He encourages his guests to graze rather than order a main course, and to this end he offers more than 30 entrée-size dishes, and some unusual salads and desserts.

If you enjoy watching chefs at work, take a seat at the counter and watch Rumpoles's wizards at work. This would also be a fun way to meet locals with whom you share an interest in creative, artfully prepared cuisine. Not surprisingly, this delightful eatery has won numerous awards, including the American Express Award for Best Specialist Restaurant in 1988–89 and again in 1990–91. Seating is both indoor and on a leafy covered terrace. An extensive wine list is offered, and many choices are available by the glass.

MODERATE

FRIDAY'S RIVERSIDE, 123 Eagle St. Tel. 832-2122.

Cuisine: CONTEMPORARY INTERNATIONAL. **Reservations:** Recommended, especially for a lunchtime window table in Friday's East. **Ferry:** Riverside Centre. **Bus:** City Circle.

$ **Prices:** Appetizers A$5–A$11 (U.S. $4–U.S. $8.80); main courses A$11.50–A$19.50 (U.S. $9.20–U.S. $15.60); luncheon buffet A$26 (U.S. $20.80). AE, BC, DC, MC, V.

Open: Sun–Fri 11am–10pm, Sat 5–10pm.

Friday's Riverside is really three contemporary-style restaurants under one roof. The attractive complex enjoys a delightful location on the north bank of the Brisbane River adjacent to the 40-story ultramodern Riverside Centre office tower. From the second-floor site, diners can watch the movement of boats of all sizes and types.

Club Friday's is an outside chargrill where the lunch and dinner menus include hamburgers, pastas, fish-and-chips, salads, seafood, and grain-fed Queensland beef. This is also a popular spot for Sunday brunch (9:30am to noon). An extensive smörgåsbord lunch of international cuisines is offered in Friday's East, and the restaurant is transformed into a nightclub at night. Friday's West, specializing in steaks and grills, is popular with those wanting a light meal or a quick snack and is open only Monday through Friday at lunch. Friday's East has the most extensive wine list.

JIMMY'S ON THE MALL, Queen Street Mall. Tel. 229-9999.

Cuisine: CONTEMPORARY INTERNATIONAL. **Reservations:** Not necessary. **Bus:** Any bus to Queen Street Bus Station.

$ **Prices:** Appetizers A$6.90–A$11.90 (U.S. $5.55–U.S. $9.55); main courses A$5.50–A$17.90 (U.S. $3.60–U.S. $6.35). Weekend and public holiday surcharge 20%. BC, MC, V.

Open: Daily 24 hours.

There are three Jimmy's, one at either end of the plaza and one in the middle. Their location in the heart of the city center and their reasonable prices contribute to their popularity. All three are casual and staffed by friendly people. The menu ranges from breakfast dishes through to lunch, dinner, and supper items. Fancy cocktails utilizing Queensland's good fresh fruit are a specialty, as is seafood, which the proprietor buys direct at the market each morning. Bagels, baguettes, and croissants can be filled with pâté, smoked salmon, prawns, or several other choices. You can also choose from nachos with melted cheese, chili sauce, and sour cream, spicy Singapore noodles, or a Weight Watcher's salad. Main courses include: sea perch, pasta, and sirloin steak.

NEWSTEAD

EXPENSIVE

ROSEVILLE, 56 Chester St., Newstead. Tel. 358-1377.
Cuisine: INTERNATIONAL. **Reservations:** Recommended.
$ **Prices:** Appetizers A$7–A$11 (U.S. $5.60–U.S. $8.80); main courses A$18–A$20 (U.S. $14.40–U.S. $16); fixed-price three-course lunch A$25 (U.S. $20); fixed-price three-course dinner A$29 (U.S. $23.20). AE, BC, DC, MC, V.
Open: Brunch daily from 11am; lunch daily from noon; dinner daily from 6pm.

It's hard to know where to start in describing this charming restaurant. The Victorian colonial house, restored by previous owners, has high ceilings, crystal chandeliers, stained-glass windows, and other earmarks of homes constructed in the early 1880s. Diners are seated in six rooms of the house and on the veranda. Outside tables have floral cloths; inside, lace tablecloths and bouquets of fresh flowers complement English and Australian antiques and an impressive collection of 16th- and 17th-century oil portraits in heavy gilded frames.

While the house is impressive, it's the 1-acre gardens that continue to win awards—300 rose bushes, 100 azaleas, and assorted other flowers and shrubs. Spring and summer (September to March) are the best seasons for a visit. Most things are in bloom then, including the century-old magnolia in front of the house.

Cuisine and service are equal to their gracious surroundings and have also won their share of awards. Tuxedoed waiters with red bow ties deliver superb gourmet dishes. You might choose something exotic such as Windsor royale—lamb brains in a light beer batter with a bourbon and pink peppercorn sauce—or a more basic dish such as roast beef and Yorkshire pudding. I can attest to the delectability of reef Sotheby, fresh filets of reef fish pocketed with sea scallops and served with a dill and white wine sauce.

MODERATE

BREAKFAST CREEK WHARF, 192 Breakfast Creek Rd., Newstead. Tel. 252-2451.
Cuisine: SEAFOOD. **Reservations:** None.
$ **Prices:** Appetizers A$5.95–A$9.95 (U.S. $4.80–U.S. $8); main courses A$13–A$19 (U.S. $10.40–U.S. $15.20); kids' meals A$6.95 (U.S. $5.60). Public holiday surcharge A$2.50 (U.S. $2) per adult. AE, BC, DC, MC, V.
Open: Lunch daily noon–2:30pm; dinner daily 6–10pm.

Breakfast Creek Wharf is located in the suburb of Newstead on the banks of Breakfast Creek, a stream that feeds into the Brisbane River. The waterfront setting is appropriate for a restaurant that specializes in fresh seafood and has a 19th-century nautical motif. Seating is both inside and out, and a ship's wheel, portholes, and wooden floors help create a briny atmosphere. The focal point of the restaurant is a full-scale reproduction of the vessel used by early explorer John Oxley.

The house specialty is the Flagship Platter, a tray for two or more people containing a combination of cold and hot seafood, including whole Moreton Bay bugs, Queensland swimmer crabs, calamari, oysters, scallops, filets of fish, and large prawns. Other popular items on the tabloid-style menu are coral trout, sea perch, barramundi, bouillabaisse, and whole lemon sole. A bottle of Lindemans Padthaway chardonnay will complement your meal. Other enjoyable white wines are Rosemount Estate chardonnay and Wolf Blass Rhine riesling.

MOUNT COOT-THA PARK
EXPENSIVE

MT. COOT-THA SUMMIT RESTAURANT, Sir Samuel Griffith Dr., Mt. Coot-tha "At the Lookout." Tel. 369-9922.
   Cuisine: INTERNATIONAL. **Reservations:** Recommended.
$ **Prices:** Appetizers A$4.90–A$11.90 (U.S. $3.95–U.S. $9.55); main courses A$13.50–A$22.90 (U.S. $10.80–U.S. $18.35); fixed-price three-course lunch A$22.90 (U.S. $18.35); kids' meals A$9.50 (U.S. $7.60); tea A$4.80 (U.S. $3.85). Public holiday surcharge 10%. AE, BC, DC, MC, V.
   Open: Morning tea daily 10–11:30am; lunch daily noon–2pm; afternoon tea daily 2:30–4pm; dinner daily 6–10pm.

⭐ Located 8 kilometers (5 miles) from the city, this restaurant offers both a splendid view of Brisbane's skyline and delicious meals served in a charming old-world atmosphere. It is housed in a renovated summer house and caretaker's cottage originally constructed by the Brisbane City Council in the 1920s. The wife of one of the park's first caretakers began serving teas to visitors more than 100 years ago, a tradition continued to the present day.

Entrées include barbecue prawns, oysters, fresh pasta, and mountain mushrooms. Main courses range from chicken and prawn roulade, steak and crayfish, pork Normandy, and Moreton Bay bugs in seafood mousse (sweet lobsterlike shellfish with a heavenly flavor). All main courses are served with vegetables or a generous tossed green salad; wonderful whole-grain rolls, baked on the premises, are accompanied by a variety of spreads. The setting is charming, the service good, and the food delicious. A taxi to Mt. Coot-tha costs about A$10 (U.S. $8).

ST. LUCIA
EXPENSIVE

CATS TANGO, 242 Hawken Dr., St. Lucia. Tel. 371-1452 or 371-1789.
   Cuisine: INTERNATIONAL. **Reservations:** Recommended.
$ **Prices:** Appetizers A$6–A$15 (U.S. $4.80–U.S. $12); main courses A$12–A$28 (U.S. $9.60–U.S. $22.40). AE, BC, DC, MC, V.
   Open: Dinner daily 5–10pm.

⭐ Cats Tango is a total experience in exotic fantasy, as well as being a very good place to eat. The restaurant is owned by a woman named Peter Hackworth, whose other talents include organizing the Cats Tango Craft Market, held at the Riverside Centre on Sunday. The name of the eatery comes from a French children's book. "It caught my fancy," Peter explains. Intricately carved Indian screens provide privacy between tables; vivid Belgian tapestries, Persian rugs, and stained glass add to a highly original, immensely uplifting atmosphere.

The menu is as creative as the decor. Each page lists an entrée, main course, and dessert from a different land. If you order from page one, the Carribean menu, you start with banana republic, "a delicate marriage of avocado and papaya, served beside tangy chicken aioli and endives." This is followed by ba ba reeba (spicy pork spareribs) and a dessert called "sugar 'n' spice and everything nice." Other pages offer French, Italian, Blackfoot Moroccan, Pritiken, Thai, Creole, African, and British fare. Portions are generous and you can, of course, mix and match your courses between countries. Costumed staff, a gypsy violinist, a belly dancer, and Kahli, the resident palmist, add to the fantasy.

MODERATE

PASTA PASTA, 242 Hawken Dr., St. Lucia. Tel. 371-1403.
   Cuisine: PASTA/DESSERTS. **Reservations:** Not required. **Bus:** Cityxpress no. 512 or others.
$ **Prices:** Full meal A$12–A$15 (U.S. $9.60–U.S. $12).
   Open: Daily 8am–midnight.

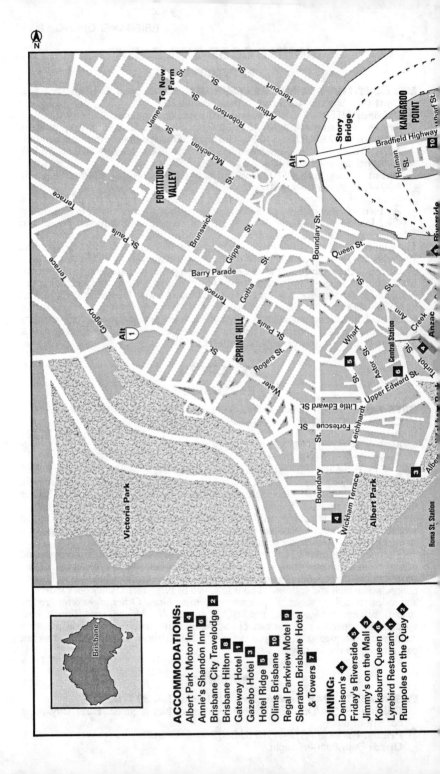

ACCOMMODATIONS:
Albert Park Motor Inn **4**
Annie's Shandon Inn **6**
Brisbane City Travelodge **2**
Brisbane Hilton **8**
Gateway Hotel **1**
Gazebo Hotel **3**
Hotel Ridge **5**
Olims Brisbane **10**
Regal Parkview Motel **9**
Sheraton Brisbane Hotel
& Towers **7**

DINING:
Denison's **4**
Friday's Riverside **5**
Jimmy's on the Mall **3**
Kookaburra Queen **6**
Lyrebird Restaurant **1**
Rumpoles on the Quay **2**

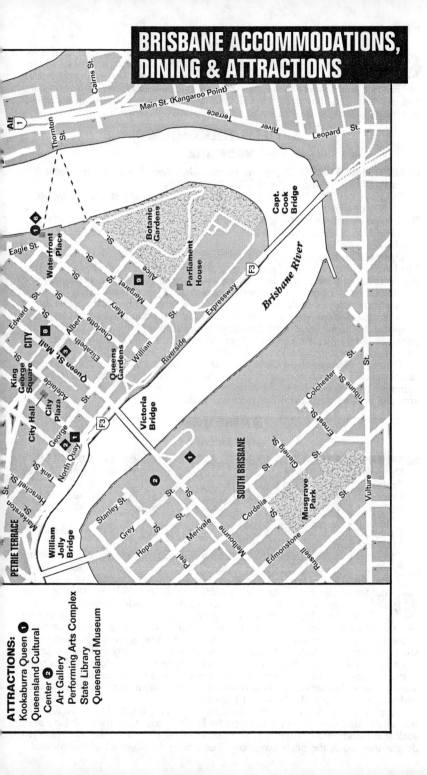

BRISBANE ACCOMMODATIONS, DINING & ATTRACTIONS

ATTRACTIONS:
Kookaburra Queen ❶
Queensland Cultural Center ❷
 Art Gallery
 Performing Arts Complex
 State Library
 Queensland Museum

Pasta Pasta is a colorful, lively spot for inexpensive pasta meals, wonderful ice cream, and fun. Everything is made on the premises: the pasta from whole-wheat semolina; the ice cream from an egg-custard base. Very fresh eggs, herbs, and produce contribute to the ultimate success of dishes. Salads and garlic bread are also available. Luscious cakes go with the ice cream, which comes in a creative assortment of flavors. You can eat in or take out. BYO.

SOUTH BRISBANE
MODERATE

LYREBIRD RESTAURANT, in the Performing Arts Complex on the south bank of the Brisbane River. Tel. 846-2434.
Cuisine: INTERNATIONAL. **Reservations:** Recommended. **Bus:** Cityxpress no. 502 or others.
$ Prices: Appetizers A$6–A$10 (U.S. $4.80–U.S. $8); main courses A$14.50–A$19 (U.S. $11.60–U.S. $15.20). Public holiday surcharge 15%. AE, BC, DC, MC, V.
Open: Mon–Sat noon–midnight.

The Lyrebird is an ideal spot for pretheater and posttheater dining. The casual bistro overlooks one of the plazas in the complex where a fountain sends up a cooling spray.

The Lyrebird offers the convenient option of a meal immediately before a performance, followed by dessert after the show. It's also handy that they sell a dozen or so very good wines by the glass, so that a concertgoing duo doesn't feel compelled to split a bottle of wine with dinner. If you dine here, you can choose curry, steak-and-kidney pie, lamb chops, a beefy hamburger, or something more elaborate such as green lobster médaillons and scallops in a puff pastry.

The nearby **Promenade Café** (tel. 840-7575) offers a less expensive, even more casual option for those who want light meals or snacks. Most seating is outside by a fountain. This inexpensive eatery is open Monday through Saturday from 10am to 4pm and until curtain time on performance nights.

SAMFORD
MODERATE

SAMFORD RESTAURANT, Main St., Samford Village. Tel. 289-1485.
Cuisine: INNOVATIVE INTERNATIONAL. **Reservations:** Recommended. **Train:** Ferny Grove, then 5-minute taxi.
$ Prices: Appetizers A$6–A$13.90 (U.S. $4.80–U.S. $11.15); main courses A$7.50–A$21.50 (U.S. $6–U.S. $17.20); "Young diners" meals A$9.50 (U.S. $7.60). AE, BC, DC, MC, V.
Open: Dinner Wed–Sun 6:30pm–midnight; tea Sun 10am–6pm; lunch Sun 11:30am–6pm.

The quality of the cuisine here is such that diners willingly make the half-hour drive to the small township of Samford 21 kilometers (13 miles) northwest of the city. Housed in a white cottage, the restaurant offers seating indoors or outdoors in a covered courtyard. Ceiling fans, fringed shades on hanging lights, and a profusion of greenery contribute to the old-world atmosphere.

Proprietress Joy Harman has designed an adventurous menu that focuses on two things: fresh seasonal produce and wonderful desserts. Most main courses are available in two sizes, so you can match your order to your appetite. For an appetizer you might like to try "oysters de joie" in a smoked cheese Mornay or thick and hearty pea-and-ham soup flavored with pita crisps. Main courses include four kinds of pasta (fettuccine carbonara is my favorite), rack of pork with a water chestnut and apricot stuffing, Snowy Mountains rainbow trout deboned and filled with Moreton Bay bugs and prawns, and aged rib filet with a béarnaise sauce.

Of all the delicious homemade desserts, Black Forest cake has evolved as the specialty of the house. Joy's version includes Bavarian cream, cherries that have been soaked in brandy and cinnamon, and "extremely rich" chocolate cake. The result is a delight that avoids the sickly sweet trap that can be the downfall of this particular dish. Other treats worth leaving room for include treacle pudding and Mandarin bread-and-butter pudding served with King Island double cream. The restaurant is BYO; a bottle shop, open daily, is two doors away. Highly recommended.

SPECIALTY DINING
DINING CLUSTERS

On the Deck, at the Riverside Centre on Eagle Street (tel. 833-2333), is an economical eatery where a dozen or so outlets sell a variety of food; seating is provided in a central area. **Designer Sandwiches** cost about A$4 (U.S. $3.20) and **Dr. Wok's** combination plate is less than A$8 (U.S. $6.40). **Aromas** sells wonderful cappuccino, and **Mediterrani** offers pastas, moussaka, pizzas, and other Southern European treats. On the Deck is open Monday to Friday 7am to 4pm and Sunday 10am to 3pm. You can dine indoors or out, and most tables have a river view. Get there on a City Circle bus or a ferry from Kangaroo Point.

LIGHT, CASUAL & FAST FOOD

If it's a quick meal in a convenient location you're after, I recommend you check out the food hall in the Transit Centre on Roma Street. **Top Chook, the Australian Pie Shop, Donut King,** and other fast-food vendors will fill you up for only a few dollars. If you like roast dinners, don't overlook the carvery, where such things as roast beef and lamb are offered for about A$6 (U.S. $4.80). Tables and chairs are provided.

WATERBORNE DINING

KOOKABURRA QUEEN, The Pier at Waterfront Place, 1 Eagle St. Tel. 221-1300.
   Cuisine: INTERNATIONAL. **Reservations:** Recommended. **Bus:** City Circle.
$ **Prices:** Cruise with morning or afternoon Devonshire tea A$15.30 (U.S. $12.25); lunch cruise A$18.60–A$44 (U.S. $14.90–U.S. $35.20); dinner cruise A$22–A$55 (U.S. $17.60–U.S. $44). Children 4–14 are charged half price. AE, BC, DC, MC, V.
   Open: Morning tea cruises Sun–Fri 10–11:30am; afternoon tea cruises Sun 3:30–5pm; lunch cruises Sun–Fri 12:45–2:15pm; dinner cruises Mon–Sat 7:30–11pm, Sun 6:30–9:30pm.
The elegant paddle wheeler, which was built in 1986 of fine Australian timber, cruises the Brisbane River while patrons enjoy fine food, live entertainment, and sightseeing. Handcrafted curved decks and sweeping staircases create a classic ambience, while the modern galleys allow chefs to prepare meals.
   The price you pay will depend on your choice of meal. At lunch this varies from the economical "snack lunch" to the midprice Aussie roast, to the pricey à la carte menu. Evening meals offer a choice of roast dinner or seafood platter. If you opt for the à la carte, you can choose between entrées (appetizers) such as blackened barramundi or crêpes filled with spinach and feta cheese served with a curry sauce. Main course offerings include Cajun chicken, noisettes of lamb with mango and mint sauce, and vegetables mille-feuille.

5. BRISBANE ATTRACTIONS

SIGHTSEEING STRATEGIES
IF YOU HAVE 1 DAY

Visit the Australian Woolshed, arriving in time for either the 11am or 2pm show. Plan to have billy tea and damper (it's served from 10:30am) and/or lunch while you're there. Allow time for browsing in their excellent craft shop. At night either attend a play, opera, or concert at the Performing Arts Complex in the Queensland Cultural Centre or take a *Kookaburra Queen* dinner cruise.

IF YOU HAVE 2 DAYS

Follow my suggestions for the first day and choose between Bunya Park and Lone Pine Koala Sanctuary on the second day. Do the walking tour as outlined in this section if the spirit moves you.

IF YOU HAVE 3 DAYS

As above for days 1 and 2, then choose between Mt. Coot-tha Park or the Art Gallery and Museum in the Queensland Cultural Centre on day 3.

THE TOP ATTRACTIONS

LONE PINE KOALA SANCTUARY, Jesmond Rd., Fig Tree Pocket. Tel. 378-1366 or 222-7278 (24-hour information).

Today wildlife parks dot the map of Australia, but when Lone Pine opened in 1927, it was the only place in the country where visitors could cuddle a koala. While the park, located 12 kilometers (7 miles) from the city, is no longer unique, it is still a good place to see, hold, and be photographed with one of the adorable balls of fur that have brought recognition to Qantas Airways and become the unofficial symbol of the nation.

For koala addicts Lone Pine is nirvana because this is the world's largest collection. More than 100 of the creatures are housed at the park, and in order to feed them all, eucalyptus leaves have to be gathered from up to 200 kilometers (124 miles) away. This bit of trivia and other koala facts are explained during a short show that is presented every afternoon. Many colorful Australian birds and other indigenous animals are also on display. If you've never seen a dingo, kookaburra, platypus, or pink-and-gray galah, this is a good opportunity. A Polaroid photo of you holding a koala costs about A$7 (U.S. $5.60). The best time to be there is around 2:30pm, because that's when the animals are fed and they're most active.

Admission: A$10 (U.S. $8) adults, A$5 (U.S. $4) children 13–17, A$3 (U.S. $2.40) children 3–12.

Open: Daily 8:45am–4:45pm. **Transportation:** Can be reached by car or by the boats operated by Koala Cruises (tel. 229-7055). A one-way river cruise costs A$11 (U.S. $8.80) for adults, A$7 (U.S. $5.60) for children 13–17, and A$6 (U.S. $4.80) for children 3–12. It departs North Quay at 1pm. Courtesy transfers are provided from inner-city hotels. The combination river cruise which includes a one-way cruise, entry into Lone Pine, and return to city by coach costs A$29 (U.S. $23.20) for adults, A$24 (U.S. $19.20) for children 13–17, and A$15 (U.S. $12) for children 3–12. Many sightseeing excursions stop at the park, or you can take public bus no. 518 from town.

THE AUSTRALIAN WOOLSHED, 148 Samford Rd., Ferny Hills. Tel. 351-5366.

⭐ You probably never thought that learning about sheep could be fun, but after you've been to the Australian Woolshed, you'll know it can be. Sheep are integral to Australia's agricultural economy. More than 155 million of them grow the wool that is one of the country's most important exports. At the Woolshed, proprietor Ken Mander-Jones explains about the different breeds, shears a sheep to the tune of "Click Go the Shears," and shows visitors the important role sheepdogs play in farm life. Spinning is also demonstrated, and a lucky volunteer gets a try at milking a cow.

During the impressive Ram Show, various breeds of sheep walk up the aisle and take an assigned place onstage. This behavior plays havoc with the widely held belief that sheep are incredibly dumb and can never be taught to do anything. After the performance you can pet a kangaroo, feed a kid goat with a bottle, and learn about koalas. The Woolshed doesn't have nearly as many of the cuddly creatures as Lone Pine, but Ken feeds his specimens while he talks about them, so they're quite active. A photo of you holding a koala costs A$6.50 (U.S. $5.20).

Lest you think my enthusiastic endorsement of this attraction is exaggerated, I quote from a letter I received recently from a reader: "Re: the Woolshed. Keep raving about it because it was great."

In addition to animal-oriented enjoyment, a craft shop offers quality Australian-made products. In 1985 this shop was voted the best of its kind in the country, and Ken and his wife, Margaret, work hard to maintain the quality and variety of goods.

The 1-hour Ram Show takes place each day at 11am and 2pm, and I suggest you go early and have billy tea and delicious damper bread with butter and golden syrup before the performance (A$2.50/U.S. $2). If you stay for lunch (served from noon to 2pm), a hearty shearer's sandwich (lamb on damper with gravy) is priced at A$5 (U.S. $4), or for about A$13 (U.S. $10.40) you can have steak and salad. If you want to experience another aspect of outback Oz, woolshed (barn) dances are held on Friday and Saturday evenings. The charge of A$26 to A$28 (U.S. $20.80 to U.S. $22.40) includes dinner.

Admission: A$8 (U.S. $6.40) adults, A$4 (U.S. $3.20) children.

Open: Daily 9:30am–5pm. **Transportation:** The Woolshed is 14 kilometers (9 miles) from the city center. You can drive or take a train to Ferny Grove. The station is 800 meters (½ mile) from the Woolshed. The other option is to join a day tour which stops there. (See "Organized Tours," below.)

BUNYA PARK WILDLIFE SANCTUARY, Bunya Park Dr., Eatons Hill. Tel. 264-1200 or 264-4606.

Another place with lots of koalas, Bunya Park is sited on 8 hectares (20 acres) of bushland to the north of Brisbane. While this spot has to be content with being home to the *second*-largest population of koalas in the world, they can justifiably boast that they are the only sanctuary not to charge a koala-cuddling fee in addition to an admission price.

Koala education and handling sessions are conducted four times daily. In addition, there are kangaroos, wallabies, pademelons, wallaroos, wombats, Tasmanian devils, and lots of colorful, noisy native birds. Visitors can hand feed these animals.

Admission: A$8.50 (U.S. $6.80) adults, A$4 (U.S. $3.20) children.

Open: Daily 9:30am–5pm. **Transportation:** A courtesy bus service is operated by Bunya Park, and there are public buses to the sanctuary.

QUEENSLAND CULTURAL CENTRE, located across the Victoria Bridge on the south side of the Brisbane River. Tel. 840-7229 or 840-7200.

The Queensland Cultural Centre is a beautiful complex of modern, low-rise buildings surrounded by imaginative pools and fountains. You may choose to wander through the area, admiring the creative use of water and the way it complements the terraced architecture of the structures, or you may wish to explore the interiors of the various theaters and museums.

The A$67-million (U.S. $53.6-million) **Performing Arts Complex** was official-ly opened by the Duke of Kent in April 1985. It contains three auditoriums for music and stage productions. The overall effect of spacious carpeted lobbies and foyers with aggregate concrete walls, glass, and stainless-steel railings is most impressive. Free tours of the three theaters leave the tour desk in the ticket sales foyer Monday through Friday at noon.

The **State Library** (tel. 840-7872) was the last building in the complex to be completed in 1988.

The Queensland Art Gallery is the permanent home of the state's extensive collection and is often the site of touring exhibitions. Fifty-minute tours are conducted by volunteers Monday through Friday at 11am and 1 and 2pm, Saturday and Sunday at 2 and 3pm. The Art Gallery Cafeteria serves light meals and snacks Monday through Friday from 10:30am to 4:30pm, Wednesday from 10:30am to 7:30pm, and weekends from 10:30am to 4pm. The Fountain Room Restaurant offers tasty cuisine and panoramic views of the river and city. Call 840-7350 or 840-7303 for more information.

The **Queensland Museum,** containing more than two million items that relate to the natural, human, and technological history of the Sunshine State, is open daily from 9am to 5pm (to 8pm Wednesday). Admission to regular exhibits is free, and prices for visiting displays vary. The Museum Cafeteria is open daily. For further information phone 840-7555.

The museums and theaters of the Queensland Cultural Centre are fully accessible to handicapped travelers. To make arrangements, phone 840-7229 or 840-7200.

If you plan to dine in this area, see the description of the Lyrebird Restaurant and the Promenade Cafe above.

Tours of the Art Gallery, Museum, and State Library are offered.

Cost: A$5 (U.S. $4) adults, A$4 (U.S. $3.20) children.

Time: Daily 10–11:30am, noon–1:30pm and 2–3:30pm. **Bus:** No. 165, 169, 175, 185, 189, or others.

MORE ATTRACTIONS

The following sights are mentioned for the benefit of visitors who can spend more than a day or two in Brisbane.

KOOKABURRA QUEEN, The Pier at Waterfront Place, Eagle St. Tel. 221-1300.

I described this atmospheric paddle wheeler in "Brisbane Dining," above, because of the meals and teas served on board, but it's worth mentioning again purely as a sightseeing attraction. Full commentary about the vessel and the places it passes is supplied over a loudspeaker on all but the evening cruises.

Admission: Any cruise A$9.90 (U.S. $7.95).

EARLYSTREET HISTORICAL VILLAGE, 75 McIlwraith Ave., Norman Park. Tel. 398-6866.

For a glimpse into Queensland's early history, walk through the gardens and colonial buildings at Earlystreet, where real pioneer-period structures have been moved onto the grounds of a stately suburban residence 6 kilometers (4 miles) from downtown Brisbane. The general store was relocated from its original location at Rocky Water Holes, the slab hut is equally authentic, and the pub was constructed out of parts saved from many celebrated hotels before they were destroyed. Typical of old-time watering holes, this building features a collection of old bottles, a traditional brass footrail, and a black-and-white tile floor. "Stromness" is a typical early Queensland home, circa 1870. The half dozen or so structures are surrounded by beautiful mature trees, some of which were growing in their present locations before John Oxley discovered Brisbane.

Admission: A$7 (U.S. $5.60) adults, A$3.50 (U.S. $2.80) children.

Open: Mon–Fri 9:30am–4:30pm, Sat–Sun 10:30am–4:30pm. **Closed:** Christmas Day and Good Friday. **Bus:** No. 8A, 8B, 8C, or 8D. **Train:** Norman Park Station, and walk 1 kilometer (½ mile).

MT. COOT-THA PARK, Mt. Coot-tha Rd., Toowong. Tel. 377-8891 or 377-8893.

A scenic wooded area only 6 kilometers (4 miles) from downtown, Mt. Coot-tha Park is the home of the **Botanic Gardens** and the **Sir Thomas Brisbane Planetarium.** In addition, the lofty open forest region affords excellent views of the city. The gardens, which include a dome-shaped glasshouse (greenhouse) with over 2,000 tropical shrubs and trees, are open daily from 9am to 5pm. In addition to the Tropical Dome, the Japanese Garden, moved to its present site after Expo 88 closed, is of particular interest. For information about the planetarium, phone 377-8896. If you want to dine at Mt. Coot-tha, read about the Summit Restaurant in "Brisbane Dining," above.

Admission: Planetarium A$6 (U.S. $4.80) adults, A$2.75 (U.S. $2.20) children under 15.

Open: Planetarium "Sky Theatre" shows Wed–Fri 3:30 and 7:30pm; Sat 1:30, 3:30 and 7:30pm; Sun 1:30 and 3:30pm. **Closed:** Late Jan–Feb 15. **Bus:** No. 39 from Ann St. in city.

BRISBANE FOREST PARK, 60 Mt. Nebo Rd., The Gap. Tel. 300-4855.
This 26,500-hectare (66,250-acre) bushland park is located only 20 minutes' drive from the center of Brisbane. Bush Ranger Tours are offered and those interested in native fauna won't want to miss Walk-about Creek Freshwater Study Centre (see "Hiking/Nature Study," below).
   Admission: Walk-about Creek A$3.50 (U.S. $2.80) adults, A$2 (U.S. $1.60) children.
   Open: Walk-about Creek Mon–Fri 9am–4:30pm, Sat–Sun 10am–4:30pm.

WALKING TOUR —— Brisbane's Heritage Trail

Start: King George Square, between Adelaide and Ann streets at Albert Street.
Finish: Treasury Building, between Queen and Elizabeth streets at George Street.
Time: 1-2 hours.
Best Times: Monday through Friday, not during rush hours when the sidewalks are crowded, or Sunday.
Worst Times: Saturday, when the stores in The Mansions are closed.

The best way to see Brisbane's impressive historic buildings is on foot. I suggest you begin at King George Square, from where there is an excellent view of:

1. **Brisbane City Hall,** which was erected of Queensland sandstone between 1920 and 1930. The nicely detailed main entrance is topped by a 91-meter (300-ft.) clock tower that affords excellent views of the city and surrounding area. Even if you don't go up in the tower, poke your head in the door and notice the marble staircase and ornate ceiling. From the Ann Street side of King George Square you can see:
2. **Albert Street Uniting Church,** built of Oamaru (New Zealand) limestone and dark brick in the Victorian Gothic Revival style. In the same block is the:
3. **Brisbane School of Arts.** The original building was constructed circa 1865. Cross Edward Street to the:
4. **Central Railway Station,** which was erected in 1901 and is a fine example of Victorian railway stations. The building is predominantly brick with white and pink sandstone trim. Be sure to notice the central clock tower and the iron gates to the entrance hall. Cross Ann Street, where you will see the:
5. **Shrine of Remembrance,** erected in honor of the Australian soldiers who died in World War I. Walk back to Edward Street and, on the corner, you will notice:
6. **The People's Palace,** which was designed by a Salvation Army architect and built as low-cost accommodation. It opened in 1911, and the elaborate cast-iron balustrades and deep verandas are typical of that time. Walk down Edward Street and notice on your left:
7. **Rowes Arcade,** which appears to be one building but is really two. The building to the left features the words "Rothwell's" and "Established 1897." The structure on the right is labeled "Rowes."

REFUELING STOP   There are several lunch and tea spots in Rowes Arcade. My personal favorite is **8. Dougalls To Go** (tel. 229-5991). It's open Monday through Thursday from 6am to 5pm and Friday 6am to 6pm. Sandwiches cost A$2 to A$3 (U.S. $1.60 to U.S. $2.40).

   Duck down Queen Street for a look at the:
9. **General Post Office,** built on the site of the convict settlement's Female Factory Prison. The northern wing was built by John Petrie in 1871–72 and the central tower and southern wing were added in 1877–79. Notice the crest within

the balustrading at the first-floor level. (Remember, in Australia the "first floor" is one aboveground.) Proceed through the GPO Arcade and across Elizabeth Street to:

10. **St. Stephen's Cathedral,** designed by well-known architect Benjamin Backhouse in the early English Gothic style. The building was begun in 1863 and completed in 1874. Adjacent to the cathedral note:

11. **Old St. Stephen's Church.** It was built in 1850 and is the oldest church in Brisbane. Walk through to Charlotte Street, turn right, and then left into Edward Street. Now walk down Edward Street to the:

12. **Botanic Gardens.** The present gardens occupy the site of the former Government Garden established in 1824 on instruction of Sir Thomas Brisbane. Of particular interest are an avenue of Bunya pines planted in the 1850s by Walter Hill, the first Colonial Botanist, and rows of weeping figs planted in the 1870s. At the George Street end of the gardens, you have a good view of:

13. **Parliament House.** The design for this building, conceived by colonial architect Charles Tiffin, was chosen in an Australia-wide competition. The French Renaissance–style building was opened in 1868. Nearby on George Street:

14. **The Mansions** was originally constructed in 1890 as a row of six terrace houses. The architects designed the building to suit local climatic conditions. Note the recessing of the main wall behind a wide veranda which provides a cooling effect to internal rooms. Continue to the corner of Queen and George, where you have a good view of the:

15. **Treasury Building.** Designed primarily in the Italian Renaissance style and built between 1885 and 1928, the building also features the verandas that are popular throughout Queensland for their cooling effect on internal rooms. Colonial architects borrowed the idea from India, where verandas were used for much the same purpose.

The Queen Street Mall begins across the street. If you're ready for a refueling stop, I suggest one of the three Jimmy's Restaurants in the Mall. (See "Brisbane Dining," above.)

ORGANIZED TOURS

If you're looking for sightseeing tours by bus I suggest you contact **Sunstate Tours,** (tel. 236-3355). **G'Day Australia Bush Tours** (tel. 891-5544) operates four-wheel-drive day tours. Also, don't overlook the possibility of doing a self-guided tour using the **Citysights** bus (see "Getting Around," above). It stops at 20 places and you can get on and off as often as you like. The fare is A$9 (U.S. $7.20) for adults and A$5 (U.S. $4) for children. Phone 225-4444 for more information.

I also recommend the **Bush Ranger Tours** offered at Brisbane Forest Park. See "Hiking/Nature Study," below.

6. BRISBANE SPECIAL & FREE EVENTS

The city's favorite festival, **Warana** (which means "blue skies" in Aborigine) is a 2-week fête. It includes parades, concerts, picnics, and lots of outdoor entertainment and is held every September, when Brisbane's weather is at its best. The energy and enthusiasm generated by Warana is impressive.

FREEPS (Free Recreation and Entertainment for Everyone in Parks) concerts, sponsored by Brisbane City Council, are held every Sunday afternoon—often in the Botanic Gardens but sometimes in the Albert Park Amphitheatre or a suburban park. FREEPS caters to all age groups with bands, dance exhibitions, jazz, country music, and holiday programs. For details, phone 225-6766 or check the local newspaper.

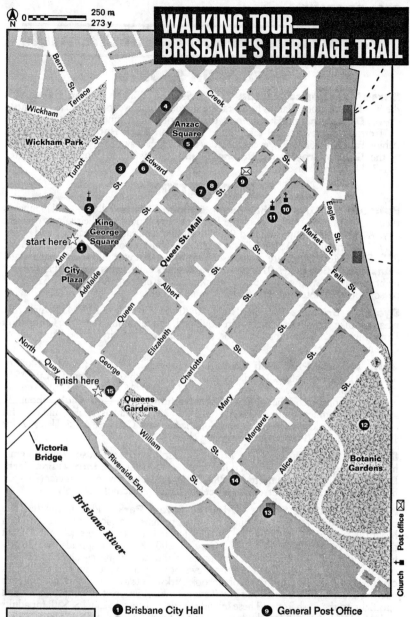

WALKING TOUR— BRISBANE'S HERITAGE TRAIL

N 0 ———— 250 m
273 y

Wickham Park
Anzac Square
King George Square
start here ☆
City Plaza
Queen St. Mall
North Quay
finish here ☆
Queens Gardens
Victoria Bridge
Brisbane River
Botanic Gardens
Riverside Exp.

Church ✝ ■ Post office ⊠

Brisbane

1. Brisbane City Hall
2. Albert Street Uniting Church
3. Brisbane School of Arts
4. Central Railway Station
5. Shrine of Remembrance
6. The Peoples' Palace
7. Rowes Arcade
8. Dougalls To Go
9. General Post Office
10. St. Stephen's Cathedral
11. Old St. Stephen's Church
12. Botanic Gardens
13. Parliament House
14. The Mansions
15. Treasury Building

7. BRISBANE SPORTS & RECREATION

SPECTATOR SPORTS

Horse/Greyhound Racing The **Brisbane Winter Racing Carnival** is the highlight of Queensland's horse-racing season. These events are held at the **Eagle Farm, Doomben,** and **Bundamba** tracks during May, June, and July.

Trotting (harness racing) takes place at **Albion Park Raceway,** Amy Street, Albion Park (tel. 262-2577), every Saturday and Wednesday evening. Greyhounds race at the **Gabba Greyhound Racing Club,** Stanley Street, Woolloongabba (tel. 391-7444), each Thursday.

RECREATION

Ballooning Lovely! **Champagne Balloon Flights** (tel. 844-6671) launches their balloons from the banks of the Brisbane River and floats their guests over the city. A 40 to 45-minute standard flight (including continental breakfast and "pink cloud" beverage) costs A$169 (U.S. $135.20), and short introductory flights cost A$95 (U.S. $76). Most flights are at sunrise. Kids under 8 aren't allowed to participate. **Sunshine Balloons** (tel. 018/72-7575) also offers daily flights over Brisbane. Every flight concludes with a champagne breakfast. The price of A$165 (U.S. $132) per person includes hotel transfers and a 30-minute flight.

Cycling **Brisbane Bicycle Hire,** 50 Albert Street (tel. 229-2433), will rent whatever bike you desire. Once you're equipped, you might like to try the Coronation Drive Bikeway, which runs along the riverbank from the city to the University of Queensland at St. Lucia.

Golf **Victoria Park Golf Club,** Herston Road, Herston (tel. 854-1406 or 852-1271), is located about 1½ kilometers (1 mile) from the city. Greens fees are A$10 (U.S. $8) for 18 holes, with club hire an additional A$12 (U.S. $9.60). Another interesting course can be played at the **Redland Bay Golf Club,** about 35 kilometers (21 miles) south of the city (tel. 206-7236). Goannas, koalas, and colorful native parrots make regular appearances on the fairways. Costs are A$15 (U.S. $12) for 18 holes and A$8 (U.S. $6.40) for renting clubs.

Grass Skiing The one thing Brisbane doesn't have is snow, so skiing on grass has become quite popular. If you'd like to try it, head for **Samford Alpine Park,** Eaton's Crossing Road, Samford (tel. 289-1581). They also have a 700-meter (763-yd.) bobsled—on grass, of course. Open weekends and public holidays only.

Hiking & Nature Study **Brisbane Forest Park** is ideal if you feel like bushwalking (hiking), birdwatching, camping, or having a picnic or barbecue in a beautiful woodland setting. The park is located 12 kilometers (7 miles) from downtown via Mt. Nebo Road, The Gap (tel. 300-4855). BFP spreads over 26,500 hectares (66,250 acres) of mountainous bushland containing eucalypt forest and subtropical rain forest and offers good views of surrounding terrain and the distant city skyline. A scenic road, the Northbrook Parkway, travels right through the park offering great sights. **Bush Ranger Tours** offers Rainforest Breakfast Tours and Spotlight on the Bush Tours. These include meals and cost A$25 (U.S. $20) for adults and A$22 (U.S. $17.60) for children under 15. Free city hotel pickups are provided. Call 300-5381 for more information.

Also located here is the popular **Walk-about Creek Freshwater Study Centre.** Admission to this center is A$3.50 (U.S. $2.80) for adults and A$2 (U.S. $1.60) for children. Brisbane Forest Park is open every day. A tearoom, restaurant, and bush crafts shop are available.

Jogging The **Botanic Gardens** in the city are a picturesque venue for your workout.

Squash Courts are available at the **Royal Queensland Lawn Tennis Associ-**

ation, Milton Road, Milton (tel. 368-2433). Open daily 6:30am to 10pm. Courts cost A$10 (U.S. $8) per hour. You can also play at the **Brisbane Squash Centre,** Waterloo Street, Newstead (tel. 252-3400).

Swimming The **Valley Olympic Pool,** 432 Wickham Terrace, Fortitude Valley (tel. 852-1231), is open Monday through Saturday from 5:30am and on Sunday from 7:30am. Closing times vary. Admission is A$1.20 (U.S. $1) for an unlimited stay.

Tennis The **Royal Queensland Lawn Tennis Association,** Milton Road, Milton (tel. 368-2433), has both grass courts and hard ones. Charges are A$10 (U.S. $8) per hour. The inner suburb of Milton is about 2 kilometers (1 mile) from downtown and is easily reached by train.

8. BRISBANE SAVVY SHOPPING

THE SHOPPING SCENE

Brisbane has good shopping facilities, including the largest central-business-district shopping center in Australia: the A$480-million (U.S. $384-million) **Myer Centre,** which completely fills the block bounded by Queen, Elizabeth, Albert, and George streets. Within the center's five levels you will find a huge department store, 250 specialty shops, eight cinemas, taverns, a food fair, and a 1,500-space parking lot.

If you want to continue your spree after going through the Myer Centre, I suggest you wander along the **Queen Street Pedestrian Mall,** which extends from Edward to George Street. Of particular interest is the **Wintergarden** complex under the Hilton Hotel.

The Mansions, located on the corner of George and Margaret streets 4 blocks south of the mall, contain interesting shops. These are open Sunday to Friday. Hours vary, but are generally from 10am to 4pm. **Paddington Circle** is a charming area of boutiques, antiques stores, galleries, craft shops, and restaurants in one of Brisbane's oldest suburbs. Information is available from **Paddington Pharmacy,** 212 Given Terrace (tel. 369-9561). Most places are open Monday through Friday from 9am to 5pm and Saturday from 9am to noon. Some close at 9pm on Thursday, and a few are open 7 days a week.

Stores in the downtown area are generally open Monday through Thursday from 9am to 5:30pm, Friday from 9am to 9pm, Saturday from 8:30 or 9am to 4pm, and Sunday from 10:30am to 4pm.

SHOPPING A TO Z
ABORIGINAL ARTIFACTS & CRAFTS

QUEENSLAND ABORIGINAL CREATIONS, 135 George St. Tel. 224-5730.

This shop sells original handcrafts and artifacts, including leather products, bark paintings, weapons, jewelry, shells, and artwork. Of particular interest is the handmade Aboriginal pottery. Sales directly benefit the Aboriginal community.

ANTIQUES

PADDINGTON ANTIQUE CENTRE, 167 Latrobe Terrace, Paddington Circle. Tel. 369-8458.

This center is the combined effort of 45 individual antiques dealers. Items range from furniture and bric-a-brac to Australiana and jewelry. Open 7 days.

BOOKS

THE MANSIONS BOOKSHOP, in The Mansions, 40 George St. Tel. 221-4965.

If you're interested in learning more about Australia, the Mansions Bookshop has a nice selection of books about Australia and by Australian authors. They also sell general fiction, biography, history, and reference books. Open Monday through Friday from 9:30am to 4:30pm and on Sunday from 11am to 4pm.

DYMOCKS, Queen Street Mall, next to the Myer Centre. Tel. 229-4266.
Easily the biggest bookstore in Brisbane, Dymocks has a huge selection of every kind of book. They tout that only the State Library has more volumes, and they're probably right. Open 7 days a week.

CRAFTS

PIERROT, 251 Arthur St., Fortitude Valley. Tel. 252-1015.
Clay, glass, wood, textiles, jewelry, and paintings await at this arts and crafts center. Open daily from 10am to 5pm.

AUSTRALIAN WOOLSHED, 148 Samford Rd., Ferny Hills. Tel. 351-5366.
Quality handcrafts are sold at the shop which is part of one of Brisbane's top sights. (See "Brisbane Attractions," above.)

THE NEEDLEWOMAN, 30 Collingwood St., Paddington Circle. Tel. 369-7959.
This shop sells everything imaginable for needleworkers, including a full range of kits, canvases, books, threads—and even heirloom sewing materials. This is the only specialized needlework shop and school in Queensland.

DEPARTMENT STORES

DAVID JONES DEPARTMENT STORE, 194 Queen St. Tel. 227-1111.
This is the granddaddy and senior partner of Australian department stores—and the oldest in the world still trading under its original name. While they sell a full range of goods, emphasis is definitely on the top end. This store is open Monday to Thursday from 8:30am to 5:30pm, Friday from 8:30am to 9pm, and Saturday from 9am to 4pm.

DUTY FREE

ORBIT DUTY FREE, 136 Queen Street Mall. Tel. 229-2922.
Like most other duty-free shops, Orbit has the usual range of duty-free items: liquor, cigarettes, perfume, cameras, and small electrical appliances.

FASHIONS

DOWN UNDER HOUSE, Riverside Centre. Tel. 832-1211.
A shop for casual clothing, Down Under House sells colorful Ken Done T-shirts, sweatshirts, shorts, aprons, and the like. Australia's best-known commercial artist has developed a worldwide following, and this is a great place to buy gifts that will be well received at home.
There's a branch at the Queen Street Mall (tel. 221-5531).

GIFTS & SOUVENIRS

BREAK OF DAY GIFT SHOP, Shop 50, 283 Given Terrace, Paddington Circle. Tel. 368-2921.
Break of Day Gift Shop has a nice selection of handmade gifts, including tapestries, pressed-flower designs, and patchwork quilts. They also sell a variety of miniatures, including doll's house furniture and accessories, cottages, and animals. The Joanna Sheen pressed flower designs and David Winter cottages are especially popular. The toiletries in Australian floral fragrances make nice gifts for friends at home.

AUSTRALIA POST SHOP, GPO, Queen St. Tel. 224-1202.

⭐ Located in Brisbane's main post office, the Australia Post Shop offers the convenience of selling gift items with purpose-designed packaging for mailing. A variety of quality Australian-made products is available.

KOALA HOMELAND, Level 1, Wintergarden Complex on the Queen Street Mall. Tel. 221-0903.

Koala Homeland sells Aussie-made gifts and souvenirs—from inexpensive to extravagant.

NATIONAL TRUST GIFT SHOP, in The Mansions, 40 George St. Tel. 221-1887.

Everything on sale here is Australian made. This includes manchester (household linens), stationery, prints, novelties, and souvenirs. Many designs are exclusive to the National Trust. The volunteers who staff the shop are helpful and friendly. Open 10am to 4pm Monday through Friday and on the first and third Sunday of the month from 11am to 4pm.

JEWELRY

QUILPIE OPALS, Lennons Plaza Building, 66-76 Queen Street Mall. Tel. 221-7369.

Named after Quilpie, a small town in Western Queensland which is the center of the boulder-opal industry, this store sells an extensive range of black, white, and boulder opals.

READERS RECOMMEND

Endors Opal Gallery, Rowes Arcade, 235 Edward St. —"We bought some opal jewelry at Endors Opal Gallery and found the people to be as helpful and knowledgeable as at Flame Opals in Sydney. Also, with your purchase they give you information about the designer of your piece as well as about the opal itself."—Patsy L. Lee, Kingwood, Texas.

MARKETS

PADDY'S MARKETS, Florence and Macquarie Sts., New Farm. Tel. 252-7211.

Here you will find 5 acres of under-cover merchandise and hundreds of individual stallholders selling everything from native Australian birds to luggage. This is the ideal place to look for army surplus, bric-a-brac, old-fashioned shoes and clothing, hard-to-find tools, books, and out-of-the-ordinary gifts. Open daily from 9am to 4pm. Paddy's bus service runs hourly from the city.

CATS TANGO PURE CRAFTS MARKET, Riverside Complex, Eagle St. Tel. 371-1452 or 371-1789.

⭐ Hundreds of arts and crafts stalls crowd the plazas and boardwalks of the Riverside Complex every Sunday from 8:15am to 3pm. Besides original wares, look for street performers and food stalls.

SPORTS EQUIPMENT

ROBINSON'S SPORTS STORE, 300 Queen St. Tel. 221-5011.

When we were last in Brisbane my husband realized he'd forgotten his swim goggles, and this is where he found a replacement pair. They also sell tennis gear, diving equipment, sports clothes, and so forth.

SWEATERS

BAA BAA BLACK SHEEP, Shop 17, Balcony Level, Brisbane Arcade, Queen St. Tel. 221-0484.

As its name implies, this shop specializes in handknitted Australian woolen products. The owner, Debra Kolkka, makes many of the items herself. Sweaters are the most popular items. Open 11am to 4pm Monday through Thursday, 11am to 6pm Friday, and noon to 1pm Saturday.

AUSTRALIAN WOOLSHED, 148 Samford Rd., Ferny Hills. Tel. 351-5366.

The Australian Woolshed sells beautiful handspun, handknitted wool garments that Aussies call "jumpers" and Americans refer to as "sweaters." For more information, see "Brisbane Attractions," above.

9. BRISBANE EVENING ENTERTAINMENT

The daily *Courier-Mail* newspaper carries entertainment information. I also suggest you pick up a copy of *Time Off*, a free weekly that is primarily a gig guide but does list cultural events and movies in addition to the performance schedules of myriad rock groups.

THE PERFORMING ARTS

MAJOR MULTIPURPOSE PERFORMANCE & CONCERT HALLS

PERFORMING ARTS COMPLEX, in the Queensland Cultural Centre. Tel. 846-4444.

This is the principal venue for Brisbane's stage productions. Within the complex, the 2,000-seat **Lyric Theatre** is designed for opera, dance, and musical comedy; the 2,000-seat **Concert Hall** handily accommodates a full symphony orchestra; and the 300-seat **Cremorne** is an experimental studio theater. For recorded information about performance schedules, dial 11-632. If you wish to purchase tickets for events at the Performing Arts Complex, call 846-4646 between 9:30am and 5:30pm. All major credit cards are accepted. The PAC also has a nationwide toll-free number (tel. 008/77-7699), and tickets can be purchased through any **Bass** ticket agency in Australia or via **Qantas** computers from the U.S.

Open: Box office Mon–Sat 9:30am–5:30pm.

THEATERS

BRISBANE ARTS THEATRE, 210 Petrie Terrace. Tel. 369-2344.

Brisbane's leading little-theater company has been playing for the city for over 50 years. Classics, musicals, comedy, Australian works, and mainstream plays are all presented. This includes the work of Shaw, Pinter, Coward, Ayckbourn, Simon, and so forth. The theater has 157 seats; Masks Bar is open for all performances. Ticket prices are usually about A$14 (U.S. $11.20).

LA BOITE THEATRE, 57 Hale St. Tel. 369-1622.

This theater in the round has been around for nearly 70 years. In the 1991 season they presented such varied productions as *Angry Housewives, A Midsummer Night's Dream, On The Verge,* and *The Three Sisters.* Ticket prices are in the vicinity of A$16 (U.S. $12.80).

PRINCESS THEATRE, 8 Annerley Rd., Woolloongabba. Tel. 891-5155.

This theater, which is the home of the TN Theatre Company, was founded in 1888 and is the third-oldest working theater in Australia and the oldest in Brisbane. Both classical productions and new Australian works are presented. The 276 seats sell for A$12 to A$24 (U.S. $9.60 to U.S. $19.20).

SUNCORP THEATRE, Turbot St. Tel. 221-5177.

The Queensland Ballet performs here, as does the Queensland Philharmonic

Orchestra. Tickets cost A$30 to A$40 (U.S. $24 to U.S. $32) depending on the performance.

THE CLUB & MUSIC SCENE

As mentioned before, Brisbane is a young person's city, and the after-dark options are aimed mainly at the under-30 set. The gig guide in the free weekly *Time Off* lists pages of rock-club engagements. In addition, discos abound. Happily, hotel cocktail lounges and friendly pubs offer an alternative for those of us looking back at 30.

No matter where you choose to have fun, be sure to try a Fourex (XXXX) or a Power's, Queensland's two most popular beers. The legal age for alcohol consumption in the Sunshine State is 18.

NIGHTCLUBS/CABARET

FRIDAY'S ON THE WATER, 123 Eagle St. Tel. 832-2122.
Friday's is a popular bar/restaurant/nightclub complex adjacent to the lofty Riverside Centre. It opens its doors Sunday through Thursday from 8pm until 3am, on Friday and Saturday until 5am. This is the place to be—especially on a Friday night—and it's quite customary to wait in line to get in. Young professionals and "uni" (university) students make up the usual crowd. The action is both indoors and out, overlooking the Brisbane River. Steely Dan, Sting, and Phil Collins are big hits here.
Cover charge: Sun–Thurs free; Fri A$7 (U.S. $5.60), Sat A$5 (U.S. $4).

RIDGE RESTAURANT, at the Ridge Hotel, 189 Leichhardt St., corner of Henry St. Tel. 831-5000.
The Ridge Restaurant is the only restaurant in Brisbane with a live dance band. Traditional tunes are played Tuesday through Saturday 6pm to midnight, and a lovely city-lights view from the ninth-floor "pozzie" (position) provides another good reason to dine here. The menu features Italian and seafood dishes.

JAZZ/BLUES

CAXTON HOTEL, 38 Caxton St., Petrie Terrace. Tel. 369-5971.
Brisbane's best-known jazz spot is the historic Caxton Hotel, which first opened in 1884. Saturday-afternoon jam sessions continue to draw large crowds, as they've been doing for more than a decade. This is the place for hot Dixieland jazz—from ragtime to swing. On Friday and Saturday nights a DJ spins Top-40 songs from the 1960s and '70s in the lounge, while sing-along and karaoke take precedence in the cocktail bar. The fun stops at midnight Monday through Thursday, 3am on Friday, and 5am on Saturday. The crowd is 25 to 40, mostly single, and all party hearty. There's a third area—and outdoor garden partially under a canopy of trees. The Australian National Marble Championship is held here the first Sunday in June. No kidding.
Admission: Mon–Fri free; Sat A$3 (U.S. $2.40).

DANCE CLUBS/DISCOS

MARGAUX'S, on level five in the Brisbane Hilton, 190 Elizabeth St. Tel. 231-3131, ext. 2577.
This nightclub has an elegant, yet relaxed atmosphere. It's open Tuesday through Thursday and Saturday from 9pm to 3am and Friday from 5:30pm to 3am. The crowd is mature, professional, and for the most part over 25. A complete range of beverages and a supper menu are offered. For the sophisticated night owl.
Cover charge: Weekend cover charge of A$8 (U.S. $6.40) is waived if you're staying at the hotel.

BRISBANE UNDERGROUND, Caxton and Hale Sts., Paddington. Tel. 369-2633.
The Brisbane Underground is a popular disco where queuing up is de rigueur. Open Wednesday through Saturday from 7pm to 3am and Sunday from 7pm to midnight.

Admission: Sun A$5 (U.S. $4).

THE BAR SCENE
PUBS

AMERICA'S CUP BAR, in the Brisbane Hilton, 190 Elizabeth St. Tel. 231-3131.

This pub has a jovial ambience and is a handy place to watch sporting events on wide-screen TV. Large yachting pictures line the walls, and sailcloth banners are extended overhead. The bar, located on the lobby level, serves up good cheer Monday through Thursday from noon to 10pm and Friday and Saturday from noon to midnight.

PORT OFFICE HOTEL, 38 Edward St., corner of Margaret St. Tel. 221-0072.

This is a popular pub housed in a lovely old colonial building; the Port Office Hotel has both indoor and outdoor seating. The historic building, which once held the original port offices for Brisbane, is now a favorite yuppie hangout. A stubbie of XXXX will set you back A$2.40 (U.S. $1.95).

BREAKFAST CREEK HOTEL, 2 Kingsford Smith Dr., Breakfast Creek. Tel. 262-5988.

This hotel, built in 1889, has won many awards for its popular beer garden and reasonably priced barbecue meals. Patrons pick their own cut and size steak. Dinner costs about A$12 (U.S. $9.60).

PIANO BARS

BRISBANE HILTON, 190 Elizabeth St. Tel. 231-3131.

The Hilton has a pleasant piano bar with a relaxed, sophisticated atmosphere. It is open Monday through Thursday from noon to 1:30pm and 5pm to midnight, Friday from noon to 1:30pm and 5pm to 1am, and Saturday from 6pm to 1am. There's no cover charge, and a complete range of beverages is available.

CHAPTER 8

SOUTHERN & CENTRAL QUEENSLAND

Sun, sand, and surf typify the southern and central Queensland covered in this chapter. In fact, the major part of the state lies inland, but it's the coastal area that attracts travelers. The famed beaches of the Gold Coast and the Sunshine Coast make them one of the most popular holiday destinations in the country. Proserpine, Gladstone, and other cities of the central and Whitsunday regions serve as jumping-off points for the fascinating Great Barrier Reef, which lies offshore. Only Lamington National Park lacks the three S's; instead, it lures visitors with birdwatching, bandicoots, and bushwalking.

The southern half of the Sunshine State constitutes an area about the size of Texas and is separated into two distinct climatic zones by the Great Diving Range. East of the mountains lies a rich coastal strip; to the west, vast dry plains stretch over great distances. Sugarcane, timber, and tourism, along with pineapples, bananas, and citrus, form the basis of the coastal economy. Inland, hardy farmers grow grain and raise cattle and sheep. Opals are found near the tiny township of Quilpie in the south, and coal is mined in the central region.

Queensland's population tends to be more decentralized than that of other parts of the country. Only half of the state's 2.4 million residents live in Brisbane, and a string of middle-size cities are found along the ocean. Queenslanders also tend to be more ethnically homogeneous than residents of other states. Most migrants come from within Australia, not from Asia and Southern Europe; therefore, little international influence is apparent.

Winter (June, July, and August) is the best time to visit. Spring and fall are pleasant too, but "the wet" season, from December through March, should probably be avoided. Central Queensland straddles the Tropic of Capricorn, and temperatures to the north can get quite hot, while the southern portion has a temperate subtropical climate. (For details, see "When to Go" in Chapter 2.)

The best source of tourist information is the **Queensland Government Travel Centre** located in each state capital and many major cities overseas.

SEEING SOUTHERN & CENTRAL QUEENSLAND

If you're traveling by public transport, Queensland Railways carries passengers up and down the coast. The Spirit of Capricorn provides daily service between Rockhampton

WHAT'S SPECIAL ABOUT SOUTHERN & CENTRAL QUEENSLAND

Beaches
☐ Gold Coast beaches, stretching for 42 kilometers (26 miles).
☐ Sunshine Coast beaches—long and uncrowded.

Ace Attractions
☐ Dreamworld, located near the Gold Coast, an enchanting down-under Disneyland.

Events/Festivals
☐ Burleigh Heads, on the Gold Coast, the site of numerous surfing championships and contests.
☐ The Gold Coast Indy Car Grand Prix every March.

National Parks
☐ Lamington National Park, one of the best places in the country to observe native fauna in its natural habitat.

Activities
☐ Surfing—what draws young people to the Sunshine Coast and, to a lesser extent, to the Gold Coast.
☐ Sailing, the big attraction in the Whitsundays.

and Brisbane. The Sunlander and luxurious Queenslander travel between Cairns and Brisbane, stopping at Nambour on the Sunshine Coast, Proserpine on the Whitsunday Coast, and Bundaberg, Gladstone, Rockhampton, and Mackay on the Central Coast.

Australian Regional Airlines supplements the routes of the major carriers, so that all places of interest in the Sunshine State are accessible by air.

McCafferty's, Bus Australia, Pioneer, and Greyhound provide frequent coach service up and down the coast from Brisbane.

If you're going to drive, contact the **RACQ** (Royal Automobile Club of Queensland), 190 Edward Street, Brisbane, QLD 4000 (tel. 07/253-2444). The trek from Brisbane to Cairns is equal to motoring from Paris to Lisbon (1,717km/1,065 miles).

1. THE GOLD COAST

The Gold Coast is the most developed, commercialized, advertised, and controversial vacation destination in Australia. Its fans point to the 300 or more days of sunshine each year, the 42 kilometers (26 miles) of golden-sand beaches, and the nonstop entertainment options. Its critics point to the rows of high-rise hotels and apartments, the general overcrowding and traffic congestion, and the constant Mardi Gras atmosphere. About 2.5 million people vacation on the Gold Coast annually. The area is especially popular with Japanese and New Zealanders.

Both admirers and critics agree that the area strongly resembles Waikiki and Miami Beach. In fact, one stretch of sand known for its rows of hotels is named after the Florida city. The Gold Coast starts about an hour's drive south of Brisbane and stretches to the New South Wales border. The center is Surfers Paradise, where many of the accommodations and entertainment venues are headquartered. Southport is the commercial center, and Burleigh Heads and Coolangatta are less congested resort areas. The whole region has a population of about 275,000.

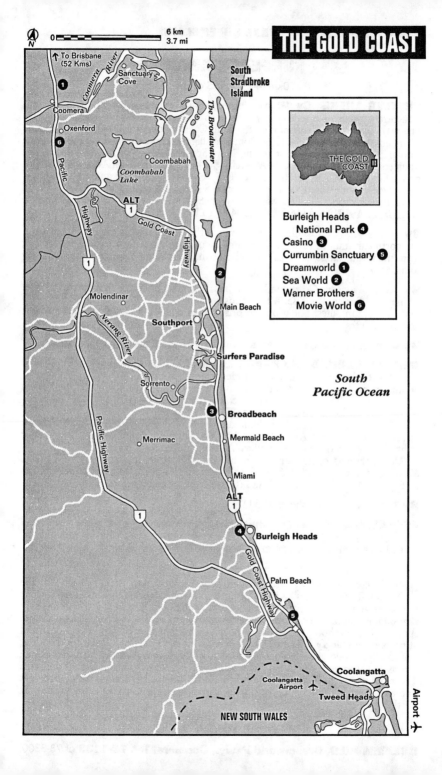

SURFERS PARADISE

70km (44 miles) S of Brisbane

GETTING THERE   By Plane   International flights arrive in Brisbane, and Coachtrans operates a half-hourly shuttle to Surfers. The fare is A$20 (U.S. $16) one-way. To contact Coachtrans on the Gold Coast, phone 075/38-8344; in Brisbane their number is 07/236-1400. Domestic flights come into the Gold Coast/Coolangatta Airport, adjacent to the New South Wales–Queensland border, and transfers to Surfers Paradise cost A$8 (U.S. $6.40). If you arrive on Australian Airlines phone Gold Coast Airport Transit (tel. 075/36-6841) to arrange a coach transfer; if you come in on Ansett or Eastwest, call Silverbrae Coaches (tel. 075/76-4000). Australian Airlines' Air Pass fares between Sydney and Gold Coast/Coolangatta range from A$131 to A$166 (U.S. $104.80 to U.S. $132.80).

By Train   It isn't possible to take a train to the Gold Coast. Travelers coming from the north can train to Brisbane and catch a coach to the Gold Coast; those arriving from the south can go as far as Murwillumbah, New South Wales, and then transfer to a coach.

By Bus   Pioneer, Greyhound, and Bus Australia offer coach service between Sydney and Surfers Paradise. A ticket costs A$63 (U.S. $50.40) and the trip takes 14 hours and 45 minutes. The trip from Brisbane costs A$10 (U.S. $8) and takes 1 hour and 20 minutes.

By Car   It takes about an hour to drive to Surfers Paradise from Brisbane.

GETTING AROUND   By Bus   The **Surfside Bus Company** (tel. 36-7666) provides regular service from Tweed Heads at the south end of the Gold Coast to Southport at the north end and many points in between. Sample fares are: Surfers Paradise to Sea World is A$1.20 (U.S. $1) for adults, A60¢ (U.S. 50¢) for children.

Another option is the **Gold Coast Tourist Shuttle** (tel. 91-1533), where a A$6 (U.S. $4.80) ticket gives adults unlimited travel for 1 day (9am to midnight); children under 14 are charged A$4 (U.S. $3.20). The shuttle connects hotels with major sightseeing and shopping destinations. A family ticket costs A$16 (U.S. $12.80).

Dreamworld operates buses from Surfers Paradise, and they cost A$9 (U.S. $7.20) for adults and A$5 (U.S. $4) for children under age 12. **Sea World's** bus costs A$6 (U.S. $4.80) for adults and A$3 (U.S. $2.40) for children.

By Taxi   For a taxi, phone 91-5111.

ESSENTIALS   Tourist information is dispensed from a kiosk in the Cavill Mall (tel. 38-4419), open Monday through Friday from 8am to 5pm, Saturday 9am to 5pm, and Sunday 9am to 4pm. The **area code** is 075.

Happily crowded onto a strip of land between the South Pacific Ocean and the Nerang River, "Surfers" is ideal for both sun-worshipers and others who like to be where the action is. Tourists fill the sidewalks at all hours. So casual is the atmosphere that bikinis and other brief resort wear worn in shopping centers barely draw a stare. As with Waikiki, hotels, souvenir shops, and entertainment centers create a carnival atmosphere. **Grundy's Paradise Centre**, with its 117 shops, 20 fast-food outlets, and multiple video-game parlors, is one focal point. **Cavill Avenue** is the main drag; it runs east-west and ends in the Cavill Mall, which is steps from golden sand and surf. The main north-south thoroughfare is the **Gold Coast Highway,** which becomes one-way south in the heart of town while **Ferny Avenue** carries the traffic one-way north.

WHAT TO SEE & DO

DREAMWORLD, Dreamworld Pkwy., Coomera. Tel. 73-1133 or 73-3300.

⭐ This is Disneyland down under. Founded by John Longhurst, a great fan of Walt Disney, the enchanting theme park offers activities closely resembling those in Anaheim and Orlando. The Australian Country Jamboree, for instance, is an Aussie version of Bear Country Jamboree performed by 22 life-size Australian animals, including Billabong Bill, a piano-playing kangaroo, and a koala chorus. Longhurst also adheres to his mentor's high standards for cleanliness and wholesomeness. The entire 84-hectare (207-acre) park is both spotless and tasteful.

Since this is Oz, the park's mascots are Kenny Koala and his girlfriend, Belinda Brown. The adorable koala couple and Coo-ee the Gum Nut Fairy circulate throughout Dreamworld, generously doling out hugs and patiently posing for pictures.

The park is divided into nine theme areas, which include natural bushland, re-created period architecture, rides, various shows, shops, restaurants, an auto museum with classic and antique cars, and an IMAX theater with a screen six stories high. It takes at least a full day to see everything.

Admission (all inclusive): A$27 (U.S. $21.60) adults, A$18 (U.S. $14.40) children 3 and up.

Open: Daily 10am–5pm. **Closed:** Christmas Day. **Directions:** Dreamworld is 20 minutes north of Surfers Paradise on Hwy. 1 and 45 minutes south of Brisbane.

CURRUMBIN SANCTUARY, on the Gold Coast Hwy., 18km (11 miles) south of Surfers Paradise. Tel. 34-1266 or 98-1645.

This 24-hectare (59-acre) park displays native birds and animals. Colorful lorikeets, which land on outstretched arms of visitors at feeding time, are Currumbin's best-known feature, but koalas, kangaroos, wallabies, dingoes, wombats, flying foxes, and other native animals are also on hand. The roos and wallabies wander loose throughout a large walk-through enclosure and can be petted and fed. This is especially fun when one has a joey in her pouch. A miniature train circles the park, but walking provides the best access to animals.

Be sure to allow time for browsing through the several shops, which sell rocks, shells, jewelry, and gemstones in addition to souvenirs. It's also a good idea to phone ahead and find out the feeding times of your favorite animals. The lorikeets usually dine between 8 and 10am and from 4 to 5pm.

The sanctuary has two snack bars.

Admission: A$11 (U.S. $8.80) adults, A$5.50 (U.S. $4.40) children.

Open: Daily 8am–5pm. **Bus:** Surfside bus to stop no. 20.

SEA WORLD, on The Spit at Main Beach, 3km (2 miles) north of Surfers Paradise. Tel. 88-2222.

Except for its plagiarized logo, there is little resemblance between this park and those in the United States. Queensland's Sea World is basically an elaborate amusement park with a marine theme. Very few of the shows include animals. Action-packed rides such as Lasseter's Lost Mine, the Corkscrew, and the Flume Ride get much more attention. Visitors at this Sea World can also ride Australia's first monorail and be taken on helicopter joy flights that range in price from A$45 to A$66 (U.S. $36 to U.S. $52.80) depending on duration. If you go, allow 4 hours to see everything.

Admission (including everything except helicopter rides): A$28 (U.S. $22.40) adults, A$18 (U.S. $14.40) children 4–13.

Open: Daily 10am–5pm. **Bus:** Surfside bus.

WARNER BROS. MOVIE WORLD, Pacific Hwy., Oxenford. Tel. 53-3999.

Located just south of Dreamworld, this attraction opened in mid-1991. It is based on the famous Hollywood movie studio and has working sets. A first in the Southern Hemisphere, Movie World offers the Police Academy Stunt Show, the Great Gremlins Adventure, Outback Action, and the Looney Tunes Studio—featuring the Warner Bros. cartoon favorites.

Themed restaurants, including Yosemite Sam's Place, Blazing Saddles Cafe, and Rick's Cafe American, offer meals and snacks.

Admission: A$29 (U.S. $23.20) adults, A$19 (U.S. $15.20) children 4–13.
Open: Daily 10am–5pm. **Closed:** Christmas Day.

SIR BRUCE CRUISES, river end of Cavill Ave. Tel. 92-0505.

This company offers a variety of calm-water cruises on the inland waterways adjacent to Surfers Paradise. The 2-hour Canal and Harbour Cruise glides past palatial waterfront residences and provides a good look at an array of yachts. This waterborne sightseeing tour also takes passengers past hotels, shopping centers, and restaurants. Complimentary fresh scones with jam and cream are served, as are tea, coffee, and soft drinks.

Admission: A$18 (U.S. $14.40) adults, A$12 (U.S. $9.60) children.
Departs: Daily 10:30am and 2pm.

GOLD COAST ARTS CENTRE, 135 Bundall Rd. Tel. 31-9500 or 91-3600.

The arts center provides a cultural retreat from the bright lights and commercial attractions of the Gold Coast. Located about 5 minutes' drive from Surfers Paradise on the banks of the Nerang River, the A$16-million (U.S. $12.8-million) complex includes two theaters and two art galleries. The Queensland Symphony Orchestra, the Queensland Ballet, and various visiting companies perform regularly. Call for tickets. The Harlequin Restaurant (tel. 319-568) in the complex serves lunch (Monday through Friday) and pretheater dinners.

Admission: Free.
Open: Art Galleries Tues–Fri 10am–5pm, Sat–Sun 1–5pm.

SHOPPING

This is a major activity in the Surfers Paradise area. **Pacific Fair,** across from the Conrad International Hotel and Jupiters Casino in Broadbeach, is Australia's only theme shopping complex and features cobbled streets and architecture designed to resemble the world's famous trading areas. Nearby, **The Oasis** is connected to the casino complex by monorail. Other places to spend your money include **Australia Fair shopping center** in Southport and the **Paradise Centre,** and **Cavill Avenue Mall** in Surfers Paradise. Most centers are open Monday through Saturday from 8:30am to 5:30pm. Some stores stay open until 9pm on Thursday night, and stores that cater to tourists are often open on Sunday. And don't forget— Dreamworld, Sea World, and Currumbin all have their own shops.

SPORTS & RECREATION

Many of the Gold Coast's fun and games are, not surprisingly, waterborne activities. **Aussie Bob's** (tel. 91-7577) can organize water sleigh rides, sea plane joy flights, waterskiing, fishing charters, windsurfing boards, and speedboat fun rides. **Budds Beach Aquatic Hire** (tel. 92-0644) rents catamarans, windsurfing boards, paddleboats, canoes, aqua bikes, and more. Boogie boards and surfboards can be rented at **Brothers Neilsen** (tel. 39-0176) at several locations in the area.

Parasailing is possible at several beaches in and around Surfers Paradise. Call Martin and Janet Vandenberg at **Gold Coast Parasailing** (tel. 91-4466) if you're ready for this thrilling experience.

Golf is also very popular on the Gold Coast. **Hooked on Golf** (tel. 075/35-7354 or 018/75-5693) will take you to a different 18-hole course every day of the week.

WHERE TO STAY

Very Expensive

HYATT REGENCY SANCTUARY COVE, Manor Circle, Sanctuary Cove, via Hope Island, QLD 4212. Tel. 075/30-1234, or toll free 008/22-2188 in Australia. Fax 075/77-8234. 247 rms and suites. A/C MINIBAR TV TEL **Transportation:** Courtesy coach and ferry service.

$ Rates: A$215 (U.S. $172) standard single or double; A$270 (U.S. $216) Regency Club; A$363–A$633 (U.S. $290.40–U.S. $506.40) 1- or 2-bedroom junior suite; A$1,100–A$1,345 (U.S. $880–U.S. $1,076) premier suite; A$1,400–A$1,645

(U.S. $1,120–U.S. $1,316) Presidential Suite; A$35 (U.S. $28) extra bed. Children under 18 stay free in parents' room. Lower midweek tariffs. AE, BC, DC, MC, V. **Parking:** Free.

Calling itself "Australia's first world-class resort," the Hyatt Regency Sanctuary Cove offers a dramatic contrast from the bright lights of Surfers Paradise. The resort is located 25 minutes from Surfers, 40 minutes from Brisbane, and 40 minutes from the Coolangatta Airport in a peaceful setting on the banks of the Coomera River. A planned residential community and village is adjacent. Five low-rise lodges are spread out across the property; three of these contain Regency Club rooms offering complimentary drinks and continental breakfast. All architecture and interiors are designed in the 1920s Australian homestead theme. Period furniture is used throughout the public spaces and bedrooms. None of the three-story buildings has a lift (elevator).

Each room has either a king bed or two doubles; all have clock radios, bathrobes, tea- and coffee-making facilities, small refrigerators, and in-room movies. Suites have their own safes. Guests receive a complimentary daily newspaper.

Dining/Entertainment: The Grange is a specialty restaurant featuring traditional cuisine; the Cove Cafe overlooks the terrace pool; tea and cocktails are served in the Veranda Bar; Michael's is a traditional Australian saloon bar; Coomeras is a poolside bar and grill restaurant.

Services: 24-hour room service, turn-down service, shoeshine, laundry, valet, concierge, and baby-sitting.

Facilities: Two outdoor pools, one freshwater and one salt (the saltwater pool has a sand bottom and sand "beach" around it); health club, gym, sauna, spa, tennis courts, squash courts, two 18-hole golf courses, and a business center.

SHERATON MIRAGE GOLD COAST, Sea World Dr., Broadwater Spit, Main Beach, QLD 4217. Tel. 075/91-1488. Fax 075/91-2299. 318 rms and suites. A/C MINIBAR TV TEL

$ Rates (including full buffet breakfast): A$358–A$424 (U.S. $286.40–U.S. $339.20) standard single or double; A$528 (U.S. $422.40) premium room; A$726–A$968 (U.S. $580.80–U.S. $774.40) ocean or executive suite; Presidential and Royal Suite rates on application; A$60 (U.S. $48) extra person. Children under 17 stay free in parents' room. AE, BC, DC, MC, V. **Parking:** Free.

The only resort hotel right on the beach in the Gold Coast area, the Sheraton Mirage also offers its guests an extensive sports/health complex, Sports Mirage, and shopping facilities across the street at Marina Mirage. Sea World theme park is steps away. I don't recommend a short stay: By the time you find your way around the 30-hectare (75-acre) resort it will be time to check out. The three-story accommodations blocks are surrounded by 2.5 hectares (6 acres) of shallow lagoons, and there is lots of lush landscaping. While guest rooms don't have balconies, the 25 Mirage Rooms have their own terrace on a lagoon and are understandably popular.

The tropical decor is stylish, impressive, and except for the deafening sound of the large fountain in the lobby, pleasant. All rooms have king-size beds or two doubles, tea- and coffee-making facilities, small refrigerators, clock radios, bathrobes, safes, in-room movies, and free daily newspapers. All have cane furnishings and quarry-tile floors; 40% have ocean views.

Dining/Entertainment: Horizons is the resort's signature restaurant; there is also a large coffee shop where large buffet-style meals are offered. Rolls is the nightclub.

Services: 24-hour room service, turn-down service, shoeshine, laundry, valet, concierge, massage.

Facilities: Two outdoor pools, including a lap pool in the health club and a huge sprawling lagoon-style pool with a swim-up bar and underwater bar stools. Health club, gym, sauna, tennis courts, spa, and hair salon.

Expensive

GOLD COAST INTERNATIONAL HOTEL, Gold Coast Hwy. and Staghorn Ave., Surfers Paradise, QLD 4217. Tel. 075/92-1200, or toll free

008/07-4020 in Australia. Fax 075/92-1180. 296 rms and suites. A/C MINIBAR TV TEL

$ **Rates:** A$195 (U.S. $156) single or double; A$450 (U.S. $360) suite; A$20 (U.S. $16) extra person. Children under 18 stay free in parents' room. Lower weekend rates. Tariffs are 10% higher in the Christmas/New Year period. No-smoking rooms available. AE, BC, DC, MC, V. **Parking:** Free.

The Gold Coast International is both luxurious and centrally located. Arriving guests enter the impressive, spacious lobby, where silk ficus trees are inset into a polished marble floor; more marble forms the staircase suspended over a reflecting pond. Tiny white lights twinkle in the trees; tribal artifacts decorate the walls; soft music comes from a white lacquer baby grand set on an island in a shallow pool.

Travertine marble also adorns the entryways and bathrooms of the sleeping quarters. The king rooms are located on the 22nd floor, and only these lack tile balconies. Half the rooms have ocean views, and all bathrooms have tub/shower combinations, phones, and hairdryers. Clock radios, in-room movies, bathrobes, tea- and coffee-making facilities, and small refrigerators are standard throughout the property. All guests receive a complimentary daily newspaper.

Dining/Entertainment: The hotel has four restaurants and a half dozen bars.

Services: 24-hour room service, turn-down service, shoeshine, laundry, valet, concierge, baby-sitting, and massage.

Facilities: Health club, gym, sauna, massage room, spa, hair salon, squash and tennis courts. The outdoor swimming pool has a cocktail bar in the middle. There's also a business center.

HOTEL CONRAD AND JUPITERS CASINO, Gold Coast Hwy., Broad-beach Island, Broadbeach, QLD 4218. Tel. 075/92-1133 or 92-8130, or toll free 008/07-4344 in Australia. Fax 075/92-8219. 600 rms, 22 suites. A/C MINIBAR TV TEL

$ **Rates:** A$180–A$230 (U.S. $144–U.S. $184) single or double; A$310–A$1,200 (U.S. $248–U.S. $960) suite; A$30 (U.S. $24) extra person. Children under 18 stay free in parents' room. No-smoking rooms available. AE, CB, BC, DC, MC, V. **Parking:** Free.

Conrad's is also a deluxe hotel but one with a very different atmosphere. Buses collect patrons from all over Surfers Paradise and bring them to play at the hotel's gaming tables and video-gambling machines—thus it has the ambience of a large Las Vegas hostelry.

The hotel is located south of the center of Surfers Paradise on its own island in the Nerang River; the beach is 1 block away, with monorail access. The hotel is the largest in Australia. More than 15 acres of landscaped grounds surround the property. Included on the 2,300-member staff are four full-time Japanese interpreters and two full-time people to look after the coach tours that stay at the hotel. All guest rooms have clock radios, tea- and coffee-making facilities, and in-room movies. Guests receive free daily newspapers.

Dining/Entertainment: The hotel has six restaurants, myriad bars, a 950-seat show room, and 24-hour gaming, dining, and imbibing facilities.

Services: 24-hour room service, turn-down service, laundry, valet, concierge, baby-sitting, and massage.

Facilities: Four tennis courts, spas, a large heated pool complex, sauna, health club, and jogging track. In the pool area, a band plays for sun worshipers from a Roman-style pavilion, and two of the three terraced swimming pools have their own fountain.

RAMADA HOTEL, Hanlan St. and Gold Coast Hwy., Surfers Paradise, QLD 4217. Tel. 075/79-3499, or toll free 008/22-2431 in Australia. Fax 075/39-8370. 403 rms and family suites. A/C MINIBAR TV TEL

$ **Rates:** A$180 (U.S. $144) single or double; A$205 (U.S. $164) family room; A$15 (U.S. $12) extra person. Children under 15 stay free in parents' room. Weekend packages available. Lower standby rates (same-day bookings for midweek accommodations). No-smoking rooms available. AE, BC, DC, MC, V. **Parking:** Free.

Located smack in the middle of Surfers Paradise, the 39-story Ramada is ideal for those who like to be where the action is. The shops and food outlets of Grundy's Paradise Centre are adjacent, and the beach is just steps away. The Ramada's spacious rooms all have tub/shower combos and hairdryers in the bathrooms, and offer a choice of either two double beds or a queen-size bed with a twin. Balconies provide a view of either the ocean to the north or the hinterland to the west.

Dining/Entertainment: Summerfield's Restaurant is open daily (A$13/U.S. $10.40 for the breakfast buffet, A$14/U.S. $11.20 for lunch).

Services: 24-hour room service, laundry, valet, and baby-sitting.

Facilities: Nine-hole putting green, parcourse, children's playground, tennis court, spa pool, outdoor swimming pool, and the Health Club which offers two steam rooms, gym equipment, and massage.

Moderate

BAHIA BEACHFRONT APARTMENTS, 154 Esplanade, Surfers Paradise, QLD 4217. Tel. 075/38-3322. Fax 075/92-0318. 30 apartments. TV TEL

$ Rates: A$80 (U.S. $64) 1-bedroom unit for one or two people; A$90 (U.S. $72) 2-bedroom unit for one or two people; A$10 (U.S. $8) extra person. Higher holiday rates. Weekly discounts. AE, BC, DC, MC, V. **Parking:** Free.

The Bahia is an ideal spot for those who wish self-contained accommodations. The 14-story building is located right on the beach 900 meters (½ mile) from the heart of Surfers Paradise. Each unit has its own washing machine and dryer, fully equipped kitchen, dishwasher, and private balcony. Accommodations are spacious. One-bedroom apartments measure 700 square feet, and the two-bedroom units, with two baths, are 1,300 square feet. Above the third floor, guests look right out over the ocean.

The Bahia is a great dollarwise value for folks who want to do their own cooking and don't mind the lack of flashy hotel amenities. Continental breakfast and other meals can be delivered to the apartments. Friendly resident managers Karen and Richard Stephens and Lynne and Kim Adamson staff the reception desk from 8:30am to 6:30pm. Guests can use the swimming pool, sauna, spa, and rooftop driving range at no extra charge. Apartments are serviced daily.

THE PAN PACIFIC HOTEL, 81 Surf Parade, Broadbeach, QLD 4218. Tel. 075/92-2250, or toll free 008/07-4465 in Australia. Fax 075/92-3747. 298 rms and suites. A/C MINIBAR TV TEL

$ Rates: A$143 (U.S. $114.40) low-view standard single or double; A$154 (U.S. $123.20) high-view standard single or double; A$242 (U.S. $193.60) corner king suite; A$440 (U.S. $352) oceanview suite; A$1,100 (U.S. $880) Pacific Suite; A$20 (U.S. $16) extra person. Peak-season rates are higher. Midweek rates are lower and special packages are available. Children under 15 stay free in parents' room. No-smoking rooms available. AE, BC, DC, MC, V. **Parking:** Free.

The Pan Pacific, which opened in 1989, is the epitome of Gold Coast accommodation. The 23-story hotel is located 50 yards from the beach, 5 kilometers (3 miles) south of central Surfers Paradise, and is connected to Jupiters Casino by a monorail. Adjacent to it is the Oasis shopping complex, which has a carousel, lots of places to spend money, and several eating options—including a McDonald's (yes, the golden arches).

The marble lobby has a very modern fountain and a pair of three-story high palm trees. Two-thirds of the rooms have ocean views, and all have at least one balcony and a pleasant sea-foam green and gray color scheme. Each bathroom has a tub separate from the shower stall, and corner king rooms and all suites have spa baths. Actually, if your budget will allow it, I highly recommend the corner king-size rooms. The view from the spa tub is great, and each has a king-size bed and lovely green marble bathroom.

Meals are served in Pelicans Restaurant and Mavericks Steakhouse,

Facilities include two outdoor pools, health club, gym, sauna, spa, running track, and tennis courts. A hair salon, gift shop, and newsagent are located in the adjacent Oasis shopping complex.

TRICKETT GARDENS HOLIDAY INN, 24-30 Trickett St., Surfers Paradise, QLD 4217. Tel. 075/39-0988, or toll free 008/07-4290 in Australia. Fax 075/92-0791. 32 apartments. TV TEL

$ Rates: A$76 (U.S. $60.80) 1-bedroom unit for one or two people; A$84 (U.S. $67.20) 2-bedroom/1-bath unit for two people; A$108 (U.S. $86.40) 2-bedroom/2-bath unit for four people; A$12 (U.S. $9.60) extra person. "Holiday Season" rates are 35% higher. AE, BC, DC, MC, V. **Parking:** Free.

Trickett Gardens is a nice serviced-apartment complex for folks who want to do their own cooking. While a little more modest than the Bahia described above, the apartments are more than adequate. Located in the heart of Surfers Paradise and close to the beach, the low-rise units, which are serviced daily, all have their own washers and dryers. Cooked or continental breakfast and other meals can be delivered to the units. A pool and spa are located in front of the building.

WHERE TO DINE

NICHOLSON'S, in the Hotel Conrad, Gold Coast Hwy., Broadbeach. Tel. 92-1133.
   Cuisine: FRENCH/INTERNATIONAL. **Reservations:** Imperative. **Directions:** 2 miles south of Surfers Paradise.

$ Prices: Appetizers A$13.50–A$23 (U.S. $10.80–U.S. $18.40); main courses A$26–A$32 (U.S. $20.80–U.S. $25.60). Public holiday and weekend surcharge 10%. AE, BC, DC, MC, V.
   Open: Dinner Tues–Sat from 6pm.

Nicholson's is the Hotel Conrad's finest dining spot, and is named after Conrad Nicholson Hilton, founder of Hilton Hotels. Its elegant atmosphere is created by gold brocade chairs; a wall-to-wall, backlit glass wine rack; and tuxedoed waiters. Fresh roses grace every table; fine china, crystal, and Swiss linens are used throughout. The gourmet à la carte food list suggests delicacies such as champagne vineyard snails, braised and served in open ravioli with fine herbs; smoked duck breast with pinkeye potatoes and a sun-dried tomato flan; traditional oxtail soup accompanied by a crisp prawn rissole; and pan-fried milk-fed veal rolled in fine herbs, with pumpkin crêpes and oyster mushrooms.

OSKAR'S GARDEN RESTAURANT, 2931 Gold Coast Hwy. Tel. 38-5244.
   Cuisine: MODERN MULTICULTURAL/SEAFOOD. **Reservations:** Recommended. **Transportation:** Surfside bus.

$ Prices: Appetizers A$8.50–A$14.50 (U.S. $6.80–U.S. $11.60); main courses A$19–A$25 (U.S. $15.20–U.S. $20). Public holiday surcharge A$3 (U.S. $2.40) per person. AE, BC, DC, MC, V.
   Open: Lunch daily noon–3:30pm; dinner daily 6pm–midnight.

This eatery, located 2 kilometers (1 mile) south of the heart of Surfers Paradise, serves delicious creative cuisine. The à la carte menu features fresh local seafood, such as salmon, prawns, lobster, and mud crab. More unusual dishes such as emu, buffalo, and pheasant are also offered. "We cook in several different styles, including Cajun, Asian, Italian, and Thai," the chef explains. All breads and pasta are made on the premises.

You might like to try their seafood salad: local seafood tossed with buckwheat noodles, chili, and sesame dressing. Or perhaps the Moreton Bay bugs baked in the stone oven and served with a chili plum sauce.

Two Oskar's restaurants are located on the Gold Coast; the other is in Coolangatta. The Surfers Paradise eatery has both inside and outside dining. Bright kelly-green fans hanging from wooden-beam ceilings complement charcoal-gray polished granite tabletops, colorful Native American–style upholstery, and a polished wooden floor. The attractive decor, good service, and wonderful food make this spot understandably popular.

YAMAGEN, in the Gold Coast International Hotel, Gold Coast Hwy. and Staghorn Ave. Tel. 92-0088.
Cuisine: JAPANESE. **Reservations:** Recommended.
$ **Prices:** Average meal A$35 (U.S. $28). AE, BC, DC, MC, V.
Open: Lunch daily noon–2pm; dinner daily from 5:30pm.

Here authentic decor and architecture complement the cuisine. Yamagen is divided into three areas: the sushi bar, the teppanyaki room, and an à la carte section. The menu, which is written in Japanese with English subtitles, includes sunomono (marinated vegetables and seasonal seafood), yakitori (bamboo-skewered chicken with teriyaki sauce), sumibiyaki (marinated beef and vegetables charcoal-grilled at the table), and tempura moriawase (a variety of fine seafood and vegetables deep-fried in soybean oil). For dessert, patrons can choose between tempura ice cream, green-tea ice cream, orange sorbet, assorted fruit, or the pineapple boat special.

FOOD FANTASY, in the Hotel Conrad, Gold Coast Hwy., Broadbeach. Tel. 92-1133.
Cuisine: BUFFET. **Reservations:** None. **Bus:** Jupiters Casino.
$ **Prices:** Breakfast buffet A$14.50–A$15.50 (U.S. $11.60–U.S. $12.40); lunch buffet A$17.50–A$18.50 (U.S. $14–U.S. $14.80); dinner buffet A$21.95–A$22.95 (U.S. $17.60–U.S. $18.40); Sun seafood brunch A$32.95 (U.S. $26.40). Weekend and public holiday surcharge 10%. AE, BC, DC, MC, V.
Open: Breakfast daily 6:30–10am; lunch daily 11:30am–1pm; dinner daily 5:30–10:30pm.

Food Fantasy is an appropriate dining spot for those who have yet to hit the jackpot. The restaurant is cheerful and overlooks the pool. Sunday lunch is a seafood smörgåsbord, which includes oysters, smoked salmon, and mussels. Quality and quantity make Food Fantasy very popular, and you'll probably have to wait in line.

Dining Clusters

Fisherman's Wharf is a waterfront complex of shops and eateries 4 kilometers (2½ miles) north of Surfers Paradise near the Sea World amusement park. The sprawling collection of low-rise buildings has an early Australian maritime theme and enjoys wonderful views out over the picturesque inland waterway, wharves, and jetties. Live entertainment is provided every day.

At one of the Fisherman's Wharf restaurants, the **Hungry Pelican** (tel. 32-7933 or 50-3073), good seafood meals, as well as steaks, salads, and sandwiches, are available self-service style. Dining is outdoors at umbrella tables, and the cost averages A$10 (U.S. $8) per person.

The fancier **Broadwater Brasserie** (tel. 71-0333 or 32-7944) offers a choice of indoor or veranda seating. All the fish on the à la carte menu comes from the port, just steps away, so the management can easily guarantee freshness. The Broadwater Brasserie is open for dinner Wednesday to Sunday night and for lunch daily. A three-course meal costs about A$30 (U.S. $24), a light lunch about A$13 (U.S. $10.40). The cocktail bar upstairs with its wonderful water view and comfy wicker chairs, makes a delightful place for a drink or snack.

Access to Fisherman's Wharf from Surfers Paradise is by boat or via the Surfside bus service.

One of the most economical places to eat in Surfers is **Grundy's Paradise Centre,** in the Cavill Mall (tel. 38-9011), where many different styles of fast food are available in the International Food Village. Seating is provided in a central area, and there's live music daily. Nearby, an illuminated merry-go-round and amusement arcade with carnival games create a lively background for dining. The area is open 7 days a week from 11am to 9pm. Dishes cost A$2 to A$8 (U.S. $1.60 to U.S. $6.40). You can pay with Bankcard, MasterCard, or VISA.

EVENING ENTERTAINMENT

In spite of everything that's available on the Gold Coast, the lure of poker (slot) machines, which are illegal in Queensland, draws many folks over the border to clubs in New South Wales. Free bus transport from Surfers Paradise to Tweed Heads is provided by **Twin Towns Services Club** (tel. 36-2277) and **Seagulls Rugby League Football Club** (tel. 36-3433). These nightspots are discussed under "Murwillumbah" in Chapter 6.

Those who elect to stay in and around Surfers Paradise can choose from a dozen or more hot discos and clubs, including **Fortunes Nightclub** at Jupiters Casino, Gold Coast Highway, Broadbeach (tel. 92-1133), which is open daily from 8pm to 3am. The sophisticated nightspot, reached by glass elevators from the gaming levels, features the latest in video, sound, and light effects. Cover charge for those not staying at the hotel is A$8 (U.S. $6.40) midweek and A$10 (U.S. $8) on weekends.

The Black Orchid Room in the Gold Coast International Hotel, at Gold Coast Highway and Staghorn Avenue (tel. 92-1200), is the site of the "Paradise Follies," a sophisticated, adult cabaret Monday through Saturday.

Melba's on the Park, 46 Cavill Avenue (tel. 38-7411), and **The Penthouse Niteclub,** Orchid Avenue (tel. 38-1388), are two more popular nightspots, both with A$7 (U.S. $5.60) cover charges. The Penthouse offers four floors of entertainment: there's a popular piano bar on the fourth floor, with disco on the first, second, and third—until 5am Monday through Saturday, until 3am Sunday.

If you like being organized, try **Gold Coast by Night Entertainment Tours** (tel. 50-3749). Transport is by stretch limousine. Tours begin at 9pm nightly and cost A$50 to A$75 (U.S. $40 to U.S. $60) per person including champagne at two places, but no other drinks or food.

The best-known dinner theater is **Dracula's Cabaret Restaurant,** at T. E. Peters Drive and Sunshine Boulevard, Miami Keys (tel. 70-1911)—"just a blood squirt from the casino." Here a four-course dinner and show, offered Tuesday through Saturday nights at 7pm, cost A$39 (U.S. $31.20) per person. This is a great spot for those who enjoy horror.

The 1,200-seat **International Showroom** on the lower level of Jupiters Casino provides another nightlife option—spectacular floor shows à la Las Vegas. Performances are scheduled for 8pm Tuesday through Friday, 7:30 and 10:15pm on Saturday, and 6:30pm on Sunday, with a Wednesday matinee at 12:30pm. For reservations, phone 92-8303, or toll free 008/07-4144 in Australia. Tickets cost A$30 (U.S. $24). Children's tickets to the matinee are A$16 (U.S. $12.80).

Gambling at **Jupiters Casino,** with its 108 gaming tables and 740 video machines, is another popular after-dark activity. Be sure to watch the crowd play two-up, an Australian game where the toss of a coin generates the kind of cheering and yelling usually associated with football contests. The casino is open 24 hours a day; minimum age is 18.

Also, don't overlook the performances at the **Gold Coast Arts Centre.** See "What to See and Do," above, for details.

BURLEIGH HEADS

91km (56 miles) S of Brisbane, 16km (10 miles) S of Surfers Paradise

GETTING THERE   By Bus or Car   Convenient bus service makes the run to and from Surfers Paradise frequently. Motorists simply follow the Gold Coast Highway.

ESSENTIALS   The **area code** is 075.

Located halfway between Surfers Paradise and the New South Wales border, the community of Burleigh Heads has a relaxed, relatively quiet family atmosphere.

WHAT TO SEE & DO

Burleigh Heads is best known as the site of various surf championships. The natural headland at Burleigh forms an ideal amphitheater from which spectators can watch skilled surfers from all over the world who come here to test their mettle against the great waves. Along with **Currumbin Alley, Kirra, Greenmount,** and **Duranbah,** Burleigh Heads is considered one of the best point breaks on the Gold Coast.

Burleigh Heads National Park is another big draw. A 3-kilometer (2-mile) graded track leads around the headland, giving sweeping views of the coast.

WHERE TO STAY

BURLEIGH BEACH TOWER, 52 Goodwin Terrace, Burleigh Heads, QLD 4220. Tel. 075/35-9222. Fax 075/56-1095. 101 apartments. TV TEL **Bus:** Stop 42.

$ **Rates:** A$65 (U.S. $52) 1-bedroom unit for one or two people; A$80 (U.S. $64) 2-bedroom unit for two people; A$20 (U.S. $16) extra person. Three-night minimum stay. Much higher holiday rates. No-smoking rooms available. AE, BC, DC, MC, V. **Parking:** Free.

Burleigh Beach Tower is just steps from a beautiful white-sand beach. Built in 1981, it has a modest lobby, small pool, and adequate spa. The apartments are furnished in a traditional decor with good-quality pieces and each has a balcony and ocean view. The kitchen is fully equipped and includes a dishwasher, while the bathroom houses a washing machine and dryer. Heating and air conditioning aren't provided, but with the Gold Coast's subtropical climate, that really isn't a problem. The only meal available on the premises is continental breakfast, but many dining spots are nearby and several eateries deliver. Weekly chamber service is included, and daily cleaning is available on request at an extra charge.

COOLANGATTA

100km (62 miles) S of Brisbane

GETTING THERE There is frequent bus service along the Gold Coast Highway to and from Coolangatta. The Gold Coast/Coolangatta Airport is nearby.

ESSENTIALS Tourist Information is available at the **Coolangatta Information Centre,** Beach House Plaza, Marine Parade, Coolangatta, QLD 4225 (tel. 075/36-7765), open Monday through Friday from 8am to 4pm and Saturday and public holidays from 9am to 3pm. The **area code** is 075.

The most southerly community on the Gold Coast, Coolangatta, like Burleigh Heads, offers beautiful beaches, relatively inexpensive accommodations, and a peaceful holiday atmosphere. Known with Tweed Heads in New South Wales as one of the "twin towns," Coolangatta is ideal for those who want to be close to the gambling and nightlife that thrive across the border. Access is also easy to the Gold Coast's other sightseeing attractions, nightlife, and shopping. Coolangatta and nearby Kirra are popular with board surfers.

WHERE TO STAY

BEACH HOUSE SEASIDE RESORT, 52 Marine Parade, Coolangatta, QLD 4225. Tel. 075/36-7466. Fax 075/36-3487. 132 apartments. TV TEL **Transportation:** Frequent public bus service.

$ **Rates:** A$95 (U.S. $76) single or double per night for stays of 3 or more nights; A$105 (U.S. $84) single or double per night for shorter visits; A$10 (U.S. $8) extra person. Rates about 20% higher during school holidays. AE, BC, DC, MC, V. **Parking:** Free.

This is a delightful spot for a self-contained holiday. Each unit at the Beach House has its own dishwasher, microwave oven, washing machine, and dryer. Ceramic-tile balconies have wonderful water views. The two-bedroom/two-bathroom units easily sleep six. The one-bedroom units have two sofa sleepers, and can also house six.

The 18-story building is across the street from a beautiful stretch of golden sand, and several eateries and shops are located in an arcade on the ground level. A supermarket, open 7 days a week, is nearby. There are an open-air squash court, a half court for tennis, a nice gym, two barbecues, a swimming pool, a spa, and two saunas.

Activities for children are provided at the Kids Club Monday through Friday. Baby-sitting can be arranged.

WHERE TO DINE

OSKAR'S ON THE BEACH, Greenmount Beach, Marine Parade. Tel. 36-4621.
    Cuisine: SEAFOOD. **Reservations:** Recommended. **Bus:** Griffith St. and walk to beach.

$ **Prices:** Appetizers A$8–A$15 (U.S. $6.40–U.S. $12); main courses A$19.50–A$22.50 (U.S. $15.60–U.S. $18). Weekend and public holiday surcharge A$2.50 (U.S. $2) per person. AE, BC, DC, MC, V.
    Open: Lunch daily noon–3pm; dinner daily 6–10pm.

It's not surprising that this dining spot won the American Express Gold Plate Award for the Best Restaurant on the Gold Coast in 1990 and 1991 along with numerous other accolades. The food and service here are really tops. You might like to try an entrée (appetizer) such as fettuccine with smoked ocean trout on a garlic cream sauce or smoked salmon and prosciutto with a peppered melon sorbet. Main courses include: whole lemon sole with fresh herb butter, seafood salad served warm with a pink peppercorn dressing, and rack of lamb with peas, carrots, mint, and a rosemary glaze.

With a wonderful beachfront setting and a view back to the high-rise skyline of Surfers, it's an ideal spot for watching the sun set. Seating is both indoors and out.

2. LAMINGTON NATIONAL PARK

45km (28 miles) W of the Gold Coast, 120km (74 miles) S of Brisbane

GETTING THERE By Car The easiest way to get to Lamington is by car. If you're traveling from Brisbane allow 2 hours for the trip. Take the Pacific Highway south to the Beenleigh turnoff. Follow the road that has the TAMBORINE/BEAUDESERT sign. After 20 minutes you will come to a small village called Tamborine. Then follow the signs to Canungra. Once in Canungra follow the signs to either O'Reilly's or Binna Burra, depending on where you're staying. Because of the windy mountain road, the trip from Canungra to O'Reilly's takes an hour; allow similar time to reach Binna Burra.

From Surfers Paradise, head west to Nerang, and then to Canungra. The New South Wales–Queensland border forms the southern boundary of the park.

By Bus The other arrival alternative is to hitch a ride on one of the day-tour buses that visit the park. Scenic Tours (tel. 07/285-1777) makes the trip from Brisbane to O'Reilly's Sunday to Friday. The Mountain Coach Company (tel. 07/848-4047, or toll free 008/07-7423 in Australia) provides daily transport to both O'Reilly's and Binna Burra from Surfers Paradise. The cost for either trip is A$32 (U.S. $25.60) return (round-trip).

ESSENTIALS The **Canungra Visitor Information Centre,** Lamington National Park Road, Canungra, QLD 4275 (tel. 075/43-5156), located 30 kilometers (18 miles) west of Nerang, is open Sunday through Friday from 10am to 4:30pm and Saturday from 10am to 12:30pm. The **area code** is 075.

One of the few Queensland attractions not located on the coast or an offshore island, Lamington National Park is a haven for those who like learning about native animals, hiking, eating hearty meals in a wholesome, family environment, and generally admiring the wonders of nature. While the park is geographically fairly close to Surfers Paradise, no two places could be experientially farther apart.

Most of the 20,000-hectare (49,400-acre) park is covered with a dense rain forest—the largest of its type in Australia. Three-thousand-year-old antarctic beech trees are found in the temperate areas of the higher altitudes, and subtropical forest thrives in the warmer valleys. The remaining 30% or so is open forest. Both types of woodland attract native birds and animals, and it's quite common to see colorful crimson rosellas, king parrots, satin bowerbirds, black-and-gold regent bowerbirds, bandicoots, sugar gliders, pademelons (a species of small wallaby), brush turkeys, and possums while walking on the 160 kilometers (99 miles) of trails that wind throughout the park. You might even happen upon a rare Albert's lyrebird, found only in this region. Because of its lofty situation on a plateau of narrow ridges, Lamington is also blessed with some 500 waterfalls.

WHERE TO STAY & DINE

Camping is permitted in certain areas. For more information contact Binna Burra Mountain Lodge (tel. 075/33-3622). Sites with power cost A$10 (U.S. $8) a day or A$60 (U.S. $48) a week. Safari tents which accommodate two to four people cost (including beds and lighting) A$30 (U.S. $24) for two people and A$48 (U.S. $38.40) for four.

O'REILLY'S GUEST HOUSE, Green Mountains, via Canungra, QLD 4275. **Tel. 075/44-0644.** Fax 075/44-0634. 52 rms (44 with bath). **Transportation:** See "Getting There," above.

$ Rates (including all meals, activities, and entertainment): A$130 (U.S. $104) per person in rooms with bath; A$95 (U.S. $76) per person in rooms without facilities. Children under 5 stay free; those aged 6–14 are charged half price. AE, BC, DC, MC, V. **Parking:** Free.

In a pocket of lofty serenity, the O'Reillys continue to introduce guests to their woodland wilderness just as older generations of their family have done since 1926. Their comfortable rustic lodge, located at an elevation of 900 meters (2,970 ft.), is approached by a road that winds up through the mountains from Canungra. While only a 2-hour drive from Brisbane and 1½ hours from the Gold Coast, O'Reilly's feels like an entirely different world. Visitors are most often met by a member of the family—usually Vince or Peter these days—and escorted to their accommodations. At the first meal they are seated at a table for six or eight and introduced to the folks they will be dining with for the rest of their stay (unless they request a change in order to sit with newfound hiking buddies). The rates include early morning tea, breakfast, morning tea, lunch, afternoon tea, dinner, and supper. Everything is made on the premises, served family or buffet style, and delicious. Drinks at the bar or with dinner are extra.

It's not unusual for small marsupials to dine along with guests—on the other side of a floodlit picture window where bread and other bits have been left for them.

A member of the family stops by each table during meals to explain the day's or evening's activities and ascertain guests' interests. Birdwatching expeditions are conducted by a resident naturalist; four-wheel-drive trips and short guided walks are intended for those whose legs aren't as nimble as they used to be. One track has been surfaced to accommodate wheelchairs. A cleverly constructed canopy walk, suspended above the rain forest, allows a unique perspective. At night, artful slide shows and educational programs highlight native animals and birds of the area, and evening walks are held to search out shy nocturnal creatures or visit glowworm grottoes. All guided walks, bus trips, and evening presentations are included in the tariffs.

Three categories of rooms are available at O'Reilly's. The most comfortable are the 36 motel-style quarters with private baths, queen-size beds, tea- and coffee-making facilities, small refrigerators, and a view of the surrounding spectacular scenery. Eight single rooms also have en suite toilets and showers. Another eight rooms rely entirely on communal bathrooms. Two rooms are suitable for handicapped travelers. Nights at this elevation can be pretty nippy, but all accommodations have electric blankets and heaters; the large rustic lounge has a lovely open fire.

There are tennis courts and a nice gift shop on the premises, and baby-sitting can be arranged. Highly recommended.

BINNA BURRA MOUNTAIN LODGE AND CAMPSITE, Beechmont, via Nerang, QLD 4211. Tel. 075/33-3622, or toll free 008/07-4260 in Australia. Fax 075/33-3647. North American sales office: tel. 408/685-8901, or toll free 800/225-9849 outside California; fax 408/685-8903. **Transportation:** Drive or take Mountain Coach Company from either Brisbane or Surfers Paradise (A$32/U.S. $25.60 round-trip).

$ Rates (including all meals and activities, based on two people sharing): A$140 (U.S. $112) per person in cabin with bath; A$98–A$117 (U.S. $78.40–U.S. $93.60) per person in cabin without private facilities. Children under 3 are free; aged 3–14 are charged half price. Weekly rates and midweek specials are lower. MC, V. **Parking:** Free.

This holiday retreat has been in business since 1933, and enjoys a scenic rain-forest site. Rustic timber, stone, and shingle accommodations offer good views of the surrounding terrain. The 22 Acacia cabins have private toilets and showers, as well as tea- and coffee-making facilities, small refrigerators, and verandas. The 12 Banksia cabins have sinks, but guests use communal bathrooms. The seven Casuarina cabins are the most basic. All three types of lodging offer heaters and electric blankets.

Home-style meals are served in the dining room which has a view of the Coomera Valley. Breakfast, morning tea, lunch, afternoon tea, dinner, and supper are included in the tariff. Guests can play pool or table tennis in the games room, where there is a cozy fire in the winter. A craft shop and tearoom are also on the premises.

3. THE SUNSHINE COAST

Like the Gold Coast, the Sunshine Coast is blessed with a benign climate and miles of beautiful ocean beaches. The Sunshine Coast starts at Caloundra, 83 kilometers (51 miles) north of Brisbane and extends to Rainbow Beach, taking in the seaside communities of Kawana, Mooloolaba, Maroochydore, Coolum, and Noosa. Unlike the popular resort area south of Brisbane, the Sunshine Coast is low-rise and laid-back. In this part of Queensland, the majority of tourists are Australians who want to enjoy the beaches and go surfing, and R and R means "rest and relaxation," not "rock and roll." Most attractions are designed for families, and much less evidence of commercialization exists. Visitors are more likely to admire the beautiful coastline of Noosa National Park than they are to dance the night away in a disco, and rides at the Sunshine Plantation are the region's tame answer to the Gold Coast's amusement parks.

NOOSA

150km (93 miles) N of Brisbane

GETTING THERE   By Plane   Travelers bound for Noosa fly into the Noosa Airport with Sunstate Airlines. Sunstate also flies into the Sunshine Coast Airport near Maroochydore, 25 minutes to the south, and a Henry's bus transfer from there costs A$7 (U.S. $5.60); the major resorts offer free shuttle service. Interstate flights also land at the Sunshine Coast Airport. An Ansett Express or Eastwest See Australia or Explore Australia Airpass ticket from Sydney costs A$154 to A$191 (U.S. $123.20 to U.S. $152.80).

By Train   You can't take a train to Noosa. The closest railway station is Cooroy, about 20 minutes to the west. The main rail depot for the Sunshine Coast is Nambour.

By Bus   SunAir Bus Service (tel. 074/43-7320) operates between the Brisbane Airport and Noosa. The fare is A$25 to A$40 (U.S. $20 to U.S. $32) depending on how many people are traveling. From downtown Brisbane it's a 2-hour-and-45-minute ride (A$16/U.S. $12.80) on Sunshine Coast Coaches (tel. 07/236-1901).

By Car   If you're driving, allow 2 hours from Brisbane. Go north on the Bruce Highway and turn east at Eumundi.

GETTING AROUND   By Bus   Noosa's public transport system, The Bus (tel. 42-8649), runs frequently throughout the township. Noosa District Bus Lines (tel. 49-1349) operates between Nambour and Noosa.

By Limousine   If you'd like your own car and chauffeur, call **Budget Chauffeur Drive** (tel. 43-6688).

By Taxi   Sunshine Coast Cabs (tel. 43-5522) is the only taxi company operating on the Sunshine Coast. Their rate is A$2.30 (U.S. $1.85) call charge and then A78¢ (U.S. 65¢) per kilometer.

ESSENTIALS   Tourist information is available at **Hastings Street Information Centre,** Hastings Street, Noosa Heads, QLD 4567 (tel. 074/47-5506), or down the coast at Tourism Sunshine Coast, Alexandra Parade, Alexandra Headland, QLD 4572 (tel. 074/43-6400, or toll free 008/07-2041 in Australia). This latter spot is open Monday to Friday 8:30am to 5pm and weekends 10am to 4pm. The **area code** is 074.

Noosa is the principal township on the Sunshine Coast and is comprised of **Noosa Heads** (restaurants and accommodations), **Noosa Junction** (business area), and **Noosaville** (riverside region and popular fishing spot). **Hastings Street** is the center of activity and main thoroughfare in this seaside resort of 17,000 residents. While the oceanfront in town has not weathered well, the coast from the Heads to **Sunshine Beach** is a long sandy paradise. Marked hiking trails and spectacular scenery are adjacent to town in Noosa National Park. The surfing here is excellent.

WHAT TO SEE & DO

The **Sunshine Plantation,** located 6 kilometers (3½ miles) south of Nambour on the Bruce Highway (tel. 42-1333), is the biggest commercial attraction in the area, and there's little chance you'll miss it as you drive up the Bruce Highway, which is inland from the Sunshine Coast. Its Big Pineapple landmark, about the size of a water tower, can be seen from quite a distance. These big things are uniquely Australian phenomena. In most cases, the big thing (banana, pineapple, trout, cow, rocking horse, and so forth) represents a local product, and a tourist center with a souvenir shop and an eatery or two has grown up around it.

In the case of the Sunshine Plantation, you can ride the sugarcane train through the plantation, take the Nutmobile to the Magic Macadamia attraction, or take Tomorrow's Harvest Tour, a flume ride through a hydroponic farm. All tours cost A$3.50 (U.S. $2.80).

The Sunshine Plantation Restaurant offers indoor and veranda seating and is open from 9am to 5pm daily. Troppo's Licensed Restaurant offers an all-you-can-eat smörgåsbord for lunch daily. Rap's Restaurant (tel. 42-1333) is open Friday through Sunday night from 6pm. The tropical market on the upper level sells everything from resort wear to local fruit, preserves, nuts, and bakery items. On the lower level, there are a souvenir shop and a plant nursery. The Sunshine Plantation is open daily from 9am to 5pm; admission is free of charge.

Farther north, the **Ginger Factory,** also known as **Gingertown** on Pioneer Road in Yandina (tel. 46-7100), is the Southern Hemisphere's largest such establishment. Visitors can watch Queensland ginger being processed into a variety of products, and a film about this industry is screened every half hour. The factory, a restaurant, and a shop selling ginger-based goods are open daily from 8:30am to 4:30pm. The ginger farm tour on the paddle steamer *Gingerbelle* along the Maroochy River departs at 11am, 1 and 3pm and costs A$8 (U.S. $6.40). Admission to the Ginger Factory is free of charge.

Among the natural sightseeing attractions, the area's beaches are number one. ✪ **Sunshine Beach,** which starts 2 kilometers (1¼ miles) south of Noosa Heads, is a marvelous uncrowded stretch of sand. Before I visited this area, I had visualized being able to drive along the coast and admire the ocean from the car window. However, this wasn't the case. The road parallels the coast but it is set back from it 100 to 500 meters (109 to 545 yd.), and water and beach are often obscured by trees and dunes. While they block the view from the road, they protect the beach from the effects of erosion. The sand grass grows close to the maximum high-tide line and holds the sand that isn't packed by tidal and wave wash. The grasses cause a protective dune to form, and eventually hearty shrubbery starts to grow inland of the berm. If it weren't for the dunes and the grasses, the relentless pounding of the waves would eventually sweep the beach away. This means that outside of the populated areas you'll have to walk through a bit of native bush or over a dune to get a good view of the ocean.

Some of the most dramatic coastal vistas are from ✪ **Noosa National Park,** a not-to-be-missed spot for anyone who appreciates natural beauty. Within the 442-hectare (1,105-acre) reserve, walking tracks provide views of rugged headlands, beautiful stretches of golden-sand beaches, and pockets of rain forest with characteristically gnarled strangler fig trees. The trails, which are well marked and easy to follow, range in length from the 600-meter (654-yd.) Palm Grove walk to the 4.2-kilometer (2½-mile) Tanglewood Track to Hells Gates, where there is a spectacular view of the rugged coast. The south end of Alexandria Bay is popular with nude sunbathers, and surfers find the best waves from Boiling Pot to Granite Bay.

The entrance to the park is located about 1 kilometer (½ mile) east of the post office in Noosa Heads—an easy 10- to 15-minute walk. A ranger is on duty to answer questions Monday through Friday from 7:30am to 3:30pm; weekend hours vary. You can also phone 47-3243. Camping is not permitted in the park, but barbecues and picnic tables are provided. Admission is free of charge.

Another popular local attraction, **Underwater World** (tel. 44-8488), is located adjacent to The Wharf complex, in Mooloolaba about a half-hour drive south of Noosa. Here visitors walk through a clear plastic tunnel and view sharks, stringrays, coral, and reef fish all around them. There's also an audiovisual theater and a touch-and-feel lagoon. Underwater World is open daily from 9am. Numerous eating options are available at The Wharf.

SPORTS & RECREATION

Some of the most popular surfing spots in Australia are located along the Sunshine Coast. Don't be surprised if dolphins surf with you at Sunshine Beach or along the coast of Noosa National Park. For current local information, stop in at or phone **Noosa Surf World** in Noosa Junction (tel. 47-3538). This shop is open daily from 9am to 5:30pm.

Four-wheel-drive day-trips to **Fraser Island** are available through several operators in Noosa, including Suncoast Safaris (tel. 47-2617). Fraser, the world's largest sand island, is 120 kilometers (74 miles) long and an average of 15 kilometers (9 miles) wide. Two-thirds of the island is state forest, the balance a national park. Camping is permitted. Suncoast's day-trip costs A$80 (U.S. $64) for adults, and A$50 (U.S. $40) for children aged 4 to 14. Children under age 4 are free. Included are pickup at any accommodation between Caloundra and Noosa, barbecue lunch, morning and afternoon teas, and ferry fees. Travel is by four-wheel drive.

The **Noosa River** is one of the popular local fishing spots where whiting and flathead can be caught year round. Bream is bountiful in May, June, and July; the best bass fishing is October through April. During the summer months (December through February), the ocean provides mackerel, tuna, black marlin, and sailfish. You can buy bait and equipment at **Davo's Bait & Tackle Shop,** 271 Gympie Terrace, Noosaville (tel. 49-8099). Open daily from 7am to 6pm. Fishing tackle and bicycles can be rented at **Noosa Sea Sports & Hire,** 4 Hastings Street (tel. 47-3426). Jetskiing, sailing, diving, yacht charters, and snorkeling can be arranged through **Seawind Charters,** Main Beach, Noosa (tel. 47-3042; mobile phone 018/73-5624). If you're interested in hot-air ballooning, contact **Balloon Aloft** (tel. 41-5020, or toll free 008/25-1481 in Australia.

WHERE TO STAY

In addition to the following properties, ☉ **Accom Noosa Holiday Accommodation,** Hastings Street, Noosa Heads, QLD 4567 (tel. 074/47-3444, or toll free 008/07-2078 in Australia; fax 074/47-2224), can arrange your own fully furnished beachfront or riverside house or condominium. Rates range from A$60 (U.S. $48) for a comfortable studio to A$350 (U.S. $280) for positively palatial digs.

SHERATON NOOSA RESORT, Hastings St., Noosa Heads, QLD 4567.
Tel. 074/49-4888, or toll free 008/07-3535 in Australia. Fax 074/49-2230. 140 rms, 29 suites. A/C MINIBAR TV TEL
$ Rates (including complimentary child care): A$190–A$275 (U.S. $152–U.S. $220) off-peak single or double; A$260–A$350 (U.S. $208–U.S. $280) peak-season single or double; A$350–A$750 (U.S. $280–U.S. $600) off-peak suite (including breakfast); A$450–A$900 (U.S. $360–U.S. $720) peak-season suite (including breakfast); A$30 (U.S. $24) extra person. Children under 17 stay free in parents' room. Special packages available. No-smoking rooms available. AE, BC, DC, MC, V. **Parking:** Free.

Located in the heart of Noosa with beachfront access, the six-story Sheraton provides the community's most luxurious accommodations. All rooms have kitchenettes, including microwaves and utensils, tea- and coffee-making facilities, small refrigerators, balconies, ceiling fans, spa baths, video players, free in-house movies, and a choice of a king-size bed or two doubles. The grounds are nicely landscaped. Facilities for handicapped travelers are available.

    Dining/Entertainment: The Sheraton offers three restaurants: the Charthouse Specialty Seafood & Grill, the Tea Tree Café, and on the beach, the Laguna Bay Beach Club. There are also four bars.

    Services: Complimentary child care for children up to 9 years of age from 8am to 5:30pm daily, laundry, valet, concierge, and 24-hour room service.

    Facilities: Pool, gym, sauna, spa, games room, and self-service laundry.

NETANYA NOOSA RESORT, 75 Hastings St., Noosa Heads, QLD 4567.
Tel. 074/47-4722, or toll free 008/07-2072 in Australia. Fax 074/47-3914. 47 suites. A/C MINIBAR TV TEL
$ Rates: A$160 (U.S. $128) 1-bedroom garden suite; A$220 (U.S. $176) 1-bedroom beachfront suite; A$295 (U.S. $236) 2-bedroom suite; A$420 (U.S. $336) 2-bedroom/2-bathroom penthouse. Children under 18 stay free in parents' room. Special packages available. Higher rates in peak season (school holidays, Easter, and Christmas). AE, BC, DC, MC, V. **Parking:** Free.

The four-story Netanya Noosa hotel is located right on the beach just a short walk from the center of town. All quarters have balconies, kitchenettes (some with microwaves), and bedrooms separate from lounge (living) rooms. While not overly spacious, the suites are well designed and have attractive, modern decors. Instead of ordinary tub/shower combinations, showers are above two-person spa baths. Hairdryers in the bathrooms and TVs and videos in all lounges and bedrooms are additional nice touches. Some rooms have private roof gardens with barbecues and hot tubs, and many have ocean views. One room has been designed for handicapped travelers. (Only this room lacks a spa bath.) All guests receive a free daily newspaper.

    Dining/Entertainment: Pavillions is a delightful à la carte restaurant with seating at umbrella tables on the terrace or indoors.

    Services: Limited room service, laundry, baby-sitting, massage, courtesy vehicle, and complimentary CDs and videos.

    Facilities: Pool, spa, sauna, and gym. Sporting goods, such as boogie boards, surf skis, and fishing rods, are available.

NOOSA INTERNATIONAL, Edgar Bennett Ave., Noosa Heads, QLD 4567. Tel. 074/47-4822. 65 apartments. A/C TV TEL

$ Rates: A$125–A$150 (U.S. $100–U.S. $120) for up to four people. Higher holiday rates. AE, BC, DC, MC, V. **Parking:** Free.

The Noosa International apartment-hotel complex is located 1.5 kilometers (1 mile) from the center of town. Since the property is away from the water, views are of surrounding foliage, not the ocean. In taking advantage of this, the owners have created a Polynesian atmosphere with the thatched roof over the pool bar and by lush, tropical plantings. The units have the advantage of being very spacious and offering full kitchens, washing machines, dryers, attractive furnishings, video recorders/players, and balconies. Bathrooms have showers only. Each apartment has a master bedroom, and the second bedroom sleeps either two adults or four children. Traffic noise is the only drawback to the well-landscaped recreation area.

Dining/Entertainment: Pierre's Restaurant offers a choice of open-air or indoor dining, and there's live music in the piano bar several nights a week.

Facilities: In addition to the two swimming pools, there are three spas and two saunas.

CASTAWAYS HOLIDAY MOTEL, David Low Way (P.O. Box 29), Noosa Heads, QLD 4567. Tel. 074/47-3488. Fax 074/47-5424. 14 apartments. TV TEL

$ Rates: A$55 (U.S. $44) single studio; A$66 (U.S. $52.80) double studio; A$77–A$88 (U.S. $61.60–U.S. $70.40) 1- or 2-bedroom apartment. Holiday rates 20% higher. No children under 10. AE, BC, DC, MC, V. **Parking:** Free.

⑤ Castaways sits by itself on the ocean side of the coastal highway 5 kilometers (3 miles) south of town. The property's units are separated from Sunshine Beach by nothing more than a small patch of native bush—just a pleasant 2-minute walk through casuarinas and honeysuckle banksia trees. The nicely landscaped grounds give Castaways an inviting appearance.

Studios lack cooking facilities, but the one- and two-bedroom apartments have full kitchens, and all furnishings are of good quality. Clock radios, tea- and coffee-making facilities, small refrigerators, in-room movies, queen-size beds, and free daily newspapers are in each apartment. Castaways doesn't have a restaurant or bar, but breakfast is served in the cabana near the attractive swimming pool, and dinner can be delivered to the rooms. There are also laundry facilities, a sauna, and a guest barbecue area. Proprietors Peter and Marea Brown make everyone feel welcome.

WHERE TO DINE

In addition to the two Noosa restaurants described below, the Sunshine Coast offers many other fine eateries. You might like to try the **Eumundi Guest House,** 1 Black Stump Road, Eumundi (tel. 42-8948), where light classical French cuisine is served in a restored Queenslander. Lunch is served on Sunday; dinner, Friday and Saturday. BYO.

Pottingers, Main Road, Montville (tel. 42-9407), is located in the Sunshine Coast hinterland, inland from the Glass House Mountains, and diners enjoy a great view on the way there. The contemporary meals have a Thai influence. Lunch is served daily. BYO.

Picnics at Fairhill, Fairhill Road, Yandina (tel. 46-8191), is known for their elegant morning and afternoon teas. Lunch is also served in these leafy surroundings. Open daily. No credit cards. BYO.

PAVILLIONS, in the Netanya Noosa Resort, 75 Hastings St. Tel. 47-4848.

Cuisine: INTERNATIONAL. **Reservations:** Recommended.

$ Prices: Appetizers A$6–A$9.50 (U.S. $4.80–U.S. $7.60); main courses A$16–A$22.50 (U.S. $12.80–U.S. $18); set three-course lunch A$12 (U.S. $9.60); breakfast from A$3.50 (U.S. $2.80). AE, BC, DC, MC, V.

Open: Lunch daily; dinner daily.

Located on the ground floor of the Netanya Noosa Resort, Pavillions offers such dishes as stir-fried lamb with garlic, chili, and mint in lettuce leaves, or fresh king prawns and oysters with peaches and chili-mint dressing. Other choices include peppered duck breast with piquant raspberry sauce, and médaillons of beef, lobster, and veal with a trio of sauces. Profiteroles are the most popular dessert. An extensive wine list is offered.

LA PLAGE RESTAURANT, Hastings St. Tel. 47-3308.
  Cuisine: FRENCH. **Reservations:** Recommended.
$ Prices: Appetizers A$6–A$13.50 (U.S. $4.80–U.S. $10.80); main courses A$18–A$20 (U.S. $14.40–U.S. $16). AE, BC, MC, V.
  Open: Dinner daily.
This sidewalk café/brasserie has an appearance and ambience to match its Gallic menu. The tile floor, bright paintings on the walls, bentwood chairs, and hanging plants help to create a casual, Mediterranean atmosphere. Local seafood is artfully used in both traditional and contemporary French dishes. You might like to try the soufflé of Moreton Bay bugs, coquilles St.-Jacques prepared with fresh, local scallops, or Australian oysters. Meat dishes include eye filet with either béarnaise sauce or a Dijon mustard glaze. In keeping with the French fare, the lamb is served pink with tomato provençale. The restaurant is BYO, and offers a messenger pickup from the Sheraton's bottle shop (liquor store).

COOLUM

15km (9 miles) S of Noosa

GETTING THERE   By Plane   Travelers bound for Coolum fly Sunstate, Ansett Express, or Eastwest Airlines into the Sunshine Coast Airport near Maroochydore 15 minutes to the south (see "Getting to Noosa," above).

By Train   You can't take a train to Coolum. The main rail depot for the Sunshine Coast is Nambour.

By Bus   See "Getting to Noosa," above.

By Car   If you're driving, allow 1¾ hours from Brisbane.

ESSENTIALS   Tourist information is available at **Tourism Sunshine Coast,** Alexandra Parade, Alexandra Headland, QLD 4572 (tel. 074/43-6400, or toll free 008/07-2041 in Australia). This office is open Monday to Friday from 8:30am to 5pm and Saturday and Sunday from 10am to 4pm. The **area code** is 074.

While international visitors have tended to stay in popular Noosa hotels, Aussies who regularly come to the Sunshine Coast have found more privacy and better values in the less-promoted coastal communities. One of these is Coolum (pop. 3,000). The focal point of the area is beautiful Coolum Beach, a long white sandy stretch with good rolling surf. The friendly township also offers a variety of shopping, dining, and accommodations options and is convenient to all Sunshine Coast sightseeing attractions.

WHERE TO STAY

HYATT REGENCY COOLUM, Warran Rd., Coolum Beach, QLD 4573. Tel. 074/46-1234, or toll free 008/22-2188 in Australia. Fax 074/46-2957. 324 suites and villas. A/C MINIBAR TV TEL **Directions:** The resort is 7 kilometers (4½ miles) from the Sunshine Coast Airport; 20 minutes south of Noosa.

$ Rates (including light breakfast): A$285 (U.S. $228) Regency Club suite; A$396 (U.S. $316.80) 2-bedroom/2-bath President's Villa; A$825 (U.S. $660) Ambassador's Club Villa; A$1,320 (U.S. $1,056) 3-bedroom/3-bath Ambassador Club residence. Children under 18 stay free in parents' room. Special packages available. AE, BC, DC, MC, V. **Parking:** Free.

This property, open since 1988, is Australia's first international-standard resort and spa. The facilities are designed for people who want to improve their health while vacationing on the Sunshine Coast. The low-rise buildings, set in 373 acres of subtropical gardens and forests, are within a short distance of the beach. However, what makes this a health resort is the Spa and Health Centre, featuring gymnasium, aerobics room, Jacuzzis, sauna, herbal wraps, massage, sun court, lap pool, and medical wing with consultation rooms.

Modeled on La Costa Resort and Spa in Southern California, the luxurious Hyatt Regency Coolum encourages its guests to learn healthy habits in the Health Management Centre and to take these new regimes home with them. Myriad beauty and cosmetic services are available for both men and women, and a wide range of sports facilities, including an 18-hole golf course, eight swimming pools, a jogging track, two ropes courses, squash courts, and nine tennis courts, is provided. Bicycles and a shuttle bus get guests around the resort. There are four restaurants and a nightclub.

COOLUM CAPRICE, 123-133 The Esplanade, Coolum Beach, QLD 4573. Tel. 074/46-2177. Fax 074/46-3559. 65 apartments. TV TEL

$ Rates: A$95 (U.S. $76) 1-bedroom unit for two people; A$105 (U.S. $84) 2-bedroom/2-bath unit for up to four people; A$120 (U.S. $96) 3-bedroom unit for up to six people. Weekly discounts. Higher holiday rates. BC, MC, V. **Parking:** Free.

Coolum Caprice is a good example of the kind of lodgings the locals like. Each of the spacious one-, two-, and three-bedroom units is tastefully furnished and has a balcony. All but the ground-floor apartments have a wonderful ocean view. Kitchens are fully equipped, and washing machines and dryers are provided. All but the one-bedroom units have walk-in closets.

The 14-story complex, across the street from the beach, lacks a restaurant and bar, but a nearby café will deliver meals. In addition, the management sells a starter pack of breakfast items for new arrivals. Two saunas, a spa, swimming pool, gym, and games room can be used by guests. Baby-sitting can be arranged.

4. THE CENTRAL COAST

Heading north from the Sunshine Coast, you enter an area that is of interest to tourists primarily because of the access it provides to offshore islands. Travelers do not flock to the central coast the way they do to other Queensland regions. Instead, the local economies are based on important agricultural and mineral production.

Maryborough (pop. 22,600) is the commercial center for a region that produces sugar, timber, dairy products, grain, fruit, and vegetables. Bundaberg (pop. 32,780) is known as "Queensland's rum city," but sugar, in fact, is the town's most significant product. Rum, like the manufacturing of sugar-harvesting equipment, is a sideline.

If you travel through this central coast region during the cane-harvesting season, July through December, you will notice the practice of burning off the fields. After dark, huge sections along the highway and in the distance are engulfed in red-orange flames; during the day, smoke from the burnt cane drifts across the highway. In either case, slow down and proceed carefully because your visibility could be impaired. And I don't suggest you inspect the fields on foot—the purpose of the burning is to remove the thick cane's leaves and drive out venomous snakes before the harvesters start cutting. You may also see cane trains chugging alongside the highway or bringing their loads through town.

Farther north, Gladstone and Rockhampton are in the Capricorn region, named for the fact that it straddles the Tropic of Capricorn. Gladstone is a major industrial center and the home of the world's largest aluminum plant. Rockhampton is the beef capital of Australia. While these cities are not totally without a charm of their own, their main interest for tourists is as a jumping-off point to islands on or near the Great Barrier Reef. Delightful Heron Island is a mere 80 kilometers (50 miles) by launch or helicopter from Gladstone. Great Keppel Island lies offshore of Rockhampton.

One-third of Australia's sugar comes from the area around Mackay, and seven mills operate in conjunction with the world's largest bulk-sugar-loading terminal. You can tour Pleystowe Sugar Mill from June to December. Mackay is 1,061 kilometers (658 miles) north of Brisbane, approximately halfway between the Queensland capital and Cooktown in the Far North region of the state. While Mackay has some nice beaches of its own, they aren't quite as special as the ones found on Brampton Island, which lies 32 kilometers (20 miles) off the coast.

GLADSTONE

600km (372 miles) N of Brisbane, 126km (78 miles) S of Rockhampton

GETTING THERE & DEPARTING By Plane or Helicopter Sunstate Airlines and **Queensland Pacific** fly to Gladstone. Helicopter flights for Heron Island leave from the Gladstone airport. Launches depart from O'Connell Wharf.

By Bus, Train, or Car Pioneer, Greyhound, and Bus Australia make the trip from Brisbane in 8 hours; a ticket costs A$57 (U.S. $45.60). Gladstone is on the main north-south train route. The Queenslander, Sunlander, Spirit of Capricorn, and Capricornian all stop there. If you're driving, head up the Bruce Highway.

ESSENTIALS The **Visitor Information Centre,** 56 Goondoon Street, Gladstone, QLD 4680 (tel. 079/72-4000), is open Monday through Saturday. The **area code** is 079.

A boomtown since the 1960s, when the potential for its harbor was realized, Gladstone (pop. 23,800) is one of Australia's most prosperous seaside cities. Handling Queensland's vast supplies of coal, as well as other minerals, wheat, and meat, Gladstone exceeds even Sydney in annual shipping tonnage.

WHERE TO STAY

Chances are that you'll arrive by air from Brisbane and connect immediately with transportation to Heron Island, but if you're driving, you may need overnight lodging. Try the following:

HIGHPOINT INTERNATIONAL, 22 Roseberry St., Gladstone, QLD 4680. Tel. 079/72-4711. Fax 079/72-4940. 54 suites. A/C TV TEL **Transportation:** Transfers to and from airport and launch to Heron Island are provided.
$ Rates: A$105 (U.S. $84) single; A$120 (U.S. $96) double; A$16 (U.S. $12.80) extra person. Reservations can be made through Flag Inns. AE, BC, DC, MC, V. **Parking:** Free.
The Highpoint International is the city's poshest hostelry. Each room in the eight-story motel has a separate lounge, fully equipped kitchen, balcony, and laundry facilities. Videos, clock radios, and tub/shower combinations are standard throughout. The Highpoint has a restaurant, bar, swimming pool, and 24-hour room service.

COUNTRY COMFORT INN, 100 Goondoon St., Gladstone, QLD 4680. Tel. 079/72-4499. 72 units. A/C MINIBAR TV TEL
$ Rates: A$75 (U.S. $60) single; A$90 (U.S. $72) double; extra person A$7 (U.S. $5.60). AE, BC, DC, MC, V. **Parking:** Free.
Conveniently located near the Visitor Information Centre in the heart of town, Country Comfort's units have all the standard amenities including coffee- and

tea-making facilities, small refrigerators, videos, and clock radios. The Brass Plum serves all meals, and there's a pool.

WHERE TO DINE

SWAGGY'S AUSTRALIAN RESTAURANT, 56 Goondoon St. Tel. 72-1653.

Cuisine: AUSTRALIAN. **Reservations:** Not necessary.

$ **Prices:** Appetizers A$4.80–A$17.50 (U.S. $3.85–U.S. $14); main courses A$14.80–A$42.80 (U.S. $11.85–U.S. $34.25). AE, BC, DC, MC, V.

Open: Lunch Mon–Fri from noon; dinner Mon–Sat from 6pm.

If you find yourself in Gladstone at lunch- or dinnertime, don't fail to sample the fare at Swaggy's. I thoroughly enjoyed my main course, which was called "jolly jumbuck" and consisted of a juicy rack of lamb baked with honey and almonds. Other dishes are "Ned Kelly's combination," "chicken Matilda," "billabong filet," "gumleaf pâté," and "swagman's surprise." Don't be put off by these folksy names—their careful preparation and presentation belie their frontier appellations. And if you're game, try the barbecued crocodile. Children's meals are available.

ROCKHAMPTON

726km (450 miles) N of Brisbane

GETTING THERE & DEPARTING   By Plane   Sunstate Airlines, Australian Airlines, and Ansett fly to Rockhampton. The Australian Airlines Air Pass fare from Brisbane to Rockhampton ranges from A$118 to A$149 (U.S. $94.40 to U.S. $119.20). Australian Regional Airline flights to Great Keppel Island leave from the Rockhampton Airport.

By Train   The Spirit of Capricorn and several other Queensland Railways trains take nearly 10 hours to reach Rockhampton from Brisbane. An economy class "sitting" ticket costs A$55.30 (U.S. $44.25).

By Bus or Car   The Pioneer, Greyhound, or Bus Australia bus from Brisbane takes either 9 or 10 hours, depending on whether you're on an express. The fare is A$63 (U.S. $50.40). If you're driving, you'll find Rockhampton on the Bruce Highway.

ESSENTIALS   The 14-meter (46-ft.) **Capricorn Spire** at Curtis Park on the main highway at the south end of town marks the exact line of the Tropic of Capricorn and is the site of the Tourist Information Office (tel. 079/27-2055, or toll free 008/07-5910 in Australia). This office is open daily. The **area code** is 079.

Rockhampton (pop. 55,700) is the beef capital of Australia, but what lures most visitors here is Great Keppel Island (see Chapter 10).

WHERE TO STAY

COUNTRY COMFORT INN, 86 Victoria Parade, Rockhampton, QLD 4700. Tel. 079/27-9933. 66 rms, 6 suites. A/C MINIBAR TV TEL

$ **Rates:** A$70 (U.S. $56) single; A$80 (U.S. $64) double; A$7 (U.S. $5.60) extra person. Lower rates through Aussie auto clubs. AE, BC, DC, MC, V. **Parking:** Free.

The Country Comfort Inn is a nine-story property where all rooms and suites have balconies, clock radios, videos, coffee- and tea-making facilities, and small fridges. The restaurant is open for lunch and dinner; there are also a coffee shop, bar, self-service laundry, and swimming pool. Room service is available 24 hours a day.

ALBERT COURT, Albert and Alma Sts., Rockhampton, QLD 4700. Tel. 079/27-7433. 44 rms. A/C TV TEL

$ **Rates:** A$50 (U.S. $40) single; A$58–A$60 (U.S. $46.40–U.S. $48) double; A$8 (U.S. $6.40) extra person. Reservations can be made through Best Western. AE, BC, DC, MC, V. **Parking:** Free.

Albert Court is a low-rise motel close to the center of town. The bathrooms have showers but no tubs. Three rooms have water beds. Coffee- and tea-making facilities, small refrigerators, and videos are standard throughout the property. A restaurant and bar are open Monday to Saturday. Guests can use the pool and self-service laundry facilities. There is limited room service.

READERS RECOMMEND

Planet Downs, *P.O. Box 420, Zillmere, QLD 4034. Tel. 07/265-5022. Fax 07/265-3978.* —*"Planet Downs is a working cattle station (ranch) with first-class accommodations. It is a family-owned and operated property consisting of 250,000 acres—about 100 miles long and 15 miles wide. There are 10,000 head of cattle and 100 horses, plus a wildlife sanctuary where guests can feed kangaroos and emus; wild koalas live on the property, too. We had a choice of watching or joining in with the daily ranch activities or playing tennis, riding horses or camels, swimming in the pool or creek, going fishing, or visiting 3,000-year-old Aboriginal cave paintings. The accommodations are extremely nice. Our room had a king-size bed, a modern bathroom, pot-belly stove, and tea- and coffee-making facilities (complete with homemade cookies). The meals, which are shared with members of the family, are great. All-in-all, Planet Downs was one of the highlights of our trip to Australia, and we heartily recommend it to your readers."*—Marj and Bob Julian, Winnetka, Ill. *Author's note:* Planet Downs has 10 suites with air conditioning and minibars. Rates, including all meals and activities, are A$410 (U.S. $328) single, A$310 (U.S. $248) per person based on double occupancy. American Express, Bankcard, Diners Club, MasterCard, and VISA are accepted. Planet Downs is located 650 kilometers (403 miles), which is a 9-hour drive, northwest of Brisbane and a 3-hour drive from Rockhampton. There is an airstrip on the property, and direct flights from Brisbane, Rockhampton, and other Queensland cities are available. Transfer by Planet Downs' four-wheel-drive vehicle from Rockhampton or Gladstone costs A$170 (U.S. $136) per person round-trip.

MACKAY

1061km (658 miles) N of Brisbane, 335km (208 miles) N of Rockhampton

GETTING THERE & DEPARTING By Plane Australian Airlines, Sunstate Airlines, and Ansett fly into Mackay. An Australian Airlines Air Pass ticket from Brisbane costs from A$152 to A$191 (U.S. $121.60 to U.S. $152.80). Australian Regional Airlines and a daily launch provide transportation to Brampton Island.

By Train Two Queensland Railways' trains, the Sunlander and the Queenslander, stop in Mackay.

By Bus A Greyhound, Pioneer, or Bus Australia ticket from Brisbane costs about A$90 (U.S. $72) and the trip takes about 13½ hours. Motorists follow the Bruce Highway.

ESSENTIALS Tourism Mackay, Nebo Road, Mackay, QLD 4740 (tel. 079/52-2677), can answer your questions. The **area code** is 079.

Pronounced "mu" (as in *mug*) "ki" (rhymes with *sky*), Mackay (pop. 50,301) is the sugar capital of the country. It is also the departure point for lovely Brampton Island.

WHERE TO STAY

FOUR DICE MOTEL, 166 Nebo Rd., Mackay, QLD 4740. Tel. 079/51-1555. Fax 079/51-3655. 34 rms, 2 suites. A/C MINIBAR TV TEL

$ **Rates:** A$70 (U.S. $56) single; A$80 (U.S. $64) double; A$140 (U.S. $112) suite;

A$14 (U.S. $11.20) extra person. Reservations can be made through Flag Inns. AE, BC, DC, MC, V. **Parking:** Free.

Located 3 kilometers (2 miles) from the city and 2 kilometers (1 mile) from the airport, this comfortable motel offers all the standard amenities: videos, clock radios, tea- and coffee-making facilities, and small refrigerators. Two rooms have a spa bath; one has a water bed. Meals are available in Pipers Grill, and there's a swimming pool. Accommodations for handicapped travelers are available.

5. THE WHITSUNDAY COAST

Surfers flock to the Sunshine Coast; night owls love the Gold Coast; and sailors are sure that the Whitsundays are their nirvana. Protected from the open sea by the Great Barrier Reef, the 74 islands in the Whitsunday Passage and the tranquil azure water between them create a mariner's perfect playground. For nonsailors, delightful resorts on seven of the islands offer myriad other pleasures and water-oriented activities. The island resorts are discussed in Chapter 10.

On the coast, most vacation-bound travelers land at the Proserpine Airport; Airlie Beach supplies lodging before and after island idylls. Seaplanes, helicopters, launches, and catamarans shuttle in and out of Shute Harbour, providing transportation to and from such getaway havens as Hayman, South Molle, and Daydream islands.

The area was named by Captain Cook when he discovered it on Whitsunday (the seventh Sunday after Easter) in 1770.

AIRLIE BEACH

297km (184 miles) S of Townsville

GETTING THERE By Plane   Australian Airlines and Eastwest Airlines fly into Proserpine, 24 kilometers (15 miles) inland. An Australian Airlines Air Pass ticket from Brisbane costs from A$158 to A$199 (U.S. $126.40 to U.S. $159.20); from Sydney the fare ranges from A$230 to A$290 (U.S. $184 to U.S. $232). Sampson's Bus (tel. 079/45-2377) transfers passengers from the airport to Airlie Beach hotels (A$11/U.S. $8.80).

By Train   Queensland Railways' Sunlander and Queenslander stop in Proserpine.

By Bus   Bus Australia, Pioneer, and Greyhound all provide service to Airlie Beach. From Brisbane the trip takes about 15 hours and costs A$103 (U.S. $82.40). From Townsville it takes about 3½ hours and costs A$38 (U.S. $30.40).

By Car   If you're driving, the trip from Townsville takes 3½ hours on the Bruce Highway.

ESSENTIALS   Tourist information is dispensed at **Mandy's Mine of Information,** first floor, The Roundabout Shops, The Esplanade and Shute Harbour Road, Airlie Beach, QLD 4802 (tel. 079/46-6848). The office is open daily. The **area code** is 079.

SPECIAL EVENTS   The Great Whitsunday Fun Race, held on the Sunday in September with the highest midday tide, is the highlight of Airlie's social season. Each boat must have a live topless figurehead, who draws much more attention than rules, protocol, or even who wins. (First prize is a bottle of rum.) The entire weekend is one of heavy-duty frivolity.

Airlie Beach, the gateway to the Whitsundays, is a laid-back beachfront community closely resembling L.A.'s Venice or San Diego's Mission Beach. The only street is chockablock with stores selling resort wear, water-sports equipment, and souvenirs.

Interspersed among these shops are agencies that book day-trips to the islands and sailing adventures. The town's population of 1,705 consists of hoteliers, restaurateurs, yacht specialists, and merchants meeting the needs of vacationers who base themselves in Airlie Beach and do a series of 1-day island excursions or who stay overnight in the community on their way to an offshore vacation.

Those in the tourist industry are joined by young people who work at the marinas or in hotels while looking for a job crewing on someone's luxury yacht. Airlie (pronounced "*a*-lee") Beach has a tropical feel and is, in fact, on the same latitude as Tahiti. Toad racing 2 nights a week draws a big crowd at the local pub, where everyone drinks stubbies—short bottles of beer served in Styrofoam holders. Shorts are the local uniform day and night in all but one or two of the better restaurants.

WHAT TO SEE & DO

Because it is protected by the Great Barrier Reef many miles to the north and east, Airlie Beach has almost no sandy stretch along its waterfront and almost no surf. Even more important, and actually *a matter of life and death,* is the presence of the deadly box jellyfish along the coast from October through April. Commonly referred to as "stingers," the jellyfish kill more humans in Australian tropical waters than sharks, crocodiles, stonefish, and all other harmful marine creatures put together. I implore you to heed signs posted on coastal beaches and close-in islands that tell you to stay out of the water during the late spring, summer, and early autumn months. Stingers can be present anywhere north of the Tropic of Capricorn, but are not a problem at the Barrier Reef islands which are far offshore.

With the exception of tours through the **Proserpine Sugar Mill** from July through November, the sights in this area are natural rather than commercial. Forget museums and historic buildings for the moment and savor some of the most beautiful scenery the country has to offer. Fly over forest-clad islands and quiet water with **Seair Pacific** (tel. 46-9133, or toll free 008/07-5157 in Australia). Their tours last 2½ to 3 hours and cost from A$130 (U.S. $104) to A$150 (U.S. $120). Included are courtesy coach pickup, a scenic flight over such beauty spots as **Whitehaven Beach,** the only long sandy stretch in the Whitsundays, water landing and takeoff on the Great Barrier Reef (which is 60km/37 miles east of Airlie Beach), a reef walking tour, snorkeling, and glass-bottom-boat coral viewing. Snorkels, masks, and reef-walking shoes are provided.

Day-trips to **Daydream** and **South Molle Islands** are also popular. The return water-taxi fare from Shute Harbour is A$16 to A$30 (U.S. $12.80 to U.S. $24). Details of the facilities in each place are in Chapter 10. Whitsunday Connections (tel. 46-6900, 46-9499, or toll free 008/07-5127 in Australia) and a half dozen other operators offer day-trips to the Great Barrier Reef, Whitehaven Beach, and Hook Island. Prices range from A$40 to A$75 (U.S. $32 to U.S. $60).

SPORTS & RECREATION

The Whitsundays are a watery playground where everyone can—and usually does—try his or her hand at yachting (sailing), scuba diving, snorkeling, fishing, or windsurfing. Bareboat (sail-yourself) charters are especially popular, as they allow total freedom. You can anchor in a sheltered inlet and stay as long as you like, explore uninhabited islands to your heart's content, visit the island resorts in the area, or raft up (tie up alongside) with newfound friends. At the same time, you have the security of checking in twice a day by radio with the people from whom you chartered the boat, and they are always on call should any problems arise.

If you're willing to trade a little privacy for less responsibility, you can rent a boat with a crew who will do all or some of the work, as you prefer.

The third option is to join a sailing adventure organized by one of the charter companies. You'll have less say in the itinerary, but the cost is lower and it's a fun way to meet people. No sailing experience is necessary.

Another possibility is a Barrier Reef dive trip, where you live aboard a boat on the reef.

Whitsunday Rent A Yacht, Shute Harbour, QLD 4802 (tel. 079/46-9232, or toll free 008/07-5111 in Australia), is one of the largest charter companies in the area. The 3- and 5-star fleet consists of yachts from 27 to 43 feet, and 34- and 35-foot motor cruisers for rent with or without a crew. You can also join a group on a Whitsunday Sailing Adventure for 5 or 7 nights; departures are Sunday and Monday at noon.

If you want a day sail, try the maxiboat *Apollo* (tel. 46-6922) or the 1962 America's Cup challenger, *Gretel* (tel. 46-6224 or 466-184). The cost of A$42 (U.S. $33.60) includes morning and afternoon tea and equipment for snorkeling and windsurfing.

The ultimate Whitsunday experience for some might be spending the day or longer on an uninhabited island. **Seair Pacific** or any of the charter companies will drop you off for a private picnic or your very own camping adventure.

WHERE TO STAY

CORAL SEA RESORT, 25 Ocean Ave., Airlie Beach, QLD 4802. Tel. 079/46-6458, or toll free 008/07-5061 in Australia. 24 rms. A/C TV TEL
$ Rates: A$95 (U.S. $76) single; A$105 (U.S. $84) double; A$45 (U.S. $36) extra person. Children under 18 stay free in parents' room. AE, BC, DC, MC, V. **Parking:** Free.

The Coral Sea Resort occupies a scenic waterfront site at the end of a peninsula less than a 10-minute walk from the heart of Airlie Beach. All but four of the rooms have an ocean view, and some quarters overlook the attractive 25-meter (27-yd.) pool and private boat jetty. A boutique, beauty salon, croquet lawn, spa, and sun deck are also on the premises. Most rooms have balconies and all have the usual coffee- and tea-making facilities.

The resort's restaurant is open Wednesday to Monday; room service is available until 9pm. In spite of the fact that the management allows nonguests to use the pool for a fee, the Coral Sea has a restful atmosphere.

WHITSUNDAY WANDERERS RESORT, Shute Harbour Rd., Airlie Beach, QLD 4802. Tel. 079/46-6446. Fax 079/46-6761. 128 rms. A/C TV TEL
$ Rates: A$75 (U.S. $60) single, A$90 (U.S. $72) single in peak season; A$99 (U.S. $79.20) double, A$109 (U.S. $97.20) double in peak season; A$18–A$24 (U.S. $14.40–U.S. $19.20) extra adult; A$7 (U.S. $5.60) extra child. Peak season is school-holiday periods and Christmas–late Jan. AE, BC, DC, MC, V. **Parking:** Free.

Whitsunday Wanderers is a Polynesian-style property where low-rise units are set in 8.5 hectares (21 acres) of lush, tropical plantings. Native lorikeets (parrots) add to the atmosphere (and make this an especially good place for those who like to be up early with the birds). Of all the rooms, the Kookaburra units with wood paneling are the coziest. Others have concrete-block walls and chenille bedspreads on a double and a single (trundle) bed. All quarters come with kitchenettes and sleep up to two adults and two children.

The unusually friendly staff offers an orientation talk and welcome cocktail daily at 3pm. They also provide free scuba-diving lessons, use of Windsurfers and paddleskis at the beach, and use of the property's other sports facilities: four swimming pools, archery, table tennis, 18-hole mini-golf course, full- and half-court tennis, volleyball, and aerobics. Whitsunday Wanderers is owned by the Proserpine Sugar Mill, where tours are conducted from July through November. All meals at the resort are served in the Wanderer's Restaurant; no room service is offered. One unit is designed to accommodate handicapped travelers.

TROPIC ISLE RESORT, 356 Shute Harbour Rd., Airlie Beach, QLD 4802. Tel. 079/46-6244. 34 rms. A/C TV TEL
$ Rates: A$35–A$70 (U.S. $28–U.S. $56) single; A$50–A$85 (U.S. $40–U.S. $68) double; A$10 (U.S. $8) extra person. AE, BC, DC, MC, V.

The three-story Tropic Isle Resort is centrally located. All units have clock radios, tea- and coffee-making facilities, and small refrigerators. Some 25 have bathtubs; others just showers. Queen-size beds are available, as is room service. Two pools, a bar, and a restaurant are also on the premises.

WHERE TO DINE

ROMEO'S ITALIAN RESTAURANT, in the Beach Shops on Shute Harbour Rd. Tel. 46-6337.
Cuisine: ITALIAN. **Reservations:** Recommended.
$ **Prices:** Appetizers A$7–A$14 (U.S. $5.60–U.S. $11.20); main courses A$11–A$24 (U.S. $8.80–U.S. $19.20). AE, BC, DC, MC, V.
Open: Lunch Mon–Fri noon–2pm; dinner Mon–Sat 6–10pm. Deli/café Mon–Sat 9am–10pm.

The mouth-watering aroma of freshly baked bread and Italian herbs led me to the delightful eatery owned by Romeo Rigo. (That's "Romeo" as in Alpha-Romeo, not as in Romeo and Juliet.) Everything is made from scratch on the premises, and only the freshest ingredients ever cross the threshold. The soup of the day simmers in a pot on one burner while Romeo adjusts the seasoning in sauces he's creating on the same huge stove. He makes the pastas and the gelati and the sorbet and the bread. And they're all delicious.

The host's ebullient personality sets the tone for the service, which is always good and never blasé. Spaghetti puttanesca (prostitute spaghetti) is a hot dish flavored with plenty of chili. Other tasty treats are veal scaloppine with white wine, fried calamari, and chicken parmigiana. If you order the white chocolate mousse for dessert, you will think you have died and gone to heaven.

Seating is outdoors on the terrace, from which there is a great view of the beach; at umbrella tables in the courtyard; or indoors at kelly-green tables with Italian-style raffia chairs. Adjacent to the restaurant, Romeo has a deli/café where you can buy pâté, quiche, fresh-from-the-oven bread, pizza, other ingredients for a memorable picnic feast, and light meals.

K.C.'S CHARGRILL, Shute Harbour Rd. Tel. 46-6320.
Cuisine: CHARGRILL. **Reservations:** Accepted only for large parties.
$ **Prices:** Appetizers from A$8 (U.S. $6.40); main courses from A$15 (U.S. $12). AE, BC, DC, MC, V.
Open: Lunch Sun noon–4pm; dinner daily 6pm–2am.

K.C.'s is not only a fun, casual site for delicious charcoal-broiled meals but also a popular local meeting place and nightspot. Whether you've been out sailing all day or lazing by the pool at your hotel, you're bound to develop an appetite when you see steaks, lamb chops, prawns, ribs, and rack of lamb sizzling away on the grill; and if you stay and socialize a while, you'll undoubtedly meet some of the friendly yachties who call Airlie Beach home. If you want to look like you belong, order a Fourex (XXXX) or Powers stubbie, which will be handed to you in a Styrofoam "cooler," and sit back and enjoy the live music that is performed nightly.

K.C.'s has a down-to-earth atmosphere, created by wooden booths, linoleum floors, and ceiling fans. It feels so tropical and funky that you almost expect to see Humphrey Bogart sitting at the bar. Meals are ordered at a desk and collected by diners; seating is both indoors and out. Portions are large and a trip to the salad bar comes with each main course. Kevin Collins, after whom the eatery was named, is no longer on the scene. Now it's host Geoff Glide who welcomes guests and keeps a loose lid on the frivolity.

EVENING ENTERTAINMENT

A big crowd gathers at the local pub, the **Airlie Beach Hotel** (tel. 466-233), on Tuesday and Thursday nights at 7:30pm for toad racing. The large cane toads chew on anything that comes close, so they're kept in cloth bags until race time and are handled with gloves. The hotel also has a disco on Tuesday, Wednesday, Thursday, and Friday from 9pm until the wee hours, a live band on Saturday night, and entertainment on Sunday afternoon. The cover charge ranges from A$3 to A$5 (U.S. $2.40 to U.S. $4).

NORTHERN & NORTHWEST QUEENSLAND

- **WHAT'S SPECIAL ABOUT NORTHERN & NORTHWEST QUEENSLAND**
- **1. TOWNSVILLE**
- **2. MISSION BEACH**
- **3. CAIRNS**
- **4. PORT DOUGLAS & MOSSMAN**
- **5. THE CAPE YORK PENINSULA**
- **6. OUTBACK & INLAND QUEENSLAND**

If you like white colonial buildings surrounded by stately coconut palms, jungle-green growth punctuated by vivid bougainvilleas, and miles of beaches edged in mangroves, you're going to love northern Queensland. While the Tropic of Capricorn actually passes through Rockhampton many miles to the south, and Mackay gives visitors their first taste of trade winds, safari suits, and a decidedly slower pace, it's Townsville, Cairns, and Port Douglas that make you want to sip a long cool drink on the veranda and wait for Clark Gable to appear.

Australians tend to divide the top half of the holiday state into two regions: North Queensland and the Far North. Townsville, capital of N.Q., is the largest city in the combined area and provides a dress rehearsal for those heading to the true tropics of the Far North. Cairns, which has been entertaining travelers since the 1920s, is the gateway to the refreshingly cool Atherton Tableland, the jungles of the Cape York Peninsula, and the wonders of the Great Barrier Reef. The international airport at Cairns also provides access to popular Palm Cove and Port Douglas—thriving tourist destinations to the north. Like Florida in the United States, northern Queensland is a lush, humid region where mangoes, pawpaws (papayas), bananas, palm trees, and jacarandas thrive. Older homes were built on stilts to provide ventilation and prevent destruction by floods and termites. Modern houses are air conditioned and close out the sun with wooden shutters.

Four climate zones running parallel to the coast divide this part of the state. To the west, the Great Artesian Basin is a flat, hot region best left to hardy folks in search of minerals. Silver, lead, copper, and zinc, for instance, come in great quantities from the mines at Mount Isa. The tablelands, to the east of the outback, are known for their rich, volcanic soils, tobacco plantations, and cattle pastures. Staghorn ferns and orchids thrive in the rain forests that grow on the edge of the tablelands near the Great Dividing Range. Seas of sugarcane characterize the coastal plains, which lead to the water's edge and the Great Barrier Reef beyond.

In northern Queensland, more than in any other area of the country, the tourist industry is prospering. Many new hotels and attractions have opened recently and services for visitors are being finely honed. Most travelers arrive during the winter months (July, August, and September), when daytime temperatures are in the high 70s and there is the least chance of rain. The wet period, December through March, is best avoided. Deadly marine stingers are a problem at coastal beaches and the islands nearest the coast from October through April or May.

WHAT'S SPECIAL ABOUT NORTHERN & NORTHWEST QUEENSLAND

Beaches
☐ The coastal communities north of Cairns, each with its own lovely stretch of sand.

☐ Mission Beach, with almost 9 miles of palm-fringed beach.

Natural Spectacles
☐ The Great Barrier Reef, a magical underwater garden that has to be seen to be believed.

☐ Daintree National Park and Cape Tribulation, featuring large areas of untouched rain forest.

Ace Attractions
☐ Great Barrier Reef Wonderland in Townsville, a must for those who want to learn about the reef.

☐ The Tjapukai Dance Theatre, comprised of talented Aborigines; they perform daily in Kuranda.

Adventurous Activities
☐ Fishing for black marlin on Lizard Island from late September to early December.

☐ White-water rafting on the Tully River.

☐ Scuba diving at the Great Barrier Reef.

Unlike the cities along the central coast of Queensland, Townsville and Cairns are both popular destinations *and* jumping-off points to the reef. Townsville is the gateway to Orpheus and Magnetic islands, and access to Lizard, Green, and Fitzroy is via Cairns. Dunk and Bedarra can be reached from either city.

SEEING NORTHERN & NORTHWEST QUEENSLAND

Queensland Railways' Sunlander and Queenslander provide transportation between Brisbane and Cairns, stopping at most coastal cities. Australian Regional Airlines and Sunstate Airlines supplement the routes of the major carriers. McCafferty's, Bus Australia, Pioneer, and Greyhound travel up and down the coast and along the major inland routes.

The **Queensland Government Travel Centres** located in Australian state capitals and **Queensland Tourist and Travel Corporation** offices overseas are the best sources of tourist information. For motoring information, contact the **Royal Automobile Club of Queensland (RACQ)**, 202 Ross River Road, Aitkenvale (near Townsville), QLD 4814 (tel. 077/75-3999), or 112 Sheridan Street, Cairns, QLD 4870 (tel. 070/51-4788).

1. TOWNSVILLE

1,439km (892 miles) N of Brisbane, 347km (215 miles) S of Cairns

GETTING THERE By Plane The city's airport is served by Australian Airlines, Australian Regional Airlines, Sunstate Airlines, Flight West, and Ansett. The cost of an Australian Airlines Air Pass ticket from Brisbane ranges from A$185 to A$231 (U.S. $148 to U.S. $184.80); from Sydney, A$256 to A$320 (U.S. $202.40 to U.S. $256). A ticket on the Airporter Bus Service into the city center from the airport costs A$6 (U.S. $4.80); if you're a traveling twosome (or more), it's cheaper to take a taxi (A$8/U.S. $6.40).

By Train The Sunlander and Queenslander trains stop on their way from Brisbane to Cairns. The Queenslander is the more luxurious of the two.

By Bus An intercity bus to Townsville from Brisbane takes about 22 hours and costs A$120 (U.S. $96). A bus to Townsville from Cairns, a 5-hour trip, costs A$40 (U.S. $32). Pioneer, Greyhound, Bus Australia, and McCafferty's cover these routes and others.

By Car Townsville is on the Bruce Highway.

ESSENTIALS   Information The **Copper Top Tourist Information Centre,** in Flinders Mall, Townsville, QLD 4810 (tel. 077/71-2724 or 21-3660), is open Monday through Friday from 9am to 5pm and Saturday and Sunday from 9am to noon. Another Information Centre located on the **Bruce Highway** is open daily from 9am to 5pm.

Orientation Townsville (pop. 120,000) is located on Cleveland Bay near the mouths of Ross River and Ross Creek. A long footpath, ideal for jogging or strolling, follows the waterfront from the breakwater near the entrance of the harbor to Kissing Point and The Rockpool, a distance of nearly 3 kilometers (2 miles).

The bare, rust-colored rock face of Castle Hill rises above the city and provides a lofty viewpoint. Flinders Mall is the focal point of the shopping precinct, and in this area and others, wonderful restored two-story colonial buildings with iron fretwork and double verandas can be found interspersed with modern structures. Townsville's James Cook University is Australia's only university in the tropics. Magnetic Island, with some small mountains of its own, lies 7 kilometers (4 miles) offshore and is, in effect, an island suburb.

Area Code The area code is 077.

A prosperous city whose port handles the minerals from Mount Isa, beef and wool from the western plains, and sugar and timber from the coastal region, Townsville also strives to attract tourists. The Sheraton Breakwater Casino Hotel is northern Queensland's only gambling venue, and Great Barrier Reef Wonderland, built in 1987 at a cost of A$20 million (U.S. $16 million), is a state-of-the-art opportunity to learn about one of the wonders of the world.

WHAT TO SEE & DO

Except for the 2.5-kilometer (1½ mile) drive from the junction of Gregory Street and Stanley Street to the top of 285-meter (941-ft.) **Castle Hill,** where a panoramic vista awaits, Townsville's major attractions all involve the water, and more specifically, the Great Barrier Reef.

THE GREAT BARRIER REEF WONDERLAND

For those who want to understand, or at least try to understand, the Great Barrier Reef, there is no better place in Australia than Townsville's Great Barrier Reef Wonderland, 2-36 Flinders Street (tel. 21-1793 or 21-2411).

The large complex includes three main areas: the largest **live coral reef aquarium** in the world, the first **OMNIMAX** theater in the Southern Hemisphere, and the first branch of the **Queensland Museum** outside of Brisbane. These attractions are contained in a covered mall, along with specialty shops, fast-food outlets, dive shops, and the departure area for outer-reef trips and Magnetic Island ferries.

The aquarium is unique to Reef Wonderland. A 20-meter (66-ft.) acrylic tunnel allows visitors to, in effect, walk through the huge tank where coral, plants, fish, and other animals have been relocated from various parts of the actual Great Barrier Reef. A predator tank, a touch tank, an aquarium theaterette, various educational displays, and a shop with an excellent selection of publications concerning the GBR are in the aquarium area. Upstairs you can see the algae turf filters, which keep the water clean in the tank, and get a bird's-eye view of marine life. The aquarium is operated by the

QUEENSLAND

N

Torres Strait
Thursday Island
Bamaga
Cape York Peninsula

Weipa

Gulf of Carpentaria

Coral Sea

5

Peninsula Development Rd.

79

Cooktown

Daintree River National Park

Mossman
Port Douglas **4**
CAIRNS
Captain Cook Hwy.

Karumba

Great Barrier Reef

South Pacific Ocean

Mission Beach **2**
Tully

Great Dividing Range

Bruce Hwy.

1 **Townsville**

6

Barkly Hwy.
Mt. Isa
Cloncurry
Flinders Hwy.
Landsborough Hwy.

66

Charters Towers
78
Hughenden

Airlie Beach **5**
Proserpine
Mackay
4

NORTHERN TERRITORY

Winton
66

6

Great Dividing Range

Clermont

Tropic of Capricorn
Longreach
Barcaldine
Capricorn Hwy.
Blackall
Emerald
66

1

Rockhampton

Gladstone
4

Liechhardt Hwy.

Bundaberg
Maryborough

Charleville
54
Mitchell
34
Warrego
Mundubbera

6

Mitchell Hwy.

Cannarvon Hwy.

Range

39

Hwy.

3
Gympie
Noosa Heads
1
BRISBANE

Cunnamulla
St. George
55
Toowoomba
Ipswich
Surfer's Paradise

71

Goondiwindi
Warwick
Lamington National Park
Coolangatta **1**

SOUTH AUSTRALIA

Newell Hwy.

2

NEW SOUTH WALES

QUEENSLAND

1 The Gold Coast
2 Lamington National Park
3 The Sunshine Coast
4 The Central Coast
5 The Whitsunday Coast

1 Townsville
2 Mission Beach
3 Cairns
4 Port Douglas & Mossman
5 The Cape York Peninsula
6 Outback & Inland Queensland

Great Barrier Reef Marine Park Authority, and knowledgeable staff are on hand to answer questions.

Great Barrier Reef Wonderland is located between Flinders Street East and Ross Creek within easy walking distance of the city center. Joint-entry admission to the three areas costs A$17.50 (U.S. $14) for adults and A$8.75 (U.S. $7) for children aged 4 to 14. Entry to the aquarium only costs A$10 (U.S. $8) for adults and A$5 (U.S. $4) for children. The OMNIMAX-only ticket is A$8.50 (U.S. $6.80) for adults and A$4.25 (U.S. $3.40) for children. This attraction is open daily except Good Friday and Christmas Day from 9am to 5pm. Phone the OMNIMAX Theatre directly (tel. 21-21-1793) for program information.

GETTING TO THE REEF

By Air   To be fully understood, the Great Barrier Reef really needs to be seen from the air. **Island Link Air Charter** (tel. 75-3866) will take you on a 1¾-hour flightseeing excursion for A$155 (U.S. $124).

By Water   **Pure Pleasure Cruises** (tel. 21-3555) offers trips to the outer reef on their 100-foot, 196-passenger Wave Piercer catamaran. Trips depart Townsville's Great Barrier Reef Wonderland every morning at 9am. The fare of A$90 (U.S. $72) for adults and A$45 (U.S. $36) for children 4 to 14 includes morning and afternoon tea, a buffet lunch, glass-bottom-boat reef viewing, snorkeling equipment, and fishing bait and tackle.

Pure Pleasure also operates trips to Orpheus Island on their 45-passenger *Cougar Cat.* The cruises are hosted by Bill and Joan Condon, and the emphasis is on friendly interaction. *Cougar Cat* departs at 9am daily and anchors off the coast of Orpheus. Guests can walk on a jetty to the beach. The fare of A$80 (U.S. $64) for adults and half price for children 4 to 14 includes morning and afternoon tea, a buffet lunch, glass-bottom-boat viewing over the reef, and snorkeling equipment. Drinks from the bar, scuba-diving lessons, and underwater-camera rental are extra.

MAGNETIC ISLAND

Only 8 kilometers (5 miles) offshore from Townsville, Magnetic is somewhat of an island suburb. Many of the permanent population of 2,000 take the 20-minute ferry ride to work daily. **Magnetic Marine** (tel. 72-7122) and **Magnetic Link** (tel. 21-1913) operate frequent services (A$12/U.S. $9.60 round-trip), and there are full-day and half-day tours. One of these, operated by Pure Pleasure, costs A$28 (U.S. $22.40) for adults and half price for children 4 to 14 and includes round-trip ferry, escorted coach tour, and lunch. While good beaches can be found on Magnetic Island, coral is sparse. For more information, see Chapter 10, "The Great Barrier Reef."

SHOPPING

Townsville's main shopping area is **Flinders Mall,** where stores are open Monday through Thursday from 9am to 5:30pm, Friday from 9am to 9pm, and Saturday from 9am to noon. **David Jones Department Store,** Australia's answer to Bloomingdale's is in the mall.

The specialty shops at **Great Barrier Reef Wonderland** are open 7 days a week and offer a nice range of souvenirs and sportswear. The work of local artisans is displayed at the **Cotters Market** held in Flinders Mall on Sunday morning from 8:30am to 12:30pm. The market also features entertainment and food stalls.

SPORTS & RECREATION

If scuba diving is your thing, **Mike Ball Watersports** (tel. 72-3022) runs courses and dive trips to the reef.

If you'd rather try your hand at landing a billfish, sailfish, or black marlin, contact **Aussie Game Fishing Agencies** (tel. 73-1912). The cost for reef fishing is about A$100 (U.S. $80) per person per day; game fishing is more expensive. Ten-meter (33-ft.) catamarans, monohull cruisers, and game boats depart Townsville at 5:30 or

6am and return by 6pm. **Australian Pacific Charters** (tel. 71-4810) and **East Coast Gamefish Charters** (tel. 21-1780) can also organize your day of angling.

The **Tobruk Olympic Pool** on the waterfront is popular from October through April, when marine stingers preclude swimming near the shore or around Magnetic Island. **The Rockpool** at the opposite end of the beachfront at Kissing Point is a rock-walled swimming enclosure which also provides safe swimming year round.

WHERE TO STAY
EXPENSIVE

SHERATON BREAKWATER CASINO-HOTEL, Sir Leslie Thiess Dr., Townsville, QLD 4810. Tel. 077/22-2333, or toll free 008/07-3535 in Australia. Fax 077/72-4741. 176 rms, 16 suites. A/C MINIBAR TV TEL **Transportation:** Courtesy shuttle bus.
$ **Rates:** A$170–A$190 (U.S. $136–U.S. $152) single or double; A$340 (U.S. $272) executive suite; A$800 (U.S. $640) Presidential Suite; A$40 (U.S. $32) extra person. Children under 18 stay free in parents' room. Lower weekend rates. Special packages available Oct–Feb. No-smoking rooms available. AE, BC, DC, MC, V. **Parking:** Free.

The Sheraton is a lovely 11-story building near the entrance to the harbor about a mile from the city center. Half of the rooms have ocean views, while the rest overlook Townsville and the marina. In spite of the fact that northern Queensland's only casino is on the premises, the hotel has an exclusive, luxurious ambience. The Lobby Lounge, with its restful periwinkle and light blue color scheme complements the marble reception area. Nine rooms have facilities for handicapped travelers.

Dining/Entertainment: Melton's, the hotel's elegant, fine-dining venue, is open for dinner Tuesday through Saturday. Keno terminals in Sails Coffee Shop, open daily, and in the Lobby Bar allow diners to continue gambling while they eat or drink. On Friday and Saturday nights a dance band plays in the Lobby Lounge.

Services: 24-hour room service, concierge, laundry.

Facilities: Pool, spa, sauna, tennis courts, gym, beauty shop.

MODERATE

TOWNSVILLE INTERNATIONAL, 334 Flinders Mall, Townsville, QLD 4810. Tel. 077/72-2477, or toll free 008/079-903 in Australia. Fax 077/21-1263. 186 rms and suites, including 7 Presidential Suites. A/C MINIBAR TV TEL
$ **Rates:** From A$100 (U.S. $80) standard single or double; A$130 (U.S. $104) deluxe single or double; A$230 (U.S. $184) Presidential Suite; A$15 (U.S. $12) extra person. Multinight packages offered throughout the year. Lower rates through Aussie auto clubs. AE, BC, DC, MC, V. **Parking:** Free.

Known as the "sugar shaker" because of its 20-story cylindrical shape, the Townsville International is a local landmark and the tallest in town. It has a convenient midcity location and is within walking distance of tourist attractions and shops. All standard rooms and executive suites have traditional furnishings. Some quarters have water views, and all standard rooms have balconies.

Raffles Restaurant is open for breakfast and lunch every day and Margeaux, with its intimate atmosphere, each night. The restaurants, as well as Rogues Piano Bar and Raffles Club Bar, are located one floor up from the ground level, which Aussies call the "first floor" and Yanks insist is the "second." A drive-in bottle store—that ubiquitous feature that is part and parcel of life in Oz—is located in back of the hotel. There's a great view from the rooftop pool.

TOWNSVILLE REEF INTERNATIONAL, 63-64 The Strand, Townsville, QLD 4810. Tel. 077/21-1777. Fax 077/21-1779. 45 rms, 2 suites. A/C MINIBAR TV TEL **Transportation:** Airport courtesy car.
$ **Rates:** A$95 (U.S. $76) single or double; A$108 (U.S. $86.40) executive double; A$125 (U.S. $100) suite; A$10 (U.S. $8) extra person. Children under 18 stay free in parents' room. Off-season (Nov–Mar) weekend discounts. No-smoking rooms available. AE, BC, DC, MC, V. **Parking:** Free.

⭐

💲 The Townsville Reef International occupies a picturesque site across the street from the Cleveland Bay waterfront approximately 1 kilometer (½ mile) from the city center. The attractive exterior of the four-story hotel is pale gray with sky-blue trim; vivid bougainvilleas add a splash of color on the front. Restful grays and beiges characterize the rooms and suites which have been made to feel personal and homey by the hotel's proprietors, Judy and Eric Baker. All quarters have balconies, and 25% have a full water view. (These rooms also get a little traffic noise, so it might be better to request a quieter side room with only a partial bay outlook.)

Large windows give Flutes, the hotel's dining venue, a lovely Cleveland Bay vista and help make the room bright and airy. Guests also have the option of dining by the pool and spa. The Bakers' willingness to help out with sightseeing arrangements, the attractive appearance of the property, and the good-value rates make this a highly recommended lodging option.

INEXPENSIVE

SEAGULLS HOLIDAY INN, 74 The Esplanade, Belgian Gardens, Townsville, QLD 4810. Tel. 077/21-3111. Fax 077/21-3133. 55 rms. A/C TV TEL
Transportation: Courtesy shuttle available.
💲 **Rates:** A$58–A$64 (U.S. $46.40–U.S. $51.20) Bay Room; A$70–A$76 (U.S. $56–U.S. $60.80) Reef Suite; A$10 (U.S. $8) extra adult; A$6 (U.S. $4.80) extra child. AE, BC, MC, V. **Parking:** Free.
Seagulls is a resort set in 3 acres of tropical landscaping on the seafront overlooking Cleveland Bay. Besides adequate rooms, 11 of which have cooking facilities, there are two pools, a restaurant, tennis courts, a playground, and laundry facilities.

THE SUMMIT, 6 Victoria St., Stanton Hill, Townsville, QLD 4810. Tel. 077/21-2122. 30 rms. A/C TV TEL
💲 **Rates:** A$60 (U.S. $48) single; A$70 (U.S. $56) double; A$10 (U.S. $8) extra person. Off-peak discounts. AE, BC, DC, MC, V. **Parking:** Free.

💲 The Summit Motel is nestled in the foothills of Castle Hill about 5 blocks from the center of town. While the walk downhill to the mall is pleasant, guests might prefer to taxi home to the striking two-story property with its cheerful peach exterior. Umbrella tables on a large sun deck and the white lattice railing seem appropriate in these tropical surroundings. Horizons Restaurant, which is closed Sunday, is open for dinner only; both breakfast and dinner can be delivered to the rooms. There are laundry facilities and a pool on the premises.

WHERE TO DINE

If the restaurants I've listed here fail to tickle your fancy, you might take a stroll down historic and slightly trendy **Flinders Street East,** where many eateries are located. Most post their menus and will be happy to let you take a peek inside.

MELTON'S, in the Sheraton Breakwater Casino-Hotel, Sir Leslie Thiess Dr. Tel. 22-2333.
Cuisine: CONTEMPORARY SEAFOOD/MEAT. **Reservations:** Recommended. **Transportation:** Courtesy bus.
💲 **Prices:** Appetizers A$12.50–A$19 (U.S. $10–U.S. $15.20); main courses A$24–A$27 (U.S. $19.20–U.S. $21.60). AE, BC, DC, MC, V.
Open: Dinner Mon–Sat 6–11pm.
Melton's is a sophisticated à la carte eatery with a menu that emphasizes fresh local seafood and prime Queensland beef. In an effort to provide light, healthy dishes, the chefs use alternative methods of cooking and employ low-sodium and low-fat recipes. You might like to start with a seafood salad served with an avocado mousse flavored with ginger and chili, a vegetable pouch on a tomato and lemongrass sauce, or king

prawns on a Pernod and garlic sauce. Main courses include loin of lamb encrusted with herbs on a yogurt sauce, poached tenderloin of beef with freshly grated horseradish, or filet of red emperor in a zucchini and thyme crust on a champagne sauce. If you don't have room for dessert, you can linger over espresso, cappuccino, Jamaican, or Irish coffee. Melton's has won several awards, including the American Express Award for The Best Restaurant in Townsville.

FLUTES, in the Townsville Reef International Hotel, 63-64 The Strand. Tel. 21-1777.
 Cuisine: INTERNATIONAL. **Reservations:** Recommended.
$ **Prices:** Appetizers A$5.50–A$11 (U.S. $4.40–U.S. $8.80); main courses A$16.50–A$23 (U.S. $13.20–U.S. $18.40); continental breakfast A$9.50 (U.S. $7.60); American breakfast A$13 (U.S. $10.40). Children's meals offered at 50% discount. AE, BC, CB, DC, MC, V.
 Open: Breakfast daily 7–10am; dinner daily 6–11pm.
Flutes overlooks Cleveland Bay and has an intimate, exclusive ambience. Soft-gray carpeting, beige rattan chairs, and pink tablecloths are complemented by trellised bougainvillea showing through large windows. Dining is limited to 14 tables. Sautéed prawns in chili-plum sauce, baked avocado with seafood, and smoked chicken supreme are sample entrées (appetizers). Main courses include coral trout topped with scallops and prawns in a creamy cheese sauce, prime beef filet, chicken Madras, and lamb médaillons sautéed in a light rosemary and mint sauce.

LUVIT, 205 Flinders St. East. Tel. 21-1366.
 Cuisine: PANCAKES. **Reservations:** Not necessary.
$ **Prices:** All dishes A$2–A$8 (U.S. $1.60–U.S. $6.40). AE, BC, MC, V.
 Open: Daily 6am–10pm.
Luvit is a pancake restaurant and coffee shop conveniently located 70 meters (77 yd.) east of the GPO on the shady side of the street. Breakfast is served until 11am. The crêpes—both sweet and savory—are popular. BYO.

EVENING ENTERTAINMENT

TOWNSVILLE CIVIC THEATRE, Boundary St., South Townsville. Tel. 71-4188, or box office 72-2677.
 With a seating capacity of 1,066, the Civic Theatre hosts a variety of performing arts, including drama, orchestral concerts, comedy, musicals, and dance. The A$4.5-million (U.S. $3.6-million) complex, completed in 1978, is an important link in the northern touring arts circuit. The box office is open Monday through Friday from 9am to 4:30pm and on Saturday from 9am to 1pm.
 Prices: Tickets A$12–A$30 (U.S. $9.60–U.S. $24).

TOWNSVILLE ART CENTRE, Stanley and Walker Sts., Townsville. Tel. 72-2549 or 72-2828.
 This historic building is the home of Dance North, one of the nine major ballet/dance companies in Australia and the only one which is regionally based.

SHERATON BREAKWATER CASINO-HOTEL, Sir Leslie Thiess Dr. Tel. 22-2333.
 Gambling at this casino is one of Townsville's most popular after-dark activities. Roulette, minidice, baccarat, blackjack, keno, craps, and two-up are played regularly. Though poker (slot) machines are illegal in Queensland, the casino has seven banks of video gaming machines. The casino operates daily from 10am to 3am. Live music, usually jazz, is offered Friday and Saturday nights. Two bars are located in the casino. A courtesy bus brings players from the city center.

THE BANK NIGHTCLUB, 169 Flinders St. East. Tel. 71-6148.
 This really was a bank at one time. Today it's a popular nightclub, open nightly,

which attracts patrons in the 18 to 30 age group. A wide range of beer and spirits (liquor) is offered.

   Admission: A$6 (U.S. $4.80) weekends, A$4 (U.S. $3.20) weeknights.

2. MISSION BEACH

1,615km (1,001 miles) N of Brisbane, 25km (16 miles) E of Tully,
140km (87 miles) S of Cairns

GETTING THERE   By Plane   You can get to Mission Beach by flying to Dunk Island on Australian Regional Airlines and catching one of the water taxis that operate a beach-to-beach service. You can also fly into Cairns and catch the Mission Beach Connection shuttle (A$33/U.S. $26.40).

By Train   The station nearest Mission Beach is in Tully, 25 kilometers (16 miles) to the west.

By Bus   Bus Australia, Greyhound, and McCafferty's buses make the trip from Townsville to Mission Beach in about 3 hours. Tickets cost A$31 (U.S. $24.80). It's a shorter trip, less than 2 hours, from Cairns (A$13/U.S. $10.40).

By Car   Motorists on the Bruce Highway should turn east at Tully and follow the signs to Mission Beach.

ESSENTIALS   The **area code** is 070.

L ittle more than a wide spot in the road, Mission Beach gives visitors a chance to see how Queensland would look had it been left relatively undeveloped. Located between Townsville and Cairns, the resort community (pop. 660) consists of 14 kilometers (9 miles) of palm-fringed beach, splendid pockets of rain forest reaching down to the coast, a significant population of rare cassowary birds, and a few tasteful low-rise resorts.

   There's really no town to speak of, just a couple of stores, some arts and crafts galleries, a Chinese take-out, a handful of casual eateries, and a real estate office. Commercial sightseeing attractions are absent, as are theaters, discos, pollution, and traffic. People come to Mission Beach to get away from those things. Instead, visitors recline on golden silica sand, walk through rain forests (where vines, creepers, palms, and ferns create a fairy-tale atmosphere), and enjoy local water sports.

   Many tourists merely pass through Mission Beach on day tours from Cairns to **Dunk Island** (see Chapter 10, "The Great Barrier Reef"). Only the lucky few know they can stay in the tiny community and take a water taxi at their leisure across the 8 kilometers (5 miles) to Dunk. There are also trips to the outer reef from Mission Beach.

   Named for the Aboriginal mission established here early this century, Mission Beach comprises several small communities that stretch north from Tam O'Shanter Point through South Mission, Wongaling, Mission Beach, and Bingal Bay. At Tam O'Shanter Point a cairn commemorates the ill-fated Cape York expedition of explorer Edmund Kennedy in 1848.

SPORTS & RECREATION

White-water-rafting enthusiasts come from all over Australia to raft the Tully and North Johnstone rivers, both within a short drive of Mission Beach. **Raging Thunder,** whose offices are at 111 Spence Street, Cairns, QLD 4870 (tel. 070/31-1466 or 51-4911), organizes trips that last anywhere from 1 to 7 days. Whether you've never tried rafting or are an old hand, this exciting experience is bound to make an impression on you. There's always plenty of water—Tully boasts Queensland's highest annual rainfall: 4,267 millimeters (171 in.).

   The full-day Tully River excursion, Australia's most popular rafting trip, costs A$109 (U.S. $87.20) per person including transfers, equipment, guides, lunch, and dinner. Departures are daily year round. A 2-day experience on the North Johnstone costs A$225 (U.S. $180), including all meals, equipment, transfers by coach and helicopter, and river guides. Departures are weekly on Wednesday from January through October. The minimum age for both trips is 13. Raging Thunder also offers sea kayaking, bicycling, canoeing, and four-wheel-drive adventures.

WHERE TO STAY

THE POINT, Mitchell St., South Mission Beach, QLD 4854. Tel. 070/68-8154, or toll free 008/07-9090 in Australia. Fax 070/68-8368. 22 suites. A/C TV TEL **Transportation:** Management provides courtesy round-trip transfers from Cairns Airport.

$ Rates: A$198 (U.S. $158.40) single or double; A$15 (U.S. $12) extra person. AE, BC, DC, MC, V. **Parking:** Free.

The Point is a deluxe resort that opened at the end of 1988. Quarters come with balconies that can be enclosed to create additional living space. All rooms have videos, hairdryers, irons, and ironing boards; king-size beds are available. The Point restaurant—where Waterford crystal and Wedgwood china are de rigueur—overlooks the pool, spa, coastline, ocean, and Dunk and Bedarra islands. A tennis court, jogging track, and water-sports facilities are provided. Guests enjoy nature walks in the rain forest.

CASTAWAYS BEACH RESORT, Seaview St., Mission Beach, QLD 4854. Tel. 070/68-7444, or toll free 008/07-9002 in Australia. Fax 070/68-7429. 54 rms. A/C MINIBAR TV TEL

$ Rates: A$108 (U.S. $86.40) single or double; A$143 (U.S. $114.40) 1-bedroom unit; A$152 (U.S. $121.60) 2-bedroom unit; A$198 (U.S. $158.40) 2-story penthouse; A$11 (U.S. $8.80) extra person. Standby rates (maximum 48-hour advance booking) are A$70 (U.S. $56) per person based on double occupancy and include meals. Other special packages available. No-smoking rooms available. AE, BC, DC, MC, V. **Parking:** Free.

Castaways is right on the beach and has a soft green exterior that blends in nicely with the surrounding palm trees and junglelike landscaping. The hostelry's design, labeled "modern Queensland," consists of three stories topped by gabled roofs and trimmed with crisp, clean white latticework. The rooms have cooling gray-and-beige decors. Spacious motel-style units are available, as are one- and two-bedroom self-contained apartments. Most quarters have balconies and water views. While there's no real surf, guests who leave their windows open can fall asleep to the sound of water lapping up on the beach. One unit is designed for handicapped travelers.

The bright, airy restaurant overlooks the pool and spa. There are also a newsagent, tour desk, and business center. Water-sports equipment (windsurfing boards, catamarans, and paddleskis) are free of charge. A 12-meter (40-ft.) game-fishing boat caters to keen anglers, and a high-speed catamaran can whisk visitors off to the Great Barrier Reef, an hour's cruise away, for an extra charge.

MISSION BEACH RESORT, Wongaling Beach Rd., Mission Beach, QLD 4854. Tel. 070/68-8288, or toll free 008/07-9024 in Australia. Fax 070/68-8429. 76 rms, 1 suite. A/C MINIBAR TV TEL

$ Rates: A$75 (U.S. $60) single; A$85 (U.S. $68) double; A$180 (U.S. $144) suite. AE, BC, DC, MC, V. **Parking:** Free.

Mission Beach Resort is a low-rise property which blends in nicely with its surroundings—in this case, a pocket of majestic rain forest. The resort is comprised of a hotel, motel, à la carte restaurant, cocktail bar, bistro, bottle shop, and a few boutiques—all set on 18 hectares (45 acres) of tropical gardens and rain forest. There are also a golf driving range, a six-hole golf course, tennis court, volleyball court, jogging track, games room, children's playground, and sports oval. Accommodations, all on the ground level, are divided into four blocks, each with its own pool, spa, and barbecue area. Some have kitchens. Tourist information is available from reception. The hotel's public bar is the center of the community's social life. Cane toad races are held on the lawn once a week.

TREEHOUSE HOSTEL, Bingil Bay Rd., Mission Beach, QLD 4854. Tel. 070/68-7137. 8 rms. **Transportation:** A courtesy bus meets all coaches in Mission Beach.

$ Rates: A$12 (U.S. $9.60) per person. A 10% discount is given to YHA members for prepaid bookings. BC, MC, V. **Parking:** Free.

Tree Tops is a 46-bed pole-framed tree house, set on a 34-hectare (84-acre) private estate. It offers views of the Pacific and a magnificent rain forest and is a quiet, secluded place for relaxing. Recreational facilities include a 12-meter (13-yd.) outdoor pool and table tennis. This hostel is a base from which regular rain forest excursions are organized. Night walks and full-day walks take place daily; 2- and 3-day treks are also available. This YHA hostel is open all day, all year.

---

3. CAIRNS

347 km (215 miles) N of Townsville, 1,786km (1,107 miles) N of Brisbane

GETTING THERE By Plane   International carriers presently flying into Cairns include Qantas, Japan Air Lines, Air New Zealand, Continental, and Air Nuigini. Australian Airlines, Ansett, Compass, Eastwest, and several regional carriers provide domestic service. A Sydney-Cairns Australian Airlines Air Pass ticket costs A$259 to A$326 (U.S. $207 to U.S. $261). Brisbane-Cairns costs A$209 to A$264 (U.S. $167 to U.S. $211). The Airport Shuttle (tel. 35-9555) from the airport into town, a distance of 6 kilometers (4 miles) will set you back A$4.50 (U.S. $3.60), or you can pay about A$10 (U.S. $5.60) for a taxi. If you're headed to accommodation on the northern beaches or in Port Douglas, Coral Coaches will get you there (tel. 98-1611 or 51-9533). The fare to Port Douglas is A$16.40 (U.S. $13.15) for adults, half price for children 3 to 14. To Palm Cove the fare is A$10 (U.S. $8). If you're in a hurry, Helijet (tel. 35-9300) can get you to Port Douglas in a matter of minutes.

Facilities in the International Terminal, which is a 5-minute walk or A$1 (U.S. 80¢) shuttle from the Domestic Terminal, include Thrifty, Avis, Budget, and Hertz car-rental counters, baggage lockers (A$2/U.S. $1.60 for 24 hours), newsagent, mailbox, showers, tourist information counter, duty-free shop, coffee shop and bar, currency exchange open for all arrivals, and free phones to a dozen hostelries. Ansa Car Rental (tel. 51-9044) provides personal pickup service. The Domestic Terminal has similar facilities, but no showers and no currency exchange. Before you leave the Domestic Terminal, take time to look at the huge ceramic-tile wall map which shows the topography of Far North Queensland; it provides a good introduction to this diverse region.

Remember, if Cairns is the last stop on your Australian itinerary, you'll need to pay a A$10 **departure tax** at the airport. The government-levied tax is payable by all persons over the age of 12 when they leave the country. Departure tax stamps can also be purchased from any post office.

By Train   At the railway station, located 1 block west of Sheridan Street on McLeod Street at Shields Street, the Sunlander and Queenslander arrive from Brisbane. The fare from Brisbane to Cairns on the Queenslander, the more posh of the two, is A$342.10 (U.S. $273.70) first class, inclusive of meals and a sleeping berth. Children 4 to 15 pay A$198.55 (U.S. $158.85). The same accommodations on the Sunlander will set you back A$212.10 (U.S. $169.70). Children pay A$126.05 (U.S. $100.85). The sitting-car fare on either train is A$114.70 (U.S. $91.80) for adults and half price for children.

By Bus   Pioneer, Greyhound, Bus Australia, and McCafferty's make the trip to Cairns from Brisbane in 24 to 26 hours. A ticket costs about A$139 (U.S. $111.20).

By Car   The Bruce Highway, which brings travelers all the way from Brisbane, ends in the middle of Cairns. Drivers who continue north do so on the Captain Cook

Highway, which takes them past the resort communities of Trinity Beach, Clifton Beach, and Palm Cove to Port Douglas. In Cairns, the Captain Cook Highway becomes Sheridan Street.

ESSENTIALS Information Tourist information is dispensed at the **Far North Queensland Promotion Bureau,** at Sheridan Street and Aplin Street, Cairns, QLD 4870 (tel. 070/51-3588), Monday through Friday from 9am to 5pm and Saturday and public holidays from 9am to 1pm. **Cairns Tour Service,** 85 Lake Street (at Shields Street), Cairns, QLD 4870 (tel. 070/51-8311), is open daily from 7am to 7pm and you can phone them from 7am to 10pm. The **area code** is 070.

City Layout The main thoroughfare is **Sheridan Street,** which becomes the Captain Cook Highway north of the city. The railway station is located 1 block west of Sheridan on McLeod Street at Shields Street. Trinity Wharf and the Marlin Jetty are the main departure points for day-trips to the reef. The Esplanade runs parallel to Sheridan Street along the waterfront.

GETTING AROUND   By Bus Local transportation is provided by four privately owned bus companies. Of these, the **Beach Bus** (tel. 57-7411), which goes along the northern beaches, is probably of most interest. Fares range from A\$3 (U.S. \$2.40) to A\$4 (U.S. \$3.20) depending on how far you're going. For example, a city-to–Palm Cove ticket costs A\$3.55 (U.S. \$2.85). The "10 tripper" and weekly passes make travel cheaper. Seven runs a day stop at Trinity, Clifton, and Palm Cove, but Kewarra service is less frequent.

By Organized Tour For sightseeing, most people either rent a car or take organized day-trips rather than using public transportation. A plethora of tour companies operate in and around Cairns. **Australian Pacific Tours** (tel. 070/51-9299 or 31-3371), **Tropic Wings** (tel. 070/35-3555), **Cairns Scenic Tours** (tel. 070/32-1381), and **Down Under Tours** (tel. 070/33-1355) are just a few of these.

By Taxi Call **Black & White** (tel. 51-5333).

The capital of the Far North is a collage of various appearances and life-styles. On one hand, it still looks like a colony in the tropics with lots of white buildings, palm trees, and bougainvilleas; on the other, evidence of its thriving tourist industry is everywhere. Since 1984 Cairns (pronounced "cans") has had an international airport, and more recently the area has acquired luxurious Sheraton, Radisson, Ramada, and Hilton hotels. Long a haven for backpackers and the budget-conscious, the community can now welcome travelers at all comfort levels.

In addition to its colonial/tropical feel and its obvious success as a tourist destination, Cairns has ethnic influences not felt in other Queensland cities. Many Southeast Asians—particularly natives of Indonesia and Papua New Guinea—have found their way to this part of Australia, and their influence, together with that of neighboring Thursday Islanders, is felt in markets, restaurants, shops, and other places.

Cairns developed first as a port serving an inland gold rush, and later as a railhead from which produce grown on the fertile Atherton Tableland and sugarcane from the coastal plains were transported to other parts of the country. While the warm climate, trade winds, lush tropical foliage, and laid-back life-style of the colorful community have been attracting tourists since the 1920s, the industry boomed in the late 1960s, when prolific game-fishing grounds were discovered offshore. Personalities such as actor Lee Marvin put Cairns on the must-visit list of dedicated anglers in search of barracuda, shark, marlin, sailfish, and tuna. In the September-through-December period, these prize catches continue to attract fishermen from all over the world. In terms of the weather, June through September is the best time to visit. Cairns (pop.

83,000) is located 17° south of the equator, approximately the same distance—and therefore with a similar climate—as the Northern Hemisphere's Hawaii, Acapulco, and Puerto Rico.

Does this collage of many styles result in a pretty picture? The answer is an overwhelming yes. Somehow upmarket tourists, backpackers, fishermen, Southeast Asian immigrants, Atherton Tableland plantation owners, descendants of colonial settlers, and sugarcane workers coexist copacetically. Even more, they contribute to Cairns's charisma. It isn't surprising that when Queensland's visitors go "troppo," forsaking jobs and extending vacations indefinitely, it's here they often choose to stay. Frankly, I was tempted myself.

WHAT TO SEE & DO

Cairns is ideally located so that day-trips from the city can reach areas as diverse as the Great Barrier Reef, the Atherton Tableland, Daintree River National Park, Cape Tribulation, Port Douglas, and the Mossman River Gorge. These spots offer some of the most beautiful scenery in Australia, which is one of the important reasons why Cairns has become so popular.

AROUND TOWN

In between excursions to places farther afield, take a wander down to the **Marlin Jetty** at the end of Spence Street (September through December) and you might see fishermen weighing in their catch of black marlin or other impressive game fish.

CAIRNS MUSEUM, in the City Place Mall, at the corner of Lake and Shields. Tel. 51-5582.

This municipal museum has interesting displays that bring local history to life. These include Aboriginal artifacts, goldfield relics, and a Chinese joss house.
Open: Mon–Fri 10am–3pm.

BOTANICAL GARDENS, 94 Collins Ave., Edge Hill. Tel. 50-2454.

The gardens, established in 1886, feature over 200 species of palm and 10,000 other plants, including ferns, orchids, fruit and nut trees, and ornamental and flowering trees and shrubs.
Admission: Free.
Open: Daily 8:30am–5:30pm.

THE ROYAL FLYING DOCTOR VISITORS CENTRE, 1 Junction St., Edge Hill, Cairns. Tel. 53-5687.

This famous medical service has its northern headquarters in Cairns, and its offices are available for visits from the public. If you go, you'll see an audiovisual presentation and hear an interesting narration on the history of this uniquely Australian phenomenon.
Admission: A$3 (U.S. $2.40) adults, A$1.50 (U.S. $1.20) children.
Open: Daily 9am–4:30pm. **Closed:** Christmas Day and Good Friday. **Bus:** Route 8.

THE GREAT BARRIER REEF

Getting There

By Boat Cairns is Queensland's best point from which to explore the wonders of the reef. Visitors have a choice of going to a platform anchored on the reef, to an uninhabited coral cay, to a coral cay with myriad tourist facilities, or to a continental island around which there is some fringing reef. This is a good time to read Chapter 10, "The Great Barrier Reef" and take a look at the "Great Barrier Reef Resorts at a Glance" chart in the appendix.

✪ **Great Adventures** (tel. 51-0455, or toll free 008/07-9080 in Australia) operates fast catamarans that depart at 8:30 and 10:30am for **Green Island,** the only inhabited coral cay on the entire Great Barrier Reef which is close enough to the coast to be visited on a day-trip. These trips cost A$55 (U.S. $44) for adults and include

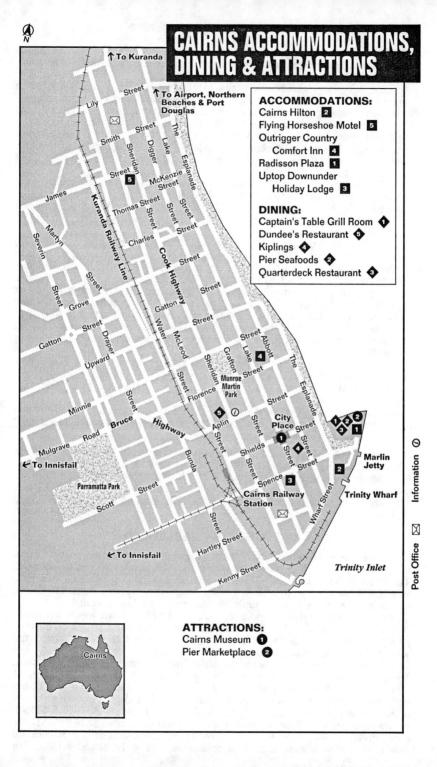

CAIRNS ACCOMMODATIONS, DINING & ATTRACTIONS

ACCOMMODATIONS:
Cairns Hilton **2**
Flying Horseshoe Motel **5**
Outrigger Country
Comfort Inn **4**
Radisson Plaza **1**
Uptop Downunder
Holiday Lodge **3**

DINING:
Captain's Table Grill Room ◆**1**
Dundee's Restaurant ◆**5**
Kiplings ◆**4**
Pier Seafoods ◆**2**
Quarterdeck Restaurant ◆**3**

ATTRACTIONS:
Cairns Museum ●**1**
Pier Marketplace ●**2**

Post Office ⊠   Information ⊘

glass-bottom-boat viewing, visiting an underwater observatory, barbecue lunch, and plenty of time for snorkeling and swimming. The cruise only, without the other items, costs A$35 (U.S. $28) for adults.

Great Adventures also operates trips to **Fitzroy Island,** a continental island covered with rain forest. Visitors here enjoy the walking tracks and exploring the fringe coral. This trip, including use of the island's swimming pool, glass-bottom-boat viewing, and a barbecue lunch, costs A$40 (U.S. $32) for adults. Without lunch and the glass-bottom boat, you'll pay A$22 (U.S. $17.60). The Two-Island Cruise, which goes to both Fitzroy and Green, costs A$60 (U.S. $48) for adults with lunch, glass-bottom-boat viewing, and entrance to the underwater observatory, or A$38 (U.S. $30.40) for the cruise only.

Another Great Adventures' trip combines Michaelmas Cay, an uninhabited coral cay, and Green Island (A$80/U.S. $64 adults). They also offer one which goes to the outer Barrier Reef and Green Island (A$100/U.S. $80 adults). All prices mentioned here include a courtesy pickup at your lodging. Children under 4 are free, and those 4 to 14 are charged half price.

If you'd rather sail than motor to the outer reef, *Ocean Spirit* (tel. 31-2920) might be the right vessel for you. The luxurious 21-meter (70-ft.) ketch goes out to Michaelmas Cay, an uninhabited coral cay, where you can snorkel, scuba dive, sun, observe the life of a large bird rookery, and view the reef from a semisubmersible boat. Trips, which accommodate up to 138 passengers, depart Marlin Marina at 8:30am daily and return at 5pm. Snorkeling gear, a delicious buffet lunch, morning and afternoon tea, guided snorkeling with a marine biologist, and pickup from your Cairns hotel are included in the price of A$95 (U.S. $76). For an additional cost you can take an introductory scuba-diving course, or if you are already certified, you can go diving.

Some tour operators offer trips that combine bus transport to Mission Beach and a launch to **Dunk Island.** This makes for a long day, in my opinion. If possible, stay overnight in Mission Beach and take the launch or a water taxi from there. (See "Mission Beach," above.)

For information on *Quicksilver,* the deluxe 300-passenger, high-speed catamaran that makes daily trips to Agincourt Reef, see "Port Douglas and Mossman," below.

By Plane ○ **Helijet** (tel. 35-9300) operates trips to the Great Barrier Reef. Their 1-hour Reef and Rainforest Discovery trip costs A$300 (U.S. $240). The Outer Barrier Reef Odyssey takes you to the Agincourt Reef, where you have lunch (on *Quicksilver,* mentioned above) and snorkel for 3 hours before returning to Cairns (A$325/U.S. $260 per person). Shorter scenic flights range in price from A$60 (U.S. $48) to A$170 (U.S. $136).

THE ATHERTON TABLELAND

Cooler weather and wonderful scenery draw tourists to the mountains west of Cairns, where tea plantations, lush rain forests, waterfalls, orchids, lakes, and butterflies await. The Atherton Tableland is only 150 kilometers (93 miles) long but contains a wide variety of scenic beauty. Situated west of the Bruce Highway from Innisfail to Cairns, the tableland includes 18 small towns dotted around the lush plateau.

Visitors can drive themselves, of course, but the best-known way to get to the Atherton Tableland is on the ○ **scenic train to Kuranda.** A hostess on the train points out such sights as the Barron River, jungle-covered Freshwater Valley, and waving cane fields. After passing through Redlynch, 11 kilometers (7 miles) from Cairns, the train starts a steep winding ascent through dramatic tropical rain forest. You pass through 15 tunnels and stop briefly for photos at Barron Falls Station, 31 kilometers (19 miles) from Cairns and 328 meters (1,082 ft.) above sea level. The trip ends at the picturesque Kuranda station, built in 1915, and covered with ferns and other tropical plants. The fare is A$28 (U.S. $22.40) for adults and A$14 (U.S. $11.20) for children aged 4 to 14 for the round-trip. A one-way ticket costs A$16 (U.S. $12.80) for adults and A$8 (U.S. $6.40) for children. Trains leave Cairns daily at 8:30am and Sunday to Friday at 9am. Returns from Kuranda are at 12:30 and 3:15pm. For reservations and to *check the timetable, which varies with seasonal demand,* phone Queensland Railways (tel. 52-6249 or 55-2222). Many sightseeing coach companies offer packages that allow you to take the train one way and the bus the other. In terms of photography, it's better to go up by train in the morning.

Wednesday, Friday, and Sunday are the most popular days to make the Kuranda trip because the **public markets** are open (7am to 1pm). At these popular flea markets you can buy everything from T-shirts and costume jewelry to local craft items, batik clothing, fresh fruit, homemade jam, and baked goods.

Another big draw is the Aboriginal dance program put on by the ✪ **Tjapukai Dance Theatre**—the brainchild of New Yorkers Don and Judy Freeman, who observed during a visit to Australia that there was no place for travelers to see native dances. The cast includes David Hudson, who is probably the best didgeridoo player in the world. The unique, exciting, educational 1-hour performance takes place in their 300-seat, air-conditioned theater at 21 Coondoo Street, Kuranda, daily at 11am and 1:30pm. Confirm show times and make bookings by calling 93-7544. Tickets cost A$13 (U.S. $10.40) for adults and half price for children. Please don't miss an opportunity to see this group—it's the only one of its kind in Australia and has won numerous significant awards, including the PATA Gold Award for Culture and Heritage. Highly recommended.

Other Kuranda attractions include the **Australian Butterfly Sanctuary** (tel. 93-7575; 10am to 3pm daily, A$9/U.S. $7.20), the **Kuranda Wildlife Noctarium** (tel. 93-7334; A$7/U.S. $5.60), and river and rain-forest cruises conducted by **Kuranda Rain Forest Tours** (tel. 93-7476; A$9/U.S. $7.20; closed January and February).

DAINTREE & CAPE TRIBULATION

The township of **Daintree,** 116 kilometers (72 miles) north of Cairns, is surrounded by the wilderness of the Daintree National Park. Several cruises operate on the Daintree River. One of these, the **Crocodile Express** (tel. 98-6120), will take you to see exotic rain forest, spooky mangrove creeks, rare birds, butterflies, and—if all goes well—at least one estuarine crocodile. The fare is A$20 (U.S. $16) for adults and half price for children. A package that includes bus transfers from Cairns, lunch, and entry to the butterfly farm in Mossman Gorge, in addition to the river cruise, costs A$70 (U.S. $56) for adults and A$30 (U.S. $24) for children.

Daintree National Park features large areas of untouched rain forest and can be explored by the self-sufficient bushwalker.

Cape Tribulation National Park, 34 kilometers (21 miles) from Daintree, is a wilderness area known for its beautiful coastline, rain forest, and clear creeks. Four-wheel-drive vehicles are required for exploring.

✪ **Australian Wilderness Safari** (tel. 98-1666) leads environmentally sensitive tours through both Daintree and Cape Tribulation national parks. Guides are well-informed naturalists. The cost of A$110 (U.S. $88) for adults and half price for children includes transfer by Quicksilver Wave Piercer from Cairns to Port Douglas, tour in air-conditioned four-wheel-drive vehicle, Daintree River cruise, naturalist guides, guided rain forest walk, the use of binoculars and reference books, morning tea, barbecue lunch, and more. If begun in Port Douglas, this day-trip costs A$99 (U.S. $79.20). Highly recommended.

WILD WORLD

If you don't have time to do a Daintree River cruise and you're dying to see a crocodile, stop at Wild World on the Cook Highway in Palm Cove, 22 kilometers (13 miles) north of Cairns (tel. 55-3669). They have 150 crocs ranging in size from hatchlings to full-grown specimens some 5 meters (16½ ft.) long.

While the crocodile show is described as "action-packed" in the brochure, I've found that the beasts are very sleepy in the winter months (June through early September). Crocodile shows, cane toad races, a cockatoo show, and a snake show take place throughout the day, so call, get the schedule, and time your visit accordingly. Admission is A$12 (U.S. $9.60) for adults and A$6 (U.S. $4.80) for children. Open daily from 9am to 5pm. If you aren't driving, the Beach Bus (tel. 57-7411) stops at Wild World.

You can also see crocodiles at **Hartley's Creek Crocodile Farm** (tel. 55-3576) 40 kilometers (25 miles) north of Cairns. It's open daily from 9am to 5pm; show time is 3pm.

SHOPPING

Shopping hours in Cairns are generally 8:30am to 5:15pm Monday through Thursday, 8:30am to 9pm on Friday, and 8:30 to 11:30am on Saturday. In addition, stores in the suburbs are open until 9pm on Thursday night; **Smithfield Shopping Centre,** corner of Cook and Kennedy Highway (tel. 38-1006), has over 40 specialty stores and is open daily. Shops in the **Pier Marketplace** are open 7 days a week, too. If you like local crafts, don't miss the **Mud Markets** held at the marketplace on Saturday and Sunday.

Bonz On The Reef, corner of Lake and Spence streets (tel. 31-4165), sells designer handknits with Australian themes for men, women, and children, as well as souvenirs and Aussie clothing. Without a doubt, ✪ **Australian Craftworks,** 20 Village Lane—off Lake Street near the Cairns International Hotel—(tel. 51-0725), is the best place in town to buy fine Australian handcrafted glass, leather, textiles, clothing, wood, ceramics, and jewelry. This shop is open 7 days a week and they will ship your purchases. In the same area at Shop 53, Village Lane, you will find **Done Art & Design** (tel. 31-5592) where the clever T-shirts, sweatshirts, and household items created by Ken and Judy Done are sold.

If you want to buy Aboriginal and contemporary art, try the **Upstairs Gallery,** on Shields Street (tel. 51-6150). You may also be interested in **City International Duty Free,** 77 Abbott Street (tel. 31-1353). Purchases can be picked up within 2 days of your departure from the country.

SPORTS & RECREATION

Raging Thunder, which offers white-water rafting on the Tully River (see "Mission Beach," above), also puts together sea kayaking trips, bicycle tours, adventure holidays, and four-wheel-drive safaris. Their offices are at 111 Spence Street, Cairns (tel. 51-4911, or toll free 008/07-9092 in Australia).

In The Wild, 49 Abbott Street (tel. 51-7777 or 53-4156), runs 1-day canoe trips costing A$75 (U.S. $60). Groups are limited to 14 people, and no one under age 6 is permitted. Tours operate daily from 7:30am to 5:30pm. Tariff includes transfers, morning tea, a tour of the Nerada tea plantation, and a smörgåsbord lunch on the banks of the Johnstone River. Their "Outrageous Russell" trip (on the Russell River) involves backpacking in for 40 minutes, then kaying out through rapids for 2½ hours. The minimum age for this experience is 14; the cost of A$49 (U.S. $39.20) includes transfers.

Open cockpit Tiger Moth scenic flights and joy rides are available from **Cairns Tiger Moth Flights** (tel. 35-9400). Cost is A$70 to A$150 (U.S. $56 to U.S. $120) for flights of 20 minutes to an hour.

Champagne Balloon Flights (tel. 51-7366) are another option. The price of A$99 (U.S. $79.20) includes scenic transfer through the Tablelands, flight, and a champagne and chicken breakfast.

Several places in Cairns will teach you to scuba dive, but **Pro Dive,** Marlin Parade (tel. 31-5255), is one of the better-known outfits. Their 6-day PADI open-water certification course costs A$375 (U.S. $300) and includes at least 3 days of diving (nine dives) on the outer reef, free pickup from your accommodation, all dive equipment, and all meals on the trip. Courses start on Monday and Thursday. Pro Dive also offers a variety of different dive trips for those who are already certified.

Contact **Cairns Reef Charter Services,** Marlin Jetty (tel. 31-4742 or 53-4803), if you want to try your luck in marlin, game, and reef fishing. Game fishing costs from A$120 (U.S. $96) per person and reef fishing from A$90 (U.S. $72) per person; calm-water fishing is A$39 (U.S. $31.20).

Bicycle rental is available at **Sheridan Street Bicycle Barn,** 61 Sheridan Street (tel. 51-7135). The price is A$6 (U.S. $4.80) for a half day and A$12 (U.S. $9.60) for 24 hours—plus a A$50 (U.S. $40) refundable deposit.

Paradise Palms, Clifton Beach (tel. 59-1166), is the most popular golf course in the area. Greens fees are A$70 (U.S. $56) and include motorized buggy (cart) and use of clubhouse. It costs A$20 (U.S. $16) to rent clubs and A$5 (U.S. $4) to rent shoes. There are also tennis courts, a practice (driving) range, a swimming pool, and assorted dining options on the premises. Transfers from Cairns cost A$10 (U.S. $8) round-trip.

You may also be interested in knowing that **bungy jumping** has been added to the long list of activities available in Cairns. Organized by A. J. Hackett (tel. 31-1119), this thrilling "antigravity" experience costs A$85 (U.S. $68) per person.

WHERE TO STAY

The main decision you have to make before booking your Cairns lodging is whether you want to be in town or on one of the northern beaches. If you want to be near the shops and departure points for Great Barrier Reef cruise boats and Atherton Tableland trains, stay in town. If being near sand and away from commercialism is a high priority, choose Yorkey's Knob, Trinity Beach, Clifton Beach, or Palm Cove. In either case, day-trip tour buses pick up at all hostelries.

IN TOWN

CAIRNS HILTON, Wharf St., Cairns, QLD 4870. Tel. 070/52-1599, or toll free 008/22-2255 in Australia. Fax 070/52-1370. 259 rms, 5 suites. A/C MINIBAR TV TEL

$ Rates: A$220 (U.S. $176) single; A$240 (U.S. $192) double; A$520 (U.S. $416) suite; A$50 (U.S. $40) surcharge for executive-floor room; A$30 (U.S. $24) extra person. Children under 18 stay free in parents' room. No-smoking rooms available. AE, BC, CB, DC, MC, V. **Parking:** A$2 (U.S. $1.60) per night.

The seven-story hotel's rooms all have water views, and many also overlook the international cruise terminal and the ferry wharf from which boats leave regularly for Green Island. Each tastefully appointed room has a balcony, either queen- or king-size bed, in-room movies, tea- and coffee-making facilities, a small refrigerator, and hairdryer. As in the Hilton in Sydney, Executive Floor rooms offer extra amenities at premium rates. All guests receive a free daily newspaper.

The main restaurant, Breezes, which overlooks the Trinity Inlet marina, provides continuous food service throughout the day. You can also get a tasty carvery lunch in the Cane Clipper, the Hilton's public bar. Of all the public spaces, the lobby level, where glass walls permit a 270° view, is the most impressive. In addition to a variety of dining choices, guests have the use of an attractive swimming pool area, as well as a health club, sauna, spa, gym, and business center.

RADISSON PLAZA HOTEL, Pierpoint Rd., Cairns, QLD 4870. Tel. 070/31-1411, or toll free 008/25-2553 in Australia. Fax 070/31-3226. 200 rms, 20 suites. A/C MINIBAR TV TEL

$ Rates: A$220–A$255 (U.S. $176–U.S. $204) single or double; A$415 (U.S. $332) junior suite; A$505 (U.S. $404) executive suite; A$900–A$1,200 (U.S. $720–U.S. $960) Presidential Suite; A$25 (U.S. $20) extra person. Children under 18 stay free in parents' room. Special packages available. No-smoking rooms available. AE, BC, DC, MC, V. **Parking:** Free.

The Radisson, with its low-rise colonial Queensland architecture, is located in The Pier complex on the Cairns waterfront. In addition to the hotel, there are about 100 shops and numerous food outlets. While most of the property has a distinct nautical theme, guests are greeted by a very lifelike crocodile in an ersatz rain forest just inside the main entrance. In this area there is also a reproduction Aboriginal cave painting.

The nautical decor in the bedrooms includes blue or green color schemes, hardwood cabinets and furniture, and verde marble bathrooms. All quarters have balconies; two-thirds have water views. Guests have a choice between king-size beds or twins; all rooms have tea- and coffee-making facilities, small refrigerators, ceiling fans, hairdryers, in-room movies, and free daily newspapers.

The Quarterdeck Restaurant serves breakfast, lunch, and dinner daily. The Captain's Table Grill Room has a panoramic view of the harbor.

Facilities include an outdoor pool, fitness center, sauna, spa, and business center.

OUTRIGGER COUNTRY COMFORT INN, corner Abbott and Florence Sts., Cairns, QLD 4870. Tel. 070/51-6188. Fax 070/31-1806. 91 rms and suites. A/C MINIBAR TV TEL

$ Rates: A$98–A$110 (U.S. $78.40–U.S. $88) single; A$117–A$132 (U.S. $93.60–U.S. $105.60) double; A$185 (U.S. $148) suite; A$10 (U.S. $8) extra person. Lower rates through Aussie auto clubs. No-smoking rooms available. AE, BC, DC, MC, V. **Parking:** Free.

This is a most attractive Queensland colonial-style motor inn with white verandas and a multigabled roof. Fifty-five of the rooms are in a two-story section and feature marble bathrooms. While these rooms aren't overly spacious, their decors are very pleasant. The 32 rooms in the four-story tower section are also bright, airy, and restful, and each has a balcony and a sitting area with a writing table.

The tropical decor of the Outrigger Restaurant includes cane furniture, potted palms, ceiling fans, shutters, and a cool marble floor. The facilities include a pool and spa.

CAIRNS COLONIAL CLUB RESORT, 18–26 Cannon St., Manunda, Cairns, QLD 4870. Tel. 070/53-5111. Fax 070/53-7072. 201 rms, 80 suites. A/C TV TEL **Transportation:** Airport courtesy car and regular shuttle service to the city center.

$ Rates: A$95 (U.S. $76) standard single or double; A$120 (U.S. $96) deluxe single or double; A$150 (U.S. $120) 1-bedroom suite with cooking facilities; A$180 (U.S. $144) VIP Suite; A$12 (U.S. $9.60) extra person. Children under 3 stay free in parents' room. AE, BC, DC, MC, V. **Parking:** Free.

The Cairns Colonial Club is located in the suburb of Manunda, 6.5 kilometers (4 miles) from the city center. The two-story property's rooms are spread over 3.2 hectares (8 acres) of tropical landscaped gardens designed to look and feel like an island resort. Of the two free-form saltwater pools provided for guests, the larger has its own beach made from sand imported onto the property; the medium-size pool is partially shaded by a mango tree that is much appreciated on hot summer days.

Two large self-service laundry rooms are provided, as are tennis courts. Two rooms are equipped for handicapped travelers. Because of the distances between blocks of lodging, room service isn't offered. Meals are served in three places: the Homestead Restaurant, Jardines, and the Poolside Cafe.

FLYING HORSESHOE MOTEL, 281-289 Sheridan St., Cairns, QLD 4870. Tel. 070/51-3022. Fax 070/31-2761. 51 units. A/C TV TEL

$ Rates: A$58 (U.S. $46.40) single, A$68 (U.S. $54.40) double; A$68 (U.S. $54.40) single with cooking facilities; A$78 (U.S. $62.40) double with cooking facilities; A$10 (U.S. $8) extra person. AE, BC, DC, MC, V. **Parking:** Free.

The Flying Horseshoe is located in the middle of motel row—an area of economical accommodations about 2 kilometers (1 mile) from the center of Cairns. The motel was built in the late 1960s by a former BOAC pilot from Yorkshire whose family coat-of-arms is the horseshoe and wings.

The present owners, Margaret and Norton Gill, offer 51 units, some with cooking facilities. All rooms have tea- and coffee-making facilities, small refrigerators, clock radios, and in-room movies. These friendly proprietors also make tour bookings for guests, serve dinner by the pool (A$14/U.S. $11.20), arrange breakfast delivery to the units, and help organize baby-sitting. Guests can use the self-service laundry. Units sleep four to six people. It isn't surprising, given the reasonable cost and friendly hosts here, that I've received numerous letters from readers complimenting the Flying Horseshoe.

UPTOP DOWNUNDER HOLIDAY LODGE, 164-170 Spence St., Cairns, QLD 4870. Tel. 070/51-3636. Fax 070/52-1211. 44 rms (none with bath). **Transportation:** Courtesy pickup from train or bus station; courtesy bus to city center.
$ Rates: A$25 (U.S. $20) single or double; A$11 (U.S. $8.80) per person in dorm. BC, MC, V. **Parking:** Free.

Uptop is an inexpensive place to stay, conveniently located only about a kilometer (½ mile) from the center of town. Guests have a choice of single or double rooms or dormitory accommodations. All quarters share bathrooms, a communal kitchen, two television rooms, a reading/writing area, swimming pool, and pool table.

A friendly atmosphere is created by the management and staff. They do day-trip bookings and provide courtesy transfers. A small shop on the premises sells food and everyone eats together at white wooden picnic tables. This is a good spot for budget travelers who want to meet others who share their style. Children under 3 aren't encouraged.

ON THE NORTHERN BEACHES

RAMADA GREAT BARRIER REEF RESORT, corner of Williams Esplanade and Veivers Rd., Palm Cove, QLD 4879. Tel. 070/55-3999. Fax 070/55-3902. 175 rms, 4 suites. A/C MINIBAR TV TEL **Transportation:** Airport courtesy coach available.
$ Rates: A$175 (U.S. $140) single; A$200 (U.S. $160) double; A$330 (U.S. $264) junior suite; A$429 (U.S. $343.20) executive suite; A$20 (U.S. $16) extra person. No-smoking rooms available. AE, BC, CB, DC, MC, V. **Parking:** Free.

The Ramada Reef Resort has the largest free-form freshwater pool in the Southern Hemisphere. It sprawls over what seems like a football field–size area on the ocean side of the four-story hotel. Stately melaleucas and palm trees grow through holes cut into the surrounding wooden decking, and a bridge is provided so that guests won't have to walk all the way around the edge. In addition to the pool and attractive landscaping, the Ramada offers a convenient location just across the road from Palm Cove Beach. The hostelry is 25 kilometers (15 miles) from Cairns.

The hotel's rooms are decorated in pleasant blue and green color schemes. All quarters have balconies and tub/shower combos; a few have king-size beds, but most have queens or twins. Etchings of local scenes by Cairns artist JoAnne Hook add a nice touch. Two rooms for handicapped travelers are available.

Tropical drinks served in the open-air bar by the pool come in punch bowl–size glasses—and no one ever complains. Meals are served in the Garden Terrace Restaurant, and poolside barbecues are popular.

Children's activities are planned during Australian school holidays, and free baby-sitting is available then, too. Besides the huge pool, the resort offers tennis courts, bicycle rental, a spa, and a business center.

THE JEWEL OF THE REEF, 1 Veivers Rd., Palm Cove, QLD 4879. Tel. 070/55-3000, or toll free 008/07-9052 in Australia. Fax 070/55-3090. 70 1- to 3-bedroom apartments. A/C TV TEL **Transportation:** Courtesy airport shuttle.
$ Rates: A$210 (U.S. $168) 1 bedroom; A$240 (U.S. $192) 2 bedroom beachfront; A$300 (U.S. $240) 2 bedroom absolute beachfront; A$360 (U.S. $288) 3 bedroom; A$420 (U.S. $336) 2 or 3 bedroom with own pool. Children under 18 stay free in parents' room. No-smoking rooms available. AE, BC, DC, MC, V. **Parking:** Free.

When Australian say "absolute beachfront," they mean right smack on the sand, and this is how they describe The Jewel of the Reef, which opened in 1989. No road or other obstacle stands in the way of guests' path to the waves. All quarters here are luxurious and fully self-contained; kitchens have dishwashers, microwaves, convection ovens, and everything else you'd expect. Every spacious apartment has a balcony, white tile floor, ceiling fans, laundry facilities, two bathrooms, and attractive modern furnishings; some have ocean views.

Three saltwater swimming pools and a spa are provided so guests can get wet even when marine stingers make the ocean unsafe (October through May). Unfortunately, the four-story building lacks a lift. A games room and baby-sitting, plus the amenities already mentioned, make this a great place for families. The Far Horizons Restaurant is open daily.

PARADISE VILLAGE RESORT, 117 Williams Esplanade, Palm Cove, QLD 4879. Tel. 070/55-3300. Fax 070/55-3991. 30 rms and suites. A/C TV TEL **Transportation:** Courtesy airport transfers.

$ Rates: A$95 (U.S. $76) standard single or double; A$135 (U.S. $108) up to four people in a 1-bedroom apartment with kitchenette; A$195 (U.S. $156) suite for up to six people; A$275 (U.S. $220) penthouse for up to seven people. AE, BC, DC, MC, V. **Parking:** Free.

Located 25 kilometers (15 miles) from the center of Cairns, Paradise Village really does have the feeling of being an intimate beachside village. Included in the attractive low-rise complex are a small post office, a bistro, an à la carte restaurant, a beauty salon, and 16 shops. The accommodations, on three levels (no lift), are connected to the bi-level shopping area by a slate and ironstone walkway. The pale blue-gray exterior is topped with a traditional Queensland corrugated-iron roof and trimmed with white railings. Parking is under cover.

Lodging is simple, but more than adequate. Colorful Ken Done comforters and posters lend a cheerful air. All quarters have their own balconies. Guests have a choice of swimming at the beach across the road (June to October, when stingers aren't present) or using the pool, where a waterfall flows from the spa. Actually, some people go in the water year round because a net is used during the stinger season. Meals are served in Cafe Paradise and at Colonies.

TROPICAL HOLIDAY INNS, 63-73 Moore St., Trinity Beach, QLD 4879. Tel. 070/57-6699, or toll free 008/07-9022 in Australia. Fax 070/57-6565. 52 apartments. A/C TV TEL **Transportation:** Courtesy transfers from airport provided. Also served by Coral Coaches and the Beach Bus.

$ Rates: A$69 (U.S. $55.20) single or double per night; A$445 (U.S. $356) single or double per week; A$8 (U.S. $6.40) extra person per night; A$50 (U.S. $40) extra person per week. Lower weekend rates. AE, BC, DC, MC, V. **Parking:** Free.

Trinity Beach is 15 kilometers (9 miles) north of Cairns Airport and south of Palm Cove. Apartments at Tropical Holiday Inns have one or two bedrooms, full kitchens, ceiling fans, laundry facilities, and balconies. There are three swimming pools and a barbecue area on the premises, and the management will help to arrange baby-sitting and day-tour bookings.

WHERE TO DINE

IN TOWN

Expensive

CAPTAIN'S TABLE GRILL ROOM, in the Radisson Plaza Hotel at The Pier, Pierpoint Rd. Tel. 31-1411.
Cuisine: SEAFOOD/CHARGRILLED MEAT. **Reservations:** Recommended.
$ Prices: Appetizers A$8–A$10.50 (U.S. $6.40–U.S. $8.40); main courses A$15.50–A$26.50 (U.S. $12.40–U.S. $21.20). AE, BC, DC, MC, V.
Open: Dinner Tues–Sat from 6:30pm–late.

Commanding a panoramic view of Trinity Bay Inlet and Marlin Marina, this upmarket dining spot specializes in grain-fed Queensland beef and fresh seafood. Preparations are modern and multicultural. Appetizers include butterfly king prawns filled with crab cake "Louisiana Style," beef carpaccio Korean style, and fresh Sydney rock oysters. For a main course you can have chargrilled Moreton Bay bugs, roast prime rib of beef carved at your table, or your choice of five different cuts of steak. Each steak is offered in two sizes. A trip to the salad bar is included with all meals, and a walk through the dessert buffet costs an additional A$6 (U.S. $4.80).

DUNDEE'S RESTAURANT, Sheridan and Aplin Sts. Tel. 51-0399.

Cuisine: SEAFOOD/STEAK/PASTA. **Reservations:** Recommended.
$ Prices: Appetizers A$9–A$15 (U.S. $7.20–U.S. $12); main courses A$12–A$30 (U.S. $9.60–U.S. $24). AE, BC, DC, MC, V.
Open: Lunch and dinner daily.

Dundee's proved to be a lucky discovery, as the restaurant specializes in grain-fed beef and has a wonderful salad bar. Steak-lovers have to make a difficult choice between T-bone, sirloin, rib filet, or rump steak, and Dundee's also offers rack of lamb, pork spare ribs, and beef kebabs. A few unusual dishes include Buffalo Humpty Doo (an eye filet of buffalo served with a delicious peanut and chili sauce) and Outback Bushman's Pie (beef and veggies covered with creamed potatoes and topped with flaky pastry). On the seafood side of things, you might like to try whole baby barramundi, Trinity Bay bugs, or whole crab. Dundee's has a large, comfortable bar above the dining area. Children are welcome at this restaurant.

Moderate

HOMESTEAD RESTAURANT, in the Cairns Colonial Club Resort, 18-26 Cannon St., Manunda, Cairns. Tel. 53-5111.
Cuisine: SEAFOOD/CHARGRILL. **Reservations:** Recommended.
$ Prices: All-you-can-eat salad bar (including soup, pasta, and bread) A$9.95 (U.S. $8); salad bar with main course A$5.95 (U.S. $4.80); main courses A$8.50–A$17.50 (U.S. $6.80–U.S. $14); children's meals A$4.75 (U.S. $3.80). Public holiday surcharge 10%. AE, BC, DC, MC, V.
Open: Dinner daily 6:30–10pm.

The Homestead Restaurant's "Salad Shack"—unlimited trips to a buffet piled high with salad ingredients, a choice of soups, several different pastas, and freshly baked bread—is extremely good value. Main courses include a variety of steaks, local seafood, and a sirloin-and-prawn combination.

KIPLINGS, on the Gallery Level of Orchid Plaza, 79-87 Abbott St. Tel. 31-1886.
Cuisine: INNOVATIVE MULTICULTURAL. **Reservations:** Recommended.
$ Prices: Appetizers A$4.80–A$12.50 (U.S. $3.85–U.S. $10); main courses A$8.50–A$18.90 (U.S. $6.80–U.S. $15.15). AE, BC, DC, MC, V.
Open: Mon–Sat 11:30am–11:30pm.

This attractive little bistro located in the heart of the central business district, across from the large white Cairns Post building, offers a wide array of ethnic specialties. You can have a Greek salad, pâté, smoked Tasmanian salmon, nachos, Indian samosas, chicken satay, Middle Eastern dips, your choice of three curries, pasta, grilled steak, or local seafood. It's a menu that would please the United Nations—and, amazingly, it's all good. Suffice it to say that if I could only have one meal in Cairns, it would be at Kiplings.

QUARTERDECK RESTAURANT, in the Radisson Plaza Hotel at The Pier, Pierpoint Rd. Tel. 31-1411.
Cuisine: INTERNATIONAL. **Reservations:** Optional.
$ Prices: Appetizer seafood buffet A$18.50 (U.S. $14.80); appetizer seafood buffet when followed by a main course A$14.50 (U.S. $11.60); appetizers A$8.50–A$11 (U.S. $6.80–U.S. $8.80); sandwiches A$6.50–A$10.50 (U.S. $5.20–U.S. $8.40); pasta A$9 (U.S. $7.20); main courses A$10.50–A$19.50 (U.S. $8.40–U.S. $15.60); dessert buffet A$5.50 (U.S. $4.40). AE, BC, DC, MC, V.
Open: Breakfast, lunch, and dinner daily 6:30am–10:30pm.

This is the Radisson's casual eatery, and it overlooks the landscaped pool area. The seafood buffet and the dessert buffet are especially good values. Certain dishes offer a "light and healthy alternative" because they are prepared with the minimum of fat and salt. These include steamed grain-fed beef sirloin served with wasabi jus, fresh "morning market" fish, and chargrilled chicken breast served with tofu tartare. If you're traveling with your offspring and they're pining for American food, you'll be glad to see the grilled cheese sandwich, BLT, and hot dog on the menu.

Main courses include baked Tasmanian salmon in rosemary and sesame-seed crust, pan-seared tropical coral trout, and Victorian lamb loin satay style.

Inexpensive

In addition to the eatery listed below, dollarwise travelers might like to know about the **Food Court** in the Pier Marketplace which is open daily until 9pm. More than a half dozen fast-food options—ranging from pizza to Chinese—are available here.

PIER SEAFOODS, in the Pier Marketplace. Tel. 31-5526.
   Cuisine: SEAFOOD. **Reservations:** None.
$ **Prices:** Light meal A$6 (U.S. $4.80). No credit cards.
   Open: Daily 9am–9pm.
This is an Australian experience you won't want to miss: your chance to eat a "croc burger." Soren Houlberg, the creator of the unusual sandwich, uses only homegrown saltwater crocodile, which he cooks while-you-wait and serves with his special sauce. Another option is the "barra burger" made from local barramundi. BYO.

ON THE NORTHERN BEACHES

CASBAH RESTAURANT, 47 Vasey Esplanade, Trinity Beach. Tel. 57-7137.
   Cuisine: FRENCH/MEDITERRANEAN. **Reservations:** Recommended.
   Transportation: Take the Beach Bus. Trinity Beach is 20km (12 miles) north of Cairns.
$ **Prices:** Appetizers A$7–A$9 (U.S. $5.60–U.S. $7.20); main courses A$14–A$25 (U.S. $11.20–U.S. $20). BC, MC, V.
   Open: Dinner daily 6pm–late.

★ The Casbah is a delightful open-air eatery across the road from the beach. Their moussaka is delicious, as are the stuffed grape leaves and the kakavia, Greek soup identical to French bouillabaisse. BYO.

COLONIES, in Paradise Village, Palm Cove. Tel. 55-3058.
   Cuisine: MEDITERRANEAN. **Reservations:** Accepted only for parties of 5 or more. **Transportation:** Palm Cove is 25km (16 miles) north of Cairns. Take the Beach Bus.
$ **Prices:** Appetizers A$7.50–A$10.50 (U.S. $6–U.S. $8.40); main courses A$11.50–A$18.95 (U.S. $9.20–U.S. $15.20); Devonshire tea A$4.50 (U.S. $3.60); average lunch A$6–A$10 (U.S. $4.80–U.S. $8). BC, DC, MC, V.
   Open: Breakfast, lunch, and dinner daily 7:30am–9pm.
Located in the whitewashed multilevel Paradise Village, Colonies offers fresh seafood prepared in Mediterranean dishes. These include marinated seafood salad, moussaka, salade niçoise, Greek salad, and various pastas. Their homemade Italian gelati is understandably popular. Diners are seated at nine tables on a pleasant terrace or at a few inside tables one level aboveground. In addition to full meals, the bistro serves espresso and Devonshire teas. One of their specialties is coffee roasted in the nearby Atherton Tablelands. BYO. Also does take-out.

EVENING ENTERTAINMENT

Cairns's after-dark scene is nothing to write home about, probably because the area caters more to families than to singles and because everyone is pooped after full-day excursions to the reef, tablelands, and so forth.

However, you will find some action at **The Playpen Nite Club,** 3 Lake Street (tel. 51-8211). Their main room is open Wednesday through Sunday nights, and there's a female stripper on Thursday. The normal cover charge of A$5 (U.S. $4) is doubled on Thursday. The Playpen's Court Jester cocktail bar is open Thursday through Monday, and hosts a male stripper on Thursday night. The cover charge is A$5 (U.S. $4), except Thursday when it's A$6 (U.S. $4.80). Samuels Saloon and Restaurant serves an all-you-can-eat buffet which is popular with backpackers. The cost is A$5 (U.S. $4) and includes a courtesy coach pickup. The Aussie Bar Hall (tel. 31-5671) is the Playpen's theater restaurant. It's presently open Monday, Wednesday, and Saturday, but may be running 7 nights a week by the time you get there. The cost of A$34 (U.S. $27.20) includes dinner and a 2-hour performance of Torres Strait and

Aboriginal dancing, fire-eating, and contemporary entertainment. Only this last section of the Playpen accepts credit cards (no Diners Club). Just to give you an idea of prices, a beer at the Playpen will set you back about A$3.40 (U.S. $2.75).

You might also enjoy **Reno Club International** in the Palm Court Center on Lake Street (tel. 52-1480 or 51-8835). The first (ground) floor is a karaoke club and there's a piano bar upstairs. Reno's is open Monday to Saturday from 8pm to 5am; there's no cover charge during the week, but it's A$5 (U.S. $4) on weekends.

EASY EXCURSIONS

Most people are quite happy basing themselves in Cairns or on the northern beaches and doing day-trips to places in the area. However, if you're interested in going farther afield, take note of the following.

Reef Endeavour is a 73-meter (241-ft.) cruise liner that departs from Cairns on 3- and 4-night trips around the Great Barrier Reef. The luxurious ship has accommodations for 156 passengers. The James Cook Cruise leaves Cairns on Saturday, returns on Wednesday, and visits Cooktown and Lizard Island. The Joseph Banks Cruise departs on Wednesday, returns on Saturday, and goes to Dunk Island and Hinchinbrook Island. Both itineraries allow ample time for snorkeling and viewing the reef through glass-bottom boats. The ship has a swimming pool, spas, gym, and sauna. Prices for the 3-night Joseph Banks Cruise range from A$690 to A$885 (U.S. $552 to U.S. $708) per person based on two people sharing; the cost of the 4-night James Cook Cruise is A$920 to A$1,180 (U.S. $736 to U.S. $944) per person based on two people sharing. The 7-night Combination Cruise is A$1,449 to A$1,858 (U.S. $1,159.20 to U.S. $1,486.40). For more information or to make reservations, contact Captain Cook Cruises, No. 6 Jetty, Circular Quay, Sydney, NSW 2000 (tel. 02/247-4548; fax 02/251-4725).

The *Coral Princess* is a 35-meter (116-ft.) cruising catamaran which accommodates up to 54 passengers. Guests can join the ship in either Cairns or Townsville for a 4-day cruise. The itinerary includes Moore Reef, Dunk Island, and Orpheus Island. For more information contact Coral Princess Cruises, corner of Aplin and Sheridan streets, Cairns, QLD 4870 (tel. 070/31-1041; fax 070/31-1442).

---

4. PORT DOUGLAS & MOSSMAN

Port Douglas: 67km (41 miles) N of Cairns
Mossman: 19km (12 miles) N of Port Douglas

GETTING THERE **By Plane** If you're in a hurry, Helijet Helicopter Service (tel. 35-9300) can get you from Cairns to Port Douglas or Mossman in a matter of minutes.

By Bus Transport from Cairns to Port Douglas and Mossman is by one of the **Coral Coaches** (tel. 98-1611 or 51-9533). The trip takes about an hour.

By Car Take the Captain Cook Highway from Cairns—and be careful, it's a little windy and not too wide.

ESSENTIALS The **area code** is 070.

The settlement at Port Douglas got off to a booming start in the late 1870s due to the fervent activity in inland goldfields. In just a few years it amassed a population of 12,000, which supported 27 hotels, two newspapers, and a Cobb & Co. coach service. However, the community declined rapidly after 1885, when the government chose to bring the railroad no farther north than Cairns. "Port," as it is known locally, was already a ghost town in 1911, when a cyclone destroyed most of the remaining buildings.

Now, more than 100 years later, the town (pop. 1,500) has been reborn as a trendy, tropical resort. Gone are the days when tourists drove through Port on their way to the Daintree National Park, Cape Tribulation, Mossman River Gorge, or Cooktown, but wouldn't have considered staying there. Now, an increasing number are basing themselves in one of the community's new or almost-new resorts. Besides its relaxed life-style and tropical ambience, Port offers a wonderful stretch of golden sand known as **Four Mile Beach.**

Nearby Mossman (pop. 1,600) is Australia's most northerly sugar town, and the gateway to the scenic Mossman River Gorge and Daintree wilderness area.

WHAT TO SEE & DO

Of all the large-scale commercial boats that take visitors to the Great Barrier Reef, **Quicksilver Connections** is the best organized, most comfortable, and enjoyable. Jim and Jo Wallace started this highly successful program in 1979; since then *Quicksilver* has carried thousands of people to where they can experience underwater wonders firsthand.

Quicksilver, a 37-meter (120-ft.) high-speed wave-piercing catamaran, carries up to 300 passengers from Port Douglas to a floating platform anchored in a lagoon at **Agincourt Reef** on the outer Barrier Reef. The platform includes both an underwater observatory and shady seating. Two semisubmersible vessels leave from the platform and cruise through vast coral canyons teeming with marine life. *Quicksilver*'s guests can also snorkel (gear is provided); marine biologists conduct guided snorkel tours. Scuba divers are escorted by an experienced dive master to two different sites. **Helijet** provides bird's-eye views of the reef at an extra charge. If your time is limited, it's possible to travel one way on *Quicksilver* and the other on Helijet. This costs A$270 (U.S. $216). Either way, it's a wonderful day.

Quicksilver also operates cruises to the **Low Isles,** a tiny, unspoiled coral cay 14 kilometers (8½ miles) from Port Douglas where passengers can go ashore by glass-bottom boat or swim and snorkel from an anchored platform. The lighthouse on the Low Isles has been in operation since 1878.

Quicksilver departs Marina Mirage, Port Douglas, daily at 10am and returns at 4:30pm. The journey to Agincourt Reef takes about 1½ hours. Marine biologists show videos and talk about the reef en route. The adult fare of A$98 (U.S. $78.40) includes an excellent buffet lunch, coral viewing from semisubmersibles, underwater observatory, snorkeling equipment (and adviser), and morning and afternoon tea. The guided snorkel tour costs A$22 (U.S. $17.60) extra and scuba diving is an additional A$65 (U.S. $52) with all equipment. The Low Isles trip leaves at 10am and returns at 4:30pm. The cost is A$55 (U.S. $44), including morning and afternoon teas, lunch, snorkeling gear, glass-bottom-boat coral viewing, and guided snorkeling and beach walk with a marine biologist. Children aged 4 to 14 are half price; those under 4 are free. Coach transfers from Cairns cost A$10 (U.S. $8). Wave Piercer cruise transfers from Cairns and Palm Cove cost A$10 (U.S. $8). To book, phone 99-5500.

If you have some extra time in Port Douglas, stop in at the **Shipwreck Museum,** on the wharf, 6 Dixie Street (tel. 99-5858). This collection of relics from historical disasters was put together by Ben Cropp, a local who has discovered more than 100 wrecks on the Great Barrier Reef. Admission is A$4 (U.S. $3.20) for adults and A$1.50 (U.S. $1.20) for children. Open daily from 9am to 5pm April through January.

Australian Wilderness Safaris into the Daintree and Cape Tribulation national parks depart from Mossman. For details see "What to See and Do," in Cairns, above.

WHERE TO STAY

IN PORT DOUGLAS

SHERATON MIRAGE PORT DOUGLAS, Port Douglas Rd., Port Douglas, QLD 4871. Tel. 070/99-5888, or toll free 008/22-2229 in Australia. Fax 070/98-5885. 297 rms, 3 suites. A/C MINIBAR TV TEL **Transportation:** Courtesy shuttle to Marina Mirage.

$ Rates (including breakfast buffet): A$375–A$500 (U.S. $300–U.S. $400) single or double room; A$570 (U.S. $456) lagoon suite; A$1,500 (U.S. $1,200)

Presidential Suite; A$1,700 (U.S. $1,360) Royal Suite; A$600–A$825 (U.S. $480–U.S. $660) 2-, 3-, and 4-bedroom Reef Mirage Villa; A$45 (U.S. $36) extra person. Children under 17 stay free in parents' room. AE, BC, DC, MC, V. **Parking:** Free.

The Sheraton Mirage Port Douglas is one of the few deluxe properties right on the beach in Far North Queensland. The hotel compound, including an 18-hole golf course, 10 tennis courts, and a 2-hectare (5-acre) swimmable saltwater lagoon, occupies an enviable spot on Four Mile Beach.

The three-story Sheraton's rooms all have king-size beds or two doubles, marble bathrooms with spa tubs and hairdryers, and spacious sitting areas. Hotel facilities include 24-hour room service, a children's activity center, a tour/travel desk, three restaurants, two cocktail lounges, and a health club with gym, steam, sauna, spa, and massage.

RADISSON ROYAL PALMS RESORT, Port Douglas Rd., Port Douglas, QLD 4871. Tel. 070/99-5577, or toll free 008/02-1211 in Australia. Fax 070/99-5559. 301 rms, 14 suites. A/C MINIBAR TV TEL **Transportation:** Airport courtesy coach from Cairns.

$ Rates: A$125 (U.S. $100) single or double; A$250 (U.S. $200) garden- or golf-view junior suite; A$340 (U.S. $272) 1-bedroom executive suite; A$440 (U.S. $352) 2-bedroom executive suite; A$20 (U.S. $16) extra person. Children under 18 stay free in parents' room and receive a 50% discount in adjacent room. Dollarwise 7-night packages available. No-smoking rooms available. AE, BC, DC, MC, V. **Parking:** Free.

One of the best values in Far North Queensland, the colonial Queensland–style Radisson is set on over 3 hectares (8 acres) of landscaped grounds. Rooms in the attractive three-story property (no lift) are not overly spacious, but offer balconies, in-room movies, free daily newspapers, queen-size beds, clock radios, tea- and coffee-making facilities, and small refrigerators. The hotel charges 23¢ for a local call—the lowest in the country.

Facilities include a large pool with swim-up bar, children's center, two tennis courts, a spa, pool table, bike rental, pitch-and-putt golf, and self-service laundry.

Room service is offered 11am to 11pm; the Guest Activities Officer runs a sports-and-crafts program for children. The restaurant serves a three-course buffet dinner for A$17.50 to A$22.50 (U.S. $14 to U.S. $18). There's live entertainment nightly. Two rooms are equipped for handicapped travelers.

REEF TERRACES RESORT, Port Douglas Rd., Port Douglas, QLD 4871. Tel. 070/99-3333. Fax 070/99-3385. 144 apartments. A/C TV TEL **Transportation:** Airport courtesy coach from Cairns.

$ Rates: A$125 (U.S. $100) 2-bedroom garden-view apartment; A$160 (U.S. $128) 2-bedroom golf-view apartment; A$20 (U.S. $16) extra person. Rates are 20% higher June–Oct. AE, BC, DC, MC, V. **Parking:** Free.

This property is next door to the Radisson Royal Palms described above and 4 kilometers (2½ miles) from the village center. Four Mile Beach is within walking distance, and the Sheraton Mirage is across the road.

Here you will find two-story, two-bedroom apartments with full kitchens, laundry facilities, ceiling fans, two bathrooms, and balconies. They are set on a lushly landscaped 4-hectare (10-acre) site adjacent to the Mirage Country Club Golf Course and include a large free-form pool, two spas, and the Terracehouse Restaurant and Cocktail Bar.

COCONUT GROVE MOTEL, 58 Macrossan St., Port Douglas, QLD 4871. Tel. 070/99-5124. Fax 070/99-5144. 22 rms. TV

$ Rates: A$50 (U.S. $40) single or double without air conditioning; A$55 (U.S. $44) single or double with air conditioning. AE, BC, DC, MC, V. **Parking:** Free.

Surely this is the only motel in Australia owned and managed by an ex–New York stockbroker. Michael Gabour does a great job at the Coconut Grove of maintaining a friendly, welcoming atmosphere. Units are clean, tidy, and basic; each has tea- and coffee-making facilities, a small refrigerator, a television, and a shower. The beach is 100 meters (110 yd.) away, and there are two freshwater pools on the premises. It's just a short walk to town and the harborfront. The Coconut Grove Licensed Restaurant serves reasonably priced meals, such as three-course dinners for A$12.50 (U.S. $10).

IN MOSSMAN

SILKY OAKS LODGE, 8km (5 miles) west of Mossman on the edge of the river gorge (P.O. Box 396, Mossman Gorge, QLD 4873). Tel. 070/ 98-1666. Fax 070/98-1983. 20 cabins. A/C MINIBAR **Transportation:** Transfers to Silky Oaks from the Cairns Airport (83km/50 miles to the south) are A$105 (U.S. $84) each way by private car. The Coral Coach costs about A$20 (U.S. $16) per person.

$ **Rates:** A$320 (U.S. $256) single or double; A$60 (U.S. $48) extra person. Children under 6 not accepted. No-smoking rooms available. AE, BC, DC, MC, V. **Parking:** Free.

Silky Oaks offers its guests much more than comfortable accommodations. It provides a unique opportunity to live amid rain forest and billabongs, spend time with an unusual couple who possess a rare understanding and respect for the environment, and be close to native animals. The lodge is surrounded on three sides by Daintree National Park and overlooks the Mossman River Gorge.

The Lodge is owned by Moss and Theresa Hunt, who were doing adventure travel on the rugged Cape York Peninsula long before it became popular. Twenty years ago theirs was one of the few vehicles to make it all the way to the top. Moss's Australian Wilderness Safaris conducts four-wheel-drive excursions into the wilderness, and when the guides encounter orphaned baby kangaroos or wallabies, they bring them back with them. These little ones add a dimension to life at Silky Oaks that is not found elsewhere. Guests can help bottle-feed the babies. The Mossman River Gorge is a haven for native birds, and books in the lodge's nature reference library help to identify them.

Accommodations at Silky Oaks are in 20 comfortable cabins built on poles among the trees near the edge of the river and overlooking the native-animal nursery. Each has a bathroom with a shower, a kitchenette, a hardwood floor, a ceiling fan, a veranda, and handcrafted colonial timber furniture. The Hunts have built a boardwalk down to the river and provide hammocks on the bank. Canoes and kayaks are also available, as are a swimming pool, tennis courts, bicycles, picnic lunches, and backpacks. Swimming in the river and hiking are popular pastimes.

Guests enjoy meals in an open-air restaurant with a river view; the lodge has a good wine list.

DAINTREE/CAPE TRIBULATION WILDERNESS AREA

HERITAGE LODGE, Turpentine Rd., Cooper Creek via Mossman, QLD 4873. Tel. 070/98-9138. 16 units. **Transportation:** The lodge is approximately 2 hours by road north of Cairns on the Captain Cook Hwy. Access by conventional vehicle is possible in all but the very worst wet weather. A Coral Coach ticket from Cairns costs A$46 (U.S. $36.80) round-trip.

$ **Rates:** A$109 (U.S. $87.20) single or double; A$10 (U.S. $8) extra person. AE, BC, MC, V. **Parking:** Free.

The lodge is located 18 kilometers (11 miles) north of the Daintree River ferry on the banks of Cooper Creek and adjoins Cape Tribulation National Park. Here 16 units are located in forest clearings. Each has a bathroom, ceiling fan, and patio. The restaurant offers all meals, and there's a bar and swimming pool. This is a great place for bushwalking (hiking), birdwatching, and swimming in nearby Cooper Creek.

WHERE TO DINE

NAUTILUS RESTAURANT, 17 Murphy St., Port Douglas. Tel. 99-5330. **Cuisine:** SEAFOOD. **Reservations:** Recommended. **Directions:** Enter from Macrossan St.

$ Prices: Appetizers A$10–A$16 (U.S. $8–U.S. $12.80); main courses A$20–A$25 (U.S. $16–U.S. $20). AE, BC, MC, V.
Open: Dinner daily 6:30pm–late.

Nautilus has been luring diners to Port Douglas for almost 40 years with its creative cuisine and careful cooking. The menu changes daily depending on market availability. Popular modern seafood dishes include fresh tiger prawns dipped in Asian spices and chargrilled, Thai fish curry with steamed rice, and stir-fried blue swimmer crab with chili, garlic, and ginger. Typical meat main courses are: grilled lamb cutlets served with beetroot chutney, chargrilled King Island rib beef with mustard-herb butter, and steamed corned beef with horseradish and creamed potatoes. These gourmet meals are served on a covered veranda or under palm trees on a garden terrace. The tropical foliage is complemented by the candlelight supplied by owners John and Carmel Forrest.

MATABUBU, Macrossan St., Port Douglas. Tel. 99-5058.
Cuisine: MODERN AUSTRALIAN. **Reservations:** Optional.
$ Prices: Appetizers A$4.50–A$7.50 (U.S. $3.60–U.S. $6); main courses A$10.50–A$16 (U.S. $8.40–U.S. $12.80). BC, DC, MC, V.
Open: Lunch Mon–Fri 10am–2:30pm; dinner Tues–Sat 6:30pm–late.

This very casual eatery is located at the foot of the steps leading up to the Nautilus Restaurant described above. This is a good place for affordable, creative meals. Starters include chilled tomato and capsicum soup with diced cucumber and ground black pepper and chargrilled tuna pieces served on a light corn fritter topped with sour cream, dill, and sun-dried tomato. As a main course you could order coral trout filet with a tomato, onion, and cucumber salad and a light pesto sauce, marinated sirloin with eggplant-and-rosemary pâté, or chargrilled boneless chicken Maryland marinated in lemon, garlic, and fresh rosemary. Toasted focaccia sandwiches are available at lunchtime, as are homemade pies, sandwiches, and salads. BYO.

SILKY OAKS LODGE AND RESTAURANT, Mossman Gorge. Tel. 070/98-1666.
Cuisine: MODERN AUSTRALIAN. **Reservations:** Recommended. **Transportation:** See Silky Oaks Lodge in "Where to Stay," above.
$ Prices: Appetizers A$10.50–A$13.50 (U.S. $8.40–U.S. $10.80); main courses A$18.50–A$39 (U.S. $14.80–U.S. $31.20). AE, BC, DC, MC, V.
Open: Lunch daily noon–2:30pm; dinner daily 6:30–9:30pm.

This is a wonderful open-air setting in which to enjoy lunch or dinner. The restaurant overlooks the Mossman River Gorge and there are lots of native birds and other animals in the area. The menu favors local seafood and only-in-Australia dishes such as prawn and buffalo brochettes and carpaccio of water buffalo. Coral trout is pan-fried with orange segments; oven-steamed barramundi is wrapped in a banana leaf with vegetables; baked lamb filet is seasoned with mustard and rosemary and wrapped in filo.

---

5. THE CAPE YORK PENINSULA

Cooktown is 334km (207 miles) N of Cairns

GETTING THERE   By Plane   Australian Regional Airlines flies from Cairns to Bamaga near the tip of the peninsula.

By Car   Surface travel is impossible during the wet season, November through May, and even in the optimum period, August through October, only those equipped with a rugged sense of adventure and an equally rugged four-wheel-drive vehicle make it to the top.

ESSENTIALS   The **Royal Automobile Club of Queensland** (RACQ) is the best source of information regarding road conditions, and **Queensland Govern-**

ment Travel Centres can provide you with a list of tour operators who offer camping safaris. The **area code** is 070.

The northernmost part of the state of Queensland is a triangle-shaped area about 1½ times the size of England. It is a land of incredible wilderness inhabited by a few hardy settlers, Torres Strait Islanders, and Aborigines. Camping tours departing from Cairns take at least 5 days to get to the tip of the Cape York Peninsula, longer if side trips are included. Along the way at least seven rivers are forded.

   Cooktown (pop. 1,000) is the last outpost of civilization before heading up the peninsula. Safaris following the **Peninsula Developmental Road,** known locally as the **Telegraph Line,** are first confronted with the up-and-down experience of dealing with high forested ridges and steep river valleys created by water flowing both east and west of the **Great Dividing Range.** Later, detours to the coast reveal spectacular sweeping beaches and evergreen rain forests that possess as many as 50 kinds of orchids and weird insect-eating plants. Farther along, crocodiles thrive in innumerable swamps and creeks. Closer to the top, fascinating termite mounds can be seen, as well as the rich bird life that inhabits the scrubland and open forest. Once at the top, weary adventurers are treated to a breathtaking view of **Endeavour Strait** and the **Torres Strait Islands.**

   This is not a trip for inexperienced, albeit enthusiastic, tourists. The lack of sealed roads, bridges, and petrol stations (the last fuel depot is in Coen)—to say nothing of man-eating crocodiles—makes this a journey to be undertaken only with a jungle-smart Aussie who knows the way and has the proper equipment. In addition to a fully outfitted four-wheel-drive vehicle, your guide will need to obtain written permission for your group to cross Aboriginal land.

WHERE TO STAY

CAPE YORK WILDERNESS LODGE, 400m (436 yd.) south of Cape York (P.O. Box 2372, Cairns, QLD 4870). Tel. 070/69-1444. Fax 070/69-1444. 24 cabins. **Transportation:** Australian Regional Airlines flies into Bamaga which is 2,782km (1,725 miles) north of Cairns and 32km (20 miles) south of Cape York. The lodge provides transfers.

$ Rates (including meals and most sporting facilities): A$238 (U.S. $190.40) single; A$400 (U.S. $320) double; A$486 (U.S. $388.80) triple. Dollarwise 7-night packages available. AE, BC, DC, MC, V.

The Cape York Wilderness Lodge is located north of the World War II airstrip at Bamaga and only 400 meters (436 yd.) from the tip of mainland Australia. Each cabin has a modern bathroom, a ceiling fan, and a balcony with a great view of the surrounding bush. Breakfast, lunch, and dinner are served in the dining room and the bar is open at mealtimes. Guests can sit around the pool, fish, take four-wheel-drive safaris, observe the incredible variety of wildlife found in the area, or do day-trips to Thursday Island. The staff provides binoculars, torches (flashlights), dinghies with outboard motors, and fishing gear and tackle.

   If you're already in Australia, you can book through Australian Airlines. In North America, call **SO/PAC** (tel. toll free 800/445-0190 in California, 800/551-2012 elsewhere in the U.S.) or **Goway Travel** (tel. 416/322-1034 in Toronto, toll free 800/663-9418 in B.C., 800/663-9107 in Alta. and Sask., 800/668-1427 in Ont. or Qué., or 800/387-8850 in Man. and the Maritimes).

---

6. OUTBACK & INLAND QUEENSLAND

Mount Isa: 900km (558 miles) W of Townsville
Longreach: 682km (423 miles) W of Rockhampton

GETTING THERE   By Plane   Australian Airlines, Ansett, and Flight West fly to Mount Isa. An Australian Airlines Air Pass ticket from Townsville to Mount Isa costs from A$307 to A$385 (U.S. $245.60 to U.S. $308). Flight West also serves Longreach.

By Train   The *Inlander* leaves Townsville Wednesday and Sunday at 6pm, arriving in Mount Isa at 11:50am the next day. The *Midlander* leaves Rockhampton Tuesday and Friday at 6:45pm and arrives in Longreach at 8:45am the next day.

By Bus   Longreach can be reached by Greyhound and McCafferty's. Bus Australia, Pioneer, Greyhound, and McCafferty's go to Mount Isa. A Townsville-to–Mount Isa ticket costs about A$81 (U.S. $64.80). A Longreach-to–Mount Isa ticket costs about A$56 (U.S. $44.80). Brisbane to Mount Isa will set you back A$135 (U.S. $108).

By Car   If you drive to Mount Isa, keep in mind that the Flinders Highway from Townsville passes through 900 kilometers (558 miles) of sparsely populated country. Motorists traveling to Longreach from Rockhampton follow the Capricorn Highway. Always check road conditions with the RACQ before setting out for any outback destination.

ESSENTIALS   **Queensland Government Travel Centres** in the capital cities throughout Australia and Queensland Tourist and Travel Corporation offices in major overseas cities have information on the outback. Another good source is **The Outback Queensland Tourism Authority,** P.O. Box 295, Blackall, QLD 4472 (tel. 076/57-4222). In addition to providing sightseeing data, these people can also make arrangements for you to stay on a working cattle or sheep station. The **area code** for Longreach is 076, and 077 for Mount Isa.

A long way from the fields of sugarcane and the tropical ambience of the coast, vast stretches of sunburned country cover more than a third of the state. This is where cattle stations, rodeos, and starkly beautiful scenery prevail, and island resorts, rain forests, and beaches seem a world away.

WHAT TO SEE & DO

Longreach (pop. 2,971) is a good place to base yourself if you wish to sample the flavor of the outback. Once there, visit the ❂ **Australian Stockman's Hall of Fame and Outback Heritage Centre,** a tribute to the people who pioneered the west. The center was built as part of the 1988 bicentennial celebration and honors explorers, pioneers, stockmen, roughriders, poets, writers, and artists. Longreach was also an early home of **Qantas Airways,** and the original hangar is still at the airport.

In the northwest section of Queensland the terrain is less hostile and dry; instead, outback scenery gives way to rolling plains. Huge stations operate throughout the region, and **Mount Isa** (pop. 23,679) is the site of one of the world's largest copper, silver, lead, and zinc mines. In addition to taking mine tours, visitors to Mount Isa can go to an underground museum and the **Royal Flying Doctor Service/School of the Air** base.

WHERE TO STAY
IN LONGREACH

JUMBUCK MOTEL, Sir Hudson Fysh Dr., Longreach, QLD 4730. Tel. 076/58-1799. Fax 076/58-1832. 36 rms. A/C TV TEL Reservations can be made through Best Western. **Transportation:** Courtesy transfer available.
$ **Rates:** A$55 (U.S. $44) single; A$70 (U.S. $56) double. AE, BC, DC, MC, V. **Parking:** Free.
All quarters here have showers, videos, coffee- and tea-making facilities, and small refrigerators. A restaurant, swimming pool, playground, and barbecue are on the premises.

IN MOUNT ISA

BURKE AND WILLS ISA RESORT, Grace and Camooweal Sts., Mount Isa, QLD 4825. Tel. 077/43-8000. Fax 077/43-8424. 56 rms. A/C TV TEL
Transportation: Airport courtesy car on request.
$ Rates: A$80 (U.S. $64) single; A$90 (U.S. $72) double. AE, BC, DC, MC, V.
Parking: Free.
Burke and Wills Isa Resort is a two-story building with all modern amenities, including water beds, queen-size beds, a swimming pool, a mini-gym, hot and cold spas, a restaurant, and facilities for handicapped travelers. Most rooms have bathtubs as well as showers; some rooms have minibars; all have tea- and coffee-making facilities and small refrigerators.

CHAPTER 10

THE GREAT BARRIER REEF

The world's greatest living structure runs along the Queensland coast from just north of Bundaberg to past the end of the Cape York Peninsula. It's a spectacular reef made of coral and surrounded by tropical fish and other marine life whose shapes and colors put so-called imaginative Hollywood moviemakers to shame. While the coral often appears inert, it is very much alive; anyone who doubts this need only watch it extend its tentacles to feed.

The reef has affected the course of Australia's history since Capt. James Cook first discovered it in 1770. Cook's expedition nearly ended in disaster when his ship, the *Endeavour,* was severely damaged when he unknowingly entered through the Whitsunday Passage and tried to find a way out across the outer reef through dense coral shoals. Many northern Queensland place names, including Cooktown, Lizard Island, Magnetic Island, and Cook's Passage, come from this 18th-century voyage. And the labels he bestowed on Cape Tribulation, Weary Bay, Hope Islands, and, finally, Providential Channel indicate the challenge the reef presented.

The Great Barrier Reef continues to amaze, inspire, and challenge the scientists who attempt to understand its fragile, yet enduring, structure and who study the myriad interrelated marine species that thrive in its environs. The reef impacts the nation's economy in the areas of shipping, fishing, and tourism, and perhaps most important, it is a source of pride for all Australians.

"It is," one Aussie explained to me, "one of the reasons we call ourselves 'the lucky country.'"

GETTING TO KNOW THE REEF

The Great Barrier Reef extends for 2,000 kilometers (1,240 miles) from Lady Elliot Island off Queensland's central coast to the Gulf of Papua near New Guinea. In the south, the outer edge of the reef is up to 300 kilometers (186 miles) offshore, and the closest coral lies about 15 kilometers (9 miles) from the coast. In the north, the reef starts about 20 kilometers (12 miles) offshore and extends for approximately 30 kilometers (18 miles). In all, it covers an area greater than that of Britain and about half the size of Texas.

NOT REALLY A BARRIER

The outer reef is not a solid wall but a system of coral shoals and individual ribbon and patch reefs upon which waves pound relentlessly. On the far side of the outer reef the Pacific Ocean is hundreds of fathoms deep. The great lagoon between the outer reef and the mainland is dotted with coral cays, continental islands, and inner patch reefs.

Coral cays are low islands formed from coral rubble and sand, created by the reef on which they stand. Over a period of time, this sedimentary debris is thrown up by

WHAT'S SPECIAL ABOUT THE GREAT BARRIER REEF

Natural Spectacles
- [ ] Coral, in a rainbow of colors and myriad assorted shapes.
- [ ] Tropical fish, whose imaginative shape is rivaled only by their vibrant hues.

Special Pleasures
- [ ] Private picnics in secluded coves.
- [ ] Candlelit dinners with tropical breezes.
- [ ] Reclining under a palm tree, and relaxing as only an island idyll allows.

Activities
- [ ] Snorkeling, scuba diving, reef walking, underwater photography, and viewing the reef from glass-bottom boats or semisubmersibles.

wind, waves, and currents onto the sheltered side of the reef top. At first a sandspit forms, and if the cay enlarges with the accumulation of more coral debris, it may become a resting site for birds; eventually, plants grow from seeds deposited in bird droppings. Vegetated cays provide ideal places for seabirds and turtles to nest and lay their eggs. Continental islands are drowned mountains rising from the continental shelf. Much larger than coral cays, they are often mountainous and wooded. Altogether the Great Barrier Reef is comprised of more than 2,600 separate reefs and over 300 islands, including small bare sand cays, 69 vegetated cays, and many continental islands.

The reef developed because 20 million years ago the waters rose around the ancient continent of Australia, creating a submerged continental shelf and an area of relatively shallow, clear, and warm water. These conditions are ideal for the growth of coral, which began building the first reefs at that time.

ARCHITECTS OF THE REEF

During the day, reef-building corals retract their polyps into their limestone skeletons. At night the polyps are extended to feed on microscopic animals that drift around in the sea. Over many thousands of years, the limestone skeletons of dead coral polyps have formed reefs. These have a veneer of living coral and provide the perfect environment for many kinds of animals such as fish, worms, sea urchins, sea cucumbers, clams, snails, sponges, crabs, shrimp, and starfish. At least 1,500 species of tropical fish live in the area of the reef, which provides them with both food and protection.

No fewer than 400 kinds of hard and soft coral comprise the Great Barrier Reef. Some of these are shaped like fans, others resemble flowers, tree branches, or mushrooms; brain coral eerily resembles its namesake. Living coral ranges in color from white to pale pink and yellow to vivid purple and red. In spite of the damage done in recent years by the crown of thorns starfish, which actually eats living coral polyps, the reef is still incredibly beautiful. Just when you think you've seen all that nature has to offer, a new shade or shape appears.

Coral colonies cluster together and form three predominant types of reefs. Long narrow ribbon reefs are found along the northern portion of the outer reef, often separated by channels. Patch reefs grow like a platform on the continental shelf, can be up to 20 kilometers (12 miles) across, are often oval or round, and frequently have a shallow lagoon in the middle. Fringing reefs form around continental islands, and because most resorts are built on this type of island, these reefs are what the majority of tourists see. The coral and marine life of a fringing reef can be just as spectacular as that found at the outer reef or on inner patch reefs.

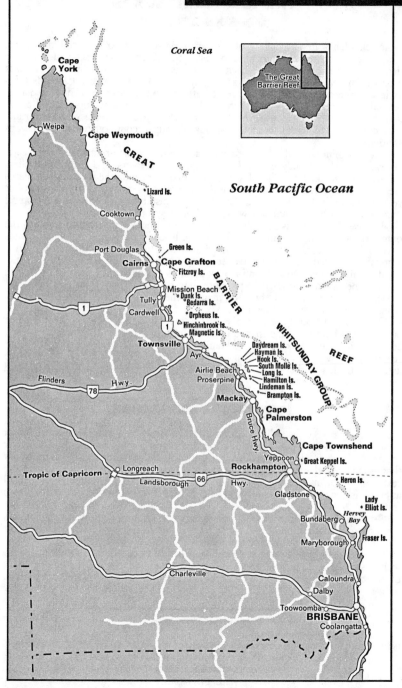

THE GREAT BARRIER REEF

N

Cape York

Weipa

Cape Weymouth

Coral Sea

GREAT

The Great Barrier Reef

Lizard Is.

South Pacific Ocean

Cooktown

Port Douglas

Green Is.

Cairns

Cape Grafton

Fitzroy Is.

Mission Beach

Dunk Is.

Tully

Bedarra Is.

Cardwell

Orpheus Is.

Hinchinbrook Is.

Magnetic Is.

BARRIER

Townsville

Ayr

Daydream Is.
Hayman Is.
Hook Is.
South Molle Is.
Long Is.
Hamilton Is.
Lindeman Is.
Brampton Is.

Airlie Beach

Proserpine

WHITSUNDAY GROUP

REEF

Mackay

Cape Palmerston

Flinders   Hwy.

78

Bruce Hwy.

Cape Townshend

Yeppoon

Rockhampton

Great Keppel Is.

Tropic of Capricorn   Longreach

Landsborough

66   Hwy.

Heron Is.

Gladstone

Lady
Elliot Is.

Bundaberg

Hervey
Bay

Fraser Is.

Maryborough

Charleville

Caloundra

Dalby

Toowoomba

BRISBANE

Coolangatta

THE ISLAND RESORTS
CHOOSING A RESORT

Nineteen islands in the vicinity of the Great Barrier Reef offer accommodations. Choosing among them is not an easy task, and it's important that you give your decision careful consideration. Each resort has its own personality and presents a particular set of options. Some are highly developed and offer a Club Med–ish variety of fun and games. Others are peaceful, secluded, do-your-own-thing places. Several cater to families; a few prohibit children. Please clarify your idea of an island paradise and pick a resort accordingly. I want you to have a wonderful time. (For complete guidelines to all 19 islands offering accommodations, see the appendix.)

Keep in mind that three islands with accommodations are actually coral cays: Green, Heron, and Lady Elliot. The first two have resorts, and Lady Elliot offers cabins and tent camping. The advantage of actually being on the reef, as these places are, is the abundance of coral that can be snorkeled over, viewed from a variety of vessels, and walked on at low tide. Coral cays are also rich with bird life and tropical vegetation. Beaches are not soft white sand but tiny bits of coral.

Because a coral cay is actually part of the reef, there is no need to travel to the outer reef for snorkeling, diving, and so forth. In contrast, some continental islands have only very small amounts of fringing coral, and a trip in the resort's boat, seaplane, or helicopter to the outer reef or an inner patch reef is required for really good coral viewing. Don't be misled by pictures of coral and tropical fish used in advertisements; the resorts they promote may be a long way from the reef. Also beware of pictures of sandy beaches; many in the vicinity of the Great Barrier Reef would be hard to walk on barefoot.

Orpheus and Lizard are examples of continental islands with excellent fringing coral reefs. In contrast, the islands in the Whitsunday group (Hayman, Daydream, South Molle, Long, Lindeman, and Hamilton) offer lots of water sports, but serious reef buffs will want to take an excursion to the outer reef or an inner patch reef to see great coral. Tidal action in the Whitsundays also limits the use of Windsurfers and catamarans.

UNDERWATER SIGHTSEEING

Nearly every resort has either a **glass-bottom boat** or a **semisubmersible** for coral-viewing excursions. This is a good alternative for nonswimmers. The driver moves the boat slowly over areas of colorful coral and gives descriptive commentary that usually includes the names of fish and other marine life. Another way to view the reef without getting wet is to go to an underwater observatory. Good ones are located at Hook Island in the Whitsundays, at Middle Island near Great Keppel, and at Green Island.

Reef walking is an additional option for nonswimmers. This is usually done on coral cays, such as Heron Island, where trained staff lead groups to whom they point out and describe the fascinating sea animals.

If you're willing to get wet, **snorkeling** provides an excellent means of seeing the wonders of the reef up close. Most resorts provide equipment and the small amount of instruction required. This isn't a tricky sport. If you can breathe, you can snorkel.

IMPRESSIONS

How can you convey the dreamlike fantasy of an undersea forest of seaweed or garden of anemones, the incredible population of tropical fishes, the coral-encrusted clams?
—ELSPETH HUXLEY

Scuba diving, on the other hand, takes a bit of practice and, done improperly, can be dangerous. Although some resorts offer a short course enabling you to do shallow dives, those who wish to dive often and deep should take instruction and get certified before leaving home. Of all the resorts, Heron caters best to divers.

If your resort has a plane and your budget can bear it, take a flight to the outer reef. It's a sight you won't soon forget.

May to October is the best time for a Great Barrier Reef holiday.

A Few Precautions

Coral cuts are nasty and can easily become infected. Resorts and dive-boat captains usually carry medication, but you might also want to have something on hand yourself. Thick-soled tennis shoes are recommended for reef walking, and some divers wear gloves for picking up thorny sea creatures.

Please **don't break off a piece of coral** to take home for a souvenir. The Great Barrier Reef Marine Park Authority prohibits doing so, for ecological reasons. The selfish sorts who do this are usually chagrined when their stolen treasure loses its color and starts to smell after being out of the water for a few hours.

You also need to be aware of the strength of **the sun** in these tropical latitudes. Reapply sunscreen each time you come out of the water and remember that your back is exposed to the sun when you're snorkeling. Many snorkelers wear a T-shirt in the water for this reason.

Box jellyfish, also known as stingers, inhabit the waters along the Northern Queensland coast from October through April or May. They are not a problem at islands that are far from shore, but close-in places such as Magnetic and Hinchinbrook islands are affected.

1. THE TROPICAL NORTH

VERY EXPENSIVE

ORPHEUS ISLAND

ORPHEUS ISLAND RESORT, 80km (50 miles) northeast of Townsville (Private Mail Bag 15, Townsville Mail Centre, Townsville, QLD 4810). Tel. 077/77-7377, or toll free 008/07-7167 in Australia. Fax 077/77-7533. 25 rms, 6 villas. A/C MINIBAR **Transportation:** The resort's seaplanes bring guests from Townsville (A$240/U.S. $192 per person round-trip) and Cairns (A$400/U.S. $320 per person round-trip).

$ **Rates** (including all meals and most facilities): A$315–A$410 (U.S. $252–U.S. $328) single terrace suite or studio; A$530–A$640 (U.S. $424–U.S. $512) double terrace suite or studio; A$150–A$180 (U.S. $120–U.S. $144) extra person; A$760 (U.S. $608) double bungalow; A$440 (U.S. $352) per person in 2-bedroom villa (minimum two, maximum four). No children under 15. AE, BC, CB, DC, MC, V.

A maximum of 74 guests can be accommodated at one time at this beautiful resort. The prohibition of television, newspapers, day-trippers, and children under 15 contributes to Orpheus's relaxed, peaceful, and private atmosphere, as do graceful palm trees, bougainvilleas, soft breezes, and a good beach. The environment is such that most folks don't bother to lock their doors, and nearly everyone eats breakfast and lunch in swimsuits or other casual attire. (In their welcome-to-Orpheus leaflet, the management requests that "swimsuits be the minimum dress.")

Once on Orpheus (11km/7 miles long, 1km/½ mile wide), guests can choose to lie by the pool, play tennis, bushwalk to lofty lookouts, have a picnic à deux on a secluded beach, snorkel over the excellent fringing reef, go windsurfing, sail a catamaran, waterski, or completely relax and do nothing at all. The open-air, native-style dining room serves all meals, and snorkeling gear, dinghies, Windsurfers, paddleskis, catamarans, and one introductory scuba lesson are available free of charge; an extra charge is made for trips to the outer reef, boat charters for deep-sea fishing, additional scuba-diving lessons, or drinks from the bar.

Those who come here usually figure out a way to extend their stay or to make a return visit. I quote from a letter I received recently from readers: "There are not enough superlative words to describe the quality of attention and abundance of great food."

Accommodations are in 23 comfortable beachfront units that feature queen-size beds draped with mosquito netting, sitting areas, ceramic-tile floors, ceiling fans, high open-beam ceilings, sound systems, and large showers. Two bungalows, slightly larger than the others, offer king-size bathtubs and private courtyard gardens. Chamber service is twice daily. The spacious two-bedroom villas, on a rise behind the other structures, offer two bathrooms and full kitchens.

Reservations in North America: Contact Utell International (tel. toll free 800/44-UTELL in the U.S., 800/387-8842 in Ontario and Québec, 800/668-1513 in the rest of Canada).

LIZARD ISLAND

LIZARD ISLAND RESORT, 241km (149 miles) north of Cairns (Private Mail Bag 40, Cairns, QLD 4870). Tel. 070/60-3999. Fax 070/60-3991. 30 rms, 2 suites. A/C MINIBAR TEL **Transportation:** Australian Regional Airlines provides transfers (A$280/U.S. $224 round-trip).

$ Rates (including all meals and most water sports): A$489 (U.S. $391.20) single; A$832 (U.S. $665.60) standard double; A$954 (U.S. $763.20) deluxe double. Children aged 6–14 receive a 50% discount. Dollarwise 7-night packages available. AE, BC, DC, MC, V.

The most northerly of Australia's island resorts, Lizard is a real tropical paradise. The surrounding fringing reef is a treasure trove of coral, beautiful fish, and giant clams; the Cod Hole, a well-known dive spot on the outer reef where huge friendly potato cod can be hand-fed and petted, is accessible (but not recommended for the fainthearted). There's a complete dive center and members of the dive team can make videos of your dive (for a fee). In addition to such year-round activities as snorkeling, scuba diving, tennis, waterskiing, secluded picnics, walking on the beach, and boating, fishing for black marlin is a popular pastime from September to December.

As on Orpheus, no television reminds guests of the real world. However, there are phones in the rooms, and there is a little less emphasis on privacy and get-away-from-it-all peace and quiet, so children over 6 are permitted. Delicious meals are served in a delightful open-air setting by staff who, like others on the island, are very attentive.

Since the resort is accustomed to catering to Americans, each of the spacious and tastefully decorated units has air conditioning, a king-size bed or two doubles, a tub/shower combination, and double sinks. Other indications that they like Yanks: pancakes on the breakfast menu and ice water on the table at meals.

Day-trips to the outer reef and fishing excursions cost extra, as do drinks at the bar and wines ordered from an extensive list. A trip to the outer reef for diving is A$110 (U.S. $88). Scuba tuition is A$100 (U.S. $80). A game-fishing boat with a crew who knows where to look for black marlin costs A$1,250 (U.S. $1,000) a day, which can be divided among four anglers.

Reservations in North America: Contact SO/PAC (tel. toll free 800/551-2012 in the U.S. and Can., 800/445-0190 in California) or Goway Travel (tel. 416/322-1034 in Toronto, toll free 800/663-9418 in B.C., 800/668-1427 in Ont. and Que., 800/663-9107 in Alta. and Sask., 800/387-8850 in Man. and the Maritimes).

BEDARRA ISLAND

BEDARRA BAY AND BEDARRA HIDEAWAY, 125km (78 miles) south of Cairns (Bedarra Hideaway or Bedarra Bay, Bedarra Island, via Townsville, QLD 4810). Tel. 070/68-8168 (Hideaway) or 070/68-8233

(Bedarra Bay). Fax 070/68-8552. 16 villas in each resort. A/C TV TEL
Transportation: Australian Regional Airlines flies to Dunk Island from Cairns
and Townsville (A$95/U.S. $76 Cairns-Dunk one-way) and transfers to Bedarra are
by launch.
$ Rates (including a 24-hour open bar, transfers from Dunk Island, most sports
facilities, and meals): A$606 (U.S. $484.80) single; A$1,064 (U.S. $851.20)
double. Seven-night packages available. No children under 15. AE, BC, DC, MC,
V.

The two resorts here, Bedarra Bay and Bedarra Hideaway, are situated at opposite
ends of the island, and are connected by a walking track. Each offers 16 split-level
villas with queen-size beds, sunken oval baths, and private balconies. The isle, only 1.5
kilometers (1 mile) from end to end, is a pocket of serene beaches and lush rain forest.
Because guests are guaranteed privacy, the resorts attract top political leaders,
business executives, and recognizable folks such as the Duchess of York and Princess
Caroline.

Both resorts have indoor-outdoor dining rooms, grand pianos, pools, spas, tennis
courts, Windsurfers, catamarans, paddleskis, snorkeling and fishing equipment, and
dinghies with outboard motors. Guests who wish to participate in motorized water
sports use the facilities at Dunk Island, which is 20 minutes away by launch. The only
additional charges are for cruises to the outer reef, game fishing, and other boat
charters. Only children over 15 are catered to (but the Duchess of York brought hers).

Like Lizard, Dunk, Brampton, and Great Keppel, Bedarra is owned by Australian
Airlines. The resorts on Bedarra are the most exclusive and provide the most security
and privacy.

Reservations in North America: Contact SO/PAC (tel. toll free 800/551-
2012 in the U.S. and Canada, 800/445-0190 in California) or Goway Travel (tel.
416/322-1034 in Toronto, toll free 800/663-9418 in B.C., 800/668-1427 in Ont. and
Que., 800/663-9107 in Alta. and Sask., 800/387-8850 in Man. and the Maritimes).

MODERATE
MAGNETIC ISLAND

More an island suburb than a resort island, Magnetic is just 8 kilometers (5 miles)
from Townsville. Two companies provide ferry service and conduct day tours:
Magnetic Marine (tel. 077/72-7122) and **Magnetic Link** (tel. 077/21-1913). The
trip takes 20 minutes and costs A$12 (U.S. $9.60) round-trip. Once you're on the
island, a regular bus service meets every ferry, as do the courtesy coaches from the
two resorts and four major budget accommodations.

Good bushland scenery and white sandy beaches are the biggest draws. Almost
75% of the island is a national park with 22 kilometers (13 miles) of walking tracks.
Many of these lead to hilltop lookouts and provide views of the 40-kilometer
(25-mile) scenic coastline. Sailing, horse riding, fishing, and parasailing are also
popular. Day-trippers can drive themselves around the island on a Mini Moke
(A$35/U.S. $28). The island's four residential areas are Picnic Bay, Nelly Bay,
Horseshoe Bay, and Arcardia. During the months of October through April, the
presence of marine stingers may preclude swimming, although Picnic Bay has a
swimming enclosure with a stinger net in place.

**LATITUDE 19 RESORT, Mandalay Ave., Nelly Bay, QLD 4819. Tel.
077/78-5200.** 73 rms, 16 suites. A/C TV TEL **Transportation:** Courtesy
transfer from ferry.
$ Rates: A$95 (U.S. $76) single or double; A$100–A$120 (U.S. $80–U.S. $96)
suite. Dollarwise packages which include meals are available. AE, BC, DC, MC, V.
If you decide to stay overnight, the guest rooms at Latitude 19 Resort have all the
modern amenities, as well as a swimming pool and tennis court.

DUNK ISLAND

Located just a short distance offshore of Mission Beach, roughly halfway between
Cairns and Townsville, this tropical continental island is 6 kilometers (3½ miles) long

and approximately 2 kilometers (1 mile) wide. Launches (45 min.) and water taxis (10 min.) bring people to Dunk from Mission Beach and Clump Point for A$16 (U.S. $12.80) round-trip. Dunk is popular with activity-loving day-trippers as well as overnight guests. (*Note:* Day-trippers can participate only in water sports and must pay for whatever equipment they use.) There's a national park camping area on the island. The best time to visit, in terms of the weather, is May through August (marine stingers sometimes preclude swimming at the beach September through April).

DUNK ISLAND RESORT, off Mission Beach. Tel. 070/68-8199. 135 rms. A/C MINIBAR TV TEL **Transportation:** Most guests arrive on one of the regularly scheduled flights of Australian Regional Airlines; there are also launches and water taxis from Mission Beach (see above).

$ Rates (including recreational facilities): A$183–A$265 (U.S. $146.40–U.S. $212) single; A$143–A$211 (U.S. $114.40–U.S. $168.80) per person based on double occupancy. Children 3–14 are half price. A$60 (U.S. $48) daily meal package for adults; A$30 (U.S. $24) daily meal package for children 3–14. Standby tariffs (purchased within 3 days of arrival) are much lower. AE, BC, DC, MC, V.

This resort can accommodate up to 380 people and, when full, is a beehive of activity. Sports and recreation options coordinated by the entertainment team in the Activities Booking Centre include trapshooting, horseback riding, golf (six holes), guided day and night rain-forest walks, birdwatching, scuba-diving courses, squash, tennis, cricket, volleyball, archery, visiting the island's farm (which supplies the resort with fresh milk and cream), snorkeling, and taking a cruise—the outer reef is the most popular destination. A trip to the outer reef on the *QuickCat* (tel. 68-7289) costs A$90 (U.S. $72) including snorkeling equipment, glass-bottom-boat ride, and buffet lunch. Kids are half price. Guests can also lie on the beach, swim in the resort's two lovely pools, or work out in the gym. There's live music nightly in the bar/lounge area and a disco Thursday through Saturday nights.

Special dinnertime and daytime children's activities for 3 to 12 year-olds are provided free of charge year round. Baby-sitting is available for a small fee. Accommodations are in three types of rooms, the nicest of which are the two-level beachfront units. Those guests who opt not to take the breakfast-lunch-and-dinner meal package can pay separately for meals in the Beachcomber Restaurant or dine in the Rainforest Brasserie, where tasty, reasonably priced meals are offered in a pleasant setting.

Reservations in North America: Contact SO/PAC (tel. toll free 800/551-2012 in the U.S. and Canada, 800/445-0190 in California) or Goway Travel (tel. 416/322-1034 in Toronto, toll free 800/663-9418 in B.C., 800/668-1427 in Ont. and Que., 800/663-9107 in Alta. and Sask., 800/387-8850 in Man. and the Maritimes).

GREEN ISLAND

✪ Just a stone's throw from Cairns, Green Island probably receives more day-trippers than any other isle in the vicinity of the Great Barrier Reef. However, it isn't just its proximity to a mainland city with an international airport that accounts for the great number of visitors. The island is a coral cay and, as part of the reef, provides several excellent coral-viewing opportunities. The Underwater Observatory has 22 windows from which you can watch the surrounding marine life, and glass-bottom boats make regular sorties. If you're willing to get wet, the snorkeling is excellent.

The 12-hectare (30-acre) island also offers the Barrier Reef Theatre, guided reef walks, fish feeding, and an outstanding collection of primitive art in Marineland Melanesia. If you're feeling lazy, stretch out under one of the coconut palms planted a century ago to provide food for shipwrecked sailors.

Great Adventures (tel. 070/51-0455) operates catamarans that make the trip from Cairns in 40 minutes for A$35 (U.S. $28) round-trip. In addition to day-trips to Green, Great Adventures offers a two-island excursion which includes both Green and Fitzroy, and a trip which goes to Green and the outer reef, and a trip which combines Green and Michaelmas Cay. For details see "Cairns: What to See and Do" in Chapter 9.

The resort on the island is temporarily closed and will reopen in late 1992.

Antipodes Tours, 9841 Airport Boulevard, Suite 820, Los Angeles, CA 90045 (tel. toll free 800/354-7471 in the U.S. and Canada) will handle reservations.

BUDGET
FITZROY ISLAND

FITZROY ISLAND RESORT, 24km (15 miles) east of Cairns (P.O. Box 2120, Cairns, QLD 4870). Tel. 070/51-9588. 8 bungalows, 128 bunkhouse beds. Bungalows: MINIBAR TV **Transportation:** Daily 45-minute trips from Cairns on Great Adventures (A$22/U.S. $17.60 round-trip).

$ Rates: A$20 (U.S. $16) bunkhouse bed; A$120 (U.S. $96) bungalow per person, based on double occupancy, including breakfast and dinner; A$10 (U.S. $8) camping facilities for two adults (A$2/U.S. $1.60 per additional adult, A$1/U.S. 80¢ per child). AE, BC, DC, MC, V.

Some of the best budget facilities in the area of the Great Barrier Reef are located on 259-hectare (640-acre) Fitzroy Island. The continental island with a coarse coral beach and modest fringing reef is known for its wooded mountains, dense rain forest, streams, and waterfalls. Bushwalking (hiking) is a popular pastime.

Accommodations are either in hostel-style bunkhouses, where 32 rooms contain four beds each and cooking and bathing facilities are communal, or in a handful of attractive two-bedroom beachfront bungalows with private baths, TVs, and small refrigerators. Each of these also has a ceiling fan, clock radio, tea- and coffee-making facilities, a hardwood floor, and porch with patio furniture. There are also campsites. To use them, obtain a camping permit from Great Adventures Visitor Centre, Wharf Street, Cairns, QLD 4870 (tel. 070/51-0455), before departure.

Island facilities include a restaurant, swimming pool, dive and snorkel equipment for rent, and glass-bottom boats.

Reservations in North America: Antipodes Tours, 9841 Airport Blvd., Suite 820, Los Angeles, CA 90045 (tel. toll free 800/354-7471 in the U.S. and Canada).

2. THE WHITSUNDAYS

VERY EXPENSIVE
HAYMAN ISLAND

HAYMAN ISLAND RESORT, 30km (18 miles) east of the Whitsunday Coast (Hayman, Great Barrier Reef, North Queensland, QLD 4801). Tel. 079/46-9100, or toll free 008/07-5175 in Australia. Fax 079/46-9410. 170 rms, 44 suites and penthouses. A/C MINIBAR TV TEL **Transportation:** Ansett Airlines flies to Hamilton Island from all major eastern Australian cities. Guests then transfer to Hayman on the resort's deluxe 35-meter (115-ft.) yacht *Sun Goddess* (A$200/U.S. $160 round-trip); champagne is served on board during the 50-minute trip, and registration is completed so that new arrivals can begin enjoying themselves as soon as they set foot on the island. The other access to Hayman Island is via water taxi from Airlie Beach.

$ Rates (including an extensive breakfast buffet): A$300–A$380 (U.S. $240–U.S. $304) double beachfront room; A$450 (U.S. $360) double Ocean View West room; A$510 (U.S. $408) double Ocean View East room; A$800 (U.S. $640) Ocean View West suite; A$950 (U.S. $760) Ocean View East suite; A$1,100–A$2,300 (U.S. $880–U.S. $1,840) penthouse. A$100 (U.S. $80) children 14–18 sharing with parents. Children under 14 stay free in parents' room. Second adjoining room occupied by children charged at 50%. Honeymoon packages available. AE, BC, DC, MC, V.

★ While the emphasis at the other deluxe resorts—Orpheus, Lizard, and Bedarra—is on the natural surroundings, Hayman Island Resort dazzles its guests with the best of man-made luxury. Instead of tropical-style accommodations and relaxed, open-air dining rooms, this hostelry offers world-class rooms and a choice of sophisticated restaurants. Even the standard accommodations have queen-size beds, video players, wall safes, water views, and 24-hour room service. Forty-four rooms remain from an earlier era, and these have showers only, but other quarters have glamorous marble bathrooms with every modern amenity.

The resort, which was completely redeveloped in 1987 at a cost of A$300 million (U.S. $240 million), covers a large area that includes six restaurants, an English club–style bar, an entertainment center, a covey of Rodeo Drive–type boutiques, a billiard room, a beautician, a hairdressing salon, an elaborate health club, tennis courts, and an absolutely breathtaking saltwater swimming lagoon that surrounds a large octagonal freshwater pool. This lagoon covers an area five times the size of an Olympic pool and is surrounded by an expanse of wooden deck, sprinkled with sumptuously comfortable sunbeds. Another oval freshwater pool is nearby. The beach was created by marine engineers, and the picturesque date palms were imported from a convent in Victoria.

Works of art, Burmese temple doors, and Persian carpets lend an air of quality and sophistication. In the formal French restaurant, La Fontaine, a pianist plays during dinner while a Louis XVI fountain bubbles away in the middle of the room.

Hayman has a nice beach and some good fringe coral; in addition, guests are transferred to nearby Langford Reef or to the outer reef for snorkeling and diving. Scuba instruction is available through the dive center. When the tide permits, catamaran sailing, parasailing, waterskiing, boardsailing, and other water sports are available. Nonpowered sports are free of charge. A children's activities program operates year round. September through November is the best time to visit. I can say with some assurance that Hayman is Australia's most luxurious resort.

Reservations in North America: Contact Ansett Airlines (tel. toll free 800/366-1300 in the U.S. and Canada), or Leading Hotels of the World (tel. 800/223-6800 in the U.S. and Canada).

MODERATE

DAYDREAM ISLAND

This 16-hectare (40-acre) Whitsunday isle, surrounded by beautiful turquoise water, is popular with both day-trippers and those wanting a longer holiday. While the beach is hard to walk on barefoot, the island's two large pools are very attractive and a plethora of water sports are offered. The Great Barrier Reef is accessible by boat, seaplane, and helicopter. Day-trippers' transportation to Daydream costs A$16 (U.S. $12.80) for adults and A$11 (U.S. $8.80) for children round-trip; once on the island day guests can use the pool at the southern end of the island, rent water-sports equipment, and play tennis. Several dining options are available, as well as showers and other amenities. Marine stingers could preclude swimming at the beach from December through April.

DAYDREAM ISLAND TRAVELODGE RESORT, located 4km (2½ miles) from Shute Harbour (Private Mail Bag 22, Mackay, QLD 4740). Tel. 079/48-8488, or toll free 008/07-5040 in Australia. Fax 079/48-8499. 301 rms, 2 suites. A/C TV TEL **Transportation:** Fly Australian Airlines or Eastwest Airlines to Proserpine, take a Sampsons bus to Shute Harbour (A$13/U.S. $10.40), and then catch a Whitsunday Water Taxi to the island (A$8/U.S. $6.40); or fly Ansett Airlines or Eastwest to Hamilton Island and get a water taxi (A$29/U.S. $23.20) from there.

$ Rates (including use of nonpowered water-sports equipment): A$143–A$158 (U.S. $114.40–U.S. $126.40) single; A$190–A$210 (U.S. $152–U.S. $168) double; A$270 (U.S. $216) larger double; A$1,000 (U.S. $800) 3-bedroom suite. A$50 (U.S. $40) adult meal plan; A$20–A$30 (U.S. $16–U.S. $24) child's meal plan. Children under 15 stay free in parents' room. Honeymoon and other packages available. Standby rates are much lower. No-smoking rooms available. AE, BC, DC, MC, V.

Daydream Island has been completely renovated since the first edition of *Frommer's Australia* was published in 1989. The previous tropical-style, slightly worn resort was dismantled and a new, modern 3-story property was built in its place. The process took 18 months and cost A$100 million (U.S. $80 million). The new Daydream opened in December 1990 and became a Travelodge in mid-1991.

Today guests are accommodated in spacious quarters, many of which have water views. Each has in-house movies, coffee- and tea-making facilities, radios, irons, ironing boards, and small refrigerators. The blocks of lodgings are surrounded by extensive picturesque lagoons and landscaping. A four-story atrium-style structure contains the Waterfall Café, Langford's Bar, the Entertainment Lounge, and Sunlovers Restaurant. There's live entertainment every night. Only overnight guests can use the large pool with swim-up bar at the north end of the island. The pool at the south end can be used by both day-trippers and house guests. At this end there are also several other dining options and a couple of shops. The two sides of the island are connected by a waterfront footpath and a path through the rain forest which covers the center.

Most water sports are at the south end of the island. Resort guests may use Windsurfers, sailboats, snorkeling equipment, spas, volleyball courts, and tennis courts free of charge. Child-care facilities are available free of charge during the day and the dinner hour. The J.D.s Club (Junior Dreamers) organizes activities for youngsters aged 5 to 14. A crèche (nursery) accommodates those under 5.

The Royal Suite and the Presidential Suite are large freestanding houses—about 2,500 square feet each—comprised of 3 bedrooms, full kitchens, 3½ bathrooms, walk-in closets, laundry facilities, and deluxe furnishings. They both have million-dollar views, too.

Reservations in North America: Contact SO/PAC (tel. toll free 800/551-2012 in the U.S. and Canada, 800/445-0190 in California, 800/235-8222 in Canada).

LINDEMAN ISLAND

As we go to press Australia's first **Club Med** is being built on Lindeman Island. Scheduled to open during 1992, it will house 500 guests and have an 18-hole golf course.

SOUTH MOLLE ISLAND

SOUTH MOLLE ISLAND RESORT, located 8km (5 miles) from Shute Harbour (Private Mail Bag 21, Mackay, QLD 4817). Tel. 079/46-9433, or toll free 008/07-5080 in Australia. Fax 079/46-9580. 202 rms. A/C MINIBAR TV TEL **Transportation:** Fly Australian Airlines or Eastwest Airlines to Proserpine, take a bus to Shute Harbour, and then catch a water taxi (A$15/U.S. $12) to the island; or fly Ansett Airlines or Eastwest to Hamilton Island and get a water taxi from there.

$ Rates (including all meals and nonpowered sports): A$155–A$190 (U.S. $124–U.S. $152) single; A$250–A$320 (U.S. $200–U.S. $256) double. Children 3–14 half price (under-3s are free). Dollarwise packages available. Standby rates are lower. AE, BC, DC, MC, V.

Another moderately priced Whitsunday island, South Molle has some modest fringe reef, as well as a nice beach, and there are excursions to the outer reef and other islands. In addition to the usual water sports, the island offers a two tennis courts, a 25-meter (27-yd.) pool, a gymnasium, a video-games room, and a nine-hole golf course (day-trippers must pay to use these facilities). After-dark activities include theme nights, talent quests, toad races, live bands, and a disco. Like Daydream, South Molle hasn't been promoted overseas and caters primarily to Australian families.

All the rooms are more than adequate. The Beachcomber rooms, each a separate bungalow with a balcony and a view, seem the best to me. The 30 Polynesian units, perched on their own hill with a good vista of surrounding clear blue water, are popular with honeymooners.

Reservations in North America: Contact Ansett Airlines (tel. 213/642-7487, or toll free 800/366-1300 in the U.S. and Canada).

3. THE SOUTHERN REEF ISLANDS

MODERATE
HERON ISLAND

HERON ISLAND RESORT, 72km (45 miles) northeast of Gladstone (c/o P&O Resorts, 10th floor, AGL House, 60 Edward St., Brisbane, QLD 4000). Tel. 07/210-0492, or toll free 008/77-7243 in Australia. Fax 07/210-0498. 109 rms and suites. **Transportation:** Lloyd Helicopter (A$313/U.S. $250.40 round-trip) or by sea (A$130/U.S. $104 round-trip) from Gladstone. Children are half price; under-3s, free. The boat takes 2 hours and the flight lasts ½ hour.

$ Rates (per person based on double occupancy and including all meals): A$115 (U.S. $92) lodge accommodation; A$178 (U.S. $142.40) Reef Suite; A$195 (U.S. $156) Heron Suite; A$225 (U.S. $180) Beach House or Point Suite. Children 3–14 half price; children under 3, free. A$45 (U.S. $36) single supplement (doesn't apply to lodge accommodation). Dollarwise dive packages available. AE, BC, DC, MC, V.

Heron Island is a true coral cay created by the Great Barrier Reef itself. The island is a mecca for nature-lovers who come to see the giant turtles that lay their eggs between late October and March, the humpback whales that skirt the island in the months of August and September, and the thousands of seabirds that make Heron their summer nesting spot. It is, of course, also immensely popular with dedicated divers who want to explore the surrounding coral and the incredible marine life that thrives in the area. The end result? The place has the atmosphere of a summer camp populated by self-indulgent adult kids who are having the time of their lives.

A national park within a marine national park, the waters surrounding the island are renowned for their abundance of protected sea life. It can be seen by reef walkers, snorkelers, or those who choose to explore in the semisubmersible. Heron and its surrounding reefs are generally considered to offer the best scuba diving in Australian waters. A team of helpful guides and instructors are available.

Accommodations for up to 300 guests are comfortable and more than adequate. The Beach House has a separate living room, a tub/shower combo, and wall-to-wall carpeting. The Point Suites are spacious and ideally located. Heron Suites and Reef Suites, with private facilities, are near the beach. Lodges, the best for thrifty travelers, can accommodate up to five people, and occupants use communal toilets and showers.

Good quality diving and snorkeling equipment is available for hire or purchase from the well-equipped dive shop on the island. One-week dive courses, starting on Sunday, are offered (A$299/U.S. $239.20) for those 15 years and over. Two of my favorite activities—sitting by the pool, which is exquisitely perched on the water's edge, and reef walking at low tide—are free of charge.

Reservations in North America: Contact P&O Resorts (tel. 408/685-8902, or toll free 800/225-9849).

GREAT KEPPEL ISLAND

Located 56 kilometers (35 miles) northeast of Rockhampton (or "Rocky," as the locals refer to it), Great Keppel Island offers a big resort with many activities, plus cabins and camping. **Australian Regional Airlines** makes the 15-minute flight from Rockhampton several times a day for A$142 (U.S. $113.60) round-trip, but most campers come to the island on the **MV *Victory*** (tel. 079/39-3144 or 079/27-2948), a 33-meter (109-ft.) catamaran that takes 25 minutes to get to the island from Rosslyn Bay, which is 44 kilometers (27 miles) from Rockhampton. It isn't unusual to see the campers, many of whom board the *Victory* bus at the Rockhampton YHA, off-loading a case of Fourex beer upon arrival at Great Keppel. Day-trippers also arrive on the *Victory* and are free to use the beach and one of the resort's pools.

GREAT KEPPEL ISLAND RESORT, P.O. Box 108, Rockhampton, QLD 4700. Tel. 079/39-1744. 190 rms, 2 suites. MINIBAR TV TEL **Transportation:** See above.

$ Rates (including most sports): A$148–A$187 (U.S. $118.40–U.S. $149.60) single; A$240–A$312 (U.S. $192–U.S. $249.60) double. Seven-night discount applies. A$55 (U.S. $44) adult meal package; A$25 (U.S. $20) child's meal package. AE, BC, DC, MC, V.

A plethora of activities and facilities is offered here: four swimming pools, two spas, 28 kilometers (17 miles) of sandy beaches, three tennis courts, two squash courts, a six-hole golf course; facilities for archery, cricket, volleyball, jumbo tennis, aerobics, catamaran sailing; sailboards, paddleskis, snorkeling gear, fishing gear, and boom-netting. And there are island cruises. The action continues on into the night with a disco, live shows, and parties.

Accommodations are in split-level Ocean View Villas with 250° views over the surrounding bays from their hillside location. Sixty of these were added during a recent A$14 million (U.S. $11.2 million) face-lift. Beachfront units also have a water view. Garden Rooms are the least expensive. Each room has its own balcony. The Keppel Kids Klub caters to children, and youngsters over 3 are supervised at a special children's dinner nightly. Additional charges are made for drinks, waterskiing, parasailing, scuba diving, and cruises to the outer Barrier Reef.

Reservations in North America: Contact SO/PAC (tel. toll free 800/551-2012 in the U.S. and Canada, 800/445-0190 in California) or Goway Travel (tel. 416/322-1034 in Toronto, toll free 800/663-9418 in B.C., 800/668-1427 in Ont. and Que., 800/663-9107 in Alta. and Sask., 800/387-8850 in Man. and the Maritimes).

WAPPARABURRA HAVEN, Great Keppel Island, QLD 4700. Tel. 079/39-1907. 12 cabins, a "tent village," and tent sites. **Transportation:** See above.

$ Rates: A$75 (U.S. $60) cabins; A$12 (U.S. $9.60) per person at the "tent village"; A$8 (U.S. $6.40) tent sites.

For travelers with thinner wallets, Wapparaburra Haven offers a dozen two-bedroom cabins with kitchenettes, as well as a "tent village" where large tents can be rented, and a BYO tent area for backpacking campers. **Keppel Campout,** another area, is limited to singles aged 18 to 35.

CHAPTER 11

THE NORTHERN TERRITORY

- **WHAT'S SPECIAL ABOUT THE NORTHERN TERRITORY**
- **1. DARWIN**
- **2. KAKADU NATIONAL PARK**
- **3. KATHERINE**
- **4. ALICE SPRINGS**
- **5. ULURU NATIONAL PARK [AYERS ROCK/MOUNT OLGA]**

Vast open spaces characterize the Northern Territory, which occupies one-sixth of the Australian continent but is home to less than 1% of the country's population. Neither the climate, the rainfall patterns, nor the quality of the soil encourages permanent settlement. As a result, 140,000 Territorians live in an area six times the size of Great Britain, or about the same size as the combined areas of Texas, Oregon, and California; lack of residents has kept the region from attaining statehood.

This is not to say that the Northern Territory is an unpopular destination. In fact, more than half a million tourists flock there every year in search of the outback made famous in *A Town Like Alice* and *Crocodile Dundee I* and *II*. Ayers Rock, the world's largest monolith, is the most popular single attraction, followed closely by Kakadu National Park (where the Crocodile Dundee movies were filmed). Many travelers feel this is the real Australia, and in a way they're right. The vast openness and harsh terrain found in the Northern Territory are unique to the island continent and are an important part of its projected image. On the other hand, most Aussies live in the green fringe of the country's perimeter.

The Northern Territory is divided into two distinct regions: the Top End and the Red Centre. Fascinating wildlife thrives in the lush, tropical environs of the Top End, which stretches from the Gulf of Carpentaria to Darwin and includes Kakadu, Arnhem Land, and Katherine. Most visitors expect to see crocodiles (and they do), but are surprised at the number and variety of water birds. The Red Centre, the area around Alice Springs and Ayers Rock, is characterized by dry reddish-brown earth, white-barked ghost gums, and clear azure-blue sky. The best time to visit either place is during "the dry," which runs from May through September. "The wet" brings monsoonal rains to the Top End from November through March, and road closures are common. During this same period, daytime temperatures can reach 36°C (97°F) in the Red Centre.

The main industry in the Northern Territory is mining. Gold, bauxite, manganese ore, copper, silver, iron ore, and uranium form the backbone of the economy. Tourism is second in importance, with beef cattle being third. (The land is so barren that 16 hectares [40 acres] are required to support one animal.)

The **Northern Territory Government Tourist Bureaus** found in Australian capital cities are the best sources of information. In North America, phone toll free 800/4-OUTBAC. While you're traveling in the Northern Territory, be sure to stop in at the **National Park Information Centres** located in Kakadu, Katherine Gorge, Simpson's Gap, and Uluru (Ayers Rock/Mount Olga). Rangers are on hand to answer

WHAT'S SPECIAL ABOUT THE NORTHERN TERRITORY

Ace Attractions
- Ayers Rock, the world's largest monolith.

Cultural Exposure
- The Northern Territory, offering many opportunities for learning about the Aboriginal culture.
- The outback way of life, including vast cattle stations, the Royal Flying Doctor Service, School of the Air, rugged individuals, and long distances between outposts of civilization.

Spectacular Scenery
- The Red Centre, a visual delight with its clear blue sky, rust-colored earth, and white-barked ghost gums.
- Katherine Gorge—gorgeous.

Film Locations
- *Crocodile Dundee I* and *II* in Kakadu National Park.

- *Quigley Down Under* near Alice Springs.
- *A Cry in the Dark* in Darwin.

Sacred Sites
- The Aboriginal cave paintings in Kakadu National Park and around Ayers Rock.

Native & Imported Fauna
- Crocodiles and waterbirds in the Top End.
- Camels roaming the Red Centre.

Activities
- Taking a camel to dinner or spending a night with a camel in Alice Springs.
- Sitting around a camp fire and enjoying a bush dinner near Alice Springs.

Shopping
- Aboriginal art and crafts at Alice Springs.

---

questions and distribute literature on the parks; films and displays enhance understanding of their historical and geological significance, as well as develop an appreciation for the local flora and fauna. The Aboriginal cave paintings at Kakadu and Uluru are the most important in the country, and Katherine has a gorgeous gorge.

SEEING THE NORTHERN TERRITORY

The Northern Territory has been self-governing since 1978, and transportation within the region has improved markedly during this time. The Stuart Highway, which follows the track first blazed by explorer John McDouall Stuart in 1861 and 1862, was finally sealed (paved) in 1987 all the way from Adelaide to Darwin; main centers of population are located along this spine. However, motorists who take this route need to remember that petrol stations are few and far between and that wandering animals (cattle, water buffalo, and sometimes camels) make night driving very hazardous. Road trains, up to three semi-truck trailers linked together, present another driving challenge. Remember, always carry plenty of water, and if you have car trouble, stay put. Don't attempt to walk to get help.

Alice Springs, located in the geographical center of the country, has regular train service. In 1980 the existing railway line, which routinely flooded out during the rainy season, was replaced with all-weather track. Both Alice Springs and Darwin are served by major airlines and coach companies.

Distances in the Northern Territory are significant: The two main centers, Darwin and Alice Springs, are 1,500 kilometers (930 miles) apart. Because of this, and the general lack of towns with tourist facilities, many visitors participate in tours that range from a day or two to a week or more. The tourist offices mentioned above have a good selection of brochures that describe these excursions. If you decide to go it alone, keep in mind that permits are required for entering Aboriginal reserves.

1. DARWIN

1,500km (930 miles) N of Alice Springs

GETTING THERE   By Plane   Flights to Darwin cost A$350 to A$439 (U.S. $280 to U.S. $351.20) from Sydney, A$259 to A$324 (U.S. $207.20 to U.S. $259.20) from Townsville, and A$197 to A$248 (U.S. $157.60 to U.S. $198.40) from Alice Springs on the Australian Airlines Air Pass fare. Darwin is served by several international carriers, including Qantas, Malaysia Airlines, Singapore Airlines, Garuda, Royal Brunei, and Merparti Airlines. The airport is 7 kilometers (4 miles) from the city center. A shuttle bus (tel. 41-1656) meets most flights (A$5/U.S. $4); a taxi to the city from the airport costs about A$9 (U.S. $7.20).

By Train   There is no train service to Darwin.

By Bus   If you take a bus, your ticket from Alice Springs will cost A$153 (U.S. $122.40) and the trip will take about 17 to 20 hours, depending on whether or not you get the express. Townsville to Darwin costs A$234 (U.S. $187.20) and takes 33 hours. Greyhound, Pioneer, and Bus Australia cover these routes.

By Car   Refer to "Seeing the Northern Territory," above. The **Automobile Association of the Northern Territory** (AANT) provides an emergency road service and free maps (tel. 81-3837).

ESSENTIALS   Information   Tourist information is dispensed at the **Northern Territory Government Tourist Bureau,** 31 Smith Street Mall, Darwin, NT 0801 (tel. 089/81-6611), and at the airport. The **area code** is 089.

Orientation   The city sits at the end of a peninsula and so is surrounded by water on three sides. Extensive mangrove swamps, a busy port, and sandy beaches are all nearby. In the downtown area, Smith Street is the main thoroughfare.

GETTING AROUND   By Bus or Taxi   The city bus system operates Monday through Saturday. The main city terminus is in Harry Chan Avenue (near the Bennett Street end of the Smith Street Mall). For information call 89-6540.

The Tour Tub provides another transport option. The bus makes the rounds of various Darwin attractions daily from 9am to 4pm. The cost is A$12.50 (U.S. $10) for an all-day ticket.

The main taxi rank is at the end of the Smith Street Mall in Knuckey Street (tel. 81-8777).

The capital of the Northern Territory, named after English naturalist Charles Darwin, has struggled for survival ever since its founding in 1869. At first, development was hampered by the settlement's isolation. Later, during World War II, the city was damaged by Japanese bombs. And, on Christmas Eve in 1974, Darwin was flattened by cyclone Tracy. In spite of these difficulties, the community has managed to prevail and today is a busy metropolis with 73,000 residents. Buildings in the city center are modern, having been built after the 1974 disaster. Prosperity is based primarily on the area's mineral wealth.

Darwin is one of Australia's most ethnically mixed places, with inhabitants from 65 or so different racial and cultural backgrounds. Chinese have historically constituted part of the population, and today they are joined by quantities of Southeast Asians, Timorese, Greeks, Italians, New Zealanders, and others.

The hot, humid climate creates a casual life-style. The walking shorts and long socks worn by men during the summer in southern cities are year-round gear in Darwin, and things tend to move at a tropical, relaxed pace.

While Darwin is an important commercial and governmental hub, its primary

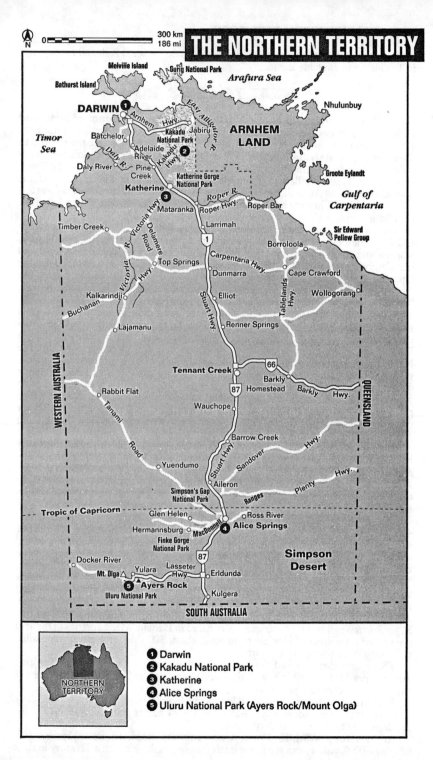

THE NORTHERN TERRITORY

0 — 300 km
186 mi

N

Melville Island
Bathurst Island
Gurig National Park
Arafura Sea

DARWIN ❶
Arnhem Hwy.
Batchelor
Adelaide River
Daly River
Daly R.
Pine Creek
Kakadu National Park ❷
Jabiru
East Alligator R.
ARNHEM LAND
Nhulunbuy

Timor Sea

Katherine ❸
Mataranka
Katherine Gorge National Park
Roper R.
Roper Hwy.
Roper Bar
Groote Eylandt
Gulf of Carpentaria

Timber Creek
Larrimah
❶
Borroloola
Sir Edward Pellew Group

Victoria Hwy.
Delamere Road
Top Springs
Carpentaria Hwy.
Dunmarra
Cape Crawford
Wollogorang

Kalkarindji
Buchanan
Elliot
Tablelands Hwy.

Lajamanu
Renner Springs

WESTERN AUSTRALIA

Tennant Creek
❻❻
Barkly Homestead
Barkly Hwy.

QUEENSLAND

Rabbit Flat
Tanami Road
❽❼
Wauchope

Yuendumu
Barrow Creek
Sandover Hwy.
Plenty Hwy.

Aileron
Ranges

Simpson's Gap National Park

Tropic of Capricorn
Glen Helen
Ross River
Hermannsburg
MacDonnell
❹ **Alice Springs**
Finke Gorge National Park

Simpson Desert

Docker River
Mt. Olga
Yulara
Lasseter Hwy.
Erldunda
❺ **Ayers Rock**
Uluru National Park
Kulgera

SOUTH AUSTRALIA

NORTHERN TERRITORY

❶ Darwin
❷ Kakadu National Park
❸ Katherine
❹ Alice Springs
❺ Uluru National Park (Ayers Rock/Mount Olga)

interest to tourists is as a jumping-off point to Kakadu National Park and for day-trips to Bathurst and Melville islands.

WHAT TO SEE & DO

Darwin has botanical gardens, the **Northern Territory Museum of Arts and Sciences,** and **Fannie Bay Gaol** (a former, incredibly primitive jail in use until 1972 and now a museum), but the most interesting thing to do is take the day-trip to **Bathurst and Melville islands.** These two places, which lie 80 kilometers (50 miles) offshore, are the home of a group of Aboriginal people known as the Tiwis. Apart from Tasmania, Bathurst and Melville are the largest islands lying off the mainland coast of Australia and together comprise some 8,000 square kilometers (3,089 sq. miles). They are separated by Apsley Strait, which is less than a kilometer wide in most places.

The day tour starts with a 20-minute flight to Bathurst Island on an Air North DC-3 Gooney Bird. Upon arrival, visitors are transferred to the village of **Nguiu,** where about 1,200 Aborigines live. A mission station was established here in 1911 and the Catholic church dates from 1941. When these islands were bombed by the Japanese in 1942, a Tiwi captured the first downed pilot. As the story goes, the Aborigine was a great fan of Western movies, and when he took his prisoner he said, "Stick 'em up, pardner, and put your hands on yer head."

After a tour of the community, tour members have a chance to shop for Tiwi Pima wood carvings, Bima Wear clothing, and Tiwi Design screen printing. The Tiwis support themselves with these handcrafts, and prices here are much lower than in Darwin shops. At morning tea, local women demonstrate weaving. The distance between Bathurst and Melville islands isn't great, but the crossing is made by dinghies with outboard motors because the waters are rife with crocodiles and deadly marine stingers. Since lunch is enjoyed next to a freshwater spring, it's a good idea to bring your swimsuit. Also handy for this trip: hat, sunglasses, camera, and sunscreen. The price of the excursion is A$220 (U.S. $176) for adults and A$165 (U.S. $132) for children and includes transportation, morning and afternoon tea, lunch, and Aboriginal land council entry fees.

The full-day tour operates April through November Monday through Saturday. A half-day tour, which includes only Bathurst Island, costs A$140 (U.S. $112) for adults and A$90 (U.S. $72) for children and operates Wednesday and Friday, March through November. For information, contact **Tiwi Tours** (tel. 089/81-5144 or 81-5115). In the U.S., Tiwi Tours is represented by **ATS/Sprint** (tel. toll free 800/423-2880, 800/232-2121 in California).

The **Darwin Aviation Museum,** on the Stuart Highway, Winnellie (tel. 47-2145), is sure to make ex-servicemen and -women feel nostalgic. The major exhibit is a B-52 on permanent loan from the U.S. Air Force. These aircraft flew in and out of Darwin from Guam and the United States from 1982 to 1990. This plane is one of only two B-52s on display outside of the U.S.—the other is in Hendon, England.

In addition, many exhibits deal with an earlier period of history. Many Americans were based in Darwin during World War II, and General MacArthur first entered Australia when he landed at Batchelor Air Field, an RAAF base, near Darwin. From 1942 to 1945 Catalinas, Liberators, War Hawks, P38 Lightnings, Mitchells, and B17 Super Fortresses flown by Americans were based in Darwin. Many airstrips in the area are named after downed U.S. pilots. In total, about 500 U.S. servicemen were killed defending or attacking from Australia.

The planes that attacked Darwin in 1942 were off the same carrier fleet that attacked Pearl Harbor. "Links with the United States are fairly solid," the president of the aviation museum explained.

The aviation museum, located 10 kilometers (6 miles) from the city, is open daily from 10am to 4pm. Admission is A$5 (U.S. $4) for adults and A$2 (U.S. $1.60) for children. Get there on a no. 5 or 8 bus.

At **Territory Wildlife Park,** Cox Peninsula Road, in Berry Springs (tel. 089/88-6000), visitors can see the animals that live in the Northern Territory in their natural habitats. Cars are left at the entrance, and an open-air shuttle takes people between enclosures. The park is spread over 400 hectares (1,000 acres), 40 minutes south of Darwin. Admission costs A$8 (U.S. $6.40) for adults; A$4 (U.S. $3.20) for children. The park is open daily from 9am to 4pm; closed Christmas Day and Good Friday. Shuker Bus Services (tel. 88-6266) provides transportation/entrance-fee packages for A$26 (U.S. $20.80) for adults and A$13 (U.S. $10.40) for children. These operate Monday through Friday, or on weekends as required.

SHOPPING

The **City Centre Smith Street Mall** is the main shopping area in Darwin. Most stores are open Monday through Wednesday and Friday from 9am to 5:30pm, Thursday from 9am to 9pm, and Saturday from 9am to noon.

Raintree Gallery, 14 Knuckey Street, sells Aboriginal craft items, as do the **Aboriginal Artists Gallery,** 153 Mitchell Street, and the **Crafts Council of the Northern Territory,** Conacher Street, Bullocky Point, near the Museum of Arts and Sciences. The **National Trust Shop,** Burnett House, 52 Temira Crescent, Myilly Point (tel. 81-2848), sells quality Australian books and gifts. It's open Monday through Friday from 10am to 3pm, except when it's closed from Christmas to New Year's.

WHERE TO STAY

All Northern Territory accommodation is subject to a 5% Tourism Marketing Duty.

EXPENSIVE

DIAMOND BEACH HOTEL CASINO, Gilruth Ave., Mindil Beach, Darwin, NT 0800. Tel. 089/46-2666. 106 rms and suites. A/C MINIBAR TV TEL
Transportation: Taxi, Tour Tub, or city bus route 6.
$ Rates: A$210 (U.S. $168) single or double; A$240 (U.S. $192) suite. AE, BC, DC, MC, V. **Parking:** Free.
This bold, contemporary, pyramid-shaped building is located on the beach about 2 kilometers (1 mile) outside town. The casino, offering all the standard games from blackjack to baccarat, is popular with groups of high-rolling Asian gamblers.

The three-story property's rooms have tub/shower combos, videos, 24-hour room service, and the other amenities you'd expect in this price range. While the presence of stingers precludes swimming at the beach much of the year, the pool, spa, sauna, gym, and tennis courts can be used year round.

SHERATON DARWIN HOTEL, 32 Mitchell St., Darwin, NT 0800. Tel. 089/82-0000, or toll free 008/89-1107 in Australia. Fax 089/81-1765. 233 rms, 12 suites. A/C MINIBAR TV TEL
$ Rates: A$205 (U.S. $164) single or double; A$245 (U.S. $196) executive floor (including breakfast); A$500 (U.S. $400) suite; A$45 (U.S. $36) extra person. Children under 17 stay free in parents' room. Tariffs are 15% higher June–Sept. No-smoking rooms available. AE, BC, DC, MC, V. **Parking:** Free.
This centrally located hotel, which opened in 1986, has 12 floors, but a somewhat confusing system of numbering them (to keep the computers happy). This little vagary aside, the hostelry has a lovely polished marble floor in the lobby, and the public rooms are very "swept up," as they say down under (meaning elegant or fancy).

All quarters have clock radios, bathrobes, hairdryers, tea- and coffee-making facilities, small refrigerators, in-room movies, either king-size or double beds, and free daily newspapers.

Mitchell's Coffee Shop is open daily from 6:30am to 11pm, and the popular Pub Bar is open from 10am to midnight; this latter spot is a friendly place for a light lunch or a drink or two. The Lobby Bar has a pianist most nights. The fine-dining venue, the

Flinders Room, is closed during the wet season. Room service is available 24 hours a day. Five rooms are equipped for handicapped travelers.

Guests can use the outdoor pool, gym, spa, business center, and hair salon.

MODERATE

ATRIUM HOTEL, corner of Peel St. and Esplanade, Darwin, NT 0800. Tel. 089/41-0755, or toll free 008/89-1102 in Australia. Fax 089/81-9025. 120 rms, 20 suites. A/C MINIBAR TV TEL

$ Rates: A$165 (U.S. $132) single studio; A$175 (U.S. $140) double studio; A$170 (U.S. $136) single 1-bedroom; A$180 (U.S. $144) double 1-bedroom; A$205 (U.S. $164) single or double 2-bedroom; A$195 (U.S. $156) single or double executive room; A$215 (U.S. $172) single or double deluxe suite; A$20 (U.S. $16) extra person. Children under 14 stay free in parents' room. Weekly rates are lower. Dollarwise packages in combination with the Red Centre Hotel at Ayers Rock. AE, BC, DC, MC, V. **Parking:** Free.

Located on the waterfront, overlooking Bougainvillea Park and the Timor Sea, this six-story hotel is just a 5-minute walk from the central business district. The Atrium offers bright, clean accommodations at affordable prices. Each room has its own kitchenette, ceiling fan, queen-size bed, contemporary furnishings, in-house videos, and clock radio. Half the quarters have harbor views. Executive and deluxe rooms have spa baths. Three rooms are equipped for handicapped travelers.

There's a nice pool and spa, as well as a children's wading pool, fitness room, self-service laundry, and barbecue area. The Jabiru Cocktail Bar is a popular meeting place; meals are served in Corellas Restaurant and Castaways, which offers al fresco dining. The dominant feature of the property is an attractive atrium—complete with pools, fountains, and tropical foliage—rising from the lobby floor. Room service is available 24 hours a day.

HOTEL DARWIN, 10 Herbert St., Darwin, NT 0800. Tel. 089/81-9211. 69 rms, 1 suite. A/C TV TEL

$ Rates: Dry season, A$65 (U.S. $52) single, A$95 (U.S. $76) double; A$11 (U.S. $8.80) extra person. Lower rates in the wet season. AE, BC, DC, MC, V. **Parking:** Free.

I like the centrally located Hotel Darwin because it's over 100 years old and is steeped in history and tropical ambience—not unlike that of the Raffles Hotel in Singapore. Opened as the Palmerston Club Hotel in 1883, it survived the 1942 bombing of Darwin but burned down later that year when soldiers rioted over the cutting of their beer ration. Quickly rebuilt, the sturdy two-story building was a command center in World War II and again during cyclone Tracy. Today the Green Room, the large central main bar where trade winds blow in through oversize sliding-glass doors, is often the site of reunions of U.S. service personnel who were there during the war. The management assured me that these returnees "don't notice many changes." (The hotel's character has not escaped Hollywood's attention. Part of the movie *Evil Angels*—called *A Cry in the Dark* in the U.S.—was filmed on the premises.)

In addition to the Green Room, there's a nice watering hole called the Kakadu Bar. (The public bar, Hot and Cold, is best avoided due to the rowdy locals who drink there.) Banjo's, the restaurant, is cooled by automatic pankas—oscillating fabric-covered panels hanging from the ceiling. There's a pool on the premises.

MARRAKAI APARTMENTS, 93 Smith St., Darwin, NT 0800. Tel. 089/ 82-3711, or toll free 008/89-1100 in Australia. 23 2-bedroom apartments. A/C TV TEL

$ Rates: A$185–A$215 (U.S. $148–U.S. $172) per apartment. AE, BC, DC, MC, V. **Parking:** Free.

The centrally located Marrakai Apartments are the ideal spot for folks who like to look after themselves. The 16-story property has spacious two-bedroom apartments that sleep up to four people. One room has a queen-size bed and the other has twins.

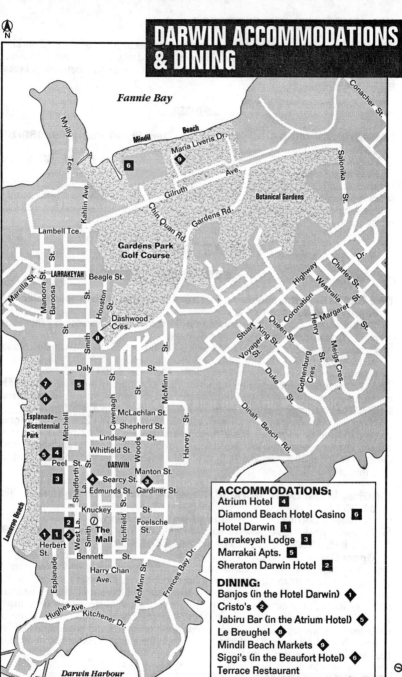

DARWIN ACCOMMODATIONS & DINING

N

Fannie Bay

Mindil **Beach**

Maria Liveris Dr.

Ave.

Gilruth

Botanical Gardens

Chin Quan Rd.

Gardens Rd.

Salonika St.

Conacher St.

Myilly Tce.

Kahlin Ave.

Lambell Tce.

Gardens Park Golf Course

LARRAKEYAH

Beagle St.

Marella St.

Manora St.

Baroosa St.

Houston St.

Dashwood Cres.

Smith St.

Daly St.

Cavenagh St.

McLachlan St.

Shepherd St.

Lindsay St.

Whitfield St.

DARWIN

Peel St.

Shadforth St.

Mitchell St.

Esplanade–Bicentennial Park

Lameroo Beach

Herbert St.

West La.

Smith St.

The Mall

Bennett St.

Harry Chan Ave.

Esplanade

Hughes Ave.

Kitchener Dr.

Searcy St.

Edmunds St.

Manton St.

Gardiner St.

Knuckey St.

Itchfield St.

Foelsche St.

Woods St.

McMinn St.

Harvey St.

Frances Bay Dr.

Stuart Highway

Coronation Dr.

Charles St.

Westralia St.

Queen St.

King St.

Voyager St.

Henry St.

Margaret St.

Gothenburg Cres.

Meigs Cres.

Duke St.

Dinah Beach Rd.

Darwin Harbour

Frances Bay

ACCOMMODATIONS:
Atrium Hotel **4**
Diamond Beach Hotel Casino **6**
Hotel Darwin **1**
Larrakeyah Lodge **3**
Marrakai Apts. **5**
Sheraton Darwin Hotel **2**

DINING:
Banjos (in the Hotel Darwin) **1**
Cristo's **2**
Jabiru Bar (in the Atrium Hotel) **5**
Le Breughel **8**
Mindil Beach Markets **9**
Siggi's (in the Beaufort Hotel) **6**
Terrace Restaurant
    (in the Travelodge Hotel) **7**
The Gourmet Deli **4**
Uncle John's Cabins **3**

Information ⓘ

The Marrakai offers a pool and spa, as well as a barbecue area and covered parking. All apartments have fully equipped kitchens with dishwashers, laundry facilities, balconies, and two bathrooms with tub/shower combinations. Room-service breakfasts are available.

BUDGET

LARRAKEYAH LODGE, 50 Mitchell St., Darwin, NT 0800. Tel. 089/81-7550 or 81-2933. Fax 089/81-1908. 56 rms (none with bath). A/C
$ Rates: A$37 (U.S. $29.60) single; A$52 (U.S. $41.60) double. AE, BC, MC, V.
Parking: Free.

Quarters in this centrally located guesthouse offer coffee- and tea-making facilities, small refrigerators, and hand basins. A comfortable television lounge, laundry facilities, a pool, and barbecue area are shared with other guests. Breakfast and light meals are available from a café on the premises.

WHERE TO DINE

EXPENSIVE

THE BEAGLE, in the Northern Territory Museum of Arts and Sciences, Fannie Bay. Tel. 81-7791.
   Cuisine: SEAFOOD. **Reservations:** Recommended, especially Thurs–Sat night. **Transportation:** Bus route 6 or taxi.
$ Prices: Appetizers A$8.50–A$15.50 (U.S. $6.80–U.S. $12.40); main courses A$15–A$25 (U.S. $12–U.S. $20). AE, BC, DC, MC, V.
   Open: Lunch Mon–Fri noon–2pm; dinner Mon–Sat 6:30–10pm.

This is a great place for lunch with a water view or dinner with a sunset view. The menu leans heavily toward seafood, which seems appropriate in this waterfront setting. The restaurant is named after the historic sailing ship HMS *Beagle*.

You might like to try oysters Kilpatrick, squid Vernon, or Top End crocodile for an entrée, and follow with Daly River barramundi or Beagle's trout platter as a main course. Drover peppered sirloin, and buffalo Arnhem are typical meat dishes. Lunch dishes cost about 20% less, and budgeteers can order the ploughman's lunch which sells for A$7.50 (U.S. $6).

SIGGI'S, in the Beaufort Hotel, Beaufort Centre, The Esplanade. Tel. 82-9911.
   Cuisine: CONTINENTAL. **Reservations:** Recommended.
$ Prices: Appetizers A$6–A$19 (U.S. $4.80–U.S. $15.20); main courses A$19–A$28 (U.S. $15.20–U.S. $22.40). AE, BC, DC, MC, V.
   Open: Dinner Tues–Sat 7–11pm.

Since it opened in 1986, this has become one of Darwin's most upmarket eateries. Dining takes place in an intimate atmosphere and waiters use silver service. The à la carte menu is changed monthly according to season and local availability. The menu and wine list are both extensive, and the food is very good. Entrées include marinated salmon and capsicums, duck terrine, and oysters gratin. Sample main courses: paupiettes of coral trout and spinach, open ravioli of lobster and bug, marinated filet of lamb. Next door to the Beaufort Centre is a performing arts complex that includes bars and conference facilities.

TERRACE RESTAURANT, in the Travelodge Hotel, 122 The Esplanade. Tel. 81-5388.
   Cuisine: INTERNATIONAL. **Reservations:** Recommended.
$ Prices: Appetizers A$6.50–A$8.50 (U.S. $5.20–U.S. $6.80); main courses A$16–A$19 (U.S. $12.80–U.S. $15.20); breakfast buffet A$15.50 (U.S. $12.40). AE, BC, DC, MC, V.

Open: Breakfast daily 6:30–10am; lunch Mon–Fri noon–2:30pm; dinner daily 6–10pm.

The Terrace offers an interesting menu. Appetizers include salmon royale, chicken liver gâteau, and chicken satay Indonesia. Main courses range from poached rainbow trout to New York–cut steak. Some low-cholesterol dishes are offered. The decor, revolving around a Kakadu theme, includes works by local Aboriginal artist Harold Thomas. (Be sure to notice the wonderful Harold Thomas mural behind the reception desk in the lobby before you ascend to the Terrace.) Live entertainment is provided 2 nights a week.

MODERATE

BANJO'S, in the Hotel Darwin, 10 Herbert St. Tel. 81-9211.
Cuisine: LOCAL SPECIALTIES. **Reservations:** Optional.
$ Prices: Appetizers A$6–A$10 (U.S. $4.80–U.S. $8); main courses A$12–A$18 (U.S. $9.60–U.S. $14.40). AE, BC, DC, MC, V.
Open: Dinner daily 7–9pm during "the dry." **Closed:** Sun–Mon during "the wet."

Banjo's has a pleasant colonial atmosphere and some unusual menu choices. Camembert Arnhem is a half round of Camembert topped with kiwi fruit and baked in a puff pastry served as an entrée. Beagle Gulf satay and peanut sambal, skewers of beef marinated in cumin and coriander served with fresh peanut sauce, reflects the ethnic influence so evident in Darwin. Mignon of buffalo Marrakai is Northern Territory buffalo filet served with a port wine and mushroom sauce.

The restaurant is named after the famous bush poet Banjo Patterson, and a quote from him appears on the menu: "And the man who goes to the Territory always has a hankering to get back there. Someday it will be civilized and spoilt, but up to the present it has triumphantly overthrown all who have attempted to improve it. It is still 'the Territory.' Long may it wave."

LE BREUGHEL, 6 Dashwood Crescent. Tel. 81-2025.
Cuisine: INTERNATIONAL. **Reservations:** Recommended during "the dry."
$ Prices: Appetizers A$8–A$17 (U.S. $6.40–U.S. $13.60); main courses A$14.50–A$18.50 (U.S. $11.60–U.S. $14.80). AE, BC, MC, V.
Open: Dinner Tues–Sun 6:30–9:30pm.

Le Breughel is a casual restaurant located on the edge of the central business district. The emphasis is on local seafood, such as scallops, calamari, and gulf bugs. Popular main courses include barramundi Creole, whole baby squid, médaillons of buffalo, and Breughel's house curry. The restaurant has a pleasant cocktail lounge for a predinner drink.

UNCLE JOHN'S CABINS, 4 Gardiner St. Tel. 81-3358.
Cuisine: SEAFOOD & OTHER TERRITORY SPECIALTIES. **Reservations:** Advisable.
$ Prices: Appetizers A$8.50–A$15 (U.S. $6.80–U.S. $12); main courses A$10–A$20 (U.S. $8–U.S. $16). AE, BC, MC, V.
Open: Dinner 6 nights a week from 7pm during "the dry" (closed either Thurs or Sun). **Closed:** Dec–Apr.

At this popular open-air seafood spot the blackboard menu changes daily to include the catch of the day. Other specialties include kangaroo, crocodile, buffalo, steak, chicken, ribs, and rabbit. This eatery is casual and centrally located. Drinks are served in the Railcar Bar.

READERS RECOMMEND

Cristo's, Mitchell St., next to the Sheraton Darwin Hotel (tel. 81-8658). —"The food was superb and the service was excellent and friendly. I think it is owned by a Greek-Australian."—Terence Fu, New York, N.Y.

BUDGET

You'd be wise to plan your trip so that you land in Darwin on a Thursday between May and October. That way you can head out to the ✪❺ **Mindil Beach Markets** and enjoy a wide variety of ethnic food at rock-bottom prices. During a recent visit I noted food stalls selling Thai, Philippine, Malaysian, Chinese, Greek, Indonesian, Laotian, Vietnamese, Portuguese, and Italian cuisine. How's that for variety? Everything I tasted was very good, and nothing was over A$4 (U.S. $3.20). This Thursday-night event is popular with the locals, some of whom bring their own tables and chairs and set them up near the beach. Entertainment ranges from a Scottish Highland band to folk guitarists. BYO if you want beer or wine with your meal. The Tour Tub provides transportation from 5:30pm (A$2/U.S. $1.60 each way) or take a public bus, route 6.

The **Gourmet Deli,** corner of Smith and Edmunds streets (tel. 41-2744), is a great place to pick up picnic supplies. Sandwiches cost A$3 to A$4 (U.S. $2.40 to U.S. $3.20). This little shop is open from 7am to 5:30pm Monday through Friday and from 8am to 2pm on Saturday. No credit cards.

Another inexpensive place to eat is the **Jabiru Bar** in the Atrium Hotel, on the Esplanade (tel. 41-0755), where a carvery lunch is offered Monday through Saturday from noon to 2pm. For only A$4.50 (U.S. $3.60) you'll have a choice of a roast meal with salad or a main course such as lasagne or curry with rice.

EVENING ENTERTAINMENT

Tickets for performances at the **Darwin Performing Arts Centre,** 93 Mitchell Street, can be obtained by phoning 81-9022.

If you're feeling lucky, the **Diamond Beach Casino** (tel. 81-7755) is open daily from noon until the wee hours. Their dress code prohibits the wearing of shorts, thongs, denim, and running shoes.

The ✪ **Hotel Darwin,** Herbert Street (tel. 81-9211), has entertainment in the Green Room lounge bar several nights a week and a disco in the Kakadu Bar on Friday and Saturday nights (no cover charge). In the Green Room a sign reads THE MINIMUM DRESS FOR THIS ROOM WILL BE SHIRT, SHORTS, SHOES, AND LONG SOCKS. I love the tropical atmosphere of the Green Room. It feels like Humphrey Bogart must be right around the corner. The Green Room closes at midnight.

The **Jabiru Bar** in the Atrium Hotel, on the Esplanade, is another great place for a drink. This popular watering hole is on the ground level of the hotel's six-story atrium, and the picturesque setting includes lots of tropical plants, flowing water, and decorative pools. The crowd includes Darwin's young professionals and overseas visitors. The Jabiru Bar is open daily 10am to midnight. A Fosters draft costs A$2 (U.S. $1.60). A can of beer will set you back A$2.80 (U.S. $2.24).

A nightclub, the **Beachcomber Nightspot,** is located in the Top End Frontier Hotel, at the corner of Daly and Mitchell streets (tel. 81-6511). The clientele is 18 to 35—"fun-loving party types." No cover charge. Open Wednesday through Sunday from 8pm 'til very late in "the dry," 9pm to 2am in "the wet." Draft beer costs A$2.50 (U.S. $2). The **Brewery Bar,** also in the Top End Frontier Hotel, is open every night and offers live entertainment and dancing. The crowd here is a little older, maybe 18 to 40. A draft costs A$2.10 (U.S. $1.70).

AN EASY EXCURSION

The **Cobourg Peninsula,** 150 nautical miles northeast of Darwin in Arnhem Land, is basically unchanged since last century when the British established a settlement on the coast. Much of the land is unexplored; Banteng cattle brought here in 1839 roam wild, as do Sambar deer, water buffalo, wild pigs, and Timor ponies. Paperbark swamps, monsoonal vine forests, mangrove swamps, open woodland forests, sandy plains, and flood plains are just some of the different kinds of terrain. Saltwater crocodiles, sharks, and marine stingers make the water around the peninsula an unlikely spot for swimming. Because of its ecological significance, two national parks have been created: Gurig National Park encompasses the land, and Cobourg Marine Park consists of the water around the peninsula. The land is owned by the Aboriginal people.

WHERE TO STAY

SEVEN SPIRIT BAY, on the Cobourg Peninsula (P.O. Box 4721, Darwin, NT 0801). Tel. 089/79-0277. Fax 089/79-0284. 24 habitats. MINIBAR TEL
Transportation: Wimray Air (tel. 41-0015) flies guests to the Cobourg Peninsula, where they are picked up by a four-wheel-drive vehicle and taken to a waiting boat in which they complete the journey to Seven Spirit Bay (A$230/U.S. $184 per person round-trip).
$ Rates (including all meals and activities): A$385 (U.S. $308) single; A$330 (U.S. $264) per person based on two sharing; A$224 (U.S. $179.20) children 3–16. Children under 3 stay free in parents' room. AE, BC, DC, MC, V.

⭐ This is a wilderness retreat like no other. A cluster of buildings offers five-star comfort for a handful of people who are keenly interested in wild places and in observing an environment yet undisturbed by man. The Aborigines have leased the land to the owners of Seven Spirits, which opened in 1990, and keep a watchful eye that their property is shown the proper respect.

Guests sleep in hexagonal "habitats" where two-thirds of the walls are floor-to-ceiling louvers, providing a 240° view of the surrounding tropical forest. Each bungalowlike habitat has coffee- and tea-making facilities, a small fridge, a minibar, telephone, two ceiling fans, two queen-size beds, lights on rheostats, designer bed linens, comfortable chairs for reading, a highly polished pine floor, iron, ironing board, torch (flashlight), hairdryer, and a pair of cotton kimonos. Each habitat has its own equally five-star bathroom just steps away and connected by a paving-stone path. Because these facilities are open-air, it's common to see little green frogs in the shower or to have a warbler build a nest within view of the loo.

This is "eco-tourism," travel for people who share an awareness of the earth's fragility. Guided walks conducted by the resident naturalist explore the microenvironments which surround this remote property. Guests can also go fishing for barramundi or giant trevally, go sailing, take a day-trip to an abandoned British settlement, go birding (285 species live in the area), study the native flora and fauna, or laze by the rock-edged saltwater pool and drink an N.T. Draught.

Meals are served in the Social Hub, a tropical building which includes the restaurant (indoor and outdoor seating), bar, reception area, lounge, photographer's darkroom, and reading area. Cobourg cuisine is a delightful blend of northern Australian ingredients prepared with a mild Southeast Asian flavor.

If you're interested in the environment and like places that are out of the ordinary, I highly recommend Seven Spirit Bay.

Reservations in North America: Contact the Robert D. Zimmer Group (tel. toll free 800/688-8414 in the U.S. and Canada).

---

2. KAKADU NATIONAL PARK

220km (136 miles) E of Darwin

GETTING THERE   By Car   You can drive to the park from Darwin via the Arnhem Highway.

By Organized Tour   If you aren't keen on driving in these remote parts, several tour operators in Darwin run trips into Kakadu. One of the better known is Australian Kakadu Tours (tel. 089/81-5144). The Kakadu Air (tel. 089/79-2411) or Brolga Air (tel. 089/71-7000) tours of Kakadu are good for folks with limited time.

ESSENTIALS   Tourist information is available at the **park headquarters** (tel. 089/79-2101), open daily from 8am to 5pm, and at Jabiru Airport (tel. 089/79-2031 or 79-2569). The **area code** is 089.

If you're driving from Darwin, be sure to stop at **Fogg Dam,** 60 kilometers (37 miles) down the Arnhem Highway, where splendid water birds glide from one lily pad to another. In this and all other areas of the park, *heed warnings to stay out of the water and do not allow children to play near the water's edge*—this is crocodile territory.

Farther along, you'll come to the **Bark Hut Inn,** where food and petrol are available. This is also a great spot for witnessing local color, in the form of the burly lads who frequent this watering hole. Most of them are buffalo hunters and look like something out of central casting.

Once inside the park, the three centers with any population are **Kakadu Holiday Village, Cooinda,** and **Jabiru.** The first two are motel and camping compounds; the latter is a small township where the people who work at the nearby Ranger Uranium Mine live. The **park headquarters** are near Jabiru, as is a small airport served by Kakadu Air and Brolga Air. Sealed roads connect the main centers, but a dirt road leads to Ubirr (Obiri Rock) and a four-wheel-drive is required to reach Jim Jim Falls.

Kakadu was declared a national park in 1979 and added to the World Heritage List in 1981.

WHAT TO SEE & DO

Kakadu National Park is famous for its Aboriginal rock art. Over 1,000 sites have been recorded, the best known being those at Obiri Rock and Nourlangie Rock—both accessible by road during the dry season. Wildlife is another attraction. Boats cruise the South Alligator River and Yellow Waters, providing a look at fascinating birds and reptiles, including crocodiles. Scenery is yet another draw. The park has saltwater swamps, wetlands, eucalyptus forests, waterfalls, and sandstone escarpments.

While many visitors see Kakadu on a day-trip from Darwin, the traveler with more time and interest should plan to spend at least 1 night. The park is about the same size as the state of Connecticut, and the points of interest are not close together.

Timing is a critical factor where a trip to Kakadu is concerned. There is no water in Jim Jim or Twin Falls until the wet season which runs from October through March. And while the rain makes Jim Jim Falls and Twin Falls overflow, it also washes out the roads. The best time to visit is between mid-June and mid-August. Outside of these months, be prepared for heat, humidity, and flies. The entry fee to Kakadu is A$8 (U.S. $6.40) per adult; there is no fee for children under 16. Permits are valid for 14 days.

Guests at the Kakadu Holiday Village usually cruise the nearby **South Alligator River** to observe local wildlife (A$24/U.S. $19.20 for 2 hours, A$54/U.S. $43.20 for 5 hours, including a barbecue lunch). Those who stay at the Four Seasons Cooinda take advantage of its proximity to **Yellow Waters,** where a similar experience is possible (A$25/U.S. $20 for 2 hours). The best viewing is in the early morning hours.

Flightseeing provides another perspective of the park. Kakadu Air operates out of Jabiru Airport and Cooinda (A$45/U.S. $36 for a half hour, A$75/U.S. $60 for an hour).

It's an easy drive to the **park headquarters, Ubirr (Obiri Rock), Nourlangie Rock,** and other points of interest. Sunset at Obiri Rock is spectacular. In addition to maintaining the information center, the rangers lead free tours in the park.

The **Wild Goose Tours** (tel. 79-2800) operate out of Cooinda. A guide takes guests across the land northwest of Cooinda, where there are vast wetlands. Birdwatchers delight in the opportunity to see thousands of geese, ducks, brolgas, egrets, ibis, jabirus, and other water birds. This 6-hour excursion also provides good insight into the Aboriginal way of life. Cost is A\$65 (U.S. \$52) for adults and A\$45 (U.S. \$36) for children under 12. Tours operate daily except Monday, June through December.

WHERE TO STAY & DINE

The number of visiting tourists tends to be higher than the number of available accommodations. My advice: Book early. And remember, a Tourism Marketing Duty of 5% is payable on all accommodation in the Northern Territory.

FOUR SEASONS KAKADU, Flinders St., Jabiru, NT 0886. Tel. 089/79-2800, or toll free 008/33-1147 in Australia. Fax 089/79-2707. 110 rms. A/C MINIBAR TV TEL

$ Rates: A\$150 (U.S. \$120) single; A\$175 (U.S. \$140) double. "Wet season" (Nov–Apr) rates are much lower. Children under 15 stay free in parents' room. AE, BC, DC, MC, V.

The Four Seasons Kakadu Hotel is shaped like a 250-meter (825-ft.) crocodile. Located in Jabiru, the hostelry offers the highest standard of lodging in the park. Open since late 1988, the Four Seasons welcomes new arrivals through a jaw-shaped portico complete with shuttered eyes. The reception area, a marble foyer, a restaurant, a coffee shop, bars, and shops are located in the head of the crocodile. Guest rooms are in the reptile's belly, and four stairways represent its legs. A swimming pool, barbecue area, and large artificial billabong (water hole) are also on the premises.

FOUR SEASONS COOINDA MOTEL, off Kakadu Hwy., Cooinda, NT 0886. Tel. 089/79-0145, or toll free 008/33-1147 in Australia. Fax 089/79-0148. 48 rms. A/C

$ Rates: A\$128 (U.S. \$102.40) single; A\$155 (U.S. \$124) double. Wet season rates (Nov–Apr) are much lower. Children under 15 stay free in parents' room. AE, BC, DC, MC, V.

The Four Seasons Cooinda has rooms and a camping/caravan area. The complex also offers a restaurant, casual open-air bistro, swimming pool, and beer garden. Since the motel has its own airstrip, it's possible to fly to this part of Kakadu and do day tours, thus eliminating the need for a car.

KAKADU HOLIDAY VILLAGE, Arnhem Hwy., Kakadu National Park, NT 0822. Tel. 089/79-0166. Fax 089/79-0147. 132 rms and 6 lodges. A/C TV TEL

$ Rates: A\$105 (U.S. \$84) single; A\$130 (U.S. \$104) double. Wet season rates are much lower. AE, BC, DC, MC, V.

Kakadu Holiday Village is 1 kilometer (½ mile) from the South Alligator River, a mistakenly labeled stretch of water: There are no alligators in this park. However, the river is inhabited by lots of crocodiles and these are viewed on the motel's boat cruises. The 7-hectare (17-acre) accommodation complex includes a motel, pool, spa, tennis court, walking track, restaurant, coffee shop, general store, caravan park, and campgrounds.

---

3. KATHERINE

350km (217 miles) S of Darwin

GETTING THERE By Plane Ansett NT and Skyport provide regular service from Darwin and Alice Springs.

By Train There is no train service to Katherine.

By Bus Pioneer, Greyhound, and Bus Australia provide regular service to

Katherine. The trip from Katherine to Darwin costs A$40 (U.S. $32) and takes 4 hours.

By Car   It takes just over 3 hours to drive from Darwin to Katherine.

ESSENTIALS   Tourist information is available at the **Northern Territory Government Tourist Bureau,** on the corner of Stuart Highway and Lindsay Street, Katherine, NT 0850 (tel. 089/72-2650), open Monday through Friday from 8:45am to 5pm and Saturday from 8:45am to noon. **Travel North,** the company that runs gorge river cruises, has an office in the BP Roadhouse, 6 Katherine Terrace (tel. 089/72-1044). (The Stuart Highway is called Katherine Terrace within the city limits.)

   The BP Roadhouse is open 24 hours a day and sells groceries, light meals, and take-out food, as well as gasoline. The **area code** is 089.

The third-largest town in the Northern Territory, Katherine (pop. 7,700) is best known for its beautiful river gorge—the focal point of **Katherine Gorge National Park**—32 kilometers (20 miles) from town. While a paved road leads out of the city to the north and south, the way to Katherine from Kakadu is partially unsealed. Nevertheless, Darwin, Kakadu, and Katherine make a convenient Top End triangle that many visitors follow.

   John McDouall Stuart, the first explorer ever to see the Katherine River in 1862, named it for the daughter of a sponsor of his expedition. Katherine has long been the center of a thriving cattle region and has recently had an increase in population due to the reopening of the nearby Tindal Air Force Base.

WHAT TO SEE & DO

Specially designed flat-bottom boats take visitors through the **Katherine River Gorge.** Birds, fish, and freshwater crocodiles are often seen, and the towering reddish-brown rock canyons above the sparkling flowing water are most impressive. Thirteen separate gorges rise from the river, but only a few are passed on the standard sightseeing excursion. These 2-hour trips cost A$17 (U.S. $13.60) for adults and A$7 (U.S. $5.60) for children, or A$32 (U.S. $25.60) for adults and A$15 (U.S. $12) for children if a bus transfer from Katherine is included. Make reservations with **Travel North** (tel. 72-1044). In addition to the 2-hour tour, they offer a Gorge Adventure Tour, which lasts 4 hours and costs A$48 (U.S. $38.40) for adults and A$23 (U.S. $17.60) for children (including transfers). Also an 8-hour excursion.

   Rental canoes are available for those who wish to see the scenic splendor on their own. Contact **Kookaburra Canoe Hire** (tel. 72-3604). Rates are A$8 (U.S. $6.40) for the first hour; a half-day rental costs from A$18 to A$27 (U.S. $14.40 to U.S. $21.60) depending on whether a one- two- or three-person canoe. Full-day hire varies from A$25 to A$45 (U.S. $20 to U.S. $36).

   Rangers are on hand at the park headquarters to answer your questions about Katherine Gorge, and their displays shed light on the wildlife in the area. I was hesitant when they said the river was safe for swimming because it is inhabited by freshwater, not saltwater, crocs, but I eventually went in and had a refreshing—and uneventful—experience.

   No matter how you choose to see the Katherine River Gorge, don't forget to bring sunglasses, insect repellent, sunscreen, and a hat or visor. Sturdy shoes are also required because it's necessary to walk about 500 meters (1,650 ft.) between stretches of the river. If you go upriver in a canoe, you'll need to ford in many places.

   Edith Falls Nature Reserve, part of Katherine Gorge National Park, is a picturesque spot for a swim in a large pool at the base of a waterfall. Camping is permitted, too. To reach Edith Falls, drive 42 kilometers (26 miles) north of Katherine and turn off at the signpost. Follow this road for another 20 kilometers (12 miles) to reach the scenic site. The admission is A$4 (U.S. $3.20) per person. Children under 5 are free.

   Katherine Low Level Nature Park, 5 kilometers (3 miles) from town via the

Victoria Highway, is an ideal riverside location for picnicking. Swimming is safe here during "the dry," but "the wet" can cause dangerous flooding and strong currents.

WHERE TO STAY

Budget travelers will be glad to know that Katherine has a **YHA hostel** located 2 kilometers (1¼ miles) south of the Stuart Highway on the Victoria Highway (tel. 089/72-2942). Charges are A$9 (U.S. $7.20) per person. Bankcard, MasterCard, and VISA are accepted.

The **Gorge Caravan Park** in Katherine Gorge National Park, NT 0850 (tel. 089/72-1253), offers another inexpensive alternative. Caravan and camping fees are A$12 (U.S. $9.60) for two adults; half price for children. Electricity costs an additional A$4 (U.S. $3.20).

All lodging in the Northern Territory is subject to 5% tax.

GARDEAN HOLIDAY VILLAGE, Giles and Cameron Sts., Katherine, NT 0850. Tel. 089/72-2511. Fax 089/72-2628. 65 rms, 18 suites. A/C TV TEL
   Directions: Located 3km (2 miles) from town center. Take a taxi.
$ Rates: A$74 (U.S. $59.20) single; A$85 (U.S. $68) double; A$94 (U.S. $75.20) executive suite; A$143 (U.S. $114.40) family suite for two adults and four children. Children under 5 stay free in parents' room. Rates are 15% lower Dec–Apr. AE, BC, DC, MC, V.

This is the town's poshest place to stay. The motel, built in 1982, has an attractive pool area as well as a bistro and an à la carte restaurant. Family and executive suites have kitchens. The motel provides covered parking, which is important in this hot climate. Baby-sitting can be arranged.

PINE TREE MOTEL, 3 Third St., Katherine, NT 0850. Tel. 089/72-2533. Fax 089/72-2920. 50 rms. A/C TV TEL
$ Rates: A$75 (U.S. $60) single; A$90 (U.S. $64) double. AE, BC, MC, V.

The Pine Tree Motel has standard rooms in a central location. Each has coffee- and tea-making facilities, a refrigerator, and other typical amenities. There are also a pool and a restaurant on the premises.

4. ALICE SPRINGS

1,500km (930 miles) S of Darwin

GETTING THERE   By Plane   Ansett and Australian Airlines both have daily flights to Alice Springs. The trip from Sydney costs A$259 to A$325 (U.S. $207.20 to U.S. $260); from Adelaide, A$199 to A$250 (U.S. $159.20 to U.S. $200). These are Australian Airlines Air Pass fares. A taxi to town from the airport costs about A$14 (U.S. $11.20), or you can pay A$7 (U.S. $5.60) for the shuttle bus (tel. 53-0310).

By Train   The Ghan makes the trip up to Alice Springs from Adelaide once a week year round (22 hours) and more frequently in the April-to-October period. Fares range from A$395 (U.S. $316) for a first-class berth and meals to A$125 (U.S. $100) for economy-class seating. This is one of Australia's nicest trains, and a winner of several tourism awards.

Australian National Holidays, 1 Richmond Road, Keswick, SA 5035 (tel. 08/212-6862), offers a very attractive package which includes travel on the Ghan from Adelaide to Alice Springs; accommodation at Ross River Lodge, Glen Helen Lodge, and at the Four Seasons motels in Alice Springs and Yulara, as well as a rental car for 8 days and some meals. The cost is A$1,385 (U.S. $1,108) per person for two adults sharing.

By Bus   A bus to Alice Springs from Adelaide takes 23 hours and costs A$156 (U.S. $124.80). The bus to Alice Springs from Darwin takes 17½ hours and costs A$156 (U.S. $124.80). Pioneer, Greyhound, and Bus Australia make the trip.

By Car   Motorists using the Stuart Highway, the only link to other centers of population, refer to "heading up the track" or "down the track." If you decide to do either, be sure to carry plenty of water with you and watch the fuel gauge. If you experience car trouble, stay with the vehicle; don't attempt to walk to find help.

ESSENTIALS   The best time to visit Alice Springs, in terms of **weather,** is from April to the end of October. The **area code** is 089.

Information   Tourist information for new arrivals is dispensed at the airport and train station 7 days a week. In town, the **Northern Territory Government Tourist Bureau** in Ford Plaza, Todd Mall, Alice Springs, NT 0870 (tel. 089/52-1299), is open Monday through Friday from 8:45am to 5pm and Saturday and Sunday from 9am to 12:30pm and 1:15 to 4pm.

City Layout   The **Todd River,** which cuts Alice Springs in two, has water in it only a few months of the year, usually December through February, but it remains a focal point of the community year round. The **central business district,** where Todd Mall is the main shopping area, lies just west of the river. Many of the new motels are located in a separate **"tourist district"** across the river and about 4 kilometers (2½ miles) from town along Barrett Drive. The Royal Flying Doctor Service base is in town, but most of the scenic sights, like Standley Chasm and Simpson's Gap, are 20 kilometers (12 miles) or more out of Alice Springs.

GETTING AROUND   By Limousine or Taxi   Alice Springs doesn't have a public bus system, but taxis are readily available (tel. 52-1877). If you want a chauffeured limousine, call **Alice Chauffeur Drive** (tel. 53-1655); they charge approximately A$50 (U.S. $40) per hour for a Ford LTD and A$80 (U.S. $64) an hour for a stretch limo.

By Coach   The *Alice Wanderer* (tel. 53-0310) is a coach that makes the rounds of the sightseeing attractions in town. Passengers get off wherever they like and then board the next bus when they're ready. The fare is A$10 (U.S. $8) for a half day and A$15 (U.S. $12) for a full day. Places on the itinerary include the Royal Flying Doctor Base, School of the Air, Camel Farm, and Vintage Auto Museum.

By Organized Tour   **AAT King's,** 74 Todd Street, Alice Springs, NT 0870 (tel. 52-5266 or 52-1700), operates the most popular full-day and half-day tours in the area. **Rod Steinert,** P.O. Box 2058, Alice Springs, NT 0870 (tel. 55-5000), offers group tours that emphasize the traditional Aboriginal life-style and expose visitors to real outback cattle stations. Transport is by 10-seater Landcruisers or coaches. Steinert and his vehicles are also available for private charter, and he can arrange a cattle-station stay or a homestay in Alice Springs for you. **Sahara 4-Wheel Drive Tours,** P.O. Box 3891, Alice Springs, NT 0870 (tel. 53-0881), operates an Aboriginal Dreamtime Culture excursion Monday, Wednesday, and Friday from February through November. Because arrangements have to be made to go on private Aboriginal land, it is necessary to book well ahead. The cost is A$110 (U.S. $88) including lunch.

SPECIAL EVENTS   The **Henley-on-Todd Regatta,** held annually in late September or early October, draws big crowds who laugh and drink beer while they watch contestants run up the dry riverbed carrying homemade bottomless boats. Another popular local event, the **Camel Cup,** is held each May.

"The Alice," as she is affectionately called by Australians, lies at the geographical center of the country, surrounded by the Macdonnell ranges and the russet-colored earth and rock formations that give this region its name—the Red Centre. Because of its Old West ambience and the beautiful scenery in the area, Alice Springs is a popular place with overseas visitors. Some say the town reminds them of Palm Springs 50 years ago, but personally, I see more of a resemblance to Sedona, Arizona, and other similar beauty spots in the U.S. Southwest.

Nevil Shute immortalized Alice Springs in his best-seller *A Town Like Alice* in 1954; the book, a wonderfully romantic story about the post–World War II reunion of an Englishwoman and a rugged outback Aussie, has subsequently been made into a film and a television series.

While Alice Springs (pop. 25,000) is a busy city with modern tourist facilities, it is also the country's consummate outback town. The Royal Flying Doctor Service and School of the Air are both based here, and the community is a source of supplies for people who live on the region's far-reaching cattle stations. Many Aborigines work as stockmen on the vast stations in this area, and reminders of their rich heritage are everywhere. Wild camels roam throughout the region, and the dry red earth, stately white-barked ghost gums, and deep-blue sky have a sense of otherworldliness to them.

Of all the artists who have tried to capture the area's beauty on canvas, the local Aborigines seem to have done it best. Albert Namatjira, a member of the Arunta tribe who grew up on the Hermannsburg Mission near Alice Springs, is the best known of the landscape watercolorists. Many others have proven their talent, not only with watercolors but also with bark painting and other crafts. Unfortunately, the Aborigines who have found a place in today's Australia constitute only a small minority, and in Alice Springs, where they constitute 25% of the population, you will see numbers of native people who, dispossessed of their traditional way of life, have found numbing consolation in alcohol.

WHAT TO SEE & DO

IN TOWN

THE ROYAL FLYING DOCTOR SERVICE (RFDS), on Stuart Terrace near the end of Hartley St. Tel. 52-1129.

The Royal Flying Doctor Service (RFDS) base provides an insight into how Australians have been able to cope with living in the outback. The RFDS was started in 1928 by the Rev. John Flynn and continues to provide medical and communications services to folks who live on isolated cattle stations. Fourteen RFDS bases exist in the country, and this is one of four (Cairns, Mount Isa, and Broken Hill are the others) that welcome tourists.

Admission: A$2.50 (U.S. $2) adults, A50¢ (U.S. 40¢) children for a half-hour tour, which includes a 10-minute video.

Open: Mon–Sat 9am–4pm, Sun 1–4pm. **Closed:** Christmas, Boxing Day, New Year's Day, and Good Friday. **Transportation:** Walk or take the Alice Wanderer (tel. 53-0310).

ALICE SPRINGS SCHOOL OF THE AIR, 80 Head St. Tel. 52-2122.

Like the Royal Flying Doctor Service, the School of the Air was devised to assist people living on isolated cattle stations in the vast, largely unpopulated regions of Australia. A total of 140 pupils, aged 4 to 12, receive their education on the airwaves emanating from this base. These children are spread out over an area two-thirds the size of Texas. Eleven other schools like this one are dotted around the country.

Tourists can visit the school and hear students receiving their lessons on the radio weekdays during the school year, which runs from February through November. Please phone beforehand and confirm that there is space available for you because sometimes they have as many as 200 guests in one afternoon. Charles and Di even stopped by in 1983. Groups of educators can make special arrangements by writing in advance to The Principal, Alice Springs School of the Air, 80 Head Street, Alice Springs, NT 0870.

Admission: A$2 (U.S. $1.60) donation requested.

Open: Feb–Nov, Mon–Fri 1:30–3:30pm. **Closed:** Dec–Jan.

NEARBY

FRONTIER CAMEL FARM, on the Ross Hwy., 8km (5 miles) from central Alice Springs. Tel. 53-0444.

Camels were imported to Australia by the first generations of white settlers, who used them for transport across the country's vast deserts. By 1907 more than 10,000 camels had been brought in. However, the advent of the railroad and motorized transport meant the animals were no longer needed. Some were destroyed, and others were set loose and thrived in the wild. Australia now has the largest population of free-ranging camels in the world—about 200,000. The Frontier Camel Farm has tame camels available for riding. They also have a very interesting camel museum. A picnic shelter with gas barbecue is available.

Admission: A$7 (U.S. $5.60) includes short camel ride, entrance to the museum and the reptile display. For opportunities for longer rides see "Sports and Recreation" and "Where to Dine," below.

Open: Daily 9am–5pm. **Closed:** Dec 25–Jan 2.

FARTHER AFIELD

SIMPSON'S GAP NATIONAL PARK, 23km (14 miles) west of Alice Springs.

This is a scenic spot in the West Macdonnell Ranges. While the parking lot at Standley Chasm (mentioned below) boasts a kiosk and souvenir shop, Simpson's Gap is totally uncommercialized. Rangers maintain the Visitor Centre, which provides information on the area's flora and fauna. A large colony of rock wallabies lives in the vicinity and can usually be seen. Available brochures describe various bushwalks and tell the way to picturesque picnic places. (Fill your basket at Le Coq en Pâté; see "Where to Dine," below.)

Admission: Free.
Open: Daily 8am–8pm.

STANDLEY CHASM, 50km (31 miles) west of Alice Springs.

Standley Chasm is a steep cleft, 9 meters (30 ft.) wide, in the Macdonnell Ranges. The towering red rock walls of the narrow gorge appear to change color when the sun is directly overhead. But while most people rush to the chasm at noon, I find the scenery along the 20-minute walk from the car park just as pretty as the midday event. The path follows a streambed and dodges around dusty-green native shrubbery and white-barked ghost gums. The wonderful rust-colored earth and mountains stand out against the cloudless blue sky. Sturdy walking shoes are a must.

Admission: A$2 (U.S. $1.60).
Open: Daily 8:30am–7pm.

GLEN HELEN GORGE, 135km (84 miles) west of Alice Springs.

This gorge, cut by the Finke River, is a wonderful spot for a swim or a walk. Glen Helen Lodge (see "Where to Stay" and "Where to Dine," below) is located at the entrance of the Nature Park.

ARLTUNGA, 111km (69 miles) east of Alice Springs in the East Macdonnell ranges.

The Historical Reserve here contains ruins of buildings that date from the late 1880s—Central Australia's gold-rush era. The Arltunga Pub, run by Gary and Elaine Bohning, is steeped in atmosphere.

ROSS RIVER HOMESTEAD, 85km (53 miles) east of Alice Springs in the East Macdonnell ranges. Tel. 56-9711.

This rustic station (ranch) is a great place for billy tea and damper, horse riding, camel riding, and more. See "Where to Stay," below, for details.

PALM VALLEY, 150km (93 miles) southwest of Alice Springs.

Palm Valley is part of the Finke Gorge National Park. A large glen of tall cabbage palms and other rare plants are unique to this area and have survived for thousands of years. This is a wilderness area, with access by four-wheel-drive vehicles only.

SPORTS & RECREATION

If you've never ridden a camel, Alice Springs is one of the best places in the world to do it. **The Frontier Camel Farm** (tel. 53-0444) offers a 1-hour Todd River Ramble that costs A$27 (U.S. $21.60) for adults and A$15 (U.S. $12) for children.

They also offer a 2-night safari called "Spend a Night With a Camel," where small groups of 4 to 10 people ride camels to a scenic spot, enjoy a delicious camp-oven dinner, and sleep out in a real Aussie "swag" (bedroll) under the stars. The next day everyone rides to historic Glen Helen Lodge (see "Where to Stay," below) and has a memorable gourmet meal at Cloudy's (see "Where to Dine," below). After overnighting (in beds) at Glen Helen, the group is transferred back to Alice Springs. This memorable experience costs A$385 (U.S. $308) including all meals, accommodation at Glen Helen, camping equipment, and vehicle transfers.

If you want to get serious and do a bona-fide trek of up to 14 days, contact **Noel Fullerton's Camel Outback Safaris** (tel. 56-0925). All excursions are geological explorations with safari guide.

If you'd like to go ballooning, phone **Aussie Balloons** (tel. 53-0544). They operate 7 days a week from April through October. Half-hour flights cost A$105 (U.S. $84) and 1-hour trips are A$160 (U.S. $128). Prices include pickup from your hotel and a traditional chicken-and-champagne breakfast before returning to Alice Springs.

Outback Ballooning (tel. 52-8723) offers a similar experience. Their 30-minute flight costs A$110 (U.S. $88) for adults and A$55 (U.S. $44) for children. The price of the 1-hour experience is A$170 (U.S. $136) for adults and A$75 (U.S. $60) for kids. "Chase and breakfast" for those who wish to join in but not fly costs A$35 (U.S. $28). A chicken-and-champagne breakfast, as well as courtesy collection from your accommodation, is included.

SHOPPING

Shopping hours in Alice Springs are Monday through Friday from 9am to 5:30pm and Saturday from 9am to noon. A few stores are also open Friday night and Saturday afternoon. The main shopping area is **Todd Mall.**

Because of the number of local artists, this part of the Red Centre is an ideal place to purchase Aboriginal art. The **Arunta Art Gallery & Book Shop,** 70 Todd Street (tel. 52-1544), has a good selection of dot paintings and watercolor scenics. They also sell art supplies and have the best selection in town of books on the Northern Territory and Aboriginal culture. They're open from 9am to 5:30pm Monday to Saturday (and sometimes Sunday from March to September).

The **Aboriginal Dreamtime Gallery,** 71 Todd Mall near Gregory Terrace (tel. 53-4203), has a large selection of dot paintings and offers free shipping and insurance worldwide. Open Monday through Friday from 9am to 5:30pm and weekends from 9am to 4pm.

✪ **Gallery Gondwana,** 43 Todd Mall (tel. 53-1577), sells only top-quality works of art. My favorite is the pottery done by the Hermannsburg craftspeople. Proprietor Roslyn Premont has written a book on Aboriginal art and is very knowledgeable on the subject. Full documentation of originality and source is provided with each piece purchased. Gallery Gondwana is open year round from 9:30am to 5:30pm Monday through Friday and from 9:30am to 3pm Saturday; also April to October from 1 to 5pm Sunday. They pack, ship, and insure paintings free of charge.

The **Outcrop Gallery,** corner of Todd Mall and Gregory Terrace (tel. 52-3662), sells souvenirs, T-shirts, and some Aboriginal goods such as boomerangs and didgeridoos. Open daily from 9am to 5pm. The **Dreamtime Art Gallery,** opposite Flynn Church, 63 Todd Mall (tel. 52-8861), sells Arnhem Land bark paintings, didgeridoos, batiks from Ernabella, and other local products. Open daily.

WHERE TO STAY

A 5% Tourism Marketing Duty is added to the cost of all accommodations in the Northern Territory.

IN OR NEAR TOWN

Expensive

SHERATON ALICE SPRINGS HOTEL, Barrett Dr., Alice Springs, NT

0871. Tel. 089/52-8000. Fax 089/52-3822. 228 rms, 7 suites. A/C MINIBAR TV TEL

$ Rates (including breakfast): A$193–A$248 (U.S. $154.40–U.S. $198.40) single or double; A$385–A$495 (U.S. $308–U.S. $396); A$50 (U.S. $40) extra person. Children under 18 stay free in parents' room. No-smoking rooms available. AE, BC, DC, MC, V. **Parking:** Free.

The Sheraton Alice Springs opened in 1985 and is located a short distance from the city center in the area known as the "tourist district." Lasseter's Casino and the Alice Springs Golf Course are just a stone's throw away. Of the rooms in the three-story hotel, all have balconies—some with a view of the Macdonnell Ranges. Most rooms have two queen-size beds and the rest have kings. All bathrooms have tub/shower combos. Twelve rooms have been specially outfitted to accommodate handicapped travelers.

Dining/Entertainment: The hotel has two dining venues: the elegant Bradshaw Room and the more casual Alice's Bistro. Drinks are available poolside, in the Lobby Bar, or in Simpson's Gap Bar.

Services: 24-hour room service, laundry, concierge, and baby-sitting.

Facilities: Two tennis courts, a gym, sauna, spa, and a large swimming pool.

Moderate

ALICE TOURIST APARTMENTS, Gap Rd., Alice Springs, NT 0871. Tel. 089/52-2788. Fax 089/53-2950. 24 apartments. A/C TV TEL **Transportation:** Courtesy coach.

$ Rates: A$60 (U.S. $48) single; A$70 (U.S. $56) double; A$75 (U.S. $60) triple. AE, BC, DC, MC, V. **Parking:** Free.

If you want to be completely self-contained, the best value in town is the two-story Alice Tourist Apartments. Owners Geoff and Fran Wilkins provide friendly service to those who stay in their attractive apartments located 2 kilometers (1¼ miles) south of the city center. All units have a combination of queen-size, single, and bunk beds, plus kitchenettes. Of the 24 units, 11 are one-bedroom and sleep four to six; the others are compact studios that sleep four. Only continental breakfast is offered (A$6/U.S. $4.80), but the Piggly Wiggly supermarket across the street is open daily. There's a pool on the premises.

ELKIRA MOTEL, 65 Bath St., Alice Springs, NT 0870. Tel. 089/52-1222. Fax 089/53-1370. 58 rms. A/C TV TEL

$ Rates: A$59 (U.S. $47.20) single in the older section, A$84 (U.S. $67.20) single in the newer section; A$72 (U.S. $57.60) double in the older section, A$84 (U.S. $67.20) double in the newer section. Children under 6 stay free in parents' room. AE, BC, DC, MC, V. **Parking:** Free.

The centrally located Elkira Motel offers adequate rooms at reasonable rates. Some 42 units are classified "deluxe," 7 of them having kitchens. The "moderate" rooms, built in 1958, are small but acceptable. Three rooms are equipped for handicapped travelers. There's a pool on the premises. The Terrace Restaurant serves à la carte dinners; the Terrace Bistro is open daily for light meals from 6am to 8pm.

FOUR SEASONS ALICE SPRINGS, Stephens Rd. just off Barrett Dr., Alice Springs, NT 0870. Tel. 089/52-6100, or toll free 008/03-0011 in Australia. Fax 089/52-6234. 140 rms. A/C MINIBAR TV TEL **Transportation:** Complimentary shuttle to town.

$ Rates: A$110 (U.S. $88) single or double; A$20 (U.S. $16) extra person. Children under 15 stay free in parents' room. AE, BC, DC, MC, V. **Parking:** Free.

Opened in 1987, the property nestles against the West Macdonnell ranges near Lasseter's Casino. Four large Aboriginal-style carved birds greet new arrivals in the entrance foyer. An open atrium rises from the reception level to the second floor, where guests dine in Ainslies Restaurant. Each of the accommodations has one queen-size bed, one single, and a tub/shower combination, as well as a clock radio, in-room movies, tea- and coffee-making facilities, and a small fridge. Room service operates 16 hours a day. The facilities include a pool, spa, and tennis courts.

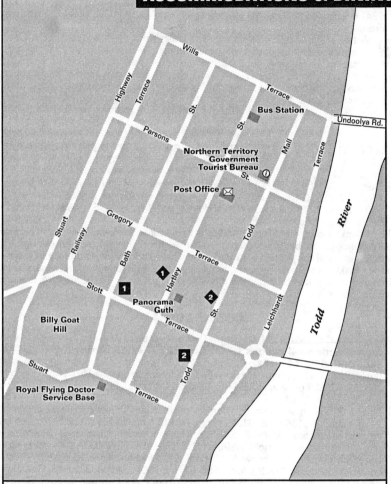

ALICE SPRINGS ACCOMMODATIONS & DINING

150 m
164 y

Wills

Highway

Terrace

St.

Parsons

St.

Bus Station

Terrace

Undoolya Rd.

Mall

Terrace

Northern Territory Government Tourist Bureau

St.

Post Office ✉

River

Gregory

Stuart

Railway

Bath

Todd

Terrace

Stott

1

1

Hartley

2

Panorama Guth

St.

Leichhardt

Billy Goat Hill

Terrace

Todd

2

Stuart

Royal Flying Doctor Service Base

Terrace

Todd

° Alice Springs

ACCOMMODATIONS:
Elkira Motel **1**
Melanka Lodge **2**

DINING:
Eranova Cafeteria **2**
The Overlander Steakhouse **1**

Post Office ✉   Information ⓘ

OASIS FRONTIER RESORT, 10 Gap Rd., Alice Springs, NT 0870. Tel. 089/52-1444. Fax 089/52-3776. 102 rms. A/C TV TEL

$ Rates: A$70–A$85 (U.S. $56–U.S. $68) single; A$90–A$105 (U.S. $72–U.S. $84) double; A$12 (U.S. $9.60) extra person. AE, BC, DC, MC, V. **Parking:** Free.

A two-story complex 2 kilometers (1 mile) from the town center, the Oasis Resort consists of units that were completely remodeled in 1987, a large octagonal swimming pool, and an attractive restaurant done in a striking salmon-and-gray decor. There's also a sauna, spa, a large aviary, another smaller pool, and plenty of garden landscaping. All quarters have balconies and some have tub/shower combos. Seven rooms are provided for handicapped travelers. Barry Partridge is a personable host; he and his staff are sure to make you feel welcome.

Budget

MELANKA LODGE, 94 Todd St., Alice Springs, NT 0870. Tel. 089/52-2233, or toll free 008/89-6110 in Australia. Fax 089/52-3819. 205 rms (50 with bath). A/C

$ Rates: A$11 (U.S. $8.80) per person in "dormitories" for four to eight people; A$13 (U.S. $10.40) double "backpacker accommodation"; A$35–A$47 (U.S. $28–U.S. $37.60) standard single or double; A$57–A$65 (U.S. $45.60–U.S. $52) deluxe single or double. AE, BC, DC, MC, V.

The Melanka Lodge offers budget lodgings in the center of town. The least expensive quarters lack private baths, but 50 refurbished "deluxe" rooms have bathrooms, TVs, clock radios, and telephones. Standard rooms have hand basins, fridges, and coffee- and tea-making facilities. Two swimming pools and a popular steak restaurant, The Hindquarter, are on the attractively landscaped premises. There are also laundry facilities and a bar.

OUT OF TOWN

ROSS RIVER HOMESTEAD, 88km (55 miles) east of Alice Springs in the East Macdonnell ranges (P.O. Box 3271, Alice Springs, NT 0871). Tel. 089/56-9711. Fax 089/56-9823. 30 cabins, also camping area and bunkhouse. A/C **Transportation:** Ground transfers provided from Alice Springs (A$35/U.S. $28 per adult round-trip; children half price). Light-aircraft transfer also available.

$ Rates (including all meals, transfers by minibus, and some activities—minimum 2-night stay): A$165 (U.S. $132) single; A$145 (U.S. $116) per person based on double occupancy; A$75 (U.S. $60) children under 13 sharing. Room-only rate—minimum stay 1 night: A$90 (U.S. $72) single; A$50 (U.S. $40) per person based on double occupancy; A$10 (U.S. $8) children under 13 sharing. Bunk- house: A$12 (U.S. $9.60) adults, A$6 (U.S. $4.80) children under 13. Camping: A$4 (U.S. $3.20) per adult, A$3 (U.S. $2.40) per child. Caravan: A$15 (U.S. $12) powered site.

I can't think of a better place to savor the flavor of the Red Centre. The original homestead here was built in 1898; it now serves as the dining room on this property which covers 24 square miles of scenic bushland in the East Macdonnell ranges. Ross River Homestead provides ample opportunity for guests of all ages to sample the activities associated with the outback without experiencing all of its discomforts.

Accommodation is in cabins built of red river gum trees; these have stone floors, air conditioning, and electric blankets, as well as en suite bathrooms. During the day, guests can ride camels or horses, or ride in a wagon pulled by Clydesdales. (Rides cost A$10/U.S. $8 for a half hour, A$15/U.S. $12 for an hour, and A$25/U.S. $20 for 2 hours.) This is also a great area for bushwalking (hiking) and birdwatching. At night there are sometimes bush dinners; meals are also served in the rustic bar or the historic dining room which features mud-and-stone walls, lace tablecloths, and a colonial decor.

Day visitors and house guests alike are invited to join in for complimentary billy tea and damper every morning. This is usually accompanied by stock-whip cracking demonstrations and boomerang throwing. If it gets too hot, folks cool off in the pool.

Reservations in North America: Austravel, 51 East 42nd Street, Suite 616, New York, NY 10017 (tel. 212/972-6880, or toll free 800/544-0212).

GLEN HELEN LODGE, 135km (84 miles) west of Alice Springs in the West Macdonnell ranges (P.O. Box 3020, Alice Springs, NT 0871). Tel. 089/56-7489. Fax 089/56-7495. 25 standard rms, 5 budget rms, 3 bunkhouses, and camping.

$ Rates: A$72 (U.S. $57.60) double standard room, A$10 (U.S. $8) child age 5 and over (children under 5 free); A$34 (U.S. $27.20) double budget room; A$10 (U.S. $8) per bed in bunkhouse. AE, BC, DC, MC, V.

Set on the bank of the Finke River, the oldest known waterway in the world, Glen Helen Lodge is renowned for the good food served in its restaurant and its beautiful scenic surroundings. Locals, as well as visitors, drive out, have dinner, and spend the night. I suggest you do the same. The lodge is built on the site of the original Glen Helen station homestead and has a relaxed, homey atmosphere, which is enhanced by open fires in winter.

The standard rooms are basic, but more than adequate. Each has an en suite bathroom, concrete-block walls, air conditioning, and a pretty patchwork-quilt bedspread.

During the day, guests swim or walk in Glen Helen Gorge which is a 5-minute walk from the lodge. A 15-minute flightseeing trip on the helicopter based here costs A$45 (U.S. $36) per person with a minimum of three people.

Award-winning Cloudy's Restaurant is open nightly for dinner, and light meals and snacks can be ordered off a blackboard menu in the bar/lounge area from 7:30am to 10pm.

WHERE TO DINE

IN TOWN

Expensive

BRADSHAW ROOM, in the Sheraton Alice Springs Hotel, Barrett Dr. Tel. 52-8000.
Cuisine: INTERNATIONAL. **Reservations:** Recommended. **Transportation:** Taxi about A$5 (U.S. $4).
$ Prices: Appetizers A$9.50–A$18 (U.S. $7.60); main courses A$20–A$32 (U.S. $16–U.S. $25.60); set menu A$58 (U.S. $46.40). 15% surcharge Sun and public holidays. AE, BC, CB, DC, MC, V.
Open: Dinner Tues–Sat 6:30–11pm.

The Bradshaw Room is an elegant spot for a special meal. The room has a colonial atmosphere, which seems appropriate since it was named in honor of Thomas Andrew Bradshaw, an English immigrant who was the post and telegraph stationmaster in Alice Springs from 1899 to 1908. Neville Weston's watercolors, displayed around the room, depict scenes from that period. In one painting, four of the Bradshaw children are shown with their Aboriginal maids at the telegraph station.

The restaurant's menu usually includes Northern Territory specialties like crocodile, kangaroo, and barramundi, as well as a surprising amount of seafood. Prawns, oysters, and scallops are offered as hot appetizers; prawns, Moreton Bay bugs, and ocean trout are main-course items. There are also a half dozen "Sheraton Cuisine" items on the menu. These are lighter, healthier dishes where the emphasis is on freshness, low sodium, and low fat. Children's menus are available. Guests select their wine from an impressive floor-to-ceiling brass wine rack. The Bradshaw Room won the 1990 Gold Plate Award for Best Silver Service Restaurant in the Northern Territory.

Moderate

THE OVERLANDER STEAKHOUSE, 72 Hartley St. Tel. 52-2159.
Cuisine: OUTBACK AUSTRALIAN. **Reservations:** Recommended for dinner.

$ Prices: Appetizers A$7.50–A$13.95 (U.S. $6–U.S. $11.20); main courses A$12.50–A$21.50 (U.S. $10–U.S. $17.20). AE, BC, DC, MC, V.
Open: Lunch Mon–Fri noon–2pm; dinner daily 6pm–late.

The Overlander Steakhouse serves generous portions of local fare in a casual Central Australian environment, where the decor includes camel saddles and farm utensils and the "dunnies" (rest rooms) are labeled "colts" and "fillies."

Both the witchety-grub soup and the kangaroo-tail soup are excellent. After the soup you can try pan-fried or barbecued barramundi, camel, kangaroo, or buffalo steaks, or a man-size 400-gram (16-oz.) beef rump steak called The Territorian. The damper bread is good, too. Dessert offerings include pavlova, apple and cinnamon crêpes, and homemade chocolate éclairs. Hosts Barb and Wayne Kraft help to create a welcoming atmosphere. There's a good wine list (my favorite is the Jim Barry 1989 Clare River Cabernet-Merlot Shiraz), or you can try the local favorite brew: NT Draught. The steak house is the home of the local bush band Bloodwood, and their music adds to the experience of dining there.

Budget

ERANOVA CAFETERIA, 72 Todd St. Tel. 52-6094.
Cuisine: BISTRO. **Reservations:** Not necessary.
$ Prices: Appetizers A$2.50–A$5 (U.S. $2–U.S. $4); main courses A$6.50–A$11.50 (U.S. $5.20–U.S. $9.20). No credit cards.
Open: Mon–Fri 8am–4pm, Sat 8am–2pm.

The central location and reasonable prices at this cafeteria contribute to its popularity. This is the place for filling breakfasts and tasty lunches that won't consume much time or money. BYO. *Note:* The Eranova will move during the life of this edition. Please check the local telephone directory for the new address if you don't find it at the location stated here.

LE COQ EN PATE, Shop 2, 12 Lindsay Ave. in the East Side Shopping Centre. Tel. 52-9759.
Cuisine: FRENCH. **Reservations:** None.
$ Prices: Picnic supplies for two A$10 (U.S. $8). No credit cards.
Open: Tues–Sun 10am–7pm.

This is the best place in town for buying cheeses, terrines, and pâtés for your picnic basket. Everything is made on the premises, including the baguettes, fruit breads, and croissants. The quiche is my personal favorite, but they also offer pies, pasties, and assorted savories. Cakes, too, are made fresh daily.

OUT OF TOWN

CLOUDY'S RESTAURANT, at Glen Helen Lodge, 135km (84 miles) west of Alice Springs in the heart of the West Macdonnell ranges. Tel. 56-7489.
Cuisine: MODERN MULTICULTURAL. **Reservations:** Imperative, well in advance, especially May–Oct.
$ Prices: Set three-course dinner A$38 (U.S. $30.40) per person. AE, BC, DC, MC, V.
Open: Dinner daily from 7pm.

This doesn't look like a place in which you'd find first-class gourmet cuisine. The rustic atmosphere and remote location makes one think more of barbecue than exquisitely seasoned sauces. However, this is where chef Mindy Byrne has chosen to work her magic. If you dine here, the entrées (appetizers) might be creamy beetroot soup with smoked salmon wasabi croutons, steamed seaweed roll with sweet ginger sauce, or quail-and-chicken salad with sesame mayonnaise. Popular main courses include lamb curry with avocado-and-watermelon salad; buttered saffron rice with octopus, orange roughy, and olives in a tomato-lemon thyme sauce; or sweet potato roasted with almond mustard seed crust and coconut spiced Asian salad. Some "desert desserts" are strawberry granita with Cointreau, lime butter tartlet, and hot freshly baked coconut cake with Japanese green-tea ice cream.

Chef Byrne is from Sydney and says her innovative menus are "the product of the influences of growing up in a multicultural society."

Up to 46 diners can be seated at Cloudy's nine tables, each of which is covered with a lace cloth and set with crystal and English bone china. The colonial ambience is further enhanced by open fires in winter.

It's an easy 1½ hour drive to Glen Helen in the daylight, but wandering stock and wild animals make the road treacherous after dark. If you dine at Cloudy's, *please stay overnight*. If you can't organize your schedule to do that, then drive out during the day and order lunch off the blackboard menu in the bar/lounge area. A smoked salmon sandwich with salad, a Greek salad, or nachos cost about A\$6 (U.S. \$4.80). It's not surprising that Cloudy's has won the Australian Tourism Commission's award for the Pursuit of Excellence.

WHITE GUMS PARK CAFE AND TEAROOM, about 25km (16 miles) west of Alice Springs. Tel. 55-0366.
   Cuisine: TEAS/LIGHT MEALS. **Reservations:** Not necessary. **Directions:** Follow the main highway out of Alice Springs headed west. Just beyond the turnoff for Simpson's Gap you will see the signpost for White Gums, which is located 1 kilometer (½ mile) south of the highway.
$ Prices: Breakfast about A\$7 (U.S. \$5.60); morning or afternoon tea A\$4–A\$5 (U.S. \$3.20–U.S. \$4); light lunches A\$5.50–A\$8.50 (U.S. \$4.40–U.S. \$6.80); desserts A\$6 (U.S. \$4.80); three-course lunch A\$24 (U.S. \$19.20). AE, BC, MC, V.
   Open: Daily 9:30am–5pm.
A delightful stop for breakfast, lunch, or morning or afternoon tea, White Gums Park Cafe and Tearoom is a contemporary eatery, which offers both inside and outside seating. The morning or afternoon tea that consists of fruit damper bread, jam, cream, and billy tea is delicious. Steak-and-kidney pie, rabbit pie, and seafood vol-au-vent are lunchtime main courses. This eatery is adjacent to a wildlife sanctuary.

SOMETHING DIFFERENT

Where else but Alice Springs could you ✪ **Take a Camel Out to Breakfast, Lunch, or Dinner?** This opportunity is presented by the Frontier Camel Farm (tel. 53-0444). The morning experience includes a 1-hour ride along the Todd River and a hearty breakfast at the Camel Farm (Monday, Wednesday, and Saturday; A\$43/U.S. \$34.40). The lunch trip is a safari to the Chateau Hornsby Winery where a barbecue lunch is enjoyed (Monday, Thursday, and Saturday; A\$65/U.S. \$52). The Take a Camel to Dinner evening includes a 1-hour sunset ride down the Todd River to Chateau Hornsby, wine tasting, and dinner (Sunday, Tuesday, Wednesday, and Friday; A\$65/U.S. \$52). Courtesy pickup at your accommodation is included. No children under 6 years.

A ✪ **bush dinner** is another Red Centre experience you won't want to miss. Offered by Tailormade Tours (tel. 52-1731) and Camp Oven Kitchen (tel. 53-1411), these include a chance to try your hand at boomerang throwing and stock-whip cracking, as well as a delicious meal served under the stars. Tailormade Tours offers their bush barbecues on Sunday, Tuesday, and Thursday (A\$60/U.S. \$48; includes refreshments). Camp Oven Kitchen operates on Monday, Wednesday, Friday, and Saturday (A\$44/U.S. \$35.20; refreshments available). Transfers included.

EVENING ENTERTAINMENT

✪ **Ted Egan,** the well-known folksinger and colorful outback character, performs at **Chateau Hornsby,** Petrick Road (tel. 55-5133), Tuesday, Thursday, Saturday, and Sunday at 8pm (show only A\$16/U.S. \$12.80; dinner and show A\$35/U.S. \$28). Because of his popularity, bookings are essential. Egan is the world-champion Fosterphone player. This instrument, in case you haven't heard of it, is an empty Fosters beer carton with some carefully placed strings attached.

If you're determined to do something conventional, try your luck at **Lasseter's Casino,** Barrett Drive, or disco the night away (from 9:30pm Friday or Saturday) in Lasseter's **Trumps Nitespot** (cover charge A$5/U.S. $4). During the casino's "happy hour," which runs from 10am to 10pm, a 7-ounce glass of wine costs A$1.20 (U.S. $1), a 12-ounce beer costs A$1.60 (U.S. $1.30), and a piña colada costs A$4.60 (U.S. $3.70). Live music is offered in **Aces Cocktail Bar** Wednesday through Sunday from 11pm to 5am. Nearby at the Sheraton, there's live entertainment Tuesday through Saturday in the **Simpson's Gap Bar.**

Bojangles Nightclub, 80 Todd Street (tel. 52-2873), is a popular watering hole in the central business district. There's live entertainment Tuesday through Saturday.

The **Araluen Arts Centre** is Alice's venue for the performing and visual arts. Check the local newspaper for schedules or call the box office (tel. 52-5022).

5. ULURU NATIONAL PARK [AYERS ROCK/MOUNT OLGA]

465km (288 miles) SW of Alice Springs

GETTING THERE   By Plane   Access to Connellan Airport, located near the Rock, is by Australian Airlines, Eastwest, and Ansett. You can also fly to Ayers Rock from Alice Springs on Alice Springs Air Charter or Skyport. Sydney-to–Ayers Rock Australian Airlines Air Pass fares range from A$269 to A$339 (U.S. $215.20 to U.S. $271.20). Adelaide to Ayers Rock costs from A$290 to A$364 (U.S. $232 to U.S. $291.20).

By Bus   Pioneer, Bus Australia, and Greyhound run service from Alice Springs (A$58 to A$87/U.S. $46.40 to U.S. $69.60; 5½ hr.) and Adelaide (A$185 to A$208/U.S. $148 to U.S. $166.40; 19 to 20 hr).

By Car   The drive to the Rock from Alice Springs is on 465 kilometers (288 miles) of paved road—south on Stuart Highway and west on Lasseter Highway.

ESSENTIALS   The **Visitor Centre,** near the Four Seasons Hotel, has excellent displays regarding the national park, its geological basis, flora, and fauna. Rangers from the Conservation Commission staff the center and provide information from 8am to 10pm daily.

In terms of the **weather,** April through October is the best time to come to this area. September and October are best for seeing wildflowers in bloom.

The **area code** is 089.

Overseas visitors and the majority of Australians refer to the world's most famous monolith as "Ayers Rock," but the rock's traditional owners, the Aborigines, call it "Uluru." The site has great cultural significance for the Aboriginal people, who believe it played an important role in their Dreamtime. The sheltered caves and overhangs around the base of the rock have acted as canvas to hundreds of generations of native artists. There are also many sacred places, and four of these are fenced off and out-of-bounds to tourists.

Uluru (Ayers Rock/Mount Olga) National Park was handed back to the Aborigines in 1985, but they lease it to the Australian government and cooperate in its management with the National Parks and Wildlife Service. Besides Ayers Rock, the park also includes the Olgas, beautiful rock formations 36 kilometers (22 miles) to the west. The Aboriginal people call this range of enormous rock domes, topped by Mount Olga, "Kata Tjuta," which means "many heads."

Ayers Rock is easily the most distinctive landscape symbol of Australia. It has been painted and photographed by millions of visitors and continues to awe all who see it. An indescribable sense of mystery fills those who watch its color change as the sun sets or rises. The rock, which stands 348 meters (1,148 ft.) above the surrounding desert, is

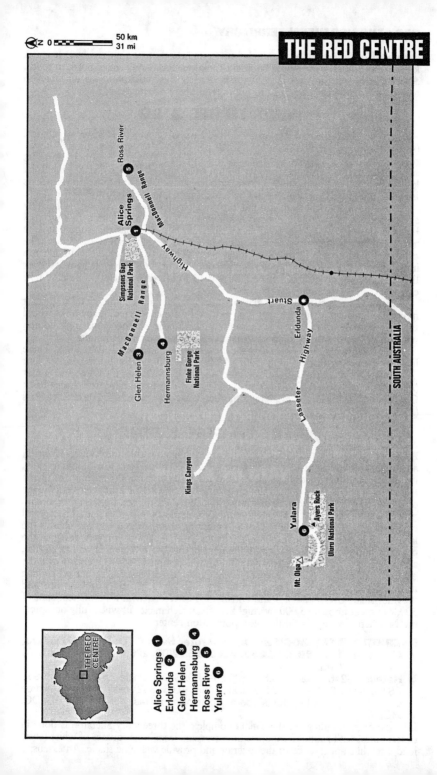

THE RED CENTRE

50 km
31 mi

Ross River

MacDonnell Range

Alice Springs ●1

Highway

Simpsons Gap National Park

MacDonnell Range

Stuart

Glen Helen ●3

Hermannsburg ●4

Finke Gorge National Park

Erldunda ●2

Lasseter Highway

Kings Canyon

SOUTH AUSTRALIA

Yulara ●6 Ayers Rock

Mt. Olga Uluru National Park

THE RED CENTRE

Alice Springs ●1
Erldunda ●2
Glen Helen ●3
Hermannsburg ●4
Ross River ●5
Yulara ●6

composed of sandstone with a high iron content—thus its rich red hue. It is 3.1 kilometers (2 miles) from east to west and 1.9 kilometers (1 mile) from north to south. Aboriginal people still live around the rock, but their community is off-limits to tourists, who are also asked not to photograph these private people.

WHAT TO SEE & DO

Rangers conduct daily walks around the base of Ayers Rock free of charge. (Admission to the park is A$8/U.S. $6.40 per person 16 years and over.) I highly recommend that you take advantage of this opportunity to learn about Uluru, its significance to the Aborigines, and its natural environment. From a distance the Rock looks like a loaf of bread plunked down on a flat surface. Only up close do you see its irregular sculptured surface, erosion patterns, caves, and rock pools.

You can, of course, walk around the Rock by yourself. If you are sufficiently ambitious to trek around the entire 9.4-kilometer (6-mile) circumference, allow 3 to 4 hours with stops. It is also possible to climb Ayers Rock, but this should not be attempted by anyone with a heart condition, asthma, fear of heights, or vertigo. The climb is 1.6 kilometers (1 mile) and takes about 2 hours round-trip if you don't run into difficulty. I don't want to put a damper on your fun, but 18 people have lost their lives on such an adventure, 5 from falls and 13 from heart attacks—so please take care.

Most tourists go to Uluru National Park solely to see the world's greatest monolith. However, I suspect that if an exit poll were conducted, many folks would say they thought the Olgas were actually prettier. The 36 enormous rock domes, which have narrow valleys between them, are a popular area for hiking.

AAT King's (tel. 56-2171) offers the most tours in and around Ayers Rock. These include the Ayers Rock Climb Tour (A$25/U.S. $20), Ayers Rock Sunrise Tour (A$25/U.S. $20), Ayers Rock Sunset Tour (A$15/U.S. $12), and the Olgas and Sunset (A$42/U.S. $33.60). AAT King's also offers a 3-day pass called the Ayers Rock Connection (A$99/U.S. $79.20) and another 3-day pass called the Ayers Rock Pass (A$85/U.S. $68).

WHERE TO STAY & DINE

All accommodations and dining facilities are contained within the **Yulara Resort,** an attractive complex located 20 kilometers (12 miles) from Ayers Rock. Built in 1984, it provides housing for tourists away from the sensitive natural environment of the Rock. Yulara, 1 kilometer (½ mile) long and approximately 1 kilometer wide, is the only land neighboring the park that is not owned by Aborigines. Because there are no nearby towns, the resort was designed to be completely self-sufficient. The central energy plant cost A$60 million (U.S. $48 million), and the desalinization plant is the largest in the Southern Hemisphere. Architect Philip Cox appropriately designed the complex to resemble a series of bedouin tents in the desert. Yulara is, and looks like, an oasis. Each of the contemporary buildings was designed both to blend in with the environment and to conserve energy. The "bull-nosed veranda," a curved awning made of corrugated iron, was inspired by colonial Queensland architecture and provides shade over balconies and corridors. The resort, with a permanent staff of 500, can accommodate 5,000 overnight guests, which makes it, when fully occupied, the Northern Territory's third-largest population center.

SHERATON AYERS ROCK HOTEL, Lasseter Hwy. (P.O. Box 21), Yulara, NT 0872. Tel. 089/56-2200. Fax 089/56-2018. 226 rms and 4 suites. A/C MINIBAR TV TEL

$ Rates: A$246–A$285 (U.S. $196.80–U.S. $228) single or double; A$385–A$420 (U.S. $308–U.S. $336) suite; A$40 (U.S. $32) extra person. Children under 18 stay free in parents' room. No-smoking rooms available. AE, BC, DC, MC, V.

Like the other buildings in the Yulara complex, the three-story Sheraton is done in desert tones, with rounded canopies of corrugated iron; large squares of white fabric lend a tentlike appearance to the exterior and provide welcome shade. An extensive collection of Aboriginal art and artifacts is on display throughout the public rooms. All rooms have a choice of a king-size bed or two doubles, and 10 rooms have been designed with the handicapped in mind.

Dining/Entertainment: The Desert Rose Brasserie is open daily from 6am to 10pm. The Kunia Room, the fine-dining venue, serves à la carte dinners Tuesday through Sunday. Drinks are available around the pool or from the Kunia Lounge.

Services: 24-hour room service, turn-down service, shoeshine, laundry, concierge, and baby-sitting.

Facilities: A free-form swimming pool, spa, children's pool, jogging course, bicycle track, and tennis courts are on the premises. There's also a viewing tower.

FOUR SEASONS AYERS ROCK, 15 Yulara Dr., Yulara, NT 0872. Tel. 089/56-2100, or toll free 008/33-1147 in Australia. Fax 089/56-2156. 100 rms. A/C MINIBAR TV TEL

$ **Rates:** A$185 (U.S. $148) single; A$225 (U.S. $180) double; A$25 (U.S. $20) extra person. Children under 15 stay free in parents' room. Lower rates Nov–Apr. AE, BC, DC, MC, V.

The Four Seasons was designed to cater to the domestic market, so rates are lower. Each modern room has one double and one single bed; bathrooms have showers, no tubs. There are a swimming pool, facilities for half-court tennis and volleyball, a restaurant, and a cocktail lounge. In addition, because Yulara is an open resort, any guest can use the facilities at either hotel. Eight rooms are provided for handicapped travelers.

RED CENTRE HOTEL, Yulara Dr. (Box 10), Yulara, NT 0872. Tel. 089/56-2170, or toll free 008/08-9622 in Australia. Fax 089/56-2320. 125 rms; 12 lodge units, 16 lodge cabins, 4 dormitories (none with bath). A/C

$ **Rates:** A$180 (U.S. $144) single or double room; A$198 (U.S. $158.40) single or double room with kitchenette; A$85 (U.S. $68) lodge unit or cabin; A$21 (U.S. $16.80) bed in dormitory. Children under 15 stay free in parents' room. AE, BC, DC, MC, V.

The Red Centre Hotel offers both standard and budget accommodation. The rooms have one single and one double bed, televisions, clock radios, coffee- and tea-making facilities, small refrigerators, and en suite bathrooms. The units, cabins, and dormitories share communal bathrooms. A swimming pool, barbecue, and laundry facilities are on the premises.

CHAPTER 12
PERTH

The most remote capital in the western world, beautiful Perth lies near the coast of the Indian Ocean, isolated from the rest of Australia. The nearest urban center, Adelaide, is 2,700 kilometers (1,674 miles) to the east. Were it not for Western Australia's mineral wealth, the city might never have gotten off the ground. As it is, the discovery of gold in the state in the 1890s helped Perth become established, and iron ore, diamonds, gold, and other minerals keep it booming today.

I lived in Perth in 1977, and whenever I go back I am reminded how much it is like my hometown, San Diego, California. The two places share a delightful Mediterranean climate, a casual, outdoorsy life-style, large parks adjacent to the city center, beautiful beaches, a love of boating—and an interest in possessing the America's Cup. In addition, both Perth and San Diego have populations of about one million, are located in the southwest corners of their respective countries and are home to people who give meaning to the phrases "laid-back" and "do your own thing."

Unlike other parts of the nation, Perth has dry summers, and what little rain the city does get tends to fall in the winter months. This is statistically the sunniest capital; temperatures average 29°C (84°F) in summer and 18°C (64°F) in winter. Just when a summer day threatens to get too warm, the Fremantle Doctor, as the stiff breeze off the ocean is known, pays a call and cools things off.

Perth's climate invites visitors throughout the year, but most come during the spring, when wildflowers bloom in profusion in the city's parks and environs. September is prime time for wildflower viewing, and if you plan to visit during this popular period, I suggest you make your reservations well in advance.

1. ORIENTATION

ARRIVING

BY PLANE

International air service is provided by **Qantas** and 13 other carriers who fly in from Africa, Britain, Europe, Hong Kong, Japan, New Zealand, and Southeast Asia.

Ansett, Compass, and **Australian Airlines** provide regular interstate service. The cost of a Sydney-Perth Australian Airlines Air Pass ticket ranges from A$345 to A$425 (U.S. $276 to U.S. $340). That trip takes 4 hours. Adelaide to Perth (3 hr.) costs A$267 to A$335 (U.S. $213.60 to U.S. $268). Melbourne to Perth (3½ hr.) costs A$305 to A$383 (U.S. $244 to U.S. $306.40). Compass Airlines often offers special fares to Perth which are lower.

Perth has separate international and domestic airport terminals located northeast of the city. The domestic terminal is 11 kilometers (7 miles) from town; the international terminal is 18 kilometers (11 miles) away. The shuttle bus to town from

WHAT'S SPECIAL ABOUT PERTH

Beaches
☐ Scarborough Beach, one of several long sandy stretches within easy reach of Perth.

Natural Spectacles
☐ Wildflowers blooming in profusion during September and October.

Parks/Gardens
☐ King's Park, affording great views of the city skyline and Swan River.

Easy Excursions
☐ Rottnest Island, only 19 kilometers (12 miles) offshore.
☐ Fremantle, a historic seaport downriver from Perth.

the international terminal costs A$6 (U.S. $4.80), or you can take a taxi for about A$18 (U.S. $14.40). The bus from the domestic terminal costs A$5 (U.S. $4); the taxi fare is about A$12 (U.S. $9.60). In the unlikely event that you need to go directly between the two terminals, that bus trip costs A$4 (U.S. $3.20). If you have questions about the Airport Bus Service, phone 250-2838.

Duty-free shops, bars, and restaurants are located in the airport's international terminal. A bank, open 1 hour before and after overseas departures and arrivals, is located on the ground floor and in the second-floor departure lounge. The major car-rental companies have staffed desks, but there isn't a tourist information counter or a post office. Showers are available, as is a baggage-storage facility.

The domestic terminal also has car-rental desks, showers, shops, bars, and places to eat. It lacks baggage lockers and a bank, but stamps are available in the newsagency/gift shop and a mailbox is located next to the shop. Both terminals have computers that supply tourist information.

When you're leaving Perth, remember to book the **Airport Bus Service** (tel. 250-2838) at least 1 hour ahead of time. If you're leaving Australia, don't forget your A$10 (U.S. $8) departure tax, which must be paid in Australian currency.

BY TRAIN

You can also arrive in Perth by train. The **Indian Pacific,** which makes the 65-hour journey from Sydney three times a week, is Australia's most popular railroad trip despite the fact that it crosses the Nullarbor Plain on the world's longest stretch of straight track past scenery that is quite monotonous. If you'd like to sample this experience, make your reservations well in advance. First-class berth and meals cost A$870 (U.S. $696). Economy-class seats cost A$292 (U.S. $233.60). The **Trans Australian** travels between Perth and Adelaide (40 hr.) twice a week. First-class berth and meals cost A$545 (U.S. $436). Economy-class berth and meals cost A$412 (U.S. $329.60). Economy sitting costs A$165 (U.S. $132). Children's fares are lower. Both trains offer a club/lounge car, as well as dining and sleeping facilities. For information regarding interstate train service in Perth, phone 326-2222 between 8:30am and 5pm.

If you're departing Perth by train, don't wait until the last minute to get to the station, because the baggage check-in counter closes 30 minutes before the train leaves.

BY BUS

Bus (coach) service from Adelaide to Perth takes 35 hours and costs A$160 (U.S. $128). Darwin to Perth takes 56 hours and costs $295 (U.S. $236). Pioneer, Greyhound, and Bus Australia provide service.

BY CAR

I really don't recommend driving across the Nullabor Plain, the incredibly long, boring, desolate stretch of road between Perth and Adelaide. If you decide to make the trip, get advice from the auto club in Perth (tel. 09/421-4444) or Adelaide (tel. 08/223-4555) before starting out.

TOURIST INFORMATION

The best source of where-to-go, what-to-see data is the **Western Australian Tourist Centre,** Albert Facey House, corner of Forrest Place and Wellington Street (tel. 483-1111). This office, open Monday through Friday from 8:30am to 5:30pm and Saturday from 9am to 1pm, is staffed by very helpful people.

InfoWest computers are dotted around the city, and an information kiosk is open during shopping hours Monday through Saturday in the Hay Street Mall.

INTERSTATE INFORMATION

The following offices are located in Perth: **Northern Territory Government Tourist Bureau,** 799 Hay Street (tel. 322-4255); **Queensland Government Travel Centre,** 55 St. George's Terrace (tel. 325-1600); **South Australian Travel Centre,** Wesley Centre, 93 William Street (tel. 481-1268).

CITY LAYOUT

The city of Perth faces the sparkling water of the beautiful **Swan River** at a point where the waterway is wide, and one has the sense of looking out at a lake more than on a river. If you take a walk along the shore, you'll probably see black swans, the symbol of Western Australia, after which Swan Lager, the state beer, is named. On weekends, these graceful birds are joined by boats of many sizes and shapes. This is a young, active, water-oriented city, and the Swan River is the inhabitants' favorite playground.

The commercial heart of the metropolis lies on the north side of the river. **St. George's Terrace,** the main street in the business district, is only 1 block beyond the grassy belt that rims the Swan. **Hay Street,** the primary shopping area, is 1 block farther from the water. **Northbridge,** across the railroad tracks, is the restaurant and nightclub region. Perth's compact city center is comprised of strikingly attractive modern high-rises juxtaposed with ornate colonial buildings. All industrial structures are located at **Kwinana,** 32 kilometers (20 miles) south, so the city is clean, relatively uncongested, and easy to get around. On its western edge, magnificent **King's Park** stretches over 404 hectares (998 acres), including open bushland, botanical gardens, lush lawns, and public facilities. Sprawling across low-rise **Mount Eliza,** the park provides a superb 270° view of the Swan River and the city skyline.

On a large-scale map, Perth appears to be located right on the Indian Ocean, but in fact it's 19 kilometers (12 miles) upstream from the mouth of the Swan, which enters the ocean at **Fremantle.** The location of the port at this distance from the city also contributes to Perth's pleasant appearance. Until 1987, Fremantle wasn't a place where you'd want to go for a walk, but restoration done in preparation for hosting the America's Cup gave historic buildings a face-lift; parks were relandscaped, new hotels and restaurants added. Today the port is a charming area with some lively, atmospheric pubs that draw the after-work crowd from Perth's high-rise office buildings.

North of Fremantle, along the shore of the Indian Ocean, wide beaches invite sunbathers, and the Fremantle Doctor gives windsurfers a thrill. **Cottesloe, Swanbourne,** and **Scarborough** are suburbs named after three of the favorite sandy stretches. Perth is sometimes called "Australia's Dallas" because it is home to many of the country's tycoons. If you'd like to see what a millionaire's row looks like down under, head for the suburb of **Dalkeith. Claremont** is a fashionable shopping district.

2. GETTING AROUND

BY PUBLIC TRANSPORTATION

Transperth, the government-run public transportation system, operates buses, local trains, and cross-river ferries. For timetable brochures, stop in at the Transperth Information Office in City Arcade (Hay Street Mall level), or the Perth Central Bus Station on Wellington Street near Queen. You can also phone Transperth (tel. 221-1211) for bus, train, and ferry information between 6am and 9pm 7 days a week. The **Transperth Sightseers Ticket** is a dollarwise value for visitors. For A$4.60 (U.S. $3.70) you can buy a ticket good for 1 day on any bus, train, or ferry within the system; a 5-day pass costs A$19.40 (U.S. $15.55). Children are half price. Tickets can be purchased at any Transperth information office or railway station.

Transperth operates free buses and trains within a city-center **"Free Transit Zone."** This area is bounded by King's Park Road, Thomas Street, Newcastle Street, the Causeway, and Barrack Street Jetty.

BY TRAIN

Electric train service started in 1990 and now links the city, suburbs, and towns which are beyond the metropolitan area. Suburban trains, including the ones to Fremantle, leave from **City Station,** Wellington Street.

BY BUS

In addition to free buses and trains within the Free Transit Zone, Transperth also operates **free City Clipper buses.** Clipper buses are easily distinguished by their blue-and-gold logo on a white background. In addition, each vehicle is color-coded red, yellow, blue, or green according to its designated route. Red and yellow Clippers run Monday through Friday from 7am to 5:30pm and Saturday from 9am to noon; blue and green Clippers operate Monday through Friday. The buses service an area bounded by Outram, Bulwer, and Plain streets and The Esplanade. A complete map of their routes is printed in the front section of city phone books.

Conducted bus excursions are offered by several companies, including Australian Pacific Tours (tel. 325-9377), Feature Tours (tel. 479-4131), Pinnacle Tours (tel. 325-9455), Great Western Tours (tel. 328-4542), and Travelabout (tel. 242-2243).

BY FERRY

Ferries across the Swan River to South Perth leave from the **Barrack Street Jetty.** This service operates daily from 7am to 7:15pm. Transperth also operates river cruises between September and early June.

BY TAXI

There are taxi stands throughout the city. Charges are A$1.90 (U.S. $1.55) at flagfall and A75¢ (U.S. 60¢) per kilometer. The flagfall goes up to A$3 (U.S. $2.40) from 6pm to 6am Monday through Friday and from 1pm Saturday to 6am Monday. The three biggest companies are **Black & White** (tel. 328-8288), **Green & Gold** (tel. 328-3311), and **Swan** (tel. 322-0111 in Perth, 335-3944 in Fremantle).

BY CAR

You can rent cars at the following offices: **Ansa International,** 351 Stirling Highway, Claremont (tel. 384-3241); **Avis,** 46 Hill Street (tel. 325-7677); **Budget,** 960 Hay Street (tel. 481-1044 for cars, 479-1919 for four-wheel-drive and minibus rental); **Capricorn,** 34 Welshpool Road, Bentley (tel. 362-4544); **Hertz,** 39 Milligan

Street (tel. 321-7777); **Letz,** 126 Grandstand Street, Belmont (tel. 478-1999); **Thrifty,** 33 Milligan Street (tel. 481-1999).

You'll find an office of the **Royal Automobile Club of Western Australia (RAC)** at 228 Adelaide Terrace (tel. 421-4444).

FAST FACTS PERTH

Airlines The following airlines have offices in Perth: Air Canada, 231 Adelaide Terrace (tel. 325-5662, or toll free 008/22-1015 in Australia); Air New Zealand, 50 St. George's Terrace (tel. 325-1099, or toll free 008/22-1111); Ansett, 26 St. George's Terrace (tel. 323-1111 or 325-0201); Australian Airlines, 55 St. George's Terrace (tel. 323-3333); British Airways, 80 William St. (tel. 483-7711); Continental Airlines, 179 St. George's Terrace (tel. toll free 008/22-2122); Garuda Airlines, 111 St. George's Terrace (tel. 481-0963); Qantas, 55 William St. or Hay Street Mall (tel. 225-2222); Rottnest Airbus (tel. 478-1322); Skywest, 26 St. George's Terrace (tel. 323-1188); United, 178 St. George's Terrace (tel. 321-2719 or 321-8747).

American Express The office is located at 78 William St. (tel. 426-3777). It's open regular business hours.

Area Code Perth telephone numbers are in the 09 area code.

Baby-sitters If you're in need of a baby-sitter, call Dial-a-Nanny (tel. 321-7485) or Dial an Angel (tel. 381-4999).

Business Hours Banks are generally open Mon–Thurs 9:30am–4pm and Fri 9:30am–5pm. Stores are generally open Mon–Wed and Fri 9am–5:30pm, Thurs 9am–9pm, and Sat 9am–5pm.

Car Rental See "Getting Around," above.

Climate See "When to Go" in Chapter 2.

Currency See "Information, Entry Requirements, and Money" in Chapter 2.

Currency Exchange Cash traveler's checks at banks or at the larger hotels.

Dentist Look in the yellow pages phone book under "Dentists—Locality Guide."

Doctor Call the Royal Perth Hospital (tel. 224-2244).

Drugstore [Chemist Shop] Pharmacity Chemist Supermart, 717 Hay Street Mall (tel. 322-6921), is open Mon–Wed and Fri 8am–6pm, Thurs 8am–9pm, and Sat 9am–5pm.

Embassies/Consulates You'll find the following consulates in Perth: Canada, 160 St. George's Terrace (tel. 322-6288); New Zealand, 16 St. George's Terrace (tel. 325-7877); United Kingdom, 95 St. George's Terrace (tel. 321-5611); United States, 246 St. George's Terrace (tel. 322-4466).

Emergencies Dial 000 to summon ambulance, fire department, or police in an emergency.

Eyeglasses OPSM Vision Center, 660 Hay Street Mall (tel. 221-2882), is open Mon–Wed and Fri 8:30am–5:30pm, Thurs 8:30am–9pm, and Sat 9am–4pm.

Hairdressers/Barbers Try Sam Rifici Hair Care, 138 Murray St. (tel. 325-3800 or 325-3020).

Holidays See "When to Go" in Chapter 2.

Hospitals Royal Perth Hospital, Wellington St. (tel. 224-2244) is centrally located.

Hotlines Crisis Care Unit, Department of Community Services; call 24 hours a day (tel. 325-1111, or toll free 008/19-9008 outside of Perth).

Information See "Tourist Information," above.

Laundry/Dry Cleaning Snow White does 1-hour cleaning at their dozen locations around Perth. The shop in the Trinity Arcade (tel. 321-5253) is convenient.

Libraries The Alexander Library Building, in the Perth Cultural Centre in Northbridge (tel. 427-3111), carries newspapers from around the world as well as a large collection of books, journals, and other library materials. The City Library is located at 27 St. George's Terrace (tel. 265-3381).

Lost Property   Lost property on trains? Call 326-2660. On buses: 426-2678.

Luggage Storage/Lockers   There are lockers in the East Perth Rail Terminal (A$1/U.S. 80¢ a day) and in the Perth City Station on the mezzanine level (A$2/U.S. $1.60 a day).

Newspapers/Magazines   The *West Australian* is the major daily.

Photographic Needs   KLIKK (camera repair) has 13 locations around Perth. The most central is in Alfred's Photographics, corner of Hay and Pier streets (tel. 325-5066).

Post Code   Central Perth addresses have a 6000 postal code.

Post Office   The General Post Office (GPO), in Forrest Place (tel. 326-5211), is open Mon–Fri 8am–5pm and Sat–Sun 9am–2pm. General-delivery mail can be picked up only Mon–Fri 9am–5pm, and some other services are also limited to these weekday hours.

Radio   Easy listening, 6KY (AM); news/weather, 810 (AM); rock, 6PM (AM), 6GL (FM), 6NOW (96FM).

Religious Services   You can attend services at the following locations: Anglican, St. George's Cathedral, 38 St. George's Terrace (tel. 325-5766); Baptist, Central Baptist Church, 10 James St. (tel. 328-6507); Buddhist, Chanh-Giac Temple, 45 Money St. (tel. 342-6069); Christian Scientist, First Church of Christ Scientists, 264 St. George's Terrace (tel. 321-5012); Church of Christ, 146 Beaufort St. (tel. 328-1499); Jewish, Temple David Congregation, 34 Clifton Crescent, Mount Lawley (tel. 271-1485); Lutheran, 16 Aberdeen St. (tel. 227-8072); Muslim, Perth Mosque, 427 William St., Northbridge (tel. 328-8535); Roman Catholic, St. Mary's Cathedral, Victoria Sq. (tel. 325-9177 or 325-9557); Uniting Church, St. Andrew's, corner of Pier St. and St. George's Terrace (tel. 321-4243 or 367-3715).

Rest Rooms   There are public toilets open 24 hours a day on the mezzanine level of Forrest Place on Wellington St. The ones on the Esplanade near Barrack St. are open 8am–7pm daily. You can also use the facilities in department stores during shopping hours and in hotels at any time.

Safety   The area adjacent to Russell Sq. in Northbridge (Milligan and Aberdeen streets) is best avoided by women on their own at night.

Shoe Repairs   While-you-wait repairs are available at the Palace Bootmakers, Westpac Arcade, 110 William St., corner of Murray St. (tel. 321-5343).

Taxes   Perth has neither a hotel tax nor a GST (Goods and Services Tax). Sales tax is included in the purchase price of merchandise.

Taxis   See "Getting Around," above.

Telegrams/Telex   Send these from the Perth GPO, 3 Forrest Place (tel. 326-5211).

Television   Channel 2, the Australian Broadcasting Corporation, is the best place to look for news, current affairs, and documentaries. The other channels are 7, 9, and 10.

Transit Info   If you have questions about local public transportation, call Transperth: 221-1211.

Useful Telephone Numbers   Seniors Information Service: 328-9155, or toll free 008/11-9087; Women's Information and Referral Exchange (WIRE): 222-0444, or toll free 008/11-9174; Gay and Lesbian Counselling Service: 328-9044.

3. PERTH ACCOMMODATIONS

Several large hotels were built in anticipation of the 1987 America's Cup, and the result today is a city with more rooms than it really needs. This oversupply means that lodging tariffs are quite reasonable, especially on weekends, when reduced rates are often in effect.

IN THE CITY CENTER

EXPENSIVE

HYATT REGENCY PERTH, 99 Adelaide Terrace, Perth, WA 6000. Tel. 09/225-1234. Fax 09/325-8899. 369 rms, 31 suites. A/C MINIBAR TV TEL
$ Rates: A$200–A$220 (U.S. $160–U.S. $176) single or double; A$400–A$900 (U.S. $320–U.S. $720) suite. Weekend discounts. AE, BC, DC, MC, V. **Parking:** Free.

Visitors enter this architectural giant, about 4 blocks from the city center, 1 block from Langley Park, and 2 blocks from the Swan River, under a clear-domed walkway. The Hyatt hosts many conferences, and delegates and their displays frequently spill over into this area.

Of the spacious rooms available at the hotel, half have water views. All have hairdryers and guests have a choice of a king-size bed, twin beds, or a double and a single.

Dining/Entertainment: The hotel is part of the Hyatt Centre, a large modern complex of eating places, shops, and offices. Two restaurants and two bars are located in the hotel.

Services: Laundry, dry cleaning, 24-hour room service, concierge.

Facilities: Squash courts, sauna, fitness center, tennis court, and a large octagonal swimming pool are on the premises.

SHERATON PERTH HOTEL, 207 Adelaide Terrace, Perth, WA 6000. Tel. 09/325-0501. Fax 09/325-4032. 396 rms, 46 suites. A/C MINIBAR TV TEL
$ Rates: A$187–A$265 (U.S. $149.60–U.S. $212) single or double; A$40 (U.S. $32) extra person. Weekend packages available. AE, BC, DC, MC, V. **Parking:** A$8 (U.S. $6.40).

The doorman in top hat and tails who greets guests at the Sheraton Hotel looks a little out of place in casual Perth. I suspect he's a prop designed to make businessmen from the eastern states feel at home. Happily, the friendly staff do not reflect his stuffy attire. The hotel, built in 1973, is located only a block or so from the city center. All rooms have a window that opens; most have king-size beds. All bathrooms have hairdryers. Quarters on the top four floors have the best view.

Dining/Entertainment: The River Room is an elegant à la carte restaurant; the Clinker Grill has a goldfields decor; and the Wandarrah is a cheerful coffee shop. Two lounge bars, a public bar, and a disco are also on the premises.

Services: Laundry, dry cleaning, 24-hour room service, concierge.

Facilities: Beauty salon, hairdressing salon, swimming pool, and sauna.

MODERATE

PERTH AMBASSADOR HOTEL, 196 Adelaide Terrace, Perth, WA 6000. Tel. 09/325-1455, or toll free 008/99-8011 in Australia. Fax 09/325-6317. 174 rms, 55 suites. A/C TV TEL
$ Rates: A$120 (U.S. $96) single or double; A$140 (U.S. $112) suite; A$15 (U.S. $12) extra person. AE, BC, DC, MC, V. **Parking:** Free.

This is a pleasant eight-story building located a couple of blocks from the heart of the city center. Rooms on upper floors in the front of the hotel overlook the Swan River. All quarters have large, bright windows and tile bathrooms with separate showers and bathtubs. The Ambassador provides the usual modern amenities. Standard rooms have either a queen-size bed or twins. Executive studios and Australian suites have king-size beds. Hallways on guest-room floors have textured grass-cloth wallpaper and little colonial-style wall-mounted lamps that give a warm, welcoming feel.

The Majestic Chinese Restaurant on the ground floor is popular with locals.

There's also a coffee shop on the second floor, offering both indoor and outdoor dining. Guests are welcome to use the large sauna and hot spa, but there is no pool.

PERTH PARKROYAL, 54 Terrace Rd., Perth, WA 6004. Tel. 09/325-3811, or toll free 008/19-8721 in Western Australia. Fax 09/221-1564. 99 rms, 2 suites. A/C MINIBAR TV TEL

$ **Rates:** A$140 (U.S. $112) single or double; A$240 (U.S. $192) suite; A$20 (U.S. $16) extra person. Children under 18 stay free in parents' room. Weekend and long-stay discounts. AE, BC, CB, DC, MC, V. **Parking:** Free.

The Perth Parkroyal is a 12-story property overlooking Langley Park and the Swan River about 4 blocks from the city center. An exclusive, private feel prevails in the Parkroyal's lobby and public spaces, and the staff gives attentive, personal service.

Pleasant light tones have been used throughout the guest bedrooms. Each room has its own balcony or patio and offers a choice of queen-size or twin beds. Bathrooms have showers only. All quarters come with clock radios, bathrobes, hairdryers, tea- and coffee-making facilities, small refrigerators, in-room movies, and free daily newspapers.

Meals and drinks are served in the Royal Palm Restaurant, Lobby Bar, and Club Lounge. Guests also have use of the hotel's spa, pool, and gymnasium.

QUALITY PRINCE'S HOTEL, 334 Murray St. Perth, WA 6000. Tel. 09/322-2844, or toll free 008/07-4444 in Australia. Fax 09/321-6314. 151 rms, 16 suites. A/C MINIBAR TV TEL

$ **Rates:** A$77–A$110 (U.S. $61.60–U.S. $88) single; A$94–A$110 (U.S. $75.20–U.S. $88) double; A$120–A$200 (U.S. $96–U.S. $160) suite; A$12 (U.S. $9.60) extra person. Weekend packages available. AE, BC, DC, MC, V. **Parking:** Free.

The Quality Prince's Hotel is located in the heart of town only a block from the Hay Street Mall and adjacent shopping areas. The hostelry has rooms on nine floors, and these are categorized either "tourist class" or "business class." None of the rooms are spacious; all offer showers only, and a choice between double or twin beds. Tourist-class quarters are on floors one to five and have modest furnishings; business-class rooms occupy loftier levels within the hotel and have upmarket decors. Studio suites have a separate lounge with a sofa sleeper and two bathrooms.

The Prince's Plaza has several pleasant drinking and dining options, including Valentine's Bistro, Valentine's Bar, and the Society Bar and Grill.

WENTWORTH PLAZA HOTEL, 300 Murray St., Perth, WA 6000. Tel. 09/481-1000. Fax 09/321-2443. 93 rms, 12 suites (some without private bath). A/C MINIBAR TV TEL

$ **Rates:** A$40 (U.S. $32) single without bath, A$60 (U.S. $48) single with bath; A$50 (U.S. $40) double without bath, A$70 (U.S. $56) double with bath, A$80 (U.S. $64) double with kitchen; A$90 (U.S. $72) apartment. Children under 12 stay free in parents' room. AE, BC, DC, MC, V. **Parking:** Free.

I take my hat off to the architects who designed the midcity Wentworth Plaza Hotel. Faced with the task of remodeling and connecting three existing hostelries, they were able to complete the job without destroying the original charm and old-world ambience. Until 1986, the three-story Wentworth Plaza was the Wentworth, the Royal, and the Bohemia—all older hotels, built in 1928, 1882, and 1879, respectively, and all in need of a face-lift.

An attractive gray-and-lavender color scheme is used throughout, and the hotel has high ceilings, large wood-framed windows that open, elaborate banisters, and lovely arches in the hallways. In the Royal section, dormer windows and slanted ceilings create an especially cozy feel. Raine Square, a complex of 40 shops, fills the courtyard between the three buildings.

It was the old-world gray exterior that attracted me to the Wentworth Plaza, and when I poked my head inside the door and saw an aviary, I knew I had found someplace special. The hotel also has four unusual restaurants and bars: Horsefeathers, The Garage, the Plaza Cafe, and Moon & Sixpence English Pub.

BUDGET

The less expensive rooms at the **Wentworth Plaza** qualify as budget digs. Even cheaper are the accommodations at the **YMCA Jewell House**, 180 Goderich Street, Perth, WA 6000 (tel. 09/325-8488, or toll free 008/99-8212 in Australia). Singles here go for A$22 to A$30 (U.S. $17.60 to U.S. $24) and doubles cost A$30 to A$40 (U.S. $24 to U.S. $32). Jewell House is located about a block from the city center next to the Royal Perth Hospital.

VICTORIA PARK

EXPENSIVE

BURSWOOD RESORT HOTEL, Great Eastern Hwy., Victoria Park, WA 6100. Tel. 09/362-7777. Fax 09/470-1789. 392 rms, 18 suites. A/C MINIBAR TV TEL **Transportation:** Free shuttle from hotel to central business district every hour.

$ Rates: A$108–A$155 (U.S. $86.40–U.S. $124) single or double; A$330 (U.S. $264) suite; A$20 (U.S. $16) extra person. Special packages available. Children under 14 stay free in parents' room. AE, BC, DC, MC, V. **Parking:** Free.

This hotel is part of a large complex which includes a convention center, Superdome, 18-hole golf course, and casino. Located on the south side of the Swan River, Burswood's lobby is topped by a 12-story cone-shaped atrium where four glass elevators whisk guests to their rooms.

Some bedrooms have king-size beds; in fact, River Suites have two king beds. All quarters have clock radios, tea- and coffee-making facilities, small refrigerators, and in-room movies. Each also has a large bath separated from the bedroom by a Japanese sliding screen. Half the rooms have a river view.

Dining/Entertainment: Windows is Burswood's fine-dining venue. The Atrium Bar is in the lobby. There are several other eating options and enough bars to make a Las Vegas veteran feel at home.

Services: 24-hour room service, laundry, concierge, and massage.

Facilities: Indoor pool, outdoor pool, gym, sauna, hair salon, gift shop, four tennis courts, spa, table tennis, bicycle rental, casino, and business center.

ON THE BEACH

EXPENSIVE

OBSERVATION CITY RESORT HOTEL, The Esplanade, Scarborough Beach, WA 6019. Tel. 09/245-1000, or toll free 008/99-9494 in Australia. Fax 09/245-1345. 331 rms, 5 suites. A/C MINIBAR TV TEL **Transportation:** Taxi to city center A$14 (U.S. $11.20); bus (route 293) A$1.60 (U.S. $1.30). Free shuttle to city center. Hotel is located 18km (11 miles) from Perth.

$ Rates: A$140–A$210 (U.S. $112–U.S. $168) single or double; A$245 (U.S. $196) Club Room; A$475–A$2,000 (U.S. $380–U.S. $1,600) suite; A$35 (U.S. $28) extra person. Lower weekend rates. Children under 18 stay free in parents' room. AE, BC, CB, DC, MC, V. **Parking:** Free.

Alan Bond is best known to Americans as the Australian who built the boat that won the America's Cup in 1983. However, in his own country, Bond is better known for his entrepreneurial ventures. The 17-story beachfront Observation City Resort Hotel is one of these. Opened in 1986, it was a good observation point for the 1987 America's Cup races.

The public rooms are done in a potpourri of styles: a waterfall and tropical plants grace one side of the lobby, while plush salmon carpeting and traditional furnishings are across the way. Each bedroom has an ocean view and a balcony. Guests have a choice of king-size beds or a queen-size bed with a single. Hairdryers and toasters are standard throughout.

Tariffs vary according to the location of rooms within the hotel. Deluxe quarters facing the beach have two sliding glass doors that open onto balconies. Superior rooms are in the middle of the hotel and have one slider. Standard rooms are at the back of the property and on the lower floors. The hotel employs a run-of-the-house policy, meaning that guests are allotted the best available room at the time of their arrival. So you might book a standard room and be given deluxe lodging. (Obviously, if you reserve deluxe that's what you get.)

Dining/Entertainment: Observation City includes the Spice Market eatery, Pines Bistro, Crusoe's Seafood Restaurant, and à la carte Ocean Room. There are six bars, plus the Club Atlantis disco and Nero's Nightclub.

Services: Free child care 8am to 6pm and coordinated children's activities every day, 24-hour room service, turn-down service, shoeshine, laundry, valet, and concierge.

Facilities: Lagoon-style pool, two tennis courts, health club, gym, child-care center, spa, sauna, and salon with masseuse and beautician.

MODERATE

WEST BEACH LAGOON APARTMENTS, 251 West Coast Hwy., Scarborough Beach, WA 6019. Tel. 09/341-6122, or toll free 008/99-9339 in Australia. Fax 09/341-5944. 69 2-bedroom apartments. TV TEL **Bus:** No. 268 or 269 takes guests into Perth, which is about 12km (7 miles) inland.

$ Rates: A$90 (U.S. $72) per apartment which sleeps four people. Rates are 25% higher Dec–Jan. No-smoking rooms available. AE, BC, DC, MC, V. **Parking:** Free.

Each of the two-bedroom units in the West Beach Lagoon has a full kitchen. They are modestly but adequately furnished; all sleep four and most have ocean views. Only an access road (no through traffic) separates this hostelry from the beach, and a nice pool provides another swimming alternative.

The Depot, a casual, family-oriented eatery, specializes in steaks. West Beach Lagoon's other dining spot, Somerset's Restaurant, has a tropical feel created by rattan furniture, slate floors, cane lampshades, and lots of green plants. Pictures of Somerset Maugham and his contemporaries line the walls, and the names of menu items are taken from his novels.

If you'd rather cook for yourself, there is a supermarket down the block.

FREMANTLE

MODERATE

TRADEWINDS HOTEL, 59 Canning Hwy., East Fremantle, WA 6158. Tel. 09/339-8188, or toll free 008/99-9274 in Australia. Fax 09/339-2266. 9 rms (none with bath), 83 apartments with cooking facilities. A/C TV TEL **Directions:** See below.

$ Rates: A$45 (U.S. $36) single without bath; A$50 (U.S. $40) double without bath; A$99 (U.S. $79.20) studio for two; A$110 (U.S. $88) 1-bedroom unit; A$125 (U.S. $100) 2-bedroom unit. Children under 12 stay free in parents' room. AE, BC, DC, MC, V. **Parking:** Free.

The Trade Winds Hotel has a bright, airy feel and tropical/colonial decor. This pleasant hostelry is located on the lower reaches of the Swan River between the Fremantle Bridge and the Stirling Bridge, with the ocean about 2 kilometers (1 mile) to the west and Perth almost 20 kilometers (12 miles) upriver. The original part of the Trade Winds was built in 1910, and the nine colonial-style quarters that remain from this era lack private bathrooms. The other 83 rooms date from 1986 and are composed of studio, one-bedroom, and two-bedroom suites. All of these have queen-size beds, fully equipped kitchenettes or kitchens, and private bathrooms. Sliding glass doors let in lots of sunlight.

Trader Morgans Bistro has a nautical flavor created by barrels, brass, and halyards. Trade Winds Lounge Bar serves snacks and lunch. Plympton, the public bar, is popular with locals who play darts and pool. The Piazza Bar offers outdoor drinking and a view of the river. Guests also enjoy the property's pool and spa.

4. PERTH DINING

IN THE CITY CENTER

EXPENSIVE

JESSICA'S SEAFOOD RESTAURANT, in the Hyatt Centre, 99 Adelaide Terrace. Tel. 325-2511.
Cuisine: SEAFOOD. **Reservations:** Recommended. **Directions:** Take any bus down St. George's Terrace to Plain St.
$ Prices: Appetizers A$9.95–A$14.50 (U.S. $8–U.S. $11.60); main courses A$19.50–A$38 (U.S. $15.60–U.S. $30.40); set two-course meal (not applicable Fri–Sat dinner) A$24.90 (U.S. $19.95); children's meal A$9.50 (U.S. $7.60). AE, BC, DC, MC, V.
Open: Lunch daily noon–3pm; dinner daily 6pm–late.

Located in the Hyatt Centre, Jessica's is easily Perth's finest seafood restaurant. Fish and shellfish are purchased daily at the market, and the menu changes depending on what's available. Because everything is fresh, the chef doesn't need heavy sauces and, instead, lets the natural flavor of the ingredients come through. On a typical night you might have a choice of grilled Exmouth red emperor, grilled Albany King George whiting filets, or barbecued Mandurah prawns with onion and herb topping. These dishes come in both entrée and main-course portions.

If you'd prefer not to have two fish courses, you could start with an entrée of fresh steamed asparagus, sautéed calves' liver with fried onions, or a bowl of homemade leek and potato soup. Bouillabaisse, served in a heavy black Dutch oven, is a favorite main-course item.

Jessica's is located across from Langley Park with a view of the Swan River. The decor has a postmodernist flavor, with a pale mint color scheme, black lacquer chairs, and polished granite tables. A pianist plays during dinner Tuesday through Saturday and for lunch on Friday. The adequate, but not extensive, wine list emphasizes Western Australian whites.

MODERATE

HORSEFEATHERS, in the Wentworth Plaza Hotel, 300 Murray St., corner of William St. Tel. 481-1000.
Cuisine: MIXED. **Reservations:** Not necessary.
$ Prices: Appetizers A$3.95–A$8.50 (U.S. $3.20–U.S. $6.80); main courses A$7.95–A$16.50 (U.S. $6.40–U.S. $13.20); continental breakfast A$8 (U.S. $6.40); cooked breakfast A$11 (U.S. $8.80). AE, BC, DC, MC, V.
Open: Breakfast, lunch, and dinner daily 7am–11pm.

Horsefeathers, located in the Wentworth Plaza Hotel, is enough to wake up anyone's senses. Described by the managers as a "food and fun emporium," the restaurant is decorated with a most amazing collection of memorabilia, including props from the television series based on the Australian classic *A Fortunate Life*.

The menu is large and equally colorful. Diners can choose from a variety of hamburgers, steaks, and sandwiches, or something more exotic like Mexican nachos, Nutty Fruity Chook, or asparagus crêpes. Horsefeathers sells the most expensive burger in town: the Saturday Night Special, which costs A$200 (U.S. $160) and includes two hamburgers, a bottle of Dom Perignon, and accommodations for two at the hotel.

BUDGET

FAST EDDY'S, corner of Murray and Milligan. Tel. 321-2552.
   Cuisine: FAST FOOD. **Reservations:** Not necessary.
$ Prices: Average meal A$7 (U.S. $5.60). No credit cards.
   Open: 24 hours.
Fast Eddy's is a budget diner's delight. The restaurant offers classic fast food such as fish-and-chips and myriad different burgers, sundaes, and shakes. More substantial fare—grilled chicken dinners, lasagne, lamb chops, and American-style spareribs—is also on the menu.

The decor is what I'd call "colonial" crossed with 1930s American: wrought-iron light fixtures, stools that swivel, and lots of pre–World War II posters. The eatery is divided into two parts, and the full menu is available only on the table-service side. Burgers, chips, and shakes served at the quick-service counter cost considerably less. BYO.

FREMANTLE

EXPENSIVE

THE OYSTER BEDS RESTAURANT, 26 Riverside Rd., East Fremantle.
Tel. 339-1611.
   Cuisine: SEAFOOD. **Reservations:** Recommended on weekends. **Transportation:** Taxi.
$ Prices: Appetizers A$10.95–A$13.95 (U.S. $8.80–U.S. $11.20); main courses A$13.50–A$29.95 (U.S. $10.80–U.S. $24); children's menu A$9.50 (U.S. $7.60). AE, BC, DC, MC, V.
   Open: Lunch daily noon–3pm; dinner daily 6pm–late.
Oyster Beds is a seafood eatery built on stilts out over the Swan River. Diners have a view of lights shining on the water and the constant parade of small boats. An informal dining area outside has a nautical decor. Inside things are a bit more formal, and the decor is pink and burgundy. The restaurant, which was formerly owned by a Perth personality who had a cooking show on television, has been a local institution for over 40 years. The new management prints the menu in both English and Japanese and attracts lots of tourists.

If you dine here, you could start with shellfish au pesto, chili squid, or brain box (crumbed brains in a pastry box "enhanced by a delicate Gorgonzola cheese sauce"). Main courses include filet of John Dory topped with scallops and prawns, crayfish Mornay, and barramundi topped with crab and mushroom sauce.

A wonderful pianist entertains Friday and Saturday nights. There's a good wine list and also a complete menu of exotic cocktails.

MODERATE

THE LEFT BANK BAR & CAFE, 15 Riverside Dr., East Fremantle. Tel.
319-1315.
   Cuisine: MULTIETHNIC/SEAFOOD. **Reservations:** Recommended, especially Fri–Sat nights and Sun lunch. **Ferry:** From Perth's Barrack Street Jetty; then walk or taxi less than 1km (½ mile).
$ Prices: Appetizers A$7.50–A$8.50 (U.S. $6–U.S. $6.80); main courses A$9–A$16 (U.S. $7.20–U.S. $12.80). AE, BC, CB, MC, V.
   Open: Food Mon–Fri noon–10pm, Sat 8–11am and noon–10pm, Sun 8–11am and noon–4pm. Bar Mon–Sat until midnight, Sun until 9pm.
Until 1970 the building which now houses the Left Bank Bar & Cafe was a private home. The atmospheric two-story was built between 1896 and 1900, and hardwood floors, potted palms, and bentwood chairs reinforce the old-world atmosphere. Wrought-iron lacework forms a railing around the balcony. Tables on the veranda have a view of the Swan River.

Sample entrées (appetizers) are chargrilled eggplant with feta cheese or fresh chili prawn cakes. Main courses include Thai chicken curry, Tex-Mex, and Shanghai

Express. This is a popular spot. On Sunday afternoon it's filled to overflowing by trendy young professionals who gather here to drink on the patio.

NORTHBRIDGE

This is Perth's dining and nightlife quarter. Your best bet is to wander James, Francis, Lake, Aberdeen, and William streets until you spot an eatery that appeals to you. You might enjoy **Spaghetti Western,** 200 William Street (tel. 227-7785), **The Fishy Affair,** 132 James Street (tel. 328-3939), the **Brass Monkey Pub & Brasserie,** corner of James and William streets (tel. 227-9596), **Cafe Valentino,** corner of Lake and James streets (tel. 328-2105), or **The Thai House,** 63 Aberdeen Street (tel. 328-6074).

If you're watching your pennies, try **The Plaka,** 87 James Street (tel. 328-1636), which serves Greek fast food until 4am.

MODERATE

TED'S, corner of Lake and Aberdeen Sts., Northbridge. Tel. 227-8520.
   Cuisine: BISTRO. **Reservations:** Optional. **Bus:** The Northbridge dining and nightlife quarter is within Transperth's Free Transit Zone.
$ **Prices:** Appetizers A$4.50–A$6.50 (U.S. $3.60–U.S. $5.20); main courses A$9.50–A$16 (U.S. $7.60–U.S. $12.80). AE, BC, MC, V (cards only with A$30 minimum purchase).
   Open: Coffee and snacks daily 10am to "way past your bedtime"; lunch daily noon–3:30pm; dinner daily 5:30pm–midnight.

"Be fed at Ted's" is the motto at this clever, casual dining spot. Everything—from the George Bernard Shaw words of wisdom on the placemat to the "Let them eat cake" comments on the menu—is witty and slightly off-the-wall.

If you're in the mood for a salad, Ted's offers "A.A.A.," artichoke, avocado, and apple with cucumber dressing, or a Thai melon salad, or English spinach with bacon, pine nuts, sun-dried tomatoes, and mustard dressing. You could also have home-style pâté, "Tex Mex" nachos, pasta carbonara, a Wall Street burger, or Torre's prime beef. There are also a wide range of coffees and teas, and "American ice cream imported from San Francisco." More than a dozen different beers are offered as well as wine, spirits, liqueurs, and teas. Go for a chuckle and a tasty meal.

BUDGET

The **Northbridge Pavillion** on Lake Street is a multiethnic food court where most meals cost A$3 to A$8 (U.S. $2.40 to U.S. $6.40). "Just Desserts" and "Miami Ice" are two of my favorite food counters; you can also have Indian, Italian, vegetarian, Moroccan, Thai, German, and Mongolian fare. The Northbridge Pavillion is open Wednesday through Saturday from 11am to 2am and Sunday from noon to 10pm. No credit cards.

COTTSLOE
MODERATE

NORTH COTTESLOE CAFE, 149 Marine Parade (corner of Eric St.), Cottesloe. Tel. 385-1371.
   Cuisine: INTERNATIONAL. **Reservations:** Recommended for a table with an ocean view. **Transportation:** Train or bus no. 70–73, 100, 101, 103, or 207.
$ **Prices:** Appetizers A$3.50–A$8.90 (U.S. $2.80–U.S. $7.15); main courses A$8.50–A$17.50 (U.S. $6.80–U.S. $14); breakfast A$1.75–A$7.95 (U.S. $1.40–U.S. $6.40). Public holiday surcharge 10%. BC, MC, V.
   Open: Daily 7am–9:30pm.

This eatery, originally an ice-cream and soft-drink kiosk, is only a few feet from the water and has wraparound windows, brick floors, wooden tables, and a canvas roof. Diners can watch windsurfers and sailors zip by as they enjoy their meal.

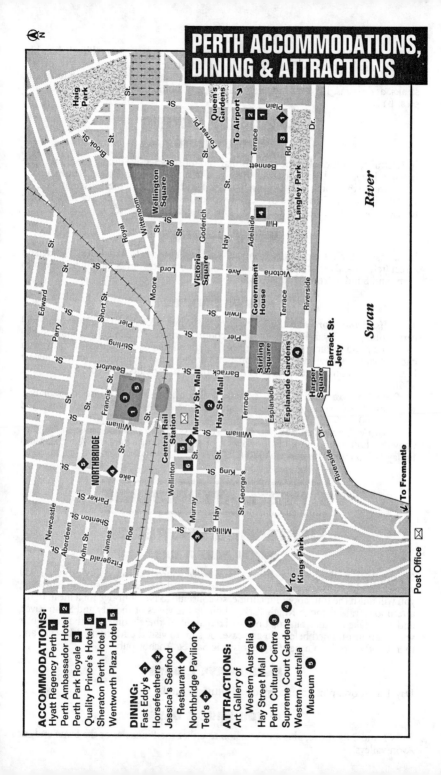

PERTH ACCOMMODATIONS, DINING & ATTRACTIONS

ACCOMMODATIONS:
Hyatt Regency Perth 1
Perth Ambassador Hotel 2
Perth Park Royale 3
Quality Prince's Hotel 6
Sheraton Perth Hotel 4
Wentworth Plaza Hotel 5

DINING:
Fast Eddy's 3
Horsefeathers 2
Jessica's Seafood
Restaurant 1
Northbridge Pavilion 4
Ted's 5

ATTRACTIONS:
Art Gallery of
Western Australia 1
Hay Street Mall 2
Perth Cultural Centre 3
Supreme Court Gardens 4
Western Australia
Museum 5

Post Office

NORTHBRIDGE

Haig Park

Wellington Square

Victoria Square

Queen's Gardens

Langley Park

Government House

Stirling Square

Esplanade Gardens

Central Rail Station

Murray St. Mall

Hay St. Mall

Harper Square

Barrack St. Jetty

Swan River

To Airport

To Fremantle

To Kings Park

Breakfast includes a choice of bacon, eggs, and sausage, or something lighter like toasted muesli (granola), fresh fruit salad, a bagel or croissant with coffee or tea. Lunch includes dishes such as calamari, king prawns, and a variety of fresh local fish, steaks, and pastas. Desserts include a full range of homemade cakes, ice creams, and pies. BYO.

SPECIALTY DINING
HOTEL DINING

In Australia, traditionally, the most formal and most expensive dining spots are in the five-star hotels, and Perth has its share of these places. The **River Room** in the Sheraton Perth Hotel, the **Ocean Room Restaurant** in the Observation City Resort Hotel, and **Windows** in the Burswood Resort Hotel are all excellent. Dinner for two costs about A$110 (U.S. $88), plus wine, and the service is impeccable.

DINING CLUSTERS

Inexpensive ethnic food is sold from stalls at the **Fremantle Markets,** Henderson Street (tel. 335-2515), which are open Friday from 9am to 9pm, Saturday from 9am to 5pm, and Sunday from 11am to 5pm.

DINNER CRUISES

The *Miss Sandalford* and the *Lady Houghton* (tel. 325-6033 for either boat) will carry you up the Swan River to the wine country, where you can enjoy a multicourse meal in a good restaurant. Sandalford or Houghton (depending on which cruise you choose) vintages flow freely on the boat and are served with dinner. The trips depart Pier 4, Barrack Street Jetty, at 6pm Friday and Saturday nights. The cost is A$45 (U.S. $36).
   Boat Torque Cruises (tel. 325-6033) also offers a dinner cruise to Fremantle with a meal served on board. This trip operates on Saturday at 7:30pm and costs A$48 (U.S. $38.40).
   Captain Cook Cruises (tel. 325-3341) offers a dinner/dance cruise to Fremantle with a buffet dinner and disc jockey on board. The cruise departs Wednesday and Friday at 7:30pm. The cost is A$30 (U.S. $24).

5. PERTH ATTRACTIONS

SIGHTSEEING STRATEGIES
IF YOU HAVE 1 DAY

Do the Perth walking tour, below, to familiarize yourself with the city center. If you visit either the Art Gallery of Western Australia or the Western Australian Museum, you will finish the tour about lunchtime, so continue to Northbridge for a meal. In the afternoon, walk through King's Park, admiring the views of the city and Swan River, and then take a train, bus, or boat to Fremantle. If there's time, do the Fremantle walking tour outlined below. In any case, be sure to visit the Maritime Museum and then treat yourself to a beer at the historic Sail & Anchor pub.

IF YOU HAVE 2 DAYS

Day 1 as above, plus an excursion to Rottnest Island.

IF YOU HAVE 3 DAYS

Days 1 and 2 as above, plus an excursion to either the Pinnacles or the Swan and/or Avon valleys.

THE TOP ATTRACTIONS

Because of its benign climate and scenic appeal, the majority of Perth's sights and activities are outdoors. Visitors would be wise to bring casual clothes and comfortable, sturdy shoes.

For 6 weeks during September and October, the southwest portion of Western Australia is covered with colorful carpets of blooming **native flora.** More than 7,000 varieties are unique to the state, and another 830 types have been introduced from other parts of Australia and from other countries. This is said to be one of the richest wildflower areas in the world. It is believed that certain flowers are found only in this corner of the nation because they are isolated by oceans on two sides and harsh desert on a third, making it impossible for seeds to spread naturally.

Of particular botanical interest are the kangaroo paws, Christmas tree, pitcher plant, dryandras, and many of the banksias, featherflowers, triggerplants, and blackboys.

Within Perth itself, King's Park is the best place for wildflower viewing, the Botanic Gardens containing a collection of 1,500 species; free guided tours are offered several days a week. It is also a good idea to venture out, either in a rental car or on a special bus excursion, to the **Darling Range** 40 minutes to the east of the city. **Westrail** (tel. 326-2222) organizes excursions. The **Western Australian Tourist Centre** (tel. 483-1111) is the best source of what's-blooming-where information.

If you're willing to go farther afield, beautiful wildflowers bloom around **Kalbarri** in the Midwest region of the state and in the vicinity of **Margaret River** in the Southwest. For information on these places, see Chapter 13. Westrail offers 5- and 6-day trips to these areas. Keen gardeners and photographers may want to contact the **Wildflower Society of Western Australia,** P.O. Box 64, Nedlands, WA 6009 (tel. 09/383-1254).

PERTH

KING'S PARK, Fraser Ave. and King's Park Rd. Tel. 321-4801.

Originally known as Perth Park, this expansive open space was renamed in 1901 to mark the accession of King Edward VII to the British throne. Spreading gently across the slopes of **Mount Eliza,** King's Park affords grand vistas of the city skyline and the Swan River. War memorials, playgrounds, the extensive **Botanic Gardens,** a restaurant, two kiosks, and walking paths are situated around the park's 404 hectares (998 acres). An information center, located between the restaurant and the huge karri log on display, is open year round daily except Good Friday and Christmas from 9am to 3pm. Free guided walking tours are available from April through October (tel. 321-4801). Bicycles can be rented from **Koala Bike Hire** (tel. 321-3061) in the parking lot behind the restaurant.

You can walk to the park from the city center or take a green Clipper Bus (for free) from the Wellington Street Bus Station or anywhere along the route.

COHUNU WILDLIFE PARK, 287A Mills Rd., Kelmscott. Tel. 390-6090.

Would you like to cuddle a koala? You can at the Cohunu Wildlife Park, which is located 26 kilometers (16 miles) southeast of Perth in the Darling Range. The holding and hugging, for which there is a charge, takes place daily at 1pm. Cohunu also has a variety of other native animals in natural surroundings, a miniature railway, and a very large walk-through aviary.

Admission: A$9 (U.S. $7.20) adults, A$4.50 (U.S. $3.60) children.

Open: Daily 10am–5pm. **Transportation:** Train or bus to Gosnells, then a A$5 (U.S. $4) taxi.

PERTH ZOO, 20 Labouchere Rd., South Perth. Tel. 367-7988.

If you haven't had your fill of native and exotic fauna, head for the Perth Zoo. Highlights here include a nocturnal house, great ape complex, walk-through aviary, and wallaby park. This is the only place in the world you can see the endangered numbat. The Harmony Farm and the Conservation Discovery Centre are especially popular with kids.

Admission: A$5 (U.S. $4) adults, A$1.50 (U.S. $1.20) children.
Open: Daily 10am–5pm. **Transportation:** Ferry across the Swan River from the Barrack Street Jetty.

UNDERWATER WORLD, Hillarys Boat Harbour, West Coast Dr. Tel. 447-7500.
Here you can walk beneath the sea in a submerged acrylic tunnel which brings you face to face with sharks, rays, octopus, and a variety of other sea life. There is also a Touch Pool where turtles, Port Jackson sharks, starfish, and squid can be handled.
Admission: A$12 (U.S. $9.60) adults, A$5 (U.S. $4) children 3–14.
Open: Daily 9am–5pm. **Closed:** Christmas Day.
Transportation/Directions: Located 20 minutes northwest of Perth. **Bus:** No. 250 from Wellington St. station, connects with bus no. 255 at Karrinyup. Takes 50 minutes; costs A$1.50 (U.S. $1.20).

FREMANTLE

"Freo," as the locals call it, was a run-of-the-mill blue-collar port area when I lived in Perth in 1977. I went there to shop at the markets, which were interesting, and felt no urge to linger in the town afterward. Not until the **Royal Perth Yacht Club** hosted the 1987 America's Cup did Fremantle get the sprucing up it needed. Today it is an area of attractive restored historic buildings, atmospheric pubs, unusual shops, and sights worth a visitor's time. While Perth, 19 kilometers (12 miles) upriver, has the appearance of a modern city, Fremantle has the hearty character of a 19th-century port. The two places are connected by frequent bus and train service, as well as **Captain Cook ferries** (tel. 325-3341). A one-way cruise ticket from Perth to Fremantle costs A$10 (U.S. $8) for adults and A$6 (U.S. $4.80) for children.

Narrow one-way streets make driving in Fremantle a frustrating experience. The best way to tour Freo is on foot, but if you leave your Reeboks at home, selected spots from the walking tour below can be reached by taxi or rental car. You might also be interested in the tram tours that operate daily in Fremantle, stopping at significant sites (tel. 339-8719). These cost A$6 (U.S. $4.80) and last 45 minutes.

WALKING TOUR 1 — Central Business District

Start: Town Hall, Hay and Barrack streets.
Finish: In Northbridge.
Time: Approximately 1 hour, not including shopping and museum stops.
Best Times: Monday through Saturday.
Worst Times: Friday through Sunday morning when the Western Australian Museum is closed; Sunday when the stores are closed and the CBD is deserted.

A stroll around Perth's central business district gives visitors an appreciation for this city which is both historically significant and progressive.
From the corner of Hay and Barrack streets you have a good view of:
1. **the Town Hall,** a convict-built Jacobean-style building. It's interesting to note that Perth, originally called the Swan River Colony, started out as a free settlement, but by 1850 the settlers realized they couldn't prosper without free convict labor. If prisoners hadn't been sent, many of the city's most interesting buildings would never have been constructed. From the Town Hall, walk east along Hay Street and turn right into Cathedral Avenue. The foundation stone for:
2. **St. George's Cathedral** was laid in 1880. A few steps past the church, you'll come out on St. George's Terrace. Turn left and, on the corner of Pier Street, you will see:
3. **the Deanery,** built in the 1850s as a residence for the first Dean of Perth. It is one of the few remaining houses of this period in Western Australia. Use the pedestrian underpass between Irwin Street and Victoria Avenue to get to the other side of St. George's Terrace.

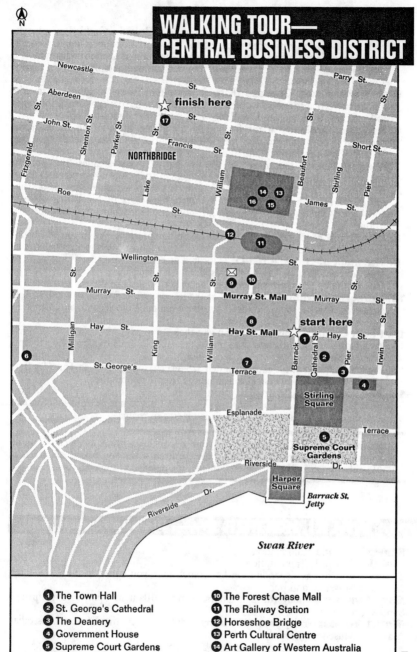

WALKING TOUR—
CENTRAL BUSINESS DISTRICT

N

finish here

NORTHBRIDGE

Newcastle St.
Aberdeen St.
John St.
Fitzgerald St.
Shenton St.
Parker St.
Lake St.
Roe St.
Francis St.
William St.
Parry St.
Short St.
Beaufort St.
Stirling St.
Pier St.
James St.

Wellington St.
Murray St.
Hay St.
St. George's Terrace
Milligan St.
King St.
William St.
Murray St.
Hay St.

Murray St. Mall

Hay St. Mall

start here

Terrace

Stirling Square

Esplanade

Supreme Court Gardens

Terrace

Riverside

Harper Square

Barrack St. Jetty

Riverside Dr.

Swan River

1 The Town Hall
2 St. George's Cathedral
3 The Deanery
4 Government House
5 Supreme Court Gardens
6 Barracks Archway
7 London Court
8 Hay Street Mall
9 The main post office (GPO)
10 The Forest Chase Mall
11 The Railway Station
12 Horseshoe Bridge
13 Perth Cultural Centre
14 Art Gallery of Western Australia
15 Western Australian Museum
16 The Alexander Library Building
17 Ted's

Post Office

4. **Government House,** opposite Pier Street, is built in the Gothic Revival style, with arches and turrets reminiscent of the Tower of London. Though Government House is the official residence of the Governor of Western Australia, it is primarily used on state occasions and to entertain members of the royal family. Toward the river from here lie the:

5. **Supreme Court Gardens** (Barrack Street and Riverside Drive), a favorite lunchtime retreat for office workers. If you detour to the park, return at this point to St. George's Terrace and, walking west, notice the Tudor-style:

6. **Barracks Archway** at the far end of the street. Built in the 1860s as the headquarters of soldier settlers, it is now a memorial to the state's early colonists. Midway between Barrack and William streets, turn into:

7. **London Court,** the most famous of Perth's many arcades; the popular collection of shops, designed in the Elizabethan style, was constructed in 1937. At both ends of the arcade, miniperformances take place when the clocks strike every quarter hour. Inside London Court, likenesses of Sir Walter Raleigh and Dick Whittington keep an eye on shoppers. Exit from London Court onto the:

8. **Hay Street Mall,** the heart of Perth's shopping precinct. When you've finished browsing, use one of several arcades to cut through to Murray Street.

9. **The main post office (GPO)** is located at Forrest Place;

10. **the Forrest Chase Mall** is Perth's newest shopping area;

11. **the Railway Station** is just across Wellington Street. Use the:

12. **Horseshoe Bridge,** which starts at the intersection of Wellington and William streets, to cross the railway tracks. This brings you out 1 block south of James Street and the:

13. **Perth Cultural Centre.** You can visit the:

14. **Art Gallery of Western Australia** (tel. 328-7233) daily from 10am to 5pm (free), and the:

15. **Western Australian Museum** (tel. 328-4411) Monday through Thursday from 10:30am to 5pm and Friday through Sunday from 1 to 5pm (free).

16. **The Alexander Library Building** (tel. 427-3111) is open Monday and Friday from 9am to 5:30pm, Tuesday through Thursday from 9am to 9:30pm, and Saturday and Sunday from 2 to 5:30pm. Admission is free of charge.

REFUELING STOP Finish off your excursion with a cappuccino or an ice-cream sundae at: **17. Ted's** on the corner of Lake and Aberdeen streets in Northbridge. See "Perth Dining," above, for details.

WALKING TOUR 2 — Historic Fremantle

Start: Fremantle Train Station.
Finish: Fremantle Train Station.
Time: 1 to 4 hours, depending on how much time you spend in the Art Centre, Maritime Museum, and pub.
Best Times: Monday through Thursday from 10am to 5pm, Friday through Sunday afternoon.
Worst Times: Friday through Sunday morning when the Western Australian Maritime Museum is closed.

A walk through Fremantle allows visitors a chance to appreciate its historic atmosphere.

From the train station, which opened in 1907, turn left onto Elder Place, then right onto Edward Place, then left onto Quarry Street. The third street on the right is James Street, which leads you to the:

1. **Fremantle Arts Centre and the Fremantle Museum,** 1 Finnerty Street (tel. 335-8244). This restored Gothic building was constructed by convicts as a Lunatic

Asylum in 1861. Today, it houses the works of many well-known Western Australian artists, printmakers, and potters and is open daily from 10am to 5pm. There are a craft shop and bookshop on the premises, as well as a tearoom which offers seating inside or outside on a leafy limestone-walled courtyard. Admission is free of charge. When you are ready to leave, head down Ord Street to High Street and turn right. Walk up High Street to:

2. **St. John's Square** where you will see St. John's Church (1882) and the Town Hall (1887). Walk down William Street to Henderson and turn right, continuing to South Terrace.

REFUELING STOP 3. **The Sail & Anchor Pub Brewery,** 64 South Terrace (tel. 335-8433), is, without a doubt, the most atmospheric spot for a drink or a meal in Fremantle. Founded as the Freemason's Hotel in 1854, this popular pub has led a colorful life. It was refurbished and renamed in 1985. The bar offers a wide selection of beers brewed both on and off the premises and traditional bar food such as ploughman's lunch, fish-and-chips, and meat pies. Breakfast, lunch, and dinner are served in a charming brasserie upstairs.

Across from the Sail & Anchor is the entrance to the historic:

4. **Fremantle Markets.** Built in 1897 for the Fremantle Municipality, these wholesale markets continued in their original function for over 70 years. The impressive size of the building indicates the vitality of Fremantle at the turn of the century. Today, arts and crafts, herbs and spices, fruit and vegetables, wooden and cane ware, antiques and bric-a-brac, and fresh seafood are sold from 140 different stalls. The 19th-century architecture provides an atmospheric background for the popular markets, which are open Friday from 9am to 9pm, Saturday from 9am to 5pm, and Sunday from 11am to 5pm. When you leave the markets walk down Essex Street until you come to the:

5. **Esplanade Hotel** on the corner of Essex and Marine Terrace overlooking the Esplanade and boat harbor. Walk along the Esplanade, past the:

6. **statue of Captain Fremantle,** after whom the colony was named, until you come to the:

7. **Western Australian Maritime Museum** on Cliff Street (tel. 335-8211). The main entrance and gallery were built by convicts in 1851 to house stores from the Commissariat Department. Today, exhibits that relate to Western Australia's maritime history, including several significant shipwrecks, are on display. These include relics from the Dutch ship *Batavia*, wrecked off the coast in 1629. The museum is open Monday through Thursday from 10:30am to 5pm and Friday through Sunday from 1 to 5pm. Admission is free of charge. As you leave the museum, walk up Cliff Street to High Street from where you will have a good view of the:

8. **Round House.** This structure, which is not round but has 12 sides, is Western Australia's oldest surviving public building. It dates back to 1831 and was Fremantle's first prison. A prime example of colonial Georgian design, the Round House, 10 Arthur Head (tel. 430-2326), is open daily from 10am to 5pm. The grounds, which include an information center, craft shop, and tearoom, afford a good view of the harbor. Admission is free of charge. From here, return to the train station on Philimore Street.

---

6. PERTH SPORTS & RECREATION

SPORTS

Australian Rules Football   Perth's team is called the West Coast Eagles. This sport is played during the winter, as is soccer, and other football codes. Local matches are played every Saturday during the season. For more information phone the Western Australian Football League (tel. 381-5599).

Cricket   This is a popular summer sport. A-grade cricket is played on weekends in summer at ovals throughout the metropolitan area. The Western Australian Cricket

Association and the Western Australian Women's Cricket Association (tel. 325-9800) can answer your questions.

Horse & Dog Racing   Regular horse races are held at Ascot Track in the summer and at Belmont Track in the winter. Trotting (harness racing) takes place at Gloucester Park most Friday nights. For more information, call the Western Australian Greyhound Racing Association (tel. 458-4600), the Western Australian Trotting Association (tel. 325-8822), or the Western Australian Turf Club (tel. 227-0777).

RECREATION

Bicycling   The longest stretch of cycleway in Australia extends along the Swan River, through King's Park, and all the way to Fremantle. The **Western Australian Ministry of Sport and Recreation** (tel. 421-4666) publishes a series of brochures that describe this ride and many others. **Koala Bike Hire,** in King's Park (tel. 321-3061), rents bikes.

Golf   Many private and public courses are within easy reach of Perth. Private clubs welcome overseas and interstate visitors with a letter of introduction from their clubs. Average greens fees for public courses are A$10 to A$25 (U.S. $8 to U.S. $20) for 18 holes. Club rental is an additional A$5 to A$15 (U.S. $4 to U.S. $12). Some popular public courses: **South Perth City Council,** Como (tel. 450-6187); **Joondalup Country Club,** Connolly (tel. 300-1538); **Burswood Park,** Burswood Resort Casino Complex, Great Eastern Highway (tel. 362-7576); and **The Vines,** Millhouse Road, Upper Swan (tel. 297-0222).

Parasailing   **Rob Thompson** (tel. 446-1835) operates from the Narrows, South Perth. A 7- to 10-minute ride costs A$28 (U.S. $22.40). The season is September through May.

Sailing   Rent a Surf Cat, a 14-foot Windrush catamaran, from **Mainsail Hire,** Coode Street Jetty, South Perth (tel. 018/927-971). The cost is A$12 (U.S. $9.60) an hour.

Swimming   The metropolitan Perth area has 19 beautiful beaches spread over less than 35 kilometers (22 miles) from South Fremantle to Mullaloo in the northern suburbs. All are within easy access of the city.
    You might share Prince Charles's preference for North Cottesloe Beach, or maybe you'd like Swanbourne, where sunning and swimming are done in one's birthday suit. City Beach and Scarborough are also popular. Mullaloo is the calmest while Trigg Island Beach is one of the better ones for surfing. Most of the Indian Ocean shoreline is patrolled by surf lifesaving clubs (lifeguards), who keep watch over those who are surfing, sailboarding, swimming, and boating.
    Beatty Park Aquatic Centre, Vincent Street, North Perth (tel. 328-4099), has a heated Olympic-size pool.

Tennis   Many tennis clubs are situated in and around Perth. The average outdoor rental cost is about A$5 (U.S. $4) an hour. Courts for hire: **Perth City Council** (tel. 265-3333); **McCallum Tennis Courts,** Fitzgerald Street, North Perth (tel. 361-2273); and **Robertson Park,** Taylor Road, Victoria Park (tel. 328-8128).

Waterskiing   Contact **Cables Water Park,** 3 Troode Street, Spearwood (tel. 418-6888 or 418-6111), if you'd like to try your hand at cable waterskiing. The fee of A$10 (U.S. $8) an hour includes skis and a life jacket. The park is open daily 10am to 6pm. They also offer mini-golf, water slides, swimming pools, and a children's playground. (Water slides are closed May to October.) Admission is A$1 (U.S. 80¢) in the summer and free in the winter.

Windsurfing   Rent a sailboard from **Mainsail Hire,** Coode Street Jetty, South

Perth (tel. 341-1542 or 367-2988). Phone before 9:30am (tel. 344-2034 or 443-1142) for same-day rentals. Boards cost A$28 (U.S. $22.40) a day.

7. PERTH SAVVY SHOPPING

Perth has extensive shopping facilities centered around the **Hay Street** and **Murray Street** pedestrian malls, which run between William and Barrack streets, and the **Forrest Chase** shopping center which runs between Murray and Wellington streets. Several arcades lead off the malls, the best known of these being **London Court,** with its Elizabethan-style facade.

Away from the city center, the suburb of **Claremont** is known for its fashionable boutiques and women's dress shops. **Fremantle,** of course, has its popular markets, which are open Friday 9am to 9pm, Saturday 9am to 5pm, and Sunday 11am to 5pm. This is the place to purchase funky clothes and handcrafted accessories.

SHOPPING A TO Z

ABORIGINAL ARTIFACTS & CRAFTS

CREATIVE NATIVE, 32-36 King St. Tel. 322-3398 or 322-3397.

This is the best place in Perth to buy contemporary and traditional Aboriginal art. This shop sells carved emu eggs, boomerangs, and other artifacts—all handmade by Aboriginal artisans.

CRAFTS

THE CRAFTS COUNCIL OF WESTERN AUSTRALIA CRAFT SHOP, first floor, Perth City Railway Station, Wellington St. Tel. 325-2799.

Here you will find the work of Western Australia's leading craft designers and makers. A wide variety of glass, leather, paper, silver, ceramics, textiles, and wood items are offered for sale. Look for the work of Sandra Black and Lesley John Wright. Open Tuesday to Friday from 10am to 5pm and Sunday from 2 to 5pm.

DEPARTMENT STORES

Perth's major department stores are **Aherns,** 622 Hay Street (tel. 323-0101), and **Myer,** in the Forrest Chase center, 200 Murray Street (tel. 221-3444).

FASHIONS

Bates Saddlery, 430 Newcastle Street (tel. 328-6988), is known for excellent horse saddles, and also sells Akubra hats, Driza-bone oilskin coats, and R. M. Williams moleskin trousers and boots. This is the place to look for Wintec and Caprilli riding saddles and riding/stockmen's clothing. Open from 8:30am to 5:30pm Monday to Wednesday and Friday, 8:30am to 8:30pm Thursday, and 8:30am to 3pm Saturday.

Similar outback clothing is sold at **R. M. Williams,** in the Carillion Centre (tel. 321-7786).

A half dozen **Purely Australian** shops are dotted around Perth, and they all sell quality T-shirts and sweatshirts emblazoned with Ken Done prints and other Aussie graphics. Most of Purely Australian's merchandise is made in Western Australia and sold nationwide. The shop at 633 Hay Street Mall (tel. 481-1027) is open Monday through Saturday from 8:30am to 9pm and Sunday from 11am to 6pm. Other P.A. stores are located in the **London Court** arcade (tel. 325-4328), **City Arcade** (tel. 321-4951), and the domestic terminal at the airport (tel. 277-6424).

St. Quentin Avenue, Claremont, is the best area for boutiques and dress shops. Look for **Liz Davenport,** whose "suitcase collection" ("designed for the traveller but a boon to every wardrobe") has made her a favorite in Australia. L.D. also has a shop at 275 Murray Street in central Perth. The **Mid 70's Boutique,** Raine Square Shopping Plaza, Murray Street (tel. 481-3262), is another popular clothing store. Look for shoes at **Pearse & Swan,** 706 Hay Street (tel. 321-6141).

FOOD

CLAREMONT FRESH MARKETS, 333 Stirling Hwy., Claremont. Tel. 383-3066.
This is the place to buy the fruits, vegetables, and other goodies for the picnic you'll take to Rottnest Island or the Swan Valley. Open 7 to 7 daily.

PERTH CENTRAL MARKETS, 100 Roe St., Northbridge. Tel. 227-5230.
Here you can buy a variety of produce, including fruit, vegetables, fish, and meat.

LIQUORLAND, 712 Hay St. Tel. 322-7487.
Going to a BYO? Pick your beverage from the extensive selection at this store.

GIFTS & SOUVENIRS

Walkabout Souvenirs, Shop 11, Forrest Place (tel. 325-2190), sells nicely framed dried wildflowers and other items typical of Western Australia. This shop is open from 9am to 9pm Monday to Saturday and 10am to 5pm Sunday. Walkabout Souvenirs also has a shop in London Court. The **Koala Bear Shop** in London Court (tel. 325-2297) sells wildflower seeds. The **National Trust Gift Shop,** 139 St. George's Terrace (tel. 321-2754), is housed in the Old Perth Boys School and offers a nice selection of Australian souvenirs and gifts. This shop is staffed by volunteers and profits are used for the upkeep of historic buildings. Open Monday through Friday from 9am to 5pm. The **G.P.O. Shop** in Forrest Place is another place to look for gifts and souvenirs.

JEWELRY

You might like to look at **Charles Edward Jewellers,** corner of Piccadilly Arcade, 704 Hay Street Mall (tel. 321-5111). They sell items which are designed and handcrafted on the premises. These include Argyle diamonds—pinks, champagne, and cognacs—from the northern part of the state. Open from 9am to 6pm Monday to Wednesday and Friday, from 9am to 9pm Thursday, and from 10am to 2pm Saturday. Diamonds from the Argyle Mine are also sold at **Kalli Brinkhaus,** 24 St. Quentin Avenue, Claremont (tel. 383-3600), and at **Swan Diamonds,** Shop 4, London Court (tel. 325-8166).

Another spot for this state's products: **Linneys,** 37 Rokeby Road, Subiaco (tel. 382-4077), where the jewelry is made of Broome pearls, Argyle diamonds, and Kalgoorlie gold. Several of their designers have won major international awards. Open from 9am to 5pm Monday to Wednesday and Friday, 9am to 8pm Thursday, and 9am to 1pm Saturday.

If it's opals you're after, try **The Opal Centre,** Shop 1–5, St. Martin's Arcade (downstairs) off London Court (tel. 325-8588). They sell both loose opals and opal jewelry, and you can tour their authentic replica working opal mine complete with life-size animated miners and full sound effects.

8. PERTH EVENING ENTERTAINMENT

THE ENTERTAINMENT SCENE

Visitors perusing the entertainment pages of *The West Australian* or *This Week in Perth* are usually surprised to see the number of concerts, recitals, and shows available in Perth and Fremantle. The **Festival of Perth,** held annually in February or March, provides a busy schedule of music, dance, film, and theater performances and complements the cultural activities that take place in the city throughout the year. "Variety" is the key word in describing Perth's after-dark activities. The city caters to a wide range of ages and interests.

THE PERFORMING ARTS

THE MAJOR CONCERT & PERFORMANCE HALLS

DOLPHIN THEATRE, at the University of Western Australia, Nedlands 6009. Tel. 380-2440 or 380-2442.

This 198-seat theater is one of several on the University of Western Australia campus. This is an intimate proscenium-arch theater, built in 1975, where the productions of the university's Dramatic Society are often staged.

Tours: On request.
Prices: A$10–A$30 (U.S. $8–U.S. $24).

HIS MAJESTY'S THEATRE, 825 Hay St. (corner of King St.). Tel. 322-2929.

One of Perth's major venues is His Majesty's Theatre, the home of the Western Australia Ballet Company and the Western Australia Opera Company. His Majesty's, which has 1,225 seats, was built in 1904 and is one of the city's most beautiful and graciously restored buildings. Displays in the stalls and dress circle foyers illustrate the theater's colorful history. Over the years many legendary figures have been associated with His Majesty's, including Dame Nellie Melba, Anna Pavlova, Percy Grainger, Yehudi Menuhin, and Dame Margot Fonteyn. State-of-the-art technology is tastefully incorporated into the Edwardian environment.

Tours: Mon–Fri 10:30am–3:30pm.
Prices: A$20–A$50 (U.S. $16–U.S. $40).

NEW FORTUNE THEATRE, on the campus of the University of Western Australia, Nedlands. Tel. 380-2441 or 380-2440.

The only theater in the world built to the known dimensions of a 17th-century Elizabethan theater is in the Arts Building on the University of WA campus. Named the New Fortune Theatre, it is a unique setting for Shakespearean drama and other theatrical performances. Without an orchestra pit, the theater seats 508.

Tours: On request.
Prices: A$10–A$30 (U.S. $8–U.S. $24).

PERTH CONCERT HALL, 5 St. George's Terrace. Tel. 325-9944.

Opened on January 26, 1973, the Perth Concert Hall is regarded as one of Australia's most acoustically perfect venues. It stands on a 1.2-hectare (3-acre) site next to Government House Gardens and has a wide view of the Swan River. Among the international orchestras that have graced this stage are the Chicago Symphony, the London Philharmonic, and the Israel Philharmonic. It is also used for other types of concerts.

Prices: A$15–A$50 (U.S. $12–U.S. $40).

PLAYHOUSE THEATRE, 3 Pier St. Tel. 325-3500 or 484-1133.

This is the home of the Western Australian Theatre Company, and a wide variety of productions is presented here. This includes classics, comedies, dramas, and musicals.

Prices: A$16–A$23 (U.S. $12.80–U.S. $18.40).

REGAL THEATRE, 47 Hay St., Subiaco. Tel. 381-1557.

The Regal Theatre, where some of Perth's best plays are staged, is a converted cinema built in the 1930s in the art nouveau style of architecture.

Prices: A$18–A$25 (U.S. $14.40–U.S. $20).

SUBIACO THEATRE CENTRE, 180 Hamersley Rd., Subiaco. Tel. 381-2633.

This intimate theater, with 302 seats, is the home of The Hole In The Wall theater company. The Hole has presented everything from Shakespeare to premieres of new Australian plays. Two Dance Plus is also located here.

Prices: A$17–A$25 (U.S. $13.60–U.S. $20).

THE CLUB & MUSIC SCENE
NIGHTCLUBS & DISCOS

X-Press is a free magazine which lists live music performances. Look for it at bars, pubs, and clubs around Perth.

The majority of Perth's nightclubs are in Northbridge. The **Arcadia,** 268 Newcastle Street at Lake Street (tel. 328-6770), is a popular club—or "super pub" as it is sometimes called. It's open Monday through Saturday from 6pm to 4am. No cover charge.

Havana, 69 Lake Street at Aberdeen Street (tel. 328-1065), is also popular with "Perth corporate workers and fashion-conscious people between 25 and 40." The admission charge to this large disco is A$6 (U.S. $4.80) after 9pm. It's open Wednesday through Sunday nights until the wee hours.

The **Berlin Club,** 89 Milligan Street (tel. 328-9870), is a very hip disco which charges A$10 (U.S. $8) entrance.

Outside of Northbridge, you can dance the night away at **Margeaux's** in the Perth Parmelia Hilton, Mill Street (tel. 322-3622). It's open from 9pm to 2am Tuesday through Saturday. A A$12 (U.S. $9.60) admission is charged on Friday. A local beer costs about A$4 (U.S. $3.20). An import will set you back about A$5 (U.S. $4). Cocktails cost from A$8.50 to A$10 (U.S. $6.80 to U.S. $8).

JAZZ

A special hotline exists for jazz fans. To find out what's on, phone **Jazzline** (tel. 271-2755).

THE BAR SCENE
COCKTAIL LOUNGES

MILLSTRASSE LOUNGE AND BAR, in the Perth Parmelia Hilton, Mill St. Tel. 322-3622.

The Millstrasse is an elegant cocktail lounge and piano bar just off the Hilton's lobby. The decor includes antiques, paintings, marble tables, and handcrafted armchairs. This is a favorite watering hole of Perth's movers and shakers. If you're feeling game, try a "Flaming Lambourgini." Millstrasse opens at 6pm Monday through Saturday.

PUBS

SAIL & ANCHOR PUB BREWERY, 64 South Terrace, Fremantle. Tel. 335-8433.

You can't leave Perth without sampling the state's own beer, Swan Lager, but at the Sail & Anchor, you might be tempted to try something more exotic. Of the 14 different draft beers on tap, four are brewed on-site. Another 45 bottled beers from around the world are also offered. Entertainment is provided at night and on weekend afternoons. This lively pub, with its old-world atmosphere, is open Monday through Saturday from 11am to midnight and Sunday from 2:30 to 7:30pm. Food is served in the bar and upstairs in a charming brasserie. A bottle of beer costs from A$3 to A$5.50 (U.S. $2.40 to U.S. $4.40). A small glass of draft costs A$2 to A$2.50 (U.S. $1.60 to U.S. $2). A glass of wine will set you back A$2.50 (U.S. $2).

Formerly called the Freemason's Hotel, the Sail & Anchor dates from 1854. The restoration of the historic property, which left the hearty seaport atmosphere intact while modernizing the facilities, received an award from the Royal Australian Institute of Architects. Highly recommended. See also the Fremantle walking tour above.

TRADEWINDS HOTEL, 59 Canning Hwy., East Fremantle. Tel. 339-8188.
This hotel, located on the south side of the Swan River between the Fremantle and Stirling bridges, offers a large outdoor patio where one can have a drink and watch the passing parade of boats. This courtyard venue is called the Piazza Bar. Drinks are also served in Plympton or Trader Morgans cocktail bars.

MORE ENTERTAINMENT
MOVIES

Lumière Cinemas, in the Entertainment Centre, Wellington Street (tel. 321-1575), presents innovative first-release films and has in the past sponsored a film festival, meet-the-filmmaker sessions, and screenings of national and international short films. Admission is A$10 (U.S. $8).
Perth also has its share of multiscreen venues. These include **Academy 1 Cinema,** Wellington Street (tel. 322-6441), **Ace Theatres,** 451 Murray Street (tel. 322-2711), **Cinecentre,** 139 Murray Street (tel. 325-2844), and **Cinema City,** 580 Hay Street (tel. 325-2377).

CASINOS

BURSWOOD RESORT CASINO, Great Eastern Hwy., Victoria Park. Tel. 362-7777.
Burswood is the city's only casino. It is open 24 hours a day and offers the traditional gambling games in a sumptuous art deco setting. The casino has 124 gaming tables, plus restaurants, cocktail bars, and a theater cabaret. Games include blackjack, roulette, baccarat, craps, minidice, money wheel, keno, minibaccarat, two-up dice, video machines and—that Aussie favorite—two-up.

9. EASY EXCURSIONS FROM PERTH

ROTTNEST ISLAND
GETTING THERE

A popular resort island located 19 kilometers (12 miles) off the coast of Fremantle, "Rotto" can be reached by air or sea. It takes only 15 minutes by light aircraft or an hour by high-speed ferry. **Rottnest Airbus** (tel. 478-1322) charges A$66.50 (U.S. $53.20) return (round-trip) for adults and A$36.50 (U.S. $29.20) for children for their flights, which depart Perth Airport. The fare on the boat **Star Flyte** (tel. 325-6033), which departs from Perth's Barrack Street Jetty, is A$35 (U.S. $28) for adults and A$10 (U.S. $8) for children. Boat Torque (tel. 325-6033) offers a package which includes transportation, a two-course lunch at the Rottnest Hotel, and a bus tour of the island for A$57 (U.S. $45.60) adults and A$32 (U.S. $25.60) for children.

WHAT TO SEE & DO

Once on the island, you can swim, snorkel, dive, cycle, windsurf, fish, or lie on one of the beaches (many of which are secluded). A golf course, tennis courts, boat rentals, and conducted tours over land and water offer more alternatives. Rottnest, which is 11 kilometers (7 miles) long and 5 kilometers (3 miles) wide, is almost completely undeveloped. The only vehicles are a few tour buses and some service trucks. Bicycles, which can be rented from **Rottnest Bike Hire** (tel. 292-5043), are the most common form of transportation. Scuba divers should contact **Diving Ventures** in Perth (tel. 336-1664 or 430-5130). The lack of population, as well as favorable environmental conditions, makes Rottnest a haven for a variety of seabirds.
The island got its name from the little marsupials that are found there. Quokkas, as

they are called, are not rats, but Dutch navigator Willem de Vlamingh didn't know that when he landed there in 1696, so he named the island Rottnest—Dutch for "rat's nest." In spite of what he perceived to be large rodents, Commodore de Vlamingh still described the low sandy isle as "a terrestrial paradise," a feeling shared by the thousands of day-trippers who flock to Rottnest today.

WHERE TO STAY & DINE

The **Rottnest Island Authority** (tel. 372-9729) can arrange accommodation for you in over 250 houses and cottages on the island. They also offer camping facilities nestled in an area of mature eucalyptus trees planted by World War I prisoners of war. In addition, Rottnest has one upmarket lodge and a traditional Aussie hotel.

ROTTNEST HOTEL, Rottnest Island, WA 6161. Tel. 09/292-5011. 12 rms.
$ Rates (including breakfast): A$65 (U.S. $52) single; A$95 (U.S. $76) double; A$20 (U.S. $16) extra person. BC, MC, V.
The Rottnest Hotel, built in 1864 and commonly known as the Quokka Arms, offers both accommodations and a lively beer garden. Brolly's Restaurant, overlooking Thomson Bay, serves breakfast, lunch, and dinner.

ROTTNEST LODGE, Rottnest Island, WA 6161. Tel. 09/292-5161. 62 units.
$ Rates (including breakfast and dinner): A$200 (U.S. $160) deluxe double; A$240 (U.S. $192) "lakeside" double. AE, BC, DC, MC, V.
This is "Rotto's" first first-class resort. Lodge units have a Mediterranean decor, including French windows. Lakeside quarters have a lounge area with a pot-belly stove and view of Garden Lake.

SWAN VALLEY
WHAT TO SEE & DO

Some of Western Australia's best wine comes from the Swan Valley, located 20 kilometers (12 miles) northeast of Perth. Originally known for their fortified wines, Swan vignerons are now producing full-bodied, or "flavorsome" (as the Aussies say), whites. Over 21 wineries in the region are open for tasting and sales, but even if you aren't interested in vineyards, this is still a good day-trip destination because of its appealing scenery and interesting historic sights.

The village of **Guildford,** classified by the National Trust, is located at the Perth end of the valley. From there, wineries, craft shops, and picturesque picnic spots fan out to the north, near such places as **Middle Swan, Henley Brook,** and **Herne Hill.** The **Western Australian Tourist Centre** in Perth has maps and information.

Two wineries in the Swan Valley operate cruises from the **Barrack Street Jetty** in Perth to the upper reaches of the river. In each case, plenty of time is allowed for tasting, and a two-course lunch (with wine, of course) is served in a pleasant spot. The *Miss Sandalford* **Vineyard Cruise** (tel. 325-6033) takes you to **Sandalford Wines,** West Swan Road, Caversham (tel. 274-5922); lunch is served at **Mulberry Farm** after a tour of historic **Woodbridge Manor House.** The *Lady Houghton* **Wine Cruise** (tel. 325-6033) takes you to **Houghton Wines,** Dale Road, Middle Swan (tel. 274-5100), and lunch is served at **Mulberry Farm Restaurant.** Both trips cost A$45 (U.S. $36).

Great Western Tours (tel. 328-4542) offers half-day coach tours of the valley. If you drive yourself on this trip, bring a picnic lunch and enjoy it under the trees at Houghton Wines. Another alternative would be to visit **Jane Brook Estate Wines,** a small boutique winery that, like other places in this area, is generous with samples. At Jane Brook, Toodyay Road, Middle Swan (tel. 274-1432), they sell a cheese, pâté, and bread platter which serves three people (A$15/U.S. $12). Proprietor David Atkinson is president of the **Swan Valley Vintners Association** and a knowledgeable source of info on this area. The Atkinsons will happily ship their product to Britain or the eastern (Australian) states for you.

Another nice spot to visit: **Evans & Tate Winery,** Swan Street, Henley Brook (tel. 296-4666). Most of the Swan Valley wineries are open for tasting and bottle sales 7 days a week.

WOODBRIDGE MANOR HOUSE, Third Ave., West Midland. Tel. 274-2432.

Located just off the Great Eastern Highway, the gracious old mansion overlooking the river dates from 1885 and is a National Trust property. Afternoon teas are available in the restored coach house on the grounds. Beverly Atkinson of Jane Brook Estate Wines also runs the Woodbridge Coach House Tea Room, which is open from noon to 4pm.

Admission: A$3 (U.S. $2.40) adults, A$1.25 (U.S. $1) children.
Open: Mon–Tues and Thurs–Sat 1–4pm, Sun 11am–5pm. **Closed:** July.

HALL COLLECTION, 105 Swan St. (at the rear of the Rose and Crown Hotel), Guildford. Tel. 279-6542.

Over 50,000 items are on display here. Many of these things are pure nostalgic Australiana, having been selected from items in common usage since the earliest days of colonial settlement. Seventy separate collections are shown, ranging from cameras, household utensils, and surgical instruments to toys, copper containers, and imported glass pieces. Where else are you likely to see Elizabethan saucepans circa 1603? Or an 18th-century lacemaker's lamp?

Admission: A$2.50 (U.S. $2) adults, A$1 (U.S. 80¢) children.
Open: Tues–Sat 10am–4:30pm, Sun 10:30am–5pm. **Transportation:** Take a bus or train to Guildford and walk 2 blocks east.

WHERE TO STAY

THE VINES RESORT, Verdelho Dr., Ellen Brook, WA 6055. Tel. 09/296-1711. 40 2- and 3-bedroom town houses. A/C TV TEL **Transportation:** The resort is 30km (19 miles) from central Perth; the management can arrange transfers from the city or airport.

$ Rates: A$185 (U.S. $148) double; A$35 (U.S. $28) extra person. Weekend and other packages available. AE, BC, DC, MC, V. **Parking:** Free.

This luxurious resort, set amid vineyards and bushland, was designed with the sports enthusiast in mind. Each spacious unit has a full kitchen and laundry facilities. The master bedroom has a queen-size bed; other bedrooms have two single beds each. The two-bedroom units have two bathrooms, and the three-bedrooms have 2½ baths.

Dining/Entertainment: Meals are served in the Vigneron Restaurant and Wine Cellar, as well as Copley's Bistro.

Services: Massage.

Facilities: 27-hole golf course, gym, eight tennis courts, squash courts, lawn bowling green, sauna, pro shop, and swimming pool.

WHERE TO DINE

ROSE AND CROWN HOTEL, 105 Swan St., Guildford. Tel. 279-8444, or toll free 008/09-0600 in Australia.

Cuisine: TRADITIONAL ENGLISH. **Reservations:** Essential. **Transportation:** Bus or train to Guildford, then walk 2 blocks east.

$ Prices: Set price menu A$20 (U.S. $16) adults; children's meal costs A1¢ per centimeter of height. AE, BC, DC, MC, V.

Open: Breakfast, lunch, and dinner daily.

The Rose and Crown Hotel offers an opportunity to dine in old-world surroundings. The Hall Collection, mentioned above, is right around the corner.

AVON VALLEY

If you've ever been to the Cotswolds in England, you may have a sense of déjà vu when you travel through the Avon Valley. The lush countryside, historic homes, and B&Bs are very appealing, and seem more British than Australian. The valley is located about 100 kilometers (62 miles) outside of Perth, which is a 1-hour drive on the Great

Eastern Highway. York, Northam, and Toodyay are the principal towns. Try to visit from April to late October, when the area is at its best; wildflowers bloom in September and October.

YORK
What to See & Do

The state's oldest inland settlement dates from 1830 and is a treasure trove of interesting turn-of-the-century architecture. Many of the current population of about 800 live in old brick cottages with white wooden verandas, and all cherish the quality of life the village affords. Vegetables come right out of the garden, fresh eggs are always available, and pollution is nonexistent.

The lack of commercialization hasn't kept York's popularity from growing. In fact, it's the absence of commercialization that draws people to the community. Most folks stroll along Avon Terrace, the town's main street, stopping to browse through arts and crafts shops and have a cup of coffee or tea at one of the many colonial-style tearooms. Bicycling along country lanes is also popular.

Some buildings of note in the area include the splendid York Town Hall, completed in 1911; the Railway Station; the Court House and Police Station; and the Residency Museum.

A **jazz festival** is held in York every September and the community hosts a large **Music Festival** in odd-numbered years. The **"Flying 50" Speed Classic** for sports and racing cars built before 1960 also draws large crowds each October.

YORK MOTOR MUSEUM, 116 Avon Terrace. Tel. 096/41-1288.
More than 100 antique and classic cars are on display at the York Motor Museum, the town's biggest attraction. Established in 1979, the York Motor Museum is now recognized as the finest collection of veteran, vintage, classic, and racing cars in Australia. The collection presents the evolution of motor transport with prime examples of the finest quality workmanship from each era. These range from an 1894 Peugeot to the race car driven by 1980 Grand Prix world champion Alan Jones.
Admission: A$5 (U.S. $4) adults, A$2 (U.S. $1.60) children.
Open: Daily 9am–5pm. **Closed:** Christmas Day and Good Friday. **Transportation:** Daily buses to York departing from East Perth Terminal. Bookings necessary.

BALLADONG FARM LIVING MUSEUM, 5 Parker Rd. Tel. 096/41-1279.
You can experience farming activities as they were in the 1831–35 period at this working farm/museum. Balladong Farm was built in 1831; the buildings have been faithfully restored. Many animals can be petted and hand-fed. Free rides on the Clydesdale horses are offered on weekend afternoons.
Admission: A$4.25 (U.S. $3.40) adults, A$2.50 (U.S. $2) children 3–14.
Open: Mon–Thurs 1–5pm, Sat–Sun 10am–5pm. (Opening times vary Dec–Feb.)

Where to Stay

If you go out to York for the day and decide to stay overnight, you won't be the first to make this on-the-spot decision. The community's charm has had a similar effect on others. Bed-and-breakfast is offered in several private homes (about A$28 to A$43/U.S. $22.40 to U.S. $34.40 per person). Contact the **York Tourist Bureau,** 105 Avon Terrace, York, WA 6302 (tel. 096/41-1301), which is open Monday through Friday from 9am to 5pm and Saturday and Sunday from 9am to 4pm, and they'll endeavor to find you a room in a cozy B&B. They also have a list of farms that accept guests.

SETTLER'S HOUSE, 125 Avon Terrace, York, WA 6302. Tel. 096/41-1096. 20 rms. A/C
$ Rates: A$73–A$104 (U.S. $58.40–U.S. $83.20) single or double; A$10 (U.S. $8) extra person. AE, BC, DC, MC, V. **Parking:** Free.
If you'd like to spend the night at an inn, I suggest the Settler's House, which has the quaint decor you'd expect from a property built in 1840. All bedrooms face a brick courtyard where flower carts, old-fashioned streetlamps, and a wisteria-covered trellis

create a colonial feel. Quarters are called after original settlers in this area, and each room contains photos and information on the person after which it is named. Four-poster and canopied beds supply atmosphere, while modern bathrooms provide convenience.

Even if you don't spend the night, drop in and have a drink in the cozy bar or a meal in the restaurant, which was at one time a Cobb & Co. coaching station. If you're hungry and hurried, grab a bite in the country-style tearoom with its pot-bellied stove. Only à la carte dinners are served in the restaurant; the tearoom is open daily from 10am to 4:30pm.

THE IMPERIAL INN, 83 Avon Terrace, York, WA 6302. Tel. 096/41- **1010.** 19 rms (4 with bath).

$ Rates: A$28 (U.S. $22.40) single; A$42 (U.S. $33.60) double; A$50 (U.S. $40) room with bath. BC, MC. **Parking:** Free.

The Imperial, located across the street from the Town Hall, was built more than 100 years ago and is rich in old-world charm. The accommodations are modest but adequate. The four rooms in the converted stables have their own bathrooms, as well as tea- and coffee-making facilities. The inn's restaurant is BYO. The historic structure's veranda was lost in a 1968 earthquake.

IRISHTOWN/NORTHAM

As long as you're in the Avon Valley, travel north to Irishtown and nearby **Buckland,** "the state's most stately home." Built in 1874 and set in magnificent landscaped gardens, the recently restored Buckland (tel. 096/22-1130) contains a priceless collection of antique furniture, silver, and paintings.

Buckland is the home of Tony and Penny Motion, a friendly, down-to-earth couple, who offer bed-and-breakfast in their wonderful mansion. Tariffs are A$60 (U.S. $48) single and A$120 (U.S. $96) double. The house and grounds are open Saturday through Wednesday from 10am to 5pm and closed from Christmas to the end of February. The admission is A$4 (U.S. $3.20).

Nearby in Northam, light lunches and dinners are served in another beautifully restored mansion. **Byfield House,** 30 Gordon Street (tel. 096/22-3380), is open Wednesday through Friday from noon to 2pm and Wednesday through Saturday from 6:30pm. This late Victorian home (1898) is classified by the National Trust of Australia. BYO.

THE PINNACLES

In the **Nambung National Park,** 260 kilometers (162 miles) north of Perth, fossilized remains of an ancient forest stretch eerily across the desert landscape. They are best approached by four-wheel drive with an experienced driver. If this day-trip destination appeals to you, I suggest you contact **Travelabout,** 61 Brady Street, Glendalough, Perth, WA 6016 (tel. 09/242-2243). Their Pinnacles day tour departs daily at 7:30am, returning about 6:30pm. The cost is about A$70 (U.S. $56) for adults and A$60 (U.S. $48) for kids. A picnic lunch is included. In spite of the Pinnacles being the destination, the highlight of the day for many is the return trip along the beach, where there are incredible sand dunes as far as the eye can see.

CHAPTER 13

WESTERN AUSTRALIA

Rugged landscapes, delicate wildflowers, and vast distances are all part of Western Australia. The nation's biggest state covers about a third of the continent and also includes goldfields, ghost towns, majestic karri forests, a seemingly endless desert, booming mining towns, and dramatic coastal scenery. The distance from the northern edge of the state to its southern side is the same as from Oslo to Madrid. Much of this land is sparsely populated: Perth houses a million of Western Australia's 1.4 million population, leaving precious few inhabitants for the remaining area, which is the equivalent of Texas, Japan, New Zealand, and Great Britain combined. Because of its size and areas of harsh terrain, travel in the state is usually limited to three or four popular regions.

One of the prettiest places is the Southwest, where wildflowers bloom in the spring, wineries produce some of the country's best vintages, and apple orchards, small farms, and B&Bs create a picture reminiscent of the English countryside. The south coast is known for its rugged cliffs and spectacular beaches on which the Southern Ocean pounds continuously. Albany and Esperance are two of the best spots for witnessing this awesome action.

Kalgoorlie and Coolgardie are the main centers in the goldfields region, which can be reached from Perth by car in 6 hours or by train (the Prospector) in 8 hours. In the 1890s, Kalgoorlie's Golden Mile was the richest square mile of gold-bearing earth in the world; gold and nickel are still mined there today. Coolgardie is an interesting ghost town. Many passengers disembark from the Indian Pacific or the Trans Australian trains en route between Perth and Adelaide to take a quick bus tour of Kalgoorlie. East of the region, the train crosses the Nullarbor Plain on the longest stretch of straight track in the world.

Kalbarri National Park and friendly wild dolphins are the main attractions in Western Australia's Midwest region. Farther north, the Pilbara is mining country where company towns such as Tom Price, Paraburdoo, and Newman exist solely because of the vast quantities of iron ore found in the Hamersley and Ophthalmia ranges. Dampier and Port Hedland are mining ports from which the iron ore is shipped. Ningaloo Reef, Australia's closest fringing reef, is located 1,081 kilometers (670 miles) north of Perth between Exmouth and Coral Bay. The Ningaloo Marine Park is popular with snorkelers and scuba divers.

Some of the most dramatic scenery in Australia is found in the rugged Kimberley region in the far north of the state. From the pearling port of Broome, 2,230 kilometers (1,383 miles) north of Perth, to the Northern Territory border, the area boasts beautiful cliffs, gorges, and plains. Even though the highway to the Kimberley is now paved, this is a remote and rough area in which to travel.

WHAT'S SPECIAL ABOUT WESTERN AUSTRALIA

Beaches
☐ Yallingup and Prevelly Park in the southwest corner of the state— beautiful beaches with wild surf.
☐ The long expanse of sand right in front of Nanga Station in the Midwest region.

Natural Spectacles
☐ The coastal scenery around Albany.
☐ The rugged landscape of the Kimberley region.

Ace Attractions
☐ Monkey Mia, in the Midwest, where wild dolphins can be petted.
☐ Wildflowers in profusion in various areas of the state during September and October.

Great Towns
☐ Margaret River, the center of an area known for excellent wineries, beautiful beaches, and pretty rural countryside.

SEEING WESTERN AUSTRALIA

The **Western Australian Tourism Commission** offices overseas and **Western Australian Tourist Centres** within Australia are the best sources of travel information. They have available several helpful booklets, including "Pubstay Holidays," "Farm & Station Holiday Experience," "Country Style," and "Wildflower Discovery."

Ansett WA, Skywest Airlines, and intercity coaches provide transport to the major centers within the state. Westrail provides both train and coach service. If you drive, it may be helpful to know that the green-and-gold route markers indicate the national highways linking capital cities. The black-on-white signs identify Route 1, the highway that completely circles the country. The blue-and-white signs indicate the state routes, and the brown signs denote tourist drives. Consult the **Royal Automobile Club of Western Australia** in Perth (tel. 09/421-4444) before setting out across this vast state.

Homestay of W.A., 40 Union Road, Carmel, WA 6076 (tel. 09/293-5347), can arrange home and farm stays throughout Western Australia.

1. MARGARET RIVER & THE SOUTHWEST

280km (174 miles) S of Perth

GETTING THERE   By Train   The New Australind departs Perth City (Central) Railway Station and takes about 2 hours to get to Bunbury, where it connects with a Westrail bus to Margaret River. For further information contact **Westrail** in Perth (tel. 09/326-2222).

By Bus   Southwest Coachlines (tel. 09/322-5173, or toll free 008/01-7033 in Australia) has direct service from Perth to Margaret River (A$24/U.S. $19.20).

By Car   Motorists headed for Margaret River follow either the Coast Road or the Southwestern Highway south from Perth and connect with the Bussell Highway at Busselton.

ESSENTIALS   Information is available from the **Augusta/Margaret River Tourist Bureau,** at Wallcliffe Road and Bussell Highway, Margaret River, WA 6285 (tel. 097/57-2147), open daily from 9am to 5pm. The **area code** is 097.

Often called "Australia's prettiest corner," the area between Busselton and Augusta is renowned for its gentle countryside, cozy accommodations, and outstanding wineries. Margaret River (pop. 1,100) is the focal point of the area, but the craft shops, beaches, vineyards, caves, and picturesque scenery that make the Southwest a favorite destination are spread throughout the region. The villages of Cowaramup, Yallingup, Karridale, and others mentioned below are all within 45 minutes of Margaret River.

WHAT TO SEE & DO

Wineries are the main attraction in this area. The best known and most visited is the **Leeuwin Estate,** Stevens Road (tel. 57-6253), where A$7 million (U.S. $5.6 million) was spent to make it one of Australia's most beautiful. Lunch is served daily in Leeuwin's à la carte restaurant, and dinner is offered on Saturday night. The winery is open daily 10am to 4:30pm; tours are at 11am, 1, 2, 3, and 4pm. Admission is A$6 (U.S. $4.80). Another dozen and a half winemakers happily open their doors for tasting and cellar sales without charge. The tourist office will give you a complete map, which is important because many of the rustic properties blend into the surrounding countryside and aren't easy to find. None of the wineries is very large, and there is no attempt here to compete with the quantities of wine produced in the eastern states. Instead, the emphasis is on creating premium-quality table wines.

Cape Mentelle (pronounced "Men-*tell*"), 3 kilometers (2 miles) west of Margaret River off Wallcliffe Road (tel. 57-2070), has won some coveted prizes for its red wines. (Its newsletter is cleverly called *Mentelle Notes.*) **Vasse Felix Winery,** Harmans South Road, Cowaramup (tel. 55-5242), has the oldest vineyard in the area. **Happ's Vineyard,** Commonage Road, Dunsborough (tel. 55-3300), produces good ports, as well as some delicious dry reds.

Besides wine tasting, you may want to visit the region's **☼ beautiful beaches and tour at least one of the caves. Yallingup** has some of the best surf in the state. **Prevelly Park,** about 8 kilometers (5 miles) southwest of Margaret River, can also get 18-foot waves, creating a challenge for windsurfers and surfboard riders. Gracetown is another good spot.

The **Jewel Cave,** 37 kilometers (23 miles) south of Margaret River, between Karridale and Augusta, is the best in the area, although **Mammoth Cave** and **Lake Cave** are also open to the public. The Jewel Cave features some unusually long straw stalactites, an underground lake, and a main cavern that is almost 100 meters (330 ft.) high and 91 meters (300 ft.) long. Tours at the Jewel Cave (tel. 58-4541) take place at 9:30 and 11:30am and at 1:30 and 3:30pm. Tours at the Mammoth Cave are at 9:30 and 11am and 12:30 and 3pm. The Lake Cave (tel. 57-7543) is open for touring at 9:30am and 1:30pm. Guided tours, which last 1 hour, cost A$5 (U.S. $4) for adults and A$1.50 (U.S. $1.20) for children under 14.

Whatever you do, don't miss the spectacular **Boranup Forest,** which starts just south of Lake Cave. Plan to drive slowly through this patch of wonderland and perhaps even have a picnic under one of the big karri trees. In the spring (September and October), the Margaret River region has one of the loveliest wildflower displays in the state.

Two local churches deserve your attention: **St. Thomas More Catholic Church,** Mitchell Street, Margaret River, is built of rammed earth and local timbers and has beautiful leadlight and stained-glass windows. The other religious structure is the little whitewashed **Greek Chapel** at Prevelly Park built in honor of the Australian, New Zealand, British, and Greek soldiers who lost their lives in Greece in World War II.

SHOPPING

The Margaret River region abounds with craft shops. Some of the better ones include **Cowaramup Pottery,** Bussell Highway, Cowaramup (tel. 55-5467), where they do glassblowing as well as stoneware, and **Happ's Pottery,** Commonage Road, Dunsborough (tel. 55-3300), which is part of the winery of the same name. At Happ's, potters work with clay dug right there on the property, and visitors are welcome to

N

WESTERN AUSTRALIA

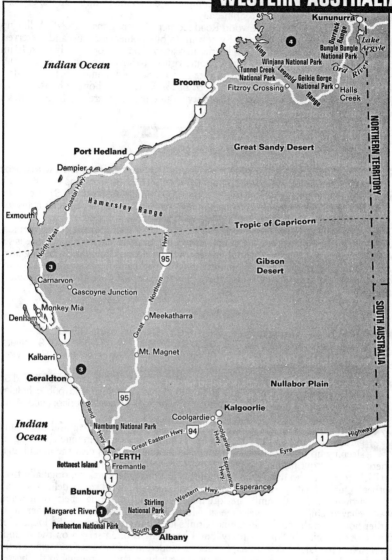

Indian Ocean

Kununurra
Durack Range
Lake Argyle
Bungle Bungle National Park
Ord River
Winjana National Park
Tunnel Creek National Park
Fitzroy Crossing
Geikie Gorge National Park
Halls Creek
Leopold Range

❹

Broome

1

NORTHERN TERRITORY

Great Sandy Desert

Port Hedland

Dampier

Coastal Hwy.

Hamersley Range

Exmouth

North West

Tropic of Capricorn

Gibson Desert

❸

Carnarvon

Gascoyne Junction

Great Northern Hwy.

95

Meekatharra

SOUTH AUSTRALIA

Monkey Mia

Denham

1

Mt. Magnet

Kalbarri

❸

Nullabor Plain

Geraldton

Brand Hwy.

95

Kalgoorlie

Coolgardie

94

Coolgardie Hwy.

Nambung National Park

Great Eastern Hwy.

Highway

1

Indian Ocean

PERTH

Fremantle

Eyre

Rottnest Island

1

Esperance Hwy.

Esperance

Bunbury

Western Hwy.

Margaret River

1

Stirling National Park

Pemberton National Park

South

❷

Albany

WESTERN AUSTRALIA

❶ Margaret River and the Southwest
❷ Albany and the South
❸ The Midwest
❹ The Kimberley

Airport

✈

watch. The mud-brick buildings in the complex are also interesting, and the gardens are pretty. Open from 10am to 5pm daily.

Rivendell Gardens, Wildwood Road (corner of Commonage Road), Yallingup (tel. 55-2090), is the place to head if you want to buy homemade jams and preserves, herbs, or flowers, or pick your own berries in season. They are open daily from 10am to 5pm, serve lunches and teas, and welcome visitors to stroll around the gallery and through the cottage and herb garden. Pete and Lu Standish named their farm after Tolkien's haven for weary travelers in *Lord of the Rings*—"a homely house east of the sea in the high pass overlooking the misty mountains . . . merely to be there was a cure."

WHERE TO STAY

MARGARET RIVER

GILGARA HOMESTEAD, corner of Caves Rd. and Carter Rd., Margaret River, WA 6285. Tel. 097/57-2705. Fax 097/57-3259. 7 rms (1 with bath).
$ Rates (including breakfast): A$75 (U.S. $60) single; A$90 (U.S. $72) double; A$110 (U.S. $88) double with bath; A$30 (U.S. $24) dinner. Special midweek rates. No children under 15. BC, MC, V.

Gilgara is a replica 1870s homestead, with a classic tin roof and encircling veranda, which offers cozy guesthouse accommodations for up to 16 people. The house is set on a 23-acre property which is 6 kilometers (4 miles) from Margaret River. Log fires, ceiling fans, and antiques help to establish the old-world ambience. Evening meals are served in the candlelit dining room. Hosts Jim and Sue Wiltshire create a welcoming atmosphere.

COWARAMUP

MERRIBROOK, Cowaramup Bay Rd., Cowaramup (P.O. Box 27 Cowaramup, WA 6284). Tel. 097/55-5490. Fax 097/55-5343. 9 chalets.
Transportation: Located 15km (9 miles) north of Margaret River. Southwest Coachlines stops in Cowaramup and hosts pick up from there.
$ Rates (including breakfast and dinner): A$108 (U.S. $86.40) per person based on double occupancy; A$158 (U.S. $126.40) single. Weekend and public holiday tariffs are higher. Weekly rates are lower. Children 4–14 are half price; under 4 are free. BC, MC, V.

Merribrook is a 65-hectare (160-acre) property with beautiful trees and gardens located on the edge of a lake. Guests are housed in nine chalets, each sleeping up to six people, which are set among the trees near the main lodge. There is good trout fishing in the lake.

Richard Firth who hails from Melbourne, and his wife Lorraine, originally from outback Queensland, are charming and helpful hosts. Richard cooks delicious meals (homegrown beef and lamb are often served). Guests bring their own wine. Well-behaved children are welcome at Merribrook and eat dinner together at an earlier hour than the adults. Predinner drinks are enjoyed in front of the lodge's log fire before the nightly "dinner party", and breakfast is often served on the veranda overlooking the lake. Recreational facilities included in the tariff are canoeing on the lake, bush bicycling around the property, trout fishing, and swimming in the heated swimming pool. There is also a wood-fired sauna and spa. Merribrook Adventures runs guided day tours which include such adventurous activities as caving, rock climbing, mountain bike tours, and abseiling (mountaineering). Guests can also use Merribrook as a base for exploring local wineries or laze around the property, enjoying its peaceful ambience. Highly recommended.

QUALITY CAPTAIN FREYCINET, Bussell Hwy. and Turnbridge St., Margaret River, WA 6285. Tel. 097/57-2033, or toll free 008/07-4444 in Australia. 62 rms. TV TEL
$ Rates: A$70 (U.S. $56) single; A$83 (U.S. $66.40) double; A$12 (U.S. $9.60) extra person. AE, BC, DC, MC, V.

All rooms have the standard amenities, plus toasters. Bathrooms have showers only. A licensed restaurant, laundry facilities, and a swimming pool are located on the premises, as are facilities for handicapped travelers.

YALLINGUP

CAVES HOUSE HOTEL, Yallingup, WA 6282. Tel. 097/55-2131. Fax 097/55-2041. 43 rms (21 with bath). MINIBAR **Transportation/Location:** Train to Bunbury, then bus; or bus direct. 300km (186 miles) south of Perth.

$ Rates (including breakfast): A$80 (U.S. $64) single without bath, A$85 (U.S. $68) single with bath; A$95 (U.S. $76) double without bath, A$105 (U.S. $84) double with bath. AE, BC, MC, V.

This 1901 hotel in Yallingup, 45 kilometers (27 miles) north of Margaret River, was almost totally rebuilt after a disastrous fire in 1930. The two-story red-brick property has an appealing old-fashioned decor and is just 1 kilometer (½ mile) from one of the best beaches in the state. Only a patch of very pretty garden separates Caves House from the water's edge. Many of the rooms have ocean views and all have coffee- and tea-making facilities, ceiling fans, and electric blankets. Most have televisions. Guests are welcome to use the tennis courts or play table tennis, croquet, or pool.

WHERE TO DINE

IN OR NEAR MARGARET RIVER

I've already mentioned several dining options—the Leeuwin Estate Winery, Rivendell Gardens, and places to stay with lovely restaurants on site. Here are a couple more ideas.

MARGARET RIVER MARRON FARM, Wickham Rd., just south of Margaret River. Tel. 57-6329.
   Cuisine: MARRON & TROUT/SNACKS. **Reservations:** Not necessary. **Directions:** 11km (7 miles) south of Margaret River.
$ Prices: Appetizers A$5–A$6 (U.S. $4–U.S. $4.80); main courses A$10–A$22 (U.S. $8–U.S. $17.60). No credit cards.
   Open: Daily 10am–4pm. Tours are given hourly 10:30am–3:30pm.
At the Margaret River Marron Farm, you can dine on marron, which are freshwater crustaceans. They also serve trout, homemade soup, sandwiches, and apple pie with cream or ice cream. Bring your own wine and enjoy the facilities on the property, which include a children's playground and spring-fed swimming hole.

ARUMVALE SIDING TEAHOUSE, Caves Rd., Karridale. Tel. 58-6745.
   Cuisine: TEA/LIGHT LUNCHES. **Reservations:** Not necessary. **Directions:** 30km (19 miles) south of Margaret River. No public transportation.
$ Prices: Light lunches A$2–A$10 (U.S. $1.60–U.S. $8). No credit cards.
   Open: Wed–Sun 10am–5pm.
This is a delightful place for afternoon teas and light lunches. The drive to this picturesque eatery takes you about 30 kilometers (19 miles) south of the Margaret River township through a patch of fairy tale–beautiful forest. Seating is provided indoors or outside in the shade of karri and peppermint trees. The menu includes Devonshire teas, sandwiches, cakes, soups, quiches, and daily specials such as lasagne or vegetarian casseroles.

2. ALBANY & THE SOUTH

402km (249 miles) SE of Perth

GETTING THERE   By Plane   Skywest Airlines has daily flights from Perth for A$141 (U.S. $112.80).

By Bus   Westrail offers coach service from Perth for A$32 (U.S. $25.60).

By Car   Using the most direct route, the Albany Highway, the road trip from Perth takes about 5½ hours.

ESSENTIALS   Tourist information is available at the **Albany Tourist Bureau,** Peel Place near York Street, Albany, WA 6330 (tel. 098/41-1088), which is open Monday through Friday from 8:30am to 5:30pm and Saturday and Sunday from 9am to 5pm. The **area code** is 098.

GETTING AROUND   The Albany Tourist Bureau runs the town's **sightseeing coaches.** Escape Tours (tel. 41-4993) operate Wednesday through Sunday year round. Half-day trips cost A$28 (U.S. $22.40) for adults and A$15 (U.S. $12) for children 3 to 11. Full-day excursions cost A$55 (U.S. $44) for adults and A$28 (U.S. $22.40) for children; the full-day price includes a picnic lunch. Contact the Albany Tourist Bureau (tel. 41-1088) to make reservations.

   Taxis (tel. 41-2125) are also available for sightseeing or other transportation.

In 1826 a military post was established on the southwest coast of Australia in order to secure England's position in this part of the world. (There were rumors that the French were thinking of launching a colonizing effort.) From that primitive settlement, inhabited by 45 men, grew Western Australia's first town. Because of its excellent natural harbor, Albany (pop. 23,000) has always been an important port and now, because of its age, it is also an important reservoir of historic buildings.

WHAT TO SEE & DO
IN OR NEAR ALBANY

The main thoroughfare, **York Street,** slopes down to the sea and is the site of many fine Victorian buildings such as the **Headmaster's House** (1880), **Albany Town Hall** (1886), and **St. John's Anglican Church** (1848).

   Not far away, you can follow the steep winding road to the top of **Mount Clarence** for a good view of the surrounding area. The **Light Horse Memorial statue** near the top is a replica of the one originally erected in Suez in 1932 in honor of Australian soldiers. It was badly damaged during the Suez crisis and the granite blocks were shipped back to Australia; bullet marks are still visible on them. **Mount Melville** also has a lookout, and a historic military fort has been reconstructed on the slopes of **Mount Adelaide,** another viewpoint.

   The most significant historic site is **Strawberry Hill Farm,** 172-174 Middleton Road (tel. 41-3735), the original home of Capt. Richard Spencer, the governor-resident in Albany in 1833. The homestead, modeled on the English estates of the 18th century, has period-style furnishings and pretty gardens. Strawberry Hill Farm is open daily from 10am to noon and 2 to 5pm except in the winter, when it's open only in the afternoon; it's closed the whole month of June. Devonshire teas are served in a cottage on the grounds (A$3.50/U.S. $2.80). Admission is A$2.50 (U.S. $2) for adults and A$1.50 (U.S. $1.20) for children.

   Some 20 kilometers (12 miles) from town, the rocky cliffs along the ocean create some of the most dramatic coastal scenery in Australia. A few of the best viewing spots are: ✪ **The Gap, Natural Bridge,** and **The Blowholes.** The holes, you'll discover, are a bit of a walk from the parking lot and they blow only in heavy seas, but the area is so pretty you won't be disappointed. Be careful because the cliffs are slippery and the winds are strong. As you might guess, Natural Bridge is a huge chunk of granite that has been eroded into the shape of a bridge, and the Gap is a steep crevasse between two cliffs.

   Nearby, tours are conducted through a former whaling station that has been converted into an impressive museum. The fate of the historic property (whaling was a major industry from the 1840s to 1978) in Frenchman's Bay, 21 kilometers (13 miles) from central Albany, hung in limbo until the Jaycees took it over in 1980. The Jaycees did a great job and put together the ✪ **Whaleworld** museum which traces the history of whaling in Albany and allows visitors to examine a boat used for chasing whales. Relics and old lithographs from the days of hand-whaling shed light on the development of whaling from the days of "iron men and wooden ships." Guided tours led by former employees (ours was a pilot who looked for whales from the air) take groups over the premises. There is also a souvenir shop and a pleasant eatery, the Whalers Gallery Restaurant. Whaleworld (tel. 44-4021) is open daily from 9am to 5pm, with guided tours on the hour from 10am to 4pm. Admission is A$4.50 (U.S. $3.60) for adults and A$1.50 (U.S. $1.20) for children.

AROUND THE SOUTHERN REGION

It isn't surprising that Albany is the focal point of Western Australia's most popular holiday region. The area offers a look at tall trees, magnificent coastal scenery, and beautiful historic buildings. Leaving Perth, most people head down the South Western Highway to **Manjimup** and **Pemberton.** These towns, just over 300 kilometers (186 miles) southeast of the capital, are in the heart of tall-timber country. Forests of towering jarrah, karri, tuart, tingle, wandoo, blackbutt, and marri trees are found throughout the region. Karri and jarrah, both superb hardwoods, predominate. About 3 kilometers (2 miles) from Pemberton, the world's highest fire lookout is built in the **Gloucester Tree,** a giant karri named following a visit by the Duke of Gloucester. You are welcome to climb the 153 rungs to the top, where a lookout platform is perched 61 meters (201 ft.) above the ground. You may also want to visit the **local trout hatchery** and drive the **Rainbow Trail,** a scenic route through splendid forest. The **Pemberton/Northcliffe Tourist Bureau,** Brockman Street, Pemberton, WA 6260 (tel. 097/76-1133), is open daily from 9am to 5pm to answer your questions and make sure you have good maps of the area.

Highway 1 is called the South Western Highway until it reaches the coast, where it is, not surprisingly, labeled the South Coast Highway. Along this road, **Walpole** and **Denmark** are a pair of attractive towns offering seaside scenery and good fishing opportunities.

Two national parks north of Albany, **Stirling Range** and **Porongorup,** have fantastic springtime (September and October) displays of wildflowers. March and April are the other optimum months for visiting this southern region of Western Australia.

SHOPPING

Nyoongah Art Shop, next to the tourist bureau on Peel Place (tel. 42-1330), sells ceramics, paintings, spears, boomerangs, and other artifacts crafted by Aborigines. Ask to see the work of artist Lance Chadd (Tjyllyungoo).

Amity Crafts, Stirling Terrace West (tel. 41-1766), has an excellent selection of homespun wool sweaters (or "jumpers," as they're called in Oz), wooden pieces, pottery, scrimshaw, hand-blown glass, and leatherwork, and they're conveniently open daily from 10am to 5pm. If you're traveling with someone who doesn't like to shop, **Alkoomi Wines** is next door, and they welcome tasters.

WHERE TO STAY

FREDERICKSTOWN MOTOR LODGE, 41 Fredericks St., Albany, WA 6330. Tel. 098/41-1600. 34 rms. A/C TV TEL
$ Rates: A$58 (U.S. $46.40) single; A$66 (U.S. $52.80) double. AE, BC, DC, MC, V.

The Frederickstown Motor Lodge has units with showers, coffee- and tea-making facilities, and fridges. The motel is situated in the town center, and some rooms have ocean views. The dining room is BYO.

ALBANY DOG ROCK MOTEL, 303 Middleton Rd., Albany, WA 6330. Tel. 098/41-4422, or toll free 008/01-7024 in Australia. Fax 098/42-1027. 81 rms and suites. TV TEL **Directions:** This motel is located 300 meters (325 yd.) down Middleton Rd. from the top end of York St.
$ Rates: A$54 (U.S. $43.20) single; A$64 (U.S. $51.20) double; A$75–A$85 (U.S. $60–U.S. $68) suite. AE, BC, DC, MC, V.

The Dog Rock is the largest and best-appointed motel in Albany. The rooms have all the modern amenities you might expect; some have bathtubs and air conditioning. There is a nice dining room on the premises, and room service is available during limited hours. The centrally located motel gets its name from a nearby granite boulder that resembles the head of a bloodhound.

APPLE TREE COTTAGE, 542 Chester Pass Rd., Albany, WA 6330. Tel. 098/41-8491. 2 rms (none with bath).

$ Rates (including breakfast): A$25 (U.S. $20) single; A$44 (U.S. $35.20) double. Three-course dinner A$11 (U.S. $8.80) extra. No credit cards.

Budget travelers get a warm welcome at the home of Pat and Kaj Nielsen. This incredibly friendly couple encourage guests to "lounge in front of the fire or sit in the garden as if this was their own home." Pat, who's Irish, and her husband Kaj, who's Danish, have two spare rooms.

WHERE TO DINE

In addition to the restaurant at Whaleworld and the tearoom at Strawberry Hill Farm, you might enjoy this casual city-center eatery.

POPPIES COFFEE SHOP, in the Mews Arcade on Lower York St. Tel. 41-7595.
   Cuisine: BREAKFAST/LUNCH/TEA. **Reservations:** Not necessary.

$ Prices: Lunch under A$6 (U.S. $4.80). No credit cards.
   Open: Mon–Fri 8am–4:30pm, Sat 9:30am–1pm.

This is my favorite place for a light meal or morning or afternoon tea. The decor is light and bright and the service friendly. You might enjoy quiche and salad, a filled croissant, or pâté with salad and toast for lunch. They also serve cappuccino, a wonderful Black Forest cake, and homemade soup—among other things. BYO.

3. THE MIDWEST

While the Southwest and the South of Western Australia are established tourist areas, the Midwest has caught the attention of travelers only in recent years. The region stretches from the shores of the Indian Ocean to the Great Victorian Desert and from Moora, 145 kilometers (90 miles) north of Perth, almost to Carnarvon. It is a sunny area, and while winter weather happily allows for tanning, summers can be just plain hot.

Geraldton (pop. 20,895) is the main center in this sparsely populated rural area and serves as a commercial base for surrounding agricultural endeavors, including grain, wool, fat lambs, pigs, and beef cattle. **Kalbarri,** an emerging resort community north of Geraldton, and **Monkey Mia,** where friendly wild dolphins allow humans to pet them, are the most interesting spots for visitors.

If you travel in the Midwest, you may notice that the oceanfront strip is referred to as the Batavia Coast, named after the Dutch ship that went aground on the offshore Abrolhos Islands in 1629. Most of the crew survived, but a subsequent mutiny resulted in the slaughter of 125 men, women, and children. Two men whose lives were spared were marooned on the mainland, thus becoming Australia's first European settlers. Their presence accounts for the number of local Aborigines with blond hair and blue eyes.

KALBARRI

661km (410 miles) N of Perth

GETTING THERE By Plane Western Airlines has flights directly to Kalbarri from Perth on Monday, Wednesday, and Friday by way of Geraldton

(A$148/U.S. $118.40 one-way). The other alternative is to fly **Ansett WA, Skywest,** or **Western** to Geraldton (A$109 to A$143/U.S. $87.20 to U.S. $114.40) and either take a local bus or rent a car for the final leg. The drive to Kalbarri from Geraldton takes about 2 hours.

By Bus   You can also take a **Westrail** coach to Kalbarri from Perth (8 hr.; A$55/U.S. $44) or join an organized coach tour from Perth which includes sightseeing and accommodation.

By Car   The drive to Kalbarri from Perth takes 7 to 8 hours. The Western Australian Tourist Centre in Perth is the best source of detailed driving data.

ESSENTIALS   Tourist information is provided at the **Kalbarri Travel Service,** Grey Street, Kalbarri, WA 6536 (tel. 099/37-1104), open Monday through Friday from 9am to 5pm, Saturday from 9am to noon, and Sunday from 10am to noon. The **area code** is 099.

The tiny seaside community of Kalbarri (pop. 820) has been discovered of late by those seeking sun, sea, scenery, and sports. The town is ideally set at the mouth of the Murchison River, and swimmers, fishermen, and boating enthusiasts have a choice of calm water or Indian Ocean rollers. I can think of few coastal sites in the country that are as beautiful as Kalbarri's: the Murchison winds its way slowly to the sea, and right at the river's mouth a long sandbar creates a tranquil estuary while breakers crash only a short distance away. Inland, the colorful gorges of the Murchison and a spectacular springtime display of wildflowers draw visitors to Kalbarri National Park.

WHAT TO SEE & DO

⭐ Coastal scenery and the magnificent gorges cut by the Murchison River as it wanders through **Kalbarri National Park** are the big attractions in this area. Some of the canyons cut into the reddish sandstone are over 130 meters (429 ft.) deep; some are very narrow and others contain pools and streams. Be sure you don't miss the **Hawkes Head Lookout, Z-bend, the Loop,** and **Meenarra Lookout.** In all, the park totals 1,000 square kilometers (386 sq. miles) of virgin bushland, and kangaroos, emus, and wild pigs are plentiful. The pigs are descended from domestic pigs introduced by a man named Harry Leever. Harry had plans to start a piggery at Lockwood Springs, but he let his animals loose to graze and they never came back. The southern boundary of Kalbarri National Park is a rabbit-proof fence that runs from the coast through all of Western Australia and neighboring South Australia. **Kalbarri Coachline** (tel. 37-1104), a subsidiary of Kalbarri Travel Service, conducts tours in the park or you can drive yourself.

South of Kalbarri, beautiful coastal cliffs have been eroded into fanciful shapes. **Madman's Gorge, Castle Cove, Grandstand Rocks,** and **Shell House** are the special spots to see.

WHERE TO STAY & DINE

PALM LODGE RESORT, Porter St., Kalbarri, WA 6536. Tel. 099/37-1008. 50 units. A/C TV

$ Rates: A$47 (U.S. $37.60) single; A$68 (U.S. $54.40) double. BC, DC, MC, V. The units at the Palm Lodge Motel have cooking facilities and other modern amenities. A restaurant and pool are on the grounds.

MONKEY MIA

24km (15 miles) E of Denham, 838km (520 miles) N of Perth

GETTING THERE   By Plane   Western Airlines operates a service from Perth to Denham on Monday, Wednesday, and Friday. Coach transfers are available to Monkey Mia. Another option is to fly to Geraldton (see "Kalbarri," above) and then rent a car for the 432-kilometer (268-mile) drive to Monkey Mia.

By Bus Kalbarri Coachline (see "Kalbarri," above) provides the only direct coach service to Monkey Mia from Geraldton or Kalbarri. **Kalbarri Air Charters** (tel. 099/37-1130) offers day tours to Monkey Mia from Kalbarri.

By Organized Tour If you want to join a group, several Perth companies conduct excursions. **Pinnacle Tours** (tel. 09/325-9455, or toll free 008/99-9069 in Australia), **W.A. Coach Service** (tel. 09/309-1680), **Westrail** (09/326-2159), and **Travelabout** (09/242-2243) are some of these.

One operator, **Peter Weiland's Flightseeing Tours** (tel. 09/361-6276), makes it possible to visit Monkey Mia on a day-trip from Perth. This option costs about A$435 (U.S. $348) and includes a flight over Perth, Geraldton, and Kalbarri, a visit to the dolphins, and lunch.

ESSENTIALS The **area code** is 099.

The only place I know in the world where you can play with *wild* dolphins is a place on Shark Bay between Carnarvon and Geraldton called Monkey Mia. Monkey Mia is a long way from anywhere, and I hesitate to tell you about it because there's never a guarantee that the dolphins will show up—but they almost always do.

The Shark Bay area can be unpleasantly windy during November and December and extremely hot until the end of March. The best time to visit this region is from late March to mid-October.

WHAT TO SEE & DO

No one is exactly sure why the Indian Ocean bottle-nosed **dolphins** first started coming to Monkey Mia in the 1960s, but six or seven of them usually turn up every day. They swim in water only a few feet deep and enjoy being petted on their sides. They seem to be as curious about humans as we are about them. A few things annoy them, such as being petted on their head and having someone touch their dorsal fin or blowhole, and the ranger on duty asks visitors to refrain from these actions. The dolphins are completely free to leave, and sometimes do for hours at a time, but so far they've always come back. The **Dolphin Welfare Centre** presents films and displays about these fascinating animals. According to the directions prepared by the Project Jonah staff, it is bad form to return a fish given to you by a dolphin. Instead, you are to "accept it with gratitude."

WHERE TO STAY & DINE

MONKEY MIA DOLPHIN RESORT, Monkey Mia (P.O. Box 119, Denham, WA 6537). Tel. 099/48-1320. Perth office: tel. 09/368-2100. Fax 099/48-1034. 36 motel units, 6 on-site vans, 18 "park homes."
$ Rates: A$95 (U.S. $76) double motel; A$40–A$60 (U.S. $32–U.S. $48) on-site vans for four or six; A$75 (U.S. $60) "park home" for four. AE, BC, MC, V.
This is the place to stay if you want to be near the water and the wild dolphins who have put Monkey Mia on the map. The motel units have private toilets and showers, tea- and coffee-making facilities, and small refrigerators. There are also four- and six-berth on-site vans which have cooking facilities, but use shared toilets and showers. The "park homes" have the best "possie" (position) right on the beach with a "beaut" water view. These mobile homes are fully furnished and have cooking facilities, but use communal bathrooms.

NANGA BAY HOLIDAY VILLAGE & CARAVAN PARK, Nanga Station, Shark Bay (c/o Post Office, Denham, WA 6537). Tel. 099/48-3992. Fax 099/48-3996. 24 motel units, 3 2-bedroom houses, 8 cabins, 15 bunkhouse rooms, caravan and tent sites. **Directions:** Nanga Station is a 40-minute drive from Monkey Mia.

$ Rates: A$77 (U.S. $61.60) motel unit; A$85 (U.S. $68) house for two people; A$45–A$55 (U.S. $36–U.S. $44) cabin; A$18 (U.S. $14.40) per person in a bunkhouse; A$10 (U.S. $8) unpowered caravan site; A$13 (U.S. $10.40) powered caravan site. Weekly discounts. BC, MC, V.

Located 50 kilometers (31 miles) southeast of Denham on Shark Bay, Nanga Station offers the widest range of accommodations in the area. The historic homestead on a half-million-acre sheep property is built of shell blocks. The station is owned by Maureen and Ted Sears, who are—and I say this with all kindness—virtual caricatures of outback Aussies. Ted's quick wit, gift of gab, and entrepreneurial talents remind one of Crocodile Dundee. Starting in business with a chicken farm at the age of 16, he has worked his way up to Nanga Station, where there are 6,000 sheep. Even more amazing, he has made this remote piece of land attractive to tourists.

At present, Nanga Station offers an 80-seat BYO restaurant (the Nanga Barn), general store (which sells liquor), take-out food shop, 24 air-conditioned motel units, three large self-contained rental houses, a caravan park, eight cabins with kitchens (but no bathrooms), 15 bunkhouse rooms that use communal bathrooms and kitchens, and a large swimming pool. Energetic Ted sees that everything is kept clean and tidy. Only the houses and motel rooms are supplied with bed and bath linen. It's very handy to bring a torch (flashlight).

The property is sited on a beautiful beach, ideal for fishing, swimming, and sunning. During the 3 weeks of shearing, which start on Boxing Day (December 26), visitors who can stand the heat and flies are welcome to go out on the station and help. March, April, and May are the best months for fishing. The week after Easter, Ted and Maureen host a huge angling competition that concludes with a hangi dinner (a New Zealand Maori-style meal where food is cooked in a pit) and a "helluva party."

4. THE KIMBERLEY

This is Australia's "last frontier:" an area about the size of California with a population of less than 15,000. A place where temperatures during "the dry" season can hit 120°F and rain during "the wet" can come at the rate of a foot a month. The Kimberley region covers the top half of Western Australia—stretching from the Northern Territory border to the Indian Ocean and from the Timor Sea to the Great Sandy Desert. The first settlers here tried to raise sheep, but the land was too barren. Today, cattle stations, each averaging over a half million acres, cover much of the land. The hardy folks who live on these outback outposts muster (round up) their livestock with helicopters, rely on the Royal Flying Doctor Service for medical care, and send their children to the School of the Air. In spite of being in Western Australia, residents of the Kimberley identify more with the Top End of the Northern Territory than with Perth *many* miles to the south, and there is a grass-roots movement to change the region's clocks to Darwin time.

Until recently, the Kimberley lacked tourist facilities, and it was the rare traveler who ventured into this remote and, in some ways, inhospitable corner of the country. However, the completion of a paved road through the region in 1986 opened the door for visitors and made it possible to tour the area in some degree of comfort. The Great Northern Highway connects the two biggest towns in the area: **Kununurra** in the East Kimberley and **Broome** in the West Kimberley. It also provides access to such beauty spots as **Windjana Gorge National Park, Geikie Gorge National Park, Tunnel Creek National Park,** and the **Bungle Bungle Range.** It is these scenic wonders and the chance to experience a real frontier that lure adventurous travelers.

Good background information on the Kimberley is contained in the January 1991 issue of *National Geographic* magazine.

BROOME

2,250km (1,395 miles) NE of Perth, 1,050km (651 miles) SW of Kununurra

GETTING THERE   By Plane   Ansett WA has regular flights to Broome from Perth and Darwin.

By Bus   Bus Australia, Greyhound, and **Pioneer** provide coach service from Perth and Darwin. Perth-Broome costs A$163 (U.S. $130.40); Darwin-Broome will set you back A$146 (U.S. $116.80).

By Car   Regular cars can travel the main highway to Broome, but motorists should first get advice from the auto club in either Perth or Darwin. Stray cattle and long road trains—several semi-truck trailers linked together—create hazards, so please take care.

By Tour   Since travel on many roads in the region, including the picturesque Gibb River Road, requires a four-wheel-drive vehicle and outback experience, I suggest you consider joining a camping tour or one that overnights in motels. **Kimberley Safari Tours** (tel. 09/323-1113), **Halls Creek and Bungle Bungle Tours** (tel. 091/68-6217; fax 091/68-6222), **Regional Safaris** (tel. or fax 091/92-1198 or tel. 091/92-1113), and **Travelabout** (tel. 09/242-2243; fax 09/242-1448) all operate well-organized excursions throughout the Kimberley. Book well in advance.

ESSENTIALS   The **Broome Tourist Bureau,** corner of Great Northern Highway and Bagot Street (tel. 091/92-2222), has maps and staff who can answer your questions. The **area code** is 091.

The pearling port of Broome (pop. 8,000) is like no other town in Australia. In addition to the pure Aborigine and white residents, there are many descendants of the Asian people who have come here since the 1880s to work the luggers. These Japanese, Chinese, Filipinos, Malays, and Koepangers often married Aboriginal women, creating an interracial society which is unique in the nation.

The architecture, too, is part Asian and part Australian. "Chinatown," Broome's business district, has changed little in the past 75 years. Most structures sport pagoda-style peaks and Chinese-red trim along with classic Aussie corrugated iron roofs and encircling verandas. In addition, colorful bougainvillea lends a tropical touch to this Asian/Aussie blend. While the pearling industry is still very important, Broome also is a supply center for the vast cattle stations which spread out from it in every direction. Cable Beach is an unspoiled stretch of sand just a few miles from town. In terms of the weather, May through October is the best time to visit. Deadly marine stingers make swimming prohibitive from November through April.

WHAT TO SEE & DO

Your Broome sightseeing should include a walk through **Chinatown** for a look at the unusual architecture. Several stores sell jewelry that incorporates locally grown pearls. Also, be sure to poke your head in the door at ◐ **Sun Pictures,** built by pearling master Ted Hunter in 1916. This "garden picture theater" seats 317 in canvas beach chairs. During "the wet" patrons sit under the cover of a tin roof, and the film is projected through the rain. The rest of the year the starry sky is the ceiling. Current movies are shown. Admission is A$7 (U.S. $5.60).

Cable Beach, which is 24 kilometers (15 miles) long, is another "must see," but I wouldn't go out of my way to do the **"Ships of the Desert" camel ride** offered there, unless they replace the extremely uncomfortable saddles that were in use the last time I tried it. It's better to walk on the beach and take pictures of the experience which is, admittedly, picturesque with the setting sun behind them. **Surf Cat rental** from a kiosk on the beach March through November (tel. 93-5551) costs A$16 (U.S. $12.80) per hour; **surfboards** cost A$5 (U.S. $4) per hour.

The **Pearl Coast Zoo** (tel. 92-1703), founded by Britain's Lord McAlpine, is a

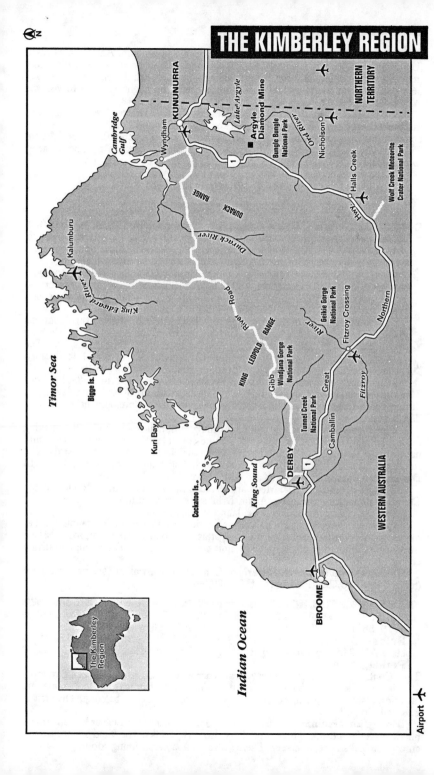

THE KIMBERLEY REGION

NORTHERN TERRITORY

WESTERN AUSTRALIA

KUNUNURRA

Wyndham

Cambridge Gulf

Timor Sea

Bigge Is.

Kuri Bay

Cockatoo Is.

Kalumburu

King Edward River

Indian Ocean

King Sound

DERBY

BROOME

Lake Argyle

Argyle Diamond Mine

Bungle Bungle National Park

Ord River

Nicholson

Halls Creek

Wolf Creek Meteorite Crater National Park

DURACK RANGE

Durack River

Gibb River Road

KING LEOPOLD RANGE

Windjana Gorge National Park

Tunnel Creek National Park

Geikie Gorge National Park

Fitzroy Crossing

Fitzroy River

Great Northern Hwy

Camballin

The Kimberley Region

N

Airport

haven for endangered species. It's open daily from 9am to 5pm. Admission is A$10 (U.S. $8) for adults and A$5 (U.S. $4) for children. The **Broome Crocodile Park** (tel. 92-1489) is open daily from April through October. Admission costs A$8 (U.S. $6.40) for adults and A$4 (U.S. $3.20) for children. You might also like to visit the **Willie Creek Pearl Farm** (tel. 92-4918).

Local tour operators conduct ✪ **excursions within the region** to such places as **Cape Leveque,** where you can visit the Beagle Bay and Lombadina Aboriginal communities and to **Roebuck Plains Cattle Station** where 10,000 cattle roam 750,000 acres. There are also Hovercraft tours of **Roebuck Bay** and **fishing excursions.**

WHERE TO STAY & DINE

In or Near Broome

CABLE BEACH CLUB, Cable Beach Rd., Broome, WA 6725. Tel. 091/92-2505, or toll free 008/09-5508 in Australia. Fax 091/92-2249. 260 rms, 3 suites. A/C MINIBAR TV TEL **Transportation:** A$10 (U.S. $8) taxi ride from town which is 6km (4 miles) away. Courtesy airport transfers are provided.

$ **Rates:** A$180 (U.S. $144) single or double; A$235 (U.S. $188) 1-bedroom bungalow for one to four people; A$285 (U.S. $228) 2-bedroom bungalow for one to six people; A$500–A$900 (U.S. $400–U.S. $720) suite. Lower off-season rates. AE, BC, DC, MC, V. **Parking:** Free.

✪ The only property in the area located adjacent to Cable Beach, this luxurious hotel features Dutch colonial furnishings from Indonesia in the sleeping quarters and antique artifacts from Asia outdoors and in the public spaces. The attractive low-rise structures on the 10 hectares (25 acres) of landscaped grounds are built in typical Broome style, combining both Asian and Australian elements. The Cable Beach Club was built in 1988 by Lord McAlpine from Britain. This gentleman fell in love with the West Kimberley region during a visit there and has contributed significantly to its development as a tourist destination.

All guest rooms are spacious and offer ceiling fans, radios, tea- and coffee-making facilities, small refrigerators, toasters, remote-control TVs, in-house movies, and hairdryers. The bungalows also have kitchenettes, irons, and ironing boards. The suites are named after Australian artists (including Sidney Nolan and Elizabeth Durack) and their original works are displayed within.

Dining/Entertainment: Meals are served in the Veranda Pearler Restaurant, the Club Restaurant, and the Asian Affair. Drinks are served in four bars.

Services: Limited room service, laundry, baby-sitting.

Facilities: Day-tour desk; in-house activities program including tennis tournaments, water-volleyball games, Surf Cat regattas, and so forth; free bikes for kids; two free-form swimming pools; a spa; 12 tennis courts; Children's Fun Club; and diving center.

Reservations in North America: Contact the Australian Destination Centre (tel. toll free 800/227-5317 in the U.S., 800/661-1236 in Canada).

THE CONTINENTAL HOTEL, corner of Weld and Louis Sts., Broome, WA 6725. Tel. 091/92-1002, or toll free 008/01-5519 in Australia. Fax 091/92-1715. 66 rms. A/C TV TEL **Transportation:** Courtesy airport pickup.

$ **Rates:** A$105 (U.S. $84) single; A$115 (U.S. $92) double; A$140 (U.S. $112) suite; A$8 (U.S. $6.40) extra person. Lower off-season rates. AE, BC, DC, MC, V. **Parking:** Free.

The "Conti" is a two-story property located across the road from Roebuck Bay and a 10-minute walk from Chinatown. Each modern room has tea- and coffee-making facilities, a small fridge, in-house movies, a ceiling fan, and a balcony. The staff is unusually friendly.

Dining/Entertainment: Pearling memorabilia makes the Lugger Bar an atmospheric place for a drink. Three other bars also serve drinks. The Weld Street Bistro is an economical self-serve eatery. There's also an à la carte dining room.

Services: Limited room service.
Facilities: Large pool, tennis court, and laundry.

In Fitzroy Crossing

FITZROY RIVER LODGE, Great Northern Hwy., Fitzroy Crossing, WA 6765. Tel. 091/91-5141. Fax 091/91-5142. 38 rms, 2 suites. A/C TV TEL
Directions: Fitzroy Crossing is 397km (246 miles) east of Broome.

$ Rates: A$80 (U.S. $64) single motel; A$95 (U.S. $76) double motel; A$60 (U.S. $48) single safari room; A$72 (U.S. $57.60) double safari room; A$10 (U.S. $8) extra person. BC, MC, V.

Located on the banks of the Fitzroy River, this lodge offers accommodation in four buildings, elevated above the flood level of the river, with parking below. These motel units offer in-house movies, coffee- and tea-making facilities, ceiling fans, small refrigerators, and en suite baths. Safari lodges have canvas sides, solid timber floors, bathrooms, small refrigerators, and coffee- and tea-making facilities. There is also a caravan park. There's a restaurant, bar, and swimming pool on the premises. Geikie Gorge is 18 kilometers (11 miles) away, and there are daily tours.

KUNUNURRA

3,192km (1,979 miles) NE of Perth, 1,050km (651 miles) NE of Broome, 525km (326 miles) SW of Katherine, Northern Territory

GETTING THERE   By Plane   Ansett WA has regular flights from Darwin and Perth. **Bus Australia, Greyhound,** and **Pioneer** provide coach service. A ticket from Darwin costs A$85 (U.S. $68). A ticket from Broome to Kununurra costs A$101 (U.S. $80.80). The Victoria Highway brings visitors from the Northern Territory, and the Great Northern Highway connects Kununurra to the West Kimberley region.

ESSENTIALS   Contact the **Kununurra Visitors Centre,** Coolibah Drive (tel. 091/68-1177). The **area code** is 091.

Barely 30 years old, the town of Kununurra came into being when the decision was made to impound the Ord River and use the water to irrigate the surrounding land. Known as the Ord River Project, this scheme has created hundreds of miles of fertile agricultural land. Man-made Lake Argyle, covering an area nine times as large as Sydney Harbour, is where the Ord's "wet" season flow is stored. Local farmers are still experimenting with various crops. Cotton, rice, and peanuts weren't as successful as it was hoped they would be, but mangoes, bananas, and melons do well.

While many of Kununurra's 4,500 residents came from other Australian states and overseas to try their hand in agriculture, a large number also came to work in the area's two highly productive diamond mines. Since these gemstones were first discovered here in 1979, Australia has become the largest diamond producing country in the world. The Argyle Diamond Mine, open since 1985, yields 34 million carats a year.

WHAT TO SEE & DO

Kununurra is the gateway to the beautiful **Bungle Bungle Range,** with its intricately sculptured chasms and beehive-shaped sandstone domes. Alligator Airways (tel. 68-1575) and Sling Air (tel. 68-1259) offer 2-hour flightseeing trips which include the Bungle Bungles, Lake Argyle, and the Argyle Diamond Mine (A$140/U.S. $112 per person). If you drive to the Bungle Bungles, you can take a Sling Air helicopter flight from there.

It is also possible to tour the **Argyle Diamond Mine** with Belray Diamond Tours (tel. 68-1014). These tours, which include a flight over the Bungle Bungles, as well as an on-site tour of the mine, operate Monday through Friday, last 5 hours and cost from A$265 (U.S. $212) per person.

Another really enjoyable experience is offered by Triple J Tours Boat Cruises (tel. 68-2682). Their jet boats cruise **Lake Kununurra** to **Lake Argyle.** Along the way you see native birds, crocodiles, and lots of beautiful scenery. The knowledgeable driver/guide provides a running commentary on the flora, fauna, the creation of the lake, how the dam was built, and so forth. Trips vary in length from 5½ to 7 hours and cost from A$65 to A$85 (U.S. $52 to U.S. $68). Children 6 to 15 are charged half price. Highly recommended.

Besides being scenic, the **Ord River** is also one of the best places in Australia to **fish for barramundi.** If this interests you, contact **Northern Explorer Safaris** (tel. 091/69-1214). Bruce Ellison and Dave Swansson, proprietors of this business, will make sure the wily barra doesn't escape your line. Lodging is at the bush camp described below.

WHERE TO STAY & DINE
In or Near Kununurra

NORTHERN EXPLORER'S BUSH CAMP, on the Ord River, 60km (37 miles) downriver from Kununurra (P.O. Box 901, Kununurra, WA 6743). Tel. 091/69-1214. Fax 091/68-2224. 6 open-air units. **Transportation:** Provided by hosts.
$ Rates (including transfers, meals, and fishing or sightseeing on the river): A$160 (U.S. $128) per person per night. AE, BC, DC, MC, V. **Closed:** During "the wet," Nov–Mar.

Perched on the west bank of the Ord River, the Bush Camp offers an experience you'll never forget. Lodging is in units which are mesh on three sides and open on the fourth. Each has twin beds, a thatched roof, a concrete-slab floor, and an electric light which operates until the generator is turned off each night. Bedding, mosquito netting around the bed, and torches (flashlights) are provided. Waking up here—on the edge of the river, under the trees, with the birds singing—is truly memorable. Shared toilets and showers are adjacent to the units. Water for drinking, showering, and cooking is pumped directly from the river. Guests dine on a patio overlooking the river and House Roof Hill. Meals are prepared on a wood-fired barbecue or in traditional camp ovens. The hosts take visitors for boat rides on the river where they can fish or just look for crocodiles, ibis, sulfur-crested cockatoos, gray night cranes, and goannas. Because of the crocs, swimming in the river isn't a good idea, but nearby there's a swimming hole with a boab tree on an island in the middle.

QUALITY INN, Duncan Hwy., Kununurra, WA 6743. Tel. 091/68-1455. 60 units. A/C MINIBAR TV TEL
$ Rates: A$90 (U.S. $72) single; A$105 (U.S. $84) double. AE, BC, DC, MC. **Parking:** Free.
Located near the center of Kununurra, this motel offers adequate rooms with modern amenities including coffee- and tea-making facilities, small refrigerators, and radios. Other facilities include a restaurant, laundry, and pool.

In Halls Creek

HALLS CREEK KIMBERLEY HOTEL, Roberta Ave. (P.O. Box 35, Halls Creek, WA 6770). Tel. 091/68-6101. Fax 091/68-6071. 44 units. A/C TV TEL **Directions:** Halls Creek is 359km (223 miles) southwest of Kununurra on the Great Northern Hwy.
$ Rates: A$60–A$80 (U.S. $48–U.S. $64) single; A$70–A$95 (U.S. $56–U.S. $76) double; A$10 (U.S. $8) extra person. AE, BC, DC, MC, V. **Parking:** Free.
All quarters here offer coffee- and tea-making facilities, small fridges, and in-room movies. Five bars serve drinks, and meals are available indoors and out. Try to be in Halls Creek on Sunday—barbecue night at this hotel. Guests can use the nice pool and spa. Scenic flights to the Bungle Bungles and Wolfe Creek Meteorite Crater operate from Halls Creek.

CHAPTER 14

ADELAIDE

One of the country's best-kept secrets, the capital of South Australia is a beautiful, well-planned city with much to offer travelers. Wide tree-lined streets, sidewalk cafés, large colonnaded colonial buildings, and grassy parks with elaborate fountains and statuary create a strong European ambience. The sunny Mediterranean climate, an old-fashioned tram rumbling down its track, and a busy public market further underscore the continental feel.

Adelaide, founded in 1836, was the only colony comprised totally of free settlers. Perhaps it is the absence of convict history that gives this city of 1.1 million its characteristic gentility. Australia's largest arts festival is held here for 2 weeks in even-numbered years, and the Festival Centre hosts a year-round program of cultural events. Adelaide's other popular happening, the annual Formula One Grand Prix, is staged the way it would be in Europe—with cars whizzing through city streets.

With the exception of Grand Prix week, Adelaide lacks the hustle and bustle of other capitals, and perhaps this is why it remains undiscovered by the majority of tourists. Wine aficionados, however, have long recognized the city's status as the gateway to the country's most prolific vineyards. German refugees were among the first settlers in this area, and they lost no time in planting grapes in the ideal climates of the Barossa Valley, the Clare Valley, and the Southern Vales. Today, two-thirds of Australia's wine comes from this state, much of it within a short drive of Adelaide.

In terms of the weather, September, October, November, March, and April are the best months to visit the Festival City.

1. ORIENTATION

ARRIVING

BY PLANE

Adelaide is served by several international and domestic airlines, including **British Airways, Qantas, Singapore Airlines, Malaysia Airlines, Ansett, Australian Airlines,** and **Kendell Airlines.** Australian Airlines Air Pass fares from Alice Springs cost from A$199 to A$250 (U.S. $159.20 to U.S. $200); from Melbourne fares range from A$127 to A$160 (U.S. $101.60 to U.S. $128). The Blue Roo fare from Sydney to Adelaide is A$190 (U.S. $152).

The major car-rental companies (**Budget, Avis, Hertz,** and **Thrifty**) have desks or contact telephones in both the international and domestic terminals. Tourist information is available, and several hotels provide phones from which you can call for reservations free of charge. On the domestic side there's a post office and a bank; in the international area you can buy stamps from a machine. Both terminals have

WHAT'S SPECIAL ABOUT ADELAIDE

Museums
- ☐ The Migration Museum, a must for anyone interested in Australia's immigrant history.
- ☐ South Australian Maritime Museum, especially about ships and the sea.

Events/Festivals
- ☐ Adelaide Festival of Arts, the country's best, held in March of even-numbered years.
- ☐ Australian Formula One Grand Prix, the first week in November.
- ☐ Barossa Valley Vintage Festival— the next is in 1993.

Unusual Transportation
- ☐ The historic Glenelg Tram, which makes frequent trips between Victoria Square and the seaside suburb of Glenelg.
- ☐ The O-Bahn Busway, a state-of-the-art means of moving.

Great Places to Visit
- ☐ The Barossa Valley, for wine tasting.
- ☐ The Adelaide Hills, for picturesque countryside and interesting villages.

showers, foreign exchange desks, shops, and places to eat. No baggage lockers are available.

Transit Regency (tel. 381-5311) provides service to major Adelaide hotels from the international and domestic terminals at the airport and from the interstate railway station located in the suburb of Keswick. The buses run daily approximately every half hour from 7am to 10pm. The fare into the city from the airport is A$3.50 (U.S. $2.80); from the train depot, the fare is A$2.50 (U.S. $2). A taxi to town from the airport costs about A$9 (U.S. $7.20).

BY TRAIN

The Trans Australian will transport you from Perth; the Ghan will deliver you from Alice Springs; and the Overland provides daily service from Melbourne. Actually, I should say "nightly," because the train departs Melbourne in the evening and takes 12 hours to get to Adelaide. Fares on the Overland are A$145 (U.S. $116) for a first-class berth, A$85 (U.S. $68) for first-class sitting, and A$42 (U.S. $33.60) for economy sitting. Call **Australian National Railways** in Adelaide if you have questions about interstate train travel (tel. 217-4086) or would like to make reservations (tel. 231-7699).

BY BUS

Greyhound's luxury express bus takes 10 hours to cross the 800 kilometers (496 miles) from Melbourne (A$45/U.S. $36). The regular service offered by Greyhound, Pioneer, and Bus Australia is a few dollars cheaper. Sydney is 1,540 kilometers (955 miles) and 22 hours away by way of the Hume and Sturt highways. That ticket costs A$125 (U.S. $100). Intercity coaches terminate at the **Adelaide Central Bus Terminal,** 105-111 Franklin Street, near Morphett Street in the city center.

TOURIST INFORMATION

Take your questions to the friendly folks at the **South Australian Government Travel Centre,** 18 King William Street, Adelaide, SA 5000 (tel. 08/212-1505). This office is open Monday through Friday from 8:45am to 5:30pm and Saturday from 8:45am to 2pm. They supply excellent maps of Adelaide and the surrounding area free of charge. The **Adelaide City Council Information Office** (tel. 203-7442) has details on events, venues, and times of Adelaide's annual program of free public concerts and organ recitals. They're open Monday through Friday from 9am to 5pm.

INTERSTATE INFORMATION

You'll find the following offices in Adelaide: **Western Australian Tourist Centre,** 1 Grenfell Street (tel. 212-1344); **Northern Territory Tourist Commission,** 9 Hindley Street (tel. 212-1133); **Queensland Government Travel Centre,** 10 Grenfell Street (tel. 212-2399); **Tasmanian Travel Centre,** 32 King William Street (tel. 211-7411); **Victorian Tourism Centre,** 16 Grenfell Street (tel. 231-4129); **New South Wales Travel Centre,** 144 North Terrace (tel. 231-4366).

CITY LAYOUT

Adelaide's orderly community plan was designed in 1836 by the surveyor general, Col. William Light. The central business district is contained in 1 square mile, and a grid pattern of streets makes it easy for visitors to find their way around. **Victoria Square** is in the center of the grid; similar, but smaller, plazas are located in each quarter. The **River Torrens** with its wide, grassy banks, separates the city center from **North Adelaide,** and a greenbelt of parkland surrounds the combined areas.

King William Street, which runs north and south, is the main thoroughfare. **Rundle Mall,** perpendicular to the main street, is a pedestrians-only shopping area; more than a dozen arcades adjacent to the mall provide space for more shops. **Rundle Street East,** with its avant-garde boutiques and ethnic restaurants, is Adelaide's answer to Greenwich Village. X-rated nightclubs and ladies of the night can be found on **Hindley Street. Adelaide Plaza,** on the banks of the river just north of the central business district, is the site of the **Festival Centre,** the city's A$30-million (U.S. $24-million) **Casino,** and the **Convention Centre.**

The mouth of the river is 10 kilometers (6 miles) to the west on the **Gulf of St. Vincent,** an inlet of the **Southern Ocean.** Of the many swimming beaches along the gulf, Glenelg is the most popular. Northwest of the city, **Port Adelaide** is both a working port and a picturesque place with an excellent maritime museum and some lively pubs. The **Adelaide Hills,** 20 minutes to the west of town, are dotted with delightful day-trip destinations. **Hahndorf** is a charming village settled by Germans fleeing Silesia in 1839. The grateful refugees named their new home after Capt. Dirk Hahn, who commanded their ship, and many original buildings and the Teutonic atmosphere remain. **Birdwood's** historic flour mill has been converted to the National Motor Museum and houses an impressive vintage-car collection.

These and other charming villages, nestled among tree-clad hills and valleys, offer craft shops and cozy bed-and-breakfasts. The Adelaide Hills are part of the **Mount Lofty Range** and encompass **Cleland Wildlife Park,** where koalas and other native animals are on display. The **Barossa Valley,** the best known of South Australia's wine districts, begins 55 kilometers (34 miles) northeast of Adelaide.

2. GETTING AROUND

BY PUBLIC TRANSPORTATION

BY BUS

Adelaide has a good system of public transportation. The **State Transport Authority** (tel. 210-1000) operates the free **Beeline Buses** around the inner city. Wait for these 99B buses anywhere you see a bumblebee on the bus stop. For timetable information, you can ring the STA Monday through Saturday from 8am to 7:30pm and Sunday from 9am to 4:15pm. They also have a **City Service Centre** on the corner of King William and Currie streets and on the platform of the Adelaide Railway Station on North Terrace. Both of these offices are open Monday through Friday from 8am to 5:30pm. Additionally, the city office is open Saturday from 8 to 11:30am and the station office is open Saturday from 8am to noon.

Adelaide Sightseeing (tel. 231-4144) operates the **Adelaide Explorer Bus** (A$14/U.S. $11.20), which takes you to a half dozen sights around town; but prospective passengers should keep in mind that the bus (a replica tram) stops at each destination only every 90 minutes. Depending on how interested you are in the various sights, you might end up wasting your valuable sightseeing time waiting for the next bus.

Premier (tel. 233-2744), **Adelaide Sightseeing** (tel. 231-4144), and **Transit** (tel. 381-5311) operate full- and half-day escorted tours.

BY TRAM

The **State Transport Authority** also runs the **Glenelg Tram,** which departs from Victoria Square and carries passengers to the seaside suburb of Glenelg. The regular price of tickets, which are good for 2 hours, is A$2.50 (U.S. $2); between 9:01am and 3pm. Monday through Friday, however, the fare is only A$1.40 (U.S. $1.15). The journey takes 29 minutes.

City and suburban buses and suburban trains are also provided by the STA. You could, for instance, take a train to Port Adelaide in order to visit the Port Dock Railway Museum or the South Australian Maritime Museum. This train runs every 30 minutes and the fare is A$2.50 (U.S. $2), except from 9am to 3pm during the week, when it's A$1.40 (U.S. $1.15). The same fares apply to buses, and budget-minded travelers will keep in mind that Day Tripper tickets are the best value. These cost A$3.80 (U.S. $3.05) and are valid from 9:01am to midnight during the week and all day on the weekends. Contact the STA at the above phone number or stop in at one of their offices for more details.

BY TAXI & CAR

Taxis operate throughout the city. The major companies are **United** (tel. 223-3111), **Suburban** (tel. 211-8888), and **Amalgamated** (tel. 223-3333). The flagfall during the day is A$1.80 (U.S. $1.45); from 7pm to 6am, it's A$2.60 (U.S. $2).

The main rental companies in the area are: **Ansa** (tel. toll free 008/07-4116 in Australia), **Avis,** 108 Burbridge Road (tel. 354-0444); **Budget,** 274 North Terrace (tel. 223-1400); **Hertz,** 233 Morphett Street (tel. 231-2856); **Thrifty,** 100 Franklin Street (tel. 211-8788).

If you need to get in touch with an auto club, contact **Royal Automobile Association of South Australia** (RAA), 41 Hindmarsh Square (tel. 223-4555).

FAST FACTS   *ADELAIDE*

Airlines   Airlines with offices in Adelaide are: **Air New Zealand,** 144 North Terrace, sixth floor (tel. 212-3544); **Air Transit,** Adelaide Airport (tel. 352-3177); **Ansett,** 142 North Terrace (tel. 233-3322); **Australian Airlines,** 144 North Terrace (tel. 217-3333); **British Airways,** 33 King William St. (tel. 238-2138); **Canadian Pacific,** 144 North Terrace, mezzanine level (tel. 216-1911); **Continental,** 50 Grenfell St., seventh floor (tel. 212-6155, or toll free 008/22-2122 in Australia); **Kendell Airlines,** c/o Ansett, 150 North Terrace (tel. 233-3322); **Malaysia Airlines,** 144 North Terrace, eighth floor (tel. 231-5320); **Qantas,** 14 King William St. (tel. 237-8541); **Singapore Airlines,** 60 Waymouth St. (tel. 238-2747); **United Airlines,** 144 North Terrace, seventh floor (tel. 231-2821).

American Express   The office, located at 13 Grenfell St., Adelaide (tel. 212-7099), is open regular business hours.

Area Code   Adelaide telephone numbers are in the 08 area code.

Business Hours   Banks are generally open Mon–Thurs 9:30am–4pm and

Fri 9:30am–5pm. Stores are generally open Mon–Thurs 8:45am–5:30pm, Fri 9am–9pm, and Sat 8:45am–12:30pm.

Car Rentals See "Getting Around," above.

Climate See "When to Go" in Chapter 2.

Currency See "Information, Entry Requirements, and Money" in Chapter 2.

Currency Exchange In addition to banks and hotels, traveler's checks can be cashed on weekends at the South Australian Travel Centre, 18 King William St. (tel. 212-1505).

Dentist Contact the Australian Dental Association emergency information service (tel. 272-8111).

Doctor Contact the Royal Adelaide Hospital, North Terrace (tel. 223-0230).

Drugstores [Chemist Shops] Burden Chemists, in the CML Building, at the corner of King William and Hindley streets (tel. 231-4701), is open Mon–Sat 8am–midnight and Sun 9am–6pm.

Embassies/Consulates New Zealand maintains a consulate at 26 Flinders St. (tel. 231-0700).

Emergencies Dial 000 to summon ambulance, fire department, or police.

Eyeglasses OPSM (Optical Prescription Spectacle Makers), 198 North Terrace or Shop 34, City Cross, Grenfell St. (tel. 223-1024), is open Mon–Fri 9am–5pm and Sat 9am–noon.

Hairdressers/Barbers Arturo Taverna, 22 Currie St. (tel. 212-5411), is open Mon–Thurs 9am–5pm, Fri 9am–9pm, and Sat 9am–noon.

Holidays See "When to Go" in Chapter 2.

Hospitals Royal Adelaide Hospital, North Terrace (tel. 223-0230) is centrally located.

Hotlines I hope you won't need to call the Crisis Care Centre (tel. 232-3300).

Information See "Information, Entry Requirements, and Money" in Chapter 2.

Laundry/Dry Cleaning Tip Top Dry Cleaners, 184 Gawler Place (tel. 232-0075), offers same-day cleaning service ("90 minutes where possible") and mending.

Libraries The State Library of South Australia is on Kintore Ave. The newspaper room is in a separate building on North Terrace.

Lost Property The STA (public transport) Lost Property Office is on the main concourse of the Adelaide Railway Station on North Terrace (tel. 218-2552). It's open Mon–Fri 9am–5pm.

Luggage Storage/Lockers There are no lockers at the Adelaide Airport. There are both small and large lockers at Australian National's train station at Keswick (A60¢/U.S. 50¢ small, A$1.20/U.S. $1 large per day or part thereof). At the Central Bus Station in Franklin St., there are luggage lockers that cost A$2 (U.S. $1.60) for 24 hours. Premier Roadlines at the Bus Station will hold luggage at A$2 (U.S. $1.60) per piece if all lockers are in use.

Newspapers/Magazines *The Advertiser* is the morning paper and *The News* comes out in the evening. *The Sunday Mail* is published Sun only; many people read the national newspaper, *The Australian*.

Photographic Needs George's Camera Store is located at 212 Rundle St. (tel. 223-3449).

Post Office The General Post Office (GPO), 141 King William St., is near Victoria Sq. (tel. 216-2222). The hours are Mon–Fri 8am–6pm and Sat 8:30am–noon. General delivery mail (poste restante) can be collected only Mon–Fri 8am–5pm. A few other services are also limited to these hours. Central Adelaide addresses have a 5000 postal code.

Radio For classical music tune to ABC-FM.

Religious Services You can attend services at the following locations: Anglican, St. Peter's Cathedral, Pennington Terrace, Lower North Adelaide (tel. 267-4551); Baptist, Flinders St. (tel. 223-4550); Greek Orthodox, 286 Franklin St.; Jewish, Temple Shalom, 39 Hackney Rd., Hackney (tel. 362-8281); Roman Catholic, St. Francis Xavier's Cathedral, Wakefield St. (tel. 231-3551); Uniting (Congregational, Methodist, and Presbyterian), Scots Church, 237 North Terrace (tel. 223-1505).

Rest Rooms Public rest rooms are located at the Central Market Arcade, between Grote and Gouger streets, at Victoria Sq., Hindmarsh Sq., and James Place (off Rundle Mall).

Safety Avoid walking along the River Torrens at night. Likewise, stay out of the side streets near Hindley St. after dark.

Shoe Repairs Mister Minit, 58 Victoria Square Shopping Centre (tel. 231-3400), offers while-you-wait service.

Taxes Sales tax where levied is contained in the retail price of goods, not added separately. There is no GST or hotel tax in South Australia.

Taxis See "Getting Around," above.

Television ABC (channel 2) is the Australian Broadcasting Commission (government) station. It offers quality dramas, documentaries, concerts, news, and so forth. SBS offers ethnic programming. Channels 7, 9, and 10 are the commercial stations and offer a variety of movies, soaps, news, and sports.

Telegrams/Telex The better hotels and the GPO offer these services.

Transit Info See "Getting Around," above.

Useful Telephone Numbers S.A. Council on the Ageing: 212-2252; Citizens' Advice Bureau: 212-4070; Youth Enquiry Service: 211-8466; Rape Enquiry Unit: 218-1212; Women's Information Switchboard: 223-1244; Gay Line: 232-0794 (7–10pm); AIDS Line: 232-0022; Lifeline: 212-3444.

3. ADELAIDE ACCOMMODATIONS

Adelaide offers lots of lodgings, but be sure to make your reservations well in advance if you plan to be in town during the Grand Prix or the Adelaide Festival. You may also be interested in the accommodations mentioned in "Easy Excursions From Adelaide," below. If you like bed-and-breakfast inns and homestays, request a copy of the booklet, *South Australian Home Style Accommodation*, from any South Australian Government Travel Centre.

IN THE CITY CENTER
EXPENSIVE

ADELAIDE HILTON, 233 Victoria Sq., Adelaide, SA 5000. Tel. 08/217-0711. Fax 08/231-0158. 380 rms, 15 suites. A/C MINIBAR TV TEL **Transportation:** Stops in front of hotel; bus adjacent.

$ **Rates:** A$215–A$248 (U.S. $172–U.S. $198.40) single or double; A$278 (U.S. $222.40) executive floor; A$385–A$990 (U.S. $308–U.S. $792) suite; A$30 (U.S. $24) extra person. Children under 18 stay free in parents' room. No-smoking rooms available. AE, BC, DC, MC, V. **Parking:** A$12 (U.S. $9.60).

The Adelaide Hilton is a luxurious 18-story hotel on picturesque Victoria Square. A doorman in top hat and tails greets guests as they enter the lobby with its polished marble floor and cascading fountain. Piano music from the adjacent Lobby Lounge fills the air. Upstairs, rooms offer a choice of king-size, queen-size, or twin beds and a green-and-beige or rust-and-beige decor. All quarters have in-room movies, clock radios, tea- and coffee-making facilities, small refrigerators, and free daily newspapers. All bathrooms have tub/shower combinations except those in the 11 specially equipped rooms for handicapped travelers. The 9th floor is reserved for nonsmokers, and the 16th floor contains the Executive Floor rooms.

Dining/Entertainment: Dining and drinking venues include the Market Place, a coffee shop just off the lobby, and The Grange, a posh à la carte eatery. Margaux's Nightclub and the Lobby Lounge are both popular, but my favorite spot in this Hilton is Charlie's Bar. I like the English pub decor, which includes pictures of lots of famous Charlies—Bronson, Brown, de Gaulle, King Charles I, and Prince Charles.

Services: 24-hour room service, laundry, valet, concierge, and baby-sitting.

Facilities: Heated outdoor pool, spa pool, tennis court, and jogging track. The court costs A$20 (U.S. $16) an hour. Also located on the premises: a unisex hair salon and a business center.

HYATT REGENCY ADELAIDE, North Terrace, Adelaide, SA 5000. Tel. 08/231-1234. Fax 08/231-1120. 369 rms and suites. A/C MINIBAR TV TEL

$ **Rates:** A$270 (U.S. $216) single or double; A$335 (U.S. $268) Regency Club (including breakfast); A$495 (U.S. $396) suite; A$30 (U.S. $24) extra person. Lower weekend tariffs. Children under 18 stay free in parents' room. No-smoking rooms available. AE, BC, DC, MC, V. **Parking:** A$15 (U.S. $12).

Located at the north end of the city center, the Hyatt Regency Adelaide, open since 1988, is part of the riverside complex that includes the Adelaide Festival Centre, the Casino, and the Convention Centre. The Hyatt offers rooms on more than 20 floors, including four floors of Regency Club accommodations. All quarters have contemporary decors, and each marble bathroom has a tub and a separate shower. All quarters include tea- and coffee-making facilities, a small refrigerator, a clock radio, bathrobe, in-room movies, and free daily newspapers. A plaza on the back of the hotel overlooks the River Torrens.

Dining/Entertainment: Fleurieu, a fine-dining restaurant, focuses on South Australia's importance as a wine-growing and culinary center. Shiki, an authentic Japanese dining spot, features four teppanyaki counters and one for tempura. The Riverside Restaurant serves breakfast, lunch, and dinner. Waves, the California-style cabaret/nightclub, offers a lively combination of video, disco, and live music. Drinks are also served in the Atrium Lounge.

Services: 24-hour room service, turn-down service, shoeshine, laundry, valet, concierge, baby-sitting, massage.

Facilities: The Hyatt Fitness Centre features a sauna, solarium, sports shop, whirlpool, plunge pool, massage room, weight and aerobics room, and juice bar—all connected to the outdoor swimming pool. There's also a business center.

MODERATE

BARRON TOWNHOUSE, 164 Hindley St., Adelaide, SA 5000. Tel. 08/211-8255, or toll free 008/88-8241 in Australia. Fax 08/231-1179. Reservations can be made through Flag Inns. 68 rms. A/C MINIBAR TV TEL

$ **Rates** (including snack-pack breakfast): A$129 (U.S. $103.20) single; A$139 (U.S. $111.20) double; A$139 (U.S. $111.20) executive room; A$15 (U.S. $12) extra person. Children under 12 stay free in parents' room. Off-season and weekend discounts. No-smoking rooms available. AE, BC, DC, MC, V. **Parking:** Free.

⑤ The Barron Townhouse is located on the edge of the city center, not far from the nightlife district. Some might find the neighborhood too lively; others might find the small hotel just their cup of tea. This is the ideal place for travelers with lots of luggage because rooms are spacious. Toasters are supplied in addition to the standard coffee-and-tea setup. Everyone has in-room movies and receives a free daily newspaper. Downstairs, Flamingo's Bistro is an informal eatery. Room service is available 24 hours. There's a nice outdoor heated pool on the fifth floor, along with a sauna. Also a hair salon.

HINDLEY PARKROYAL, 65 Hindley St., Adelaide, SA 5000. Tel. 08/231-5552. Fax 08/237-3800. 177 rms and suites. A/C MINIBAR TV TEL

$ **Rates:** A$190 (U.S. $152) single or double; A$240 (U.S. $192) suite; A$500 (U.S. $400) executive suite. Children under 15 stay free in parents' room. Weekend rates about 50% lower. No-smoking rooms available. AE, BC, DC, MC, V. **Parking:** Free.

Located in the central business district, this property opened under a different name in late 1989. The Southern Pacific Hotel Corporation took over at the end of 1990, adding this property to its upmarket Parkroyal Collection. Guests enter the marble-floored lobby where there is an attractive fountain. Sebastians, the lobby bar, is just inside the front door. All bedrooms have light wood interiors complemented by muted earth tones and modern furnishings. Standard rooms have either two double beds or one queen, a clock radio, tea- and coffee-making facilities, a small refrigerator, in-room movies, free daily newspapers, irons, and ironing boards. There's 24-hour room service, a heated outdoor pool, a well-equipped gym, a spa, a sauna, and a nice business center. Meals are served in Cafe Mo, which is casual, and the fancier Oliphants.

Serviced Apartments

APARTMENTS ON THE PARK, 274 South Terrace, Adelaide, SA 5000. **Tel. 08/232-0555,** or toll free 008/88-2774 in Australia. Fax 08/223-3457. 50 2-bedroom apartments. A/C MINIBAR TV TEL **Bus:** No. 161.

$ **Rates:** A$140 (U.S. $112) single or double; A$10 (U.S. $8) extra adult; A$5 (U.S. $4) extra child. Lower weekly rates. No-smoking rooms available. AE, BC, CB, DC, MC, V. **Parking:** Free.

This apartment complex is located on the southern edge of the city center overlooking a scenic greenbelt. Each of the fully furnished units has a full kitchen, two bedrooms, a separate lounge and dining area, and a washing machine and dryer. Built in 1987, the modern lodging offers a choice between a beige-and-apricot or beige-on-beige color scheme. Baby-sitting can be arranged, and there's a spa on the premises. Valet and breakfast service can be arranged.

THE MANSIONS APARTMENTS, 21 Pulteney St., Adelaide, SA 5000. **Tel. 08/232-0033,** or toll free 008/88-8292 in Australia. Fax 08/223-4559. 51 apartments. A/C TV TEL

$ **Rates:** A$85 (U.S. $68) studio, single or double; A$98 (U.S. $78.40) 1-bedroom unit, single or double; A$108 (U.S. $86.40) executive 1-bedroom; A$10 (U.S. $8) extra person. Rates are 70% higher during Grand Prix. AE, BC, MC, V. **Parking:** A$8 (U.S. $6.40).

The Mansions Apartments was the first "high-rise" apartment building in Australia. It is now one of those exceptional values I look forward to sharing with you. All spacious studio and one-bedroom units have full kitchens and attractive decors. The property was built in 1912, and the high ceilings and traditional furnishings underscore the old-world atmosphere.

The apartments are ideally sited in the city center near North Terrace and within a short walk of museums, the Festival Centre, and the Rundle Mall. Shops and eating places are located in the Renaissance Arcade on the street level. A sauna and spa are on the premises.

A Bed-and-Breakfast Inn

ADELAIDE'S BED AND BREAKFAST, 239 Franklin St., Adelaide, SA 5000. Tel. 08/231-3124. 5 rms (1 with bath). TV

$ **Rates** (including continental breakfast): A$65–A$75 (U.S. $52–U.S. $60) single; A$80–A$90 (U.S. $64–U.S. $72) double. AE, BC, DC, MC, V. **Parking:** On street, limited time, free.

This is a cozy five-bedroom B&B in the heart of the city. Proprietors Deidre and Tony Difalco rate tops for personal service. Their bed-and-breakfast is in a sandstone block building that dates from the 1870s. Each of the rooms has a high ceiling, fireplace, and Victorian decor. My favorite, number five, is a quiet double with an iron-and-brass headboard. Antique armoires and dressers are used throughout, as are fluffy comforters and ceiling fans. Don't worry if you failed to pack your robe: The hosts supply them. Cooked morning meals are provided for an extra charge.

BUDGET

BRECKNOCK HOTEL, 401 King William St., Adelaide, SA 5000. Tel. 08/231-5467. Fax 08/410-1968. 10 rms (none with bath). A/C

Transportation: Located 4 blocks from Victoria Sq. Tram stops in front of hotel.

$ Rates (including continental breakfast): A$30 (U.S. $24) single; A$45 (U.S. $36) double; A$60 (U.S. $48) triple. AE, BC, DC, MC, V. **Parking:** Free.

The Brecknock was built in 1851 and has been in the Moore family since 1901. Today it is run by Kyran (Kerry) Moore and his Canadian wife, Trisha, who has refurbished each of the rooms with period wallpaper and homey touches. High ceilings and stained-glass windows add to the hotel's charm. Each room has a sink, an electric blanket, and coffee- and tea-making facilities. The guests enjoy sitting down to breakfast together and exchanging travel tips. Downstairs, they serve great hamburgers in C J's Bistro and you can get an inexpensive pub meal in the front bar. There's also a cook-your-own barbecue area.

IN NORTH ADELAIDE

MODERATE

HOTEL ADELAIDE, 62 Brougham Place, corner of O'Connell St., North Adelaide, SA 5006. Tel. 08/267-3444, or toll free 008/88-8244 in Australia. Fax 08/239-0189. 129 rms, 11 suites. A/C MINIBAR TV TEL **Transportation:** 1km (½ mile) north of the city on bus routes 181, 182, or 222.

$ Rates: A$140 (U.S. $112) single or double; A$175 (U.S. $140) suite; A$195 (U.S. $156) executive floor; A$10 (U.S. $8) extra person. Children under 14 stay free in parents' room. Lower weekend rates. AE, BC, DC, MC, V. **Parking:** Free.

Because it has been renovated, few would guess that the Hotel Adelaide, located 3 blocks north of the River Torrens, is more than 25 years old. The lobby has a contemporary reception counter, the cocktail lounge is off to one side, and a floating staircase leads to the mezzanine level. Bedrooms have an unusual French Provincial decor, including gray carpeting, rose-and-gray bedspreads, and lavender draperies with sheer white festoons for privacy. Each room has coffee- and tea-making facilities, a small refrigerator, a clock radio, in-room movies, and free daily newspapers. Closet space is a bit limited. The hotel's suites are each named and decorated in recognition of one of Adelaide's sister cities: Christchurch, New Zealand; Austin, Texas; Penang, Malaysia; and Himeji, Japan. I think the designer of the Texas suite was inspired by the television show "Dallas."

More than half the rooms and suites have an excellent view of the city or surrounding hills. The hotel is within walking distance of the Festival Centre and the central business district. The Brougham Restaurant on the top of the nine-story hotel has an especially nice vista. Twenty-four-hour room service is available. Facilities include an outdoor pool, business center, hair salon, two restaurants, two bars, and a newsagent.

GLENELG

MODERATE

RAMADA GRAND HOTEL, Moseley Sq. (P.O. Box 600), Glenelg, SA 5045. Tel. 08/376-1222, or toll free 008/88-2777 in Australia. Fax 08/376-1111. 226 rms and suites. A/C MINIBAR TV TEL **Transportation:** The tram from Adelaide takes 29 minutes and stops in front of the hotel.

$ Rates: A$105–A$187 (U.S. $84–U.S. $149.60) single or double depending on floor; A$132–A$252 (U.S. $105.60–U.S. $201.60) grand suite; A$154–A$209 (U.S. $123.20–U.S. $167.20) junior suite; A$286–A$572 (U.S. $228.80–U.S. $457.60) Royal suite; A$20 (U.S. $16) additional charge for ocean view; A$20 (U.S. $16) extra person. Children under 12 stay free in parents' room. No-smoking rooms available. AE, BC, DC, MC, V. **Parking:** A$4 (U.S. $3.20).

Located on the beach in the seaside suburb of Glenelg, this Ramada opened in late

1990. Many rooms overlook the ocean and the pier. All offer tea- and coffee-making facilities, small refrigerators, in-house movies, hairdryers, 24-hour room service, and modern furnishings. Meals are served in The Quarterdeck, which has a nautical theme, in Calypso's, where cane chairs and ceiling fans impart a tropical feel, and in Charlotte's, where the ambience is old-world Australian. The Pier and Pines is the popular front bar; Horizons is the piano bar. There's a nice outdoor pool, a spa, sauna, and gym.

4. ADELAIDE DINING

Adelaide has more restaurants per capita than any other city in the country—and some of the best. This means a good selection for visitors who want to try the local offerings. Greek and Italian food is especially popular, due to the large number of immigrants from these countries. Because of South Australia's dominance of the wine industry, diners can look forward to choosing from extensive lists.

The citizens of Adelaide feel strongly about preserving their architectural heritage, so it's not surprising that several dining spots are housed in historic structures.

For a description of dining possibilities at Mount Lofty House in the Adelaide Hills, see "Easy Excursions," below.

IN THE CITY CENTER
EXPENSIVE

FLEURIEU, in the Hyatt Regency Hotel, North Terrace. Tel. 238-2381.
   Cuisine: MODERN FRENCH. **Reservations:** Recommended well ahead, especially for dinner Fri–Sat.
$ **Prices:** Appetizers A$12–A$13.50 (U.S. $9.60–U.S. $10.80); main courses A$27–A$48 (U.S. $21.60–U.S. $38.40); fixed-price six-course menu ("Le Menu Dégustation") A$50 (U.S. $40). AE, BC, DC, MC, V.
   Open: Lunch Mon–Fri noon–2pm; dinner Mon–Sat 6–10:30pm.
This is easily Adelaide's grandest dining option. Located on the upper lobby level of the Hyatt, Fleurieu's has a view of the adjacent casino and convention center complex. However, the important thing here is the cuisine—small portions of carefully crafted, artistically presented food. You might like to start with carpaccio of venison with pickled cherries and bone marrow crouton or warm smoked salmon with poached quail eggs and dill hollandaise. Main courses include médaillon of ocean trout with cucumber in fine ravioli, rognonade of lamb with persillade on fine beans, and braised veal head with spring onions and lime. Save room for the Grand Dessert. The service is excellent, as you might expect in this price range.

MODERATE

JASMIN INDIAN RESTAURANT, 31 Hindmarsh Sq. Tel. 223-7837.
   Cuisine: NORTH INDIAN. **Reservations:** Recommended.
$ **Prices:** Appetizers A$4–A$5.90 (U.S. $3.20–U.S. $4.75); main courses A$9.50–A$11.90 (U.S. $7.60–U.S. $9.55); lunch buffet A$13.50 (U.S. $10.80); dinner buffet A$20 (U.S. $16). Weekend and public holiday surcharge A$1 (U.S. 80¢) per person. AE, BC, DC, MC, V.
   Open: Lunch Tues–Fri noon–2:30pm; dinner Tues–Sat 5:30–9:30pm.
Jasmin is a family affair. Amrik Singh is the proprietor and his mother is the chef. Located a block south of the Rundle Mall in a cozy cellar pozzie, the place has a simple and attractive decor, including Indian tapestries and paintings. The low ceiling makes things a little noisy, but that's a small price to pay for the delicious northern Indian food. Beef vindaloo is the house specialty, but those who like chicken tandoori, malabari beef, curry, lamb korma, and

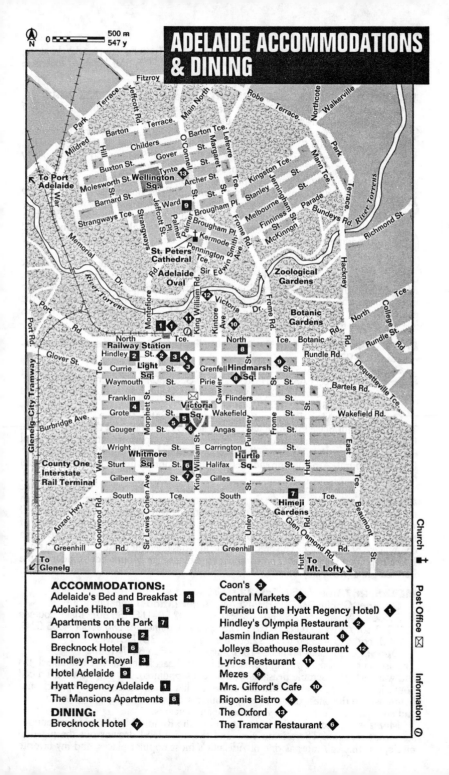

ADELAIDE ACCOMMODATIONS & DINING

0   500 m
    547 y

Church ■✝

Post Office ⊠

Information ⊙

prawn sambal won't be disappointed. Traditional breads—chapati, paratha, bhatura, and pappadum—are available. The wine list, a notebook full of labels, is extensive and reasonably priced.

JOLLEYS BOATHOUSE RESTAURANT, Jolleys Lane. Tel. 223-2891.

Cuisine: MODERN AUSTRALIAN. **Reservations:** Recommended, especially if you want one of three tables on the balcony.

$ Prices: Appetizers A$7.50–A$8.50 (U.S. $6–U.S. $6.80); main courses A$13.50–A$15 (U.S. $10.80–U.S. $12); set two-course lunch A$21 (U.S. $16.80); set three-course lunch A$27 (U.S. $21.60). Sunday and public holiday surcharge A$5 (U.S. $4) per person. AE, BC, DC, MC, V.

Open: Lunch daily noon–2:30pm; dinner Wed–Sat 6:30–10pm.

Set on the south bank of the River Torrens, Jolley's Boathouse affords diners a wonderful view of boats and black swans. This spot is a must for a leisurely lunch on a sunny day, especially if you can nab one of the three al fresco tables on the balcony. The inside seating is also airy and bright. Crisp cream-colored cloths complement the blue backs of the director's chairs. The brick floor and open-beam ceiling add to the pleasant ambience.

You could start with goat cheese, charred capsicum, eggplant, zucchini, and black olives on dried tomato damper or a salad of chargrilled octopus with chili sambal. Main courses include duck leg and lentil curry with jasmine rice and pickles, fresh fish, and a seafood stir-fry with coriander, lemongrass, and noodles. Try the passionfruit ice cream or the rich chocolate cake with double cream for dessert. This is a good spot for a pretheater meal as the Festival Centre is nearby.

LYRICS RESTAURANT, in the Adelaide Festival Centre, King William Rd. Tel. 216-8720.

Cuisine: INTERNATIONAL. **Reservations:** Recommended.

$ Prices: Appetizers A$5–A$11 (U.S. $4–U.S. $8.80); main courses A$16–A$18 (U.S. $12.80–U.S. $14.40); lunch buffet (Le Quick Lunch Parisien—includes wine) A$20 (U.S. $16). AE, BC, DC, MC, V.

Open: Lunch Mon–Fri noon–3pm; dinner Mon–Sat 6–9:30pm.

This is a pleasant place for lunch with a view across Elder Park and the River Torrens. It's also a handy spot to eat dinner before attending a performance at the Festival Centre. At night, the floor-to-ceiling windows capture the floodlit majesty of St. Peter's Cathedral. A pianist provides entertainment during lunch and dinner several times a week.

The à la carte menu presents a variety of creative dishes. Sample entrées include sugar-cured Tasmanian ocean trout with lime mousseline, duck liver terrine with muscat grape jelly, and warm salad of baby octopus with sun-dried tomato and basil vinaigrette. Mains include rack of lamb with a herb crust and parsnip purée, sirloin of beef with mushroom ragoût, and supreme of chicken filled with spinach served on a champagne beurre blanc. The pretheater menu is designed for those with limited time. If you're going to order wine, I recommend the Henschke Mount Edelstone from the Barossa Hills (A$19.70/U.S. $15.76).

MEZES, 287 Rundle St. Tel. 223-7384.

Cuisine: GREEK/MEDITERRANEAN. **Reservations:** Imperative.

$ Prices: Appetizers A$3.50–A$8.50 (U.S. $2.80–U.S. $6.80); main courses A$13.50–A$16.50 (U.S. $10.80–U.S. $13.20); dinner for two about A$55 (U.S. $44); corkage A$3.50 (U.S. $2.80) per bottle. AE, BC, DC, MC, V.

Open: Lunch Tues–Fri noon–2pm; dinner Tues–Sun 6:30–10pm.

This isn't a traditional Grecian bistro, and if your heart is set on checked tablecloths and waiters who resemble peasants, you'll be disappointed. Instead, it's what I'd call nouvelle Greek cuisine. Both modern dishes (like quail stuffed with spinach and hummus) and the ones you are already familiar with (spanakopita, dolmas, moussaka, and so forth) are served here. And they're all delicious.

Mezes is located 3 blocks from the end of the Rundle Mall in an unpretentious storefront location. There is no view and the noise level drowns out the piped-in music, but this still rates as one of Adelaide's most popular places, and my favorite

Greek restaurant in the area. The proprietor is Anthony Kathreptis; brother Elias is head chef, and Mum lends a hand in the kitchen a few days a week. Licensed and BYO (bottled wine only).

RIGONIS BISTRO, 27 Leigh St. Tel. 231-5160.

Cuisine: ITALIAN. **Reservations:** Recommended.
$ Prices: Appetizers A$3.50–A$7.50 (U.S. $2.80–U.S. $6); main courses A$8.50–A$13.50 (U.S. $6.80–U.S. $10.80); antipasto bar (lunch only) A$9.50 (U.S. $7.60). AE, BC, DC, MC, V.
Open: Lunch Mon–Fri noon–2:30pm; dinner Mon–Fri 5:30–10pm.

Tucked away on a narrow lane west of King William Street in the central business district, the restaurant brings the flavors of old-world Italy to present-day Australia. The blackboard menu, which changes daily, often includes lasagne della casa, vitello arrosto (baby veal pot-roasted in white wine, herbs, and butter), pesce persico (marinated perch filets lightly pan-fried in butter and sage), and fettuccine carciofi salsicle (fettuccine tossed with artichokes and Italian pork sausage). In addition, there's an extensive salad bar with a variety of antipasti.

The bistro has a casual atmosphere created by Italian travel posters, Michelangelo "sketches," and autographed black-and-white photos of personalities who've dined in this popular place—including Liza Minnelli and Andy Williams. Wooden tables are set on a rust-colored tiled floor. Licensed and BYO.

BUDGET

MRS. GIFFORD'S CAFE, at the Migration Museum, 82 Kintore Ave. Tel. 223-1935.

Cuisine: VEGETARIAN. **Reservations:** Recommended.
$ Prices: Light lunch A$7.50–A$9.50 (U.S. $6–U.S. $7.60); coffee or tea and cake A$4.50 (U.S. $3.60). BC, MC, V.
Open: Lunch and teas daily noon–5pm.

This is a delightful spot for a light lunch in the shade on a brick patio or inside a former schoolhouse which dates from the 1860s. The blackboard menu offers such items as spring rolls, stuffed mushrooms, and a cheese and fruit platter. Good wines are available by the glass.

KENT TOWN
EXPENSIVE

CHLOE'S, 36 College Rd., Kent Town. Tel. 362-2574 or 363-1001.

Cuisine: CREATIVE FRENCH. **Reservations:** Recommended.
$ Prices: Average appetizer A$12 (U.S. $9.60); average main course A$20 (U.S. $16); dinner for two about A$80 (U.S. $64). Lunchtime prices much lower. AE, BC, DC, MC, V.
Open: Lunch Mon–Fri noon–2:30pm; dinner Mon–Sat from 7pm.

This grand 1880s mansion, located in a suburb on the edge of the city center, has been faithfully restored by proprietor Nicolas Papazahariakis, who named his restaurant after his daughter. A meal here is a memorable experience.

Diners at Chloe's are seated in one of four rooms. All have 14-foot ceilings and elaborate chandeliers. Museum-quality oil paintings by Australian artists of the late 1800s are on display. Much of the stained glass in and around the doors is original, and the color scheme is true to the period.

The same attention to detail evident in the decor is obvious in the preparation and presentation of the restaurant's food. While the menu changes every 3 months, sample entrées include smoked mackerel tartare, marinated quail salad, and cassoulet of rabbit filet. For a main course, you have a choice of duck with wontons, braised lamb loin, saddle of kangaroo, supreme of chicken with tortellini and a light tarragon sauce, or cornets of trout. Desserts include warm pear and almond tart, vacherin of rhubarb, and petite creams of mascarpone with poached satsuma plums.

While the house and the cuisine are impressive, the center of attention at Chloe's is the 20-page wine list, which offers a choice of 600 different domestic and imported vintages. Nicholas started collecting wine in 1971, when he came to Australia; his cellar is now stocked with more than 22,000 bottles.

NORTH ADELAIDE

MODERATE

THE OXFORD, 101 O'Connell St., North Adelaide. Tel. 267-2652.
  Cuisine: MODERN AUSTRALIAN. **Reservations:** Recommended, especially for lunch and dinner Fri and dinner Sat. **Bus:** No. 182, 222, 224, 226, 228, or 229.
$ Prices: Appetizers A$6.50–A$7.90 (U.S. $5.20–U.S. $6.35); main courses A$12.50–A$14 (U.S. $10–U.S. $11.20). AE, BC, DC, MC, V.
  Open: Lunch Mon–Fri noon–3pm; dinner Mon–Sat 6–10pm or later.

If you can only eat one meal in Adelaide, let it be at the Oxford. The restaurant is housed in an 1870s building which has recently been renovated and now has a modern European appearance. Crisp white cloths cover the tables laid with simple white crockery (pottery) dishes. The single sheet menu arrives on an aluminum clipboard. The very high ceiling, hardwood floor, open kitchen, and wait staff comprised of students from the nearby university contribute to the agreeable ambience.

Chef Louis Thyer works wonders with the fresh, local ingredients. Order the Oxford fries to munch on while you decide what your other courses will be. I highly recommend the linguine with braised duck, parmesan cheese, black pepper, and basil. This dish comes in both an entrée (appetizer) and main course size. You might also like to try kangaroo sashimi and tofu salad with wasabi and ponzu dressing, braised lamb shank with tomato pie, or red-cooked spatchcock with ginger, lemon, and chili paste. The berry sorbet dessert is excellent. The wine list is extensive. I like the 1988 Hollick Cabernet-Merlot from the Coonawarra wine district, among others.

SPECIALTY DINING

A MOVEABLE FEAST

The Tramcar Restaurant (tel. 410-0044), Adelaide's answer to the *Orient Express,* is a 60-year-old tramcar that has been totally refurbished with brocade seats, fringed lampshades, and etched-glass panels. This atmospheric vehicle makes the 11.4 kilometer (7 mile) run between Victoria Square in central Adelaide and the seaside suburb of Glenelg. Along the way, up to 42 people can enjoy dinner (A$39 to A$49/U.S. $31.20 to U.S. $39.20) Tuesday through Sunday, lunch A$25/U.S. $20) or afternoon tea (A$16/U.S. $12.80) Wednesday through Friday and Sunday, or brunch A$25/U.S. $20) on Sunday. Children under 13 are charged about half price. Book well in advance.

DINING CLUSTERS

At the rear of the **City Cross Arcade,** which leads off Rundle Mall, there's an extensive **Food Plaza,** where many kinds of quick meals (Chinese, seafood, and Italian, for instance) can be purchased take-out style and eaten at tables provided in a central area. Food is sold during the day Monday through Friday, on Friday night, and up until noon on Saturday. You can eat well for A$8.50 (U.S. $6.80). A similar place, this one selling the cuisine of 12 different countries, is adjacent to the Central Markets between Gouger and Grote streets. The **International Food Plaza** is open Monday through Thursday from 11am to 4pm and Friday, Saturday, and Sunday from 11am to 9pm. Again, meals cost less than A$10 (U.S. $8).

Speaking of the ✪ **Central Markets,** this is an excellent place to buy cheese, bread, pâté, salami, fresh fruit, and so forth to put in the picnic basket you'll take on day-trips to the Barossa Valley or Adelaide Hills. The markets (tel. 203-7494) are open

Tuesday from 7am to 5:30pm, Thursday from 11am to 5:30pm, Friday from 7am to 9pm, and Saturday from 7am to 1pm.

LIGHT, CASUAL & FAST FOOD

The front (public) bar and the cocktail bar at the **Brecknock Hotel,** 401 King William Street (tel. 231-5467), serves very inexpensive counter meals Monday through Saturday from noon to 2pm and from 6 to 9pm. Roast beef and vegetables and similar staples cost less than A$6 (U.S. $4.80).

Homesick Yanks may want to head for the golden arches—yes, **McDonald's**— in Rundle Mall and at 44 Hindley Street (tel. 231-9565). Another familiar sight, **Pizza Hut,** can be found at 9 Hindley Street (tel. 231-2281).

My personal favorite budget dining spot in Adelaide is **✪ Hindley's Olympia Restaurant,** 137-139 Hindley Street (tel. 231-9093). Traditional Greek food is served by an exceptionally friendly staff. The gyro wrapped in pita is delicious and the portion is large. Likewise, the horiatiki salata (Greek-style green salad) is big enough to share with a friend. Three-course meals cost about A$15 (U.S. $12).

READERS RECOMMEND

Caon's Restaurant, 19 Leigh St. Tel. 231-3011.—*"The seafood there was superb, and the waiters so friendly. I would have gone back the next day to eat there again, but unfortunately it was Sunday and they were closed. Reservations are definitely recommended."*—Terence Fu, New York, N.Y.

5. ADELAIDE ATTRACTIONS

SIGHTSEEING STRATEGIES

IF YOU HAVE 1 DAY

Start out at the Migration Museum, then walk over to the Festival Centre and either take a tour of the facility or just admire the view from the surrounding plaza. In the afternoon, take a train to Port Adelaide and visit the South Australian Maritime Museum. When you get back to town, either hop on a Glenelg tram and make the short journey to Adelaide's most popular seaside suburb or take the Tramcar Restaurant, which travels the same route, and have dinner along the way.

IF YOU HAVE 2 DAYS

Follow my suggestions for day 1 and take a tour of the Barossa Valley and its many wineries on the second day. Several coach companies, listed under "Getting Around," above, conduct such excursions. Of course, this can also be done as a self-drive trip, but remember that Australia's drinking-driving laws are strictly enforced.

IF YOU HAVE 3 DAYS

Day 1 and 2 as above. On the third day do a trip through the Adelaide Hills. Tour the National Motor Museum in Birdwood, browse through the shops in Hahndorf, visit Cleland Wildlife Park, and stop for a meal or tea at Mount Lofty House.

IF YOU HAVE 4 DAYS

On the fourth day, visit Tandanya Aboriginal Cultural Institute first, then browse through the Central Markets. In the afternoon choose two out of the following three activities: the O-Bahn Busway to Tea Tree Plaza or Paradise Interchange; a visit to Carrick Hill; or a craft-shopping excursion to the Jam Factory.

IF YOU HAVE 5 DAYS

On day 5 tour another nearby wine region, such as the Clare Valley or McLaren Vale.

THE TOP ATTRACTIONS

It's a pleasure to explore Adelaide and its environs. The city is still slightly off the beaten path of the average overseas traveler, so visitors enjoy a sense of being the first to discover certain sights, shops, and scenic vistas. Most of the area's attractions are low-key and noncommercialized, in keeping with its innate gentility. This isn't a place in which to rush from point to point. Instead, I suggest you slow down, put on some casual clothes, sample one of the local vintages, and proceed to wander along the banks of the River Torrens, and through craft shops, wineries, and picturesque villages.

THE MIGRATION MUSEUM, 82 Kintore Ave. Tel. 223-8748 or 223-8940.

It is impossible to separate Australia's history from the dramatic impact made by immigrants. From the first boatload of convicts in 1788 through to the present time, Australia's story is a story of migration. The British who came in the 19th century suffered untold hardships. The ethnic groups who have arrived in great numbers since World War II have had their own trials. At this museum, the stories of individual new arrivals are told in a personal way that develops understanding of the nation's multicultural society. The Migration Museum is housed in the former Destitute Asylum, and the empty cells that once held women and children add impact to the skillfully designed exhibits. In addition to the permanent displays, changing exhibitions present the history of cultural traditions of different groups. This is a hands-on, experiential museum. *Highly recommended.*

Mrs. Gifford's, a vegetarian restaurant, is located in the courtyard of the museum. For details, see "Adelaide Dining," above.

Admission: Free. Guided tours cost A$3.50 (U.S. $2.80) for adults and A$2 (U.S. $1.60) for children.

Open: Mon–Fri 10am–5pm, Sat–Sun and public holidays 1–5pm. **Closed:** Christmas Day and Good Friday. **Transportation:** Part of the North Terrace Cultural Precinct, the museum is easily reached on foot from the central business district.

THE ADELAIDE FESTIVAL CENTRE, King William Rd. Tel. 216-8760.

Ideally located between the city center and the River Torrens, the Festival Centre is comprised of three auditoriums: the 1,978-seat Festival Theatre, the 612-seat Playhouse, and the 350-seat Space Theatre. Also located in the center, the Silver Jubilee Organ is the largest transportable concert-hall organ in the world. The instrument was built in Austria and paid for by public subscription to commemorate the Silver Jubilee of the reign of Queen Elizabeth II. An outdoor amphitheater, an art gallery, Lyrics Restaurant (see "Adelaide Dining," above), the Playhouse Bistro, and a piano bar are also part of the complex.

Even if you don't take a tour of the center, walk over and look at the view. From the plaza, the vista to the north includes the River Torrens, its grassy banks, a gazebo, and St. Peter's Cathedral. To the south, one sees the city, with its graceful mix of colonial and modern structures.

Admission: The 45-minute guided walk costs A$3 (U.S. $2.40).

Open: Mon–Sat 9am–5pm, Sun 2–5pm. Tours, which start at the box office foyer, are offered Mon–Sat at 11am and 2pm. **Transportation:** Located near the intersection of King William Rd. and North Terrace, the center is easily reached on foot from the city center.

SOUTH AUSTRALIAN MARITIME MUSEUM, 126 Lipson St., Port Adelaide. Tel. 240-0200.

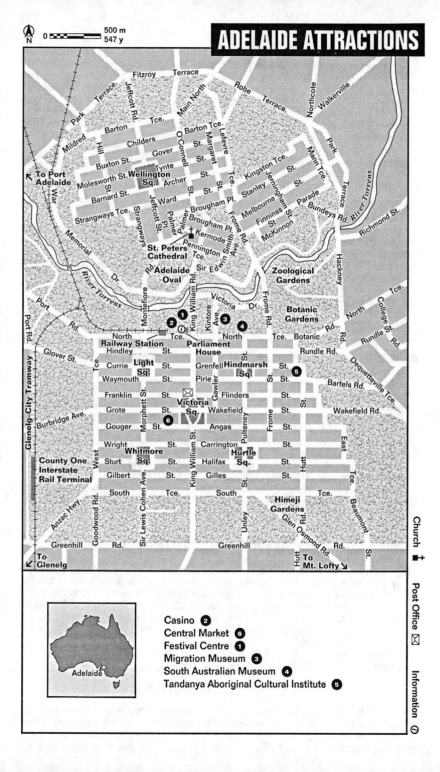

ADELAIDE ATTRACTIONS

0 — 500 m
— 547 y

Church ✝

Post Office ⊠

Information ⓘ

Casino ➋
Central Market ➏
Festival Centre ➊
Migration Museum ➌
South Australian Museum ➍
Tandanya Aboriginal Cultural Institute ➎

★ Located in Port Adelaide, 15 kilometers (9 miles) from the city center, the museum commemorates 150 years of maritime history. Most of the exhibits are housed in the 1850s bond store at 126 Lipson Street, but the total museum encompasses a lighthouse that dates from 1869 and two vessels moored alongside no. 1 wharf—all within a short walk. Inside the bond store, a replica of the 54-foot ketch *Active II* is fully rigged, with its sails ready to raise. A re-created penny arcade and seaside pier help establish the 19th-century port atmosphere. While the museum lacks dining facilities, the Lipton Tea Rooms are only steps away.

Admission: A$6 (U.S. $4.80) adults; A$3 (U.S. $2.40) children.
Open: Tues–Sun 10am–5pm most of the year; daily during South Australian school holidays and public holidays. **Closed:** Most Mon and Christmas Day. **Bus:** Bus no. 153-157 from North Terrace in the city to Stop 40 (Port Adelaide).

SOUTH AUSTRALIAN MUSEUM, on North Terrace between the State Library and the Art Gallery. Tel. 223-8911.

The museum focuses on the state's natural history and anthropological background. It is well known for its excellent collection of Aboriginal artifacts, but because of very limited space, only a fraction of these items can be displayed at any one time. The contrast of styles between this traditional museum and the state-of-the-art Migration Museum is dramatic.

Be sure to visit the gift shop, which sells a wide range of books, cards, and other quality merchandise.

Admission: Free.
Open: Daily 10am–5pm. **Closed:** Christmas Day and Good Friday. **Directions:** Within easy walking distance of the city center.

CARRICK HILL, 46 Carrick Hill Dr., Springfield. Tel. 379-3886 or 379-3158.

Carrick Hill is a real treat for those who like antiques, grand old homes, and fine art. The house was built in 1939 for Sir Edward and Lady Hayward, who bought oak paneling, an ornate Jacobean staircase, fireplaces, and windows of a Tudor mansion that was going to be demolished in Staffordshire, England, and had them shipped to South Australia. Designed to incorporate these items, Carrick Hill was built in the style of an English manor house of the late Elizabethan period. The house is set in English-style gardens and surrounded by Australian bushland.

A tearoom on the premises serves morning and afternoon teas and light lunches.

Admission: A$5 (U.S. $4) adults, A$2.50 (U.S. $2) children.
Open: Wed–Sun 10am–5pm. Guided tours start at 11am, noon, 2 and 3pm.
Closed: July. **Transportation:** Take bus no. 171 (Mitcham) from city center. Get off at Stop 16 (Maitland St./Fullarton Rd.). Walk along Fullarton Rd. which becomes Carrick Hill Dr. (.5km/⅓ mile).

TANDANYA ABORIGINAL CULTURAL INSTITUTE, 253 Grenfell St. Tel. 223-2467.

★ This is a venue for Aboriginal art, culture, and activities. Changing exhibits provide a glimpse into the past and present life of Australia's native people. Guides are available to answer questions and give informal tours. Films and occasional live performances take place in the on-site theater. The work of Aboriginal artists and books about this mysterious culture are sold in a shop on the premises. The building was originally Adelaide's power-generating station. Cafe Tandanya serves "the flavour of Australia."

Admission: A$4 (U.S. $3.20) adults; children under 14 free.
Open: Mon–Fri 10:30am–5pm, Sat–Sun noon–5pm.

MORE ATTRACTIONS

The **O-Bahn Busway** is a new transport technology involving buses running on concrete tracks. The vehicles travel up to 100kmph (62 m.p.h.) and pass through lots of pretty scenery along the 12 kilometers (7½ mile) route from Adelaide to a major shopping center at Tea Tree Plaza. If you'd like to take this ride, board bus no.

540-549 at the intersection of Grenfell Street and James Place. More information is available from the STA (tel. 210-1000).

NEARBY ATTRACTIONS

GLENELG

Why not spend a pleasant morning or afternoon making a trip to the seaside suburb of Glenelg? You can start with a 29-minute tram ride from Victoria Square that will take you through the southern parklands and right out to the coast.

While there you can tour the HMS *Buffalo* and enjoy a walk along the beach. The **Old Gum Tree,** under which Governor Hindmarsh read the 1836 proclamation making South Australia a colony, is on MacFarlane Street. The **Glenelg Tourist Information Centre** (tel. 08/294-5833) can answer your questions.

HMS BUFFALO, Adelphi Terrace, Patawalonga Boat Haven. Tel. 294-7000.

You can visit the full-size replica of the HMS *Buffalo* which was built from the original plans, drawn in 1813. This is the ship that brought the first settlers to South Australia in 1836. Today the *Buffalo* contains a small maritime museum and a seafood restaurant.

Admission: A$2.50 (U.S. $2) adults, A90¢ (U.S. 75¢) children.

Open: Mon–Fri 9am–5pm, weekends and public holidays 10–5pm. **Transportation:** Glenelg Tram.

6. ADELAIDE SPORTS & RECREATION

SPORTS

Auto Racing Adelaide becomes Grand Prix City every November, when the **Australian Formula One Grand Prix** takes place. The 3.78-kilometer (2½-mile) street circuit includes the city and eastern parklands. It's a weeklong carnival with street parties, wine and beer festivals, shows, parades, and concerts. This is the perfect place for those looking for some high-octane fun.

Cricket The Adelaide Oval is the site of national and international matches during the summer months.

Football Australian Rules Football has a large following. Venues include the Adelaide Oval and Football Park, West Lakes.

Horse Racing Main tracks are Victoria Park Racecourse and Morphettville Racecourse. The prestigious Adelaide Cup is held at Morphettville in May.

RECREATION

Ballooning **Balloon Academy,** Bagshaw Road, Kersbrook (tel. 389-3195), will take you up, up, and away over Adelaide or the Barossa Valley. The price of A$185 (U.S. $148) includes a 1-hour flight, champagne celebration, and ground transfers. Flights are scheduled for very early in the morning or late afternoon.

Bicycling Adelaide's parklands and recreational areas are popular with cyclists, who turn out in droves on the weekends. Rent your cycle from **Action Hire,** 400 King William Street (tel. 211-7060). Rates for a 10-speed are A$1.50 (U.S. $1.20) per hour, A$6 (U.S. $4.80) per half day, and A$12 (U.S. $9.60) per day. They also have tandems. Action is open 7 days a week from 9:30am to 5pm. You can also rent a bike in Glenelg at **Bike & Beach** (tel. 294-1477). **The Department of Recreation and Sport** (tel. 234-0844) publishes a brochure which shows the cycleways through the O-Bahn Park. **Mapland,** 12 Pirie Street (tel. 226-3895), is also a good source of maps.

Canoeing   The Murray River is an ideal place for paddling a canoe. Contact the **Department of Recreation and Sport** (tel. 234-0844) to get their excellent *Canoe Guide,* which suggests routes and gives safety tips and other information.

Hiking & Jogging   The banks of the **River Torrens,** just north of the city center, invite visitors to put on their Nikes and get some exercise. Likewise with the parklands that surround Adelaide. If you wish to go farther afield, I suggest you contact the **Department of Recreation and Sport** (tel. 234-0844) and request a set of their *Jubilee Walks* brochures. You might also ask them about the **Heysen Trail,** a 1,600-kilometer (992-mile) walking track, which starts 80 kilometers (50 miles) south of Adelaide and goes to the Flinders Ranges by way of the Adelaide Hills and the Barossa Valley.

Houseboat Cruising   The Murray River winds along the New South Wales–Victoria border and eventually finds its way to South Australia, where it enters the sea east of Adelaide. The river is a popular place for houseboating. The best place to rent such a vessel is in **Berri,** a riverfront community 3 hours northeast of Adelaide. Contact Garry and Cheryl Von Bertouch at **Swan Houseboats** (tel. 085/82-1622). Ski boats, dinghies, and canoes can also be hired and pulled behind the houseboat. Tariffs vary depending on the time of year and size of vessel, but an average 3-night rental for an eight-berth boat would be around A$500 (U.S. $400).

7. ADELAIDE SAVVY SHOPPING

Adelaide's **Central Markets,** behind the Hilton Hotel between Gouger and Grote streets, are a great place to buy fresh fruits and vegetables, pâté, cheese, and bread to pop into a picnic basket. Even if that isn't your style, the markets are a colorful slice of life that shouldn't be missed. Stallholders tout their goods above the din created by bargaining shoppers. The markets, held in a huge warehouselike structure, are open on Tuesday from 7am to 5:30pm, Thursday from 11am to 5:30pm, Friday from 7am to 9pm, and Saturday from 7am to 1pm.

In contrast to the chaos of the Central Markets, **Rundle Mall,** the city's main shopping precinct, seems relatively orderly at most times. Friday night, however, is an exception. This is the only evening that working people can shop, and the mall becomes a beehive of activity.

SHOPPING A TO Z
ABORIGINAL ARTS & CRAFTS

Adella Gallery, 27-29 Gilbert Place, off Currie Street (tel. 212-2171 or 212-3600), has a nice selection of authentic Aboriginal art and crafts, as well as Aboriginal-designed T-shirts and other clothing items. This is the place to look for carved emu eggs by well-known artist Bluey Roberts and western desert art by Kaapa Napajima and Paddy Carroll. Opals and opal jewelry are also sold here. This shop is open regular hours and after hours by arrangement.

CRAFTS

L'Unique, in the Renaissance Arcade, Shop 6, 21-27 Pulteney Street (tel. 223-1328), and Shop 54, City Cross Arcade, off Rundle Mall (tel. 231-0030), sells beautiful South Australian pottery, jewelry, glass, and sculpture. The ✪ **Jam Factory Craft Centre,** 169 Payneham Road, St. Peters (tel. 362-5661 or 362-4542), also has a very good selection of locally made craft items. This award-winning shop, located only a few minutes from the city center, also provides an opportunity to watch craftspeople at work. Exhibits in the gallery change monthly. You might also like to browse at the **Jam Factory City Style,** 74 Gawler Place (tel. 223-6809). **Quality 5 Crafts,** Shop 47 City Cross Arcade, corner of James Place (tel. 212-3340), sells glass, wood, leather, pottery, and other South Australian handcrafts, too.

DEPARTMENT STORES

In addition to the many smaller and medium-size stores, Adelaide has a **David Jones Department Store**—Australia's answer to Bloomingdale's and Marshall Field's. **Myer** and **John Martins** are the other department stores.

FASHIONS

Adelaide is the home of the **R. M. Williams Company,** makers of what locals refer to as "bush gear." If you're looking for kangaroo-leather boots, moleskin pants, Driza-bone coats, or Akubra hats, head to the R. M. Williams shop on Gawler Place. **Morrisons,** 203 Rundle Street (tel. 223-4327), sells similar apparel.

FOOD

Haigs, corner of King William Street and Rundle Mall, is the favorite chocolate shop of Adelaidians. An exotic confection called "freckles" is especially recommended. **Ditters,** King William Street, is also a local institution; it sells nuts, dried fruit, and the like.

GIFTS/SOUVENIRS

Lawrences, 111 Rundle Mall, has a good selection of stuffed animals, boomerangs, T-shirts, and so forth.

JEWELRY

At least 90% of the world's gem-quality opals come from South Australia, so it's not surprising that Adelaide is a good place to buy these stones. Prices are lower than in other cities and a good selection is available. At **Opal Field Gems,** third floor, 29 King William Street (tel. 212-5300), you can view a 10-minute film about opals, watch the cutting, and shop. (Note that this store does not stay open on Friday night as do others in the city.) **Opal Gem Mine,** 5 Rundle Mall, and 142 Melbourne Street, North Adelaide (tel. 267-5525 or 211-7440), has a simulated opal mine and is another good place to shop.

WINE

Buy your bottle at **Watermans,** King William Street, or at the **Bottle Barn,** 150 Payneham Road, Evandale (nearly opposite the Jam Factory).

8. ADELAIDE EVENING ENTERTAINMENT

Adelaide hosts Australia's largest performing arts festival in March of even-numbered years, one which covers the literary and visual arts as well as dance, theater, opera, and music. The Australian Opera, Peter Schreier, the Royal Philharmonic, Vienna Chamber Orchestra, and the national premiere of John Adams's landmark opera *Nixon in China* are just a few of over 500 attractions and performances to be presented February 28 through March 21, 1992. More than a million attendees were recorded at 40-plus venues around the city in 1990.

THE PERFORMING ARTS

MAJOR CONCERT HALLS & ALL-PURPOSE AUDITORIUMS

ADELAIDE FESTIVAL CENTRE, King William Rd. Tel. 216-8600 or 211-8999 for recorded information 24 hours a day; 213-4788 for the box office; 213-4777 to buy tickets over the phone from the BASS Booking Agency.

The **Festival Theatre** accommodates opera, ballet, drama, and orchestral concerts. The **Adelaide Symphony Orchestra** plays in the Festival Theatre, and the **Playhouse** is the home of the **State Theatre Company.** Experimental dramas are often done in the **Space Theatre.** For more details about the Festival Centre, see "Adelaide Attractions," above. The box office is open Monday to Saturday 9:30am to 8:30pm; tickets can be purchased over the phone Monday to Saturday 9am to 6pm.

Prices: Ticket prices vary depending on the event—A$3.50–A$50 (U.S. $2.80–U.S. $40).

THEATRES

ARTS THEATRE, 53 Angas St. Tel. 212-5777.

This theater was constructed in 1964 and is the home of the Adelaide Repertory Theatre. This company presents a season of six productions a year, ranging from drama to comedy. A sample of the playwrights whose work is performed is Neil Simon, Alan Ayckbourn, Noël Coward, Agatha Christie, and Terence Rattigan.

The theater is also the home of the Metropolitan Musical Theatre Company who presents two musical comedy productions a year. A venue for both amateur and professional theater, the Arts Theatre is walking distance from the Hilton and other hotels and restaurants. The theater seats 501.

Prices: A$12 (U.S. $9.60) for amateur shows; more for professional productions.

HER MAJESTY'S THEATRE, 58 Grote St. Tel. 212-6833.

Located opposite Adelaide's famous produce markets in the heart of the city, Her Majesty's is a landmark theater venue with 1,000 seats. Presentations here include drama, comedy, smaller-scale musicals, dance, opera, and recitals. Tickets can be purchased through all BASS ticket outlets or on Dial 'n Charge (tel. 213-4777). All major credit cards are accepted.

Prices: Tickets generally A$10–A$30 (U.S. $8–U.S. $24).

THE CLUB & MUSIC SCENE

DANCE CLUBS/DISCOS

MARGAUX'S, on the lobby level in the Hilton Hotel, 233 Victoria Sq. Tel. 217-0711.

Margaux's is a popular disco Wednesday through Saturday nights. Live music is played on Sunday. The nightclub opens at 9pm and attracts an "over 25" crowd.

Admission: A$9 (U.S. $7.20); free for hotel guests.

LE ROX, 9 Light Sq. Tel. 231-3234.

This nightclub is popular with the 18- to 28-year-old crowd who are "alternative to modern." Only open Friday and Saturday night 9pm to 5am. Live music is offered on Friday night. A wide range of drinks is served, but no food.

Admission: A$6 (U.S. $4.80).

THE BAR SCENE

PUBS

OLD LION, 163 Melbourne St., North Adelaide. Tel. 267-3766.

This is a restored brewery hotel built in 1850 with several different bars. Patrons can watch as ales and lagers are produced, and they can sample the Old Lion brew in the Brewery Ale House Bar. The Tavern Bar is also fun.

THE PORT DOCK, 10 Todd St., Port Adelaide. Tel. 240-0187.

The Port Dock has three bars: the Upstairs Bar, the P.O.S.H. Bar, and the Long Bar. Four beers are brewed on the premises and pumped to the bars by traditional English beer engines. The Port Dock is a great place to go on Sunday, when they host a big crowd from 11am to 10pm. The hotel was first licensed in 1865 and has a handsome decor.

EARL OF ABERDEEN, 316 Pulteney St., corner of Carrington St. Tel. 223-6433.

This is a restored 19th-century, colonial-style pub. It is popular with the city's businesspeople and yuppies. Excellent food is served here. The hotel's Gazebo Restaurant is renowned for its aged steaks and huge range of beers from Australia and around the world.

OLD BOTANIC HOTEL, 309 North Terrace, corner of East Terrace. Tel. 223-4411.

This is a favorite watering hole for university students. There's sidewalk dining during summer (December through February).

PIANO BARS

FEZBAH BAR, in the Festival Centre, King William Rd. Tel. 216-8730.

In the Fezbah Bar you might hear anything from hot jazz to 1950s rhythm and blues. You could also happen upon a dance cabaret, South American rhythms, or the big-band sound.

LOBBY BAR, in the Hilton Hotel, 233 Victoria Sq. Tel. 217-0711.

The Lobby Bar, located in the Hilton, is a good spot for people-watching accompanied by pleasant piano music.

MORE ENTERTAINMENT

Adelaide's after-dark options range from slightly sedate to positively X-rated. For strip clubs and raunchy nightspots head for Hindley Street.

CASINOS

ADELAIDE CASINO, North Terrace. Tel. 212-2811, or toll free 008/88-8711 in Australia.

The focal point of the city's nightlife is the Adelaide Casino with its old-world atmosphere. It is built in the shell of the historic railway station and over the existing train tracks just north of the city center. The Hyatt Regency and the Adelaide Convention Centre are nearby. Besides the predictable gaming tables, the casino has five bars and a buffet restaurant called The Pullman (lunch Monday to Friday A$19/U.S. $15.20; lunch Saturday A$21/U.S. $16.80; brunch Sunday A$21/U.S. $16.80; dinner Monday to Friday A$23.50/U.S. $18.80; dinner Saturday and Sunday A$25.50/U.S. $20.40). The casino is open 24 hours daily.

9. EASY EXCURSIONS FROM ADELAIDE

BAROSSA VALLEY

WHAT TO SEE & DO

South Australia is the country's chief wine-producing state and the Barossa is the best-known grape-growing region within the state. The area was settled by Silesian refugees, who planted the first vines in 1847. Today 40 wineries are in operation and the "wine valley" continues to have a German flavor. In addition to visiting wineries, you can poke around in craft shops, admire historic churches, and enjoy the beauty of the valley. **Tanunda** is the focal point of the area, but smaller villages are dotted along the highway from **Lyndoch** to **Nuriootpa.**

Several companies offer conducted tours of the Barossa. If you are driving, this scenic valley is the ideal place for spontaneous travel from one winery to another, stopping for photography, a picnic, or maybe even a nap as the spirit moves. Another alternative is to rent a bike, take the train to Gawler, and cycle through the Barossa. There is no public transportation between wineries.

The wine region of the valley starts 45 kilometers (28 miles) northeast of Adelaide and extends for about 20 kilometers (12 miles). The area is approximately 11 kilometers (7 miles) wide. Data on the wineries and detailed maps are available at the **Barossa Valley Information Centre,** 66 Murray Street, Nuriootpa, SA 5355 (tel. 085/62-1866), which is open Monday through Friday from 8:30am to 5pm and weekends from 9:30am to 1:30pm.

The impressive old buildings that house the wine-making operations in the Barossa Valley are a bonus for visitors to the area and set the region apart from Australia's other wine districts. Happily for South Australia, the immigrants who developed this industry built picturesque castles and châteaux to live in and from which to operate their businesses.

CHATEAU YALDARA WINERY, Lyndoch. Tel. 085/24-4200.

Built of yellow sandstone, the grand house contains valuable period furniture and crystal chandeliers. Extensive collections of porcelain and objets d'art can be viewed on daily house tours.

Chateau Yaldara, the second-largest family-owned winery in the Barossa, was founded in 1947 by emigrant German vintner Hermann Thumm. He bought the ruins of an 1876 flour mill and used the old European-style buildings as the beginning of his estate. In addition, tours of the château and winery, wine tasting, and bottle sales are available to visitors. Like most wineries in this area, Chateau Yaldara has a generous tasting policy.

Admission: Free.

Open: Mon–Fri 8:30am–5pm, Sat–Sun 9am–5pm. The Garden Bistro serves lunch noon–2pm; teas and snacks 10am–4pm. Phone ahead to check the times of scheduled tours.

CHARLES CIMICKY WINES, Lyndoch. Tel. 085/24-4025.

This is another interesting property to visit. A castlelike structure holds the winery and the tasting and sales rooms.

Admission: Free.

Open: Daily 10am–4pm.

BAROSSA SETTLERS WINERY, Trial Hill Rd., Lyndoch. Tel. 085/24-4017.

This winery is located in an old stone horse stable built in 1860. This small property is owned by Joan and Howard Haese.

Admission: Free.

Open: Mon–Sat 10am–4pm, Sun 1–4pm.

WOLF BLASS, Sturt Rd., Nuriootpa. Tel. 085/62-1955.

This is an extensive wine-tasting complex with a Germanic style that incorporates an interesting museum on wine making and the history of the Barossa. This winery consistently produces some of Australia's greatest red wines—the black label vintages have international reputations.

Admission: Free.

Open: Mon–Fri 9:15am–4:30pm, Sat–Sun noon–4:30pm.

PENFOLDS, Nuriootpa. Tel. 085/62-0389.

This is one of the largest wineries in the valley, with a storage capacity of 22.5

million liters (5.85 million U.S. gallons). This winery got its start in 1844, when Dr. Christopher Rawson Penfold, a medical doctor, planted a few grapes in the Adelaide foothills so that he could make wine for his patients. Today the winery building covers an area of over 3 hectares (7½ acres).
Admission: Free.
Open: Tours Mon–Fri 10am, 11am, 1:30pm, 2:30pm; tasting and sales Mon–Fri 9am–5pm, Sat 10am–5pm, Sun 1–5pm.

SEPPELTS, Seppeltsfield. Tel. 085/62-8028.
The business was founded by Joseph Seppelt, an immigrant from Silesia, who purchased the land in 1851 to grow tobacco. The winery and storage buildings are built of bluestone and surrounded by attractive gardens. Barbecues are provided in nice picnic areas.
Admission: A$2 (U.S. $1.60).
Open: Tasting and sales Mon–Fri 8:30am–5pm, Sat 10:30am–4:30pm, Sun 11am–4pm.

WHERE TO STAY

BAROSSA MOTOR LODGE, Murray St., Tanunda, SA 5352. Tel. 085/632-988. Fax 053/63-3653. 40 rms, 2 suites. A/C MINIBAR TV TEL
$ Rates: A$70 (U.S. $56) single; A$77 (U.S. $61.60) double; A$84 (U.S. $67.20) suite; A$8 (U.S. $6.40) extra person. Reservations can be made through Flag Inns. AE, BC, DC, MC, V. **Parking:** Free.
It may be that after a day of tasting, you'll decide to stay overnight in the Barossa Valley rather than return to Adelaide. If that's the case, you might consider this motor lodge. All quarters have coffee- and tea-making facilities, small refrigerators, clock radios, and queen-size beds. There are also accommodations for handicapped travelers. A restaurant and a barbecue are on the property. Guests also have the use of a pool, sauna, half-court tennis, spa, and playground. Baby-sitting can be arranged.

CHATEAU YALDARA ESTATE, Barossa Valley Hwy., Lyndoch, SA 5351. Tel. 085/24-4268. 34 rms, 1 suite. A/C MINIBAR TV TEL
$ Rates (including continental breakfast): A$70 (U.S. $56) single; A$80 (U.S. $64) double; A$10 (U.S. $8) extra person. Reservations can be made through Flag Inns. AE, BC, DC, MC, V. **Parking:** Free.
This motel is near the Chateau Yaldara Winery. All units have single and double beds, showers, and more than adequate furnishings. Tariffs are higher for rooms with the best views of surrounding countryside. A bar, restaurant, playground, and pool are all on the premises.

TANUNDA HOTEL, 51 Murray St., Tanunda, SA 5352. Tel. 085/63-2030. Fax 085/63-2165. 10 rms (6 with bath). A/C TV **Transportation:** Bus no. 910 from Adelaide.
$ Rates: A$42–A$53 (U.S. $33.60–U.S. $42.40) single; A$49–A$59 (U.S. $39.20–U.S. $47.20). AE, BC, DC, MC, V. **Parking:** Free.
The hotel was built of local stone by the early settlers in 1846, and its first liquor license was granted the next year. It was rebuilt after being partially destroyed by fire in 1895, with more renovations following in 1945. Today it is an impressive building with a long veranda supported by wrought-iron columns and lacework that were brought over from England. The Tanunda's popular bars are open 7 days a week, and meals are served in several different restaurants, ranging from very casual to elegant. All quarters have tea- and coffee-making facilities and small refrigerators. Six have telephones, showers, and toilets.

LAWLEY FARM, Krondorf Rd. (P.O. Box 103, Tanunda, SA 5352). Tel. 085/63-2141. Fax 085/63-3734. 6 suites. A/C TV TEL **Transportation:** Bus to Tanunda, then taxi.
$ Rates (including breakfast): A$82 (U.S. $65.60) single; A$100–A$118 (U.S. $80–U.S. $94.40) double; A$21 (U.S. $16.80) extra person. BC, MC, V. **Parking:** Free.

⭐ 💲 At this cozy property, Sancha and Bruce Withers invite guests to stay in "The Barn," "The Cottage," or "The New Cottage" on their 3 acres of native trees and orchard. The Cottage and the Barn date from 1850; all lodging offers old-world charm and scenic surroundings. Each has limited cooking facilities, an en suite bathroom, a clock radio, and either a king- or queen-size bed. There are laundry facilities, a spa, and a games room with pool table on the property; baby-sitting can be arranged. Breakfast can be served in your room or in the elegant old farm dining room. Hosts can arrange "insider" visits to wineries.

ADELAIDE HILLS

To the east and southeast of Adelaide, tree-clad slopes and valleys and pretty hills dotted with picturesque villages provide a rural getaway for visitors. The **South Australian Government Travel Centre,** 18 King William Street, Adelaide, SA 5000 (tel. 08/212-1505), is the best source of tourist information and maps.

BIRDWOOD

⭐ Located 46 kilometers (28 miles) east and slightly north of Adelaide, Birdwood is best known for its historic flour mill, which has been restored and now contains the **National Motor Museum**—the best collection of cars (both antique and classic) and motorcycles under one roof anywhere in Australia. Also included in the complex are cottage-style tearooms, a small museum, a gift shop, a playground, and an extensive picnic area alongside the upper reaches of the River Torrens. The museum (tel. 085/68-5006) is open daily from 9am to 5pm, except Christmas Day. The admission price of A$6 (U.S. $4.80) for adults and A$3 (U.S. $2.40) for children includes a ride on a tiny train pulled by a miniature steam engine. There is no public transportation to Birdwood. Either drive yourself or join a coach tour that includes this attraction on its itinerary.

HAHNDORF
What to See & Do

Hahndorf, 25 kilometers (15 miles) from Adelaide, was settled in 1839 by Lutherans fleeing religious persecution in the eastern provinces of Prussia. They named their town after Capt. Dirk Hahn, who brought them to Australia in his ship, the *Zebra*. Today the village, which retains its German appearance and atmosphere, is included on the World Heritage List as a Historical German Settlement. As you walk around town, notice **St. Paul's Lutheran Church,** erected in 1890. In the late 19th century, brides sometimes arrived at this church in a wagon wearing the traditional black wedding gown and a wreath of green and white leaves in their hair. Today, couples married in St. Paul's are often the fourth or fifth generation of their family to do so.

The Wool Factory, Hahndorf Handcrafts, and **Bamfurlong Fine Crafts**—all within walking distance of each other on Main Street—have an extensive range of fine Australian-made gifts and souvenirs. Tourist information and bookings are available through the **Hahndorf Tourist Association** (tel. 389-6724).

Where to Stay

HAHNDORF INN MOTOR LODGE, 35A Main St., Hahndorf, SA 5245. Tel. 08/388-1000, or toll free 008/88-2682 in Australia. 19 rms. A/C TV TEL **Transportation:** Mount Barker Bus Lines stops in Hahndorf.

💲 **Rates:** A$55 (U.S. $44) single; A$62 (U.S. $49.60) double; A$86 (U.S. $68.80) deluxe double; A$6 (U.S. $4.80) extra person. Tariffs are higher during Easter week and school holidays. Reservations can be made through Best Western. AE, BC, DC, MC, V. **Parking:** Free.

If you decide to stay overnight in this charming community, you'll find this motor lodge to be quite comfortable. All rooms have showers and the standard modern motel amenities, plus toasters. Two rooms have private spas, and a pool, spa, sauna, and laundry facilities are provided for all of the guests.

APPLE TREE COTTAGE, P.O. Box 100, Oakbank, SA 5243. Tel. 08/388-4193. 2 cottages. A/C **Directions:** 35-minute drive to Oakbank from Adelaide; 7 minutes from Hahndorf; less than an hour from the Barossa Valley.

$ **Rates** (including breakfast): from A$110 (U.S. $88) double; A$35 (U.S. $28) extra person. Weekly rates are lower. Higher rates during Grand Prix. No-smoking rooms available. No credit cards. **Parking:** Free.

⭐ If you're looking for cozy accommodation, here are two self-contained cottages, 1 kilometer (½ mile) apart, surrounded by 150 acres of scenic countryside. Owned by Gai and Brenton Adcock, Apple Tree Cottage, which sleeps up to five guests, and Gum Tree Cottage, for up to four, have won several tourism awards. Apple Tree, circa 1860, overlooks a lake on the Adcocks's cattle stud and apple orchard. It is furnished with antiques and has a stone fireplace in the living room. Guests enjoy using kerosene lamps, snuggling under patchwork quilts, and discovering lavender bags beneath their pillows. Gum Tree Cottage, built of stone and red gum, also has an open log fireplace and superb country views from the windows. Both cottages' kitchens are fully equipped, so visitors can cook for themselves, or go out to local restaurants. The Adcocks either fuss over guests or leave them in absolute privacy—as the guests prefer. This is a great place for rowing a boat across the lake, birdwatching, fishing, or lazing in a hammock.

Where to Dine

Several nice places for lunch or tea are located on Hahndorf's Main Street. **Stewart's Coffee Shoppe,** near Gumnut Antiques (tel. 388-1083), is a tiny spot with only a half dozen tables, but they serve an excellent Devonshire tea. For a tasty German-style meal accompanied by a wide range of German beers, wines, and schnapps, try the restored **German Arms Hotel,** 69 Main Street (tel. 338-7013). **Tony's Bistro,** across the road, serves Italian cuisine.

MOUNT LOFTY
What to See & Do

The summit of Mount Lofty, 20 minutes southeast of Adelaide, provides a panoramic view of the city, suburbs, beaches, valleys, and surrounding hills. It is also the location of one of the area's several bushfire lookout towers. The Adelaide Hills have been badly burned several times and careful watch is kept, especially during the hot, dry summer months.

Nearby, off Summit Road in Crafters, native birds and animals are displayed in a natural bush setting at **Cleland Wildlife Park** (tel. 339-2444), where visitors can hold a koala. The park is open daily from 9:30am to 5pm, but koala cuddling is allowed only from 10am to noon and 2 to 4pm. A small charge is made for photography. Admission is A$5.50 (U.S. $4.40) for adults and A$3.50 (U.S. $2.80) for children. Cleland Wildlife Park is included in the itinerary of several coach tours from Adelaide. If you're driving, take Greenhill Road or the South Eastern Freeway and turn into Summit Road. It's well signposted. Cleland is closed on Christmas Day and "extreme fire danger days." A kiosk and licensed restaurant are on the premises.

Where to Stay

MOUNT LOFTY HOUSE, 74 Summit Rd., Crafters, SA 5152. Tel. 08/339-6777. Fax 08/339-5656. 27 rms, 3 suites. A/C TV TEL **Transportation:** Chauffeured limousines available for airport transfers and sightseeing. Guests could also take coach to Crafters, then walk 1km (½ mile) or phone to be picked up.

$ **Rates** (including continental breakfast): A$195 (U.S. $156) single; A$195–A$245 (U.S. $156–U.S. $196) double; A$280 (U.S. $224) deluxe double; A$380–A$495 (U.S. $304–U.S. $396) suite; A$30 (U.S. $24) extra person. Weekend and other packages available. AE, BC, DC, MC, V. **Parking:** Free.

⭐ Commanding a spectacular view of the Piccadilly Valley and surrounding hills, Mount Lofty House is an elegant English-style country house poised near the summit of the 725-meter (2,393-ft.) peak. Built between 1852 and 1858, it has had many distinguished owners. It was all but destroyed by fire in 1983, and only the efforts of Ross Sands, an Adelaide architect, rescued it from the ashes. Ross and his wife, Janet, bought the remains of Mount Lofty House shortly after the fire and have painstakingly restored it. Today it offers tasteful lodging as well as dining in both formal and informal venues.

Overnight guests will find that their room is individual in layout and decor, including original works of art and old-world furnishings. Eight rooms have fireplaces. Each has a tub/shower combination, some have spa baths, but none has coffee- and tea-making facilities. Rooms offer queen- and king-size beds, or a pair of doubles. One room has its own conservatory; the Piccadilly Suite affords a wonderful view of the valley. The grounds of this grand manor house include a swimming pool and pleasant gardens. Mount Lofty House is a member of the exclusive Relais & Châteaux group and has won several Australian awards.

Dining/Entertainment: For meals, guests can choose between Piccadilly, the casual dining room and Hardy's, the formal dining area. In addition, predinner drinks are available in Tiers and tea is served in the Arthur Waterhouse Lounge (all of these are described in detail below).

Services: Turn-down service, laundry, baby-sitting, and massage.

Facilities: Pool and tranquil gardens.

Where to Dine

Guests of Mount Lofty House are not the only ones who have access to its beautiful dining venues. Nonresidents can enjoy lunch, dinner, and teas 7 days a week. Additionally, brunch and high tea are served on Sunday. A sample lunch in the casual **Piccadilly** room might start with an entrée of avocado and mango salad with mild curry vinaigrette, followed by a main course of roasted filet of kangaroo with eucalyptus jus and, for dessert, perhaps a tuille basket filled with vanilla-seed ice cream and blackberries on a blackberry coulis. This typical three-course meal would cost about A$24 (U.S. $19.20).

Hardy's, with its marble fireplace, fine crystal, high ceiling, and fresh flowers, is Mount Lofty's fine-dining room. Menus change seasonally, but dinner in this elegant environment could include mille-feuille of scallop and ginger "soup," followed by a main course of gin-marinated venison with pumpkin pie and gin glaze or grilled Atlantic salmon with cucumber jewels on a dill and Pernod cream. Dessert could be apple with brandied caramel crème and tuille basket of walnut-and-caramel ice cream or coeur à la crème with blackberry coulis and frosted blackberries. This typical dinner costs about A$42 (U.S. $33.60) per person, plus wine selected from an extensive list.

Predinner drinks are enjoyed in **Tiers,** the posh, cozy little cocktail bar with its dark woodwork and rust-colored burlap wall covering. The **Arthur Waterhouse Lounge** is a superbly appointed room where traditional furnishings, original oil paintings, high ceilings, and polished-brass fixtures re-create the gracious colonial life. A picture window in this room frames a beautiful view of the Piccadilly Valley.

CHAPTER 15
SOUTH AUSTRALIA

- **WHAT'S SPECIAL ABOUT SOUTH AUSTRALIA**
1. **KANGAROO ISLAND**
2. **OUTBACK SOUTH AUSTRALIA**
3. **THE COONAWARRA WINE DISTRICT**

South Australia is the "wow" state: It produces most of the nation's *w*ine, has vast expanses of outback terrain, and is home to lots of wonderful *w*ildlife. For travelers interested in these things, that adds up to a wow.

The Barossa Valley, discussed in Chapter 14, is the best known of the winery regions, but vineyards can also be found in other areas. McLaren Vale is the most prolific of the Southern Vales, located just south of Adelaide. The Clare Valley, 135 kilometers (84 miles) north of the capital, produces excellent red and white table wines. Sevenhill Cellars in Clare was started by two Jesuit priests in 1848 and still operates today. Coonawarra, due north of Mount Gambier near the Victoria border, is another wine-making district.

Vineyards are also found along the Murray River where most of the nation's bulk wine is produced. The Riverland is also known for citrus production. The town of Berri, 3 hours from Adelaide and 2 hours from Mildura (Victoria), is a popular vacation center.

The Yorke and the Eyre peninsulas, west of Adelaide, produce large quantities of grain and have beautiful, unspoiled coastlines. These agricultural gulf lands are in sharp contrast to the two-thirds of the state that is desertlike. From Port Augusta northward, very little rain falls and temperatures soar. It isn't surprising that in Coober Pedy, where it can be over 50°C (122°F) in the summer, most folks choose to live underground. Were it not for a rich supply of opals, this town would no doubt cease to exist. Likewise with Olympic Dam, the site of huge copper and uranium mines. While touring these outback areas is fun, 72% of the state's population chooses to live in Adelaide.

The Flinders Ranges, northeast of Port Augusta, are a spectacularly scenic area of peaks and gorges. Wilpena and Arkaroola are tiny rural communities that provide facilities and services to those who explore the area by four-wheel-drive, on horseback, or on foot.

The second "w" in wow stands for wildlife, and visitors whose interest lies in this area should head for Kangaroo Island. In addition to friendly kangaroos and wallabies, the occasional wombat, and lots of koalas, Australia's third-largest island also has colonies of seals, sea lions, and fairy penguins.

SEEING SOUTH AUSTRALIA

South Australia is four times the size of the United Kingdom. Several regional airlines, including Kendell, Air Transit, State Air, Air Kangaroo Island, and Albatross Airlines provide links between cities and towns. The Stuart Highway cuts the state in half diagonally and connects Port Augusta with Alice Springs in the Red Centre. While this road is now sealed, the trek between these two places is not without some hazards. Anyone considering this journey should seek advice from the **Royal Automobile Association of South Australia (RAA)** in Adelaide. The **South Australian Government Travel Centres** located in major Australian and overseas cities are the best source of tourist information. If you like off-the-beaten-path accommodations, ask them for a booklet entitled *Farm & Country Holidays,* which gives details on farms around the state that welcome visitors.

WHAT'S SPECIAL ABOUT SOUTH AUSTRALIA

Offbeat Oddities
☐ Coober Pedy, where people live underground to avoid the heat (and flies).

National Parks
☐ Flinders Chase National Park, on Kangaroo Island, a treasure trove of native fauna.

Regional Food & Drink
☐ The wine regions: the Barossa Valley, the Clare Valley, McLaren Vale, and the Coonawarra.

Activities
☐ Houseboating on the Murray River.
☐ Hiking and camping in the Flinders Ranges.

Beaches
☐ Seal Bay, on Kangaroo Island, home to a colony of sea lions.

1. KANGAROO ISLAND

110km (68 miles) S of Adelaide

GETTING THERE By Plane Albatross Airlines, Kendell Airlines, and Air Kangaroo Island fly to Kingscote from Adelaide, and Air Kangaroo Island also flies into Penneshaw and American River. The round-trip fare is A$110 (U.S. $88).

By Boat If you prefer to go by sea, the *Sea Link Ferry* takes 1 hour to cross the 16 kilometers (10 miles) from Cape Jervis on the tip of the mainland to Penneshaw. This trip costs A$52 (U.S. $41.60) round-trip for people and A$110 (U.S. $88) round-trip for cars. The *Sea Link* operates year round. Connecting bus service from Adelaide to Cape Jervis (tel. 08/251-3181) is provided at an extra charge of A$11 (U.S. $8.80). The other boat is the *Island Seaway,* which leaves from Port Adelaide three times a week and takes 6½ hours to get to Kingscote. The fare is A$25.50 (U.S. $20.40) each way for passengers and A$136.30 (U.S. $109.05) each way for cars. In addition, the fast passenger ferry *Valarie Jane* makes the 14-kilometer (8¾-mile) crossing from Cape Jervis to Penneshaw in 30 minutes and costs A$48 (U.S. $38.40) round-trip.

ESSENTIALS Area Code The area code for the communities on Kangaroo Island is 0848.

Information The **Kingscote Tourist Information Centre,** Kingscote, Kangaroo Island, SA 5223 (tel. 0848/22-640), is open Monday through Friday from 9am to 5:30pm and Saturday from 9am to noon. If you drop into this office, you'll probably meet Allen Tucknott, whom I dubbed "Mr. Kangaroo Island" after watching him in action for a couple of days. Cheerful Allen runs the office, leads bus tours of the island, owns the taxi company, and owns the bus company. While he seems like a dinky-di (true blue) Aussie, this former shearer was actually born in England. If you visit Kingscote, you're bound to meet Allen.

In addition, hotel and motel operators on the island are well versed in the area's attractions and will most likely be able to answer your questions.

Island Layout Kangaroo Island is 156 kilometers (97 miles) long and 57 kilometers (35 miles) wide at the widest point. The distance across at the narrowest point is only 2 kilometers (1 mile). The total population is 4,200, with more than half of these residents located in one of three towns: Kingscote (pop. 1,800), Penneshaw (pop. 250), and American River (pop. 200). The others are on scattered farms.

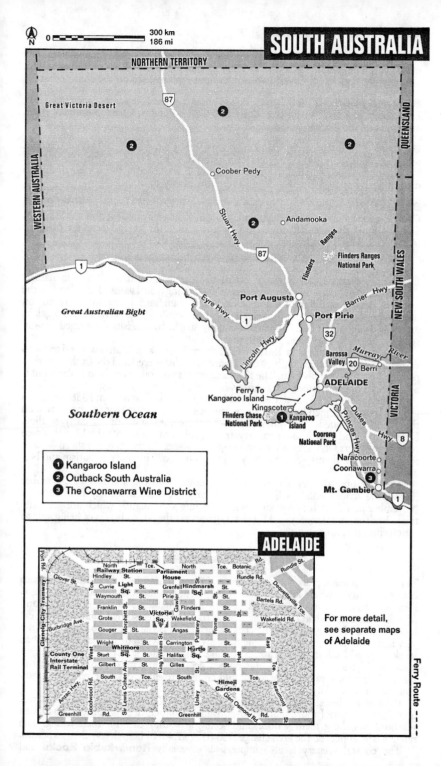

SOUTH AUSTRALIA

NORTHERN TERRITORY

WESTERN AUSTRALIA

QUEENSLAND

300 km
186 mi

Great Victoria Desert

Coober Pedy

Andamooka

Stuart Hwy.

Flinders Ranges

Flinders Ranges
National Park

NEW SOUTH WALES

Flinders

Eyre Hwy.

Port Augusta

Barrier Hwy.

Great Australian Bight

Lincoln Hwy.

Port Pirie

32

Murray River

Barossa
Valley

20

Berri

ADELAIDE

VICTORIA

8

Southern Ocean

Ferry To
Kangaroo Island

Kingscote

Flinders Chase
National Park

Kangaroo
Island

Coorong
National Park

Dukes Hwy.

Princes Hwy.

Naracoorte

Coonawarra

Mt. Gambier

❶ Kangaroo Island
❷ Outback South Australia
❸ The Coonawarra Wine District

ADELAIDE

North Tce.

Glenelg–City Tramway

Glover St.

Railway Station

Hindley St.

Currie **Light Sq.** St.

Waymouth St.

Franklin St.

Grote St.

Gouger St.

Wright St.

Whitmore Sq. St.

Sturt St.

Gilbert St.

South Tce.

Greenhill Rd.

Burbridge Ave.

County One
Interstate
Rail Terminal

Anzac Hwy.

Goodwood Rd.

Sir Lewis Cohen Ave.

Morphett St.

West St.

Parliament House

Grenfell St.

Pirie St.

Gawler

Victoria Sq.

Wakefield St.

Angas St.

Carrington St.

Halifax St.

Gilles St.

South Tce.

King William St.

North Tce.

Hindmarsh Sq. St.

Flinders St.

Pulteney St.

Frome St.

Hutt St.

Hurtle Sq. St.

Himeji Gardens

Unley Rd.

Greenhill Rd.

Botanic Rd.

Rundle St.

Rundle Rd.

Bartels Rd.

Wakefield Rd.

East Tce.

Dequetteville Tce.

Beaumont St.

Glen Osmond Rd.

For more detail,
see separate maps
of Adelaide

Ferry Route – – –

While most people live on the north side of the island closest to the mainland, the most fascinating wildlife is found in Flinders Chase National Park on the west end. Seal Bay and Kelly Hill Caves, two other popular places, are on the south coast.

GETTING AROUND   By Bus   Public buses connect Kingscote, American River, Penneshaw, Seal Bay, Vivon Bay, Kelly Hill Caves, Flinders Chase, Admiral's Arch, and Remarkable Rocks.

By Car   The towns on the island are connected by a total of 1,600 kilometers (992 miles) of roads, only 300 kilometers (186 miles) of which are sealed (paved). Since all but the main thoroughfares are reminiscent of a washboard, those who decide to drive from point to point will do well to allow plenty of time.

By Taxi   If you don't want to rent a car from Budget or Kangaroo Island Rental Cars or bring yours from the mainland, you can sightsee by taxi (at about A$35/U.S. $28 an hour) or take day tours run by the motels or an independent operator (A$54/U.S. $43.20, including lunch and all entrance fees).

Of all the places I can think of in Australia to witness native fauna in natural surroundings, none is more impressive than Kangaroo Island. The island is the home of dozens of different kinds of birds and mammals. The animals are not on display, per se, but can easily be seen in the wild. While koalas, echidnas, and galahs are what I like about K.I., others are equally struck by the island's rugged coastal scenery, beaches, caves, and good fishing.

The island was named in 1802 by English explorer Capt. Matthew Flinders, who was grateful for the large numbers of kangaroos he discovered and the fresh meat they provided for him and his men. The K.I. kangaroo is not found on the mainland but is a subspecies of the Western Gray variety. In general, K.I. roos are larger and less timid.

The island was officially settled by the South Australia Company in 1836. Since this group's trip was funded by Henry Kingscote, it's not surprising that the main town on the island is named—you guessed it—Kingscote. In spite of its early settling, Kangaroo Island was known to very few people until after World War II, when returned soldiers were set up with farms on the island. Today there are sheep—more than a million of them—everywhere you look. The No. 2 industry is tourism and No. 3 is fishing.

The best time to visit K.I. is during November and the first half of December (before the school holidays begin). If you can't get there then, any time between November and March is pleasant, but avoid July and August, which are generally rainy. Midsummer (January and February) guests get the added bonus of being able to watch sheepshearing.

WHAT TO SEE & DO

The most important place for you to go on Kangaroo Island is   ✪ **Flinders Chase National Park,** where koalas can be seen perched in the forks of eucalyptus trees. Flinders Chase also has scads of kangaroos and wallabies, and they're so tame and friendly that a fence had to be built around the picnic area so that humans could eat lunch without having their sandwiches swiped. This is the first place I ever petted a joey in his mama's pouch, and I remember my surprise when he jumped out and then stuck his head back in for a drink. If you like wildlife, this is one park you shouldn't miss. You'll also see lots of Cape Barren geese, some emus, and lots of native birds—like galahs, rainbow lorikeets, and crimson rosellas. If you're very lucky, you could even see a platypus.

If I had to choose between Flinders Chase and   ✪ **Seal Bay,** I'd be in a real quandary, because I thoroughly enjoyed walking among the magnificent Australian sea lions, watching them snooze, and seeing how they care for their young. The rangers who supervise the area charge A$3 (U.S. $2.40) to help defray their expenses.

The coastal scenery is also impressive, especially **Remarkable Rocks** and

Admiral's Arch, and while caves just aren't my thing, I believe the ones at Kelly Hill are very good. Tours are conducted at 11am, noon, 1:30pm, and 3:30pm. Admission is A$3 (U.S. $2.40). **Stokes Bay** and **Emu Bay** are good beaches on the north side of the island, but don't swim at Pennington Bay because of dangerous currents.

WHERE TO STAY

A good selection of motels is described below. If you're a diehard romantic and would prefer sleeping in a self-contained farmer's cottage, or perhaps even a lighthouse, I suggest that you contact **Australian Odysseys** (tel. 0848/31-019). Standards vary and prices range from A$26 to A$55 (U.S. $20.80 to U.S. $44) for each property.

IN KINGSCOTE

WISTERIA LODGE, 7 Cygnet Rd., Kingscote, SA 5223. Tel. 0848/22-707, or toll free 008/08-8211 in Australia. Fax 0848/22-200. 20 rms. A/C MINIBAR TV TEL

$ Rates (depending on time of year): A$70–A$85 (U.S. $56–U.S. $68) single; A$80–A$110 (U.S. $64–U.S. $88) double; A$10–A$15 (U.S. $8–U.S. $12) extra adult; A$8–A$12 (U.S. $6.40–U.S. $9.60) child under 12. Money-saving packages (including transportation to the island, transfers, meals, and day tours) available. Reservations can be made through Flag Inns. AE, BC, DC, MC, V.

⑤ The Wisteria Lodge is a modern motel that opened in 1986. The hostelry is located across the road from Nepean Bay, and each room has a sea view. Recreational facilities include a swimming pool, spa, playground, half-court tennis, and bike rental; meals are served in the Beachcomber Restaurant. Deluxe rooms offer spa baths and queen-size beds.

OZONE HOTEL, The Foreshore (Box 145), Kingscote, SA 5223. Tel. 0848/22-011, or toll free 008/08-3133 in Australia. Fax 0848/22-249. 36 rms. TV TEL

$ Rates: A$62 (U.S. $49.60) single; A$75 (U.S. $60) double; A$5 (U.S. $4) extra person. Off-season rates are lower. No-smoking rooms available. AE, BC, DC, MC, V.

The Ozone is the best known of the K.I. lodging alternatives. The historic hotel has 36 rooms, all with attached bathrooms, and enjoys a central location on the waterfront. In fact, it gets its name from the smell of the nearby sea. It is the social center of the island and offers an à la carte restaurant, a casual bistro, and a couple of friendly watering holes. A swimming pool, sauna, and spa are available to guests.

GRAYDON HOLIDAY LODGE, 16 Buller St., Kingscote, SA 5223. Tel. 0848/22-713. 7 self-contained units. TV

$ Rates: A$58 (U.S. $46.40) single or double; A$8 (U.S. $6.40) extra adult; A$5 (U.S. $4) extra child. Rates are 15% higher during holiday periods (Oct–Mar). BC, V.

Graydon Holiday Lodge offers one- and two-bedroom units that sleep up to seven people. The all-brick property, which opened in 1986, is located a 5-minute walk from the shopping area and 1 minute from the waterfront. Each unit has a clock radio, kitchen, ceiling fan, and electric blankets. Laundry facilities are on the premises and baby-sitting can be arranged.

IN AMERICAN RIVER

Located 37 kilometers (23 miles) from Kingscote, American River is popular with fishermen who come looking for whiting from October through March. The area lacks a beach, but the black swans on Pelican Lagoon are a picturesque sight. Wild wallabies abound and have even been known to take a swim in the pool at the American River Resort.

AMERICAN RIVER RESORT, Wattle Ave., American River, SA 5221. Tel. 0848/33-052. 27 rms. TV TEL

$ Rates: A$75 (U.S. $60) single; A$85 (U.S. $68) double; A$10 (U.S. $8) extra person. BC, MC, V.

All rooms here offer electric blankets, clock radios, coffee- and tea-making facilities, and small refrigerators. There are also a sauna, spa, swimming pool, restaurant, and bar. Charming hosts Lyn and Marty Ryan also offer a full complement of escorted island tours and can arrange fishing excursions. Facilities for the handicapped are available.

IN PENNESHAW

The most appealing of the three resort communities, Penneshaw is located 58 kilometers (36 miles) from Kingscote and 32 kilometers (20 miles) beyond American River. It has the best beach of the three towns but, while being closest to the mainland, is farthest from island attractions.

SORRENTO RESORT, North Terrace (P.O. Box 352), Penneshaw, SA 5222. Tel. 0848/31-028. Fax 0848/31-204. 27 units. TV

$ Rates: A$74 (U.S. $59.20) single; A$89 (U.S. $71.20) double; A$10 (U.S. $8) extra person. Rates are 10% higher Oct–May. Dollarwise packages available. AE, BC, DC, MC, V.

Most of the units here have sea views. The Village units at the back of the property are separate A-frames with cooking facilities; modern motel rooms face the water, where a colony of fairy penguins resides. A swimming pool, spa, sauna, half-court tennis, bar, and restaurant are on the premises. Proprietor Jack Boyd offers packages that include transportation to the island and local touring.

WHERE TO DINE

In addition to the restaurants that are part of the above accommodations recommendations, you might try the following:

MUGGLETON'S, Penneshaw. Tel. 31-151.
  Cuisine: MODERN AUSTRALIAN. **Reservations:** Recommended.
$ Prices: Three-course dinner for two A$48 (U.S. $38.40).
  Open: Summer daily 8am–9pm; rest of the year daily 9am–7pm.

Sandra and Rowan Muggleton have restored an 1890s building near the water that was completely derelict. Half of it is now a general store, and the other part they've made into a charming little eatery. Dimity-print cloths, plants, and Sandra's antique-doll collection from England have transformed the room into a most appealing spot. Devonshire teas include cranberry jam made from wild island berries, local dairy cream, and homemade scones. The blackboard menu at lunch usually features fresh fish and homemade pasta. Pecan pie is the specialty dessert. If you're there during the summer, typical dinner offerings include grilled barramundi served with cream, mustard, and shallot sauce or grilled deep-sea perch served with avocado, banana, and orange-juice sauce.

2. OUTBACK SOUTH AUSTRALIA

South Australia has the distinction of being the country's driest state. Two-thirds of it gets almost no rainfall and experiences very hot temperatures. The Stuart Highway leads north from Port Augusta and cuts the region in half. While this is a memorable trip, it should not be undertaken by people who lack outback driving experience. The town of Woomera, 485 kilometers (300 miles) north of Adelaide, supports the Woomera Weapons Testing Range, a restricted area that spreads from the highway across the Great Victoria Desert into Western Australia. The opal towns of Andamooka and Coober Pedy lie to the north.

COOBER PEDY

854km (529 miles) NW of Adelaide, 689km (427 miles) S of Alice Springs

GETTING THERE   By Plane or Bus   Kendell Airlines has regular flights to Coober Pedy from Adelaide (A$226/U.S. $180.80). If you opt for **bus** transport (Greyhound, Pioneer, or Bus Australia), the trip from Adelaide to Coober Pedy will cost A$80 (U.S. $64) and take about 12 hours.

ESSENTIALS   The **area code** is 086.

I've been to a lot of strange places in my life and, quite honestly, I think Coober Pedy is one of the strangest. The town, with its population of just over 2,000, is out in the middle of nowhere. Were it not for the fact that most of the world's supply of gem-quality opals are mined here, the town wouldn't even be a wide spot in the road. As it is, Coober Pedy is inhabited by rough-and-ready Aussies and immigrants (some legal and some not) from about 40 different nations who live here in the hopes of striking it rich. Aborigines constitute about 10% of the population.

If you approach Coober Pedy by air, which you probably should, you can't help but notice what look like huge gopher holes all around the town. This moonscape is created by miners who continuously drill new holes, leaving behind the many dozens that proved to be a disappointment. Once you're on the ground, it's easy to understand why most residents live in dugout houses to escape the extreme heat, dust, and flies. There are two underground churches and two underground motels. The town itself consists of a few motels, some casual restaurants, shops in which opals are sold, and the necessary service-type businesses. These places are all within walking distance of one another on the main highway, and the only other roads are those that lead to the mounds and holes created by those who search for opals.

Unlike other mining areas in Australia, Coober Pedy is not dominated by one huge company. All mining is done by individuals, and anyone can stake a claim. Even visitors can "noodle" through the dirt around the top of a shaft looking for a small stone that others have failed to see. This free-for-all system of mining attracts colorful characters who add to the town's Wild West atmosphere. Many eccentric old miners, for instance, camp by their staked territory to prevent claim-jumpers from "night mining."

WHAT TO SEE & DO

Once in Coober Pedy, excursions are conducted by Tom Compagna, proprietor of **Coober Pedy Tours** (tel. 086/72-5333). These cost A$10 (U.S. $8) and provide a look at an underground home and a visit to an underground church. They also take passengers to visit a working mine and explain a bit of the history and technique involved. Opals were discovered here in 1915, and the miners soon started building dugout houses because they realized that their underground workplaces were considerably cooler than the camps they were living in on the surface.

Another tour takes visitors to see the harsh and desolate countryside that surrounds the town.

The **Old Timers Mine,** in the Crowders Gully area of Coober Pedy (tel. 72-5555), provides another opportunity to learn about opals and the people who search for them. It's open Monday through Saturday from 8:30am to 6pm and Sunday from 11am to 6pm. Admission is A$3 (U.S. $2.40) for adults and A$1 (U.S. 80¢) for children.

WHERE TO STAY

DESERT CAVE, Hutchison St., Coober Pedy, SA 5723. Tel. 086/72-5688. Fax 086/72-5198. 50 rms. A/C MINIBAR TV TEL
$ **Rates:** A$108 (U.S. $86.40) single; A$119 (U.S. $95.20) double; A$12 (U.S. $9.60) extra person. AE, BC, DC, MC, V. **Parking:** Free.

⭐ The Desert Cave, located directly opposite the bus depot, has the distinction of being the world's only underground hotel "of international standard." Both aboveground and underground lodging is offered. All units have modern motel amenities, including in-room movies and coffee- and tea-making facilities, and a swimming pool, spa, sauna, hair salon, gift shop, and restaurant are available to guests.

OPAL INN HOTEL MOTEL, Hutchison St. (P.O. Box 223), Coober Pedy, SA 5723. Tel. 086/72-5054. 82 rms (70 with bath).
$ **Rates:** Hotel room A$25 (U.S. $20) single, A$35 (U.S. $28) double; motel room A$60 (U.S. $48) single, A$65 (U.S. $52) double; A$5 (U.S. $4) extra person. AE, BC, DC, MC, V. **Parking:** Free.

All rooms here are aboveground. In the original hotel, the quarters lack bathrooms. The motel rooms come with clock radios, coffee- and tea-making facilities, and small refrigerators. A restaurant and laundry facilities are on the premises.

WHERE TO DINE

It isn't surprising, given the large Greek population, that gyros, salad with feta cheese, and moussaka are all easy to come by in Coober Pedy.

TRACES, corner of Hutchinson St. and Wright St., Coober Pedy. Tel. 72-5147.
Cuisine: CHARCOAL GRILL/GREEK. **Reservations:** Not necessary.
$ **Prices:** Appetizers A$3–A$8 (U.S. $2.40–U.S. $6.40); main courses A$8–A$15 (U.S. $6.40–U.S. $12). Half-price meals for children. BC, MC, V.
Open: Daily 4pm–late.

⭐ Traces serves excellent Greek food including "yiros" (gyros), mezes (mixed meat platters), Greek salads, tzatziki (yogurt with garlic and cucumber), shashlick, and taramosalata. They also offer several cuts of chargrilled steak, omelets, and seafood. On Saturday night after 10:30pm, the restaurant turns into a disco. Children are welcome. Also does take-out.

---

3. THE COONAWARRA WINE DISTRICT

381km (236 miles) SE of Adelaide, 424km (263 miles) NW of Melbourne

GETTING THERE By Plane Kendell Airlines and O'Connors Air Services have nonstop flights from Adelaide and Melbourne to Mount Gambier, 61 kilometers (38 miles) to the south of the Coonawarra.

By Car Motorists following Highway 1 (the Princes Highway) from Victoria turn north at Mount Gambier and follow the signs to Penola. Those coming from Adelaide have a choice between the coastal Highway 1 or Highway 8 (the Dukes Highway).

By Bus Bond's Coach Company stops in Coonawarra, but there aren't any coach tours or public transportation within the district.

ESSENTIALS Area Code The area code is 087.

Information The **Penola Tourist Information Centre and John Riddoch District Interpretation Centre,** Arthur Street, Penola, SA 5277 (tel. 087/37-

2855), can provide maps and brochures, and has for sale a very informative book, *Your Guide to Penola and Coonawarra*, by Annette Balnaves. The tourist center is housed in the Old Mechanic's Institute built in 1869. It's open daily 10am to 4pm.

GETTING AROUND   This is a destination that requires a rental car, because there are no local public buses or coach tours of the wineries.

The Coonawarra is South Australia's, and maybe even Australia's, most elite wine area. The Jimmy Watson Trophy, the country's most important wine award, has been won by Coonawarra wines 5 of the last 8 years. Wineries such as Rouge Homme, Mildara, Lindeman's, Hollick, and Katnook Estate have also won other recognition, including Robert Mondavi's International Winemaker of the Year. There are 16 wineries in an area which is 12 kilometers (7½ miles) long and only 2 kilometers (1 mile) wide. They produce predominantly red wines, cabernet sauvignon being the most prestigious. All are open to the public for bottle sales and tasting.

There really is no town of Coonawarra—at least not in the sense of stores or gas stations—just a small post office, a motor inn, and a half dozen wineries. There's a bit more at Penola (pop. 1,250) 10 kilometers (6 miles) to the south; Naracoorte (pop. 4,700), 41 kilometers (25 miles) to the north, is a booming metropolis by comparison. The majority of wineries are located between Penola and Coonawarra.

In addition to wineries, the Coonawarra area offers several lovely historic buildings, some unusual caves, a wonderful wool museum, and lots of scenic countryside. Penola was founded in 1838 and is the oldest town in southeast South Australia. Mother Mary MacKillop, soon to become Australia's first saint, came to Penola in 1861 to be governess for her uncle's children and later taught school there.

WHAT TO SEE & DO

Wineries are what brings visitors to the Coonawarra. Happily they are not far apart, and all welcome the public to taste their products. Following are just a few of the 16 in the area.

IN COONAWARRA

ROUGE HOMME WINES, Main Penola/Naracoorte Rd., Coonawarra. Tel. 36-3205.
Be sure to visit this award-winning winery. In 1988 Greg Clayfield, manager of Rouge Homme, won the Robert Mondavi International Winemaker award. The winery, established in 1954, specializes in red table wines, specifically shiraz and cabernet.
Admission: Free.
Open: Daily 10am–4pm.

MILDARA WINES, Main Penola/Naracoorte Rd., Coonawarra. Tel. 36-3380.
Mildara specializes in both red and white wine and grows several kinds of grapes including cabernet sauvignon, shiraz, merlot, cabernet franc, malbec, pinot noir, pinot meunier, and chardonnay. Visitors are welcome to use the barbecue and picnic facilities, and tours are available by appointment.
Admission: Free.
Open: Mon–Fri 9am–4:30pm, Sat and public holidays 10am–4:30pm.

SEPPELT, Main Penola/Naracoorte Rd., Coonawarra. Tel. 37-2613.
Formerly Hungerford Hill Wines, Seppelt is a large winery specializing in premium

red and white table wines, as well as champagne and fortified wines. There are a playground and picnic facilities on the premises.

Admission: Free.
Open: Mon–Fri 9am–5pm, Sat–Sun 10am–5pm.

JAMES HASELGROVE WINES, Main Penola/Naracoorte Rd., Coonawarra. Tel. 37-2734.

This is one of the newer wineries, having been established in 1981. Dry and sweet white wines and dry red wines are the specialty. Wine Tasters Lunch is offered Friday through Monday from noon to 3pm. See "Where to Dine in Coonawarra," below.

Admission: Free.
Open: Daily 9am–5pm.

IN PENOLA

YALLUM PARK, 8km (5 miles) west of Penola on the Millicent Rd. Tel. 37-2435.

This Victorian mansion is, in fact, a living museum. The owners, Mr. and Mrs. Clifford, still live there and open for tours by appointment. The two-story homestead, built in 1880, is set on 2,000 acres. If you visit here, be sure to notice the original William Morris wallpapers. The acid-etched glass window next to the front door came from England by ship and was carried from Port McDonald by bullock cart. Mr. Clifford's father bought the house in 1914. The house is closed when the grandkids are visiting because they play in all the rooms.

Admission: A$2 (U.S. $1.60) adults, A$1 (U.S. 80¢) children under 15.
Open: By appointment.

IN OR NEAR NARACOORTE

NARACOORTE CAVES, 12km (7½ miles) southeast of Naracoorte. Tel. 62-2340.

Guided tours of the Blanche Cave, the Victoria Fossil Cave, and the Alexandra Cave are offered daily at regular intervals. There are also a campground, walking tracks (trails), a kiosk, and an interpretive center within the Naracoorte Caves Conservation Park.

Admission: A$3.50–A$5 (U.S. $2.80–U.S. $4) per guided cave tour.
Open: Daily; first tour 9:30am, last tour 3:30pm.

THE SHEEP'S BACK, MacDonnell St., Naracoorte. Tel. 62-1518.

Located in an historic 1860 flour mill, exhibits in this wool museum illustrate the history of the sheep and wool industry in this part of Australia. I think a visit here is essential for developing a sense of place and beginning to understand what the lives of the region's early settlers were like. The National Trust, which owns and operates the property, has done an excellent job of creating displays which provide a glimpse into the personal lives of shearers and homesteaders. There's a small craft shop on the premises.

Admission: A$2 (U.S. $1.60) adults, A$1 (U.S. 80¢) children.
Open: Daily 10am–4pm.

WHERE TO STAY

IN COONAWARRA

CHARDONNAY LODGE, Penola Rd. (P.O. Box 15), Coonawarra, SA 5263. Tel. 087/36-3309. Fax 087/36-3383. 24 rms. A/C TV TEL

$ Rates (including light breakfast): A$73 (U.S. $58.40) single; A$85 (U.S. $68) double; A$12.50 (U.S. $10) extra adult; A$8.50 (U.S. $6.80) children under 15. AE, BC, DC, MC, V. **Parking:** Free.

Surrounded by vineyards on one side and extensive lawns on the other, the spacious rooms here all offer one queen-size bed and two singles. Each also has coffee- and tea-making facilities, a small fridge, a clock radio, a toaster, electric blankets, and windows that open. Two units were designed for handicapped travelers.

It's not surprising that Chardonnay Lodge, open since 1985, has won numerous state and regional awards. Its red-brick exterior, stained-glass windows, and gracious grounds set it above other lodging offered in the area. Hosts Anne and James Yates provide a sincere welcome and are well prepared to answer questions about local attractions.

Meals are served in an attractive dining room, where the wine list includes more than 85 Coonawarra wines. An exhibition of paintings by regional artists adds interest to this room. A children's meal is served between 5 and 8:30pm, if parents wish to dine alone later. There are also a swimming pool, playground, self-service laundry, and wine gallery. Room service is available from 7:30am to 8:30pm. Baby-sitting can be arranged.

HONEYSUCKLE RISE COTTAGE, .2km (200 yd.) off Main Rd. on Lucindale Rd., Coonawarra, SA 5263. Tel. 087/36-3311. 1 cottage, sleeps four. TV
$ Rates (including light breakfast): A$130–A$140 (U.S. $104–U.S. $112) for two. **Parking:** Free.

⭐ Located a stone's throw from the Leconfeld Winery, this attractive stone cottage is set among picturesque vineyards. Two double beds, one upstairs one down, and a full kitchen make this a desirable lodging option. The charming decor and comfortable appointments are the creation of Americans Dennis and Bonnie Vice.

IN PENOLA

COONAWARRA MOTOR LODGE, 114 Church St. (P.O. Box 161), Penola, SA 5277. Tel. 087/37-2364. Fax 087/37-2543. 12 rms. A/C MINIBAR TV TEL
$ Rates: A$66 (U.S. $52.80) single; A$76 (U.S. $60.80) double; A$9 (U.S. $7.20) extra person. 10% winter discount June–Aug with minimum 2-night stay. Reservations can be made through Flag Inns. AE, BC, DC, MC, V. **Parking:** Free.
This modern motel is adjacent to a building which dates from 1868 and today houses a restaurant. All guest rooms feature tea- and coffee-making facilities, a small refrigerator, electric blankets, in-room movies, queen-size beds, and clock radios. Eleven units offer bathtubs. Meals are served in the atmospheric Bushman's Restaurant. A wine shop, tasting room, swimming pool, and self-service laundry are also on the premises.

WHERE TO DINE
IN COONAWARRA

CHARDONNAY LODGE, Penola Rd. Tel. 36-3309.
Cuisine: INTERNATIONAL. **Reservations:** Recommended.
$ Prices: Appetizers A$7–A$10.50 (U.S. $5.60–U.S. $8.40); main courses A$14.80–A$19 (U.S. $11.85–U.S. $15.20). AE, BC, DC, MC, V.
Open: Breakfast daily 7:30–9am; snacks and teas daily 8:30am–5pm; lunch daily noon–2pm; dinner daily 6–8:30pm or later; children's menu daily 5–8:30pm.
Local produce is given an international flavor in the dining room of the Chardonnay Lodge motor inn. Dinner guests can start with smoked fish in a savory cream sauce with crisp potato pikelets, beef satays with spicy soy sauce and a timbale of long grain and wild rice, or a platter of yabbies with coconut dressing. Main courses include turban of trout filet with a ginger and cucumber sauce, kangaroo filet pan-fried and served with sherry sauce and pickled walnuts, and beef eye filet filled with oysters and diced bacon, served on a Roquefort sauce.

Quiche, filled croissants, other light meals, and Devonshire teas are available throughout the day. The work of local artists, on display in the dining room, is for sale. The extensive wine list includes 85 Coonawarra wines.

JAMES HASELGROVE WINES, Main Penola/Naracoorte Rd. Tel. 37-2734.

Cuisine: INTERNATIONAL. **Reservations:** Recommended.

$ Prices: Appetizers A$4–A$5 (U.S. $3.20–U.S. $4); main courses A$8.50–A$10 (U.S. $6.80–U.S. $8); ploughman's lunch A$9 (U.S. $7.20). AE, BC, DC, MC, V.

Open: Lunch Fri–Mon noon–3pm.

This is the only winery in the Coonawarra district with a restaurant on the premises. Your light lunch here could start with pumpkin soup, followed by eggplant parmigiana, or you could have a traditional ploughman's lunch. Chocolate auslese trifle makes a nice dessert.

IN PENOLA

BUSHMAN'S INN, in the Coonawarra Motor Lodge, 114 Church St. Tel. 37-2364.

Cuisine: INTERNATIONAL. **Reservations:** Recommended, especially evenings and weekends.

$ Prices: Appetizers A$7.50–A$11.50 (U.S. $6–U.S. $9.20); main courses A$14–A$17.50 (U.S. $11.20–U.S. $14). AE, BC, DC, MC, V.

Open: Lunch daily noon–2pm; dinner daily 6:30–8:30pm.

This historic building which dates from 1868 has been a hotel, a private home, and a museum. Today it is an atmospheric spot to enjoy lunch or dinner. The colonial ambience is enhanced by antiques and lace cloths. For lunch, you could have pasta, a filled croissant, or a main course such as curry puffs with chili chutney or rabbit-and-pork pie. Dinner entrées (appetizers) include crumbed lamb brains in lemon-parsley sauce, smoked salmon and avocado salad, and marinated calamari. The main course selections include prawn curry, King George whiting caprice, and kangaroo steak with herbed butter. There's a nice selection of wines by the glass as well as a complete wine list.

MELBOURNE

Australia's second-largest city takes itself seriously. Men and women in conservative suits march through the central business district on their way to offices where the nation's financial decisions are made. Massive Victorian bluestone buildings and wide, tree-lined boulevards create a sense of permanence that predominates over the modern appearance of glossy high-rise towers. Unlike the residents of other Australian capitals with more relaxed lifestyles, pedestrians stride purposefully and tend to look slightly somber. In these ways and others, Melbourne is more like London than Sydney, Brisbane, or Perth.

The oft-quoted remark "Sydney is made of plastic, while Melbourne is made of stone" sums up the sentiments of Melburnians toward their archrival. Another old Australian saw claims that in Melbourne one is asked "What school did you go to?" while in Sydney, questioners want to know "How much money do you make?"

While these remarks polarize the two cities unrealistically, there's no denying that Melbourne's metropolitan persona is unique. Changeable and sometimes inclement weather has helped to foster a citizenry interested in the arts; sophisticated shopping and dining venues have been developed to meet the requirements of the financially successful; and old-guard Melburnians have fought to retain the Victorian architecture, English-style parks and gardens, and turn-of-the-century tram system that contribute so much to the city's air of stability, reserve, and tradition.

Melbourne's cultural and financial roots were born in the 1850s, when the city boomed as the result of a huge gold rush in the Victorian hills. Following the rush, business and manufacturing continued to thrive as a result of the availability of skilled labor and an excellent natural harbor. By the end of the century, the city was clearly established as the business and cultural capital of the colony. Its British origins were dramatically diversified after World War II by changed immigration policies, which brought in large groups of immigrants from Italy, Greece, Turkey, and elsewhere—adding a vibrant cosmopolitan flavor to the city. These industrious new arrivals further increased the community's prosperity.

This is not to say that the residents of Melbourne (pronounced "*Mel*-bun") don't know how to have a good time. They are the country's most avid supporters of Australian Rules football and follow local teams with something approaching religious zeal. In addition, the entire country stops on the first Tuesday in November to watch horses at Flemington Racecourse compete in the Melbourne Cup and to observe the standard-setting partying that accompanies the race. In early March the city celebrates Moomba, a 10-day carnival whose Aboriginal name translates to "let's get together and have fun."

WHAT'S SPECIAL ABOUT MELBOURNE

Local Transport
- [ ] Melbourne's trams, an atmospheric and convenient mode of getting around.

Ace Attractions
- [ ] The Victorian Arts Centre—to see a production and visit the Performing Arts Museum.

Shopping
- [ ] Toorak and South Yarra, offering dozens of fashionable boutiques.
- [ ] The Queen Victoria Market, selling almost everything imaginable.

Museums/Galleries
- [ ] The National Gallery of Victoria, one of the country's best.

Parks/Gardens
- [ ] The Royal Botanic Garden and Treasury Gardens, both lovely spots for a walk.

The Dandenongs
- [ ] The Dandenongs—a day-trip designed for flower fans.

Monuments
- [ ] The Shrine of Remembrance, honoring fallen soldiers and providing a good view of the city.

Zoos/Wildlife Parks
- [ ] The Melbourne Zoo—the best in the nation.
- [ ] Healesville Sanctuary, for native fauna in natural settings.

Events
- [ ] Melbourne Cup Day, the first Tuesday in November.

Day-Trip Destinations
- [ ] The National Wool Museum in Geelong.
- [ ] Queenscliff, where time's stood still.

1. ORIENTATION

ARRIVING

BY PLANE

More than 25 international and domestic airlines fly into this capital city's **Tullamarine Airport,** providing overseas access and frequent connections to all Australian states and territories. Australian Airlines' Blue Roo fare from Sydney to Melbourne is A$140 (U.S. $112); from Brisbane A$210 (U.S. $168); from Adelaide A$130 (U.S. $104); from Perth A$305 (U.S. $244); from Hobart A$138 (U.S. $110.40).

Tullamarine lacks tourist information, but some hotels provide free phones for reservations. A **Westpac Bank** is open for all arriving and departing flights, and baggage lockers are available at a cost of A$2 (U.S. $1.60) per day. Duty-free shops are located in the international area, and there are one restaurant and several snack bars in case you get hungry. Showers are also available. Stamps are sold in the gift shop, and a mailbox is provided for dropping off those last-minute postcards. The big four—**Thrifty, Budget, Avis,** and **Hertz**—all maintain car-rental counters.

Melbourne's Tullamarine Airport is 22 kilometers (14 miles) northwest of downtown. Transport into the city is provided by the **Skybus Coach Service,** which takes 30 to 35 minutes and costs A$8.50 (U.S. $6.80) for adults and half price for children. The service operates every half hour, 7 days a week, from the airport to the Skybus terminal, 58 Franklin Street (tel. 335-3066). Complimentary transfers are provided to city hotels Monday through Friday from this terminal, and luggage lockers are available. A taxi to the city center from the airport costs about A$20 (U.S. $16).

Departing Passengers When you're leaving Melbourne, remember to book the Skybus Coach Service (tel. 335-3066) ahead of time and, if you're leaving the country, have your departure tax (A$10/U.S. $8) ready.

BY TRAIN

Melbourne is also well served by interstate trains. The **Melbourne Express** provides overnight rail transport from Sydney. A first-class berth costs A$180 (U.S. $144); the fare for first-class sitting is A$120 (U.S. $96); the economy sitting fare is A$85 (U.S. $68). The **Intercapital Daylight** train also takes 12½ hours; tariffs are A$120 (U.S. $96) first class and A$49 (U.S. $39.20) economy. The **Overland** and **Daylink** will get you to and from Adelaide, and the **Canberra Link** provides a combination of rail and coach service to the nation's capital. For train information and reservations, call 619-5000 Monday through Saturday from 8am to 8pm and Sunday from 10am to 6pm. Interstate trains come into the Spencer Street Station.

BY BUS

Major bus companies connect Melbourne with other Victorian communities and all state capitals. Sample fares: Sydney to Melbourne on the Hume Highway, 14 hours, A$52 (U.S. $41.60); Sydney to Melbourne along the coastal Princes Highway, 18 hours, A$52 (U.S. $41.60); Canberra to Melbourne, 9 hours, A$48 (U.S. $38.40).

Some interstate buses arrive at the bus terminal on the corner of Franklin and Swanston streets and others come into the bus terminal at the Spencer Street Station. New arrivals can either take a tram or taxi from this depot to their final destination.

BY CAR

If you drive to Melbourne from Sydney, the trip will take 12 hours using the **Hume Highway** and about 2 days, with stops, along the more scenic **Princes Highway.**

TOURIST INFORMATION

Start your visit to Melbourne by calling in at the **RACV—Victorian Tourism Centre,** 230 Collins Street, Melbourne, VIC 3000 (tel. 03/650-1522). The staff can answer your questions, make bookings, and arm you with maps and brochures. This office is open Monday through Friday from 9am to 5:15pm and Saturday from 9am to noon.

For information on **free events** in Melbourne throughout the year, contact **F.E.I.P.P.** (Fantastic Entertainment in Public Places) at 23 Heffernan Lane (tel. 663-8307).

INTERSTATE INFORMATION

For interstate information, contact the following tourist centers: **ACT Tourism Commission,** 102 Elizabeth Street (tel. 654-5354); **New South Wales Travel Centre,** 388 Bourke Street (tel. 670-7461); **Northern Territory Government Tourist Bureau,** 415 Bourke Street (tel. 670-6948); **Queensland Government Travel Centre,** 257 Collins Street (tel. 654-3866); **South Australian Government Travel Centre,** 25 Elizabeth Street (tel. 614-6522); **Tourism Tasmania,** 256 Collins Street (tel. 653-7999); **Western Australian Tourist Centre,** 35 Elizabeth Street (tel. 614-6833).

CITY LAYOUT

Melbourne (pop. three million) lies on the north side of the Yarra River, just a few kilometers north of **Port Phillip Bay.** The central business district, where **Swanston Street** is the main thoroughfare, is bounded by the river on one side and **Spencer, Victoria,** and **Spring streets** on the others. Finding your way around is simplified by a straightforward grid system and the repeated use of street names. If you walk north from the **Yarra,** you will cross—in this order—**Flinders Street, Flinders Lane, Collins Street, Little Collins Street, Bourke Street, Little**

Bourke Street, Lonsdale Street, Little Lonsdale Street, and **Latrobe Street.**

Parks and gardens lie around the edges of the city center. **Queen Victoria Gardens** and **King's Domain** are just across the river on the east side of **St. Kilda Road,** which is the southern continuation of Swanston Street. **Treasury Gardens** and **Fitzroy Gardens** start at Spring Street, the central business district's eastern boundary.

NEIGHBORHOODS IN BRIEF

Greater Melbourne sprawls over 6,110 square kilometers (2359 sq. miles). For comparison, Greater New York covers 3,950 square kilometers or 1,525 square miles. Within this area are a number of distinct ethnic communities and pockets of historical and scenic interest.

Carlton   Italian restaurants line Lygon Street in the inner suburb of Carlton.

Richmond   Many Vietnamese live and operate businesses in the vicinity of Bridge Road in Richmond. Swan Street has Greek restaurants.

Chinatown   Sited in Little Bourke Street between Swanston and Exhibition streets.

Prahran   Greek eateries are located along Chapel Street in the suburb of Prahran (pronounced "pran"). After Athens, in fact, Melbourne is the second-biggest Greek city in the world, but because of the larger population, the presence of this ethnic group isn't as evident here as it is in Adelaide.

St. Kilda Road   This wide, tree-lined boulevard with trams rumbling down the middle, is the site of the Victorian Arts Centre, including the Melbourne Concert Hall, the Theatres Building, and the Performing Arts Museum. The National Gallery is adjacent.

St. Kilda   At the end of this grand avenue, the waterfront suburb of St. Kilda is known for its red-light district and cake shops, or "tarts and tortes," as Melburnians say.

Toorak   Where old money lives.

South Yarra   Popular with newly moneyed yuppies.

FARTHER AFIELD

The Yarra River winds down into Melbourne from the heavily forested slopes of the **Dandenong Ranges,** which lie 35 kilometers (22 miles) east of the city. The western suburbs are located on the edge of a huge volcanic plain that extends through western Victoria to the South Australia border.

The **Bellarine Peninsula** and the **Mornington Peninsula** curve around **Port Phillip Bay,** creating a calm waterway for port facilities and pleasure boating. **Phillip Island,** 1½ hours south of Melbourne, is the site of the renowned nightly penguin parade.

2. GETTING AROUND

BY PUBLIC TRANSPORTATION

The **Metropolitan Transit Authority** operates trains, trams, and buses that run throughout the city and suburbs. Generally speaking, trams cover the inner city, while trains and buses go farther afield. One ticket is interchangeable among the three different modes. If you want to travel on a tram, you can buy a ticket on board or in a train station. If you stay in the inner neighborhoods, the price is A$1.20 (U.S. $1) for a short journey, A$1.80 (U.S. $1.45) for a 3-hour ticket, or A$3.20 (U.S. $2.60) for an all-day ticket, which is good from 5:30am to midnight—when all transport stops.

A brochure that gives detailed route information is available at the Met office in the **Flinders Street Station** or at **The Met Shop,** 103 Elizabeth Street (tel. 617-0900).

Discount Passes The **Anywhere Travelcard,** selling for A$6.90 (U.S. $5.55), is a dollarwise deal if you plan to leave the inner neighborhoods. It's good for 1 day on any bus, train, or tram in the system.

If you're going to be in Melbourne for an extended period, you might want to get a **Weekly Travelcard,** which costs A$13.80 (U.S. $11.05) for the inner neighborhoods and A$27.60 (U.S. $22.10) for the entire system. With this comprehensive card, another adult and up to six children can travel free with you on weekends.

BY BUS

A compromise between public transportation and an escorted tour, the **City Explorer** (tel. 650-1511) allows you to travel around the city on a double-decker bus, stopping at as many sights as you choose. The loop route starts at Flinders Street Station on the hour from 10am to 4pm. You may get off at the Museum of Victoria, the Old Melbourne Gaol (which we non-British types spell "jail"), Queen Victoria Market, Melbourne Zoo, Lygon Street, and Cook's Cottage in Fitzroy Gardens. You stay as long as you like in each place and reboard the next bus. Tickets cost A$13 (U.S. $10.40) for adults and A$6 (U.S. $4.80) for children. Ticketholders are entitled to discounted admissions to the zoo, gaol, National Gallery, and Performing Arts Museum.

For trips farther afield, you can get intercity coach information at the following numbers: **Greyhound** (tel. 664-7888); **Pioneer** (tel. 668-2422); **Bus Booking Centre,** 14 Spencer Street near Flinders (tel. 629-1113 or 629-3848).

BY TRAM

Melbourne's green-and-yellow trams have become a much-loved symbol of the city. While most communities around the world have phased out this type of transport, the Victorian capital, with over 700 vehicles and 325 kilometers (200 miles) of track, is still expanding its system. The old cars have become collector's items. Elton John wants one to use as a summer house in his Berkshire garden; three of the cars run on a tourist line along the Seattle waterfront. The going price for a complete 1920s W-class tram is now about A$10,000 (U.S. $8,000), and it costs over A$20,000 (U.S. $16,000) to transport one of them to North America.

In the mid-1980s, a local artist came up with the idea of turning the trams into canvases in motion. The City Council agreed and six artists were commissioned to create "tramurals." The head-turning designs range from the delights of a Melbourne summer to mythical creatures, and in this conservative city it isn't surprising that the works of art have met with mixed reviews.

Point of information: When standing at a tram stop, hail the tram which you want to get on, and pull the left-hand cord once when you wish to disembark.

BY TAXI

Cabs are available throughout the city and cost A$2.60 (U.S. $2.10) at flagfall and A62¢ (U.S. 50¢) a kilometer from 6am to 7pm; the per kilometer charge is A71¢ (U.S. 60¢) from 7pm to midnight and A78¢ (U.S. 65¢) from midnight to 6am. (There's also an extra A$1 (U.S. 80¢) flagfall charged from midnight to 6am.) The charge for telephone bookings is A60¢ (U.S. 50¢). Two local companies are **Silver Top** (tel. 345-3455) and **Embassy** (tel. 329-9444).

BY CAR

Several good reasons for using public transportation quickly become evident to the innocent visiting motorist who tries to drive in Melbourne. The most obvious reason is a wacky local law about turning right; add to this the generally grumpy attitude of behind-the-wheel Melburnians, the absence of parking lots and spaces, and the double-digit figures hotels charge for parking at their property, and you'll be turning in your rental car faster than you would have believed possible. However, if you want a car for a day-trip outside the city, here's a list of the rental companies:

Ansa International, 245 Peel Street, North Melbourne (tel. 326-6339, or toll free 008/33-1041 in Australia), **Avis,** 400 Elizabeth Street (tel. 663-6366); **Budget,** 21 Bedford Street, North Melbourne (tel. 320-6333); **Hertz,** 97 Franklin Street (tel. 663-6244); **National,** corner of Peel and Queensberry Street, North Melbourne (tel. 329-5000); **Thrifty,** 390 Elizabeth Street (tel. 663-5200).

If you should want to contact the **RACV** (Royal Automobile Club of Victoria), it is located at 422 Little Collins Street (tel. 607-2137), and is open Monday through Friday from 9am to 5pm. Present your home-country auto-club membership card.

BY BICYCLE

Extensive bike paths wind through the city and suburbs. Many bookstores sell *Melbourne Bike Tours,* which is published by the State Bicycle Committee (tel. 60-2315) and describes 20 of the most popular routes. You can rent a bike from one of the **Hire a Bicycle** rental stores (tel. 801-2156) Monday to Friday 11am to 5pm and weekends from 10am to 5pm. Costs are A$4 (U.S. $3.20) for a half hour, A$5.50 (U.S. $4.40) for 1 hour, A$9 (U.S. $7.20) for 2 hours, and A$16 (U.S. $12.80) for a full day.

FAST FACTS MELBOURNE

Airlines   The following airlines have offices in Melbourne: **Air New Zealand,** 154 Swanston St. (tel. 654-3311 or 650-2288); **Ansett Airlines,** 465 Swanston St. (tel. 668-2222 or 668-1211); **Australian Airlines,** 50 Franklin St. (tel. 665-1333 or 665-3333); **British Airways,** 330 Collins St. (tel. 602-3500); **Canadian Airlines,** 500 Collins St. (tel. 629-6731); **Compass,** 267 Collins St. (tel. 650-6888); **Continental,** 469 Latrobe St. (tel. 602-5377); **Eastwest Airlines,** 215 Swanston St. (tel. 663-2422); **Kendell Airlines,** contact Ansett (tel. 668-2222); **Qantas Airways,** 114 William St. (tel. 602-6026 or 602-6111); **United Airlines,** 233 Collins St. (tel. 654-4488 or 602-2544); **UTA French Airlines,** 459 Collins St. (tel. 62-2982 or 614-2041).

American Express   The office, at 105 Elizabeth St. (tel. 608-0333), is open regular business hours.

Area Code   Melbourne telephone numbers are in the 03 area code.

Baby-sitters   Melbourne Occasional Child Care Centre, 104 A'Beckett St. (tel. 329-9561). They charge A$2.50 (U.S. $2) an hour.

Business Hours   Stores are generally open Mon–Thurs 9am–5:30pm, Fri 9am–9pm, and Sat 9am–12:30pm. Two large department stores, David Jones and Myer, are open Thurs night. Both are located in the Bourke Street Mall.

Banks are generally open Mon–Thurs 9:30am–4pm and Fri 9:30am–5pm.

Car Rentals   See "Getting Around," above.

Climate   See "When to Go" in Chapter 2.

Currency   See "Information, Entry Requirements, and Money" in Chapter 2.

Currency Exchange   Cash travelers' checks at banks or the larger hotels.
Dentist   Dental emergency service (tel. 341-0222).
Doctors   If you're sick or injured and it is an emergency, go to the "casualty" department of the Royal Melbourne Hospital (tel. 342-7000).
Drugstores [Chemist Shops]   Galleria Pharmacy, Galleria Plaza, corner of Bourke and Elizabeth streets (tel. 670-3644), is open Mon–Thurs 8:30am–5:30pm, Fri 8:30am–6:30pm, and Sat 10am–1pm (and they stock electrical adapters, if you need one). O'Neale's Pharmacy, 206 Bourke St. (tel. 663-3339), next to the Village Cinema, is open daily 9am–9pm.
Embassies/Consulates   The following countries maintain consulates in Melbourne: Britain, 90 Collins St. (tel. 650-4155); Canada, 1 Collins St. (tel. 654-1433); New Zealand, 60 Albert Rd., South Melbourne (tel. 696-0399); United States, 24 Albert Rd., South Melbourne (tel. 697-7900).
Emergencies   Dial 000 to summon ambulance, fire department, or police in an emergency.
Eyeglasses   O.P.S.M. (Optical Prescriptions Spectacle Makers), 82 Collins St. (tel. 650-3599), can make you new glasses.
Holidays   See "When to Go" in Chapter 2.
Hotlines   Lifeline (tel. 662-1000); Alcoholics Anonymous (tel. 429-1833); CASA (Centre Against Sexual Assault; tel. 344-2210).
Information   See "Information, Entry Requirements, and Money" in Chapter 2.
Laundry/Dry Cleaning   Brown Gouge Dry Cleaners is located in the Flinders Street Railway Station (tel. 614-3342), and in the Myer Department Store (tel. 661-2639).
   The South Yarra "8 to 8" Laundromat, 326 Toorak Rd., South Yarra (tel. 824-4892), is open daily 8am–8pm.
Libraries   The State Library of Victoria is located at 328 Swanston St. between Latrobe and Little Lonsdale (tel. 669-9888).
Newspapers/Magazines   Melbourne has two major morning newspapers, *The Age* and *The Herald-Sun. The Australian,* distributed throughout the nation, is also widely read.
Photographic Needs   Ted's Camera Stores are scattered throughout Melbourne and the suburbs. The best locations for tourists based in the city are 239 Elizabeth St. (tel. 600-0711), and 600 Collins St. (tel. 629-4366).
Post Office   The General Post Office (GPO) is on the corner of Bourke and Elizabeth streets (tel. 660-1355). It's open Mon–Friday 8am–6pm. There is also a limited service 9am–noon Sat and public holidays. Central Melbourne addresses have a 3000 postal code.
Religious Services   You can attend services at the following locations: Anglican, St. Paul's Cathedral, Flinders St. (tel. 650-3791); Baptist, Collins Street Baptist Church, 174 Collins St. (tel. 650-1180); Jewish, Melbourne Hebrew Congregation Synagogue, Toorak Rd., South Yarra (tel. 266-2255); Presbyterian, Scots Church, 99 Russell St. (tel. 650-9903); Roman Catholic, St. Patrick's Cathedral, Albert St., East Melbourne (tel. 662-2233); Uniting (Congregational, Methodist, and Presbyterian), Wesley Uniting Church, 148 Lonsdale St. (tel. 662-2355).
Safety   Avoid St. Kilda late at night and do your strolling in the city's parks and gardens before it gets dark.
Shoe Repairs   Mister Minit, corner of Lonsdale and Elizabeth streets (tel. 663-4704), offers while-you-wait service. He's open Mon–Thurs 9am–5:30pm, Fri 9am–9pm, and Sat 9am–1pm.
Taxes   Taxes on retail items are included in the price. There are no hotel taxes in Melbourne.
Taxis   See "Getting Around," above.
Useful Telephone Numbers   Travellers' Aid: 654-2600; Monash University Student Union: 565-4000; Melbourne University Student Union: 341-6973; Latrobe University Student Union: 347-2319; Student Services Australia: 348-1777; Student Counselling and Advice Bureau: 380-5253; The Also Foundation (for gay men and lesbians): 650-7711; Gay Advisory Service: 489-2059; Lesbian Lines: 416-0850;

Women Who Want to Be Women: 589-5039; Women's Information and Referral Exchange: 654-6844; Zonta Club of Melbourne (tel. 809-1084).

Weather   For a forecast call 1196.

3. MELBOURNE ACCOMMODATIONS

As you might expect in a city the size of Melbourne, a good selection of lodgings is available. Reservations are fairly easy to come by on weekends, when visiting businesspeople have gone home, but weekday room reservations should be made well in advance.

The high-powered executives who come to the nation's financial center expect international-class hostelries, and Melbourne gives them a good selection from which to choose. All are in the central business district; two offer old-world charm; most charge top rates midweek and offer good value in weekend packages. Moderate lodging is evenly distributed between the city center and inner suburbs. Additionally, a good choice between hotels and serviced apartments is offered.

The following price categories apply in this chapter: Very expensive—more than A$320 (U.S. $256) for a room for two people; expensive—A$190 to A$319 (U.S. $152 to U.S. $255.20); moderate—A$101 to A$189 (U.S. $80.80 to U.S. $151.20); inexpensive—A$70 to A$100 (U.S. $56 to U.S. $80); budget—less than A$70 (U.S. $56).

IN THE CITY CENTER
VERY EXPENSIVE

HYATT ON COLLINS, 123 Collins St., Melbourne, VIC 3000. Tel. 03/ 657-1234, or toll free 008/33-9494 in Australia. Fax 03/650-3491. 580 rms and suites. A/C MINIBAR TV TEL

$ Rates: A$350 (U.S. $280) superior single or double; A$385 (U.S. $308) deluxe; A$420 (U.S. $336) Regency Club; A$700–A$2,000 (U.S. $560–U.S. $1,600) suite; A$50 (U.S. $40) extra person. Children under 18 stay free in parents' room. Lower weekend rates. Weekend packages available. Tariffs are 10% higher Nov 1–10. No-smoking rooms available. AE, BC, CB, DC, MC, V. **Parking:** A$18 (U.S. $14.40) per night.

Hyatt on Collins is not only the largest hotel in Melbourne, it's also the newest in this price category and the one most open to the public. Throughout the Hyatt, brass, lacquer, and polished marble create a modern, slightly showy, atmosphere. In the lobby shop you can buy handy items like a A$210 (U.S. $168) shoehorn and an attaché case for A$1,440 (U.S. $1,152).

Each of the superior and deluxe guest bedrooms has the same amenities and decor: camel-and-gray color schemes, modern marble-topped furniture, either a king-size bed or twins, and hairdryers. The Regency Club on the top four floors of the hotel offers upgraded rooms and a complimentary continental breakfast. Prices vary according to the view.

Dining/Entertainment: The Plane Tree Cafe Restaurant is open for breakfast, lunch, dinner, and supper. Max's is a glitzy seafood eatery where the Romanesque decor includes black lacquer and gold chairs. Bar Deco is done in black and white; Monsoon's is a hot disco catering to the over 25s.

Services: 24-hour room service, turn-down service, shoeshine, laundry, valet, concierge, baby-sitting, massage.

Facilities: The City Club includes a gym, indoor pool, spa, plunge pool, aerobics classes, and flotation tanks. Like the tennis court, which costs A$15 (U.S. $12) an hour, there is a charge for the other exercise and fitness facilities. The Business Centre on the ground floor is convenient for traveling executives.

MENZIES AT RIALTO, 495 Collins St., Melbourne, VIC 3000. Tel. 03/620-9111, or toll free 008/33-1330 in Australia. Fax 03/614-1219. 243 rms, 11 suites. A/C MINIBAR TV TEL

$ Rates: A$320–A$343 (U.S. $256–U.S. $274.40) single or double; A$385–A$430 (U.S. $308–U.S. $344) Courtyard and Executive suites; A$550 (U.S. $440) Premier Suite. AE, BC, DC, MC, V. **Parking:** A$16 (U.S. $12.80) per night.

The hotel was created by connecting two 19th-century buildings—the Rialto Building and the Victorian Winfield Building. In 1984, under the watchful eye of the National Trust, all but the front section of the Winfield Building was razed and replaced with a brick structure complementing the facade of the Rialto. The space between the buildings was glassed in, turning the bluestone footpath into a covered courtyard. First-class accommodations were fitted into both structures; the preserved front section of the Winfield Building became a charming drawing room–style lounge called the Edinburgh Bar; the front of the Rialto Building, dating from 1890, was turned into tasteful shops; and the courtyard was designated the Portego, a Venetian word for "meeting place."

The hostelry offers every modern amenity along with wonderful old-world ambience. All quarters are spacious and have traditional furnishings. All have hairdryers, terry robes, bathroom scales, in-room movies, and the normal coffee- and tea-making facilities, plus toasters. More than half the rooms open onto the atrium between the buildings.

Dining/Entertainment: Dining options vary from the formal Chandelier Room to the Cafe Rialto Coffee Shop. Breakfast, teas, snacks, and drinks are offered daily in the convivial atmosphere of the Portego.

Services: 24-hour room service, turn-down service, concierge, baby-sitting, and laundry.

Facilities: On the premises: a hair salon, chemist shop (drugstore), dentist, doctor, and business center. Recreational facilities include an indoor pool and spa on the ninth floor.

REGENT HOTEL, 25 Collins St., Melbourne, VIC 3000. Tel. 03/653-0000, or toll free 008/31-1123 in Australia. Fax 03/650-4261. 311 rms, 52 suites. A/C MINIBAR TV TEL

$ Rates: A$308 (U.S. $246.40) single or double; A$440–A$748 (U.S. $352–U.S. $598.40) suite; A$900–A$1,900 (U.S. $720–U.S. $1,520) Penthouse, Premier, and Royal suites; A$30 (U.S. $24) extra person. Lower weekend rates. Weekend packages. Children under 18 stay free in parents' room. AE, BC, CB, DC, MC, V. **Parking:** A$10 (U.S. $8) per night.

The Regent Hotel offers the town's top accommodations. If you stay here, you'll find little fault with this superior high-rise. Designed by I. M. Pei and built in 1981, the hotel is entered from a plaza set back from busy Collins Street, so that peace and quiet start before guests even get in the front door. The lobby, with its reception desk, Green Room Lounge, and Black Swan Bar, is one level above ground. The rest of the hotel is located from the 35th to 50th floors, with the intervening space occupied by offices.

The Regent offers spacious rooms decorated with Italian designer fabrics in muted tones. The rooms have Portuguese marble bathrooms, "Regent robes," hairdryers, views of the city through floor-to-ceiling windows, daily complimentary newspapers, and nightly complimentary mineral water. King-size beds are available. All the modern amenities, including toasters, are provided. The hotel's best suites are on the 50th floor. These include the Royal and Premier suites, which combine elaborate decor with facilities for entertaining in style, and eight theme suites, each with a distinctive atmosphere created by appropriate furnishings and fittings. A well-trained staff provides service reminiscent of fine European hostelries, and the overall ambience is one of understated elegance and good taste.

Dining/Entertainment: Spectacular views are enjoyed by the dining spots on the 35th floor: Le Restaurant and Café La. The Atrium, encircled by a waterfall almost two stories high, is a casual eatery on the base of the 15-story space around which walkways lead to guest bedrooms.

Services: 24-hour room service, turn-down service, valet, shoeshine, concierge, baby-sitting, and massage.

Facilities: The hotel's Health Studio includes a gym, spa, sauna, and solarium. There are also a business center, hair salon, and newsagent.

WINDSOR HOTEL, 103 Spring St., Melbourne, VIC 3000. Tel. 03/653-0653, or toll free 008/00-3100 in Australia. Fax 03/654-5183. 171 rms, 19 suites. A/C MINIBAR TV TEL

$ Rates: A$325 (U.S. $260) standard single or double; A$375 (U.S. $300) superior room; A$410–A$880 (U.S. $328–U.S. $704) suite. Dollarwise weekend packages. Children under 12 stay free in parents' room. AE, BC, DC, MC, V. **Parking:** A$10 (U.S. $8) per night.

Another Melbourne property with old-world atmosphere, the Windsor Hotel enjoys the distinction of being the oldest deluxe property in Australia. Built in 1883, it has an eye-catching Victorian facade that includes two statues on the top of the front doorway, Hope and Charity. Inside, the original cage-style lifts just off the lobby have been turned into phone booths. Over the years, the Windsor has hosted many famous people, including the Duke of Windsor, after whom the hotel was renamed in 1920.

The Windsor is located on the eastern edge of the central business district across from Parliament House. Its rooms all have traditional furniture and modern amenities. Deluxe rooms are larger, have walk-in closets, the best views, and king-size beds.

The hotel is owned by the National Trust and run by Oberoi Hotels International, which operates prestigious properties throughout the world.

Dining/Entertainment: The Grand Dining Room is the most impressive part of the hotel. A$4 million (U.S. $3.2 million) was spent to restore and reglaze the original domed skylights with stained glass. Chandeliers were also reproduced from original photographs. Dining in these surroundings is made more elegant with the use of the finest crystal and silver.

Services: 24-hour room service, concierge, valet, laundry.

Facilities: Business center.

Reservations in North America: Preferred Hotels and Resorts (tel. toll free 800/323-7500 in the U.S. and Canada).

EXPENSIVE

BANKS HOTEL, corner of Flinders Lane and Spencer St., Melbourne, VIC 3000. Tel. 03/629-4111, or toll free 008/03-9099 in Australia. Fax 03/629-4300. 204 rms and suites. A/C MINIBAR TV TEL

$ Rates: A$210 (U.S. $168) single or double. Lower rates through Aussie auto clubs. Lower weekend rates. Children under 12 stay free in parents' room. No-smoking rooms available. AE, BC, DC, MC, V. **Parking:** Free.

This nine-story downtown hotel opened in late 1990 and quickly developed a reputation as the friendliest place to stay in the vicinity of the CBD. The staff all seem to have taken their training from television's Mister Rogers—and their smiling faces and helpful attitude are much appreciated by the guests who stay there. All quarters have very modern furnishings, tile baths, queen-size or twin beds, and floor-to-ceiling windows. Each also has a clock radio, bathrobe, hairdryer, tea- and coffee-making facilities, a small refrigerator, free daily newspaper, iron, ironing board, umbrella, and video player.

Dining/Entertainment: Breakfast, lunch, and dinner are served in Gnomes Restaurant. The cocktail bar is adjacent to the lobby.

Services: Courtesy car, 24-hour room service, turn-down service, shoeshine, valet, concierge, and baby-sitting.

Facilities: Heated outdoor pool, small gym, sauna, complimentary mountain bikes with helmets, video library, and self-service laundry.

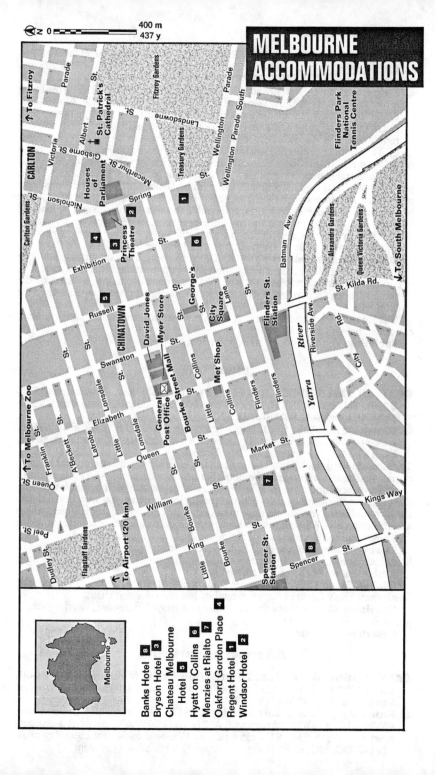

MELBOURNE ACCOMMODATIONS

Banks Hotel 8
Bryson Hotel 3
Chateau Melbourne Hotel 5
Hyatt on Collins 6
Menzies at Rialto 7
Oakford Gordon Place 4
Regent Hotel 1
Windsor Hotel 2

THE BRYSON HOTEL, 186 Exhibition St., Melbourne, VIC 3000. Tel. 03/662-0511, or toll free 008/33-3104 in Australia. Fax 03/663-6988. 298 rms and 65 suites. A/C MINIBAR TV TEL

$ Rates: A$215 (U.S. $172) superior single or double; A$230 (U.S. $184) king room; A$260 (U.S. $208) queen suite; A$330 (U.S. $264) king suite; A$440 (U.S. $352) executive suite. Lower weekend rates. Lower rates through Aussie auto clubs. Long-stay rates. Children under 12 stay free in parents' room. No-smoking rooms available. AE, BC, DC, MC, V. **Parking:** Free.

This 22-story property, located in Melbourne's theater district, offers city views from all but the lowest floors. The lobby, with its wood parquet floor and comfortable upholstered chairs, has a welcoming feel. Each bedroom is bright (the large windows don't open) and has a homey ambience. Executive suites have remote-control draperies, bidets, spa baths with city views, king-size beds, three phones, two TVs, large living rooms, and double showers. Queen suites have many of the same features and seem to me to be the best value. Superior rooms offer clock radios, hairdryers, tea- and coffee-making facilities, in-room movies, free daily newspapers, queen- or king-size beds, irons, and ironing boards.

Dining/Entertainment: Bobby McGee's, the hotel's restaurant, is open daily from 6:30am to midnight. This dining spot, where the costumed staff do zany stunts, is popular with kids and their parents. The entertainment lounge upstairs of the restaurant is open 5pm to 3am 7 days a week. The weekend cover charge is waived for house guests.

Services: 24-hour room service, turn-down service, shoeshine, laundry, valet, concierge, baby-sitting, and massage.

Facilities: Outdoor pool, sauna, and gift shop.

MODERATE

CHATEAU MELBOURNE HOTEL, 131 Lonsdale St., Melbourne, VIC 3000. Tel. 03/663-3161, or toll free 008/33-1006 in Australia. Fax 03/662-3479. 159 rms. A/C MINIBAR TV TEL

$ Rates: A$150 (U.S. $120) single or double; A$20 (U.S. $16) extra person. Weekend discounts available. Children under 12 stay free in parents' room. AE, BC, DC, MC, V. **Parking:** A$10 (U.S. $8).

The Château Melbourne is an 18-story building ideally located in the central business district and near Chinatown. The hotel has an unusual decor—a combination of French provincial and a couple of other styles—but you may well be so pleased with the spaciousness of the quarters and the central location that you won't even notice the surroundings. Every standard room has a balcony; deluxe lodging is larger and has a better city view. All rooms have hairdryers, clock radios, tea- and coffee-making facilities, small refrigerators, free daily newspapers, and in-room movies.

The front entrance of the hotel is sheltered by an attractive maroon awning, and a half dozen stairs lead up to glass doors. Six elaborate crystal chandeliers are the most noticeable feature of the small carpeted lobby.

Dining/Entertainment: Dinner and breakfast are served in the Lonsdale Restaurant; Elly's Cocktail Bar off the lobby has red velveteen chairs.

Services: 24-hour room service, turn-down service, shoeshine, valet, concierge, and baby-sitting.

Facilities: Pool, sauna.

A Serviced Apartment

OAKFORD GORDON PLACE, 24 Little Bourke St., Melbourne, VIC 3000. Tel. 03/663-5355, or toll free 008/33-1180 in Australia. Fax 03/663-5794. 59 apartments. A/C MINIBAR TV TEL

$ Rates: A$150 (U.S. $120) single studio; A$178 (U.S. $142.40) 1-bedroom unit; A$225 (U.S. $180) 2-bedroom unit; A$328 (U.S. $262.40) split-level 3-bedroom apartment; A$15 (U.S. $12) extra person. Weekend packages. Long-stay rates. AE, BC, DC, MC, V. **Parking:** Nearby A$8 (U.S. $6.40) per night.

These apartments provide a pleasant alternative for those wanting something other than standard hotel accommodations. The property, originally constructed in 1884, offers studio, one-, two-, and three-bedroom apartments, all with full kitchens including dishwashers. The south block features contemporary furnishings in old-world rooms with high ceilings, built-in wooden bookcases, and marble kitchen counters. Apartments in the north block have a modern appearance, and because it is farther from Little Bourke Street, this might be the quieter of the two sections. An iron and ironing board are provided in all units. Two-bedroom quarters have their own washing machines and dryers.

Dining/Entertainment: The Terrace Cafe and Bar is a casual eatery located between the four-story accommodations blocks. Here tables are set around a huge palm tree, and other green plants create a garden feel; a retractable glass roof makes possible year-round al fresco dining. Breakfast is offered daily; lunch and dinner are served Monday through Friday.

Services: Laundry, turn-down service.

Facilities: A heated saltwater pool is provided for guests between the north and south blocks. A spa, sauna, and small gym are also available. A hair salon is on the premises; a supermarket is only a block away.

CARLTON

MODERATE

THE TOWNHOUSE HOTEL, 701 Swanston St., Carlton, VIC 3053. Tel. 03/347-7811, or toll free 008/33-3001 in Australia. Fax 03/347-8225. 105 rms. A/C TV TEL **Transportation:** 5 minutes by tram no. 1 or 15 from the city center.
$ Rates: A$129 (U.S. $103.20) single or double; A$147 (U.S. $117.60) executive floor; A$200 (U.S. $160) suite; A$15 (U.S. $12) extra person. Children under 12 stay free in parents' room. Lower weekend tariffs. AE, BC, DC, MC, V. **Parking:** Free.

This is one of the best values in this cost category. Located in the inner suburb of Carlton, the five-story hotel's rooms are quite spacious. A few have tub/shower combos, but most have just large shower stalls. Guests have a choice of three color schemes: rust, light green, or beige. Some rooms have minibars.

This part of Carlton is a mixed neighborhood with both commercial and light industrial activity; a fire station is across the street from the hotel. Lincoln Park, a grassy patch with a fountain, lies to one side. Lygon Street, with its plethora of dining options and boutique shopping, is a block away.

Dining/Entertainment: Breakfast and dinner are served in Kaynes, where the attractive decor includes cane chairs and exposed-brick walls. Doctor Jazz, as the name implies, is a popular jazz club on the premises.

Services: 24-hour room service, laundry, baby-sitting, and secretarial service.

Facilities: Pool, sauna, barbecue area, and business center.

SOUTH YARRA

MODERATE

A Bed-and-Breakfast Hotel

THE TILBA, 30 W. Toorak Rd. at Domain St., South Yarra, VIC 3141. Tel. 03/867-8844. Fax 03/867-6567. 15 rms (all with bath). TV TEL **Transportation:** 10 minutes by tram from city center.
$ Rates (including breakfast): A$125–A$170 (U.S. $100–U.S. $136) single or double. No children under 12 allowed. AE, BC, DC, MC, V. **Parking:** Free.
Closed: Last week of Dec, first week of Jan, Easter week.

An eye-catching Federation-period building trimmed with just the right amount of gingerbread, the Tilba is located near St. Kilda Road and across the street from Fawkner Park. Proprietors Gayle and Bruce McGregor have decorated their bedrooms with antiques, ceiling fans, and period accessories such as Victorian shaving mirrors. Each has a shower; two have bathtubs. Rooms have been created from a grand residence and its former loft and stable, which date from 1907. "Pocket parlors" provide breathing space for those whose quarters seems close.

A beautiful stained-glass window over the cedar stairway, the subdued sand-colored decor, and a profusion of potted palms give the Tilba a light, airy feel, which is both welcoming and elegant. Housemaids wear black-and-white uniforms; classical music is piped throughout the public rooms at a pleasing volume. The inn's typical clientele includes visiting professors, ballerinas, artists, authors, businessmen, and travelers—all of whom share an interest in staying somewhere very special.

NORTH MELBOURNE

MODERATE

A Serviced Apartment

CITY GARDENS APARTMENTS, 335 Abbotsford St., North Melbourne, VIC 3051. Tel. 03/320-6600. Fax 03/329-2174. 124 units. TV TEL **Transportation:** 12 minutes by tram from city center.
$ Rates: A$110 (U.S. $88) single or double studio; A$120 (U.S. $96) 1-bedroom unit; A$130 (U.S. $104) 2-bedroom unit; A$185 (U.S. $148) Victorian town house for one to four; A$195 (U.S. $156) 3-bedroom unit for one to six; A$8 (U.S. $6.40) extra adult. AE, BC, DC, MC, V. **Parking** Free.

Spread out over 4 acres of grounds, the two-story Victorian town houses have camel-colored brick exteriors with black wrought-iron lace trim. Inside, these very spacious two- and three-bedroom dwellings have high-quality furnishings and appointments. Each has its own carport and courtyard with barbecue.

City Gardens also offers studio, one-bedroom, and two-bedroom apartments with more modest, but still adequate, interior decors. Like the town houses, all have washing machines and dryers, and only the studios lack dishwashers. All accommodations are two-story, except the studios. Chamber service is provided weekly and is available more frequently at an extra charge. A grocery store is across the road, and the Melbourne Zoo and North Melbourne City Council swimming pool are in the vicinity.

BUDGET

QUEENSBERRY HILL YHA HOSTEL, 78 Howard St., North Melbourne, VIC 3051. Tel. 03/329-8599. Fax 03/326-8427. 83 rms. **Transportation:** Tram no. 55 north along William St. or tram no. 19 or 59 traveling north along Elizabeth St.
$ Rates: From A$15 (U.S. $12) per person in a dorm; from A$51.30 (U.S. $40.80) for a room; A$7.20 (U.S. $5.80) extra person. No-smoking rooms available. MC, V. **Parking:** Free.

Forget your previous notions about youth hostels. This state-of-the-art budget facility, open since August 1991, offers 24-hour access, a licensed cafeteria, rooms with en suite toilets and showers, wheelchair access, Laundromat, foreign currency exchange, and full travel agency services. Each member has their own bedside security locker and can use the self-catering kitchen. The hostel is located 1.4 kilometers (1 mile) from the CBD; Queen Victoria Market is nearby.

EAST MELBOURNE

INEXPENSIVE

MAGNOLIA COURT BOUTIQUE HOTEL, 101 Powlett St., East Melbourne, VIC 3002. Tel. 03/419-4222. Fax 03/416-0841. 25 rms and suites (all with bath). A/C TV TEL **Transportation:** 10-minute walk, or short tram ride, to city center.

$ **Rates:** A$95 (U.S. $76) single; A$100 (U.S. $80) double; A$120 (U.S. $96) deluxe double; A$145 (U.S. $116) suite; A$15 (U.S. $12) extra adult; A$7 (U.S. $5.60) extra child. AE, BC, DC, MC, V. **Parking:** Free.

Magnolia Court is located on a quiet residential street in an area of Melbourne known for its charming terrace houses. The oldest part of the property dates from 1858. Proprietor Travers Humphreys has painted the three-story building in its original Victorian colors—dark and light green—and cast-iron posts with Victorian iron lacework support the second-floor veranda. The sunny breakfast room is popular with residents of the nearby and much-pricier Hilton Hotel as well as with the Magnolia Court's own residents.

During the morning meal and at other times of the day, the host chats with guests and helps to plan their sightseeing excursions and dining experiences. This personal attention makes the place feel like a B&B, but the bedrooms are much more reminiscent of a quality motel. All the modern motel amenities—coffee- and tea-making facilities and fridges—are provided. There are laundry facilities and a spa on the premises. After 8pm, Travers locks the front door and guests use their own keys. No elevator. Breakfast is the only meal offered, and there isn't a bar or a lounge.

A Serviced Apartment

ALBERT HEIGHTS EXECUTIVE APARTMENTS, 83 Albert St., East Melbourne, VIC 3002. Tel. 03/419-0955. Fax 03/419-9517. 36 apartments. A/C TV TEL **Transportation:** 10-minute walk to central business district or tram no. 42.

$ **Rates** (including a light breakfast on the first morning): A$95 (U.S. $76) single; A$100 (U.S. $80) double; A$15 (U.S. $12) extra adult; A$10 (U.S. $8) extra child. Weekly and weekend rates lower. AE, BC, DC, MC, V. **Parking:** Free.

Albert Heights offers apartments in a neat brick building. Each unit has a full kitchen with a microwave (no conventional oven), cooking utensils, dishes, and cutlery. Iron and ironing boards are also supplied, as are hairdryers and bathroom scales. Modern furnishings take their place in a black-and-gray color scheme. Each apartment sleeps four: two in the bedroom and two in the living room on a divan with a trundle.

Albert Heights is everything midprice lodging should be: clean, attractive—and, in this case, an ideal spot for folks who want to do their own cooking. The management make themselves available in the small reception foyer, should you have any questions. Chamber service is available Monday to Saturday, and there are a hot spa and a laundry on the premises. Baby-sitting can be arranged.

A Bed-and-Breakfast

GEORGIAN COURT GUEST HOUSE, 21 George St., East Melbourne, VIC 3002. Tel. 03/419-6353. Fax 03/416-0895. 32 rms (most without bath). **Transportation:** 15-minute walk from city center; 1 block from tram route. It's on the street behind the Hilton Hotel.

$ **Rates** (including continental breakfast): A$60 (U.S. $48) single; A$70 (U.S. $56) double; A$20 (U.S. $16) surcharge for larger, period-style room with private bathroom; A$20 (U.S. $16) extra adult; A$10 (U.S. $8) extra child. AE, BC, MC, V. **Parking:** Free.

Built in 1870, the Georgian Court retains much of its original appearance. White columns support a porte cochère and a balcony in front. The dining room and guest lounge have high ceilings, period antiques, and an old-world atmosphere. The accommodation section is a modern addition, so bedrooms, while adequate, are quite plain with cream-colored brick walls and simple pine furniture. Each room has coffee- and tea-making facilities and a clock radio. Guest may rent small refrigerators and TVs. The modern shared bathrooms are kept clean and tidy. There are a pay phone and laundry facilities on the premises. Dinner is available at an extra charge.

4. MELBOURNE DINING

Melbourne is renowned throughout Australia for its number and variety of fine dining establishments. These restaurants, bistros, grand hotel dining rooms, delis, and cafés are a reflection of the ethnic origins of the city's residents and its well-heeled heritage. Close to 1,500 eatery options covering 60 different national cuisines are listed in the yellow pages. Be sure to book early for all but the budget spots and remember that BYO means you must bring your own beer or wine if you intend to drink. Be aware that many local restaurants are closed on Sunday.

IN THE CITY CENTER
EXPENSIVE

FLOWER DRUM, 17 Market Lane. Tel. 662-3655.
   Cuisine: CANTONESE. **Reservations:** Recommended.
$ Prices: About A$110 (U.S. $88) for two, plus drinks. AE, BC, DC, MC, V.
   Open: Lunch Mon–Fri noon–3pm; dinner daily from 6pm.
The Flower Drum is owned by Gilbert Lau, who serves tasty traditional Cantonese dishes complemented by innovative cuisine. Baked squab with Chinese wine is marinated for a full day and served with a sauce made from its own juice. "Phoenix nest quail" consists of stir-fried boneless quail served in a nest of finely shredded fried potatoes. The Peking duck, which must be ordered 24 hours in advance, is delicious.
   Yum cha lunches, where diners choose individual servings from trolleys that are pushed around the room by staff, are very popular. A wide variety of cocktails and a reasonable number of wines are available.

LE RESTAURANT, in the Regent Hotel, 25 Collins St. Tel. 653-0000.
   Cuisine: INTERNATIONAL. **Reservations:** Recommended.
$ Prices: Appetizers A$15–A$23 (U.S. $12–U.S. $18.40); main courses A$23–A$40 (U.S. $18.40–U.S. $32); six-course "Menu Dégustation" A$100 (U.S. $80) per person including wine. AE, BC, DC, MC, V.
   Open: Dinner Tues–Sat 7pm–midnight.
Le Restaurant, on the 35th floor of the Regent, commands a superb view of Melbourne and the distant Dandenong Ranges. Its cool green contemporary decor creates a sophisticated ambience, complemented by outstanding service and cuisine.
   Diners make their selections from an à la carte menu that changes daily to include fresh produce and seafood, or they can elect to have the multicourse set menu. A typical meal might start with warm salad of squab, venison, and hare with lentils, baked tomato, and balsamic vinaigrette or smoked Tasmanian salmon with rémoulade of celeriac and parsnip chips.
   Main-course possibilities include médaillons of Victorian venison and breast of pigeon on stir-fried savoy cabbage and ocean trout and white veal with goose-liver wontons and basil butter. Iced mint yogurt can be served between courses to freshen your palate, and fresh spring berries glazed with a Cointreau sabayon make a nice light dessert.

MELBOURNE OYSTER BAR RESTAURANT, 209 King St. Tel. 670-1881.
   Cuisine: SEAFOOD. **Reservations:** Recommended.
$ Prices: Dinner for two about A$100 (U.S. $80); less for lunch. AE, BC, DC, MC, V.
   Open: Lunch Mon–Fri noon–3pm; dinner daily from 6pm.
This restaurant has a nautical decor in keeping with its menu offerings. It is located one floor above street level in a city-center location. Tuxedoed waiters and live organ music create an atmosphere that is a little dated but still elegant. Diners can dance between courses every night of the week.
   In addition to regular menu items such as scallops provençale, seafood kebab, and oysters prepared five different ways, the "chef's suggestions" list daily fresh offerings. These might include barramundi filet, John Dory, trevally, or crayfish—prepared

Mornay, thermidor, Newburg, or Mexican style. The specialties of the house are seafood platters, served on a plate big enough to hold a Thanksgiving turkey. A separate dessert menu lists several flambéed dishes, including crêpes Suzette and crêpes Jamaican. Quite a few liqueurs and liqueur coffees are available.

This restaurant is one of several owned by Nick Kadamani, who calls himself "Mr. Seafood." You might also like to know about his casual **Oyster Bar Bistro,** located on the ground floor, where the same food is available at lower prices.

MIETTA'S, 7 Alfred Place. Tel. 654-2366.
   Cuisine: FRENCH. **Reservations:** Recommended.
$ Prices: Appetizers A$15–A$24 (U.S. $12–U.S. $19.20); main courses A$24–A$32 (U.S. $19.20–U.S. $25.60); less at lunch. Fixed-price two-course lunch A$15 (U.S. $12); fixed-price three-course dinner A$35 (U.S. $28). AE, BC, CB, DC, MC, V.
   Open: Lunch Mon–Fri from noon; dinner Mon–Sat from 7pm.

It is indeed ambitious to describe Mietta's in the space allotted here. This restaurant is generally acknowledged to be the finest in Melbourne and, perhaps, the country.

The restaurant is located in a narrow lane running between Collins and Little Collins in the central business district. The German Club originally occupied this building in 1886, and it became the Naval and Military Club in 1918; as such, it was host to senior military personnel during World War II. In the 1960s the building was sold and made into a hotel until it was rescued by Mietta O'Donnell and her partner, Tony Knox, in 1984. They hired Suzanne Forge, expert on Victorian restorations, to bring their building back to its former glory. They also traveled to London with antiques dealer Graham Geddes to obtain furnishings. Done in classic Victorian pastel colors, the main dining room is in the original German Club ballroom. Mahogany balloon-back chairs surround ample tables set with fine damask and silver. Lavish floral arrangements top pedestals, and a pair of 12-foot blackamoor figures stand guard by the door.

Petite Mietta presides over the grandeur like a mother hen. Her watch includes the kitchen, where first-class French cuisine is prepared by chef Romain Bapst. Sample entrées include terrine of leek and salmon, warm winter salad of pheasant with crêpes; wild field mushrooms and cassolette of grilled prawns, bugs, and scallops. For a main course you might like to try boned oxtail formed into a mould surrounded by sautéed beef filet, stuffed gnocchi, and vegetables; or roast lobster combined with pigeon leg stuffed with foie gras and pigeon breast roasted pink. Desserts? How about crème brûlée of mangoes with sabayon or a miroir of passionfruit mousseline. No matter what you order, it will be delicious.

MODERATE

ELECTRA GREEK TAVERN, 195 Lonsdale St. Tel. 663-4760.
   Cuisine: GREEK. **Reservations:** Recommended on weekends. **Transportation:** Tram from Swanston St.
$ Prices: Appetizers A$4–A$8 (U.S. $3.20–U.S. $6.40); main courses A$10–A$17.50 (U.S. $8–U.S. $14); fixed-price two-course lunch or dinner A$25 (U.S. $20). AE, BC, DC, MC, V.
   Open: Mon–Fri noon–midnight, Sat–Sun 5pm–midnight.

Lonsdale Street in the heart of the city is lined with Greek eateries, and one of my favorites is the Electra Greek Tavern where proprietor Nick Spanos, who immigrated from Mykonos in 1982, serves traditional Grecian fare and wonderful seafood. His restaurant, while informal, is decorated with more imagination than is sometimes found in ethnic eateries. Shades of gray, exposed stone walls, green plants, and white lattice trim create an attractive environment for enjoying the fresh fish that Nick buys at the wholesale market and from fishing friends 5 days a week. He gets his delicious desserts from his brother, who owns the Medallion Cake Shop up the street. While they're all good, I especially endorse the galaktoboureko. Greek music fills the room on Friday and Saturday nights after 7:30pm. Licensed and BYO.

LUCATTINIS, 22 Punch Lane. Tel. 662-2883.
 Cuisine: ITALIAN. **Reservations:** Recommended.
$ Prices: About A$62 (U.S. $49.60) for two. AE, BC, DC, MC, V.
 Open: Lunch Mon–Fri noon–2:30pm; dinner Mon–Sat from 6pm.
Lucattinis is an old-fashioned Italian restaurant at the top end of Chinatown in a lane off Little Bourke Street. The owner and his efficient staff have many years of experience in the hospitality trade and it shows. The pasta is excellent, and the wide range of dishes includes traditional veal saltimbocca, fish, chicken, and lamb. The wine list is adequate.

MASK OF CHINA, 115-117 Little Bourke St. Tel. 662-2116.
 Cuisine: CHINESE. **Reservations:** Recommended, especially on weekends.
$ Prices: About A$70 (U.S. $56) for two. AE, BC, DC, MC, V.
 Open: Lunch Sun–Fri noon–3pm; dinner daily 6–11pm.
The Mask of China continues to collect awards for its distinctive Chiu Chow cuisine and its consistently high standards. With its trademark of a Chinese opera mask, the decor is more art deco than traditional, but the food on the plate is what counts. The cuisine is similar to Cantonese, but it uses less oil and relies on the development of natural flavors and textures. Fine seafood is a specialty and the game dishes on the menu are well worth trying also—the marinated soy goose in particular. BYO.

SHARK FIN INN, 50 Little Bourke St. Tel. 662-2681 or 662-2552.
 Cuisine: CHINESE. **Reservations:** Recommended.
$ Prices: Appetizers A$2.40–A$7 (U.S. $1.95–U.S. $5.60); main courses A$9.80–A$30 (U.S. $7.85–U.S. $24); banquets A$23.50 (U.S. $18.80), A$28 (U.S. $22.40), A$32 (U.S. $25.60). AE, BC, DC, MC, V.
 Open: Lunch Mon–Fri noon–3pm, Sat 11:30am–3pm, Sun 11am–3pm; dinner daily 5:30pm–1:30am.
The Shark Finn Inn has won several awards since it opened in 1982 and is one of the most popular spots in the city. The attractive decor includes pink tablecloths, dusty rose napkins, an exposed-brick wall, and a realistic picture window–size backlit nighttime photograph of Hong Kong.
 An extensive menu includes both preset "banquets" and à la carte offerings of creative Cantonese cuisine. Should you dine here, give strong consideration to the hot pots (perhaps bone marrow, Chinese mushrooms, and abalone with vegetables) and the daily specials incorporating seasonal produce. BYO.
 A "sister" restaurant, the **Shark Fin House,** is located at 131 Little Bourke Street (tel. 663-1555).

SOUTH MELBOURNE
EXPENSIVE

ROGALSKY'S, 440 Clarendon St. Tel. 690-1977.
 Cuisine: FRENCH. **Reservations:** Recommended.
$ Prices: About A$110 (U.S. $88) for two. AE, BC, DC, MC, V.
 Open: Lunch Tues–Fri from noon; dinner Tues–Sat from 6:30pm.
One of Melbourne's outstanding restaurants, Rogalsky's has amassed a vast collection of awards. For an entrée, how about boned quail prepared Peking style, served on small pancakes with scallions and preserved vegetables? Or Atlantic salmon marinated in lemon juice dressed with virgin olive oil and sea salt. Main courses include beef filet marinated in red wine and stuffed with tapenade, roasted and served on tomato pasta; crisp roasted duck breast with the braised leg in a tangy orange glaze served with vegetable stir-fry; and pan-fried filet of deep-sea fish with an herb crust served on an eggplant purée. If you leave room for dessert, try the wild strawberry soufflé with a pineapple ice-cream sandwich.

MODERATE

THE VIC RESTAURANT, in the Theatres Building at the Victorian Arts Centre. Tel. 617-8180.

Cuisine: INTERNATIONAL. **Reservations:** Recommended. **Transportation:** Any tram down Swanston St.

$ **Prices:** Appetizers A$5.50–A$8.50 (U.S. $4.40–U.S. $6.80); main courses A$14–A$16.50 (U.S. $11.20–U.S. $13.20); buffet lunch per person A$29.50 (U.S. $23.60). Public holiday surcharge 15%. AE, BC, DC, MC, V.

Open: Lunch Mon–Sat noon–2:30pm; pretheater meals Mon–Sat 5:30–8pm, dinner Mon–Sat 8–11:30pm.

Vic's is a convenient place for dining before or after a performance. The modern evening menu features light fare with a slight foreign flavor. Before a show you might have an entrée of puff parcel of lamb's brains, followed by waterzooi of chicken. The streamlined supper menu is limited to lighter fare such as creamy field mushroom soup, English spinach salad, spicy beef noodles, or a selection of cheeses. Framed costume sketches are displayed on the Vic's walls, and an Italianate painted ceiling floats high overhead. An adjacent coffee shop is open 6 days a week from 11am to 4pm.

CARLTON

MODERATE

CHALKY'S, 242 Lygon St., Carlton. Tel. 663-6100.

Cuisine: INTERNATIONAL. **Reservations:** Recommended. **Transportation:** Bus no. 203 traveling north on Russell St. or tram no. 1, 15, 21, or 22 traveling north on Swanston St. (alight at stop 12).

$ **Prices:** Appetizers A$8–A$9 (U.S. $6.40–U.S. $7.20); main courses A$16–A$18 (U.S. $12.80–U.S. $14.40); dollarwise set menus with various prices. AE, BC, DC, MC, V.

Open: Fri–Sat 24 hours, Sun–Tues noon–1am, Wed–Thurs noon–3am.

Chalky's is located in a pair of historic terrace houses in the Italian sector of Melbourne 1 kilometer (½ mile) from the CBD. The cozy decor in each of three dining areas is created by used-brick walls, wooden open-beam ceilings, and quarry-tile floors. The eatery feels a little like a wine cellar, which is appropos, since John Chalker is a wine expert and his list is extensive.

This is a spot you definitely don't want to miss. With his chef, Michael Sanz, "Chalky" challenges the local restaurant scene with his forward thinking. At one time only entrées (appetizers) were served, so patrons could sample many different flavors in one meal. (Thanks to reader Neal L. Rosenberg of New York for advising me that this had changed.) Now the menu, which is altered seasonally, is more traditional in format. Here are some of the treats that are offered: avocado topped with wafer-thin slices of sugar-cured Tasmanian salmon, virgin olive oil, and freshly cracked black peppercorns; barbecued quail marinated in champagne, five spices, and herbs; and steak-and-kidney pie—diced eye filet, mushrooms, onion, and kidney cooked in red wine and topped with pastry. All delicious. BYO and licensed.

LA SPAGHETTATA, 238 Lygon St., Carlton. Tel. 663-6102.

Cuisine: ITALIAN. **Reservations:** Recommended on weekends. **Transportation:** Bus no. 203 traveling north on Russell St. or tram no. 1, 15, 21, or 22 traveling north on Swanston St. (alight at stop 12).

$ **Prices:** Appetizers A$8.50–A$12.90 (U.S. $6.80–U.S. $10.35); main courses A$10.80–A$19.50 (U.S. $8.65–U.S. $15.60). AE, BC, DC, MC, V.

Open: Lunch daily noon–3pm; dinner daily 5–11pm or later.

The proprietors of La Spaghettata caught my attention with a boast printed on their napkins: "The best spaghetti house in Australia." The casual decor, including red-and-white-checked tablecloths and exposed-brick walls, made a good first impression. Outside seating under red, white, and green umbrellas, as well as the friendly and prompt service, also scored points. Sicilian-born proprietors Tony and Santino Cattafi stop at each table to chat with their patrons. The eatery is usually filled with the pleasantly noisy hum of happy diners, and it's easy to see that La Spaghettata is popular with locals, especially students from the nearby university.

Blackboards list specials and homemade desserts that are available in addition to regular menu items. All pasta is made on the premises and, the hosts claim, people come from all over to have the spaghetti marinara. I chose the spaghetti carbonara from the list of nearly two dozen pastas and thoroughly enjoyed it. Happily, I took the waitress's advice and ordered the generous entrée size instead of the huge main course. Chicken parmigiana or cacciatore, veal parmigiana or scaloppine, tournedos Rossini, and prime eye filet are also on the menu. Desserts include zabaglione freddo, profiteroles with hot chocolate sauce, and strawberries Romanoff. BYO.

FITZROY
MODERATE

AMBROSIA, 363 Brunswick St. Tel. 417-7415.
Cuisine: GREEK. **Reservations:** Advisable Thurs–Sat. **Transportation:** Tram no. 10 or 11 traveling east on Collins St.
$ Prices: Appetizers A$4–A$6.90 (U.S. $3.20–U.S. $5.55); main courses A$10.90–A$13.80 (U.S. $8.75–U.S. $11.05). BC, MC, V.
Open: Dinner daily 6:30pm–midnight.

No less than two dozen eateries line Brunswick Street in Fitzroy, which is Melbourne's newest trendy dining neighborhood. Unlike Lygon Street in Carlton where most spots serve Italian fare, Brunswick Street's offerings are definitely multiethnic. At Ambrosia, winner of the 1991 *Cheap Eats* Bent Fork Award, a clever trompe l'oeil creates the sense of being in a Greek café. Wooden chairs with hemp seats, wooden tables, the tile floor with mosaic border, and ceiling fans enhance the Mediterranean ambience. Patrons at the 15 or so tables can choose such traditional dishes as saganaki ("pan-fried sheep's cheese"), tzatziki (yogurt and cucumber dip), barbecued baby octopus, chicken souvlaki, Greek sausage, and baklava. Licensed and BYO.

ST. KILDA
MODERATE

JEAN-JACQUES BY-THE-SEA, 40 Jacka Blvd., St. Kilda. Tel. 534-8221.
Cuisine: FRENCH SEAFOOD. **Reservations:** Recommended, especially Fri–Saturday nights and Sun lunch. **Transportation:** Take tram no. 96 or 15 to Luna Park stop and walk toward the sea.
$ Prices: Appetizers A$9.50–A$15.50 (U.S. $7.60–U.S. $12.40); main courses A$16.50–A$32 (U.S. $13.20–U.S. $25.60). Set-price lunch or dinner: two courses A$19.50 (U.S. $15.60); three courses A$26 (U.S. $20.80). Snack menu: A$6.50–A$16.50 (U.S. $5.20–U.S. $13.20). 10% Sun surcharge. 15% public holiday surcharge. AE, BC, DC, MC, V.
Open: Lunch and dinner daily 11am–late; snacks Mon–Sat 11am–11pm, Sun 3–11pm.

Jean-Jacques By-the-Sea is literally a stone's throw from the beach in Melbourne's favorite seaside community. Inside dining in slightly art deco surroundings is possible 7 days a week year round. The informal, contemporary eatery is located in the former beach changing rooms, remodeled and refined by proprietors Jean-Jacques and Susan Lale-Demoz.

The cuisine is French with a strong emphasis on seafood. Oysters are the specialty of the house. You might also like to try escargots de mer (periwinkle snails with garlic butter), moules à la crème anisette (mussels cooked in white wine with a dash of Pernod), la chaudée de langouste (crayfish chowder with fresh fennel), or friture d'encornets (fresh calamari, deep-fried). The current favorite item is "Fondue Chinoise," which is a selection of the choicest fish and shellfish cooked in a court bouillon at the table.

If you're watching your pennies, **Jean-Jacques Bistro and Takeaway**, right on the water at the other end of the building, is a glorified fish-and-chips shop with outside dining. BYO. Très cheap.

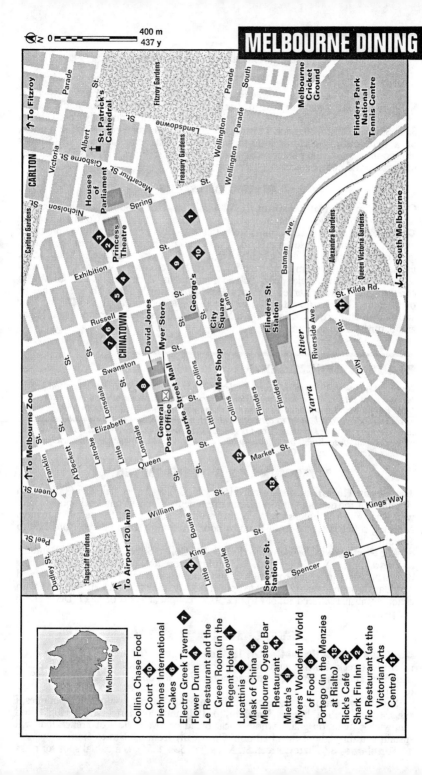

MELBOURNE DINING

400 m
437 y

To Fitzroy

CARLTON

Carlton Gardens

Fitzroy Gardens

St. Patrick's Cathedral

Houses of Parliament

Landsdowne

Treasury Gardens

Melbourne Cricket Ground

Flinders Park National Tennis Centre

Princess Theatre

CHINATOWN

George's

City Square

David Jones

Myer Store

Flinders St. Station

St. Kilda Rd.

Alexandra Gardens

Queen Victoria Gardens

To South Melbourne

To Melbourne Zoo

General Post Office

Bourke Street Mall

Met Shop

Yarra River

Riverside Ave.

Batman Ave.

Market St.

Kings Way

To Airport (20 km)

Flagstaff Gardens

Spencer St. Station

Collins Chase Food Court 10

Diethnes International Cakes 6

Electra Greek Tavern 7

Flower Drum 4

Le Restaurant and the Green Room (in the Regent Hotel) 1

Lucattinis 3

Mask of China 5

Melbourne Oyster Bar Restaurant 14

Mietta's 9

Myers' Wonderful World of Food 8

Portego (in the Menzies at Rialto) 13

Rick's Café 12

Shark Fin Inn 2

Vic Restaurant (at the Victorian Arts Centre) 11

Melbourne

SPECIALTY DINING
LATE-NIGHT

⭐ **Mietta's Lounge,** 7 Alfred Place (tel. 654-2366), is one floor below Mietta's, the deluxe restaurant described earlier. A cross between a salon and a central European coffeehouse, the lounge is a popular meeting spot daily from 11am to 3am. Since it is both a bar and a bistro, you could stop in for a cup of coffee, a drink, or a light meal. Great for after-theater dining. The entertainment on Sunday afternoons ranges from poetry readings to opera, and includes jazz, classical pianists, magicians, and comedy acts.

DINING CLUSTERS

One wouldn't normally think of a A$200-million (U.S. $160-million) hotel as the place to go for a budget bite, but it is in the case of the Hyatt on Collins's **Collins Chase Food Court,** 123 Collins Street (tel. 657-1234). For a minimum amount of money, you can purchase a variety of food items and enjoy them under the vaulted glass dome covering the 400-seat plaza area. **Perfect Balance** serves health food, including beverages from their fresh-juice bar; **Hanzleman's** will tempt you with Viennese pastries and cakes; **Mr. Tchoo** offers quality Asian fare, as does **Sushi Q;** can you guess what is served at **Fasta Pasta? Bloom's New York Deli** has its own seating. **The Lone Star Diner** also serves American food. The **Chase Bar** and **Galah Bar** provide drinks. Open Monday to Thursday 7am to midnight, Friday and Saturday 7am to 2am.

READERS RECOMMEND

Myers' Wonderful World of Food, Little Bourke St. (tel. 66-111) "The greatest food fest in Melbourne awaits you in a department store. Myers' Wonderful World of Food in the store on Little Bourke Street is a food lover's paradise where you can snack your way around the globe. Prices range from rock-bottom to astronomical. This gigantic bazaar is always mobbed, and since there are no tables or chairs, food is generally consumed on the spot. But don't be turned off by the madhouse. Brings bags, load up, and create your own banquet heaven elsewhere." —Connie Tonken, Hartford, Conn.

MORNING OR AFTERNOON TEA

The **Green Room,** in the Regent Hotel, 25 Collins Street (tel. 653-0000), is an elegant spot for morning or afternoon refreshments. Located one level aboveground with a view of the hotel's entrance, this is also a good place for people-watching. Morning coffee is served from 10am to noon; afternoon tea is offered from 2:30 to 5:30pm.

The **Portego,** in the Menzies at Rialto, 495 Collins Street (tel. 620-9111), and the **Lounge,** in the Windsor Hotel, 103 Spring Street (tel. 653-0653), are two other delightful spots in which to have a cuppa. Afternoon tea at the Windsor is served Monday through Saturday from 2 to 5pm and costs A$19 (U.S. $15.20). High tea with chamber music is offered Sunday from 2:30 to 5:30pm at a cost of A$27 (U.S. $21.60) per person.

LIGHT, CASUAL & FAST FOOD

Diethnes International Cakes, 185 Lonsdale Street (tel. 663-2092), is a wonderful little Greek bakery with seating where they sell incredible pastries, cakes, marzipan, and—my favorite—almond horseshoes. It's open 7 days a week from 9am to 1am.

Should you get hungry while shopping in South Yarra's fashionable boutiques, I suggest you grab a bite at **Traffles,** 311 Toorak Road (tel. 827-6046). Good sandwiches made on grainy whole-wheat bread or lovely slices of French loaf will sustain you throughout the afternoon. Open daily from 6:30am to 6pm.

Topolinos, 87 Fitzroy Street, St. Kilda (tel. 534-4856), is a casual spot for pizza and pasta. It's located near the red-light district, but because this is conservative Melbourne, you'll hardly notice. Open from 5pm to 5am Monday to Friday and 5pm to 6am Saturday and Sunday. Also does take-out and delivers.

A MOVABLE FEAST

THE COLONIAL TRAMCAR RESTAURANT. Tel. 696-4000 or 696-0374.
    Cuisine: INTERNATIONAL. **Reservations:** Reserve *well* ahead. After 6:30pm, call mobile phone (tel. 007/33-2900). **Transportation:** The tram departs from and returns to stop 12 on South Bank Blvd.
$ Prices: Luncheon four-course meal A$60 (U.S. $48); early dinner three-course meal A$50 (U.S. $40); late dinner five-course meal A$75 (U.S. $60). All drinks included.
    Open: Luncheon daily 1pm; early dinner daily 5:45pm; late dinner daily 8:30pm.
This is a way of combining good eating with an atmospheric ride around the city. The fully refurbished 1927 vehicle trundles along the tracks of Melbourne's scenic thoroughfares while guests enjoy Pullman-style silver service and champagne. Seats covered in plush velvet, warm light glowing from brass lamps, and fresh flowers help to transport diners to another era. Stabilizers ensure a smooth ride, and one-way windows have been installed so that the passing scenery can be enjoyed without the distraction of curious gazes.

    The multicourse menu changes regularly and includes a choice between two entrées, main courses, and desserts. For example, following an appetizer of duck-liver bigarade, you select either seafood en cocotte Matthew Flinders or Victoria broth for an entrée. The main offerings might be tenderloin of beef Sherwood or supreme of chicken colonial. A platter of Victorian cheeses is offered, followed by a choice of desserts such as apple crêpe Port Arthur or coupe kallista. Coffee, mints, and liqueurs are served at the end of the meal.

BREAKFAST/BRUNCH

    Rick's Caffé, 412 Collins Street between Queen and William streets (tel. 670-2280), presents a pleasant alternative to pricey hotel breakfasts. The Humphrey Bogart–Lauren Bacall poster at the entrance, the white cane furniture, and casual dusty rose and white decor set the scene for a relaxed and inexpensive meal. American pancakes cost A$2.90 (U.S. $2.35); eggs Benedict and omelets will set you back less than A$7 (U.S. $5.60). Rick's is open Monday through Friday from 7am to 4pm. In addition to breakfast, lunch is offered 11:30am to 3pm, and afternoon tea is served from 3 to 4pm.

5. MELBOURNE ATTRACTIONS

Visitors enjoy the conservative, almost old-world, ambience of the city while they ride trams and wander through leafy parks and gardens. This is also a good spot for serious shoppers, those who enjoy fine dining, and theater buffs. In between sightseeing excursions and shopping trips, be sure to allow time for a traditional afternoon tea.

SIGHTSEEING STRATEGIES

IF YOU HAVE 1 DAY

Start out at the National Gallery of Victoria, and then, if you're a theater buff, visit the nearby Performing Arts Museum. After lunch, do the walking tour suggested in this section and have afternoon tea at the Windsor Hotel. In the evening, travel to Phillip Island to see the fairy penguins.

IF YOU HAVE 2 DAYS

Day 1 as above, then on day 2 visit the Queen Victoria Market in the morning and the Melbourne Zoo in the afternoon. In the evening dine on Melbourne's tramcar restaurant or eat in one of the city's myriad ethnic dining spots.

IF YOU HAVE 3 DAYS

On the third day, do a day-trip to the Yarra Valley. Visit Healesville Sanctuary, have lunch at Fergusson's Winery, and stop for tasting at some of the other wineries in the area. This can be a self-drive excursion or you can join a coach tour.

IF YOU HAVE 4 DAYS OR MORE

On the fourth day, do an excursion to Queenscliff with a stop at the National Wool Museum in Geelong. If there's time, stop at historic Werribee Park on the way back.

THE TOP ATTRACTIONS

NATIONAL GALLERY OF VICTORIA, 180 St. Kilda Rd. Tel. 618-0222.

⭐ The National Gallery contains an excellent collection of Aboriginal, colonial Australian, Asian, and European works. Be sure not to miss Tom Roberts's *Shearing the Rams,* one of the best-known paintings of its period. Also look for Sidney Nolan's *Burke and Wills at the Gulf* and Arthur Streeton's *The Purple Noon's Transparent Might.* Frederick McCubbin and Russell Drysdale are also represented. For more information, The Gallery Shop sells a good selection of books about Australian art and artists. If you're fond of stained glass, note the ceiling in the Great Hall.

The Gallery Restaurant offers an à la carte menu. A kiosk sells snacks.

Admission: A$5 (U.S. $4) adults, A$2 (U.S. $1.60) children. Free tours conducted throughout the day (Mon 11am and 2pm; Tues–Fri 11am, noon, 1, 2, and 3pm; Sat–Sun 2 and 3pm).

Open: Daily 10am–5pm. **Closed:** Christmas Day and Good Friday. **Transportation:** Take any southbound tram on Swanston St. to stop 12.

RIPPON LEA, 192 Hotham St., Elsternwick. Tel. 523-9150.

Located in the suburb of Elsternwick 8 kilometers (5 miles) from the city center, Rippon Lea is a great Victorian house surrounded by 5.3 hectares (13 acres) of landscaped gardens. The first owner of the property was Sir Frederick Thomas Sargood, who started construction of the 15-room Romanesque-style house in 1868. By the time he died, in 1903, the mansion had grown to 33 rooms. In the 1930s the house underwent major alterations and a swimming pool and ballroom were added. Responsibility for Rippon Lea was assumed by the National Trust in 1974. While the house, with its polychrome brickwork, spacious rooms, and stained glass is interesting, it's the gardens that are most deserving of a visitor's attention. A fully restored conservatory, a lake, and a lookout tower are adjacent to a fernery, an orchard, and extensive flower and shrubbery displays.

The tearoom is open only on weekends, public holidays, and during school vacation periods.

Admission: A$6 (U.S. $4.80) adults, A$3 (U.S. $2.40) children.

Open: Daily 10am–5pm. Guided tours of house 11am–3pm. **Closed:** Christmas Day and Good Friday. **Transportation:** Bus no. 602 from corner of Latrobe and Elizabeth streets; get off at stop 45, or train to Rippon Lea Station (Sandringham Line) from Flinders Street Station platform 10/11, or tram no. 67 to stop 40 and walk up Hotham St.

PERFORMING ARTS MUSEUM, Victorian Arts Centre, 100 St. Kilda Rd. Tel. 617-8325.

If you're a theater buff, you'll enjoy the Performing Arts Museum located in the Concert Hall in the Victorian Arts Centre. The museum's collection includes costumes worn by Dame Nellie Melba; props and sets from various drama, dance,

MELBOURNE ATTRACTIONS

z 0   400 m / 437 y

To Fitzroy

CARLTON

CHINATOWN

Carlton Gardens

Parade

Albert St.

Victoria

Nicholson St.

Gisborne St.

Macarthur St.

Houses of Parliament

Princess Theatre

Exhibition St.

Russell St.

Swanston St.

David Jones

Myer Store

George's Lane

City Square

St. George's

Spring St.

Landsdowne

Wellington Parade

Wellington Parade South

Parade South

Fitzroy Gardens **9**

3

8

St. Patrick's Cathedral **7**

Treasury Gardens

Melbourne Cricket Ground

Flinders Park National Tennis Centre

Batman Ave.

Alexandra Gardens

Queen Victoria Gardens

St. Kilda Rd.

4

5

To South Melbourne

Riverside Ave.

City Rd.

River

Yarra

Flinders St. Station

Collins St.

Little Collins St.

Flinders St.

Flinders St.

Market St.

Kings Way

Spencer St. Station

Spencer St.

Met Shop **6**

General Post Office

Bourke Street Mall

Elizabeth St.

Lonsdale St.

Latrobe St.

A'Beckett St.

Little Lonsdale St.

Queen St.

William St.

King St.

Little Bourke St.

Bourke St.

Bourke St.

Franklin St.

Queen St.

Peel St.

Dudley St.

Flagstaff Gardens

To Melbourne Zoo

2

1

To Airport (20 km)

Melbourne

Bourke Street Mall **6**
Cook's Cottage **3**
Fitzroy Gardens **9**
Museum of Victoria **2**
National Gallery of Victoria **5**
Queen Victoria Market **1**
St. Patrick's Cathedral **7**
Treasury Gardens **8**
Victorian Arts Centre (includes Performing Arts Centre) **4**

and music performances; artistic show posters; and other sight-and-sound displays that permit insight into the world of entertainment.

The Treble Clef Coffee Shop is next door to the museum.

Admission: A$2.50 (U.S. $2) adults, A$1.30 (U.S. $1.05) children.

Open: Mon–Fri 11am–5pm, Sat–Sun noon–5pm. **Transportation:** Any southbound tram on Swanston St. to stop 12.

THE MUSEUM OF VICTORIA, corner of Latrobe and Russell Sts. Tel. 669-9888.

Included in this museum are exhibits relating to natural history, science, technology, sociology, and astronomy. The pièce de résistance is Phar Lap, Australia's most famous racehorse, whose stuffed body is on view.

Admission: A$3 (U.S. $2.40) adults, A$1 (U.S. 80¢) children.

Open: Daily 10am–5pm. **Transportation:** Any northbound tram on Swanston St. to Latrobe St.; walk across Swanston St. Or take any train on the City Loop to Museum Station.

MELBOURNE ZOO, Elliott Ave., Parkville. Tel. 347-1522.

Opened in 1862, the Royal Melbourne Zoological Gardens is one of the oldest and finest in the world, with over 3,000 animals housed in natural surroundings. Of most interest to overseas visitors are the native fauna, including koalas, kangaroos, wallabies, wombats, emus, and so forth. The Platypusary provides a good look at one of Oz's stranger natives, and the walk-through Butterfly House is also of particular importance. If you go to the zoo, take time to look at the Gorilla Rainforest exhibit, the rare snow leopards, and the Syrian bears. The underwater seal viewing and arboreal primates exhibits are other highlights.

Two licensed restaurants and several take-out facilities offer meals and snacks.

Admission: A$10 (U.S. $8) adults, A$5 (U.S. $4) children 4–14.

Open: Daily 9am–5pm. Free guided tours available 10am–3pm weekdays and 11am–4pm weekends. **Transportation:** Mon–Sat tram no. 55 or 56 traveling north on William St. to stop 23; Sun, tram no. 68 traveling north on Elizabeth St. to stop 23.

MORE ATTRACTIONS
PARKS & GARDENS

Be sure to visit at least one of Melbourne's parks and gardens. The **Royal Botanic Gardens,** 2 kilometers (1 mile) south of the city off St. Kilda Road (tel. 655-2341), is best for serious green thumbs who want to see a variety of plant life, most of it identified with labels. The gardens are landscaped with sweeping lawns and ornamental lakes, which make them a pleasant place for strolling. Free guided walks leave from the Visitor Centre Sunday and Tuesday to Friday at 10 and 11am. The botanic garden's kiosk serves Devonshire teas. To get there, catch a tram on route 8 traveling south on St. Kilda Road and alight at stop 21.

Nearby in **King's Domain,** you can visit **Latrobe's Cottage** (tel. 654-5528), Victoria's first Government House. The cottage was built in England and brought out by ship in 1839. It's owned by the National Trust; admission is A$4 (U.S. $3.20) for adults and A$3 (U.S. $2.40) for children. The cottage is closed on Friday and open 11am to 4:30pm other days. Just across Birdwood Avenue, the **Shrine of Remembrance,** which honors Australia's fallen soldiers of World Wars I and II, Korea, and Vietnam, provides a good view of the city. From the top of the steps you can see right up Swanston Street to the landmark CUB (Carlton United Breweries) sign at the north edge of town. King's Domain is stop 12 on a route 15 tram traveling south down St. Kilda Road.

Treasury Gardens with its lush lawns, lies to the east of the central business district. **A memorial to John F. Kennedy** is located next to the lake. **Cook's Cottage,** built in 1755, is in **Fitzroy Gardens** off Wellington Parade (tel. 419-8742). The tiny bungalow was transported from the village of Great Ayton, England, in 1934 to mark Victoria's centenary, but today researchers have raised doubt about whether the English explorer ever actually lived in it. Admission is

A$2.50 (U.S. $2) for adults and A$1.20 (U.S. $1) for children. It's open daily from 9am to 5pm. Treasury Gardens and Fitzroy Gardens can be reached by a route 75 tram traveling east along Flinders Street. Alight at stop 14 for Treasury Gardens and at stop 14A for Fitzroy Gardens.

TOURS

Local organized tours are offered by several companies including **Melbourne Sightseeing** (tel. 670-9706), **AAT King's** (tel. 650-1244), and **Australian Pacific Tours** (tel. 650-1511).

WALKING TOUR — The East End of the CBD

Start: On Collins Street at Spring Street.
Finish: On Little Collins at Spring Street.
Time: Allow approximately 1 hour, not including shopping stops.
Best Times: Monday through Friday.
Worst Times: Weekends, when the CBD is deserted.

Don your Reeboks and see the city on foot, starting at the top of Collins Street, Melbourne's most interesting thoroughfare. Begin at:

1. **The elegant Old Treasury Building,** at the intersection of Spring and Collins streets, dating from 1857. The impressive neoclassic structure is built of brick and bluestone and faced with freestone. As you walk down Collins, the classy:

2. **Regent Hotel** (see "Melbourne Accommodations," above) is on your left, and the:

3. **Melbourne Club,** a bastion of conservatism, is on your right. Continue downhill past the fashionable boutiques that give this area the name "the Paris end of Collins Street." On the corner of Russell and Collins, note the large:

4. **Uniting Church and the Scots Church,** both very pretty. The Scots Church, built in 1841, was originally quite plain; however, when gold-rush money poured into the city 10 years later, the church acquired Gothic trimmings.

5. **Georges Department Store,** 162-168 Collins Street, is a Melbourne institution and, some say, Australia's most elegant department store. Even if you don't want to shop, this posh pit stop is handy to keep in mind. In addition to the necessary plumbing fixtures, the second-floor women's rest room has a diaper-changing room, telephones on which you can make local calls free of charge, and comfy couches. If you're hungry or thirsty, there's a charmingly staid tearoom on the third floor. Turn right as you come out of Georges and you'll see the:

6. **Baptist Church,** which dates from 1845.

7. **The Town Hall** (1867), on Collins and Swanston, and:

8. **St. Paul's Cathedral** (1891), 1 block to the south, provide a sharp contrast to the modern:

9. **City Square** between them. Waterfalls, canopies, flowers, and periodic free concerts make this a popular place for brown-bagging office workers. Continue down Collins Street and turn right into the:

10. **Block Arcade** (1892). Pause to admire its intricate mosaic floor and high domed ceiling before crossing Little Collins Street. Enter the:

11. **Royal Arcade** and wait just inside to see the mythical figures Gog and Magog (inside the dome) strike the hour. Walk north and you will emerge on the:

12. **Bourke Street Mall** just opposite the huge Myer department store. If you passed up the pit stop at Georges, David Jones has a nice women's lounge on the third floor. Keep your wits about you in the *pedestrian* mall, because trams run down the middle of it. At the east end of the mall, turn left onto Swanston Street and then right onto Little Bourke Street. You'll find yourself in the midst of colorful:

13. **Chinatown.** Walk east to Spring Street and turn right. Pause to admire the handsome:

14. State Parliament House, which dates from 1856. Guided tours are conducted Monday through Friday when the House is not sitting; phone 651-8362 for information.

REFUELING STOP If you're ready for a cup of tea or something stronger at this point, I suggest you take yourself to the wonderful **15. Windsor Hotel,** which faces Spring Street between Bourke and Little Collins. They've been pampering the city's weary visitors since 1883. (See "Melbourne Dining," above, for information.)

---

6. MELBOURNE SPORTS & RECREATION

SPECTATOR SPORTS

Cricket During November through March, everyone's attention turns to cricket and tennis. For on-the-spot insight into cricket, tour the **Melbourne Cricket Ground** and its large collection of memorabilia. The MCG's museum contains trophies, stamps, and postcards commemorating great batsmen, bats signed by victorious teams, pennants, famous players' old equipment, and so forth. The Australian Gallery of Sport and Olympic Museum, which includes portraits of well-known teams and players, is also located at the Melbourne Cricket Ground. The gallery is open daily from 10am to 4pm (tel. 654-8922). Admission costs A$5 (U.S. $4) for adults and A$2 (U.S. $1.60) for children. Guided tours of the MCG complex, Brunton Avenue, are available (tel. 650-3001). To get there, take tram no. 48 or 65 to the Hilton Hotel and walk across the park to the members' entrance.

Football Melburnians love their spectator sports, especially **Aussie Rules football,** which reigns supreme from late March to September. The **Victorian Football League's** season ends with the **Grand Final,** sort of a Super Bowl down under. For an estimated 65% of the four million people in the state of Victoria and thousands more from interstate, Grand Final day—the last Saturday in September—is not simply the climax of the Victorian Football League's season, it is the high point of the year.

Horse Racing Horse racing is a year-round passion. The **Melbourne Cup,** the country's richest race, is run on the first Tuesday in November. The **Victorian Racing Museum,** dedicated to the history of horse racing in Australia, is located at the **Caulfield Racecourse.** It contains racing trophies, paintings, photographs, saddles, silks, and even scales. The museum is open Tuesday and Thursday and on race days from 10am to 4pm or by appointment (tel. 572-1111).

Tennis The **Australian Open Tennis Tournament** is played at the **Flinders Park National Tennis Centre,** on Batman Avenue (tel. 655-1244), each January. The A$70-million (U.S. $56-million) complex, built in 1987, has a retractable roof over center court for all-weather play. Guided tours, which cost A$3 (U.S. $2.40) for adults and A$1.50 (U.S. $1.20) for children, are offered Tuesday through Friday from April through September.

RECREATION

Bicycling Extensive bike paths wind through the city and suburbs. Many bookstores sell *Melbourne Bike Tours,* which is published by the **State Bicycle Committee** (tel. 60-2315), and describes 20 of the most popular routes. You can rent a bike from one of the **Hire a Bicycle** rental stores (tel. 801-2156) Monday to Friday 11am to 5pm and on weekends from 10am to 5pm. Costs are A$4 (U.S. $3.20) for a

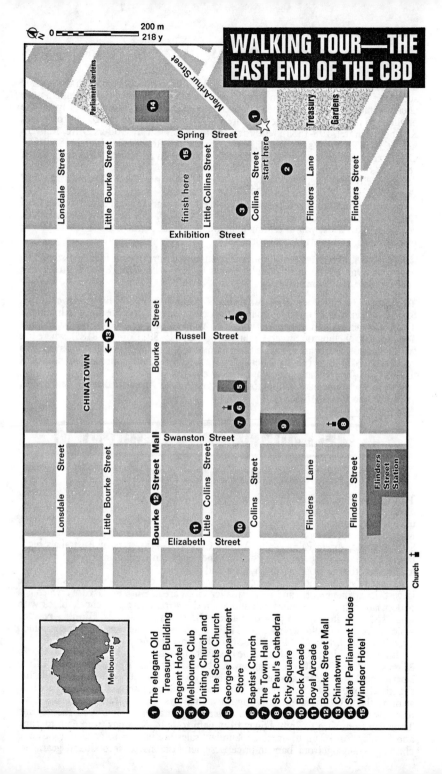

WALKING TOUR—THE EAST END OF THE CBD

0   200 m
     218 y

Parliament Gardens

MacArthur Street

Treasury Gardens

1 start here

Spring Street

15

Lonsdale Street

Little Bourke Street

finish here

Little Collins Street

Collins Street

2

Flinders Lane

Flinders Street

3

Exhibition Street

Bourke Street

4

Russell Street

13

CHINATOWN

5

6

7   9

8

Swanston Street

Bourke 12 Street Mall

Little Bourke Street

Little Collins Street

Collins Street

Flinders Lane

Flinders Street

Flinders Street Station

Lonsdale Street

11

10

Elizabeth Street

Church

Melbourne

1 The elegant Old Treasury Building
2 Regent Hotel
3 Melbourne Club
4 Uniting Church and the Scots Church
5 Georges Department Store
6 Baptist Church
7 The Town Hall
8 St. Paul's Cathedral
9 City Square
10 Block Arcade
11 Royal Arcade
12 Bourke Street Mall
13 Chinatown
14 State Parliament House
15 Windsor Hotel

half hour, A$5.50 (U.S. $4.40) for 1 hour, A$9 (U.S. $7.20) for 2 hours, and A$16 (U.S. $12.80) for a full day.

Golf   The city's best-known course, **Royal Melbourne,** is located in the bayside suburb of Black Rock, 24 kilometers (15 miles) from the center of town. This is a posh enclave, but if you're a member of an equally elite club at home, you may get the privilege to play. Other notable links are **Keysborough Golf Club,** Hutton Road, Keysborough (tel. 798-1333); **Malvern Valley Golf Club,** Golfers Drive, Malvern (tel. 563-1877); and **Yarra Bend Park,** Yarra Bend Road, Fairfield (tel. 481-0171). Greens fees are about A$10 (U.S. $8); club rental is an additional A$10 (U.S. $8). If you need further information, contact the **Australian Golf Union,** 155 Cecil Street, South Melbourne (tel. 699-7944), or the **Victorian Golf Association,** 17 Bardolph Street, Burwood (tel. 889-6731).

Several companies specialize in personalized golf tours to local clubs. **Koala Golf Day,** 125 Beach Road, Sandringham (tel. 598-2574), can help you decide which course to play, assist you in renting equipment, obtain permission for you to play at private clubs, and provide transportation.

Jogging & Walking   Melbourne's parks and gardens are ideal for stretching your legs. One of the most popular places is the 4-kilometer (2½-mile) track that encircles **King's Domain.**

Tennis   The **Flinders Park National Tennis Centre,** on Batman Avenue (tel. 655-1244), with its 20 courts is open to the public when it isn't hosting a tournament. They rent rackets and shoes. You may also want to play at **Collingwood Indoor Tennis,** 100 Wellington Street, Collingwood (tel. 419-8911 or 419-8185), where five synthetic grass courts are available from 6am to midnight. Court rental costs A$18 to A$30 (U.S. $14.40 to U.S. $24) per hour. Rackets, balls, and shoes are an extra A$4 (U.S. $3.20). The sauna and spa are free of charge.

For further information, contact the **Lawn Tennis Association of Australia,** St. Kilda Road (tel. 510-3137).

7. MELBOURNE SAVVY SHOPPING

THE SHOPPING SCENE

Throughout Australia, people talk about Melbourne as being *the* place to shop. The number and variety of its stores are renowned. However, in terms of the items visitors usually seek, namely gifts and souvenirs, it probably isn't any better than Sydney. Melbourne's specialty is designer clothing. Perri Cutten, Trent Nathan, Prue Acton, Sally Browne, Adele Palmer, and Anthea Crawford—the stars of Australia's high-fashion scene—all operate boutiques in the Victorian capital, many of which are located on Toorak Road in South Yarra and Toorak.

The city's main shopping area, however, is in the central business district. The largest department stores and many smaller shops are in **Bourke Street,** which is a pedestrian mall between Elizabeth and Swanston streets. Arcades, chockablock with small specialty stores, also provide interest. Be sure to notice the **Block Arcade,** which runs from **Collins Street** to **Little Collins,** and the **Royal Arcade,** which stretches from **Little Collins Street** to the **Bourke Street Mall.**

Like other cities in Oz, Melbourne has its share of markets. The **Queen Victoria Market** (tel. 658-9800), covering several blocks between **Peel, Victoria, Elizabeth,** and **Therry streets** on the northern edge of the city center, is a wonderful, slightly chaotic feast for the senses. Wares of every kind, plus fresh produce, are sold at more than 600 stalls. You can buy souvenirs, toys, clothes, furniture, bric-a-brac, leatherware, all kinds of food—almost everything imaginable. It is open Tuesday and Thursday from 6am to 2pm, Friday from 6am to 6pm, Saturday from 6am to 1pm, and Sunday from 9am to 4pm. On Sunday, sales are limited to general goods and clothing—ranging from bargain-price designer fashions to secondhand gear. Get there on a route 55 tram traveling north along William Street. Alight at stop 13. Or take any northbound tram on Elizabeth Street; alight at Victoria Street corner.

You might also like to browse through the **Art and Craft Market,** held on the St. Kilda Esplanade, St. Kilda, on Sunday from 9am to 4pm.

At the **Jam Factory,** 500 Chapel Street, South Yarra (tel. 826-0537), 55 specialty shops are ensconced in historic bluestone buildings.

SHOPPING A TO Z
ABORIGINAL ARTIFACTS & CRAFTS

Aboriginal Handcrafts, located at 125-133 Swanston Street on the ninth floor (tel. 650-4717), is the place to go if you're looking for boomerangs, bark paintings, carvings, didgeridoos, and so forth. Open Monday to Thursday from 10am to 4:30pm and Fri from 10am to 5pm, this shop is largely run by volunteers, and profits are used to meet the needs of Aboriginal people.

BOOKS

Hill of Content Bookshop, a member of the Collins Booksellers Group, at 86 Bourke Street (tel. 654-3144), has a good selection. Open daily, except public holidays. Other **Collins Bookshops** are located at 115 Elizabeth Street and 401 Swanston Street.

CRAFTS

⭐ **The Meat Market Craft Centre,** 42 Courtney Street (corner of Blackwood), North Melbourne (tel. 329-9966), is really a former meat market that has been converted into a center where craftspeople can work and sell their wares. This is an excellent place to buy high-quality Australian handcrafts, including ceramics, leather, glass, metal, textiles, and wood. Rotating exhibits focus on particular talents. Go Monday through Friday if you want to watch artisans at work. These include a bookbinder, milliner, jeweler, silk printer, and basket weaver. This special place is open Tuesday through Sunday from 10am to 5pm.

DEPARTMENT STORES

Myer, 314 Little Bourke Street (tel. 066-111), is the nation's biggest department store, and **David Jones,** 310 Bourke Street, also has an ample selection. Collins Street hosts **Georges Department Store,** 162 Collins Street, a posh place popular with suburban matrons (the ones who wouldn't consider coming into town without their hats and white gloves). Because of the number of exclusive boutiques, the eastern portion of this attractive avenue is known as "the Paris end."

DUTY FREE

Downtown Duty Free, 128 Exhibition Street (tel. 650-3258 or 663-3144), sells the usual range of duty-free items—Cartier watches to Sony cameras and Kodak film to Wild Turkey bourbon. Downtown also has stores on Collins Street and Swanston Street. Open Monday to Saturday.

FASHIONS

If you're in the market for a Driza-bone coat or an Akubra hat, try **Thomas Cook,** 60 Hoddle Street, Abbotsford (tel. 416-1333), or **Morrisons,** 462 Chapel Street, South Yarra (tel. 241-8255), or **R. M. Williams,** Shop 3, State Bank Galleria, Elizabeth Street (tel. 670-7400).

The following shops sell designer clothing: **JAG** (Adele Palmer), 459 Toorak

Road, Toorak (tel. 241-2301), and the New Dendy Centre, 26 Church Street, Brighton (tel. 592-0396); **Sue Grant,** 60 Church Street, Brighton (tel. 59-2022); **Sally Browne,** 27 Toorak Road, South Yarra, and 207 Bridge Road, Richmond (tel. 427-0166); **Trent Nathan,** 68 Toorak Road, South Yarra (tel. 867-5515), and 1080 High Street, Armadale, (tel. 500-0822); **Anthea Crawford,** 1071 High Street, Armadale (tel. 824-7765); and **Perri Cutten,** 1083 High Street, Armadale (tel. 822-3984).

If you decide to wander down Toorak Road, Toorak, check out the **Liz Davenport** shop on the corner of Tintern Avenue; as you walk east there's **Crabtree & Evelyn, Sports Image, Benetton,** and **Henry Buck's** (men's clothes). Cross the street at Grange Road and take a look in **Sports Girl.**

The **Como Centre** on the corner of Toorak Road and Chapel Street in South Yarra has a **Done Art & Design, Pierre Cardin, Morrisons,** and many others. Another 55 specialty stores are steps away in the **Jam Factory** on Chapel Street.

In addition to these retail shops, factory outlets are also dotted around the city. Since these tend to change location and open and close faster than you can say "such a deal," I recommend that dedicated bargain hunters sign up with a pro. **Pamm's Shopping Tours,** 10 St. Andrews Street, Brighton (tel. 592-6555), or **Melbourne's Shopping Tours,** 9 Tennyson Street, Richmond (tel. 428-2007), will get you where you want to go.

FOOD

Acland Street, St. Kilda, is renowned for its number of cake shops. Since many of these are owned by European Jewish immigrants, many foreign languages are heard throughout the neighborhood. Stroll down **Lygon Street** in Carlton if you like Italian sights and sounds. Several shops sell foodstuffs.

GIFTS & SOUVENIRS

The **Australian General Store,** 1227 High Street, Armadale (tel. 822-2324), and at Collins Place, 45 Collins Street (tel. 650-2075), and **Mainly Australian,** in the Royal Arcade (tel. 654-5919), both have a good selection. In addition, you should look at **Yarrandoo Souvenirs and Native Art,** Shop 11, 147 Exhibition Street (tel. 650-2461), and Shop 8, Collins Place, 45 Collins Street (tel. 650-2050). The Collins Street location is open Monday through Friday from 9am to 6pm, Saturday from 9am to 4:30pm, and Sunday from 10am to 3pm. Yarrandoo specializes in Aboriginal craft items, but also sells other souvenirs and gifts. The **National Trust Shop,** at Rippon Lea, 192 Hotham Street, Elsternwick (tel. 532-8298), also has nice things.

JEWELRY

Gemtec Australia, third floor, 136 Exhibition Street (tel. 654-5733), and **V. F. Trainor & Sons,** third floor, 289 Flinders Lane (tel. 654-8361 and 650-2129), both sell opals.

However, the most interesting place to shop for these stones is **Altmann & Cherny,** corner of Little Collins and Exhibition streets (tel. 650-9685). They are open from 9am to 5:30pm Monday through Friday and from 9am to 2pm Saturday and have a large selection of opal jewelry. Mr. Cherny travels to Coober Pedy and Lightning Ridge, where he buys rough-cut opals which he makes into jewelry. Even if you don't want to shop, stop in and look at "Olympic Australis"—the largest precious-gem opal in the world. It was found in Coober Pedy, South Australia, in 1956 and is valued at over A\$2 million (U.S. \$1.6 million). It weighs 3,540 grams and is listed in the *Guinness Book of World Records.* Altmann & Cherny also cut and supplied the Andamooka opal presented to Queen Elizabeth II in 1954.

SHEEPSKIN PRODUCTS

Victoria's Farm Shed is your best bet. (See comments below under "Easy Excursions From Melbourne.")

8. MELBOURNE EVENING ENTERTAINMENT

THE ENTERTAINMENT SCENE

Melbourne offers a variety of nightlife options, ranging from hot discos to high-quality performing arts. The best source of current what's-on information is the "EG," the "Entertainment Guide" included in *The Age* each Friday.

Half-price day-of-performance tickets can be purchased for live entertainment events, including dance, drama, and opera, at the **Half-Tix Kiosk** in the Bourke Street Mall (tel. 650-9420 and 649-8888). The booth is open Monday from 10am to 2pm, Tuesday to Thursday from 11am to 6pm, Friday from 11am to 6:30pm, and Saturday from 10am to 2pm. Tickets must be paid for in cash.

THE PERFORMING ARTS

MAJOR MULTIPURPOSE PERFORMANCE & CONCERT HALLS

VICTORIAN ARTS CENTRE, 100 St. Kilda Rd. Tel. 684-8484 or 11-500 for ticket purchase.

The three theaters and the Concert Hall of the Victorian Arts Centre on the south bank of the Yarra River are the focal point of the city's cultural life. The **State Theatre** seats 2,079 people on three levels. The motorized stage is large enough for elaborate productions of opera, ballet, musical comedy, or variety. The Australian Ballet Company, Australian Opera Company, Victoria State Opera, and many visiting companies perform here. The **Playhouse,** which seats 888, is designed for drama productions and is used most of the year by the Melbourne Theatre Company. The **George Fairfax Studio,** accommodating 420, is a multipurpose auditorium with flexible seating. It is used for experimental theater and late-night cabaret.

A 115-meter (380 ft.) spire on top of the **Theatres Building,** open since 1984, makes it the city's most identifiable landmark. Likewise, the round shape of the adjacent **Melbourne Concert Hall,** which opened 2 years earlier, makes it easy to spot. The excellent acoustics of this large hall, seating 2,677, are created by 30 Plexiglas shells suspended above the stage and 22 wool banners hanging along the walls on both sides. The Melbourne Symphony Orchestra and the State Orchestra of Victoria, as well as visiting orchestras, play in the Concert Hall. Luciano Pavarotti, Joan Sutherland, and Isaac Stern have also performed here.

Overseas visitors can make reservations for "An Evening at the Victorian Arts Centre" by contacting **ATS/Sprint** (tel. toll free 800/232-2121 in California, 800/423-2880 in the rest of the U.S.). The "Evening," offered Monday through Friday, includes a guided tour of the center, pretheater dinner with wine in the Vic Restaurant and the performance of your choice. (For details of the Vic Restaurant, see "Melbourne Dining," above.) The cost ranges from U.S. $71 to U.S. $126 per person, depending on what type of performance is selected. Other options, available Monday through Saturday, include dinner and a show, a show and supper, or champagne and chocolates at the interval. The standard booking fee is U.S. $12. Reservations can be made up to 12 months in advance.

Tours: Guided 1-hour tours of the theaters and Concert Hall and their adjacent foyers are offered Sun–Fri at noon and 2:30pm. These cost A$4 (U.S. $3.20) Mon–Fri and A$4.50 (U.S. $3.60) Sun and public holidays. Backstage tours, available Sun at 12:15 and 2:15pm, cost A$9 (U.S. $7.20). Children under 12 aren't allowed on the backstage tour. Phone 684-8151 9:30am–5pm for further information.

Prices: Ticket prices for shows in the State Theatre A$40–A$73 (U.S. $32–U.S. $58.40); in the Playhouse A$30–A$35 (U.S. $24–U.S. $28); in the Studio A$15–A$20 (U.S. $12–U.S. $16); in the Concert Hall A$35–A$40 (U.S. $28–U.S. $32).

THEATERS

ATHENAEUM THEATRE, 188 Collins St. Tel. 650-3504 or 650-1500 for tickets.
This building dates from the 1880s, and is currently undergoing renovation to return it to its original appearance. The theater opened in 1924 and was, at one time, a cinema. The 884 seats are arranged on three levels. Performances vary from drama to musical theater—and often include Shakespeare.
Prices: A$16–A$40 (U.S. $12.80–U.S. $32).

COMEDY THEATRE, 240 Exhibition St. Tel. 662-2222 or 662-2644 for tickets.
The Comedy Theatre opened in 1928, but there's been a theater on this site since the founding of Melbourne. The theater, with 1,008 seats, has an intimate feel and a Spanish rococco–influenced architecture. The wooden beam ceiling is original. Musicals and plays are the normal fare, although comedians and dances companies do sometime rent the theater for their performances.
Prices: A$30–A$44 (U.S. $24–U.S. $35.20).

HER MAJESTY'S THEATRE, 219 Exhibition St. Tel. 663-3211.
The original theater on this site, built in 1886, burned in 1928. Her Majesty's as it is today is a combination of the original Victorian front, saved from the fire, and the art deco interior from the 1934 rebuilding. This is a large venue—1,600 seats— usually used for short-run musicals. *Cats*, which ran for 12 months in 1988, was the last big success.
Prices: Tickets vary depending on show.

THE MALTHOUSE, 113 Sturt St., South Melbourne. Tel. 685-5111.
The Malthouse is a relatively new theater complex comprised of The Merlyn (maximum 500 seats) and The Beckett (maximum 200 seats) theaters. It is the home of The Playbox Theatre Centre of Monash University, a theatrical production company. This group's primary artistic focus is on contemporary Australian theater.
Prices: A$18–A$28 (U.S. $14.40–U.S. $22.40).

THE PRINCESS THEATRE, 163 Spring St. Tel. 639-0022 or 663-3300 to purchase tickets.
This lovely Victorian theater is currently hosting Andrew Lloyd Webber's *The Phantom of the Opera* and will continue to do so through the end of 1992 or early 1993. The all-Australian cast has received rave reviews and drawn an audience from across Australia and New Zealand. The 1,471-seat theater, designed by well-known colonial architect William Pitt, opened December 18, 1886. It was first renovated in 1922, and was overhauled again in 1989 prior to the opening of *Les Misérables*. It has a dramatic marble staircase, beautiful murals on an ornate plaster ceiling, and a stained-glass window that dates from 1901.
Prices: *Phantom* tickets cost A$20–A$60 (U.S. $16–U.S. $48). The booking office is open Mon–Sat 9am–6pm. Visitors without tickets to this sold-out show can queue for returns prior to the performance; however, if you want to be sure to get a seat, I strongly suggest purchasing tickets well ahead of time.

RUSSELL STREET THEATRE, 19 Russell St. Tel. 654-4000.
This 394-seat proscenium-arch theater is the home of the Melbourne Theatre Company (M.T.C.). Live theater was established here in 1953.
Prices: Ticket prices A$23–A$29 (U.S. $18.40–U.S. $23.20).

SIDNEY MYER MUSIC BOWL, King's Domain, Alexandra Ave. Tel. 617-8360 or 617-8211.
This venue is a huge outdoor entertainment area used for opera, jazz, and ballet in warm months and ice skating in the winter. It was presented to the people of Melbourne in 1959 by the Sidney Myer Charity Trust at the request of Mrs. Sidney Myer, widow of the founder of Australia's biggest department store. In 1980, it was handed over to the control of the Victorian Arts Centre Trust.
Prices: Vary according to the performance.

ST. MARTIN'S YOUTH ARTS CENTRE, 44 St. Martin's Lane, South Yarra. Tel. 867-2477.

Established in 1956, St. Martin's is a venue for live productions by and for young people. The Irene Mitchell Studio seats 80; the Randall Theatre has a capacity of 350.
Prices: Ticket prices vary.

THE CLUB & MUSIC SCENE
COMEDY CLUBS/CABARET

THE LAST LAUGH COMEDY ZOO/LE JOKE, 64 Smith St., Collingwood. Tel. 419-8600.

⭐ The Last Laugh Theatre Restaurant is one of the original comedy clubs in Melbourne and features the best new wave, contemporary, and cabaret acts. It is open Tuesday through Saturday most of the year and nightly during November and December. Dinner is served at 7:30pm; the show starts at 9pm. Le Joke, upstairs, is open only Friday and Saturday nights. Dinner at 7pm; shows at 8:30pm and midnight.

Admission: Le Joke, dinner and show A$28–A$32 (U.S. $22.40–U.S. $25.60), show only A$15 (U.S. $12). The Last Laugh, dinner and show A$37–A$42 (U.S. $29.60–U.S. $33.60), show only A$20–A$22 (U.S. $16–U.S. $17.60). Tues half-price dinner and show (A$17/U.S. $13.60). Special offer to readers of *Frommer's Australia*: 20% off dinner-and-show price Wed–Thurs (excluding Nov–Dec).

CRAZY HOUSE, 169 Exhibition St. Tel. 663-2566.

This cabaret restaurant opens Tuesday through Saturday nights at 6:30pm. The admission charge includes dinner, a show, and dancing afterward. The show starts at 7pm.

Admission: A$32–A$37 (U.S. $25.60–U.S. $29.60).

THE COMEDY CLUB, in the Hilton Hotel, 192 Wellington Parade, East Melbourne. Tel. 419-3311.

Comedy and cabaret acts appear here Wednesday through Saturday. The doors open at 7:30pm; the acts start at 8:30pm. There are music videos and dancing after the show. Closes at 1am.

Admission: A$15 (U.S. $12) cover charge.

COCKTAIL LOUNGES

GREEN ROOM, in the Regent Hotel, 25 Collins St. Tel. 653-0000.

The Green Room has comfortable lounge furnishings and is an ideal place for pre- and posttheater imbibing. Located on the lobby level, one floor aboveground, the Green Room serves drinks and light suppers until 1am during the week and until 3am on Friday and Saturday. A pianist plays soothing music after 8pm.

The hotel's **Black Swan Bar** on the same level is a sophisticated spot specializing in vintage champagnes and still wines. It's open Monday through Saturday from 5pm to midnight. The **Atrium** and the adjacent **Piano Bar** on the 35th floor provide other options.

THE PORTEGO, in the Menzies at Rialto, 495 Collins St. Tel. 620-9111.

The Portego is a picturesque courtyard with an atrium-style roof joining the historic Rialto and Winfield buildings. Cocktails are served from noon to midnight or later.

MIETTA'S LOUNGE, 7 Alfred Place. Tel. 654-2366.

⭐ Mietta's Lounge (see "Specialty Dining," above) is popular with show-biz types and the after-theater crowd. The Victorian drawing-room decor creates a pleasant environment for drinks and good conversation, and is open from 11am to 3am. On Sunday afternoon literary, theatrical, and musical events are scheduled. Phone or look in the "EG" to see what's on while you're in town.

DANCE CLUBS/DISCOS

King Street is nightclub row in Melbourne.

LAZAR MELBOURNE, 240 King St. Tel. 602-1822.

Open Wednesday to Sunday, this is one of Melbourne's most popular dance spots catering to a well-dressed over-25 crowd. A maximum of 2,000 merrymakers can be accommodated on three floors of what was once a warehouse. Live music is offered Friday, Saturday, and Sunday nights. In addition to the disco areas, there's also a piano bar. Dinner is offered 7 to 10:30pm; supper 10:30pm to late.

Admission: Wed free, Thurs and Sun A$5 (U.S. $4), Fri–Sat A$14 (U.S. $11.20). Restaurant patrons get free entry to disco any night.

MONSOON'S INTERNATIONAL NIGHTCLUB, in the Hyatt on Collins, 123 Collins St. Tel. 657-1234.

Open Thursday through Saturday night from 9pm to 3am, Monsoon's attracts a cross section of well-heeled patrons. These include visitors and locals who are members of this upmarket nightclub. The glittery Asian decor includes works of art commissioned in Tokyo. Snacks and supper are offered, as well as a full range of beverages.

Admission: Thurs A$8 (U.S. $6.40), Fri A$12 (U.S. $9.60), Sat A$15 (U.S. $12). The admission charge is waived for house guests.

BOBBY MCGEE'S ENTERTAINMENT LOUNGE, in the Bryson Hotel, 186 Exhibition St. Tel. 662-0511.

Located upstairs of the popular Bobby McGee's Restaurant, the Entertainment Lounge is open daily from 5pm to 3am. The disco is popular with the 22 to 35 crowd after work and a younger set after 10pm. Complimentary hors d'oeuvres are served from 5 to 8pm Monday through Friday and drinks are sold two for the price of one during this time. The dance music starts at 9pm.

Admission: Fri–Sat A$5 (U.S. $4); free for house guests.

JAZZ

LIMERICK ARMS HOTEL, 364 Clarendon St., South Melbourne. Tel. 690-2626.

One of the best places in the city for jazz is the Limerick Arms. The pub dates from 1855 and is a cozy spot with a relaxed atmosphere. Live jazz bands—modern, improvised, contemporary, funk, blues, Latin—perform nightly. Food is served, in addition to beer, wine, and a wide range of spirits (hard alcohol). The pub opens at 11am and closes at midnight or 1am. The music starts about 9pm during the week and 10pm weekends.

Admission: A$5–A$10 (U.S. $4–U.S. $8) depending on who's performing.

THE BAR SCENE

PUBS

CRICKETERS BAR, in the Windsor Hotel, 103 Spring St. Tel. 653-0653.

This is one of several bars in Melbourne named and decorated in honor of the city's summer passion. Cricketers is an English-style pub popular with locals. Glass cases hold cricket memorabilia; plush green walls, green carpeting, and handsome mahogany woodwork create a traditional feel.

MAC'S HOTEL, 34 Franklin St. Tel. 663-6855.

Dating from 1853, Mac's is thought to be the city's oldest operating pub. It was originally a goldfield's coach terminus with stalls for over 100 horses and an ample yard for wagons. A special lockup was provided for the gold, along with accommodations for the gold escort. All that remains of this era is a watering trough at the front door. Mac's great claim to fame occurred on November 11, 1880, the day outlaw Ned Kelly was hanged. Emotions ran high, and one of the biggest fights ever seen in Melbourne broke out, nearly destroying the hotel.

THE LOADED DOG, 324 St. George's Rd., North Fitzroy. Tel. 489-8222.
Melbourne has some of the niftiest old pubs in the country. If you like to drink brewed-on-the-premises beer, head for the Loaded Dog. This pub brewery makes several interesting boutique beers. The decor includes a large fiberglass dog that leans on the bar with a frothy glass in its paw. The Loaded Dog is open Monday to Wednesday from noon to midnight, Thursday and Friday from noon to 1am, Saturday from 11am to 1am, and Sunday from noon to 10pm. Meals are served Monday through Saturday from noon to 2pm and 6 to 8pm.

YOUNG & JACKSONS (also known as the Princes Bridge Hotel), corner of Flinders and Swanston Sts. Tel. 650-3884.
This is another landmark watering hole. It is known for its nude painting of Chloe. It was painted in Paris in 1875 and brought to Melbourne for the Great Exhibition in 1880. In 1908 the painting was purchased by Henry Young and Thomas Jackson and given a place in the bar. Chloe holds a special place in the hearts of customers, not the least of whom are the many servicemen who have paid tribute to her over the years. Some of them have painted replicas, and today Chloe look-alikes are dotted around the world.

OTHER ENTERTAINMENT
GAMBLING

There are no casinos or poker machines in Victoria.

TABARET, in the Menzies at Rialto, 495 Collins St. Tel. 612-2900.
This gaming and wagering facility offers specially designed video games of chance. Using PATs (player activated terminals), participants "play" and bet on various sports, including golf, tennis, 10-pin bowling, football, and basketball. All transactions are conducted using plastic cards. Open daily from 11am to 3am or later.

9. EASY EXCURSIONS FROM MELBOURNE

DANDENONG RANGES
WHAT TO SEE & DO

Only 40 kilometers (25 miles) east of Melbourne lie the beautiful forest-clad hills of the Dandenong Ranges. Here is an opportunity to see native bush at its best and to tour several spectacular gardens. You can drive yourself or take a conducted excursion. The **Mount Dandenong Tourist Road** starts at **Upper Ferntree Gully** and winds its way through the villages of **Sassafras, Olinda, Mount Dandenong,** and **Kalorama** to **Montrose.** If you follow this route, plus make a detour through the **Sherbrooke Forest** to **Kallista,** you will see a good sample of the local scenery. Craft shops and tearooms are dotted around the area.

THE RHODODENDRON GARDENS, OLINDA, The Georgian Rd., Olinda. Tel. 751-1980.
This garden where thousands of "rhodies" and azaleas are planted in a 40-hectare (100-acre) setting of native and exotic trees deserves special attention. September through December is the best time to visit. A 3-kilometer (2-mile) planned walk leads you past incredibly colorful displays and to viewpoints from which you can see the Yarra Valley and beyond. A tearoom and small shop are on the property, and the staff are very helpful. (On my first visit, the sky opened up just after we arrived and one of the gardeners, hearing my accent and noting my disappointment at not being able to tour the grounds, took me around in his service vehicle.)

Admission: A$5.50 (U.S. $4.40) adults; children under 15 free.

Open: Daily 10am–4:30pm (5:30pm during daylight saving time). **Closed:** Christmas Day and Good Friday. **Transportation:** Train to Upper Ferntree Gully and bus no. 698 along the Mount Dandenong Tourist Road to Olinda.

THE WILLIAM RICKETTS SANCTUARY, Mount Dandenong Tourist Rd., Mount Dandenong. Tel. 751-1300.

This garden features clay figures which are one man's vision of the Aboriginal Dreamtime. They were created by 92-year-old sculptor William Ricketts and are set among 6 hectares (15 acres) of fern gullies, rockeries, waterfalls, and stately mountain ash trees.

Admission: A$4.50 (U.S. $3.60) adults, A$1.50 (U.S. $1.20) children 10–14; under 10, free.

Open: Daily 10am–4:30pm. **Transportation:** Train to Croydon and bus no. 688 to the sanctuary or as directed for the Rhododendron Gardens, above.

BONSAI FARM, Mount Dandenong Tourist Rd., Mount Dandenong. Tel. 751-1150.

It's also fun to see what's on display at the area's commercial garden nurseries. This place specializes in traditional and Aboriginal bonsai.

Admission: Free.

Open: Wed–Sun 11am–5pm. **Transportation:** See William Ricketts Sanctuary, above.

TESSELAAR'S TULIP FARM, Monbulk Rd., Silvan. Tel. 737-9305.

From mid-September to mid-October, the show garden here is a photographer's delight. Hyacinths, ranunculi, daffodils, azaleas, rhododendrons, fuchsias, and cinerarias bloom in profusion, in addition to an amazing display of tulips. Four windmills and a coffee shop selling sweet Dutch treats complete the scene. Tulip bulbs are for sale year round.

Admission: During the Tulip Festival A$8 (U.S. $6.40) adults; free for children under 16 accompanied by an adult.

Open: Daily 10am–5pm during the Tulip Festival (mid-Sept to mid-Oct); rest of the year Mon–Fri 8am–4:30pm and Sat–Sun 1–5pm. **Transportation:** Train to Lilydale and bus no. 679.

PUFFING BILLY, Belgrave Station, Belgrave. Tel. 754-6800 (Mon–Fri) or 870-8411 (recorded information, 24 hours).

The Dandenongs' best-known attraction is an antique steam train called Puffing Billy, which operates on a scenic 13-kilometer (8-mile) route from Belgrave to Emerald Lake. Passengers riding in open carriages have a good view as the train passes through forests and fern gullies and over a wooden trestle bridge classified by the National Trust. Puffing Billy has been operating for nearly 90 years, with the same engines pulling the same cars over the original tracks. Recorded information about the train's timetable, which varies seasonally, is available 24 hours a day and other questions are answered Monday through Friday during business hours.

Admission: A$11.50 (U.S. $9.20) adults, A$7.70 (U.S. $6.20) children 4–14.

Operates: Daily, except Christmas Day. **Transportation:** Trains from the Flinders Street Station in the city carry passengers to Belgrave. The Puffing Billy Station is a short walk from the Belgrave Station.

WHERE TO STAY

BURNHAM BEECHES COUNTRY HOUSE, Sherbrooke Rd., Sherbrooke, VIC 3789. Tel. 03/755-1903. Fax 03/755-2539. 50 rms and suites. TV TEL

Transportation: Drive from Melbourne, 45 minutes. Transfers by helicopter and limousine can be arranged.

$ Rates: A$250–A$315 (U.S. $200–U.S. $252) single or double; A$425–A$685 (U.S. $340–U.S. $548) suite; A$36 (U.S. $28.80) extra person. AE, BC, DC, MC, V. **Parking:** Free.

A fine country house provides lodging to well-heeled travelers near Sherbrooke Forest in the heart of the Dandenongs. Burnham Beeches was built in 1932 for Alfred Nicholas, cofounder of the company that developed the Aspro (aspirin) formula in Australia. Set on 22 hectares (55 acres), the classic art deco–style house is listed by the National Trust. The impressive Alfred Nicholas Memorial Gardens, once part of the property, are adjacent.

Burnham Beeches is popular with Australian executives in need of a weekend retreat and, ironically, with midweek business conferees. With the exception of a few original art deco rooms, guests are housed in attractive modern quarters with either queen-size or king-size beds. Of the new rooms, 20 have spa baths and all offer terry robes and fresh flowers. King and queen suites are comprised of two spacious rooms. All quarters have views of the surrounding forest and gardens and feature top-quality fabrics in luscious hues such as dusty rose, mint green, mauve, and lapis lazuli blue. One of the seven suites boasts a balcony large enough for a garden party, and the Alfred Nicholas Suite features an antique mahogany grand piano. Children under age 10 "are not encouraged."

Dining/Entertainment: The formal dining room has large windows overlooking gardens of trees and shrubs. Tuxedoed waiters present award-winning dishes created by chef Stephen Goodlad. The wine list is extensive. A three-course dinner costs about A$132 (U.S. $105.60) for two, plus drinks. All meals and morning and afternoon tea are open to nonstaying guests.

Facilities: The most popular recreation in this area is walking through the beautiful countryside and next door to see the gardens. Bicycles are supplied for those who are a bit more energetic. There's also an indoor pool, sauna, spa, and tennis courts on the premises.

THE YARRA VALLEY
WHAT TO SEE & DO

Another good day-trip, which can be combined with an excursion to the Dandenongs, is a trip to the Yarra Valley. The area is known for its bucolic scenery and vineyards, including those of Domaine Chandon. A dozen wineries are open for tasting and cellar-door sales along the road from **Lilydale** to **Dixon's Creek** and in the vicinity of **Healesville** and **Seville.** Good detailed maps are available from the **RACV** in Melbourne. The maps are free of charge if you're a member of an auto club in your home country and remember to bring your membership card.

If you'd like to glide over the wineries in a colorful balloon, contact **Balloon Aloft** (tel. 059/65-2449, or toll free 008/02-8568 in Australia). Flights operate daily November through May.

HEALESVILLE SANCTUARY, Badger Creek Rd., Healesville. Tel. 059/ 62-4022.

⭐ Healesville Sanctuary is one of the best places in Australia to observe native fauna. The open-plan zoological park is home to 1,800 specimens of 200 species of the country's most unusual animals. You can come face to face with a number of these creatures, at the same time enjoying the surrounding eucalyptus bushland. Many colorful birds are attracted to feeding tables set around the grounds; others are housed in walk-through aviaries. The sanctuary was started in 1921 by Sir Colin MacKenzie, knighted for his study of native wildlife. It continues to be an important center for the preservation of endangered species and for its educational programs. A café serves light meals, and picnic grounds are provided. Highly recommended.

Admission: A$10 (U.S. $8) adults, A$5 (U.S. $4) children 4–14.

Open: Daily 9am–5pm. **Transportation:** Trains from Flinders Street Station carry passengers to Lilydale, where buses connect to Healesville Sanctuary.

WHERE TO STAY

SANCTUARY HOUSE HEALESVILLE, Badger Creek Rd., Healesville, VIC 3777. Tel. 059/62-5148. 12 units. A/C TV **Transportation:** See Healesville Sanctuary, above.

$ Rates: A$50–A$60 (U.S. $40–U.S. $48) single; A$55–A$70 (U.S. $44–U.S. $56) double; A$10 (U.S. $8) extra person. AE, BC, DC, MC, V. **Parking:** Free. Located 400 meters (440 yd.) north of the sanctuary, each room at this motel offers electric blankets, clock radios, coffee- and tea-making facilities, and small refrigerators. A public telephone, casual restaurant, pool, spa, sauna, and half-court tennis are on the premises.

WHERE TO DINE

FERGUSSON'S WINERY, Will's Rd., Yarra Glen. Tel. 059/65-2237.
   Cuisine: AUSTRALIAN. **Reservations:** Recommended, especially Sun.
Transportation: Drive or join coach tour from Melbourne that stops here for lunch.
$ Prices: Appetizers A$5–A$9 (U.S. $4–U.S. $7.20); main courses A$10.50–A$15.50 (U.S. $8.40–U.S. $12.40); 5-course Sun lunch A$38 (U.S. $30.40). BC, DC, MC, V.
Open: Lunch daily noon–5pm.

Fergusson's Winery is open daily for tasting, but delicious meals are the biggest draw. Louise Fergusson presents innovative country cuisine in a charming restaurant which features cathedral ceilings and picturesque views across the vineyards. Australian timbers are used extensively in the pole construction and in the tables, chairs, and benches in the restaurant.

Lunch is served every day, but try to go on Sunday when the Fergussons offer their renowned five-course extravaganza. This meal consists of delicious aged Charolais beef roasted on a turning spit and incredible salads, side dishes, and desserts prepared by Louise, a graduate of La Varrenne Culinary School in Paris and a representative of the successful 1980 Australian Culinary Olympic Team.

PHILLIP ISLAND
WHAT TO SEE & DO

PHILLIP ISLAND PENGUIN RESERVE, Summerland Beach, Phillip Island. Tel. 059/56-8691 or 56-8300.

The nightly parade of fairy penguins on Phillip Island is one of the best-known tourist attractions in Australia. Every evening at dusk the little tuxedo-clad birds swim ashore and scamper across the beach to their sand-dune burrows. They are the smallest of the penguin species, measuring only about 33 centimeters (13 in.) high. A platform has been constructed that permits visitors to get a good view of the birds. Flash pictures are not allowed because they frighten the penguins. Be sure to wear very warm clothes, as it can get mighty chilly down by the water while you're waiting for the penguins to appear. Walking shoes are also essential.

A kiosk selling take-out food opens 1 hour before the penguins arrive.
Admission: A$6 (U.S. $4.80) adults, A$2 (U.S. $1.60) children under 14.
Open: The Visitor Centre opens at 10am; penguins arrive at sunset. **Transportation:** Phillip Island is 1½ hours by car from Melbourne. If you don't want to drive, several tour companies conduct daily excursions. If you choose to use public transportation, take a train to Frankston and change to a Stony Point train; once in Stony Point, catch a ferry to Cowes on Phillip Island. The penguin parade takes place on the opposite side of the island. Check train and ferry schedules with the MET office before starting out.

TYNONG
WHAT TO SEE & DO

VICTORIA'S FARM SHED, Princes Hwy., Tynong. Tel. 056/29-2840.
On your way to Phillip Island or after visiting the Dandenongs, you might want to stop at Victoria's Farm Shed. In an informative 1-hour show, various breeds of sheep and cattle are paraded in front of the audience, sheepshearing is demonstrated, and a cow is milked. Afterward, visitors move outside where they can

see sheepdogs working. A shop on the premises sells sheepskins and wool products at very reasonable prices.

A snack bar serves light meals, and a licensed restaurant offers a tasty barbecue lunch of prime beef steak, fish, or lamb with salads, damper, and dessert.

Admission: Normally A$9 (U.S. $7.20) adults, A$4.50 (U.S. $3.60) children, but the proprietors will deduct 20% if you tell them you're using this book.

Open: Daily 9am–5pm; shows daily 10:30am and 2pm year round; sometimes an extra show at 3:30pm Nov–Mar. **Transportation:** Drive (71km/44 miles east of Melbourne) or take a Melbourne Sightseeing coach tour (tel. 03/670-9706).

AROUND PORT PHILLIP BAY

Day-trippers from Melbourne have a choice of following the Princes Highway around the west side of Port Phillip Bay to Werribee and Geelong or taking the Nepean Highway, which goes along the east side of the bay and ends at Portsea. Those with the time to overnight along the way can combine the two options.

My suggestion for those with only 1 day: Start early, drive directly to Geelong, visit the wool museum, continue to Queenscliff on the Bellarine Peninsula, have lunch and explore a bit, and visit Werribee on the way back to Melbourne. If you have more time, stop at Werribee as you head south, have lunch and visit the wool museum in Geelong, have dinner and overnight in Queenscliff. The next day, take the ferry from Queenscliff to Sorrento, explore the Mornington Peninsula, and either return to Melbourne, stay overnight at one of the two properties described below, or catch a ferry from Stony Point to Phillip Island.

The **Peninsula Princess** car and passenger ferry (tel. 052/52-3171 or 52-2344) makes about a dozen trips a day between the Bellarine and Mornington peninsulas. The crossing takes 35 to 40 minutes. The one-way fare for a car and up to five passengers is A$40 (U.S. $32); pedestrians pay A$5 (U.S. $4).

QUEENSCLIFF
What to See & Do

In the 1880s the seaside town of Queenscliff at the head of Port Phillip Bay became a fashionable place for wealthy Melburnians to go for a holiday. Steamers made regular trips, carrying Victorian ladies and gentlemen, and a number of grand hotels were built to accommodate them. However, the community's heyday came to an end with the advent of motorcars early in this century. The vehicles opened up new destinations, and Queenscliff's popularity took a nosedive. The place remained of little interest to travelers until recently, when it was rediscovered as a pleasant weekend escape from the city. A few of the old hotels have been restored to their former glory and, with other mid-19th-century buildings, create a sedate, old-world atmosphere. This is also a good excursion for those who enjoy the smell of salt air, beaches, water sports, and clifftop walkways with panoramic views of Bass Strait. Queenscliff (pop. 3,700) is located 103 kilometers (64 miles) from Melbourne. You can drive there in about 1½ hours, taking the Princes Highway out of Melbourne and picking up the Bellarine Highway in Geelong.

Where to Stay & Dine

MIETTA'S QUEENSCLIFF HOTEL, 16 Gellibrand St., Queenscliff, VIC 3225. Tel. 052/52-1066. Fax 052/52-1899. 21 rms (none with bath). **Transportation:** Train to Geelong, bus from Geelong Station to Queenscliff.

$ Rates: A$95 (U.S. $76) per person Sun–Fri (including breakfast and either lunch or dinner from the simpler menu); from A$160 (U.S. $128) per person (including breakfast and dinner in the main dining room with wine). Other packages available. AE, BC, DC, MC, V. **Parking:** None available off-street.

⭐ This Mietta's is run by Patricia O'Donnell, sister of Mietta O'Donnell, whose superb eatery I described in "Melbourne Dining," above. The hotel, with a view of the water, was restored with the same attention to detail apparent in Mietta's restaurant. The public rooms are a joy—whether you dine, take tea, have a drink, or relax by the fire with a book. The "pink sitting room" has Chinese carpets and a pair of flowered wingback chairs in front of the fireplace. The "little sitting room" at the front of the house has a view of a park that slopes down to the seaside. In the "large sitting room" books, chess, and jigsaw puzzles are left out for guests.

The bedrooms have authentic period decors, including iron-and-brass headboards, hardwood floors, high ceilings, and Oriental carpets. Number 27, a spacious room with a working fireplace and a bay window, is my favorite. Since the hotel is a popular weekend escape for Melburnians, midweek rates are lower. Even if you don't stay overnight, stop by and have a drink or afternoon tea at the hotel. It's charming.

Dining/Entertainment: Superb gourmet cuisine is served in three areas: the formal main dining room, with crisp white tablecloths and an elaborate brass chandelier; the delightful courtyard dining room with its marble-topped tables from the Raffles Hotel in Singapore; and at umbrella tables in the garden.

VUE GRAND HOTEL, 46 Hesse St., Queenscliff, VIC 3225. Tel. 052/52-1544. Fax 052/52-3471. 32 rms (all with bath). TEL **Transportation:** See above.

$ Rates (including dinner and breakfast): A$140 (U.S. $112) per person. Weekend and other packages available. AE, BC, DC, MC, V.

The Vue Grand Hotel, which dates from 1864, is a two-storied Victorian hostelry that has also been restored. The bedrooms have contemporary decors, but the public spaces are replete with period splendor. An indoor pool has taken the place of the original stables. There are also a gym and a spa.

GEELONG

What to See & Do

THE NATIONAL WOOL MUSEUM, corner of Moorabool and Brougham Sts. Tel. 052/26-4660.

If you've heard someone say "Australia was founded on the sheep's back" and not understood what they meant—here's your chance to find out. Displays in this wonderful museum explain the importance of sheep farming in Australia—then and now—and provide historical background. Videos show sheepdogs working; visitors can feel several different fleeces; and there's a chance to experience a shearing shed. It's especially interesting to follow the path of the fleece from the sheep's back to a finished wool garment.

The museum is part of the National Wool Centre which also includes several stores selling Australian clothing and souvenirs, a deli, and Lamby's Bistro—an à la carte restaurant. The building which houses this significant center, the Dennys Lascelles Woolstore, dates from 1872.

Admission: A$5.50 (U.S. $4.40) adults, A$2.80 (U.S. $2.25) children under 16.

Open: Daily 10am–5pm. **Closed:** Christmas Day and Good Friday. **Transportation:** Geelong is a 45-minute drive from Melbourne. There's also regular train service, and the museum is a 10-minute walk from the station.

WERRIBEE

What to See & Do

WERRIBEE PARK MANSION, K Rd. Tel. 03/741-2444.

Here is a 60-room Italianate mansion built in 1877 by Scottish squatters Thomas and Andrew Chirnside. Known as "the palace in the paddock," this great house was, at that time, without rival in the colony. Today it stands on 130 hectares (325 acres) of bushland fronting the Werribee River. There is a free-range zoo adjacent.

Admission (to the mansion only): A$5 (U.S. $4) adults, A$2.50 (U.S. $2) children 5–14.

Open: Daily 10am–3:45pm (4:45pm weekends, public holidays, and during daylight saving time). **Closed:** Christmas Day. **Transportation:** Werribee is a 30-minute drive from Melbourne. You can also take a train and catch a connecting bus to Werribee Park.

MORNINGTON PENINSULA
What to See & Do

Long a playground for Melburnians, the Mornington Peninsula offers safe beaches on Port Phillip Bay, rugged cliffs overlooking Bass Strait, coastal parks, and hinterland hills. A chair lift whisks passengers to the summit of 305-meter (1,006 ft.) Arthur's Seat, the highest point on the peninsula. If you prefer to drive, a good road winds to the top from Dromana. There are tourist information centers in Dromana on the Nepean Highway (tel. 059/87-3078), and on Ocean Beach Road in Sorrento (tel. 059/84-2247).

Where to Stay

DELGANY COUNTRY HOUSE HOTEL, Nepean Hwy., Portsea, VIC 3944. Tel. 059/84-4000. Fax 059/84-4022. 34 rms. A/C TV TEL **Transportation:** Portsea is 100km (62 miles) southwest of Melbourne and 4km (2½ miles) from the ferry dock in Sorrento. To reach by public transport, take a train from Melbourne to Frankston and bus no. 788 from there.

$ Rates (including continental breakfast): A$170 (U.S. $136) standard room single or double midweek; A$230–A$345 (U.S. $184–U.S. $276) executive, deluxe, or grand suite midweek; A$240 (U.S. $192) standard room single or double on a weekend; A$330–A$495 (U.S. $264–U.S. $396) suite weekend. Dollar-saving packages available. AE, BC, DC, MC, V. **Parking:** Free.

⭐ This grand mansion, built in 1927, was inspired by ancestral castles with Roman arches and Tudor battlements, and this character is still present today. In addition to the years when it was a residence, Delgany has been a military hospital and, later, a school for the deaf. In 1989 it opened its doors as an elegant country-house hotel.

Totally restored to its former splendor, the house is set in 12 acres of private gardens abutting the Portsea golf course. Each room is tastefully furnished. Some have fireplaces and spa baths. The drawing room has a grand piano, a huge open fire, and manor-house furnishings.

Dining/Entertainment: A meal at this country house is a memorable experience. Hermann Schneider has moved his Two Faces Restaurant, for many years a leading Melbourne dining spot, to Delgany. Now the same gourmet cuisine is available to house guests and nonstaying guests who book far enough in advance. Fixed-price lunches served Monday through Saturday noon to 2:30pm cost A$32.50 to A$40 (U.S. $26 to U.S. $32). Sunday lunch and nightly dinners are à la carte.

Facilities: Outdoor heated pool, two tennis courts, and croquet lawn.

WARRAWEE HOMESTEAD, 87 Warrawee Rd., Balnarring, VIC 3926. Tel. 059/82-1729. 5 rms (2 with bath). **Directions:** Balnarring is 1 hour southeast of Melbourne.

$ Rates (including breakfast): A$135 (U.S. $108) double with bath, A$125 (U.S. $100) double with shared bathroom. Midweek and weekend packages. Discounts for extended stays. AE, BC, DC, MC, V. **Parking:** Free.

⭐ This is a great place to get a sense of what it might have been like to live in colonial Australia. Warrawee Homestead was built in 1860 on a large farming property and later became a Cobb & Co. stopover. Today the house has a very pretty dining room with lace tablecloths, a big open fireplace, period furnishings, and the original Baltic pine floor. There's a sunny enclosed veranda where guests can relax, and the whole place has a real sense of history.

My favorite room is the honeymoon suite with an en suite bathroom and a brass four-poster bed. Accommodations are offered nightly year round and all meals are provided for house guests. Nonstaying guests can enjoy lunch, dinner, or afternoon tea on weekends year round and Tuesday through Sunday during December and January. A two-course lunch costs A$35 (U.S. $28); three-course dinners cost A$45 (U.S. $36); afternoon teas cost A$7.50 (U.S. $6).

VICTORIA

Victoria occupies only 3% of the country, but there is a lot of variety within its borders. In addition to 1,300 kilometers (806 miles) of coastline, the state has desert in the west, a major river to the north, and mountains in the east. In between are forests, wine- and fruit-growing regions, and cities with rich gold-rush histories.

The mighty Murray River has its origins in the snowcapped high country of the northeast, and its course forms the border with neighboring New South Wales. The Murray's valleys produce prime vineyards and orchards. Mildura, Swan Hill, and Echuca are gracious riverfront towns where visitors can catch a ride on a paddle steamer.

The Grampians, in the western portion of the state, are scenic mountains popular with rock climbers, bushwalkers, and campers. The area has many rock shelters containing Aboriginal paintings. Good roads crisscross Grampians National Park, and there is vehicular access to lookout points, lakes, waterfalls, and wide valleys. From June through November native flora puts on a colorful display, and all year long fauna, including kangaroos, koalas, and over 200 species of birds, are abundant. Hall's Gap, the center of the Grampians, is a 3-hour drive from Melbourne.

The Great Ocean Road follows the coastline southwest of the state capital. Those who make this curvaceous trip are rewarded with outstanding ocean views. The shore on the eastern half of Victoria is less dramatic, but that doesn't prevent Wilsons Promontory National Park from being a favorite recreation area. The "Prom," as it is known, is 230 kilometers (143 miles) from Melbourne.

The center of the state was populated by hopeful gold miners in the 1850s. Relics of this era can be seen throughout places like Ballarat and Bendigo.

SEEING VICTORIA

Intrastate train and coach service in Victoria is provided by **V/Line,** 67 Spencer Street, Melbourne, VIC 3000 (tel. 03/619-5000). This includes a wide network of interurban trains and an even more complete service of buses which extend beyond the rail network. V/Line also offers day tours and overnight excursions (03/619-8080) to such places as Ballarat and the Great Ocean Road. Kendell Airlines (03/688-2222 or 670-2677) is the principle intrastate air carrier. Sunstate Airlines flies to Mildura. Both V/Line and Kendell offer passes that are money-saving values for those traveling extensively within Victoria.

While the vast majority of Victoria's four million residents live in Melbourne, some live on farms throughout the state and welcome visitors. If you fancy a farmer as a host, contact the **Victorian Host Farm Association,** c/o Trish Beare or Don

WHAT'S SPECIAL ABOUT VICTORIA

Ace Attractions
☐ Ballarat's Sovereign Hill Goldmining Township, where history is re-created.

Natural Spectacles
☐ The Twelve Apostles, highlight of the wonderful coastal scenery along the Great Ocean Road.

Activities
☐ Mildura, where you can ride down the mighty Murray River on a paddle wheeler.

☐ Snowy River National Park, in the eastern part of the state, a great place to go horseback riding.

Beaches
☐ Lakes Entrance on the southeast coast—a seemingly endless stretch of ocean beach separated from an inland waterway by a row of sand dunes.

MacDowall, 332 Banyule Road, View Bank, VIC 3084 (tel. 03/457-5413; fax 03/457-6725). In the U.S., bookings can be made through **SO/PAC** (tel. toll free 800/551-2012 in the U.S. and Canada, 800/445-0190 in California). If you wait and make arrangements after your arrival in Victoria, you'll pay from A$120 to A$200 (U.S. $96 to U.S. $160) for two including meals and lodging. The all-inclusive rate, which includes all meals, morning and afternoon tea, full-time hosting, accommodations, district tours, transfers from the nearest rail or bus station, and farm tours and activities, ranges from A$246 to A$286 (U.S. $196.80 to U.S. $228.80) for two people sharing. If you book in the U.S., prices are higher.

Victoria's Tourism Centre, 230 Collins Street, Melbourne, VIC 3000 (tel. 03/650-1522), is the best source of tourist information. Pick up maps and motoring details at the **RACV,** 422 Little Collins Street, Melbourne, VIC 3000 (tel. 03/607-2137).

1. BALLARAT

113km (70 miles) W of Melbourne

GETTING THERE   By Plane   There is no air service to Ballarat.

By Train   V/Line trains carry passengers from Melbourne in just under 2 hours (A$30.40/U.S. $24.35 round-trip in first class). At the station, visitors can catch a shuttle bus to Sovereign Hill and the Gold Museum (see below).

By Bus   V/Line also offers coach service to Ballarat, and many sightseeing companies, including Australian Pacific Tours (tel. 03/650-1511), Melbourne Sightseeing (tel. 03/670-9706), and AAT King's (tel. 03/650-1244), conduct day tours from Melbourne.

By Car   The Western Highway connects Ballarat and Melbourne.

ESSENTIALS   Tourist information is dispensed at **Ballarat Tourism,** 39 Sturt Street, Ballarat, VIC 3350 (tel. 053/32-2694). This office is open Monday through Friday from 9am to 5pm and Saturday and Sunday from 10am to 4pm. Ballarat's **area code** is 053.

SPECIAL EVENTS   The Royal South Street Eisteddfod, which focuses on music and the dramatic arts, is held every September/October. The Ballarat Begonia Festival in early March celebrates the city's floral emblem.

The history of Victoria's largest inland city (pop. 90,000) is inextricably intertwined with the discovery of gold in 1851. The area had been used as sheep and cattle pasture since 1838, and by the middle of the 19th century a small township had developed. However, after blacksmith Thomas Hiscock found gold, hopeful miners from as far away as California flooded the region. Within 2 years, Ballarat had a population of nearly 40,000, including many Chinese who labored as cooks and at other auxiliary jobs in the goldfields. The difficulty of accessing the gold, some of which was under four layers of basalt, created a machinery- and equipment-manufacturing industry that has sustained the community since the last mine closed in 1918.

Today, Ballarat's economy continues to be based on heavy industry, but the city also has a strong interest in the arts.

WHAT TO SEE & DO

The main attraction for visitors is Sovereign Hill, a re-created colonial town where you can pan for gold and get a taste of life in the mid-19th century. Ballarat also has many splendid old buildings. Ask at the tourist office for a brochure describing a walking tour which will lead you past the many significant local buildings.

SOVEREIGN HILL GOLDMINING TOWNSHIP, Main St. Tel. 31-1944.

This is clearly the city's—and, for that matter, the state's—top attraction. Sovereign Hill is a living museum covering the period 1851 to 1861: Buildings are based on drawings, photographs, and plans of their original counterparts.

The township consists of three sections: the **Red Hill Gully Diggings,** showing early mining equipment and dwellings; **Main Street,** featuring shops and businesses that were in Ballarat in the 10 years following the discovery of gold; and the **Mining Museum,** consisting of steam-driven surface installations and impressive underground displays.

At Sovereign Hill visitors can shop in stores that are historically accurate both in their design and in the goods they stock. Children can be observed studying in two Victorian-era schoolhouses. (Primary classes from anywhere in the state can book for a 2-day program based on the 1850s curriculum.) You can pan for gold, see how the early miners lived, and contrast that with the living conditions of the Chinese workers. You can have your picture taken in old-fashioned clothes, take a Cobb & Co. coach ride, and watch craftspeople such as blacksmiths, potters, and tinsmiths at work. Local folks in period costumes are on hand to answer questions. The guided tour of the underground mine takes about 45 minutes, but several hours are required to walk through the whole township. This is—in short—Australia's Williamsburg.

There are several eating options at Sovereign Hill. In addition to an à la carte dining room, there's a family restaurant, a kiosk, a bakery selling freshly made wares straight from a wood-fired oven, and two coffee shops.

Admission (including the Gold Museum described below and the underground mine): A$13.70 (U.S. $11) adults, A$6.60 (U.S. $5.30) children under 16; tots under 5, free; A$38 (U.S. $30.40) family pass (two adults and up to four kids).

Open: Daily 9:30am–5pm. **Closed:** Christmas Day.

GOLD MUSEUM, Bradshaw St. Tel. 31-1944.

Across the street from the township is the high-security Gold Museum, where samples of alluvial gold, gold nuggets, and gold coins are on display. Exhibits depict life in the Ballarat area before the discovery of gold. There is also a major display on the Eureka story (see below).

Admission: A$3 (U.S. $2.40) adults, A$1.60 (U.S. $1.30) children.

Open: Sun–Fri 10am–5:20pm, Sat 12:30–5:20pm.

EUREKA STOCKADE PARK AND DIORAMA, Stawell St. South, at Eureka St.

This park commemorates an important event in Australia's history. During the

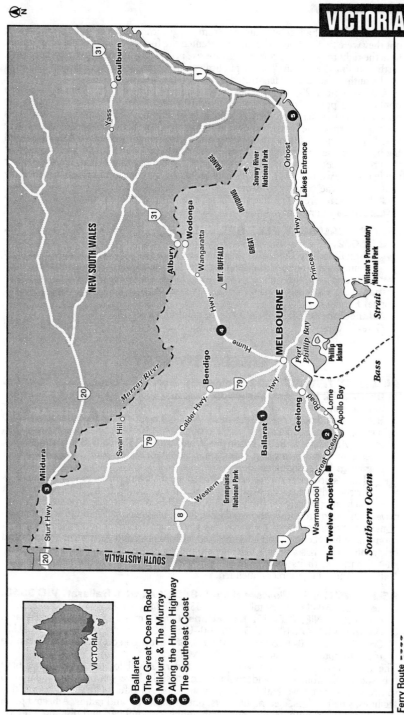

VICTORIA

Ferry Route ----

VICTORIA

1 Ballarat
2 The Great Ocean Road
3 Mildura & The Murray
4 Along the Hume Highway
5 The Southeast Coast

gold rush, miners had to buy a license from the government every month, whether or not they were finding gold. The miners resented the fee, especially because they didn't have the right to vote. The corrupt and abusive police conducted regular license hunts, further fueling dissension. When a publican guilty of murdering a miner was acquitted by the authorities, the miners rioted at his hotel.

On November 29, 1854, thousands of miners burned their licenses in a huge bonfire. The police countered with a ruthless license hunt. A few days later, the poorly armed miners gathered behind a stockade and were attacked by soldiers bearing firearms. The battle was over in 15 minutes, but 30 miners and 5 soldiers were killed. This incident forced the government to do something about the situation, and the hated licenses were replaced with "miner's rights," which cost only a fraction of the previous fee and included the privilege of voting. In other words, the diggers lost the battle but won the war. The Eureka Stockade is significant because it is the only civil battle in the country's history.

Admission: Free. The diorama has a coin-operated commentary.
Open: 24 hours a day.

CITY OF BALLARAT FINE ART GALLERY, 40 Lydiard St. North Tel. 31-5622.

Established in 1884, this was the first provincial gallery in Australia. The foundation stone for the building was laid in 1887 to commemorate Queen Victoria's Golden Jubilee. Here you will find a comprehensive collection of Australian art, especially from the colonial period and the Heidelberg School, and the original Eureka flag.

Admission: A$2 (U.S. $1.60) adults; children under 15, free.
Open: Tues–Fri 10:30am–4:30pm, Sat–Sun 12:30–4:30pm. **Closed:** Good Friday and Christmas Day.

WHERE TO STAY

BALLARAT TERRACE, 229 Lydiard St. North, Ballarat, VIC 3350. Tel. 053/33-2216. 3 rms. Directions: Located 100m (110 yd.) from the Ballarat Rail Station.

$ Rates (including a cooked breakfast): A$80 (U.S. $64) single occupancy; A$100 (U.S. $80) two people in the "maid's room"; A$110 (U.S. $88) two in the "brass room"; A$130 (U.S. $104) two in the "front room"; A$20 (U.S. $16) extra person. All rooms are no-smoking. Teenage children only (at adult tariff). BC, MC.
Parking: By arrangement; free.

There's no better way to experience Ballarat's history than to stay in one of its lovely old homes. This restored terrace house dating from 1889 presents just such an opportunity. Evelyn and Bernie Ebbs offer three bedrooms, each with private bathroom, to those who would like to sample gracious Victorian accommodations. The hosts go out of their way to assure their guests' comfort. The charming rooms have high ceilings and are furnished with English and Australian antiques and bric-a-brac. One has a private balcony and fireplace. Breakfast is served in the lovely guests' parlor with its open fire and cozy atmosphere. The house is listed by the National Trust. Highly recommended.

BELL TOWER INN, Western Hwy. (1845 Sturt St.), Ballarat, VIC 3350. Tel. 053/34-1600, or toll free 008/03-2978 in Australia. Fax 053/34-2540. 75 rms. A/C MINIBAR TV TEL Directions: 6km (4 miles) west of central Ballarat.

$ Rates: A$72–A$105 (U.S. $57.60–U.S. $84) single; A$79–A$130 (U.S. $63.20–U.S. $104) double; A$10 (U.S. $8) extra person. Reservations can be made through Flag Inns. AE, BC, DC, MC, V.

The Bell Tower is for those who prefer modern motel lodging. Five rooms have tub/shower combinations and cooking facilities; 39 have spa baths in addition to showers. The rest have bathrooms with showers. All offer coffee- and tea-making facilities, small fridges, electric blankets, queen-size beds, and radios. A heated pool, spa, sauna, playground, tennis court, trampoline, cocktail bar, and restaurant are on the grounds. The restaurant is closed Sunday.

WHERE TO DINE

THE BONSHAW, corner of Tait St. and Ross Creek Rd., Sebastapol. Tel. 35-8346.
   Cuisine: INTERNATIONAL. **Reservations:** Recommended. **Location:** On the outskirts of Ballarat.
$ Prices: Dinner for two about A$48–A$57 (U.S. $38.40–U.S. $45.60). AE, BC, DC, MC, V.
   Open: Dinner Tues–Sat from 6:30pm.
Here is a good place for well-prepared French dishes such as snails in garlic butter and spinach au gratin, as well as steak, lobster (in season), and chicken, pork, and veal dishes. The Bonshaw, located in a historic building, has a pleasant atmosphere and offers good service and an extensive wine list.

ALIBIS, 10 Camp St. Tel. 31-6680.
   Cuisine: MODERN AUSTRALIAN. **Reservations:** Recommended.
$ Prices: Dinner about A$65 (U.S. $52) for two; lunch and meals served in the wine bar cost less. AE, BC, DC, MC, V.
   Open: Lunch Tues–Fri noon–2pm; dinner Tues–Sat from 6:30pm; wine bar to 1am.
This eatery is housed in a bluestone and brick building which dates from the 1850s, and consists of a ground-floor restaurant and a cellar wine bar and bistro. Chef Simon Donoghue's expertise is evident in the creative cuisine he presents. This ranges from traditional fare, such as steak, to multicultural dishes like Creole gumbo and innovative pasta preparations. Save room for dessert.

---

2. THE GREAT OCEAN ROAD

Torquay: 94km (58 miles) SW of Melbourne
Port Campbell National Park: 285km (177 miles) SW of Melbourne

GETTING THERE **By Plane** There are no airports along the Great Ocean Road.

By Train V/Line has regular service to Geelong and Warrnambool with connecting coaches along the Great Ocean Road.

By Bus V/Line coaches provide service along the Great Ocean Road.

By Car This scenic road is best enjoyed by car, which allows for stopping at the various viewpoints. It is completely paved, wide enough to be safe, and well signposted.

ESSENTIALS Bell's Beach, just a few kilometers southwest of Torquay, is the site of the annual Surfing World Championships. The **Park Information Centre,** at Port Campbell National Park (tel. 055/98-6382), has an interesting display and audiovisual show about the area. It's open daily from 10am to 5pm. The primary resort towns along the Great Ocean Road offering dining and lodging are Lorne (pop. 935) and Apollo Bay (pop. 1,162). Both also offer opportunities for surfing, fishing, golf, and bushwalking. The region's **area codes** are 052 and 055.

The rugged Southern Ocean crashes onto the coast of Victoria from one side of the state to the other, but only for a couple hundred kilometers does a highway maintain close proximity with the sea. This portion that follows the shoreline is called the Great Ocean Road. It begins in Torquay, 94 kilometers (58 miles) southwest of Melbourne, and ends near Peterborough, some 200 kilometers (160 miles) later. The scenic route has been compared to California's coastal Highway 1 and the drive along the Italian Riviera.
   Construction of the road was begun after World War I, as a memorial to those

who'd lost their lives and to provide employment for returned soldiers. The going was rough. Equipment was sent overland by train to Dean's Marsh, and from there it was taken by wagons pulled by teams of 14 horses. It took 2 days to travel the 25 kilometers (15 miles) to Lorne. The workmen complained of low wages and rough conditions, but they did experience one pleasant windfall: A coastal steamer ran aground near the town of Kennet River in 1924 and had to jettison its cargo. Among the things that floated to shore were 50 barrels of beer and various cases of spirits; no work was done for the following 2 weeks. While building the road was a struggle, it was finally completed in 1932. In addition to providing coastal access to tourists, it has made viable the fishing industry in Lorne and Apollo Bay.

WHAT TO SEE & DO

In some places the road skirts high cliffs well above the ocean; at others, it descends to sea level and curves along sightly sand beaches. One of the most spectacular areas is known as the **Twelve Apostles**—a row of great stone pillars emerging from the sea just a short way offshore. These sentinels are part of **Port Campbell National Park,** as are the other unusual features created by the sea from limestone cliffs: **Loch Ard Gorge** and **The Arch.** (Another landmark, London Bridge, collapsed into the sea in 1990.) This stormy coast has claimed 163 sailing ships. While they can't be seen from land, the wrecks can be explored with scuba gear. (Because they have been declared historical sites, nothing may be removed from them.)

READERS RECOMMEND

Otway Ranges Deer and Wildlife Park, *Great Ocean Rd., Princetown. Tel. 055/98-3151 or 37-5262. "On the way to the Twelve Apostles, this place is well worth a visit. You can hand-feed wallabies and kangaroos. It's shortly before the Twelve Apostles and well signposted. Closed Tuesday."*—Wendy Gross and Bev Wybrow, Toronto, Canada.

WHERE TO STAY

IN LORNE

CUMBERLAND LORNE CONFERENCE & LEISURE RESORT, 150–178 Mountjoy Parade, Lorne, VIC 3232. Tel. 052/89-2400, or toll free 008/03-7010 in Australia. Fax 052/89-2256. 51 1-bedroom, 35 2-bedroom, and 12 penthouse apartments. TV TEL **Location:** On the main road in Lorne, which is 142km (88 miles) southwest of Melbourne.

$ Rates: A$165–A$185 (U.S. $132–U.S. $148) 1-bedroom apartment; A$205–A$225 (U.S. $164–U.S. $180) 2-bedroom apartment; A$285 (U.S. $228) penthouse. Lower off-season rates (May–Aug). Dollarwise midweek packages. Jan rates are higher. No-smoking rooms available. AE, BC, DC, MC, V. **Parking:** Free.

This resort, which opened in late 1989, is the ideal place for families who want to enjoy all the recreational opportunities available in Lorne. It's located in the heart of the community, near all activities. Each modern spacious apartment has a full kitchen, washing machine and dryer, spa bath, two televisions, in-room movies, and a balcony with patio furniture. More than half have ocean views. Each block of apartments is named for a shipwreck which occurred in the vicinity of the Great Ocean Road.

Dining/Entertainment: Chris' Restaurant, a casual bistro with indoor and outdoor seating, is open from 11am to midnight during the week and 9am to midnight on weekends. Both local seafood and ethnic fare are offered. Horizons, the more elegant à la carte dining spot, is open Friday and Saturday nights year round and Monday through Saturday during December and January.

Services: Baby-sitting can be arranged.

Facilities: Heated indoor pool, table tennis, billiards, gym, sauna, two squash courts, two tennis courts, and children's center. Bicycles, surf skiis, surfboards, and windsurfing boards can be rented. The children's activity program includes beach games, movies, clowns, face painting, walks, and picnics. The resort's shopping plaza has 14 specialty shops, a beauty salon, bank, and post office.

MOTEL KALIMNA, Mountjoy Parade (Great Ocean Rd.), Lorne, VIC 3232. Tel. 052/89-1407. 25 rms. TV TEL
$ Rates: A$70 (U.S. $56) single; A$95 (U.S. $76) double; A$10 (U.S. $8) extra person. Off-season rates are lower. Reservations can be made through Best Western. AE, BC, DC, MC, V. **Parking:** Free.

At Motel Kalimna, a low-rise property, private balconies face the sea. A cocktail bar, restaurant, swimming pool, laundry facilities, tennis court, barbecue area, and games room are on the premises.

IN APOLLO BAY

APOLLO INTERNATIONAL MOTOR INN, 37 Great Ocean Rd., Apollo Bay, VIC 3233. Tel. 052/37-6100. Fax 052/37-6066. 24 rms. A/C TV TEL
$ Rates: A$68 (U.S. $54.40) single; A$80–A$115 (U.S. $64–U.S. $92) double; A$15 (U.S. $12) extra adult; A$12 (U.S. $9.60) child under 12. Surcharge on Sat night, Christmas, Easter, Melbourne Cup weekend, and during public and school holidays. Reservations can be made through Flag Inns. AE, BC, DC, MC, V. **Parking:** Free.

It may look like just another red-brick motel, but it's really much more. Six rooms have spa baths in very large bathrooms. There are also six two-story family units, and all quarters have small refrigerators, toasters, electric blankets, art deco interiors, hairdryers, and coffee- and tea-making facilities (with teapots!). The property, which opened in early 1991, also offers a pool, spa, and guest laundry.

CLAERWEN COUNTRY HOUSE RETREAT, P.O. Box 174, Apollo Bay, VIC 3233. Tel. 052/37-6334. Fax 052/37-6127. 5 rms. **Location/ Transportation:** On hilltop, 6km (4 miles) inland from the coast. Drive or charter a helicopter. There's a helipad on the property.
$ Rates (including all meals, wine, and drinks): A$220 (U.S. $176) per person per 24-hour stay. A$40 (U.S. $32) surcharge for sole occupancy. Surcharge for stays of less than 2 days. No children under 12. BC, MC, V. **Parking:** Free.

This is gracious country living at its best. Claerwen consists of a beautiful modern home, purpose-built to accommodate guests. Each of the five spacious rooms has its own bathroom with shower, terry robe, slippers, hairdryer, electric blanket, and wonderful view of surrounding verdant hillsides dotted with sheep and the coast beyond. One room has a king-size bed, two have queens, and two have twin double beds. Hosts Pam and Ron McCallum are charming, friendly, and helpful. They prepare picnic lunches or guests can dine in. Everyone enjoys three-course dinners together around a large blackwood table. Almost everything is homemade; apples, peaches, and other fruit are grown on the property. There's a swimming pool and a spa in the garden and a tennis court and four-hole golf course steps away. Tom Selleck stayed here for 2 weeks during the filming of *Quigley Down Under*. To avoid disappointment, book this property at least 1 month in advance.

NEAR WOOLSTHORPE

QUAMBY HOMESTEAD, Caramut Rd., Woolsthorpe, VIC 3276. Tel. 055/69-2395. Fax 055/69-2472. 7 rms and suites. A/C MINIBAR TV **Location:** 32km (19 miles) north of Warrnambool.
$ Rates (including afternoon tea, dinner, and breakfast): A$138 (U.S. $110.40) per person; A$215 (U.S. $172) 2-day package per person (including two dinners, two breakfasts, and a picnic-hamper lunch). Lower rates for extended stays. No children under 16. BC, V. **Parking:** Free.

Quamby is a wonderful historic homestead where guests sleep in cottages and other buildings on a 66-acre property surrounded by sheep and pretty gardens. The location is ideal: just a short distance from both the Great Ocean Road and the Grampians. Hosts Kent and Cathy Lamont enjoy telling guests about William

Lindsay, the immigrant from Scotland who cleared and drained 30,000 acres here in 1854. By the 1870s, the property had grown to 70,000 acres and was the largest cattle station in Victoria. Unfortunately, the Lindsay grandchildren gambled and drank away their inheritance and died penniless, and Quamby was in ruins when it was sold in 1983. Today it has been beautifully restored and provides a good chance to experience rural life and understand an important aspect of Australia's history.

All buildings are white with blue trim and surrounded by English-style gardens and lawns. Guests sleep in queen-size iron and brass beds with colonial-style doonas and awaken to the sound of native birds, peacocks, and sheep. All accommodations have en suite bathrooms. Breakfast is served on the veranda of the main homestead. Dinner is offered in a former parlor, now called The House of Lindsay's Restaurant. Tasty four-course dinners, included in the tariff for house guests, are available to nonstaying guests on Friday and Saturday night. These cost A$35 (U.S. $28). Diners may bring their own wine or choose one from the Quamby list.

Hosts will happily make arrangements for you to watch shearing (September to December) or tour other local gardens and homesteads.

WHERE TO EAT
IN LORNE

THE PIER RESTAURANT, at the town pier. Tel. 89-1119.
 Cuisine: SEAFOOD/STEAK. **Reservations:** Recommended on weekends.
$ **Prices:** Appetizers A$6.50–A$11.50 (U.S. $5.20–U.S. $9.20); main courses A$9.50–A$23 (U.S. $7.60–U.S. $18.40); snacks A$2.50–A$5 (U.S. $2–U.S. $4); kids' meals A$5–A$8.50 (U.S. $4–U.S. $6.80). BC, MC, V.
 Open: Nov–Easter daily 9am–10pm. Sometimes open weekends at other times of the year. Breakfast until 11:30am; lunch until 3pm; teas and snacks throughout the day; kids' meals until 7pm; other dinners until 10pm or later.

This is a very picturesque spot in which to dine. The Pier, as the name suggests, is right on the water, and the bubble-gum pink picnic tables under a lattice roof provide a 180° view of the coastline. Additional seating is available inside. BYO.

THE ARAB RESTAURANT, 94 Mountjoy Parade. Tel. 89-1435.
 Cuisine: INTERNATIONAL. **Reservations:** Recommended.
$ **Prices:** Appetizers A$5.50–A$9.50 (U.S. $4.40–U.S. $7.60); main courses A$12–A$17.50 (U.S. $9.60–U.S. $14). No credit cards.
 Open: Year round.
This popular bistro has been pleasing customers since it first opened in 1956. Black-and-white photos on the wall show "bathing beauties" in the restaurant as it was then. Host Sammy Gazis writes the daily offerings—seafood, chicken, and steaks—on a blackboard menu. The specialty of the house is chicken Kiev. Diners, seated at wooden tables, can watch their meal being prepared in the open kitchen. There is limited seating outdoors, and two levels inside.

IN APOLLO BAY

THE BAY LEAF GOURMET DELI, 131 Great Ocean Rd. Tel. 37-6470.
 Cuisine: CAFE. **Reservations:** None.
$ **Prices:** Breakfast, lunch, and snacks A$2.75–A$7.50 (U.S. $2.20–U.S. $6). No credit cards.
 Open: Daily 8am–2:30pm. Breakfast is served all day.
 Closed: Aug.

The Bay Leaf serves the best breakfast for miles around—maybe the best in Australia. Whether you choose eggs Benedict, buckwheat pancakes with blueberries and maple syrup, or a crumpet with honey, you won't be disappointed. Lunchtime fare includes such items as tortellini with ham and mushrooms; smoked salmon, avocado, and cream cheese on rye; or hot roast beef and salad sandwich. There are seven tables inside and two outside. Some locals just drop in for a cappuccino or a cup of Twinings tea and read the magazines which are provided. Not licensed. Highly recommended.

3. MILDURA & THE MURRAY

544km (337 miles) NW of Melbourne, 400km (248 miles)
NE of Adelaide, 297km (184 miles) S of Broken Hill

GETTING THERE By Plane Kendell and Sunstate Airlines provide service to Mildura from Melbourne, Adelaide, and Broken Hill. The flight from Melbourne takes 1½ hours. Sunstate and V/Line offer a package deal called SUNTRAK which combines air travel in one direction with train or coach travel the other way. Contact V/Line for more information (tel. 03/619-8080).

By Train V/Line's *Vinelander* provides overnight rail service, leaving Melbourne at 9:45pm on Tuesday, Thursday, Friday, and Sunday and arriving in Mildura the next morning at 7:30am. A first-class berth costs A$101 (U.S. $80.80); a first-class seat is A$61.60 (U.S. $49.30) and an economy seat is A$44 (U.S. $35.20).

By Bus V/Line's Sun Link service operates daily and combines coach and rail travel. Passengers travel to Bendigo by a fast InterCity Express train. The journey to Mildura is completed on a double-decker coach. The fare is A$50.70 (U.S. $40.60) first-class sitting, A$44 (U.S. $35.20) economy-class sitting.

By Car The drive from Melbourne takes 7 hours.

ESSENTIALS Information Information is dispensed at the **Mildura Tourist Information Centre,** Langtree Mall, Mildura, VIC 3500 (tel. 050/23-3619), Monday through Friday from 9am to 5pm and Saturday and Sunday from 10am to 4pm. Day tours in and around Mildura are offered by **Ron's Tourist Centre,** 41 Deakin Avenue (tel. 050/21-1166). Mildura's telephone **area code** is 050.

Orientation Americans feel right at home in Mildura which the Chaffeys patterned after U.S. cities: Avenues run north and south and numbered streets run east and west. Deakin Avenue is the main thoroughfare.

I n the Aboriginal language, the word *mildura* means "dry red earth," which brings to mind much of Australia's landscape. Thousands of miles of inland terrain are rust-colored and barren. In the case of Mildura, however, this isn't true. When the natives named the area, it *was* indistinguishable from the land around it, but subsequently the largest irrigation scheme in the country has created 22,000 fertile hectares (54,340 acres) that produce wine and table grapes, olives, many types of citrus fruit, avocados, and melons. These horticultural achievements are possible because of the town's location on the banks of the Murray River and the know-how of California's Chaffey brothers—George and W. B. (William Benjamin).

The Chaffeys honed their skills in Etiwanda and Ontario, California, where they developed large-scale irrigation programs. George, the older of the two, was an engineer, and W. B. had a talent for business ventures. In 1887 they were invited by Alfred Deakin, a member of Victoria's Parliament, to transform the red earth along the Murray River into prime growing land. George Chaffey designed two triple-expansion pumping engines, and while they were being manufactured in England, newly arrived settlers set about clearing hundreds of hectares of scrub, erecting fences, and digging many kilometers of channels. By 1890 Mildura had 3,000 residents and 2,500 hectares (6,175 acres) of vines, citrus, and stone fruit. One pump continued operating until 1955; the other lasted until 1959. Today the oasislike community (pop. 19,360) is the heart of one of Australia's most important fruit-growing regions.

WHAT TO SEE & DO

ATTRACTIONS

MILDURA ARTS CENTRE, 199 Cureton Ave. Tel. 23-3733.

The Mildura Arts Centre consists of **Rio Vista** (the former home of W. B. Chaffey), the **Regional Art Gallery,** and a 400-seat **theater.** The grand house, built in 1890, is interesting both for itself and items of local history it contains. The dining room and smoking room are just as they were when the Californian was in residence. A variety of equipment used by the pioneers in this area is on display on the front lawn, including one of Chaffey's original pumping engines. This 6-meter-high (20-ft.), 750-horsepower engine transformed Mildura from a waterless wasteland into the most densely populated rural production center in Australia.

Admission: A$2 (U.S. $1.60) adults; children, free.

Open: Mon–Fri 9am–5pm, Sun 2–4:30pm. **Closed:** Christmas Day and Good Friday.

MILDURA WORKINGMAN'S CLUB, Deakin Ave. Tel. 23-0531

Another point of interest in Mildura is the Workingman's Club, where the bar is nearly the length of a football field and has 27 beer taps. According to the *Guinness Book of World Records,* this is the Southern Hemisphere's longest.

Admission: Free.

Open: Mon–Sat 9am–noon.

GOLDEN RIVER ZOO, Flora Ave. Tel. 23-5540.

Set on 14 hectares (35 acres) of lush Murray River frontage, this privately owned zoo is well worth a stop. Visitors walk through large enclosures where native animals roam freely and can be petted and fed. Daily animal shows—times vary. Paddleboat cruise to the zoo departs Mildura Wharf at 9:50am and returns at 3pm. Snacks are sold from a kiosk on the grounds.

Admission: A$9.50 (U.S. $7.60) adults, A$4.75 (U.S. $3.80) children.

Open: Daily 9am–5pm. **Closed:** Christmas Day. **Directions:** 4km (2½ miles) from city center down 11th St.

FRUIT & WINE PRODUCTION

The original settlers sun-dried their fruit because they couldn't get it to Melbourne markets before it spoiled. This changed when the railroad was put through to Mildura in 1903, but dried fruit remains an important product in this area. The packing companies located here are among the world's largest. You can tour the **Mildura Cooperative Fruit Company Proprietary Ltd.** on the Calder Highway at Irymple (tel. 24-5203). In town, the **Sunraysia Dried Fruits and Healthfood Centre,** 33 Deakin Avenue (tel. 23-1760), shows a video on the industry and sells an amazing array of the product. The center is open Monday through Friday from 9am to 5:30pm and Saturday from 9am to noon. Light lunches and morning and afternoon teas using the local products are available.

The area's wineries also welcome visitors. **Mildara Wines Limited,** Wentworth Road, Merbein (tel. 25-2303), 11 kilometers (7 miles) northwest of Mildura, is open Monday through Friday from 9am to 5pm, Saturday from 11am to 4pm, and Sunday from noon to 4pm. Tours cost A$1 (U.S. 80¢). **Lindeman's,** the largest winery in the Southern Hemisphere, is located 30 kilometers (18 miles) from Mildura in Karadoc (tel. 24-0303); tastings, sales, and inspections are Monday through Friday from 9am to 5pm and Saturday from 10am to 1pm. (In both cases guided tours are Monday through Friday only.)

THE MURRAY RIVER

The Murray River provides a number of activities for visitors. To begin with, you can watch the action as boats pass through the river's **Lock 11.** If you have a bit more time, why not take a 2-hour cruise on the PS *Melbourne* (tel. 23-2200)? This steam-powered paddle wheeler, built in 1912, leaves from the Mildura Wharf Sunday through Friday at 10:50am and 1:50pm and Saturday at 1:50pm. It is still driven by its original steam engine and boiler. The fare is A$14 (U.S. $11.20) for adults and A$6 (U.S. $4.80) for children 5 to 15 years; under 5 are free. A kiosk on board sells snacks and teas. Cruises don't operate on Christmas Day.

Longer excursions are possible on the paddleboat *Coonawarra,* which makes regular 3- and 5-day trips on the Murray and Darling rivers. Under the leadership of charming Capt. Leon Wagner, the romantic paddleboat offers modern accommodations and tasty meals for up to 36 people. Stops are made along the way at such points of interest as the Mildara Winery and the Golden River Zoo. Locks are navigated en route to ports of call in Victoria and South Australia, and time is allowed for relaxing, bushwalking, and enjoying the fresh air and scenery along the way. The paddleboat *Coonawarra*, 98 Seventh Street, Mildura, VIC 3000 (tel. 23-3366, or toll free 008/03-4424 in Australia), is the last remaining historic paddleboat offering accommodated cruises on the river. The fare is A$390 (U.S. $312) per person including all meals for the shorter trip and A$650 (U.S. $520) for 5 days. Children 3 to 14 years are charged A$155 (U.S. $124) for 3 days and A$260 (U.S. $208) for the 5-day trip.

The Murray is fed by the Darling River, which starts in Queensland, and the Murray-Darling system constitutes the longest river in Australia. Because the land is so flat, it is also one of the world's slowest rivers. When there is a flood in Queensland, it takes the water 3 months to reach Victoria and South Australia, so people have plenty of time to protect their riverfront property.

WHERE TO STAY

CHAFFEY INTERNATIONAL MOTOR INN, 244 Deakin Ave., Mildura, VIC 3500. Tel. 050/23-5833. 32 rms. A/C MINIBAR TV TEL
$ Rates: A$70 (U.S. $56) single; A$80 (U.S. $64) double; A$10 (U.S. $8) extra person. Reservations can be made through Flag Inns. AE, BC, DC, MC, V.
Parking: Free.

This is a modern two-story property. In addition to its 32 rooms, the Chaffey has a cocktail lounge, restaurant, spa, pool, laundry, and playground. All quarters have coffee- and tea-making facilities, small refrigerators, in-room movies, and clock radios. Room service is offered, and facilities for handicapped travelers are available.

MILDURA GRAND HOTEL, Seventh St., Mildura, VIC 3500. Tel. 050/23-0511, or toll free 008/03-4228 in Australia. Fax 050/22-1801. 105 rms, 7 suites. MINIBAR TV TEL
$ Rates: A$40 (U.S. $32) budget single; A$55 (U.S. $44) budget double; A$55 (U.S. $44) standard single, A$67 (U.S. $53.60) standard double; A$88 (U.S. $70.40) "Grand Room" single, A$103 (U.S. $82.40) "Grand Room" double; A$110 (U.S. $88) "VIP" single, A$130 (U.S. $104) "VIP" double. Bed-and-breakfast and dinner-bed-and-breakfast packages available. AE, BC, DC, MC, V.
Parking: Free.

The Grand Hotel, located across the street from the train station, is a charming reminder of an earlier, more elegant era. Each room in the two-story, 19th-century hostelry has a private bathroom (20 have tubs), in-rooms movies, free daily newspaper, and coffee- and tea-making facilities; some "VIP" rooms have their own spa baths. A swimming pool, spa, and sauna are sited in a charming garden setting. Meals are served in the dining room, and teas and drinks are available in a number of different bars and lounges or around the pool. Large open fires warm these public areas in the winter. Room service is provided 24 hours.

4. VICTORIA/NEW SOUTH WALES: ALONG THE HUME HIGHWAY

If you're driving, the fastest route from Melbourne to Sydney is the Hume Highway, a distance of 840 kilometers (520 miles). Most vacation travelers break this 12-hour journey with an overnight stay, but truck drivers and businesspeople in a hurry go nonstop. In Chapter 6, I described the northern end of the trip through the Southern Highlands outside of Sydney. Albury and Goulburn, both in New South Wales, are other logical places to pause. The turnoff to Canberra, the nation's capital, is at Yass if you're coming from the south and just past Goulburn if you're coming from the north.

WANGARATTA

WHAT TO SEE & DO

AirWorld, on Greta Road in Wangaratta, Victoria (tel. 057/21-8788), 233 kilometers (144 miles) north of Melbourne, is worth a look if you're interested in antique aircraft. This aviation museum contains some 37 very old civil and military planes—most in flying condition. Some are the last of their type left in the world. Antique bicycles are also on display. A 200-seat restaurant is on the premises. AirWorld is open daily from 9am to 5pm; admission is A$6 (U.S. $4.80) for adults and A$4 (U.S. $3.20) for children. There is no public transportation to this attraction.

ALBURY-WODONGA

Straddling the border and the Murray River, 305 kilometers (189 miles) north of Melbourne, the twin towns of Albury, New South Wales, and Wodonga, Victoria, provide a convenient point at which to break the Melbourne-Sydney drive. Tourist information on New South Wales and Victoria is available from **The Crossing Place Tourist Information Centre,** Wodonga Place, Albury, NSW 2640 (tel. 060/21-2655). Open Monday to Thursday from 9am to 6pm, Friday from 9am to 10pm, Saturday from 9am to noon, and Sunday from 9am to 5pm. They also provide a 24-hour phone service.

WHAT TO SEE & DO

The **Regional Art Gallery,** 546 Dean Street, contains the city's art collection and a group of Australian photographs. The **Albury Regional Museum,** Australia Park, Wodonga Place (tel. 060/21-4550), is housed in the Old Turks Head Inn, which dates from 1854. It's open daily from 10:30am to 4:30pm. Admission is free of charge. The **Botanical Gardens** would be an ideal place to stretch your legs.

WHERE TO STAY & DINE

ALBURY GEORGIAN MOTOR INN, 599 Young St., Albury, NSW 2640. Tel. 060/21-8744, or toll free 008/02-8273 in Australia. Fax 060/21-8320. 19 rms, 5 suites. A/C MINIBAR TV TEL **Location:** 1km (½ mile) from rail station and 3km (1½ miles) from airport on Hume Hwy.

$ Rates: A$64 (U.S. $51.20) single; A$69 (U.S. $55.20) double; A$85 (U.S. $68) suite; A$12 (U.S. $9.60) extra person. AE, BC, CB, DC, MC, V. **Parking:** Free.
Each room in this two-story motel has a tub/shower combination, queen-size bed, clock radio, hairdryer, tea- and coffee-making facilities, and a small refrigerator. A restaurant is on the grounds and room service is available 15 hours a day. There's a pool and a spa; baby-sitting can be arranged.

HUME COUNTRY GOLF CLUB MOTOR INN, 736 Logan Rd., Albury, NSW 2640. Tel. 060/25-8233. Fax 060/40-1203. 21 rms, 4 suites. A/C TV TEL

$ Rates: A$55 (U.S. $44) single; A$65–A$70 (U.S. $52–U.S. $56) double; A$95 (U.S. $76) suite; A$15 (U.S. $12) extra person. Tariffs are 10% higher on public holidays. AE, BC, DC, MC, V. **Parking:** Free.
This is a fairly new motel adjacent to a golf club. All rooms have toasters in addition to the standard facilities. The four VIP suites have two-person spas. Pool and laundry facilities are available to guests. The golf-club complex includes a 27-hole course, modern locker rooms with showers, a pro shop, a day-and-night golf driving range,

100 poker (slot) machines, a bistro for quick meals, a cocktail lounge, and a restaurant. Many rooms in the motel have golf-course views.

HUME MOTOR INN, 406 Wodonga Place, Albury, NSW 2640. Tel. 060/21-2733. Fax 060/41-2239. 40 rms, 5 suites. A/C TV TEL

$ **Rates:** A$63 (U.S. $50.40) single; A$70 (U.S. $56) double; A$84 (U.S. $67.20) suite. A$5 (U.S. $4) surcharge on public holidays. AE, BC, DC, MC, V. **Parking:** Free.

At this two-story motel, the licensed, à la carte restaurant is open daily and there's a pool and playground. Some rooms have queen-size beds and clock radios. All offer tea- and coffee-making facilities and small refrigerators. Baby-sitting can be arranged.

GUNDAGAI
WHAT TO SEE & DO

You might want to stop briefly in Gundagai, New South Wales, 491 kilometers (304 miles) north of Melbourne and 386 kilometers (239 miles) south of Sydney, to see the **"Dog on the Tuckerbox" memorial,** 8 kilometers (5 miles) north of town, which is celebrated in a popular Australian folk song, "The Road to Gundagai." **Rusconi's Marble Masterpiece,** a miniature cathedral made of 20,000 pieces of NSW marble, is worth a look, too. It's on display at the **Tourist Information Centre** on Sheridan Street.

GOULBURN
WHAT TO SEE & DO

Even if I didn't tell you that Goulburn is the center of a wealthy farming district, you might guess it when you see the high-rise horned ram that towers over the **Big Merino Tourist Complex** on the Hume Highway (tel. 048/21-5477). This all-inclusive pit stop is located 681 kilometers (422 miles) north of Melbourne and 196 kilometers (121 miles) south of Sydney. It consists of a 24-hour petrol (gasoline) station, a large gift and souvenir shop, a 400-seat Agrodome, the Billabong Restaurant, the 24-hour Viennaworld Restaurant, and an ice-cream parlor.

Several times a day Australia's top 20 ram breeds are presented in shows in the Agrodome. The 1-hour entertainment also includes a shearing demonstration and information on the wool industry. Admission is A$6 (U.S. $4.80) for adults and A$3 (U.S. $2.40) for children. Many woolen items are sold in the complex's shop.

WHERE TO STAY

LILAC CITY MOTOR INN, 126 Lagoon St. (Hume Hwy.), Goulburn, NSW 2580. Tel. 048/21-5000. 28 rms. A/C TV TEL

$ **Rates:** A$68 (U.S. $54.40) single; A$75 (U.S. $60) double; A$7 (U.S. $5.60) extra person. Lower rates through Aussie auto clubs. AE, BC, DC, MC, V. **Parking:** Free.

Should you decide to break your Melbourne-Sydney trip in Goulburn, the Lilac City Motor Inn is a nice two-story motel with a restaurant, room service, and the standard amenities. Facilities for handicapped travelers are available.

5. THE SOUTHEAST COAST

The **Princes Highway** follows the perimeter of Victoria and New South Wales, connecting Melbourne and Sydney over a route of 1,080 kilometers (670 miles). Unlike the speedy Hume Highway trip, this journey is best done over a 2-day period. You may want to take longer, of course, especially if you stop to play golf, go boating, or enjoy the beaches. I described the coast from Sydney to the state border in Chapter 6. The highlights of the Victorian portion are Lakes Entrance, 319 kilometers (198 miles) east of Melbourne, and the Snowy River National Park, due north of Orbost.

LAKES ENTRANCE

A series of interconnecting lakes and lagoons and a long expanse of beach make Lakes Entrance (pop. 4,100) a popular summer resort. The town is at the eastern end of the Gippsland Lakes: Lake King, Lake Victoria, Lake Wellington, Lake Reeve, and others provide a wonderful playground for boaters, waterskiers, windsurfers, and fishermen. (Boats of all shapes and sizes can be rented in Lakes Entrance. Cruises and fishing excursions are also available.) The inland waterway is separated from the ocean by a thin sliver of sand dunes, and a footbridge allows surfers, swimmers, and sun-worshipers access to a seemingly endless stretch of beach.

Lakes Entrance is the base for Australia's largest commercial fishing fleet. Even if you don't choose to break your Melbourne-Sydney journey at this point, do pause at **Jemmy Point,** 2 kilometers (1 mile) west of town on the Princes Highway, to admire the view.

WHERE TO STAY & DINE

BANJO PATTERSON MOTOR INN, 131 Esplanade (Princes Hwy.), Lakes Entrance, VIC 3909. Tel. 051/55-2933. 23 rms. A/C TV TEL

$ Rates: A$60–A$85 (U.S. $48–U.S. $68) single; A$60–A$118 (U.S. $48–U.S. $94.40) double. Rates are highest Christmas–end of Jan and Easter week. Reservations can be made through Best Western. Lower rates through Aussie auto clubs. AE, BC, DC, MC, V. **Parking:** Free.

Three of the rooms at the Banjo Patterson Motor Inn have spa tubs and all are equipped with radios, videos, coffee- and tea-making facilities, and small refrigerators. A restaurant and swimming pool are on the premises, and room service is available.

ABEL TASMAN MOTOR LODGE, 643 Esplanade (Princes Hwy.), Lakes Entrance, VIC 3909. Tel. 051/55-1655. 12 rms. A/C TV TEL

$ Rates: A$45–A$82 (U.S. $36–U.S. $65.60) single; A$50–A$81 (U.S. $40–U.S. $64.80) double. Rates are highest Christmas–end of Jan and Easter week. AE, BC, DC, MC, V. **Parking:** Free.

The Abel Tasman Motor Lodge is a two-story motel with modern amenities and a pool. All rooms offer radios, coffee- and tea-making facilities, small refrigerators, and toasters.

SNOWY RIVER NATIONAL PARK

Adventurous travelers who don't mind driving on unsealed (unpaved) roads have the option of leaving the Princes Highway and wandering up through the foothills of Victoria's high country. The **Barry Way** follows the course of the Snowy River, passing through the rustic townships of **Buchan** and **Gelantipy.** The wilderness scenery in this area is breathtaking. One of my most vivid mental pictures of Australia was formed when I walked down to the river, at a point just south of the New South Wales border, and discovered that the banks were covered with colorful California poppies. Besides being a beautiful drive, this route is also a shortcut to **Jindabyne,** the gateway to Thredbo and the Snowy Mountains (see Chapter 6).

WHAT TO SEE & DO

The **Buchan Caves** (tel. 051/55-9264) are open to the public with several tours daily between 10am and 3:30pm. Both Fairy and Royal caves are easily accessible and highly decorated with delicate calcite formations. Cave tours cost A$5 (U.S. $4) for adults and half price for kids 5 to 16. A kiosk sells snacks. The road to Buchan is sealed all the way from the coast.

Horseback riding is a popular activity in this area. If you're interested, contact **Snowy River Trail Rides,** R.M.B. 4030 Buchan Bruthen Road, Buchan, VIC 3885 (tel. 051/55-9245). Rides cost A$14 (U.S. $11.20) per hour. Longer trail rides in the Snowy River country cost A$80 (U.S. $64) a day (all inclusive) for 2- to 10-day rides. These take place November to May.

Paul and Judi Sykes of **Snowy Mountain Rider Tours,** Karoonda Park,

Gelantipy, VIC 3885 (tel. 051/55-0220), host guests at their property and do day rides from there. These cost A$100 (U.S. $80) a day. They also organize longer, more adventurous trail rides, which involve camping for 4 or 5 nights. These cost A$400 to A$500 (U.S. $320 to U.S. $400) and take place from November to March. Between the spectacular scenery, Judi's good cooking, and the pleasure of riding and sleeping out where, according to Banjo Patterson, "the night stars fairly blaze," this could be the thrill of a lifetime.

TASMANIA

Australia's only island state looks more like New Zealand than mainland Oz. It's green and mountainous in some places; green and pastoral in others. It's sparsely populated, has cool, wet winters, and is a great place for growing apples.

There are several good reasons why you should spend the time and money to visit Tasmania. The first is wilderness scenery. Because it is so isolated, Tasmania's bush remains very much the way it was when Abel Tasman first sighted the island in 1642. Dense rain forests, jagged mountains, alpine meadows, stands of Huon pine trees that predate European exploration, lush valleys, and wild rivers await adventurous souls. Some of them can be viewed from the main roads, but the best are stashed away where only those willing to hike, climb, raft, or canoe will ever see them. South West National Park and the rugged West Coast are magnets for those who like roughing it.

This is not to say that the "holiday island" is only for athletes. In addition to beautiful wilderness scenery, Tasmania is well known for its colonial buildings. While other states have pulled down many of their Victorian and Edwardian structures, this kind of "progress" has eluded out-of-the-way Tassie. Cozy bed-and-breakfast inns, quaint tearooms, and appealing eateries are housed in historic buildings. In this respect, Tasmania resembles England.

Were I packing for a trip to Hobart or Launceston right now, I'd leave room in my suitcase for all the handcrafts I know I'd buy. Many talented artisans are drawn to the island's slow way of life and appreciation of nature. While some of their products are sold on the mainland, the selection and prices offered in local craft shops are unmatched in other states. Pottery, wooden items created from Tasmanian trees, and hand-blown glass pieces are especially attractive.

In addition to wonderful wilderness, a plethora of colonial buildings, and crafts, the island state offers excellent trout fishing on more than 3,000 lakes. Arthur's Lake, Lake Sorell, and Great Lake, all in the central region, are three of the anglers' favorites. If you like eating seafood, but aren't interested in catching it, a large commercial fleet keeps local restaurants well supplied.

Seafood is only one aspect of Tasmanian cuisine. Visitors here can also look forward to cheese, cream, game, beef, fruit, vegetables, and wine that are some of the best Australia has to offer.

Nothing in the state's appearance hints at its early violent and cruel history. First settled by Europeans in 1803, Tasmania was primarily a penal colony where convicts lived in terrible conditions and toiled hard until the last transportations in 1852. Unfortunately, this isn't the worst aspect of the island's story. The white settlers hunted the local Aborigines like animals.

SEEING TASMANIA

Tasmanians are very hospitable hosts who will make you glad you took the time to visit. Try to go between mid-September and May, when the weather is at its best. The best sources of tourist information are the Tasmanian Travel Centre offices located in most Australian capitals and in Hobart, Launceston, Devonport, and Burnie. Be sure

WHAT'S SPECIAL ABOUT TASMANIA

Buildings
☐ Colonial buildings, some functioning as B&Bs.

Ace Attractions
☐ Port Arthur, the remains of a penal colony.
☐ Wilderness scenery, much of it on the World Heritage List.

Shopping
☐ For crafts—excellent selection and good prices.

Regional Food & Drink
☐ Tasmanian wine, both red and white.

☐ Fruits and vegetables, freshly picked in season.
☐ Seafood—including salmon, crayfish, trout, and oysters.

Activities
☐ Camping, hiking, and fishing in beautiful bushland settings.
☐ Sailing, a popular summer pastime.

Saturday Selections
☐ The Salamanca Market in Hobart, for arts and crafts.

to pick up a copy of *Travelways,* Tourism Tasmania's free tourist tabloid, which is several cuts above the norm.

In addition to many air services, Tasmania can be reached by two different boats across Bass Strait. The *Abel Tasman* ferry carries more than 800 passengers, with or without their cars, from Melbourne's Station Pier to Devonport on the island's north coast. The ship has all modern conveniences, and unless rough seas are encountered, the trip is comfortable and enjoyable. Facilities include a cafeteria, buffet bistro, fine-dining room, pool, sauna, and disco. The *Abel Tasman* sails on alternate evenings at 6pm from Devonport and Station Pier, arriving the next morning at 8:30am. Reservations can be made with TT-Line (tel. 03/644-5233 in Melbourne, 004/23-0333 in Devonport, or toll free 008/03-0306 in Australia). You can also make reservations for the *Abel Tasman* by phoning SO/PAC (tel. toll free 800/551-2012 in the U.S. and Canada). Fares vary according to the time of year. The "holiday" period (mid-December through January) is the most expensive; "shoulder" season (mid-September through mid-December and February through late April) fares are lower; the "bargain" period is from late April through mid-September. One-way adult fares range from A$83 to A$295 (U.S. $66.40 to U.S. $236) depending on the type of accommodations required. These vary from hostel-type lodging to deluxe suites with en suite bathrooms.

The other way to cross Bass Strait is by *SeaCat Tasmania,* a high-speed catamaran service from George Town in Tasmania to Port Welshpool in Victoria. Actual crossing time is 4½ hours from coast to coast. This vessel can carry up to 350 passengers and 84 cars. Fares, based on the time of year you want to travel, range from A$109 to A$120 (U.S. $87.20 to U.S. $96) one-way. RoadCat coaches will get you from Melbourne to Port Welshpool (a trip which takes about 3 hours) and from George Town to Launceston (40 minutes) for an additional charge. For more information on SeaCat Tasmania and RoadCat coaches, call toll free 008/03-0131 in Australia.

Transportation on the island is provided by **Airlines of Tasmania, Tasmanian Redline Coaches,** and **Hobart Coaches** which go to all sizable towns. The **Tassie Pass** for Redline Coaches is a dollarwise value for those who plan to travel extensively. It costs A$120 (U.S. $96) for 14 days of unlimited travel or A$99 (U.S. $79.20) for 7 days. Hobart Coaches offers an **Explorer Travel Pass** which costs A$100 (U.S. $80) and is valid for 10 trips within 30 days of issue. Because the state is relatively small, fly/drive packages (such as the ones offered by Australian Airlines) are popular. The travel time by car from Devonport on the north coast to Hobart on the south is less than 4 hours. Launceston to Hobart takes just under 3 hours. The **RAC**

(Royal Automobile Club of Tasmania), corner of Murray and Patrick streets, Hobart (tel. 38-2200), is the best source of driving data.

---

1. HOBART

198km (123 miles) S of Launceston

GETTING THERE   By Plane   Air New Zealand provides regular service from New Zealand, and Eastwest Airlines, Ansett, and Australian Airlines carry passengers from the mainland. A Sydney-Hobart Australian Airlines Air Pass ticket costs from A$176 to A$215 (U.S. $140.80 to U.S. $172); a Melbourne-Hobart Blue Roo fare is A$138 (U.S. $110.40). The trip from the airport to the city center takes about 30 minutes and costs A$17 (U.S. $13.60) by taxi and A$5 (U.S. $4) by Redline Coach (tel. 34-4577).

By Train   Tasmania lacks passenger train service.

By Bus   If you cross Bass Strait on the *Abel Tasman,* you can get a connecting **Redline Coach** to Hobart. This ticket costs A$32 (U.S. $25.60). If you cross on the *SeaCat,* **RoadCat** coaches will transport you to Hobart. **Hobart Coaches** provide service, too.

By Boat   Hobart is a favorite port of call for cruise ships.

By Car   It takes about 3 hours to drive from Launceston to Hobart.

ESSENTIALS   Information   Tourist information is available at the **Tasmanian Travel Centre,** 80 Elizabeth Street, Hobart, TAS 7000 (tel. 002/30-0250 or 002/30-0211), Monday to Friday from 8:45am to 5pm and Saturday from 9am to noon. Hobart's **area code** is 002.

City Layout   Hobart is perched astride the River Derwent on the south coast of the state. The central business district is on the west side of the water, and pleasant residential suburbs fan out across the way. Mount Wellington (1,270m/4,191 ft.) rises up behind the city. The Derwent empties into Storm Bay only 20 kilometers (12 miles) or so downstream. The open sea is about 50 kilometers (31 miles) farther on.
  The main thoroughfares, Campbell, Argyle, Elizabeth, Murray, and Harrington streets, slope down to the busy harbor, where boats of all sizes and shapes can be seen at Victoria Dock and Constitution Dock. The Tasman Bridge and regular passenger ferries reach across the River Derwent.

GETTING AROUND   Hobart's Metropolitan Transportation Trust (tel. 71-3232) operates a system of buses throughout the city and suburban areas. Single MTT fares range from A90¢ to A$1.30 (U.S. 75¢ to U.S. $1.05); Day Rover passes, good anytime on weekends and between 9am and 4:30pm and after 6pm during the week, cost A$2.20 (U.S. $1.80). All tickets can be purchased directly from the drivers.

SPECIAL EVENTS   On any given day, the city's harbor is a busy place, but the Sydney-to-Hobart Yacht Race, which starts in Sydney on December 26, fills this area to overflowing and creates a carnival atmosphere. The race takes anywhere from 2 to 4 days, and the sailors and their fans stay on to celebrate the New Year in Hobart.

History and a picturesque harbor make the capital of the island state (pop. 200,000) the appealing place that it is. Second in age only to Sydney, Hobart has wonderful stone buildings surrounding the waterfront and little colonial cottages lining the narrow lanes of **Battery Point.** The harbor, which once hosted tall sailing ships,

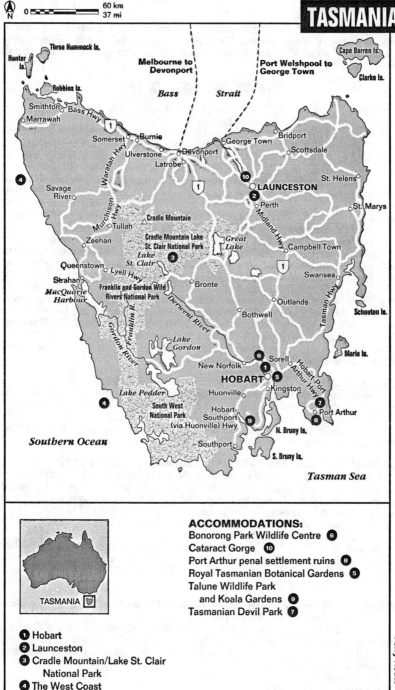

TASMANIA

0 — 60 km / 37 mi
N

Three Hummock Is.
Hunter Is.
Robbins Is.
Smithton
Marrawah
Somerset
Burnie
Ulverstone
Devonport
Latrobe

Melbourne to Devonport
Port Welshpool to George Town

Bass Strait

Cape Barren Is.
Clarke Is.

Bass Hwy
Waratah Hwy

George Town
Bridport
Scottsdale

4

Savage River
Tullah
Cradle Mountain
Zeehan

10
LAUNCESTON
2
Perth
St. Helens
St. Marys

Murchison Hwy

Cradle Mountain Lake St. Clair National Park
Great Lake
Lake St. Clair
3

Midland Hwy

Campbell Town
Swansea

Queenstown
Lyell Hwy
Strahan
MacQuarie Harbour

Franklin and Gordon Wild Rivers National Park
Bronte

Bothwell
Outlands

Tasman Hwy

Schouten Is.

Gordon River
Franklin R.
Lake Gordon

Derwent River

Maria Is.

Lake Pedder
4

New Norfolk
6
Sorell
1
HOBART
5
Kingston

Hobart-Port Arthur Hwy

7 Port Arthur
8

South West National Park
Huonville
Hobart-Southport (via Huonville) Hwy
9
N. Bruny Is.
Southport
S. Bruny Is.

Southern Ocean

Tasman Sea

ACCOMMODATIONS:
Bonorong Park Wildlife Centre 6
Cataract Gorge 10
Port Arthur penal settlement ruins 8
Royal Tasmanian Botanical Gardens 5
Talune Wildlife Park
   and Koala Gardens 9
Tasmanian Devil Park 7

TASMANIA

1 Hobart
2 Launceston
3 Cradle Mountain/Lake St. Clair
   National Park
4 The West Coast

Ferry Route - - - - -

today provides shelter for yachts from all over the world. The city is not without modern high-rise hotels, but the 1840s warehouses of **Salamanca Place,** now converted to shops and dining spots, have much more impact on the overall atmosphere.

WHAT TO SEE & DO

It's easy to understand why Hobart is popular with sailors. The surrounding coastline is a maze of bays, channels, coves, peninsulas, and smaller islands.

For the best view of the area, make the 22-kilometer (13-mile) drive to the top of ✪ **Mount Wellington.** From this lofty vantage point you can see the irregular coast with its many bays, coves, and peninsulas. If you don't want to drive, join one of the day- or half-day tours offered by the Tasmanian Travel Centre.

When you return to sea level, take time to walk around **Battery Point,** an area of colonial stone cottages located just south of the harbor. (You can reach Battery Point on a route 53 or 55 bus.) The point gets its name from a battery of guns set up on the promontory in 1818. Today, antiques shops, tearooms, atmospheric pubs, and cozy restaurants are interspersed among historic homes. Most of these houses are modest, but **Narryna,** 103 Hampden Road (tel. 34-2791), is a good example of how the upper classes lived in early Hobart. **Van Diemen's Land Folk Museum,** located within the Georgian dwelling, is open Monday through Friday from 10am to 5pm and Saturday and Sunday from 2 to 5pm. The museum is closed during July. Admission is A$4 (U.S. $3.20) for adults and A$1 (U.S. 80¢) for children. Also in Battery Point, the **Maritime Museum of Tasmania,** Secheron Road (tel. 23-5082), is worth a stop. It's open Monday through Friday and Sunday from 1 to 4:30pm and Saturday from 10am to 4:30pm, with an admission fee of A$2 (U.S. $1.60) for adults. The **National Trust** conducts walking tours of Battery Point on Saturday mornings at 9:30am. Contact the tour organizer, Miss D. Henslowe (tel. 23-6236), or the **Tasmanian Travel Centre** (tel. 30-0250) for more information.

RUNNYMEDE, 61 Bay Rd., New Town. Tel. 28-1269.

History buffs will love this gracious colonial home, built in 1836, and now the property of the National Trust. The house is furnished in period antiques.

Admission: A$4 (U.S. $3.20) adults, A$1.50 (U.S. $1.20) children.

Open: Daily 10am–4:30pm. **Closed:** July, Good Friday, and Christmas Day. **Bus:** Lutana, route 20.

CADBURY CHOCOLATE FACTORY, Claremont. Tel. 49-0111.

For a change of pace, take a cruise on the *Derwent Explorer* and visit the Cadbury Chocolate Factory in suburban Claremont. Along the way you'll pass the **Naval Base, Government House,** and other landmarks. You must reserve ahead of time for factory tours by calling the Tasmanian Travel Centre (tel. 30-0250 or 30-0211).

Admission: Tour A$7 (U.S. $5.60) adults, A$3.50 (U.S. $2.80) children 6–15; younger children not admitted unless carried.

Tours: Mon–Thurs 9, 9:30, and 10:30am, Fri 9 and 9:30am. **Closed:** Mid-Dec to late Jan. **Transportation:** Phone the Cruise Company (tel. 34-9294). Boat fare is A$17 (U.S. $13.60) adults, A$8 (U.S. $6.40) children 5–15; under 5, free of charge. **Bus:** Route 38 or 41.

ROYAL TASMANIAN BOTANICAL GARDENS, on the Domain near Government House. Tel. 34-6299.

If you like flowers, trees, and shrubs, visit the Royal Tasmanian Botanical Gardens. Established in 1818, the gardens are known for their Fern House and Cactus House. Colorful seasonal blooming plants are housed in the Conservatory. A restaurant provides lunch and teas.

Admission: Free.

Open: Daily 8am–4:45pm.

BONORONG PARK WILDLIFE CENTRE, Briggs Rd., Brighton. Tel. 68-1184.

If you're interested in native fauna, visit Bonorong Park Wildlife Centre which is about 25 minutes' drive north of Hobart. The 6-hectare (15-acre) park houses native Tasmanian animals in a bush setting. The Bush Tucker Shed serves lunches, billy tea, and damper.

Admission: A$4 (U.S. $3.20) adults, A$2 (U.S. $1.60) children under 17.

Open: Daily 9am–5pm. **Closed:** Christmas Day. **Transportation:** Bus no. 125 or 127 or drive north on Route 1 to Brighton. Well signposted.

SHOPPING

The Hobart area is a great place to shop for Tasmanian crafts. I hope you'll be in town on Saturday because the ✪ **Salamanca Market,** held from 8:30am to 2pm, is a treasure trove of items made from native woods, pottery, and glass. Many of the goods available from 200 colorful stalls are identical to those sold in the adjacent **Salamanca Place** shops; the only difference is the price.

The **National Trust Shop,** 33 Salamanca Place, sells tasteful souvenirs and gifts. It's open Monday through Friday from 9:30am to 5pm and Saturday from 9:30am to 1pm. Other places to browse or buy: **Handmark Gallery,** 77 Salamanca Place (tel. 23-7895); the **Spinning Wheel,** 69 Salamanca Place (tel. 34-1711); and the **Wilderness Society Shop** (tel. 34-9370), 31-35 Salamanca Place. **Aspect Design,** 79 Salamanca Place (tel. 23-2642), sells the work of jeweler Jon de Jonge and other Tasmanian artisans. Be sure to notice the Richard Clements glass bottles.

The main shopping area of Hobart is centered around the **Elizabeth Street Mall** between Collins Street and Liverpool Street. **The Cat and the Fiddle Arcade,** located between the mall and Murray Street, houses interesting boutiques and shops. Store hours are Monday through Thursday from 9am to 6pm, Friday from 9am to 9pm, and Saturday from 9am to noon.

SPORTS & RECREATION

Tasmania is the ideal place for those who like a lot of action. At least a dozen operators will happily help you get organized for hiking, rafting, climbing, or canoeing. Contact **Peregrine Adventures** (tel. toll free 008/33-1124 in Australia) if you'd like to raft the Picton or Huon River. They also offer 5-, 11-, and 13-day raft trips on the Franklin River for those with more experience.

Bushventures, 54 Princes Street, Sandy Bay (tel. 23-6910), conducts four-wheel-drive excursions that last from 1 to 6 days. Their 4-day Franklin River/World Heritage Area tour is especially popular. These operators and others can be contacted directly or through any Tasmanian Travel Centre. For information on Tasmania's wilderness regions, contact the **Department of Parks, Wildlife, and Heritage,** 134 Macquarie Street (tel. 30-8011).

Half-, full-day, and longer cycling trips are organized by **Brake-Out Cycling Tours,** 300 Park Street, Newtown (tel. 28-5022). **Trout Fishing Safaris of Tasmania,** 2/45 Lansdowne Crescent, West Hobart (tel. 34-7286), will happily take you to where the fish are biting. Daily all-inclusive charges are A$190 (U.S. $152) per person for two or more and A$250 (U.S. $200) solo. No trips during June or July.

✪ **Par Avion,** Cambridge Aerodrome (tel. 48-5390), operates scenic flights over wilderness areas in the southern portion of the state. This is an ideal way to witness Tassie's mountains, rivers, plains, beaches, and dense bush (A$130/U.S. $104). Those who want something a bit more experiential can join the trip that lands at Port Davey on the coast of South West National Park for a tour by boat and a barbecue lunch. The cost is A$295 (U.S. $236) for adults and A$236 (U.S. $188.80) for children 3 to 14 years.

The **Royal Hobart Golf Club,** Seven Mile Beach (tel. 48-6161), is an 18-hole championship course open to members of overseas clubs. "Ladies and gentlemen" pay A$25 (U.S. $20) to play here.

An extensive network of walking tracks (trails) is located on the slopes of Mount

Wellington. These afford wonderful vistas of the surrounding area as well as pleasurable hiking. Pick up a copy of the *Mt. Wellington Day Walk Map and Notes* from the **Department of Environment and Planning's Tasmap Centre,** ground floor, Lands Building, 134 Macquarie Street (tel. 30-3382).

WHERE TO STAY

In addition to modern hotels and motels, Hobart and the surrounding area offer a nice selection of homestays. If you'd like to stay overnight with a Tasmanian family either in town or on a farm, contact **Homehost Tasmania Proprietary Ltd.,** P.O. Box 550, Rosny Park, TAS 7018 (tel. 002/44-5442; fax 002/44-7181). Bed-and-breakfast prices range from A$44 to A$52 (U.S. $35.20 to U.S. $41.60) single and from A$68 to A$74 (U.S. $54.40 to U.S. $59.20) double per night. Rates are lower May to September. In some cases, guests share bathroom facilities with their hosts; in others, private en suite facilities are provided. A few properties are totally self-contained (meaning entirely separate quarters with a kitchen).

Hosts belonging to the **Country Accommodation Association** also welcome visitors to their country homes and host farms. Ask at any Tasmanian Travel Centre for a brochure. Another option, **"colonial accommodation,"** refers to lodging in a building or cottage built on its present site before 1901. Interiors are true to the period and contain either genuine antiques or reproduction furniture. Tasmanian Travel Centres also have literature on this island-state specialty.

EXPENSIVE

SHERATON HOBART HOTEL, 1 Davey St., Hobart, TAS 7000. Tel. 002/35-4535. Fax 002/23-8175. 222 rms, 12 suites. A/C MINIBAR TV TEL
$ Rates: A$260 (U.S. $208) single or double; A$370 (U.S. $296) executive suite; A$50 (U.S. $40) extra person. Children under 18 stay free in parents' room. No-smoking rooms available. AE, BC, CB, DC, MC, V. **Parking:** Free.

The Sheraton Hobart is a posh property overlooking the city's picturesque harbor. More than half of the rooms in the 12-story hotel, which opened in 1987, have a view of the water and wharves. The attractive lobby has a polished-marble floor, pale gray walls, and a large curved window that frames the activity on Victoria and Constitution docks. Colorful sails are suspended from the top of a four-story atrium.

All quarters are spacious and have polished-granite bathrooms. Ten executive suites have separate bedrooms with harbor views, and large bathrooms that feature separate showers and tubs, bathroom scales, hairdryers, and terry robes. An additional half bath is off the lounge. Eight rooms are equipped for handicapped travelers.

Dining/Entertainment: The Gazebo Coffee Shop and Atrium Cocktail Lounge also enjoy a nice vista. Sullivans is the fine dining room.

Services: 24-hour room service, turn-down service, laundry, valet, concierge, baby-sitting, and massage.

Facilities: A heated indoor saltwater pool and a sauna. Gym equipment and massage are available in the Health Club. There are also a unisex hair salon, business center, and newsagent.

WREST POINT HOTEL CASINO, 410 Sandy Bay Rd., Hobart, TAS 7005. Tel. 002/25-0112, or toll free 008/03-0611 in Australia. Fax 002/25-3909. 264 rms, 14 suites. A/C MINIBAR TV TEL **Transportation:** The hotel is located 3 km (2 miles) south of the city center. A taxi costs about A$5 (U.S. $4), and there is bus service.
$ Rates: A$94 (U.S. $75.20) Garden View room; A$105 (U.S. $84) River View room; A$205–A$242 (U.S. $164–U.S. $193.60) tower double; A$280 (U.S. $224) junior suite; A$380 (U.S. $304) executive suite; A$30 (U.S. $24) extra adult. One child sharing with parents stays free. Reservations can be made through Flag Inns. No-smoking rooms available. AE, BC, DC, MC, V. **Parking:** Free.

Built in 1973, the tower of the Wrest Point Hotel Casino is almost as much a landmark in Hobart as Mount Wellington. Located on the waterfront in the suburb of Sandy Bay, the 17-story hotel is easy to recognize on the skyline. Wrest Point is popular with those who like to gamble, as its large casino is open 7 days a week.

Most of the rooms are in the tower, which is round and creates pie-shaped quarters. A choice of bed sizes is offered. All have good views. Less expensive lodging is in the low-rise Motor Inn River View and Motor Inn Garden View sections. Ten rooms are designed for handicapped travelers. Hint: Don't use the telephone here; charges are the highest I've encountered anywhere in the country.

Dining/Entertainment: The hotel offers a wide range of dining and drinking choices. These include a 24-hour coffee shop, the River View Lounge in the keno area of the casino, an Asian eatery, and a posh revolving restaurant on the top of the tower.

Services: 24-hour room service, shoeshine, valet, concierge, baby-sitting, and massage.

Facilities: Indoor pool, spa, gym, tennis court, sauna, mini-golf, and Ping-Pong. Beauty and hair salons are on the premises. Also a business center—and, of course, a casino.

MODERATE

ISLINGTON ELEGANT PRIVATE HOTEL, 321 Davey St., Hobart, TAS 7004. Tel. 002/23-3900. 8 rms (all with bath). TEL **Directions:** Islington is located 3 km (2 miles) from the city on the way to Mount Wellington. Take the A6 Hwy. from the airport to Davey St. It's important to stay in the right-hand lane and go straight ahead when road turns left. There are buses to/from the city.

$ Rates (including continental breakfast): A$65 (U.S. $52) single; A$95 (U.S. $76) double; A$120 (U.S. $96) suite. No children. BC, MC, V. **Parking:** Free.

Islington is a delightful hostelry created from a gracious private home built in 1845. The hosts are Hayden and Judith Oxley. Throughout the Regency mansion, antiques, cedar woodwork, and elegant furnishings contribute to an air of gentility, calm, and tradition. French doors open onto a charming garden where breakfasts are served. Guests sleep in queen-size beds, read free daily newspapers, and have the covers turned down for them at night. Islington is located on an avenue of stately old-world homes. The view of Mount Wellington is lovely, and a swimming pool and tennis court are on the grounds.

Serviced Apartments

SALAMANCA INN, 10 Gladstone St., Hobart, TAS 3000. Tel. 002/23-3300, or toll free 008/03-0944 in Australia. Fax 002/23-7167. 40 1- and 20 2-bedroom apartments. MINIBAR TV TEL **Bus:** Sandy Bay Rd.

$ Rates: A$144 (U.S. $115) 1-bedroom apartment single or double; A$168 (U.S. $134.40) 2-bedroom apartment for up to four people; A$25 (U.S. $20) extra adult; A$15 (U.S. $12) each child aged 3–14. Weekend and long-stay packages. AE, BC, DC, MC, V. **Parking:** Free.

It isn't surprising that the Salamanca Inn won the Tasmanian Tourism Award in 1990. The all-suites property offers pleasant apartments right around the corner from Salamanca Place and within walking distance of most attractions. All quarters have modern furnishings, full kitchens (including dishwashers), queen-size beds, in-room movies, and hairdryers. Facilities on the premises include a complimentary self-service laundry, an indoor pool, spa, and a cheerful restaurant called Gladstones. Baby-sitting can be arranged. Room service is offered during restaurant hours.

WOOLMERS INN, 123 Sandy Bay Rd., Hobart, TAS 7005. Tel. 002/23-7355, or toll free 008/03-0780 in Australia. Fax 002/23-1981. 15 1- and 16 2-bedroom apartments. TV TEL **Bus:** Sandy Bay.

$ Rates: A$90 (U.S. $72) single or double; A$14 (U.S. $11.20) extra adult; A$8 (U.S. $6.40) extra child. Rates are 10% higher Christmas–Jan. AE, BC, DC, MC, V. **Parking:** Free.

Woolmers Inn is located 2 kilometers (1 mile) south of the city. Their cozy units have one or two bedrooms and fully equipped kitchens. Bathrooms contain tub/shower combinations and laundry facilities. The two-story complex has an attractive red-brick colonial-style exterior. One unit can accommodate handicapped travelers. Baby-sitting can be arranged. There's an eight-ball table in the house bar.

In Richmond

PROSPECT HOUSE, Main Rd., Richmond, TAS 7025. Tel. 002/62-2207.
Fax 002/62-2551. 10 rms, 1 suite (all with bath). MINIBAR TV **Transportation:** Drive or bus from Hobart.
$ Rates: A$90 (U.S. $72) single; A$100 (U.S. $80) double; A$120 (U.S. $96) suite; A$20 (U.S. $16) extra person. AE, BC, DC, MC, V. **Parking:** Free.

Located 26 kilometers (16 miles) from Hobart, Prospect House is primarily known for its restaurant, but it also offers 10 rooms in the original convict-built barn and haylofts. Quarters have antique furnishings and modern bathrooms. The property is set on 8 hectares (20 acres) of grounds, where there is a tennis court. Hosts Mike and Shauna Buscombe, direct descendants of the original owner, are sure to make you feel welcome. See "Where to Dine," below, for details about Prospect House's award-winning fare.

BUDGET

WELLINGTON LODGE, 7 Scott St., Glebe, Hobart, TAS 7000. Tel. 002/31-0614. 5 rms (1 with bath). TV **Bus:** No. 2.
$ Rates (including breakfast): A$45–A$57 (U.S. $36–U.S. $45.60) single; A$58–A$70 (U.S. $46.40–U.S. $56) double; A$20 (U.S. $16) extra person. No smoking. No children under 12. BC, MC, V. **Parking:** Free (on street).

Eric Littman hails from Glasglow, Scotland, and Martyn Jones is originally from Staffordshire, England. Together they purchased, painted, and restored this late Victorian house (ca. 1900). Their friendly service is reason enough to stay here. One room has its own shower; the other four rooms share two bathrooms. Throughout the house there are hardwood floors. All quarters have wicker chairs, nice spreads with matching draperies, and coffee- and tea-making facilities; two have iron beds and three have wooden beds.

WHERE TO DINE

Tasmania is renowned for its fresh seafood, including king crab, oysters, crayfish, salmon, and other equally wonderful treats. If you choose from the following recommendations, you will also encounter some great game and wonderful wine lists. Prices are considerably lower than they would be for comparable cuisine on the mainland.

EXPENSIVE

DEAR FRIENDS, 8 Brooke St. Tel. 23-2646.
Cuisine: TASMANIAN. **Reservations:** Recommended.
$ Prices: Appetizers A$12.50–A$15 (U.S. $10–U.S. $12); main courses A$19.50–A$26 (U.S. $15.60–U.S. $20.80); fixed-price two-course lunch A$16 (U.S. $12.80); five-course Discovery Menu A$38 (U.S. $30.40). Surcharge Sun and public holidays 10%. AE, BC, DC, MC, V.
Open: Lunch Thurs–Fri; dinner Mon–Sat.

Dear Friends has been awarded Best Restaurant in Tasmania every year except one since it opened in 1984. This no doubt pleases proprietor Geoff Copping, who is actively involved in all aspects of the centrally located dining spot. The restaurant is located one level aboveground—what Aussies call the first floor—and, while there isn't a view, paintings done by Tasmanian artists make the walls interesting.

The specialty here is Tasmanian produce. This includes game, seafood, and beef. You might start with carpaccio of King Island beef with virgin olive oil, slithers of fresh parmesan, baby capers, and dusted with black pepper. Another popular entrée (appetizer) is chargrilled quail served boned on a Rösti potato with shredded vegetables and a citrus and currant glaze. Main courses include deep-sea salmon with

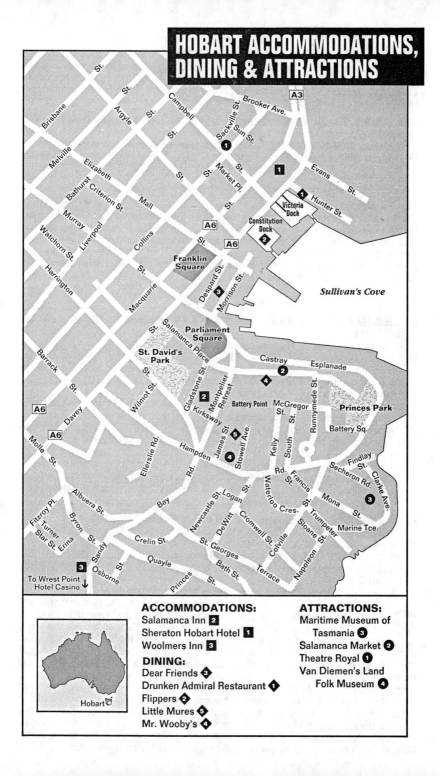

HOBART ACCOMMODATIONS, DINING & ATTRACTIONS

ACCOMMODATIONS:
Salamanca Inn **2**
Sheraton Hobart Hotel **1**
Woolmers Inn **3**

DINING:
Dear Friends **3**
Drunken Admiral Restaurant **1**
Flippers **2**
Little Mures **5**
Mr. Wooby's **4**

ATTRACTIONS:
Maritime Museum of
Tasmania **3**
Salamanca Market **2**
Theatre Royal **1**
Van Diemen's Land
Folk Museum **4**

Hobart

a herb crust served on a champagne sauce, filet of highland beef cooked pink and served with a peppercorn and red wine reduction, and a duo of game—venison and hare served with a red currant reduction, two vegetable purées, and crisped leeks. Tasmanian cheeses and local stone fruit, poached and served in a liqueur of sauternes and lemon, are among the dessert offerings.

THE POINT, in the Wrest Point Hotel Casino, 410 Sandy Bay Rd. Tel. 25-0112.
  Cuisine: TASMANIAN/AUSTRALIAN. **Reservations:** Recommended.
$ **Prices:** Dinner for two about A$100 (U.S. $80); three-course City Lights dinner A$39.50 (U.S. $31.60); fixed-price three-course lunch A$21.50 (U.S. $17.20). AE, BC, DC, MC, V.
  Open: Lunch daily noon–2pm; dinner daily 6:30–9:30pm.
The Point is the revolving restaurant on the 17th floor of the Wrest Point Hotel Casino, and it serves up spectacular harbor and mountain views as well as tasty lunches and dinners. The à la carte menu includes entrées such as homemade venison sausages on lentils, duck liver in juniper berry sauce, and Tasmanian smoked trout. Sample main courses: paupiette of sea-run trout, diced filet of venison, and pan-fried John Dory filets. If you can manage dessert, typical offerings are crêpes Suzette and apple beignets served with vanilla ice cream.

MODERATE

DRUNKEN ADMIRAL RESTAURANT, 17-19 Hunter St., Old Wharf. Tel. 34-1903.
  Cuisine: SEAFOOD. **Reservations:** Recommended.
$ **Prices:** Appetizers A$6.50–A$13.90 (U.S. $5.20–U.S. $11.15); main courses A$13.90–A$22.90 (U.S. $11.15–U.S. $18.35). Sun and public holiday surcharge 15%; Sat surcharge A$2 (U.S. $1.60) per person. AE, BC, MC, V.
  Open: Dinner daily 6–11pm or later.
Situated opposite the Sheraton Hotel on the waterfront, the Drunken Admiral is decorated with colorful sailing memorabilia from the colonial period. Tasmanian oysters are presented four ways: natural, grilled with garlic and butter, baked with chablis and cheese, and barbecued Aussie-style with bacon, homemade sauce, and a "dash o' grog." Drunken Admiral fish stew "ain't no ordinary stew. It's a little of everything the fishmonger had to sell at the docks this morning." Buccaneers revenge is squid, scallops, trevalla, John Dory, and mussels, pan-fried with tomatoes, onions, garlic, and olives. The salad bar is spread out in a sailing dinghy. This is a popular spot. Book early.

LITTLE MURES, 5 Knopwood St., Battery Point. Tel. 23-6917.
  Cuisine: TASMANIAN. **Reservations:** Recommended. **Bus:** No. 53 or 55.
$ **Prices:** Appetizers A$5.50–A$9.50 (U.S. $4.40–U.S. $7.60); main courses A$17.50–A$26 (U.S. $14–U.S. $20.80); fixed-price three-course lunch A$18.50 (U.S. $14.80); fixed price three-course dinner A$23.50 (U.S. $18.80). AE, BC, DC, MC, V.
  Open: Lunch Mon–Fri from noon; dinner Mon–Sat 6pm–late.
Little Mures was formerly known as Mures Fish House, but the management decided to add some vegetarian dishes and some beef and venison numbers—thus the name change. The other news here is that this is now Tasmania's first totally nonsmoking licensed restaurant. It's located in the historic Battery Point area of Hobart. The former colonial cottage, renovated by George and Jill Mure in the early 1970s, has an Australia-wide reputation for presenting fine meals. In addition to the seafood specialties, including Tasmanian king crab, Angasi oysters, and crayfish, diners now also enjoy such dishes as vegetable curry, venison médaillons, and beef filet. The crayfish bisque is wonderful, as is the gravad lax (thin slices of sugar-cured sea trout). For dessert, try profiteroles au chocolat or "proper English trifle." Mures Upper Deck opened in late 1987 on Victoria Dock (tel. 31-2121) and specializes in Tasmanian seafood. Open daily noon to midnight. Personally, I prefer the atmosphere of the cottage. Highly recommended.

MOORILLA ESTATE WINE CENTRE, 655 Main Rd., Berriedale. Tel. 49-2949.

Cuisine: TASMANIAN. **Reservations:** Advisable anytime, essential Sun. **Bus:** No. 33, 35, 36, or 42.

$ Prices: Light lunches A$6.50–A$12 (U.S. $5.20–U.S. $9.60); three-course "Grapepickers Lunch" A$16 (U.S. $12.80); samples of five wines and Tasmanian cheese A$5 (U.S. $4). AE, BC, DC, MC, V.

Open: Lunch and wine tasting daily 10am–5pm.

Open since late 1990, the Moorilla Wine Centre in Berriedale (about 10km/6 miles from Hobart) is a delightful place for a light meal and some wine tasting. There is both inside and outside dining, all surrounded by extensive vineyards. Handsome proprietor/chef David Quon formerly ran a Japanese restaurant in Salamanca Place. Under his care, Sakura won heaps of awards. Now he's turned his talent to this wine center which, besides serving delicious food and wine, also sells bottles of wine which can be shipped worldwide. You might like venison pie, Tasmanian oysters, or game terrine. The Grapepickers Lunch is a sampler of Tasmanian fare. Be sure to try some Lactos cheese from Tassie's northwest coast. There are special events during harvesttime (April).

MOUNT NELSON SIGNAL STATION TEA HOUSE, 700 Nelson Rd., Mount Nelson. Tel. 23-3407.

Cuisine: TASMANIAN. **Reservations:** A good idea at lunch, especially to get a window table on the veranda. **Transportation:** Bus no. 57, 58, or 59 from Franklin Sq. or A$8 (U.S. $6.40) taxi.

$ Prices: Appetizers A$4.50–A$8 (U.S. $3.60–U.S. $6.40); main courses A$8.50–A$13.50 (U.S. $6.80–U.S. $10.80); afternoon tea A$6–A$9.50 (U.S. $4.80–U.S. $7.60). Public holiday surcharge 10%. AE, BC, DC, MC, V.

Open: Daily morning tea, lunch, and afternoon tea 9:30am–5pm.

What a delightful spot this is! Perched on the top of Mount Nelson with an uninterrupted view of water and islands as far as you can see. In 1811 Governor Macquarie ordered a flagstaff and guardhouse erected here. From 1830 to 1877 there was a semaphore station, from which messages were transmitted between Hobart and Port Arthur. The restaurant is housed in the cottage of the chief signalman. Today, there's indoor and outdoor seating and diners are treated to delicious local produce. Entrées (appetizers) include smoked salmon pâté and smoked trout. Sample main courses: Atlantic salmon-and-shrimp crêpes and King Island ham salad. For afternoon tea I suggest scones with Tasmanian jam and King Island cream or Lady Nelson's Delight—warm chocolate sponge sandwich filled with ice cream and topped with hot chocolate fudge sauce. Proprietress Frances Farrington is a charming hostess.

In Richmond

PROSPECT HOUSE, Main Rd., Richmond. Tel. 62-2207.

Cuisine: TASMANIAN. **Reservations:** Recommended, especially Fri–Sat dinner and Sun lunch. **Transportation:** Drive or bus.

$ Prices: Appetizers A$9.50 (U.S. $7.60); main courses A$19.50 (U.S. $15.60). BC, MC, V.

Open: Lunch daily noon–2pm; dinner daily 7–9pm.

Prospect House is located in the village of Richmond, less than a half hour's drive from the center of Hobart. Built around 1830, the house exudes colonial country charm. The two dining rooms both have marble fireplaces, high ceilings, and Oriental rugs. The restaurant is renowned for its gourmet cuisine and has won many awards. On a typical evening the entrées might include salad of quail tossed with a medley of warm fig dressing, and hare-and-prune pie accompanied with crème fraîche and homemade tomato relish. Sample main courses: smoked loin of lamb, aged venison marinated and lightly baked, and oven-poached river trout. The wine list is extensive. Prospect House is owned and operated by the great great grandson of the original owner, Michael Kestell Buscombe, and his wife, Shauna.

In Woodbridge

WOODBRIDGE HOTEL, Channel Hwy., Woodbridge. Tel. 67-4604.
Cuisine: TASMANIAN. **Reservations:** Essential. **Transportation:** Drive, 30 minutes south of Hobart.

$ **Prices:** Appetizers A$5.50–A$15.50 (U.S. $4.40–U.S. $12.40); main courses A$10–A$17.50 (U.S. $8–U.S. $14); Tasmanian platter of local specialties and tastes of six wines A$20 (U.S. $16); wine tasting A$1 (U.S. 80¢) each taste or A$5 (U.S. $4) for any six; kids' meals A$3–A$4 (U.S. $2.40–U.S. $3.20). Sun and public holiday surcharge 10%. BC, MC, V.
Open: Lunch daily noon–2pm; dinner Mon–Sat 6:30–8:30pm; wine tasting and Tasmanian platter Mon–Sat 11am–10pm and Sun 11am–7pm.

One doesn't normally look for great cuisine in a country pub, but this place is definitely an exception. The Woodbridge Hotel is owned by four generations of the Gawith family. Mom and Dad formerly ran the Ozone Hotel in Queenscliff, Victoria, and son Hugh has worked at several well-known restaurants around Melbourne, including the legendary Mietta's. Hugh is the head chef at the Woodbridge, and he's turning out meals that are equal to Melbourne's best. The blackboard menu changes daily, but frequently features such items as crayfish bisque; duck liver, orange, and brandy pâté; plaited lamb filet with berry demi-glaze; and baked green crayfish with beurre blanc.

Meals are served in a casual room that overlooks the D'Entrecasteaux Channel or on an outdoor covered patio. In addition to dining, guests enjoy wine tasting—the Woodbridge offers Tasmania's largest selection of Tasmanian wines—and bottle sales.

BUDGET

On Salamanca Place, there's a little Greek place called the **Parthenon. Flippers** is a floating fish-and-chips shop on Constitution Dock. Both of these spots are popular with budget diners.

✪ ⑤ **Mr. Wooby's,** at the rear of 65 Salamanca Place (tel. 34-3466), is named after a man who owned a "goody stall" on the wharf in the 1870s. It was a ramshackle structure, but despite this, he locked it each evening with a huge padlock obtained from the convict prison at Port Arthur. Needless to say, the sweets stall is long gone, but the name of the proprietor and a little of his eccentricity live on in Mr. Wooby's eatery. Reading material and board games are provided for patrons, and some folks regularly while away an afternoon or evening in this casual café. Once a jam factory, the building has thick stone walls with exposed girders; rafters show in the low ceiling. Proprietor John Addison retired after 40 years with Telecom (Australia's AT&T) and now enjoys being the host and chef. The eatery is open Monday during the day, Tuesday through Thursday from 9am to midnight, and Friday and Saturday from 9am to 2am. Three courses cost about A$13 (U.S. $10.40), but you might just want soup, pâté, some pasta—or a game of checkers. You can be served beer and wine only if you order a meal. No credit cards.

EVENING ENTERTAINMENT

THE PERFORMING ARTS

THEATRE ROYAL, 29 Campbell St. Tel. 31-0899 for information, 34-6266 for tickets.

The Theatre Royal was built in 1837 and is the oldest remaining live theater in Australia. It was substantially restored after a 1984 fire. It has what Laurence Olivier described as "perfect" acoustics and an elegant late Victorian decor. Tasmanian professional and amateur companies and professional companies from mainland Australia and overseas perform regularly. The theater seats 747 on three levels—stalls, dress circle, and upper circle (what Americans would call the orchestra section, mezzanine, and balcony or upper mezzanine). Shows include dance, drama, comedy, revue, music theater, concerts, puppetry, and mime.

Tours: Daily at 10am during the summer, for A$4 (U.S. $3.20).

Prices: A$3–A$39 (U.S. $2.40–U.S. $31.20), depending on the type of performance.

THE CLUB & MUSIC SCENE

REGINE'S NIGHTCLUB, at the Wrest Point Hotel Casino, 410 Sandy Bay Rd. Tel. 25-0112.

Regine's is open 7 nights a week from 9pm to 3am (sometimes 4am on Friday and Saturday) and is popular with those who are "young and young at heart." The decor is reminiscent of the '60s and there's an open fire in the winter. Karaoke is a big crowd pleaser on Friday and Saturday nights, and is the only live music offered. A wide range of beverages and snacks is served.

Admission: A$5 (U.S. $4) cover charge Fri–Sun.

THE BAR & PUB SCENE

SPINNAKER LOUNGE, in the Sheraton Hotel, 1 Davey St. Tel. 35-4535.

The Spinnaker is what I call an "upmarket public bar." It has the friendliness of a traditional pub and a clean and bright decor. This is a good place to chat with locals and also an inexpensive spot for counter lunches. The entrance to the Spinnaker Lounge is on the side of the hotel.

ATRIUM LOUNGE, in the Sheraton Hotel, 1 Davey St. Tel. 35-4535.

The Atrium Lounge is a sophisticated watering hole and a good spot for a drink with a view of waterfront activity. Live music is offered.

KNOPWOOD'S RETREAT, 39 Salamanca Place. Tel. 23-5808.

Located near the waterfront in the historic Battery Point area, Knopwood's Hotel is a favorite local tavern and wine bar. The clientele is comprised of artists, poets, laborers, politicians, political activists, and other interesting folks. They enjoy the late Victorian atmosphere, al fresco seating, and live music, which varies from jazz and blues to rock and roll. Knopwood's opened in 1829 as a tavern/brothel for whalers. Such personalities as Joseph Conrad and Roald Amundsen have called in for a drink. Some 145 different beers and wines are offered.

MORE ENTERTAINMENT

WREST POINT CASINO, in the Wrest Point Hotel Casino, 410 Sandy Bay Rd. Tel. 25-0112.

This casino was Australia's first legal gaming club. It continues to be a popular place with those who like to play blackjack, roulette, minidice, two-up, craps, baccarat, keno, and so forth. The table games in the main casino are open from 1 pm to 3am Monday through Thursday, 1pm to 4am Friday and Saturday, and from noon to 3am Sunday. Video gaming machines are available from noon every day in both the main casino and the Riverview Lounge.

EASY EXCURSIONS

PORT ARTHUR

I suggest you take a day to drive out to Port Arthur, where you can tour the remains of the penal colony. If you've got the time, stop in the historic village of **Richmond** and at the **Tasmanian Devil Park** on the way. The rural scenery is also most enjoyable.

Richmond is only 26 kilometers (16 miles) northeast of Hobart and is the site of the country's oldest bridge (1823), a gaol (jail) that dates from 1825, and several old churches including St. John's Roman Catholic (1837) and St. Luke's Church of England (1834–36). In addition to these colonial structures, Richmond offers a plethora of cozy tearooms, craft shops, galleries, and antiques stores. The riverbank is a nice spot for a picnic. If you're interested in overnight accommodations or gourmet fare, see my descriptions of Prospect House in "Where to Stay" and "Where to Dine," above.

The **Tasmanian Devil Park,** Port Arthur Highway, Taranna, 80 kilometers (50 miles) from Hobart (tel. 50-3230), presents an opportunity to see some of the fauna unique to the island state. In the wild, Tasmanian devils are vicious animals, but tame devils are a feature of this attraction. The park is open daily from 9am to 5pm. The admission is A$6 (U.S. $4.80), with children paying half price.

The ruins of the penal settlement at **Port Arthur,** 100 kilometers (62 miles) southwest of Hobart, are Tasmania's number-one tourist attraction. While the grounds are now peaceful—one could almost say picturesque—from 1830 to 1877 Port Arthur was the site of one of the country's harshest convict institutions. The infamous settlement was located on the **Tasman Peninsula,** which is connected to the rest of Tasmania by a narrow strip of land called **Eaglehawk Neck.** To keep the prisoners from escaping, guards and savage dogs kept a constant vigil across this path, and the authorities circulated rumors that the surrounding waters were shark-infested. As you pass Eaglehawk Neck, stop and look at the blowhole and other coastal formations, including **Tasman's Arch, Devil's Kitchen,** and the **Tesselated Pavement.**

At Port Arthur, visitors can tour the remains of the church, guard tower, hospital, commandant's residence, model prison, asylum, and several other buildings. Because these structures have been damaged by fire and vandalism over the years, it is best to take a walking tour with a guide who describes what they originally looked like and what purposes they served. The audiovisual show presented in the visitor center also provides valuable background information. The admission to the Port Arthur Historic Site (tel. 50-2363) is A$7.50 (U.S. $6) for adults and A$2 (U.S. $1.60) for children 5 to 15. Horse-drawn tours of the site, ghost tours, and cruises to the **Isle of the Dead,** off the coast of Port Arthur are also available.

Where to Stay & Dine

PORT ARTHUR MOTOR INN, Port Arthur Historic Site, Port Arthur, TAS 7182. Tel. 002/50-2101, or toll free 008/03-0747 in Australia. Fax 002/50-2417. 35 rms. MINIBAR TV TEL **Transportation:** Daily Hobart Coaches from Hobart.

$ Rates: A$72 (U.S. $57.60) single; A$85 (U.S. $68) double; A$13 (U.S. $10.40) extra person. Children under 12 stay free in parents' room. AE, BC, DC, MC, V. **Parking:** Free.

Should you decide to stay overnight, this motor inn has comfortable rooms and a restaurant overlooking the historic site of the penal settlement. All quarters have clock radios, coffee- and tea-making facilities, and small refrigerators. Guests may use the self-service laundry and playground.

Evening Entertainment

For entertainment, you might want to view the original version of the 1926 silent movie *For the Term of His Natural Life,* which is screened nightly at 7:30pm November through April at the **Broad Arrow Tea House and Coffee Shop,** on the historic site (tel. 50-2242). The cost is A$4 (U.S. $3.20) for adults and half price for children 6 to 16 years. The film is also available on in-house video to guests at the Port Arthur Motor Inn all year. Much of the film was shot on location at Port Arthur.

THE HUON VALLEY & THE CHANNEL COAST

Another delightful day-trip route leads southwest from Hobart and takes visitors past apple orchards to craft workshops, a wildlife park, and wonderful water views. Blooming cherry, pear, and apple trees are a bonus on this drive September through early November. The trees are laden with apples in March, and cherries are for sale in January.

Take Highway B64 from Hobart to the **Apple Industry Museum** (tel. 66-4345), which is just past Grove. Located in a former apple-packing shed, the displays here provide insight into an era when people in the once-thriving apple industry worked by candlelight and earned about 50¢ a week. The museum is open daily from 9:30am to 5pm. Admission is A$2 (U.S. $1.60) for adults and A$1.50 (U.S. $1.20) for children under 16.

Continue down the east side of the Huon River on Highway B68, the Channel Highway. Just before the town of Cygnet, look for the **Cygnet Pottery** (tel. 95-1957). It's open Tuesday through Sunday from 10am to 5pm and is a great place to learn about this craft and perhaps purchase a piece or two.

Continue south until you come to Highway C626. Turn left (east) and drive 7 kilometers (4 miles) to **The Deepings** (tel. 95-1398), where you can watch woodturner Adrian Hunt at work. (Adrian and his wife, Roslyn, also offer country accommodations.) Be sure to notice the Deepings Dolls. Return to the Channel Highway and go south to Highway C627. Turn left and stop at the ✪ **Talune Wildlife Park and Koala Gardens** (tel. 95-1775) where former science teacher Mike Jagoe has assembled a large collection of native animals. Because this is not a huge commercial operation (and because Mike is an extremely friendly "bloke"), visitors can hold, pet, and feed lots of different creatures. Admission is A$3.50 (U.S. $2.80) for adults and A$1.50 (U.S. $1.20) for children. Open daily from 9:30am to 5pm.

Further along C627 you'll come to **Winterwood Winery** (tel. 95-1864) where fruit wines, as well as grape wines, are made. Next is **Woodbridge Hill Handweaving Studio** (tel. 67-4430) where you can watch Anna Maria Magnus at her loom.

As you continue toward the coast, you'll see really pretty **views of the D'Entrecasteaux Channel.** Just north of Woodbridge, you have the option of stopping at the **Woodbridge Hotel** for wine tasting, lunch, dinner, or overnight lodging. (See "Where to Dine," above, for more information.) The return to Hobart from Woodbridge takes about 35 minutes.

2. LAUNCESTON

198km (123 miles) N of Hobart

GETTING THERE   By Plane   The flight to Launceston from Melbourne takes 55 minutes and costs A$107 to A$135 (U.S. $85.60 to U.S. $108) if you use Australian Airlines' Air Pass Fare. Airlines of Tasmania will fly you up from Hobart for A$65 (U.S. $52). Coach transfer to the city from the airport costs A$5 (U.S. $4).

By Train   There are no passenger trains in Tasmania.

By Bus   If you take the *Abel Tasman* ferry across Bass Strait, the drive from Devonport takes about 1½ hours, and the bus fare is about A$13 (U.S. $10.40). If you take the *SeaCat*, **RoadCat** coaches will take you to Launceston. A Tasmanian Redline Coaches or Hobart Coaches ticket from Hobart costs about A$16 (U.S. $12.80).

By Car   Hobart is less than 3 hours away by car on Highway 1.

ESSENTIALS   Information   The ever-efficient **Tasmanian Travel Centre** dispenses tourist information and books tours from their office on the corner of St. John and Paterson streets (tel. 003/37-3111). They're open Monday through Friday from 8:45am to 5:30pm and Saturday (Sunday, too, in the summer) from 9 to 11:30am. The **Royal Automobile Club of Tasmania** doles out maps and answers questions from their headquarters on the corner of York and George streets (tel. 31-3166). Launceston's **area code** is 003.

City Layout   A pedestrian shopping mall is on Brisbane Street between St. John and Charles streets. The **Town Hall** is located 2 blocks north on Civic Square. **City Park,** on the northeastern edge of the central business district, makes a pleasant spot for a picnic.

Tasmania's second city is sited at the head of the Tamar River, 50 kilometers (31 miles) inland from the state's north coast. Surrounded by hills, Launceston is the center of a lush, green farming region. Because of its easy access from the mainland, it is a handy place for visitors to start their exploration of the state. Often referred to as the Garden City, Launceston (pop. 92,000) has many fine parks and some excellent examples of colonial architecture.

WHAT TO SEE & DO

⭐ **Cataract Gorge,** the result of violent earthquakes that ruptured Tasmania about 40 million years ago, is a scenic area with walking trails, picnic grounds, and splendid gardens located 10 minutes from central Launceston. The South Esk River flows through the gorge, which is traversed by a suspension bridge and a chair lift. Whether you go to hike or to photograph the view, you won't be disappointed. The hike to the Duck Reach Power Station takes about 45 minutes and should be attempted only by those with sturdy footwear; other walks are shorter and easier. The Gorge Restaurant serves meals and teas. Walkers should pick up the *Guide to Cataract Gorge Nature Walks* from the Tasmanian Travel Centre.

WAVERLEY WOOLLEN MILLS, Waverley Rd. Tel. 39-1106.

This business was established in 1874 and is still operating on the same site 5 kilometers (3 miles) northeast of town. On the tour, visitors see how animal fibers are turned into quality woolen garments. Hats, caps, ties, skirts, bush shirts, blankets, and jackets are sold on the premises. Teas and light lunches are available.

Admission: Tour of mill and auto museum (see below) A$6 (U.S. $4.80) adults, A$3 (U.S. $2.40) children.

Open: Tours daily 9am–5pm.

NATIONAL AUTOMOBILE MUSEUM OF TASMANIA, Waverley Rd. Tel. 39-3727.

This museum shares the Waverley site and gives visitors a chance to see classic cars undergoing restoration, as well as completely restored vehicles. Children particularly enjoy the model car collection.

Admission: A$4 (U.S. $3.20) adults, A$2 (U.S. $1.60) children under 14.

Open: Daily 9am–5pm. **Closed:** Christmas Day.

OLD UMBRELLA SHOP, 60 George St. Tel. 31-9248.

Of the local colonial buildings, the Old Umbrella Shop—now used as the National Trust Gift Shop and Information Centre—is one of the more interesting. The facade of the shop, which dates from the 1860s, remains unchanged. Umbrellas used during the last 100 years are on display. Notice, too, the Union Bank building one block west on the corner of St. John and Paterson streets. Its Doric columns and wrought-iron work are impressive.

Admission: Free.

Open: Mon–Fri 9am–5pm, Sat 9am–noon.

NEARBY ATTRACTIONS

ENTALLY HOUSE, Hadspen (15km/9½ miles) from Launceston. Tel. 93-6201.

This is another historic property of note. Built around 1820, the lovely Georgian colonial house, once the home of a Tasmanian premier, is furnished in period antiques. The surrounding grounds contain pretty gardens, a glasshouse (greenhouse), many mature trees, and a display of horse-drawn vehicles. Refreshment are sold on the premises.

Admission: A$4 (U.S. $3.20) adults, A$1.50 (U.S. $1.20) children.

Open: Daily 10am–12:30pm and 1–5pm.

WHERE TO STAY

EXPENSIVE

LAUNCESTON INTERNATIONAL HOTEL, 29 Cameron St., Launceston, TAS 7250. Tel. 003/34-3434, or toll free 008/03-0123 in Australia. Fax 003/31-7347. 165 rms and suites. A/C MINIBAR TV TEL

$ Rates: A$198 (U.S. $158.40) single or double; A$330–A$650 (U.S. $264–U.S. $520) suite; A$10 (U.S. $8) extra person. Children under 14 stay free in parents' room. Weekend packages. Weekend tariffs about 50% lower. No-smoking rooms available. AE, BC, DC, MC, V. **Parking:** Free.

Located in the heart of the city center, this hostelry is Launceston's most elegant. All rooms have clock radios, terry robes, hairdryers, tea- and coffee-making facilities, small refrigerators, in-room movies, and free daily newspapers. Standard rooms have two double beds.

Dining/Entertainment: Jackson's International Tavern is a popular watering hole. On the Avenue is an upmarket coffee shop. Vintages Bar adjoins Cameron's, the hotel's fine-dining venue (see "Where to Dine," below).

Services: 24-hour room service, turn-down service, shoeshine, laundry, valet, concierge, baby-sitting, and massage.

Facilities: Self-service laundry, business center, hair salon, and gift shop.

MODERATE

ALICE'S PLACE, 17 York St., Launceston, TAS 7250. Tel. 003/31-7481. 1 cottage. TV
$ Rates (including breakfast ingredients): A$100 (U.S. $80) single or double; A$20 (U.S. $16) extra person. No credit cards. **Parking:** Free.

Like Ivy Cottage, located next door and described below, Alice's Place is owned by Helen Poynder. However, this attractive spot, which sleeps four, isn't actually old. An expert in restoring colonial buildings, Helen created Alice's Place from bits and pieces of historic places that were being razed, doing much of the work herself. The result is charming quarters that are a bit roomier than those of Ivy Cottage and share the same wonderful garden. Alice's Place has its own washing machine and dryer, while the cottage next door has just a washing machine.

COLONIAL MOTOR INN, 31 Elizabeth St., Launceston, TAS 7250. Tel. 003/31-6588, or toll free 008/03-0111 in Australia. Fax 003/34-2765. 64 rms, 3 suites. A/C MINIBAR TV TEL
$ Rates: A$110 (U.S. $88) single or double; A$160 (U.S. $128) suite; A$18 (U.S. $14.40) extra person. Lower weekend tariffs. Children under 12 stay free in parents' room. No-smoking rooms available. AE, BC, DC, MC, V. **Parking:** Free.
The Colonial Motor Inn combines old-world ambience with traditional comfort and facilities. In fact, the Old Grammar School has been incorporated into the complex, but those who desire tried-and-true standard motel lodging will feel right at home here. Rooms have attractive furnishings and modern amenities including clock radios, hairdryers, tea- and coffee-making facilities, small refrigerators, in-room movies, and free daily newspapers. The Quill and Cane Restaurant was once a big schoolroom; Rosie's Tavern, central Launceston's liveliest nightspot, was formerly the boys' gymnasium.

IVY COTTAGE, 17 York St., Launceston, TAS 7250. Tel. 003/31-8431. 1 2-bedroom cottage. TV
$ Rates (including breakfast ingredients): A$95 (U.S. $76) single or double; A$20 (U.S. $16) extra person. No credit cards. **Parking:** Free.

This is one of the most interesting places at which I have ever stayed. Proprietor Helen Poynder has restored the Georgian cottage (ca. 1840) with loving attention to detail. The two bedrooms not only are furnished with antiques but are replete with accessories and fascinating bric-a-brac—for example, period clothing and a wonderful doll collection. Guests stay here on their own, cook for themselves, and come and go as they please. Helen lives nearby and is happy to answer questions and chat, but she also respects her guests' privacy. The slate-floored kitchen is equipped with absolutely everything you might need for preparing a meal, and the hostess urges visitors to take fresh herbs from the garden as required. The bathroom has a wonderful claw-foot tub with a metal shower surround. Two working fireplaces, games and books, and a cheerful, old-world flower garden are other pluses.

BUDGET

LLOYD'S HOTEL, 23 George St., Launceston, TAS 7250. Tel. 003/31-4966. 18 rms (all with bath).

$ **Rates** (including breakfast): A$30 (U.S. $24) single; A$48 (U.S. $38.40) double. BC, MC, V. **Parking:** Free.

Lloyd's is an older-style property where the emphasis is on booze, not beds. However, the rooms all have private bathrooms, with guests sharing coffee- and tea-making facilities and a television lounge. The central location is a bonus.

WHERE TO DINE
EXPENSIVE

CAMERON'S, in the Launceston International Hotel, 29 Cameron St. Tel. 34-3434.

Cuisine: TASMANIAN. **Reservations:** Recommended.

$ **Prices:** Appetizers A$11–A$17 (U.S. $8.80–U.S. $13.60); main courses A$22–A$28 (U.S. $17.60–U.S. $22.40); Tasmanian Gourmet Experience A$50 (U.S. $40). AE, BC, DC, MC, V.

Open: Lunch Mon–Fri; dinner Mon–Sat.

Cameron's won Tourism Tasmania's Fine Dining Award 6 months after it opened in 1990, and it's not surprising. Chef Bret Hanson treats Tasmania's produce with respect and creativity. In addition, meals are served in an attractive room with an gold-and-beige decor, windows which overlook Cameron Street, and a faux fountain in the center of the room. Candlelight makes Bret's dinners even more enjoyable. I suggest you arrive early enough to have an apéritif in Vintages Bar, which adjoins the restaurant.

You might start with tiger prawns and a broccoli timbale, or a mussel soufflé on a beurre rouge, or whole quail filled with a medley of fruit and a bush honey sauce. Main courses include bouillabaisse, loin of veal poached and served on a bouquet of vegetables, and pillows of scallops on coconut and lemon-leaf sauce.

MODERATE

FEE & ME, 36 The Kingsway (corner of York St.). Tel. 31-3195.

Cuisine: TASMANIAN. **Reservations:** Recommended.

$ **Prices:** Appetizers A$8–A$12 (U.S. $6.40–U.S. $9.60); main courses A$14.50–A$23 (U.S. $11.60–U.S. $18.40). BC, MC, V.

Open: Lunch Tues–Fri from noon; dinner Tues–Sat from 6pm.

This is an attractive brasserie where the decor includes cane chairs, exposed brick walls, and black-and-white tablecloths. Windows overlook the street. Sample entrées are chargrilled quail, chili oysters, and scallops with goat cheese and pesto. Sample mains include trevalla with leeks and mushrooms, roast duckling, and a mixed grill. The wine list is extensive.

THE OWL'S NEST RESTAURANT, in the Penny Royal Watermill Motel, 145-160 Paterson St. Tel. 31-6699.

Cuisine: TASMANIAN. **Reservations:** Recommended.

$ **Prices:** Appetizers A$7.50–A$9.50 (U.S. $6–U.S. $7.60); main courses A$14–A$19 (U.S. $11.20–U.S. $15.20). AE, BC, DC, MC, V.

Open: Dinner daily 6–9pm.

The Owl's Nest offers an interesting menu based on fresh local products. All dishes are available in either entrée or main-course portions. These include smoked salmon and cucumber salad, sweetbreads in a seeded mustard sauce, barbecue quail with peppercorns, tomato and basil fettuccine, and honey duckling with orange sauce. The Owl's Nest, which has a colonial decor, is adjacent to a historic 19th-century water mill that has been reconstructed on the grounds. It's a 10-minute walk to the city center.

SHRIMPS, 72 George St. (corner of Paterson St.). Tel. 34-0584.

Cuisine: SEAFOOD. **Reservations:** Recommended.

$ Prices: Dinner for two about A$65 (U.S. $52). AE, BC, DC, MC, V.
   Open: Lunch Mon–Fri noon–2pm; dinner Mon–Sat from 6:30pm.
It's impossible not to notice Shrimps. The outside of the building is pumpkin with a red metal roof and forest-green trim. Its style is classic Georgian and it was, in fact, built in 1824 and restored in 1980. A sign near the door says it is "a fine example of one of the few classical Georgian corner buildings in Launceston."
   If you dine here, you'll choose between fresh Tasmanian mussels, oysters Tzarina which are served with crème fraîche, abalone tempura, and more unusual dishes such as a Spanish seafood omelet. Save room for dessert.

VICTORIA'S TASSIE FARE RESTAURANT, in City Park, corner of Tamar and Cimitiere Sts. Tel. 31-7433.
   Cuisine: INTERNATIONAL. **Reservations:** Recommended.
$ Prices: Complete meal A$7–A$19 (U.S. $5.60–U.S. $15.20). AE, BC, MC, V.
   Open: Mon–Sat 10:30am–late, Sun 11am–4pm.
This is a charming coffee shop with oversize windows looking out on the park. Drop in for a sinfully delicious dessert, such as chocolate mousse, apple Danish, or chocolate-rum-and-mint cream puffs. For lunch you could have quiche and salad, several different kinds of pasta, or one of their creative sandwiches.

BUDGET

MICHELLES LUNCHBAR, 2 Paterson St. Tel. 34-1095.
   Cuisine: LIGHT LUNCHES. **Reservations:** Not necessary.
$ Prices: Light lunch for one A$5 (U.S. $4). No credit cards.
   Open: Mon–Fri 7am–4pm, Sat 8am–noon.
Michelles is a little deli in the city center near the corner of Paterson and George streets. This is a great stop to pick up sandwiches to take on a picnic.

SHOPPING

The **National Trust Shop,** in the Old Umbrella Shop mentioned above, sells interesting gift items, and you also don't want to miss the **◑ Design Centre of Tasmania,** on the corner of Tamar and Brisbane streets (tel. 31-5506). Wonderful craft items, ranging from wood to glass—all made by Tasmanians—are sold in this attractive gallery on the edge of City Park. It's open Monday through Friday from 10am to 6pm, Saturday from 10am to 1pm, and Sunday from 2 to 5pm.
   If you're in Launceston on a Sunday, you might want to go to the **Yorktown Square Market,** located at the rear of the Launceston International Hotel. This is an ideal place for buying local craft items. The market is open from 9am to 2pm.

3. CRADLE MOUNTAIN/ LAKE ST. CLAIR NATIONAL PARK

LOCATION   Cradle Mountain/Lake St. Clair National Park is located in the northwest quadrant of the state. Queenstown is on approximately the same level as the park's southern border. Devonport is 85 kilometers (53 miles) north of the park. Lake St. Clair is 173 kilometers (107 miles) northwest of Hobart.

GETTING THERE   By Plane   An airstrip is located near Cradle Mountain Lodge at the north end of the park. Par Avion (002/48-5390) will fly you there from Hobart. Two passengers can travel for A$380 (U.S. $304); four people will pay A$450 (U.S. $360). Devonport Aviation (tel. 004/27-9777) provides transfers from Devonport. These cost A$70 (U.S. $56) per person if there are two passengers and A$50 (U.S. $40) per person when there are three. If you're coming from Launceston, the Launceston Flying School and Charter Service (tel. 003/91-8477) will fly you to Cradle Mountain. Three passengers pay A$160 (U.S. $128); five pay A$240 (U.S. $192).

By Train   There are no passenger trains in Tasmania.

By Bus   Tasmanian Wilderness Transport (tel. toll free 008/03-0505 in Australia) operates coach service from Devonport (2 hr.) and Launceston (3 hr.). From either place the one-way fare is A$35 (U.S. $28) and the round-trip costs A$65 (U.S. $52). They also provide transfers from Hobart to Lake St. Clair (3 hr.; A$35/U.S. $28 one-way; A$65/U.S. $52 round-trip). Hobart to Cradle Mountain via Strahan costs A$70 (U.S. $56) one-way.

By Car   Motorists can enter the park on only two roads: From the north you can drive to Dove Lake and Waldheim Chalet; from the south you can drive to Derwent Bridge and Lake St. Clair. The drive from Devonport to Cradle Mountain takes 1½ hours; from Launceston about 2½ hours.

ESSENTIALS   The **Visitor Information Centre** near Cradle Mountain Lodge has displays which tell about the World Heritage Area, as well as brochures, posters, and booklets about the geography, flora, and fauna of the region. It's open from 9am to 5pm daily. The **area code** is 004.

Tasmania has many beautiful wilderness areas, but it is generally agreed that the national park, encompassing both Cradle Mountain and Lake St. Clair, is one of the most spectacular regions. The 1,545-meter (5,100-ft.) mountain dominates the north end, and the long, deep lake is located in the most southerly section. Between them lie steep mountains, flat plains, dozens of lakes, several rivers, majestic forests, and scenic valleys. **Mount Ossa** (1,617m/5336 ft.), the state's highest point, is sited in the center of the park. The **World Heritage Committee** added Cradle Mountain/Lake St. Clair National Park to their list of the world's most precious places in 1982.

WHAT TO SEE & DO

Don't leave the area until you've driven the 8 kilometers (5 miles) from Cradle Mountain Lodge down to ✪ **Dove Lake.** The view of this beautiful body of water and Cradle Mountain is picture-postcard material. The lake, encircled by rugged mountains, was formed by a glacier.

I also recommend that even the least athletic folks take the less than 10-minute walk from the lodge to Pencil Pine Falls.

A daily program of walks and outdoor activities is planned by the staff at **Cradle Mountain Lodge** (see below). These range from short excursions to longer, more arduous hikes. The guided walks, abseiling (mountaineering), rock-climbing excursions, and trout-fishing trips are open to registered guests, including campers. A nominal charge is levied for activities requiring equipment. Many people, of course, prefer to go off on their own, and this is perfectly all right as long as they are properly equipped and aware of safety essentials.

The most popular hiking trail in the park is the **Overland Track,** an 80-kilometer (50-mile) route that links Cradle Mountain and Lake St. Clair. The trek takes 5 to 10 days. The trail passes through almost every type of country—from highland moors to dense valley rain forests. Every summer hundreds of people of various ages and countries make this hike. An Overland Track fee of A$15 (U.S. $12) must be paid to the rangers before you can start the walk. Lodging is in huts spaced out along the way. Even in the summer, hikers must be prepared to deal with sudden inclement weather. **Cradle Mountain Huts** is the name of a company that organizes guided versions of the Overland Track. Their fee of about A$1,000 (U.S. $800) per person includes transfers to/from Launceston, meals, guiding, and accommodations in their huts along the track. Trips last 6 days. Contact them at 003/31-2006, or through any Tasmanian Travel Centre.

Between June and October it is possible to cross-country ski in the park. Swimming is a popular pastime in summer.

At the southern end of the park near Derwent Bridge, there's a ranger station and campgrounds. Day hikes can be done from here, and **Lakeside St. Clair Wilderness Holidays** (tel. 002/89-1137) offers cruises on Lake St. Clair (A$16/U.S. $12.80).

WHERE TO STAY & DINE

CRADLE MOUNTAIN LODGE, P.O. Box 153, Sheffield, TAS 7306. Tel. 004/92-1303, or toll free 008/03-0377 in Australia. Fax 004/92-1309. 4 lodge rms (none with bath), 76 cabins. **Transportation/Directions:** See above.

$ Rates: Lodge rooms A$87 (U.S. $69.60) single, A$104 (U.S. $83.20) double; A$20 (U.S. $16) extra adult; A$14 (U.S. $11.20) child under 15; under 4, free of charge. Pencil Pine cabins A$140 (U.S. $112) single or double; extra adult/children as above. Spa cabins A$180 (U.S. $144) single or double (no children). Cradle Campground A$10 (U.S. $8) site for two people; A$15 (U.S. $12) bunkhouse bed; A$7.50 (U.S. $6) bunkhouse bed for a child. Meal package (full breakfast and five-course dinner) A$46 (U.S. $36.80) per person per day. BC, MC, V. **Parking:** Free.

If you love the outdoors, but have no desire to sleep in a tent; enjoy hiking, kayaking, and canoeing, but want a hot shower and a clean bed at the end of the day; like eating next to a roaring fire, but don't want to wash dishes, this is the place for you. This remote mountain lodge has comfortable rooms, good food, friendly staff, and big open fireplaces—all surrounded by magnificent scenery. The two-story timber building, with a peaked roof and verandas where hikers remove muddy boots before going inside, looks like an inn you'd find in the Alps.

Pleasant rooms with shared facilities are located in the lodge, and cozy cabins are spread across the grounds. Each modern wood cabin has a pot-bellied stove, bathroom (with above-mentioned hot shower), small kitchen, and comfortable bed. Spa cabins are carpeted and have spa tubs as well as showers.

Hearty meals are served in the big dining room in the lodge, which is just rustic enough to be invigorating. Rather than choosing from a published wine list, guests are free to make their selection from the well-stocked wine cellar. Drinks are served in a country-style tavern, where a welcoming fire blazes in a stone fireplace. At night, wild animals from the nearby forests come right up on the verandas to claim the edible goodies left out for them. This is a great opportunity to see opossums, wallabies, and Tasmanian devils up close.

Nonstaying guests are welcome and can enjoy meals and teas in the lodge. Hot breakfast costs A$10 (U.S. $8) and continental is A$6 (U.S. $4.80). Lunches, ordered from a blackboard menu, range from A$7 to A$12 (U.S. $5.60 to U.S. $9.60). Five-course family-style dinners are A$26 (U.S. $20.80). Morning and afternoon teas cost A$3 (U.S. $2.40).

In the United States you can make reservations for Cradle Mountain Lodge through **P&O Resorts** (tel. 408/685-8902, or toll free 800/225-9849).

LEMONTHYME LODGE, off Cradle Mountain Rd., Sheffield, TAS 7306. Tel. 004/92-1112. Fax 004/92-1113. 12 rms (none with bath). **Transportation:** Lemonthyme Lodge is located 70km (43 miles) southwest of Devonport. The management can provide transfers, or you can take the Tasmanian Wilderness Transport coach (A$35/U.S. $28) which will drop you 8km (5 miles) from the lodge and the management will pick you up. If you're driving, phone for specific directions.

$ Rates (including breakfast): A$66 (U.S. $52.80) single; A$88 (U.S. $70.40) double. Children under 14, half price; under 4, free. Three-course dinner A$22 (U.S. $17.60). AE, BC, MC, V. **Parking:** Free.

Open since late 1990, this remote lodge offers comfortable accommodations for those who really want to get away from it all. Each room has simple pine beds (one double and a set of bunks) which were handmade on the property by Darryl (Devil Dundee) Stafford and his partner, Ted Burtt. These colorful characters also built the lodge itself, which is the largest log cabin in the Southern Hemisphere. It's constructed of ponderosa pine and set on 109 acres. All meals are served in a rustic dining room where there is a big open fire. Guests help themselves to complimentary coffee and tea throughout the day; the bar operates on the honesty system.

If you stay here, you can take walks in the surrounding bush, go fishing, go on four-wheel-drive trips (A$60/U.S. $48 including lunch), or drive over to Cradle Mountain. However, what you'll probably remember the most is getting to know real Aussie bush folks and experiencing pristine wilderness.

4. THE WEST COAST

Strahan: 296km (184 miles) NW of Hobart,
245km (152 miles) SW of Devonport

GETTING THERE By Bus Tasmanian Wilderness Transport (tel. toll free 008/03-0505 in Australia) provides service to Strahan from Hobart on Saturday. The trip departs at 9am, stops at Lake St. Clair for 2 hours, and arrives in Strahan at 4:45pm. The cost is A$55 (U.S. $44) one-way; A$85 (U.S. $68) round-trip. TWT also provides service from Devonport on Tuesday, Thursday, and Saturday. It takes about 5½ hours and costs A$50 (U.S. $40) one-way and A$80 (U.S. $64) round-trip. The low-season (Easter through November) schedule is slightly different.

Tasmanian Redline Coaches provide service from Hobart to Strahan Monday through Saturday, departing at 8:30am and arriving at 4:15pm. The fare is A$31.20 (U.S. $25) one-way.

By Car The drive from Hobart to Strahan takes about 4½ hours without stops. From Devonport, allow about 3½ hours. While the roads are paved and well marked, I don't recommend that you do either trip after dark.

ESSENTIALS Information about the World Heritage Area is available at the **Ranger Station,** Customs House, Strahan (tel. 004/71-7122). It's open Monday through Friday from 8am to 5pm. The **area code** is 004.

Tasmania's West Coast is an area of steep mountain ranges, deep gorges, swift rivers, rain forest, and wilderness. It is a region of sharp contrasts—the "moonscape" at Queenstown is the result of intensive mining and industrial activity; the pristine Franklin and Gordon rivers are included in a World Heritage Area. Strahan, sited at the head of Macquarie Harbour, is a historic port and the starting point for cruises through the harbor to the Gordon River.

WHAT TO SEE & DO

Gordon River cruises depart Strahan Wharf daily at 9am. The half-day trip returns at 1:30pm after traveling through Macquarie Harbour and down the Gordon River. A stop is made at Heritage Landing, where passengers get a taste of rain forest. During January, there is also a half-day cruise at 1:45pm.

The full-day trip returns at 3pm and follows the itinerary of the half-day trip with an additional stop at Sarah Island where there are ruins of a penal settlement which was abandoned in 1833. The fare for the half-day trip (including morning or afternoon tea) is A$37 (U.S. $29.60) for adults and A$19 (U.S. $15.20) for children 4 to 14 years. The full-day fare (including tea) is A$42 (U.S. $33.60) for adults and A$22 (U.S. $17.60) for children. Lunch can be purchased on board the vessel.

Bookings can be made with Gordon River Cruises, P.O. Box 40, Strahan, TAS 7468 (tel. 004/71-7187; fax 004/71-7317), or any Tasmanian Travel Centre.

While the cruises are the main attraction in the area, it is also possible to do jet boat rides, go flightseeing in a seaplane that lands on the Franklin River, do four-wheel-drive tours, and go fishing. In Zeehan, 42 kilometers (26 miles) to the north, the **West Coast Pioneers Memorial Museum** is worth a stop. It's open daily, and admission is free of charge.

WHERE TO STAY & DINE

FRANKLIN MANOR, The Esplanade, Strahan, TAS 7468. Tel. 004/71-7311. Fax 004/71-7267. 13 rms (all with bath). TV TEL **Transportation:** See above.

$ Rates (including breakfast): A$98 (U.S. $78.40) double, A$120 (U.S. $96) double with spa bath. BC, MC, V. **Parking:** Free.

⭐ This is easily one of the nicest B&Bs in Australia. Built in 1890—Strahan's heyday—for the harbormaster, the house was restored in 1988. Today it is owned by gracious hostess Bernadette Woods, who immigrated from Ireland in 1983 and formerly was the manager at Cradle Mountain Lodge. All rooms have tub/shower combinations, tea- and coffee-making facilities, beautiful comforters and coordinated draperies, heaters, electric blankets, iron or brass queen-size beds, clock radios with cassette players, and small refrigerators. Quarters are spacious, have old-world decors, handcrafted timber cabinets, and large windows that make them sunny. Four also offer large spa baths.

Gourmet meals, prepared by chef Paul Chan, are served in two atmospheric dining rooms. Three-course dinners cost A$25 (U.S. $20). The handsome Huon pine bar in the foyer and the wine cellar operate on the honesty system. Diners choose what they want and note their selection in a notebook. An adjacent lounge is where coffee is served after dinner and guests relax throughout the day. Taped classical music, an open fire, and large arrangements of dried flowers contribute to the charm of this room.

Bernadette fixes picnic lunches for those going on day-trips and is a good source of information on things to do in the area. Highly recommended.

GORDON GATEWAY CHALETS, Grining St., Strahan, TAS 7468. Tel. 004/71-7165. 10 1-bedroom units. TV

$ Rates: A$77 (U.S. $61.60) single or double off-season (May–Dec); A$88 (U.S. $70.40) single or double in season. BC, MC, V. **Parking:** Free.

These modern units are located on a hill and have excellent views of the harbor. Each has a full kitchen, a bathroom with shower, contemporary furnishings, and local Huon pine and blackwood timbers. Electric blankets, in-house movies, and cozy comforters are standard in all units. Breakfast is provided on request at an additional charge. Guests have the use of a self-service laundry, and there's a playground for children. One unit is designed for disabled travelers.

CHAPTER 19
CANBERRA

Canberra is unique in Australia. Other cities were founded near the mouth of a river whose natural harbor could be made into port facilities. Canberra isn't even on the coast. Other cities survived because minerals, particularly gold, were discovered nearby. Canberra has no mineral wealth. Other cities were founded in the 19th century and grew gradually and naturally. Canberra, begun in 1913, was carefully planned before the first brick was laid.

Why is the nation's capital different? The story begins with federation in 1901. As soon as Queen Victoria agreed to the establishment of the Commonwealth of Australia, the need for a site for the national government became an issue. Archrivals Sydney and Melbourne each wanted to become the federal capital. To appease them, Australian leaders chose to follow the U.S. example of a federal district, and in 1908 a place between the two cities was chosen. The Australian Capital Territory (ACT), was at that time nothing more than a sheep-grazing region. The work of creating a capital out of the bush began in 1911 with an international competition for a city plan. Walter Burley Griffin, a Chicago landscape architect and contemporary of Frank Lloyd Wright, won the contest with his design. In 1913 the federal capital was named Canberra—an Aboriginal term for "meeting place."

1. ORIENTATION

ARRIVING

BY PLANE

Canberra is well served by the daily flights of Ansett and Australian Airlines. An Australian Air Pass fare from Sydney costs from A$76 to A$96 (U.S. $60.80 to U.S. $76.80); the flight lasts 40 minutes. The same discounted fare from Melbourne is A$108 to A$135 (U.S. $86.40 to U.S. $108), and that flight takes 55 minutes.

The **Canberra Airport** has car-rental desks, a gift shop, and a newsagent (a kiosk where magazines and newspapers are sold), but it lacks lockers, showers, a money exchange, and a post office. Stamps are sold at the newsagent's and a mailbox is provided for your cards and letters. A bar and bistro are available.

The Canberra Airport is about 10 minutes from the city center. A taxi costs approximately A$10 (U.S. $8).

BY TRAIN

You might also want to consider taking the train to Canberra. Countrylink's Canberra Express and Southern Highlands Express make the journey from Sydney in 5 hours; the fare is A$42.50 (U.S. $34) first class and A$30 (U.S. $24) in economy. Children are

WHAT'S SPECIAL ABOUT CANBERRA

Museums
- ☐ The Australian National Gallery, a treasure trove of the nation's art.
- ☐ The National Science and Technology Centre, a hands-on science center.

Monuments
- ☐ The Australian War Memorial, a tribute to those who gave their lives.

Activities
- ☐ Cycling on Canberra's many miles of bike paths.

Parks/Gardens
- ☐ The city's extensive greenbelts and parklands.
- ☐ The Australian National Botanic Gardens, the best collection of native flora.

Ace Attractions
- ☐ Parliament House on Capital Hill.

Buildings
- ☐ The High Court of Australia, an impressive concrete-and-glass structure.
- ☐ The Telecom Tower, providing a lofty viewpoint.

Man-made Spectacles
- ☐ Lake Burley Griffin, contributing significantly to the city's overall beauty.

Local Specialties
- ☐ The embassies of many foreign governments.

---

half price. For more information phone Countrylink (tel. 02/217-8812, or toll free 008/04-3126 in Australia). V/Line provides service from Melbourne. The Capital Link and Canberra Link are a combination of train and coach travel. The fare is A$56.50 (U.S. $45.20) first class and A$44 (U.S. $35.20) economy. Children pay a little more than half fare. For further details call V/Line (tel. 03/619-5000, or toll free 008/13-6109 in Australia). Canberra's **Railway Station** (tel. 239-0133) is about 3 kilometers (2 miles) southeast of Capital Hill.

BY BUS

A Countrylink coach ticket from Sydney to Canberra costs A$24 (U.S. $19.20) for adults and A$15 (U.S. $12) for children; the trip takes 4 to 4½ hours. Pioneer and Greyhound tickets cost the same; Bus Australia charges A$21 (U.S. $16.80). A Pioneer or Greyhound ticket from Melbourne to Canberra costs A$48 (U.S. $38.40). Several sightseeing bus companies in Sydney, including AAT King's and Australian Pacific Tours, offer day-trips to Canberra. Intercity buses arrive at the **Jolimont Tourist Centre,** corner of Northbourne Avenue and Alinga Street, in Civic.

BY CAR

The ACT is located within the state of New South Wales. Sydney is 306 kilometers (190 miles) to the northeast, and Melbourne is 651 kilometers (404 miles) to the southwest. If you drive from Sydney via the **Hume and Federal highways,** the trip will take 3½ to 4 hours.

TOURIST INFORMATION

The **ACT Tourism Commission** (tel. 06/245-6464) dispenses information and books accommodation from their information center on Northbourne Avenue, Dickson (just south of Morphett Street). The office is open daily from 8:30am to 5pm. A fast-food eatery and souvenir shop is located next to the information center.

A host of free events—from concerts to competitions—are part of the annual

Canberra Festival held in March. The 10 days of frivolity end on Canberra Day (a local public holiday), which is always the third Monday in March.

CITY LAYOUT

Walter Burley Griffin's plan for Australia's capital has stood the test of time. Canberra is an attractive, carefully designed city that functions well both as the seat of the federal government and as a desirable place to live. The Chicago architect did not envisage that 290,000 people would one day inhabit his city, but because parks, gardens, and open space were important to him, the many residents of this model metropolis consider themselves lucky. In addition to the planned greenbelts, those who live in Canberra enjoy excursions into the surrounding Australian Capital Territory, which remains a sparsely populated, rural region.

Griffin had not seen the site for the capital when he created his prize-winning design, but it's hard to imagine him having done any better even if he had. **Capital Hill,** where the **Parliament House** opened in 1988, is the center of a hub from which more than a half dozen avenues radiate. Each of these broad, tree-lined streets leads to a traffic circle from which more roads emanate, like spokes in a wheel. Around each hub, the streets form a pattern of concentric circles. This unusual traffic plan is one of the hallmarks of Griffin's design. The other notable feature is the man-made lake he stipulated, created by damming the Molonglo River. Today, **Lake Burley Griffin** contributes to the overall beauty of the city and provides its residents with a welcome recreation area.

Not everyone admires Canberra. Some say the city is so well planned that's it's boring and sterile. Others complain that the circular street system is hard for newcomers to navigate. Personally, I appreciate the capital's treasure trove of museums and galleries and find the fresh, modern architecture a pleasant change from that of other Aussie cities. Admittedly, I have gotten lost in the spokes going from one hub to the other, and you might be wise to use public transportation or take taxis. Because this is a horizontal, rather than a vertical, city, the distance between points of interest precludes walking. However, if you are fit, you can tour the area of greatest national importance on foot: The major sights are located in the **Parliamentary Triangle,** a pie-shaped wedge whose boundaries are **Kings Avenue, Parkes Way,** and **Commonwealth Avenue.** While extensive walking isn't practical, cyclists can rent a bike and move around Canberra on its 120 kilometers (74 miles) of bicycle paths. Commonwealth Avenue leads across the lake to City Hill, which is the commercial heart of the capital. **Northbourne Avenue** is the main thoroughfare in this central business district, known officially as **Canberra City,** and locally as **"Civic."** Separate centers for national and municipal functions were part of Walter Burley Griffin's plan. The **Telecom Tower** on **Black Mountain** and the viewpoint on **Mount Ainslie** provide spectacular wide-angle vistas of the entire region. The best time to visit Canberra is in spring (September through November) or autumn (March to May).

2. GETTING AROUND

BY PUBLIC TRANSPORTATION
BY BUS

Several bus companies offer escorted sightseeing tours of Canberra. These include **ACTION** (tel. 251-6566), **Murrays** (tel. 295-3677), and **Monarch** (tel. 259-1686). Those who wish a bit more independence might prefer to use the **Canberra Explorer,** a bus that makes 19 stops on a 25-kilometer (15-mile) route around the city (tel. 295-3611 or 295-3677). Passengers can get off and stay as long as they like at each attraction and reboard the next bus. Buses run every hour 7 days a week. The fare of A$9 (U.S. $7.20) for adults and A$5.50 (U.S. $4.40) for children includes full commentary. Another option is to stay on the bus as it makes its complete 1-hour circuit (and then go back later on your own to the places that interest you); this costs A$4.50 (U.S. $3.60) for adults and A$3 (U.S. $2.40) for children. **Canberra Cruises** (tel. 295-3544) offers 1- and 2-hour cruises on Lake Burley Griffin. These cost A$8 (U.S. $6.40) for 1 hour and A$12 (U.S. $9.60) for 2 hours; children are charged half price.

A network of public buses is run by ACTION (tel. 251-6566). The basic fare is A$1.40 (U.S. $1.15) for adults and half price for kids. Dollarwise **day-tripper tickets** cost A$4.60 (U.S. $3.70) for adults and A$2.30 (U.S. $1.85) for children 5 to 15. Route maps and timetables are available at City Walk on Northbourne Avenue between London Circuit and Alinga Street, Civic, or at the ACT Tourism Commission office mentioned above. The *Bus Book,* which contains complete timetables and route maps, costs A$1.95 (U.S. $1.60). You can phone ACTION for information Monday through Saturday between 6:30am and 11:30pm and Sunday 8:30am to 6:30pm.

BY TAXI OR CAR

Aerial (tel. 285-9222) is Canberra's only taxi company. **Budget** offers chauffeur service (tel. 259-1144, or toll free 008/33-3052 in Australia). See "City Layout," above. **Car** rental can be arranged through Budget (tel. 248-9788 or 257-1305), Hertz (tel. 249-6211), National (tel. 247-8888), or Thrifty (tel. 247-7422).

 CANBERRA

American Express The office at Centrepoint, Shop 1, 185 City Walk (corner of Petrie Plaza), Canberra City (tel. 247-2333), is open Mon–Fri 9am–5:15pm and Sat 9am–noon.

Area Code Canberra's area code is 06.

Baby-sitters All Suburbs Baby Sitting Agency is at 21 Gillies St., Curtin (tel. 281-3027). The 3-hour minimum costs A$22 (U.S. $17.60); additional hours cost A$5.50 (U.S. $4.40).

Business Hours Offices are open Mon–Fri 9am–5:30pm. Many stores stay open on Fri nights until 9pm and are open Sat. The City Market section of the Canberra Centre is open daily.

Car Rentals See "Getting Around," above.

Climate See "When to Go" in Chapter 2.

Currency See "Information, Entry Requirements, and Money" in Chapter 2.

Currency Exchange Cash traveler's checks at banks (Mon–Fri 9:30am–4pm), at American Express (see above), or at Thomas Cook (on Bunda St. near Ainslie St.) Mon–Fri 8:45am–5:15pm and Sat 9am–noon.

Dentist Canberra lacks a dental emergency referral service. Two dentists with conveniently located offices are Dr. A. W. Bubear, City Walk Arcade, Canberra City (tel. 247-8400), and D. R. Robertson, City Walk Arcade, Canberra City (tel. 248-0161).

Doctor The Capital Medical Centre, 73 London Circuit, Canberra City (tel. 257-3766), is open Mon–Fri 8:30am–5pm.

Drugstores The Canberra City Pharmacy, corner East Row and Alinga St., Canberra City (tel. 248-5469 or 248-6491), is open daily.

Embassies/Consulates British High Commission, Commonwealth Ave., Yarralumla (tel. 270-6666); Canada High Commission, Commonwealth Ave., Yarralumla (tel. 273-3844); U.S. Embassy, Moonah Place, Yarralumla (tel. 270-5000).

Emergencies Police, fire, ambulance: 000.

Eyeglasses OPSM Express, lower ground floor, The Canberra Centre (tel. 249-7344), is open Mon–Thurs 9am–5:30pm, Fri 9am–9pm, and Sat 9am–3pm.

Hairdressers/Barbers Cataldo's Salon, 55 Northbourne Ave. (street level, the Melbourne Bldg.), Canberra City (tel. 247-2877 or 299-6666), or Unisex Hair Salon, 4 Garema Place, Canberra City (tel. 248-0352).

Holidays See "When to Go" in Chapter 2.

Hospitals Royal Canberra Hospital North (tel. 243-2111); Accident & Emergency Department (tel. 243-2169 all hours).

Hotlines Lifeline (tel. 257-1111); Rape Crisis Centre (tel. 247-2525); Drug/ Alcohol Crisis Line (tel. 245-4545 all hours); Suicide Prevention (tel. 02/331-2000); Poison Information Centre (tel. 243-2154).

Information See "Tourist Information," above.

Laundry/Dry Cleaning 60-Minute Dry Cleaners, Bailey's Corner, Canberra City (tel. 248-0521).

Libraries The National Library (tel. 262-1279 or 262-1111) is open Mon–Thurs 9am–9pm, Fri–Sat 9am–4:30pm, and Sun 1:30–4:30pm. "Beyond the Foyer" guided tours are conducted weekdays at 2:15pm.

Lost Property Inquire at local police station.

Luggage Storage/Lockers At the train station in Kingston there is a luggage storage room. Each item left costs A$1.50 (U.S. $1.20).

Newspapers/Magazines Canberra's daily newspaper is the *Canberra Times.*

Photographic Needs One Hour Photos, 132 City Walk, Canberra City (tel. 247-2669), can do film processing, take passport photos, sell film, and so forth.

Police See "Emergencies," above.

Post Office Canberra Post Office, Alinga St., Canberra City (tel. 248-5211), is open Mon–Fri 9am–5pm.

Radio Classic hits, 2CC 1206 AM or 2CA 1053 AM; classical music, ABC 102.3 FM; rock, 104.7 FM or 106 FM.

Religious Services Anglican, All Saints, 1 Bonney St., Ainslie (tel. 248-7420); Baptist, Kingston (tel. 295-9470); Catholic, St. Christopher's Cathedral, 55 Franklin St., Forrest (tel. 295-9555); Jewish, National Jewish Memorial Centre, National Circuit, Forrest (tel. 295-1052); Presbyterian, St. Andrew's Church, State Circle, Forrest (tel. 295-3457); Uniting Church, Wesley Centre, Sydney Ave., Forrest (tel. 295-3680).

Rest Rooms Near city bus exchange, City Hill, London Circuit.

Safety Canberra is generally quite safe. However, it's always a good idea to stay out of parks and dimly lit places at night.

Shoe Repairs Cavallo Nero, Master Boot and Shoe Repairs, first floor, Canberra Centre, Canberra City (tel. 257-5248).

Taxes No GST. No hotel tax. No sales tax added to purchases.

Taxis See "Getting Around," above.

Telegrams/Telex Send these from the post office.

Television Channel 3 (Australian Broadcasting Company): news, current affairs, educational programs, and entertainment. Channels 7, 9, and 10: sports, entertainment, news, and so forth.

Transit Info ACTION timetable information 251-6566.

Useful Telephone Numbers Citizen's Advice Bureau (tel. 248-7988); Australian National University (tel. 249-2229); Lesbian Line (tel. 247-8882 or 247-9001); Gay Contact (tel. 247-2726); Women's Information and Referral Centre (tel. 245-4650 or 245-4654).

3. CANBERRA ACCOMMODATIONS

Australia's national capital offers a good range of lodging at prices that are lower than those of many other big cities. Since many people come to Canberra for business during the week, weekend tariffs are often less expensive.

IN THE CITY CENTER

EXPENSIVE

CAPITAL PARKROYAL, 1 Binara St., Canberra, ACT 2601. Tel. 06/247-8999, or toll free 008/02-0055 in Australia. Fax 06/257-4905. 287 rms, 6 suites. A/C MINIBAR TV TEL

$ Rates: A$250 (U.S. $200) standard single or double; A$285 (U.S. $228) deluxe room; A$450–A$800 (U.S. $360–U.S. $640) suite; A$20 (U.S. $16) extra person. Lower weekend tariffs. Children under 15 stay free in parents' room. No-smoking rooms available. AE, BC, DC, MC, V. **Parking:** Free.

The centrally located Capital Parkroyal is part of the National Convention Centre Complex and overlooks Glebe Park. The impressive garden setting includes pools, watercourses, and fountains. All rooms have clock radios, terry robes, hairdryers, tea- and coffee-making facilities, small refrigerators, in-room movies, and free daily newspapers. The majority of rooms have either one queen-size bed or two doubles. Deluxe quarters have king-size beds. Five rooms were designed for handicapped travelers.

Dining/Entertainment: Two restaurants, Blundell's and the Glebe Cafe, and two bars offer meals and drinks.

Services: 24-hour rooms service, turn-down service, laundry, valet, concierge, and baby-sitting.

Facilities: Pool, health club, gym, sauna, and business center.

IN YARRALUMLA

EXPENSIVE

HYATT HOTEL CANBERRA, Commonwealth Ave., Yarralumla, ACT 2600. Tel. 06/270-1234, or toll free 008/22-2188 in Australia. Fax 06/281-5998. 249 rms and suites. A/C MINIBAR TV TEL

$ Rates: A$260 (U.S. $208) single or double; A$298 (U.S. $238.40) deluxe single or double; A$350 (U.S. $280) Pavilion Terrace (Regency Club) quarters; A$650 (U.S. $520) executive suite; A$1,100–A$1,500 (U.S. $880–U.S. $1,200) Diplomatic Suite; A$40 (U.S. $32) extra person. Children under 18 stay free in parents' room. Weekend packages. No-smoking rooms available. AE, BC, DC, MC, V. **Parking:** Free.

★ This is the capital's most posh hotel. It is ideally sited in the shadow of the new Parliament House and between Lake Burley Griffin and the Parliamentary Triangle. The hotel, which opened in March 1988, is a renovation of the Hotel Canberra, a historic landmark built in 1924. The gracious ambience of the National Trust building was preserved while luxurious lodging and dining facilities were installed. All staff wear 1920s-style outfits, and the hotel has the low-key atmosphere usually associated with a country club.

Some 39 rooms are located in the original two-story section; these have small windows and tend to be a little dark. The majority of lodging is in the new four-story section, and these rooms are spacious, have pleasant beige/cocoa-color decors, and marble bathrooms with separate tub and shower stall. Each offers a radio, terry robe, hairdryer, tea- and coffee-making facilities, small refrigerator, in-room movies, free daily newspapers, and king-size or twin beds. Deluxe rooms on the fourth floor of the north wing have the best lake views.

Dining/Entertainment: Meals and drinks are served in The Promenade Cafe, The Tea Lounge, The Oak Room (winner of the 1990 Australian Tourist Commission Award for fine dining), Speaker's Corner, and Griffin's.

Services: 24-hour room service, turn-down service, shoeshine, laundry, valet, concierge, and massage.

Facilities: Business center, indoor pool, extensive fitness center with daily aerobics classes, gym, sauna, spa, tennis court, and bike rental.

IN DICKSON

MODERATE

**CANBERRA INTERNATIONAL HOTEL, 242 Northbourne Ave., Dickson,
ACT 2602 Tel. 06/247-6966,** or toll free 008/02-6305 in Australia. Fax
06/248-7823. 152 rms and suites. A/C MINIBAR TV TEL **Bus:** No. 382 or 431.
$ Rates: A$180 (U.S. $144) single or double; A$190 (U.S. $152) executive suite;
A$215 (U.S. $172) 1-bedroom unit; A$240 (U.S. $192) 2-bedroom unit; A$10
(U.S. $8) extra person. Children under 12 stay free in parents' room. Lower
weekend rates. Reservations can be made through Flag Inns. AE, BC, DC, MC, V.
Parking: Free.
Before the Capital Parkroyal and the Hyatt were built, Canberra International was the
city's most prestigious address. The three-story hotel offers standard rooms and one-
and two-room suites, 10 of which have kitchens. All quarters have hairdryers, irons,
ironing boards, in-room movies, free daily newspapers, clock radios, tea- and
coffee-making facilities, and small refrigerators. Two rooms are equipped for
handicapped travelers.
Dining/Entertainment: Meals and drinks are served in the Garden Terrace
Restaurant, the Gazebo Cocktail Bar, and the Lemon Tree Brasserie.
Services: 24-hour room service, laundry, valet, and baby-sitting.
Facilities: Outdoor pool and gift shop.

IN GRIFFITH

MODERATE

**THE DIPLOMAT INTERNATIONAL MOTOR INN, Canberra Ave. and Hely
St., Griffith, ACT 2603. Tel. 06/295-2277,** or toll free 008/02-6367 in
Australia. Fax 06/239-6432. 68 rms and suites. A/C MINIBAR TV TEL **Bus:** No.
371.
$ Rates: A$105 (U.S. $84) single or double; A$150–A$170 (U.S. $120–U.S.
$136) suite; A$10 (U.S. $8) extra person. Lower weekend rates. Children under 18
stay free in parents' room. AE, BC, DC, MC, V. **Parking:** Free.
The white contemporary Mediterranean–style hotel is about 3 kilometers (2 miles)
from the Parliamentary Triangle and about 6 kilometers (4 miles) from Civic. Most
rooms face onto a multilevel atrium and are spacious and modern. Two-thirds have
tub/shower combinations; all have hairdryers, clock radios, in-room movies, tea- and
coffee-making facilities, and small refrigerators.
Dining/Entertainment: Meals are served in The Casablanca, an informal
eatery at the base of the atrium.
Services: Room service during limited hours and baby-sitting.
Facilities: An outdoor pool and sauna.

IN KINGSTON

MODERATE

**KINGSTON COURT SERVICED APARTMENTS, 4 Tench St., Kingston,
ACT 2604. Tel. 06/295-2244.** Fax 06/239-9499. 36 apartments. A/C TV TEL
Bus: No. 352.
$ Rates: A$100 (U.S. $80) single; A$110 (U.S. $88) double; A$10 (U.S. $8) extra
adult; A$5 (U.S. $4) extra child. AE, BC, DC, MC, V. **Parking:** Free.
Kingston Court is a good choice for those who want the comforts of home.
Each 100-square-meter (1,000-sq.-ft.) unit has its own washing machine, dryer,
kitchen with dishwasher, and balcony or courtyard. Quarters are cleaned only
twice a week, but towels are changed daily. Kingston Court is located 1 kilometer (½

mile) from the Parliamentary Triangle and about 6 kilometers (3½ miles) from Civic. Telopea Park is across the street. The only drawback is that this three-story building has no lift (elevator). A pool, a gas barbecue, and half-court tennis are provided on the premises.

IN BRADDON

MODERATE

OLIMS CANBERRA HOTEL, corner of Limestone and Ainslie Aves., Braddon, ACT 2601. Tel. 06/248-5511, or toll free 008/02-0016 in Australia. Fax 06/247-0864. 126 rms and suites. TV TEL **Bus:** No. 385.

$ Rates: A$95 (U.S. $76) standard room single or double; A$115 (U.S. $92) deluxe room single or double; A$140 (U.S. $112) suite; A$15 (U.S. $12) extra person. Reservations can be made through Flag Inns. AE, BC, DC, MC, V. **Parking:** Free.

The Olims Canberra was remodeled not long ago, and thankfully, the original section was retained. The old Ainslie Hotel, which opened its doors in 1927, was known for its high, pitched gables and attic windows—a style called "English deco." The building was classified by the National Trust in 1981, and more than A$5 million (U.S. $4 million) has subsequently been spent in upgrading and extension efforts.

Today 37 standard rooms remain in the original part and the rest are in a tasteful addition. (Only standard rooms lack air conditioning and minibars.) All quarters are very spacious and nicely furnished. The 33 suites are on two levels, with kitchen and lounge (living room) downstairs and bedroom and bathroom upstairs. Standard rooms offer a choice of twin or double beds; in the new section, kings, queens, and twins are available. Some rooms overlook the attractive central courtyard. The hotel's bistro/carvery is open 7 days a week for moderately priced lunches and dinners. The restaurant serves breakfast and dinner Monday through Saturday. There's also a beer garden and a bottle shop. Civic is just over a kilometer away. Room service is available 24 hours a day.

IN ACTON

MODERATE

UNIVERSITY HOUSE, on the campus of The Australian National University, Balmain Crescent, Acton (GPO Box 1535, Canberra, ACT 2601). Tel. 06/249-5211. Fax 06/249-5252. 154 rms and suites. TEL **Bus:** No. 434.

$ Rates: A$53 (U.S. $42.40) single without bath, A$85 (U.S. $68) single with bath; A$95 (U.S. $76) twin with bath; A$100 (U.S. $80) suite or West Wing apartment; A$150 (U.S. $120) 2-bedroom flat with bath and kitchen. AE, BC, DC, MC, V. **Parking:** Free.

Whether you have business at ANU or not, University House is a pleasant and out-of-the-ordinary place to stay. It's conveniently located within 2 kilometers (1 mile) of the city center. All rooms offer telephones, a small refrigerator, toaster, and coffee- and tea-making facilities. Some quarters have televisions and kitchenettes. Meals are served in the Bistro and the Cellar. University House has a billiards room and offers bicycle rental. Tennis courts and a jogging track are nearby.

IN O'CONNOR

BUDGET

CANBERRA MOTOR VILLAGE, Kunzea St., O'Connor, ACT 2601. Tel. 06/247-5466, or toll free 008/02-6199 in Australia. Fax 06/249-6138. 38 motel units, 44 powered sites. **Bus:** No. 381.

$ Rates: A$73 (U.S. $58.40) single; A$84 (U.S. $67.20) double. On-site vans A$62 (U.S. $49.60). Powered sites A$20 (U.S. $16). Lower rates through Aussie auto clubs. AE, BC, DC, MC, V. **Parking:** Free.

The Canberra Motor Village offers motel lodging, on-site vans, and camping sites. The 38 motel units all have private bathrooms, televisions, and telephones; some have cooking facilities and some have air conditioning. The Motor Village is located about 5 kilometers (3 miles) northwest of Civic.

4. CANBERRA DINING

IN THE CITY CENTER
MODERATE

CHARCOAL RESTAURANT, 61 London Circuit. Tel. 248-8015.
   Cuisine: INTERNATIONAL. **Reservations:** Imperative.
$ Prices: Appetizers A$4.90–A$13.90 (U.S. $3.95–U.S. $11.15); main courses A$12.90–A$18.50 (U.S. $10.35–U.S. $14.80). AE, BC, DC, MC, V.
   Open: Lunch Mon–Fri noon–2:30pm; dinner Mon–Fri 5:45–9:30pm, Sat 6–9:30pm.

This well-established Canberra favorite has been serving thick, juicy steaks to bureaucrats and their buddies for 28 years. Diners can choose either King Island sirloin or rump, T-bone, filet mignon, carpetbag steak (eye filet with a pocket of oysters), pepper steak, or steak Dianne. Other dishes offered include chicken Kiev, Creole blackened fish, Snowy River trout, and curry pot. The central location no doubt adds to the popularity of the Charcoal Restaurant. Things can get really busy for lunch when every red leatherette chair is occupied. Good wine list. Book early.

WAFFLES PATISSERIE, 50 Northbourne Ave. Tel. 247-2913.
   Cuisine: CAFE. **Reservations:** Recommended.
$ Prices: Appetizers A$4–A$6.50 (U.S. $3.20–U.S. $5.20); main courses A$8–A$11.50 (U.S. $6.40–U.S. $9.20). AE, BC, DC, MC, V.
   Open: Daily 8am–well past midnight.

At Waffles, tasty dishes are served by a friendly staff in a pleasant atmosphere. The peach-and-gray decor and large windows create a light, airy feel. Technically, this is a "licensed pâtisserie," which means they specialize in pastry—in this case waffles—and are licensed to serve alcoholic beverages, but that's only half the story. Waffles are the specialty at breakfast, but a selection of eggs and cereals is also available. Pasta, burgers, and open sandwiches are served for lunch, as are many kinds of dessert waffles. Waffles also does take-out.

BUDGET

GUS' CAFE, next to the Centre Cinema, Garema Arcade, Bunda St. Tel. 248-8118.
   Cuisine: LIGHT CONTINENTAL. **Reservations:** Not necessary.
$ Prices: Homemade soup with bread A$4–A$5 (U.S. $3.20–U.S. $4); main courses A$4–7.50 (U.S. $3.20–U.S. $6); desserts A$1.60–A$4 (U.S. $1.30–U.S. $3.20). Sun and public holiday surcharge A50¢ (U.S. 40¢) per person. 10% discount to readers of *Frommer's Australia*. No credit cards.
   Open: Daily 7am–midnight.

Gus' is a popular local hangout. Canberrans congregate here to read the newspaper, meet friends, and munch on things like focaccia (Italian flat bread), Black Forest cake, and carrot cake. The cheesecake, made fresh every morning by proprietor Goronwy Price, is also excellent. If you're ready for a meal, I recommend homemade Hungarian goulash with noodles or knodel (dumplings). Seating is both indoors and out, and magazines and board games are provided for use while you sip your cappuccino. BYO.

IN YARRALUMLA

EXPENSIVE

THE OAK ROOM, in the Hyatt Hotel Canberra, Commonwealth Ave. Tel. 270-1234.
 Cuisine: MODERN AUSTRALIAN. **Reservations:** Recommended.
$ **Prices:** Appetizers A$14–A$20 (U.S. $11.20–U.S. $16); main courses A$25–A$30 (U.S. $20–U.S. $24); set-price three-course lunch A$31.50 (U.S. $25.20). AE, BC, DC, MC, V.
 Open: Lunch Mon–Fri noon–2pm; dinner Mon–Sat 7–10pm.

This elegant restaurant won the Australian Tourist Commission's 1990 award for "Best Fine Dining Restaurant," and it isn't hard to understand why. Chef Gary Hague creates interesting dishes that are neither too simple nor too belabored. Entrées (appetizers) include a medley of marinated raw seafood, enhanced by fresh basil around a crisp autumn salad and green wasabi; tender South Australian lobster tail lightly pan-fried in herb butter and surrounded by a champagne and wild mushroom beurre blanc; or Oriental-flavored beef tartare accompanied by a red currant ginger sauce and served with warm oven-baked buckwheat blinis. Mains are equally creative. The menu changes monthly.

Guests entering the dining room walk past extensive wine cellars—white to the left, red to the right—into the oak-paneled room, divided into intimate spaces. One room with 10 tables has been designated no-smoking; the other room has eight tables. Both areas have fireplaces and art deco decors. Three private dining rooms are ideal for politicians and others needing privacy.

IN BRADDON

MODERATE

BURPS B.Y.O., 9 Lonsdale St. Tel. 247-8300.
 Cuisine: MIXED ETHNIC. **Reservations:** Recommended on weekends. **Bus:** No. 431, 381, 382, 383, 384, or 385 (get off at Cooyong St.).
$ **Prices:** Appetizers A$4.50–A$10.50 (U.S. $3.60–U.S. $8.40); main courses A$9.50–A$14.50 (U.S. $7.60–U.S. $11.60); two courses A$11.50 (U.S. $9.20); three courses A$15 (U.S. $12); Kids Biz A$6.50 (U.S. $5.20); corkage A$1 (U.S. 80¢) per bottle or six-pack. BC, MC, V.
 Open: Lunch Tues–Fri noon–2:30pm; dinner Mon–Sat 6pm–late.

Diners at Burps have the sense of eating in a contemporary art gallery. One wall is dark green; one is yellow; one is lavender, and another is mauve. Framed art and photos hang from a single black strip which encircles the room. Chairs and tables are simple and modern. Black metal shades on hanging lights also contribute to the artists' studio/gallery feel.

The restaurant opened in 1990 and has enjoyed considerable success. Good food and very reasonable prices seem to be the key. Guests have the choice of ordering freely from the à la carte menu or choosing selected items at the set prices mentioned above. You might like the linguine vongole, Creole-style okra and eggplant gumbo, or Savannah-style southern fried chicken. Desserts include sweet pumpkin pie with fresh cream and golden mapled pecan pie. BYO. (There's a bottle shop two doors up the street.)

IN ACTON

MODERATE

VIVALDI RESTAURANT, in the Arts Centre on the campus of The Australian National University. Tel. 257-2718.
 Cuisine: CONTEMPORARY AUSTRALIAN. **Reservations:** Recommended on weekends. **Bus:** No. 434.

$ Prices: Appetizers A$5.90–A$12.50 (U.S. $4.75–U.S. $10); main courses A$14.90–A$17.90 (U.S. $11.95–U.S. $14.35). AE, BC, DC, MC, V.
Open: Mon–Fri noon–10pm; Sat 6–10pm.
This restaurant has an appealing casual ambience created by lots of green plants, cane springback chairs, exposed brick walls, and (ersatz) marble tables. It's licensed and BYO, and most diners arrive toting their bottles. The clientele includes politicians, university staff, and local residents. The printed menu is the same for lunch and dinner, but at lunchtime there's also a blackboard menu announcing such dishes as boned rainbow trout filled with seafood mousse and spinach fettuccine tossed with prosciutto, black olives, and roasted red capsicum. If you order from the printed menu, you could start with angel-hair pasta with duckling, asparagus, snow peas, and emerald capsicum butter, and follow that with turkey breast and smoked salmon wrapped in spinach puff pastry with smoked salmon hollandaise. Vivaldi boasts a large no-smoking section, which the management is hoping to expand.

WITHIN THE PARLIAMENTARY TRIANGLE

MODERATE

THE LOBBY RESTAURANT, King George Terrace. Tel. 273-1563.
   Cuisine: INTERNATIONAL. **Reservations:** Recommended. **Bus:** No. 352, 357, 358, or 359.
$ Prices: Appetizers A$7.50–A$9 (U.S. $6–U.S. $7.20); main courses A$16.50–A$17.50 (U.S. $13.20–U.S. $14). AE, BC, DC, MC, V.
   Open: Lunch Mon–Fri noon–2:30pm; dinner Wed–Fri 6:30–9pm.
The Lobby, located close to Capital Hill, is a popular haunt for politicians and others with government business on their minds. Entrées include a selection of terrines and pâtés served with homemade chutney, and spiralli and tortellini pasta cooked with Italian sausage, chili, olives, and basil. Main courses are eclectic: whole boned Snowy Mountains trout, a selection of satays on a bed of salad, and escalopes of fallow deer in a red wine, leek, and bacon sauce. Desserts include forest berry pudding with crème à l'anglaise, and strawberries Romanoff (in season, of course).

BUDGET

HIGH COURT CAFE, in the High Court Building. Tel. 270-6828.
   Cuisine: INTERNATIONAL. **Reservations:** Not necessary. **Bus:** No. 234, 350, 352, or 358.
$ Prices: Appetizers A$2–A$5.50 (U.S. $1.60–U.S. $4.40); main courses A$3.85–A$9.50 (U.S. $3.10–U.S. $7.60). Children's portions half price. Prices slightly higher on weekends and public holidays. No credit cards.
   Open: Daily 9:45am–4:15pm.
This café, which overlooks a wide grassy area and Lake Burley Griffin, is a good spot for a morning or afternoon tea break or a light lunch while you're sightseeing. For lunch you could have pasta, a ploughman's platter, pan-fried sea perch, or something classically Aussie like a meat pie and chips. For tea, be sure to try their fluffy scones with your cuppa.

PUBLIC DINING ROOM, in Parliament House. Tel. 277-3990.
   Cuisine: AUSTRALIAN. **Reservations:** Not accepted.
$ Prices: Carvery lunch A$7.50 (U.S. $6); other lunch items A$3.50–A$9 (U.S. $2.80–U.S. $7.20). Prices slightly higher weekends and public holidays. BC, MC, V (with A$10 minimum purchase). **Bus:** No. 231, 234, 235, or 777.
   Open: Daily 9am–5pm; carvery 11am–2pm.
This cafeteria is a handy and inexpensive place to eat lunch or just enjoy a beer after you've toured Parliament House. There's indoor and outdoor seating and it's all very light and bright. The menu reads like a list of archetypical Australian dishes: fish-and-chips, sausage rolls, meat pies, roast meat with "veg," and, for dessert, lamingtons, of course.

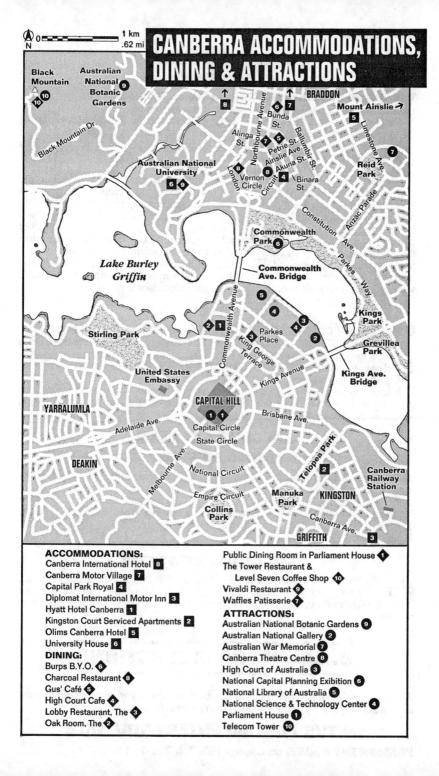

CANBERRA ACCOMMODATIONS, DINING & ATTRACTIONS

ACCOMMODATIONS:
Canberra International Hotel **8**
Canberra Motor Village **7**
Capital Park Royal **4**
Diplomat International Motor Inn **3**
Hyatt Hotel Canberra **1**
Kingston Court Serviced Apartments **2**
Olims Canberra Hotel **5**
University House **6**

DINING:
Burps B.Y.O. **6**
Charcoal Restaurant **8**
Gus' Café **5**
High Court Cafe **4**
Lobby Restaurant, The **3**
Oak Room, The **2**

Public Dining Room in Parliament House **1**
The Tower Restaurant &
    Level Seven Coffee Shop **10**
Vivaldi Restaurant **9**
Waffles Patisserie **7**

ATTRACTIONS:
Australian National Botanic Gardens **9**
Australian National Gallery **2**
Australian War Memorial **7**
Canberra Theatre Centre **8**
High Court of Australia **3**
National Capital Planning Exibition **6**
National Library of Australia **5**
National Science & Technology Center **4**
Parliament House **1**
Telecom Tower **10**

ON BLACK MOUNTAIN
EXPENSIVE

THE TOWER RESTAURANT, Telecom Tower. Tel. 248-6162.
Cuisine: INTERNATIONAL. **Reservations:** Imperative.
$ **Prices:** Appetizers A$13 (U.S. $10.40); main courses A$23 (U.S. $18.40); buffet lunch A$24.50 (U.S. $19.60); fixed-price two-course lunch A$23.50 (U.S. $18.80); fixed-price three-course lunch A$27.50 (U.S. $22). Weekend and public holiday surcharge 10%. AE, BC, DC, MC, V.
Open: Lunch daily noon–3pm; dinner daily 6pm–midnight.

For dining with a view, the top spot in town is the revolving restaurant on the Telecom Tower located on Black Mountain. The Tower Restaurant occupies a lofty site 54 meters (178 ft.) above the top of the mountain. Sunset is my favorite time here, but whether you dine during the day or at night, the view is spectacular. Happily, the food is also good. There is a fixed menu at lunch, but you may also choose à la carte. For dinner, you might start with broccoli and vegetable terrine, seafood tartlets, or warm quail salad. Main courses include boned loin of lamb, Atlantic salmon cutlet on leek purée topped with lemon and dill butter, and kangaroo filets flamed in brandy and served with pepper cherries. The wine list, which features maps of Australia's wine-producing regions, is both interesting and educational.

BUDGET

LEVEL SEVEN COFFEE SHOP, in the Telecom Tower. Tel. 248-6162.
Cuisine: FAST FOOD. **Reservations:** Not necessary. **Transportation:** Drive or taxi (weekends). **Bus:** No. 904 (Mon–Fri).
$ **Prices:** Quick lunch A$8 (U.S. $6.40) or less. AE, BC, MC, V.
Open: Daily 9am–9pm.

This inexpensive eatery is a good spot for a quick bite while you savor the view from the lofty lookout. No fancy fare. Sandwiches, burgers, soft drinks, and so forth. Snacks in the Tower Kiosk cost even less.

SPECIALTY DINING
DINING CLUSTERS

Glebe Park A La Carte, 15 Coranderrk Street, Civic (tel. 247-2753), is a light, airy food court with eight outlets serving various kinds of food. You can eat lunch or dinner for A$5 to A$6 (U.S. $4 to U.S. $4.80). One entrance faces the plaza of the National Convention Centre. **Pasta Palace, Flaming Wok, Ali Baba,** and the others are open daily from 11am to 8:30pm. The brewery/tavern stays open until 11pm.

LIGHT, CASUAL & FAST FOOD

★ **My Mother's Favourites,** Shop 5A, City Market, Bunda Street, Civic (tel. 247-8840), sells wonderful muffins which could be the basis of a picnic breakfast in your hotel room. Proprietor David Cox stays open daily from 9am to 5pm.

5. CANBERRA ATTRACTIONS

As the national capital, Canberra has a wealth of impressive government buildings and is, in many ways, a repository of the country's treasures.

IN THE PARLIAMENTARY TRIANGLE

PARLIAMENT HOUSE, on Capital Hill. Tel. 277-7111.

⭐ Since it opened in 1988, Parliament House has become Canberra's number-one attraction. The building was designed by the New York firm of Mitchell, Giurgola, and Thorp (Thorp is an Australian) and is the culmination of the city plan conceived in 1912 by American Walter Burley Griffin. Like Griffin, the New York architects entered their design for the building in an international competition—and won. The new Parliament House would have pleased Griffin, for he urged that when it was eventually constructed, it should be functionally as well as symbolically "the people's house." In keeping with this idea, the architects created a structure with extensive access to the public. The design of the building is very distinctive. It merges into the top of Capital Hill; only a national flag the size of a double-decker bus rises above the natural curve of the hill. The grass lawns that cover the roof can be used for picnicking and play 24 hours a day. The view from this roof can only be described as "spectacular." No doubt it gives egalitarian Aussies some satisfaction knowing they can walk over the heads of their representatives.

Free 50-minute guided tours are offered throughout the day. You can also wander through on your own or rent a 40-minute Acousti guide (A$3/U.S. $2.40). You must make reservations for gallery tickets ahead of time if you want to observe Parliament in session. Write to: The Sargeant of Arms, Joint House Department, Parliament House, Canberra, ACT 2600, or phone 06/277-4889. There's a bookstore off the foyer and a post office on the first floor. The Public Dining Room is an inexpensive self-serve eatery. See "Canberra Dining," above, for details.

Admission: Free.
Open: Daily 9am–5pm. Guided tours 9am–4pm when Parliament isn't sitting.
Bus: No. 231, 234, 235, or 777.

HIGH COURT OF AUSTRALIA, overlooking Lake Burley Griffin, Parkes Place. Tel. 270-6811.

The High Court was opened by Queen Elizabeth II in May 1980. The impressive 40-meter-tall (132-ft.) concrete-and-glass building overlooks Lake Burley Griffin. Several interior features are of note: These include the large tapestry in Courtroom One in which symbols of each state are incorporated, and the various native timbers, donated by the states, which lend elegance to the courtrooms. You must stay at least 10 minutes if the court is in session. It is most likely to be in session on Tuesday, Wednesday, and Thursday of the first 2 weeks of the month.

Admission: Free.
Open: Daily 9:45am–4:30pm. **Bus:** No. 234, 350, 352, or 358.

AUSTRALIAN NATIONAL GALLERY, Parkes Place. Tel. 271-2502 or 271-2411.

⭐ This attraction is next door to the High Court and linked by a pedestrian bridge. It features permanent and special exhibitions of Australian and international art. These are displayed in 11 galleries over three floors, with sculptures in the garden. You might want to look for Jackson Pollock's *Blue Poles,* Monet's *Haystacks at Noon* and *Waterlillies,* and de Paolo's *Crucifixion.* Among the most interesting Australian works is Sidney Nolan's Ned Kelly collection.

Admission: A$3 (U.S. $2.40) adults; children under 15, free. Free guided tours daily.
Open: Daily 10am–5pm. **Closed:** Good Friday and Christmas Day. **Bus:** No. 234, 350, 352, or 358.

NATIONAL LIBRARY OF AUSTRALIA, Parkes Place. Tel. 262-1111.

The National Library is the information resource for the nation. It houses over five million books, as well as huge collections of paintings, maps, manuscripts, films, music, newspapers, and oral histories. In addition to reading rooms, the library offers a bookshop specializing in Australian literature, history, and biography, and souvenirs. Dining facilities include a self-service bistro and a restaurant. Both are licensed.

Admission: Free.
Open: Reading rooms Mon–Thurs 9am–9pm, Fri–Sat 9am–4:45pm, and Sun 1:30–4:45pm. Exhibitions daily 9am–4:30pm. Guided tours Mon–Fri. **Closed:** Christmas Day and Good Friday. **Bus:** No. 350, 352, or 358.

NATIONAL SCIENCE AND TECHNOLOGY CENTRE, between the High Court and the National Library, King Edward Terrace. Tel. 270-2800.
This is a hands-on science center, open since 1988, which is enjoyed by kids and their parents. Some 150 interactive exhibits deal with the mysteries of science and demonstrate their day-to-day use. Topics include waves, robotic dinosaurs, force, sound, light, earthquakes, communications technology, and mathematics. The NSTC is a joint Australia-Japan bicentennial project with substantial input from the Japanese government and business community, as well as Australian entities. Meals and snacks are served in a cafeteria and bistro.
Admission: A$6 (U.S. $4.80) adults, A$3 (U.S. $2.40) children 4–16; under 4, free of charge.
Open: Daily 10am–5pm. **Closed:** Christmas Day. **Bus:** No. 350, 352, 358, or 777.

NATIONAL CAPITAL PLANNING EXHIBITION, Regatta Point, Commonwealth Park. Tel. 246-8797 or 257-1068.
⭐ Even though it is across the lake from the other attractions, the National Capital Planning Exhibition is still within the Parliamentary Triangle. Here are excellent displays and a film that explain Canberra's origin and design. This is a must for anyone who wants to understand the full scope of the city. The Planning Exhibition also provides a good point from which to view Lake Burley Griffin, the Captain Cook Memorial Water Jet, and the Carillon. A kiosk and licensed restaurant serve meals and snacks.
Admission: Free.
Open: Daily 9am–5pm. **Closed:** Christmas Day. **Bus:** No. 905.

OUTSIDE THE PARLIAMENTARY TRIANGLE

Because Canberra is the nation's capital, 70 countries maintain embassies here. While you can't go inside most of them, it's fun to drive past and note the ethnic architecture. Many of the embassies are located in the suburb of Yarralumla. The **Embassy of the United States,** on Moonah Place (tel. 270-5000), is built in the style of colonial Williamsburg. The architecture of the **India High Commission,** Moonah Place (tel. 273-3999), was inspired by the Moghuls. The **Greek Embassy,** on the corner of Empire Circuit and Turrana Street (tel. 273-3011), is a modern derivative of classic Greek style. The **Embassy of Thailand,** on the corner of Empire Circuit and Adelaide Avenue (tel. 273-1149), has a sloping roofline that rises to points on either end, which is characteristic of sacred Siamese Buddhist buildings. You may also be interested in the High Commissions of **Britain** (tel. 270-6666), **Canada** (tel. 273-3844), and **New Zealand** (tel. 273-3611), all located on Commonwealth Avenue.

AUSTRALIAN WAR MEMORIAL, at the head of Anzac Parade on Limestone Ave. Tel. 243-4211.
⭐ Until the new Parliament House opened, the War Memorial was Canberra's top attraction, drawing more than one million visitors a year. I hope you'll take time to tour this impressive collection of historical artifacts and displays that tell about the wars in which Australia has been involved. I can think of few other experiences that offer as much insight into the country. It is a sobering but not depressing experience. The Aussies have served alongside America in many conflicts, and seeing these experiences from their point of view is fascinating. Don't miss the displays relating to Gallipoli, the World War I bloodbath in which so many Anzac (Australia and New Zealand Army Corps) troops lost their lives.
Admission (including guided tours): Free.
Open: Daily 9am–4:45pm; guided tours Mon–Fri 10:30am and 1:30pm. **Closed:** Christmas Day. **Bus:** No. 302 or 303.

TELECOM TOWER, Black Mountain Rd. Tel. 248-1911.
The Telecom Tower, which rises 195 meters (644 ft.) above the summit of Black Mountain, is the loftiest spot in town for getting a bird's-eye view of the landscape.

For the admission fee visitors are whisked up to an enclosed viewing gallery, which is 58.5 meters (193 ft.) aboveground, and to two open viewing galleries, which are 62 and 66 meters (205 and 218 ft.) in the air. Those who dine in the revolving Tower Restaurant (see "Canberra Dining," above) are entitled to a refund of their admission charge. There's also a coffee shop on level 7 and a kiosk.

Admission: A$2 (U.S. $1.60) adults, A50¢ (U.S. 40¢) children under 17.
Open: Daily 9am–10pm. **Bus:** No. 904 (Mon–Fri).

AUSTRALIAN NATIONAL BOTANIC GARDENS, located on the slopes of Black Mountain. Tel. 267-1805.

These gardens contain the world's best collection of Australian native flora. More than 6,000 species are under cultivation, and excellent printed guides (available at the Information Centre) help visitors find their way around. In addition, walks of various lengths are marked, and plants along the way are labeled.

Admission: Free.
Open: Daily 9am–5pm. **Closed:** Christmas Day. **Bus:** No. 434 or 904.

6. CANBERRA SPORTS & RECREATION

SPORTS

Rugby League is the most popular local sport. Matches are held at Bruce Stadium, Battye Street, Bruce (tel. 253-2111).

RECREATION

Ballooning   **Balloon Aloft** (tel. 285-1540) will take you up, up, and away on an unforgettable sunrise trip over the city. One-hour flights cost A$175 (U.S. $140) per adult and A$120 (U.S. $96) per child. The price includes a champagne picnic. Half-hour flights cost A$120 (U.S. $96) for adults and A$80 (U.S. $64) for kids and include champagne or orange juice and a flight certificate.

Bicycling   Rent a bike from **Mr. Spokes,** at the lake ferry terminal, Acton Park (tel. 257-1188), and take advantage of Canberra's 120 kilometers (74 miles) of cycleways. Some picturesque paths follow the shore of Lake Burley Griffin; others head out through the suburbs. It costs A$5 (U.S. $4) an hour to rent a bike. Mr. Spokes is open daily. **Glebe Park Bike Hire,** Glebe Park, Coranderrk Street, Civic (tel. 249-6861 or 249-7633), rents bikes for A$4 (U.S. $3.20) an hour or A$12 to A$16 (U.S. $9.60 to U.S. $12.80) for a full day. Open daily from 9:30am.

Boating   Contact **Dobel Boat Hire Pty. Ltd.,** on the north side of Lake Burley Griffin and just east of Commonwealth Avenue, Acton Jetty, Acton (tel. 249-6861), if you want to rent catamarans, paddleboats, sailboards, rowboats, or other vessels. Rates start at A$6 (U.S. $4.80) an hour.

Golf   The closest 18-hole course to the city center is the **Yowani Country Club,** located on the Federal Highway in the suburb of Lyneham (tel. 241-2303 or 241-3377). Greens fees are A$25 (U.S. $20) for 18 holes and A$15 (U.S. $12) for nine. Club rental costs an additional A$6 to A$12 (U.S. $4.80 to U.S. $9.60). You *must* book in advance.

Swimming   The 50-meter (54½-yd.) indoor heated pool at the **Australian Institute of Sport,** Leverrier Street, Bruce (tel. 252-1111), is open to the public at certain times of the day. This facility is about 8 kilometers (5 miles) northwest of Civic. Adults pay A$3 (U.S. $2.40) to swim.

Tennis   The **National Tennis and Squash Centre** is located on Federal Highway in Lyneham (tel. 247-0929). Squash courts cost A$9.20 to A$11 (U.S. $7.40 to U.S. $8.80) an hour depending on when you want to play. Tennis courts rent for A$12 to A$14 (U.S. $9.60 to U.S. $11.20). There are also courts at the Australian

Institute of Sport (see "Swimming," above). Court rental is A$15 to A$20 (U.S. $12 to U.S. $16) an hour inside and A$8 to A$10 (U.S. $6.40 to U.S. $8) an hour outside.

7. CANBERRA SAVVY SHOPPING

The **Canberra Centre,** which fills 4 square blocks between City Walk and Ballumbir Street between Petrie Street and Akuna Street in Civic, is the city's best place to shop. Some 150 specialty stores of all types fill the three-story atrium which, because of the amount of glass used, feels like a conservatory. **David Jones** and **Grace Bros.** are the major department stores. You'll also find a **Target, Venture,** and **Supa Barn** here. The **City Market** section, which includes a butcher shop, bakery, fruit and vegetables sellers, deli, and several fast-food outlets, is open from 9am to 6pm Monday through Thursday, from 9am to 9pm Friday, and from 9am to 5pm Saturday and Sunday. The rest of the stores are open from 9am to 5:30pm Monday through Thursday, Friday from 9am to 9pm, and Saturday from 9am to 4pm.

My favorite shop is the ✪ **Craftsman's Collection** on the first floor of the center (tel. 257-4733). The crafts sold here are made of Australian materials, by Australians, in Australia. These include pottery, jewelry, glass pieces, and wood items. Be sure to notice the Dingo Pottery and Mathew Larwood's glass work.

8. CANBERRA EVENING ENTERTAINMENT

THE PERFORMING ARTS

THE CANBERRA THEATRE CENTRE, London Circuit, Civic Sq., Civic. Tel. 243-5711 or 257-1077 for tickets, or toll free 008/04-1041 in New South Wales.
This is the best-known venue for the performing arts. A wide range of productions—from rock to Shakespeare—takes place here. The theater, built in 1965, has 1,189 seats. Check the Saturday *Canberra Times* for what's-on information.
Prices: A$30–A$39 (U.S. $24–U.S. $31.20).

THE CLUB & MUSIC SCENE

MADDIES, in the Kingston Hotel, 73 Canberra Ave., Griffith. Tel. 295-6844.
This is a disco which is popular with the 18- to 25-year-old crowd. It's open nightly from 9pm to the wee hours. A can of Fosters costs A$2 (U.S. $1.60).
Admission: Thurs–Sat A$3 (U.S. $2.40); other nights free of charge.

CANBERRA TRADESMEN'S UNION CLUB, 2 Badham St., Dickson. Tel. 248-0999.
There's something for nearly everyone in this large club, which is located 4 kilometers (2½ miles) north of Civic. The Canberra Bicycle Museum, with about 60 unusual bicycles, is on display here. You can also have dinner in one of 10 restored trams, and there are rooms full of poker and card machines—191 in all. Housie (bingo) is played about 20 times a week, and there are four snooker tables. Naturally, a wide range of drinks is available at several different bars. A "tinnie" (can) of Fosters will set you back A$1.70 (U.S. $1.40). The hours at present are Monday to Wednesday from 9:30am to 12:30am, Thursday to Saturday 9:30am to 3am, and Sunday 9:30am to 1:30am, but they hope to be open 24 hours soon—perhaps by the time you get there.
Admission: Free.

DORETTE'S BISTRO, 17 Garema Place, Civic. Tel. 247-4946.

⭐ There's no doubt about why Dorette's is a popular place. There's live music here every night; the modern Australian food is good (if you choose to eat); and the ambience is that of a small European bistro. Jazz is king 5 nights a week, but Wednesday is reserved for classical music, and Sunday is just for folk and blues. The music starts at 8pm during the week and at 9pm on Friday and Saturday.

Dorette's is located on the first floor (one level up from ground) overlooking the fountain in Garema Place which is a pedestrian plaza. The decor includes ceiling fans, large modern oil paintings, and wooden tables and chairs. Lunch is served daily from noon to 2pm; dinner daily from 6 to 10pm; light suppers daily from 10pm to midnight or later. You don't have to eat, but there's a A$15 (U.S. $12) per person minimum charge for those occupying dining tables on Friday and Saturday nights. No minimum applies to the cocktail tables.

Admission: Thurs–Sat A$2–A$4 (U.S. $1.60–U.S. $3.20).

APPENDIX

A. AN AUSSIE/YANKEE LEXICON

According to the encyclopedia, Britain, Canada, South Africa, New Zealand, Australia, and the United States—as well as a few other places—are all English-speaking countries. While this is true in theory, those of us who have traveled in these lands know that communication difficulties do arise because of the use of idioms, colloquial expressions, and the difference in accents. Personally, I've never experienced a serious language problem down under. Rather, I've found our choice of words to be a built-in ice breaker, an excuse to start a conversation.

This is not to say I've never embarrassed myself or caused a few giggles. I remember the time I was at the home of a new Aussie acquaintance and asked to use *the bathroom*. I was shown the way down the hall, but once inside, realized the one piece of plumbing I needed was nowhere in sight. I obviously didn't know that in Australia the bathroom is a room in which there is a bathtub, and I should have asked for *the toilet*.

Then there was the time I verbally blasted the chap who asked me if I'd go to a *hotel* with him. I'd have responded differently if I'd realized that in Oz, hotel is synonomous with *pub* and he was just inviting me to have a drink.

New Zealanders share many expressions with their cousins across the Tasman, but aren't immune from oral errors. A Kiwi who requests to be *knocked up* will get the same quizzical response in Sydney that he'd receive in San Francisco or New York. He will only be asking to be awakened, but Aussies and Yanks will think of a much more physical act.

However, these down-under relatives share bemusement when they hear Americans talk about *rooting* for the home team. They'd *barrack* for their favorite squad and do their rooting in the bedroom.

The following list of Aussie words and expressions is intended to save you a few red-faced moments, to help you order what you want to eat, and get you where you're going.

Air conditioning Refers to both heating and cooling the air
Aussie An Australian
Barby Barbecue
Bathroom Where one bathes
Beetroot Beets
Billabong Water hole in a usually dry river
Billy Tin container used for boiling water over an open fire
Billy tea Tea boiled over an open fire
Biscuits Cookies
Bloke Guy, man
Bon bons Cylindrical party favors containing a prize similar to that found in a box of

Cracker Jack (U.S.), Christmas crackers (N.Z.)
Bonnet Hood of a car
Boot Trunk of a car
Boxing Day The day after Christmas
Brasserie A casual restaurant
Bum Backside (if you mean a guy who's down on his luck, say "tramp")
Bushranger Outlaw, bandit
Bushwalking Hiking (U.S.), tramping (N.Z.)
Chemist shop Drugstore
Cobber Friend
Cozzie, bathing costume, swimmers, togs Swimsuit
Crook Sick

Cuppa Cup of . . , tea
Drover Cowboy
Dunny Slang for toilet, but really an outhouse
Esky Styrofoam cooler (U.S.), chilly bin (N.Z.). A large esky is often called a "car fridge."
Chips French-fried potatoes
Chook Chicken
Doona Quilted eiderdown cover
Entrée Smallish first course; appetizer
Fair dinkum True, real, genuine
Fancy-dress party Costume party
Fête A function to raise money for a charity, church, school or similar
Flog Sell
Footpath Sidewalk
Footy Football
Frankfurt or saveloy Hot dog
Galah A noisy pink-and-gray native parrot, anyone who talks a lot, especially foolishly
Gaol Jail
German sausage Bologna
Gidday or g'day Hello (good-day)
Greenies Ecology-minded activists
Grog Booze
Gumboots Waterproof rubber boots (U.S.), Wellingtons (Britain)
Hotel Public licensed hotel, a pub, a bar
Ice block Popsicle
Jackeroo Male apprentice ranch hand
Jilleroo Female apprentice ranch hand
Joey Baby kangaroo in the pouch
Jumbuck Sheep
Jumper Pullover sweater (U.S.), jersey (N.Z.)
Kerb Curb
Knickers Underwear, undies
Lift Elevator
Lollies Candy (U.S.), sweets (Britain)
Loo Toilet
Mackintosh A rubberized raincoat
Main course Entrée
Mate Friend (not spouse)
Matilda Slang for swag (see *swag* below)
Napkin or nappy Diaper

Newsagent A kiosk where magazines and newspapers are sold
One off One of a kind
Oz Australia (the Lucky Country)
Poker machine Slot machine
Pom or Pommie Person from England
Pozzie Position, location
Prawn Shrimp
Queue Line, waiting in line
Return ticket Round-trip ticket
Rubber Pencil eraser (the one used for birth control is a "condom")
Sandshoes Sneakers
Serviette Napkin
Sheila Female (slang)
Shout Treat someone to a drink, buy a round
Silverbeet Swiss chard
Silverside Corned beef
Singlet Sleeveless undershirt
Sister Nurse
Snags Sausages (U.S.), bangers (N.Z. and Britain)
Station Ranch
Strides Trousers
Stubby Short, brown bottle of beer
Swag A bundle or roll carried across the shoulders
Swagman A man who travels about the country on foot, living on his earnings from occasional jobs. Such a person often carries his possessions in a swag.
Ta Thank you
Telly Television
Tinny Can, as in "a tinny of beer"
To call To visit
To ring To phone
Thongs Jandals (N.Z.), flip-flops (Britain)
Troppo, bonkers Mentally disturbed
Tucker Food
Ute Pickup truck
Wireless Radio (also known to younger Aussies as a "trannie")
Wowser Prude, killjoy
Yabby An Australian freshwater crayfish
Yank American
Yarn Conversation

B. MENU SAVVY

Balmain bug An edible crustacean first discovered in Sydney Harbour and named after a Sydney suburb. Similar delicacies found around Brisbane are called Moreton Bay bugs.

Barramundi Large freshwater fish found in the northern part of Australia; giant perch

Beetroot Beets

Billy tea Tea boiled over an open fire

Biscuit Cookie

Capsicum Bell pepper

Carpetbag steak A thick cut of beef stuffed with oysters

Chips French-fried potatoes

Coral trout A popular eating fish found in the vicinity of the Great Barrier Reef

Crayfish A freshwater crustacean; crawfish

Damper A type of bread made from a simple flour-and-water dough with or without a leavening agent and cooked in the coals of an open fire or in a camp oven

Entrée A smallish first course; appetizer

Frankfurt, saveloy Hot dog

German sausage Bologna

Jewfish A popular saltwater eating fish

John Dory A thin, deep-bodied popular food fish found in Australian waters

Lamingtons Pieces of sponge cake covered with chocolate icing and shredded coconut

Main course Entrée

Meat pie A two-crust pie filled with stewed cubed or ground meat (usually beef) and gravy

Mud crab A large edible crab found in the mangrove regions of New South Wales and Queensland

Pavlova A large soft-centered meringue filled with whipped cream and garnished with fruit

Pawpaw Papaya

Prawn Shrimp

Rockmelon Cantaloupe

Roast dinner Roast beef or leg of lamb served with potatoes and other vegetables which have been cooked with the meat

Salad bar A buffet of prepared salads such as potato, three-bean, coleslaw, and so forth

Scone A biscuit, often served with jam and clotted cream

Silverbeet Swiss chard

Silverside Corned beef

Snags Sausages (U.S.), bangers (N.Z. and Britain)

Tomato sauce Catsup

Vegemite A yeast-based vegetable extract used as a spread on bread

Witchetty grubs Large white edible larvae of certain Australian moths and beetles

Yabby An Australian freshwater crayfish

C. METRIC MEASURES

LENGTH

1 millimeter (mm)	=	.04 inches (*or* less than 1/16 in.)
1 centimeter (cm)	=	.39 inches (*or* just under ½ in.)
1 meter (m)	=	39 inches (*or* about 1.1 yards)
1 kilometer (km)	=	.62 inches (*or* about ⅔ of a mile)

To convert kilometers to miles, multiply the number of kilometers by .62. Also use to convert kilometers per hour (kmph) to miles per hour (m.p.h.).

To convert miles to kilometers, multiply the number of miles by 1.61. Also use to convert from m.p.h. to kmph.

CAPACITY

1 liter (l)	=	33.92 fluid ounces	=	2.1 pints	=	1.06 quarts
	=	.26 U.S. gallons				
1 Imperial gallon	=	1.2 U.S. gallons				

To convert liters to U.S. gallons, multiply the number of liters by .26.

To convert U.S. gallons to liters, multiply the number of gallons by 3.79.

To convert Imperial gallons to U.S. gallons, multiply the number of Imperial gallons by 1.2.

To convert U.S. gallons to Imperial gallons, multiply the number of U.S. gallons by .83.

WEIGHT

1 gram (g)	=	.035 ounces (*or* about a paperclip's weight)
1 kilogram (kg)	=	35.2 ounces
	=	2.2 pounds
1 metric ton	=	2,205 pounds (1.1 short ton)

To convert kilograms to pounds, multiply the number of kilograms by 2.2.

To convert pounds to kilograms, multiply the number of pounds by .45.

AREA

1 hectare (ha)	=	2.47 acres		
1 square kilometer (km²)	=	247 acres	=	.39 square miles

To convert hectares to acres, multiply the number of hectares by 2.47.

To convert acres to hectares, multiply the number of acres by .41.

To convert square kilometers to square miles, multiply the number of square kilometers by .39.

To convert square miles to square kilometers, multiply the number of square miles by 2.6.

TEMPERATURE

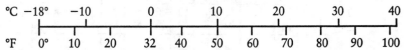

To convert degrees Celsius to degrees Fahrenheit, multiply °C by 9, divide by 5, and add 32 (example: 20°C × 9/5 + 32 = 68°F).

To convert degrees Fahrenheit to degrees Celsius, subtract 32 from °F, multiply by 5, then divide by 9 (example: 85°F − 32 × 5/9 = 29.4°C).

D. MILEAGE CHART

	Sydney	Surfers Paradise	Port Hedland	Perth	Mount Isa	Melbourne	Mackay	Kununurra	Hobart*	Darwin	Canberra	Cairns	Broken Hill	Brisbane	Ayers Rock	Alice Springs	Albany	Adelaide
Adelaide	1475	2028	3847	2720	2734	747	2100	3248	999	3261	1230	2858	513	1992	1597	1555	2675	
Albany	3791	4305	2105	409	4773	3422	4377	3735	3674	3735	3905	5135	2790	4269	3636	3594		2675
Alice Springs	2831	3106	3289	3639	1179	2302	2391	1693	2554	1706	2785	2307	1670	3026	446		3594	1555
Ayers Rock	2873	3552	3737	3681	1625	2344	2837	2139	2596	2152	2827	2753	1712	3472		446	3636	1597
Brisbane	1031	80	5289	4314	1847	1718	1010	3659	1970	3672	1315	1710	1479		3472	3026	4269	1992
Broken Hill	1161	1559	4531	2835	2105	861	1783	3363	1113	3376	1100	2345		1479	1712	1670	2790	513
Cairns	2636	1790	4570	5180	1128	3039	700	2940	3291	2953	2938		2345	1710	2753	2307	5135	2858
Canberra	302	1235	5646	3950	2724	651	2325	4400	903	4233		2938	1100	1315	2827	2785	3905	1230
Darwin	4095	3752	2510	4206	1825	4008	3037	880	4260		4233	2953	3376	3672	2152	1706	3735	3261
Hobart*	1141	2074	5338	3719	3070	252	2971	4247		4260	903	3291	1113	1970	2596	2554	3674	999
Kununurra	4096	3739	1630	3326	1812	3995	3024		4247	880	4400	2940	3363	3659	2139	1693	3735	3248
Mackay	2061	1090	3654	4422	1212	2719		3024	2971	3037	2325	700	1783	1010	2837	2391	4377	2100
Melbourne	889	1822	5286	3467	2818		2719	3995	252	4008	651	3039	861	1718	2344	2302	3422	747

	Adelaide	Albany	Alice Springs	Ayers Rock	Brisbane	Broken Hill	Cairns	Canberra	Darwin	Hobart*	Kununurra	Mackay	Melbourne	Mount Isa	Perth	Port Hedland	Surfers Paradise	Sydney
Mount Isa	2734	4773	1179	1625	1847	2105	1128	2724	1825	3070	1812	1212	2818		4973	3442	1927	2396
Perth	2720	409	3639	3681	4314	2835	5180	3950	4206	3719	3326	4422	3467	4973		1696	4393	3996
Port Hedland	3847	2105	3289	3737	5289	4531	4570	5646	2510	5338	1630	3654	5286	3442	1696		5369	5692
Surfers Paradise (Gold Coast)	2028	4305	3106	3552	80	1559	1790	1235	3752	2074	3739	1090	1822	1927	4393	5369		933
Sydney	1475	3791	2831	2873	1031	1161	2636	302	4095	1141	4096	2061	889	2396	3996	5692	933	

*Distances are in kilometers. To convert to miles: $\frac{km}{1} \times \frac{5}{8}$ miles.
*Road distance to Hobart excludes Melbourne-Devonport ferry journey.
*Source: Australian Tourist Commission.

E. GREAT BARRIER REEF RESORTS AT A GLANCE

	Island	Access	Description	*Rating/ Coral	Beaches	Accommo- dations	Sports/ Activities	Day Trips	Comments
Far North	Lizard	Cairns	continental is; mountainous	3 fringe	white sand	exclusive deluxe resort; fine dining	all sports with good facilities; marlin fishing; scuba instruction, diving	no	no children under 6; marine research facility; near outer reef & "Cod Hole"
	Green	Cairns	coral cay; tropical	3 on reef	fine coral sand	being redeveloped, may open in 1992	snorkeling and scuba diving	yes	good underwater observatory and guided reef walks; glass-bottom boats
	Fitzroy	Cairns	continental is; mountainous; tropical	1 fringe	coarse coral	mid-price lodgings; camping; backpacker hostel	fishing; bush walks; scuba-diving instruction	yes	rain forest with streams, waterfalls, wild orchids, butterflies
North	Dunk	Cairns; Townsville; Mission Beach	continental is; tropical	1 fringe	sand	large, relaxed resort	all sports including horseback riding; outer reef trips; bush walks; farm	yes	family resort; national park; rain forest; free child care ages 3–12
	Bedarra	Dunk Is.	continental is; tropical	1 fringe	sand	2 small exclusive resorts; tariff includes open bar	some sports; motorized sports at Dunk	no	hideaway for the rich and famous; no kids under 16
	Hinchin-brook	Townsville; Cardwell	continental is; large, tropical rugged	1 fringe	sand	small unsophisticated resort	outer reef trips; bush walks	yes	national park; wildlife; dense rain forest, waterfalls; mangroves; wilderness

	Island	Access	Type	Reefs	Beach	Accommodation	Activities	Airstrip	Notes
North (cont.)	Orpheus	Townsville; Cairns	continental is.; bush to tropical	3 fringe	white sand	exclusive, informal; good dining	snorkling, scuba; tennis; bush walks; outer reef trips	no	no children under 12; ideal honeymoon spot; giant clam research facility
	Magnetic	Townsville	continental is.; hilly, rocky	1 fringe	white sand	motels	cycling; horseback riding; bush walks; fishing	yes	considered suburb of Townsville close to mainland
Whit-sunday	Hayman	Airlie beach; Hamilton Is.	continental is.; tropical	2 fringe	soft sand, tidal	five-star luxury; multiple fine-dining options	water sports; outer reef trips; scuba instruction	no	world-class resort; patch reef nearby; easy access
	Daydream	Shute Harbour; Proserpine	continental is.; tropical	1 fringe	coarse coral, tidal	modern resort built in 1990	water sports; outer reef trips	yes	free child care, popular with families
	South Molle	Shute Harbour; Proserpine	continental is.; tropical	1 fringe	tidal, sand	large resort with various types of lodging	water sports; tennis; golf; outer reef trips; scuba; walking paths	yes	free childcare; many activities; good for families with small children
	Long	Shute Harbour; Proserpine	continental is.; tropical	1 fringe	tidal, sand	midprice	water sports; scuba; bush walks	yes	popular with 18–35 market; rain forest
	Hook	Shute Harbour; Proserpine	continental is.; tropical	2 fringe	coarse sand & coral	budget	underwater observatory; snorkeling	yes	dangerous currents preclude swimming at southeast passage; excellent sailboat anchorage

	Island	Access	Description	*Rating/Coral	Beaches	Accommodations	Sports/Activities	Day Trips	Comments
Whitsunday (cont.)	Hamilton	Shute Harbor; Brisbane; Cairns	continental is.; dry bush	1 fringe	modest; tidal	large varied; some high-rise; numerous food outlets	water sports; outer reef trips	yes	easy access via island's jet airport
	Lindeman	Shute Harbor; Proserpine Hamilton	continental is.; wooded slopes, bush	2 fringe	tidal	Club Med Village	bush walks; water sports	yes	Club Med new in 1992
Central	Brampton	Mackay	continental is.; wooded; mountainous	2 fringe	fine white sand	informal, relaxed	water sports; reef walks at low tide	yes	Kangaroos on golf course; rain forest
	Great Keppel	Rockhampton; Yeppoon	continental is.; large, hilly	1 fringe	fine white sand	resort; camping cabins	all sports; adjacent underwater observatory	yes	popular with young people; disco; easy access
	Heron	Gladstone	coral cay; tropical	3 on reef	coarse sand & coral	comfortable resort; budget; midprice	water sports including snorkeling, scuba; scuba instruction; birdwatching; guided reef walks	no	outstanding coral reef; marine research facility; turtle-nesting sanctuary
	Lady Elliot	Bundaberg; Brisbane	coral cay; tropical	3 on reef	coral sand	camping and cabins	water sports; scuba instruction; guided walks; diving	yes	very little development; southern end of reef

*Ratings: 3 = excellent; 2 = good/fair; 1 = fair/poor
Compiled by Richard Adams

INDEX

GENERAL INFORMATION

DESTINATIONS

KEY TO ABBREVIATIONS: B&B = Bed & Breakfast; B = Budget; E = Expensive; GH = Guest House; I = Inexpensive; M = Moderate; PL = Pub Lodging; SA = Serviced Apartment; VE = Very Expensive; * = an Author's Favorite; $ = Super Value Choice

NOW, SAVE MONEY ON ALL YOUR TRAVELS!
Join Frommer's™ Dollarwise® Travel Club

Saving money while traveling is never easy, which is why the **Dollarwise Travel Club** was formed 32 years ago to provide cost-cutting travel strategies, up-to-date travel information, and a sense of community for value-conscious travelers from all over the world.

In keeping with the money-saving concept, the annual membership fee is low—$25 for U.S. residents and $35 for residents of Canada, Mexico, and other countries—and is immediately exceeded by the value of your benefits, which include:

1. Any TWO books listed on the following pages;
2. Plus any ONE Frommer's City Guide;
3. A subscription to our quarterly newspaper, *The Dollarwise Traveler;*
4. A membership card that entitles you to purchase through the Club all Frommer's publications for 33% to 40% off their retail price.

The eight-page **Dollarwise Traveler** tells you about the latest developments in good-value travel worldwide and includes the following columns: **Hospitality Exchange** (for those offering and seeking hospitality in cities all over the world); and **Share-a-Trip** (for those looking for travel companions to share costs).

Aside from the various Frommer's Guides, the Gault Millau Guides, and the Real Guides you can also choose from our Special Editions, which include such titles as **Caribbean Hideaways** (the 100 most romantic places to stay in the Islands); and **Marilyn Wood's Wonderful Weekends** (a selection of the best mini-vacations within a 200-mile radius of New York City).

To join this Club, send the appropriate membership fee with your name and address to: Frommer's Dollarwise Travel Club, 15 Columbus Circle, New York, NY 10023. Remember to specify which single city guide and which two other guides you wish to receive in your initial package of member's benefits. Or tear out the pages, check off your choices, and send them to us with your membership fee.

FROMMER BOOKS
PRENTICE HALL TRAVEL
15 COLUMBUS CIRCLE
NEW YORK, NY 10023

Date_____

Friends: Please send me the books checked below.

FROMMER'S™ COMPREHENSIVE GUIDES
(Guides listing facilities from budget to deluxe, with emphasis on the medium-priced)

☐ Alaska	$14.95	☐ Italy	$19.00
☐ Australia	$14.95	☐ Japan & Hong Kong	$17.00
☐ Austria & Hungary	$14.95	☐ Morocco	$18.00
☐ Belgium, Holland & Luxembourg	$14.95	☐ Nepal	$18.00
☐ Bermuda & The Bahamas	$17.00	☐ New England	$17.00
☐ Brazil	$14.95	☐ New Mexico	$13.95
☐ California	$18.00	☐ New York State	$19.00
☐ Canada	$16.00	☐ Northwest	$16.95
☐ Caribbean	$17.00	☐ Puerta Vallarta (avail. Feb. '92)	$14.00
☐ Carolinas & Georgia	$17.00	☐ Portugal, Madeira & the Azores	$14.95
☐ Colorado (avail. Jan '92)	$14.00	☐ Scandinavia	$18.95
☐ Cruises (incl. Alaska, Carib, Mex, Hawaii, Panama, Canada & US)	$16.00	☐ Scotland (avail. Feb. '92)	$17.00
		☐ South Pacific	$20.00
☐ Delaware, Maryland, Pennsylvania & the New Jersey Shore (avail. Jan. '92)	$19.00	☐ Southeast Asia	$14.95
		☐ Switzerland & Liechtenstein	$19.00
☐ Egypt	$14.95	☐ Thailand	$20.00
☐ England	$17.00	☐ Virginia (avail. Feb. '92)	$14.00
☐ Florida	$17.00	☐ Virgin Islands	$13.00
☐ France	$15.95	☐ USA	$16.95
☐ Germany	$18.00		

0891492

FROMMER'S CITY GUIDES

(Pocket-size guides to sightseeing and tourist accommodations and facilities in all price ranges)

☐ Amsterdam/Holland	$8.95	☐ Minneapolis/St. Paul	$8.95
☐ Athens	$8.95	☐ Montréal/Québec City	$8.95
☐ Atlanta	$8.95	☐ New Orleans	$8.95
☐ Atlantic City/Cape May	$8.95	☐ New York	$12.00
☐ Bangkok	$12.00	☐ Orlando	$12.00
☐ Barcelona	$12.00	☐ Paris	$8.95
☐ Belgium	$7.95	☐ Philadelphia	$11.00
☐ Berlin	$10.00	☐ Rio	$8.95
☐ Boston	$8.95	☐ Rome	$8.95
☐ Cancún/Cozumel/Yucatán	$8.95	☐ Salt Lake City	$8.95
☐ Chicago	$9.95	☐ San Diego	$8.95
☐ Denver/Boulder/Colorado Springs	$8.95	☐ San Francisco	$12.00
☐ Dublin/Ireland	$10.00	☐ Santa Fe/Taos/Albuquerque	$10.95
☐ Hawaii	$12.00	☐ Seattle/Portland	$12.00
☐ Hong Kong	$7.95	☐ St. Louis/Kansas City	$9.95
☐ Las Vegas	$8.95	☐ Sydney	$8.95
☐ Lisbon/Madrid/Costa del Sol	$8.95	☐ Tampa/St. Petersburg	$8.95
☐ London	$12.00	☐ Tokyo	$8.95
☐ Los Angeles	$8.95	☐ Toronto	$8.95
☐ Mexico City/Acapulco	$8.95	☐ Vancouver/Victoria	$7.95
☐ Miami	$8.95	☐ Washington, D.C.	$12.00

FROMMER'S $-A-DAY® GUIDES

(Guides to low-cost tourist accommodations and facilities)

☐ Australia on $40 a Day	$13.95	☐ Israel on $40 a Day	$13.95
☐ Costa Rica, Guatemala & Belize on $35 a Day	$15.95	☐ Mexico on $45 a Day	$18.00
		☐ New York on $65 a Day	$15.00
☐ Eastern Europe on $25 a Day	$16.95	☐ New Zealand on $45 a Day	$16.00
☐ England on $50 a Day	$17.00	☐ Scotland & Wales on $40 a Day	$18.00
☐ Europe on $45 a Day	$19.00	☐ South America on $40 a Day	$15.95
☐ Greece on $35 a Day	$14.95	☐ Spain on $50 a Day	$15.95
☐ Hawaii on $70 a Day	$18.00	☐ Turkey on $40 a Day	$22.00
☐ India on $40 a Day	$20.00	☐ Washington, D.C., on $45 a Day	$17.00
☐ Ireland on $40 a Day	$17.00		

FROMMER'S CITY $-A-DAY GUIDES

☐ Berlin on $40 a Day	$12.00	☐ Madrid on $50 a Day (avail. Jan '92)	$13.00
☐ Copenhagen on $50 a Day	$12.00	☐ Paris on $45 a Day	$12.00
☐ London on $45 a Day	$12.00	☐ Stockholm on $50 a Day (avail. Dec. '91)	$13.00

FROMMER'S FAMILY GUIDES

☐ California with Kids	$16.95	☐ San Francisco with Kids	$17.00
☐ Los Angeles with Kids	$17.00	☐ Washington, D.C., with Kids (avail. Jan '92)	$17.00
☐ New York City with Kids (avail. Jan '92)	$18.00		

SPECIAL EDITIONS

☐ Beat the High Cost of Travel	$6.95	☐ Marilyn Wood's Wonderful Weekends (CT, DE, MA, NH, NJ, NY, PA, RI, VT)	$11.95
☐ Bed & Breakfast—N. America	$14.95	☐ Motorist's Phrase Book (Fr/Ger/Sp)	$4.95
☐ Caribbean Hideaways	$16.00	☐ The New World of Travel (annual by Arthur Frommer for savvy travelers)	$16.95
☐ Honeymoon Destinations (US, Mex & Carib)	$14.95		

(TURN PAGE FOR ADDITONAL BOOKS AND ORDER FORM)

0891492